INSTITUTES OF ELENCTIC THEOLOGY

FRANCIS TURRETIN

Photograph from the frontispiece of volume 1 of
Turretin's *Institutio theologiae elencticae* (1696),
courtesy of *La Bibliothèque publique et universitaire de Genève*.

INSTITUTES OF ELENCTIC THEOLOGY

BY

Francis Turretin

Pastor in the Church and Academy of Geneva
and S. S. Professor of Theology

TRANSLATED BY

George Musgrave Giger

Princeton University

EDITED BY

James T. Dennison, Jr.

Westminster Theological Seminary
in California

VOLUME 2
ELEVENTH THROUGH SEVENTEENTH TOPICS

P&R

P U B L I S H I N G

P.O. BOX 817 • PHILLIPSBURG • NEW JERSEY 08865-0817

The editor acknowledges permission from Harvard University Press to use excerpts from the Loeb Classical Library.

Juvenal and Persius. Translated by G.G. Ramsey. 1979.

Seneca, *Moral Essays*. Translated by John W. Basore. 1970.

Virgil, *Aeneid*. Translated by H. Rushton Fairclough. 1974.

Suetonius, *Lives of the Caesars*. Translated by J.C. Rolfe. 1970.

All Scripture quotations are from the King James Version (1611).

Manufactured in the United States of America.
Typesetting by Thoburn Press, Box 2459, Reston, Virginia 22090.

Library of Congress Cataloging-in-Publication Data

Turrettini, François, 1623–1687.
Institutes of elenctic theology.

Translation of: Institutio theologiae elencticae.
Includes bibliographical references.
Contents: v. 1. First through tenth topics.
—v. 2. Eleventh through seventeenth topics.
1. Reformed Church—Doctrines—Early works to 1800.
2. Theology, Doctrinal—Early works to 1800. 3. Catholic Church—Controversial literature—Early works to 1800.
I. Giger, George Musgrave, 1822–1865. II. Dennison, James T., 1943– . III. Title.
BX9421.T7913 1992 230'.42 92-10128
ISBN-10: 0-87552-451-6 (v. 1)
ISBN-13: 978-0-87552-451-1 (v. 1)
ISBN-10: 0-87552-452-4 (v. 2)
ISBN-13: 978-0-87552-452-8 (v. 2)

Primogenito filio, J. T.
et
Primogenitae filiae, Kristin

Laudemus novissimum Agnum!

TABLE OF CONTENTS

Tables of Abbreviations and Transliteration

General Abbreviations

*	Corrected citation
+	Citation cannot be identified or located as cited by Turretin
AA	Josephus, *Against Apion*. Translated by H.St.J. Thackeray. Cambridge: Harvard University Press, 1926.
ACW	*Ancient Christian Writers*. New York: Newman Press, 1946- .
AJ	Josephus, *Antiquities of the Jews*. Translated by H.St.J. Thackeray, R. Marcus and L.H. Feldman. Cambridge: Harvard University Press, 1928-31.
ANF	Alexander Roberts and James Donaldson, eds., *Ante-Nicene Fathers*. Grand Rapids: Wm. B. Eerdmans Publishing Co., 1969-73.
BT	I. Epstein, ed., *The Babylonian Talmud*. London: Soncino Press, 1935-52.
CCSL	*Corpus Christianorum, Series Latina*. Turnholt: Brepols, 1953- .
CG	Augustine, *City of God*. Translated by Demetrius B. Zema and Gerald G. Walsh. New York: Fathers of the Church, 1950-54.
CI	Augustine, *Christian Instruction*. Translated by John J. Gavigan. New York: Cima Publishing Co., 1947.
CR	*Corpus Reformatorum*. Berlin: C.A. Schwetschke, 1834- .
CSCO	*Corpus Scriptorum Christianorum Orientalium*. Paris: Reipublicae, n.d.
Cochrane	A.C. Cochrane, *Reformed Confessions of the 16th Century*. Philadelphia: Westminster Press, 1966.
FC	*Fathers of the Church*. Washington, D.C.: Catholic University of America Press.
Hefele	Charles J. Hefele, *A History of the Councils of the Church*. 5 vols. New York: AMS Press, 1883/1972.
ICR	John Calvin, *Institutes of the Christian Religion*. 2 vols. Edited by John T. McNeill. Translated by Ford L. Battles. Philadelphia: Westminster Press, 1960.
JW	Josephus, *The Jewish War*. Translated by H.St.J. Thackeray. Cambridge University Press, 1926-29.

LCC	John Baillie, John T. McNeill and Henry P. Van Dusen, eds., *Library of Christian Classics*. Philadelphia: Westminster Press, 1953-66.
Lauchert	Friedrich Lauchert, *Die Kanones der Wichtigsten Altkirchlichen Concilien*. Frankfurt am Main: Minerva, 1896/1961.
Mansi	Giovan D. Mansi, *Sacrorum Conciliorum*. Paris: H. Welter, 1901-27.
NPNF1	Philip Schaff, ed., *Nicene and Post-Nicene Fathers, First Series*. Grand Rapids: Wm. B. Eerdmans Publishing Co., 1956.
NPNF2	Philip Schaff and Henry Wace, eds., *Nicene and Post-Nicene Fathers, Second Series*. Grand Rapids: Wm. B. Eerdmans Publishing Co., 1952.
PG	Jacques Paul Migne, *Patrologiae . . . series Graeca*. Paris: J.-P. Migne, 1857-87.
PL	Jacques Paul Migne, *Patrologiae . . . series Latina*. Paris: Garnieri Fratres, 1878.
ST	Thomas Aquinas, *Summa Theologica*. 3 vols. New York: Benzinger Brothers, 1947-48.
Schaff	Philip Schaff, *Creeds of Christendom*. 3 vols. Grand Rapids: Baker Book House, 1931.
Schroeder	*Canons and Decrees of the Council of Trent*. Translated by Henry J. Schroeder. St. Louis: Herder, 1941.
VD	Robert Bellarmine, "De Controversiis: Prima Controversia Generalis —De Verbo Dei," in *Opera Omnia*. Vol. 1. Neapoli: Josephum Giuliano, 1856.

Hebrew Transliteration Table

א	'	ל	l
ב	bh	מ	m
בּ	b	נ	n
ג	gh	ס	s
גּ	g	ע	'
ד	dh	פ	ph
דּ	d	פּ	p
ה	h	צ	ts
ו	v	ק	q
ז	z	ר	r
ח	ch	שׂ	s
ט	t	שׁ	sh
י	y	ת	th
כ	kh	תּ	t
כּ	k		

Greek Transliteration Table

α	a	σ, ѕ	s
β	b	τ	t
γ	g	υ	y
δ	d	φ	ph
ε	e	χ	ch
ζ	z	ψ	ps
η	ē	ω	ō
θ	th	ῥ	rh
ι	i	ʽ	h
κ	k	γγ	ng
λ	l	γκ	nk
μ	m	γξ	nx
ν	n	γχ	nch
ξ	x	αυ	au
ο	o	ευ	eu
π	p	ου	ou
ρ	r	υι	yi

Scripture Abbreviations

Old Testament

Genesis	Gen.
Exodus	Ex.
Leviticus	Lev.
Numbers	Num.
Deuteronomy	Dt.
Joshua	Jos.
Judges	Jdg.
Ruth	Ruth
1 Samuel	1 S.
2 Samuel	2 S.
1 Kings	1 K.
2 Kings	2 K.
1 Chronicles	1 Ch.
2 Chronicles	2 Ch.
Ezra	Ezr.
Nehemiah	Neh.
Esther	Est.
Job	Job
Psalms	Ps.
Proverbs	Prov.
Ecclesiastes	Ecc.
Song of Solomon	Cant.
Isaiah	Is.
Jeremiah	Jer.
Lamentations	Lam.
Ezekiel	Ezk.
Daniel	Dan.
Hosea	Hos.
Joel	Joel
Amos	Am.
Obadiah	Ob.
Jonah	Jon.
Micah	Mic.
Nahum	Nah.
Habakkuk	Hab.
Zephaniah	Zeph.
Haggai	Hag.
Zechariah	Zech.
Malachi	Mal.

Apocrypha

Tobit	Tob.
Judith	Jud.
Wisdom of Solomon	Wis. Sol.
Ecclesiasticus or Son of Sirach	Sir.
Baruch	Bar.
1 Maccabees	1 Mac.
2 Maccabees	2 Mac.

New Testament

Matthew	Mt.
Mark	Mk.
Luke	Lk.
John	Jn.
Acts	Acts
Romans	Rom.
1 Corinthians	1 Cor.
2 Corinthians	2 Cor.
Galatians	Gal.
Ephesians	Eph.
Philippians	Phil.
Colossians	Col.
1 Thessalonians	1 Thess.
2 Thessalonians	2 Thess.
1 Timothy	1 Tim.
2 Timothy	2 Tim.
Titus	Tit.
Philemon	Philem.
Hebrews	Heb.
James	Jam.
1 Peter	1 Pet.
2 Peter	2 Pet.
1 John	1 Jn.
2 John	2 Jn.
3 John	3 Jn.
Jude	Jd.
Revelation	Rev.

ELEVENTH TOPIC

THE LAW OF GOD

FIRST QUESTION

Whether there is a natural law, and how it differs from the moral law. The former we affirm; the latter we distinguish.

Necessity of disputing.

I. As the doctrine concerning the law of God (the discussion of which we now enter upon with the favor of God) properly belongs to the theologian, so it has a multiple use in theology. (1) For the direction of life—as a perfect rule of God's right over man and of man's duty towards God. (2) For a knowledge of sin—because as sin is illegality (*anomia*), from no other source than the law can its truth and heinousness be ascertained (Rom. 3:20). (3) For preparation for grace—that from the declaration of man's sin and misery, the necessity of saving grace may be unfolded and a desire for it excited in us (in which sense it is called "a schoolmaster unto Christ," Gal. 3:24).

Etymology of the word "law."

II. Now law is called by the Hebrews *twrh* (from the verb *yrh*) signifying in the Hiphel "to teach" because by it all are put in mind of their duty. The Greeks call it *nomos* (from *nemein*) which denotes both "to rule" and "to distribute" because according to its prescription men ought to be governed and each one's own is given to him. The Latins either derive it from *legendo* (according to Isidore, *Etymologiarum* 2.10 [PL 82.130]) because, as Cicero obeserves, it is usually read when enacted that it may become known to all or is exposed on public tablets to be read (*Laws* 2*.5.11 [Loeb, 16:384-85]); or inasmuch as *legere* is put for *deligere* because in it is contained a choice of things to be done and avoided; or finally from *ligando* (as Thomas Aquinas, ST, I-II*, Q. 90, Art. 1, p. 993 and most of the Scholastics after him hold), because it binds and fastens men as it were by a chain. It may be in reference to this that in Scripture "laws" are frequently called "bonds" (Ps. 2:3; Jer. 5:5).

Its equivocal sense.

III. However, it is used in different ways in Scripture: either broadly, for the whole word of God (Ps. 1:2; 19:7, 8)—now for all the books of the Old Testament (Jn. 10:34; 1 Cor. 14:21), then for the Mosaical books alone—or the Pentateuch as distinct from the Psalms and the Prophets (Lk. 24:44; Rom. 3:21); or strictly, for the Mosaic dispensation in opposition to the New Testament dispensation (Heb. 7:12; Jn. 1:17); or for the covenant of works exclusively in contradistinction to the covenant of grace (Rom. 6:14); or for "the rule of things to be done and avoided, which God has prescribed to rational creatures under the sanction of rewards and punishments." It is to be particularly examined in this sense.

It is divided into natural and positive.

IV. Now this law of God is divided in general into natural and positive. As the right of God is twofold (one natural, founded in the perfectly just and holy nature of God; the other positive, depending on the will of God alone in which he also shows his own liberty), so there is a positive law of God built on the free and positive right of God (with respect to which things are then good because God commands them). Hence God was free either not to give such a law or to institute otherwise (such as the law relating to food and the symbolical law given to Adam [Gen. 2:16, 17] and the ceremonial laws of the Old Testament, in which there was no moral goodness or evil per se, but only from the command of God). There is another (natural) founded on the natural right of God, with regard to which things are not called just because they are commanded, but are commanded because they were just and good antecedently to the command of God (being founded on the very holiness and wisdom of God). And such is its nature that (the creation of man being supposed) it must have been given to him, since it prescribes to him indispensable duties to be performed by all, always and everywhere.

Natural is taken either broadly or strictly. Statement of the question.

V. However, natural law is again taken in two ways: either broadly and improperly (inasmuch as it is extended to inanimates also and brutes and denotes nothing else than the most wise government of the providence of God over creatures and the most efficacious direction to their ends). In this sense, Ps. 119:91 (where it treats of the motion of the heavens and the stability of the earth) says, "All things continue this day according to thine ordinances: for all are thy servants"; "He hath also stablished all things for ever and ever: he hath made a decree which shall not pass" (Ps. 148:6). In the latter, he is speaking of the works of creation: by this law plants grow, beasts generate and every animal has his own desires (*hormas*) and spontaneous instincts. Or natural law is taken strictly and properly for the practical rule of moral duties to which men are bound by nature. Concerning this law, it is here inquired whether there is such a natural law of God obtaining among all (as the rule of justice and injustice) antecedently to the positive laws of men; or whether justice and virtue depend upon man's will alone and spring from the consent of human society and are to be measured by each one's own utility. The orthodox affirm the former; libertines the latter.

VI. For just as of old Carneades and the Cyrenaics (following Aristippus) denied all natural justice, pretending that "nothing is just and base by nature, but by law and custom" (*mēden einai physei dikaion ē aischron, alla nomō kai ethei*, [Diogenes] Laertius, *Lives of Eminent Philosophers: Aristippus* 2.93 [Loeb, 1:220-21]). This was also the opinion of Epicurus, in reference to whom Gassendi says many things ("Philosophiae Epicuri Syntagma," in *Opuscula Philosophica* [1658], 3:3-94). So there are not wanting many in our day who, treading in their footsteps, think that no rule of right and wrong is given by nature, but that it depends only upon the free determination of man and is to be measured by each one's own advantage (as man is by nature free from every law and has no other rule of right and good than the preservation of himself and the defense of his life and limbs). Calvin testifies that this impious error (with many others) is held by the libertines (*Contre le secte des Libertins*, CR 35.144-248). Hobbes approaches them on this subject in his *Elementa philosophica de cive* (1647).

VII. But the orthodox speak far differently. They affirm that there is a natural law, not arising from a voluntary contract or law of society, but from a divine obligation being impressed by God upon the conscience of man in his very creation, on which the difference between right and wrong is founded and which contains the practical principles of immovable truth (such as: "God should be worshipped," "parents honored," "we should live virtuously," "injure no one," "do to others what we would wish them to do to us" and the like). Also that so many remains and evidences of this law are still left in our nature (although it has been in different ways corrupted and obscured by sin) that there is no mortal who cannot feel its force either more or less. Now they wish this law to be called natural, not because it has its origin from bare nature (since it depends upon God the supreme lawgiver), but because it becomes known from the aspect of creatures and the relation of man to God, and the knowledge of it is impressed upon the mind by nature, not acquired by tradition or instruction.

The origin of the natural law is not to be sought in the Noahic precepts.

VIII. Thus the origin and foundation of this law ought not to be sought (as the Jews falsely seek it) from "the seven precepts" which they maintain were given to Adam and Noah, by which all posterity should be bound: (1) not worshipping idols; (2) not blaspheming the name of God; (3) not committing theft; (4) avoiding incest and foul lusts; (5) appointing judges and magistrates; (6) not shedding blood; (7) not eating the members of a living animal, or flesh with the blood (which is its life). Besides their being founded upon tradition alone (which cannot be said of the natural right), they are not all simply moral and of perpetual observance, but some are ceremonial and positive (such as that about not eating blood); nor do they draw out whatever belongs to natural right, although from it they can be deduced as conclusions from their own principles.

But from the right of nature.

IX. But it must be drawn from the right of nature itself, founded both on the nature of God, the Creator (who by his holiness must prescribe to his creatures the duties founded upon that right), and on the condition of rational creatures themselves (who, on account of their necessary dependence upon God in the genus of morals, no less than in the genus of being, are bound to perform or avoid those things which sound reason and the dictates of conscience enjoin upon them to do or avoid).

In how many ways the right of nature may be used.

X. The right of nature, however, is here used by us, not broadly and improperly (as by lawyers for "that which nature teaches all animals" [*Corpus Iuris Civilis, I: Institutiones* 1.2, p. 1]) as distinguished from the law of nations which all nations use; and from the civil law which each state or community has determined for itself (because as reason does not belong to brutes, so neither are they properly capacious of right or wrong), but strictly and properly for that which has reference only to rational creatures. The lawyers include this under the law of nations. It is rightly described by common practical notions, or the light and dictation of conscience (which God has engraven by nature upon every individual, to distinguish between virtue and vice, and to know the things to be avoided and the things to be done).

XI. Now of these notions, some are primary (which we call principles), others secondary (called conclusions). The principles are those which (being known of themselves and immovable in all, founded on the common good) by the help of reason beget conclusions from themselves. These are reduced to the foundation of the common good; are either more near, immediate and (as they say) of the first dictation of nature (which are proximately gathered from the principles and readily come into knowledge); or mediate and more remote (which by remoter consequence and with greater difficulty are deduced from the principles). The former admit of no variety; the latter of a great variety in this corrupted nature. Although in these conclusions, this law has been in many ways corrupted after sin both by natural corruption, by wrong education, and by vicious custom (by which the basest vices and crimes sometimes receive the name of virtues and obtain praise which the most iniquitous laws and most depraved morals of certain nations plainly testify); still this does not prevent its always remaining the same among all, as to its first principles and the immediate conclusions thence deduced.

Proof that there is a natural law: (1) from Scripture.

XII. Many arguments prove the existence of such a natural law. First, the voice of Scripture asserts that "the Gentiles which have not the law" (to wit, the written law of Moses) as the Jews "do by nature the things contained in the law, and are a law unto themselves: since they show the work of the law written in their hearts, their conscience also bearing witness, and their thoughts the meanwhile accusing or else excusing one another" (Rom. 2:14, 15). And "that which may be known of God" (*to gnōston tou theou*) is said to be manifest in the Gentiles "for God hath shewed it unto them" (Rom. 1:19*). But how could that truth be said to be revealed in the Gentiles (that although they have not the law, still they do the things contained in the law; not by previous doctrine and instruction, but by nature; that they are a law unto themselves and bear the work of the law written in their hearts [to which the conscience bears witness by approbation or accusation in good or evil deeds]) if this depended upon the mere will of man and was not in them by nature itself and indeed impressed and fixed in them by God?

2. From the consent of nations.

XIII. Second, the consent of nations, among whom (even the most savage) some law of the primitive nations obtains, from which even without a teacher they have learned that God should be worshipped, parents honored, a virtuous life be led and from which as a fountain have flowed so many laws concerning equity and virtue enacted by heathen legislators, drawn from nature itself. And if certain laws are found among some repugnant to these principles, they were even with reluctance received and observed by a few, at length abrogated by contrary laws, and have fallen into desuetude.

3. From the conscience of each one.

XIV. Third, the conscience of each one dictating the good to be done and the evil to be shunned; and which, as by observation, it exhibits to us practical principles, as universal rules of things to be avoided and omitted. So by consciousness (*syneidēsin*), it makes an application and test of itself to that rule. Hence arise distresses of conscience which at the sight of sin and the sense of divine judgment, trembles all over and torments the sinner as if by familiar, unremitting furies, and night and day inflicts punishment upon the most abandoned. Thus Cicero speaks, "The wicked are punished, not so much by judgments, as by anguish of conscience and the torment of crime" (*Laws** 1.14.40 [Loeb, 16:340-41]). Now whence these scourgings and terrible avengers, except from the natural law impressed upon man which knows that this is "the judgment of God, that they which commit such things are worthy of death" (Rom. 1:32)? Hence according to Cicero, it is called "the law not written, but born, in which we are not taught but made, not instructed by precepts, but imbued by nature" (*On Behalf of Milo* 10 [Loeb, 16:16-17]). By others it is termed *empsychon dikaion* ("the living right") and *agraphon theou nomimon* ("the unwritten law of God").

4. From God's government over man.

XV. Fourth, the rule and government of God over man; for if the creature as a creature must depend upon the Creator and be governed by him physically, it is even most absurd (*asystaton*) that the rational creature as rational should not be in subjection to him in the genus of morals and not be governed by him suitably to his nature (i.e., by moral means) by the establishment of a law. Hence it follows either that man ought to have been created independent by God (which is absurd) or that he has a natural law impressed upon him, in accordance with which he may be ruled by him.

5. From absurdities.

XVI. Fifth, the various absurdities by which the opposite opinion is pressed. For if nothing is just by nature, but that only which can be made to minister to human advantage, it follows that men are born for themselves and not for the glory of God or for the good of society (of which there is by nature in them an earnest desire), which the wiser heathen themselves acknowledge could not be said. (2) All things would be equally lawful: to hate God as well as to love him; to kill parents as well as to honor them; and each one's own will would be to him for a reason and a law, so that he might do whatever he pleased (whether this does not pave the way to atheism, anyone can readily understand). (3) This moral right and government of God being taken away, all the foundations of right will be removed; all the laws of men which could have flowed from no other source, and thus all government, honesty and order in human society will perish and the world be turned into mere confusion and villainy.

6. From the testimonies of the heathen.

XVII. Sixth, the testimonies of the most illustrious heathen philosophers, who bravely opposed themselves to that impious opinion (such as Plato, Aristotle and the Stoics). Even Cicero sufficiently proves this in his books on the laws. He demonstrates by various weighty arguments "that we are born to justice, and that right is not established by opinion, but by nature" (*Laws* 1.10.28 [Loeb, 16:328-29]); that Socrates deservedly execrated the man who first drew a distinction between utility and nature, for he used to complain that this error was the source of all human vices, since if this were true all justice and piety would be swept from the world. "For if nature does not ratify law," says he, "then all the virtues may lose their sway. For what becomes of generosity, patriotism or friendship? Where will the desire of benefitting our neighbors, or the gratitude that acknowledges kindness, be able to exist at all? For all these virtues proceed from our natural inclination to love mankind. And this is the true basis of justice, and without this not only the mutual charities of men, but the religious services of the gods, would be at an end; for these are preserved, as I imagine, rather by the natural sympathy which subsists between divine and human beings, than by mere fear and timidity" (ibid., 1.15.43, pp. 344-45). Hence in *The Republic* (3.22 [Loeb, 16:210-11]), as quoted by Lactantius, "True law," says he, "is right reason conformable to nature, universal, unchangeable, eternal, whose commands urge us to duty, and whose prohibitions restrain us from evil" (Lactantius, *Divine Institutes* 6.8 [FC 49:412; PL 6.660]). And afterwards: "This law cannot be contradicted by any other law, and is not liable either to derogation or abrogation. Neither the senate nor the people can give us any dispensation for not obeying this universal law of justice. It is not one thing at Rome, and another at Athens; one thing today, and another tomorrow; but in all times and nations this universal law must forever reign, eternal and imperishable. It is the sovereign master and emperor of all beings. God himself is its author, its promulgator, its enforcer. And he who does not obey it flies from himself, and does violence to the very nature of man" (ibid., pp. 412-13; PL 6.660-61).

Sources of solutions.

XVIII. From the cauterization of conscience (1 Tim. 4:2) in the wicked ("who, being past feeling [*apēlgēkotes*] have given themselves to work all uncleanness," Eph. 4:19) can indeed be gathered the suppression of the natural law as to the second act or exercise; but not its extinction and destruction as to the first act or the principle; also insensibility of conscience as to duty, not however as to punishment.

XIX. If various wicked laws obtained among the heathen, repugnant to the natural law (such as those sanctioning idolatry, human sacrifices [*anthrōpothysian*], permitting theft, rapine, homicide, incest), they do not prove that no light of reason was granted to men by nature, as Selden improperly infers (*De Iure Naturali et Gentium* 6, 7 [1640], pp. 75-94). Rather they prove only that men with leisure ill employed have wickedly abused the conceded light and, by struggling against and striving with all their might to extinguish it, were given over to a reprobate mind.

XX. Although various practical notions have been obscured after sin and for a time even obliterated, it does not follow either that they were entirely extinguished or that they never existed at all. For the commonest principle (that good should be done and evil avoided) is unshaken in all, although in the particular conclusions and in the determinations of it good men may often err because vice deceives us under the appearance and shadow of virtue.

XXI. What is natural ought indeed to be universal and to be the same as to foundation and principle, but not always as to the things principiated: as reason and intelligence are indeed natural, but yet do not exist in the same manner and degree in all (since some are more sharp-sighted than others).

How the natural law differs from the moral law given by Moses.

XXII. If it is asked how this natural law agrees with or differs from the moral law, the answer is easy. It agrees as to substance and with regard to principles, but differs as to accidents and with regard to conclusions. The same duties (both toward God and toward our neighbor) prescribed by the moral law are also contained in the natural law. The difference is with regard to the mode of delivery. In the moral law, these duties are clearly, distinctly and fully declared; while in the natural law they are obscurely and imperfectly declared both because many intimations have been lost and obliterated by sin and because it has been variously corrupted by the vanity and wickedness of men (Rom. 1:20-22). Not to mention other differences: as that the natural law was engraven upon the hearts of men, the moral on stony tables; the former pertains to all universally, the latter only to those called by the word; the former contains nothing except morality, the latter has also certain ceremonials mingled with it.

XXIII. Hence is easily gathered the reason why God wished to recall that law by Moses, to deliver it to his people *viva voce*, and proclaimed it in a solemn manner, committing it to writing and comprehending it in the decalogue. For although in upright nature there was no need of such a promulgation, still (after sin) so great was the blindness of mind, such the perversity of will and disturbance of the affections that only remains of this law survived in the hearts of all (like rubbed pictures of the same, which on that account ought to be retouched by the voice and hand of God as by a new brush). Hence there were weighty causes for that promulgation. (1) That the natural law might be confirmed more and more, lest the remaining traces might gradually be obliterated by the vanity and wickedness of men or be considered as their uncertain and doubtful opinions. (2) That it might be corrected in those things in which it had been corrupted by the fall. (3) That it might be supplemented in those things which were wanting in it and had been obliterated. (4) That the necessity of a mediator might be understood and a desire for him be enkindled more strongly every day on account of the weakness of man and of the law in the flesh (Rom. 3:20; 8:3; 10:4). (5) That the people of Israel might be joined by this law into one republic and be separated from all other nations (Dt. 4:6, 7; Ps. 147:19, 20; Rom. 9:4).

Second Question: The Nature of the Moral Law

Are the precepts of the decalogue of natural and indispensable right? We affirm.

I. There can be four questions concerning the moral law. (1) What is its nature? (2) What are its parts? (3) What is its use? (4) What about its abrogation? In reference to its nature, there is a dispute concerning its immutability and perfection. In reference to its parts, there is a dispute concerning the division of the precepts and their genuine sense. In reference to its use, there is a dispute concerning its use either absolute or relative, as to the various states of man (in nature, in sin and in grace). In reference to its abrogation, in what sense may it be said to have been abrogated and in what sense not?

Statement of the question. Whether it is of natural and indispensable right.

II. The first question about the nature of the moral law refers to its indispensability. For the sake of clarity (1) we must premise a distinction of terms often occuring in this argument. Obligation is the right of the law over man on account of which the man who is under law is bound to obey it. Dispensation is when, in any case in which the law really prevails and obliges, the obligation of the law is taken away from some man in particular, the rest remaining under obligation. A declaration or interpretation of law is when it is declared that the law does not bind in a particular case. Irritation is when a law is abolished before it can perfectly bind; abrogation when that is simply abolished and taken away which has already perfectly bound; derogation when it is partly taken away and partly remains.

III. (2) We must distinguish between simple precepts (i.e., merely moral) belonging to natural right and mixed precepts (moral and ceremonial, partly of natural and partly of positive right; as the fourth commandment concerning the Sabbath, which is moral as to the genus of public worship, but ceremonial as to the circumstance of the defined time; and the fifth, which is moral as to the prescribed duty and the promise of longevity, but ceremonial as to the appended promise of the land of Canaan).

The right of dominion and government.

IV. (3) We must observe that the right of God (as far as regards creatures) is either of dominion (which includes the right of possessing, disposing and using creatures, as a lord or proprietor, who is able to use and enjoy his own property at pleasure); or of government (which properly refers to rational creatures whom he governs as ruler and legislator; to whom belong legislation, judgment and execution, so as to have the power of enacting laws, of judging in accordance with them and of carrying out the sentence pronounced). This right is commonly distinguished into natural and positive: the former, according to which he must prescribe to rational creatures their duties (the opposites of which imply a contradiction because they are not founded simply on the divine will, but on the perfection, eminence, holiness and rectitude of the divine nature); the latter, however, according to which he freely and from his mere good-pleasure prescribes such duties as he either was able not to prescribe, or the opposites of which antecedently to the open intimation of the divine will, he might have willed and enjoined without any prejudice to his perfection and holiness, and without embarrassing contradiction.

V. Therefore, whatever things have so close a connection with the nature, perfection, eminence and holiness of God (that he cannot command their opposites without prejudice to his nature and which involve a contradiction as commanded) belong to that natural right. It is certain that God cannot deny himself, or do or command anything contrary to his own holiness and perfection. So God cannot command the hatred of himself, blasphemy and lying; or relieve man from the dependence and obedience due to him because this would be to say that God is not God (i.e., the first cause and absolute Lord). These are what Bradwardine calls "prior reasonables" (*De Causa Dei Contra Pelagium* 1.18 [1618], pp. 220-24), which are such naturally antecedent to the divine will. However, all those things of which it cannot be said that God was not by necessity of nature bound to the other part of the contradiction (or in which we know that God can make or has actually made some change in the obligation) belong to positive right. Such were the symbolical law given to Adam and the ceremonial laws of the Old Testament (which depended on the free will of God). Here also the permission of sin is usually referred.

VI. Besides the uncreated natural divine right (called primary) founded immediately upon the very nature and holiness of God (the contrary of which he could not will nor command without denying himself), another is granted (created and secondary), founded on the nature of things (according to the constitution established by God and the mutual suitableness or fitness of things to each other). On the hypothesis of the order instituted by God (according to which he willed such to be the nature of things), it is necessary. Still it cannot be regarded as of the same necessity with the first, nor do the duties flowing from it have an equal degree of obligation. For the former is immutably absolute; nor is there any case in which God can relax it because thus he would appear to deny his own nature, on which it is based. Hence he never could command or approve hatred of himself, idolatry, perjury and falsehood. But the latter (although containing the natural rule of rectitude, because it supposes a certain state of things) could in certain cases (the circumstances of things and persons being altered) be changed, but only by his authority who established it. For example, murder and stealing (forbidden in the sixth and eighth commandments) could become lawful, some circumstance being changed—for instance, a divine command or public authority being given. In this respect, it can be referred to positive right; not indeed absolutely and simply such and merely free (which has no foundation except in the will of God alone), but relatively, inasmuch as (although based upon the order of things and created nature), it can still admit of a change in accordance with the wisdom of the legislator, who established that order.

VII. From this distinction of the divine right flows the distinction of the precepts (to be held here). For those things that have so close a connection with the nature of God that (the rational and governable creature being posited) he cannot but be bound to do them (such as that he should subject himself to and reverence God; should have him for his one only God; and the like), without controversy belong to natural right. But those which flow from the free good will of God and which he was perfectly free to establish or not establish, ought to be referred to positive right. With regard to this, almost all are agreed. But concerning the particular distinction and enumeration of these and those, all do not equally agree. Some refer those to natural right which others think belong to positive right.

Indispensability with respect to God and ourselves.

VIII. (4) Immutability and indispensability can be understood in two ways: either absolutely and simply with respect to God as well as to us; or comparatively and relatively with respect to us and not to God. Some are absolutely indispensable by God as well as by us; others, however, relatively with respect to us because, since we are not lords or judges, but subjects and accused (*hypodikoi*), we cannot add to or take anything away from the law. Yet this is not the case with respect to God, who, as supreme Lord and lawgiver, could in certain cases dispense with some law given by himself without sin.

IX. The question then returns to this—whether the precepts, not of the ceremonial and forensic law (which are evidently of mutable positive right), but of the moral law (not according to the appendages, but according to substance) are of natural right, whether primary or secondary (not merely positive) and so are necessary (not only hypothetically from the sanction of the divine will, but absolutely on the part of the thing) and incapable of being dispensed with, not only by men but also by God.

Three opinions on the nature of the law.

X. In reference to this question, there are three more celebrated opinions: two extreme, asserting the dispensability or indispensability of the commands; the third (a middle one) maintaining them to be partly dispensable and partly not. The first holds that the moral law in all its precepts is dispensable; it is founded, namely, on positive right alone, which depends upon the free will of God. This law, therefore, he can change at pleasure. This opinion is held: (1) by many of the Scholastics (Occam, in 2 q. 19+; Gerson, "De Vita Spirituali Animae," 1 in *Opera Omnia* [repr. 1987], 3:5-16; Peter of Ailly, in 1. q. 14+; Almayno, *Acutissimi clarissimi . . . Moralia*, Pt. 3.15 [1525], pp. 103-4 and their followers, impelled especially by a rash desire to expunge the second precept from the decalogue and by the power which they claim for their pope of dispensing with the precepts of God); (2) by the Socinians, who insist upon dispensability principally for this reason—that they may prove the imperfection of the Mosaic Law and the necessity of its correction. These are joined by those of our party who maintain that the moral goodness and wickedness of things flows from no other source than the free will of God; so that things are good and just only because they are commanded, not commanded because they were just antecedently. Thus there is nothing to hinder his commanding the contrary to them if he wishes. The second and middle opinion maintains that three precepts of the first table are indispensable; that the fourth, however, is partly dispensable; and that all the others of the second table are dispensable (as Scotus and Gabriel [Biel], who therefore take away those precepts from the natural law strictly so called). To them some of our men approach, who maintain that certain moral precepts of the decalogue which flow absolutely from the nature of God are absolutely indispensable (such as the first, second, third, seventh and ninth), but the others, depending upon the free will of God (as the fourth partly, and the fifth, sixth, eighth and tenth), although immovable and indispensable as to us, still are dispensable as to God (who can for certain reasons command the contrary and yet do nothing repugnant to his own nature). The third is the opinion of those who hold that the moral law as to all its precepts is simply indispensable because it contains the intrinsic reason of justice and duty; not as proceeding from the law, but as founded on the nature of God and arising from the intrinsic constitution of the thing and the proportion between the object and act, compared with right reason or the rational nature. Thomas Aquinas, with his followers (ST, I-II, Q. 100, Art. 8, pp. 1045-46), Altissiodorensis, Richard of Middleton, Peter Paludanus and many others, thinks thus.

XI. This last is the more common opinion of the orthodox. We also follow it with this limitation however—all the precepts are not equally based on the primary right of nature, but some flow absolutely from the nature of God and command such things as God wills most freely indeed but yet necessarily (and so necessarily and immutably that he cannot will the contrary without a contradiction). However, other precepts depend upon the constitution of the nature of things (the free will of God coming in between) so they should not be thought to hold an equal degree of necessity and immutability. Although a dispensation properly so called does not have place in them, still a declaration or interpretation is sometimes given concerning them, the circumstances of the things or persons being changed (as will be seen hereafter).

Indispensability of the precepts is proved: (1) from the necessary dependence of man upon God.

XII. The following reasons establish our opinion. First, there is a necessary and indispensable dependence of the rational creature as such in the genus of morals and in order to right reason, in virtue of which he cannot but be bound to obey God and be in subjection to him (for otherwise he would not be a creature, which is absurd). Therefore, there is in God, naturally and antecedently to his free will, the right of subjecting the rational creature to himself and of binding him to obedience (which he cannot deny, nor can he decree the opposite without a contradiction). Now that such a right belongs to him is evident both from the independence, preeminence, perfection and supreme dominion of God, and the similar attributes which build up such a right. Also from equality because there is a necessary and essential natural dependence of the creature upon God in the genus of being and of the second cause (in virtue of which the creature cannot exist and operate without God, nor can God cast off the care of him and leave him to himself). Therefore, the moral dependence of the rational creature upon God (as the first truth and perfect holiness) is no less necessary and immutable than the natural dependence of each creature.

XIII. Nor is it an objection that God was impelled to the production of the creature by no necessity, but by mere liberty. For although all things out of God are in this sense contingent (i.e., such as he could have abstained from creating); still from the hypothesis, he wills and acts necessarily in and about those things which he wishes to exist, so that he cannot act or will otherwise. The words of Cajetan refer to this: "Although the divine will is simply free, outwardly; still on the exercise of one free act he can be necessitated to another; as if he wills to promise absolutely, he is necessitated to fulfil the promise; if he wills to speak and reveal, he is bound to reveal the truth; if he wills to govern, he must govern justly; if he wills to have subjects using reason, he must be their legislator" (1am. 2ae, q. 100, artic. 8+). So on the hypothesis of the existence and action of the creature, God must necessarily conserve and concur with it, as long as he wills it to be. Thus, the rational creature being made, it was necessary for some law to be established by God, which he is bound to obey. For that the creature should be and not be under God; or be under God and not be governed by him; or be governed without law and a just law, is contradictory.

2. From the nature of the things commanded.

XIV. Second, if all the precepts of the law are dispensable and founded only upon positive right, God was perfectly free to make or not make them; yea, he could even command the contrary without any repugnancy. In those things which are by nature indifferent (*adiaphora*), he who has the right to command has also the right to forbid and so command the opposite. Thus God on this hypothesis could not only give no law to the rational creature about loving and worshipping him, but could also lay down the contrary concerning hating and blaspheming him; not believing any god; or not believing him to be just, good, omnipotent and the like; not obeying him; worshipping strange gods, yea, even the Devil himself. Thus the most horrible sins (hatred of God, atheism, blasphemy and the like) would become praiseworthy for the very reason that they would fall under the precept, their character would be changed and they would no longer be sins. The proposition of such monstrous absurdities is their own sufficient refutation. For who does not see that God cannot do such things without denying himself and doing violence to his own nature? For as he is true and holy, it is repugnant to his nature to command what is false and base. Now if he would command the hatred of himself (or atheism and idolatry), he would command dreadful and most base falsehoods against his own truth and holiness. In vain is the reply that the will of God is the supreme rule of justice and cannot be ruled by anything else. It is one thing for it to be such extrinsically (which we grant), another intrinsically (which we deny, as has been proved in Topic III, Question 18).

3. From the difference between the moral and the ceremonial law.

XV. Third, if all the precepts of the moral law are dispensable, there would be no difference between it and the ceremonial law; nor any greater obligation to obedience or greater sin of transgression in reference to the one than to the other. So he will contract no lesser guilt before God who has eaten swine's flesh or who has touched a corpse, than he who has blasphemed God or committed murder. But that this is by far the most absurd, both the nature and the thing evinces and Scripture itself clearly teaches, when (a comparison being instituted between the sacrifices of the law and the works of piety and mercy, the ceremonial and moral worship) it so often testifies that with God the one is of no value in comparison with the other.

4. From the conformity of the moral law with the eternal law of God.

XVI. Fourth, the moral law (which is the pattern of God's image in man) ought to correspond with the eternal and archetypal law in God, since it is its copy and shadow (*aposkimation*), in which he has manifested his justice and holiness. Hence we cannot conform ouselves to the image of God (to the imitation of which Scripture so often exhorts us) except by regulating our lives in accordance with the precepts of this law. So when its observation is enjoined, the voice is frequently heard, "Be ye holy, for I am holy." Now this law is immutable and perpetual. Therefore the moral law (its ectype) must necessarily also be immutable.

5. From the identity of the moral with the natural law.

XVII. Fifth, the moral law is the same as to substance with the natural, which is immutable and founded upon the rational nature; both because the sum of the law (which is exhausted by the love of God and of our neighbor) is impressed upon man by nature and because all its precepts are derived from the light of nature and nothing is found in them which is not taught by sound reason; nothing which does not pertain to all nations in every age; nothing which it is not necessary for human nature to follow in order to attain its end. Therefore it ought to be of perpetual right because the rational nature is always the same and like itself. Hence what is founded upon it must also be such. If by the sin of man the rational nature was changed in the concrete and subjectively, the law was not forthwith altered in the abstract and objectively.

Sources of solution.

XVIII. The natural law cannot be said to have undergone a change by the division of lands and the ownership of possessions and goods introduced by the law of nations. No natural law commands a community of goods or prohibits their distribution. If all things are said to have been common from the beginning, this is to be understood not so much positively (as if God had enacted a law making all things common) as negatively (because nothing was expressly determined concerning it, since there was as yet no necessity for it). Afterwards a distinction and ownership of goods was justly introduced with the authority of God, to prevent controversies, to restrain external violence and to afford certainty to inheritances and make a distinction in conditions (without which human society could not exist).

XIX. Nor by the introduction of slavery; while before, by the primeval law, all were free. They were not otherwise free than inasmuch as they were free from criminality. When this entered, slavery passed upon all. For he who assails another's liberty deservedly loses his own. Nor if the law of nature makes all men equal with regard to nature does it follow that they are equal with regard to qualities and external condition. Nor by prescription and usucapion by which one obtains dominion over another's property, if the owner has not demanded it within a certain space of time. They do not give the right to another's property if the owner is unwilling (which is repugnant to natural equity). They only concede that what belonged to another before, when it is considered as abandoned by the former owner, may become the property of another. Although the master of the deposited right may not have expressly by pact or donation transferred it to the depositary, still he may be considered as having made it over by implication because he neglected and deserted it. Nor by the retention of a sword which the infuriated owner claims in order to perpetrate homicide; for it is not retained in order that its ownership may be wrested from the lawful owner and for the sake of gain, but to prevent homicide, which each one is bound by natural right to hinder as far as he can (because he who does not prevent an evil deed when he can is just as guilty as the doer). Besides it is not equitable that he should be master of his own property who is not master of himself.

XX. God did not dispense with the second commandment when he ordered the cherubim above the mercy seat and the brazen serpent to be made. These figures were not personal religious images, representing some subsisting substance (since there was no similarity of nature between the cherubim and angels, between the brazen serpent and Christ); rather they were only symbolic and emblematic, to adumbrate duty and qualities. They were not to be regarded as the object and means of worship (in which sense images are prohibited), but to be regarded only as a sacred sign which God employed to shadow forth certain mysteries to us. Therefore although they pertained to religion, they were not on that account the objects of religion or of worship. The same can be said of the brazen serpent, which was indeed a symbol or type of Christ, but not an image.

XXI. The fourth commandment is moral and perpetual as to the substance of the thing commanded (to wit, that some solemn external worship is due to God and that a certain time should be devoted to it; not as to the particular determination of the seventh day [a matter of positive right], which moreover as ceremonial could be changed, as will be shown more at length in its proper place). If the Maccabees fought on the Sabbath, this was not done by a dispensation from the law, but in virtue of its declaration and true interpretation (according to which arbitrary works are indeed prohibited, but not necessary works, such as the lawful defense of one's self against enemies, which Christ himself often confirms). "What man," says he, "shall there be among you, that shall have one sheep, and if it fall into a pit on the sabbath day, will he not lay hold on it, and lift it out?" (Mt. 12:11). "The sabbath was made for man, and not man for the sabbath" (Mk. 2:27*). Hence he healed a man on the Sabbath, and the disciples of Christ, being hungry, plucked ears of corn on the Sabbath.

XXII. When Christ commands us to "hate" parents (Lk. 14:26), he does not dispense with the fifth commandment, but unfolds its true sense and points out both the subordination of the second table to the first and man to God. Thus the word *to misein* is not to be understood absolutely and simply for hatred properly so called and expressed, but comparatively for a lesser and diminished love, to teach us that no necessities should have such power over us as to seduce us from the duty of piety; that God must be loved and worshipped above all; so that if the love of parents is incompatible (*asystatos*) with the love of God, we should be ready to relinquish parents rather than deny God and know that it is always better to obey God rather than men. Thus "to hate" is often used for "to love less" (as Jacob is said to have "hated Leah" [i.e., loved her less, Gen. 29:31, 33]); for we must not consider Jacob to have been so cruel as to have hated her. That it is to be so understood in this place is evident from a comparison with Mt. 10:37 where it is explained by "to love less": "He that loveth father or mother more than me, is not worthy of me."

XXIII. The sixth commandment, about homicide, was not dispensed with when Abraham was ordered to kill his own son. The command was only exploratory, not absolute. Neither if he had killed him by God's command would he have violated the law concerning homicide because he would have done it empowered by a public authority (to wit, the command of God). However, the law does not condemn homicide of every kind. For the magistrate is bound to punish the guilty, and every private person has the right to kill an unjust aggressor and robber for the sake of preserving life (a moderate use being made of the lawful right of protection); only homicide committed by a private person unjustly and without authority is condemned. Moses' act cannot be considered a homicide against the law because God had approved of it by a dispensation (Ex. 2:12). Moses was a public person, having already an internal call. The same may be said of Phineas, who was furnished with public authority and had an internal, if not an external, call to do it. The self-murder (*autocheiria*) of Samson was not simply against the law, because it was not done by a private impulse only (which is condemned), but by a peculiar instinct and inspiration of him who has an absolute right over life and property (and so can claim our lives or another's whenever he pleases). That such was the case here is proved: (1) by the prayers (which were heard) which he addressed to God for obtaining extraordinary strength for that last act; thus they proceeded from faith. (2) By that divine strength supplied to him, furnished with which he overturned so prodigious an edifice. Hence Augustine properly remarks that the Spirit (who wrought a miracle by him) had secretly commanded this (CG 1.21 [FC 8:54; PL 41.35]). (3) By the testimony of the apostle who among the examples of faith instances Samson (Heb. 11:32), which surely he would not have done if in this act he had sinned and violated the law.

XXIV. When he bids "whosoever shall smite thee on thy right cheek, turn to him the other also; and if any man take away thy coat, let him have thy cloak also" (Mt. 5:39, 40*), Christ does not change the implanted law of nature, which teaches us to repel injury and force by force. Rather he only condemns retaliation (*to antipeponthos*) when to the defense of one's self is added revenge and an equal or greater injury. These words must be understood proverbially and hyperbolically, not according to the letter (*kata to rhēton*); for Christ himself did not turn the other cheek to the one smiting him (Jn. 18:23), nor did Paul (Acts 23:3). The meaning then is that it is better to be ready to suffer new injury, than to return an equal injury or recompense evil for evil; and that too under the pretext of a divine law concerning retaliation. Thus the adversative (as often elsewhere) includes under it a comparison.

XXV. God did not command Hosea to commit whoredom contrary to the law (Hos. 1:2), but commanded him to take a wife of whoredoms. That this is to be understood parabolically rather than historically is testified by the rule of Augustine, who holds that Scripture is to be understood figuratively as often as it either commands a vice or prohibits a virtue, and by the scope of the prophets, which was to rebuke the people for their spiritual fornication. This he could not have done if he had enjoined such things upon them. Finally, the words themselves prove it: "take unto thee a wife of whoredoms and children of whoredoms." The same children could not have been taken with the mother and have been begotten of her. Therefore, the sense is—take unto thee a whore in place of an argument, propose it to the people of Israel and apply this simile of the wife of whoredoms to the Israelites for they are devoted to spiritual fornication (viz., idolatry). If the names of the wife and her father are mentioned by the prophet, it is not to be considered a true history because it is evident from the parable of Lazarus that this was not universal. Besides, for the sake of argument, suppose these things did occur historically, still it would not follow that the prophet was commanded to commit whoredom. The latter is one thing; it is quite another to marry a whore. However there is nothing to hinder the execution (as well as the command) from being emblematic.

XXVI. Simultaneous polygamy is repugnant to the primeval institution of marriage (in which God created one man and one woman that two, not more, might be in one flesh). This is also confirmed by Christ while rebuking the facility of gaining divorces. He says "from the beginning it was not so" (Mt. 19:8). It is also confirmed by the testimony of the wiser heathen, among whom it was considered infamous for a man to have two wives at the same time. Whatever Ochino may say in its defense (*A Dialogue of Polygamy* [1657]), it is undoubtedly unlawful in itself and opposed to natural law. All do not agree as to what should be thought of the patriarchs who were polygamists. Some hold that they had a special dispensation and moral permission from God according to which he remitted for them the law which he had enacted from the beginning in order that the promise concerning the multiplying of the seed of Abraham might be more speedily fulfilled. Otherwise it can hardly be conceived how so many and such men would so frequently and so perseveringly have entered upon a manner of life displeasing to God and sought the blessing of offspring in that which perverted the rules of natural and divine right. And they think they can decide more easily by this—that polygamy is itself certainly contrary to natural law (second in rank) and respectable nature (which the change of events and circumstances of persons may lawfully alter occasionally), but not contrary to law (first in rank) that is absolutely indispensable. But because such a dispensation cannot be proved from Scripture and rests only upon probable reasons, others think it better to acknowledge only a tolerance here and a physical permission of deed; not a moral permission of right, according to which he neither simply approved, nor absolutely and formally permitted it as lawful. Rather he only winked at and tolerated it as a weakness and fault for his own reasons. Hence it might be lawful in the court of earth (so as to obtain immunity from civil and ecclesiastical punishments among men), but not in the court of heaven before God.

XXVII. Although the Scriptures do not censure polygamy in the patriarchs, it does not follow that it was lawful. For various other things are also related in

Scripture (and are not blamed) which cannot be separated from sin: as the incest of Lot, the suicide (*autocheiria*) of Saul, and the like. But that it was not approved by God can be gathered *a posteriori* from the dire calamities with which he castigated polygamists for their conduct. We know the domestic cross imposed upon Abraham on this account; the quarrels and strivings of Jacob's wives; what David suffered from the crimes of his children (the issue of polygamy); and how dear was its cost to Solomon.

XXVIII. Although the patriarchs had not known that they sinned through polygamy, still this does not hinder their having sinned from ignorance. They supposed that to be lawful for all which everywhere prevailed; the evil habit (which had grown strong in them) obscuring or obliterating the memory of the primeval institution, so that they did not recognize it to be a sin. Nor does it follow that they were dead in the guilt of that sin of ignorance, because they never repented of it. If they did not expressly and formally repent of it, yet they sought its pardon implicitly when they sought the pardon of all sins (even of secret sins). Nor was a special repentance to be exacted of them for this act more than for the other acts of which we do not read that they repented. Otherwise we do not read that Noah repented of his drunkenness; or Lot of incest; or others for other sins. Still we do not doubt that they obtained the pardon of all their sins from God through faith in the Messiah. If many pious persons commit numerous sins out of ignorance and error (of which they never distinctly repent), this does not prevent their seeking and obtaining the pardon of them—saying with David, "cleanse thou me from secret faults" (Ps. 19:12). Why may we not say the same of the ancient polygamists?

XXIX. As to divorce, God neither simply commanded nor permitted it, but only wished to restrain by fixed laws the facility of divorces which prevailed among the Jews against the natural law of marriage, so as to regulate the mode of an unlawful thing, not however to make it lawful. Hence Christ says that God "permitted" or "tolerated" it "because of the hardness of heart of the Jews" (Mt. 19:8).

XXX. If marriages within the prohibited degrees did take place among the children of Adam (between brothers and sisters in the beginning, necessity so demanding), this was done not so much by a dispensation (properly so called) of the law as by its declaration. Most of the Jewish teachers have recourse here to the indulgence of God as if God had indulged those first human beings in this, although they were corrupt. But an indulgence inconsistent with natural right and virtue cannot have place because God never indulges in doing evil. Others (as Augustine) allege necessity here: "since there were none except those born of these two, the men took their sisters to wife, which by as much as it is the more ancient, necessity compelling, by so much did it afterwards become the more worthy of condemnation, religion forbidding" (CG 15*.16 [FC 14:450-51; PL 41.457-58]). Yet neither is this fully satisfactory. God himself was the cause of that necessity, who might easily have altered this state of things by creating more pairs that men might not be reduced to the necessity of violating the natural right. Others get rid of the difficulty better by making a distinction between the primary and absolute natural right (based immediately upon the very nature of God); and the secondary natural right (founded on the nature of things and having place only in a certain state of things, as the law forbidding theft supposes a division of things). Such marriages are indeed repugnant to the posterior natural right in a certain state of things (or constituted nature) after the multiplication of the human race and are unlawful by nature, on account of the reverence for blood. In sister and brother (who are the flesh and image of the parent), the parent is himself to be reverenced; also natural modesty forbids it. Hence the Gentiles themselves call such marriages "by no means holy and hated by God" (*mēdamōs hosia kai theomisē*, Plato, *Laws* 8.838 [Loeb, 11:156-57]). Diodorus Siculus says that it is "the common custom of men (*koinon ethos anthrōpōn*) not to join brothers with sisters" (Diodorus Siculus, 1.27 [Loeb, 1:84-85]). For the daily dwelling and eating together would never exist without a suspicion of illicit amours and would give occasion to lusts and adulteries, if such marriages were to be allowed. However they were not repugnant to the primary and absolute natural right. Otherwise God (who does not deny himself) could never dispense with it; nor could he ever (not even in the beginning of the world) have either instituted or approved such a connection. Therefore as the constitution of things depends upon the will of God, he could in certain cases (if not absolutely, yet relatively and in a certain state of things) change it, so far forth as he knew it to conduce to the preservation of human society. Because he willed that all should be born of one blood, such a conjunction was necessary then in nature about to be constituted. Now although the union of parents with children never can be lawful, it is not the case with the marriage of brothers with sisters. The reverence of children towards their parents is absolute and intrinsic and can never be removed. That of sisters towards brothers is only extrinsic and relative, inasmuch as they are only the image of their parents. Thus there is nothing to hinder this respect from being restrained by God, in order that it may not clearly manifest itself in this or that person whom she is to marry.

XXXI. The same must be said of the law of the Levirate (Dt. 25:5) by which the brother of the deceased was bound to take the wife of his brother in order to raise up seed for him. If it is understood of the husband's brother properly so called (or of the full brother, as the Jews evidently understood it, Mt. 22:24, 25), it was undoubtedly a peculiar case in which God wished to favor the preservation of the tribes and families of his people. The whole difficulty will be removed if it is extended wider to the nearest kinsman outside of the prohibited degrees, as not a few learned men without improbability maintain, especially Calvin (*Commentaries on the Four Last Books of Moses, Arranged in the Form of a Harmony* [ed. C.W. Bingham, 1854], 3:103-4, on Lev. 18:16). Nor does the word *ybmh* stand in the way. It signifies either a blood relation both on the father's and mother's side or a marriage relation (such as Boaz was to Ruth, the Moabitess, Ruth 3:9).

XXXII. A dispensation was not made of the law of theft by the Israelites bearing away the vessels of the Egyptians: (1) because the Egyptians willingly granted those vessels, "for the Lord gave the people favor in the sight of the Egyptians, so that they lent unto them such things as they required. And they spoiled the Egyptians" (Ex. 12:36*). Nor did they demand them from them as they departed; nay, they drove them out with their vessels "while they were urgent upon the people, that they might send them out of the land in haste" (Ex. 12:33). So the Israelites cannot be said absolutely to have taken the property of others without their consent. (2) God, as supreme Lord (yea, as a just judge), justly transferred the goods of the Egyptians to the Israelites as the wages of their former services and of that severe bondage with which the Egyptians oppressed them (free by nature); even as a judge permits the creditor to take pledges in the house of the debtor or puts him into the possession of his property. Now that cannot be called theft which is done by the authority of a judge. (3) Nor assuredly can the Egyptians themselves be considered the lawful owners in the court of heaven with God, but only usurpers (as also other wicked men, although in the forum of earth and with men they are esteemed such). Now although the Israelites did not return what they had borrowed, they cannot on that account be called thieves because they might have had the intention to restore the property, if God had commanded them.

XXXIII. Although it was not lawful to move a sickle into a neighbor's standing corn, still the liberty was formerly lawfully granted to a passing traveller, either to pluck ears of corn from the field or grapes from a vineyard for the sake of satisfying hunger (Dt. 23:24, 25*). This was done not by dispensing with the law of theft, but by its true interpretation for it was a work of necessity, permitted by the supreme Lord for the purpose of binding men more closely in the bonds of love. If these acts have any indecency in themselves, they cease to be such when the divine command (or instinct or vocation) intervenes, imposing such a necessity or conceding liberty.

XXXIV. Though men can dispense with their own laws, this is not so with God and the moral law. Human laws are positive, binding only on the part of the legislator, not on the part of the thing. On the contrary, the moral law is of natural right, binding in itself and on the part of the thing.

THIRD QUESTION: THE PERFECTION OF THE MORAL LAW

Is the moral law so perfect a rule of life and morals that nothing can be added to it or ought to be corrected in it for the true worship of God? Or did Christ fulfill it not only as imperfect, but also correct it as contrary to his doctrines? The former we affirm; the latter we deny against the Socinians, Anabaptists, Remonstrants and papists.

Opinion of the Socinians, Anabaptists and Remonstrants.

I. In this question we have to deal with various parties. First, with the Socinians, who maintain that the commands of Christ differ from those of Moses and that Christ supplemented and increased the moral law (as imperfect) by various additions and corrected it as less right in certain particulars. Hence they hold that various corrections and additions to the law were made by Christ in reference to particular precepts of the decalogue (by which they are made perfect). For example, with regard to the first, a certain form of prayer defined in the Lord's prayer and the religious worship of Christ, as the Mediator; with respect to the second, the avoidance of idols or images; with regard to the third, the prohibition of oaths even in true affairs; with regard to the fourth, the abrogation of the Sabbath, as far as the substitution of another day is concerned; with regard to the fifth and the second table in general, the love of our enemies; with regard to the sixth, the prohibition of anger and revenge, whether private or public; with regard to the seventh, the prohibition of unchaste looks, of divorce except in case of adultery, of impurity and obscenity; with regard to the eighth, the prohibition of avarice, and the giving of superfluous wealth to the poor; with regard to the ninth, the prohibition of vain and trifling conversation, unjust censures; with regard to the tenth, the prohibition of lust, not only that we should not delight in it, but not even conceive it in our minds. With respect to new commandments, they pretend these were given by Christ in addition to the decalogue, the principal of which are three: (1) the denial of ourselves; (2) the bearing of the cross for Christ's sake; (3) the imitation of him (cf. concerning these "Of the Prophetic Office of Christ: Precepts Added to the Law," 5.1, 2 in *The Racovian Catechism* [1818], pp. 173-249; Ostorodt, *Unterrichtung . . . hauptpuncten der Christlichen Religion* 22 [1612], pp. 149-52; Volkelius, *De vera Religione* 4.21 [1630], pp. 298-301). Their object is: (1) to establish the impious dogma of Christ as Savior not by ransom (*lytron*), but by doctrine; (2) to build up the justification of men by works, not indeed by the merit of works (in which they differ from the papists), but by the gracious acceptation of them; (3) to prove that the reward of the soul's immortality did not exist under the Old Testament economy, but was delivered by Christ. Second, the Anabaptists and Remonstrants follow them. The former in the Frankenthal Colloquy (*Protocoll . . . alle Handlung des gesprechs zu Franckenthal . . . J. Mayer*, Art. I, 10, 11 [1571], pp. 14-15) and Embden Colloquy (*Protocol . . . handelinge des gesprecks tot Embden . . .* G. Goebens, Art. 4 [1579], pp. 50-127); the latter in their apology ("Apologia pro confessione sive declaratione," 12 in Episcopius, *Operum Theologicorum* [1656], Pt. II, pp. 178-81). Here they approve the Socinian thesis concerning the imperfection of the law and on that hypothesis make and defend various additions. In chapter 13, they treat at large of the three precepts added by Christ, especially the first (ibid., pp. 181-82).

Of papists.

II. The Manichaeans had played the same game before, between whom and the orthodox the same question was agitated. Thus Augustine says they taught that Christ partly supplemented the moral law by the commands in Mt. 5, partly destroyed it (*Reply to Faustus Manichaean* 19 [NPNF1, 4:239-52]). This is refuted by Augustine throughout that book. From their muddy pools the Mohammedans seem to have derived that expression in the Koran: Moses introduced a less perfect law, Christ a more perfect, but Mohammed a most perfect (Azoa 12+). The papists err here also (not for the same reason), asserting the imperfection of the law. Hence Bellarmine teaches that Christ made the imperfect law perfect (or certainly the perfect law more perfect) and that between the law and the gospel there is the same difference as between an inchoate and perfect doctrine ("De Justificatione," 4.3 *Opera* [1858], 4:572-74). Maldonatus obstinately contends that the old law was corrected by Christ, those things being added which were wanting for gospel perfection (*Commentary on the Holy Gospels: Matthew* [1888], 1:154 on Mt. 5:21). Against all these, the orthodox however think the moral law so perfect as to need no addition or correction, but only a genuine interpretation, and whatever is said to have been added is either false and gratuitous, or contained before in the law, either explicitly or implicitly.

Statement of the question.

III. The subject in controversy is not whether the law needed illustration, confirmation and vindication against the corruptions of the scribes and Pharisees, and the perverse judgments of men (for this we readily grant and will demonstrate in what follows). Rather it is whether it had need of additions or corrections, as if imperfect or incorrect. Our opponents affirm, while we deny. The importance of the question is great because the object of our opponents is no other than to transform the gospel into a new law, and so to establish the righteousness of works in the place of the righteousness of faith.

The perfection of the law is proved.

IV. The arguments of the orthodox are: First, "the law is perfect" (Ps. 19:7), not only relatively and with regard to its age under the Old Testament, but also absolutely with regard to nature; and so perfect as not only to contain all things to be done, and there is no defect in these (Genebrardus, *Psalmi Davidis* [1606], p. 71 on Ps. 18 [19]:9, and Lorinus testifying on this passage), but also to be capable of no addition to or detraction from it (according to Dt. 4:2; 12:32). (2) It is perfect extensively as to parts because it adequately embraces in the love of God and our neighbor all that is due to them (as Christ teaches in Mt. 22:37); intensively as to degrees because it demands not any, but the most perfect love and a greater than which cannot be conceived; and finally as to perfect use and effect because it can grant to its observers life and happiness—"If a man do these things, he shall live in them" (Lev. 18:5). This could not be said if they needed either addition or correction.

V. Second, Christ "came not to destroy but to fulfil the law" (Mt. 5:17). Here *plērōsai* does not mean to make the imperfect perfect or to correct the faulty (which would rather be to destroy [*analysai*] it), but according to Hebrew usage to do what is commanded. Thus Christ fulfilled the law not by addition or correction, but by observation and execution. He fulfilled the law in three ways: either as a doctrine by faithful preaching, solid confirmation and powerful vindication; or as a rule (*normam*) by a full and consistent keeping of it; or as a type by a perfect consummation, by exhibiting in himself the truth of the types and prophecies and the body of its shadows.

VI. Third, Christ in the New Testament did not introduce (either by himself or by his apostles) any other precepts of the law than those which had been given by Moses (Mt. 22:37; Rom. 13:9). He gave no other explanation of them than had been given before by the prophets. Hence the commandment of love is called by John "old and new" (1 Jn. 2:7, 8): old with regard to its first promulgation in the Old Testament; new with regard to its renovation and illustration in the New.

VII. Fourth, the law could not be supplemented or corrected without convicting it of imperfection and faultiness (and so charging that faultiness upon God, the author of the law). Even the thought of this is impious.

VIII. Fifth, the "denial of ourselves," "bearing the cross" and "imitation of Christ" were already commanded under the Old Testament. For when we are entreated to love God above all things are we not by that very command charged to deny ourselves for God's sake and to patiently bear the cross imposed upon us by him? And when the imitation of God is so frequently prescribed, is not the imitation of Christ (who is true God) also commanded by it? Besides, the imitation of Christ lies in the practice of the moral virtues, the rule for which is to be sought only in the law. This is also confirmed by various examples in the Old Testament: as to denial—by Abraham leaving his country and getting ready to sacrifice his son; the Levites slaying their brothers (Ex. 32); Job blessing God in adversity (Job 1:21, 22); Moses, Daniel and his friends disdaining all pleasures (Heb. 11:25, 26; Dan. 1:8ff.). Note also the following: as to "bearing the cross"—by Moses (Heb. 11:25, 26), the prophets under Ahab (1 K. 18:4), Zechariah (2 Chron.

24:20-21), the friends of Daniel (Dan. 3), the Jewish church under Antiochus (Ps. 44; Heb. 11:33-38). As to the "imitation of Christ," by believers conducting themselves after the example of God.

Sources of solution.

IX. It is one thing to correct the law itself; another to clear it of the false interpretation of the scribes and Pharisees. One thing to introduce an entirely new sense into the law; another to introduce only a new light by unfolding what lay concealed in the law and was not attended to by teachers (and so by explaining, to declare; and by vindicating, to restore). Christ did the latter, not the former (Mt. 5). He does not act as a new lawgiver, but only as an interpreter and vindicator of the law given by Moses. He opposes his sayings not to the sayings or writings of Moses, but to those of the scribes and Pharisees (which they boasted of having received from ancient teachers). This is clear: (1) from the proposition of Christ where he speaks of the righteousness of the Pharisees—"except your righteousness shall exceed the righteousness of the scribes and Pharisees" (Mt. 5:20). Therefore his intention was to set aside the righteousness of the Pharisees and not that enjoined by the law of Moses. (2) From the manner of speaking he does not say, "It is written in the law of Moses"; or "the law or Moses has said to you," but "ye have heard" (viz., from the scribes or Pharisees) "that it was said in old times" or "by them of old time." And thus he shows that he discards only the traditions of the elders (Mt. 15:2, 3) and not the law of Moses. (3) From the example adduced concerning the love of neighbors (Mt. 5:43) and the hatred of our enemies, which was not said by Moses, who commands even the opposite (Lev. 19:18; Ex. 23:4, 5), and Solomon after him (Prov. 25:21, 22), but by the Jewish teachers and elders of the Pharisees. (4) From the things themselves either commanded or forbidden by Christ (which we will hereafter prove were contained either explicitly or implicitly in the law); and from others which he rejects, which were not in the law (as will appear from what follows).

X. In whatever way the words *errethē tois archaiois* are understood—either subjectively to mean the same as *hypo tōn archaiōn* ("said by them of old time") as our Beza holds (*Annotationes maiores in Novum . . . Testamentum* [1594], Pars Prior, p. 31 on Mt. 5:21) and after him Piscator; or objectively, which pleases others following Syrus (*?Saint Ephrem Commentaire de l'Evangile Concordant* [trans. L. Leloir, 1954], CSCO 145:55-57) and seems more suitable, to mean *pros tous archaious* ("said to the men of old time"), it does not follow that they were said by Moses to the ancient Israelites of his day. For that word refers promiscuously to all ancestors and the meaning of our Lord is no other than that the Jewish teachers (corrupters of the law) were accustomed to preface the precepts corrupted by them with this specious phrase, "it was said in old times" (i.e., the precepts inculcated by them were not new, but old and long ago delivered by the elders of the Jews). Therefore the antithesis instituted by Christ is not between himself and Moses (or the law delivered by him), but the glosses of the Pharisees upon the law of Moses by which they restricted it too much and falsely interpreted it. He does this in order to show that the letter and the meaning of the law had been violated by them and not by him (although he was charged with it by his enemies).

Mt. 5:21, 27, 31, 33, 38.

XI. Although Christ cites the words of Moses (Mt. 5:21, 27, 31, 33, 38), yet not in the Mosaic but Pharasaical sense. The words indeed were common, but the meaning was different. The Pharisees most erroneously explained the words of Moses by restricting them to external acts alone, whereas they extend to internal motions also (which Christ teaches by unfolding the true and genuine sense of the law). Christ therefore corrects various things expressed in the law, but not reduplicatively (as there expressed). Rather he corrects as they were usually explained by the scribes and Pharisees (not according to the meaning of Moses, but according to their own private opinion [*pareisaktō*]; not implanted [*emphytō*] and genuine [*gnēsiō*], but spurious [*hypobolimaiō*]).

Mt. 5:33, 34.

XII. The law is not corrected by Christ in reference to the third command about oaths (Mt. 5:33, 34). He only explains and vindicates it against the corruptions of the Pharisees, who restricted the general prohibition of "taking the name of God in vain" to the perjury of him who swore in the name of God. They gave loose rein to trivial and rash oaths in daily conversation and also to oaths by creatures, as if sin was not committed against the law or the lawgiver by swearing rashly and lightly (or even falsely, provided it was not in the name of God, but in the name of some creature), but by perjury alone and in not fulfilling or not performing the oaths. Indeed he was bound who had sworn by the name of God or by a gift consecrated to God, but not he who had sworn by a temple, altar and the like (Mt. 23:16-18). Such oaths could be made and violated with impunity. Christ refutes these false glosses, showing that neither vain and rash oaths are lawful, nor those which are taken by any creatures whatsoever. In this way, he adds to and corrects nothing in the law. For the law does not prohibit only perjury, but also light and rash oaths, when it forbids the taking of the name of God *lshv'* ("in vain"). The Socinians (and Grotius shouldering them) falsely confound this term with *lshqr* ("in a falsehood" or "lie"—concerning which Lev. 19:12 treats), as if perjury alone was condemned. But it has a far wider reference and is rightly extended to the vanity and levity of rash oaths. Hence the Septuagint renders it by *epi mataiō;* and Aquila by *eis eikē;* the Targum by *lmgn'*, the same as the Hebrew *chnm* ("gratuitously" and without cause). Although the name of God is taken in vain by perjury, still it can often be taken in vain without perjury (viz., in rash and trivial oaths).

XIII. Oaths also by creatures are sufficiently prohibited by the law in the Old Testament, both implicitly (by referring the oath to God alone as an act of worship [*latreias*] due solely to him—"thou shalt fear the Lord thy God, and serve him, and thou shalt swear by his name," Dt. 6:13; 10:20; cf. Is. 65:16) and explicitly (by condemning oaths taken by those who are not gods—"they have sworn by them that are no gods," Jer. 5:7). The nature of the oath also proves this. It is the formal calling upon God as a witness, whether explicitly or implicitly. The conditions required in the object are omniscience, omnipresence and omnipotence (which fall upon no creature). Nor do examples stand in the way, if there are any such oaths in the New Testament. They are of deed, not of right; of practice, not of law (which was nowhere given for taking an oath by creatures).

XIV. What Christ adds, *hōlōs* ("swear not at all" and is confirmed by Jam. 5:12), cannot be understood absolutely and universally of every oath, as if we should not simply swear, which would be repugnant both to the nature of the thing (which is good in itself and necessary and as such commanded for the confirmation of the truth and the end of all controversy, Heb. 6:16) and to the practice of Christ himself and the apostles, who sometimes used oaths. Rather it must be understood relatively—concerning rash and light oaths or those conceived by creatures (of which he was speaking in this place). The added explanation clearly teaches this. He says, "swear not at all; neither by heaven, nor by the earth" (i.e., that no perverse formulas of such an oath in use among the Jews were to be employed). James condemns these by a general reference when he adds, "neither by any other oath" (5:12). Otherwise if he had intended to proscribe all oaths entirely, he ought to have added "neither by God." Therefore the universal particle is falsely separated from the species of oath added (or is referred to the genus and substance of the oath), not to the form of it expressed by Matthew. Nor do the words added by Christ, "let your communication be, yea, yea; nay, nay" prove the contrary. Christ does not speak absolutely and universally of all conversation; or of extraordinary practice; or of cases of necessity, when the conscience is to be cleared, a neighbor to be assisted and the glory of God to be promoted. He speaks of the ordinary habit and practice in lighter cases and of familiar conversation in which a simple affirmation or denial and "yea, yea; nay, nay" (*to nai nai, ou ou*) ought to be sufficient. Here three things are commended: (1) simplicity of speech, in opposition to the habit of swearing; (2) truthfulness, as opposed to falsehood and equivocation; (3) constancy and fidelity, as opposed to fickleness and inconstancy. As to "whatsoever is more than these" (*to perisson*) said to be "of evil" (*ek tou ponērou*), it cannot be extended to the necessary and just additions in weightier oaths and pertaining to the glory of God, or the salvation of a neighbor, or our own, permitted and enjoined by God, but must be referred only to superfluous, unnecessary additions at variance with that simplicity and truthfulness of words, occurring in light and rash oaths.

XV. The sixth command about homicide is not corrected but vindicated in Mt. 5:21. The Pharisees explained it only of external homicide, punishing it capitally. Christ, however, extends it to the internal motions of wrath and to insulting speech, imposing upon them eternal punishments indeed, but diverse as to degree, in allusion to the different degrees of capital punishments inflicted by the Jews (concerning which see Topic IX, Question 4, Section 17). Thus Christ teaches that the sixth commandment is improperly restricted in the Pharasaic school to actual slaughter because this alone was capitally punished among men, while it is extended also in the court of God (in which we must render account not only of deeds, but also of words and thoughts) to those things which otherwise are removed from the punishments usually inflicted by men.

XVI. Although Christ quotes the words of the law concerning retaliation (occurring in Ex. 21:24: "an eye for an eye, and a tooth for a tooth") and opposes to them his own opinion ("resist not evil," Mt. 5:39), he does not on that account correct them, as if he meant to abolish simply all vengeance. For he himself as God ordained the magistrate and armed him with the sword for a terror and punishment of evildoers (Rom. 13:3). He himself, when smitten on the cheek, did not offer the other, but resisted evil by asserting his own innocence and rebuking the injustice of his adversaries (Jn. 18:23), which Paul also imitates (Acts 23:3). Rather he only refutes the gloss of the Pharisees who transferred to private revenge what had been sanctioned by the law of Moses in reference to the public vengeance of the magistrate. Christ wishes his followers to act far differently, so that they ought to prefer their injuries to be doubled than to avenge them themselves. Moses had already taught this: "Thou shalt not avenge, nor bear any grudge against the children of thy people, but thou shalt love thy neighbor as thyself" (Lev. 19:18), undoubtedly because (as he elsewhere says) "To the Lord belongeth vengeance, and recompense" (Dt. 32:35). The law of retaliation can still, however, have a place in its own sense; not precisely and formally, but with regard to moral estimation.

XVII. The words of Christ about "turning the other cheek to one smiting, and relinquishing the cloak to one suing" (Mt. 5:39, 40) are not to be understood so much positively as if the cheek should be actually presented and the cloak let go (which neither Christ himself nor Paul observed when smitten) as negatively (i.e., concerning the not resisting and avenging ourselves by a private, irregular and unnecessary resistance); not literally and according to what is spoken (*kata to rhēton*), but figuratively and hyperbolically according to the sense (*kata to noēton*) concerning enduring another injury rather than avenging the former. So that we must attend here not to the words, but to the sense and scope; not to the species of the command, but to the genus concerning patience (*peri tēs hypomonēs*) and forbearance (*anexikakias*). Therefore culpable resistance, arising from revenge, is forbidden here, but not that of lawful defense and unblamable protection.

XVIII. Christ did not correct the seventh commandment about adultery, when he extended it to desire and looks (Mt. 5:28), but unfolds the true sense of the law. As spiritual, it regards not only external but also internal motions, so that the last commandment concerning covetousness also proves this (against the Pharisees, who restricted this law to the external act alone of fornication).

XIX. The command of Christ concerning the "not putting away of a wife, saving for the cause of fornication" agrees with the law of Moses. In Dt. 24:1, the uncleanness (*aschēmon pragma*) can be best referred to this and with the first institution related by Christ (Mt. 19:4, 5). Nor are the words "writing of divorcement" used by Christ in the sense which they have in the law, but as explained by the Pharisees. (1) The Pharisees usually spoke categorically and imperatively, "give her a writing of divorcement" (*Dotō autē apostasin*), whereas the words of Moses are hypothetical: "when a man hath taken a wife . . . then let him write her a bill of divorcement, and give it in her hand, and send her out of his house" (Dt. 24:1). (2) Moses has a restriction in his permission of divorce "on account of some uncleanness" (*'rvth dbhr*). But the Pharisees are without any limitation: "whosoever shall put away his wife, let him give her a writing of divorcement" (as if the putting away of a wife in any manner did not at all conflict with the law, provided the formula of dismission was observed and the husband, by the usual writing, ordered her to take her own things and go about her business). (3) The Pharisees also falsely wrested the words of Moses to an approval of divorce, since there was only a toleration and permission. This did not of itself institute it, but only set bounds to it incidentally on account of the hardness of heart of the Jews (Mt. 19:7, 8). Hence Christ in place of *tou eneteilato* (which the Pharisees had used) adds the word *epetrepsen* ("he permitted") not that it might be allowed by a moral dispensation, what was only such by a forensic and civil; or by a relaxation of right, what was only by a relaxation of punishment; or as to freedom from blame in the internal court of conscience, what was free only from punishment in the civil and external court.

XX. The command to love our neighbor cannot be said to have been corrected by Christ with regard to the object, as if the object of love was more restricted under the Old Testament (viz., the neighbor of the same covenant and religion), but in the new extended more wisely to embrace all men universally, even enemies. For in each there is the same command of love, the same object, the same form and the same end, the same love, both extensively as to object and intensively as to manner or degree. By the "neighbor" (whose love the law prescribes) is not meant only a Jew and fellow countryman, but also any stranger; yea, even an enemy, in which sense the Egyptians are called "neighbors" (Ex. 11:2) and the Philistines (Jdg. 14:20). So an enemy is also reckoned under the name of neighbor, when it is clearly said, "Thou shalt not avenge, nor bear any grudge against him" (Lev. 19:18). Solomon commands to "give bread to a hungry enemy; and if he be thirsty, to give him water to drink" (Prov. 25:21*), after the example of Elisha (2 K. 6:22). Yea, God commands that we should "help an enemy's beast of burden and bring him back to the way" (Ex. 23:4, 5). Finally, our neighbor is one against whom we ought not to bear false witness and whose wife and goods we must not covet (expressions applicable not to some only but to all men). It is not an objection that in Mt. 5:43, 44 it is said (as if drawn from the law), "thou shalt love thy neighbor, and hate thine enemy," because Christ there refers to the addition of a Pharisaical gloss, not to an imperfection of the law (which neither now has nor ever had this). The law of retaliation given under the Old Testament did not restrict the command of love because it treats of the right of the magistrate, not of the duties of love; of the punishments to be inflicted upon the guilty by a judge, not of private revenge.

XXI. If the Israelites are forbidden to intermarry, to make covenants with and even to pity the seven Canaanite nations (Ex. 34:12; Dt. 7:2): (1) it does not follow that they were commanded to hate them. There is a medium between friendship (implying an agreement in mind and in duties) and hatred; nor is mercy towards them prohibited absolutely, but only relatively (with regard to the vengeance of God respecting them, who ought to be slain by his express command, and indeed for this reason—that they might not be a snare to his people). (2) The command does not concern hatred, but concerns their destruction because God had devoted them to death as his enemies on account of their dreadful crimes. (3) This was not to be done simply, but then only when they had refused peace (Dt. 20:10). (4) In the New Testament, this also holds good, not only when we are forbidden to pray for those who sin unto death (1 Jn. 5:16), and to bid him Godspeed who brings in another doctrine (2 Jn. 10), but also because wars are allowed.

XXII. (2) The commandment of love was not corrected by Christ as to mode and intensity whether we consider God or our neighbor. With respect to God, there can be no greater love than that with which we are bidden to love God as the highest good, not only on account of the blessings he bestows upon us, but also on account of his excellency (than which there is no greater). With respect to our neighbor, the love is susceptible of no degree because we are commanded to love him as ourselves. The command of the gospel that we should lay down even life for our brethren (1 Jn. 3:16) does not prove that we ought to love our neighbor more than ourselves, so that the measure of Christian love may be greater than legal love. (a) The command to lay down life for a brother was not unknown under the Old Testament, as appears from the example of Moses wishing to die for the people; and of David for Absalom (2 S. 18:33); of the three friends prepared to die for David (2 S. 23:13-17). Nor was this unknown to the heathen themselves, as is evident from the examples of those who devoted themselves to death for their country and did not refuse to die for their friends—as Damon and Pythias, Pylades and Orestes (which Paul himself confesses, Rom. 5:6, 7). (b) The mark of comparison ("as ourselves") is not to be understood canonically (*kanonikōs*), but exemplarily (*paradeigmatikōs*). Nor does it exhibit the measure and rule according to which we ought to love our neighbor, but only the example, and such indeed that a more intense does not commonly exist because by nature we are prone to love ourselves (Eph. 5:29). Thus he who lays down his life for a brother, does not love that brother more than himself, but as himself because he does what he would wish to be done for himself in like case. (c) He who lays down his life for a brother does indeed love his own life less than the other's safety; but he does it both because that other's safety is far more valuable than temporal life and especially because the glory of God is concerned in it; yea, even our own safety, which we ought to love more than our own life. Hence this life is willingly to be lost in order to obtain the eternal.

XXIII. The commandment of love is not called "new" by Christ (Jn. 13:34) and "the law of Christ" (Gal. 6:2) absolutely and simply as to the substance of the command (which was the same in both). It is called new relatively and comparatively (with regard to the mode) because renovated by Christ and restored to its former splendor (since it had become almost antiquated by the evil habits of men) and illustrated and sanctioned by new reasons and motives (such as both the example of Christ and his greatest blessings; since if he loved us so greatly, we ought in turn, in order that love may be paid by love, to delight as a recompense of love both in him and our brethren on account of him, 1 Jn. 4:11). It is new also with regard to duration because it is perpetual and eternal.

XXIV. It cannot be said that anything was added by Christ to the precepts of the moral law as to essentials. Not to the first, either a new method of praying (proposed in the Lord's prayer) because the command to worship and adore God necessarily embraces prayer. Although the Lord's prayer as to form was instituted by Christ, it has nothing as to matter and things to be sought which is not expressed in the prayers of the saints in the Old Testament. Not a new worship of Christ and of the Father in him because the adoration of Christ was both commanded frequently in the Old Testament (Ps. 2:12; 45:11; 97:7; Ex. 23:20-25) and confirmed by various examples—of Abraham (Gen. 18:23), of Jacob (Gen. 48:16), of Daniel (Dan. 9:17). Yea, no prayer was offered by the patriarchs except in the name of Christ (at least impliedly), inasmuch as they rested upon the divine promises whose foundation was the Messiah (2 Cor. 1:20).

XXV. Not to the second commandment, by the prohibition not only of the worship of images and idols, but also their fabrication and the frequenting of places consecrated to idols. This very thing had already been commanded under the Old Testament when they are ordered to burn the idols of the heathen, destroy their altars and hew down their groves (Ex. 23:24; Dt. 12:2, 3). Nay, they were forbidden to use the names of idols in their conversation (Ex. 23:13; Ps. 16:4); even fellowship with idolators is regarded as dangerous to religion (Dt. 7:2, 3).

XXVI. Not to the third commandment, either by invoking Christ to witness as the searcher of hearts (Rev. 2:23). As Christ was adored under the Old Testament as coeternal and coessential with the Father, so his name was sworn by (Is. 45:23; Rom. 14:11). Or by the absolute prohibition of oaths, since (as was said before) the discourse of Christ in Mt. 5 is not to be understood absolutely and simply, but with a limitation as to the subject matter (i.e., those rash and perverse forms of swearing by creatures used in daily conversation). Not to the fourth commandment, by the abrogation of the Sabbath, because (as will be afterwards proved) it was abrogated only as ceremonial, not as moral.

XXVII. Not to the fifth commandment, by respect for magistrates, masters and husbands (who ought to be obeyed as fathers). It is certain that under the name "fathers" in the Old Testament are also included both magistrates, masters and husbands (Gen. 41:43; 45:8; Job 29:16; 2 K. 5:13). These should use their power moderately and paternally, not despotically (Dt. 5:20, 21; 17:15; 24:1; Mal. 2:14, 15). Not to the sixth commandment, by the prohibition of anger and insults towards a brother and of vengeance of individuals. As to the former, the law by prohibiting homicide prohibits whatever may lead to it, both outward injuries and insults and inward movements of anger and hatred. As to the latter, private revenge only is prohibited by Christ in accordance with the law, but not public, which cannot be separated from the office of magistrate (Rom. 13:1, 2).

XXVIII. Not to the seventh commandment, by forbidding unchaste looks, divorce (saving for the cause of adultery) and all lust and obscenity of speech. All these were already embraced in the law (embracing under one species the entire genus) by forbidding all impurity (either of deed or word), and the tenth precept concerning covetousness more strongly confirms this very thing. However, divorce (as was said before) was not permitted or commanded by the moral law, but only tolerated by the forensic law on account of the hardness of heart (*sklērokardian*) of the people.

XXIX. Not to the eighth commandment, by prohibiting avarice and luxury in food and dress, for both were already forbidden in the law: the former (Ex. 20:17; 22:25; Ps. 119:36; Is. 3:17); the latter (Dt. 21:20; Prov. 23:20; Is. 3:16, 17; 5:11, 12). Not to the ninth commandment, by the prohibition of all lies, slander and informing, because these also occurred in the law and were prohibited elsewhere (Ps. 15:3; 101:5). Not to the tenth commandment, by the command not to turn the mind to the coveted thing, because Paul teaches that all concupiscence in general is condemned (Rom. 7:7, 8) and so all its species and degrees. In one word, all the additions proposed by our opponents are either contained under the commandments themselves (as species under their genus, parts under the whole, effects under causes, consequents under antecedents and the reverse); or they are heterogeneous in reference to them, foreign to their design and subject or even opposed to them (as is evident from what has been said).

XXX. What is in no way contained under the love of God and our neighbor, neither explicitly nor implicitly, neither as to the letter, nor as to the sense, may well be said to have been added to the law. But self-denial, the bearing of the cross and the imitation of Christ are contained in the law; if not expressly, at least impliedly and as to sense. We cannot love God with all our heart without being prepared to deny ourselves, bear the cross for his sake and imitate Christ, who is true God.

XXXI. Although the law treats expressly only of the duties towards God and our neighbor, yet under them are necessarily contained the duties towards ourselves. We cannot love God with all our heart without every kind of holiness; nor will we rightly love our neighbor as ourselves, unless we regulate the love of ourselves by the law of God.

XXXII. Christ is compared to Moses (Heb. 2:1-3), not in legislation (as if he was a new lawgiver more perfect than Moses; for so he is rather opposed, since it is said the law was given by Moses, but grace and truth came by Jesus Christ, Jn. 1:17), but partly as to the kind of doctrine (which in the one case was legal, in the other evangelical), partly in dignity and glory (by which Christ infinitely surpassed Moses).

XXXIII. Although the law does not directly and formally enjoin repentance (because it holds out no hope of pardon to the sinner and thus it properly belongs to the gospel), still materially and indirectly it is related to it because in it is prescribed the rule of right living and what is pleasing to God (which is the design of repentance).

Fourth Question

May anything be added to the moral law in the way of counsel? We deny against the papists.

What is evangelical counsel? The opinion of papists.

I. This question (lying between us and the papists) differs from the preceding. There the dispute was about precepts; here the dispute is about counsels. They define counsels "to be good works not enjoined upon, but demonstrated to us by Christ; not commanded, but commended" (cf. Bellarmine, "De Monachis," 2.7 *Opera* [1857], 2:228). These are called by them "evangelical" and "of perfection" (*perfectionis*) because they are set forth and encouraged in the gospel as a more perfect law and lead to a greater perfection of holiness (those who bind themselves by a special desire to the keeping of them). Hence they are made by them to differ from the precepts: (1) on the part of the matter, which in counsels is far more difficult and perfect than in the precepts; (2) on the part of the subject, because the counsels pertain only to a certain order of men; the precepts, however, to all universally; (3) on the part of the form (or observation) arbitrary in counsels, but in precepts necessary; (4) on the part of the end and effects, because they obtain a greater and more excellent reward (viz., a golden) and a higher degree of happiness above the keeping of the precepts. Now although they are not agreed as to the number (some making more, others fewer), still there are three principal ones upon which they build up the monastic life, continence, obedience and poverty. To these the three vows imposed upon monks correspond: of perpetual continence, regular obedience and voluntary poverty.

Of the orthodox.

II. On the other hand, the orthodox do not deny that there are certain indifferent works left to each one's own will in the Scriptures, and with respect to which counsels may be given in the word of God, not improperly distinguished from the precepts necessarily to be obeyed: such as Paul's counsel concerning a virgin's marrying or not marrying (1 Cor. 7:26, 36); concerning the use of wine with regard to Timothy (1 Tim. 5:23*). Still they are of such a nature that they are not of themselves pleasing to God and when neglected, deserve no punishment; nor when observed, any reward. But they deny that there are any such counsels about moral things, since these fall under commands properly so called, not under counsels. Again they acknowledge that there are diverse precepts—some universal (binding all men without exception, as the command to love God and our neighbor); others special—suitable to certain persons in a particular state and manner of life (such as the duties of magistrates, parents, husbands and the like); still others private—imposed upon particular individuals (as the command given to Noah to build an ark and to Abraham to offer up his son). But they deny that any of these fall under counsel, since they were expressly commanded.

Statement of the question.

III. The question therefore returns to this—whether in the gospel anything has been added, not by way of precept, but way of counsel; not about indifferent, but about moral things; not with respect to all, but to some only; not to secure the perfection of Christianity only, but to the attainment of a certain more perfect state and to establish the merits of supererogation. The adversaries affirm; we deny.

Proof of the nonexistence of evangelical counsels.

IV. The reasons are: (1) there is no morally good work which is not contained in the moral law and so does not therefore fall under the precept (since indeed it is a most perfect rule of all rectitude and perfection and nothing can pertain to the moral perfection of man of whatever degree which is not included in the love of God and our neighbor). (2) Whatever falls under counsel in moral things, falls also under precept. For what God counsels, by that very act he commands. Hence counsel is used for command (Prov. 1:30; Lk. 7:30; Acts 20:27; Rev. 3:18). (3) Whatever conduces to the perfection of the Christian is not only encouraged or commended, but commanded by Christ: "Be ye perfect, even as your Father is perfect" (Mt. 5:48). (4) What are thrust forward as evangelical counsels are either commanded in the word (such as the love of enemies [Mt. 5:44; Rom. 12:20]; the suffering of injuries [Mt. 5:39]; chastity or even celibacy, if the gift of continence is possessed and it is required for any reason [1 Cor. 9:5]; voluntary poverty for the sake of Christ and the gospel [Lk. 14:33; Mt. 16:24]); or they have been invented by men without the authority of the word and rest upon no other ground than that of voluntary worship (as regular obedience, which is repugnant to the liberty in which Christ has established us [Gal. 5:1] and according to which we ought no longer to be made the servants of men [1 Cor. 7:23]; perpetual continence, because Christ testifies that this is not a gift belonging to every one [Mt. 19:11] and by the apostle he commands, "If they cannot contain, let them marry: for it is better to marry than to burn" [1 Cor. 7:9]; voluntary poverty, such as is recommended by the papists, because no one without a special call or necessity ought to throw away his resources [Mt. 19:21, 27], lest he tempt God [Mt. 4:7] or be compelled to neglect charity towards his neighbor [Eph. 4:28]).

Sources of solution.

V. The mandate given by Christ to the proud young man (boasting of his perfect observance of the law Pharisaically), "if thou wilt be perfect, go and sell all thou hast, and give to the poor" (Mt. 19:21), was not a counsel of perfection, but "a personal and explanatory comment" to rebuke his pride and unveil his hypocrisy. Nor is it proposed by way of counsel (which he was at liberty to follow or not), but by way of precept (to the keeping of which he was bound). (2) The perfection here proposed is not a perfection of glory (which he was to obtain above others), but a perfection of righteousness, to be obtained in this life by a zeal in good works (as if he had said, if you wish to show that you are perfect, as you boast yourself to be, you ought to prove it by this trial, by selling all things; as is evident from the question of the young man and Christ's answer to it). (3) What Christ says ("one thing thou lackest") does not evince that Christ approved of what the young man had said about the perfect keeping of the law. Otherwise he would not have refused to obey the command of Christ. Rather it was only exploratory, that the latent hypocrisy might be uncovered. (4) Although the command to sell all is not general and common, it does not follow that it is a counsel because it can be a special precept and personal testing (*peirastikon*) proposed for certain reasons. (5) Christ is said to have "loved him" (Mk. 10:21). This does not imply that the young man spoke the truth when he professed to have kept all the commands of the law from his youth up. The sorrow produced by the command of Christ sufficiently proves that his love to God was not perfect. Rather it was a sign of benevolence (on account of the desire he expressed to obtain eternal life), and the zeal employed in fulfilling the law (although he was not without his faults).

VI. When the apostle opposes judgment to commandment (*gnōmēn epitagē*, 1 Cor. 7:25) and says that he has no commandment (*epitagēn*) or mandate concerning virgins, but gives his judgment (*gnōmēn*) or "opinion and counsel" (as the Vulgate renders it), he does not favor the evangelical counsels of the papists. He treats of a matter free and indifferent which neither done nor omitted brings on any guilt. For whether the virgin marries or not, she does not sin in the least (since each state can be pleasing to God, if purely lived in). (2) Nor if Paul adds, "he doeth better that giveth her not in marriage" (*kreisson poiein*, 1 Cor. 7:38), does he mean so much a virtuous and moral good (since according to Paul himself "if a virgin marry she hath not sinned" [1 Cor. 7:28] and "marriage is honorable in all" [*timios gamos en pasi*, Heb. 13:4]) as a useful and suitable good (on account of the various trials which matrimony brings with it and especially in reference to that time, on account of the impending persecutions which they could meet better as single persons than as married). The apostle intimates this in v. 28, "such shall have trouble in the flesh," and v. 35, "this I speak for your own profit" (*pros to ymōn sympheron*). (3) If "she" is called "happier who abides in a state of celibacy" (1 Cor. 7:40), this must not be understood of a more perfect degree of glory, but concerning the condition in this life because she is exposed to fewer afflictions and temptations.

VII. The eunuchs mentioned in Is. 56:3, 4 to whom is promised a place "within the walls of Jerusalem and a name better than of sons and of daughters" (v. 5) are not voluntary eunuchs (making themselves such by any vow), but natural or made so by violence, to whom under the New Testament (provided they cultivate piety) admission is promised into the temple and city of God (i.e., into the church) and the illustrious name of sons of God (which is better than children because it is eternal)—notwithstanding the forensic law concerning eunuchs by which (under the Old Testament) they were excluded from the congregation of the Lord (Dt. 23:1, 2). Because therefore the law promised fruitfulness to the obedient, childless (*ateknoi*) eunuchs might think their zeal would be in vain, especially since they were stigmatized and excluded from the privileges of the people. Thus what they lacked in this respect, God says he would make up to them by better blessings, if they would be faithful so that their labor should not be lost. Thus under "strangers and eunuchs" Isaiah embraces all who seem to be unworthy of being reckoned by God among his people, either because they were excluded from the covenant or because they carried a certain mark of disgrace separating them from the people of God (whom he addresses in order that they may not despair, because "God is no respecter of persons: but in every nation he that feareth him is accepted with him," as Peter says in Acts 10:34, 35).

VIII. They who are said to "have made themselves eunuchs (*eunouchizein*) for the kingdom of heaven's sake" (Mt. 19:12) do not denote those who from counsel vowed perpetual celibacy whether it would happen that they would burn or not. They could not be exculpated from blame because it is better to marry than to burn. Rather it denotes those who impose upon themselves voluntarily the necessity of remaining in celibacy and of preserving such a state of life that they may serve God better and promote his cause, as long as God may grant them the gift of continence. This limitation is gathered from v. 11 where the Lord testifies that all are not capable of celibacy and so marriage is necessary to some; also from v. 12 when he says, "he that is able to receive it, let him receive it," where he exhorts to continence those who are conscious of possessing the gift (and as long as they have it).

IX. Some apostles were unmarried, but not in consequence of a vow (the liberty of entering the married state remaining unimpaired if circumstances should demand it, 1 Cor. 9:5). Others remained married even after their call (1 Cor. 9:5; Lk. 4:38). They indeed left all things (as it is said in Mt. 19:27), but they were those things which might hinder their following Christ. To number among these their wives is disgraceful both because they themselves followed Christ (Lk. 8:2, 3) and because we read of their constantly adhering to their faithful husbands. As to property (if they had relinquished it), they would have done it not by counsel, but by the command of Christ (Jn. 1:40; Mt. 9:9). But the gospel teaches that they did not give up their ownership in it, as those who retained their houses and ships (Mt. 8; Jn. 19, 21), but by abstaining from the ordinary use of them and from their occupations in order that they might devote all their time to the ministry.

X. The gratuitous preaching of the gospel (concerning which Paul speaks in 1 Cor. 9:12, 15) was not indeed enjoined by a common command; otherwise it would not have been lawful for him or others to receive wages. Rather it rested upon him from his singular call (in accordance with the circumstances of men and of places) in order to the proper performance of the apostolic functions imposed upon him by Christ (on account of the false apostles [his rivals] who did this in order to recommend themselves to the churches). The glory which on this account he claims for himself (v. 15), he opposes to the calumnies of the false brethren (as if he made a gain of the gospel); not as if he had done an undue and supererogatory work, but inasmuch as he had diligently and faithfully executed the office entrusted to him.

XI. When Christ enjoins upon the young man the duty of following him (Mt. 19:21), he does not give a counsel, but a command to all in common because no one can have a hope of salvation unless he follows Christ (1 Pet. 2:21), although from a particular cause it is peculiarly adapted to him.

Fifth Question: The Division of the Precepts of the Decalogue

Are four precepts rightly assigned to the first table and six to the second? We affirm.

Statement of the question.

I. The question is not whether the precepts are more or fewer than the number ten (for concerning this all are agreed). Hence the name "decalogue" was given to the law on account of the ten words. The question is not whether these ten precepts may be divided into two tables (for this also is granted). But how are they to be distributed; and how many and which ones belong to each table (for concerning this the opinions of divines vary)?

II. Some assign five precepts to each table: as Josephus, "Moses brings forward two tables containing ten written precepts, five on each" (AJ 3.5*.8 [Loeb, 4:364-65]) whom Philo follows (*The Decalogue* 12.50 [Loeb, 7:30-31]) and, of the fathers, Irenaeus (*Against Heresies* 2.24* [ANF 1:395]). But this is false because Christ comprehends the fifth precept under the second table (Mt. 19:18); and Paul also when he calls it the first commandment of the second table with promise (Eph. 6:2). For in the first table, a promise is given in the second precept. Also the nature of the thing proves it because some are duties of religion towards God (prescribed in the first table), others of love and reverence for superiors (prescribed in the second table).

III. Some assign only three precepts to the first table, throwing the first and second into one and dividing the tenth into two: a division made by Clement of Alexandria (*Stromata* 6.16 [ANF 2:511-12]) and Augustine (*Quaestionum in heptateuchum*, Q. 71 [PL 34.620-21] and Letter 55, "To Januarius" [FC 12:276]) and adopted by the papists and Lutherans. Finally, others claim four for the first and six for the second table; the opinion of the Chaldee Paraphrase on Ex. 20 and most of the fathers: Origen, Athanasius, Ambrose, Chrysostom and others (whom we also follow). Let us only observe with our men that this is a controversy concerning which we are not to contend bitterly and pertinaciously with anyone, provided the teaching of the whole decalogue be preserved and the number of precepts be unmutilated. The papists do the latter here, joining the second commandment, about graven images, to the first, about not having other gods, as if it was only an appendix or explanation of the first. They are even also accustomed to expunge it from their breviaries so that the people may not know it. This is the reason why some of our party have zealously defended that division and adhered to the received opinion (relying principally upon the following arguments).

IV. First, unless our division holds its place, the duties of religion towards God (contained in the first table) will be confounded with the duties of justice and love towards our neighbor (contained in the second table). For the first four precepts have respect to the worship and love of God; the last six, however, have respect to love towards our neighbor.

V. Second, the first and second precepts differ in meaning; therefore, they also differ in order. The former refers to the object (*to on*) of worship (that the true

God may be worshipped); the latter to the mode (*to poion*) of worship (that he be not worshipped by images). Hence one could be violated without a violation of the other, when the true God is worshipped as the object, but with an unlawful worship, as to manner (as the Israelites who worshipped Jehovah in the calf, Ex. 32).

VI. Third, the tenth precept is falsely divided into two because it is comprehended under the one common name of covetousness and the same kind of sin is prohibited. Hence Moses puts the coveting of the house before the coveting of the wife (Ex. 20:18); but reverses the order (Dt. 5:21), which he ought not to have done, if they were two distinct precepts. Paul refers to this precept as only one, not as two: "I had not known lust, except the law had said, Thou shalt not covet" (Rom. 7:7).

Sources of solution.

VII. Although under the prohibition of other gods in the first precept is contained also the prohibition of idols (inasmuch as they constitute the object of worship), it does not follow that the second does not constitute a distinct precept because then they are viewed under a different relation (*schesei*) with regard to the mode of worship. Nor do they denote only idols or representations of fictitious gods, but also images of the true God. In order therefore that the worship of images (or of God by images) might not be considered lawful, God most wisely willed to forbid it by a peculiar precept. Nor does it help them to say that images can best be called other gods because whoever religiously worships an image does not worship the true God, but a false one, even the Devil himself (according to Paul, 1 Cor. 10:20). For although consequently and eventually, the worship of images terminates on false gods or the Devil, still not according to the mind and intention of the worshippers (who sin here not in the object, but in the manner of worship).

VIII. Although the promise and threatening added to the second precept can be extended to all the precepts in general (with regard to those who keep God's commmands), yet it is well annexed to this command in particular for a peculiar reason (because the people at that time were inordinately given to idolatry), in order that they might the more diligently keep themselves from it, both by the hope of the promise and by the fear of the threatening.

IX. Although Moses uses two words to prohibit covetousness (*chmdh* and *th'vh* in Exodus and Deuteronomy), it does not follow that he intended to make a twofold precept; for in the second also (which is only one), he uses two words for the prohibition of image worship (*shchh* ["bow down"] and *'bhdh* ["serve"]), which he does not for the sake of distinction, but of greater emphasis.

X. Although covetousness is different as to degrees (one original, another actual; one without, another with a previous consent of the will), still it is the same as to species which is prohibited by this precept. Nor, if the objects materially considered are diverse, do they differ formally because they are contained under the formal relation of the possessions of others. If the precepts were to be multiplied according to the diversity of coveted things, there would have to be not two, but many more.

XI. The division of the decalogue as to matter (or things commanded or prohibited) can be so instituted. In general, the worship of God is commanded and whatever is opposed to it is forbidden. However the worship of God is either immediate (containing the duties which are immediately rendered to God) or mediate (when duties to our neighbor are performed on account of God). The immediate is contained in the first table and is either internal (consisting in both retaining the true object of worship by worshipping the one God alone—sanctioned by the first precept; and in worshipping him in a lawful manner—mentioned in the second); or external (and this either private, to be rendered by everyone always and everywhere, taught in the third; or public in the sanctification of the Sabbath, contained in the fourth). The mediate is likewise internal and external: external both in the duties of superiors towards inferiors and of the latter towards the former (the subject of the fifth precept); and in the duties of neighbors towards neighbors, such as the conservation of life and safety (taught in the sixth); of chastity and marriage (in the seventh); of property or possessions (in the eighth); of fame and truth (in the ninth). Internal is the rectitude of all the affections and desires (included under the tenth).

Sixth Question: The Rules of Explanation and of Observance of the Decalogue

What rules are to be observed in explaining and keeping the precepts of the decalogue?

The first rule of explanation of the law.

I. Two things come under this question. First, concerning the rules of explanation of the decalogue, that the genuine sense of the precepts may be held against the perverse judgments of men who interpret them preposterously. Second, concerning the rules of obedience, that we may know what the law demands of us. As to the first, the following rules are to be observed in the explanation of the law.

II. First, "the law is spiritual, respecting not only the external acts of the body, but the internal motions of the mind." It is evident both from Paul (who in Rom. 7:14 testifies that "the law is spiritual") and from the nature of the lawgiver himself. He is not a human and earthly lawgiver who, since he has fleshly eyes, attends only to the external deeds striking the senses, nor does he take notice of counsels and intentions (except insofar as they manifest themselves outwardly); hence his interdicts are violated only by flagitious actions. Rather he is a divine and heavenly lawgiver whose eye nothing escapes and who regards not so much the external appearance as the purity of the heart. Thus he speaks to the soul no less than to the body and demands an internal no less than an external obedience. Christ plainly teaches this when he extends homicide to hatred of a brother and adultery to lust and looks (Mt. 5:22, 28).

Rule 2.

III. Second, "in affirmative precepts, negative, and in negative, affirmative are contained." As in Scripture there are more things than words, so in the precepts and interdicts there is always more than is expressed in words. Not that the law is to be considered as a Lesbian rule (to be made to mean anything), but that we may search more deeply into the meaning of the lawgiver and embrace those things which are mutually connected or depend upon each other. Hence since a good precept cannot be performed by the law without its opposite evil being avoided (nor a prohibited evil be shunned without its opposite good being performed), it follows that in the affirmative precepts negative are contained, and in the negative affirmative; so that those which are expressly negative are impliedly affirmative and vice versa. And so virtues are commended when vices are forbidden. Not that virtue is to be placed in the abstinence from vice alone (as is commonly said), for we must proceed farther (viz., to the contrary duties and deeds). Thus in the precept "thou shalt not kill" reason sees nothing else than that we must abstain from every evil deed, but it is certain that in addition love is recommended that we should cherish our neighbor's life in every way we can. Reason demands this because God forbids us to assail or injure a brother by injustice because he wishes his life to be dear and precious to us. Thus we should exert all our efforts to preserve it. So when theft is prohibited, beneficence is enjoined. If God commands us to honor our parents and promises a reward to those reverencing them, it forbids us by that very thing to injure them and intimates that he will not go unpunished who acts differently.

Rule 3.

IV. Third, "in all the precepts synecdoche is to be acknowledged" by which in one proposed species all under the same genus are understood, and by one prohibited vice others of the same kind analogous to it (and whatever bear upon or lead to it) are prohibited. Thus in the precept "thou shalt not commit adultery" is prohibited every affection for another's wife; to lust after her (Mt. 5:28) and all illicit desires are forbidden. Under homicide, all angry feelings are included. What are most base and capital in each species of sin are forbidden, under which all the others are included, either because they flow thence or because they lead at length to it; or because what appear the smallest to men are in the most accurate judgment of God rated more severely. This is not done, therefore, to excuse or exclude lesser sins, but that a greater detestation of sin may be impressed upon our minds. For the flesh endeavors to dilute the foulness of sin and to cover it under specious pretexts; for example, anger and hatred are supposed to be so execrable when these terms are used, but when they are prohibited under the name of homicide, we understand better in how great abomination they are held by God.

Rule 4.

V. Fourth (belonging to the same), "in the effect, the cause, in the genus, the species, in the related, the correlative is included." He who wishes or prohibits anything, also wishes or prohibits that without which it cannot be or is not usually done. So in the prohibition of adultery are prohibited all illicit desires and their springs—intemperance and all incitements of them. Thus while the law enjoins chastity, it requires also its nurse—temperance and moderation in eating. When children are commanded to honor their parents, parents are in turn commanded to cherish their children paternally and to bring them up in the nurture of the Lord. Under the word "parents" are understood all superiors—magistrates, masters, teachers, pastors—to whom in turn the duties are prescribed which they are bound to perform towards inferiors.

Rule 5.

VI. Fifth, "the precepts of the first table take the preference of those of the second" as to necessary internal and external acts, when they both cannot have place at the same time. Thus the love of our neighbor ought to be subjected to the love of God. We are bound to hate father and mother for Christ's sake (Lk. 14:26), when the love of parents is incompatible (*asystatos*) with the love of Christ. Human commands are to be neglected when opposed to the commands of God (Mt. 10:37; Acts 4:19). But in turn "the ceremonial of the first table yields to the moral of the second because God desires mercy and not sacrifice" (Hos. 6:6), i.e., moral worship principally and primarily as better and of itself necessary; the ceremonial, however, only secondarily on account of the moral. Hence we ought not to be so anxious about the former as about the latter.

Rule 6.

VII. Sixth, "some precepts are affirmative" (ordering things to be done, sins of omission); "others negative" (prohibiting things to be avoided, sins of commission). "The former bind always, but not to always, the latter bind always to always." The virtues and duties commanded by the affirmative precepts cannot be exercised every moment together at once, and suppose certain conditions (which being absent, there is no place for them); for example, parents are not always alive or near us, so that we can render them their due respect. But the vices and crimes prohibited can be committed lawfully in no article of time. Here however, we must make an exception of the general affirmative command to love God (which obliges always and to always) because there is no time or place or state in which man can be exempted from the duty of loving God.

Rule 7.

VIII. Seventh, "the beginning and end of all the precepts is love." Hence love is called the "end" and "fulfilling" (*plērōma*) of the law (1 Tim. 1:5; Rom. 13:10). Love discharges all the claims of God's beneficence and of man's obedience. As all God's blessings flow from love and are contained in it, so all man's duties are included in love. The love of God is the fullness of the gospel; the love of man is the fullness of the law. God is love and the mark of the sons of God is none other than love (Jn. 13:35). However as the object of love is twofold (God and our neighbor), so a twofold love is commanded: of God in the first table of the law; of our neighbor in the second. That is called "the first and great commandment"; this "the second like to it." The love of God is rightly called the "first" commandment because as there is nothing before God, so his worship ought first to be attended to by us in order that all things may begin from and end in it. It is called "great" (a) with regard to the object because conversant with the greatest and infinite object (viz., God); (b) with regard to the subject because it demands all the powers and faculties of man, that we love God with all our mind and heart and strength; (c) with regard to amplitude and extension, because it shuts up all things in its embrace and flows into all the actions of man, for nothing can be pleasing to God except it be done for his sake. The second is said to be "like" unto it, not with regard to importance, but (1) with regard to quality because both in the love of God and of our neighbor sincerity and purity of heart are required; (2) with regard to authority because each is commanded by God and tends to his glory; (3) with regard to punishment because the violation of either table exposes to eternal death; (4) with regard to connection and dependence because they are so strictly connected with each other that neither can be fulfilled without the other (for as God cannot be loved without a love for our neighbor made after his image, so neither can our neighbor be loved without the love of God, who created him). "If a man say, I love God, and hateth his brother, he is a liar: for he that loveth not his brother whom he hath seen, how can he love God whom he hath not seen" (1 Jn. 4:20)?

The first rule of observation of the law.

IX. The rules of obedience due to the law are also diverse. First, the whole law must be fulfilled by the whole man. For as God prescribes to us the entire law as to all its precepts without any division of them, so he demands the whole man and not a half to keep it; not only externally as to the body, but also internally as to the soul and all its powers (as nothing of the precepts should be omitted by us that we may remain in all things which are written). As the whole man is under the law to God, no part of it can or ought to be withdrawn from his obedience. Whatever is in man (whether in the mind or in the will and affections; whether in soul or in the body) may worship and be in subjection to God. This is also demanded by the strictest justice of the lawgiver and the nature of good (which ought to be perfect) and by the formula of the legal covenant.

Rule 2.

X. Second, a fourfold perfection is required in obedience. First, with regard to the principle, that it be true and sincere, consisting not only in the mouth or external motion of the body, but which has its seat in the soul and arises from a purified heart and faith unfeigned (*anypokritō*): "the end of the commandment is charity out of a pure heart, and of a good conscience, and of faith unfeigned" (1 Tim. 1:5). Second, with regard to the object or parts, that it be universal, not with regard to this or that command, but with regard to all. For he who sins in one thing is guilty of all; nor is he to be considered as having fulfilled the law who has not remained in all the things which are written. Third, with regard to degrees, that it be intense and perfect, so that nothing can be added to it. Hence Bernard says the measure of loving God is "to love him without measure" (*De Diligendo Deo* 1.1 and 6.16 [PL 182.974 and 983]). Fourth, with regard to time and duration, that it be perpetual and constant from the beginning unto the end, so that we rest not only in one or another act of the law, but remain through our whole life in those things which are written.

Rule 3.

XI. Third, that as the internal obedience is far better than the external, the moral than the ceremonial, so to no purpose is the latter rendered without the former. Hence the grievous complaints of the prophets who rebuke the people for their impiety because they separate those things which God has joined together by an indissoluble bond, are content with external and ceremonial worship and show no anxiety about the internal and morals (cf. Is. 1:15-18; 58:1-4; 66:1-4; Mic. 6:7; and frequently elsewhere).

Rule 4.

XII. Fourth, as the precepts do not have an equal degree of importance and necessity, so neither is the obedience to be reckoned of the same order and value; nor is all disobedience of the same demerit, but contracts a greater or lesser guilt. The omission of a command is one thing; opposition to it another; forgetfulness, neglect and contempt are different. Neglect proceeds from the languor of slothfulness, but contempt from the swelling of pride. Hence the exaltation of the despiser increases guilt and turns his fault into a crime. In easier things contempt is more worthy of condemnation and the act less praiseworthy. In more difficult things obedience is the more acceptable as violation is the more heinous.

Seventh Question: The First Commandment

Is God alone to be worshipped and invoked? Or is it lawful to invoke and religiously worship deceased saints? We affirm the former and deny the latter against the papists.

I. By the first precept "thou shalt have no other gods before me," the true object of religious worship is sanctioned. Not only is atheism forbidden (which acknowledges and worships no God) and polytheism (which makes for itself gods without number), but also all superstition and idolatry in the object (by which what is not God is esteemed and served as God [Gal. 4:8] whether it be a mere figment of man, such as most of the fictitious gods of the Gentiles were, or a really existing thing, but created and finite, to which the religious worship of faith, adoration, and invocation due to God alone is in any way paid). The papists sin in many ways about this: by the religious worship of creatures, angels, saints, relics, the host of the Mass, and of the pope himself. Thus they are guilty of not one kind of idolatry. And thus we must dispute concerning the most important head of religion in controversy between us. We have spoken before of the worship of angels (Topic VII, Question 9); now we treat of the invocation of saints.

Statement of the question.

II. The question is not whether the saints piously dying in the Lord are to be held in any respect and honor. We do not deny that they are to be honored by us according to the degree of their excellence, both by thinking highly of them as servants of God most happy and admitted into the fellowship of the Lord and by cherishing their memory with a grateful and pleasant recollection (Lk. 1:48; Mk. 14:9), extolling their conflicts and victories, preserving their doctrine, celebrating and imitating their virtues (Heb. 12:1), praising God in and for them and giving him thanks for raising up such for the good of his church. Rather the question is whether they are to be reverenced with religious worship properly so called. This our opponents wish; we deny. At the outset, we oppose the calumnies of the papists who slander us as despisers and enemies of the saints because we repudiate the worship of them (as if disgrace were thrown upon the saints when what belongs to God and Christ alone is not attributed to them). Now although their memory is very sacred to us, still we think that care should be diligently taken that they be not worshipped to the injury of God. Nay, we think grievous injury is done to them by those who turn them into idols and abuse the friends of God to provoke him to jealousy. Nor do we hesitate to assert if they could see from the heights of glory what is done here, they would not only refuse the worship offered to them, but also testify the greatest indignation towards such undutiful worshippers.

III. The question is not about invocation improperly so called; or social, civil and loving address, customary among living men (belonging to the second table). Rather the question is about invocation properly so called and religions of piety, commanded in the first table as the principal part of religion (frequently put by way of synecdoche for the whole worship of God [Rom. 10:13], under which our adversaries embrace the universal worship of saints). According to them this worship consists partly within in the judgment concerning them (because they know our necessities and can assist us), partly in confidence in them (because they also wish to do so), partly without in the sacrifices and invocations presented to them, in the festivals and temples consecrated to them. The question is whether they are to be reverenced, not with that respect of love and fellowship exhibited to holy men of God in this life on account of imitation, but with a sacred worship of piety on account of religion (as Augustine expresses it, *Reply to Faustus the Manichaean* 20.21 [NPNF1, 4:261-63]). This we deny; the papists affirm.

IV. The question is not whether the saints are our mediators and intercessors with God. This belongs to another question to be taken up when we discuss the intercession of Christ. Rather the question is whether they are to be invoked as our mediators and intercessors. Nor only as intercessors who may obtain for us by their prayers and merits the blessings asked from them; but as the bestowers of them (which the papists, although they dissemble, still maintain, as will appear from the examples of prayers directed to saints given below).

V. The question, therefore, comes back to this—whether the worship of adoration and of invocation is due to God alone, to the exclusion of all creatures of whatever order and dignity; or whether it cannot be rendered also to angels and saints (not militant, but triumphant). The papists maintain the latter; we assert the former.

Opinion of the papists.

VI. The opinion of the papists is gathered not only from their practice, but also from its sanction by the Council of Trent, the decree concerning the invocation of saints and the veneration of relics: "It enjoins upon the same to teach the invocation of saints, the honor of relics, and the use of images; and charges those who teach otherwise with holding an impious opinion" (Session 25, Schroeder, pp. 215-17). Bellarmine says, "The holy, whether angels or men, are invoked piously and usefully by the living" ("De Sanctorum Beatitudine," 1.19 *Opera* [1857], 2:451). The Roman Catechism advocates the invocation of saints, by various arguments, and especially by this: "that they assiduously labor in prayers for the salvation of men, and God bestows upon us many blessings on account of their merit and for their sake" (*Catechism of the Council of Trent* [ed. J.A. McHugh and C.J. Callan, 1923], p. 371). Perronius endeavors to prove the invocation of saints to be not only useful but also necessary (*Reply of the . . . Cardinall of Perron to the Answeare of the . . . King of Great Britaine* [1630/1975]). Maldonatus says "that the error of those, who afford no religious honor except to God, is impious and ignorant" (*Commentary on the Holy Gospels: Matthew* [1888], 1:174 on Mt. 5:34). Hence so earnestly do the Expurgational Indexes labor to destroy whatever (either in books or in the writings of the fathers) pertains to the worship of God alone. From the books of Vatablus, they erase "who believe in God will be saved, but who do not will perish" (*Bibliorum sacrorum* [1584], 2:63 on Is. 8:32). From the Index of Athanasius they erase, "God alone is to be adored and no creature." From Augustine, they destroy "the saints are to be honored by imitation, not by adoration" (*Of True Religion* 55 [108] [LCC 6:280; PL 34.169]); and "against those who say, I do not worship images, but by them I am drawn to that which I ought to worship" ("In Psalmum CXIII* Enarratio: De altera parte," 3, 4 [PL 37.1483]).

VII. As to their practice, there is no one who does not know that this worship is placed among the principal parts of the popish religion; that saints are honored by temples, chapels, altars, images, rayed heads, Masses, festivals, tapers, that gifts and sacrifices are offered to them, prayers addressed to them, oaths taken by them, vows made to them, hope of salvation and confidence placed in them. Thus they are invoked, not only as intercessors, but also as protectors from evil and bestowers both of grace and glory. Thus invocation is directed to all the saints: "Also ye happy hosts of souls in heaven; Let present, past and future ills from us be driven" (cf. "Festa Novembris: Ad Vesperas," in *Breviarium Romanum* [1884], 2:817). And to the apostles: "O happy apostles, deliver me from sin, Defend, comfort and lead me into the kingdom of heaven" (*Hortulus Animae* [1602], pp. 450-51). Also: "I seek to be saved by you in the last judgment." To Peter: "O Shepherd Peter, mild and good, receive My prayers—from bonds of sin my soul relieve; By that great power which unto thee was given Who by thy word dost open and shut the gate of heaven" ("Festa Junii: SS. Petri et Pauli," in *Breviarium Romanum* [1884], 2:499). To the elder James: "O James hasten To blot out my wickedness, Giving me the gift of righteousness From the leaven of malice" (*Hortulus Animae* [1602], p. 294). The same thing could easily be shown of the other apostles and saints. Hence it most clearly appears that they are not only invoked as intercessors to pray for us, but also as bestowers of good in whom therefore hope and confidence should be placed. For this reason they order to invoke in the article of death whatever saint anyone has been most devoted to in life, after this manner: "O most glorious Saint or Saintess, N., I have always reposed in the particular hope and confidence while I have lived, succor me now struggling in this time of extreme necessity" (*Hortu. ani.* +). This is especially evident with respect to the blessed virgin, to whom they not only frequently ascribe divine names and articles (when they call her "Goddess, Mistress, Queen of Heaven, Mother of Mercy, Redemptress, Our Omnipotent Mistress, the Refuge of sinners"), but also worship internal as well as external. This can be proved by innumerable examples; even the *Psalterium Marianum* composed by Bonaventure (and never censured by the Roman church, not even by the *Expurgatory Indexes*) most clearly proves. In it the ascriptions of the psalmist to God are impiously transferred to the virgin. See what we have said in "De Necessaria Secessione Nostra ab Ecclesia Romana" (in *Opera* [1848], 4:31-50); and Downame* (*A Treatise concerning Antichrist* [1603], Part I, 5.1, 2, pp. 313-41); and especially Drelincourt (*De l'honneur qui doit estre rendu à la Saincte etii Bien-heureuse Vierge Marie* [1643]).

VIII. To understand their meaning more fully, however, we must observe that worship in general among the papists is the honor due from an inferior to a superior. Three things are required for it. (1) An act of the intellect by which we apprehend the excellence of any one. (2) An act of the will by which we internally bow to it and desire to testify its excellence and our subjection. (3) An external act by which we bow the head or bend the knee or exhibit any other sign of subjection. Hence they infer three kinds of adoration or worship according to the kinds of excellence. These they also make three: divine, to which the kind of worship they call "latria" answers; human, which is placed in the various dignities, powers and degrees of men, to which *cultus civilis* or that of human observance corresponds; intermediate, arising from grace and glory and answering the third kind of worship, which they call "dulia." The latter is either simple (afforded to saints and angels) or "hyperdulia" (given to the humanity of Christ considered apart, although united to the Word; and to the blessed virgin, which they hold to be religious).

IX. Although we do not deny that a diversity of worship is not improperly constituted according to the diversity of excellence in the objects; and we readily grant that by reason of the uncreated and infinite and the created and finite excellence, there can be a twofold worship (the one religious due to God alone, the other civil given to creatures; which again can be considered either with respect to this earthly state, in all the offices of reverence, love and respect due to men [although they may be strangers to the faith]; or with respect to the heavenly state, with which honor we regard the household of faith, whether living by a communication of duties, or dead by love, praise, memory, imitation, etc.), still we do not think that without serious error religious worship is divided into various degrees, but hold it to be one only, peculiar to God alone and incommunicable to all creatures.

X. Nor can the distinction into latria and dulia help this error. (1) It rests upon no solid foundation; not on the propriety of the words, because the signification of *latreias* and *douleias* is promiscuous with profane writers. Hesychius sets forth *latreian* by *douleian* (*Hesychii Alexandrini Lexicon* [1861], 3:16); Glossator, *douleia latreia, latreuō douleuō.* From the force of the word, *douleia* means more than *latreia.* The latter marks only the obedience and worship of a hireling (*latris ho epi misthō douleuōn*), but the former the subjection of a slave and servant who owes himself entirely to his master. Not on the use of the Scriptures; for although in the New Testament the word *latreias* is never used except for the worship due to God alone, the same is also often set forth by the word *douleias* (as in Gal. 4:8; 1 Thess. 1:9; Mt. 6:24; Rom. 12:11; 14:18; Eph. 6:7). The Septuagint applies *latreia* to human respect (Dt. 28:48; Lev. 23:7); a servile work not to be done on the Sabbath is called *latreuton*; Paul always calls himself a *doulon* of Christ and never a *latreutēn*. Not on the authority of the fathers, for although Augustine made a distinction between *latreian* and *douleian*, his intention was not to divide religious worship into two degrees: one pertaining to God and the other to the saints. Rather his intention was only to distinguish servitude into that which is due to God alone and which for the purpose of teaching he calls *latreian* (and elsewhere the servitude of religion) and that which is due to men, which he calls peculiarly dulia. "But that servitude" (i.e., in opposition to the latria due to God) "which is due to men, according to which the apostle teaches slaves that they ought to be obedient to their masters, he is wont to call by another name, to wit dulia" (CG 10.1 [FC 14:116; PL 41.278]). Our opponents are forced to confess that the distinction is unwritten (*agraphon*) and that the Hebrew as well as the Greek words are used promiscuously (Bellarmine, "De Sanctorum Beatitudine," 1.12 in *Opera* [1857], 2:441; Vasquez, *Commentariorum ac Disputationum in Tertiam Partem*, I, Disp. 93.1 [1631], pp. 625-27).

Invocation of saints is rejected by Ex. 20:3 and Mt. 4:10.

XI. For the worship of God alone (against the invocation of saints and the worship of creatures), the orthodox contend: First, with express command of God by which he forbids having any other gods before himself—"thou shalt have no other gods before me" (Ex. 20:3) or as the Septuagint has it "besides me" (*plēn emou*). Here the Lord decrees that nothing should be religiously worshipped except himself, the alone and supreme God. For that is said to be God to us and to be regarded as God whatever we adore and serve with religious worship, whatever that may be otherwise, either in itself or with us—namely because we transfer to it the honor which belongs to God alone. This is confirmed by Christ disputing against Satan: "Thou shalt worship the Lord thy God, and him only shalt thou serve" (Mt. 4:10). Now although the exclusive particle "alone" does not occur in Dt. 6:13 and 10:20 (whence the quotation is made), yet necessarily from the nature of the thing it is included (as it is expressed in 1 S. 7:3, "serve him only" [*lbhdv*], and in the cited place is expressed by *monon* by the Septuagint, which the Vulgate follows here). And if there was no other reason, the expression of the Savior is sufficient for us to conclude that religious worship must be paid to God alone. Nor can it be replied here that the exclusive is added only to the latter words where the verb *latreuō* occurs, not to the former, in order to indicate that religious worship indeed is common to God and the saints, but *latreian* belongs to God alone. Since the same species of worship is designated by adoring and serving, if the exclusive particle is added to one, it is understood to be added to the other also. Finally, Satan does not seek *latreian*, but *proskynēsin* ("All these things will I give thee," says he "if thou wilt fall down and worship me" [*ean pesōn prokynēsēs moi*]). Since Christ refuses this to him, by that very thing is unconquerably testified that *proskynēsin* as well as *latreian* is due to God alone.

2. From the defect of precept and example.

XII. Second, invocation of saints has neither a precept, nor promise, nor example in Scripture for its foundation. Thus it is nothing else than a corrupt and damnable will-worship (*ethelothrēskeia*). Invocation of God is indeed everywhere urged, but mention is nowhere made of the invocation of creatures. Yet the word "to pray" is often put simply for to pray to God because no other lawful invocation than that of God can be granted. Bannes does not question this: "The Scriptures neither expressly nor impliedly teach that prayers should be made to the saints" (2.2, q. 1, Art. 10+); thus Eck (*Enchiridion of Commonplaces* 15 [trans. F.L. Battles, 1979], pp. 119-21); Salmeron (*Commentari in evangeliam historiam et in Acta Apostolorum*, Disp. VII [1602-04], 15:456-67 on 1 Tim. 2). Cotton says, "As to a command concerning the invocation of saints, the church never taught that any existed except so far forth as we are ordered to obey the church" (*Institutio Catholica* 1.16* [1616], p. 91). Bellarmine says, "A command is not required, when necessity itself impels us" ("De Sanctorum Beatitudine," 1.20 in *Opera* [1857], 2:461). But he takes for granted that there is a necessity for such worship; yea, since whatever is without faith is sin, such worship (which we never read to have been instituted by God) must be corrupt. As to examples, they acknowledge that under the Old Testament dispensation the invocation of saints was not indulged, because they hold that they were not then received into heaven, but were still in limbo. Under the New Testament, however, we read of no address either to the virgin or the apostles or any saints (which affords a clear argument of its impropriety).

3. Because they are without the knowledge, power and will requisite in the one invoked.

XIII. Third, invocation supposes faith (Rom. 10:14) in the invoker; knowledge, power and will in the one invoked: knowledge to know all our necessities and everywhere hear our prayers (mental as well as oral) and be truly a searcher of hearts (*kardiognōstēs*); power to be able to succor those in distress; will, to will to assist us and demand this worship to be paid to them. Now these belong to God alone (the only searcher of hearts [*kardiognōstēs*]), who alone is the object of faith and omniscient, the only omnipotent one, who calls to himself and opens his ears to the prayers of suppliants. As to the saints, on the contrary, we have no proof of their knowledge, less of their power, none of their will; nor more of their mediatorial and intercessory office. Rather they themselves are unwilling for that to be exhibited to them which they know is due to God alone. Augustine expresses this when he gives the reason why angels do not wish to be thus adored—"they are our fellow servants, Rev. 19:10" (*Reply to Faustus the Manichaean* 20.21 [NPNF1, 4:262; PL 42.385]). Indeed, Scripture (which often ascribes to God alone omniscience, heart-searching [*kardiognōsian*] and omnipotence, 1 K. 8:39; 2 Ch. 6:30; Rev. 2:23; Jer. 17:10) clearly proves that these cannot belong to creatures and frequently ascribes to the saints an ignorance of the affairs of earth (Is. 63:16; Ecc. 9:6; 2 K. 22:20).

XIV. Nor can this defect be supplied (as the papists wish) either by the imaginary mirror of the Trinity, which they feign (as if the saints, seeing all things in the essence of God saw all things done here)—because as it is gratuitously invented without Scripture, it is rejected with the same facility with which it is proposed. It displeased not a few of the distinguished papists: Lombard, Thomas Aquinas, Altissiodorensis, Bannes, Estius and many others. Nor if the saints see the face of God seeing all things (i.e., enjoy immediate vision of him) does it follow that they see all things in God. Otherwise they would not be ignorant of the day of judgment (which however is the case). Besides that mirror will be either natural or voluntary; if the former, nothing at all will be hidden to them, no less than to God (to say which is impious); if voluntary, they will see in God no other things than those which he is pleased to represent (and who can say what they are?). Or by a revelation of God since he reveals to the saints the prayers and thoughts of believers; for besides such a revelation being thrust forward in vain when Scripture is silent, why should such a circuitous course be chosen when God calls us directly to himself? And what would be the use of God's revealing to the saints our necessities and prayers that they might offer them to him again? If God sometimes willed to reveal to prophets the thoughts of the heart in order that they might perform their duty (as was done to Elisha, 2 K. 5:16), it does not follow that this is ordinarily done to the saints since Scripture says nothing about it, nor do they have any duty towards men, to perform which such knowledge would be necessary. Or by the gift of beatitude, in virtue of which they can behold from heaven the affairs of earth (as Coster wishes, *Enchiridion controuersarium* 14 [1586], pp. 417-38). It is falsely assumed both that such a vision is granted and that it increases the blessedness of the saints. Nor can either the example of Stephen (to whom, by an extraordinary dispensation, it was granted to see Christ in heaven) or of Paul (caught up into the third heaven and hearing there unutterable things) prove that the saints living in heaven see the thoughts of the heart (which belongs to God alone).

4. Because it is idolatrous.

XV. Fourth, all religious worship and invocation (directed to any other than God) is idolatrous for that is truly called idolatry by which the creature is worshipped "beyond the Creator" (*para ton ktisanta*) or "he being passed by" (Rom. 1:25), when they are worshipped "which by nature are no gods" (Gal. 4:8), which no one denies is rightly said of the saints. Hence Gregory Nazianzus calls idolatry "the transference of adoration from the Creator to creatures" (*metathesis tēs proskynēseōs apo tou pepoiēkotos epi ta ktismata*, Oration 38, "On the Theophany," 13 [NPNF2, 7:349; PG 36.325]), and Thomas Aquinas defines idolatry as "the giving of divine honor to a creature" (ST, II-II, Q. 94, Art. 3, p. 1598). Nor can the idle distinctions and incrustations obtruded by the papists remove so great a crime. They deny that they offer the supreme worship due to God, but only a subordinate (to the saints, not as to God, but as the friends of God). (a) They falsely invent degrees of religious worship (which is one alone and indivisible). (b) This was the limitation of the Gentiles, who distinguished between the supreme God (to whom supreme worship was due) and those holding a middle and inferior place (to whom inferior worship was also paid). (c) The Arians and Nestorians did not adore Christ as God (whom the former held to be a created god, the latter a man divided from the person of the *Logos*) and yet they were charged with idolatry by the fathers. (d) Who would excuse an adulteress saying that she furnished her body to another, not as to a husband, but as to a friend of her husband? And yet all religious worship is as peculiar to God alone as conjugal benevolence is due to the husband alone: since it is evident that our communion with God is frequently shadowed forth by wedlock, and idolatry by adultery and fornication. (e) The worship which the adherents of Rome pay to creatures does not differ from divine worship, neither as to the internal worship of confidence and hope, which they place in them, nor as to the external worship of adoration and invocation, which they offer them, as was seen above and we have proved elsewhere (Disputation 2, "De Necessaria Secessione nostra ab Ecclesia Romana," Section 16, 17ff. in *Opera* [1848], 4:40-42). Hence if they make a distinction in words to deceive the more simple, nevertheless it remains really the same in practice.

5. It rests upon a doubly false foundation.

XVI. Fifth, the invocation of the saints rests upon a doubly false foundation. The first is that they are our mediators and intercessors with God, who can obtain temporal and spiritual benefits for us not only by their prayers but also by their merits. Since this is most false and most dishonoring to Christ (as we will show in the proper place), whatever is built upon it must necessarily be false and fictitious. The other is the canonization or apotheosis of the saints by which the saints to be invoked by the church (introduced into heaven by the pope with certain ceremonies, especially with the golden ladder) are declared to be such as ought to be worshipped and invoked. But this impious fabrication of god-making (*theopoiias*), by which an earthly insignificant man, who is not certain of his own salvation, wishes to pronounce concerning that of another, and sacrilegiously to constitute himself the distributor of heavenly blessings, is a pure imitation of impure Gentilism and Jewish superstition, having no foundation either in Scripture, or in pious antiquity, as a long time ago divines remarked and incontestably proved (see John Prideaux, "Oratio xiii, De Canonizatione Sanctorum," in *Viginti-duae Lectiones . . . accesserunt Tredecim Orationes* [1648], pp. 120-28 and Hospinius, *De Festis Iudaeorum et Ethnicorum . . . de origine* 6 [1674], pp. 34-37). Not to say now that many fictitious saints are worshipped, who either never existed or are anything but blessed.

6. From the testimonies of the ancients.

XVII. Sixth, the invocation of saints was unknown to the apostolic church and to the first ages of Christianity. It is evident from the testimonies of the most ancient fathers. Justin Martyr says, "Hence we adore God alone and joyfully serve you in other things" (*First Apology** 17 [FC 6:52; PL 6.354]). The church of Smyrna denies that "she can worship any other" in Eusebius (*Ecclesiastical History* 4.15 [FC 19:241; PG 20.359]). Irenaeus says, "Him alone it behooves the disciples of Christ to worship" (*Against Heresies* 5.22 [ANF 1:550; PG 7.1183]). Tertullian says, "What we worship is the one God" (*To Scapula* 2 [FC 10:151; PL 1.777] and *Apology* 17 [FC 10:52; PL 1.431]). Epiphanius says, "The holy church of God does not adore a creature" (haeres. 69+). Athanasius says, "A creature adores not a creature, adoration belongs to the deity alone" ("Contra Arianos, Oratio tertia," *Opera Omnia* [1627], 1:394). Gregory of Nyssa: "He who adores a creature, although he may do it in the name of Christ, is an idolator, giving the name of Christ to an idol" (*Oratio Funebris de Placilla Imperatrice* [PG 46.891]). Gregory Nazianzus: "Neither worshipping any above nor under (*mēd' hypersebontes, mēd' hyposebontes*); for the former cannot be done, the latter is wicked and impious" (*Oratio* 22.12 [PG 35.1143-44]). And that the saints were neither worshipped nor invoked by them at that time can be proved by various arguments. No mention is made of temples, altars, images, festivals or offerings dedicated to deities (as is seen everywhere among our adversaries); that in the public worship of the church, they sang hymns to the one and only God; that in explaining the first commandment and the Lord's prayer, they did not (like the Romanists) make equal mention of religious prayers to the departed; that the canonization of saints was unheard-of and unknown among them; that most of them thought the souls of the saints existed out of heaven until the resurrection of the body; that the pagans nowhere charged the Christians with the worship of deities before the fourth century; that to the pagans worshipping God in the highest, ministers in the second place, they so constantly responded as to deny sternly that they adored any other but the supreme God alone, nor did they anywhere distinguish the worship of God from the worship of ministers; and other things of the same kind which clearly prove that such worship was unknown in the first ages (cf. the collection by the celebrated Daille, *Adversus Latinorum de cultus religiosi obiecto* 3 [1664], pp. 340-581). And if error gradually crept in through the progress of time (becoming apparent about the year 370 A.D.), there were not wanting those who strenuously opposed it. It was condemned by the Council of Laodicea, Canon 35 (Hefele, 2:317) and the Third Council of Carthage, Canon 23 (Lauchert, p. 166). It was opposed by Epiphanius against the Collyridians invoking the virgin (*Panarion* 79 [PG 42.739-55]) and by Augustine, who maintained that "they should be honored on account of imitation," not "adored on account of religion, with the worship of love and fellowship" (*Of True Religion* 55 [108] [LCC 6:280; PL 34.169) (such as is due to fellow servants and fellow citizens), not of religion (such as belongs to God) (cf. *Reply to Faustus the Manichaean* 20.21 [NPNF1, 4:261-63]).

7. From the testimonies of our opponents.

XVIII. Seventh, not a few of our opponents agree with us here. Cassander mentions the various errors on this head ("De Articulis Religionis . . . consultatio," Art. 20 and 21 in *Opera* [1616], pp. 963-81). Vives ingenuously confesses that many "Christians very often sin in a good thing, venerating saints and saintesses no otherwise than God; nor do they see in many things what is the difference between their opinion concerning the saints and what the Gentiles thought concerning their deities" (*Saint Augustine of the Citie of God . . . with . . . comments of Ludovicus Vives* [1620], p. 320). Cardinal Richelieu acknowledges that the primitive church did not invoke saints before the fourth century and maintains that the Catholic church does not absolutely bind Christians actually to pray to the saints (lib. 3, cap. 4 of his method, p. 410+). Thus he attempts to remove the stigma of idolatry from his church; but in vain, since this is confirmed by multiple sanctions and by continuous practice.

Sources of explanation.

XIX. From the civil addresses of the living to the religious invocation of departed saints, the consequence does not hold good. Among the living there is a mutual interchange of duties; between the living and dead there is none (Is. 63:16; Ecc. 9:5, 6*). The former rests upon God's command and promise and the commended examples of the saints of the Old and New Testament; the latter, however, is destitute of these. The former is merely the effect of social and mutual love; the latter is religious, a primary part of the worship due to God alone. That rests upon the love alone of the living; this upon the merits also of the dead. Nor if deceased saints now possess greater love, do they on that account wish to be invoked by us; yea, by way of retort, much less than in this life they permitted it (Acts 10:25, 26; 14:11-15), since they now know more perfectly that such honor is due to God alone. And if they could be addressed by us either by the voice or by letter (because they were with us sojourners in an earthly country), they ought not to be invoked in their heavenly country, which is far distant from us. If there is the same reason for the invocation of the saints and the salutations of the living, why did Paul (who so often orders some to pray for others) never command us to invoke the saints? And why do we not read of his praying either to Stephen or the blessed virgin or any other? To no purpose, therefore, do the Wallenburg brothers, Meth. Aug. c. 32+, and Bishop Condomensis (Jacques Bossuet, *An Exposition of the Doctrine of the Catholic Church* [1685]) attempt to persuade us that the papists invoke deceased saints in no other way than the Reformed invoke living saints—that they may pray for us. The protestation is contrary to the fact and the thing itself cries out that to seek pardon, protection, salvation, deliverance from evils (and the like) is far different from seeking their intercession. Nor can the intention of the church be obtruded here, when the words themselves prove the contrary (unless we wish to allow her to trifle with us by thinking one thing and speaking another, which no one would say).

XX. It is one thing for Jacob to wish (when he says that he desires "his name to be named on them," Gen. 48:16) that Ephraim and Manasseh, the sons of Joseph, should be named by his name and be two heads of tribes among the sons of Joseph (as Tostatus, Ribera, Cajetan, Cornelius a Lapide, Arias Montanus and others acknowledge; as the Scripture elsewhere expresses it, Is. 4:1); quite another for him to wish to be invoked by them after his death (which we deny).

Job 5:1.

XXI. When Eliphaz advises Job to turn to some one of the saints, he does not speak of deceased saints, but calls the living to witness of whom he denies that he can bring forward any saint agreeing with him in affirming that God afflicts the innocent and just (as the antithesis teaches and the series of the context). When Job calls upon his friends, by *r'y* ("companions" whose pity he implores, 19:21) angels or saints in heaven are not meant (since they were not his companions and familiars), but they who were formerly his companions and friends, whose sympathy (*sympatheian*) he seeks. Hence in the following verse he complains of the same friends, not intending to complain of angels. "The messenger," "the interpreter," "one among a thousand" (referred to in Job 33:23) mean no other than the angel of the covenant (Christ). To him alone can belong the predicates of having mercy, praying for deliverance, showing unto man his uprightness, interceding with the exhibition *khphr* (*lytrou*) "of a ransom" (*'lyw*) to him (i.e., the Father). For Christ alone can say, "I have found a ransom" (*mts'thy khphr*). Thus the ordinary gloss explains the text.

XXII. Invocation differs from commemoration. Moses does not address Abraham, nor fly to his protection (Ex. 32:13), but directs his prayers to God that (mindful of his covenant entered into with the patriarch) he may mercifully pardon their calf-worshipping posterity.

XXIII. The councils adduced by Bellarmine (held 400 years after the time of the apostles) could not introduce any new doctrine of religion not found before in Scripture, nor promulgated in the primitive church through so many years. They show rather what was done (the shades of superstition thickening) than what ought to be done.

XXIV. It is evident that no father can be found in the first three centuries as a patron of this invocation. Under Origen (as it seems, a good interpreter, but a bad theologian, according to Jerome), the opinion of intercession began to creep in among the teachers. Still not immediately did anyone invoke saints or teach that they should be invoked, until gradually (partly from the Platonic philosophy and the remains of Hellenism; partly from poetic and oratorical license and hyperbolical eulogies and apostrophes) Basil, Gregory Nyssa, Gregory Nazianzus (among the Greeks) and Ambrose (among the Latins) opened the door wider to this error. Sixtus Senensis very appropriately remarks: "We should bear in mind that the words of haranguers are not to be taken with the same strictness with which they come at first to the ears of the hearers. For speakers often utter hyperboles either influenced by a regard to places, times or persons, or carried away by the impulse of their feelings and the flow of the oration" (*Bibliotheca Sancta*, 6, annot. 152 [1575], 2:174). The fathers also frequently declare that the saints were invoked rather than that they should be invoked; or they employ a hypothetical invocation, only hesitatingly and with a limitation in these terms—"as I think," "unless I am deceived," "if the dead have any feeling," "if they have a care for us"—and when they do not express this condition it must be understood as implied.

Eighth Question: The Worship of Relics

Should the bodies of saints and relics be adored with religious worship? We deny against the papists.

Statement of the question.

I. Worship of relics is an appendix to the worship of saints. It is believed to pertain not a little to the honor of the saints that their bodies (or at least their bones, ashes, girdles, garments and similar relics) should be religiously worshipped. Although indeed the Sophists of the present day (endeavoring to cover and encrust the turpitude of this relic-worship [*leipsanothrēskeias*]) deny that the adoration due to God is paid to them, but only veneration and honor; still it is certain that it was sanctioned by the authority of the Second Council of Nicea in these words: "Adoring bones, ashes, garments, blood, and sepulchers, still we do not sacrifice to them" (Actione 4, Mansi, 13:47). Baronius says that he was sent by Clement VIII "to search for and worship the venerated body of Cecilia" (*Annales Ecclesiastici* [1868], Annus 821, 14, 14:15). Vasquez proves that "images and relics are to be adored in the same manner" (*De Cultu Adorationis*, Bk. 3, Disp. 4.1, 2 [1594], pp. 216-18). The Catechism of Trent approves of an oath by relics, which no one can deny is an act of religion (*Catechism of the Council of Trent* [trans. J.A. McHugh and C.J. Callan, 1923], p. 386). But under whatever name (whether worship is designated by adoration or veneration), it is certain that it is religious to them.

II. Now although we think the bodies of the saints with their relics should not be cast aside and made sport of, but should be decently buried (not only because they are the relics of men who ought to obtain honorable burial by a certain privilege of nature; but also because of believers and saints whose memory ought to be blessed in the church); yet we deny that they should receive religious worship. We deservedly turn away from the superstition by which (through sheer fraud to make sport of the people) the relics of the apostles are shown, while their writings are concealed. The relics are mute and there is no danger of their muttering anything against the pope, but the apostolic writings strangle the papacy and overthrow idolatry.

Arguments against the worship of relics. (1) The silence of Scripture.

III. Our arguments are: (1) Scripture has sanctioned such worship nowhere either by command or promise or example. As often as in the Old or New Testament the examples of the dead are commemorated, their bodies are said to have been committed to the earth without any ostentation or religious veneration. Thus dying Jacob and Joseph ordered their bones to be carried out of Egypt to Canaan that they might rest with their fathers; but nowhere do we read that they were adored or kissed, nor were they placed in a tabernacle or carried about in processions or placed upon altars (all which are constantly practiced in the Roman church). And how could the Israelites be induced to kiss or carry about relics when (according to the law of Moses) he was considered polluted who had only touched a corpse. God himself is said to have buried and concealed the body of Moses (Dt. 34:6) in order that the Israelites might not abuse the relics of so great a man to idolatry. It is very consistent with this that there was no other cause of the contest between Michael and Satan (mentioned in Jd. 9) than that Satan wished to draw forth the dead body of Moses, which Michael wished to conceal and keep hidden. The disciples carried the body of Stephen, the first martyr, to its burial and made great lamentation over it (Acts 8:2), but we read of no one prostrating himself on his bier or paying religious worship to his bones.

2. Mt. 23:29 opposes it.

IV. (2) Christ rebukes "the Pharisees and scribes, hypocrites, because ye build tombs of the prophets, and garnish the sepulchres of the righteous" (Mt. 23:29) in the meantime despising their doctrines. No less are they to be censured who worship and venerate their dead bodies lying in sepulchers. Paul protests that henceforth he knows no man "not even Christ after the flesh" (2 Cor. 5:16, to wit, that he may bestow all his zeal and labor upon seeking and possessing him according to the spirit). Now who would deny that they who seek and worship the relics of Christ and the saints, wish still to know them according to the flesh? Thus it is expressly forbidden "for the living to go to the dead" (Is. 8:19).

3. *It is useless and idolatrous.*

V. (3) Such worship is not only useless (being exhibited to inanimate things and wanting all sense), but also idolatrous and superstitious (cannot be given to them without sacrilege, as due to God alone). Nor does the encrustation of our opponents avail, denying that they give to relics an absolute religious worship (strictly and properly so called or latreutic [*latreuticam*] adoration, proper to God alone), but only a relative and douleutic (*duleuticam*). Scripture does not recognize the difference between the adoration of latreia, douleia (absolute and relative), but claims religious adoration simply for God alone. Nor will God judge according to those ingenious but idle distinctions and intentions of prevaricating men (which the common people know nothing of), but according to the rule prescribed in his word.

4. *It is exposed to impostures.*

VI. (4) That worship is exposed to a thousand frauds and impostures; while instead of the true relics of Christ and the saints, a thousand suppositious and adulterated relics are obtruded and the bodies of many are worshipped on earth, whose souls are tormented in hell (as Augustine said). An example is given by Socrates concerning a certain Ammonius (a monk and robber) who was worshipped as a saint for a long time (*Ecclesiastical History* 7.14 [NPNF2, 2:160]). Gregory of Tours testifies "that in the coffin of a certain saint were found roots, teeth of moles, bones of mice and claws of foxes" (*Historia Francorum* 9.6 [PL 71.485]). At Zurich in a most costly box (in which the relics of a saint and the rules of martyrs were supposed to be deposited) were found (when opened at the Reformation) some particles of a burnt side, also a rope 12 cubits long and ribs of a cat or of a similar animal, and nothing besides. Our Geneva can bear witness to a not dissimilar fraud. Before the Reformation, we boasted of two special relics: the brain of Peter and the arm of Anthony. What was said to be the brain of Peter was afterwards shown to be a pumice stone and the arm of Anthony to be the hip of a stag. Cassander does not deny "that for the sake of avarice to allure the simple people, false relics were substituted, and feigned miracles reported, and superstition nourished by these miracles" ("De Articulis Religionis . . . consultatio," Art. 21 ["De Veneratione reliquiarum"] in *Opera* [1616], p. 973). If, however, we would enumerate such frauds, innumerable examples of them occur everywhere. From this it clearly appears with how great license the clergy insulted and trifled with the miserable common people; yea, it would seem altogether incredible that they could have been seduced by such base and so continual impostures, unless the thing itself proclaimed it (cf. Calvin, *Advertisement Tresutile . . . inventoire de . . . reliques* [CR 34.405-452] and Hospinian, "De Origine . . . Reliquiarum," in *De Origine Templorum* [1681], pp. 92-122). Therefore as many as worship relics, worship they know not what. For after the detection of so many frauds and impostures, what certainty can there be that they are the relics of the saints they pretend to be?

5. It was unknown to the ancient church.

VII. (5) Relic worship (*leipsanothrēskeia*) was unknown to the first ages of Christianity. This can be seen even from this—they most carefully buried the bodies of martyrs and saints, which they would not have done if they supposed they ought to be adored. Eusebius testifies this was done by the church of Smyrna with the bones of Polycarp (*Ecclesiastical History* 4.15 [FC 19:242]). No mention of such worship paid to relics occurs in the books of the most ancient theologians, where not only opportunely, but also almost necessarily it would have to be mentioned. The pagans never charged our people with such worship for 300 years, as they did afterwards. Reliquiaries, such as are now constantly worn as arms and protection by Romanists, were then wholly unknown. Now from these and many other similar arguments (which you may find collected by the celebrated Daille, *Adversus Latinorum de cultus religiosi obiecto* 4 [1664], pp. 582-703), it appears clearer than the noonday sun, that in those first ages the worship of relics was entirely unknown and unheard-of; that it was introduced only in the following ages and indeed successively and by degrees.

By what degrees introduced.

VIII. At first ecclesiastical assemblies began to be held at the sepulchers of the martyrs and indeed on the day of their suffering; not however to worship and invoke them, which the epistle of Smyrna expressly denies, but "that the minds of their followers might be aroused by illustrious examples to the way of their predecessors" (cf. Agobard, *Liber de Imaginibus Sanctorum* 18 [PL 104.215]). Basil confirms this (*Homily 19* [PG 31.507-26]). Augustine writes: "To excite imitation, Christian people celebrated the memory of the martyrs in connection with religious solemnities" (*Reply to Faustus the Manichaean* 20.21 [NPNF1, 4:262; PL 42.384]) which thus far were devoid of superstition. But in the course of time the seeds of superstition were gradually sown. Under Constantine the Great the digging up and translation of relics from more obscure to more celebrated sepulchers began to take place. Indeed this was appointed by the emperor with a proper intention and praiseworthy zeal. As he desired to transfer the various external ornaments (which had conciliated any respect and authority for the heathen religion) to the Christian religion (that he might render it more acceptable not only to Christians but also to the heathen, as Eusebius tells us in his *Life of Constantine* 2.40 [NPNF2, 1:510]); so since he saw the heathen transferring with great pomp and solemnity the bodies of kings and other distinguished men (if they had been buried in somewhat obscure places) to more splendid monuments (yea, even to deposit them in magnificent temples), he thought that this honor ought to be shown much more properly to the bodies and relics of the holy apostles of God, martyrs and others. When however the bodies and relics of saints began to be exhumed and removed, presently a persuasion entered the minds of men that the martyrs and other saints were the columns, towers and guards of that country, city, place where their relics or bodies were deposited (as Basil tells us, *The Long Rules*, Question 40 [FC 9:313-14]). Another superstition immediately followed this, that the bodies of saints and other relics should no longer be buried under the altar, but be placed on them and prostituted to veneration. Hence arose the carrying around of the relics that they might be held in greater admiration. And because various miracles were wrought at the sepulchers of the martyrs, they began to invoke there not only God, but also the martyrs themselves; yea, even to worship their relics. Thus the error gradually grew and increased to the most superstitious worship and the grossest idolatry.

Sources of explanation.

IX. The miracle divinely performed at the bones of Elisha (2 K. 13:21) confirmed the faith of his preceding prophecy concerning the coming irruption of the Moabites, but does not favor the religious worship of his body. Hence neither before nor after that miracle do we read of anyone having visited the sepulcher of Elisha or kissed his bones adoringly. Again, that was a real miracle and free from all false suspicion (which no one can say concerning the pretended miracles of relics).

X. The touch of Christ's garment was an extraordinary symbol of miraculous healing (Mt. 9:21). Yet on this account neither was any other symbol of divine miracles religiously worshipped by any pious person, nor is there the same reason of the garment of Christ (clothed with which he willed to use for a demonstration of his divine power) and the popish relics (which either uncertain or separated from the living Christ, cannot have the same virtue and efficacy).

XI. The "shadow" of Peter (Acts 5:15) and the "handkerchiefs" and "aprons" of Paul (which healed the sick, Acts 19:12) were likewise symbols of extraordinary cures. But that on account of this symbolical office they should be adored, neither the apostles commanded nor does it appear to have been done by anyone. Did Peter, who would not be adored by Cornelius when living, wish to order the adoration of his carcass? Or would he suffer that before his shadow or aprons (pertaining not at all to his essence) men should prostrate themselves in reverence?

XII. The translation of the bones of the patriarchs tended to confirm their faith towards the promise of God concerning the possession of the land and the Messiah who was to be born in it. Yet it had nothing to do with the religious worship of their bones (which were again buried).

XIII. If Vigilantius did that one thing in order to set himself in opposition to the growing superstition in the worship of relics, he could not therefore be justly accused of heresy by Jerome (*Against Vigilantius* [NPNF2, 6:417-23]) or be associated with the Gnostics and Eunomians (from whose opinion he most widely differed). That Jerome dealt most unjustly with him in this, Erasmus himself cannot conceal, when he says that he was so much enraged against him as to be compelled to desire more modesty in him (as if he denied that martyrdom was to be endured or thought that the blood of the martyrs should be trodden underfoot and was to be worthy of no honor at all; while he only denied that the relics of martyrs should be worshipped). In this thing, we do not hesitate to say that we agree with Vigilantius. But if he nourished certain errors on other heads of doctrine (as Jerome charges him, how truly is not sufficiently clear), we confess that there is nothing common to us with him.

Ninth Question: The Second Commandment—The Worship of Images

Is it lawful to religiously worship images of God, the holy Trinity, Christ, the virgin and other saints? We deny against the papists.

I. There are two principal questions concerning sacred images: (1) concerning the worship of them—should they be worshipped and reverenced? (2) concerning their use—should they at least be made and placed in temples and other sacred places? We now discuss the former and will afterwards take up the latter.

Statement of the question.

II. The question is not whether images may be made which ought to be valued by us (whether we regard the artist, material or antiquity, or even on account of the prototype, if he is a man of some reputation, dear to us). Rather the question is Should any religious worship (whether called adoration or veneration) be paid to images of God and the saints made by the hand of men? Among our opponents, there is no agreement on this point, some roundly showing adoration, others however, to avoid odium, urging only veneration. But this is an empty distinction. Since religious worship is only one and does not admit of various species, it is equally such by whatever name it may be designated.

III. Second, the question here does not concern the mode of exhibiting worship to images, but in what manner images ought to be adored. This is done in order to examine the varying and adverse opinions of papists themselves who, like the builders of ancient Babel, are divided in their tongues and fiercely fight with each other—whether they are to be adored properly and per se (so that they may limit the adoration between themselves, as some hold); or, on the other hand, only analogically, improperly and with reference to the example and prototype (as others think). Whether with the same worship as the prototype (as not a few); or with a different and inferior worship (as others). Rather the question only concerns the truth of worship—whether any religious worship ought to be paid to them. This the papists constantly maintain; we, however, deny.

IV. The opinion of the papists can be gathered in no better way than from the decree of the Council of Trent. For although here, as elsewhere, they speak hesitatingly and ambiguously, so as to satisfy as far as possible each of the dissenting parties; yet they sufficiently disclose their meaning, when they appeal to the Second Nicene Council and approve whatever was sanctioned in it concerning the worship of images. The words are in Session 25, where bishops are commanded to "teach the invocation of the saints, honor of relics, and use the images, and charge those who teach otherwise with thinking impiously; that which was sanctioned against the opposers of images by the decrees of councils, especially of the Second Nicene Council" (Schroeder, pp. 215-16). Now everybody knows that this council (held in the year 787 and considered ecumenical by them) expressly sanctioned the adoration of images. Hence it anathematizes those who even for a little while doubt whether images should be adored. "We think the images of the glorious angels and saints ought to be adored. If anyone, however, is not so disposed, but labors and hesitates about the adoration of images worthy of veneration, the holy and venerable synod anathematizes him" (Second Council of Nicea, Actione 7 in Mansi, 13:743). However since to some the word "adoration" might appear too strong and they would be disposed to say in milder terms "that images should be reverenced," the Synod thus inveighs against them: "All who profess to venerate sacred images, but refuse adoration, are proved to be hypocrites by holy father Anastasius"; and he says that "they dishonor the saints" (Actione 4, Mansi, 13:597). Since, therefore, the Council of Trent approves whatever was sanctioned in that Synod, it is clear that its opinion was the same.

V. Second, this is confirmed by their daily practice in which it is evident that they prostrate themselves before images, kiss them, burn incense to them, erect altars, offer prayers, make vows, institute sacred festivals and make use of similar parts of adoration and worship. And that no one may suppose that only the people sin in that practice while the principal divines think differently, it is not difficult to show that their views correspond with this practice. Hence Thomas Aquinas wishes the worship of *latreia* to be given to the cross of Christ, no less than to Christ himself. "Since, therefore, Christ ought to be adored with the adoration of *latreia*, it follows that his image ought to be adored with the same adoration" (ST, III, Q. 25, Art. 3*, p. 2155). As usual, Cajetan follows him and Gabriel Biel —"If there are images of Christ, they should be adored with the same kind of adoration as Christ, viz., that of latreia" (*Canonis Misse Expositio* 49 [ed. H. Oberman and W. Courtenay, 1965], 2:264). A majority of divines embrace this opinion: Alexander [of Hales], Bonaventure, Richard [of Middleton], Paludanus, Capreolus, Castro, Canisius, Turrianus and many others, whom Vasquez counts up to thirty (*De Cultu Adorationis*, Bk. 2, Disp. 8.3 [1594], p. 133). He indeed contends with the greatest earnestness that all inanimate things can be adored with the worship of *latreia*—yea, even straw and the rays of the sun, under which the devil lies concealed (ibid., Bk. 3, Disp. 1.2, 3, pp. 183-89). Bellarmine wishes images to be worshipped, not only on account of the prototype (or thing signified), but also on account of themselves so that the veneration may be terminated upon the image ("De Reliquiis et Imaginibus Sanctorum," 21 *Opera* [1857], 2:499-500). Pertinent here is the fact that in a solemn and public worship, the cross itself is invoked in the hymn, sung in adoration of it on the Wednesday before Easter, for while the priest, uncovering the cross, says, "Behold the wood of the cross" and the choir responds, "Come let us worship"; the prayer is addressed to it, "Hail, O Cross, our only hope, in this time of Passion, increase righteousness to the pious, and bestow pardon on the guilty." And that no one may suppose that this is said metonymically of the crucifix, it is immediately distinguished expressly from it: "thou alone wast worthy to bear the price of the world." Thus in *Pontificale Romanum*: "The cross of the apostolic legate will be on the right hand, because *latreia* is due to it, and the sword of the emperor on the left" ("Ordo ad recipiendum Imperatorem," *Pontificale Romanum Clemente VIII* [1700], p. 645).

VI. I confess that this opinion does not please some among the papists, who hold that no worship ought to be given to the images of God, but that they should be esteemed only for history and the memory of past things. Not that the image itself should be adored, but only the exemplar itself before the image. This was the opinion of Gregory the Great, who praises Serenus, Bishop of Marseilles, for condemning the worship of images, but blames him for breaking them: "We praise you wholly for having prohibited their adoration, but blame you for having broken them; it is one thing to adore a picture, another to learn through the history of a picture what ought to be worshipped" (Letter 13, "To Serenus" [NPNF2, 13:53; PL 77.1128]). With him agree [William] Durand, Bishop of Mimatum (*Rationale* [1481], Bk. IV, Quart. Canonis, fo. 64), Gerson, Chancellor of Paris ("Declaratio defectum Virorum Ecclesiasticorum," n. 67 in *Opera Omnia* [1987 repr.], 2:318), Holchot, Tostatus and others on Dt. 4 ("Preclarum . . . super Deuteronomium," in *Opera* [1507-31], pp. 11-15). Nor is it doubtful that the more devoted and sharp-sighted papists incline to this opinion. But that it cannot be considered as the received opinion of the Roman church is evident, not only from Bellarmine and others, who fiercely reject it as rash and heretical, so that Baronius (on the year 794) says that they were insane who thought thus (*Annales Ecclesiastici* [1868], Annus 794, 13:255-79) and Sirmondus calls this the "heresy of the Gauls" (cf. *Concilia Antiqua Galliae* [1629/1970], 2:191-92); but especially from the Council of Trent, which expressly sanctions the worship of images.

The worship of images is rejected: (1) from the law.

VII. However, the orthodox impugn it. First, from the law because it contains an express prohibition, when the Lord clearly teaches us neither to make images for the sake of religion, nor to adore and worship them. "Thou shalt not make unto thee any graven image, or any likeness of any thing that is in heaven above, or that is in the earth beneath, or that is in the water under the earth: thou shalt not bow down thyself to them, nor serve them" (Ex. 20:4, 5*). This is confirmed: "ye shall make you no idols nor graven image, neither rear you up a standing image, neither shall ye set up any image of stone in your land, to bow down unto it" (Lev. 26:1; cf. Dt. 4:15). In these places they are forbidden to make not only a "graven image" (*phsl*), but also any "likeness" (*thmvnh*) whatever (even painted), expressing or representing by copy any shape, whether in heaven or on earth or under the earth. Could anything ever be more strictly forbidden than that every image (which may be used for religious worship) is here interdicted? Or was anything ever more manifestly violated than this commandment is in the Romish communion?

VIII. To no purpose is it here objected (in order to escape the force of this argument): (1) that this is a precept of positive right, binding only the Jews and not a natural precept by which all are bound, as Vasquez tries to escape (*Commentariorum ac Disputationum in Tertiam Partem . . . Thomae*, I, Disp. 104*.2* [1631], p. 678) and Ambrosius Catharinus ("Disputatio: De Cultu et adoratione Imaginum," in *Ambrosius Catharinus: Ennarationes, Assertationes, Disputationes* [1964], pp. 121-22), with whom Grotius agrees. The contrary is testified to both by the immediate and proximate end of the precept, which is of moral and perpetual right (viz., that the true God should be worshipped purely and uncorruptedly without any idolatry), and by its two parts—the first concerning idol-making (*eidōlopoiia*) because it is impossible and wicked to represent God by an image; the other concerning idol-worship (*eidōlolatreia*), which is simply forbidden (Dt. 4:15). Again, by the frequent repetition in the New Testament (even after the abrogation of the ceremonial law, Acts 15:20; 1 Jn. 5:21) and often in both epistles to the Corinthians. Third, the precept is known by nature, whence Paul convicts the Gentiles by it (Acts 14:11-18, 17:22-31; Rom. 1:18-23). This is confirmed by the history of many nations which would not allow the introduction of images (cf. *Plutarch's Lives: Numa* 8.7-8 [Loeb, 1:332-35]; Tertullian, *Apology 25 [FC* 10:77-81; Tacitus, *Germania* 9 [Loeb, 1:144-45]). Fourth, many of the adversaries acknowledge this with us: Bellarmine, ??"De Cultu Sanctorum," 7 in *Opera* [1857], 2:535-37; Suarez, "Commentaria . . . in tertiam partem D. Thomae," Q. 25, Art. 3*, Disp. 54, Sect. 7 in *Opera Omnia* [1856-78], 18:647).

IX. Second objection. It refers to idols, of things not existing (such as the false deities of the Gentiles) and not to the images of existing things. For this reason they think *phsl* should be translated by *eidōlon* and not by *eikona*. But that this is a fruitless way of extrication is evident: (1) because the word *phsl* is said of every representation, hence the Septuagint translates it now *eidōlon* (as in Exodus) then *glypton* (as in Dt. 4:16 and 5:8), then *eikona* (Is. 40:18, 20); the Chaldee renders it by *tslm'* ("image"). (2) Although the word *phsl* may be somewhat restricted, the word *thmvnh* (indeed with the mark of universality) ought to include every image necessarily, unless we wish a representation not to be an image and vice versa. (3) The Vulgate version rejects this distinction in Dt. 4:16 when it renders "sculptam similitudinem, aut imaginem masculi" and in Is. 40:18 "quam imaginem ponteis ei?" (4) The distinction between *eidōlon* and *eikona* is falsely taken for granted. Although in theological and ecclesiastical use idol is understood for the most part in a bad sense (and even in a good sense) for any representation; yet it is certain that in grammatical use they have the same signification and are used promiscuously for any representation. Hence the Glossator has *eikōn, eidōlon.* In Cicero, "image" and "idol" differ only in this—one is Greek, the other Latin. Says he, "Empty images of an atom, which they term idols" (*De Finibus* 1.6.21 [Loeb, 17:22-23]). So everywhere in Diodorus, Polybius, Plutarch and other approved authors, the status of kings, emperors and others is called *eidōla.* Among ecclesiastical authors they are frequently confounded so that *eidōlon* is used for a simple image, and in turn image for idol. (5) Although they may differ in this, that in everyday use idol is taken more strictly and image more widely (so that indeed every idol is an image, but not in turn every image an idol, unless some relation of divinity is added to it, whether as to representation or as to worship), it is certain that nowhere have they been thus distinguished from each other, as the papists maintain, as if an idol was only of things not existing, and an image of things existing. Uniformly (among profane writers) idol is used of existing things. In the Scriptures indeed images of the true God are called idols (as the golden calf is called an "idol" [Acts 7:41] and its worshippers idolaters, which nevertheless was formed to represent the true God): thus the idol of Micah (Jdg. 17:3, 4) and the calves of Jeroboam (1 K. 12:28). Again in the law God prohibits not only the images of false things, but also of things existing whether in heaven or on earth, etc. He does not say of those things which are not, but "which are." So every created thing becomes an idol when religious worship is paid to it. The brazen serpent became an idol when the Israelites wished to burn incense to it. The statue of Nebuchadnezzar was an idol when set up for adoration. Most idols of the Gentiles were images not of false things, but of truly existing things (viz., either of the stars or of men or of animals). An "idol" is said "to be nothing" (1 Cor. 8:4), not subjectively (by reason of existence) or objectively (with regard to representation), but with regard to efficacy and formally (because it is not the true God).

X. Third objection. In the law not all images are forbidden, but those which are made for the adoration of latria and are considered "as gods." We answer that the words of the law reject such an explanation. They forbid not only latria, but also dulia to be given to images, for the Hebrew word (*th'bhdhm*) signifies "serve them" (which is *douleuein*). (2) If only images esteemed as gods are forbidden, it would thus refer to the object of worship, not to the mode (and so the first commandment would be confounded with the second). (3) If the objection holds good, the Gentiles might easily be freed from the crime of idolatry. They often professed that they did not consider their idols as gods. Celsus says "who but a perfect child considers these (viz., representations) to be gods?" (*tis gar allos ei mē panta nēpios tauta hēgeitai theous*, Origen, *Contra Celsum* 7.66 [trans. H. Chadwick, 1965], p. 446; PG 11.1509). Arnobius introduces the heathen saying, "You err and are mistaken, for we consider neither the bronze, nor the materials of gold and silver to be of themselves gods, and religious deities; but we worship the gods by them" (*The Case Against the Pagans* 6.17 [ACW 8:470; PL 5.1199-1200]). They speak in the same manner in Lactantius (*Divine Institutes* 2.2 [FC 49:97-101]). Augustine mentions and refutes this subterfuge. "They seem to themselves to be of a purer religion, who say, I neither worship the image, nor demons, but through the bodily appearance I behold the sign of that which I ought to worship" (*Psalm 115 [113].6 [4]* [NPNF1, 8:552; PL 37.1483]). "I worship not this visible thing, but the divinity dwelling there invisibly" (*Ennaratio in Psalmum CXIII* ["In Psalmum CXIII Alterum: De altera parte," 3] PL 37.1483). Neither would the Israelites have been idolaters of the golden calf, which they did not suppose to be God. For who can believe them to have been so stupid as to believe the work of their own hands to be that of God who had led them out of Egypt? They intended merely to form for themselves a representation of him that they might worship the true God in this image (according to Aaron himself, who calls the feast consecrated to this idol "the feast of Jehovah," Ex. 32:5). Nor is it an objection that they said to Aaron "make us gods" because it is well known that in Scripture the names of the things signified are often given to the signs.

XI. Hence it is evident that our adversaries can in no way free themselves from the crime of idolatry brought upon them by the law. While they attend to this and feel themselves pressed by such an express command, they turn their indignation against the law of God itself with a sacrilegious boldness and impiety unheard-of before, by expunging it from the number of the rest that it may not trouble them (if not from Scripture itself). Since this was not in their power, still they expunge it from the offices, the breviaries and other formulas of the divine law which are given to the people (which is verily a clear argument of a desperate cause).

2. Because image-worship is idolatrous.

XII. Second, the religious worship of images (never commanded or approved by Scripture) cannot be freed from the crime of idolatry. According to the usage of Scripture and of the ancient church, an idol is every image made for the sake of religion. Therefore he worships idols who bends and bows down before images (Is. 2:8, 9) or adores them in themselves with any religious worship properly so called whatsoever (which, under whatever name it may come, is due to God alone). Yea, they who worshipped images not indeed in themselves, but in the image of the prototypes, are called "idolaters" (as the Israelites in the worship of the golden calf [Ex. 32:4, 5] and in the worship of the two calves set up by Jeroboam in Dan and Bethel [1 K. 12:28]). For Ahab afterwards introduced the worship of Baal and of the false gods by images (1 K. 16:32, 33), who on that account is said to have done evil more than all who were before him. The same thing is said of the idol of Micah (Jdg. 17:3), which was sanctified to Jehovah and whose priest is described as the priest of Jehovah (Jdg. 17, 18). Thus the Gentiles (although they adore the prototype in presence of images) are justly condemned no less as idolaters. Finally that cannot help being idolatrous worship by which God is worshipped in a manner not due, but unlawful and forbidden. To no purpose is the objection here, that the images themselves are not worshipped by themselves (which would be idolatrous), but only in relation to the prototype or the prototype in them. For besides the fact that not a few of them wish the image itself to be worshipped properly and by itself (as something sacred) and to regulate the worship itself and not only that it may represent the exemplar (as Bellarmine teaches, "De Religuiis et Imaginibus Sanctorum," 20, 22 in *Opera* [1857], 2:498-99, 500-01), the words of the law expressly forbid all worship of images, whether absolute or relative. Where indeed has God instituted the relative worship of latria, whose proximate object is the creature and remote object God? Were not the calf-worshipping Israelites of old (and so the pagans themselves) ready to encrust their idolatry with the same distinction? Again, if a relation (*schesis*) to the prototype would take away from the crime of idolatry, there never could be any idolatry about images of the deity. For they could not be worshipped as images without a relation to the prototype which they represent.

3. Because they can be worshipped neither on account of themselves, nor on account of the exemplar.

XIII. Third, if images could be religiously worshipped, it would be either on account of themselves or of the exemplar. But neither can be said. Not on account of themselves, because they are beneath the dignity of man which are made and preserved by the care of men (as being inanimate things subject to the hand and fancy of the artificer); hence so often the worship of images is forbidden because they are the workmanship of men's hands (Ps. 115:8; Is. 40:18; Jer. 10:14; Hab. 2:18, 19). Not on account of the exemplar, either God or the saints, because God does not wish to be worshipped in an image (in which he has not put his name) and cannot be represented by a material image; and the saints must not be worshipped either by themselves or by images.

4. Because it was unknown in the ancient church.

XIV. Fourth, the worship of images was unknown in the Christian church during the first four centuries. This appears from the various testimonies of the fathers impugning it: Origen, *Contra Celsum* 3.40 and 7.70 (trans. H. Chadwick, 1965), pp. 155-56 and 384-85; Tertullian, *Apology* 12 (FC 10:41-42) and *De Idolatria* (ed. J.H. Waszink and J.C.M. van Winden, 1987); Clement of Alexandria, *Exhortation to the Heathen* (ANF 2:171-206); Lactantius, *Divine Institutes* 2.1 (FC 49:94-97); Epiphanius (cf. Jerome, Letter 51, "Epiphanius to John of Jerusalem" [NPNF2, 6:89]); Jerome, Letter 57, "To Pammachius" (NPNF2, 6:112-19); Augustine, *Ennaratio in Psalmum CXIII* (PL 37.1483). (2) From the Elibertine Council (Council of Elvira) where we have this express decree: "Pictures ought not to be in churches, nor any object of worship or adoration be painted on the walls" (Canon 36, cf. Mansi, 2:11). (3) The fathers constantly throw up to the pagans the worship of images and the Gentiles (answering the Christian charge that this is a disgrace) never bring forward the worship of images as practiced by Christians to remove or at least mitigate the odium of their superstition in reference to idols (which undoubtedly they would not have omitted, if any such custom had then existed among the Christians). They not only make no such reply, but upbraid them with the want of altar and images as the greatest impiety. To purge themselves from this charge, so far are the Christians from referring in the slightest degree to any use or worship of images among them that they rather employ various reasons to prove that it is impossible or unlawful and useless to make images of the deity. The Jews in their disputations with the Christians never charged them with the worship of images (which they held in the greatest detestation). Different fathers condemned the pictorial art, either as absolutely unlawful or as vain and useless. From these and similar reasons, it is indisputably gathered that in the primitive church the worship of images did not as yet prevail (which the celebrated Daille proves in his usual solid manner, *De Imaginibus* 1, 2 [1642], pp. 1-244). (4) Not a few of the papists confess this. Cassander: "it is certain that in the beginning of the preached gospel for a considerable time among the Christians especially in churches there was no use of images" ("De Articularis Religionis . . . consultatio," Art. 21 ["De Imaginibus"] in *Opera* [1616], p. 974). And afterwards: "Now how strongly opposed to all veneration of images the ancients in the beginning of the church were, Origen alone declares" (ibid., p. 975). "At length," says he, "pictures were admitted into churches as expressing the history of events or bearing the likeness of holy men" (ibid., p. 974). Erasmus says, "Even to the age of Jerome there were men of approved piety, who introduced no image into the temples neither painted, nor sculptured, nor woven, nor indeed of Christ" ("Symbolum sive Catechismus," in *Opera* [1704/1962], 5:1187). In the same place: "For no constitution, even human, commanded that images should be in temples; and as it is easier, so it is safer to remove all images from temples" (ibid., p. 1188). Lilius Gyraldus: "That certainly I will not pass over, we, I say Christians, as formerly Romans, were without images in what is called the primitive church" ("Historiae deorum gentilium syntagma," 1 in *Opera* [1696], p. 15). Polydore Virgil testifies "that almost all the ancient fathers condemned the worship of images on account of their fear of idolatry, than which no crime can be more execrable" (*De rerum inventoribus* 6.12 [1671], pp. 417-18). Add to these words the following in which he teaches that Moses inculcated nothing more strongly than that the people should not venerate anything made with hands; and that the prophet said, "Let all be confounded, who adore graven images" (ibid., p. 418). The Index Expurgatorius (with the sanction of the Council of Trent) ordered this phrase to be erased.

XV. However, after the fourth century, near the beginning of the fifth, Paulinus, Bishop of Nola, and Severus (Sulpicius), Bishop of Bituricensis, introduced certain historical pictures into the basilicas which they erected. This was not done that they might be images of that which is religiously worshipped, nor that the pictures themselves might be religiously worshipped; but only that they might be historical and commemorative symbols and also ornaments of the basilicas, as is evident from Letter 13 of Paulinus to Severus (ACW 36: 134-59). Since however by degrees from the use of images, the worship of them was introduced by some, it happened that in the beginning of the sixth century, Serenus, Bishop of Marseilles, and Gregory I, the Roman, decided to meet this superstition, though in different ways. The former by taking them away entirely; the latter, however, by retaining them indeed, but diligently instructing the people that they were useful only as remembrancers and should not in any way be adored. Hence writing to Serenus, he says, "We praise your zeal that nothing manufactured can be adored, but we judge that you ought not to have broken the images themselves" (Gregory the Great, Letter 13, "To Serenus" [NPNF2, 13:53; PL 77.1128]). Since, however, from the retention of images, their worship gradually returned and superstition creeping in by little and little, it prevailed both in the east and the west. Various decrees were made by the emperors concerning the removal of images: by Leo III, the Isaurian, in the year 726; by Constantine VI Caballinus, called Copronymus; his son who (338 bishops of the east being assembled at Constantinople in the

Seventh Ecumenical Council) had a decree passed against the worship of images in the year 754; by Christophorus and Nicephorus, emperors, in the year 775; by Leo IV in the year 780. However although Irene, wife of Leo IV, ruling over the east, strove to restore by her youthful son the images with which he was greatly pleased, in the general Council of Nicea, which sanctioned their worship in 787 contrary to the Constantopolitan; still there were many emperors in the east who did not cease to oppose it—Nicephorus I and Stauratius in 810; Leo V Armenus in 814; Michael II, Balbus and Theophilus in 824, 829, 830, 832; Michael III, Porphyrogenitus, in 866. See the *Decreta Imperialia* concerning the worship of images.

XVI. But more especially in the west, Charles the Great was so indignant at the decree of the Second Nicene Council that he not only in a special treatise (very recently reproduced) entitled *Capitulare de Imaginibus* (PL 98.989-1248) (that this is the true and genuine offspring of the author, whatever Baronius and Bellarmine may allege to the contrary, even the testimony of Hincmar, Archbishop of Rheims [cf. "Opuscula et Epistolae . . . ad causam Hincmarii Laudunensis" PL 126.360; cf. PL 98.997-98], alone and the prolix letter of Pope Adrian [*Epistola Adriani Papae ad beatum Carolum Regem De Imaginibus*, PL 98.1247-92] to Charles in reply, abundantly demonstrate) most learnedly impugned the worship of images against the false Synod of Nice, but also assembled a Council at Frankfort in the year 794 which condemned the Nicene and enacted a severe decree against the worship of images. That from this time, the presidents of the western church constantly repudiated entirely all veneration of images is so clear that Baronius and the editors of the Library of the Fathers (*Patrum Bibliothecam*) confess (although unwillingly) that the most distinguished writers of that age held this opinion: among them is Agobard, Bishop of Lyons; Claudius of Turin; Jonas of Aurelia (Orleans) who indeed rebukes Claudius for his intemperate zeal in removing images, but agrees with him that they should in no way be adored (*De Cultu Imaginum* 1 [PL 106.305-42]; cf. Walafridus Strabo, *De Ecclesiasticarum rerum exordiis et incrementis* (PL 114.919-66). This was more strongly confirmed in the Synod of Paris by Louis I (the Pious), son of Charles, held in the year 825, in which the worship of images was again condemned. Hence Pithou: "Indeed if we seriously desire the truth, our men" [he means the French] "very lately began to be fond of images" ("Praefatio," *Historia Miscellae a Paulo Aquilegiensi Diacono* [1569], p. [6]). How many and how great commotions, however, were excited from the eighth century about the erection and worship of images between the image-breakers and the image-worshippers, both in the east and in the west, have been fully recounted by the illustrious Plessaeus in *Mysterium iniquitatis seu historia papatus* (1611) and Forbes in *Instructiones Historico-theologicae* 7.12 (1645), pp. 563 [363]-356 [368]. The latter in a historical narration concerning images brought down from the time of the Council of Frankfort even to the 13th century, shows the constancy of the French and Germans even to that age in rejecting images (cf. also Daille, *De Imaginibus* [1642]).

XVII. Before the Council of Trent, many among the papists inveighed against the veneration of images and the notorious abuses springing from their use, as William Durand, Bishop of Mimatum, John Billet (a Parisian Divine), Gerson, Biel and others. Yea, while the Council was sitting, Sebastian, Elector of Mainz, held a provincial council in which it was decreed that images should be set up in temples not for adoration or worship to be paid them, but to recall those things only to remembrance which ought to be adored (cf. Sarpi, *Historie of the Council of Trent* 3 [1620], p. 296). Also Catharine de Medici, Queen of France, in the year 1561 sent a letter to Pius IV, in which among other things she seeks "that the use of images forbidden by God, and condemned by the sainted Gregory should be removed forthwith from the place of adoration" (cf. Thuanus, *Historiarum sui temporis* 28 [1625], p. 563). In the year 1562, by his command, Valentinus and Sagiensis (Bishops), Butillerius, Espensaeus, and Picherellus were chosen to consult concerning the plan of entering into union with the Protestants. Among other things, this was proposed: "that the representations of the Holy Trinity should be removed from the temples, that crowns and garments should not be placed upon images, vows and offerings should not be made to them, they should not be carried around in supplications; that the sign of the cross should be no longer worshipped." However from that time (after the sanction of the Council) the worship of images prevailed everywhere in the Roman church. Still there were always some (and are still many among them) who are ashamed of such gross idolatry. Hence so many distinctions, pretexts and disguises are invented to cover up this superstition and to remove the odium of so great a crime (with which however they cannot satisfy even themselves). Yea, Bellarmine concedes, "If we treat of the thing itself, that images can be worshipped improperly and by accident, with the same kind of worship, with which the exemplar is worshipped; but as to the manner of speaking to the people, it ought not to be said that any images should be adored with latria" ("De Reliquiis et Imaginibus Sanctorum," 22, 23 in *Opera* [1857], 2:500-01). As if it was wrong to say what nevertheless it is right to do.

XVIII. Fifth, the dissent of papists, and their various and uncertain (yea, inextricable) opinion concerning the adoration of images sufficiently prove the falsity of the doctrine. While some hold that images should receive the same worship as the exemplar (viz., the images of God, Christ and the cross, the worship of latria; the images of the blessed virgin, that of hyperdulia; and those of the saints, that of dulia—as Thomas Aquinas with his followers and many of the Scholastics), others however assign an inferior worship to that of the exemplar (as Bellarmine and others); some that they should be worshipped properly and by themselves; others only by accident, analogically and relatively to the exemplar. Since therefore there is no agreement as yet among the worshippers of images (as to whether they ought truly and properly to be adored and with what kind of worship), such worship is falsely prescribed to the people, calculated to bring them into the most imminent and constant danger of idolatry. For who is there either among the people (nay, even among the learned) who either understands such distinctions or can rightly apply them when understood; so as by an abstraction of mind, while bowing before an image, not to give it any proper, but only a relative and analogical worship; or a worship only inferior to its prototype? Who on the other hand does not see that in practice the theoretical distinctions devised by divines to escape a too horrible idol mania are confounded? Bellarmine, indeed, could not conceal this, and speaking of the distinction between "relative and absolute latria," says, "They who contend that images should be adored with latria, are compelled to use the most subtle distinctions, which scarcely they themselves understand, much less the uninstructed people" (ibid., 22, p. 500).

Sources of explanation.

XIX. It is one thing "to bow down at God's footstool" (i.e., towards the ark, so called as the symbol of God's glorious presence); another, however, to worship the footstool itself. The former we grant, but not the latter. Nor is the contrary proved by Ps. 99:5 where the psalmist commands: "Worship, or prostrate yourselves at his footstool" (*hshthchvv lhdhvm rglyv*), as in v. 9 "at his holy hill" (*lhr qdhshv*) where the "place of worship" is proposed, not the object; as the Chaldee renders it, "Worship ye in the house of his sanctuary"; and the Septuagint translates the same words in Ps. 132:7, "Bow down at the place in which his feet stand" (*proskynēsomen eis ton topon*). (2) The pious are commanded to bow down towards the temple (Ps. 5:7) and yet all will confess that it was not to be worshipped.

XX. From the cherubim and the brazen serpent the consequent does not hold good to images. The one is a symbol, emblem and type of something (as the brazen serpent was a type of Christ); the other an image. (2) Neither the cherubim, nor the brazen serpent was adored (Vasquez himself confessing). God indeed promised that he would answer Moses from between the cherubim (Ex. 25:22), but nowhere commands him to worship them; nor were they set up for worship, since they were out of sight of the people above the ark in the holy of holies. As to the brazen serpent, so far from there being any obligation to worship it, it was even thrown down and broken in pieces by King Hezekiah, since the Jews began to worship it (2 K. 18:4). The Israelites were therefore healed, not by a religious worship of this serpent, but by looking at it according to the command of God. No objection can arise from its high position because the relation of type and the necessity of seeing demanded that. For both the sun and the planets are placed on high and yet not for worship.

XXI. The adoration of an angel, often occurring among the patriarchs, does not favor the worship of images, because they adored the uncreated angel, who not only belonged to Jehovah, but was Jehovah himself (as is clearly evinced by the circumstances of the passages and has been shown elsewhere, Topic VII, Question 9, Section 22).

XXII. When the apostle says that "Jesus Christ had been evidently set forth before the eyes of the Galatians, crucified among them" (Gal. 3:1), he does not speak of the fashioning of images of the crucifix (which were made either by the brush of the painter or the chisel of the sculptor), but of the preaching of the gospel, by which he is exhibited to us as crucified. Paul sets before himself no other object of teaching than Christ crucified (1 Cor. 2:2) and the word *proegraphē* used by the apostle means nothing else.

XXIII. The honor of the image does not pass over to the prototype and exemplar, unless he himself (who is the exemplar) has so willed or ordained. But if on the contrary he has prohibited any image of himself to be made or to be honored, he is treated injuriously if anyone goes against his will. This we maintain has been done by God here. Nor can a good intention be sufficient here, because the goodness of a work is to be judged not by the intention of the performer, but by the command of the legislator.

XXIV. From the worship of the "name of God" (prescribed in Ex. 20:7 and Phil. 2:10), the consequence does not hold good to the worship of images for then the name is not taken precisely for the syllables and letters, but for the thing itself signified by the name. In this sense, the Hebrews were accustomed to call God himself *shm* ("name").

XXV. Although we read that Christians before the time of Constantine the Great used the sign of the cross, but unreal (*anyparktō*) and only formed in the air by a certain motion of the fingers, as appears from Tertullian, *The Chaplet* 3 (FC 40:237; PL 2.80), it was not done according to any law of Scripture, but by custom alone (as he confesses in the same place). Nor did they employ this sign as in adoration or as operative *ex opere operato* (as Bellarmine falsely maintains, "De Reliquiis et Imaginibus Sanctorum," 30 *Opera* [1857], 2:512), but only as a distinguishing sign and mark by which Christians might mutually know each other and that what was thrown up to them as a reproach (their worship of the crucified) might be ascribed to his glory (according to Masius, *Iosua imperatoris histori illustrata* [1574], pp. 313-27, on Jos. 22). Hence Minucius Felix says, "Crosses, we neither worship nor desire; you evidently who consecrate wooden gods, adore wooden crosses, as perhaps parts of your gods" (*Octavio* 29 [ANF 4:191; PL 3.346]). If Constantine the Great in the heavenly vision (which portended victory by the sign of the cross) was so moved by these words *En toutō nika* ("by this conquer") as to make a standard in the form of a cross; and if his mother, Helen, is said to have found the wood of the cross at Jerusalem, in the year 326 (which even the silence of Eusebius alone ought to make us greatly suspect); we do not therefore read that any worship was rendered to the cross. Ambrose expressly refutes this. "Helen," says he, "found a title; she adored the king, the wood not at all, because this is a pagan error and the vanity of the impious" (*Funeral Oration on the Death of Theodosius* 46 [FC 22:327; PL 16.1464]). If afterwards images of the cross were gradually introduced into the Christian oratories (although repugnant to many pious persons), they were not yet objects of adoration, but symbols of Christian faith, until in later times, and especially about the eighth century in the false Nicene Council under Irene, this worship was sanctioned.

Tenth Question

Whether not only the worship but also the formation and use of religious images in sacred places is prohibited by the second commandment. We affirm against the Lutherans.

I. In the preceding question we treated of the worship of images. It remains to inquire further concerning their use—whether by the precept concerning images, besides the adoration, the making of them is also prohibited. Here we come into collision not only with papists, but also with Lutherans who (although they are opposed to and condemn the worship of images as unlawful and superstitious) endeavor to defend the making of images (*eikonopoiian*) and their use in sacred places as legitimate (if not for worship, at least for history and as the reminders of events).

Statement of the question.

II. The question is not whether all images of whatever kind they may be (even for a civil and economical use) are prohibited by God (as if the plastic [*plastikē*] art and all pictures as well as statues were condemned). Although this was the opinion of some of the ancients, Jews as well as Christians (as appears from many passages of Clement of Alexandria, Tertullian and others who thought that all use of images should be absolutely interdicted in order to withdraw Christians the more easily from the dreadful idol-mania of the Gentiles), still that this is a false opinion even the structure of the tabernacle and temple alone can teach (in which various figures of cherubim, oxen and other things were ingeniously wrought by skillful artists under the direction of God). Thus we do not condemn historical representations of events or of great men, either symbolical (by which their virtues and vices are represented) or political (impressed upon coins). But we here treat of sacred and religious images which are supposed to contribute something to the excitation of religious feeling.

III. The question is not whether it is lawful to represent creatures and to exhibit with the pencil historical events (either for the sake of ornament or for delight or even for instruction and to recall [*mnēmosynon*] past events) for this no one of us denies. Rather the question is whether it is lawful to represent God himself and the persons of the Trinity by any image; if not by an immediate and proper similitude to set forth a perfect image of the nature of God (which the papists acknowledge cannot be done), at least by analogy or metaphorical and mystical significations. This the adversaries maintain; we deny.

IV. Finally, the question is not whether it is lawful to have in our houses representations of holy men for a recollection of their piety and an example for imitation. Rather the question is whether it is right to set them up in sacred places; for instance in temples and oratories, not for worship and veneration, but for strongly impressing believers and exciting their affections by bringing up past things (which the Lutherans hold with the Council of Frankfort; we deny).

Proof that the use of images is unlawful. (1) From the second precept (Ex. 20).

V. The reasons are: First, God expressly forbids this in the second commandment, where two things are prohibited—both the making of images for worship and the worshipping of them. Nor can it be replied (a) that such images are meant by which men endeavor to express the essence of God; not, however, those by which either God or the saints are represented in appearance. The falsity is evident from this—that there would be no necessity of prohibiting this because no one is so simple and insane as to wish to represent the spiritual essence of God by any external and corporeal symbol. If we would speak accurately and philosophically, not even the smallest essence of the creature can be set forth, but only the external lineaments. (b) Nor can it be replied that it refers only to images of false gods. Moses himself clearly explained not representing God (Dt. 4:12); yea, even God himself (the best interpreter of his own law) intimates this (Is. 40:18). Hence the Israelites representing God by the image of a calf were sharply rebuked and heavily punished (Ex. 32). Pious kings of the Jews no less than of the heathen removed idols, even as God had laid both commands upon his people that they should demolish the altars of the Canaanites, break the statues and not make molten gods for themselves (Ex. 34:13, 17).

2. From the nature of God.

VI. Second, God, being boundless (*apeiros*) and invisible (*aoratos*), can be represented by no image: "To whom will ye liken God? or what likeness" (or "image" as the Vulgate has it) "will ye compare unto him" (Is. 40:18). Paul refers to this in Acts 17:29: "Forasmuch then as we are the offspring of God, we ought not to think that the Godhead is like unto gold, or silver, or stone, graven by art and man's device." Hence God in promulgating the law wished to set forth no likeness of himself, that the people might understand that they must abstain from every image of him as a thing unlawful; yea, even impossible: "Take ye therefore good heed unto yourselves; (for ye saw no manner of similitude on the day that the Lord spake unto you . . . lest ye corrupt yourselves, and make you a graven image, the similitude of any figure, the likeness of male or female" (Dt. 4:15, 16*). This the apostle condemns in the Gentiles "who changed the glory of the incorruptible God into an image made like to corruptible man, and to birds, and fourfooted beasts, and creeping things" (Rom. 1:23). Indeed this was not unknown to various Gentiles, who thought it unlawful to wish to represent the deity by an image. Plutarch: "He (Numa) however, forbids any image of God, like man or any animal; nor was there before among them any sculptured or graven representation of God. Indeed during all those preceding 160 years they continually built temples and erected sacred buildings, or shrines; still they made no corporeal representation, judging that it was not holy to liken better things to worse, and that God could be apprehended by us in no other way than by the mind alone" (*Plutarch's Lives: Numa* 8.7-8 [Loeb, 1:334-35]). Thus Antiphanes: "God is not discerned by an image, is not seen by the eyes, is like to no one, wherefore no one can learn him from an image" (*De Deo*+). And Herodotus: "The Persians have neither statues nor altars, and think those who make them insane, because they do not (like the Greeks) think the Gods to be the offspring of men" (Herodotus, 1.131 [Loeb, 1:170-71]).

3. Because it is connected with the danger of idolatry.

VII. Third, that ought to be distant from sacred places which does not belong to the worship of God and is joined with danger of idolatry. Now images in sacred places do not belong to the worship of God, since indeed God has expressly removed them from his worship by the law and they are connected with the most imminent danger of idolatry. For men (especially uneducated men prone by nature to superstition) are moved to the worship of them by the very reverence for the place, as experience shows. As Brochmann properly acknowledges, "Rather ought all images of whatsoever kind to be removed than that we should permit them to stand in a public place for the sake of religious worship against the express command of God" ("De Lege," 7, Q. 1 in *Universae theologicae systema* [1638], 2:46). In vain is the reply made here that indeed the occasion of sin per se is prohibited, not likewise that which is by accident; otherwise the sun ought to be taken away from the heavens since it has afforded the occasion of idolatry to innumerable persons. Therefore the abuse should be removed, but not the lawful use of them. For the abuse indeed ought not to take away the legitimate use, if any such is granted from the appointment of God (which the adversaries suppose; we deny). Second objection: that only worship makes images unlawful, from which Lutherans profess that they shrink. We answer that although they are not expressly worshipped by them (as by the papists) by bowing the knee and burning incense to them or offering prayers, still they cannot be said to be free from all worship; if not direct, at least indirect and participative because they hold that by images and the sight of them they conceive holy thoughts concerning God and Christ (which cannot but belong to the worship of God, so that thus they really worship God by images). Finally, if they are not worshipped by them, they can be worshipped by others (namely by papists if they enter their churches) and so render the use of them in churches unlawful (exposed to the danger of idolatry) by which idolaters are confirmed in their error and innumerable persons—not only unbelieving Jews and Mohammedans, but believing Christians—are scandalized.

VIII. Our ancestors cannot therefore be blamed for their zeal at the time of the Reformation in causing all images to be removed from sacred places. They did nothing here which was not commanded by God (Num. 33:52; Dt. 7:5; Ezk. 20:7) and confirmed by various examples of kings and emperors. In destroying idols and purging all sacred places of every kind of idolatry, the latter labored diligently, as was done by Hezekiah, who "removed the high places, and brake the images, and cut down the groves, and brake in pieces the brazen serpent that Moses had made: for unto those days the children of Israel did burn incense to it" (2 K. 18:4). For this reason various emperors obtained the name of "image-breakers" (*iconoclastarum*).

Sources of explanation.

IX. Although God sometimes manifested himself in a visible form and in such an appearance is described to us in Scripture (when members and bodily actions are ascribed to him), it does not follow that it is lawful to represent him by an image. (1) The same God who thus appeared nevertheless strongly forbade the Israelites to fabricate any representation of him (to wit, God could employ speech, bodies and symbols, in order to testify his special presence; yet not on that account may man make unto God an image and statue in which he may exhibit himself to man). (2) Those bodily appearances were exhibited only in vision, shadowing forth not the essence of God, but in some measure his works and external glory; indeed extraordinary not ordinary, temporal not perpetual, not presented openly to all, but shown to individuals, especially in the spirit. Therefore they have nothing in common with images. (3) It is one thing to speak metaphorically concerning God in accommodation to our conceptions; another to form a visible representation of him as if true and proper and exhibit it publicly to the eyes of all.

X. The making of images is not absolutely interdicted, but with a twofold limitation—that images should not be made representing God (Dt. 4:16), nor be employed in his worship. Therefore to make images and to worship them are not to be regarded in the second commandment only as means and end, but as two parts of the divine prohibition. Images are prohibited not only inasmuch as they are the object or the means of worship, but inasmuch as they are made simply for the sake of religion or are set up in sacred places.

XI. From a mental image to a sculptured or painted image, the consequence does not hold good. The former is of necessity, since I cannot perceive anything without some species or idea of it formed in the mind. Now this image is always conjoined with the spirit of discernment by which we so separate the true from the false that there is no danger of idolatry. But the latter is a work of mere judgment and will, expressly prohibited by God and always attended with great danger of idolatry. Hence it is falsely asserted that it is no less a sin to present images of certain things to the mind or to commit them to writing and exhibit them to be read, than to present them to the view when painted. For there is a wide difference between these things.

XII. The consequence does not hold good from the figures of the temple at Jerusalem to the images of Christians. The former were commanded and the latter not; those typical and fulfilled in the New Testament, these not; the former placed almost out of sight of the people and danger of adoration, which cannot be said of the latter. Nor is Christian liberty to be brought up here (which is not the license of doing anything whatsoever in relation to the worship of God, but is the immunity from the malediction of the law and the slavery of ceremonies). Since the former figures pertained to these, they also are to be considered as equally abrogated in the New Testament.

XIII. So far from images being rightly called "books of the common people" and aids to piety and religious devotion, the Holy Spirit testifies that they are "teachers of vanity and lies" (Jer. 10:8; Hab. 2:18). There is another book to be consulted by all (learned as well as unlearned) which makes us wise and learned (to wit, Scripture, which is to be continually read and meditated upon by believers that they may be made wise unto salvation). But the pope takes this away from the people that they may be involved in inextricable error and that he may not be convicted by it. He substitutes other dumb books by which ignorance is not removed but nourished because he does not fear that they will mutter anything against it. So while for teachers he gives stones, the people are turned into stones and become no wiser than their teachers. Hence Augustine treats of the images of Peter and Paul (by occasion of which certain persons fell into error): "Thus forsooth they deserved to err, who sought Christ and his apostles not in the sacred writings, but on painted walls" (*The Harmony of the Gospels* 1.10 [NPNF1, 6:83; PL 34.1049]). (2) It would have been bad for the Jews to whom God denied those books (to whom nevertheless as more simple they were more necessary).

XIV. Whatever may be said of the utility of images in sacred places cannot and ought not to be opposed to the command of God forbidding them. That is taken for granted, not proved. Sacred signs are the sacraments, not images. The ornaments of churches are the pure preaching of the word, the lawful administration of the sacraments and holiness of discipline. The means for keeping the mind attentive are the presence and majesty of God himself and the difficulty and excellence of sacred mysteries.

XV. It is not sufficient to cast images out of the heart by the preaching of the word unless they are removed also from sacred places (where they cannot remain without danger of idolatry).

Eleventh Question: The Third Commandment

Whether every oath so obliges the conscience that we are bound to keep it by an inevitable necessity. We distinguish.

The question concerning the obligation of an oath is disposed of by three propositions.

I. To the third commandment belongs the celebrated question concerning the faith of an oath; or what and how great is the obligation of an oath; and in what cases we can violate or are bound to keep plighted faith. We reach the determination of this question in three propositions.

1. Proposition: an unlawful oath is not binding.

II. First, every oath repugnant to the law of God and the lawful obedience to magistrates (concerning things either unlawful or impossible) does not bind the swearer to a performance of it. An oath ought not to be a bond of iniquity and no one ought to be compelled to do anything iniquitously. The apostolic maxim ought always to hold good here, "It is better to obey God rather than men" (Acts 5:29). Here belongs that trite saying of Isidore of Seville: "In wicked promises break your faith, in a base vow change the purpose, do not perform what you have incautiously vowed" (actually, cf. Rudolf of Liebegg, *Pastorale novellum* 4.14, v. 1058 [Corpus Christianorum, Continuo Medaevalis 55:223]). And of the other Isidore (of Pelusium): "It is better in those things which have atrocity of wickedness, well to rescind bad promises than badly to seem to keep an oath" (*ameinon gar en tois enagesi ta kakōs epangelthenta lyein kalōs, ē to dokein enorkein kakōs*, *Book IV, Letter* 96, PG 78.1160). Hence the oath of David was unlawful and consequently not obligatory—swearing with fervor that he would put to the sword the whole house of Nabal on account of the denial of food (1 S. 25:22, 23); of Herod promising the head of John the Baptist to a most depraved woman (Mt. 14:7); of the Jews who pledged themselves to the destruction of Paul (Acts 23:21). Such oaths not only do not bind (because an evil thing receives no power from an oath), but if observed increase guilt. For then two sins are committed: one as a deed considered by itself, the other against religion from the abuse of the name of God (inasmuch as the proposed evil is sought to be strengthened by the authority of God). Of this kind are monastic vows which, as they are made badly, so they are worse if observed and are lawfully revoked.

III. There are various vicious oaths of this kind. (1) As to matter, they concern either unlawful or impossible things. (2) As to persons who cannot swear (such as children, idiots, fools, the intoxicated, madmen) or who cannot otherwise use the judgment of reason (such also are they who are not masters of themselves, but under the power of others [as children, slaves, women, etc.] who bind themselves to anything, they to whom they are in subjection being unwilling), they are not bound by an oath, but ought to rescind it according to the command of the Lord (Num. 30:4), even though taken under pretext of worship and religion. Thus when the formal reason of an oath is taken away, the oath ceases by reason of the event. This is the case with those who have sworn to obey a master or prince who afterwards ceases to be such.

2. Proposition: an oath concerning a lawful and possible thing binds.

IV. Second proposition: Every oath concerning a lawful and possible thing which can be performed without detriment to religion, to the obedience due to magistrates and the salvation of our neighbor ought to be kept without treachery and deceit; even if extorted by violence or fear, or connected with temporal injury and involving loss to the swearer. Such an oath was made with the invocation of the divine name, which is not to be profaned. Its truth rests upon the express words of Scripture: "Ye shall not steal, neither deal falsely, neither lie one to another. And ye shall not swear by my name falsely" (Lev. 19:11, 12). "Thou shalt not forswear thyself, but shalt perform unto the Lord thine oaths" (Mt. 5:33). "He that sweareth evil" (i.e., an evil of loss which he sees to be injurious to his property, not of fault) "and changeth not, shall dwell in the mountain of the Lord" (Ps. 15:4). Although the injury done takes away the obligation with respect to the man doing the injury (since no right is founded upon injustice), still the obligation made to God remains (which without irreverence and injury to God cannot be considered as void). And here is the case of a man forced to an oath by robbers, concerning the payment of a redemption price, who either ought not to swear or religiously to observe the oath made because the oath was made to God (who cannot be trifled with). (2) It is not made simply by an unwilling person, but it is a mixed action in which there is something voluntary (between the payment of the money and the redemption of his life, he chooses the better). (3) The thing promised is possible and private to which religion and truth is always to be preferred. Nor can it be said that thus robbery and rapine would be encouraged if the robber is paid what he has violently extorted. This is done by accident, for the traveller who has sworn neither assists robbers, nor approved their conduct, but redeems his life by paying what he had promised under oath. He can however meet this evil as far as in him lies by revealing the robbery to a magistrate. Nor is it any hindrance if he has sworn silence to the robber in addition. That is an oath concerning an unlawful thing which has the appearance of some collusion with the robbers. If this were not at all the case, still it hinders justice, confirms the depraved in their wickedness and affords to a neighbor the occasion of falling into peril of life (and thus in many ways sins against piety, justice and charity).

V. This very thing is confirmed by the example of the Israelites toward the Gibeonites. Although they had confirmed by an oath the covenant made with the former (deceived by their treachery as if they were strangers from most remote places), they did not rescind the oath when their treachery and deceit was afterwards found out, but fulfilled it in good faith (although they belonged to those nations whom God had devoted to destruction): "We have sworn unto them by the Lord God of Israel: now therefore we may not touch them. This we will do to them; we will even let them live, lest wrath be upon us, because of the oath which we sware unto them" (Jos. 9:19, 20*). And that no one might condemn this as not meeting with God's approbation, the joyful and miraculous victory testifies that he was pleased with it (Jos. 10:13). And when Saul (a hundred years afterwards) put to death certain of the Gibeonites, God testified how greatly he was displeased by sending a famine. This perjury could be atoned for only by the hanging of seven sons of Saul (2 S. 21:1ff.).

VI. As the religious force of an oath belongs to the divine court, so it does not come under the human court. Hence to no class or order of men is conceded the power to absolve from an oath: either from the whole by dispensation (which is a simple breaking of the bond) or in part by breaking it by a commutation (which is the transference of the bond from one matter to another).

3. Proposition: sworn faith is to be kept even with heretics.

VII. Third proposition: plighted faith is to be kept even with heretics and infidels. It is opposed to the opinion held by papists that faith is not to be kept with heretics (which both in a former age and in ours was the foundation of the dreadful massacres and slaughters of Protestants). The first authors of this perfidy were the Roman pontiffs themselves, who not only entertained this opinion, but both openly professed and approved it by their practice. (1) Against excommunicated emperors, kings and princes (who were regarded by them as infidels) with whom neither they themselves kept faith, nor did they wish others to keep faith. This was begun by Gregory III against Leo III (the Isaurian), the Iconoclast. (2) Against infidels (strangers to religion), as is evident even from the single example of Uladislaus, King of Poland, against Amurathes, the Turk, who, instigated by Cardinals Julian (Cesarini) and Francis (Condulmaro), violated a covenant and broke plighted faith. (3) Against pretended heretics, as was done towards John Hus and Jerome of Prague in the Council of Constance. This is strongly held and pressed by the Jesuits of the present day.

VIII. I confess that some of the papists (who are ashamed of such an infamous dogma) seem averse to this detestable opinion; yea, deny that it is a dogma of the popes. But the futility and falseness of this declaration appears even from the single decree of the Council of Constance: "The present holy Synod declares that no prejudice is generated against the catholic faith or ecclesiastical jurisdiction or that an obstacle can or ought to be interposed by any safe-conduct, granted by an emperor and other secular princes to heretics, or those reported to be heretics (thinking thus to recall them from their errors), no matter with what obligation they may have bound themselves, to prevent a competent and ecclesiastical judge (notwithstanding the safe-conduct) from inquiring concerning the errors of such persons and otherwise proceeding dutifully against them and punishing the same, as far as justice demands, if they obstinately refuse to recant their errors: even if relying upon the safe-conduct they may have come to the place of trial, while otherwise they would not have come; nor does the promiser remain bound by his promise" (Council of Constance, Session 19, Mansi, 27:799). This was also immediately confirmed in practice against John Hus and Jerome of Prague, who contrary to the plighted faith and imperial passport of Emperor Sigismund, were nefariously burned. Nor ought the Council of Trent (Session 15*, Schroeder, pp. 116-18) in the safe-conduct given to Protestants to have derogated in this particular from the Council of Constance by name and the axiom concerning the breaking of faith with heretics, unless otherwise she had acknowledged this to be a constant dogma of the Romish communion. Nor did Thomas Aquinas hold a different opinion, maintaining that "a heretic should be delivered up to the judges, notwithstanding faith and an oath" (II-II, q. 97, art. 1+). *Cardinal* Toletus says, "They who are held bound by the chain of friendship or oath to another are freed from such bond, if the person has fallen under excommunication" (*Instructio Sacerdotum* 1.13.7 [1628], 1:47). Now all heretics are *ipso facto* excommunicated. This is confirmed by Azorius (*Institutiones morales*, Pt. I, 8.13 [1613], pp. 529-34) and the Directory of the Inquisition where it is taught that "all those, who are held bound to another by any kind of obligation are then wholly freed, when they, to whom they have bound themselves, have fallen into heresy" (p. 3, q. 129+). This punishment, says the author of *De amisso jure obligationem*, produces many effects; nor do we hesitate to mention some. First, he with whom a heretic has deposited something will not be bound after the heresy is established to return the deposit. Again a Catholic wife will not be obliged to restore a debt to a heretical husband. Add to these that the keepers of citadels, forts or of states will not be bound to restore them to a heretical master, nor to guard them in his name. Finally, all vassals are freed by right itself from every obligation, even the sanction of an oath by which they had bound themselves to their lords. Thus Cardinal Simancas: "It also belongs to the punishment and hatred of heretics that plighted faith should not be kept with them . . . Catholics ought to have no intercourse, no peace with heretics. Wherefore faith given to them even confirmed by an oath, against the public good, the salvation of souls, divine and human laws, ought in no manner to be kept" (*De Catholicis Institutionibus* 56.52 [1613], pp. 529-34). Pertinent here are the impious decrees of popes concerning the liberation of subjects from the oath of fidelity to princes, either on account of heresy or excommunication. Nor does the mystery of Jesuitical equivocations and of dispensation of oaths have any other effect than to deceive men by so eluding all agreements and covenants that scarcely anyone can safely make a contract with them. How much more straightforward this opinion of Charles V, who, when solicited to break the faith plighted with Luther as a heretic, nobly responded, "Even if from the whole world faith should be banished, still it ought to remain immaculate with an emperor." This is also the opinion of the orthodox supported by the weightiest reasons.

IX. First, to keep faith is an act of truth, justice and fidelity. He that keeps faith does what he says, the characteristic of truth. He does what he has promised and to which he is bound, the characteristic of fidelity. He restores to another what is his due according to the promise, the characteristic of justice.

X. Second, it is lawful to swear faith to infidels, therefore also to keep faith with them as appears from the examples of Abraham making a covenant with Abimelech (Gen. 21:23, 24), of Isaac (Gen. 26:26), of Jacob (Gen. 31:53), of the spies with Rahab (Jos. 6:22), of the Israelites with the Gibeonites (Jos. 9:15). The condition of heretics cannot be worse.

XI. Third, God most severely punished such perjuries in the sons of Jacob against the Shechemites (Gen. 34 and 49:5-7), in Saul on account of the Gibeonites (2 S. 21:1-9), in Zedekiah against Nebuchadnezzar (2 Ch. 36:11-13; Ezk. 17:11-21); in Uladislaus, King of Poland, against Amurathes, the Turk; in Rudolph of Swabia, against the emperor Henry IV.

XII. Fourth, marriages with infidels are not to be broken on account of infidelity and heresy, nor plighted faith to be broken on this account (1 Cor. 7:13, 14); therefore no other covenant whatsoever because in such cases a religious pledge intervenes.

XIII. Fifth, faith plighted even to enemies is to be kept by the law of nature and of nations (as appears from the illustrious examples of Regulus, Agesilaus and others). Now under that law come infidels and heretics, no less than enemies themselves.

Twelfth Question

Whether it is lawful to use ambiguous equivocations and mental reservations in oaths. We deny against the papists and especially the Jesuits.

Statement of the question.

I. To understand the state of the question, observe: (1) that we do not speak of the rhetorical use of equivocations, for rhetoricians frequently use these in the figure called antanaclasis and *plokē;* also ironically, as in the common epigram: "Who can deny the descent from Aeneas' great line of our Nero? One his mother took off, the other one took of his sire" (Suetonius, *Lives of the Caesars*, Book IV: Nero, 39.2 [Loeb, 2:158-59]). In Scripture the same word is often taken in a different sense in the same place (Jn. 1:10; Mk. 8:35). Nor do we speak of the logical use which often obtains in disputations and other proving (*peirastikois*) discourses instituted for the purpose of exercising and strengthening the mental powers against sophisms. Rather we speak of the theological and moral use in giving testimony, either in a trial or in the case of confession; and whether besides the grammatical or logical ambiguity which often occurs either from the doubtful meaning of the words or from the structure of a discourse or from the various disposition of circumstances, another theological use is to be admitted under some pretext of limitation by which we profess one thing with the mouth, keep another shut up in the breast, in order that the investigations of judges may be escaped and the truth concealed.

II. The question does not concern a limitation proposed, either explicitly or implicitly; nor a limitation supposed, which can be readily gathered from the mutual consent of the speakers or from other plain circumstances. No one denies that such limitations or logical restrictions which may be elicited from the proposed or are supposed and understood on both sides are lawful and free the discourse from falsehood and perjury. But the question concerns a limitation supposed only and secretly understood by the speaker, amounting to a verbal or real equivocation. The verbal is when the words used themselves are of ambiguous sense and are received in that sense by the swearer (which he desires to conceal from the hearers that they may be accepted by them in a different sense). As if anyone being asked, "Is Peter at home?" should reply, "He is not" (i.e., "he is not eating"). Mental is when the words employed have one simple sense, but by a tacit restriction or interpretation (which he keeps to himself) they are changed into another (which was the nature of the reply of Francis of Assisi, who being asked in what direction a certain murderer who had passed by him had gone, thrusting his hands into his sleeves, answered he did not pass in this direction—meaning that he had not passed through his sleeves). In this manner, many of the Jesuits hold that a priest being asked whether he is a priest (if he should either be asked by one not a judge or has a reasonable cause for dissembling the truth), can answer that he is not a priest, provided he means that he is not a priest of Baal or that he is not a priest as to tell this to another.

III. The question returns to this—whether equivocation and ambiguity (not rhetorical or logical from the indifferent signification of words or the construction of a sentence or a collation of circumstances; but moral, intended to deceive, which reserves in the mind a limitation proposed in no intelligible manner, nor supposed and understood on both sides, but reserved within the breast of him only who speaks) can have place either in a trial or in case of a confession or in the common conversation of men, and excuse from falsehood and (if confirmed by an oath) from perjury. Our opponents affirm; we deny.

IV. The ancient heretics were masters of equivocations. On account of them, the Basilidians were rendered infamous. They taught that faith was to be dissimulated or denied by perjury so that martyrdom might be escaped (cf. Irenaeus, *Against Heresies*, 1.24* [ANF 1:350; Eusebius, *Ecclesiastical History* 4.7 [FC 19:215-18]). The Priscillianists followed the same thing after them, concerning whom Augustine says, on account of their contaminations and basenesses to be concealed, had among their dogmas these words: "swear, commit perjury, betray not a secret" (*De Haeresibus* 70 [PL 42.44]). The shuffling (*kybeia*) of Arius is also well known. He evaded the examination of Constantine concerning the Nicene faith (cf. Nicephorus, *Ecclesiasticae Historiae* 8.51 [PG 146.205-10]). In a former age the Jesuits (masters of all perfidy) recalled the same dogma as it were from the pit. Although not willingly but almost unwillingly, they brought it forward and have it among the secrets of their society, still in their writings they do not disguise it and sufficiently approve it by their deeds. The open defenders of this art are Cardinal Toletus (*Instructio Sacerdotum* 4.21 [1628], 1:578-83), Suarez ("Commentaria in secundam . . . Thomae: De Virtute et Statu Religionis," Tract. 5*, 3.10, 11 in *Opera Omnia* [1856-78], 14:697-701), Lessius (*De iustitia et iure*, Chap. 47, Dub. 6, Sec. 35 [1617], p. 688), Emmanuel Sa (*Aphorismi* [1607], pp. 291-98 on *juramentum* and pp. 345-46 on *mendacium*), Sanchez (*De praeceptis decalogi* 6 [1738], pp. 281-87), Gregory of Valentia, ad 2.2, q. 110+ and many more—Azorius, Maldonatus, Parsons, Eudaemon-Johannes (*Ad actionem . . . apologia pro . . . Garneto* [1610]), who professedly and laboriously pleads this cause. To all these ought to be added Garnett himself, who in practice and defense before judges approved this art, as can be seen in *Actio in H. Garnetum . . . proditione* (published by Camden in 1607) and in King James I, *An apologie for the oath of allegiance* (1609). All these belong to the order of Jesuits. With them agree Navarrus, the Canonist (*Enchiridion sive Manuale Confessariorum* 12 [1584], pp. 187-221), Bannes (*Scholastica Commentaria in Secundum S. Thomae* [1614], 4:96 on II-II, Q. 62, Art. 2, Dub. 8), Gloss of Canonical Law, in cap. ne quis 22 qu.+, Vincent Candidus (*Illustres Disquisitiones Morales*, Disp. 26, Art. 3, Dub. I [1639], 2:267) and many others.

V. Now although Becanus protests that injustice is done to himself and his allies because they teach that we ought to speak and answer sincerely, candidly and free from all equivocation; yet it can easily be seen that he in his usual way tergiversates and sports with equivocation. He maintains that an accused person is not bound to confess the truth, if the judge in his interrogations does not observe the legitimate process of right. Now the judge is considered as not adhering to the order of right when he interrogates concerning a concealed crime (about which there is neither a report against the accused, nor a competency of the judge, nor a full proof). In such a case, he holds that the accused does not lie if he denies the crime to have been committed by him; if, namely, the crime is still concealed as if the order of right depended upon the estimation of the accused himself.

VI. Still we must confess that not a few boldly and openly reject and oppose this impious dogma: such as Malderus in his *Tractatus de Restrictionum Mentalium Abusu* 4 (1625), pp. 20-32; Sepulveda in his little work "De Ratione Dicendi Testimonium in Causis" (in *Opera* [1780], 4:375-413); Paul (?François) Sylvius, a Duacene (Douai) theologian, and especially John Barnes, a Benedictine, who published a special treatise *Dissertatio contra aequivocationes* (1625) with the approbation of the theological faculty of Paris, which approved his doctrine by the consent of Thomas Aquinas, Scotus, Gerson, Lombard, Cajetan, Soto and all the Scholastics of distinction.

VII. This opinion the orthodox constantly follow. For although Becanus calumniously says that he may for a little while withdraw the nefarious doctrine of the Jesuits from the eyes of his readers, by ejecting the liquor as it were of a cuttlefish, he ascribes to us "that we strenuously use this art, and calumniously charge upon them what we ourselves do" (*Manuale controversiarum* 5.21 [1750], pp. 582-83), whom Brochmann follows ("De Lege," 6, Q. 4 in *Universae theologicae systema* [1638], 2:36-37). That they boldly lie is clear from the constant teaching and practice of our men. Nor does what each brings forward from Beza favor the calumny that he asserted in his *Confession* (in the year 1556) "that the body of Christ is truly and really present in the supper" (*A briefe and pithie summe of Christian Faith made in forme of a Confession* [1589], pp. 129-30). We hold to a true and real presence and perception of Christ to believers in the supper, although we reject a corporeal and capernaitic presence.

Proof from Heb. 6:16 that it is not lawful to use equivocations in oaths.

VIII. Our reasons are: (1) an oath ought to be an end of all controversy according to the apostle (Heb. 6:16); but where there is equivocation, controversies are rather multiplied than ended, since nothing appears whence the other party may ascertain whether it is done in good faith or not. Nor does the distinction of a competent or incompetent judge hold good here (who may proceed or not juridically), so that we must not equivocate before a judge proceeding juridically, but we may before an incompetent one. For even among enemies faith must be kept, nor are we to consider to whom, but by whom we have sworn. And although in a certain case, as Thomas Aquinas acknowledges, it is not only lawful, but also praiseworthy "to keep secret the truth, when you are not bound to bring it forward; still it is lawful in no case, says he, to declare a falsehood to anyone" (ST, II-II, Q. 69, Art. 2, p. 1490). For as Lombard says—with whatever art of words anyone swears, still God (who is a witness of the conscience) so receives it as he to whom it is sworn understands it (*Sententiarum*, 3.39.10 [PL 192/2.838]). Thus a simple asseveration is to be estimated not by a concealed reservation, but by the agreement of the distinct enunciation with the thing proposed by the interrogator (provided it be directed to him). Nor does it make any difference whether he addresses a competent judge or an enemy or a friend. For as a mendacious writing does not borrow truth from the reader, so neither does a false assertion from any auditor.

2. Because Scripture condemns it.

IX. (2) Scripture openly condemns this art when it rebukes those who speak peaceably to their neighbor with their mouths, but in heart lie in wait (Jer. 9:8) and those who walk in craftiness (2 Cor. 4:2). Hence he wishes us to renounce the hidden things of dishonesty and commands us (by manifestation of the truth) "to commend ourselves to every man's conscience in the sight of God" (*ta krypta tēs aischynēs peripatountōn en panourgia*). To no purpose is the objection that they do not everywhere and without distinction permit equivocation, but when a just necessity for concealment so requires that when you truly respond, still you may escape his conscience who has no right to know the secret. It is taken for granted that there is a just necessity for using such equivocation which cannot be without a falsehood. Although therefore they are unwilling that it ought to have a place, either in things of faith or in contracts (by which there might be a prejudice to others), or in morals (as in the common intercourse of life when truth is required among friends), but either in necessary defense to escape some great loss or to obtain a good of no little importance, elsewhere they extend it further "in any other act of utility or virtue" (as Garnett says) where "a mental reservation is considered expedient and zealous" (as Sanchez* maintains). "In the cause of religion in times of persecution, anyone can, and perhaps is bound," says Parsons, "to equivocate." In other things, however, by this remarkable doctrine, we can escape many sins, as Navarrus says. In this way according to them it will be lawful to equivocate when and as often as we like, as Mason (*The New Art of Lying, Covered by Iesuites under the Vaile of Equivocation* 3 [1624], pp. 41-54) rightly shows from the various cases of themselves. Everyone sees how dangerous this would be in the church, the state and in the reciprocal intercourse of individuals.

3. Because it is repugnant to divine right—natural and civil.

X. (3) This is repugnant to the divine, natural and civil right: to the divine, which forbids us to do evil that good may come; to the natural because it is a false signification, contending against nature and connected with an intention to deceive; to civil because this being established colloquys, oaths, contracts, commerce would be suspected and nothing would be safe and secure.

4. Because it imposes upon the magistrate.

XI. (4) It is wrong to impose upon a magistrate and to elude his questions by ambiguous answers (which the Jesuistical equivocations do because they so impose upon God, who stands over judges, and in whose name they act, 2 Ch. 19:6). Thus all decisions of magistrates are dissolved, since by equivocation neither the truth can be found nor controversies decided nor the guilty punished and the innocent acquitted.

5. Because a mental reservation is a grievous sin.

XII. (5) Mental equivocation cannot be employed without the most grievous sin. (a) It is a direct and manifest lie since one thing is concealed in the breast, another brought forward with the lips (and that too with the intention of deceiving) and the words are as much against the mind and conscience of the witness as against the thing itself. Nor does he escape who says that there is no falsehood here because the equivocator enunciates what is false, not indeed with the desire of deceiving but of preserving himself. He who thinks otherwise than as he speaks deceives another and intends to deceive, says Toletus (*Instructio Sacerdotum* 8.54 [1628], 2:1081-82), for he speaks in such a way as to produce a different opinion in the mind of another (which is to deceive). Nor does the circumstance of this being done to escape help the matter; for howsoever the primary end may be to escape danger, the intermediate is that you may escape by deceiving. A robber will say that he goes prowling about, not that he may despoil the traveller, but to consult for his own necessities. The judge will answer, "I do not condemn you because you had a regard for yourself, but because you wished to rob in order to do this, for evil is not to be done that good may come." (b) The nature of an oath is violated by such simulation (which is to give the most solemn testimony to others, which cannot be done when we unfold nothing certain by words, but something feigned and deceitful). (c) It is a grievous injury towards God to adduce his testimony (although feignedly) to prove a falsehood. (d) Thus the gate would be thrown open to all lies. There is nothing, says Azorius, so false that it cannot be freed from all falsehood if we retain at will something concealed in the mind. For we can easily deny that we have whatever is asked of us, understanding (namely) to give and to deny that we have done or seen what we have (to wit, in this sense, that we may tell it to others). It cannot be replied that one compound and total statement is made by a vocal statement and a mental restriction in which there is no falsity, it being lawful for man to compose his declaration from vocal and mental terms. Although such a mixed speech can in some way be admitted (when the believer speaks with himself or with God alone, who perceives whatever is in our minds equally as well as if expressed in words), still it cannot have place in testimony given before men because a mental reservation testifies nothing to the hearers. Of whatever kind therefore it may have been, it does not cease to be a lie and if confirmed by an oath, perjury (since that which in the testimony is signified by the vocal declaration is repugnant to the understanding of the witness).

6. Because a verbal equivocation is unlawful.

XIII. (6) A verbal equivocation is no less unlawful in an oath both because nothing certain is testified (without which the oath at least is worthless) and because it misleads and deceives the hearers (which is opposed to the nature of an oath) and because an oath of this kind confirming a lie is manifest perjury from the nature of the thing and from the very intention of the swearer (and is a profanation of the divine name). Nor is the relation of perjury or falsehood taken away if injury would be done to us or we are interrogated in an illegal manner (as if it were right for us to consult our own interest provided we speak ambiguously). For no injury done to us by men can justify the doing injury to the divine name (such as is done in a lie and still greater in perjury).

7. It is opposed to the example of Christ and the saints.

XIV. (7) The example of Christ, the apostles and martyrs affords the strongest argument here. We never read of their using equivocations. Although Christ, when once asked, held his peace to testify that he laid down his life of his own accord; still when he replied to the high priest and Pilate, he spoke openly (Jn. 18:19) and is said to have witnessed a good confession (1 Tim. 6:13). Thus the apostles conducted themselves in Acts before the Jews and Gentiles. The martyrs, when dragged before the tribunals of unbelieving judges, never eluded their interrogations or answered ambiguously.

8. It is pressed with various absurdities.

XV. (8) The opinion of our opponents is weighed down by many of the greatest absurdities. For if it is lawful to make true an enunciation clearly false by an added limitation (which anyone may mentally conceive at pleasure), it will follow: (a) that to no purpose has God enacted laws against falsehood and perjury, since there is no one to whom such a mental limitation may not afford help immediately; (b) that the devil is not the father of lies, or that he never lied since he must always have such a reservation; (c) that the martyrs were not only fools, but injurious both to the truth and themselves, since everyone is bound especially in peril of life to employ every lawful defense by which to extricate himself (which according to this Jesuitical hypothesis might easily have been done). (d) All confidence is taken away from trials, covenants and contracts, whether public (between princes or states) or private in ordinary dealings, if a mental reservation lies concealed, perverting and rendering doubtful all things. Since, therefore, this cunning-in-the-perversion-of-justice (*strepsodikopanourgia*) labors under so many and so great absurdities, it clearly appears with how much reason not only the orthodox, but also the more sincere papists have thus far rejected and opposed so rank and preposterous a fiction.

Sources of explanation.

XVI. It is one thing to pass over in silence something true; another to speak something false. It is not a lie when the truth is hidden by silence, but when by speaking a falsehood is educed; as Augustine answers the Priscillianists who excused falsehood by the example of the patriarchs (*To Consentius: Against Lying* 23 [NPNF1, 3:491]). Abraham could be silent about something true when he did not call Sarah his wife (Gen. 12:18) because he was not asked precisely this, nor was it necessary for him of his own accord to declare it; but he said nothing false when he called her his sister because "indeed," says he, "she is my sister, she is the daughter of my father" (Gen. 20:12). Again, the examples of the saints are recorded in the Scriptures, but are not therefore praised; nor are we to live by examples, but by laws. Hence Augustine: "When we read these things in the Holy Scriptures, not on this account because we believe them to have been done, should we also believe that they ought to be done, lest we violate commands, while we everywhere follow examples" (ibid., 21 [NPNF1, 3:489-90; PL 40.531]).

XVII. The promises and threatenings which have a tacit condition do not favor Jesuitical equivocation. Although it is tacit and not expressed, still it was not unknown to those to whom they were proposed (as the threat of destruction made by Jonah to the Ninevites [3:4] included a limitation known by all, unless they should repent; this very thing the Ninevites understood and therefore did repent). So Samuel, while he professes that he had come to Bethlehem to sacrifice unto the Lord (1 S. 16:5), says something which he was about to do and actually did, but he did not tell what he was about to do further because there was no need.

XVIII. Christ did not equivocate when he said "that he would not go up to the feast" (Jn. 7:8), while nevertheless he had determined tacitly to go up (as he did a short time afterwards). He does not say simply that he will not go up, but relatively with respect to a certain time. "I go up not yet [*Egō oupō anabainō*]" because, to wit, his own determined time or appointed hour of going up had not yet come, as he immediately adds. Therefore he put off and did not deny his going up. Thus he simply says that he does not know the day and hour of judgment (Mk. 13:32) without any mental reservation, but he means this according to his human nature as the Son of man. The gesture of Christ by which his disciples going to Emmaus (Lk. 24:28) were led to believe that he would go further does not imply any equivocation, but a concealment of his purpose which belonged to prudence, not to equivocation. "The Lord determined to go further," says the Jesuit Barradius, "unless he should be restrained by his disciples" ("De discipulis petentibus Emmaus," *Commentaria in Concordiam et Historiam Evangelicam* 8.12 [1622], 4:309). "The truth did not deceive," says Ribera. "If they had not detained him, he would undoubtedly have passed by and gone further."

1 K. 3; Jn. 6:6.

XIX. Examination to elicit the truth differs from a subterfuge to palliate a lie. The first is confirmed by the practice of Solomon in the case of the harlots and of the

Savior with Philip, whom he asked concerning bread, "proving him; for he himself knew what he would do" (Jn. 6:6). Hence it is evident that explorations differ widely from equivocations and prudently trying anyone or concealing an intention are just as far from lying as they depart from Christian sincerity who patronize a lie. In proving, it is allowable to conceal the truth; but to lie, to deceive, to perjure yourself that you may more safely prove, is not allowable.

XX. The fictions of physicians to soothe madmen always have an understood modification (most known in practice) so that it is evident from the thing concerning which it is treated and the end which they propose—that they do not feign to deceive, but only narrate fictions that they may consult the weakness of the diseased person. An explanation being made at the end of the business, not a perfidious imposture of equivocation heals all things.

XXI. When it is asked what must be done in the peril of a prince of our country or to preserve the chastity of a wife or mother or to escape the severity of an overbearing tyrant in personal danger or to divert a robber and assassin from a harmless traveller; a certain and just subterfuge for escaping cannot be accounted an equivocation (which cannot be employed without sin). Let us rather hear Firmus, Bishop of Tagaste, who being asked about a man sought by officers, "I will neither tell," said he, "nor will I lie" (Augustine, *On Lying** 23 [NPNF1, 3:468; PL 40.504]). And the woman on the rack: "I do not wish to deny in order that I may not perish, but I am unwilling to lie in order that I may not sin" (Jerome, Letter I, "To Innocent" [NPNF2, 6:1; PL 22.327-28]). Therefore we must do our duty leaving the rest to the providence of God, who knows how to protect the innocent without the help of sin.

THIRTEENTH QUESTION: THE FOURTH COMMANDMENT

Whether the first institution of the Sabbath was in the fourth commandment; and whether the commandment is partly moral, partly ceremonial. The former we deny; the latter we affirm.

Etymology of the word "Sabbath."

I. For the easier understanding of the most vexed question concerning the Sabbath, some things must be premised—both concerning the etymology of the word and concerning its various significations. The true derivation of the word (for there is no necessity for mentioning the worthless and absurd conjectures of many) is from the verb *shbhth* (i.e., "to cease" or "to rest"), which relates either to the existence of a thing, when it ceases to be and fails (as is said of the manna [Jos. 5:12] and of joy [Is. 24:8]) or to the operation of an agent when he ceases to work and is put for "he rested" and "stopped working." This is the proper signification in Gen. 2:3 when God is said to have blessed the seventh day because "in it" (*bhv shbhth*) "he had rested." Therefore that day is called *shbhth* and *yvm shbhth*. The Greeks render it by *pauein*, *anapauein* and *katapauein*; the noun *shbhth* by *anapausin* (as Josephus, *Against Apion* 2.27 [Loeb, 1:302-3], and the Septuagint frequently do also). Otherwise they retain the Hebrew word, as also the New Testament writers, who abstained from a translation of it as a word well known and so distinguish it from a profane and common rest (as was the case with many other Hebrew words, "Hosanna," "Pascha," "Immanuel," etc.).

Its manifold significations.

II. The use and the meaning of the word is manifold. The peculiar and primary (upon which all the others depend and which is understood here) is that by which it is put for each seventh day of the week and that too from the event—God after finishing the creation of things ceased from the creation of new species and determined that this should be set apart for the rest of man afterwards in memory of the thing; so that not only in imitation of God should they rest on it from bodily and secular works, but also employ it for divine worship. Accordingly for the same reason all the solemn feasts of the Jews were designated by the name "Sabbath," although they did not fall upon the seventh day (Lev. 23:32 and elsewhere), because they were kept almost in the same manner as the weekly Sabbath. Third, the first and last day of each festival (which lasted many days) is called a Sabbath because both were equally solemn. Here belongs the "second Sabbath after the first (*deuteroprōton*)" (mentioned in Lk. 6:1), so called either because it followed next after the feast of the Passover (which is the first from the second [*apo tēs deuteras prōton*] in the computation of Pentecost, as the great Scaliger holds); or because it was the last day of the feast (which as it was in order the posterior and second Sabbath, so in dignity it was equally the first or great Sabbath as the first day of the feast, which was solemn on account of the public assembly congregated on it; as if you should call it the first secondarily repeated). The latter is more agreeable to Beza and others. Fourth, the Sabbath is also taken synecdochically for the week itself, which the seventh day concluded: "I fast twice (*nēsteuō dis tou sabbatou*) in the week" (Lk. 18:12); also *mia sabbatōn* (1 Cor. 16:2) is put for the first day of the week.

A threefold Sabbath: temporal, spiritual and eternal.

III. Again a threefold Sabbath is mentioned in the Scriptures: temporal, spiritual and eternal or heavenly. The temporal is that which God prescribed to the Old Testament believers, which again was either annual (viz., each seventh year) in which he ordered the Israelites to leave the land uncultivated that it might have its own rest also (Lev. 25:2) and the forty-ninth year, which was the year of Jubilee (which was a Sabbath of seventh years, Lev. 25:8); or monthly, of the new moon; or of each first day; or weekly, of which we speak here. (2) The spiritual consists in that peace of conscience enjoyed by believers and cessation from sinful works which they ought to seek after through the whole course of their lives (which is referred to in Heb. 4:1, 3). (3) The eternal and heavenly is that by which, being received into heaven most perfectly freed both from sin and from the labors and troubles of this life, we rest eternally in God: "There remaineth a rest for the people of God" (Heb. 4:9, viz., a heavenly rest under which eternal happiness is usually shadowed forth).

First question: concerning the origin of the Sabbath.

IV. Two things particularly are sought concerning the Sabbath which are embraced under this question: (1) concerning its first origin or institution; (2) concerning its nature and use, or what is the nature of its obligation, moral or ceremonial? Both these are the subjects of controversy among divines and they dispute with great zeal even in our day. We will set forth our own opinion here in accordance with the judgment of the more learned.

Statement of the question.

V. As to the former, the question does not concern the author of the Sabbath, for all agree in referring its institution to God alone; rather it concerns the first beginning and origin of this institution—whether we must trace it back to the very cradle of the world or refer it to the promulgation of the law on Mount Sinai. Most of the Reformed embrace the former opinion (see a list of them in Walaeus and Rivet); some others follow the latter opinion. Now although each is supported by its own reasons (not to be despised) and the dissent is not fundamental, still we judge the first to be the truer and more suitable to the words of Scripture and to it we adhere, relying principally upon the following argument.

The institution of the Sabbath before the law is proved: (1) from Gen. 2:3.

VI. First, God is said immediately after the end of creation to have blessed and sanctified the seventh day: "And God blessed the seventh day, and sanctified it; because that in it he had rested from all his work which God created and made" (Gen. 2:3). These words are too clear to be turned by any distinction to the support of the contrary opinion. For God cannot be said to have blessed the seventh day and sanctified it unless by the institution of the Sabbath. That day was blessed for no other end than that it might be consecrated to the worship of God in memory of the divine rest from the works of creation. Therefore God is said to have blessed and sanctified it because by sanctifying he blessed it, separating it from secular and common use and dedicating it to divine worship; so that afterwards it might be sanctified by men in the public exercises of piety and the solemn worship of God.

VII. Of no force are the following objections. (1) This is said proleptically by Moses to show the equity, not the beginning of the command; so that God may be said to have sanctified this day, not when he ceased from his works, but when he gave the manna or when he delivered the law by Moses. We answer that although the Scriptures sometimes use a prolepsis, we are never to have recourse to it unless driven by necessity. But here there is no necessity for a prolepsis and many reasons stand in the way of its adoption. First, as God is said to have rested from his works on this seventh day properly and historically (not proleptically), so also to have blessed and sanctified it. These things are proposed in the same connection and ought to be understood concerning the same seventh day of creation; not of another similar day (which also the thrice repeated demonstrative article *h* indicates). Second, on the supposition of a prolepsis, the sense of the words of Moses will be: God, after the six days' work was finished, rested on the seventh day; therefore after the lapse of two thousand four hundred and fifty-three years, he blessed a similar day and sanctified it to sacred uses. Everyone sees this to be harsh and forced. Third, no solid reason can be adduced why Moses in a simple narration of history or of events (two thousand years before they occurred) determined to insert something which took place only in his own time. It would plainly tend to obscure rather than explain the history he was composing, not even the slightest intimation of such a prolepsis being introduced.

VIII. Objection two: that sanctification and blessing are to be understood with regard to the intention and destination, not with regard to the execution. We answer that he is said to have blessed the day in the same way that he rested upon it. Now he did not rest only in intention because he intended to do it, but really because he ceased from his works. (2) The destination was not then at length made on this day, but from eternity. Thus God might be said to have sanctified the day of the Passover and Pentecost because he then intended to sanctify them. Objection three: "Although God then blessed the seventh day, it does not follow that he then enjoined the observance of it upon Adam" for God does not forthwith command us to keep those things which he blesses. To bless and to sanctify are the acts of God, not ours; while a precept pertains to the actions of men. We answer that since blessing and sanctification are not done with respect to God, but to man, it is hence plain that God for no other end sanctified that day (i.e., separated it from a common and dedicated it to sacred use) than that it might be religiously observed by man.

2. From Ex. 16:23, 25.

IX. Second, in Ex. 16:23 mention is made of the Sabbath as already known and observed among the Israelites in the giving of the manna before the promulgation of the law. They are ordered to gather a double quantity on the sixth day, to support them on the sixth and on the seventh days, which day was the Sabbath of the Lord. "This is that which the Lord hath said, Tomorrow is the rest of the holy sabbath unto the Lord: bake that which ye will bake today"; and "six days ye shall gather it; but on the seventh day, which is the sabbath, in it there shall be none" (v. 26); and "See, for that the Lord hath given you the sabbath, abide ye every man in his place, let no man go out of his place" (viz., to gather manna) "on the sabbath. So the people rested on the seventh day" (v. 29, 30*). This could not have been said unless the Sabbath had already been instituted and commanded by God. Nor ought it to be objected that it was not instituted until just when the Lord said "tomorrow is the Sabbath." In whatever way it is read, whether tomorrow "is" (as most of the interpreters have it) or tomorrow "will be" (in the future), neither of which occurs in the Hebrew, this does not denote the first institution of the Sabbath, but only its confirmation and an exhortation to observe it properly. Nor ought the institution of so solemn a day to have been so obscurely made, but ought to have had also a solemn and clear declaration of the divine command.

3. From Ex. 20:8.

X. Third, the words of the fourth commandment ("Remember the sabbath day, to keep it holy") plainly imply that this law was not then given for the first time, but only renewed after it had fallen as it were into desuetude, that they should exercise particular care in this matter and not afterwards be unmindful of this command (as they had been before). The following words confirm this view where he repeats the reason for its institution adduced in Gen. 2:2, 3 concerning the rest of God and the blessing and sanctification of the seventh day (which sufficiently indicates that the Sabbath was then instituted when that reason applied). Hence Calvin says, "From this passage it is elicited by probable conjecture that the sanctification of the Sabbath was prior to the law. Certainly what Moses had narrated before (that they were forbidden to gather manna on the seventh day) seems to have been taken from a received knowledge and use. And since God gave to the saints the rite of sacrifice, it is not credible that the observance of the Sabbath was omitted" (*Commentaries on the Four Last Books of Moses* [1853], 2:439-40 on Ex. 20:11).

4. From Heb. 4:3, 4.

XI. Fourth, from Heb. 4:3, 4 where the apostle, about to prove that there remains a Sabbatism (i.e., a rest for the people of God into which believers will enter by faith as unbelievers will be excluded from it on account of unbelief), shows that the words of Ps. 95:11 (which he quotes: "As I have sworn in my wrath, if they shall enter into my rest") must necessarily be referred to this. Since the Scriptures speak of only three Sabbatisms of God—the first, after the work of creation; the second, after the introduction of his people into the land of Canaan; the third, as to the spiritual and eternal rest of believers and the blessed—the words of David cannot be referred either to the first rest of God (into which he entered from the beginning and which he prescribed to men by his example) or to the second (which he procured for them by the introduction of his people into the land of Canaan under Joshua) because both have long ago passed by. They must necessarily be understood of that third rest promised to believers in the gospel through grace and to the saints in heaven through glory. Thus the sense of the words (otherwise involved) is plain: "For we who believe," says he, "enter into the rest of God, as if he had said, and so have I sworn in my wrath, if they shall enter into my rest" (for although the words of the psalm are threatening, yet they include a promise by way of consequent; as in the commands of God, every command includes a prohibition and every prohibition a command). To prevent anyone from saying that these words should be referred either to the rest of God (which he took after the work of creation in Gen. 2:3), he adds *kaitoi ergōn* ("although the works were finished from the foundation of the world") to show that this could not be understood of the rest of which Moses speaks in the same place (because it had long ago passed by). That it could not be understood of the rest of Canaan, he subjoins, "For if Joshua had given them rest" (to wit, that true and saving rest in which happiness consists) "then he would not afterward have spoken of another day" (v. 8). Hence he concludes in v. 9, "There remaineth therefore a rest for the people of God" (i.e., a rest differing from the former ones).

XII. It cannot be objected here that the rest of which the apostle speaks in vv. 3 and 4 has nothing in common with the Sabbath instituted by God because it must be understood of the rest of God (i.e., peculiar to him and not of men). The rest of God does not exclude, but necessarily includes in this passage the rest or Sabbath of men. For no reason can be assigned why the apostle should except that rest from the laying of the foundations of the world, if it pertained in no manner to men and if under the rest of God he did not understand that which he had by his own example prescribed to men. (2) If the Sabbath of men is not here included, it will follow that Paul omitted the Jewish Sabbath (which he could not do without prejudice to the reasoning he employed) because it might have been objected to him that there was another Sabbath besides that on which God rested and that which the Israelites enjoyed after the possession of Canaan (to wit, the ordinary weekly Sabbath).

5. From the religion of the fathers.

XIII. Fifth, the piety and religion of the ancient fathers confirm this very thing. Since it is of natural and perpetual right that certain times should be set apart for the solemn worship of God, Adam and the holy patriarchs must have had some sacred and stated days in which to worship God and remember his blessings in the creation of heaven and earth.

And if there were then sacred days, it is right to suppose that this day instituted by God was observed, rather than some other days of which Scripture says nothing. To no purpose is the objection that they might have had other days besides this day. For since this is nowhere said, it is rejected just as easily as it is asserted. Nor without temerity are other times imagined which are nowhere mentioned; and that time passed by of whose sanctification such express mention is made before the law.

6. From the traces of a Sabbath among the Gentiles.

XIV. Sixth, not obscure monuments are extant among the heathen, both of the number seven in general as sacred and of the recurring seventh day held sacred among them. This seems not so much to have been drawn from the custom of the Jews (whose religion was despised by the Gentiles) as received from the tradition handed down from their fathers (*patroparadotō*) and conveyed to them by long use. Hence Clement of Alexandria: "Not only the Hebrews, but also the Greeks hold each seventh day to be sacred" (*alla kai tēn hebdomēn hieran, ou monon hoi Hebraioi, alla kai hoi Hellēnes isasi*, *Stromata* 5.14 [ANF 2:469; PG 9.161-62]). He proves this from Hesiod, Homer, Linus and Callimachus, by whom the seventh day (*hebdomē*) is called the "sacred day" (*hieron ēmar*). By Philo, it is called the "public feast" (*heortē pandēmos*) belonging to all the Gentiles equally (*Flaccus* 14 [116] [Loeb, 9:366-67]). Josephus says, "There is no city anywhere of the Greeks nor of the barbarians, to which the observance of the seventh day, in which we rest, has not reached" (*Against Apion* 2.282 [Loeb, 1:404-7]). Saturday is called "the sacred day" by Tibullus (*Tibullus* 1.3*.18 [Loeb, 206-7]; cf. more authorities in Eusebius, *Preparation for the Gospel* 13.13.677c [ed. E.H. Gifford], 2:732).

XV. Although God is said to have made known the command concerning the Sabbath through Moses (an emphatic arresting of attention being premised, Ex. 16:29; 31:13; Ezk. 20:12; Neh. 9:14), it does not follow that it had not already been instituted from the beginning. Not only what is at first instituted is said to be given, but also what is renewed (if perchance it has been obliterated or neglected) or what is clearly and distinctly promulgated in a new and more remarkable manner. Thus in Ps. 147:19, God is said to have given his statues and his judgments unto Israel and not to have dealt so with any nation; not absolutely and simply because the Gentiles bear the work of the law written on their hearts (Rom. 2:15), but relatively and comparatively with respect to the revelation made in his word. The Sabbath is said to have been made known in the same way as the law and the precepts and statutes (which are said to have been commanded by Moses). These are connected together in Neh. 9:14. Yet no one can deny that that law (to wit, the moral law) had been given before as also the statutes and various ceremonial precepts in the institution of sacrifices and of circumcision.

XVI. Things given commonly to all may be given specially to certain ones, with an emphatic distinction (and indeed as a sign of the sanctification of them). If these had been given at first in common and by negligence omitted or forgotten, they were afterwards restored to particular persons and commended for special reasons (as is the case here). Although therefore the Sabbath in its first institution had uses common to all and a general design (namely to celebrate the memory of the creation, contemplating the works of God and the performance of public worship of God), it nevertheless had special ends with respect to the

Israelites. Just as the rainbow (which was in other respects a natural sign) was made the sacramental sign of a thing which it had not before indicated (although it had existed). Thus what had been the sign of one blessing could (when blessed and instituted anew) be a special sign to those to whom the blessing had been enlarged. In this sense, the Sabbath is said to have been given to the Israelites as a special sign that they might be separated from other nations (Ex. 31:13; Ezk. 20:12), especially from the Egyptians, by a true worship of God (which otherwise was a common sign).

XVII. Although upright and holy Adam in his state of innocence ought every day to have worshipped God and contemplated his works, still this would not have prevented his having a certain stated time for the solemn and public worship of God—by ceasing, not indeed from works of righteousness and praise (which ought to have been continual), but from his daily labors in cultivating paradise (to which he was bound also to apply himself according to the command of God—although without weariness and fatigue, as was afterwards the case on account of sin).

XVIII. Although in the life of the patriarchs no express mention is made of a Sabbath kept by them, it does not follow that it was not at all known or observed by them. Theirs is a compendious narrative in which it is not necessary that all things pertaining to them should be found. It was sufficient for the Holy Spirit to touch upon those things which bore upon his purpose (namely, to confirm the promises made to them concerning the blessed seed, and to weave together their genealogy to exhibit the truth of history). So no mention is made of the Sabbath observed in the time of the Judges and of Samuel. But the inference would be false that it was not observed. (2) We do not read of the patriarchs observing any stated times for the public worship of God. Yet their piety forbids our doubting that they had certain sacred and fixed days consecrated to the worship of God. Now no other days could have been more fit than the seventh day of the week, which for a peculiar reason had been blessed and sanctified by God for the rest of man like the rest of God.

The second question, concerning the morality of the Sabbath.

XIX. The second question treats of the morality of the Sabbath—whether the fourth commandment, sanctioning the sanctification of the Sabbath, is moral and perpetual; or only ceremonial and constituted for a certain time. In reference to this, there are three principal opinions of theologians—two extreme and a third between the two. The first is that the command is simply moral and perpetual (held by the Jews). With them agreed the old Ebionites, Cerinthians, Apollinarians and others (called by the common name of Sabbatarians), who maintained that the seventh day ought to be kept sacred now as well as formerly. Eusebius mentions that they were condemned for heresy by the ancient church (*Ecclesiastical History* 3.27, 28* [FC 19:184-86]). They do not differ from those, who even now in our day hold that this precept is absolutely moral as the other precepts of the moral law and thus is of perpetual observance. The second asserts that it is merely ceremonial and so entirely abrogated by Christ. This was the opinion of the ancient Manichaeans and of the Anabaptists and Socinians of the present day (who hold that it was so abrogated as to pertain in no way to Christians). The Racovian Catechism answers: "It was taken away under the New Testament as other ceremonies" (*Racovian*

Catechism [1818], p. 219). And Volkelius: "The fourth precept of the decalogue concerning the Sabbath, formerly given to the Israelites, is ceremonial, not moral, and moreover has nothing to do with the discipline of Christ" (*De vera Religione* 4.14 [1630], p. 250). Others also are pleased with this opinion. The third (and mean) holds this precept to be mixed (i.e., partly moral, partly ceremonial; moral as to substance [viz., the necessity of divine worship on a stated and certain time], but ceremonial as to circumstance [viz., the special determination of the seventh day]). This is the opinion of the orthodox, and we will demonstrate its truth by three propositions.

First proposition: the fourth precept is not wholly moral.

XX. First, the fourth precept is not in all its parts moral and perpetual. It is proved both against the Jews and the Christians who urge its absolute morality still. First, against the Jews, from the nature of moral things: moral precepts strictly so called belong to the law of nature conformed to the image of God and to the notions of good and evil, virtue and vice (which have their origin in nature itself and by themselves conduce to good morals and so are of eternal and immutable right). Such, however, is not the determination of the seventh day, since it (whether considered simply [*haplōs*] in itself) is neither good nor holy; or comparatively is no better than the determination of another day, except on account of the authority alone of the one commanding. (2) From the precept itself (in which is prescribed the determination of public worship to the seventh day, which being a mere circumstance of time is for that reason to be considered mutable, and so ceremonial and positive, not moral). (3) From the design of the precept, for among other ends it also had the relation of a sign and type (which therefore ought to be abrogated in their own time). A sign when it is called a sign of the covenant made between God and the Israelites (Ex. 31:13; Ezk. 20:12, 20); a sign not indicative only of present grace, but also sealing future grace; not only that Jehovah is the God of the Jews, but also the God sanctifying them. A type because it is called with other ceremonies "a shadow of things to come" (Col. 2:16, 17) (to wit, shadowing the twofold rest which believers obtain in Christ). This rest is first spiritual both in quiet of conscience from the terror of divine wrath and in cessation from our evil works (referred to in Mt. 11:28; Rom. 5:1; Heb. 4:3; Is. 58:13, 14). Hence the spiritual worship of the New Testament is wont to be described in the style of the Holy Spirit (who loves to express as far as possible the mysteries of the gospel in legal terms) by the celebration of the Sabbath (Is. 56:2; 66:23). Next this rest is celestial (to wit, a rest not only from all sin, but also from all the toils and miseries of this life, Ps. 95:11; Heb. 4:10; Rev. 14:13). (4) Sabbaths are frequently enumerated by the prophets among the other festivals and ceremonies of the Jews (which, however, were of mere ceremonial and positive right and observed only from command and on account of it). Therefore the precept concerning the Sabbath also is related to them as to some part of it.

XXI. Second, against the Christians: (1) because all ceremonies and types as such were taken away by Christ; therefore also that which is ceremonial in the Sabbath. And that there is some such thing in it Christ testifies when he reckons it in the same class with other legal ceremonies, such as the institution of the showbread and the service (*leitourgia*) of the priests in the temple (Mt. 12:3-5). In the same passage, the Sabbath is included by him under the term "sacrifice" and that too of "sacrifice" as contradistinguished from "mercy" (Mt. 12:7, 8). (2) Our Lord testifies, "the sabbath was made for man, and not man for the sabbath, therefore, the son of man is Lord also of the sabbath" (Mk. 2:27, 28). Thus its sanction is of a different nature from the other precepts, subject even to the Son of man who has the power to abrogate it with respect to that which is merely positive (which cannot be said of the others). (3) The apostle expressly declares this when he says, "Let no man therefore judge you in meat, or in drink, or in respect to an holyday, or of the new moon, or of the sabbath days, which are a shadow of things to come; but the body is of Christ" (Col. 2:16, 17). Here (a) he connects the observance of Sabbaths with other ceremonials as something of the same kind with the distinction of food, of holydays and new moons. (b) He calls all these "a shadow of things to come (*skian tōn mellontōn*)" where the words *ha esti* are not so much diacritical (*diakritika*) as etiological (*aitiologika*), giving the reason why the Sabbaths should no longer be kept, because "they are a shadow of things to come." (c) He opposes Christ to them as the body in whom and by whom the thing signified was accomplished. In vain is the reply that weekly Sabbaths are not meant, but the various others prevailing among the Jews (which were typical). [1] What ought to be proved is taken for granted. The words of the apostle do not admit it because, since they are general and treat of Sabbaths in the plural without any limitation, they ought also to be extended to all; nor does it become us to restrict what the apostle has not restricted. [2] Festivals are here distinguished from Sabbaths. [3] The Sabbaths are specially meant (which were sanctioned by the fourth commandment) which frequently recurred and whose observance the Jews and Sabbatarians among the primitive Christians insisted upon. Still, however, it would be wrong to infer that the Sabbath is therefore merely ceremonial, as those who are of the opposite opinion thence argue (because what is ceremonial in a certain respect ought not immediately and so mutably to be such in all its parts, as will hereafter be proved more fully). (4) From an absurdity: if this precept is in all its parts moral and perpetual, then we are still at this time (under the New Testament) bound to the particular observance of the seventh day, nor could a transference of it have been made to the Lord's day.

Sources of explanation.

XXII. Although the command concerning the Sabbath is contained in the decalogue, it does not follow that it is in all its parts moral. The decalogue is not only a compendium of the moral law, but in it is given the foundation of the whole Mosaic Law (whose parts were three: moral, ceremonial and forensic). Hence besides the moral law (which is principally delivered here), there is given also the root of all the ceremonies (of which the divine worship of that time consisted) in the first table, as in the second the foundation of the Jewish polity and its judicial laws. We must therefore distinguish here between the thing commanded and the circumstance of the thing: the thing commanded is moral; the circumstance of the thing, however, is ceremonial (or at least merely positive).

XXIII. The Sabbath is called "a perpetual covenant" (*bryth 'vlm*, Ex. 31:16, 17), not by reason of absolute perpetuity, but as comparative and periodic on account of its continual observance under the Old Testament. The word *'vlm* is often used for a remarkable duration, but limited according to the nature of the thing. In this sense, it is applied to circumcision (Gen. 17:13), to the showbread

(Lev. 24:8), to the offerings of the first fruits (Num. 18:19), to the priesthood (Num. 28:23); and everywhere the word *'vlm* is used for the time of the legal economy up to the Messiah. It is used even for a shorter duration, for instance, for the time of Jubilee. The servant, it is said, "shall serve forever" (Ex. 21:6, that is, unto the Jubilee).

XXIV. From the fact that the law concerning the Sabbath was given before the fall (that that day might be sanctified by man after the example of God), it is well inferred that it is moral as to a principal part, but it does not immediately follow that it is such absolutely and simply. Not whatever God commanded or forbade Adam is of itself and in itself morally good and evil (which is evident even from the eating of the tree of the knowledge of good and evil).

XXV. The immutability of God and the constancy of his decrees makes those things which are of the natural right of God (or were decreed by him forever) to be also perpetual and unchangeable; but there is not the same reason for those things which are of positive right and were instituted only for a certain time (such as was the Mosaic Sabbath as to the circumstance of time and the mode of observation prescribed to the Jews).

Second proposition: the fourth precept is not merely ceremonial.

XXVI. Second proposition: the fourth precept is not in every part ceremonial. The reasons are: (1) it is a precept of the decalogue, in which the moral law is contained; therefore no precept of it is merely ceremonial. (2) Its end is moral, both the first (viz., the public and stated worship of God consisting in the consideration and contemplation of his works; also in the public exercises of religion, which cannot be accomplished without the determination of a certain stated and fixed day devoted to that worship) and the subordinate (to wit, the cessation from servile work for the relaxation of servants and of brutes). (3) The duty prescribed is moral (to wit, the sanctification of the Sabbath by separating that day from others, and consecrating it to sacred uses—namely, the exercises of piety and worship towards God and of love towards our neighbor). (4) The reason and motive of the precept from the example of God proposed to us for imitation (to wit, his rest on that day and sanctifying it is moral; we therefore cannot be conformed to it except by a performance of the moral duty answering to it).

XXVII. (5) The nature of the precept concerns things which become a rational nature as such and are agreeable to natural principles and right reason. For as a rational creature is bound to worship God (not only with the internal service of the soul, but also external of the body; not only private, but also public in the communion of saints), so right reason teaches that nothing is more suitable than to consecrate some stated and fixed time in a certain convenient cycle for publicly worshipping and celebrating the praises of God, who has gratuitously given our being to us, all that we possess and the whole of time itself. (6) We never read of the abrogation of this precept in the New Testament. Since Christ confirmed the whole moral law as pertaining to Christians and binding them at all times, by this very thing he should be considered to have confirmed this precept also. And since certain days have always been sanctified and devoted by the Christian church to public assemblies and the solemn worship of God, it is abundantly evident from this that the observance of this precept should be considered as moral and of perpetual right. Otherwise if the precept were merely moral, it would not be lawful now to observe any Sabbath, no more than to introduce by the back door other ceremonies which God has abrogated under the New Testament (and everyone sees how absurd this is).

Sources of explanation.

XXVIII. The precept concerning the Sabbath ought to be viewed in two ways: either absolutely and in itself (as to the substance of the command); or relatively (as to the Mosaic economy of the Old Testament and as to the precise circumstance of time; also the special reasons and ends for which it was given to the Israelites). Although in this latter respect it may be called a "sign" of the particular dispensation of that covenant (Ex. 31:13; Ezk. 20:12) and thus may have something ceremonial, it does not follow that it is a mere ceremony or that the precept considered in itself pertained only to that economy.

XXIX. Although the command concerning the particular place of worship was ceremonial, it does not follow that the command concerning the particular time is equally ceremonial, for there is here a manifold difference between the place and the time. (1) Mention is made in the decalogue of the observance of time, but not of a determination of place; therefore the circumstances of religion are not equal. (2) The necessity and utility of a certain place for worship is only physical and accidental to religion. It has nothing to do with the promotion of religion whether God is worshipped in an open place or in a church or underground or in a public or private place. But the necessity of the time, whether indeterminate or determinate, is far greater because it is moral and theological (whether we speak separately of the whole portion or the duration or the frequency, and much more if we speak of these together). There is no doubt that the greater portion of time (either as to duration or as to frequency or as to both) in the exercises of religion conduces to progress in piety and that he is more pleasing and acceptable to God who spends such time in sacred worship, than he who spends time rarely and briefly (provided other things are equal). (3) The determination of a time for sacred exercises is necessary because it is impossible that at one and the same time we can attend to worldly affairs and at the same time worship God. Therefore, in order that these may not hinder us from being free for divine worship as long and as often as it is required, such a determination is absolutely demanded. Yet nothing like this can be said of the place because in one and the same place (namely at different times), we can worship God and carry on worldly business. The determination of the place being made, it is not necessary that worship should be given there, if no determination of time has been made.

XXX. Although the weekly Sabbath (considered in reference to the Mosaic economy) and the ceremonial adjuncts (namely with regard to the particular observance of the seventh day and its scrupulous and exact observance, prescribed in the Old Testament) were a shadow of things to come and may properly be said to have been abrogated under the New Testament; it does not follow that the Sabbath itself considered in itself and absolutely is equally ceremonial and so has been abrogated. In Col. 2:16, 17, Paul speaks of the Sabbath in the former sense (in which sense the false apostles pressed it); but not in the second. In the same manner, he speaks of meat and drink, not absolutely and simply (because then it would follow that no moral precept was given about meat and drink and on that account gluttons and wine-bibbers are no more to be condemned now, than the observers of new moons), but relatively and comparatively, with reference to the law of food (which prescribed a distinction of foods, which has now been taken away under the New Testament).

XXXI. Although the institution of the Sabbath as to the determination of a certain day does not flow from the nature of God and is not founded absolutely upon the primary natural right of God, but depends upon his will and so is rather based upon his positive right, it does not follow that it cannot be moral and perpetual by reason of the secondary right natural to us. What is positive to God can be natural to us (as has already been seen).

Third proposition: the fourth precept is partly moral, partly ceremonial.

XXXII. Third proposition: the fourth precept, concerning the Sabbath, is partly moral and partly ceremonial. Ceremonial can be viewed in three ways: (1) in the designation of the seventh day, which, as it was changed under the New Testament, ought to have been ceremonial. (2) In the sanctification of that day, its strict and rigid observance from evening to evening, both privative (by the cessation from all servile work, according to which it was not lawful either to kindle a fire, prepare and cook food or walk and go on a journey) and positive (in the performance of various ceremonial works, partly common to other days—such as the continual sacrifice and circumcision—partly peculiar to that day—as for instance the sacrifices of that day for the whole church, the two lambs of the first year, the two tenth deals of flour mingled with oil [Num. 28:8, 9] and the showbread to be placed in the temple every Sabbath [Lev. 24:7, 8]). (3) In the typical signification of that day, to shadow forth the grace of sanctification and from it the spiritual and heavenly rest in Christ (of which Paul speaks in Col. 2:16, 17).

XXXIII. The moral also consists in three things: (1) in the appointment of public meetings for the worship of God on a certain and fixed time and day. (2) In the sanctification of the day itself, both privative by a cessation from the works of our ordinary calling so that we may have leisure for sacred meditation and divine worship (works of charity and necessity, however, being excepted); and positive, by the solemn and public worship of God in the congregation of the church. (3) In the relief of servants and beasts, for whom God had regard (that they might not be broken down by continued labor), and that servants themselves also might attend to sacred things.

Whether the determination of one day out of seven pertains to the morality of the Sabbath. Statement of the question.

XXXIV. Here, however, a new question arises about this morality (also the subject of dispute among the orthodox): whether from the force and analogy of this precept there belongs to it not only the determination of a certain time and an indeterminate day for public worship, but also the designation of one day out of seven in the weekly cycle, which, recurring in each seven-day period, ought necessarily to be observed. Concerning this: (1) it is not inquired about the suitableness of the thing—whether it was convenient and agreeable to reason for it to be so designated (for all agree that one day out of seven could rightly be instituted for the worship of God and was not instituted without various weighty reasons); rather the question concerns the necessity—whether it was absolutely necessary from the nature of the thing that this should be so arranged from the force and analogy of the precept. (2) The question does not concern the moral strictly so called. This is natural to God, being founded in his nature and holiness and flowing from his image (the contrary of which he cannot command nor dispense with without a contradiction). In this sense, all agree that the designation of such a day is not natural to God and that he was free to select either one out of seven or out of eight or out of ten days for his worship; and that he was not bound to the other part of the contradiction from any necessity of his nature. Rather the question treats of the moral broadly so called, which, although positive on the part of God, still is natural to us inasmuch as it suits the rational nature and the relation of man and his duty to God.

XXXV. Although the dispute is here carried on problematically on both sides (the bond of faith and love remaining unbroken, nor are weighty reasons wanting to the distinguished men who support the negative), still we do not hesitate to say that we incline to the affirmative with others and that the reasons brought forward for it seem to us the more convincing.

XXXVI. First, from the nature of the thing. For since it is natural and moral not only that man should worship God publicly with some external service (and indeed in the communion of saints and in a public assembly), but also that some time should be set apart for this purpose, it ought to be equally natural that there should be some fixed determination of that time, both as to frequency and as to duration (which could not be done by any other than the most wise God, the author of the worship and of time). Since, then, he determined to define that day in the law which in his wisdom he knew to be most in accordance with this purpose and most suitable (six days being left to man and keeping one only for himself in the weekly cycle), he who would now refix that day and substitute another in its place would in a measure raise himself above God and profess to be wiser than he (which would be a proof not only of the greatest rashness, but also of intolerable pride and profane impiety).

XXXVII. Second, if from the force and analogy of the precept, it is not rightly inferred that one day out of seven should be consecrated to divine worship, no certain number or circle of days could have been limited by any divine precept, since mention is made of no other number anywhere in any other precept (and everyone sees this is absurd). Nor is the objection of any force that it is enough that a day sufficient for exhibiting gratitude to God may be gathered from the force of the precept. The precept does not treat only of a sufficient day, but of one day out of seven (which is not ours to change).

XXXVIII. Third, the apostles in the change of the seventh day still retained the hebdomadal cycle, that they might select for public worship one out of seven days. However, they would not have done this unless they had recognized this as invariable and moral. And no one has ever been found among Christians who dared to attempt any change here. Nor ought it to be said that this was the result of Christian liberty and prudence. Although the change of the seventh day to the first was made from Christian liberty, it does not follow that the retention of one day out of seven was equally absolutely free and positive, depending merely upon their will.

Sources of explanation.

XXXIX. The determination of one day out of seven is no more repugnant to Christian liberty than the designation of a certain and stated day for divine worship. For whether one out of seven or eight or ten be selected, always a certain discrimination would be observed. Therefore, when the apostle teaches that under the New Testament the difference of days was taken away (Rom. 14:5, 6; Gal. 4:10) and rebukes the Galatians for keeping days and months, this must be understood of the ceremonial distinction of days (such as prevailed among the Jews under the Old Testament, when it constituted a part of divine worship and had to be laboriously and strictly observed; or such as prevailed among the Gentiles who thought some days to be more holy and fortunate than other days in themselves, and which on that account they were accustomed to distinguish into black and white, lucky and unlucky). Otherwise if all observation of days is absolutely and simply condemned, it would not be lawful now to observe any day at all devoted to the worship of God. Nor could Paul have enjoined it upon Christians to come together upon the first day of each week and make collections (1 Cor. 16:2).

XL. Although believers are bound to worship God on each day of the seven (and thus our whole life ought to be a continual Sabbath), it does not follow that a stated day in the seven should not be consecrated to God. It is evident that public worship could not be performed every day, both on account of weakness of the flesh and on account of the necessity of animal life (which demands the various works of man for its conservation). Thus the Sabbatism of this life is distinguished from the heavenly (which will be perpetual and constant because we will rest from our labors, being then freed from all the miseries and necessities of this life).

XLI. Although from the force of the precept one day out of seven must necessarily be kept as a moral and perpetual duty, it does not follow that the observance of the seventh day (sanctioned in this precept) is equally moral. The precise determination of the seventh day is merely free and accidental to worship; for whether on the seventh or the sixth or any other day of the week the worship of God is attended to, it is all the same provided he is worshipped. But the determination of one day is necessary and conduces in a high degree to the worship of God, for we do not think God can be worshipped conveniently and sufficiently unless one day in seven be consecrated to him.

XLII. That this was the opinion of Calvin can be clearly gathered from his discourses on the ten commandments. In discourse five: "If we would be fervent in the worship of God, as we should be, not one day in seven would be selected, but every day it would be fitting without a written law; since then such and so great is our infirmity, we recognize that polity to have been given not only to the Jews, that there should be a certain day for assembling together, but also to us and that this is common to us with them" ("Sermon Five on Deut. 5:12-14" in *John Calvin's Sermons on the Ten Commandments* [ed. B.W. Farley, 1980], pp. 108-9). So in the sixth discourse: "When it is said, six days shalt thou work, the Lord shows that it ought not to seem grievous to us for him to set apart some one day, when he grants us six in place of one" ("Sermon Six on Deut. 5:13-15," ibid., p. 117). Near the end he adds: "God does not treat with us by his supreme right, but is content if we consecrate one day to him or if that day should serve us through the whole seven" (ibid.).

XLIII. This may also be gathered from the *Institutes* when he says that "he does not so dwell upon the septenary number of days as to bind the church to its invariable observance" (ICR 2.8.34, p. 400). There his design is not so much to condemn the destination of one day in seven to public worship (which elsewhere with sufficient explicitness he approves) or to refer it to merely human and free polity, as to combat here the Jewish superstition of those who Judaized in its observance. The words which follow have the same reference: "Thus all the triflings of false prophets vanish, who in former ages imbued the people with a Jewish notion, affirming that nothing but the ceremonial part of this command has been abrogated, which they call the appointment of the seventh day, but that the moral part of it still remains (to wit, the observance of one day in seven). And yet this is nothing else than changing the day in contempt of the Jews, while they retain the same opinion of the holiness of the day." Here it is certain that he does not attack any of the Reformed (with whom he never had any controversy on this point), but certain papists and Scholastics who thought that they had a sufficient regard for evangelical freedom, if they taught the appointment of the seventh day as ceremonial to be abolished (and in the meantime taught that one day out of seven should be kept in the same way as the Jews kept their Sabbath). Hence he adds, "They, who adhere to their constitutions, far surpass the Jews in a gross and carnal superstition of Sabbatism."

XLIV. Peter Viret, a colleague of Calvin, follows the received opinion and discusses it fully (*Exposition familiere sur les dix Commandemens* [1554], pp. 260-314). Nor did Beza think differently: "The fourth precept concerning the sanctification of each seventh day, as to the day of the Sabbath and the legal rites, was ceremonial; as to the worship of God it belonged to the immutable moral law and in this life is a perpetual precept" (*Annotationes maiores in Novum . . . Testamentum* [1594], Pars Altera, p. 634 on Rev. 1:10). Afterwards: "Therefore assemblies on the Lord's day are of apostolic and truly divine tradition, so however that the Jewish cessation from all work should by no means be observed, since this would plainly be not to abolish Judaism, but only to change the day" (ibid., p. 635). The same is the opinion of Peter Martyr: "We here omit the mystery of the number seven . . . and this only we notice, that one out of every seven days is to be devoted to God" (*Loci Communis*, Cl. 2.7.1 [1583], p. 241). And afterwards: "Just as it is perpetual and eternal that as long as the church exists on earth, she is bound to support her ministers . . . so, that one day in the seven should be consecrated to divine worship, is well settled and firm" (ibid.). Bucer: "This also is certainly our duty publicly to sanctify one day in the seven to religion. Who, therefore, does not see how healthful it is to the people of Christ, that there should be one day in the week so consecrated to sacred religious exercises that in it no other work is right than to meet in sacred assemblies?" ("De Regno Christi," 1.11* in *Martini Buceri Opera Latina* [ed. F. Wendel, 1955], 15:82). Zanchius: "The precept is moral inasmuch as it commands us to consecrate one day out of seven to external divine worship" ("De Quarto Praecepto," in *Opera Theologicorum* [1613], 4:650). Of the same opinion were Fayus (cf. "Theses in quartum legis," 33*.9* in *Theses Theologicae in Schola Genevensi* [1586], pp. 65-66 [40]); Junius ("De Politiae Mosis Observatione," 8 in *Opera Theologicae* [1613], 1:1914); Paraeus (*Miscellanea Catechetica* [1600], pp. 175-76); Alsted (*Theologia Catechetica* [1622], pp. 568-93) and many others.

FOURTEENTH QUESTION: THE LORD'S DAY

Whether the institution of the Lord's day is divine or human; whether it is of necessary and perpetual or of free and mutable observance. The former we affirm and the latter we deny (as to both parts).

What is the Lord's day?

I. The Lord's day (*kyriakē hēmera*) in Christian usage is applied to the first day of the week, appointed for the public worship of God in memory of Christ's resurrection. Now it is so called not so much with regard to the efficient (as if it was formally instituted by Christ himself, as the Lord's Prayer and the Lord's Supper are designated by the apostle, 1 Cor. 10:21). As will be seen afterwards, no argument can be given for such institution. With regard to the end, it was instituted in memory of the resurrection of Christ, which took place on this day (Mt. 28:1); and for his honor and worship (as that is called "the Lord's altar," "the Lord's festival" which was instituted for his worship), and the ancients call temples dedicated to divine worship *Kyriakas* (or "the Lord's").

The origin of the Lord's day. Statement of the question.

II. Concerning this day, there are two principal questions: (1) what is its origin; (2) what is the necessity of its observance? As to the first, it is not asked whether a change was made of the seventh day to the first by abrogation of the Jewish Sabbath (for this is granted among Christians who acknowledge that this change could be made by him who is Lord of the Sabbath), but both ought to be made and was made most fittingly; that former day (on account of its ceremonial part and what on that account pertained to the legal economy) ought to be abrogated that another might be substituted in its place: another, however, could not be more appropriately introduced under the new covenant than that which is now called the Lord's day (on account of the resurrection of our Lord Jesus Christ on this day, the recollection of which is most justly to be celebrated always in the Christian church, since on it was most fully accomplished the work of our redemption and of the new creation); that this might be a public monument of the abrogated ceremonial law and of the distinction which ought to exist between the Jews and Christians. Rather the question concerns the principle and origin of this change—whether it was only of human and political (or ecclesiastical) or of divine ordination.

III. Here the opinions of theologians vary. Some refer it to canonical right (as the papists do, who gather from it also the necessity of unwritten traditions). There are some among the latter who (according to Azorius, *Institutionum morales*, Pt. II, 1.2 [1613], pp. 12-16) contend for its divine authority (as Anchoranus, Panormitanus, Angelus Sylvester). Others refer it to political ordination (as the Remonstrants, who in their Confession allege that the distinction of days was removed under the New Testament, and the Socinians, who assert that its observance is arbitrary, cf. *Racovian Catechism* [1818], p. 220). Others ascend to a divine ordination, so that either Christ himself may be said to have immediately and expressly instituted that day, which Junius holds ("Praelectiones in Geneses," in *Opera Theologica* [1613], 4:26-27 on Gen. 2:1, 2) and some others with him; or mediately only inasmuch as the apostles inspired of God (*theopneustoi*) sanctioned it in the Christian church by precept, example and their own practice. This is the more common opinion of the orthodox and to this we adhere.

IV. They who refer the origin of the Lord's day to Christ rely most especially both upon the resurrection of Christ (who by rising on this day from the dead seems to have consecrated it to his worship in memory of that fact) and on the various appearances made after the resurrection on this day when he showed himself to his assembled disciples (Jn. 20:19, 26; Rev. 1:10); also by the effusion of the Holy Spirit upon the apostles which is held to have occurred on this day. Although these things may with probability be said and seem to have given occasion for the institution of this day, still they cannot make a strong and solid argument to prove it because it would require some express command (or the example of Christ).

V. Far more properly, therefore, is it said to be of apostolic institution. They substituted the Lord's day for the Sabbath and commended it to the churches, not without the special influence of the Holy Spirit by whom they were infallibly directed to prescribe such things as not only conduced to faith and morals, but also to the good order (*eutaxian*) of the church and the performance of divine worship. Now there are three passages in particular from which this institution is gathered: (1) from Acts 20:7—"And upon the first day of the week, when the disciples came together to break bread, Paul preached unto them, ready to depart on the morrow." Why are the apostles said to have assembled for the preaching of the word and the administration of the eucharist, on this rather than on any other day (or on the well-known Sabbath of the Jews), unless at that time the custom of holding stated meetings had prevailed, the ceremony of the Jewish Sabbath by degrees vanishing? Nor ought it to be said that *mian sabbatōn* here designates not the first day of the seven, but only one (i.e., some one of the seven) because it is used in no other sense (Lk. 24:1; Mk. 16:2). What is adduced from Lk. 5:17 (cf. 8:22) does not apply here because it is one thing to say *en mia tōn hēmerōn* (which denotes an indeterminate time), another to say *en tē mia* with the article which determines the day.

VI. (2) From 1 Cor. 16:1, 2, where not only the apostolic practice but also a precept is introduced: "Now concerning the collection for the saints, as I have given order to the churches of Galatia, even so do ye. Upon the first day of the week let every one of you lay by him in store, as God hath prospered him, that there be no gatherings when I come." The apostle wishes collections to be made by believers upon each first day of the week (viz., on which their public assemblies ought also to be held), which he draws from the custom of the Jews who, according to Philo (cf. *The Special Laws* I. 14.76-78 [Loeb, 7:145]) and Josephus (AJ 18.312 [Loeb, 9:180-81]), on each Sabbath on which they were accustomed to assemble used to make collections in the synagogues of tithes and other voluntary offerings, afterwards sent to Jerusalem for the use of the temple and the Levites. On account of the persecution of the Jews, the advent of many strangers, and their continual zeal in propagating the gospel, the church at Jerusalem was greatly pressed by want and the apostle wishes believers to take up collections for their benefit. As therefore he orders collections on each first day of the week, so he also is considered by parity of reason to have ordained the public assemblies in which they were accustomed to be made (or to have approved them by his vote as already ordained).

VII. (3) From Rev. 1:10, where John says that "he was in the Spirit on the Lord's day"; not verily on the Jewish Sabbath because he undoubtedly would have named it; not on some one day only of the seven because thus the title would be ambiguous, calculated to confuse rather than explain; but on that day on which Christ had arisen, on which the apostles were accustomed to assemble to perform sacred worship and on which Paul had ordered collections to be made, as was the custom in the primitive church. Since he speaks of that day as known and observed in the church, there is no doubt that it had been distinguished by this name from the received usage of the church. Otherwise, who among the Christians would have understood what John meant by this appellation, if he intended to designate some other day?

VIII. Second, he alone could change the Sabbath (either immediately and by himself or mediately by the apostles) who is Lord of the Sabbath (Mt. 12:8). It was most fitting that the day of worship should be instituted by him under the New Testament (by whom the worship itself had been instituted and from whom all blessing in all worship is to be expected).

IX. Third, if the Lord's day was constituted neither by Christ nor by the apostles, the condition of the Christian church under the New Testament would be worse than of the Jews under the Old. Under the Old Testament a day was appropriated to rest from secular labor in which to servants and beasts of burden was granted a breathing time from servile work (Dt. 5:14), such as would not exist under the New Testament. Everyone sees this to be absurd, since far better is our condition in comparison with their state who were pressed down by the unbearable (*abastaktō*) yoke of the law.

X. Fourth, if the institution of the Lord's day is only of human ordination (whether political or ecclesiastical, as a human constitution circumscribed the necessity of public worship), it could be rescinded as easily as it was enjoined. Nor could the necessity of its observance be so strongly pressed, for thus a profane person might dispense with it, not attend to prayer and assemblies, and anyone might excuse himself for doing or neglecting anything, if nothing could be elicited from the Scriptures to bind the conscience besides a human appointment. Prudently, therefore, and piously (in addition to the uniform and uninterrupted tradition of the church), the apostolic sanction and practice is urged that it may be evident that the church has done nothing in an affair of so much importance which she has not received from inspired men (*theopneustois*) and which on that account is not of necessary observation.

XI. Fifth, it is favored by the authority of the fathers who were nearest the age and times of the apostles. Among whom is Ignatius (Pseudo-Ignatius, "Ad Magnesianos," 9.4 in *Patres Apostolici* [ed. F.X. Funk, 1913], 2:125; "Ad Trallianos," 9.5, ibid., 2:104-7); Justin Martyr (*First Apology** 67 [ANF 1:185-86]); Dionysius of Corinth, according to Eusebius (*Ecclesiastical History* 4.23* [FC 19:259]); Melito, according to the same (Eusebius, ibid., 4.26, p. 262); Irenaeus (*Against Heresies* 5.23* [ANF 1:551-52]); Tertullian (*Chaplet* [FC 40:237, 256]); Origen (cf. *In Exodum Homilia* 7.5-6 [PG 12.345-47]) and not a few others. Here belongs the law enacted concerning it by the Emperor Constantine the Great (cf. Eusebius, *Life of Constantine* 4.18 [London: 1845], pp. 189-90), repeated and confirmed by succeeding emperors—Theodosius, Valentinian, Arcadius, Leo and Anthemius*—by whom the most severe penalties were imposed upon those who exhibited spectacles on this day or gave themselves up to pleasure, as may be seen in the "Codex de feriis" (cf. *Corpus Iuris Civilis, II: Codex Iustinianus* 12.9 [ed. P. Krueger, 1968], p. 128).

XII. Most of our men assert the same thing. Calvin says: "It is very probable that the apostles retained in the beginning the day already observed, afterwards forced by the Jewish superstition substituted another in the place of the one abrogated" (in Acts 20+). Bucer says: "The Lord's day was consecrated to sacred acts by the apostles themselves" ("De Regno Christi," 1.11* in *Martini Buceri Opera Latina* [ed. F. Wendel, 1955], p. 82). So Beza maintains that this tradition is truly divine and made by the apostles at the suggestion of the Spirit: "The services of the Lord's day therefore, which Justin also in the *Second Apology* (sic!) expressly mentions, are of apostolic and truly divine tradition" (*Annationes maiores in Novum . . . Testamentum* [1594], Pars Altera, p. 635 on Rev. 1:10). So Gallasius, a colleague of Calvin and Beza: "We have received this as established, that the Lord's day should be substituted in place of the Sabbath, not by men, but even by the apostles, that is, by the Spirit of God, who directed them" (*In Exodum Commentaria* [1560], p. 195 on Ex. 31). Not otherwise Fayus: "Deservedly therefore we might have said that the apostles under the guidance of the Holy Spirit substituted it for that seventh legal day which was the first in the creation of the former world" (cf. "Theses in quartum Legis," 33*.12* in *Theses Theologicae in Schola Genevensi* [1586], p. 66 [40]). Of the same opinion are Bullinger (*A Hundred Sermons upon the Apocalips* [1561], pp. 29-30 on Rev. 1:10); Gualterus, homi. 162+ (on Mt.); Junius ("Praelectiones in Geneses," in *Opera Theologica* [1613], 1:26-61 on Gen. 2); Piscator in *Aphor explic. Aphor.* 18+; Perkins, Ames, Hyperius (*In Epistolam D. Pauli ad Romanos et . . . ad Corinthos* [1583], pp. 331-32 on 1 Cor. 16:2); Wallaeus (*Dissertatio de Sabbatho* 7* [1628], pp. 147-88); Voetius (*Selectae Disputationes* [1667], 4:760-61) and not a few others.

Sources of explanation.

XIII. Although the Lord's day may be said to be of apostolic institution, the authority upon which it rests is nevertheless divine because they were influenced by the Holy Spirit no less in sacred institutions than in setting forth the doctrines of the gospel either orally or by writing. Divine ordination is, therefore, rightly claimed here; not indeed formally and immediately by the institution of Christ, but mediately by the sanction and practice of the inspired (*theopneustōn*) apostles.

XIV. Although certain ordinations of the apostles (which referred to the rites and circumstances of divine worship) were variable and instituted only for a time (as the sanction concerning the not eating of blood and of things strangled [Acts 15:20]; concerning the woman's head being covered and the man's being uncovered when they prophesy [1 Cor. 11:4, 5]) because there was a special cause and reason for them and (this ceasing) the institution itself ought to cease also; still there were others invariable and of perpetual observance in the church, none of which were founded upon any special occasion to last only for a time by which they might be rendered temporary (such as the imposition of hands in the setting apart of ministers and the distinction between the offices of deacon and pastor). Since the institution of the Lord's day was of this kind, from this we infer that the intention of the founders was that the observance of this day should be of perpetual and immutable right.

XV. The constitutions of emperors and the canons of councils about the observance of the Lord's day do not prove that it was only of human ordination because they did not sanction it first, but confirmed and established it by their own authority as already instituted by the apostles that no one might presume to violate it with impunity. This was done by them most piously, both on account of the Gentiles and on account of the impious Christians by whom they were unwilling that this day should be profaned (and who without constitutions of this kind might think themselves free and unrestrained in their violation of it).

XVI. The Scripture passages usually adduced against the divine institution of the Lord's day (Rom. 14:5; Gal. 4:10; Col. 2:16) do not overthrow our argument. (1) In all these passages, the observance of some day for the purpose of religion (from the order of Christ) is no more condemned or denied than the choice of some particular food for the use of religion from the institution of Christ. And no one would say that the selection of bread and wine in the Supper for a religious use is either unlawful or not instituted by Christ. (2) The apostle expressly speaks of that regard for days (Rom. 14:5, 6) which at that time gave offense to Christians; but the observance of the Lord's day (which the apostle himself teaches prevailed at that time in all the churches, 1 Cor. 16:1, 2), could not afford the occasion of offense to anyone. (3) They treat of the Jewish distinction of days, which belonged to the slavery of weak and beggarly elements (Gal. 4:9), inasmuch as it had something typical and ceremonial and brought back the rigor of the law (which has now no place with respect to the Lord's day).

XVII. Christian liberty cannot be said to be lessened by this opinion. It is not liberty, but an unchristian license for anyone to think he is freed from the observance of any precept of the decalogue and from a divine and apostolic sanction. Experience teaches too well that license and the negligence of sacred things grows more and more, where a proper regard is not shown for the Lord's day.

XVIII. However, above all things, we must observe this—that we should not be so anxious to investigate the primary origin of this day as its careful and serious sanctification. Whatever opinion anyone may wish to follow (for we suffer each one to enjoy his own judgment), this should be strictly and inviolably taken care of by all—that according to the command of Christ, believers keep themselves clear of profanations, seriously devote themselves to the sacred exercises of piety and observe this consecrated day in a holy manner. Concerning the necessity and mode of its observance we will treat in what follows.

Second question: concerning the observance of the Lord's day. The necessity of it proved.

XIX. Concerning the observance of the Lord's day also there is not a little controversy. Some (in excess) incline to a too great rigor and severity and thus approach Judaism. Others on the contrary (in defect) use too great relaxation, which opens the door to profanity and license. The middle way, however, seems to us to be the safest. We unfold it by two propositions: the first teaches the necessity, the second the mode of its observance.

XX. First proposition: (1) the observance of the Lord's day is not necessary per se as a part of divine worship or a grace of mystical signification, but still it is necessary with regard to the preservation of good order (*eutaxias*) and apostolic and ecclesiastical polity. It cannot be called a part of worship in itself, but only an adjunct and circumstance of it because the gospel and rational (*logikos*) worship of the New Testament is no longer restricted to certain places or times (as under the Old Testament), but can be performed everywhere and always in spirit and truth. Still it is necessary according to God's arrangement by reason of the polity always to be preserved in the church, for without a certain day neither order nor decorum will exist in the church, but there will be mere confusion in ecclesiastical assemblies. (2) It was not instituted from any peculiar reason for a particular church of one time, but generally for the church of all times. As the apostles (who sanctioned this by their own example and precept, 1 Cor. 16:2; Acts 20:7) were universal ambassadors, so they had regard to the good of the whole church in this sanction. And as it was received even in the age of the apostles, so it was constantly retained by all the churches (as is evident from ecclesiastical history). (3) There can be no reason for a change since, as the memory of Christ's death, so also the memory of his resurrection ought to be perpetual in the church (1 Cor. 11:26; 2 Tim. 2:8). (4) It was afterwards confirmed by the various canons of ecumenical councils and by the many edicts and laws of the emperors.

XXI. Now although we readily grant that if he pleases God (who is the Lord of the Sabbath) can change this first day into any other of the seven, still we do not think that this is lawful for any mortal, after so constant and general an observance of this day. Nor if cases can be granted, in which the public exercises of piety cannot be performed on this day, does it follow that this observance is only temporal and mutable; for this is not done spontaneously, but from necessity (which has no law).

XXII. If the ancient Christians observed for some time the Sabbath also in connection with the Lord's day, so that they held sacred assemblies on that day and thought it wrong to fast on it, as we gather from *Constitutions of the Holy Apostles* (2.59 [ANF 7:422-23]) and from Socrates (*Ecclesiastical History* 6.8* [NPNF2, 2:144]), this pertained to the decent burial of the synagogue. It is evident that the festivity of the Sabbath, even when kept, was considered far inferior to the Lord's day. This appears even from this—that among the errors of the Ebionites (on account of which they were condemned by the church), they were convicted of this also, that they celebrated the Lord's day and the Sabbath together (in Eusebius, *Ecclesiastical History* 3.27* [FC 19:184]). Note also the Council of Laodicea, whose words are these: "It is not becoming for Christians to Judaize and to rest on the Sabbath, but to work on that day, preferring to rest on the Lord's day, as Christians, provided they can" (which seems to have been added on account of servants who had heathen masters) "and if they are discovered to be Judaizers, let them be anathema by Christ" (Canon 29, Mansi, 2:569).

And the mode.

XXIII. Second proposition: the mode of the right observance of the Lord's day resolves itself into two parts—first, what may be called privative and consists in rest or cessation from all servile work; the other, which is positive, and is concerned with the sanctification of that rest by the religious worship of God.

XXIV. The rest required is not one of ease and idleness, much less of feasting and gluttony, of shows and dances and other profane practices condemned by Paul in Rom. 13:13. It is the Sabbath of Jehovah, not a feast of Ceres, Bacchus or Venus. Rather the rest is a cessation from all works of our ordinary and worldly vocation which can call us away from divine worship. Thus we must abstain on that day: (1) from all those works which are strictly and properly called servile, usually done by servants and serving men (to wit, as much as it can be done through immediate necessity); (2) from our works which pertain to the uses of this life in natural and civil affairs and properly refer to our own gain and advantage. This is gathered from the opposed concession, for as he grants six days to us that we may labor and do all our work in them, so on this day he enjoins a cessation from such work that no obstacle may be put in the way of divine worship. And further here belongs the memorable law of Leo and Anthemius, extant in the "Codex de feriis," whose words we are not ashamed to quote: "We decree the Lord's day to be always so honorable and to be reverenced that it should be free from all executions, no admonition should be given to anyone, no exaction of bail be made, the officer should be silent, summons lie hid. Let that day be free from judicial examinations, let the rough voice of the crier be still, litigants cease from controversy" (*Corpus Iuris Civilis, II: Codex Iustinianus* 12.9 [ed. P. Krueger, 1968], p. 128). And afterwards: "Nor relaxing the rest of this religious day, do we suffer anyone to be occupied with obscene pleasures, theatrical shows, circus plays, and the mournful spectacles of wild beasts should have no patronage on that day, and if our birth day should fall upon it, the celebration of it should be deferred" (ibid.).

XXV. Here, nevertheless, are excepted: (1) those works which directly regard the worship and glory of God (Mt. 12:5; Jn. 5:8, 9), for in this case those works which are in their nature servile pass into the nature of sacred works—nor are they so much our works as God's; (2) works of charity and of mercy which are reckoned among the duties of piety (Mt. 12:10, 12; Jn. 5:9; 9:14; Lk. 13:15); (3) the works of common honesty, because as always, so on this day above others, we ought to carry ourselves and to act honestly and decorously; (4) works of necessity, which are neither feigned nor designedly produced, but imposed upon us by providence (Lk. 14:5); not only absolute and simple, that may be called necessary only (which we can in no way be in want of), but modified and relative so that those things may be reckoned necessary not only which are required absolutely for the existence or support of life, but also those which conduce to our living better. Hence some great advantage and emolument accrues to us or our neighbor if they are done or some great disadvantage and loss if they are omitted. "The sabbath" (as Christ testifies in Mk. 2:27) "was made for man and not man for the sabbath."

XXVI. Therefore, we do not think that in this cessation believers are bound to Judaical precision which some (more scrupulous than is just) maintain was not revoked, so that it is lawful neither to kindle a fire, nor to cook food, nor to take up arms against an enemy, nor to prosecute a journey begun by land or sea, nor to refresh themselves with innocent relaxation of the mind and body, provided they are done out of the hours appointed for divine worship, nor to have any diversion, however slight, to any things belonging to the advantages or emoluments of this life. For although this opinion bears on its face a beautiful appearance of piety (and undoubtedly with good intention is proposed by pious men to procure the better sanctification of this day, usually so basely profaned), still it labors under grievous disadvantages; nor can it be retained without in this way bringing back into the church and imposing anew upon the shoulders of Christians an unbearable yoke (*abastakton*), repugnant to Christian liberty and the gentleness of Christ and opposed to the sweetness of the covenant of grace by agitating and tormenting the consciences of men through infinite scruples and inextricable difficulties (nearly driving to desperation).

XXVII. The other part of the observance of the Lord's day pertains to the sanctification of the rest which is employed in sacred assemblies and in the stated and public worship of God. For although sacred assemblies for the public exercises of piety can and ought to be frequented on other days also by everyone (as far as their business will allow) and every pious person is bound in duty to his conscience to have privately his daily devotional exercises, still on this day above others a holy convocation ought to take place (as was the custom on the Sabbath, Lev. 23:3) in which there may be leisure for devout attention to the reading and hearing of the word (Heb. 10:25), the celebration of the sacraments (Acts 20:7), the psalms and prayer (Col. 3:16; Acts 1:14), to alms and help to the poor (1 Cor. 16:2) and in general to all that sacred service pertaining to external and stated worship.

XXVIII. And all agree that to this we should most especially devote ourselves, the many other controversies here waged, either curious or by no means necessary and useful, being removed. The Synod of Dort has reference to this, maintaining "that this day ought so to be appropriated to divine worship, that we should rest on it from all servile works (with the exception of those which charity and pressing necessity demand) and from all pleasures of such a kind as could hinder divine worship" ("Post-Acta, of Na-Handelingen, Sec. 164" in *Acta of Handelingen der Nationale Synode . . . 1618 en 1619* [1987 repr.], pp. 941-42). And "lest the people on the Lord's day after 12 o'clock, distracted by other labors and profane exercises, should be kept away from the afternoon meetings, it wishes the magistrates to be asked to prohibit by more severe edicts all servile or daily works and especially plays, drinking together and other profanations of the Sabbath, in which the afternoon (especially in the town) is accustomed for the most part to be passed, so that in this way also they may better be drawn to those afternoon meetings and so learn to sanctify the entire Sabbath day" (ibid.). For no other reason did God in the Law and the Prophets so strongly urge and recommend the sanctification of the Sabbath and threaten to punish so severely its violation and profanation. For although these had a primary reference to the Jews, yet we cannot doubt that in their own manner they had a reference to Christians also inasmuch as they included a moral duty and one of perpetual observance.

Sources of explanation.

XXIX. Although the conscientious regard for and distinction of days (and of other typical ceremonial times of the Old Testament) has been taken away under the New, as also straightway is forbidden the superstitious distinction of days and times (prevailing among the heathen), it does not follow that the Sabbath of the Lord transferred from the seventh day to the first (and freed from the typical use and economical strictness of the Old Testament) was on that account abrogated.

XXX. He who does works of necessary charity and mercy on the Sabbath does not profane it. He would be guilty of the basest superstition and hypocrisy who, under this pretext, would desert a neighbor in trouble. He ought to help whom he can and to serve God according to his ordination. For the Sabbath is said to have been "made for man" that he may in a special manner consult his own salvation by performing the duties of piety to God and of love to his neighbor; "not man for the Sabbath," as if he ought to neglect necessary charity or mercy towards himself or neighbor through a superstitious regard for the Sabbath.

XXXI. The cessation from all servile work and carnal pleasure ought not to be pressed to the neglect of the spiritual practice of true holiness. It ought not to be pressed on account of itself, as if it were a part of worship or as if the day itself were holier than others, but as the condition and help of private and public exercises to be performed thus. Therefore, this doctrine is very far from leading men to the opinion that they have done their duty remarkably well if, the desire for true piety and holiness being left, they devote themselves to a scrupulous and absolute cessation from all work. We seek the means on account of the end and the condition on account of the principal work (to wit, rest on account of the spiritual exercises of true piety and holiness). Therefore no more ought the practice of the Sabbath to be burdened with those consequences from the accidental abuse of men, than the practice of sacred reading, the hearing of the word, prayers and the sacraments, which are open to the same abuses, although no one would deny that these are moral duties of perpetual observance.

XXXII. The accommodation of the fourth precept to the peculiar state of the Jews (which was in the observance of the seventh day from the beginning of creation) did not render this precept ceremonial anymore than the promise to give the land of Canaan to the people of Israel makes the fifth commandment ceremonial; nor the preface, where the bringing of the people out of Egypt is mentioned, makes all the precepts ceremonial. Indeed, we grant that a somewhat stricter observance of the Sabbath was commanded in those times, accommodated to the training and servitude of the times, which does not obtain in all ages. However, this does not hinder the observance itself from being moral and common to all ages.

Fifteenth Question: Festivals

Whether it belongs to the faith in the New Testament that besides the Lord's day there are other festival days properly so called whose celebration is necessary per se and by reason of mystery, not by reason of order or ecclesiastical polity only. We deny against the papists.

Statement of the question.

I. Festivals are stated days recurring every year or week or month, separated from others for the sake of religion and piety and, as it were, consecrated by a certain law to the public worship of the deity. No one doubts that there were many under the Old Testament, since a distinction of days was a part of the ceremonial law. But the question is whether they ought to have a place in the Christian church. This is the question between us and the papists, who, as in other things, have retained various rites of the Jews. Here they have interpolated Judaism or rather paganism itself (in which it is known that there were more festival days distinct from common days), burdening Christianity with such a mass of festivals as to embrace the greater portion of the year.

II. The question is not whether the memory of God's blessings to us and the mysteries of Christ wrought to acquire salvation for us ought to be perpetual in our minds and continually reflected upon by us. For this all allow and it is done daily by the preaching of the word and the administration of the sacraments. Rather the question is whether for the recollection and solemn and public commemoration of those singular benefits and mysteries particular festival days, sacred to God, annually recurring, should be celebrated every year by Christians. This we deny.

III. The question is not whether anniversary days may be selected on which either the nativity, or circumcision, or passion, or ascension of Christ, and similar mysteries of redemption, may be commemorated, or even on which the memory of some remarkable blessing may be celebrated. For this the orthodox think should be left to the liberty of the church. Hence some devote certain days to such festivity, not from necessity of faith, but from the counsel of prudence to excite more to piety and devotion. However, others, using their liberty, retain the Lord's day alone and in it, at stated times, celebrate the memory of the mysteries of Christ, with whom "the dissonance of things of this kind does not take away the harmony of faith," as Augustine+ formerly remarked of a fast. Rather the question is whether some days are more holy and sacred than others and a certain part of divine worship ought to be celebrated under the reason of mystery and not only as related to ecclesiastical order and polity (as Bellarmine maintains, "De Cultu Sanctorum," 3.10 *Opera* [1857], 2:541-47 and is the doctrine and public practice of the papists). On the contrary, we deny that those days are in themselves more holy than others; rather all are equal. If any sanctity is attributed them, it does not belong to the time and the day, but to the divine worship. Thus the observance of them among those who retain it, is only of positive right and ecclesiastical appointment; not, however, necessary from a divine precept.

IV. First, festivals properly so called (which are of the necessity of faith, obligatory of themselves and under the relation of mystery) ought to be commanded by the divine word because the right of prescribing his own worship belongs to God alone (who in his word has omitted none of the things which he judged necessary to his church). But such festivals we nowhere read as having been either instituted or kept by Christ or his apostles. Nor can an unwritten (*agraphos*) tradition be brought up here, since no place can or ought to be allowed it in matters of faith and practice, as has already been demonstrated. Second, this brings back the Old Testament distinction of days, abrogated in the New Testament and condemned by Paul (Rom. 14:5, 6; Gal. 4:10; Col. 2:16). It introduces into the church under other names and a specious appearance both the superstition and idolatry of the old heathen.

V. Third, the ancients confess that festivals were kept neither from the institution of Christ nor of the apostles, but from choice and custom. There is a noteworthy passage in Socrates where, speaking of the disagreement of the Eastern and Western churches about the observance of Easter (which was the first festival day begun to be kept in the Christian church), he says expressly, "Neither the apostles, nor the gospel itself imposed the yoke of slavery upon those who yielded to the doctrine of Christ, but left the festival of Easter and others to be celebrated according to the free and impartial judgment (*tē eugnōmosynē tōn euergetēthentōn timan katelipon*) of those who had received on such days blessings" (*Ecclesiastical History* 5.22 [NPNF2, 2:130; PG 67.627-28]). And he adds: "Neither the Savior nor the apostles commanded it to be observed" (ibid., p. 627). "For," he subjoins, "the apostles proposed not to enact laws concerning the celebration of festivals, but to prescribe to us the method of piety and of right living" (ibid.). Nicephorus repeats this (*Ecclesiastical History* 12.32 [PG 146.847-54]).

VI. Fourth, in the papacy these festivals sowed the seeds of deadly superstitions, making festival days in themselves more holy than others, cherishing the opinion of work wrought (*operis operati*), attaching to them merit and the expiation of sins, consecrating them to the saints and so connecting them with the worship of latria, since (according to Durandus) festivals also belong to latria (cf. *Sententias theologicas Petri Lombardi Commentariorum*, Bk. 3*, Dist. 38, Q. 1 [1556], p. 234). Finally they make so many festivals and distract the mind with such difficult trifles and scruples that great men in the papacy (overcome by their tediousness) have most bitterly complained. Let Nicholas de Clemangis be heard ("De novis celebratibus non instituendio," *Opera Omnia* [1613/1967], pp. 155-56). Among other things, he proves that some old festivals were better abolished on account of their great abuse, than new ones instituted. He complains that so many things are read and spoken in the churches about the saints that now the reading of the Holy Scriptures is altogether omitted. Peter Ailly among other things advises the chief ecclesiastics of the Council of Constance "to take care not to appoint so many new festivals, that besides the Lord's day and the greater festivals instituted by the church it might be permitted to work after the service had been heard, both because often on festivals sins are more multiplied in taverns, dances and other lascivious amusements which ease teaches: and because the working days are hardly sufficient for procuring the necessaries of life" (*de Reform. Eccles.*+). Polydore Virgil writes: "As much as it was formerly the custom to institute festivals, so much now it seems better that they should be rendered antiquated; since a great many men barefacedly employ that rest of festivals not in praying, but in increasing every day more and more all kinds of corruptions of good morals" (*De rerum inventoribus* 6.8 [1671], p. 396). Erasmus confirms the same thing (*In Novum Testamentum . . . annotationes* [1522], p. 48 on Mt. 11). Pope Urban VIII himself in his Bull, published in the year 1642, having endeavored to restrict the number of festivals, among other things confesses: "The festivals instituted at first to glorify the deity, in the progress of time inimical man has corrupted and converted into great offence to him and the grievous loss of souls" (Bull 759, "Pro observatione festorum," in *Bullarium . . . sanctorum Romanorum Pontificum* [1868], 15:206).

Sources of explanation.

VII. Although the Lord's day is sacred to God, it does not follow by an equal reason that other festivals can be consecrated to God. (1) The Lord's day was instituted and kept by the apostles themselves; other festivals were ordained only by the fathers. (2) The Lord's day as to genus is commanded so that one day in seven should be set apart for the public worship of God (although not as to species). On the contrary, these festivals were commanded in neither way.

VIII. The practice of the Jews, who kept the feast of Purim in Esther and the Feast of Dedication in memory of the temple purged by Judas Maccabaeus (mentioned in Jn. 10:22), does not immediately prove that this custom ought to prevail in the Christian church (on account of the difference between the Old and New Testament economy). It shows only that on certain days (annually recurring) there may be a public commemoration of the singular benefits of God, provided abuses, the idea of necessity, mystery and worship, superstition and idolatry be absent.

IX. Paul does not intimate that the Feast of Pentecost was to be kept by him necessarily (Acts 20:16), but only that he must hasten to be present in Jerusalem on the day of Pentecost on account of the gathering of the Jews (that he might have a fuller opportunity and chance to preach and turn many to Christ).

X. It is one thing to make mention of the conception, nativity, death, resurrection and ascension of Christ on certain days in discourses to the people and thus to embrace the opportunity of exhorting, consoling, instructing Christians to edification, piety, patience and holiness. It is another, however, to make and by established law to impose necessarily upon Christians festivals sacred to God and the saints, to constitute these a part of religion and of divine worship as more holy than other days. The former can sometimes be employed with advantage according to the circumstances of time, place, persons and things (provided abuse, superstition and idolatry are absent, as was not rarely done in the primitive church); but the latter is not lawful both because it belongs to God alone (and not to men) to prescribe what belongs to divine worship and because religious worship is not to be paid to any creatures, but to God alone.

XI. A thing can be called "holy" either absolutely (with regard to some inherent sanctity) or relatively (with regard to its destination to a sacred use); either by divine or human appointment. There are no days to which any quality of inherent sanctity may be attached of which they are not capacious (nor if it could be attributed to them, could this be done by the operation of men, who can communicate internal sanctity to nothing). We do not deny relative sanctity to certain days by reason of their destination to sacred uses, which (if it proceeds from God, as formerly on the Sabbath day and on the festivals established among the Jews) was a true relative sanctity by reason of the divine will. But if from men, in no way can sanctity be ascribed to days, except in relation to the things done on them and on account of the purpose for which the cessation from our works is enjoined.

XII. By the feast (of which the apostle speaks in 1 Cor. 5:7, 8), he does not mean a stated day on which the memory of Christ's passion should be celebrated, but the whole time commencing with our regeneration; not only for seven days (as the Passover of the Jews), but the whole time of our life. This is evident because he is speaking of the paschal feast, when having slain a lamb, unleavened bread is eaten. Now in the New Testament, Christ, the Lamb of God, having been once slain (whose efficacy remains forever), our unleavened bread of sincerity and truth ought to last through the whole course of life.

XIII. If some Reformed churches still observe some festivals (as the conception, nativity, passion and ascension of Christ), they differ widely from the papists because they dedicate these days to God alone and not to creatures. (2) No sanctity is attached to them, nor power and efficacy believed to be in them (as if they are much more holy than the remaining days). (3) They do not bind believers to a scrupulous and too strict abstinence on them from all servile work (as if in that abstinence there was any moral good or any part of religion placed and on the other hand it would be a great offense to do any work on those days). (4) The church is not bound by any necessity to the unchangeable observance of those days, but as they were instituted by human authority, so by the same they can be abolished and changed, if utility and the necessity of the church should demand it. "For everything is dissolved by the same causes by which it was produced," the lawyers say. In one word, they are considered as human institutions. Superstition and the idea of necessity are absent.

XIV. If some days with certain churches are designated by the names of apostles or martyrs, it is not to be supposed that they were instituted for their worship or should be terminated on their honor, as the papists do. Hence Bellarmine asserts "that the honor of the festivals immediately and terminatively pertains to the saints" ("De Cultu Sanctorum," 3.16 *Opera* [1857], 2:555). Rather they are referred to the memory of the saints by whom Christ built up his church for our advantage (to the worship, however, and honor of God alone, who conferred upon the apostles and martyrs whatever thing worthy of praise they possessed, did or underwent). They neither invoke nor burn incense to them, but to God alone, whom they invoke. They give thanks on account of the benefits redounding to us by their ministry and example. Hence we cannot approve the rigid judgment of those who charge such churches with idolatry (in which those days are still kept, the name of the saints being retained), since they agree with us in doctrine concerning the worship of God alone and detest the idolatry of the papists.

XV. However although our churches do not condemn that practice simply as evil, yet since sad experience has shown that the institution of festival days received into the papacy from a false jealousy (*kakozēlia*) of the Jews or of the heathen gave occasion to the abominable idolatry which continues and increases in the papacy, not without weighty reasons have they preferred to abolish that usage in their reformation (that no contagion might be contracted, but that they might carefully shun the danger from that source). For in religion, when even the slightest departure takes place from the commands of God and men wish or suppose a thing to be lawful for them, all safe things are to be feared. Indeed it has been found by experience that from insignificant beginnings wonderful progress was made in superstition and idolatry in the papacy as to the worship of images, invocation of saints, purgatory, the sacrifice of the mass, prayers for the dead, etc. Thus it seems better to lack some useful good (but less necessary), than from the use of it to incur the imminent danger of any great evil.

Sixteenth Question: The Fifth Commandment

May children withdraw themselves from the power of their parents and marry without their consent? We deny against the papists.

I. Among others in relation to the fifth precept, this question concerning the honoring of parents is agitated between us and the papists. In many ways, the latter weaken this precept, maintaining that children, against the consent of their parents, may not only contract marriage, but even adopt a monastic life. Therefore, two points must be discussed here. First, whether children (the parents being unwilling) can in any way withdraw themselves from their power. Second, whether without their consent it is right for them to marry.

How parents are to be honored.

II. That the first question may be more easily settled, we must see what is meant by "the honor" due to parents from their children (since many things are contained in it). (1) Love, which they ought to bear to them and want of which (*astorgia*, "without natural affection," Rom. 1:31) is reckoned among the most detestable crimes. For if our neighbor is to be loved, who is a greater neighbor to us than father and mother whose flesh we are? Again if kindnesses bestowed upon us ought to conciliate our love to the bestower, from whom have we received more or greater benefits than from our parents (from whom as instruments of divine power we have received whatever we are and have)? (2) Reverence, which is due to them both on account of preeminence (*hyperochēn*) (because they are superior and children inferiors; and inferiors owe honor to superiors) and on account of their authority (*exousian*) and power over children, which they have by reason of generation and education. Since this is the highest, it demands special honor; to which, as abominable sins, are opposed contempt (Lev. 20:9; Dt. 27:16; Prov. 20:20), despising and mocking (Prov. 15:5; 30:17). (3) Obligatory and voluntary obedience (Eph. 6:1; Col. 3:20; 1 Tim. 3:4; Tit. 1:6); but this ought to be "in the Lord," i.e., so that obedience to God be not compromised and God's authority be recognized. For if they command anything contrary, then it is certain that the children are not bound to obey, because "it is better to obey God than men" (Acts 5*.29*). (4) Gratitude; not verbal only, but also real, in offices necessary to the support of life in all things which depend upon them (which is called by the Greeks *antipelargia*, "mutual love"). Storks are accustomed to rear, in turn, their old parents, as Aristotle mentions (*De historia animalium* 9.13 [1552], p. 216). The apostle and Christ commend this trait (1 Tim. 5:4, 16; Mt. 15:4, 5), so that they ought not to be ashamed in case of a deficiency of servants to render servile duties and obedience to them.

Statement of the question.

III. The question is Can children shake off the subjection and obedience due to parents and withdraw themselves from paternal authority? This the papists hold, maintaining that children can (the parents being unwilling) freely devote themselves to a monastic life. Thomas Aquinas says, "After the years of puberty children can bind themselves by a religious vow without the will of parents" (ST, II-II, Q. 88, Art. 9, p. 1574). Bellarmine confirms this ("De Monachis," 36 *Opera* [1857], 2:290-92). On the contrary, we deny it.

Children cannot take upon themselves a vow against the wish or knowledge of their parents.

IV. First, Christ expressly condemns this in the Pharisees who, under the pretext of piety and of a vow, maintained that children could justly refuse the offices due to parents. "Whoever," they said, "shall say to his father or mother, it is a gift, by whatsoever thou mightest be profited by me; and honor not his father or his mother, he shall be free" (Mt. 15:5*, 6*). For although this obscure passage has given rise to various interpretations, yet all agree in this—that they thought the offices due to parents could be withheld under the pretext of religion and the worship of God. This may be understood of a gift which the child had presented to God for the sake of a father and under this pretext refused to help a needy parent; as if he had said, it is a gift by whatsoever thou mightest be assisted by me, i.e., I have consecrated to God all that by which thou mightest otherwise have been helped in this need by me (or from my goods) and on that account I can no longer devote it to your use. This absolves me from the right which you have over me and from all honor and office due to you, as Beza (*Annotationes maiores . . . Novum . . . Testamentum* [1594], Pars Prior, p. 92 on Mt. 15:5) and Scaliger interpret it. Or it may be understood as Masius in c. 6 Judic.+ and many other learned men prefer (and is more pleasing to us). The formula of a vow and oath is here described by which the rebellious son devotes to God whatever proceeding from him could profit his father. The sense is this: I swear that I will not show you any kindness, no more than it is not lawful to use things sacred to God, in which class I place as if by an express vow whatever help I might give you—"gift" or as in Mk. 7:11, "Corban" (supply "it is"), i.e., a thing devoted to God and sacred, which it is not right to touch anymore; "whatsoever will profit you from me," i.e., will or could profit (for *to ōpheleisthai* is here a verb implying power [*dynētikon*]) and "will no longer honor his father or his mother" by any assistance afterwards (supply "he will be free" or "should no more honor" that they may be the words of the Pharisees forbidding the child to assist his parent that they may have a share with the son). This seems to be intimated in Mk. 7:12: "And ye suffer him no more to do ought for his father or his mother." That this is the true meaning of the passage appears from the rites of the Jews, with whom such formulas of oaths and vows were frequent. They often occur in the Talmud: "Let all this be Corban, by which I might be useful to thee" (*qrbhn sh'ny nhnh lk*) or "it is a sacred thing" (namely, which it was not lawful to touch) "whatever proceeding from me could profit thee" (*qrbhn khl mh dhthhn' mny*) (*Babylonian Talmud: Seder Nashim* [ed. I. Epstein, 1936], passim). However because the Pharisees held such vows ratified (regard being had to sacred offerings, which they made of more account than the command to honor parents), so they are said to have made the commandment of God of none effect by their tradition, by withdrawing children from the power of parents. For this reason they are severely rebuked by Christ and with them all their followers.

V. Second, the honoring of parents prescribed in the law cannot consist with this opinion, which withdraws children from the reverence due them in an affair of the greatest importance (viz., in choosing such a kind of life as calls them away from the obedience due to them). Yea, it takes them away from duties which by nature they are indispensably bound to perform. Nor does it help the matter to say that the obedience due to God, the Father of spirits, ought to be placed before the obedience due to carnal parents. Although we willingly grant this, it does not follow that he is free and untrammeled to devote himself to a monastic life. The obedience due to God is not involved here (or rather is repugnant to it) since he forbids us to be the servants of men (1 Cor. 7:23).

VI. Third, children are not independent. Therefore they cannot decide for themselves, their parents being unwilling. Hence the law considers that vow void which a virgin has vowed in her father's house in her youth, if the father disallow her (Num. 30:4). Nor does the objection have any force that it refers only to girls who have not reached the years of puberty. The law does not limit this, but speaks in general of virgins who are in the house of their father. It is evident that in law such a liberty is not granted to girls.

VII. Fourth, this opinion (by taking away the obedience of children) overthrows nature herself and destroys human society altogether. For who would labor to nourish and bring up children if, after all the care and anxiety, they are strangers (not our own) and by a certain right (or rather Turkish tyranny) are torn away from their parents, who cannot enjoy the comfort and obedience which they expected from them, especially in old age when these duties are more necessary to them.

VIII. Fifth, Canon 16 of the Council of Gangra opposes this impiety. "Whatever children," it says, "depart from their parents under the pretext of divine worship and do not accord to them due reverence, let them be anathema" (Mansi, 2:1103). To no purpose does Bellarmine try to show that this is to be restricted to those who desert needy parents, in extreme necessity, and against their will take upon them vows of any religious order of life. The canon speaks absolutely and without any limitation; nor is it lawful to restrict the obedience due to parents to extreme necessity.

Sources of explanation.

IX. The example of Abraham called out from his home and relatives by God (Gen. 12:1) cannot favor either the wickedness of children withdrawing themselves from the power of parents or of the men-stealing Jesuits who tear them with impunity from the bosom of their parents. (1) Abraham was already married and no longer under the guardianship of his father. (2) He had a special divine command, which is not the case here. (3) He went away from idolators, but these depart from Christian parents. (4) He did not assume vows of celibacy (or of obedience to any man) to lessen the paternal power; yea, not against but with the consent and to the gratification of his father, he went out from his home.

X. When the Levites are said to "have said unto their father and to their mother, we have not seen them, and to their brethren, we do not know them" (Dt. 33:9), it is shown indeed that they are worthy of praise who, in order to obey God expressly commanding anything, have a regard neither for blood nor marriage relations. This can be referred either to the law where a priest is forbidden to go in and defile himself with the dead body of his father or his mother (Lev. 21:10, 11), as if he did not know them; or to the deed of the Levites where they were to slay all the guilty irrespective of persons (Ex. 32:25-28); or to the trials which they ought to conduct without respect of persons. But it has no reference to those who (contrary to the command of God to honor parents) desert them in order to enslave themselves to other men.

XI. If the spouse is told "to forget her own people and her father's house" (Ps. 45:10), it has no reference to denying the obedience due to parents, but that she may understand (from the law of marriage instituted from the beginning by God) that parents are to be left so that she may cleave to her husband. The duty of believers (who are bound to renounce the world, the flesh and the old Adam) is mystically represented that they may be indissolubly united to Christ.

XII. When Christ commands us to hate parents for his sake (Lk. 14:26), he does not wish the binding duties of piety to be denied them, which are founded in nature and are indispensable. The command must be understood comparatively, so that the love of parents should yield to divine love (as when the commands of parents are opposed to the obedience due to God, we should postpone them to the commands of God).

XIII. Although Christ does not permit him whom he orders to follow him to bury his father (Lk. 9:59, 60), in order to teach that a divine call is to be preferred to the burying of a parent, i.e., to the offices due to parents, it does not follow that a child (not called by Christ, without necessity, the parent being unwilling) may take a vow withdrawing himself forever from the authority of parents. It is one thing to follow Christ calling; another to embrace a monastic life without such a call and through will-worship (*ethelothrēskeian*). It is one thing to leave dead parents (especially if they are also spiritually dead) to be buried by the dead; another to throw off parents living spiritually and temporally and to devote one's self to fictitious parents often dead in sins.

Second question: concerning the necessity of the consent of parents to the marriage of children.

XIV. The second question refers to the consent of parents for marriage—whether children have the right to contract marriage, their parents being unwilling. It is necessary not only to restrain youthful license (which indulges itself more than is right on this subject, mutually entering into a marriage contract, yea, and sometimes into the state, the parents either unconsulted or even unwilling), but also on account of the papists, whose opinion is too favorable to this disorder. "It is not to be doubted that clandestine marriages made with free consent, are legal and true marriages, as long as the church has not made them void; and forthwith they are rightly to be condemned and the holy synod pronounces them accursed, who deny that they are true, and who affirm that the marriages of children without the consent of their parents, are void, and that parents can make them void or ratify them" (Session 24.1, "Reform of Matrimony," Schroeder, p. 183). Bellarmine holds the consent of parents to be of honesty, but not of necessity ("De Sacramento Matrimonii," 19 *Opera* [1858], 3:824-26).

XV. On the contrary, the orthodox maintain that the consent of parents in the marriages of children is not only of honesty, but also of necessity, so that without it the marriages are not legitimate and may also be broken. On the state of the question observe: (1) the question here is not whether the parental authority extends so far that it can compel unwilling children to marriage and to make matches for them without their consent; for this is denied on both sides. (2) It does not concern insane and maniacal parents or captive in a far distant region, who cannot give their consent. Rather it concerns sane and free parents, who can use their rightful power. (3) It does not concern children freed and in their majority, who have already gone from under parental power (whom no one doubts to be independent), but especially concerns minors, who are still in every way constituted under parental authority. (4) It is not whether any dissent of parents can hinder or render void a marriage. We confess that where parents morose and avaricious and through sheer obstinacy will not consent to the proper marriage of children and cannot give sufficient reasons for their dissent after the request has been made by their children that the latter are not absolutely bound to their will, but it is right for them to apply to a superior power to whom a judgment concerning the justice or injustice of the dissent belongs. Thus the matter being well considered, they may determine what the children ought to do and consult their interest by supplying in this point the defect of the consent of the parents. But this is the special question—whether children, without the consent or knowledge of their parents, may lawfully marry, their consent not being sought or expected. This we deny.

The necessity of the consent of parents proved: (1) from the law, Eph. 6:1.

XVI. The reasons are: (1) from the fifth commandment, for that honor consists principally in the obedience due to them and since it is to be rendered to in all things "in the Lord," according to the command of Paul (Eph. 6:1), marriage cannot be excepted, which is of so great importance to settling the condition and fortune of the whole life and which, as the most difficult thing, exceeds the age, understanding and judgment of children. How can they be said to obey them in all things, who in the most momentous case pay no regard to them?

XVII. (2) From the special passages pertaining here in which precepts are given to parents concerning the settling of children in marriage. "Thou shalt not take of their daughters unto thy sons" (Ex. 34:16); "thy daughter thou shalt not give unto his son, nor his daughter shalt thou take unto thy son" (Dt. 7:3); "Take wives for your sons, and give your daughters to husbands" (Jer. 29:6); "So then he that giveth his virgin in marriage doeth well; but he that giveth her not in marriage doeth better" (1 Cor. 7:38). Now how could such things be said unless the children were in subjection to parental power, especially in the contraction of marriage?

3. Ex. 22:16, 17.

XVIII. (3) There is an express law concerning a daughter seduced and defiled who is not married, unless the father has assented: "If a man entice a maid that is not betrothed, and lie with her, he shall surely endow her to be his wife" (Ex. 22:16). This is repeated in Dt. 22:29. Nevertheless that this was not to be understood absolutely, but with the condition of the consent of the father, it is immediately added, "If her father utterly refuse to give her unto him, he shall pay money according to the dowry of virgins" (Ex. 22:17). Nor is Bellarmine's objection of any force that it treats not of a marriage already contracted, but of a future marriage on account of the preceding rape ("De Sacramento Matrimoni," 20 *Opera* [1858], 3:826-30). The force of the argument always remains. If it is left in the power of the father, whether he is willing to give the defiled daughter in marriage to her defiler (requesting it), assuredly in the marriage of a daughter the necessary consent of the parent is supposed. Yea, it binds even more strongly; for if this holds good with respect to a debauched daughter (whose dishonor seems to be covered by marriage), how much more with respect to an untouched and pure daughter? The same thing is proved from parity, as was seen before from Num. 30:4. The father can make void the daughter's vow; therefore also a marriage. If a vow, which is a promise made to God, comes under the parental will, how much more a promise made to men?

4. From the practice under the Old and New Testaments.

XIX. (4) From the continuous practice and the examples of the Old and New Testaments. Abraham sought Rebecca for his son (Gen. 24); Hagar a wife for Ishmael (Gen. 21:21); Jacob from Laban (Gen. 29:21). See similar examples in Caleb promising his daughter (Jdg. 1:12); in Samson seeking a wife from his parents (Jdg. 14:3); in the Israelites binding themselves to the Benjamites for this—that they would neither give their sons nor receive daughters from them (Jdg. 21:7); in Tamar answering Amnon according to law and custom, referring her disposal in marriage to her father—"speak unto the king for me" (2 S. 13:13).

5. Because children are not independent.

XX. (5) They who are not their own masters cannot determine for themselves. Children who are under parental power are not independent. (a) They are reckoned among the goods of parents as being from the parents and owing themselves to them (Job 1:2, 10, 12). (b) It was lawful for parents in extreme poverty to sell them into servitude (Ex. 21:7). (c) The vow of a daughter is rendered void by a father because she is under his power (Num. 30:5). For if it is not lawful to dispose of the goods of parents without their consent (if no power is given to the son of making away with money or of selling property), how can it be lawful for him to dispose of himself? What is nefarious as to the property in a farm that in persons is far more to be condemned (as an alienation would be made of a thing belonging to another). We punish thieves who steal money and furniture from their owners; but the theft is greater in a thing far more valuable.

6. From the absurd consequences.

XXI. (6) The opinion of our opponents is urged with the greatest absurdities. Not only is the divine law concerning honor to parents violated, the authority of fathers weakened, public morality flowing from the law of nature trampled upon, but also (the father being unwilling) an heir is introduced, domestic peace disturbed, while (against the will of the father) the young bride (who ought to be in the place of a daughter) is brought in and the safety of children (who on account of their age cannot yet consult for themselves) is placed in imminent danger. Devoid of counsel, inexperienced and untried, the latter are easily captivated by allurements and entangled in miserable marriages. The window is even opened to lust, since with the hope of matrimony many virgins are easily enticed to fornication.

7. From the civil laws.

XXII. (7) The civil laws written with the highest agreement both by ancient lawyers and by the emperors are too well known to be ignored, too clear to be obscured, too sacred to be rightly abolished. "Natural and civil reason persuades this," says an emperor, "that the consent of parents ought first to be obtained" (Justinian, *Institutes*, 1.10 ["De Nuptiis"] [ed. P. Birks and G. McLeod, 1987], p. 4). Not even to widows (although freed) does he allow this under the twenty-fifth year, nor to a soldier (to which class of men many privileges are conceded): "A soldier, if a minor, does not contract matrimony without the will of the father." Paulus says: "It cannot hold good, unless all agree together, as well those who unite as well as those under whose power they are" (*Corpus Iuris Civilis, I: Digesta* 23.2.2 ["De Ritu Nuptiarum"] [ed. P. Krueger, 1955], p. 330). Ulpianus says, "If the father is out of his mind, the grandfather sane, the opinion of the latter is to be inquired" (ibid., 23.2.9, p. 331). However, the reasons are to be noticed which are added in the civil law. (a) The paternal power is to be pressed, on account of which children are not their own masters. (b) The succession of inheritance, that an heir be not introduced against the wish of the father. (c) The affection of parents, which is presumed to take the best counsel for a child (for whom it prepares everything willingly) and from whose offspring it hopes for continual remembrance. (d) The judgment of infirm children.

XXIII. Most of the popish canonists do not decide otherwise. See the testimonies of Euaristius, Leo I, Pelagius, Urban V, Nicholas (of Cusa) and others in Espensaeus ("De clandestinis matrimoniis," *Opera omnia* [1619], pp. 633-55). He has compiled many things on this opinion from the fathers and the Gentiles themselves. Zanchius and Gherardus ("De conjugio, coelibatu et similibus argumentis," in *Loci Theologici* [1869], 7:54-55) ought also to be consulted, who collect many pertinent passages from Gratian, Cassander, Erasmus, Vives, Groper, Beatus Rhenanus.

Sources of explanation.

XXIV. If Esau took a wife without consulting his parents, so far is this from confirming the validity of such marriages that it rather the more strongly proves their invalidity. It was most bitter to the parties and had a dreadful end. However, if Isaac did not declare it void, this is to be attributed either to parental indulgence (which tolerates many things in children which it cannot alter) or to the obstinacy of Esau, who could not be drawn away from the unjust and unlawful consort. Still the argument from fact to right is not valid. Nor are we to be guided here by examples, but by laws. The same must be said of the apocryphal example of Tobit which is brought forward.

XXV. What God has joined together man cannot separate; but God cannot be regarded as the author of that union made only by violating his laws. If an ecclesiastical blessing comes in, it cannot ratify the marriage. For either by deceit or evil arts, it is extorted from the church; or when injury to it is granted by its corrupt ministers, which (when it is made void) ecclesiastical authority is not weakened but asserted.

XXVI. The expression that man ought to leave his parents and cleave to his wife does not avail except for true and lawful marriages. So close is the bond in these that if parents or the wife must be left, it is better to cleave to the wife. And yet in a wicked connection, how could the Lord seem to have absolved children (manifestly rebellious and obstinate) from the right of paternal power?

XXVII. Although marriages without the consent of parents (as being clandestine) are unlawful (even if the blessing of the church and copulation has taken place), they are not always actually rescinded. This arises from the paternal indulgence that greater evils may be avoided, not from justice. It is one thing however to seek the right; another to seek forbearance (*epieikeia*) or the remission of the right in any case. With respect to the latter is to be understood whatever is said by some orthodox theologians and lawyers about such clandestine marriage where copulation has taken place. Otherwise, if by illicit intercourse the right of making such marriages void would be taken away from the parent, occasion would be afforded to innumerable rapes and lusts, and the gate would be opened to every rake for seducing respectable virgins and trampling underfoot parental power. Nor is it a hindrance that a virgin, who has lost her virginity, is forced to be without a husband and thus injury would be suffered. She ought to impute that to her own folly, which may make others more cautious and that they suffer themselves not to be ruined. Nor ought they to complain of the injury received from the parent, but of the misery they have brought upon themselves.

XXVIII. There is not at all the same reason for slaves and children here. Between the slave and his master, the obligation is merely civil, but between parents and children it is natural. Servants belong to masters only by possession, but children belong to parents by generation. Hence there is not an equal necessity for the master's consent in the marriages of slaves, as for the parent's in the marriage of children. Again, if slaves are property (as formerly), they can marry without the will of the master neither by divine nor civil laws. Hence power is given to the master of giving a wife to his slave (Ex. 21:4; Lev. 25:44).

XXIX. Although there may be the consent of the contracting parties in such marriages and the intention of the minister, still there is wanting the lawful consent. This is not only attended to with respect to the contracting parties, but also with respect to those in whose power they are. If a son is free, he is not forthwith absolutely independent (*autoexousios*) and master of himself. Otherwise, how could a father sell his son (Ex. 21) and how could a father make void the vow of a daughter, or a husband the vow of a wife (Num. 30)? If he can in no way alienate the goods of parents, how much less himself?

Seventeenth Question: The Sixth Commandment

Are the rights of war and punishment contained under this commandment? Are suicide (autocheiria) *and duelling prohibited? The former we deny; the latter we affirm.*

I. Because various cases can occur in which homicide can either be lawful or unlawful and to be condemned, hence arises the question—What is prohibited in the sixth precept, "Thou shalt not kill," and what is not?

1. Judicial homicide is not prohibited.

II. First negatively (*kat' arsin*), judicial homicide is not prohibited, committed by the public magistrate against private persons whom he punishes with the sword or the gallows or in any other way. The magistrate is armed with the sword for the purpose of avenging evil (Rom. 13:4; 1 Pet. 2:14). This pertains not only to the heathen magistrates then in power, but to all magistrates as such, whether believers or not. Yea, it has a special reference to believers, who as guards of both tables ought to attend to the observation of the law. This could not be done if it were not allowed them to punish the guilty. For where there is no fear of punishment, crime is encouraged. Thus the Anabaptists and Socinians have failed, who endeavor in this respect to wrest the sword from the Christian magistrate.

III. Nor does the duty of the magistrate alone claim this, but public tranquility and peace demand it. This could never be preserved if the sword could not be unsheathed against the guilty, so that the state might be cleared of such wretches.

IV. This public right is not opposed either by the command of God, which respects private persons (not magistrates and ministers of God clothed with public authority), or by Christian charity, which can love the persons and punish the crimes. It would be a violation of the law of charity to leave the desperately wicked unpunished as pernicious to the republic and injurious to the good. Nor is it opposed by the prophecy concerning the wolf dwelling with the lamb (Is. 11:6). This does not refer to the duty of magistrates, but to believers. It consists of this—that they who were before cruel and fierce, after putting on the yoke of Christ should grow mild and live peacefully together. Nor is it opposed by the words of Christ, "resist not evil" (Mt. 5:39, 40), because they treat only of private vengeance, not public (which should be exercised in the name of God, who asserts that vengeance belongs to him). This is the meaning of Paul's words, "Recompense to no man evil for evil" (Rom. 12:17). Nor is it opposed by Mt. 26:52: "All they that take the sword shall perish with the sword." It is one thing to take the sword without its being given (as all do who from private vengeance seize it and are here condemned), another to use it lawfully when given by God (which magistrates do). Nor is it opposed by the fact that Christ did not condemn the adulteress (Jn. 8:11) because Christ did not act as a magistrate or judge on earth, but as a minister of the circumcision (Rom. 15:8). Nor is it opposed by the parable concerning not rooting up the tares (Mt. 13:29, 30) because hypocrites are meant by the tares, not the openly wicked. Nor does it treat of the office of magistrates and political punishment, but of the administration of ecclesiastical discipline, in the exercise of which he does not wish his people to be so rigid, lest with hypocrites they root out believers themselves.

The right of war is proved against the Socinians and Anabaptists.

V. We maintain the same thing concerning the right of war, against the Socinians and Anabaptists, who think it is abolished under the New Testament. Hence Smaltzius: "We deny that it is lawful to carry on wars and hold that it is unworthy of Christian piety" (*Refutatio Thesium D. Wolfgangi Frantzii*, Disp. VI [1614], p. 393). On the contrary, we maintain that the right of war belongs to the magistrate and can be lawfully exercised by him in a just and necessary war. Unjust and hasty wars, undertaken without just and necessary cause from mere ambition or avarice in order to extend the boundaries of an empire, we detest as mere highway robberies.

(1) From the Old Testament.

VI. The reasons are: (1) it was lawful under the Old Testament; therefore it ought to be lawful under the New, since there is the same reason of both as far as this is concerned. Nor is the objection of Socinus of any force—that it was lawful formerly because God in many ways declared that he did not disapprove of it at that time; but under the New Testament in no way (either by Christ or by his apostles) did he approve of the repulse of invaders connected with their destruction. From the very fact that Christ did not take away, but confirmed, the authority of the magistrate, he also approved of the right of carrying on war, since it pertains to the magistrate to defend his subjects against unjust violence (which certainly cannot sometimes be done without war). Besides these do not fall under political law, but under the moral and natural law, which was confirmed by Christ.

(2) From the New Testament.

VII. Second, the same right is repeatedly approved in the New Testament. First, by John the Baptist, who (preparing the way of the Lord) sanctioned military discipline by laws (Lk. 3:14). He exhorted the soldiers who asked him what they ought to do in order to escape the wrath to come and obtain eternal life; he did not order them to give up their military profession (which they would have to do entirely if it was wicked and unlawful per se), but that remaining in it, they should be content with their wages and do violence to no man. It does not help the matter to say that John speaks only of the manner of warring rightly and of the military office and not of the office of candidates for eternal life. For if the military life is hateful to God under the New Testament, John would not have prescribed a rule for that life, but would have simply condemned it and exhorted them to change their manner of life. Thus the faith of the centurion is mentioned by Christ (Mt. 8:10), the piety of Cornelius by Luke (Acts 10:1) and is adorned by the testimony of an angel (cf. Acts 10:7). Nor does Paul refuse to employ a military guard for his safety and protection (Acts 23:17-31).

(3) From the office of the magistrate.

VIII. Third, the office of the magistrate necessarily demands this. To him has been given the sword as the avenger of crimes (Rom. 13:4; 1 Pet. 2:14). Now if small robberies are rightly punished (committed against a few), how much more severely should the great and public robberies be punished of those who endeavor to lay waste a state and to devastate regions? He is bound to undertake the defense of his subjects and to have a care for the public tranquility and safety; to guard the laws against the contumacious and open enemies who strive to destroy them (which cannot be done without just war).

(4) From Revelation.

IX. Fourth, the Apocalypse records and approves various wars of the pious under the New Testament, which the circumstances of the passages sufficiently prove are to be understood not only spiritually, but also concerning external war and the real effusion of blood. Nor ought it to be said that here only the wars of infidels, Gog and Magog (which have no reference to Christians), are mentioned. These mutually follow each other; for if those former offensive wars are unjust, these latter defensive wars are just.

Sources of explanation.

X. What is said of New Testament believers does not invalidate the right of war: "They shall beat their swords into plowshares, and their spears into pruninghooks" (Is. 2:4). "Messiah will cut off the chariot from Ephraim, and the horse from Jerusalem, and the battle bow shall be cut off" (Zech. 9:10). It is one thing to speak of the spiritual and internal peace of the kingdom of Christ to be procured by Messiah; another to speak of the political and external peace which does not have a place here. For Christ testifies that "he did not come to send peace, but a sword" (Mt. 10:34). The meaning of these prophecies is no other than that the propagation of the kingdom of Christ is to be accomplished not by carnal weapons, but by the preaching of the gospel and the power of the Holy Spirit alone. But it cannot be inferred that it is not lawful for the magistrate to carry on wars for just and necessary causes because the gospel does not abolish governments or magistracies.

XI. Although the arms of the apostles (with which they were to fight against Satan, the world and the flesh) are said to be spiritual, not carnal (2 Cor. 10:4), because they were ordered to war against the world not by external force, but by the preaching of the word alone (Mt. 28:19); and the arms of believers are no other than prayers and tears in spiritual war, it does not follow that the right of the sword and of carnal weapons does not belong to the magistrate. As the calling of the apostles and of believers does not take away the office of the magistrate, so the spiritual arms with which believers fight do not take away the carnal which the magistrate uses.

XII. The private duty of believers is one thing, the public duty of a magistrate another. Believers ought to be prepared to pour out their own blood rather than that of others because to them the right of the sword and of war is not granted. But it is different with the office of the magistrate, since God has armed him for the avenging of wickedness and the defense of the state and the church. He has granted to him also the right of waging necessary wars.

XIII. The objections drawn from Mt. 5:39 and similar passages do not prove that every war is simply unlawful. (1) Nothing new is there commanded which cannot be shown to have been commanded in the Old Testament (where nevertheless war is approved). (2) What is said there is said to private persons—how far in any way they may indulge their affections and perturbations. It is not said to the public authority ordained of God, a revenger to execute wrath upon him that doeth evil (Rom. 13:4). Thus the hatred of enmity and of sheer revenge is prohibited there, not the care of justice.

XIV. James teaches indeed that the origin and cause of wars is evil because it is always unjust on one side (4:1), but it does not follow that every war is evil on both sides. It is frequently lawful for the magistrate to repel again and avenge by force offensive injury.

2. Defensive homicide is not forbidden.

XV. Second, defensive homicide is not forbidden when anyone, for the purpose of defending his own life against a violent and unjust aggressor (keeping within the limits of lawful protection), kills another. To be considered as lawful protection, it is necessary: (1) that the aggressor unjustly assails and falls upon us; (2) that the defender be placed beyond all blame, while every other way of escaping morally by speaking or flying or yielding is shut against him; (3) that the defense be made during the very attack and not after it is over; (4) that nothing is done by him either under the impulse of anger or with the feeling and desire of revenge, but with the sole intention of defending himself.

XVI. The reason is clear. Although it is not lawful to return like for like and to avenge oneself, still to repel force by force and to defend oneself belongs to natural and perpetual right (especially where the aggression is simply violent and destitute of all public authority) even unto the slaying of the aggressor (although not intended by itself, but inasmuch as we cannot otherwise defend our lives and free ourselves from his unjust oppression). Nor do civil laws alone approve this, as is evident from the Codex to the Cornelian law and to the Aquilian law: "All laws and all rights allow the repelling of force by force" (cf. *Corpus Iuris Civilis, I: Digesta* 48.8 ["Ad legem Corneliam de sicariis"] [ed. P. Krueger, 1955], pp. 852-53 and ibid., 9.2.45 ["Ad legem Aquiliam"], p. 162). But God himself is found to have intimated this clearly in the law where a case of private defense is set forth from which a judgment can be formed concerning the practice of that law: "If a thief be found breaking up" (in the very act) "and be smitten that he die, there shall no blood be shed for him" (Ex. 22:2). If the sun be risen upon him, there shall be blood shed for him if doubtless the slayer could discover that he had come only for the purpose of stealing and not of killing.

XVII. However such defense is wrongfully extended to the preservation or recovery of honor (oftentimes imaginary), whose idol the devil (who is a murderer from the beginning) has set up in the world that offering may be made to it with human blood; both because honor can be recovered, but life never; and because such slaughter would pertain not to lawful defense, but to unlawful revenge. But it is properly referred: (1) To the defense of life, whether our own or our neighbor's, especially when they are bound to us by a somewhat closer tie (as our parents, wives, children, friends and the like). For he who does not repel an injury from another when he can is as much to blame as he who commits it. Still the person acting can be such, as is (for example) a father or a prince, so that it is more becoming for the one attacked to suffer death itself than to repel injury by such a defense. (2) It is referred to the defense of chastity, either our own or another's (as the examples of brave virgins stand forth, who killed those attempting to violate their chastity, when they could in no other way escape). Just as many laws permit the father or the husband to kill with impunity the violator of a daughter or wife taken in the act (*ep' autophorō*).

XVIII. Blameless protection is not prohibited in Rom. 12:19, but private revenge (as the words themselves show: *mē heautous ekdikountes*). Nor does he who justly defends his own life do it by private undertaking, but by the public authority of the law of nature. The injunctions to love our enemies do not take away the necessary defense of life because the foundation of the love of neighbors is the love of ourselves. The passage in Mt. 26:52 in which our Lord orders Peter, "Put up again thy sword into his place: for all they that take the sword shall perish with the sword" does not take away just self-defense. This had the appearance not so much of defense (which would have been useless against so great a multitude) as of revenge. Again, he had not waited for the command of the Lord (who had no need of such a defender), but acted precipitately.

3. Casual homicide is not prohibited.

XIX. Third, casual homicide is not prohibited, whether committed personally or by another, provided it be in no way intended and treachery and guilt be absent (such as is described in Dt. 19:4, 5). Hence asylums and cities of refuge were appointed for such, to which murderers might retreat, lest the Goel (or avenger of blood), carried away by fury before the cause was known, should slay the innocent. But this is falsely extended in the papacy to wretches of all kinds and voluntary homicides, ravishers of virgins and the like, to whom they wish an asylum to lie open in sacred places.

Affirmatively, all private homicide is forbidden.

XX. Affirmatively (*kata thesin*) private manslaughter is prohibited when committed by private authority and wicked treachery, or from hatred and studied vengeance or from any other evil motive: whether by force or cunning, by the sword or by poison; whether directly by oneself or indirectly by another (as David had Uriah killed by others). Hence Abraham would not have sinned against this law if, in accordance with the command of God, he had slain his own son. He would have done it by the supreme authority of him who has the right of life and death over all.

XXI. There is a threefold reason of the sanction: divine, natural and civil. Divine, because since man is the image of God, it cannot be destroyed without manifest and sacrilegious injury to God (the archetype and the sole arbiter and Lord of our life). Natural, because since all things by their own nature seek self-preservation, they are deservedly to be considered enemies of the human race who deprive men of life. Civil, because civil society (which is damaged by other wickednesses) is by the crime of homicide straightway disturbed and overthrown.

Under which suicide is comprehended.

XXII. Under homicide condemned by the law, we include: (1) self-murder (*autocheirian*, so highly praised by the Stoics) of those who desert this post without the will of the supreme commander. By this precept is prohibited self-murder (*autophonia*) no less than the murder of others (*heterophonia*). For although the second table seems to terminate on our neighbor, still it must be considered to pertain no less to man with respect to himself, since each one is nearest to himself. Yea, since each one is bound to love his neighbor as himself and to defend his life as his own, for the very reason that he is forbidden to do violence to the life of a neighbor, is he far more strongly prohibited from doing injury to his own life.

XXIII. That suicide (*autocheirian*) is a most heinous sin appears from the following reasons. A suicide (*autocheir*) sins against God by trampling on his authority, who alone is Lord of life; on his goodness, who has so kindly preserved him thus long among the living; on his providence, whose order he endeavors to disturb. He sins against himself by violating the natural inclination prompting each one to love himself, and cherish and preserve his own flesh (Eph. 5:29). He sins against the state by destroying one of her citizens; against his family by violently tearing away its member and (perhaps the chief) plunging all his relatives into disgrace, grief and mourning; against the church and religion by branding the Christian system with ignominy, causing grief to all, scandal to the good and occasion of scoffing to enemies. It is opposed to the law of nature, which binds each one to self-preservation; and to confidence and piety in God, which ought to receive all evils, either resting upon or threatening us, as from God; to wisdom because this crime is reached not so much by reflection as by fury and wild impulse. Not even Seneca could deny this: "A wise man ought not to assist in his own punishment: it is folly to die through fear of death" (*Epistle* 70 [Loeb, 2:60-61]). It is opposed to justice because man is no more lord of his own than of another's life. He is a servant who has a master, a soldier who has a general. He is placed in his station; he ought not to be irregular (*leipotaktēs*) or to leave at his own pleasure, but to be discharged by another. This is expressed in the best way by Epictetus himself, who orders men to wait until God gives the sign (*ekdechesthai ton theon*) and discharges us from this service (*Discourses* 1.9.16 [Loeb, 1:68-69]). It is opposed to fortitude because it arises from an impatience of evil sent or from fear that it will be sent, whether in order that it may be removed or escaped. Hence Augustine properly says that it does not belong to magnanimity and that he is deservedly said to have a greater soul who can bear a life of trials rather than fly from it (CG 1.22* [FC 8:54]). It is opposed to the consent of the wiser among the heathen, Greeks as well as Romans: Pythagoras, Plato, Aristotle, Seneca, Cicero and others, who confess it to be wicked. Here pertain the examples of self-murder (*autocheirias*) recounted in the Scriptures, which are ascribed only to the abandoned: in Saul (1 S. 31:4); Ahithophel (2 S. 17:23); Judas Iscariot (Mt. 27:5; Acts 1:18).

Sources of explanation.

XXIV. The example of Samson (Jdg. 16:30) does not favor suicide (*autocheiria*) because in the ruins of the house which he threw down he buried himself no less than others. This was a singular deed, perpetrated by the extraordinary influence of the Holy Spirit, as appears both from the apostle (Heb. 11:34), who says that he did this by faith and from the prayers which he offered to God for obtaining extraordinary strength for this act and from their being heard (Jdg. 16:28). God increased his strength and bestowed the desired success that he might thus be an illustrious type of Christ causing the great destruction of his enemies by his own death and breaking the tyrannical yoke resting upon the neck of his people. Finally, the design was not private revenge simply, but the vindication of the glory of God, of religion and of the people, since he was a public person and raised up by God from the people as an avenger.

XXV. Nor do the examples of Eleazar, the brother of Judas Maccabeus, who crept under an elephant and, crushed by it, died (1 Mac. 6:43-45); and of Razis (killing himself with his own sword, 2 Mac. 14:41, 42) favor it because they are drawn from the Apocryphal books. Nor is it to be called generosity, but the height of timidity for anyone voluntarily to rush upon his own total destruction on account of an uncertain evil. Nor do the examples of those who wished to encounter extreme dangers for their country or friends and to purchase the tranquility and safety of others by their own death belong here. It is one thing to expose oneself to dangers from the pressure of necessity and in answer to a special divine call; another to kill oneself. Nor ought he to be considered a suicide (*autocheir*) who lays down his life for another, for then Christ's laying down his life for us would have been a suicide (*autocheir*) (which no one would say).

XXVI. The act of those who blow up themselves with their ships (as is sometimes done by sailors who, reduced to extremity, have their own ship set on fire in order that they might not be brought under the tyranny of enemies; nor the warlike instruments, in their power, be turned by the enemy to the destruction of their native country and that the same works might inflict injury upon the enemy, by taking themselves away together with the ship), although approved by certain theologians (or taken out of the sphere of suicide [*autocheiria*] because they did not design their own destruction, but the slaughter of the enemy and the good of their country), yet by us and many others cannot be approved at all. By this act they directly and voluntarily bring death upon themselves as a physical and moral cause; thus they cannot escape the crime of self-murder (*autophonōn*). Besides in it they oppose confidence in God by limiting his providence, as if with him there were not a thousand ways for escaping even when we suppose that we are shut up on all sides. They oppose Christian prudence because they weigh certain and present destruction with an uncertain chance and event and hold the former to outweigh the latter. They might, although almost conquered, come out superior; the enemy might spare their lives; some might save their lives by swimming away or in some other manner. They oppose fortitude, for it is bravery not basely to leave our post from desperation of victory or safety, but to fight even to the very last. They oppose love and kindness towards miserable persons: the old, the weak, the sick, children—whom the enemies themselves might spare and for the most part are accustomed to spare. Therefore such cannot be acquitted of guilt according to the rule of the apostle (not to do evil that good may come); nor can any laws either of war or of the state stand opposed to the divine sanction. Although such may sometimes be excused from so much, still they cannot be excused from the whole, whether they may be said to do it as private persons or as public servants. Nor can public authority bind us in opposition to the divine authority. Nor can any disadvantage done to the enemy or advantage to the country be so great as to absolve the conscience here. Nor can the intention of injuring the enemy be wholly abstracted from the most certain knowledge of destroying himself together with the enemy and of bringing indubitable death upon himself.

XXVII. It is good to render to God what has been given by him, but when that is both demanded of us and is restored in due manner; not however when it is neither demanded nor restored in due manner. We grant that death is sometimes better than life; but inflicted by others, not brought upon ourselves. Death can be lawfully wished for, but not sought. As life is received only at the divine will, so neither ought it to be laid down except by his command. To despise that most dreadful messenger (*to phoberōtaton*) from God is brave; but voluntarily to rush upon it is rash and insane (which Aristotle, *Nichomachean Ethics* 3.8 [Loeb, 19:163-71], teaches to be not bravery but cowardice). Nor if the love of country, the safety of others, the desire of immortality can impel to the brave endurance of death sent against us, they ought to have the same influence in inviting it when unsent.

XXVIII. It is one thing to suffer death, to permit the murder of oneself; yea, even to present oneself bravely to it at the call of God. It is another to kill oneself. The former in some circumstances is lawful and Christ, the martyrs and heroes did something like it; but not the latter likewise.

XXIX. "The giving of the body to be burned" of which Paul speaks (1 Cor. 13:3) is not a rash and useless act by which anyone voluntarily and unnecessarily exposes himself to death for the cause of God. Rather it is necessary and holy by which he meets martyrdom at the call of God, nor refuses that call either by lying or by denying the truth on account of love; either for his relatives or for the world, when it is his lot to be carried to the tribunals of pagans by the enemies of the gospel.

2. Unlawful duels.

XXX. Second, duelling is prohibited; not every single combat or fight between two, such as is the necessary defense of life against an unjust aggressor (which has been approved by us before); not one engaged in by public authority for the common good (as was the single combat of David and Goliath); but a fight between private persons, directly and willingly entered into, by appointment or agreement, with danger of slaying or of mutilation, which we think is simply to be condemned, as much in the accepter as in the challenger, although the challenger is more guilty. It directly assails this precept: "Thou shall not kill."

XXXI. No reason can be given, which can make duelling honorable and lawful. Not the defenses of worldly honor and the avoidance of disgrace because that honor is false and prevails only among worthless men (the wounding of which takes nothing away from the true fortitude, which is not to be preferred to the honor due to God). Nor can there be any danger of real disgrace when he who refuses to accept a challenge gives as the reasons the divine prohibition, and the danger of the soul (with which no loss of honor is to be compared). Besides wounded honor can be better and more easily healed than the death of the injurer. Not the defense of goods because our own life and another's ought not to be exchanged with other temporal goods. Not the manifestation of truth or the purgation of crime because since there is no promise of God which wills to give testimony to the truth in this way, thus to consult his extraordinary providence (or appeal to it) is nothing else than to tempt God by a diabolical invention. Not the execution of vengeance because vengeance is denied to private persons. They would thus be judges in their own case while it is lawful to public persons only and that in a legal way. How the Jesuits (Lessius, Amicus, Escobar and others) favor this diabolical art is evident from the extracts of their moral theology published in the year 1666 (Proposi. 11, 12, 15, 16+).

3. Anger and hatred.

XXXII. Third, not only is external homicide and whatever pertains to it forbidden; but also (since the law is spiritual) anger, hatred, the desire of revenge, envy, contumely and whatever is opposed to the true and sincere love of our neighbor or his legitimate defense. All these are condemned not only in the New Testament (Mt. 5:21), as Socinians falsely maintain, but were also prohibited and condemned in the Old (Lev. 19:17, 18; Zech. 8:16, 17). For although only effective and external homicide was capitally punished by the forensic law (Lev. 24:17), affective and internal homicide in the sight of God comes under the same head.

XXXIII. However, because under negative precepts affirmative ones are contained, we are bound by this law to the defense, aid, love, kind treatment of our neighbor, the desire for concord and peace (Rom. 12:18). For it is not sufficient that we injure no one, rather we must give to everyone his due. It is not enough not to kill anyone, but we must in addition study to preserve our neighbor's life in whatever lawful way it can be done. And as a lamp is extinguished in a twofold manner (either by blowing it out or by not supplying it with oil), so the life of our neighbor is destroyed either by a violent extinction or by an iniquitous withdrawal of the alms and assistance by which it might have been preserved.

Eighteenth Question: The Seventh Commandment

What is forbidden and what is enjoined by the precept concerning not committing adultery?

I. As by the sixth precept both our own and our neighbors' lives are entrusted to us, so by the seventh both our own and others' virtue. A threefold reason is assigned: divine, because since God is holy, it is just that man created in the image of God should lead a holy and consequently also a chaste life (since chastity is a part of holiness); natural, because since the conjunction of male and female pertains to the right of nature, it must necessarily be directed in accordance with the rule of right reason, lest nature herself remain unbridled (thus there is no nation in the world which has not approved matrimony and condemned promiscuous intercourse); civil, because as by the distinction of families political good order (*eutaxia*) is maintained, so the disturbance of the same by promiscuous lusts overthrows republics and brings destruction upon houses.

Under adultery all illicit intercourse is synecdochically forbidden.

II. Therefore, by this precept all lewdness and wantonness of whatever kind is forbidden under the word "adultery" (which is one of its grossest forms, most injurious to human society and contumelious to our neighbor) as comprehended by way of synecdoche. Thus here is condemned all illicit intercourse outside of marriage. Under which is included, first, adultery properly so called, the violation of another's bed, whether one of the parties is unmarried or both are married (in which way the adultery is doubled by the violation of a twofold bed). (2) Fornication in general and simple (of two unmarried persons), which, although among the heathens looked upon as a venial sin (or rather as no sin at all—as also among the papists), still is frequently expressly condemned as a heinous sin in the Old as well as in the New Testament (Dt. 22:28; 23:17, 18; 1 Cor. 6:18; Heb. 13:4; Rev. 21:8). The apostle marks its seriousness because he who commits fornication makes his body one with a harlot, sins against his own body, profanes a temple of the Holy Spirit and pollutes a vessel of grace (1 Cor. 6:16). Hence we gather the extent of the criminality of those who defend public brothels against human and divine laws (as is done in the papacy where such establishments are publicly tolerated; yea, even taxes and tributes are drawn from them; although God formerly forbade the wages of a harlot and the price of a dog to be brought into the temple, Dt. 23:18). Espensaeus complains about this ("De Continentia," 3.4 *Opera Omnia* [1619], pp. 732-35), while others defend this infamous cause (as Emanuel Sa, Toletus and various casuists among the papists). Bellarmine confesses that brothels are necessary evils for avoiding greater sin; but here the apostolic rule ought to obtain, evil must not be done that good may come. If in the Old Testament there are said to have been harlots (as in the time of the patriarchs and of Solomon), they are not on that account approved or proposed for imitation. The example of Solomon (revelling in lust) is not to be pressed, as it was vicious. Rather we are to imitate the zeal of Josiah reforming the worship of God and especially destroying brothels (2 K. 23:7); and also of Louis IX (called Sanctus), who expelled actors from his kingdom and destroyed houses of prostitution.

Incest.

III. (3) Incest which is committed between persons connected by consanguinity or affinity, if the degrees prohibited in both kinds of relationship are settled by the law of God, not by the legislation of men. (4) Rape, when a girl is forcibly carried from the house of her father for the purpose of lust, whether she struggles against or assents to it. For then violence is done at least to the father from whom his property is violently wrested. (5) Concubinage, when anyone has intercourse with a woman living in his house; not with marital affection, but only for the sake of convenience (who can even be dismissed, so that the children are not considered either as legitimate or heirs). This is a species of whoredom; yea, it is rather worse, for this bespeaks only a transient act, but concubinage adds permanency to the condition. Hence the apostle makes a direct antithesis between marriage and whoredom (Heb. 13:4) because all concubinage outside of lawful marriage is whoredom. However although it prevailed under the Old Testament among the patriarchs, it cannot therefore be made honorable or be imitated. We live by rules, not by examples; nor are the defects and blemishes of the saints, recorded by the sacred writers, on that account approved; nor if they are excused by the canonical law, can they consequently be excused by the divine law.

Sin against nature.

IV. (6) The sin against nature and those horrible crimes expressed by the words "sodomy" and "bestiality" (of which mention is made in Lev. 20:13 and Rom. 1:27, which are not even to be named among Christians, although even now they prevail too much in various places to the disgrace of the Christian name).

Obscenity; dancing.

V. (7) All unchaste obscenity, existing as well in the heart by evil thoughts and depraved concupiscence and condemned by Christ (Mt. 5:28), as expressed by obscene words and immodest gestures. We do not doubt that under these are contained the painting of the face and the loose and lascivious dress of the body, when lewdness flows (*aselgeia*) from the soul into the clothing, from the conscience to the surface: dances and lascivious motions, demoralizing scenic representations and stage plays (usual now); intoxication, habitual drunkenness, gluttony and the like (which are so many different allurements and incentives to this kind of illicit intercourse). It is certain that all these are comprehended under this interdict, since they are frequently condemned in the Scriptures as characterizing the heathen and the children of this world (Rom. 13:12, 13; Eph. 4:19; 1 Pet. 4:3; 1 Jn. 2:15, 16). They are wrong for Christians to indulge in, who ought not to be conformed to this world (Rom. 12:2), but are bound to regulate their whole lives in accordance with sobriety, temperance, modesty and holiness (Tit. 2:12; Rom. 13:13).

VI. Nor if the apostle wishes Christians to abstain from all impurity and lasciviousness (Eph. 5:3, 4; 1 Thess. 4:3), does it follow that this was prohibited only under the New Testament and is an addition made by Christ to the moral law. It is evident that the holiness commanded in the law excludes every kind of impurity, internal of the heart as well as external of the body. But here is gathered only that this duty is commanded no less by the gospel than by the law and in the former is more strongly confirmed what had already been forbidden in the latter, which can be proved further by various passages (Prov. 6:25, 26; Job 31:1, 9; Gen. 39:7, 9; Jer. 5:8, 9). Nor if the wise man seems to allow the young man to walk in the ways of his heart and in the sight of his eyes (Ecc. 11:9), does he approve this as lawful. Rather he speaks ironically, immediately altering his tone and adding, for all these things God will bring him into judgment.

Polygamy.

VII. (8) Polygamy, not successive (which is lawful), but simultaneous (which is a sin). (a) It is against the first institution of marriage (Gen. 2:23, 24), to which Christ recalls the Jews. God made and joined together one man and one woman and sanctioned by an edict that two (not three or more) should be one flesh; also that the man should cleave to his own wife, not to wives; nor are they to be separated whom God has joined together (Mal. 2:15; Mt. 19:5). (b) It is a sin against the nature of conjugal love, which is so peculiar and singular that it cannot receive a third person into participation of the same thing (as experience teaches in conjugal jealousy). (c) Against the nature of the marriage contract, by which neither has power over his or her own body (1 Cor. 7:4). Hence he is convicted of injustice and treachery who joins himself to another (Mal. 2:14). (d) Against the command of Paul, who wishes each wife to have her "own husband" (*ton idion andra*). Hence a wife is called an adulteress who becomes the wife of another while her husband is still living (Rom. 7:2, 3) because matrimonial fidelity ought to be reciprocal. This cannot be the case if one can have many husbands or one husband many wives. (e) Against that united care of offspring which the end of marriage requires (which is divided in polygamy). (f) Against the peace of the family because innumerable strifes arise from it (Lev. 18:18), as was seen in the house of Jacob (Gen. 30) and of Elkanah (1 S. 1:6).

VIII. The legality of polygamy cannot be gathered either from the example of the patriarchs of the Old Testament, who were polygamists and to whom polygamy ought to have been permitted. We are to be governed by laws and not by examples. (b) If it was permitted, it was either by an ethical permission of right through a particular dispensation on account of infirmity because they were still babes, to whom many things are allowed which are denied to adults (and this now ceases under the New Testament); or, what is more likely, by a permission of the deed (i.e., through mere tolerance, not through approbation) so that in this way they might be free from civil punishment in the earthly court, but not likewise from the divine punishment in the court of heaven (from which they had to be freed by the grace of God, by the intervention of their repentance, either explicit or at least implicit); see above Topic XI, Question 2, Section 27, 28. Or from this that God gives laws concerning the inheritances of polygamists (Dt. 21:15, 16). Although he gives laws to polygamists, still he does not on that account approve polygamy itself; as he gives a law concerning the not bringing the hire of a whore into the house of the Lord (Dt. 23:18), yet he does not approve of the hire itself. He gives a law concerning the election of a king and yet does not approve of the desire of the people (1 S. 8:6, 7). Or from this, that a man who may be married ought to raise up seed to his dead brother (Dt. 25:5). The reference is to brothers dwelling together, i.e., who were not both married.

IX. Because lawful intercourse (found in virtuous union) is a remedy for the irregular lusts and illicit intercourse forbidden by this precept, the lawful use of marriage instituted by God is enjoined in those who are unwilling or unable to contain themselves so that there may be a lawful and undivided conjunction of two in one flesh, by the just consent not only of the contracting parties, but also of those in whose power they are and without which the nuptials are clandestine and *ipso jure* null; full, not extorted by force or deceit (which refers to rape); sincere, not fraudulent, since it ought to be an inseparable connection, not only of bodies, but also of souls and of property to be regularly dissolved by death alone (Rom. 7:2, 3).

X. Modesty, chastity (whether in celibacy or in marriage), purity, sobriety and all virtues pertaining to the true sanctification of the body and soul (whose leader is temperance) are also commanded, by which the reason restrains lust and all the force of the concupiscible appetite and teaches them to obey her.

Nineteenth Question: The Eighth Commandment

What is forbidden and commanded by the precept concerning not stealing? Is usury of all kinds contained under it? We deny.

I. As by the two preceding precepts the persons and bodies of neighbors (or their lives and chastity) were guarded, by this eighth precept their goods (or property) are placed in safety. The design is that each one's own may be rendered to him, since injustice is an abomination to God.

The reason of the precept is threefold.

II. There is a threefold reason for this sanction no less than the preceding. (1) Divine, because since God is no less the bestower of goods than the Creator, whoever does not wait for these things from his bounteous hand, but seizes them by injury, greatly offends God himself. (2) Natural, because since the distinction of property (according to which some possess more, others fewer things) is of natural right the usurpation of another's possession cannot but be a grievous sin, repugnant to natural right. (3) Political, because (the license of thieves and robbers prevailing) the public peace and tranquility (the bond of human society) is weakened.

Theft and its various kinds are condemned.

III. Theft in general is here forbidden, which is commonly defined as the illegal appropriation of what belongs to another; or the unlawful use (the owner being unwilling) of what belongs to another, whether by treachery or violence. This, however, is not only simple, but qualified: also various and multiple according to the diversity of objects. For if it is the appropriation of a sacred thing, it is called "sacrilege"; if of public goods belonging to the state, "peculation"; if of a person in another's power (whether he be free or a slave), "man-stealing." Here belong highway robbery, extortion of money by threats, cheating: to each of which their own punishments are assigned by the civil laws.

IV. To theft belong also reductively all deceits, frauds and overreaching in contracts, measures, weights, monies, monopolies and all evil arts and trickery by which another's property is appropriated. Yea, they are guilty of the theft in the sight of God who devote themselves to indolence and depraved ease (which is the cushion of the devil) and who, in their callings, professions and ministries, are negligent and unfaithful—who unjustly steal the wages allowed them, performing lazily and imperfectly the work entrusted to them.

V. Here belongs avarice also, the root of all evils (1 Tim. 6:9, 10). It consists in an insatiable desire of gain and accursed thirst of gold; or an inordinate love of riches, which is incompatible (*asystatos*) with the love we owe to God and to our neighbor. "Ye adulterers and adulteresses, know ye not that the friendship of the world is enmity with God?" (Jam. 4:4). Hence it is characterized by the apostle by the detestable crime of idolatry (Eph. 5:5) because by it man is led (the deity being neglected) to place his whole confidence and trust in riches as his highest good.

VI. And hence it is evident that this vice was prohibited not just under the New Testament (as the Socinians with the Anabaptists maintain, as if it were an addition made to the law by Christ) in this—that the possession of riches even beyond necessity was allowed under the Old Testament, but under the New is restricted to those things which are necessary simply to support life (as in the *Racovian Catechism* [1818], p. 247). It is frequently interdicted in the Old Testament, not only by this and the tenth precept (where the coveting of the goods of a neighbor is forbidden), but is also condemned elsewhere (Ex. 18:21; 22:25; 23:8; Lev. 19:13; 25:46; Dt. 16:19; Ps. 62:10; Is. 5:8; Jer. 6:6, 7; 22:17; Ps. 119:36). Nor is the possession of riches unlawful per se, provided they are acquired in lawful ways and we use them as means, not enjoy them as an end (as is done by many believers who are said to have abounded in wealth even under the New Testament, such as Joseph of Arimathea [Mt. 27:57], Cornelius the centurion [Acts 10:2], Tabitha [Acts 9:36] and similar persons). If it is said that the rich can hardly enter into the kingdom of heaven (Mt. 19:23), this is not on account of riches, but on account of the abuse of them. This is clear from Mk. 10:24 where they who trust in riches are condemned. Hence riches are called "unrighteous mammon" (Lk. 16:9); not properly by reason of itself, but accidentally by reason of the possessors because they are too frequently unjustly acquired and badly used. And "deceitfulness" (*apatē*) is ascribed to them (Mt. 13:22), not per se, but with respect to the mind by which they are possessed. In this sense, worldly care and the choking of the word is also attributed to them, not in relation to the riches themselves, but to the mind of the possessor who, anxious with care, chokes in himself the seed of the word and suffers it not to take root in his heart. Therefore avarice consists not in the execution but in the disposition; not in the riches, but in the desire for and unlawful use of them.

Is usury lawful?

VII. Here belongs the celebrated question concerning usury, reckoned by some among the species of theft. Is any kind of usury lawful? We must say a few words about it in order that we may see what is taught about it in the word of God. Usury is the gain which is demanded over and above a mutual exchange, whether it be money or produce or any other thing. It is so called from use because it is obtained by the use of money; by the Greeks *tokos*, from *tiktō* ("I bring forth") because it is as it were the birth of money lent out. The Hebrews were accustomed to designate it by two words: *thrbhyth* from *rbhh* ("he multiplied") because by usury the principle itself is multiplied and grows; and *nshk* from the root *nshk* ("he has bitten") because like a serpent it bites and bruises the unwary.

VIII. With regard to the question, there are two principal opinions: the one of those denying, the other of those affirming usury. The canonists here defend the negative and think all usury should be absolutely condemned (Gratian, "Decreti," Pt. II, Causa XIV, Q. 3 in *Corpus Iuris Canonici* [ed. A. Friedberg, 1955], 1:734-35). The Scholastics and the followers of the Master of Sentences agree (Peter Lombard, *Sententiarum* 3.37.3 [PL 192/2.832]). Also some of the Lutherans; yea, even of our men—Zwingli, Musculus, Aretius; and various Anglican theologians—Jewel ("De Usura," *Works of John Jewel* [1848], 8:252-61), Lancelot Andrews, (Thomas) Wilson and others. The orthodox commonly embrace the affirmative and hold that usury is lawful, on the basis however of certain distinctions.

IX. First, usury is to be distinguished. One kind is biting and immoderate and fraudulent, which without any regard for equity and Christian charity, is unmercifully exacted from every borrower—even a poor and reduced person or one who has suffered some great loss in his property which renders him (without any fault of his own) unable to repay. Another is moderate and helping in which such moderation is used as is conducive to the necessity, advantage and gain acquired (or usually acquired) by the benefit of a loan of both the lender and the borrower. It answers to Christian equity according to the mode prescribed by the magistrate in relation to the places, times and persons (for these vary in different countries and among different people). Second, they who let out money on interest are either moneylenders and usurers professedly (who do this alone or not); or those who only lend money on interest or even sometimes gratuitously; or such as can or cannot trade with their own money honestly—whether because they are without the power or talent for doing it or because they are wholly devoted to public offices, either sacred or political. Third, they who borrow temporarily as either poor or rich or at least moderate circumstances. They either receive the loan for necessary uses to the support of themselves and family or for their own advantage and gain.

Statement of the question.

X. These principles being laid down, we say that the question is not about biting usury (which we consider unjust and unlawful), but about moderate and reasonable usury; not about those who practice usury as a profession and do that alone, that by assessments and usury they may benefit themselves to the disadvantage of others (for we think this art should be stigmatized and such moneylenders and brokers, who follow this kind of life, and like leeches suck out the blood of the poor, are most justly condemned); but about those who have a regard for others' interests as well as their own. These exact so honest an interest from those from whom it can rightfully be exacted as to be ready gratuitously to assist the poor with their own money (and actually do it); or who are somewhat unfit (whether on account of age or through incapacity or on account of other business) to increase their property by the use of their own money. Not concerning the poor and needy who for necessary and unavoidable uses borrow money on interest—for to contract for and to demand usury from these we hold to be unjust; but concerning others who are wealthy or at least in moderate circumstances, who borrow money in order to increase their own property and who from negotiations with money can receive any advantage and gain. From them, we maintain, it is just and lawful to demand a certain interest.

Proof that all usury is not unlawful.

XI. First, because it was lawful under the Old Testament to take usury from strangers (Dt. 23:20), which could not have been done if it had in it intrinsic baseness; for what is by itself and by its own nature evil cannot become lawful in relation to any object. Nor can it be said either: that only the seven nations devoted to destruction are meant (because it treats of strangers in general as distinguished from brethren, i.e., from the Jews), for as they had the power of exacting usury from the Jews, so it was fair that the Israelites should have the same privilege so that commerce might be carried on between them (this is equality); or that it is only a permission of the deed, not of the right, not as something lawful, but as less evil (like the bill of divorcement). This is taken for granted, not proved, nor are express evils to be done or permitted by sanction in order that good may come.

XII. Second, if usury was absolutely unlawful, Christ would not under that figure have a spiritual duty from the lawful use of talents (Mt. 25:14-30) without any intimation of disapprobation, such as he was accustomed to employ in other parables drawn from a disapproved practice (as in Lk. 16:8). Nor would John the Baptist have directed the publicans who hired the tributes from the Romans at a certain price (Lk. 3:13) only to exact nothing beyond what was just without making a change in their manner of life.

XIII. Third, all practice of usury is neither prohibited in the law, nor is it opposed to equity and honesty. Yea, it is founded (1) upon necessity and utility because without usury commerce, the principal support of human society, can neither subsist nor be carried on. Now can a thing be charged with injustice without which human society cannot exist and which, taken away, all negotiations and dealings of men would cease? (2) Upon natural equity because it is fair that he who receives benefit from another's money should make him also a sharer in that by the help of which he gains this benefit, as a due compensation. (3) Upon just gratitude, for what another rightly owes, that the other rightly receives. He who gains by a loan the right of gratitude owes some recompense (*antidōron*); for the right of nature demands that we should be grateful to those who oblige us, not only by words, but also in fact. (4) Upon Christian charity, which requires each head of a family to provide for his own (1 Tim. 5:8), and parents are bound to lay up for their children (2 Cor. 12:14). However if anyone should assist others with his own money and neglect his own, he would never increase his own means. (5) From a comparison with other contracts, which have a place in society and are approved by all; for example, of implanting reciprocal use (*emphyteuseōs*), hiring (*antichrēseōs*), accommodations, etc. If from the letting of a house and a farm and the lending of utensils, anyone gains advantage, why not equally from the borrowing of money? (6) Besides there are constitutions of emperors and of kings by which limitations are established for lawful usury; cf. "De usuris et fructibus," *Corpus Iuris Civilis, I: Digesta* 22.1 (ed. P. Krueger, 1988), pp. 320-24; "De usuris," ibid., *II: Codex Iustinianus* 4.32 (ed. P. Krueger, 1967), pp. 171-73.

Sources of explanation.

XIV. Against usury is not opposed (1) the prohibition of usury in Ex. 22:25*-27 and Lev. 25:35-37*. It is restricted manifestly to the poor and destitute, so that it may appear that there is a different reason for the rich: "If thou lend money to any of my people that is poor," i.e., to him who among the people is miserable and needy, having nothing wherewith to relieve himself (as it is more clearly set forth, "If thy brother be waxen poor . . . take thou no usury of him," Lev. 25:35, 36*; cf. Dt. 15:7-9). If elsewhere it seems to be extended to all the Israelites indiscriminately (as "Unto thy brother thou shalt not lend upon usury," Dt. 23:20), the interdiction is either to be explained from parallel passages of Exodus and Leviticus, in which it is manifestly restricted to the poor. This is not obscurely intimated when mention is made of "usury of victuals," namely, which would be received by him who takes a loan for his sustentation that he may have wherewith to live. If it applies without exception to all the Hebrews, the law will be forensic peculiar to this people so that the society of the Israelites might be more closely connected together by this bond (such as were not a few others concerning slaves, pledges, fields, gleaning and the like, which have no force now under the New Testament).

XV. (2) Nor is it against this—that he is praised as just who does not put out his money to usury (Ps. 15:5; Ezk. 18:8). It refers to usury of all kinds, otherwise it would be repugnant to Moses, who permits some kinds of usury. Rather it is opposed to biting and wicked usury by which the creditor, disregarding all equity, burdens and oppresses his debtor by exacting either too much or too rigidly that which the law wished proscribed.

XVI. (3) Nor is what Christ says ("lend, hoping for nothing again," Lk. 6:35) opposed to this because there is indeed commanded what is to be done, not what is only to be done (viz., that we should also assist the poor and needy, from whom nothing can be expected). (b) If the words of Christ were to be taken strictly, it would follow that not even the principal should be sought from anyone because we are commanded "to lend, hoping for nothing again" (*daneizein mēden apelpizontes*): thus no less the principal than interest. That this however would be unjust absolutely and universally, no one can deny. (c) The design is to encourage benevolence towards the poor that on them also when necessity presses something may be expended, even if there is no hope either of gain or even of the principal. It was not without reason that Christ spoke of this kind of loan because it is ordinarily neglected by us. Nor on this account should the word *dote* be substituted for *daneizete* since it seems to be pure benevolence, not a loan. In a loan, the obligation to return always remains in the receiver (although on the part of the giver there ought not to be a prosecution of his right); while he who receives alms is not bound to repay. Besides such a loan can properly be called not only a gift (*dōrēma*), but also a loan (*daneisma*) on account of the great reward which the Lord promises to him—he who gives to the poor, lends to the Lord. (4) Some explain it as if it were written *mēdena apelpizontes* ("making no one despair") referring to persons and not to things (drawn from the Syrian Interpreter who translates it "lend, and do not cut off the hope of a man"—which agrees with the parallel passage "from him that would borrow of thee, turn not thou away" [*ton thelonta apo sou daneisasthai mē apostraphēs*], Mt. 5:42), nor cut off him from the hope of a loan, whatever may be his circumstances, looking to the reward laid up for us with God. Others, not badly, explain according to the force of the word *apelpizein* ("despairing nothing") as if your kindness were lost or your money badly bestowed; as if you would receive nothing in return because great will always be your reward with God, if men do not neglect their duty.

XVII. Although money of itself seems to be barren, yet it can be made productive by use; as a field and a farm is rendered fertile not by itself, but under human industry. Nor by lawful usury is the same thing reckoned twice or a double payment demanded, since the money loaned is one thing, the interest hoped for from it another; as a farm is something different from the emolument gained from the farm.

XVIII. Christ overthrew the tables of the moneychangers in the temple and cast them out, as also the buyers and sellers (Mt. 21:12), not so much because it is unlawful to buy and sell and to exchange money, as that the house of prayer ought not to be made a place of merchandise. However, they are blamed for having made the house of God a den of thieves and this is not said so much with respect to them, as that by bringing their wares into the temple (with the connivance of the priests), they ministered to the rapacity of the latter, since from that moneychanging and merchandise, they increased their own gains.

XIX. The axiom of canonists—"that every loan ought to be gratuitous"—cannot be simply admitted of a loan properly so called. A man's duty ought not to be injurious to anyone. Nor is it more fair to use gratuitously the money of another in an affair of our own than his house or carriage; so that he obtains no profit or emolument and your surplus (*perisseuma*) supplies his deficiency (*hysterēma*); so that to him there is oppression (*thlipsis*), while there is recreation (*anesis*) to you.

XX. The name of usurer has become infamous. The art is not only illiberal, but also dishonest when anyone professes the art of usury and opens a public establishment; or when he exacts immoderate interest, condemned by the civil laws; or when impatient of delay he follows up his right too rigidly towards the poor (for here the highest right often is the highest injustice, under which name the moneychangers are related to have been called deservedly "Jews" and "Longbeards," who gnaw the people and especially the poor with the most oppressive usury and gorge themselves with their blood by receiving from everyone promiscuously, by which they are not only secure concerning the principal but also of inordinate interest, even from those who beg bread from door to door, from servants without their master's knowledge, from children unknown to their parents). These professedly exercise the art of usury for the very purpose of enriching themselves by it (whom it could be wished were cast out of Christian states as public pests and plunderers of society). But this does not apply to those who by good arts and under equitable conditions established by the civil law, endeavor to make the money which they have at home productive.

XXI. The crime unjustly charged by the papists and especially the Jesuits (as Baile, cf. "De l'usure," in Andre Rivet, *Sommaire de toutes les controverses touchant la religion* [1615], pp. 1240-46) upon our Calvin as a patron of usury because he did not absolutely disapprove of usury, is more justly laid upon themselves by the Jansenists. They permit and practice almost every kind of usury and these very dishonest (see [Pascal], *The Provincial Letters* [1657] and Amadeus Guimenius, "Tractatus de Usuris," *Opusculum singularia* [1664], pp. 158-73). But it is more wonderful that Lancelot Andrews, a great divine, should be so greatly excited because in a certain epistle and on Ezk. 23, he defends usury ("De Usuris, Theologica Determinatio," *Opuscula quaedam* [1629], pp. 109-38). Indeed we cannot but wish for equity in so great a man, who casts so unjust an accusation upon Calvin. For the latter spoke so sparingly and moderately about usury that he could not conceal his preferring to answer nothing on this subject and adds so many precautions that anyone can easily see how little he deserves the calumnies of his opponents.

"I have not yet tried," he says, "what fit reply can be given to the question proposed, but from the peril of others I have learned, with how great a danger that thing is connected; for if we condemn usury altogether, we put a tighter noose upon conscience than the Lord himself wished; if we allow it in the smallest degree, forthwith under that pretext many will seize an unbridled license" (Epist. 383+; cf. "Quaestiones Iuridicae: De Iusuris," CR 38.245-49). And since he had said that usury was not condemned by any testimony of Scripture, he adds a little after, "It were desirable to banish from the world all usury, and so the very name itself." He confirms the same thing on chapter 18 of Ezekiel (*Commentaries on . . . Ezekiel* [1948], 2:225-26 on Ezk. 18:5-9). If more is desired, consult the very celebrated Voetius (*Selectae Disputationes*, Pt. IV [1667], pp. 555-89).

XXII. The virtues commanded by this precept are (1) contentedness (*autarkeia*) or acquiescence in one's lot, so that each one attending to his calling should live by his own honest labor (Gen. 3:19) and, content with his own condition, should not covet that of another (1 Tim. 6:6; Heb. 13:5). (2) Economy and frugality. (3) Sincerity and justice in all dealings that we may live always without treachery and deceit (*aneu dolou kai apatēs*) and give to each one his due. (4) Liberality towards the poor and needy, that we may not only not unjustly seize the goods of our neighbors, but also liberally bestow our own upon him as often as necessity and occasion demand.

Twentieth Question: The Ninth Commandment

Whether a lie under any pretext can be rendered virtuous and lawful. We deny against the Socinians.

I. As our neighbor ought not to be injured by deed, so neither should he be injured by word. This injury is forbidden by the ninth precept, concerning "not bearing false witness against our neighbor." Testimony simply against our neighbor is not forbidden, since oftentimes trials demand it and we are bound to it from a regard to justice; but only "false testimony" is prohibited, by which injury is done in any way to the life, honor or property of a neighbor. Also whatever is repugnant to the veracity and sincerity which ought to prevail among men (which is usually expressed by the word "lie") is forbidden.

What is a lie?

II. A lie is defined by Augustine as "a voluntary enunciation of what is false for the purpose of deceiving" (*On Lying* 5 [NPNF1, 3:460; PL 40.491]); but more accurately by others "the testimony by which a man speaks differently from what he thinks." Although the intention to deceive constitutes a more perfect kind of lying, it is not always required in a lie, provided there is a will of enunciating what is false. Thomas Aquinas well explains, "The nature of a lie is taken from formal falsity (viz., according to this) that the person has the will of enunciating what is false" (ST, II-II, Q. 110, Art. 1, p. 1664). And a little afterwards: "That one, however, intends to establish a falsity in the opinion of another, by deceiving him, does not belong to the species of a lie, but to its perfection" (ibid.). Thus two things are always required in a lie: (1) that the enunciation be false, contrary to the truth of the thing; (2) that there be a will of enunciating what is false and so the speech be contrary to the thought. Hence they hold that the word *mentiri* is equivalent to *contra mentem ire.* A person can speak what is false and yet not lie because through ignorance he believes it to be true and his speech does not contradict his thought.

Threefold lie.

III. The lie prohibited by the ninth precept is commonly distinguished as to its object into pernicious (which is told with the intention of injuring and tends to the injury of a neighbor); jocose (told for the purpose of amusement); and officious (intended to promote the benefit of others). Concerning the first, all agree that it is a grievous sin, but concerning the last two (and especially the last) a controversy is moved by the Socinians, who maintain that they are either venial or no sins (with whom agree some laxer casuists, who take them out of the category of sin). However although we recognize a distinction between these lies (as that the pernicious is more criminal, the other two more light), still we consider them true sins condemned by the law of God.

Whether there can be any lawful lie.

Scripture condemns all lies.

IV. First, lying without any exception is everywhere condemned in Scripture as a sin abominable to God (Ps. 5:6; Prov. 6:17, 19; 12:22; Eph. 4:25; Col. 3:9), as promoted by the instigation of the Devil, the father of lies (Jn. 8:44), injurious to the majesty of God, the author and such a lover of truth that he can neither lie, nor by any dispensation ever give the power of lying; yea, has expressly forbidden and decreed severely to punish it (Prov. 19:5, 9; 21:28).

Because it is evil in itself.

V. (2) What is evil according to itself in its own kind can in no way be made good and lawful. Now every lie is evil in itself, falling under undue matter. It is a disorder both of the liar in himself because it is against the order of nature of his speech (the interpreter of the mind plainly disagrees with the mind) and against his neighbor because each one owes a regard for the truth to his neighbor, from natural obligation and that of divine right. "Words," says Thomas Aquinas, "are naturally signs of thought, it is therefore unnatural and undue for anyone to signify by words that which he has not in his mind." So Durandus, "Words were instituted, not that men might deceive each other by them, but to convey their opinions to others; therefore it is an undue act for anyone to use words to signify what he does not have in his mind" (*Sententias theologicas Petri Lombardi Commentariorum*, Bk. 3, Dist. 38, Q. 1.8 [1556], p. 244). The Philosopher (Aristotle) concludes that a lie is in itself wicked and to be avoided (*Nichomachean Ethics* 4.7.6 [Loeb, 19:240-41]). No lie therefore can be granted so officious as not to be inofficious to the liar, since it has both an intrinsic formal disorder (*ataxian*) and a deformity contrary to nature and the law of God. What however is in itself and intrinsically evil, cannot be rendered good by the consideration of any end, even the best. For good things are to be obtained properly and a good end is to be sought by good means; nor can any circumstances change a thing in itself evil.

VI. (3) If a pernicious lie only is sinful, its illegality (*anomia*) would be drawn only from its end. Which is false, because in itself the very deformity and disorder (*ataxia*) of the lie (viz., in the divorce of the mind and tongue, which ought to be the interpreter of the mind) makes up its illegality (*anomia*). (4) If a lie could be justified by its end (namely by the intention to benefit a neighbor), so also thefts which would be officious might be justified, when one would wish to benefit a neighbor by stealing. However no one would say this because the apostolic rule ought to obtain here: "Evil must not be done that good may come" (Rom. 3:8).

VII. Augustine frequently inculcates this. "All lying is sinful, although he does not sin so much who lies with the will of benefitting as he who lies with the will of injuring" (*Enchiridion* 6 [18] [FC 3:383; PL 40.240]), which he repeats (ibid., 7 [22], p. 389; PL 40.243). "To say that any lie is just is to say that there are some just sins, and consequently that there are some just things which are unjust" (*To Consentius: Against Lying* 15 [31] [NPNF1, 3:495; PL 40.539]). He more fully discusses this in the two books: *On Lying* (NPNF1, 3:457-77) and *To Consentius: Against Lying* (NPNF1, 3:481-500). Gregory says, "Every lie is iniquitous, because whatever is at variance with the truth, is at variance with equity. Nor may the life of anyone be defended by the fallacy of lying, lest he injure his own soul, who strives to give life to another's body" (*Morals on the Book of Job* 18.3*.5 [1845], 2:320; PL 76.40-41 on Job 27:34).

Sources of explanation.

VIII. Although God commended the Egyptian midwives who lied to Pharaoh (Ex. 1:17-21), he did not on that account reward their lie, but their good feeling and pity towards the infants because they preferred to expose themselves to the indignation of the king than to obey his cruel command. "The deceit was not rewarded in them, but the benevolence; the kindness of mind, not the iniquity of lying," as Augustine says (*To Consentius: Against Lying* 15 [32] [NPNF1, 3:495; PL 40.540]). For two acts are here to be distinguished: the one by which they refused obedience to the tyrannical edict of the king, proceeding from the fear of God (which is commended); the other of the lie, by which they excused themselves and lied, proceeding rather from pusillanimity and a servile fear of the king than from the fear of God (which was sinful). God therefore in his benignity, by pardoning the sinful act, wished the good deed to be rewarded, to show how pleasing their piety and pity was to him, although it was not free from blemishes. It can also be said with some that these midwives did not lie because what they said might have been true—that the Hebrew women were lively and strong and were delivered ere the midwives came in unto them.

IX. Whatever we read of having been done by holy men is not forthwith to be imitated as if lawful. Although they were holy, it is evident that they did not live without sin. Hence neither the lie of Jacob, nor of the harlot Rahab, can render a lie lawful. If God blessed Jacob lying (Gen. 27:20), it does not follow that his lie was approved, because the blessing followed the faith which he gave to the word of God, that the elder should serve the younger (Gen. 25:23). It was not however given on account of the vice and fault clinging to the faith. Nor is the lie of Rahab ascribed by the apostle to faith (Heb. 11:31), but to a kind and honest act by which she took in and preserved the spies, although she employed wicked means to save them. Therefore the blessing she obtained from God was not a reward of the lie, but of the love towards the people of God and of her faith towards the men whom she hospitably received. Thus in similar deeds we must always distinguish the virtue of the action from the spots and blemishes cleaving to it and the manner in which it is done; the weakness of man from the goodness of God. The former in the best actions always mixes something faulty from the latter, which by pardoning the fault graciously rewards the good. As therefore it pleased God that the son of Moses should be circumcised, without approving of the violent manner of doing it (which Zipporah adopted, Ex. 4:25), so it pleased God that the midwives abstained from infanticide, that Rahab consulted the safety of her guests, that Michal preserved the life of her husband, David (1 S. 19:17), Jonathan the life of his friend (1 S. 20:6, 28), although the mode of doing these good works by falsehood was not free from criminality in his sight.

X. It is no more lawful to bear false testimony in favor of a neighbor than against him, as it is no more lawful to pervert justice in favor of a widow and orphan than against them (Lev. 19:15). As we are bound "to speak the truth in love" (*alētheuein en agapē*), so we are bound "to love in speaking the truth" (*agapan en alētheia*) and even to the altars. Yea, although no more specious pretext can be put forward for falsehood than the glory of God and the vindication of divine truth, still God rejects this and does not wish it to be employed in defending his cause: "Will ye speak wickedly for God? and talk deceitfully for him?" (Job 13:7). Since God is very truth itself, he ought not to be defended with a lie, nor arms be borrowed for him from the Devil.

XI. Although sometimes such difficulties lie in the way of men, that being in a great strait they prefer to sin against truth than against love; although in that case they are excused from so much, yet they cannot forthwith be excused from the whole, as if they were free from all blame. Whither pertain these words of Augustine: "A lie is not to be considered as no sin because we can sometimes benefit someone by lying. For we can also profit another by stealing" (*Enchiridion* 7 [22] [FC 3:389-90; PL 40.243-44]). Therefore if a lie benefits any, it is not on that account to be attributed to the nature of a lie, but to the goodness and providence of God, which frequently disabuses the sins of men to some good thing.

XII. Elisha did not lie to the Syrian soldiers, because he said nothing which was not true as to the eventuality of the thing (2 K. 6:19). To those inquiring the way in which they might find Elisha, he answers, "This is not the way" (since he was going to Samaria) "neither is this the city" (from which he had already gone out). He promises indeed to bring them to the man whom they sought, which he really fulfilled by leading them to Samaria where they recognized the prophet.

XIII. When Micaiah persuades the king to go to war (1 K. 22:15), he does not speak so much affirmatively and prophetically as ironically and imitatingly (*mimētikōs*); not according to his own opinion, but that of the king and the false prophets; not to deceive them, but to teach them that they were deceived (for afterwards, when he was adjured by the king to tell him nothing but what was true in the name of the Lord [vv. 16, 17], he spoke far differently), which the king sufficiently perceived either from his greatness or manner of speaking. No lie can also be ascribed to Jeremiah in favor of the king (Jer. 38:27) because he related to the princes what was true (to wit, that the king had been asked by him not to thrust him again into the old prison in the house of Jonathan, which Jeremiah had really solicited from the king, as is evident from Jer. 37:15, 20 and 38:15, 16, that he might not be delivered into the hands of his enemies. However, it is one thing to pass over in silence an unnecessary part of the truth; another to tell what is false as if it were true. The former is lawful, not the latter.

XIV. Simulation is threefold: (1) of fraud and malice; (2) of caution and design; (3) of instruction and trial. The first, when a virtuous exterior is made to cover vice within; the second, employed in warlike stratagems and approved by God (concerning which cf. Jos. 8:5-7); the third, employed not to deceive, but to explore and teach, such as often occurs in the society of men. Such was the situation of the angels who pretended a purpose of passing the night in the streets in order to excite a desire in Lot to receive them under his roof. Such was true of Christ, who pretends that he wishes to go farther (Lk. 24:28). He did not do this to deceive his disciples, but to try them whether they ardently desired to have his company. Besides this pretense (*prospoiēsis*) is to be understood not so much formally as materially because Christ did that which one pretending to go farther is accustomed to do. He proceeds some steps beyond the destined place that he might excite their prayers and arouse a warmer desire for him (as parents when about to depart are accustomed to call forth the prayers of children, friends of friends). It can also be said that Christ intended to go farther and would have done so if he had not been detained by the prayers of his disciples.

XV. It is gratuitously supposed that God suggested a falsehood to Samuel, when he orders him to tell Saul that he had come to Bethlehem to sacrifice (1 S. 16:2). For although he was to come with another purpose in view (to wit, to anoint David), yet that did not hinder his coming there both for the purpose of sacrifice and of celebrating a feast. Now it is one thing not to set forth all the ends of anything; another to state a false end. The former was suggested to Samuel by the Lord, not the latter. Nor when one end is stated, are others denied.

XVI. When Paul says that he did not know that Ananias was the high priest (Acts 23:5), the sense can consist in the highest degree with his words without any mark of a lie. This is true whether he is said to have spoken ironically (as some hold, because from his furious manner of speaking, he saw nothing in him worthy of the high priest, nor did he conduct himself as such towards himself); or said this seriously (as others better) because he really was not the high priest, but had obtruded himself into the office of the true high priest (whether of Ishmael or of Joseph, as there was a great anarchy [*anarchia*] at that time, so that every day there were high priests or there were not); or because he had been absent so long from Jerusalem that the new high priest was unknown to him as yet. From his seat, he could not gather this because they were not in the temple or in the house of the high priest and were sitting in the ordinary place of the council (and perhaps in disorder and confusion).

XVII. Parables are falsely brought forward in support of lies. A parable is not introduced to signify that which is said, but to signify that is which is represented by what is said. Hence not on account of the material is it proposed, but on account of its formal, and (as Jerome well expresses it, *Commentarius in Ecclesiasten*, CCSL 72.357 on Ecc. 12:9, 10) they have one thing in the marrow, they promise another on the exterior. It differs therefore in many ways from a lie. (1) As to origin, because every lie proceeds either from an evil mind or deviates from good to evil; a parable, however, from a good mind persisting in good. (2) As to form, because a lie has an intrinsic contrariety to the mind of the speaker; a parable has not. (3) As to end, because a lie is told to deceive; a parable to teach. (4) As to effects, because by a lie a false notion is produced in the mind of the hearer; by a parable, on the contrary, a true one. The same can be said concerning apologies in which not a history but a type is set forth; nor is anything represented as a fact; nor is that which is set forth meant although false and invented, but another thing altogether and indeed true.

XVIII. We conclude with Augustine, "Whoever thinks there is any kind of lie which is not sinful, deceives himself grossly, when he thinks he is an honest deceiver of others" (*On Lying* 21 [42] [NPNF1, 3:477; PL 40.516]). And to the same: "Either therefore lies are to be shunned by doing rightly or to be confessed with repentance; not however since they abound by living unhappily, are they to be increased also by teaching" (*To Consentius: Against Lying* 21 [41] [NPNF1, 3:500; PL 40.547]).

Twenty-First Question: The Tenth Commandment

What concupiscence is prohibited by the tenth precept? Are the incipient motions sins? We affirm.

Concupiscence threefold: natural, good and bad.

I. God has planted two principles in the mind of man: the avoidance of evil and the desire of good; the irascible (*to thymikon*) and concupiscible appetite (*to epithymētikon*). Viewed in the genus of being and physically, these are neither good nor bad, but mean and indifferent, drawing all their moral goodness and evil from the quality of the objects about which they are exercised. Hence concupiscence at one time is praised as good, when occupied with a good and lawful object (in which sense "the Spirit" is said "to lust against the flesh" [Gal. 5:17] and Paul wishes believers to covet spiritual gifts [1 Cor. 12:31]). At another time, it is condemned as inordinate and vicious, when it has an unjust and unlawful object. At yet another time, as middle and natural, it is neither praised nor blamed.

It is either original or actual.

II. Depraved and inordinate concupiscence (of which we now treat) can be viewed either as to source and habit (called original concupiscence, spoken of in Jam. 1:14, 15, as frequently original sin is termed concupiscence by Augustine). The Jews were accustomed to denote this by *ytsr hr'* ("evil deceit") and the Scholastics commonly call it "tinder." Or it can be viewed as to depraved acts and motions and is called "actual." This again is either determinate by a formal and settled consent of the will (as they call delectation) or indeterminate and titillating in its first motions, proceeding no further than a velleity and suggestion.

III. Since the precept about not coveting is general, it ought to be extended to all depraved and inordinate concupiscence, original and habitual as well as actual—whether this is determinate and voluntary or still indeterminate and only titillating. This is true in order that the perfect purity and holiness of the lawgiver may be noted (which will suffer not even the smallest taint of depraved concupiscence in man, but demands righteousness and holiness of every kind).

Whether original concupiscence is contained under the tenth precept.

IV. Two questions are here plied by the papists. The first concerns original and habitual concupiscence; the second concerns its incipient motions. As to the first, they deny that concupiscence or tinder is prohibited by the law of God because they do not consider it to be a sin. The Council of Trent asserts "that concupiscence remains in the baptized, yet that this concupiscence, which the apostle sometimes calls sin, is not so in itself and is so denominated not because it is truly and properly sin in the regenerated, but because it arises from sin and inclines to sin; and whoever thinks differently, let him be accursed" (Session 5, Canon 5, Schroeder, p. 23). But the orthodox think concupiscence is both properly sin and is prohibited by the law.

Proof that it is contained under it.

V. First, from the words of the law which expressly prohibit concupiscence, indeed in general and indefinitely, so that all inordinate concupiscence may be understood, not only in act, but also in habit and in root. Also we must not limit what the law does not limit. Second, the end of the law implies this, i.e., to exact from man perfect holiness, not only as to act, but also as to habit. For as it requires both kinds of holiness (habitual and actual), so it ought to prohibit both kinds of concupiscence (actual and habitual). Third, depraved and evil concupiscence is not of God, but of the world (1 Jn. 2:16). It ought therefore to be interdicted by the law, which forbids every vice.

VI. Fourth, Paul expressly asserts that it is forbidden by the law and is sin. "I had not known sin, but by the law: for I had not known lust, except the law had said, thou shalt not covet" (Rom. 7:7). He does not simply deny that lust was known to him, but that he knew it to be sin (which at length he did know by the law forbidding it). Thus he supposes lust to be sin because forbidden by the law; not only actual, but also habitual. For he immediately adds, "sin" (undoubtedly lust forbidden by the law) "taking occasion by the commandment, wrought in me all manner of concupiscence" (Rom. 7:8). He confirms this in Rom. 7:9, 11, 13, 17, 20 where he calls the same thing "sin," "indwelling sin" and "exceeding sinful"; also "a law in my members warring against the law of my mind, and bringing me into captivity to the law of sin" (Rom. 7:23). Now who can believe that Paul would so often and so expressly have called that sin, if it was not true sin and properly so called, but only because it flowed from sin and inclined to sin (as the Council falsely maintained)? On the contrary, who does not see that his intention was to ascribe to it a true relation of sin which he had known from the written law alone, the light of reason not reaching so far in the heathen? See above Topic IX, Question 11, Section 20 and 21.

Sources of explanation.

VII. Although the law proximately and immediately prohibits only acts and is enunciated by words signifying actions, this does not hinder the habits and principles of sins from being prohibited under them (such as original sin and habitual concupiscence). Yea, this ought to be intimated even necessarily because causes are included in their effects and principles in what flows from them. Thus the axe may be laid at the root of sin and perfect holiness be demanded of man.

VIII. Although original sin is indeed taken away in the renewed as to guilt by justification, so that there is no condemnation to them (Rom. 8:1), and as to dominion by sanctification, that it may no more reign in them; yet it always remains in them as long as they dwell in this mortality as to presence and inhabitation. Thus it is to be continually crucified and mortified in them.

IX. When James says "lust brings forth sin" (1:15), he does not deny that it is sin because he does not here discuss when it begins to be (or to be considered sin in the sight of God), but when it emerges to the light and is consummated by a deed. He concerns himself only with this—to teach that the root of our destruction is in us. So far is it from being lawfully inferred from this that lust is not sin that by necessary consequence its sinfulness can thence be elicited. The effect ought to correspond with the cause; nor could lust bring forth actual sin unless it is itself sin.

Whether its first motions are sins.

X. The other question relates to the first motions of concupiscence (which the papists deny are prohibited here because they are not sinful). They call "first motions" those which arise stealthily, but without a deliberate judgment of the mind and a formal consent of the will. On that account, they are accustomed to call them *propatheian* since they differ from determinate and deliberate affections which are with the consent of the will and are on that account called "tarrying" because the mind and will rest in them with pleasure. They think that these only are prohibited by the law because they are voluntary and in our power; not the others, since they are neither free nor in our power and thus are not sins. Toletus speaks thus on Rom. 7 and others with him. On the contrary, as we think concupiscence is evil in its root and forbidden by the law, so also as to all the acts and motions springing from it, whether they follow or precede the formal consent of the will.

Proved to be sins.

XI. First, it condemns those motions of lust which a man could know only by the written law, as the apostle testifies. Now the voluntary motions of concupiscence were not unknown to the heathen themselves as depraved and inordinate. Hence that of Seneca: "A man becomes a brigand before he stains his hands with blood" (*De Beneficiis* 5.14.2 [Loeb, 3:328-29]). Also Juvenal: "For he who secretly meditates a crime within his breast has all the guiltiness of the deed" (*Satires* 13.209-10 [Loeb, 260-61]). (2) Such motions are not consistent with the holiness and purity which God demands from us and the required perfection of loving God with the whole heart and all the strength; therefore they cannot but be depraved and lawless (*anomoi*). (3) Other motions are now forbidden by the other precepts in which the law so prohibits external acts that it also condemns internal acts because it is spiritual. So he is called an adulterer by Christ who looks on a woman to lust after her (Mt. 5:28); and according to John, "whosoever hateth his brother is a murderer" (1 Jn. 3:15). If therefore such motions only are forbidden, nothing new would be commanded or prohibited by this precept above the rest (which is absurd). For although we do not deny that this precept was added to the others by way of a general rule for declaring and applying them more expressly in the court of conscience, yet the distinction of the precepts necessarily demands something further to be designed, which can be nothing else than the habit of concupiscence with its first motions. Thus it may be shown how much the divine law differs from human laws (which regard only external acts and do not rise to the source of evil).

Sources of explanation.

XII. Although the involuntary (*to akousion*) (what is involuntary and a positive volition) is not sin, it does not follow that nothing can have the relation of sin which is not voluntary (*hekousion*) formally and strictly from a deliberate movement and consent of the will. For thus neither original sin, nor sins of ignorance, would be true sins. Rather it suffices that it be called voluntary broadly because it affects the will and inheres in it. Therefore although the first motions are not voluntary in the former sense, still they are properly so called in the latter because they affect the will and are placed under it.

XIII. Although such motions are not in our power, still they are not the less inordinate because neither is any good work in our power (whose omission, however, is nonetheless sinful and inordinate). Therefore the law does not attend to the ability of man, but to his duty; not what he can or cannot, but what he is bound to do in morals.

XIV. The motions of concupiscence cannot be called natural except with respect to the corrupt nature whence they flow; not however with respect to a sound and unimpaired nature. If Adam had never sinned, he would never have felt such motions (which cannot be free from vitiosity).

Twenty-Second Question: The Use of the Law

What and how many are the uses of the moral law according to the various states of man? Can it bind to obedience and punishment together? We make distinctions.

I. We said that four things were to be considered principally concerning the law: its nature, parts, use and abrogation. Concerning the first two, we have already treated. Now we must speak of its use, without the knowledge and practice of which all speculation about the law would be in vain.

The use of the law twofold: absolute and relative. Absolute that it may be the rule of things to be done and avoided.

II. A twofold use of the law may be laid down—absolute and relative. The former regards the law in itself; the latter regards the law in relation to the various states of man. The absolute (which obtains in every state of man) is that it may be a unique, full and certain rule of things to be done and avoided by each of us as well towards God as his neighbor. Thus there is no work truly and properly good and acceptable to God which does not agree with the law and is not prescribed by it; and whatsoever is not commanded nor forbidden by it is to be considered in its own nature indifferent and left to the freedom of man, unless this freedom has been restricted by some positive law.

Proof of its perfection: (1) from the equity of the law.

III. That it is a most perfect rule of action, we gather from its various attributes. (1) From its equity, because the more equitable a law is, the more perfect it is; for equity is the mind of the law. Now so great is its equity that it is both the aim and rule and end of all laws; and the very nations most bitterly opposed to the Jews have not denied that their laws were derived from it. On this account, it has a wider extent because it stands in need of no correction, as human laws do. For none are so fair as not to need their own restrictions or exceptions (in certain cases) from the infinity of particular cases which occur. But there is no case so special, no circumstance so extraordinary, as not to come under some rule and determination (either general or particular) in the word of God. "The judgments of the Lord are true and righteous altogether" (Ps. 19:9).

(2) From its majesty.

IV. (2) From its regal majesty, which flows from its equity; for the greater the equity of a law, the greater its sway. On this account the law of nature (the fountain of all other laws, because it is most equitable) is also the most majestic. James calls it "royal" (*basilikēn*, 2:8) (a) because it belongs to the supreme king and lawgiver, who is able to save and destroy (Jam. 4:12), who has power to bind and loose the consciences of men; (b) because it is superior to the others, judging all other laws and being judged by none.

(3) From its universality.

V. (3) From its universality and extent, which is gathered both from its object, embracing all the duties of man (human laws enjoin external duties, but the law of God enjoins internal as well as external, so that there is no virtue which is not here commanded, no vice which is not forbidden); from its subject, which informs and directs (because it composes and regulates the whole man and all the human faculties and functions, by speaking to the soul no less than to the body); from its end (because it has no other object than to make man cleave to God and live happily).

(4) From its immutability.

VI. (4) From its immutability, because it remains forever nor ever will be destroyed (Ps. 119:89; Mt. 5:18). Human laws are often changeable on account of their excessive rigor or strictness. On this account, it was ingeniously said by the Philosopher (Aristotle) that the laws of kings had to be accommodated to the times like shoes to the feet because the slightest variation of circumstances or accidents sometimes requires a variation of laws. But this is not the case with God's law because he foresees all circumstances most contingent and all cases which can occur. On this account, he so arranges his laws as to embrace all cases and circumstances.

(5) From its holiness.

VII. (5) From its holiness, because it is a most clear image of God. God has so represented his own mind in his law that each one can contemplate (as in a mirror) the living and accurate reflection of the holiness of God. This further appears both from the end of the law, which is to make the internal principles and external operations of men to adhere to God by the bond of holiness, and from its effects, because the law of God inspired by the Holy Spirit and written upon the heart is the most efficacious instrument of holiness. Hence the word of God is said to be "very pure" (*tsrvphh m'dh*, Ps. 119:140) and "the commandment of Jehovah" is said to "be pure" (Ps. 19:8).

Relative use in the instituted state.

VIII. The relative use is manifold according to the different states of man. (1) In the instituted state of innocence, it was a contract of a covenant of works entered into with man and the means of obtaining life and happiness according to the promise added to the law. Although express mention is not made of a promise made to obedience (but only of a punishment), still it may be sufficiently inferred from the latter because it is not very probable that God would have threatened our first parent with punishment (if he should sin) and not have added any promise of a reward (if he should obey); or that he promised less in reference to a reward than he had threatened in reference to a punishment. Yea, the tree of life itself was a seal that there would be conferred upon him eternal life, which is opposed also to the eternal together with temporal death denounced in Rom. 6:23. This has already been proved in Part I, Topic VIII, Question 5.

In the destitute state.

IX. (2) In the destitute state of sin, the use of the law cannot be "justification" because it was weak in the flesh. It is not said to have been given for life, but "because of transgressions" (Gal. 3:19). Still there is a threefold use of the law. (a) For conviction, when it brings man to a knowledge of sin and convinces him of his guilt—"by the law is the knowledge of sin" (Rom. 3:20). Thus it is like a mirror in which we see our blemishes. (b) For restraint, restraining and checking men by its commands and threatenings, so that they who feel no regard for justice and rectitude unless compelled (while they hear its direful sanctions) may be restrained at least by the fear of punishment. In this sense, it is like a bit, holding sinners within the bars of external discipline that the world may not become a den of robbers. In this respect, Paul says "the law is not made for a righteous man, but for lawless and disobedient [*ataktois*], for the ungodly and for sinners" (1 Tim. 1:9). Whither pertains another use of the law accidentally (viz., of provocation and of the increase of sin, inasmuch as the law by restraining sin like a bit not only does not reduce its rebellion and contumacy, but rather increases and irritates on account of the perversity of the sinner who strives after what is forbidden). Hence it is said to have been given "that sin might abound" (Rom. 5:20) and elsewhere sin is said to be made "exceeding sinful" by it (*kath' hyperbolēn hamartōlon*, Rom. 7:13). (c) For condemnation, when it denounces upon the convicted sinner the divine malediction by the dreadful sentence which it thunders in his ears: "Cursed is he who continues not." Hence the apostle calls it "the ministration of condemnation" (2 Cor. 3:9), and he says that "it worketh wrath" (Rom. 4:15) and then it is like a whip, tormenting and scourging the conscience guilty of sin.

In the restored state.

X. (3) In the restored state of grace, it has a varied use with respect to the elect, both before and after their conversions. Antecedently, it serves (a) to convince and humble man so that (his own misery and weakness being felt) he despairs of himself and renounces confidence in his own righteousness and merit and rests upon the mercy of God alone. (b) To lead men to Christ, not indeed primarily and by itself (because the law does not know Christ), but by the accident of grace, inasmuch as it impels man (cast down and despairing of his own strength) to seek the remedy of saving grace. Under this relation (*schesei*), it is called by Paul "a schoolmaster" unto Christ (Gal. 3:24) and Christ is called "the end of the law" (Rom. 10:4). Not the end of destruction and abolition (because the law remains also in the gospel, as will be shown hereafter), but of perfection and of complement (because Christ was bound to fulfill it in himself and in us) and of intention (because he is the mark to which it is directed and on account of whom the law was given). Not indeed in its own nature and on the part of the thing, for the end of the law in this respect was the justification of the just man, but on the part of God giving the law to sinful man that he might be prepared for Christ; that his weakness (*astheneia*) being seen from the law, he might more clearly know the necessity of a mediator and also more ardently seek him.

XI. It not only antecedently prepares the elect man for Christ, but consequently also directs him already renewed through Christ in the ways of the Lord; serving him as a standard and rule of the most perfect life, to which he knows he is called by Christ and which he ought diligently to pursue (1 Tim. 1:5). Before, it was an instrument of the spirit of bondage to throw down and bruise man, but afterwards it becomes the instrument of the Spirit of adoption to promote sanctification. Thus the law leads to Christ and Christ leads us back to the law; it leads to Christ as the redeemer and Christ leads to the law, as the leader and director of life. In this way, man in his integrity and as just was under the blessing of the law; corrupt, he comes under its curse; regenerated, he comes under its direction. Concerning this latter use of the law, we will treat more fully in Question 23.

XII. Here belongs the question concerning the obligation of the law—whether it binds to obedience and punishment at the same time. It arose from the opinion of Cargius concerning the imputation to us of Christ's passive obedience only and not of his active obedience. For since the law did not bind sinners to obedience, but only to punishment, Christ (substituted in our place) owed only punishment for us and not obedience. On the state of the question take notice: (1) that it is not inquired in general whether the law obliges to obedience and to punishment. For since it enjoins obedience under the promise of a reward and forbids disobedience under the threatening of punishment, it evidently binds man to both. Rather the question concerns the manner—whether at the same time or successively and in what order it binds. (2) The question is not whether in every state the law binds at the same time to both. In the innocent state, the law bound to obedience, but not to punishment because it would have been unjust to bind to punishment him who had not sinned. In the state of grace, it binds the believer only to obedience, not to punishment because there is no condemnation to those who are in Christ (Rom. 8:1), whose transgressions are forgiven (Ps. 32:1). Rather the question concerns the state of sin—whether in it the sinner is bound to both (which we assert).

XIII. First, from the twofold condition of sinful man, who is both a creature and a sinful creature. As a creature, he owes to God obedience forever and never can be discharged from it. As a sinner, he owes punishment. To the former he is bound on account of a present and future debt; to the latter he is bound on account of the past disobedience; to the former primarily and of itself, to the latter secondarily and accidentally on account of sin.

XIV. Second, if the law does not oblige the sinner to obedience, then God by the sin of man would be divested of his right to require obedience from him. Also man would not sin in disobeying because where there is no law there is no transgression.

Source of explanation.

XV. This is not the case with the state of integrity because in it there was only one relation (*schesis*) of man (to wit, inasmuch as he was a rational creature, owing obedience to his Creator), but in the corrupt state another relation was added to that first—guilt by sin. Hence although in the first state the law bound only to obedience (so that man obeying would be free from punishment), it does not equally follow that in the state of sin (in which man has become liable to punishment) he is freed from obedience. As both relations (*schesis*) are found in the sinner, both are here to be conjoined (as rebellious subjects, worthy of punishment on account of rebellion, do not cease to remain bound to perpetual obedience to the ruler).

XVI. Although the law binds sinful man to punishment and obedience at the same time, it does not follow that man is held under obligation to pay the same thing twice. The law binds to present and future obedience; punishment, however, is demanded only for sin already committed and an act of obedience once violated.

XVII. When it is said that by the suffering of punishment, a sin of omission is expiated, it ought not to be understood in the sense that the sin had not been committed and that man had done whatever he was bound to do (which is repugnant to the truth). Rather inasmuch as by the penal endurance he is freed from the curse resting upon him on account of sin (nor can such punishment anymore be placed upon him to be undergone), the remission therefore granted to him takes away indeed actual guilt, but does not on this account give him a right to life.

XVIII. The obligation to obedience is either natural, which man owes to God as a rational creature (which is eternal and indissoluble and remains even in heaven); or federal, by which each one is not only bound to obey the law, but to fulfill it under the relation (*schesei*) of a covenant—to deserve eternal life, either for himself or for another one. Christ, by the former obligation, owed obedience to God for himself as man; but he was not bound by the latter (except for us) because he had no need through it to merit eternal life for himself (which he obtained in virtue of the hypostatical union). This will be shown in its place when we treat of the obedience of Christ.

Twenty-Third Question: The Abrogation of the Moral Law

Whether the moral law is abrogated entirely under the New Testament. Or whether in a certain respect it still pertains to Christians. The former we deny; the latter we affirm against the Antinomians.

I. From the third use of the law (which we called directive) arises the proposed question lying between us and the Antinomians, who maintain that there is no use of the law any longer under the New Testament. On this account, they hold that the Scriptures of the Old Testament do not belong to Christians (concerning which we treated Part I, Topic II, Question 8).

II. In order to apprehend properly the state of the question, we must ascertain in what sense the law may be said to have been abrogated and in what sense not. First, the question does not concern the use of the law as to justification—whether we are still bound to the law in order to acquire life. Since this is impossible after sin, in this sense it may even be said to have been abrogated: "By the deeds of the law there shall no flesh be justified" (Rom. 3:20) and "As many as are of the works of the law, are under the curse" (Gal. 3:10). Second, the question does not concern its curse because by Christ under this relation (*schesei*), it is abrogated with respect to believers: "Christ hath redeemed us from the curse of the law, being made a curse for us" (Gal. 3:13). Third, the question does not concern restraint and rigor (which was the case under the Old Testament) because we are no longer under that servile training and dispensation in which the spirit of bondage exercised its power. Rather we are under the gospel economy, in which the Spirit of adoption reigns (Rom. 8:15); by which the yoke of Christ is made easy (Mt. 11:30) and his commandments not grievous (1 Jn. 5:3). But the question only concerns its directive use—whether we are now freed from the direction and observance of the law. This the adversaries maintain; we deny.

Proof that the law is not abrogated as to direction.

III. First, Christ "did not come to destroy but to fulfill the law" (Mt. 5:17). Therefore as it was not abolished but fulfilled by Christ, neither is its use among us to be abolished. Luke wants us to hear Moses and the prophets: "They have Moses and the prophets, let them hear them" (16:29). If they are to be heard, their commands must therefore be obeyed also. If this is said by Christ to the Jews of his time, it ought forthwith to be understood of them to the exclusion of others. He does not give here a special, but a general precept to all who desire to escape the place of torment. Now what was the case with the Jews in reference to this, the same is the case with Christians. Also the practice of what is here proposed as a precept is by Peter commended generally to Christians (2 Pet. 1:19 and frequently elsewhere).

IV. Second, Christ and his apostles confirm and recommend it to be observed by all (Mt. 22:36-40). Paul says, "Owe no man anything, but to love one another: for he that loveth another hath fulfilled the law" (Rom. 13:8, 9). Love is called by John the old and new commandment (1 Jn. 2:7, 8). Third, "faith does not make void but establishes the law" (Rom. 3:31). Hence the gospel is often designated by the name law: "the law of the Spirit of life" (Rom. 8:2); "the royal law of liberty" (Jam. 2:8, 12). "For I through the law am dead to the law, that I might live unto God" (Gal. 2:19) through the law of Christ, to the law of Moses. For it has the relation of a covenant, which is not only to be understood imitatively (*mimētikōs*) in relation to the mind of the Jews (because the gospel gives truly and perfectly to us what the Jews falsely sought in the law [viz., justification and safety], in which sense even faith is called "the work of God," Jn. 6:29), but also properly (because the gospel is not without the law, which is now set forth in a certain sweeter manner, but nevertheless always binds man to obedience). Fourth, the moral law is of natural and immutable right (as was proved above). On this account, it pertains equally to all men in whatever state so that they cannot be released from their subjection to it.

The necessity of the law proved. (1) With respect to the covenant of grace. (2) With respect to God, the Father. (3) With respect to Christ. (4) With respect to the Spirit.

V. Finally, the law is necessary in many ways to Christians. (1) With respect to the covenant of grace (under which believers live), which contains not only the promise of grace and salvation on God's part, but also carries with it the stipulation of obedience on man's part, so that just as God promises to be our God in love and protection, we in turn are his people by worshipping and obeying him (Jer. 31:33; 2 Cor. 6:16, 17). (2) With respect to God the Father, who receives us into his family and holds towards us the relation (*schesin*) of Father and Lord, to honor and worship whom we are indispensably bound (Mal. 1:6; 1 Pet. 1:15, 16). (3) With respect to Christ, who, as he sustains a twofold person towards us (of surety and priest, to satisfy for us by fulfilling the law; and of head and king, to work and fulfill the law in us by his Spirit), so he demands a twofold virtue from believers to be united and conformed to him (faith, which embraces the promise of grace and the merit of the surety; and love, which imitates the holiness of the head by obeying his commands). Hence his death is not only the price of our redemption (*lytron*), by which he made a most full satisfaction for us, but also "the model for our imitation" (which is set before us) "that we should follow his steps" (1 Pet. 2:21). (4) With respect to the Holy Spirit, who consecrates us for temples to himself in which he may dwell (1 Cor. 3, 4); who has the name and office of Consoler and Sanctifier, that as by the office of Paraclete he consoles us against the curse of the law, so as the Spirit of sanctification, he confirms and sanctions the necessity of the obedience to the law.

5. With respect to grace.

VI. (5) With respect to grace (now conferred upon us here), which demands that obedience (Tit. 2:14) as the fruit of that seed; gratitude for benefits received (Pss. 116:12; 130:4; Lk. 1:74) and the mark at which it aims, as is evident in election (Eph. 1:4), in redemption, (Tit. 2:14), in calling (1 Pet. 1:15; 2:9), in justification (Ps. 85:9; Gal. 2:20; Ps. 130:4), in regeneration (2 Cor. 5:17; Rom. 6:14). (6) With respect to the glory which we expect, to which the obedience due to the law stands related as a means to the end, without which we cannot attain unto it (Jn. 3:5; Mt. 5:8; Heb. 12:14); the way to the goal (Eph. 2:10; Phil. 3:14); the seed to the harvest (Gal. 6:7, 8) and the first-fruits to the mass (Rom. 8:23)—yea, as the principle part of happiness. Hence arises the necessity of good works to glory; not of merit, but of means. No one can be glorified in heaven who has not been sanctified on earth by the pursuit of holiness and obedience to the law.

6. With respect to glory.

Sources of explanation.

VII. It is one thing to be under the law as a covenant to acquire life by it (as Adam was) or as a schoolmaster and a prison to guard men until the advent of Christ; another to be under the law as a rule of life, to regulate our morals piously and holily. It is one thing to be under the law inasmuch as it is opposed to the gospel as to rigid and perfect exaction of obedience and the terrible curse with which it threatens sinners; another to be under the law inasmuch as it is subordinated to the gospel, as to sweet direction. In the former sense, Paul says "We are not under the law, but under grace" (Rom. 6:14) as to the federal relation and as to malediction and rigor because Christ by his merit has freed us from that and by his Spirit taken us away from this. But in the latter sense, we always remain bound to it, although for a different end. In the first covenant, man was bound to do this in order that he might live (to deserve life); but in this he is bound to do the same (not that he may live, but because he lives) to the possession of the life acquired by Christ and the testimony of a grateful mind (as the apostle in the same place exhorts believers to obedience).

VIII. The law is compared by Paul to "a dead husband" (Rom. 7:2, 3), not simply, but relatively with regard to the sway and rigorous dominion it obtained over us and the curse to which it subjected sinners; but not with regard to liberation from the duty to be performed to it. Thus the law threatening, compelling, condemning, is not "made for a righteous man" (1 Tim. 1:9) because he is impelled of his own accord to duty and is no longer influenced by the spirit of bondage and the fear of punishment (Rom. 8:15; Ps. 110:3), but the law directive and regulative of morals is always laid down for him and he ought to be under it. "If ye be led of the Spirit, ye are not under the law" (Gal. 5:18, viz., compelling and cursing), but under it directing, inasmuch as the Spirit works that law upon our hearts (2 Cor. 3:2; Jer. 31:33). On this account, the law is called the Spirit of life (Rom. 8:2).

IX. It is one thing to speak of the duration of the legal economy, another to speak of the duration and use of the doctrine delivered in it. The former ought to have been changed and to cease (and has really ceased); not so, however, the latter. Christ speaks in the former sense in Lk. 16:16, when he says, "The law was until John," but not in the latter. Nor if the economy is taken away, ought the doctrine accommodated to that economy to be taken away entirely, but only according to the relation (according to which it was peculiar to that economy).

X. It is one thing for the law not to be imposed upon Christians, another for an intolerable yoke (*abastakton*) (viz., the observance of circumcision and of legal ceremonies) not to be imposed on them. The former is not removed from Christians, but only the latter: "Why tempt ye God to put a yoke upon the neck of the disciples, which neither our fathers nor we were able to bear" (Acts 15:10)? It is evident from the occasion of these words (related in v. 5) that certain ones rose up who said "that it was needful to circumcise Christians, and to command them to keep the law of Moses" (to wit, the ceremonial, as we gather from vv. 20, 28, 29, elsewhere called the "yoke of bondage" [*zygos douleias*], Gal. 5:1; or the moral with an undue end, as if Christians must seek from it life either wholly or at least partly; thus it can well be called an "unbearable yoke" [*zygos abastaktos*] on account of the weakness of the flesh because no one can be justified by it, Rom. 8:3). So that yoke can be taken off as far as it was intolerable (*abastakton*) (to wit, as to the strict severity [*to akribodikaion*] of the law, the compulsion and curse annexed to it), although it remains as to the necessity of obedience.

XI. What is a cause of itself and in its own nature of the increase and multiplication of offenses, ought not to be retained in use among Christians. But the law does not increase sin (in this sense) because sin follows not from the laying down of the law as such, but only from its transgression. On this account, it is said to increase sin accidentally (Rom. 5:20) not only because it declaratively manifests it, but also occasionally inasmuch as sin, taking occasion by the commandment, wrought concupiscence (Rom. 7:8, to wit, by irritating it, so that it becomes more furious against the restraining commandment, like an ungovernable horse becoming the more enraged against his rider the tighter he draws the bit). Hence the violation of the known law draws after it a heavier guilt.

XII. When the law is called the "letter that killeth, and the ministration of death and condemnation" (2 Cor. 3:6-9), it is to be understood not of itself and in its own nature, but accidentally on account of man's corruption; not absolutely and simply, but relatively when viewed as a covenant of works, in opposition to the covenant of grace; or in respect to the legal economy and teaching considered precisely in itself, apart from the promises of grace and in contradistinction to the gospel ministration (compared with it there by the apostle). In this sense, it may well be called "the letter" because it indeed shows duty, but does not fulfill it; orders, but does not help; commands, but does not operate and is said to be "made void" (*katargeisthai*) in respect to that economy, because that old covenant ought to be abrogated. Yet it cannot be called so absolutely (under the relation of a rule and a standard).

XIII. The liberty of Christ frees us from the yoke of the cursing law, from the tyranny of the Devil and from the bondage of sin. It does not release from the necessity of rendering obedience to God, which is indispensable from every creature as such and especially from redeemed sons. Yea, the chain of our duty binds so much the more strongly, as we are connected with God by more names. Thus liberty from sin implies necessarily the service of grace; being made free from sin, we become the servants of righteousness (Rom. 6:18). True liberty consists in this—that we be subject to God, for "to serve him is to reign." "The liberty of the spirit," therefore, differs from "the license of the flesh." The latter is in truth incompatible (*asystatos*) with the law, but the former is in the highest degree consistent with it and inseparable from it: "As free, and not using your liberty for a cloak of maliciousness, but as the servants of God" (1 Pet. 2:16); "Ye have been called unto liberty; only use not liberty for an occasion to the flesh" (Gal. 5:13).

XIV. What was given to the Jews as Jews can be for the use of the Jews alone; but what is given to the Jews as covenanted (or as the people of God simply) does not refer to them alone, but to all those who hold the same relation of people of God. The law was not given to the Jews in the first sense in every way, but in the latter; for now at this day it speaks to us (Rom. 7:7; 1 Cor. 9:8). Nor if it is said to have been given by Moses (Jn. 1:17) does it follow that under the gospel of Christ it has no place. Moses is not opposed to Christ, but subordinated (as a servant to a master and he who is in a house to him who has a right over the house as the builder and governor of it).

XV. Moses also can be viewed in two lights: either generally and indefinitely as a teacher of the whole church; or particularly and definitely as a leader of the people and legislator of Israel, having a regard for its interest. In the latter sense, the law (brought in by Moses) pertained to the Jews alone, but in the former is extended to all no less than the law of nature (of which it is a compend). And thus the diverse opinions of the orthodox about the use and obligation of the Mosaic law can be reconciled. Some hold that it belonged to the Jews exclusively (as Zanchius and Musculus); others, however, assert that it referred to all (as Pareus and others). The latter consider Moses and the law under the first notion; the former, however, under the second.

Twenty-Fourth Question: The Ceremonial Law

What was the end and the use of the ceremonial law under the Old Testament?

The Mosaic law threefold: moral, ceremonial, forensic.

I. The law given by Moses is usually distinguished into three species: moral (treating of morals or of perpetual duties towards God and our neighbor); ceremonial (of the ceremonies or rites about the sacred things to be observed under the Old Testament); and civil, constituting the civil government of the Israelite people. The first is the foundation upon which rests the obligation of the others and these are its appendices and determinations. Ceremonial has respect to the first table determining its circumstances, especially as to external worship. Civil has respect to the second table in judicial things, although it lays down punishments for crimes committed against the first table.

Foundation of the distinction.

II. The truth of this distinction appears from the diversity of the names by which it is designated in the Scriptures. The moral law is for the most part expressed by *mtsvth* ("precepts"), the ceremonial by *chqym* ("statutes") and the judicial by *mshptym* ("judgments"), which the Septuagint renders by *entolas*, *dikaiōmata* and *krimata*. "I will speak unto thee all the commandments, and the statutes, and the judgments, which thou shalt teach them" (Dt. 5:31); so also in 6:1, 20; 7:11; and Lev. 26:46. Sometimes however these words are synonymous and used promiscuously (Ezk. 5:6; 20:11, 16, 18). But the distinction appears principally from the nature of the thing and the office of the law (whose it is to settle the order according to which man is joined to God and his neighbor). Now man is joined to God first by a certain internal and external likeness—in love and justice, holiness and truth, whose rule the moral law delivers. Again by the external signification and testification of those acts of divine worship (marks and symbols being employed) whose use the ceremonial law prescribes. Finally, what duty man owes to man, the civil law (applied more distinctly to the Israelites) explains. The moral law regards the Israelite people as men; the ceremonial as the church of the Old Testament expecting the promised Messiah; the civil regards them as a peculiar people who in the land of Canaan ought to have a republic suiting their genius and disposition.

Difference between the moral law and others.

III. Hence arises a manifold difference between the moral law and others both in origin (because the moral is founded upon natural right and on this account is known by nature; but the others upon positive right and on this account are from free revelation) and in duration. The former is immutable and eternal; the latter mutable and temporary. In regard to object, the one is universal embracing all; the others particular applying only to the Jews (the civil, indeed, inasmuch as it regarded them as a distinct state dedicated to God; the ceremonial, however, referring to their ecclesiastical state and state of minority and infancy). In regard to use, the moral is the end of the others, while the others are subservient to the moral. Thus far we have spoken of the moral; now we must discuss the ceremonial.

What is the ceremonial law?

IV. The ceremonial law is the system of God's positive precepts concerning the external worship in sacred things, prescribed to the ancient church, either for the sake of order or of signification. It is so called from the object about which it is conversant (viz., the sacred ceremonies or rites that were formerly to be observed in the external worship of God). This is so whether the word ceremony is derived from the Etruscan *cerus*, meaning "holy," as *sanctimonia* from *sanctus* (according to Joseph Scaliger and Dionysius Gothofredus in *notis ad Festum+*); or from Ceres which (because the Gauls occupied Rome, they preserved the eternal fire and the vestal virgins) was called the sanctuary of the Roman people and the receptacle of the Roman sacred vessels. The Romans, for the sake of renumeration, called their sacred rites *caeremoniae* from Ceres (according to Valerius Maximus, *Factorum et Dictorum Memorabilium* 1.1.10 [ed. C. Kemp, 1966], p. 6; cf. Florus, lib. 1, cap. 13+). Or (what is more probable) from the Hebrew *chrm* which signifies a thing sacred and devoted to God.

V. It is marked by various names—now by *chqym* (as *mshptym* marks the judicial and *mtswth* the moral); then by "the law of commandments in ordinances" (*nomon tōn entolōn en dogmasi*, Eph. 2:15) because its precepts are ordained (*dedogmena*) (sanctioned by the will of God) having no goodness except from the divine appointment; then by "carnal commandment" (*entolēn sarkikēn*, Heb. 7:16) and "carnal ordinances" (*dikaiōmata sarkos*, Heb. 9:10) because they are occupied with prescribing external and corruptible things (which are called carnal in the Scriptures); then by "weak and beggarly elements" (*stoicheia asthenē kai ptōcha tou kosmou*, Gal. 4:9) because they were the first rudiments and, as it were, the alphabet of the Jewish church. During her infantile state, she ought to have been instructed in them and able to do nothing by herself either for justification or for salvation.

Origin of ceremonies.

VI. Ceremonies are external rites and sacred accidents of the worship of God. They are not of themselves the worship of God, but concomitant adjuncts and assistants by signification, exercise, work and decorum. Their rise and foundation is drawn from the nature and condition of man, who, since he is a "ceremonial animal" (according to Melanchthon), cleaves to and is affected by external ceremonies and rites. Also since he consists of soul and body and in both ought to glorify God, he demands external rites by which he may compose the motions of his body to the worship of God and be carried from sensible and earthly things to spiritual and heavenly things. Hence in the state of integrity certain external symbols and ceremonial rites were not wanting: such as the tree of life set apart above the others for a sacrament of the covenant and of the promises; and the tree of the knowledge of good and evil, which alone was separated from the many as a symbol of trial; such also was the sanctification of the Sabbath. But after sin, the necessity of these rites increased, not only for good order (*eutaxian*) and a bond of holy society and of pious communion under God (for the sealing of the covenant, both as to the presence and blessings of God and as to the testimonies of our gratitude and the marks of our duty to God), but especially to shadow forth the person and offices of the Mediator, without whom no approach can be made to God.

VII. Hence arose the institution of the ceremonial law, of which there are many very important reasons in which we should acquiesce besides God's most holy will. (1) The condition of the church, which, still constituted in its childhood and infancy (on account of the small portion of the Holy Spirit given to it, Gal. 4:1), was to be instructed by figures of this kind, since it was not ordinarily able to receive greater light. (2) The nature of the Israelite people, who, being a stiff-necked people and very prone to the idolatry and profane worship of the Gentiles, were to be guarded by ceremonies of this kind and restrained as it were within certain barriers, to prevent their falling into other worship. (3) The turpitude and heinousness of sin, which was to be shown in order that man (convicted of it) might be excited to seek a remedy which was found in purifications and sacrifices. (4) The necessity and efficacy of grace, which ought to be shadowed forth by various types.

The general end of the ceremonial law—good order; the special end with respect to the moral law.

VIII. Therefore a manifold end no less than use of the ceremonial law can be observed. (1) General (to wit, good order [*eutaxia*]), that in it the people might have an external form of public worship and religion of which God could approve. (2) Special, again various according to its different relations (*schesin*), either in relation to the moral law or to the Israelite people or to grace. For with respect to the moral law, its end was to subserve the former table by a prescription of legitimate external worship and will-worship (*ethelothrēskeiōn*) and to aid the moral law in convincing men of their impurity, weakness and guilt.

With regard to the people.

(3) With regard to the people, it was to serve for distinguishing them from other people and to bind them more strongly together among themselves. On this account, it is called a "middle wall of partitions" (*mesotoichon*, Eph. 2:14) by which the Israelites were separated from other nations, who moreover had no commerce with them; yea, exercised mutual hatred and enmity from this cause. Hence it is called by the apostle in the same place "hatred" (*echthra*) or "enmity" (i.e., the occasion of hatred and variance between them). Thus it was like a schoolmaster which led the people away from companionship with the Gentiles (from their idolatry and impurity) and conducted them to God and more strictly bound them to worship him as their own God peculiarly and so to be occupied with this laborious worship, that there might be no time or hour free for them either to invent new worships or accept such as were employed by others.

With regard to grace.

IX. With regard to the covenant of grace, there was a use of the law to show its necessity by a demonstration of sin and of human misery; of its truth and excellence by a shadowing forth of Christ and his offices and benefits; to seal his manifold grace by its figures and sacraments; to keep up the expectation and desire of him by that laborious worship and by the severity of its discipline to compel them to seek him; and to exhibit the righteousness and image of the spiritual worship required by him in that covenant. Undoubtedly three things are always to be specially inculcated upon man: (1) his misery; (2) God's mercy; (3) the duty of gratitude: what he is by nature; what he has received by grace; and what he owes by obedience. These three things the ceremonial law set before the eyes of the Israelites, since ceremonies included especially these three relations. The first inasmuch as they were appendices of the law and the two others as sacraments of evangelical grace. (a) There were confessions of sins, of human misery and of guilt contracted by sin (Col. 2:14; Heb. 10:1-3). (b) Symbols and shadows of God's mercy and of the grace to be bestowed by Christ (Col. 2:17; Heb. 9:13, 14). (c) Images and pictures of duty and of the worship to be paid to God in testimony of a grateful mind (Rom. 12:1). Misery engendered in their minds humility, mercy, solace and the duty of gratitude, sanctification. These three were expressly designated in the sacrifices. For as they were a "handwriting" on the part of God (Col. 2:14) representing the debt contracted by sin, so they were a shadow of the ransom (*lytrou*) to be paid by Christ (Col. 2:17; Heb. 10:5, 10) and pictures of the reasonable (*latreias logikēs*) and gospel worship to be given to God by believers (Rom. 12:1; 1 Pet. 2:5).

X. Still it is certain that the first and most principal relation (*schesin*) of this law was to Christ. As he was the aim and foundation of all the promises and oracles (2 Cor. 1:20), so he was the body and truth of all the types and figures (Col. 2:17). These were "a shadow of things to come; but the body is of Christ" (*skia tōn mellontōn, to de sōma tou Christou*). They are called a "shadow" both physically (as it is opposed to the body because as a shadow is the sign of a body, so ceremonies were the shadows of Christ to be exhibited; as a body is the cause of the shadow, on the other hand Christ was not the cause of the institution of these rites; as the shadow of itself has and can have no force, but the power belongs to the body, so all the efficacy is from Christ—but ceremonies of themselves are vain and dead) and artificially for an obscure and rude delineation of a thing, opposed to the perfect image (*eikona*) of a thing (in which sense it is used by the apostle, Heb. 10:1). However, it was most wisely arranged by God that since for the most weighty reasons he willed to put off the advent of the Messiah for many ages, he might not only be promised and predicted in the oracles, but also represented in types, only until the time of the reformation (*diorthōseōs*) should come and the sun of righteousness arise. It was also arranged by God that his ancient people by these shadows and oracles might sustain themselves in the hope of the coming Messiah and so under these images might have a foretaste of the heavenly grace to be manifested in Christ; and that the believers of the Old Testament from these marks might more readily and certainly recognize the Messiah (as represented) and their faith be more confirmed by beholding the fulfillment of the shadows in the body and of the figures in the truth.

Whether the ceremonial law was given from wrath to wrath.

XI. And hence we may easily gather what we must decide concerning the question agitated by some in our day—whether the ceremonial law (prescribed after the making of the calf [*moschopoiian*]) had a use significative of and sealing the guilt and curse still binding believers and so was given from wrath to wrath, both for aggravating and sealing the bondage of the fathers under the guilt of wrath and of the curse (as some hold). Or—whether it principally respected Christ and was given as a type of good things to come, to raising up the minds of believers (as others think). For as there was a twofold relation (*schesis*) of that law which must be carefully attended to (the one legal, referring to the covenant of works and its violated law; the other evangelical, by which it was referred to the covenant of grace, and its Mediator), so we must reason concerning it in different ways according to that double relation (*schesin*). For with regard to the former, there is no doubt that it had the use of discovering sin, sealing its guilt and threatening the wrath and curse of God impending on account of sin. In this sense, Paul says that the "handwriting" was against us and by them was made a remembrance (*anamnēsin*) of sins. But when the latter is attended to, it is certain that even in it were symbols and seals of the grace of God in Christ by which believers could be supported in the hope of good things to come and be confirmed against the sense of sin and God's anger.

XII. However, these relations (*scheseis*) are so connected that whoever wishes rightly to understand the nature of the Old Testament economy and the use of the ceremonial law, ought always to join them together; nor can they be wrested asunder except at a heavy expense of the truth. For as he who would attend to the evangelical relation (*schesin*) alone (the rigor of the law as a schoolmaster being disregarded) would not understand the character of the Old Testament, which consisted principally in this; so he who would press the legal relation too much (the evangelical neglected and not sufficiently considered) would seem not a little to obscure the grace of God exercising itself under that dispensation and to depress and weaken too much the faith and consolation of the fathers. Hence the middle seems to be the safest way here—that we may always keep in view both these relations (*schesin*). Nevertheless the legal must be the inferior, subservient to the evangelical and constituting the less principal end of that whole dispensation; the evangelical, however, must be the primary, as containing the special and ultimate end of God in that economy.

XIII. Hence it cannot be absolutely said that the ceremonial law was given from wrath to wrath, to seal and aggravate the bondage of the fathers under guilt and the curse; and that sacrifices were not a remedy for sin, but a handwriting (*chirographum*); and like things of this kind by which the rigor of the legal pedagogy is set forth. For although these things can be said in a sound sense as to the legal relation (*schesin*) considered strictly in itself (nor do we think any controversy should be carried on among brethren on that account, if such were their meaning), they cannot, however, be received absolutely and simply, if the ceremonies are considered relative to the evangelical relation (*schesin*) from which they ought never to be separated. For if it is true (as cannot be denied) that God under these wished to adumbrate and seal to us gospel mysteries and the saving grace of Christ (which the apostle so often and so expressly inculcates in the epistle to the Hebrews, and the types and sacraments necessarily demand), how can that law be said to have been given from wrath to wrath and to seal and aggravate the guilt and bondage of the fathers? Or can we think that what had so grateful and sweet a use was given for so oppressive and severe an end? And if the sacrifices sealed Christ's future expiation itself to a freedom even then efficacious, how can they be said to have sealed guilt resting upon the fathers with a troublesome rebuke to their consciences?

XIV. The contrary opinion cannot be established from the law being called an "unbearable yoke" (*abastakton*, Acts 15:10). This is meant of the law of itself considered in opposition to the gospel. In this sense, it is a ministry of death and condemnation which loaded the conscience with laborious observances. Nor can this opinion be established from it in subordination to the gospel, in which sense it was a schoolmaster unto Christ (Gal. 3:24); or from its being described by the weak and beggarly elements of the world (Gal. 4:9), to which the apostle attributes weakness and unprofitableness (*to asthenes kai anōpheles*, Heb. 7:18). Paul does not speak of ceremonies in their legitimate use according to the institution of God under the Old Testament, but of them as now abrogated and deadened by Christ; or considered per se, aside from their typical relation, separated (namely, from Christ) as the Judaizers considered them; or from the law being said to have had a shadow of good things to come and not the very image of the things (Heb. 10:1). It is certain that the apostle speaks of the law in itself considered simply, apart from Christ the Mediator. In this sense, no one denies that it had only the shadow of good things to come and could not expiate sin or appease the conscience. But this does not hinder it from being referred to Christ to shadow forth his grace; yea, the words of the apostle manifestly lead us to this.

XV. Nor is it gathered any better from Col. 2:14 where it is called the hand writing (*chirographum*) against us, which seems to mark the sealing and reproaching of the guilt still resting upon believers. This is said only in respect to the legal relation (*scheseōs*), which ought by no means to be so urged, as to blot out the evangelical. Otherwise Paul had falsely said, "Circumcision is a seal of the righteousness of faith" (Rom. 4:11). According to the former, it may well be said to have been a handwriting because in it was the confession of sin and of guilt; not abolished by the legal victims (as was evident in their repetition), but to be abolished by the death of Christ alone. According to the latter, it was a figure of the substitution of the Mediator in our place and of the guilt transferred to him and thus of the liberation to be received through him and of the remission already obtained in virtue of the sacrifice that was to be offered. Hence it is that Paul does not simply say that the handwriting is *enantion* ("contrary" to us), but *hypenantion* ("subcontrary," i.e., in a certain manner contrary). To wit, against the fathers under that legal relation and inasmuch as they were sinners, it was the handwriting of sin and of the guilt incurred by it and of the punishment deserved; still inasmuch as they were believers, it contained the favorable symbols and seals of the grace even then bestowed upon them according to the evangelical relation, which was the principal and ultimate and that by which the former was tempered to the consolation of believers that they might not be reckoned as still under guilt, who were made over to Christ in virtue of the agreement made and the future payment.

XVI. Moreover the multitude of ceremonies and figures was a proof of the imperfection under which they labored. At the same time, it brought before their minds and eyes the supreme perfection of Christ, to shadow forth which there was need of so great variety that what could not be fully represented by one picture might be brought out by many exhibiting the same object considered in different relations (*schesei*). The same Christ was adumbrated by the kings, prophets and priests with reference to his threefold office: by the priest offering, in reference to his eternal Spirit or divinity; by the victim offered, in reference to his human nature; by the altar of whole burnt offerings, in reference to his satisfaction; by the altar of incense, in reference to his intercession, etc. The same Spirit by the water of purification, by the anointing oil, by the sacred fire was signified in reference to his various operations. Hence what were divided in the types were joined together in the antitype. Concerning this, judgment ought to be made not from one or another separately, but from all considered connectedly because there was no adequate type fully covering the antitype, but all were partial and inadequate.

XVII. As however the same mystery was often represented under various figures and ceremonies, so the same figure was often used to adumbrate different mysteries, especially when these mysteries were subordinated and had a mutual relation (*schesin*) to each other. Thus the tabernacle was a type of Christ (Jn. 1:14), of the church and of believers (Eph. 2:20) and of heaven (Rev. 11:1, 2). The sacrifices were figures of the expiatory sacrifice of Christ (Heb. 10:5, 6) and of the spiritual sacrifices and thanksgivings of believers (1 Pet. 2:5). The priests represented Christ, who is the chief high priest of the New Testament (Heb. 9, 10); the ministers of the gospel, who ought to minister (*leitourgein*) to God (Rom. 15:16), and believers, who are made a "royal priesthood" (1 Pet. 2:5; Rev. 1:6). The

Passover was not only a memorial of the passage of the angel through Egypt and of deliverance from Egypt, but a symbol of the future redemption by Christ from the bondage of Satan and sin; and a figure of the passage of believers from slavery to liberty, from death to life (1 Cor. 5:7).

Inability of ceremonies to expiate sin.

XVIII. And hence we may clearly gather against the Jews that the use and end of the ceremonial law was not the justification and sanctification of sinful man (because "the law made [*eteleiōsen*] nothing perfect, but the bringing in of a better hope did; by the which we draw nigh unto God," Heb. 7:19) since it was concerned only with a carnal commandment and things earthly and corporeal, "which could not make the conscience perfect [*teleiōsai*]" (Heb. 9:9). It reached no further than to "the purifying of the flesh" (v. 13), i.e., the external and ceremonial, which the apostle shows at length (Heb. 10:1-4). It is easily proved: (1) generally from "the nature of that law, which had a shadow of things to come" (Heb. 10:1) and not the very image of the things and so could not make the "comers thereunto perfect." (2) Specially, from the imperfection of the ceremonies, which had no proportion either to the sins (which, as moral, can be expiated and purged out only morally by a victim having a moral relation, i.e., from the highest love and most perfect obedience presenting itself to God, such as Christ alone is) or to God, to whom satisfaction ought to be made. Being a Spirit, he also demands a spiritual and rational victim to make satisfaction to him; nor would his wisdom or justice allow sins to be taken away by brute and material blood, but required a rational victim to take away the guilt contracted by a rational creature and that the rebellion against infinite majesty should be settled by an infinite price and satisfaction. The imperfections of the ceremonies had no proportion to man, for whom expiation ought to be made because sin ought to be punished in the same nature in which it was committed. Hence the apostle expressly asserts, "It is not possible that the blood of bulls and of goats should take away sins" (Heb. 10:4)—not only from the appointment of God, but from the nature of the thing (since in those sacrifices continually renewed there was rather a remembrance [*anamnēsis*] again made of sins every year, vv. 2, 3).

XIX. If expiation is somewhat frequently attributed to those sacrifices, it does not follow that they truly and properly expiated. This is to be referred only to a typical and ceremonial expiation by which the impurity of the flesh was taken away (i.e., sin committed against the law), not however to a real and spiritual expiation from the guilt and pollution of sin properly so called (which purged the conscience, as the apostle expresses it in Heb. 9:14). Therefore a twofold effect of that law must be attended to: the former (external and carnal), the taking away of carnal impurity by which one was kept away from the ecclesiastical assemblies, such as was contracted by the touching of things prohibited by the ceremonial law; the latter sacramental (to wit, the signifying and sealing of the grace and all the benefits to be obtained from the Mediator). With respect to the latter, cf. "Disputatio . . . De Satisfactionis Christi," Pt. VI, Section 4 in *Opera* (1848), 4:564.

Ceremonies are viewed either in regard to the persons, or etc.

XX. Now these ceremonies can be distributed into various classes: (1) in regard to the persons by whom the sacred rites were performed; (2) in regard to the sacred things themselves which ought to be done; (3) in regard to the places in which they ought to be celebrated; (4) in regard to the times in which they ought to be performed. The sacred persons were of two kinds: some called sacred commonly; others for a special reason. Of the former kind were all those initiated by the sacrament of circumcision (by which mark the people dedicated to God were separated and distinguished from profane nations). This rite prefigured the taking away of our native corruption, the restoration of the image of God to us, our implanting in Christ and the sealing of the divine covenant.

XXI. Of the latter kind are they whose ministry God used for the government of his church. They were both the ordinary and extraordinary ministers. The latter were those who, to build up the church and to establish order in it at first or to restore it when it had fallen and so predict future things, were immediately raised up (such as the prophets). Hence by visions, dreams and the internal inspiration of the Holy Spirit, they were prepared for prophesying. The ordinary were they who being mediately called were bound to preserve the order established in the church by performing the sacred rites (such as the priests and Levites). The former sprung by a perpetual series of succession from the family of Aaron, exercised their office in the tabernacle, placed their hands upon the people and blessed them invoking the name of God. Among them the chief high priest was pre-eminent, whose particular consecration, particular dress and particular office constituted him a peculiar type of Christ. They were specially called "Levites" who (employed for sacred things in place of the first-born, Num. 18) served the priests in cleaning the holy vessels, slaughtering and washing the animals, placing the bread and other similar duties.

Nazarites.

XXII. The Nazarites are also reckoned among the sacred persons, although they had nothing to do with sacred things. Some of them were such by a vow (referred to in Num. 6:2-8); others by birth and by divine command (as Samson, Samuel, John the Baptist). The latter's peculiar sanctity adumbrated the perfect purity of Christ, who was a true *nzyr* of God (antonomastically such), separated (*aphōrismenos*) from others. In him is truly found in a mystery what occurred in the Nazarites as to the letter since indeed he abstained from all defilement which could taint his most perfect holiness. He had no communication with the dead works of sin and his life was a continual example of sobriety and temperance and of all the other virtues. He devoted himself to his office with such zeal as to prefer it to all the duties of relationship.

Sacred things: offerings.

XXIII. Sacred things were those which were exempted from profane uses and (sanctified by the word of God) were destined to sacred uses, such as offerings or sacrifices. Those were the offering of inanimate things which (sprung from the earth) ministered to man either food for life or spice for cheerfulness or medicines for cure. Of the first kind, bread and wine; of the second, oil and salt; of the third, frankincense was presented, by which both Christ's benefits towards us and the gifts of the Spirit were designated as well as our duty towards God and the testimony of a grateful mind (Mal. 1:11).

Sacrifices.

XXIV. Sacrifices especially belong here for they constituted a great part of the ceremonial law. Not because they had been of free use which could either be offered or not without a neglect of due worship (as some maintain); for that they had been prescribed by God is sufficiently and more than sufficiently gathered even from this—that Abel is said to have offered by faith (Heb. 11:4). Now faith is founded upon the word of God and God is said to have borne witness to those sacrifices, thus testifying that they were pleasing to him. Now in the matter of religion, nothing pleases him except what he has himself commanded; thus all will-worship (*ethelothrēskeia*) is condemned (Col. 2:23). But their institution was more clearly and solemnly renewed by Moses. Sacrifices, too, were living victims, exhibited by the believer and offered by the priest to God, according to the rites prescribed by him. Their integrity and soundness (*holoklēria*), as they signified Christ, the immaculate lamb and the mark of perfection at which in this life we must aim, so the offering of them designated first the sacrifice of Christ offered for us and then also our reasonable service (*logikēn latreian*). There were two principal species of them. For some were hilastic (*hilastica*) or propitiatory for sins committed (which adumbrated the expiatory sacrifice of Christ offered for us on the cross for a sweet-smelling savor [*eis osmēn euōdias*] to expiate our sins [Eph. 5:2] and the consecration of ourselves, body and soul, made in Christ to the Father, Rom. 12:1). Others were eucharistic for benefits either expected or received, which were the types of the spiritual sacrifices of prayers and praises to be offered every day to God and of the love to be exercised towards our neighbors (Heb. 13:15, 16).

XXV. Sacrifice is sometimes taken widely for any religious action instituted by God that we may offer our own to him for his glory and be joined in a closer fellowship with him. In this sense, it could exist even before sin, and the end was to testify, seal, preserve and increase communion with God, man returning thanks, acknowledging his indebtedness and taking all he has and placing it before God to testify a thankful soul and to obtain the blessings he still needs. But it strictly denotes the offering and slaying of a victim for the expiation of sin by the shedding of its blood (*haimatekchysian*) and death; thus only after sin could it take place. Since the evils of blame and of punishment, introduced by sin, were to be removed and the good things which man had lost to be procured by a satisfaction to divine justice and the appeasing of his wrath, the shedding of blood and the death of the victim in sacrifices was necessarily required to adumbrate more efficaciously the sacrifice of Christ by his accursed death and the shedding of his most precious blood.

Sacred places.

XXVI. Third, because place and time come under sacred things, on this account, they also pertain to the ceremonial law. A sacred place is one in which God exhibited his presence by some visible symbol and publicly commanded himself to be worshipped there. Even before the building of the tabernacle and the temple, this is called "the face of the visible God," "the house of God" and "the gate of heaven" (Gen. 16:13; 28:17). For as the law orders sacred assemblies, so also places of assembly were to be selected in which those things might be more conveniently and opportunely done for which the assemblies were convened. This choice depended not upon the pleasure of men (who often feign a divinity where there is no proof of it), but upon God, who selects and sets them apart both by a manifestation of himself (where, as it were, by a flash of lightning, he the most clear, yea, very light itself, turns the eyes of all upon himself) and by a declaration of his will. This local adhesion was necessary under the Old Testament where the external and ceremonial worship required a certain place also, to which it might be confined. But now under the gospel, where the knowledge of God is diffused throughout the whole world, it has become accidental and indifferent because our worship is restricted to no place. Neither on Mount Gerizim nor in Jerusalem only is he worshipped in spirit and in truth (Jn. 4:23). It is lawful to lift up holy hands to God everywhere (1 Tim. 2:8).

The tabernacle, the temple.

XXVII. That place was made known to Moses by the ordination of God. First, the movable tabernacle which he was commanded to build for this purpose. On this account, it was commonly called the "tabernacle of assembly" and "of testimony." Afterwards in the time of Solomon, it was changed to a fixed and immovable temple. It was a figure (1) of Christ, in whom dwells all the fulness (*plērōma*) of the Godhead bodily (*sōmatikōs*, Col. 2:9), in which alone God could rightly be recognized and worshipped, who by his humanity dwelt among (*eskēnōsen*) us as in a tabernacle (Jn. 1:14; Heb. 10:20; Jn. 2:19). (2) Of the church, out of which there is no salvation (Rev. 11:2), which is the tabernacle of God in the Spirit (Eph. 2:22) and the house of the living God (1 Tim. 3:15). (3) Of believers, who bear about with them the earthly tabernacle of the body made with hands, which is by degrees dissolved (2 Cor. 5:1; 2 Pet. 1:14). They are the temple of God (1 Cor. 3:16; 6:19) in whom Christ dwells by faith (Eph. 3:17). (4) Of heaven and of glory (Rev. 11:19; 21:3, 22).

XXVIII. Its unity signifies the unity both of Christ, the head, and of his mystical body or church. Its division into sanctuary, holy place and double court, in Christ can represent the body (answering to the court), the soul (answering to the holy place) and the deity (answering to the sanctuary); in the church can represent its three conditions: the visible church, into which hypocrites and profane persons can enter (answering to the court); the invisible and church of the elect, still on earth, into which believers and the elect alone like the legal priesthood are admitted, that they may render reasonable service (*logikēn latreian*) to God, where they still need the light of the word for their direction, the food of the sacraments for their nourishment and the incense of prayers; and the church of the saints on high, who admitted into heaven as the sanctuary of God enjoy intimate communion with him (Heb. 9:24). Or it may represent the state of nature, grace and glory: in man, his three parts—the external senses, which apprehend the sensibles (*ta aisthēta*), which are in the court; the intellect and mind, which gains acquaintance with intelligibles (*ta noēta*), which are in the holy place; and the heart or conscience, which embraces the credibles (*ta pista*), which are in the holy of holies (which eye hath not seen, nor ear heard); in the revelation of God, the three degrees: by works, corresponding to the court because they lie open to all promiscuously; by the word, corresponding to the holy place because destined for the church alone; and by face, corresponding to the holy of holies and given to the beatified saints alone.

XXIX. The apt connection of the tabernacle by bands and fastening figured the body of the church fitly joined together (*synarmologoumenon*) and compacted (*symbibazomenon*) from Christ the head and believers, his members (Eph. 4:16). The change of it into the temple designated the mutable form of the Jewish polity, which was first movable and ambulatory in the desert, then under Solomon obtained rest. This the temple designated, analogous indeed to the tabernacle in its parts and furniture, but in stability, splendor and grandeur far surpassing it. Again in the tabernacle was rightly exhibited the image of the mutable state both of the ancient church and of the whole human life. In the temple, however, both the Christian and the triumphant church were exhibited. On this account, the Jews alone worked on the tabernacle, while Gentiles, Tyrians and Sidonians also worked on the temple.

Ark of the covenant.

XXX. The ark of the covenant (contained in the tabernacle and temple, in which the tables of the law were deposited—a mercy seat of golden work covered by the cherubim resting upon it) signified: (1) Christ, upon whom God has erected the throne of grace (Heb. 4:16); in whom he manifests himself as reconciled to us; whom he has set forth to be a propitiation for us in his blood (Rom. 3:25); in whom are hid all the treasures of wisdom and knowledge (Col. 2:3) and the tables of the law are laid up, since the law of God is written upon his heart (Ps. 40:8); in whom the oracle (*logion*) of God is found because, as the Word (*Logos*) of the Father, he utters his oracles and reveals his will to us; unto whom the angels minister and to contemplate more closely his glory and mysteries the cherubim stoop (*parakyptousi*) and prostrate themselves (1 Pet. 1:12). (2) The church, in which God has set up his throne and wished the sacred tables to be kept; where he shows himself present in grace and appeased in Christ, the true propitiation; where he utters his oracles through the word; where angels, as ministering spirits, stand continually near believers and watch for their salvation; where the rod of discipline and of the cross, with which he exercises us, is joined with the manna of consolation and of life, with which he supports us.

The twofold altar.

XXXI. The twofold altar (of whole burnt offerings and of incense) represented the two parts of the priestly office of Christ, which ought to be fulfilled in his twofold state: satisfaction, in the offering of his body and the shedding of his blood in the state of humiliation; and his intercession in heaven, in the state of exaltation, by a living and continual representation of his sacrifice, adumbrated by the golden censer in which incense was burned upon the altar (Rev. 8:3). "We have an altar," says the apostle, "whereof they have no right to eat which serve the tabernacle" (Heb. 13:10). A passage was made from one to the other: on the brazen altar, sacrifice ought first to be offered, before the incense could be offered; so the satisfaction must go before the intercession for without a satisfaction all prayers are useless. Christ is our altar: on the cross, by immolation; in heaven, by intercession; on the table, by commemoration.

The table, the candlestick, the altar of incense.

XXXII. In the holy place, three things were seen particularly: the table, where the showbread was placed; the candlestick, on which the candles were lighted; and the altar of incense, where incense was burned. To these correspond in the church, the light of the word by which he enlightens us; the bread of life with which he feeds us; and the sacred worship which he demands of us by the offering of prayers and other spiritual sacrifices. The light of faith shines on the candlestick; the life of hope is fed at the table; and the fire of love is supplied from the altar.

The brazen laver.

XXXIII. The brazen laver in which the priests were bound to wash their hands and feet before they approached the altar and performed the sacred rites was a sign of the special purification required in those who draw near to God, whether they hold the special office of ministers of God or the common office of believers. Thus it was evident that no one can rightly engage in the worship of God, unless by faith in Christ he has been purged entirely of the guilt of sins and in part at least from the pollution (Jn. 13:8; Heb. 10:22; Tit. 1:15, 16).

Sacred times, the continual sacrifice.

XXXIV. Finally, sacred times are those in which the blessings of God, whether past or future, are publicly spoken of and celebrated. To these belong: (1) the continual sacrifice, accustomed to be offered every day (morning and evening) with the attendant duty, which signified both the eternal power and efficacy of Christ's sacrifice and the daily prayers of the pious and the worship of the grateful to God through Christ.

Festivals.

XXXV. Second, festivals of a threefold kind: weekly, monthly and annual. The weekly was the festival of the seventh day, called the Sabbath, to put us in mind both of the creation of the world and of Christ redeeming and sanctifying us as well as beginning his rest in us. The monthly were called "new moons" celebrated on the first of each month, yet without intermission of external works. This taught that all months and their changes were sanctified in us by Christ.

XXXVI. The annual were those which recurred either every year or only after a certain number of years. Of the anniversary festivals, the most solemn were those three in which every male was ordered to appear in the sight of the Lord, not without a gift (viz., the Passover, Pentecost and the Feast of Tabernacles). Although they were instituted for a recollection of past blessings (as the Passover in commemoration of their deliverance from Egypt; Pentecost for a calling to mind the blessing of the given law; and the Feast of Tabernacles in memory of the divine protection in the desert), still they had a conjoined adumbration and promise of the spiritual benefits to be conferred by Christ. The Passover adumbrated the liberation from Egypt and the liberation from the power of hell and the immolation of Christ (1 Cor. 5:7; 1 Pet. 1:18, 19). Pentecost adumbrated the mission of the Holy Spirit and the writing of the law upon the tables of the heart by the same Spirit (2 Cor. 3:2, 3; Jer. 31:33). The Feast of Tabernacles indicated the wandering of the pious man through this desert world to his heavenly country (Heb. 13:14).

XXXVII. The feasts recurring after an interval of certain years were the Sabbatical year, returning each seventh year, in which the intermission of cultivation was allowed; the Jubilee, on the fiftieth, in which there was besides a manumission of slaves, a remission of debts, and a restitution of goods sold. This is a symbol of the gospel Jubilee promulgated by the gospel of Christ which is truly the acceptable year of the Lord (Is. 61:1-3). All our spiritual debts (namely sins) are remitted through Christ (Rom. 8:1; Col. 2:14); freedom from sin, Satan and death given to us (Lk. 1:74; Rom. 6:13); and the goods lost through Adam restored.

In a word, full deliverance from all evils and perfect and everlasting rest under Christ is granted.

XXXVIII. Let these things be said in passing and strictly concerning ceremonies and their use, especially the typical and ceremonial. For to discuss them fully and to explain the mysteries of all the ceremonies would be the subject not of a few pages but of a large treatise (which does not fall within our scope and belongs rather to didactic than to elenctic theology).

Twenty-Fifth Question: The Abrogation of the Ceremonial Law

Was the ceremonial law abrogated under the New Testament? When and how?

Statement of the question.

I. The ceremonial law can be viewed in two ways: either with regard to doctrine and signification; or with regard to obligation and observance. The question is not whether it was abrogated as to doctrine. We confess that it still remains and is useful in many ways among Christians; and that the mystical truth, hidden under this shell, is always the same and of perpetual necessity. Hence on account of that analogy, the names are always retained (the ancient state being changed) and circumcision, sacrifices, altars, incense are attributed to Christians, not because these rites ought to prevail under the gospel, but because the truth of these figures always remains (in which we have the things adumbrated by these signs). Rather the question is whether it was abrogated as to obligation and obedience and whether believers are still in subjection to the ceremonial law (as the Jews of old) and are bound to keep it (as the Jews maintain). This was the opinion not only of the Jews of old (and is of those in our time), but also of the Judaizing false apostles in the time of the apostles. They urged the observance of ceremonies as necessary, rashly confounding the law with the gospel, Moses with Christ. However we, with the apostles and the whole church, deny it.

The abrogation of the ceremonial law proved: (1) from Gen. 49:10.

II. The reasons are: (1) because the Mosaic economy (of which the ceremonial law was the principal part) ought to be changed, therefore the ceremonial law ought also to be abrogated. Now that the former was to be changed is demonstrably gathered against the Jews from the oracles of the Old Testament. (a) From Gen. 49:10, where it is said, "The sceptre shall not depart from Judah, nor a lawgiver from between his feet, until Shiloh come." In some measure, here is asserted the necessity of the legal economy, designated by the scepter and lawgiver, until the advent of the Messiah, who is expressed by *shylh* (as if it were *'shr lh*—"whose is" the kingdom). Thus, he being manifested, its abrogation is necessarily supposed. For if it was to remain until Christ, there ought to be no place for it after him. The objections of the Jews will be refuted when we treat of the advent of the Messiah.

(b) From Jer. 31:31, 32*.

III. (b) From Jer. 31:31, 32*, where a new covenant and a new law is promised in those last days (i.e., under the New Testament): "Behold, the days come, that I will make a new covenant with the house of Israel, and with the house of Judah; not according to the covenant that I made." Not only is the truth and certainty of the change marked because where a new covenant is said to be made by that very fact the former is made old (Heb. 8:13), but also the cause of the change is indicated, the violation (namely, of the former covenant), and the manner, by an internal writing of the law. And that no one might object with the Jews that it is called new by reason of the confirmation and coalition of the old (not as to the institution of a new), it is expressly asserted that "it will not be according to that which he had made with their fathers." This necessarily implies a diversity of covenants, if not as to substance, certainly as to economy.

(c) From Dan. 9:27.

IV. (c) From Dan. 9:27, where it is said, "The Messiah shall cause the sacrifice and the oblation to cease, and seal up prophecy." This cannot be understood without the abrogation of the legal economy. And from Jer. 3:16, 17: "In those days, they shall say no more, the ark of the Lord, neither shall they visit it." If mention was no more to be made of the old ark, which was (as it were) the center of the old economy, then the whole of that economy was to become old. Nor does what is added in v. 17 concerning the glory of Jerusalem and the return to Canaan stand in the way of this opinion. This is to be understood spiritually and mystically concerning the church, not literally concerning the earthly Jerusalem (which was to be destroyed).

(d) From Ps. 110:4.

V. (d) From Ps. 110:4, where a new priest is promised according to the order of Melchizedek, who was not only to spring from a different tribe, but also to perform his office in a different manner, without successor and substitute; not for a time, but forever. Hence the apostle infers, "The priesthood being changed, there is made of necessity a change also of the law" (Heb. 7:12, 13). "For if," says he, "perfection were by the Levitical priesthood, what further need was there that another priest should rise after the order of Melchizedek, and not be called after the order of Aaron?" (Heb. 7:11). The same thing is gathered from all those passages in which it is said that the worship of God will be spread through the whole world (Mal. 1:11; Is. 54:5* and elsewhere), which could not take place under the old economy.

(e) From the end of the legal economy.

VI. (e) From the end of that economy and of ceremonies. For the causes and reasons of the introduction of the law being changed, the laws also are changed. [1] That law was like a "schoolmaster" to lead unto Christ and keep believers in expectation of good things to come, until the time of the restoration (*diorthōseōs*) or the time appointed (*prothesmias*) of the Father (Gal. 4:2), in which the church should be adult and emancipated. Now when Christ, who is the father and head of the church, appeared and the church itself had been brought by him to adult age, there was no need of a schoolmaster, as the apostle proves in Gal. 4:1-3. [2] The law was a "middle wall" (*mesotoichon*) separating the Jews from the Gentiles, but the distinction of nations having been taken away by Christ, there is no more any use for that party wall and Paul expressly testifies that Christ broke it down (Eph. 2:14). [3] The law was a handwriting (*cheirographon*) against us, not only by unveiling sin, but by sealing both the guilt and condemnation of the sinner. But our debt having been paid and sins expiated by Christ, the handwriting is destroyed and taken away; yea, affixed also to the cross, as the apostle elegantly expresses it (Col. 2:14). [4] That law had a shadow of future things (Heb. 10:1) because all its rites (as has been seen) had this special end, to adumbrate Christ and his offices and benefits. But shadows vanish before the rising sun; there is no room for figures when the truth is set forth; and there is no need of candles in the light of day. These are so incompatible (*asystata*) with each other that to wish to retain the shadows under the New Testament would be to deny that advent of Christ because they were employed as signs of his coming (which indeed could truly be done before his advent, but afterwards only falsely and uselessly). [5] The law was a guard (*phroura*) under which the people were detained that they might not turn aside to the profane worship of the Gentiles and be mixed with them (Gal. 3:23), by the spirit of bondage which obtained among them. But now believers, called to gospel liberty and gifted with the Spirit of adoption, as a willing people (Ps. 110:3) could no longer be held under that guard.

(f) From the change of things, persons and places.

VII. (f) Because the persons, things and places required for a strict observance of the ceremonial law should be changed and were actually changed. Therefore the law itself also should be abrogated, as it is abrogated. As to persons, the law was introduced only for the Israelites and had no reference to other nations. But now all peoples and nations are called to the economy of saving grace and that people is rejected. Here belong those various passages of the prophets which speak of the rejection of the Jewish nation and the calling of the Gentiles (Dt. 32; Lev. 26; Hos. 2; Is. 2; 49; 54; 60; 66). Formerly only one of the tribes (to wit, the Levitical) was admitted to the sacred ministry; but now another priesthood has arisen after the order of Melchizedek from the tribe of Judah. Priests are taken not only from the Jews, but also from the Gentiles themselves (Is. 66:21; 1 Pet. 2:5; Rev. 1:6). Formerly sacrifices were external and carnal, but now spiritual sacrifices are demanded (Rom. 12:1; Mal. 1) and God declares that he sometimes rejects and is opposed to the old sacrifices (Is. 1:12; Hos. 6:6; Mic. 6:7; Pss. 50 and 51; Is. 58 and 66). Yea, Ezk. 20:25 calls them "statutes that were not good," whereby man cannot live, undoubtedly both in themselves as to the impossibility of justification and sanctification and relatively to the abuse of the Jews, who separated ceremonies from moral worship. Formerly the sacred worship was confined to a certain part of the world and to one place, outside of which it was not lawful to perform sacred rites; but now the temple of God is everywhere. In the catholic church, it is lawful everywhere to lift up holy hands to God (1 Tim. 2:8) and true worshippers are no longer bound to appear in Jerusalem or on Mount Gerizim to worship because they can adore God everywhere in spirit and in truth (Jn. 4:21, 23). Hence it is said that an altar shall be erected in the midst of the land of Egypt (Is. 19:19), which would have been wrong under the Old Testament, under which religious worship is symbolized. It is predicted that incense shall be offered in every place unto God (Mal. 1:11), which could not be done under the law. Hence Eusebius proves conclusively that the observance of the ceremonial law has become impossible after the calling of the Gentiles (*Proof of the Gospel* 1.3.6 [trans. W.J. Ferrar, 1920], 1:20); nor can God, the most wise legislator, be conceived to have wished to impose such a law upon nations remote from the place chosen by the Lord (as if God wished the Indians, the Europeans, and the Britons, divided through the whole world, even now to go up to Jerusalem three times in each year). For what city (I will not say what temple); nay, what region could be capable of containing all these? What altars could be sufficient for receiving the victims? What region could furnish victims for so many worshippers?

(g) From the destruction of the temple.

VIII. (g) Nor only of right ought that law with the whole Mosaic economy to be abolished; but it has also actually been abolished. For indeed the temple being destroyed and Jerusalem levelled to the ground (which was the seat of worship), the whole nation miserably dispersed and scattered through the whole world, it is impossible for that law to be observed according to God's prescription. Neither an altar nor a temple occurs where worship is performed; nor is there a priest and sacrifices; nor any reason of the old polity and the distinction of the tribes and families; and indeed for so many ages, which divine providence would never have suffered if indeed those ceremonies ought to have continued. Nor can the Jews reply that these are indeed signs of an angry God which they experienced at other times (as in the Babylonian and Egyptian captivity) and as they were delivered from these, so they can also be recalled from this, the last exile. The present dispersion of the Jews is vastly different from their other captivities. The time of them was fixed; but by no means is this fixed. So much has already flowed by as has surpassed the time appointed for the others not twofold or fourfold, but tenfold; not of 70 years or of one or two centuries, but of sixteen centuries already passed. In the others, the temple and Jerusalem (although corrupt) were still standing; but now they are totally destroyed. In the others, the distinction of tribes remained, but here no true distinction can be granted, whatever the circumcised may babble. In the others, there were prophets and priests; but now they are wholly wanting.

(h) From the synodical decree, Acts 15.

IX. (h) The synodical decree (Acts 15) openly confirms this abrogation when it maintains that nothing further should be imposed upon Christians beyond abstinence from things strangled and from blood and from meats offered to idols (vv. 28, 29). From this it is clearly gathered that with the exception of these three, all other ceremonies and the observance of the ceremonial law are abrogated (as the use of circumcision which the false apostles urged and gave occasion for the Council at Jerusalem). For what reason, however, that decision was made and how it is to be understood, will be spoken of hereafter.

The mode of abrogation is noted: de jure and de facto.

X. The manner and time of the abrogation must be inquired into. The manner is considered first when the force of the law and the foundation of obligation is taken away (which was done by the death of Christ, in which he destroyed—not only destroyed, but took wholly out of the way—the handwriting that was against us, a full payment of debts having been made, Col. 2:14). Second, *de facto*, when really and actually the law ceases to bind and is abrogated with respect to man. The former was done at the same time and once; the latter however successively and by degrees. In the former, the abrogation was made meritoriously and causally; in the latter, formally and effectively.

XI. Hence three times (*tempora*) of the ceremonies must be accurately distinguished: first, in which they are alive; second, in which they are dead; third, in which they are deadly. The first, with regard to the divine institution, in which way they were not only lawful, but useful and necessary under the Old Testament. In this sense, circumcision is spoken of as a seal of the righteousness of faith (Rom. 4:11), and a great value is ascribed to it (Rom. 3:2), which can be applied to the other ceremonies from parity of reasoning. The second, with regard to accommodation (*synkatabaseōs*) and human tolerance, in which manner (now abrogated according to right by the death of Christ), they have become dead and indifferent. Nevertheless they could still sometimes be observed for the benefit of weak Jews, provided it was done from love only and not from necessity. The third, with respect to the abuses of the Jews and false apostles by whom they were pressed under the gospel as necessary to salvation (with the idea of merit), in which manner they were made pernicious and destructive. As to the first, they are observed as necessary according to the command of God. As to the second, they are suppressed as nothing and indifferent (1 Cor. 7:19; Rom. 14:3, 4). As to the third, they are condemned as deadly and noxious (Gal. 5:4). The first extends from the sanction of the law even to the time of correction (*diorthōseōs*) and the death of Christ; the second from the death of Christ even to the full manifestation of the gospel and of Christian liberty; the third from the promulgation of the gospel and the destruction of the temple unto the end of the world.

XII. However this abrogation was not a simple abolition by which something so ceases to be that nothing succeeds it. Rather it was a consummation of perfection (Heb. 8:6) by which something more perfect succeeds that which is imperfect (as the light of the sun, the daybreak, and the adult, the infantile age). Thus, undoubtedly, to circumcision in the letter (*en grammati*) succeeded circumcision in the spirit; to brute victims of bulls and of goats, the heavenly and rational victim (namely, the Lamb of God); to immolation made by mere man (and he a sinner) immolation by Christ, the God-man (*theanthrōpō*) (and most holy); to earthly things, things heavenly; to a mortal priest, an immortal and celestial; to a sanctuary worldly and made with hands, a sanctuary heavenly and not made with hands (*acheiropoiēton*); to purity of the flesh, purity of conscience; to a carnal and external worship, a reasonable (*latreia logikē*) and spiritual worship (Rom. 12:1; 1 Pet. 2:5).

Sources of explanation.

XIII. That which is of natural divine right is immutable, being founded upon the unchangeable holiness of God; but not equally that which is of positive divine right founded on the will of the legislator (who as he gave the law for his own reasons, can also change it, if he pleases). The ceremonial law is not of natural right, but only of positive; it is not commanded because just, but is just because commanded.

XIV. The abrogation of the ceremonial law is not repugnant to the constancy and immutability of God because he did not give it to remain forever, but only for a time. Thus the law was changed according to the immutable will of God, who neither began to will what he willed, nor left off willing what he willed, but fulfilled the counsel which he had taken of governing his minor church for a certain time by such a law, until Christ having appeared, the gospel economy should succeed to govern its adult age.

XV. Not more repugnant to it are the facts that circumcision is called an "eternal covenant" (Gen. 17:7) and that the law was to continue forever. A perpetuity, not absolute, but limited and periodic is meant; so designated because it ought to continue, not for some years only, but during the whole time of the Mosaic economy until the rectification (*diorthōsin*, Heb. 9*:10). The word *ʿlm* is often elsewhere used for a long duration, but still limited (as mention is made of the ministry of the Levites as perpetual [1 S. 1:22] which was only for 50 years; and the servant who bound himself to his master until the Jubilee was said to be about to serve him *lʿlm* "forever," Ex. 21:6). It can also be said that ceremonies are spoken of as perpetual, not with respect to the signs in themselves, but with respect to the things signified and the spiritual truth adumbrated by them, which remains ever the same. Hence circumcision is said to be made in Christ (Col. 2:11) and the true passover is given to us in him (1 Cor. 5:7).

XVI. The prophetic oracles which seem to promise a restoration of the legal economy under the Messiah with a return to their native country and the rebuilding of Jerusalem and of the temple are not repugnant to it (Dt. 30:1-5; Ezk. 37:24, 25; 40; 41). Many of these can be referred to the return from the Babylonian captivity. Hence it is not surprising that the restoration of the temple, altar and other things pertaining to it should be spoken of. If they are understood of the state of the church under the Messiah (as they certainly ought to be so far extended in order that their full meaning may be gained), the expressions are not to be pressed literally because they are symbolical, not proper; typical, not literal; to be explained spiritually and not carnally. Israel is to be restored, not according to the flesh and letter, but according to the promise and spirit (Rom. 9); the holy city, not Jerusalem, but the church; the worship to be renewed, not carnal, but spiritual—designated, however, according to the state of the times and the comprehension of the nation by carnal, to which the Jews were specially attached. Just as the prophets call prayers incense, the conversion of the Gentiles the going up to Jerusalem, adoration the offering of incense, the knowledge of God visions and dreams. Therefore, as often as the prophets speak of the return of the people to their native country and of its restitution, this can be understood in part literally (for the return from captivity); in part mystically and symbolically (concerning the constitution of the church of the New Testament, described by legal terms). That they cannot be understood simply literally is sufficiently evident from this—that they have not been fulfilled thus far and cannot be fulfilled, the temple having once been destroyed, Jerusalem devastated and the nation scattered.

XVII. If the apostles observed ceremonies after the death and resurrection of Christ, they did not do so from necessity, but from charity, to accommodate themselves to the weakness of the Jews; partly that they might show that they were not opposed to the law of Moses (as the evilly-disposed wickedly calumniated Paul); partly that they might gain the Jews over to Christ (1 Cor. 9:20); partly to give the synagogue a decent burial. This is clearly evident even from the fact that although in dealing with weak brethren they wished to use ceremonies for a time, still when they were dealing with the obstinate false apostles and adversaries, they constantly repudiated them. Paul, who wished Timothy to be circumcised (Acts 16:3), still (disputing against the false brethren who plotted against his liberty) was unwilling to circumcise Titus (Gal. 2:3, 4), that he might not give them an opportunity of cavilling. On this account, he severely reprimanded Peter because he had Judaized (cf. Augustine, Letter 82, "To Jerome" [FC 12:399]).

XVIII. Paul's vow about shaving his head (Acts 18:18) was not an act of religion (as if he had promised something to God according to the law as a part of necessary worship), but of charity, in order to accommodate himself to the weak showing that he was not a despiser of the law, but "was made all things to all men," 1 Cor. 9:22). "Not by deceitfully doing all the evil deeds of men, but diligently applying the medicine of mercy to all the evils of all others, as if they were his own," as Augustine says (Letter 82, "To Jerome" [FC 12:414; PL 33.288]).

XIX. It is one thing for some external rites to be granted in the church; another, however, to retain the ceremonial law. External rites are necessary in the church for the sake of good order because all things ought to be done in it "decently and in order" (1 Cor. 14:40). Yet they differ widely from the ceremonial law because that signified Christ as about to come, these not at all. This was a necessary part of the divine worship; those are only the supports and adjuncts of worship. In reference to them, these cautions should always be observed: (1) that no rites be prescribed with an opinion of their necessity and merit; (2) that they do not have an equal obligation upon the conscience with the divine laws, as if damnable guilt were incurred from any violation of them whatsoever (although that may happen without a contempt of the enjoiner and the scandal of others); (3) that these rites be not so multiplied as to press Christians by a servile yoke and bring them back as it were into Jewish bondage.

XX. The apostolic sentence concerning abstinence from things strangled and from blood (Acts 15:20) was not of perpetual, but of temporary right. This is proved: (1) from the end and aim which was the cause of the institution (which was temporary, viz., the peace of the church, by a tolerance of the weak among the Jews who, accustomed to ceremonies, should by degrees be weaned from them); (2) from the manner of decision by which they both gratified the Gentiles (absolving them from the ceremonies of the law) and desired to satisfy the Jews (enjoining certain ceremonies upon the Gentiles that for the sake of concord they might indulge them a little, until Christian liberty became better known, especially because the Jews professed to be opposed to the Gentiles particularly on this account); (3) because all distinction of food was wholly abrogated under the New Testament (as appears from Rom. 14:14; 1 Cor. 8:8; 10:27; Col. 2:21; 1 Tim. 4:3). And so much the stronger does the argument bind that Paul himself, who was present at the synod and knew and explained its intention best, wrote these things after the synod. Now how could the apostle so clearly and expressly have taken away such distinction without any exception, if the apostolic sanction had been considered by him to be of perpetual right? Yea, since the latter law restricted the former, we ought not to doubt that that law was considered by him as already abrogated or as about to be abrogated. If this sanction is renewed after the epistle to the Corinthians was written (Acts 21:25), it is to be understood in no other way than from the apostolic institution and ordination for a certain time, not in perpetuity; (4) by the judgment and authority of the church which, under a fuller knowledge of Christian liberty, gradually changed and abrogated that law (concerning which see Augustine, *Reply to Faustus the Manichaean* 32.13 [NPNF1, 4:336]).

XXI. The following do not prove the perpetuity of that sentence: (1) that it was made by apostolic authority—because the things pertaining to good order (*eutaxian*) were also sanctioned by them (1 Cor. 14:33). (2) That it is sanctioned under the title of necessity because it is not a necessity absolute and simple, but relative and hypothetical (with reference to the time and for the sake of avoiding scandal). (3) That it is joined with the prohibition of fornication, which is altogether of perpetual right—because not fornication itself can be understood, but meretricious food; or the price of lust, so that the word pollution (*alisgēmatos*) should be repeated (*apo koinou*), denoting the pollution of meat and drink (from Dan. 1:8). And if it be referred to fornication itself, it does not follow that it belongs to the same class because often dissimilars are joined together and morals with ceremonials (as in Ezk. 18:6; Lk. 1:6; 1 Tim. 3:2). Here he speaks of "sacrifices to idols," abstinence from which is not of the same necessity with fornication because it is sometimes lawful to partake of things offered to idols, but to commit fornication is never lawful. Therefore, morals can be joined with positives, especially when such are considered to be of the same kind in the estimation of men (as fornication was considered by the pagans as almost an indifferent thing or at least as a very slight fault, especially among the Greeks; among whom to commit fornication, as Comicus says, was not a disgrace). (4) That this law was enacted before Moses (Gen. 9:4)—because many ceremonial things prevailed before Moses, as sacrifices and circumcision. (5) That the reason of the law is moral and perpetual, that men, accustoming themselves to human blood, might not grow too cruel—because a moral reason does not always argue a moral law, as the observance of the seventh day has a moral reason from the rest of God, still it is not moral. Besides that reason had something forensic about it, accommodated to the hardness and sternness of the Jewish nation and in relation to that time, when before the flood they were wholly given up to violence and crime (Gen. 6:5).

XXII. (6) Nor finally that it was confirmed by the Synod of Gangra (Canon 2, NPNF2, 14:92) and the Council of Trullo* (Canon 67 [NPNF2, 14:395]) and by the emperor Leo in the fifth century and was for a long time observed in the Christian church. Hence Tertullian related among the trials of the Christians "the offering to them blood sausages" (*Apology* 9 [FC 10:33; PL 1.376]); as at this day the Armenians observe this law and there are some Protestants who think it should be retained. Human authority ought not to outweigh the divine, of which the ancients were destitute. The long continued observance of this law arises from the perverse explanation of the passage and its being agreeable to the ignorance and false zeal (*kakozēlia*) of those who know not how (or are unwilling) to distinguish between things (*kata ti*) instituted on account of another thing (and in a certain sense) and those which are to be observed simply and on their own account.

Twenty-Sixth Question

Whether the judicial law was abrogated under the New Testament. We make distinctions.

Ends of the individual law.

I. The forensic or judicial law concerned the civil government of the people of God under the Old Testament and contained a body of precepts concerning the form of that political rule. There were various ends of it. (1) The good order (*eutaxia*) and legitimate constitution of the Jewish polity, which should be a true theocracy (*theokratia*), as Josephus calls it. (2) The distinguishing of that state and nation from all other people and states and that that polity might be the seat of the church and the place for the manifestation of God. (3) The vindication of the moral and ceremonial law from contempt, and so the enforcer of respect and obligation towards both. (4) The adumbration of the spiritual kingdom of Christ.

Three opinions concerning its abrogation.

II. There are three opinions about its abrogation: the first in defect (of the Anabaptists and Antinomians, who think it is absolutely and simply abrogated as to all things). On this account, whatever reasons are drawn against them from the Old Testament for the right of the magistrate and of war; for the division of inheritances and the like, they are accustomed to resolve with this one answer—that these are judicial and pertain to the Israelite people and the Old Testament, but are now abrogated under the New. The second, in excess, of those who think that law is still in force and should be retained and that Christian states are to be governed like the Jewish (which was the opinion of Carlstadt and Castellio, with whom the Lutheran Brochmann agrees). Both wander from the truth. The former because thus many moral things would be abrogated which are contained in the forensic law. The latter because thus many typical things would have to be observed which are most foreign to the reason of our times. The third, of the orthodox, who, holding a middle ground, relieve the matter by a distinction, both according to what has been abrogated and according to what is still in force.

III. In that law various ends must be distinguished. For inasmuch as it was a distinction of the Jewish state from the Gentiles and a type of the kingdom of Christ, it is simply abrogated because there is no longer any distinction between the Jews and the Gentiles in Christ (Gal. 3:28; Eph. 2:14). As the Jewish state and polity has been destroyed, so there is no need of a type to adumbrate the future kingdom of Christ, since it has already come. But as to the good order (*eutaxian*) or form of government of the Israelite people, it cannot be said to have been abrogated, unless relatively. Undoubtedly those things are to be accurately distinguished which in the law were of particular right (which peculiarly applied to the Jews in relation to time, place and Jewish nation: such was the law concerning a husband's brother, the writing of divorcement, the gleaning, etc.) from those which were of common and universal right, founded upon the law of nature common to all (such as the laws concerning trials and the punishment of crimes, widows, orphans, strangers and the like, which are of moral and common right). As to the former, they may well be said to have been abrogated because the Jewish polity having been taken away, whatever had a peculiar relation to it must also necessarily have ceased. But as to the latter, it still remains because it enters into the nature of the moral and perpetual law and was commanded to the Jews not as Jews simply, but as men subject with others to the law of nature. For distinguishing those things which are of common and particular right, a threefold criterion can be employed. (1) That what prevails not only among the Jews, but also among the Gentiles (following the light of right reason) is of common right. Thus the Greeks, Romans and others had their own laws in which are many things agreeing with the divine laws (which even a comparison of the Mosaic and Roman law alone, instituted by various persons, teaches). (2) What is found to be conformed to the precepts of the decalogue and serves to explain and conform it. This is easily gathered, if either the object and the matter of the laws or the causes of sanctioning them are attended to. (3) The things so repeated in the New Testament that their observance is commended to Christians.

Sources of explanation.

IV. In the laws founded upon the common right or the law of nature, the substance of the precept must be distinguished from its circumstances. Some, both as to substance and as to circumstances, are of common right; others, however, are as to substance of common right, but as to circumstances of particular right. The former are perpetual in all parts; the latter, on the other hand, only relatively. Thus in the laws concerning the punishment of crimes, the substance of the punishment is of natural right, but the manner and degree of punishment is of particular right and on that account mutable.

V. Whatever forensic laws are mixed with types are in their own nature changeable and so have been abrogated of right because their causes and foundations are temporary, not perpetual. Such are the laws concerning the right of primogeniture (Dt. 21:17), asylums (Dt. 19:2), the Jubilee, the not sowing of fields with different kinds of seed, the not wearing garments of wool and linen and the like. Although they might have had a political end also, they still (because they were typical) cease to bind on that very account.

VI. The forensic laws accommodated to the genius and reason of the Jewish polity were not only made useless to Christians living under a different polity, but neither can, nor ought to be observed any longer (such as the Levirate law, the law of jealousy, the law of the selling of a son [Ex. 21], the law concerning the rest of fields, dividing the land of Canaan between the tribes and the like). These had a peculiar relation (*schesin*) to the Israelite people and its government. This having been taken away, they can have no further use.

VII. The polity having been abolished, the laws must necessarily be abolished upon which that polity was founded. They are of positive right and referred simply to the Jewish state; but not forthwith the others founded in natural right and appendages to the decalogue. Therefore, the forensic law as to general determinations, founded upon the moral law, is not abrogated; but as to special determination, which concerned the state of the Jews, is abrogated.

VIII. The forensic law may be viewed either formally, as it was enacted for the Jews (and so is abrogated); or materially, inasmuch as it agrees with the natural law and is founded on it (and thus it still remains).

IX. Although the best and wisest laws (as far as the state of that people was concerned) were sanctioned by God, it does not follow that on this account they ought to be perpetual. God, from positive and free right, could give them for a certain time and for certain reasons, to some one nation, which would not have force with respect to others. What is good for one is not immediately so for another.

X. What is better than others in every way (in both the abstract and the concrete and both negatively and affirmatively) is to be preferred to the others. But the forensic law is better than other laws, not affirmatively, but negatively because it was determined to certain circumstances which do not now exist. Then again it is better than human laws (simply as human), but not inasmuch as they are founded upon the natural law, whose source is God. Therefore, when the Roman laws are preferred to the Mosaic, they are not preferred simply as enacted by men, but as derived from natural and common right they can be more suitable to places, times and persons.

TWELFTH TOPIC

The Covenant of Grace and Its Twofold Economy in the Old and New Testaments

First Question
The origin and meaning of the words bryth, diathēkēs, foedus, epangelias *and* evangelium *used here.*

Necessity for treating the covenant.

I. The nature and use of the law (which goes before the covenant of grace) having been unfolded, we must now treat of the covenant itself. Since it is of the greatest importance in theology (being as it were the center and bond of all religion, consisting in the communion of God with man and embracing in its compass all the benefits of God towards man and his duties towards God), our highest interest lies in rightly knowing and observing it. Hence the discussion of it demands peculiar accuracy (*akribeian*), that the truth may be confirmed against the errors by which Satan has endeavored in almost every age to obscure and corrupt this saving doctrine.

***Etymology of the word* bryth.**

II. That the nature of the covenant may be more easily understood, a few things must be premised concerning the origin and meaning of the words used in Scripture to designate it and commonly employed by theologians. By sifting these, not a little light can be thrown upon the various difficulties occurring here. By the Hebrews, covenant is expressed by the word *bryth* (of uncertain etymology). Some derive it from the root *brh* either as signifying "to eat" (because in the making of covenants feasts were usual); or rather as denoting "to choose" (because the persons, things and conditions under which the covenant was made, were chosen). Hence the Jews are called "the children of the covenant" (Acts 3:25), "the people of God," "a chosen generation" (*genos eklekton*, 1 Pet. 2:9), for here there is a mutual election both on the part of God choosing men for a people and on the part of men choosing God for their God (as it is expressed in Jos. 24:22, 25). Others derive it from *brr* ("he has purified" and "declared") because by a covenant the faith and sincere friendship of the contracting parties is confirmed and declared. Others, with more propriety, deduce it from the root *br'* which in the Piel signifies "he cut in pieces"; or from the root *bthr* of the same meaning by a metathesis of the letters *th* and *r*. Scripture uses this word when it mentions confirmed covenants (Gen. 15:10; Jer. 34:18) because in making a covenant, the animal was cut in two and they passed between the parts of the slain victims, signifying that the violators of the covenant should be in like manner cut in pieces (as is evident from Gen. 15:10, 17). Among the Arabians, it is *'qsm* which signifies to divide into parts and "to cut in pieces." It also signifies "to swear" because covenants were ratified by victims cut in pieces (as Cyril of Alexandria, *Contra Julianum* 10 [PG 76.1054] ascribes this custom to the Chaldeans). Hence "to strike" and "to cut a covenant," the Hebrews call *krth bryth*. This suits the gospel covenant very well. It is founded on Christ being dead (as is said in Gal. 3:17, "the covenant was confirmed in Christ" [*diathēkē kekyrōmenē eis Christon*])—the covenant begun in Christ wounded and smitten and even in that divided immaculate Lamb in whom God was reconciling the world unto himself (2 Cor. 5:19); and through whom passing (as it were), he confirmed and ratified that covenant.

Signification of diathēkē.

III. Among the Greeks, the word "covenant" is commonly expressed by *diathēkē*. This can indeed be referred to every covenant and agreement. It is frequently taken in this sense (Lk. 1:72; Acts 3:25; 7:8; Rom. 9:4; Gal. 3:15; 4:24; Eph. 2:12; Heb. 8:6, 8, 9). But it peculiarly denotes a testamentary disposition with a federal agreement. It bears this signification in Mt. 26:28, in 1 Cor. 11:25 and especially in Heb. 9:15, 16, where Paul says, "Christ is the mediator of the new testament, that by means of death, for the redemption of the transgressions that were under the first testament, they which are called might receive the promise of eternal inheritance." However this was not done without authority as the Septuagint (which the apostle follows here) translates the word *bryth* by *diathēkē* rather than by *synthēkēn* (which denotes a simple agreement). The covenant of grace partakes both of a testament and of a covenant. Hence it is not improperly called "a covenant by a testament," "a testamentary covenant" and a "federal testament." It is a covenant because after the manner of a covenant there was an agreement between parties and conditions were laid down on both sides, both on the part of God and on the part of man, and there was a mediator to reconcile the discordant parties. But it is also a "testament" (1) because it is a covenant in which an inheritance is promised (which necessarily demands the antecedent death of the testator, since he only then is reckoned an heir who obtains the goods by an intervention of the will of the disposer). Since therefore the covenant (*diathēkē*) is a promise (*epangelia*) of this kind (in virtue of which the inheritance is discerned), it must necessarily be testamentary. On this account, the apostle adds, "For where a *diathēkē* is [to wit, by which an inheritance is promised, i.e., a testament], there must also of necessity be the death of the testator." (2) Because for our advantage only was this covenant made, as in a testament the advantage not of the testator but of the heirs is regarded; nor is God reconciled concerning mutual benefits, but concerning his own alone. (3) Because although conditions are set forth on both sides, they are entrusted for execution to the virtue and fidelity of only one party (namely, of God). Hence it is founded upon the mere grace of God and upon no disposition and merit of man (as will be fully proved in the proper place).

Whether the word* diathēkēs *denotes only a "testament" in the New Testament. Whether it does not also mean a "covenant."

IV. Hence it is easily gathered what must be determined on the question (agitated by some) concerning the use of the word *diathēkēs*—whether according to the usage of the New Testament and especially of Paul, it signifies only a testament and not also a *synthēkēn* or covenant and agreement. For since the signification of *diathēkēs* is promiscuous in profane and sacred authors, as much for a testament as for a covenant, no solid reason can be adduced why the relation of testament alone ought to have place with Paul, to the exclusion of the relation of covenant. Henry Stephens (Estienne) defines *diatithemai* by *testari* and *pacisci* (*Thesaurus Graecae Linguae* [ed. K. Hasse, 1831-65], 2:1349). Budaeus agrees; he asserts that *diathēkēn* is used promiscuously for a testament and a covenant: *Diatithemai, anti tou syntithemai, paciscor* ("Commentarii linguae Graecae," *Opera Omnia* [1557/1969], 4:704-5). Hesychius explains *diathēkēn* by *synōmosian* (*Hesychii Alexandrini Lexicon* [1858], 1:487), which is used only in the making of a covenant. The Septuagint interprets the word *bryth* by *diathēkēn* where no other signification than that of an agreement and covenant can hold good (1 S. 11:1; Gen. 31:44).

V. If the passages in the New Testament where the word *diathēkēs* occurs are carefully examined, they not only do not exclude the signification of a covenant (*synthēkēs*), but also often necessarily demand it. In Lk. 1:72 and Acts 3:25 mention is made of a *diathēkēs* made with the fathers in Abraham. From Gen. 17:10, 11, it cannot be denied to have had the relation of a covenant. Hence the covenant sealed by that sacrament is called "the covenant of circumcision" (*diathēkē peritomēs*, Acts 7:8). In Rom. 9:4, *diathēkai* are said to belong to the Jews, surely not testaments (which were not many), but covenants (which are often renewed). In Gal. 4:24, "these are the two *diathēkai*" ("covenants," to wit, the legal and evangelical). The proof that it does treat of these will be given hereafter. And as often as Christ is called the Mediator *diathēkēs* in Hebrews (chaps. 8 and 9) and his blood the blood *diathēkēs*, although the testamental relation is connoted, the federal relation (*schesis*) cannot and ought not to be excluded because there are properly no sureties of testaments; but between adverse parties a mediator is appointed to reconcile them and to unite them with each other by a covenant.

VI. It must indeed be acknowledged that the testamentary notion is principally urged here by the apostle (Heb. 9:15), that the necessity of the death and satisfaction of Christ (as the testator) may be more clearly set forth and the efficacy of grace (to which all things must be ascribed in the covenant of grace) more strongly demonstrated. But this is not to be understood exclusive of the federal relation which demands faith and obedience on man's part. Since this is clear of itself and is not denied by our brethren, the controversy waged concerning it appears useless and settles itself, if both relations (*schesis*) (the testamentary and federal) are attended to here; the former indeed as the principal and primary; and the latter as secondary and subservient to the former.

***Why called* foedus.**

VII. Among the Latins, the word *foedus* is referred to various sources. Some, as Festus, think it comes from *feriendo* because in making a covenant the victim was struck and slain, a like destruction being imprecated upon him who should first violate the covenant (*Sexti Pompei Festi De Verborum Significatione* [1975], p. 84). Livy explains the manner of this when he gives the formula of the covenant entered into between the king of the Roman people and the dictator of the Albans (*Livy* 1.24 [Loeb, 1:82-83]). Virgil says, "And each with each made covenant over the sacrifice of swine" (*Aeneid* 8.641 [Loeb, 2:102-3]). Others more fitly supposed it is so called from *fides* (as Isidore holds because in a covenant faith intervened, cf. *Etymologiarum* 8.2 [PL 82.296]). Hence Ennius, according to Varro, said *fidus* for *foedus* (*On the Latin Language* 5.86 [Loeb, 1:82-83]); as indeed a covenant is entered into for no other reason than that faith may exist between the parties.

Its different meanings.

VIII. Now there is not the same signification attached to God's covenant in the Scriptures. It denotes properly a pact and agreement entered into between God and man, consisting partly in a stipulation of duty (or of the thing to be done) and partly in the promise of a reward (which is the meaning in Gen. 17:2 where God is said to wish to make a covenant with Abraham). At one time it is taken improperly for a simple promise (as the promise not to destroy the world again by a flood is called a covenant, Gen. 9:9). At another time, it is taken metonymically for the symbols and sacraments of a covenant: as circumcision is called a covenant (Gen. 17); the eucharistic "cup" is said to be "the new testament in the blood of Christ" (Lk. 22:20), i.e., a sign and seal of it; then for "the tables of the covenant" laid up in the ark (1 K. 8:21); again for the "covenanted people," as the people of God are called "the holy covenant" (Dan. 11:28, 30); and for the Messiah, the foundation of that covenant, in whom it is made with us ("I will give thee for a covenant of the people," Is. 49:8). But we, dismissing the improper significations, attend here to the proper signification, when we dispute concerning the covenant.

IX. Now this covenant is called "the covenant of grace" both causally because it proceeds from grace strictly so called (such as had place towards the sinner, Lk. 1:54, 55, 72, 74; Eph. 1:6; Tit. 3:4) and materially because all things in this covenant are gratuitous and thus even the conditions (Jer. 31; Ezk. 36); and finally because by it God wished to manifest the riches of his grace (Eph. 2:7). It is also called "evangelical" because it is the object of evangelical doctrine (Rom. 1:16, 17); "new" not only because it succeeded the old covenant of works and because in a far more illustrious manner it was renewed in Christ under the New Testament, but also because it is eternal, immutable and never to be abrogated (Heb. 8; Jer. 31, 32).

Why the covenant is called a "promise."

X. Besides these words, the words *epangelias* and *euangeliou* also often occur to designate the covenant of grace. First, it is called *epangelia* (or "promise") indeed by way of eminence (*kat' exochēn*); not only because it is of God and not of men, but also because it is the most excellent of all, as being alone saving. Thus it is distinguished from the promise given to Abraham concerning his fleshly seed in Isaac (Rom. 9:9; Gal. 4:23) and concerning the inheritance of the land of Canaan (on that account called "the land of promise," Heb. 11:9) and from all the other earthly promises given to the Israelite people. Yea, it is even distinguished from the promise added to the law concerning the giving of life to the doer (which, the laws having been once violated, became void through the fault of man). It peculiarly denotes the gospel promise concerning the Messiah and the spiritual and eternal benefits to be bestowed by him. "For the promise that he should be the heir of the world, was not through the law" (Rom. 4:13, 14); and "if the inheritance be of the law, it is no more of promise" (Gal. 3:16-18) (to wit, the evangelical). Hence believers, to whom these benefits promised in Christ belong, are called "the sons of promise" (Rom. 9:8) and the Holy Spirit, who is given to us in virtue of that promise and who seals it in our hearts, is called "the Spirit of promise" (Eph. 1:13); yea, also "the promise of the Father" (Acts 1:4). Not only in the singular does the Scripture speak of the promise, but in the plural of "promises" (Gal. 3:16, 21), either to denote its excellency or because once made, it was frequently renewed to the fathers.

XI. Not without reason did the Holy Spirit wish to designate the covenant of grace under the name of "promise," because it rests entirely upon the divine promise. In this it wonderfully differs, not only from all human covenants (which consist of a mutual obligation and stipulation of the parties), but from the covenant of works (which although it also had its own promise on the part of God to the doers and so was founded on the goodness of God, still it required obedience on the part of man that it might be put into execution). But here God wished the whole of this covenant to depend upon his promise, not only with regard to the reward promised by him, but also with regard to the duty demanded from us. Thus God performs here not only his own part, but also ours; and if the covenant is given for the happiness of only the one party, it is guarded and fulfilled by the fidelity of only one party. Hence not only God's blessings fall under the promise, but also man's duty; not only the end, but also the means and conditions leading us to it (as will be shown in the proper place).

***Why called* evangelium.**

XII. Any "good and joyful tidings" whatsoever are called by the Greeks *euangelion* and by the Hebrews *khshrh twbhh*. Yet that is eminently (*kat' exochēn*) ascribed in Scripture to the news (the most pleasing of all) concerning the happy advent of Christ to the world, the covenant of grace made in him and the salvation obtained through him. It is not, however, used always with the same meaning. Sometimes it denotes (broadly and in general) the gratuitous covenant made in Christ. In this sense, Paul speaking of the ancient people, says, "They have not all obeyed the gospel" (Rom. 10:16); and it is said, "The gospel was preached to them that are dead" (1 Pet. 4:6). Sometimes it is put strictly and in particular either for the promise and the doctrine concerning Christ about to come (in which sense, Paul says, "The gospel was preached before unto Abraham when the promises were given to him," Gal. 3:8); or more properly for the doctrine of Christ manifested and the fulfillment of all the promises (in which sense it is everywhere used in the New Testament for the doctrine of the mission of Christ or the completed gospel and is oppo. d to the *epangelia*, which denotes simply the doctrine of the promise of Christ in the Old Testament). It is called the "promised gospel" (Rom 1:1, 2), although this distinction is not perpetual. For as the doctrine of the Old Testament is called "gospel" as well as that of the New Testament (as we have already said), so the doctrine of the New Testament is called no less *epangelia* or "the promise" than that (Gal. 3:14; 2 Tim. 1:1).

XIII. There are many other very emphatic synonymous words used to express this covenant, as "the oath" (Lk. 1:73) because God interposed his oath in this covenant to represent its immutability (which had not been done in the former covenant, Heb. 6:17; 7:21); "the sure mercies promised to David" (Is. 55:3) because founded upon the mere mercy and grace of God and upon no merit in man; "the law of faith" (Rom. 3:27) because in it faith is prescribed to us as a condition of the covenant; "quickening spirit and the ministration of righteousness" (2 Cor. 3:6, 9) because in it the righteousness of ages in Christ is promised to us for justification and the quickening Spirit of Christ for sanctification.

Question Two: The Nature of the Covenant of Grace

Who were the contracting parties; who is the mediator; what are the clauses of the covenant—both on God's part and on man's?

I. As God wished in every age to have a church in which he might dwell and which might cherish communion with him for the fruition of happiness, so it pleased him to institute that communion in no other way than that of a covenant in which there is a mutual approach of the contracting parties to each other and a close and familiar union (which proves on the part of God his wonderful condescension [*synkatabasin*], through which he was willing to let himself down from the incomprehensible splendor of his majesty to the most miserable state of his creatures; and on the part of man the extraordinary dignity to which the grace of God exalts them, that from the lowest depths of misery they should be admitted to the communion and glory of God blessed forever).

II. Although properly and strictly speaking, there can be no covenant between God and man because there is no room for a contract (which takes place between equals), nor any obligation of God, but a spontaneous communication of himself (as was proved in Part I, Topic VIII, Question 3), still God by singular grace willed to enter into a covenant with man, in the sense of what lawyers call a "quasi-contract."

III. He entered into a twofold covenant with men: first, a legal covenant (or one of works) with innocent man; another of faith and evangelical with fallen and sinful man. By the former, God promised eternal life to the man perfectly fulfilling the law and threatened the sinner with death according to the clauses, "do this and live" and "cursed is he who continueth not." By the latter, he promises to the believer safety in Christ and on account of Christ. The former was made with Adam before the fall and in him with all men (concerning which see Part I, Topic VIII, Question 3). The latter was entered into with the elect in Christ after the fall.

IV. That first covenant having been broken by the fall of man, God might (if he had wished to deal in strict justice with our first parents) immediately after their sin have delivered men over to death and no one could justly have expostulated with him on that account. But it did not please him to use that supreme justice towards the whole human race; rather moved with pity, he devised and instituted a remedy for such great misery by graciously sanctioning a new covenant in Christ, in which we have the method not only of escaping from that misery, but also of attaining unto most perfect happiness. This remedy (or method) justice demanded, wisdom found out and mercy and power procured in Jesus Christ, the only begotten Son of God, our Mediator, the foundation of that covenant.

What is the covenant of grace?

V. This covenant of grace is a gratuitous pact entered into in Christ between God offended and man offending. In it God promises remission of sins and salvation to man gratuitously on account of Christ; man, however, relying upon the same grace promises faith and obedience. Or it is a gratuitous agreement between God offended and man offending, concerning the bestowal of grace and glory in Christ upon the sinner upon condition of faith. In reference to this, two things must be attended to: (1) its nature; (2) its properties. To understand the nature, four things especially must be explained: (a) who is the author of the covenant; (b) who are the contracting parties; (c) who is the Mediator and what are his offices here; (d) what are the things covenanted or the clauses of the covenant, both on the part of God by the promise and on the part of man by the stipulation of duty.

***God, the author of the covenant, moved by his mere good pleasure* (eudokia).**

VI. (1) The author and principal efficient of this covenant is God, influenced to make it by his mere goodness and free good will (*eudokia*). Hence in Scripture it is everywhere called the "covenant of God" and never the covenant of man for he alone thought about it (man not only not thinking about it, but intent upon everything else, being at enmity with God in mind and in works). He alone had the power, as the supreme Lord and prince, of contracting with the creature and dispensing with that supreme right by which (according to the covenant of works) he could have punished the sinner himself without any hope of pardon. He alone could raise up fallen, lost man and save him by substituting a new covenant in the place of the former. However he is so its author that the glory is to be ascribed wholly to himself alone, nor did any impelling cause out of himself move him to institute it—neither the merit nor the misery of man. For if innocent man could merit nothing with God, how much less the guilty sinner? And if the misery of fallen angels did not impel God to save them, why should the misery of fallen men have the rather impelled him to their redemption? Therefore the good will (*eudokia*) alone of a God of mercy and his gratuitous love was the leading cause (*proēgoumenē*) of that covenant (which Zachariah calls in his song "tender mercy" [*splanchna eleous*, Lk. 1:78] and Paul "the exceeding riches of his grace" [*hyperballonta plouton charitos*], Eph. 2:7).

VII. As this work is eternal, it is common and undivided to the whole Trinity with this distinction, however—that each person has his own proper and peculiar mode of operation here, agreeable to this saving economy (1 Pet. 1:2). God, the Father, concurs in it because he first instituted this method of communicating himself and gave his Son in virtue of that constitution (Jn. 3:16). He invites to communion with him, first by the prophets, then by his Son, finally by his apostles and ministers and sends the Holy Spirit to apply the covenant (Gal. 4:6). God, the Son, both as the cause and foundation of the covenant through his own blood (Mt. 26:28; Eph. 1:3, 4) and as the matter of it (because promised in this covenant and the angel of the same, Mal. 3:1); or internuncio and executor and thus as Mediator between God and men (1 Tim. 2:5; Heb. 9:15) and the surety for men (Heb. 7:22). God, the Spirit, as the cause together with the Father and the Son, and the matter (because promised, Gal. 3:14) and the witness (Rom. 8:16) and the earnest of the heavenly inheritance (Eph. 1:14; 2 Cor. 1:22).

VIII. The instrumental causes are both the word and sacraments and the ministers of each. The word, not of the moral law (to wit, directly and of itself) because it is the ministration of death and the letter killing the sinner (2 Cor. 3:6), but of the gospel, which thence also takes its name because in it is revealed both the grace of God and the righteousness of Christ (Rom. 1:16, 17). The sacraments because on the part of God they are signs representing the substance of the covenant and seals, sealing the same (Rom. 4:11), and moral instruments by which it is applied to us. On our part, however, they are restipulations by which we bind ourselves to God (1 Pet. 3:21) and external marks or symbols of confederation. The ministers are as ambassadors and servants by whom God addresses us and invites us to the covenant (Mt. 23:3; Heb. 1:1) and as legates by whom he authoritatively stipulates with us (2 Cor. 5:20).

The contracting parties: God offended.

IX. The contracting parties or the subject of the covenant are three: God offended, man offending and Christ, the Mediator, reconciling offending man to God offended and angry. God acts here not as in the covenant of nature (inasmuch as he is Creator and Lord) because sin abolished that natural communion which joined the creature with the Creator; nor inasmuch as he holds a lofty and infinite preeminence (*hyperochēn*) over created things because man (guilty of sin and smitten with a feeling of it) could not have borne so great majesty, much less the angels who are compelled to cover their faces before it (Is. 6:2); nor as legislator and the rigid exactor of moral perfection from him because this could not be expected from a corrupt creature; nor can the sinner approach in any way a most just and holy God except as he is a merciful Father and Redeemer—as offended, indeed, but as to be appeased, who through his love of benevolence wished to reconcile offending men to himself (Rom. 5:8; Eph. 2:4).

Man offending.

X. Man is not viewed here simply as a creature or as an upright and just creature (as in the first covenant), but as an offending sinful creature; as man dead in sin, helpless, a child of wrath, alienated from God and his life; and indeed inasmuch as he is conscious of his own misery, smitten with a sense of it and so legally "heavy laden" (Mt. 11:28). Thus here the relation (*schesis*) of sinner is not simply to be considered, although it is the previous condition required in the object; otherwise this covenant should be extended to each and every sinner. That this cannot be said the thing itself cries out and the decree of reprobation sufficiently proves; but it must necessarily be joined with the relation (*schesei*) of the contrite sinner to believe in virtue of the free election of God.

The Mediator.

XI. Third, Christ, the Mediator, here comes in, reconciling offending man with his offended God. In the first covenant (because there was as yet no variance between God and man), there was also no need of a mediator; but in the latter, it was so necessary on account of the intervention of sin that without him no covenant could exist between God and man: God on account of his own justice not enduring guilty man and man on account of his unrighteousness being unable to approach God. In this the wonderful mercy of God towards man manifests itself, through which he not only willed to think of entering into a covenant, but even gave a Mediator (without whom it could not have been made). Now this Mediator ought to be God and man, partaking of both: man indeed, that he might suffer and die, because only by suffering and a bloody death could sin be expiated and the sinner restored to favor (Col. 1:20, 22; Heb. 2:14, 15); but God, that his death might have an infinite value, surpassing the measure of a creature, and that having overcome death he might live forever with his people and, standing between both, he might first do in nature what he was bound to effect afterwards in grace.

XII. And it seems superfluous to inquire here whether this covenant was made with Christ as one of the contracting parties and in him with all his seed (as the first covenant had been made with Adam and in Adam with his whole posterity—which pleases many because the promises are said to have been made to him [Gal. 3:16] and because, as the head and prince of his people, he holds the first place among all, so that nothing can be obtained except in him and from him); or whether the covenant was made in Christ with all the seed so that he does not so much hold the relation of a contracting party as of Mediator, who stands between those at variance for the purpose of reconciling them (as seems to others more appropriate). It is superfluous, I say, to dispute about this because it amounts to the same thing. It is certain that a twofold pact must be attended to here or the two parts and degrees of one and the same pact. The former is the agreement between the Father and the Son to carry out the work of redemption. The latter is that which God makes with the elect in Christ, to save them by and on account of Christ under the conditions of faith and repentance. The former was made with the surety and head for the salvation of the members; the latter was made with the members in the head and surety.

The pact between the Father and the Son is proved.

XIII. The pact between the Father and the Son contains the will of the Father giving his Son as a *lytrōtēn* (Redeemer and head of his mystical body) and the will of the Son offering himself as a sponsor for his members to work out that redemption (*apolytrōsin*). For thus the Scriptures represent to us the Father in the economy of salvation as stipulating the obedience of his Son even unto death, and for it promising in return a name above every name that he might be the head of the elect in glory; the Son as offering himself to do the Father's will, promising a faithful and constant performance of the duty required of him and restipulating the kingdom and glory promised to him. All these things are plainly gathered from the Scriptures.

XIV. Of this agreement express mention is made in Lk. 22:29: "I appoint unto you a kingdom, as my Father hath appointed unto me." In it the Father is set forth as calling the Son and committing the work of our salvation to him: "Behold my servant, whom I uphold; mine elect, in whom my soul delighteth" (Is. 42:1); "I the Lord have called thee in righteousness, and will hold thine hand, and will keep thee, and give thee for a covenant of the people, for a light of the Gentiles" (v. 6). "I give thee for a covenant of the people, that thou mayest be my salvation unto the end of the earth" (Is. 49:6, 8). This vocation is extended to the three parts of the mediatorial office: to the priesthood (Ps. 110:4); to prophecy (Is. 61:2); to the kingdom (Ps. 2:8). The law of the covenant is established by the Father that he should be a covenant of the people and a light of the Gentiles and lay down his life for the sheep: "This commandment have I received of my Father" (Jn. 10:18). A promise was added to that law by the Father, not only of perfection and help in the execution of duty (Is. 42:6, 7) and of a happy issue of his work by the approval of God (Is. 49:1-6, 8), but also of pay and a reward in spiritual seed and the exaltation granted to him: "When thou shalt make his soul an offering for sin, he shall see his seed, and the pleasure of the Lord shall prosper in his hand" (Is. 53:10). The acceptance on the part of the Son consists in this—that to this will of the Father and law of the covenant he voluntarily submitted himself by becoming surety for us: "A body hast thou prepared for me" (Heb. 10:5), i.e., thou hast devoted me as thy servant, giving me a body by incarnation. "Then said I, Lo, I come to do thy will, O God, it is a pleasure to me, and thy law is in my heart" (Heb. 10:7). Nor did the Son only take this upon himself, but also actually performed it, made of a woman, made under the law (Gal. 4:4). "I have kept my Father's commandments and abide in his love" (Jn. 15:10) and restipulates his own glory and the salvation of his body. "I have glorified thee on the earth: I have finished the work which thou gavest me to do. And now, O Father, glorify thou me with thine own self, with the glory which I had with thee before the world was" (Jn. 17:4, 5); "keep through thine own name, those whom thou hast given me. Sanctify them through thy truth: thy word is truth" (vv. 11*, 17).

Three periods of that covenant: (1) In destination.

XV. Now that covenant can be considered in three periods. (1) With regard to destination, when from eternity in the counsel of the most holy Trinity he was given as a sponsor and Mediator to the church. To this those words of the supreme Wisdom refer, who, speaking of herself, says, "I was anointed from everlasting" (Prov. 8:23), i.e., by my own and my Father's will (which is one), I was appointed to perform the office of Mediator in time. Note also the words of Peter when he says that "Christ was foreordained before the foundation of the world" (1 Pet. 1:20); also "I will declare the decree; the Lord hath said unto me, Thou art my Son; this day I have begotten thee. Ask of me, and I shall give thee the heathen for an inheritance" (Ps. 2:7*, 8). Here Christ describes the eternal destination (made in the decree of God) of himself, who is the eternally begotten Son of God and on that account alone capable of undertaking so great an office as King of the whole church.

2. In the promise.

(2) With respect to the promise, while immediately after the fall of man, God (being now offended on account of sin) offered himself for the actual performance of those things which he had promised from eternity; and thus was actually appointed Mediator and declared to be such in the word and according to that suretyship. He began to do many things pertaining to the office of Mediator, whether with regard to prophecy (acting as an interpreter of the divine will, both immediately by himself manifesting himself to the fathers as the angel of the covenant; or mediately by his ministers whom he influenced by his Spirit, 1 Pet. 1:10, 11; 3:19) or with regard to his kingdom (acting as the leader and chief of his people, 1 Cor. 10; Jos. 5:13) or with regard to the priesthood (interceding for his elect in virtue of his future ransom, Job 33:24).

3. In execution.

(3) With regard to the execution, in his incarnation by which he took upon himself our flesh that he might accomplish in it the work of our salvation. The writer of Hebrews refers to this when he institutes an antithesis between the legal sacrifices

and the alone most perfect sacrifice of Christ: "Wherefore when he cometh into the world, he saith, Sacrifice and offering thou wouldest not. Then said I, Lo, I come to do thy will" (10:5, 7*).

XVI. However, as the Mediator stood between the parties at variance, he ought to act with both: on the part of man with God, by the encouragement of all those things which were owed by men; and on the part of God with men, by a solemn promise that all things promised by God would most assuredly be fulfilled. With the offended God, he ought to act for men by making satisfaction for their sins and interceding for them with the Father to obtain the Spirit with his gifts; engaging, as to the past, a full payment of all debts and in fact paying that ransom (*lytron*) by his obedience and death; and as to the future, a sincere and constant keeping of the covenant afterwards, perfecting virtue in them by his Spirit. With offending men, however, on the part of God, as the legate of the Father by declaring his good will concerning their salvation, signifying his mission to the work of redemption, demanding faith in the promises and obedience to his commands as the duties and conditions of the covenant (and in turn promising all the benefits of the covenant), engaging for the absolutely certain bestowal of all those things not only by the word of the gospel and the sacraments, but especially by the pouring out of his own blood, by which he sealed this new covenant before God and by the efficacy of the Holy Spirit, by which he ratified it in us. Thus a twofold obstacle to a covenant had to be removed. On the part of God, his enmity on account of man's sin and on the part of man, his enmity on account of the righteousness of God; God was to be reconciled to man and man to God. Christ effected the former by the merit of his blood, by which he satisfied for us and reconciled God to us; the latter by the efficacy of the Spirit, by which he sanctifies and converts us and by converting, reconciles us to God. And thus he perfectly fulfilled what had to be done either on God's part with us or on man's part with God, unto a full consummation of the covenant of grace.

The things covenanted: on the part of God that he would be our God.

XVII. The things covenanted are either on God's part or man's. On God's part, the promised blessings; on the part of men, the duties prescribed to them. Both are set forth in general or in particular. In general, they are contained in the formula of the covenant in which God promises to be our God and demands that we should be his people. They are expressed indeed in the fewest but weightiest words, embracing whatever is promised by God to man or demanded from man (as will clearly appear from a little more distinct consideration of that formula); as much with regard to the promise of blessing and the testimony of love as with regard to the exaction of worship and duty—two things included here. With regard to the promise, it is such and so great that it is deservedly called the soul and substance of the covenant, the foundation and compendium of all the other promises given to believers in the Scriptures; than which there is nothing higher, fuller, sweeter or more firm. On this account, it is proposed not only once or twice, but most frequently as often as the covenant was either instituted at first or renewed under the Old as well as under the New Testament. It was made at first with Abraham ("I will be a God unto thee, and to thy seed after thee," Gen. 17:7, 8); confirmed to the people of Israel (Ex. 20:2; 29:45; Dt. 5:2, 3, 6); repeated to the Jews in the Babylonian captivity (Jer. 24:7; 30:22; Ezk. 11:20);

reiterated after the captivity (Zech. 13:9); renewed under the New Testament from the prophecy of Jer. 31:33 (cf. 2 Cor. 6:16; Heb. 8:10); which is also to be fulfilled in celestial glory ("Behold the tabernacle of God is with men, and he will dwell with them, and they shall be his people, and God himself shall be with them, and be their God," Rev. 21:3). And thus it is the greatest of all the blessings of God to believers in grace as well as in glory. Hence not undeservedly does the psalmist say, "Blessed is the nation whose God is the Lord" (Ps. 33:12).

What is implied in the promise that God shall be our God.

XVIII. But that the genuine sense of this may be understood, it is not to be taken broadly inasmuch as it signifies the authority, care and dominion of God. For thus he is the God not only of believers, but also of men in general; yea, even of all creatures in respect to creation and government and nothing singular and extraordinary would be promised to his people above other nations. Rather it is to be taken strictly inasmuch as it implies a federal relation and that gracious communion by which God communicates himself to the sinner to bestow upon him immortal life and happiness (as that formula is wont to be explained everywhere). So if he is the God of all providence, he is the God of believers by grace; if the God of creatures in the world by authority and power, he is the God of his people in the church by benevolence and love and by the blessings he bestows upon them.

All saving benefits are included here, but four principally.

XIX. Now although these are innumerable, still they can be referred to these four principal ones. (1) Reconciliation and communion with God by which he is not only at peace with us, but also gives himself to us that ever after he may be ours as much essentially (*ousiōdōs*) (as to his nature and attributes) as hypostatically (*hypostatikōs*) (as to the persons and personal operations). (2) Communion of goods, that all the good things of God and whatever pertain to him may be ours. (3) Conformity to God by a participation of the divine nature and transformation into his image. (4) The constancy and eternity of the love of God and of our union with him. Since these are of great importance in this argument, they ought to be explained a little more fully.

1. Reconciliation and union with God that he may be our God in nature and attributes.

XX. I say that we ought first to mark reconciliation and communion with God because he cannot be called ours except as appeased; and from an angry judge is made a merciful Father who not only deigns liberally to bestow his goods upon us, but gives himself to us that we may be able afterwards to glory in him as our God and portion (Ps. 16:5; 73:26; 119:57; Hos. 2:23). He gives himself to us as a husband who betrothed us unto himself in eternal mercies (Hos. 2:19; Cant. 2:16); as a father who adopts us into his family (2 Cor. 6:18); as a ruler and king who selects us for his chosen (*periousion*) people, with whom he makes an offensive and defensive covenant that he may protect us with his shield against the assaults of all our enemies. God so gives himself to us as to be ours as to all the attributes (conducing to our advantage and salvation). They are well said to be ours by fruition and use because their salutary effects flow unto us. Ours is the wisdom of God for direction; the power of God for protection; the mercy of God for the remission of sins; the grace of God for sanctification and consolation; the justice of God for the punishment of enemies; the faithfulness of God for the execution of promises; the sufficiency of God for the communication of all manner of happiness. And as sin brought innumerable evils upon us, we find a remedy for all in the divine properties: wisdom heals our ignorance and blindness, grace our guilt, power our weakness, mercy our misery, goodness our wickedness, justice our iniquity, the sufficiency and fulness of God our poverty and indigence, fidelity our inconstancy and fickleness, holiness our impurity and life our death.

In the persons.

XXI. God is ours personally, inasmuch as the individual persons are ours and give themselves to us for accomplishing the work of redemption: the Father electing, the Son redeeming, the Holy Spirit sanctifying. He becomes our Father by adoption when he receives us into his own family and regards, cherishes and loves us as sons (1 Jn. 3:1). The Son becomes ours by suretyship when he offers himself as the surety to make satisfaction for us and as the head, to rule over and quicken us. He becomes ours as a Prophet, revealing salvation by the light of his doctrine; our Priest, who purchases it by his merit; and our King, who applies it (when acquired) by the efficacy of the Spirit. The Holy Spirit becomes ours when he is sent to us and gives himself to us as a sanctifier and consoler that he may dwell in us as his temples and enrich us with his blessings, light, strength, joy, liberty, holiness and happiness. Thus our communion is with the Father and the Son and the Holy Spirit (1 Jn. 1:3; 2 Cor. 13:14). Hence baptism, which is a seal of the covenant, is administered in their name so that we may be consecrated as sons of God, the Father, as members of the Son and as temples of the Holy Spirit and enjoy the blessings flowing from each person—the mercy of the Father, the grace of the Son and the power of the Holy Spirit.

2. The communication of goods.

XXII. (2) God is ours by reason of the communication of goods. He cannot be our God without all things belonging to him becoming ours; and as all things belong to God, ours also are all things in heaven and on earth: "All things are yours," says Paul, "and ye are Christ's; and Christ is God's" (1 Cor. 3:21, 23*). Ours are God's creatures on the earth to serve us; the angels in heaven to guard us (heaven as our native land); the earth as a place of pilgrimage, the world as an inheritance given to us with Abraham (Rom. 4:13). Thus all God's promises are ours—of the present life as well as of the future; and the goods of God are ours—of grace as well as of glory: "The Lord God is a sun and shield: the Lord will give grace and glory: no good thing will he withhold from them that walk uprightly" (Ps. 84:11). A sun of all manner of blessing for the communication of good things; a shield of invincible protection for the repelling of evils, so that we may rightly infer with Paul that nothing can hurt us because God is for us ("If God is for us, who can be against us?" Rom. 8:31); and with David that we shall want nothing because God is our shepherd ("The Lord is my shepherd; I shall not want," Ps. 23:1)—because he denies nothing to those who fear him, but grants all things liberally and blesses us with all spiritual blessings (Eph. 1:3). "Christ is all in all" in grace (Col. 3:11); "God will be all in all" in glory (1 Cor. 15:28); "He that overcometh shall inherit all things; and I will be his God, and he shall be my son" (Rev. 21:7).

3. Conformity to God.

XXIII. (3) God is ours in respect of conformity. Since he is not satisfied with pouring out upon us the salutary effects of his properties, but wishes further to impress upon us their mark and likeness (as far as a finite creature can bear it) that we may be "partakers of the divine nature" (2 Pet. 1:4) and be like to it (which is the most perfect mode of communion). As the sun sending its rays into a crystal or any diaphanous body makes it lucent, so as to shine like the sun, thus the Father of lights irradiates us with his light, not only to scatter the darkness of error, vice and misery, but also to communicate his light to us and make us shine like so many suns. Hence it is said "the righteous shall shine forth as the sun in the kingdom of their Father" (Mt. 13:43). The words of Paul refer to this when he says that "we, with open face beholding as in a glass" of the gospel "the glory of the Lord, are changed into the same image from glory to glory" (2 Cor. 3:18); and "we shall be like him; for we shall see him as he is" (1 Jn. 3:2), i.e., no communion can be held with God except on the basis of conformity to him. The latter is twofold, both in holiness and moral virtues (that we should be holy, just, patient, merciful and perfect as God is, Mt. 5:48; 1 Pet. 1:15); and in life and happiness (that we may enjoy his immortality and glory—"because I live, ye shall live also," Jn. 14:19); "Thou art the same, and thy years shall have no end. The children of thy servants shall continue, and their seed shall be established before thee" (Ps. 102:27, 28). The invincible argument of Christ belongs here when he demonstrated from the formula of the covenant the immortality of the soul and the resurrection of the body against the Sadducees because he is called "the God of Abraham, Isaac and Jacob" (Mt. 22:32*), even after their death. "God however, is not the God of the dead, but of the living." Two things are necessarily supposed here: first, that this formula of the covenant implies a communication of life and immortality, so that as many as are received into communion of it should be made like to him in this particular—God living forever cannot hold communion with the dead. Hence it was necessary that the patriarchs should always live in some part of themselves, since God calls himself their God even after their death. Second, the covenant was not made with only one part of man, but with the whole man so that the benefits of the covenant ought to pertain to the whole man. Hence follows the necessity of the resurrection of the body, that believers may become partakers in soul and body of life and happiness.

4. Eternity of good things.

XXIV. Now because these good things (although excellent) could not make us perfectly happy (unless perpetuity was added to them), by this very promise God wished to commend the constancy of his love and the eternity of the blessings. Since Jehovah bespeaks eternity in its own conception when he promises to be our God, by that very thing he intimates that he will be ours forever. So that as long as God will be God (and he will be so forever), he will also be our God that we may forever enjoy his communion and happiness. The psalmist declares, "This God is our God for ever and ever" (Ps. 48:14). This is undoubtedly the strongest argument for the consolation and confidence of believers against all temptations and an inviolable support of faith. If God will be ours forever, what further can we fear of evil or expect of good since we shall be conquerors in him forever?

XXV. Moreover, in addition to that general promise contained in the formula of the covenant, many other special promises founded upon and flowing from it are included: such as the bestowal of the Holy Spirit (Ezk. 36:27); the remission of sins (Jer. 31:34); regeneration, designated by the inscription of the law (Jer. 31:33); adoption (2 Cor. 6:18); the taking away of a stony heart and the giving of a new and fleshly heart (Ezk. 36:26); perseverance (Jer. 32:40), the peculiar blessing of this covenant because it ought to be inviolable and eternal; all the spiritual blessings of grace and glory (Gen. 12:3; Gal. 3:8, 9, 14; Acts 3:26; Eph. 1:3). All these are usually designated by the word "salvation," which implies not only the possession of life (which had a place in the first covenant), but also deliverance from death (which had been introduced by sin). This is carried out in four parts, opposed to the same parts of death to which we had become liable by sin: (1) justification, which frees us from the impending curse; (2) sanctification, taking away the defilement and corruption in which we lay dead; (3) consolation and peace of conscience, sustaining us against the afflictions of life and the terrors of conscience (which in Scripture come under the term death); (4) eternal glorification, delivering us safe from eternal death and bringing us to complete happiness.

The duties required of man in the covenant.

XXVI. As that formula of the covenant is mutual with the blessings promised by God to the covenanted (including also the duties required of man), we must see now what these are. They are set forth in the Scriptures in general and in particular: in general, when God wishes that inasmuch as he promises to be our God, we in turn should be his people—"I will be their God, and they shall be my people" (Jer. 31:33). Here the relation between God and us is designated, implying a mutual exchange of benefits and duties, so that if God is our husband, we should be his chaste and faithful spouse; if he is our Father, we should be sons; if a King and Redeemer, we should be his peculiar people who live as the ransomed of the Lord. However as all God's blessings towards us are comprehended in this one promise alone, so all man's duties towards God are prescribed in this single condition (which indicates together and at once both what they ought to be and what they are bound to do).

What it is to be the people of God: the duties—separation from the world and consecration to God.

XXVII. To be the people of God is not only to be subjected to his dominion and to depend upon and be governed by him (for thus all men universally are his people), but to cleave to him in worship and obedience, so as to be nothing, to have nothing, to be capable of and do nothing which is not of God, i.e., which may be referred to his glory. Thus is designated first, separation from the world and consecration to God—that inasmuch as we are not our own masters, but belong to him who created and redeemed us and gave himself for us, so we should no more live to ourselves, to Satan, to sin and the world, but to him alone. As from him we are what we are, so to him should be referred what we are and are capable of. As God chose us while other men were left, to make a covenant with us and take us to himself for a people, so we (all others being dismissed) are bound to select him alone as our God, to worship and follow him alone (which the Holy Spirit so often urges: Dt. 7:6, 7; 26:17, 18; 1 Cor. 6:19, 20; 2 Cor. 5:14, 15; 6:17, 18; Rom. 14:7-9). Now this consecration ought to be such that we should dedicate ourselves both in body and soul to God as temples and spiritual sacrifices (Rom. 12:1; 1 Cor. 3:16, 17), so that our minds should be God's (to know him), our wills to worship him, our affections to love him, our eyes to contemplate his wonders, our ears to hear his voice, our mouths to celebrate his glory, our hands to do his work and all our members to be instruments of righteousness unto God for his glory (Rom. 6:13). Thus whatever we have either good or honorable or wise or virtuous ought to be devoted to the glory and worship of God.

Worship and obedience.

XXVIII. (2) Worship and obedience that we should be anxious in worshipping him religiously and alone, so as to do zealously whatever we can either to advance his kingdom or promulgate his truth or defend his good cause or fulfill his commands, that thus we may respond to his call and manifest our gratitude for his benefits. For these things are mutually connected with so indissoluble a bond that they neither can nor ought to be separated. In vain do we hope that God will be our God, unless in turn we are his people and bear witness to the love of the Father, unless we give the obedience of children to him. In vain do we hope that he will bestow the promised blessings, unless we perform the duties required of us.

In faith and repentance.

XXIX. Now these are the two principal duties demanded—faith and repentance. The former embraces the promises; the latter fulfills the commands; the one answers to the promise of grace—"Believe and thou shalt be saved"; the other is commanded by the evangelical law—"Walk before me, and be thou perfect" (Gen. 17:1). For as there are two special benefits of the covenant on God's part (the remission of sins and the writing of the law upon the heart), so on the part of man two duties ought to answer to them—faith, which applies the pardon of sins to itself; and repentance (or the desire of sanctification), which reduces the law written upon the heart to practice by walking in its statutes (which Christ intimates, "Repent ye, and believe the gospel," Mk. 1:15).

XXX. Although these two duties are commanded by God as works due from man, still they are also promised by him as his gifts. Thus they are here to be considered at the same time both as the duties of man and as the blessings of God: "I will put my spirit within you, and cause you to walk in my statutes" (Ezk. 36:27). It is the singular privilege of this covenant above the covenant of nature that the conditions themselves depend upon the grace of God and pass over into promises. This is the reason why it cannot be made void as the first covenant (which was founded upon man's strength), but remains efficacious and eternal. It depends entirely upon God and all things in the covenant are gratuitous (as also the very conditions). What these conditions are and what relation they bear, the following question will teach.

Third Question

Is the covenant of grace conditional and what are its conditions?

Occasion of the question.

I. This question was occasioned in a former age by the controversy about justification against the papists and was agitated among the evangelicals themselves, some of whom denied that the promises of the gospel (or of the covenant of grace) are conditional, while others affirmed that they are; those holding the former position that the law might not be confounded with the gospel and the promises of each; those holding the latter, however, that the necessity of faith and holiness might not be impaired and libertinism introduced. But it is easy to reconcile these views by laying down some distinctions.

Statement of the question.

II. (1) Condition is used either antecedently and *a priori*, for that which has the force of a meritorious and impulsive cause to obtain the benefits of the covenant (the performance of which gives man a right to the reward); or concomitantly and consequently *a posteriori*, for that which has the relation of means and disposition in the subject, required in the covenanted. (2) A condition is either natural, flowing from the strength belonging to nature; or supernatural and divine, depending upon grace. (3) The federal promise is twofold: either concerning the end or the means, i.e., either concerning salvation or concerning faith and repentance (because each is the gift of God). (4) The covenant can be considered either in relation to its institution by God or in relation to its first application to the believer or in relation to its perfect consummation.

III. These things being laid down, we say first, if the condition is taken antecedently and *a priori* for the meritorious and impulsive cause and for a natural condition, the covenant of grace is rightly denied to be conditioned. It is wholly gratuitous, depending upon the sole good will (*eudokia*) of God and upon no merit of man. Nor can the right to life be founded upon any action of ours, but on the righteousness of Christ alone. But if it is taken consequently and *a posteriori* for the instrumental cause, receptive of the promises of the covenant and for the disposition of the subject, admitted into the fellowship of the covenant (which flows from grace itself), it cannot be denied that the covenant is conditional. (a) It is proposed with an express condition (Jn. 3:16, 36; Rom. 10:9; Acts 8:37; Mk. 16:16 and frequently elsewhere). (b) Unless it was conditional, there would be no place for threatenings in the gospel (which could not be denounced except against those who had neglected the prescribed condition)—for the neglect of faith and obedience cannot be culpable, if not required. (c) Otherwise it would follow that God is bound in this covenant to man and not man to God (which is perfectly absurd and contrary to the nature of all covenants, in which there always is a mutual agreement and a reciprocal obligation because the contracting parties are bound on both sides—as between a husband and wife, a king and his subjects, etc.).

IV. Second, if the promises of the covenant are understood concerning the end, no one can deny that they are conditional because they are always made under the condition of faith and repentance. But if they are taken for the promises concerning the means (to wit, concerning faith and regeneration or repentance), they certainly cannot be conditional, but are simple and absolute because otherwise there would be granted a progression into infinity and the condition of the condition would always be demanded (which is absurd).

V. Third, if the covenant be viewed in relation to the first sanction in Christ, it has no previous condition, but rests upon the grace of God and the merit of Christ alone. But if it is considered in relation to its acceptance and application to the believer, it has faith as a condition (uniting man to Christ and so bringing him into the fellowship of the covenant). If, however, in relation to its consummation with faith (obedience and the desire of holiness), it has the relation of condition and means because without them no one shall see God.

Source of explanation.

VI. Although the covenant of grace be conditional, the promises of the law and the gospel are not therefore to be confounded. There always remains a manifold difference: (1) in the matter, because the legal condition is an entire and perfect obedience to the law (Rom. 10:5), but the evangelical is faith (Rom. 10:9; Jn. 3:16)—not perfect and free from all blemish, but living and sincere (1 Tim. 1:5; Jam. 2:14); (2) in origin, because the legal condition should be natural, flowing from the strength belonging to nature, but the evangelical is supernatural, depending upon grace. The former is only commanded, but not given or promised; but the latter is both commanded and promised and also given (Jer. 31:33; Jn. 6:45; Eph. 2:8). (3) In the end, the legal condition has the relation of a meritorious cause (at least congruously and improperly) of the promised thing (namely, of life)—"Do this and live." Thus life is granted to him because he has done and on account of his own obedience; but the evangelical condition cannot properly be called the cause of salvation, much less merit, because it is the pure gift (*charisma*) of God (Rom. 6:23). It may only be called an instrument by which the thing promised is apprehended (Acts 26:18; Rom. 5:17) and without which it cannot be obtained (Heb. 11:6).

VII. If the covenant of grace was said to depend upon an unstable human condition, its efficacy and immutability would be overthrown. But because the condition is supernatural and divine (produced by the efficacy of omnipotent grace), so far is it from being weakened by it that on the contrary it is more and more strengthened. According to Paul, "It is of faith, that it might be by grace; to the end the promise might be sure to all the seed" (Rom. 4:16). The covenant does not rest upon a condition in us, but upon the mere grace of God and his inviolable faithfulness and the infinite merit of Christ.

VIII. When Christ answers the young man inquiring what he must do to inherit eternal life ("Keep the commandments," Mt. 19:17), he does not mean to teach that the same obedience is demanded in the same manner in both covenants. In his answer to the man, he did not act as an interpreter of the covenant of grace, but of the Mosaic Law, that he might convict this boastful legalist (wishing to be saved by the law) of his own inability and thus bring him to the Mediator.

IX. Although the covenant of grace is set forth under the notion of a testament (which is suspended upon no condition, in respect to which all the duties of man which have the relation [*schesin*] of conditions are blessings of God, falling under his promises), still this is no reason why it should not also have a federal relation, according to which it is called "a covenant by a testament" (as was said before), and contain conditions on the part of man.

2. Question: What are the conditions in the covenant of grace?

X. Second, here arises the question—What are the conditions in this covenant and under what relation (*schesei*)? Is faith alone to be called the condition of the covenant of grace; or, with it, repentance and the obedience of a new life? And as to faith indeed, the question is not whether it is a condition of this covenant (Scripture so clearly asserting this, Jn. 3:16; Rom. 1:16, 17; 10:9), but (a) What relation does it here hold? (b) Does it alone perform this office?

How faith is a condition.

XI. As to the former when we say that faith is a condition of the covenant, we do not mean it absolutely and according to its nature and essence. It is contained under obedience as being commanded by the law (just as the other virtues) and so it cannot be contradistinguished from it. Hence it cannot be accepted for righteousness or the obedience of the law because such a judgment would not be in accordance with the truth (since faith is only the smallest part of that righteousness). Rather it must be considered relatively and instrumentally, inasmuch as it embraces Christ and applies to him for righteousness and through him obtains the right to eternal life. First, it is distinguished from the works of the law (which could not be done if it were taken absolutely because thus it is a work of the law). Second, faith (taken instrumentally) can consist only (a) with the grace of God (for which nothing but a reception is required, which is the proper action of faith, Rom. 5:17; Jn. 1:12); hence Paul says, "It is of faith that it might be by grace"; for all the other virtues seem to give something to God, but this alone is purely receptive—"for by grace are ye saved through faith" (Eph. 2:8); boasting is excluded by the law of faith (Rom. 3:27). (b) Faith can consist only with the condition of sinful man because in the first moment of justification there is nothing in him except faith which can please God. (c) Faith can consist only with the satisfaction and righteousness of the Mediator because he applies that to himself. (d) Faith can consist only with eternal life as the gift and inheritance of God because faith apprehends this in the gospel (Rom. 3:24, 25; 1 Cor. 1:30; Eph. 1:3, 4; 2:8). (e) Faith can consist only with the promises of the gospel, which sets life before man, not as to be acquired (like the law), but as already purchased. Third, Christ is our righteousness (1 Cor. 1:30; 2 Cor. 5:21), in whom we have redemption and life. Therefore it cannot be ascribed to faith materially (inasmuch as it is a work), but instrumentally (inasmuch as it is the hand apprehending).

XII. Now in this covenant faith is opposed to righteousness or obedience, not on this account that they cannot subsist together (since it alone is true faith which is efficacious through love or obedience), but that they cannot stand together causally (since the causality of each is distinguished in its total species—the one meritorious and principal, the other only organic and instrumental). Righteousness gives, faith receives; righteousness consists in the mutual love of God, faith in a persuasion of God's love. Hence what is taken away from the one is ascribed to the other, not by reason of the same causality, but by reason of the effect because faith in the covenant of grace is to us in the place of works, i.e., obtains for us (although in a different genus of cause) what works ought to have done in the covenant of nature.

XIII. That it may be known further how faith has the relation of a condition in this covenant, we must know that faith does not bear this relation except in reference to Christ (inasmuch as it is the means and instrument of our union with Christ which reconciles him to us: "I ascend to my Father and your Father; to my God and your God," Jn. 20:17). Thus we cannot be received into God's covenant except we are united to Christ, who is the foundation of the covenant and the bond of our union with God. However, because it is of great importance for us to know whether our faith is truly a faith of union, this can be perceived not so much *a priori* as *a posteriori* (from its operations). If it excites in us a fervent love of Christ (Cant. 5:10, 16; Phil. 3:8; Jn. 1:14; 21:15); a burning desire to enjoy him (Pss. 42:1; 84:1, 2; Phil. 1:23); a separation from all things earthly and carnal hindering our union to Christ, such as "the love of sin and of the world" (Hos. 4:8; Rom. 6:2; Mt. 10:37; 1 Jn. 2:15, 16; Jam. 4:4). Hence the gospel merchant sells all things for that most precious union (Mt. 13:46); Moses prefers the reproach of Christ to the treasures and honors of Egypt (Heb. 11:25, 26); the disciples leave all things to follow Christ (Mt. 19:27). It produces a presumption of one's [un]righteousness because "they that be whole need not a physician, but they that are sick; and Christ came not to call the righteous, but sinners to repentance" (Mt. 9:12, 13); unbelief, impenitency, other sins of this kind and works of the flesh are incompatible (*asystata*) with Christ (Rom. 8:1, 10). Especially if it produces two acts following together with that union immediately and necessarily. Hence, on the part of Christ, a sense of his love through the consolation of the Holy Spirit, who, by sealing adoption in our hearts, persuades us that we are the sons of God, heirs of God and fellow-heirs with Christ; that Christ dwells in us and has become ours (Rom. 8:15, 16; 1 Jn. 3:24). On our part, the mutual consent of our love through a desire of sanctification by which as Christ loves us, we in turn love him; as he gives himself for us, we give ourselves entirely to him, so that we no longer live to ourselves, but in the faith of the Son of God who loved us and gave himself for us (Gal. 2:20; 2 Cor. 5:15). The spouse pathetically describes this, "My beloved is mine, and I am his" (Cant. 2:16).

XIV. In order that this consent may be true, it ought not to be a consent concerning the future (such as that of those who put off their conversion from day to day), but concerning the present, so that if today we hear the voice of Christ, we harden not our hearts, but receive the offered grace; not distinguishing between Christ as Redeemer and Lord, as surety and head, between the blessings and duties (as is done by those who willingly embrace the merit of Christ, but are unwilling to be in subjection to his dominion; are willing to enjoy the blessings, but not to be bound to the duties), but joining the whole Christ with his duties and benefits and receiving him not only as a surety, but also as a head; not only for righteousness, but also for sanctification; for a Savior to redeem, but also for a Lord to govern (and whom we are bound to obey in all things); not exceptive and conditional (such as theirs who consent to Christ and his gospel, but when the cross and persecution come recede and are scandalized), but total and absolute, so that without any limitation we follow Christ in every condition (not only triumphant and glorious in heaven, but also suffering and nailed to the cross on earth) wherever he may lead us, prepared both to live and to die with him. Thus our communion with Christ will be true and saving and with all the blessings of Christ: fellowship in the same Spirit (Rom. 8:9; 1 Cor. 6*:17); "in the same life" (Gal. 2:20); "in the same righteousness" (2 Cor. 5:21; Jer. 23:6); "in the same glory and inheritance" (Jn. 17:21, 24; Rom. 6:8; 8:17). And as we receive the good things of Christ in communion with him, so in turn Christ expects from us love (Jn. 21:17; 1 Pet. 1:8) and subjection (Eph. 5:24; Mt. 11:29; Ps. 2:11; 110:3)—sincere, full and constant.

XV. Thus we have demonstrated how faith is a condition in this covenant. Now we must see whether it performs this office alone or whether other virtues are with it, particularly repentance. Concerning this, the orthodox dispute among themselves—some denying and others affirming. We think the matter may be readily settled by a distinction, if we bear in mind the different senses of a condition. It may be taken either broadly and improperly (for all that man is bound to afford in the covenant of grace) or strictly and properly (for that which has some causality in reference to life and on which not only antecedently, but also causally, eternal life in its own manner depends). If in the latter sense, faith is the sole condition of the covenant because under this condition alone pardon of sins and salvation as well as eternal life are promised (Jn. 3:16, 36; Rom. 10:9). There is no other which could perform that office because there is no other which is receptive of Christ and capable of applying his righteousness. But in the former, there is nothing to hinder repentance and the obedience of the new life from being called a condition because they are reckoned among the duties of the covenant (Jn. 13:17; 2 Cor. 5:17; Rom. 8:13).

XVI. Second, the condition is either antecedent to the acceptance of the covenant (which holds the relation of the cause why we are received into it) or subsequent (holding relation of means and the way by which we go forward to its consummation). In the former sense, faith is the sole condition of the covenant because it alone embraces Christ with his benefits. But in the latter sense, holiness and obedience can have the relation of a condition because they are the mean and the way by which we arrive at the full possession of the blessings of the covenant. If they do not have causality either with respect to justification (or eternal life flowing from it), still in other respects they pertain to this covenant both as inseparable attendants of true and sincere faith because "faith ought to be effectual through love" (Gal. 5:6), as the qualities of those to be saved (Mt. 5:8; 25:35, 36; Heb. 12:14), as fruits of the Spirit in Christ (Rom. 8:2, 9, 10) and marks of our conformity with Christ (Rom. 6:4, 5; Col. 3:1; Eph. 2:4, 5), as proofs of our gratitude towards God (Tit. 2:14), as testimonies of our sonship (1 Jn. 3:3; Rom. 8:15) and as duties which the rational creature owes to God (Lk. 17:10).

XVII. There is not the same relation of justification and of the covenant through all things. To the former, faith alone concurs, but to the observance of the latter other virtues also are required besides faith. These conduce not only to the acceptance of the covenant, but also to its observance. For these two things ought always to be connected—the acceptance of the covenant and the keeping of it when accepted. Faith accepts by a reception of the promises; obedience keeps by a fulfillment of the commands. "Be ye holy, for I am holy." And yet in this way legal and evangelical obedience are not confounded because the legal is prescribed for the meriting of life, the evangelical, however, only for the possession of it. The former precedes as the cause of life ("Do this and thou shalt live"); the latter follows as its fruit, not that you may live but because you live. The former is not admitted unless it is perfect and absolute; the latter is admitted even if imperfect, provided it be sincere. That is only commanded as man's duty; this is also promised and given as the gift of God.

FOURTH QUESTION

How do the covenants of works and of grace agree with and differ from each other?

The covenants of works and of grace agree.

I. The covenants of works and of grace agree in various particulars: (1) in their author, who in each case is God, to whom alone belongs the right of making a covenant with the creature; (2) in the contracting parties, God and man; (3) in the general end, the glory of God; (4) in the extrinsic form, because a restipulation is annexed to each; (5) in the promise, which is life and happiness, heavenly and eternal.

And differ: (1) in the author.

II. But they differ in many more particulars. (1) As to the author, for although God is the author of both covenants, still he must be viewed in different relations (*schesei*): in the first as Creator and Lord, in the second as Redeemer and Father; in the first, he was impelled by love and benevolence towards an innocent creature; in the latter, by special mercy and grace towards a miserable creature.

2. In the contracting parties.

III. (2) As to the contracting parties between whom the covenant was made. For in the first, they were only two (God and man), nor was there any need of a mediator because as yet they were not at variance with each other. In the other (entered into after the fall), a mediator was necessarily required to make peace and reconcile men to God and God to men. On this account, that is called the "covenant of friendship" and this the "covenant of reconciliation" (which supposes a preceding disagreement which ought to be settled).

3. In the foundation.

IV. (3) As to the foundation, the former rested upon man's own obedience and the strength of nature or free will, since man was placed in the hand of his own counsel. But the latter is built upon Christ and his obedience. Hence he is called a "covenant of the people" (Is. 49:8). Nor is man any longer in the hand of his own counsel (placed in which he immediately fell), but in the hand of God, by whose power he is most effectually guarded forever (1 Pet. 1:5).

4. In the promise.

V. (4) As to the promise, not in this—that the former promised only perpetual happiness (but to be enjoyed in paradise) as some hold, not sufficiently considering the nature of that covenant, for heavenly happiness and life was promised no less in the first than in the second covenant (as has been proved in Volume I, Topic VIII, Question 6). Rather the difference consisted in this—that in the first only life was promised, i.e., a state perfected by an accumulation of all blessings; but in this, salvation was promised which (together with life) brings a deliverance from sin and death. The first promised life as a due reward (Rom. 4:4); the other as the gift of God (Rom. 6:23).

5. In the condition.

VI. (5) As to the prescribed condition—in the former, works ("do this and live"); in the latter, faith ("believe and thou shalt be saved"). The former consisted in man's giving a perfect righteousness; the latter in his receiving the infinite righteousness of God. The one was carried out in the court of justice, in which either a sentence of acquittal was pronounced upon the just or a sentence of condemnation upon the sinner (because there was no hope of pardon); the other in the court of mercy, where a sentence of absolution is pronounced upon sinners (but believing and penitent).

VII. Nor can it be objected here that faith was required also in the first covenant and works are not excluded in the second (as was said before). They stand in a far different relation. For in the first covenant, faith was required as a work and a part of the inherent righteousness to which life was promised. But in the second, it is demanded—not as a work on account of which life is given, but as a mere instrument apprehending the righteousness of Christ (on account of which alone salvation is granted to us). In the one, faith was a theological virtue from the strength of nature, terminating on God, the Creator; in the other, faith is an evangelical condition after the manner of supernatural grace, terminating on God, the Redeemer. As to works, they were required in the first as an antecedent condition by way of a cause for acquiring life; but in the second, they are only the subsequent condition as the fruit and effect of the life already acquired. In the first, they ought to precede the act of justification; in the second, they follow it.

6. In the end.

VIII. (6) As to the end—for the end of the first was the declaration of justice; but of the second, the manifestation of the mercy and exceeding love of God. In that, the strict severity (*to akribodikaion*) of the lawgiver and Judge played its part, by which there was no room for repentance or for pardon. But in this, the forbearance (*epieikeia*) of the Father appears—he opened the way to grace and the salvation of the sinner.

7. In manifestation.

IX. (7) As to manifestation—for as the former was made in the state of nature, so it was known by nature and impressed upon the consciences of men (in which the work of the law was written, Rom. 2:14, 15). But the second, a mystery, is entirely hidden, which reason cannot discover, unless it is made known to us by a supernatural revelation (because it depends upon God's good will [*eudokia*] alone and his most free purpose). Therefore it could become known to no one except by a revelation from God himself. Hence Christ says that flesh and blood could not reveal it, but only the Father who is in heaven (Mt. 16:17). The mysteries of the gospel are said to be "such as eye hath not seen" (1 Cor. 2:9).

8. In order.

X. (8) As to order, the covenant of works precedes and the covenant of grace follows. From this to that, there is granted an appeal from the throne of justice to the throne of mercy. Hence the violator of the covenant of nature has a remedy in the covenant of grace, but the violator of the covenant of grace has no further remedy or hope of pardon because there is no other covenant by which he can be reconciled to God. On this account, the sin against the Holy Ghost is unpardonable because it is committed against the covenant of grace.

9. In extent.

XI. (9) As to extent, the first was universal, made with all men in Adam. Hence there is no mortal who is not by nature under the covenant of works (as each individual bears the work of the law, which is the contract of that covenant, written on his conscience, Rom. 2:14). But the latter is particular, made with the elect alone and those to be saved in Christ (as will hereafter be proved).

10. In effects.

XII. (10) As to effects, the first gave matter for glorying to man when he observed it; but the second excludes all glorying of man because it is founded upon the grace of God alone—"boasting is excluded, not by the law of works, but by the law of faith" (Rom. 3:27). The first after the fall became terrible, striking terror into the conscience; but the latter is gracious and saving. The first genders to bondage, the other to freedom. In the first, God from Mount Ebal thunders curses in the ears of sinners, but in the second as it were from Mount Gerizim blessings are promulgated. The first drives men away from God because by it no one can approach him; but the latter calls men back to God and opens a way to the throne of mercy, coming to which with confidence we can find help in every time of need.

Fifth Question: The Unity of the Covenant of Grace

Was the covenant of grace one and the same as to substance under each dispensation? We affirm against the Socinians, Anabaptists and Remonstrants.

I. This most important controversy is waged by us with the ancient and modern Pelagians (to wit, the Socinians, Remonstrants, Anabaptists and others who deny the identity of the gratuitous covenant). They hold that the fathers of the Old Testament were not saved by the gratuitous mercy of God in Christ, the Mediator (God-man, *theanthrōpō*) through faith in him about to come.

Opinion of the Socinians.

II. The Socinians express their opinion in the Racovian Catechism where they assert that in the law of Christ two promises are contained (which were not contained in the law of Moses)—eternal life and the Holy Spirit, "Nowhere will you discover in the law of Moses, either eternal life or the gift of the Spirit promised to those obeying the precepts of the law, as it is evident they are promised in the law given by Christ" (*Racovian Catechism* 5 [1652], p. 113). Socinus clearly confirms this: "We say, therefore, that the new covenant brought most openly to us the promise of eternal life; moreover the promise of remission of sins. Finally the promise to be obtained by all believers, of the Holy Spirit. Since that old covenant wants and wanted all these and proposed earthly happiness, it is easy to recognize the superiority of the new covenant in this respect" (*de Officio Christi*+). Volkelius labors to prove the same thing by various arguments (*De vera Religione* 3.11 [1630], pp. 56-72) and also Smaltzius (*De Divinitate Jesu Christi* 2 and 7 [1608], pp. 3-7 and 25-29). Still they do not deny that the fathers of the Old Testament were saved or would be saved in eternal happiness. "Not to be guilty of dissimulation," says Smaltzius, "we firmly maintain, even if no open promise occurs of eternal life in the old covenant, that it would be given at some time or other to all those, who ever trusted in God and obeyed him" (ibid., 7, p. 27). Volkelius agrees with him (ibid.). Nor do they deny that God pardoned their sins, although he had not promised it nor signified his intention to do so (Socinus, *De Iesu Christo Servatore*, Pt. III. 2 [1594], pp. 228-50; "Tractatus de Justificatione," 3* *Opera Omnia* [1656], 1:604-9), and that the fathers had some knowledge and hope of eternal life, although not promised to them (Smaltzius, *De Divinitate Jesu Christi* 7 [1608], pp. 25-29); that Christ and grace and salvation in Christ had been preached under the Old Testament. Socinus in his *Praelect.*+: "Now it is certain, that Christ not only really was and is our savior, but it was also predicted by the prophets, as we learn, among other passages, from chap. 23 and 33 of Jeremiah." But on this account, they do not hold either that the ancients looked to Christ or were saved in the hope of his coming. The same one: "In this I disagree with you, that you seem to concede, that the pious under the Old Testament, looked to Christ in those ceremonies and sacrifices in which he was

Covenant of grace = same under each dispensation

typified, and were saved in the hope of his coming, a thing of which I can in no way persuade myself" (Socinus, "Ad amicos epistolae: ad Matthaeum Radecium," *Opera Omnia* [1656], 1:377). Hence they distinguish between the faith of those times and ours, so that that was a faith in God simply and this a faith also in Christ. Smaltzius: "Nor was that faith in Jesus Christ, but in God and his promises" (*Refutatio Thesium D. Wolfgangi Frantzii*, Disp. 12 [1614], p. 459); and Volkelius holds that the faith of the ancients and ours differs in three things and especially "that now we are commanded to believe as much in Christ as in God; but that formerly such a faith by no means was exercised is evident even from the fact that Christ was not then manifested" (*De vera Religione* 4.3 [1630], p. 176).

Of the Remonstrants.

III. The Remonstrants do not differ from the Socinians. Arminius indeed properly places the agreement of both testaments in the one and same matter of both (to wit, the obedience of faith required in both and the inheritance of eternal life promised through the imputation of the righteousness of faith, and the gracious adoption in Christ) ("Disputation XIII: On the Comparison of the Law and the Gospel," *Works* [1956], 1:539-48). The one object is Christ. The difference is in some accidentals which detract nothing from the substantial unity. But his followers speak differently. The apologists call the question concerning faith in Jesus Christ ("whether and how it had a place under the Old Testament") "absurd, ambiguous and useless and there is certainly no passage where it appears that that faith was commanded or flourished under the Old Testament" ("Apologia pro confessione sive declaratione . . . Remonstrantes," 7 in Episcopius, *Operum theologicorum* [1665], Pt. II, p. 155). At length they distinguish the manner of revelation (clear or obscure) and say that faith in Jesus Christ was taught in the Old Testament neither openly and directly, but yet indirectly and obscurely comprehended and involved in the faith of the general favor and grace of God. They say the same thing concerning the promise of eternal life: "From this it is easy to gather what must be determined concerning the famous question, did the promise of eternal life have a place in the old covenant or rather was it comprehended in the covenant itself? For if special promises seem to be expressed in that old covenant, we must confess that no clear promise of eternal life can be found in them. If anyone thinks differently, it is his place to point out where it can be found, which I think cannot be done. But if there seem to be general promises, it must be confessed on the other part that they are such that the promise of eternal life should not only seem to come under, but also by the intention it ought to be believed to have come under them" (Episcopius, "Institutiones theologicae," 3.4.1 *Opera theologica* [1678], p. 156).

Of the Anabaptists.

IV. Many Anabaptists fall into the same error, as is evident from the Frankenthal Colloquy where they speak of the Israelite people as if they were a herd of swine, whom they jestingly say were fattened on this earth by the Lord without any hope of heavenly immortality (*Protocoll . . . Frankenthal*, Art. 15, 16 [J. Meier, 1573], pp. 292-335). They maintain that only temporal goods and earthly promises were granted to them. This was also the impious notion of Servetus, against whom Calvin solidly disputes (ICR, 2.10 pp. 428-49).

Statement of the question.

V. From these things the state of the question can clearly be gathered. The question is not: (1) whether the covenant of grace was various as to accidentals and the different modes and degrees of dispensation and manifestation (for we confess that under this relation [*schesei*] there is a multiple difference between the Old and New Testament or the old and new economy, as will be proved in its proper place). Rather the question is whether it was the same as to substance and the essential parts of the covenant, i.e., both as to the covenanted themselves and as to the federal pact consisting in the mutual obligation of the parties. Whether the same Mediator (Christ) in both; the same faith in Christ; promises of the same spiritual and heavenly blessings; the same way of reconciliation and salvation—the economy and administration only of the covenant varying. This our opponents deny; we affirm.

VI. The question is not whether the fathers of the Old Testament were saved, whether their sins were pardoned, whether they had any hope of eternal life, whether Christ was predicted to them. Most of our adversaries do not dare deny this. Rather the question is whether they looked to Christ and were saved in the hope of his coming. Whether promises not only temporal, but also spiritual and heavenly concerning eternal life and the Holy Spirit were given to them. And whether the same covenant entered into with us in Christ had already been contracted with them, although more obscurely and reservedly. This they deny; we assert. We maintain that Christ was not only predicted but also promised to the fathers and by his grace they were saved under the Old Testament no less than we are saved under the New; nor was any other name given under heaven even from the beginning from which salvation could be hoped for (Acts 4:12) and that too according to the inviolable promise of the gratuitous covenant.

The identity of the covenant is proved: (1) from the Scriptures.

VII. The reasons are: First, in general, the Scriptures teach that the covenant of grace (which God contracted with us in the New Testament) is the same with the covenant previously made with Abraham. Hence Zachariah says in his song, "God visited and redeemed his people, as he spake by the mouth of his holy prophets, which have been since the world began: to perform the mercy promised to our fathers, and to remember his holy covenant; the oath which he sware to our father Abraham" (Lk. 1:68, 70, 72, 73). And Peter addressing the Jews concerning the days of Christ (which had been predicted by all the prophets) says, "Ye are the children of the prophets, and of the covenant which God made with our fathers, saying unto Abraham, And in thy seed shall all the kindreds of the earth be blessed" (Acts 3:25). Paul mentions by name the promise of the gospel: "The Scripture, foreseeing that God would justify the heathen through faith, preached before the gospel unto Abraham, saying, In thee shall all nations be blessed" (Gal. 3:8). Hence he brings forward the justification of Abraham by faith as an example for us (Rom. 4:3) and exhibits him as "the father of the faithful" to the Jews as well as the Gentiles (which could not have been done if the covenant was not identical). This is confirmed by the fact that he calls the promise given to Abraham "the covenant that was before confirmed of God in Christ" (*diathēkēn prokekyrōmenēn hypo tou Theou eis Christon*, Gal. 3:17).

2. From the identity of the covenant of grace.

VIII. Second, in particular, from all the parts of the covenant of grace which were the same in both cases. Such is the clause of the covenant that God will be our God and the God of our seed; for as it had already been proposed to Abraham (Gen. 17:7) and renewed to Moses in a vision (Ex. 3:15) and frequently in legislation, confirmed in the captivity and after it (Ezk. 36:28), so no other was proposed in the covenant of grace as the foundation of all blessings, spiritual as well as celestial (Mt. 22:32; 2 Cor. 6:16; Rev. 21:3).

3. From the identity of the Mediator.

IX. Third, the identity of the Mediator (given in the Old and New Testament), the foundation of the covenant. He is the blessed seed of the woman who would bruise the serpent's head (Gen. 3:15 compared with Heb. 2:14 and Rom. 16:20), the seed of Abraham in whom all the nations of the earth were to be blessed (Gen. 22:18, viz., Christ—cf. Gal. 3:16); in the Old Testament "the angel of Jehovah's presence" (Is. 63:9), "the angel of the covenant" (Mal. 3:1), "a covenant of the people and of the Gentiles," i.e., its Mediator (Is. 42:6; 49:8), who bore the griefs of his people and was smitten for their sins (Is. 53:5, 6). In the New Testament, he is the Mediator between God and men (1 Tim. 2:5); the Mediator of the New Testament and of a better covenant (Heb. 8:6; 9:15); "the same yesterday, today and forever" (Heb. 13:8); by whose grace the fathers, no less than we, were saved (Acts 15:10, 11); to whom all the prophets bore testimony (Acts 10:43); the one sole name given under heaven by which we can be saved (Acts 4:12); the Way, the Truth and the Life, so that no one can come to the Father except by him (Jn. 14:6).

X. The objection to Heb. 13:8 is vain. Christ is said to be "the same yesterday, today and forever," and it is supposed either that it treats of his doctrine, not concerning his person and the covenant made in it. If a doctrine is eternal, therefore also the person who delivers it and the covenant proposed in it is eternal. Or it is supposed that "yesterday" denotes the day of his flesh before his ascension and "today" the time after his ascension. This is repugnant to the aim of Paul, which is to exhort to constancy of faith, the argument being drawn from the identity and perpetuity of the gospel doctrine, of which Christ as Mediator is the object. Or that by "today" and "yesterday" is denoted a thing new and recent which commenced not very long ago (as men are said to be of "yesterday" in Job 8:9 and among the Greeks *ephēmeroi* ["beings of a day"] on account of the shortness of their lives). The expressions are very dissimilar. To be *mthmvl* ("from yesterday and the day before") depresses human nature. But here Christ is said to have been yesterday and to be today and forever through all the differences of time, to denote his glory and eternity. Nor is he only said to be yesterday, today and forever, but the same, i.e., not different, either now or then or afterwards; but always and everywhere the same Jesus Christ. This could not be said if Christ had not even from the beginning been the Mediator of the covenant of grace and the Prophet and teacher of the church.

XI. Acts 15:11 cannot be understood of the apostles compared with the converted Gentile believers and not with the fathers of the Old Testament (as they maintain). For Peter had spoken proximately of the fathers and so the following words are fitly referred to them—"But we believe that through the grace of the

Lord Jesus Christ, we shall be saved, even as they (*kath' hon tropon kakeinoi*)." (2) The design of Peter demands this. He wishes to prove that the yoke of the ceremonial law is not to be placed on the necks of the Gentiles for this reason—that the fathers themselves could not bear it, but were saved by the same grace of Christ as we. (3) If the apostles had wished to join themselves with the Gentiles in the manner of salvation, they would not have said we believe that we are saved even as they; but rather vice versa, they even as we. It did not become the apostles to follow the Gentiles and to set these before themselves as an example in the manner of salvation, but the contrary. (4) Nor is it absurd for Peter (discoursing concerning the manner in which the Gentiles should obtain salvation) to end with an argument taken from the fathers, because there is one method of salvation for all. If the yoke of the law was insufferable (*abastakton*) to the fathers, it is rightly inferred that the Gentiles are not to be subjected to that yoke.

XII. It is also falsely alleged that the words "There is none other name under heaven given among men, whereby we must be saved" (Acts 4:12) refer only to the time in which Christ was manifested and cannot be extended to the past. The words themselves disprove this interpretation. They do not assert that there is now no name given to men whereby they can be saved, but that no name is given among men (*en anthrōpois*) in all time. The thing itself demands this. For since no salvation can be granted to the sinner without a mediator (and there is no mediator except Christ), it follows either that the fathers had no salvation or that they were saved by Christ. Nor if the words are used in the present, are the past or the future excluded; but this is done that the truth of the mediation of Christ may be predicated of all time.

XIII. The words "from the foundation of the world" (*apo katabolēs kosmou*, Rev. 13:8) are not to be separated from those which immediately precede ("the Lamb slain") and to be joined with "the book of life" by transposition (as is the case in Rev. 17:8). (1) There is no necessity for such a transposition doing violence to the series of the discourse, which flows far more smoothly when we thus read—"whose names are not written in the book of life of the Lamb slain from the foundation of the world"—than according to the wish of our opponents—"whose names are written from the foundation of the world in the book of life of the Lamb slain." For as the book of life is said "to be the book of life of the Lamb" (Rev. 21:27), it ought not to be torn away from the words "of the Lamb slain" (*arniou esphagmenou*). (2) "The Lamb slain" is nowhere put by itself, but mention is always made either of the time from which or of the persons for whom (or for what causes) he was slain. (3) It is most properly said "slain from the foundation of the world"; not in himself, but intentionally, in the decree of God; objectively, in the promises of the word and the faith of the fathers; typically, in sacraments and sacrifices. (4) Even granting that the words are to be so explained, the force of the argument is not destroyed because no one can be written in the book of life, except in Christ slain (or in his death).

4. From the identity of condition.

XIV. Fourth, there is in each case the same condition of the covenant (to wit, faith) by which they obtained salvation. It is evident in Abraham, whose faith is said to have been imputed for righteousness (Gen. 15:6) and is proposed to us for an example (Rom. 4:11; Gal. 3:6-8); in David (Ps. 116:10 compared with 2 Cor. 4:13); in the ancient worthies whose faith is celebrated throughout Heb. 11. Here belongs what is said in Hab. 2:4, "The just shall live by faith," where mention is made not only of faith, but also of justification, suspended on faith (Rom. 1:17). Hence Peter testifies, "To Christ give all the prophets witness, that through his name whosoever believeth in him shall receive remission of sins" (Acts 10:43). Nor can it be objected that the faith of the ancients was general in God, not special in Christ (the Savior), because the opposite is evident from many considerations. (a) No faith can be saving unless founded upon Christ. (b) He speaks of the faith by which they looked to God as their God (Heb. 11:16) and to heaven as their native country. Now this cannot be done without Christ. (c) Of the faith by which they looked to Christ himself and preferred his reproach to all treasures (Heb. 11:26). (d) Not only a general but also a special command of faith in Christ is found in the Old Testament (Ex. 23:20, 21; Dt. 18:18, 19; Ps. 2:12; Is. 53:1, 5). If the faith of the ancients were not the same as ours, it would be improperly proposed to us for imitation (Heb. 12:1, 2; Rom. 4:12). Paul could not argue with sufficient strength from the faith of the father of believers and his justification to ours (Gal. 3:6, 7; Rom. 4:16).

5. From the identity of the promises.

XV. Fifth, the same spiritual promises were given to them with us, although often under the shell and veil of temporal things. This is evident (a) in general, as to the promises from Acts 13:32—"we declare unto you glad tidings," says Paul, "the promise made unto the fathers." Hence it is evident that the gospel preached by Paul did not differ from the promises made unto the fathers and on this account the more that Paul (the most faithful herald of the promises) taught nothing other than what Moses and the prophets had taught (Acts 26:22). In particular, certain spiritual blessings are conferred upon believers under the New Testament which had already been promised and given to Abraham (Acts 3:25, 26; Gal. 3:8, 9): as the gift of the Holy Spirit (Gal. 3:14; Ezk. 36:26, 27); justification and remission of sins (Gen. 15:6; Ps. 32:1; Is. 43:25; Jer. 31:33; Acts 10:43); sanctification (Dt. 30:6; Ezk. 36:26; Ps. 51:12); eternal life, both from the federal promise, in which Christ clearly teaches that eternal life and the resurrection are included (Mt. 22:31, 32), and from the inheritance given to Abraham and his seed, which is no other than eternal life (Gal. 3:18; Heb. 9:15); from the "city which has foundations" and the heavenly country which the fathers waited for (Heb. 11:10); from the life promised to believers (Is. 55:3). Hence Job knows that his Redeemer lives (Job 19:25); David is persuaded of his own resurrection and life (Pss. 16:10; 22:26); Daniel awaits the resurrection to eternal life (12:1, 2).

XVI. It cannot be objected: (1) as to the promises concerning Christ in the Old Testament that they were indeed given to the fathers, but not for the fathers; rather for the believers of the New Testament, as the promises of the calling of the Gentiles were given to the ancients, but only for the times of the New Testament. (a) It is absurd that the prophets should have given such promises to believers and that believers heard them and did not apply them to themselves. For they were oppressed by the same evils as others for whom they are supposed to have been made and equally needed the same remedy. Since they were sent to the ancient people in order to sustain them in the hope of a Messiah about to come and of the salvation to be obtained through him, who does not see that such promises were given to the fathers for their consolation? (b) The promises belonged to them in the same manner as the adoption, glory, the covenants, the giving of the law and the service of God (Rom. 9:4). Now these latter belonged properly to the ancients. (c) If the promises did not pertain to them, they could not and ought not to have applied them to themselves, as was done by Abraham (Gen. 15:6), who also was justified in this way (Rom. 4:4); by Jacob (Gen. 49:18); by David (Pss. 16, 23, 40, 110, 118 and frequently elsewhere); by Isaiah (Is. 9:6—"Unto us a child is born, unto us a son is given") and by the whole Israelite church (Is. 53:11); throughout, by Jeremiah (Jer. 23:5, 6; Mic. 5:2). Peter could not have said all the prophets give witness that whosoever "believeth in him shall receive remission of sins" (Acts 10:43), no one either of Old Testament or New Testament believers being excepted; nor Paul that Christ is made a Mediator for the redemption of the transgressions that were under the first testament that they which are called might receive the promise of eternal inheritance. (d) The relation of the calling of the Gentiles (which evidently conduced in no way to the salvation of the Jews) differs from that of the advent of the Messiah and of grace in Christ (without whom no hope of salvation could have shone upon them).

XVII. (2) No better is the objection that the prophecy adduced by Christ in Mt. 22:32 was too obscure to be perceived by believers; or that it is not a general promise of a future life, but a special promise referring to Abraham, Isaac and Jacob by name (as Volkelius says, *De vera Religione* 3.11 [1630], pp. 56-72). Although the promise of eternal life is somewhat obscurely set forth in that prophecy (when compared with the clearness of the New Testament promises), it does not follow that it could not be perceived by the fathers, as far as it could minister to their consolation. Yea, unless it had been an evident and clear proof, the Sadducees would not have held their tongues (which they did not do on account of the authority of the speaker, but from the evidence of reason). Nor can it be called a special grace to the patriarchs, because it is extended to their seed (Gen. 17:7). Otherwise the proof of Christ against the Sadducees would neither have been sufficiently firm, nor could the psalmist call that nation blessed whose God is the Lord (Ps. 33:12).

XVIII. (3) It is added falsely that the fathers are said to have looked for a city having foundations (Heb. 11:16); not because promised to them, but because accommodated to their wishes and suitable to their deeds and because it was credible that God would give it to his worshippers (as the same Volkelius says and the *Racovian Catechism*, "Of Christ's Prophetic Office" [1652], p. 114). For what can be the hope founded upon no word? Yea, since it is proposed as an act of faith, it necessarily supposes and has regard to a promise. Hence they are said to have "died in faith," "to seek and desire a country" (Heb. 11:13, 14, 16). And how can that be sought and desired which is not known, since there is no desire of a thing unknown? Nor is the evanescent and doubtful opinion which the Gentiles (not having hope, Eph. 2:12) could conceive of immortality to be confounded with the sure and infallible hope of eternal life which the fathers had from the word.

XIX. (4) In vain is Job 19:25 said to treat of a temporal deliverance from the troubles which the man of God suffers; and concerning the vision or clearer knowledge of God's power, wisdom and providence (as in Job. 42:5, "Now mine eye seeth thee")—although this is the opinion of the Jews and also of some Christians. For many things prove that Job looked farther and consoled himself (against his troubles and the preposterous judgments of men about him) by his belief in the resurrection and in eternal life. (a) He expects this benefit from *g'l* (his Redeemer). Now *g'l* is no other than Christ. (b) He expects it at the time of the last judgment for he says, "I know that my redeemer liveth, and that he shall stand at the latter day upon the earth." (c) He expects it only after his death, after his body had been gnawed and destroyed by worms, since indeed after his skin has been laid aside and his body destroyed by worms, he should be restored entire and in his flesh see God. (d) This vision cannot be referred simply to the knowledge of the power and providence of God (of which he speaks in 42:5). Here Job hears God addressing him directly and experiences his presence nearer than before, exciting in him serious compunction. This would not have consoled him much, nor could it certainly persuade him of his restoration. Nor if it could have persuaded him, could it have begotten in him so much joy and fulness (*plērophorian*) of faith. Therefore it is more properly understood of the beatific vision, by the hope of which he consoled himself in his troubles and through which (secure of eternal salvation) he expected with the utmost certainty his own resurrection.

XX. Not more truly is it contended that Daniel does not treat of the universal resurrection of the dead (Dan. 12:2) because it is referred only to "many." Rather it concerns the restoration of the Jewish people from the terrible calamity they were on the point of suffering under Antiochus, denoted by "that time" (namely concerning which he had spoken thus far, which was the time of Antiochus). (1) The words themselves prove the opposite since they treat of a resurrection properly so called from the dust of the earth and such as will be to everlasting life or to everlasting shame; but a temporal deliverance cannot be said to be to eternal life, since believers are still exposed to death; nor to everlasting shame, since men can repent. (2) It is not necessary that that time mentioned in Dan. 12:1 should be understood of the time in which Antiochus was about to persecute the church most severely. That phrase is often taken without any reference to the preceding (as in Mt. 3:1; 4:1) and the *beth* can mean "after" (as in Jos. 5:5). Thus the meaning is, after that deliverance of the people through the death of Antiochus, another far more illustrious will succeed through Michael (i.e., Christ) so nevertheless that terrible calamities will precede and then happy resurrection will follow. That time, therefore, which followed the death of Antiochus was the gospel time in which Christ should perform the work of the church's redemption. This is so because first, it is contained in the two advents of Christ; and second, the whole is here comprehended by the Holy Spirit (because he does not give a continuous series of things and times, but only mentions the remarkable changes in the state of the church). Therefore there is denoted here: (a) the time of Christ's first advent and what he would do in favor of his church; (b) the time of the second advent in the resurrection or the completion of happiness (12:2). Now it ought not to seem surprising if a transition is here made from the first to the second coming of Christ and times far distant from each other are connected together on account of their similarity (as in Mt. 24 the destruction of the temple and the world are joined together). Thus the salvation of the church is most properly connected with the last resurrection because in the world all things are confused; nor does the matter of salvation occur anywhere unless we raise our minds there. Moreover the "many" are here put for "all" (as frequently elsewhere).

6. From the identity of the sacraments.

XXI. Sixth, the sacraments (the seals of the covenant) were the same in both testaments as to substance, signifying and sealing Christ and his benefits. It is evident both with respect to the ordinary (to wit, circumcision, which is called a seal of the righteousness of faith [Rom. 4:11] and the Passover, which is fulfilled in Christ [1 Cor. 5:7]); and with respect to the extraordinary (the passage of the sea and the deluge which answer to our baptism [1 Cor. 10:1, 2; 1 Pet. 3:20]; the manna and the water from the rock, answering to the Eucharist [1 Cor. 10:3, 4]). And hence arises the change of names (often occurring here) by which the names of the New are given to the sacraments of the Old Testament and vice versa. To the fathers is ascribed baptism and the feast (1 Cor. 10:1-4); to us circumcision (Col. 2:11, 12), the Passover (1 Cor. 5:7), sacrifices (Heb. 9). This, however, could not be done by enallage (*enallagē*) unless there was a certain identity. Now it cannot be with respect to the sign because the signs are diverse. Therefore it ought to be with respect to the thing signified, which in all the sacraments was always the same (namely Christ with his benefits; in whom the types and sacraments, no less than the promises, are yea and amen, i.e., obtain their realization and fulfillment).

XXII. Nor is the objection of our opponents to be entertained—that the ancients eat the same food with each other and not with us. This is repugnant to the design of Paul, which is to compare the ancients with Christians and from the examples (both of the sacraments and the benefits bestowed upon them and of the sins and punishment of the Israelites) to argue to a parity of punishments, if they had an equality of sins. Still (1) this argument would have no force if the Israelites were compared only with each other and not with us. (2) It is repugnant to the words of Paul by which he teaches that Christ was even then known to the ancients when he says that the rock which followed them was Christ and that they tempted Christ in the desert (1 Cor. 10:9). (3) In vain would the apostle speak of baptism if it was not true that the sacraments of the Old and New Testaments were the same at least analogically and as to substance.

7. From the use of the law.

XXIII. Seventh, the very law of Moses (under which the fathers were) instructed them concerning the covenant of grace and prepared and stimulated them to embrace it (which could not have been done if the covenant of grace had not already gone into effect). On this account, the law is called a "schoolmaster unto Christ" (Gal. 3:24) and Christ the end of the law (Rom. 10:4). This is readily demonstrated from its three parts: (a) from the moral, because by convincing the fathers of sins committed against the law (Rom. 3:19, 20; Gal. 3:19) and on account of them subjecting them to the divine curse (Gal. 3:10), it excited and stimulated them to seek and embrace the expiation and pardon of sins in Christ (Gal. 3:24); (b) from the forensic, inasmuch as it constituted the polity of the Israelites until Christ (Gen. 49:10) and sealed (as it were) by an impressed mark the nation from which the Messiah was to spring; (c) from the ceremonial, because the ceremonies of the law were types and figures of Christ who was to come, adumbrating his sacrifice for sins and confirming the minds of believers concerning the enjoyment of it (Col. 2:17; Heb. 9 and 10).

Sources of explanation.

XXIV. The gospel (meaning the doctrine of the grace of God in Christ) is used in two ways: either for the gospel promised or *epangelia*; or for *euangelismō* or the gospel completed and manifested. In the former sense, it was under the Old Testament; in the latter only in the New. In this respect, it is said to have been "kept" secret in preceding ages (Rom. 16:25), not absolutely and simply, since in the same book it is said to have been promised and manifested by the prophetic Scripture (Rom. 1:2), but relatively: (1) as to natural knowledge because flesh and blood does not reveal this; (2) as to its promulgation among the Gentiles because God permitted them to walk in their own ways and made known to them nothing about Christ; (3) as to its fulfillment among the Jews because he reserved its fulfillment not for their times, but for ours. The apostle, therefore, does not mean that the gospel was altogether unknown under the Old Testament, but when compared with the light of the New Testament, by which he made it more clearly known and to more persons (Eph. 3:5).

XXV. The "beginning of the gospel," inasmuch as it denotes the gospel history concerning the ministry of John the Baptist and the birth of Christ (in which sense it is spoken of in Mk. 1:1) is one thing. Another is the beginning of the doctrine concerning the grace of God in Christ. In this sense, it did not just then begin in the New Testament, but in the Old Testament it was declared by Moses and the prophets (as in the same place it is confirmed by prophetic testimonies, Mk. 1:2, 3).

XXVI. The Law and the Prophets are said to have "prophesied until John" (Mt. 11:13) as to the manner of dispensation, not as to federal substance, as if the legal covenant only had been in the Old Testament. For the Law and the Prophets with the promulgation of the law always had the promises of grace, but they treat only of the legal and prophetic ministry in opposition to the evangelical, especially as to clearness of manifestation. The ministering persons or things administered are not opposed, but only the different modes in which the same things were administered—before by prophecy (*prophēteian*) or a somewhat obscure mode of teaching, symbolically (namely) and enigmatically; afterwards by the gospel (*euangelismon*), a clear and open mode of teaching. Therefore the thing and the mode of the thing (*to hon kai to poion*) ought not to be confounded here.

XXVII. It is one thing for the covenant of grace to be renewed and to be set forth in a clearer manner; another for it to be made anew, since it was not before. The former is said (Jer. 31:33), not the latter because the same clause of the covenant had already existed in the covenant with Abraham. Nor is it unusual in Scripture style to speak of a certain thing being made when it is more clearly and efficaciously manifested (as the commandment of love is called "new" [Jn. 13:34; 1 Jn. 2:8], not absolutely, because it had already been proposed in the law, but relatively because inculcated anew, based upon new promises and sanctioned by a new example). Thus "the strength of God is said to be made perfect in weakness" (2 Cor. 12:9), i.e., to be demonstrated as perfect and a friend to be borne in adversity; and the stars are said to rise at the setting of the sun, i.e., to become apparent.

XXVIII. It is one thing not to see Christ exhibited in the flesh; another not to perceive the benefits and fruits of his mediation. Peter says the former was denied to the fathers when he says, Unto them it was revealed that not unto themselves, but unto us they did minister those mysteries (1 Pet. 1:12), because

Christ was to be manifested at length in our times, not in theirs. But on that account, the latter was not denied to them because the power of Christ's death, however far distant, could exert its efficacy over them for the expiation of sins and in producing peace of conscience (as moral causes are wont to act before they are).

XXIX. Although God has provided some better thing for us than for the Old Testament fathers (Heb. 11:39, 40), as to the complement of the promises and the manifestation of the Messiah (in which sense the eyes of the disciples are said to be blessed who saw those things which kings desired to see and did not see, Lk. 10:23, 24), it does not follow that they did not have the same substance of the covenant with us since God willed to be their God no less than ours. Therefore it is said "they without us" (i.e., separated from us, *chōris hēmōn*) "should not be made perfect," because they were saved by the same merit, the same righteousness and grace of Christ. But they could be made perfect "before us" in the way of order and of time.

XXX. Although Christ brought life and immortality to light by the gospel (2 Tim. 1:10), it does not follow that it was not absolutely known under the Old Testament. (1) Paul does not speak of an absolute and simple manifestation among all, but "among the Gentiles." Hence he immediately adds, Whereunto I am appointed a preacher and a teacher of the Gentiles. (2) He teaches (v. 9) that that grace was not new when he says it was given before the world began (*pro chronōn aiōniōn*), both by eternal destination and by temporal promise. (3) He does not speak properly of the promise of eternal life, but of the procurement of it by the actual merit of Christ, which was peculiar to the New Testament.

XXXI. When the apostle says, "The law made nothing perfect" (Heb. 7:19), he does not take the law broadly for the Mosaic economy, as if the ancients were not made perfect under the Old Testament as to the possession of grace and glory. Rather he views the law strictly and in opposition to the gospel because the moral law could neither justify nor sanctify, since it was weak in the flesh (much less ceremonial law).

XXXII. If the same one asserts "that the way into the holiest of all was not yet made manifest, while as the first tabernacle was yet standing" (Heb. 9:8), he does not mean to deny that the fathers under the Old Testament were received into heaven, which the example of Enoch and the reasoning of Christ (Mt. 22:32) abundantly prove. Rather he wishes to intimate two things: (1) that the ceremonies such as were before appointed by the tabernacle, could not of themselves open a way to heaven on account of their weakness and inefficacy; (2) as long as these ceremonies existed, that approach to heaven (or the method and mode of it) was more obscure and was not so clearly set forth, as was done when Christ appeared and the ceremonies were abolished. Now the consequence does not hold good from a negation of the mode to a negation of the thing. It is one thing not to be in any manner laid open; another not to be clearly and fully revealed. The apostle says this, not that—for *to pephanerōsthai* indicates the full manifestation of a thing (which was denied under the Old Testament).

XXXIII. The old covenant is taken in two ways: either for the covenant of works or the legal covenant strictly understood, made with our first parents before their fall and afterwards renewed in the desert; or for the second covenant, of grace, made with our first parents after the fall and confirmed in the Mosaic economy. The new is taken either in general for the covenant of grace or for the covenant of grace illustrated in the New Testament. Hence a double opposition of the Old and New covenants must be accurately distinguished: the one by reason of substance, if they are taken in the first sense; the other as to the accidents or the accidental mode of dispensation, if taken with the second meaning. For although as to the shell of the letter, the Mosaic covenant would seem to be legal because only under the condition of one's own obedience (and that too perfect, without any forbearance [*epieikeia*]) did it promise life, still as to the intention of the lawgiver and as to the end of the law again promulgated, it led to the coming Messiah—and so it is rightly said to belong to the covenant of grace. In this sense, the old covenant is called "antiquated" only as to the mode of administration, not as to the thing administered; as to the accidents of the covenant, not as to its substance; as to the external observance of the additions annexed to the covenant, not as to the internal form of the covenant itself.

XXXIV. The "promises of the new covenant" are said to be "more excellent" (Heb. 8:6), relatively, not simply. Not with regard to the substance of the promises, but with regard to the mode both of setting them forth more clearly, of enlarging them and more efficaciously impressing them and of extending them to the Gentiles also. Therefore that preeminence (*hyperochē*) of the New Testament is wholly in the mode, not in the thing, and has relation to the nonessentials (*ta epousiōdē*) and not to the essentials (*ousiōdē*) of the covenant. For more excellent promises as to matter cannot be granted than were made to Abraham, Isaac and the other fathers.

XXXV. It is one thing for "the righteousness of faith now" (i.e., under the gospel economy) to be simply manifested (*phanerōtheisan haplōs*); another to be manifested without law (*phanerōtheisan chōris nomou*) (i.e., by another word than that of the law, namely the word of the gospel). The former is not asserted by Paul (Rom. 3:21), but the latter. He says that righteousness was "witnessed" (*martyroumenēn*) by the law and the prophets. Nor can it be said to be witnessed (*martyroumenēn*) as future, not as present (as destined for the believers under the New Testament) and not for the fathers. Thus it would follow either that no one of the fathers was justified (which the examples of Abraham, David and others prove to be false) or that they were justified in a different way than by the righteousness of faith (as Paul asserts, Rom. 4).

XXXVI. Although Moses was the mediator of the old covenant, Christ is not excluded from this office even in the Old Testament, because Moses was only a typical mediator and a mere messenger between God and his people; but Christ is a real and true peacemaker (*eirēnopoios*), reconciling the Father to us by his merit; the same yesterday, today and forever; in the Old Testament indeed without flesh (*asarkos*), but in the New incarnate (*ensarkos*).

XXXVII. The faith of the fathers was not only "the believing that Christ was to come," but "the believing in Christ who was to come" (Acts 19:4, 5). They could not, however, believe in him except as he was promised (namely as the Messiah and only Savior, out of whom there can be no salvation). Now although Christ did not as yet exist physically as incarnate, still he existed from the beginning morally (with regard to destination and promise as to be incarnate). On that account, by the efficacy of his divinity, he could even then bestow his benefits upon believers. The faith which was to be revealed under the New Testament (Gal.

3:23) was an objective faith. It is believed by reason of clearer manifestation, not subjective by which it is believed.

XXXVIII. As faith and the word are related, the faith in Christ ought to have been such as was the word of the Old Testament concerning Christ. Now the word of the Old Testament teaches Christ and testifies of him (Jn. 5:39), yet it does so somewhat obscurely. On account of the promises and types of him who was about to come, their faith therefore was also in him, but more obscurely and less enlightened. The same thing, therefore, was always known and proposed as the object of faith, but the mode was less clearly discovered before the advent of Christ than after it (as the knowledge of all future things is less evident than the knowledge of the past and the intuition of the present; but the greater degree of light being denied, the lesser is not therefore denied).

XXXIX. The mode of redemption by the death of the Messiah could not have been wholly unknown to the fathers, since it was so often indicated both by verbal oracles and types (real as well as personal); consult the following passages—Pss. 22, 69; Is. 53, 63; Dan. 9:27; Zech. 12:10. Christ himself teaches from the Old Testament that he ought to be manifested and thus to enter into his glory (Lk. 24:26). The same was beheld in the paschal lamb, in each of the two goats (Lev. 16:5ff.) and everywhere in the sacrifices: all which the fathers must have received without faith and have believed that sins could be expiated by the blood of bulls. Then their faith would have been lower than the light of the pagans themselves, who had no such belief. Or we must maintain that they perceived in these spiritual meaning and that all referred to the Messiah.

XL. If the two disciples at Emmaus were still fascinated with the opinion of a worldly kingdom to be established by Christ on earth (Lk. 24:21) and did not think of the cross on which Christ was to suffer, it does not follow that all believers thought the same or that nothing concerning the death of Christ had been revealed to the fathers. For this was a fault in the subject, not a defect in the object. It had been with sufficient clearness predicted in the Old Testament and taught by Christ, if they had wished to attend to it. Their faith, therefore, could be true as to the object, but still mixed with error; derived not from the Scriptures (according to which he convinces them, Lk. 24:27), but from the erroneous opinion of the Jews concerning an earthly kingdom of Christ (Mt. 20:21).

XLI. If the apostles sometimes imagined for themselves an earthly and carnal kingdom of Christ, it did not proceed so much from ignorance as from blindness (*ablepsias*) and rashness (*propeteias*). On account of this, they either did not always think of this mystery or by various carnal affections were drawn to incorrect views or sometimes said what was far different from what they really knew. In many other cases (from the same cause), they often transgressed what they knew to be their plain duty; as when they wished to repel men asking help from Christ and wanted fire to be sent from heaven upon the Samaritans; when they did not wish to go up to Jerusalem and the like.

XLII. If Peter reprehends Christ speaking of the cross (Mt. 16:22), the cause of this reproof (*epitimēseōs*) was not an absolute ignorance of the mystery of redemption or of his death. For they had heard John testifying that he was the Lamb of God taking away the sin of the world. Christ himself most expressly predicted the destruction of the temple of his body and his remaining until the third day in the sepulcher (Jn. 2:19; Mt. 12:39, 40, besides the oracles of the prophets). Rather it was the ordinary impetuosity (*propeteia*) and zeal (*thermotēs*) of Peter which often impels a man to utter what is foreign to what he has most clearly discovered because at the moment he does not recall it to mind.

XLIII. The amazement and consternation of the disciples is not prejudicial either to the revelation or to the faith and knowledge of others. They did not understand what they could and ought to understand and what the pious before and near them well understood according to the measure of faith (Mt. 26:12). And if the mystery could not then in any way be understood, the disciples did not sin in not understanding it (since no one is bound to such an impossibility, of which nevertheless they were guilty); yet they were frequently severely rebuked by Christ (Mt. 16:23; Lk. 24:25, 26). Nor was there a need for believers to know those mysteries with other eyes than those of faith (with which they saw the body in the shadows, the nucleus and the truth in the prophecies).

XLIV. Although God promised corporeal goods by Moses in the Old Testament, still he did not promise them to the exclusion of spiritual (which are frequently promised—Ex. 34:6, 7; Lev. 26:12, 41, 42, 44; Dt. 18:15ff.; 30:2, 3, 6, 11, 12). Yea, they are embraced with sufficient clearness in the formula of the covenant. Indeed these corporeal goods themselves were the evidences and symbols of the spiritual (Rom. 4:12ff.; 1 Cor. 10:1-3; Heb. 11:8-10). Express mention is made of eternal life (Is. 45:17; Dan. 12:2; Ps. 16:11), although it was neither so clearly revealed, nor to so many as now.

XLV. The gift of the Holy Spirit is promised under the New Testament; not simply, as if it was absolutely wanting in the old church (against the declaration of these passages, Pss. 51:11, 12; 143:10; Is. 44:3; 59:21; Ezk. 36:27; 39:29; Hag. 2:5), but relatively, inasmuch as it was dispensed both more sparingly and to fewer persons and, as it were, drop by drop. Now it flows in great abundance and like a river inundates the whole church (Jn. 7:39). What was visibly begun on the day of Pentecost (Acts 2:17, 18) ought to be continued invisibly under the kingdom of Christ even until the consummation of the ages.

Sixth Question: The Extent of the Covenant of Grace

Was the covenant of grace ever universal, either as to presentation or acceptance? We deny.

Occasion of the question.

I. This question relates to the object of the covenant of grace, agitated with us by the patrons of universal grace (although in different ways and for a different end). For in order that they may sustain (*diaphylattein*) their thesis (*thesin*) concerning the universality of grace, they are bound to maintain the universality of the covenant by which grace is dispensed. Thus there is no mortal who does not come under that covenant in his measure and with whom it is not made. They draw an argument from the universality of Christ's death, which they place as a foundation under the covenant of grace. For they think Christ died for all that God might obtain the power of contracting a new covenant with the human race.

Opinion of the Remonstrants.

II. The Remonstrants in the declaration of their opinion about this set forth their opinion thus: "Christ by the merit of his death thus far reconciled God, the Father, to the whole human race, that the Father on account of that merit, without injury to his own justice and truth, could and willed to enter into and sanction a new covenant of grace with sinners and men exposed to damnation" (cf. *Acta Synodi Nationalis . . . Dordrechti* (1620), Pt. I, pp. 115-16, on Article 2, "Concerning the Death of Christ"). Now this new covenant, they maintain, was so made with the whole human race that no nation and no individual ought to be said to be excluded from it. "The nations living under the Old Testament, although the covenant was not revealed to them in the same manner as to the Jews, ought not forthwith to be considered as having been absolutely excluded from the covenant, who in some way at least are called that they may seek God. Yea, to them, equally with the Jews, the spiritual gifts of the covenant were exposed, if they would only fulfil the conditions—that they would turn themselves to the God of Israel" (Corvinus, *Defensio Sententiae D. Iacobi Arminii . . . adversus . . . Tileno* 3 [1615], p. 98). And afterwards: "Although many nations are destitute of the ordinary preaching of the gospel, and, indeed, according to the will of God, still such are not absolutely cut off from the grace of the gospel" (ibid., pp. 105-6). Also: "We willingly grant that no one as to himself is born absolutely a stranger to the covenant" (Corvinus, *Petri Molinaei novi anatomici* [1632], p. 440).

And of the universalists.

III. Not only the Lutherans agree with them on this point, but also some of our men who hold to universal grace. Testard says, "That covenant God first made with Adam after his fall, and in him with the whole human race to be propagated, then after the flood he renewed with Noah, and in him with the whole human race to be restored, afterwards permitting the nations to walk in their own ways, with Abraham and his family until the kingdom of Christ, when, the distinction between Jews and Greeks being taken away, in the third place, he established it with the whole human race" (*Eirenikon*, Th. 112 [1633], pp. 82-83). On this account, he had said, "God entirely concealed the grace of the new covenant neither from any nation nor indeed from any individual" (ibid., Th. 111, p. 82). And he adds there are three species of calling: the first real, by works, treated of in Ps. 19:1; Mt. 5:45; Acts 14:17; 17:26; the second verbal, by the gospel; the third internal, by the Spirit (ibid., Th. 113, pp. 83-84). No different is Amyrald: "The degree of love and mercy by which God was induced to make such a covenant with sinners, bears upon them all equally. The consequent, therefore, is that it should be considered to have been made with all men" ("Theses Theologicae de Tribus Foederibus Divinis," 34 *Syntagma Thesium Theologicarum* [1664], p. 220).

IV. Now because that covenant can be viewed in two ways (either with regard to its promulgation or external presentation in objective grace; or with regard to its bestowal or internal reception in subjective grace), some maintain that this covenant is universal in both respects. They assert that sufficient objective and subjective grace is given to each and all that they may be saved if they will (as the Socinians and Remonstrants and others who fight along with Pelagianism). However others extend the universality of the covenant only to objective and not to subjective grace (such are some among us who embrace universal grace).

Common opinion of the Reformed.

V. But the common and received opinion among the Reformed is different. They hold to a particularity of the covenant (no less than of saving grace) that although what is extended to many may be called general (especially under the New Testament, the distinction of nations being taken away), still it never was universal with each and all, but particular only with the true elect members of Christ. Further they think that covenant may be regarded in two ways: either as to internal essence; or as to external dispensation. The former answers to the internal calling and the invisible church of the elect (which is constituted by it). The latter, however, answers to the external calling and the visible church of the called. In the latter respect the covenant is regarded only as to promulgation and presentation by the external call; and as to external benefits, which flow from that presentation, in the preaching of the word; the administration of the sacraments and the participation in sacred things (of which as many as in the people or in the church retain the same profession, become partakers; and thus it is extended even to many reprobates who remain in the visible church). In the former respect, it is further extended to the acceptation and conferring and reception of all federal benefits and internal communion with Christ by faith. In this sense, it pertains to none other than the elect, who are really partakers of the covenant according to God's intention, in whom he fulfills the very conditions of the covenant and to whom he not only offers but actually confers the benefits of the covenant. In whatever manner this covenant is regarded, they deny it to be universal, not only as to acceptation and bestowal, but as to promulgation or presentation (which although at one time wider and more general, still never was absolutely universal, nor can be so called).

Statement of the question.

VI. Hence the statement of the question is clearly gathered. (1) The question does not concern the event and the saving fruit of the covenant; whether all will be saved in virtue of the covenant of grace (for they with whom we argue confess that innumerable persons perish and are without the benefits of the covenant). But the question concerns the purpose and intention of God in sanctioning the covenant of grace—whether he regarded each and all (as they hold) or only certain persons (which we maintain). (2) The question is not whether the call to faith, made by the word, is universal (for our opponents [*hoi ex enantias*] cannot deny that it was particular at least under the Old Testament). But the question is whether there is a real call through the works of nature by which all are summoned to the covenant of grace. This they assert and we deny. (3) The question is not whether without Christ men may ever either be saved or could be saved. For they acknowledge that there is no other means of salvation. Rather the question is whether without a knowledge of Christ adults could obtain salvation. This we deny and they affirm. (4) Finally, the question is not whether God is every day bestowing upon individuals various blessings by which he testifies his goodness and grace to miserable sinners. For this is agreed upon by all. But the question is whether these blessings are saving, flowing from the covenant of grace and the merit of Christ, and are dispensed by God, as Father and Redeemer, with the intention of their salvation. This they assert; we deny. Thus the question returns to this—Is the covenant (made by God in Christ with men) universal and entered into with each and all—first in Adam, then in

Noah and lastly in Christ; if not as to the event of the thing, at least as to the destination and intention of God; if not as to the reception and use of objective and subjective grace, at least as to its presentation? They affirm; we deny.

The particularity of the covenant of grace is established: (1) From its destination.

VII. The particularity of the covenant of grace appears from various considerations. (1) From its destination because there was no universal purpose and will in God to pity the whole human race, but a particular will to select and appoint unto salvation a certain number from the common corrupt mass (as has been proved in full, Volume I, Topic IV, Question 17). Therefore, as no such covenant was decided upon in the counsel of God, so neither was it made in time.

2. From its procurement.

VIII. Second, from the procurement because the satisfaction of Christ (which procures this covenant for us and on which as a foundation it rests) was particular, to be made only for those in whose place (according to the ordination of God) he was bound to substitute himself as surety. They were given by the Father to be redeemed as his (the Son's) seed, people and body, sons of promise. He was given by God (as Mediator and head) to obtain redemption for them and according to the ordination of God, he merited not only salvation and glory for them, but also the grace of the Spirit, regeneration and faith (as will be proved in the proper place).

3. From the promises of the covenant.

IX. Third, from the promises of the covenant because to them alone the covenant of grace belongs to whom the promises expressed in it belong. Now they belong not to each and all, but only to the elect and believers, upon whom the blessings comprehended under those promises are conferred. For those promises are absolute, not conditional, springing from the mere grace of God, not depending on any condition in man. This not only the notion of a testament given to that covenant indicates, but also the nature of the promises, which not only concern the end, but also the means and conditions themselves (which thus exclude every condition). And although the promise of the covenant is conditionally proposed and applied to individuals, it does not follow that the promise itself depends upon man's will and so is not absolute. That conditional promise is a consectary of an absolute promise and it is thus commanded as the duty of man that it may be produced at the same time and at once in the elect as the gift of God.

X. To no purpose is the objection made here that the covenant of grace ought to be considered either as absolute upon the performance of the condition or as conditional (i.e., that it regards those from whom a condition not as yet fulfilled is demanded). It is taken for granted that the covenant of grace was also entered into with those from whom God only wishes to demand the condition annexed to it and not to effect it in them. This is repugnant to the nature of the covenant of grace, which differs from the legal; the latter promises life under a condition which it exacts from man, but does not effect in him. The former promises salvation upon condition of faith which it both demands from and works in man (as clearly appears even from Jer. 31:31-33 where remission of sins and regeneration [or the writing of the law upon the heart] are reckoned as blessings of the covenant). Now although it may be called conditional in a certain sense (inasmuch as it has a condition subordinated to it, although to be absolutely fulfilled by God, by whose intervention the thing promised is granted), still it is properly absolute, both *a priori* (because it has no cause except the perfectly free will of God) and *a posteriori* (because God determined to give to all the elect certainly and infallibly the condition itself without another condition). No one (except absurdly) will say that this can be extended to those whom God hated from eternity and decreed to pass by (by granting them neither his word nor faith, the two means of salvation).

4. From the promulgation of the covenant.

XI. Fourth, from the promulgation of the covenant because that never has been universal (as it ought to have been if the covenant had been universal). How can the covenant be said to have been made with those to whom a knowledge of it has never reached and to whom it was never revealed? Now that not only innumerable persons, but also nations have been without that knowledge, under the Old Testament as under the New Testament is clearer than the noonday sun, since they were destitute of the word, the sole herald of the covenant of grace. As to the Old Testament, who does not know that God restricted this covenant only to the family of Abraham and the Israelite people, all other peoples of the world being excluded (who on that account are called "Lo-ammi, not my people" [Hos. 1:9; Rom. 9:25]; "strangers to the covenants" [Eph. 2:12]; to whom he did not give his statutes as unto Jacob [Ps. 147:19, 20], but whom "he suffered to walk in their own ways" [Acts 14:16]). Now who will say that to such belonged the covenant of grace, which was the peculiar property of the people of Israel? Or that God would have left for so many ages all nations (with the exception of one people) in that thickest darkness in which they lay without any preaching of the word (the only object of faith and means of salvation) if he had willed them to be included under the covenant of grace? On the contrary, does not this dispensation strongly prove that this covenant was so particular to the people of God, as that other nations were excluded from it? And as to the times of the New Testament, although we grant that it has a far greater extension, being indiscriminately extended to all nations, Gentiles as well as Jews; still it is certain that it never has been universal, so that all without exception are called to the covenant of grace. Innumerable men and peoples exist at the present day who are shrouded in the darkness of paganism, who have never heard anything of Christ and of the covenant of grace: "How then shall they call on him in whom they have not believed? and how shall they believe in him who has not been preached to them?" (Rom. 10:14).

XII. Futile is the objection to Ps. 147:19, 20 that the words are to be understood, not absolutely (as if the nations were deprived of all revelation from God, since he did not leave himself without witness [*amartyron*] with respect to them, Acts. 14:17), but comparatively because it was not such and so great as he had given to the Jews. Thus the comparison and the antithesis is with respect to the mode rather than the thing; or because to the Jews was given a revelation, attended by the power of the Spirit, which was denied the Gentiles. For (1) whatsoever the revelation of nature may be, it differs not only in degree but in species from the revelation of the word, since it leads to the Creator, but not to the Redeemer. It testifies of the existence, power, wisdom, providence and beneficence of God towards living creatures (*ta biōtika*); but not of saving grace and the good will of God in Christ (which is a mystery hidden from all the past ages). (2) It is taken for granted that a comparison is made between the revelation accompanied by the Spirit and that destitute of him. For it treats of the external revelation of God's statutes made to Israel and absolutely denied to other nations. Thus the distinction is not between the denying or conferring of the Spirit, but in the conferring and denying of an external revelation of objective grace.

XIII. With no greater show of reason is it said that Paul speaks of the Gentiles not absolutely, but as compared with the Jews (Eph. 2:12) and regards them not as they were by nature (guilty of having violated the first or natural covenant alone), but as they are after impenitence, guilty of having despised and most contemptuously rejected kindness. It is clear that the apostle's design is not to compare them with the Jews, but to set forth only what they were absolutely and considered in themselves before the preaching of the gospel. Otherwise what is said in the beginning of the chapter (that they are dead in sins) must also be understood comparatively (which no one will say). It is also gratuitously supposed that before the gospel was heard, they had contracted the guilt of having violated another covenant than that of nature because as many as are not under grace are under the law and thus under the covenant of works.

XIV. Nor does what is added have any force—if the gospel is not preached everywhere, it is owing to the negligence of men who are wanting in their duty or to the righteous judgment of God, punishing in this way the unbelief of parents who formerly (when it was offered to them) made themselves unworthy of it. For from whatever source the deficiency may arise, it is a fact that the gospel has never been preached to multitudes who, therefore, have no knowledge either of Christ or of the covenant of grace. Now if God seriously intended their salvation, if he willed to extend the covenant of grace to them, why was he unwilling that it should be revealed to them? Why did he not correct the negligence of men, which he undoubtedly foresaw? Again when it is said that God deprives people of the light of the gospel because their parents rendered themselves unworthy of it by their unbelief, two things are assumed which need proof. First, that the gospel has already been offered to all people without exception (which no one would readily say of the inhabitants of the New World). Second, that God willed in this way to punish in the children unbelief of their parents (which can hardly be admitted by those who deny the imputation of sin).

5. From the knowledge of Christ.

XV. Fifth, from the knowledge of Christ because the covenant of grace cannot be extended to those to whom a knowledge of Christ, as Mediator (in whom it was made), has never reached. Such are all those who are destitute of the gospel word, who therefore cannot have faith in Christ, excited by the hearing of the word alone (Rom. 10:17). Nor can it be replied that no one indeed can be saved without Christ; but it does not immediately follow that a knowledge of Christ (at least a distinct knowledge) is necessary to all for salvation. These two things are so connected that they cannot be separated with respect to adults. Christ does not save except as known and apprehended by faith (Is. 53:11; Jn. 6:29, 40; 17:3). Otherwise what need would there be of the gospel, if salvation could reach us without a knowledge of Christ? Nor is this crude doctrine confirmed either by the example of infants, who are saved by Christ without a knowledge of him. It is clear that they are not capable of having it on account of their age (which cannot be said of adults); or of the believers of the Old Testament, who were saved without at least a distinct knowledge of Christ. Besides being a gratuitous supposition that they were without the knowledge of Christ (the opposite of which was proved in the previous question), the divines with whom we treat do not deny that at least under the New Testament a distinct knowledge of Christ is necessary. And since multitudes still at this day are without it, it cannot be said that they were included in the covenant of grace, which is founded upon Christ.

6. From the sealing of the covenant.

XVI. Sixth, from the sealing of the covenant, which is particular; whether the external by the sacraments (which are the peculiar property of the church) or the internal by the Spirit (Eph. 1:13), given only to the members of Christ. Nor thence can you properly infer—therefore also the covenant belongs to the called who are in the church and not only to the elect. For the offering of the sealing is one thing, the real application of it another. The former is common to all the called; the latter special to believers. So far is the covenant from being sealed for salvation unto unbelievers that on the contrary their own condemnation is sealed because they pronounce judgment upon themselves.

7. From the absurdity of confounding nature with grace.

XVII. Seventh, if each and all are invited to the covenant of grace by a universal call, nature is confounded with grace; knowledge (*to gnōston*) with faith (*tō pistō*); and we must ascribe to the voice of nature and of creatures, the preaching of the divine mercy manifested in Christ alone by the Scriptures. And since universal objective grace is vain and illusory without subjective grace, we must either say that sufficient strength is restored to each and all, by which they can (if they will) obey God and be received into the covenant (which is nothing else than to sacrifice to the idol of free will and wholly to abolish discriminating grace, against Paul; as if something is or can be in us which is our own [according to Pelagius] and does not proceed from the unmerited grace of God, 1 Cor. 4:7; or that God intends something under an impossible condition which neither man can have of himself, nor does God, who alone can, will to bestow upon him).

Sources of explanation.

XVIII. So far is the first gospel promise (Gen. 3:15) from being universal, that its particularity can be clearly gathered from various considerations. (1) It treats of the "seed of the woman," not simply and in its whole extent (in which sense it denotes men as such), but comparatively and in contradistinction to the seed of the serpent (to wit, those between whom, with the serpent and his seed, there should be enmity), which should bruise the head of the serpent (i.e., would destroy the kingdom and works of the Devil and free us from his power), whose heel only the serpent injures. Now this pertains only to Christ and those "who are Christ's" (Heb. 2:14, 15), to wit, to the seed taken individually and antonomastically, to whom this primarily belongs; secondarily, to the seed taken collectively for his mystical body or believers, "for whom," "in whom" and "by whom" the head of the serpent and after the head, the seed, is bruised or trampled upon by his power. (2) In the New Testament, this is explained of believers to the exclusion of others (Rom. 16:20; 1 Jn. 2:14; 5:4, 18; 2 Cor. 2:14; Heb. 2:14, 15; Rev.

12:11). (3) The wicked are called the seed of the serpent. Therefore they cannot be contained under the seed of the woman. Hence everywhere Scripture calls them "children of the wicked one" (*hyious ponērou*, Jn. 8:44; 1 Jn. 3:8; Acts 13:10); "generation of vipers" (Mt. 3:7); not indeed properly and physically (which does not apply even to the evil spirits themselves, who have no seed), but figuratively and morally, by way of imitation and likeness because they do the works of the Devil and obey him, in whom he powerfully and effectually works (Eph. 2:2), making them like himself both by instilling wickedness and impiety and by inheriting destruction. Now who will say that they are the seed of the woman between whom and him there is a perpetual enmity; who watch for and bruise his heel; and who not only do not bruise the head of the serpent, but in whom the serpent thrusts forth both head and venom?

XIX. Nor can it be replied here: (1) that either all men are the seed of the woman (for although this could be said in a broad sense and physically, still not morally and strictly in contradistinction to the seed of the serpent, as it is here taken); (2) or that the wicked cannot be called the seed of the serpent or the children of the Devil (because from serpents only serpents are procreated)—this is to be understood only figuratively and morally, so that here a conformity, not of species but of wickedness and malediction, is to be attended to; (3) or that it is contrary to the command of Christ and the duty of Christians to exercise enmity against men. This does not terminate upon their persons, but upon the venom; and therefore so far is it from being abhorrent to the disposition of Christians and the command of Christ, that no one can maintain the name of believer and regulate himself by the commands of Christ without hating the evil in the wicked and those in whom it is reduplicatively (as it is in them and as they are such). (4) Or that a victory was indeed prepared by Christ for all, but the incredulity of men prevents their obtaining the fruit of it (namely that all might be united to Christ and enjoy his victory, if they would exercise faith in God, rather than in their enemy). It is absurd to say that a victory is prepared for those who have never heard anything either about the victor or the victory; or its fruit or of the manner of gaining possession of it; yea, could not even hear on account of age. Again, what is it for a victory to be prepared for them under the condition of believing (i.e., of now conquering), since faith is our victory (1 Jn. 5:4)? Third, a victory cannot be said to be prepared for those who do not perceive its fruit, since it has this reference—not only that Christ bruises the head of the serpent for them, but also in them (i.e., that he works faith in them to conquer the Devil). Fourth, it cannot be said that it was permitted them to enjoy the victory, if they had believed. Whatever was about to be depended upon the antecedent decree of God, according to which he selected some from unmerited love and reprobated others by just hatred. Hence they did not make themselves the seed of the serpent through unbelief; but since they already belonged to the seed of the serpent by sin and the decree of reprobation, they made themselves still further such by their actual sins.

XX. Although the promise made to Noah (or the covenant entered into with him, Gen. 6:18) as to the preservation of the world from a flood was universal (extending even to the brutes, Gen. 9:10, 11), it does not follow that the covenant of grace (renewed with him as to eternal salvation) was of the same extent, since it is expressly limited to the seed, with whom at length Japheth (or his posterity) was to be associated (Gen. 9:26). Ham and Canaan were excluded from it and devoted to destruction (Gen. 9:25). Yea the nations who were to spring from the sons and grandsons of Noah are so separated from each other that many also depart from the church (Gen. 10:11, 12). Nor if the covenant of grace was included and shadowed forth in that general promise, ought it immediately to be universal. Nothing is more frequent than to adumbrate something particular by a universal; for instance, the waters of the flood are the symbol of baptism (1 Pet. 3:21); the first creation, the type of the second.

XXI. All men coming into the world are illuminated by Christ by reason of his divinity (inasmuch as he is the Word and the Son of God) by the light of nature, through the common notions (*koinas ennoias*) and indistinct conceptions (*prolēpseis*), impressed upon them. But the same thing cannot be said of Christ economically considered (inasmuch as he is Mediator and God-man [*theanthrōpos*]) as if he illuminated all by the light of grace. This is the privilege of believers, who are in the church and rejoice in the light of the word and Spirit. Jn. 1:9 treats concerning the former and not the latter relation (*schesei*).

XXII. That is always true which can be affirmed, whether affirmed concerning a fact or not, but only in that sense in which it can be affirmed. But what cannot be affirmed, except on the positing of some condition (which, being denied), is not true. For example, it can indeed be affirmed that the pagans are commanded and bound to believe the gospel, if it were announced to them; but it is not true that they are commanded and bound to believe the gospel, although not announced to them. It can indeed be affirmed that Christ died for them, if the gospel should be announced to them and if on hearing the gospel they would repent and believe, because then they would belong to the elect and the covenanted. But it cannot be affirmed (nor is it true) that Christ died for them, even if they do not believe or repent, or hear the gospel; for then the argument is drawn from the conditional to the absolute.

XXIII. Although he has given various testimonies of his goodness and patience to the pagans (by which they ought to have been excited to glorify him continually as their Creator and to give thanks to him for so many benefits received), it does not follow that the mercy and placability of God were revealed to them. If any generic and confused knowledge of the divine placability could be held, it is not immediately to be inferred that a distinct and specific knowledge is possessed by them (by which the mind of the sinner can be elevated to a certain and true confidence of the pardon of his sins and of eternal salvation). For without Christ and his satisfaction (which cannot be gathered from the light of nature), it cannot possibly be held. Besides the covenant of grace does not consist only in a revelation of placability, but of actual reconciliation (*katallagēs*) whether made or to be made. Nor is it sufficient for salvation to know that God is placable, unless we know that he had really been appeased or certainly will be.

XXIV. Although God did not leave himself among the Gentiles entirely without proof of his existence, providence and beneficence through the temporal blessings he has bestowed upon them (Acts 14:17), it cannot be lawfully concluded that the knowledge of saving grace was given to them (unless we wish to confound nature with grace and to make fruitful showers and seasons heralds of the gospel, against the testimony of the apostle—"God suffered them to walk in their own ways," to wit, by depriving them of the light of his word and saving knowledge of Christ). Now it is one thing to testify his beneficence and forbearance (*anochēn*) towards men by the giving of bodily goods or by a suspension and delay of merited punishment (arising from the goodness and wisdom of God, the Creator and governor, in the order of nature); another to show his mercy in the remission of sins and the communication of spiritual and eternal goods (which cannot be done without Christ). The former was granted to the Gentiles and not the latter. Our Calvin excellently teaches this on the passage: "We must see," says he, "how these two things agree with each other. For if God testified of himself, he did not suffer, as far as was in his power, the world to err. I answer: this kind of testimony, of which mention is made, was such as could deprive men of excuse, but was not sufficient for salvation. For the expression of the apostle is true, that by faith they understood the world was made by the word of God; and yet a faith derived not from the mere sight of heaven and earth, but from the hearing of the word. Hence it follows that men cannot be brought to a saving knowledge of God, except by guidance of the word. Nor yet does this prevent them from being inexcusable even without the words, who although naturally deprived of light, still have blinded themselves by their own wickedness" (*Acts of the Apostles* [trans. J.W. Fraser, 1966], 2:13, on Acts 14:17), as Paul teaches in Rom. 1.

XXV. When Paul says, "God hath made of one blood all nations of men . . . that they should seek the Lord, if haply they might feel after him, and find him" (Acts 17:26, 27), he intimates indeed that God had so manifested himself in nature by creation and providence and by the various blessings which he continually conferred upon them, that they ought to have been incited to seek (i.e., to know and worship him as their author). But it cannot be concluded that God did this with the design and end that men should seek him savingly (i.e., to fly to him and seek his grace). (1) Such a seeking supposes faith in the seeker (Heb. 11:6), which is not given without the word (Rom. 10:17). (2) It treats of such a seeking which can be made as if by feeling (i.e., in the midst of darkness), which cannot be said of that which is made either by invocation and prayers or with the desire of living holily and uprightly (which is done by the light of faith and of the divine word). (3) Paul accommodates his discourse to those whom he addresses (to wit, the Gentile philosophers—the Stoics and Epicureans—whose questions for the most part concerned the existence and providence of God; nor did they proceed further). He shows therefore that there are so many proofs of the existence and providence of God that he might even be felt by the blind; nor should they any longer refer either to fate or fortune, but regard God alone, the Creator and preserver of the world. (4) The apostle calls that dispensation with respect to the Gentiles "the times of ignorance" (Acts 17:30), which he opposes to the external revelation of the word made in the New Testament (in which he commands all to repent), which could not be said if he had given to them a revelation sufficient for salvation. Nor if he says "God commandeth all men everywhere to repent" does it follow that the call is universal under the New Testament with respect to each and all; no more than when Paul says, "The gospel was preached to every creature which is under heaven" (Col. 1:23) can it be inferred that even then in the time of Paul the gospel was preached to each and all. Thus is intimated only the generality of the call to all people and persons indiscriminately, in opposition to the Old Testament (under which it was restricted to a single nation).

XXVI. The passages of Paul urged here (Rom. 1:19, 20; 2:4) were examined in Volume I, Topic I, Question 4; cf. also Topic IV, "Of Predestination," Question 17, where the various objections belonging here are answered.

XXVII. The covenant of grace ought not to extend as widely as the covenant of nature (although its blessings are enlarged) because grace ought to be compared with the fall; not in extent, as if they were of equal breadth (in which sense all would be saved in Christ even as many as perished in Adam), but in intensity and efficacy. Thus it is true that where sin abounded, there grace much more abounded because it is more to save one than to lose a thousand.

XXVIII. If Adam represented all in the covenant of nature and in his fall, it does not follow that it was equally the case in the restitution and the covenant of grace. The force of the representation ceased in the fall, when he precipitated himself and his posterity into destruction. Hence he does not sustain anymore a public, but a private character and thus the covenant was made with him and his posterity; not all, but with those who belong to Christ and are included under the seed of the woman.

XXIX. The promises of the covenant of grace are not absolutely and simply universal because in the Old Testament they were not promulgated to all (Dt. 7:7, 8; Ps. 147:19, 20; Acts 14:16; 17:30). Nor are they promulgated in the New Testament, since it is plain that the gospel was preached successively and there are still many nations to whom that preaching neither formerly, nor at this day, has reached. Rather the promises are only relatively and limitedly universal from the twofold manner of the divine dispensation; the one external as to obligation (which is extended indiscriminately to classes of individuals, although not to individuals of classes); the other internal (as to application and fruit) with respect to all and each believer, without distinction of nation, sex or age and condition. Hence frequently that universality is restricted to believers from the Jews and Gentiles (Rom. 3:22, 23; 10:12; Acts 10:43; 13:43; Jn. 3:16). And the nature of the promises (which can only be received by faith) demands this (Gal. 3:14; Rom. 4:13). Now all men have not faith (2 Thess. 3:2), but only the elect (Tit. 1:1, 2). And these are the true and proper object of them, who on that account are called "the children of promise" (Rom. 9:6, 7).

XXX. Nor can it be said that the promises are universal of themselves and from the intention of God, inasmuch as God seriously wishes all to be saved and to come to the knowledge of the truth; but that all do not obtain it, is accidental on account of the wickedness and unbelief of men, who obstinately resist the Holy Spirit and hinder his operation. For it is falsely supposed that God seriously intends the salvation of all; this cannot be said of those whom he reprobated from eternity and to whom he wishes to give neither the gospel nor faith, without which the promise can neither be known nor received. (2) Although it is true that men resist the Holy Spirit and hinder his work, it is no less true that God does not furnish to all that grace by which the resistance of the heart may be taken away; that this is the special gift of God (Mt. 13:11; Rom. 11:7), which destroys the universality of the promise.

XXXI. Although the federal promises are not absolutely universal, the foundation of consolation (and certainty of salvation) is not on that account overthrown as no sure inference can be drawn from a particular. They always have their own universality with respect to all believers. In this respect, an argument can solidly be drawn for the consolation of believers by a practical syllogism (whose major is founded on Scripture and minor is built upon the testimony of the believer's heart) in this way: the gospel promises pertain to each and all believers; now I believe; therefore they pertain to me also. (2) So far is consolation from being strengthened by the absolute universality of promises that it is the rather weakened and diminished. Since on that hypothesis, the promises pertain to believers and unbelievers promiscuously (to those to be saved and to be damned), no solid consolation and assurance of salvation can exist here. For what foundation of consolation can be in that which is common to those who will be saved and to those who will be lost?

XXXII. That Calvin's opinion did not differ from the common and received is most clearly gathered from his various writings. "Now Pighius may vaunt that God willed all to be saved, since not even the external preaching of the doctrine, which is far inferior to the illumination of the Spirit, is common to all" (*Concerning the Eternal Predestination of God* [trans. J.K.S. Reid, 1961], p. 109). "If he wished his will to be known to all, why has he not published his law to the nations; why did he keep the light of life shut up in a narrow place" (ibid., p. 108)? "While I say that reconciliation is offered to all, I do not mean as if that grace, by which God reconciles the world to himself, has reached all" (ibid., p. 149). And a little after: "Why did he not will the gospel to be preached to all indifferently from the beginning of the world? Why for so many ages has he suffered so many nations to wander in the shades of death?" (ibid.). This then is confirmed: "Now 'God wishes all to be saved' is not to be anxiously disputed because these two things mutually cohere, salvation and the knowledge of the truth; now answer, if God willed to make known his truth to all, why has his pure truth never reached to so many nations from the time that the gospel began to be published? Again why has he not opened the eyes of all equally, when the interior illumination of the Spirit, vouchsafed only to a few, is necessary to faith?" (*Calumniae Nebulonis*, CR 37.293; cf. also ICR, 3.22.2, p. 934 and 3.24.15, pp. 982-83; *The Second Epistle of Paul . . . to the Corinthians and . . . Timothy* [trans. T.A. Smail, 1964], pp. 205-20 on 1 Tim. 2).

Seventh Question: The Twofold Economy of the Covenant of Grace

Why did God will to dispense the single covenant of grace in different ways? In how many ways was it dispensed? And what was its economy?

I. The substantial unity of the covenant of grace has been proved before. Now its economical diversity is to be explained. For as the manifold (*polypoikilos*) wisdom of God shines forth wonderfully in the works of nature and in their extensive variety, disposition and diverse government; no less (yea, more clearly) does it shine forth in the works of grace and especially in the varied dispensation of the new covenant. It had various forms and as it were faces, on account of the varied economy of the mystery of Christ (who is its foundation), which God so willed to administer as to propose it at first somewhat obscurely and then more clearly; first in the promise and then in the fulfillment. Hence a twofold economy of it was instituted—the one old, which is usually termed that of the Old Testament, which promised Christ about to come; the other, the new, called the

one covenant dispensed in different ways?
9:5 - grace is common to the covenant (of Christ)

New Testament, which announces Christ as manifested and incarnate and dead. In the former, God spoke to the fathers at sundry times and in divers manners (*polymerōs kai polytropōs*). In the latter, however, he hath spoken unto us by his Son (Heb. 1:2).

Why God dispensed the covenant of grace in divers manners. (1) His mode of acting demanded it.

II. If it is asked, Why did God will to institute such a dispensation of the covenant, the sole will of God can here be abundantly sufficient to bridle curiosity. In the meantime, there are not wanting various wise reasons for this counsel. (1) God's mode of acting seems to demand this. He does not accomplish great things together and at once (which however he might easily do), but successively and by various steps that thus his wisdom and power may be the more clearly perceived. So the covenant of grace (deservedly called the greatest work of God and worthy of the highest admiration) he willed to perfect and promulgate by degrees in order that it might have its beginning and increments before its full consummation should follow. Nor was it agreeable to the wisdom of God that so great light (as is in the gospel) should be poured out together and at once and by one impulse as it were, but by degrees and by strictures; like the sun, which not in one moment, but gradually ascends to the meridian. The apostle teaches this in a few but expressive words when he says, "God at sundry times (*polytropōs*) and in divers manners (*polymerōs*) spake in time past unto the fathers" (Heb. 1:1). The former denotes "the various modes of revelation" under the Old Testament; the latter the different degrees by which he manifested himself unto the fathers.

2. The condition of the church.

III. (2) The condition of the church demanded it. For as he willed to lead it along through various ages, so he determined to deal with it in diverse ways. Therefore while it was in infancy and had not reached maturity, it was to be treated as an infant (Gal. 4:1). Thus God, as it were lisping, gave it the smallest measure of revelation, and kept it under the first elements and rude figures which were afterwards to make way for a fuller revelation, when it had advanced and arrived at adult age.

3. The dignity of the Messiah.

IV. (3) The dignity of the Messiah and the excellence of the work to be accomplished by him. As he (not immediately from the beginning for the weightiest reasons, but at length in the fulness of time) was to be manifested, it was suitable to propose his image beforehand to excite a desire for him and to keep their minds in the desire and expectation of him, lest they might grow weary by too long a delay. It was just to reserve the open declaration of so great a mystery for Christ (the chief Prophet) that he might more clearly explain the distinction between Moses (the servant) and Christ (the Master); between the symbolic teacher (teaching the first elements) and the heavenly teacher (revealing all secrets). Finally, a conviction of man's weakness ought to precede that the necessity of grace and a more ardent desire for the Savior (by whom it was to be brought) might be more clearly known and excited.

4. The nature of things.

V. (4) The nature of the things, for since they were still future and prophecies before their fulfillment are wont to be somewhat obscure (at least as to the manner of fulfillment), it is not to be wondered at that at first they were set forth more obscurely and then more clearly, the nearer the time of fulfillment approached. Thus the light increased more and more. There was a progress in revelation: prophet handed on to prophet, and he received the lamp of the gospel by which the church might be illuminated, adding a new measure of light. The same promises are repeated and illustrated. The more the time of fulfillment presses on, the clearer and fuller they become. Before the law given by Moses, the promise was somewhat obscure; from the giving of the law until the times of the prophets less obscure; from the times of the prophets until John the Baptist, clearer; after the preaching of John clear; after the coming of Christ most clear. Thus from the beginning, the Messiah was promised only as the seed of the woman (Gen. 3:15); afterwards as the son of Abraham (Gen. 12:2); to spring from Judah (Gen. 49:10); and in the tribe of Judah from the family of David (2 S. 7:13, 14). Afterwards various circumstances concerning the condition of his mother were added, that she would be a virgin (Is. 7:14); concerning the place of his nativity (Mic. 5:2); concerning the time (Dan. 9:24-27); his twofold state of suffering and glory (Is. 53); his forerunner (Mal. 3:1); and other adjuncts which shed more and more light upon the promise.

VI. Nor without a weighty reason was it that this mystery was so much the more obscurely set forth as the times were farther distant from the coming of Christ. (1) It was fitting that the times should be the darker, the farther they were from the rising of the sun of righteousness. (2) The nearer the coming of Christ approached, the more earnestly ought the minds of men to be excited in expectation of him. (3) The nearer the church was to her commencement, the more uninstructed she was and therefore needed to be taught by the ruder elements.

The Old Testament stretches from Adam to Christ.

VII. Further the diversity of that economy is wont to be comprehended in two parts called the Old and New Testament (as was said before). The former extends from Adam to Christ; the latter extends from Christ to the end of the world. Whatever in the dispensation of that covenant was typical (connoting imperfection and the confession of a ransom [*lytrou*] not as yet paid) pertains to the Old Testament. Whatever indicates redemption actually purchased by Christ, that is peculiar to the New. I am aware that a threefold division (*trichotomian*) is more acceptable to some so the administration of the covenant of grace may be considered: (1) under the promise before the law, from the first gospel until Moses (which they hold to have been a promise of mere grace and freedom without any yoke and burden of the accusing law); (2) under the law, from Moses to Christ (where they wish the Old Testament at length to begin whose inheritance was the land of Canaan); (3) under the gospel, where the New begins. But we do not think that the received opinion (which retains the twofold [*dichotomian*] division and designates the first economy before Christ under the notion of the Old Testament) ought to be discarded. In accordance with Scripture usage, the promise is not only referred to the time before the law, but is extended to all the ages following under the law until Christ. This is gathered from the following passages: Acts 2:39; 7:17; 13:32; Lk. 1:72; Rom. 9:4; Eph. 2:12. And the term "Old Testament" is not restricted to the Mosaic economy, but is extended to the whole dispensation which preceded Christ from the fall of man and the promise given to him (2 Cor. 3:14). Hence Christ is called the Mediator "appointed for the redemption of the transgressions that were under the first testament" (Heb. 9:15); not only under the law, but even from the beginning of the world. In Heb. 8:13, the Old Testament is called whatever has "waxed old," not only the ceremonies first introduced by Moses, but sacrifices and circumcision, which prevailed before the law was written.

VIII. If for a peculiar reason the covenant of the Old Testament is sometimes attributed to the Mosaic economy, it does not follow that the Old Testament had then at length begun. The same religion prevailed in both, before and after the law, sacrifices, circumcision and many other things—which constitute the Old Testament. But it was done for the purpose of great confirmation because then the confirmation of the ancient together with the new rites approached a certain form of sacred things. The period was so enriched with that solemn renewal of the covenant (and by many additions) that it was far more perfect and seemed as it were to absorb all that went before. In this sense, circumcision (which was long before Moses) is said to have been given by Moses (Jn. 7:22). Often in Scripture that is said to be made which is renewed and proposed in a more illustrious manner, as was said before concerning the making of a new covenant in the last days. Hence the explanation of the passages Dt. 5:2, 3; Jer. 31:32; Gal. 4:24 is easy. In these texts, the beginning of the covenant (or Old Testament) seems to be made from Moses and the covenant made by him with the Israelites in Horeb. There the reference is not to the thing itself, but only to the mode of the thing; not that it should be denied that God made a covenant with the fathers (which is so often asserted elsewhere; yea, whatever God did to Israel, he did in virtue of the covenant given to the fathers, Ex. 2:24); but only to intimate that it had not as yet been made in this manner and form; and with such an apparatus (by speaking to them from the midst of thunderings and lightnings) giving them a law written with his own hand, with the addition of so many rites.

IX. When Paul says the Old Testament was "dedicated with blood" (Heb. 9:18, 20), he does not wish that its origin should be referred only to the shedding of blood (*haimatekchysian*) spoken of in Ex. 24:6 (as if it was as yet recent). Besides the fact that this consecration could have been already made by the shedding of blood (*haimatekchysian*) in the patriarchal sacrifices, if it be referred to Ex. 24, it will denote only a solemn dedication, not the first institution, as that also can be said to be *enkainizesthai*, which at length is solemnly dedicated, although the thing itself had existed long before. *Enkainia* can therefore be understood of any dedication, whether the first or repeated (1 Mac. 4*:56*, 59*; Jn. 10:22; Heb. 10:20).

X. If the covenant of grace (contained under the bare promise made to Adam) is said by theologians to have received more federal relation (*schesin*) in the time of Abraham and a more perfect character of a testamentary disposition in the time of Moses, it does not follow from this that the fathers before the law were excluded from the embrace of the Old Testament; or that the Old Testament should be restricted only to the typical promise of the land of Canaan. Rather it means that the progress of the revelation of the covenant of grace may be marked and the infancy and rudiments of that economy (which were before the law) may be distinguished from its more perfect constitution. Although under the Old Testament in a certain period of it the inheritance of the land of Canaan was given to Israel, this does not impair the complete nature of the Old Testament, which embraces whatever was typical and ceremonial in that dispensation even from the very beginning of the world.

The first age of the church from Adam to Abraham.

XI. However, that we may speak distinctly of that twofold economy, the former (that of the Old Testament) may be considered under three periods or stages: from Adam to Abraham; from Abraham to Moses; from Moses to Christ. The first period extends from Adam to Abraham. In this time, the sum of the covenant of grace was contained in the briefest, but still most clear words of the first gospel (*protevangelii*) or first promise: "The seed of the woman shall bruise the head of the serpent" (Gen. 3:15). By this, the faith of the first parents was supported, the substance of the oracle being this—A certain one will at some time arise who will snatch from perdition those with whom God had made a covenant, that he will be bruised by the one through whose deceit they had fallen into this calamity. In this the wonderful mercy of God shines forth, which willed to propose on the spot the remedy of grace to Adam for healing the wound received from Satan. Thus where the poison of sin grew, there he might meet the antidote (*alexipharmakon*) of grace (which physicians tell us is often observed in nature, especially in a poisonous flower and its antidote placed near each other).

XII. The thing itself strongly proves that this prophecy referred to Christ. Nor will we here waste time on the Vulgate version, which substitutes the feminine pronoun for the masculine, so as by a manifest corruption the passage may be applied to the blessed virgin. Instead of *hv'*, they suggest we should read *hy'* (as with wicked fraud Guido Fabricius Boderianus endeavored to corrupt the passage in the Antwerp interlinear royal copies). The sounder papists themselves pressed by the force of truth have acknowledged it (as Pagninus, Arias Montanus, Vatablus, Isidore Clarius, [Franciscus] Lucas Brugensis and innumerable others). It is evident that this is contrary to the authority of all the approved manuscripts; to the most ancient versions of the Chaldee Paraphrase; of the Septuagint; to grammatical analogy, which cannot allow a feminine relative to be referred to a masculine noun (*zr'*) and to a verb (*thshvphnv*) of the same gender; contrary to the nature of the thing ascribed to this subject, which is such that it altogether surpasses human strength (to wit, the bruising of the serpent's head, i.e., the destruction of Satan's empire), everywhere in Scripture claimed by Christ.

XIII. Therefore by the "seed of the woman" we infer that Christ is antonomastically and principally meant. (1) To him is not opposed another seed as before, but a particular antagonist (namely the serpent) whose head was to be bruised by that seed to intimate a certain particular single combat. (2) The manner of the fight and of the victory is such as can belong to no one except God; a victory over the Devil, who could be overcome neither by man himself (already overcome), nor by an equal angel, but by God alone. (3) The Scriptures refer to Christ the same promise of the blessed seed made to Abraham: "He saith not, And to seeds, as of many; as of one, And to thy seed, which is Christ" (Gal. 3:16). (4) The fulfillment of this prophecy is everywhere in the New Testament claimed for Christ (Jn. 12:31; 14:30; Lk. 10:18; Col. 2:15; Heb. 2:14, 15; Rom. 16:20; 1 Jn. 3:8; Rev. 12:8, 9).

XIV. Now Christ is said to be about to bruise "the head of the serpent" inasmuch as he ought to abolish the tyranny and entire power of the Devil given to him through sin (designated by the head of the serpent, as the venom of the serpent is principally in the head and this being wounded and bruised it can injure no more). A symbol of this bruising was that wonderful power granted to the disciples of Christ, of which Luke speaks: "Behold, I give unto you power to tread on serpents and scorpions, and over all the power of the enemy: and nothing shall by any means hurt you" (10:19); cf. what is attributed to the pious, "Thou shalt tread upon the lion and adder" (Ps. 91:13). This however is not accomplished together and at once, but by various degrees. First, "in himself" for us. Then "in us" and by his power through us. "In himself" (1) by his incarnation and death, by which he so most fully satisfied divine justice and expiated our sins as to take away from Satan all right of accusing men afterwards: "Through death he destroyed him that had the power of death" (Heb. 2:14, 15); "He made a show of principalities and powers openly, triumphing over them in the cross" (Col. 2:15); (2) by his resurrection and ascension, in which (as the conqueror of death and the sepulcher) "he led captivity captive" (Eph. 4:8); (3) by the preaching of the gospel, concerning which he says, "I beheld Satan as lightning fall from heaven" (Lk. 10:18, 19); (4) by his final advent when Satan and the false prophet are to be cast into the lake of fire and brimstone (Rev. 20:10). "In us" by the operation of the Spirit, by which believers are said to "overcome the wicked one" (1 Jn. 2:14; Rev. 12:11): (a) in calling, by which they are turned from Satan to God, from the power of darkness to the kingdom of light (Acts 26:17, 18; Col. 1:13); (b) in justification and sanctification, which frees us from the guilt and dominion of sin, by which Satan exercised his tyranny over us (Rom. 8:1, 31-33; 1 Jn. 5:18); (c) in the final resurrection and last judgment, by which Satan will be bruised under our feet (Rom. 16:20) and thrown headlong into eternal fire (1 Cor. 15:54, 55; Rev. 20:10, 14; Mt. 25:41).

XV. However, this victory to be gained by Christ over Satan ought not to be bloodless and without a struggle, for his heel was to be bruised by the serpent ("thou shalt bruise his heel"). On both sides, there must be a fight, but very dissimilar. Christ seeks and bruises the head of the serpent, namely overthrows the kingdom of Satan. But the serpent can only reach and bite the heel (i.e., prostrate the humanity and flesh of Christ, by which he trod the earth, through temptations, persecutions and death); still not with destruction because he soon arose and came forth victorious; so that here the sufferings must necessarily be joined together with the glory about to follow. The same thing is also beheld in believers. God indeed permits that old serpent to bite the heel of believers (i.e., to vex them in body and in the goods of the body by temptations, when he sifts them [Lk. 22:31], by afflictions and crosses [Rev. 2:10; 12:13-15] and by death, as he is a murderer from the beginning); but the heart and head he cannot strike because he has no power over the soul and salvation.

XVI. Although, indeed, it cannot be doubted that Christ is primarily and by way of eminence (*kat' exochēn*) to be understood here by "the seed of the woman," yet since the word "seed" is collective, usually embracing not one, but more individuals (and ought to be so taken when referring to the seed of the serpent), we are not to reject the opinion of those who maintain that in the former case it should be taken collectively, so as to be extended to all believers who are Christ's and who have a part in that promise; but nevertheless that in the collection some one may be prominent who is the author of so great a work. Thus the whole church is here included (the head with the members), but with this difference—that to Christ it is attributed primarily and principally; to the others secondarily and dependently; to him primitively and eminently; to the rest participatively and in an inferior degree; to him as the conqueror and leader, by whose power all things are performed; to the rest as soldiers who fight under his standard and whom he called to receive the fruit of victory. This was the opinion of our Calvin with many others who on this account are most unjustly traduced by the Lutherans (as if he Judaized on this subject and overturned that first gospel promise because he takes the seed of the woman, not individually, but collectively). He expressly states that "it is necessary to come to the one Head, that we may discover to whom the victory belongs" (*Commentaries . . . on Genesis* [trans. J. King, repr. 1946], 1:170-71 on Gen. 3:15), which he frequently confirms in his *Institutes* (ICR, 1.14.18, pp. 176-78 and 2.13.2, pp. 476-78).

XVII. From all this, we readily gather that the primeval promise given to our first parents (although somewhat obscurely) contained as in a compendium the principal parts of the covenant of grace and of the gospel. Although in those words is not expressly set forth the answer or restipulation of believers; still they contain a manifestation of the obligation of the worship and obedience to be rendered by them to God, which it also appears was rendered when the name of the Lord is said to have been called upon (Gen. 4:26). Besides, the promise on God's part necessarily demands faith on man's part; hence the faith of Abel, Enoch and Noah is celebrated by Paul (Heb. 11:4-7). Nor did the propitiatory (*hilastika*) sacrifices in those first times offered to God by the pious (not without God's command) have a different reference, since they were offered in faith (which is founded upon the word of God) that they might sustain themselves in the hope of a redemption to come.

The second age, from Abraham to Moses.

XVIII. The second age stretches from Abraham up to Moses, the deliverer of the people and promulgator of the law. In this era, since the recollection of the divine promise was almost obliterated in the minds of men and the contagion of idolatry had contaminated even the holy race of Shem and the family of Terah (Jos. 24:2), God (having selected and called Abraham) renewed the covenant with him and his seed, engaging that the Messiah should be born of his posterity and demanding faith and obedience in turn from him (Gen. 22*:18; 17:1, 2).

XIX. The promise was not only of temporal and earthly blessings, the multiplication of his seed and the rendering his name illustrious and the possession of the land of Canaan; but principally of spiritual and heavenly blessings, included in the benediction pronounced upon Abraham—"In thee shall all the families of the earth be blessed" (Gen. 12:3). "In thee," i.e., "in thy seed," as it is explained in Gen. 22:18 and 26:4. Now this benediction embraces all kinds of salutary goods (Eph. 1:3) (as the malediction opposed to it included every kind of evil). That it is evangelical, both the nature of the thing itself proves and the voice of the apostle teaches, when he refers it (1) to justification—"The Scripture foreseeing that God would justify the heathen through faith, preached before the gospel unto Abraham, saying, In thee shall all nations be blessed" (Gal. 3:8*); and "Christ hath redeemed us from the curse of the law, being made a curse for us: that the blessing of Abraham might come on the Gentiles through Jesus Christ" (Gal. 3:13, 14); (2) to adoption—"If ye be Christ's, then are ye Abraham's seed, and heirs according to the promise" (Gal. 3:29) and "We, as Isaac was, are the children of promise" (Gal. 4:28); (3) to conversion—"Ye are the children of the prophets, and of the covenant which God made with our fathers, saying unto Abraham, And in thy seed shall all the kindreds of the earth be blessed. Unto you first God, having raised up his Son Jesus, sent him to bless you, in turning away every one of you from his iniquities" (Acts 3:25, 26*); (4) to the promise of the Spirit (Gal. 3:14); (5) to glorification; hence it is said the Gentiles will sit down with Abraham in the kingdom of heaven (Mt. 8:11; Lk. 16:23) and the elect are called "blessed of the Father" (Mt. 25:34).

XX. The seed on whom that blessing should be conferred is not the natural only, but the mystical and blessed seed (namely, Christ) according to the apostle: "To Abraham and his seed were the promises made. He saith not, And to seeds, as of many; but as of one, And to thy seed, which is Christ" (Gal. 3:16). And the thing itself necessarily demands this because the seed is such as that in it all the families of the earth should be blessed and Abraham become the father of many nations (which cannot be said of Isaac, but only of Christ). Such a seed that "faith in it should be imputed for righteousness" (Gen. 15:6), i.e., bring with it justification, which is fulfilled only in Christ ("in whom the promises are yea and Amen," 2 Cor. 1:20). In Christ, therefore, the nations were to be blessed both "by and on account of him" who acquired that blessing by his merit; and "in him and with him," i.e., in virtue of the mystical union which believers have with him, so that the unity of the seed may be marked, not strictly of the person, but of a certain mystical body, united by faith under Christ, the head, from whom the remaining members are denominated.

XXI. Finally the federal promise (in which all the rest are contained) is that "God would be a God unto him, and to his seed after him" (Gen. 17:7), concerning the meaning and extent of which we have already spoken. Moreover God was not content with expressing that promise in words, but wished to give it additional confirmation in multiple ways, so that its immutability might be declared (Gal. 3:15, 17). Now there was a threefold ratification (*kyrōsis*). The first by the solemn rites of those entering into covenant in the dissection of animals and the passing between them (Gen. 15:10-18), which we are taught was the customary manner of making covenants (Jer. 34:18). The second, by the sacrament of circumcision added to the promise (Gen. 17:9-14). The third, by a solemn oath "wherein God, willing more abundantly to show unto the heirs of promise the immutability of his counsel, confirmed it by an oath" (Heb. 6:17, 18 with Gen. 22:16).

XXII. Conditions of the covenant are also proposed. First, faith by which he is said to have "believed in the Lord" (Gen. 15:6). Second, conversion and the desire of sanctification: "Walk before me and be thou perfect" (Gen. 17:1). Both of these is sealed and taught in the sacrament of circumcision and wonderfully exerted their power in the father of believers. (a) Faith, when he embraced the promise concerning the seed (Gen. 12:4-6); expected from him all good times, not only temporal, but especially spiritual and eternal (which therefore was justifying faith). Its virtue was increased by the circumstances that he believed things so difficult and almost incredible: the possession of a land held by a most powerful nation, while he was a single individual; offspring, himself and Sarah being now stricken in years; the blessing of all nations in his seed, yet never seen by him; the strength of this faith Paul graphically describes (Rom. 4:18-21). (b) His obedience was remarkable in two things: [1] in going out from the house of his father and from his own country, not knowing whither he went (Heb. 11:8); this is the highest glory of obedience to follow God calling and leading, to go whither you know not and when you are ignorant as to whether it will be well or evil with you. [2] In the "offering up of his son" (Heb. 11:17; Gen. 22:2), the greatest and most grievous trial of all; not only to lose an innocent, beloved and only son, but to kill and butcher him with his own hands, so that he who had been a father in giving life, should become a murderer (*homicida*) to take it away. And that promptly and without delay, the knife being passed through each member, to tear him to pieces after the manner of a sacrifice and to offer him as a whole burnt offering, so that he might be entirely consumed; and that too after the thing had been premeditated, three whole days being occupied with such thoughts. It seemed a sacrilege rather than a sacred thing, contrary to all divine and human law, against the light and influence of nature itself, against the promise given concerning the blessed and blessing seed, and thus against the eternal faith and salvation of Abraham and all the covenanted. And yet he obeyed and was prepared from faith in the resurrection of the dead to offer even such a son (Heb. 11:19), which remarkable obedience obtained for him the name of "friend of God" (Is. 41:8; Jam. 2:23).

XXIII. There was a manifold difference between the economy of this age and the preceding. The former is more properly called by the name of promise, the subsequent by the name of covenant. For in this the condition of obedience is perspicuously and expressly set forth, which in that was only implicitly contained. The one had indeed sacrificial rites, but the other was sealed by the sacrament of circumcision as by a peculiar seal. The former was proposed to the human race in common and indefinitely; the latter was particularly restricted to Abraham and his posterity. In the former, the promises were not so clear, nor was there such an express mention made of the calling of the Gentiles, nor anyone proposed as the father of the covenanted (who moreover is called the heir of the world [Rom. 4:13*, 16, 17] because he had as his own sons the world, i.e., all nations, to whom the blessing was to come).

The third age, from Moses to Christ.

XXIV. The third age of the church and of the Old Testament economy extends from Moses to Christ or from the promulgation of the law in the desert until the manifestation of the Messiah. In this interval of time, the appearance of things was far different. Then was the Israelite republic reared by Moses for whose benefit the covenant of grace had not only the relation of promise and covenant, but a more perfect and testamentary form which was ratified by the blood of victims (Ex. 24:6-8), as the symbol of the blood of Christ (Mt. 26:28). Before, the covenant had been restricted to certain persons and families only; but by Moses it was enlarged both objectively (since it was established with an entire and numerous nation) and subjectively, on the part of the covenant itself ratified by many solemnities, not only with the Passover and other sacraments, but with very many other things—especially with sacrifices (figures of the death of Christ) and new prophecies coming in concerning Christ to be revealed in his own time. Thus after the seed of Abraham grew up into an entire nation, God most clearly manifested himself to it in the deliverance from Egypt; not only as *'l shdy* (Gen. 17:1, i.e., as omnipotent and self-sufficient) that no one might doubt concerning the fulfillment of his promises; but also as *yhvh* (Ex. 6:2, 3), who, with eternity and immutability of essence, would maintain constancy and fidelity in carrying out his promise concerning the deliverance of the people from the Egyptian captivity (which subsisted with the fulfillment itself).

The author of the promulgation of the law.

XXV. In this interval, the law was promulgated. Its author was God, that one lawgiver, who can save and destroy (Jam. 4:12), who has the right of dominion over the conscience and who by taking Israel for a people to himself, in a special manner proved himself to be their God; and indeed the whole sacred Trinity in the one Godhead of which we are bound to acknowledge and worship an equal majesty and glory; but in a peculiar manner the Son, as the leader and governor of the people. For the same angel who appeared to Moses in the burning bush, afterwards gave him the law (Acts 7:38). That he was not a created angel clearly appears from his speaking in the person of Jehovah (which belongs to no angel or delegate) when he calls himself the God of Abraham, Isaac and Jacob. And such things are ascribed to him as cannot be said of a created angel (as that he should not be provoked, for he will not pardon) since the name of God is in him (Ex. 23:20, 21). Hence he is elsewhere called "the angel of his presence" by way of eminence (*kat' exochēn*, Is. 63:9), and "of the covenant" (Mal. 3:1) and for this cause the Israelites are said to have tempted Christ (1 Cor. 10:9, to wit, that angel in the pillar of cloud and fire).

Angel ministers.

XXVI. The less principal or instrumental causes were created angels (as stipulators) who attended the supreme lawgiver for his greater glory as witnesses of all the things done and as ministers, by whose intervention not only the thunders and lightnings and those terrible signs which attended the promulgation of the law were produced, but also the voice of God speaking was put into an intelligible form. In this sense, the law is called "the word spoken by angels" (*logos lalētheis di' angelōn*, Heb. 2:2). It is said to have been "ordained by angels in the hand of a mediator" (*diatageis di' angelōn en cheiri mesitou*, Gal. 3:19), i.e., commanded, digested, enacted and promulgated by the ministry of angels. To this the words of Stephen refer where he asserts that the Israelites received the law "by the disposition of angels" (*eis diatagas angelōn*, Acts 7:53) whether by *diatagas* are understood (with some) bands disposed in military order of angels attending their commander (which seems to be meant when it is said, "Jehovah came from Sinai, he came with ten thousand of saints," Dt. 33:2); or (as others hold) *diatagē* is put here for a "command," "ordination" and "sanction" (as in Rom. 13:2). Thus the sense is, the law was received at the regulations of angels, to whom, as ministers and heralds, the Son of God had committed its promulgation. To these, however, Moses (an external and visible minister) was added, who as to the external dispensation could bear the relation of mediator, but such as would be only typical, as the redemption (*lytrōtēs*) was typical (Acts 7:35), as a servant in the house of God (Heb. 3:2, 5) and a mere ambassador between God and the people (Dt. 5:31).

Manner of giving the law.

XXVII. The manner of giving the law was majestic and terrible, not only on account of the barriers placed around the mountain (that free access should be given to no one)—the punishment of death was denounced upon him who should attempt to ascend the mountain or to touch it (Ex. 19:13)—but also from the horrible signs and prodigies which attended the presence of God on the mount (Ex. 19:16-19; Heb. 12:18, 19), by which not only the people but Moses himself trembled all over and openly acknowledged that he exceedingly feared and quaked (*ekphobon kai entromon*, Heb. 12:21). This intended nothing else than to indicate the tremendous majesty of the lawgiver and to designate the nature of the law, by which no approach unto God can be given to the sinner; yea, it is nothing else from itself than a minister of death and condemnation.

Whether the decalogue is the covenant of grace.

XXVIII. And hence we can clearly gather what is to be determined about a question here agitated by some—whether the decalogue promulgated on Mount Sinai contained nothing except the covenant of grace and its pure stipulation. For since from what has already been said, it is evident that the manner of this lawgiving (*nomothesias*) was terrific, smiting with fear their consciences and by the severity of its threatenings removing them from the sight of God, everyone sees that this was not the manner (*schēma*) or the genius of the covenant of grace (which exhibits God to us as appeased and recalls sinners to itself by the sweetness of its promises). Besides, the law (contained in the decalogue) is of natural right, founded on the justice of God; while the covenant of grace is of positive and free right, founded on his good pleasure (*eudokia*) and mercy. The latter sets forth a surety, promises remission of sins and salvation in his satisfaction; not only demands but also effects obedience. But in the decalogue, no mention either of a surety or promise of salvation to be given to sinners occurs; but a bare promise of life to those doing and a threatening of death to transgressors. Hence the law of works (comprised in the decalogue) is everywhere contradistinguished by Paul from the law of faith and the promise of grace (Rom. 3:27; Gal. 3:17, 18) for as the law is not of faith (Gal. 3:12), so neither is faith of the law. So great is the contrariety between these two means that they are wholly incompatible (*asystata*) with each other.

XXIX. This we do not say, as if we wished either to deny that the covenant of grace had then been made with the Israelites (which is expressly taught in Dt. 5:2 and is easily inferred, both from its sanction given in Ex. 19:5 and from its solemn confirmation and ratification alluded to in Ex. 24:8, 9 where mention is made of the sprinkling of the blood of victims and the approach of the elders to God). Or as if we supposed the decalogue had nothing in common with the covenant of grace and was nothing else than the covenant of works itself, renewed for the purpose of recalling the people to it, that they might seek life from it. For since the law was made weak in the flesh after sin (Rom. 8:3), the way to life by it became altogether impossible for man. Hence Paul testifies that the law was not given that it might give life (Gal. 3:21) or that the promise first given might be abrogated (Gal. 3:17), but "on account of transgressions," that sin being uncovered by it, the necessity of grace might be the more clearly seen.

XXX. Thus it is rightly said that the decalogue belonged to the covenant of grace; yea, in a measure flowed from it inasmuch as it was promulgated from the counsel of God that it might serve him—both antecedently as a schoolmaster, by convincing of sin, bringing to it men smitten with fear of death and despairing of themselves; and consequently as a rule, prescribing the measure of obedience and holiness demanded by God in the covenant of grace. Thus God willed that there should be in the decalogue various connections with the covenant of grace to recall the people to it, in order that from a knowledge of their own weakness and the terrible denunciation of death, they might not wholly despair of the grace of God. Even the preface (in which he professes himself to be the God of his people, who led them out of Egyptian bondage) and the promises annexed to the second and fifth precept, teach this with sufficient clearness.

XXXI. Meanwhile it pleased God to adminster the covenant of grace in this period under a rigid legal economy—both on account of the condition of the people still in infancy and on account of the putting off of the advent of Christ and the satisfaction to be rendered by him. A twofold relation (*schesis*) ought always to obtain: the one legal, more severe, through which by a new promulgation of the law and of the covenant of works, with an intolerable yoke of ceremonies, he wished to set forth what men owed and what was to be expected by them on account of duty unperformed. In this respect, the law is called the letter that kills (2 Cor. 3:6) and the handwriting which was contrary to us (Col. 2:14), because by it men professed themselves guilty and children of death, the declaration being written by their own blood in circumcision and by the blood of victims. The other relation was evangelical, sweeter, inasmuch as "the law was a schoolmaster unto Christ" (Gal. 3:24) and contained "the shadow of things to come" (Heb. 10:1), whose body and express image is in Christ. Hence, as much of trouble and vexation as that economy brought in its former relation (*schesin*), so much of consolation and of joy it conferred in the latter upon pious men attending to it and seeking under that bark and veil the spiritual and evangelical truth (which the Holy Spirit taught them by a clearer revelation). God supplied more and greater helps according to the time, not only by promises and oracles often repeated, but also by more expressive types and more perfect shadows and figures, in which they had a more exact delineation of the thing itself and a more accurate picture (*programma*) of Christ crucified before their eyes as it were in types.

The twofold economy of the covenant under the Old Testament: (1) external, its matter and form.

XXXII. According to that twofold relation, the administration can be viewed either as to the external economy of legal teaching or as to the internal truth of the gospel promise lying under it. The matter of that external economy was the threefold law—moral, ceremonial and forensic. The first was fundamental; the remaining appendices of it. The form was the pact added to that external dispensation, which on the part of God was the promise of the land of Canaan and of rest and happiness in it; and, under the image of each, of heaven and the rest (*sabbatismou*) in him (Heb. 4:3, 9); or of eternal life according to the clause, "Do this and live." On the part of the people, it was a stipulation of obedience to the whole law or righteousness both perfect (Dt. 27:26; Gal. 3:10) and personal and justification by it (Rom. 2:13). But this stipulation in the Israelite covenant was only accidental, since it was added only in order that man by its weakness (*adynamian*) might be led to reject his own righteousness and to embrace another's, latent under the law.

The end.

XXXIII. The end of that economy (by way of negation [*kat' arsin*]) was not the justification of man. By reason of the moral law, they could easily know their own sins, by which they became guilty (Rom. 3:20); the irritation of their lusts (Rom. 7:7);

the impossibility of fulfilling the moral law (Rom. 8:3); the curse of the law, which it denounced against the least transgression (Gal. 3:10). By reason of the ceremonial law, they knew that the end of that economy was not the justification of man (1) from the nature of the ceremonies, which was wholly worldly and carnal, having nothing in common with the conscience; (2) from their repetition and iteration, such as the justification which consists in not remembering of sins (Heb. 8:12); (3) from their condition, both because they were mutable, which would not have been the case if sinful man could have been made perfect by them, and because they were as figures and shadows (*hypodeigmata*) of good things to come (Heb. 10:1; Col. 2:17). But affirmatively (*kata thesin*), it was: (1) in order that by it the people might have an external form of religion approved of God; (2) that it might be a servant to the covenant of grace and Moses to Christ (Rom. 10:5, 6), that by that economy the spiritual economy might be presented, which should have solitary place in the New Testament (God here acting after the manner of illustrious artists, who before putting their hand to the work, are accustomed first to draw a rude outline with the pencil of the idea [*skiagraphian*] of it conceived in the mind [*hōs en typō*]); (3) to render the gospel or yoke of Christ more easy by its burdensomeness (Mt. 11:28, 29).

Marks and effects: (a) the promise of Messiah's coming.

XXXIV. The marks and effects of that economy were external: (a) the promise of the Messiah about to come, and the delaying of the satisfaction to be made for us. For although he was promised in oracles and graphically shadowed forth in various types, yet neither was he to be incarnate during that whole period nor was he to pay the ransom (*lytron*) required for our redemption. In this sense, Peter says it was revealed unto the prophets that not unto themselves, but unto us they did minister the things which are now reported unto us concerning the sufferings of Christ and the glory that should follow (1 Pet. 1:10-12). And hence it is rightly said that everlasting righteousness had not as yet been brought (Dan. 9:24), that sins remained without a true expiation, until they should be destroyed by the satisfaction of Christ. Not that they still rested upon believers (from whom they were transferred to Christ, the surety), but because they existed in their relations to the surety, upon whom they rested for expiation; nor were they taken away until the payment was made.

(b) Obscurity.

XXXV. (b) Obscurity because the sun of righteousness not having as yet arisen, only a prophetic word was given like a candle shining in a dark place (2 Pet. 1:19). The time of the Old Testament was a time of night, but the time of the New, the day (which dawned upon us). Hence the ceremonies were like a veil covering the mysteries, which the apostle teaches us was adumbrated by the veil over the face of Moses (2 Cor. 3:13) because Moses there allegorically denotes the whole economy of the Old Testament. This was also signified by the veil of the tabernacle and of the temple, preventing the Israelites from entering and beholding the most holy place.

(c) Bondage.

XXXVI. (c) Bondage or servile condition, by which the ancient church was in subjection to the law, the pact of slaves (Gal. 4:24, 25), which (with respect to those who sought salvation by the law) was absolute and total; but to those who beheld Christ in it, only relative (as in Egypt the Israelites, who did not think of deliverance, were altogether slaves; those, however, who accepted it in faith were indeed slaves in body, but not in soul). Hence Paul says, "A child differeth nothing from a servant" (Gal. 4:1) and Christ calls them "laboring and heavy ladened" (*pephortismenous kai kopiōntas*, Mt. 11:28)—the words indicating a servile labor and yoke, such as formerly belonged to the Israelites in Egypt. The bondage was on this account the more grievous both because (like Pharaoh's taskmasters), it exacted fulfillment and yet did not supply the strength for it, and because it threatened the least transgression with punishment and indeed with the divine malediction itself. Now this servitude was confirmed by the elements of the world (*stoicheia tou kosmou*), i.e., ceremonies (so called on account of their rudeness and imperfection) under which they were ordained and which (on account of that immense multitude of rites, which they were bound to perform under severe threatenings) oppressed the worshippers. In this respect, they are called "the yoke of bondage" (Gal. 5:1) and an intolerable burden (*abastakton*, Acts 15:10).

And the spirit of bondage, Rom. 8:15.

XXXVII. This bondage, the spirit of bondage attended (adjusted to the servile economy, Rom. 8:15), which commonly wrought a servile fear of God, the judge, and a dread of punishment. From this a continual anxiety and solicitude as it were by the law and its threats sounded daily in their ears (more than alacrity) by the doctrine of grace preached sparingly and somewhat obscurely; not that believers were absolutely destitute of the spirit of adoption (as is afterwards said), but because it excited emotions suitable to that condition, in which the heir being still a child did not differ much from a servant.

(d) Rigor and severity.

XXXVIII. Hence (d) rigor and severity arose from the legal discourses frequently mingled and the promises of grace repeated somewhat rarely and obscurely; also through compulsion, by which they were impelled to duty through fear of punishment rather than from the love of God and of righteousness; Moses continually like a hard master with his rod, not so much persuading as extorting obedience. Here belongs the terrible apparatus under which the law was given, by which not only the people, but Moses himself also is said to have been terrified (Heb. 12:21). That rigor was not without purpose; the wantonness of Israel could hardly otherwise be thoroughly tamed, whom Moses and the other prophets so often reproached for its hard neck and adamantine heart.

(e) Purity of flesh.

XXXIX. (e) To that economy belonged eternal purity of the flesh or immunity from carnal guilt, purged of which (from the institution of the law) they could freely mingle in public assemblies and perform public worship together with others, such as consisted in the observance of ceremonies (Heb. 9:13); in contradistinction to this is purity of conscience and immunity from the spiritual guilt of sin. Here comes in the immunity from temporal punishments in the court of earth which (as to sins not committed with uplifted hand) was granted through the sacrifices, which (without relation either to repentance or faith) restored men to their rank and rendered them free from all forensic punishment. As to spiritual punishment in the court of heaven, freedom from it could not be obtained by the sacrifices of beasts as such; for between the guilt (which was moral) and the satisfaction, there had been no proportion, but only by them as figures and types.

Adjuncts: (1) weakness.

XL. Finally, the adjuncts were various: first, weakness and imperfection because this economy had no true ransom (*lytron*) for sin (but only a type of it), nor the accompanying power of the Spirit to subdue the flesh and furnish strength to fulfill the law. Thus by it as such no one could be saved causally, i.e., either be justified (Acts 13:39; Heb. 10:1, 2) or be sanctified (Heb. 9:14, 15) or obtain life, because it was a ministry of condemnation and death (2 Cor. 3:6, 7; Heb. 7:18). Under this name Paul testifies that this economy was not "faultless" (*amempton*, Heb. 8:7), to wit, "on account of its weakness and unprofitableness" (*dia to autēs asthenes kai anōpheles*, Heb. 7:18).

(2) Mutability.

XLI. Second, mutability and abrogation because it embraced things earthly, carnal, perishable and in their very nature corruptible—consisting only in meats and drinks and divers washings and carnal ordinances (*dikaiōmasi sarkos*), which could not sanctify the conscience, and were not to continue forever; but were imposed until the time of reformation (*mechri kairou diorthōseōs*, Heb. 9:9, 10). Hence an abrogation (*athetēsis*) must take place on account of its imperfection (Heb. 7:18), especially a more perfect economy succeeding; as when the sun rises, there is not more need of candles or lighted torches.

(3) Glory and splendor.

XLII. Third, the glory and splendor with which this economy was instituted, which shone forth most of all in the magnificent apparatus and illustrious miracles which God willed should attend the promulgation of the law. Hence Paul calls this a "glorious ministration" (2 Cor. 3:7, 9). But that glory was both terrifying, inspiring with fear, not only the people, but also Moses himself, who is said to have trembled (*entromos*) on account of it (Heb. 12:21); and mutable and transient, as being worn out (*katargoumenē*) and antiquated (2 Cor. 3:11). This appeared in the glory of the countenance of Moses, which was to be done away (2 Cor. 3:7).

2. The internal dispensation. It contained Christ and promises temporal and spiritual.

XLIII. Such was the external dispensation of the Old Testament. The internal, latent under it, pertains to the substance of the covenant of grace and of the gospel promise. This was also administered in different ways and by various degrees. On God's part, it contained both Christ himself (the foundation of the covenant promised in the oracles and lying under the types of ceremonies) and his sufferings, crucifixion, death and glory (obscurely indeed and hidden). Hence the gospel is said to have been formerly a hidden mystery (Rom. 16:25) because obscurely proposed under the various veils of figures, but still so that through them it could be seen (as was done by Moses, Heb. 11:26); and promises (temporal as well as spiritual), which the formula of the covenant ("I am thy God") includes in itself. Temporal, as the inheritance of the land of Canaan and the earthly blessings (given in detail, Dt. 28) which were promised in it to the faithful worshippers of God; less principally and secondarily on account of the disposition of the Israelite people (still children and more affected by carnal than spiritual things); but spiritual primarily and principally, as absolutely necessary to salvation.

XLIV. Now although that revelation of grace was somewhat obscure and sparing as to mode (being wholly enigmatical and specular, and such that Christ could be beheld in it only under a veil—as formerly Moses, 2 Cor. 3:7), still it was sufficient as to substance. Hence the knowledge of the ancients and their faith was founded upon it (although it varied as to circumstances and mode and might be called implicit in this sense and confused), by which the thing indeed is known, but not in such a way that it is also known as to all (which distinguishes it from other things). We wish this to be understood of the state of the church of the Old Testament and not of particular persons (as Abraham, Moses, David and others who enjoyed a richer knowledge of the divine mysteries). Still it did not differ as to substance and no less saved them, than faith under the New Testament saves us. For Christ saves, not as perfectly known and according to all circumstances, but as truly and seriously apprehended.

What it was: (1) remission of sins; (2) adoption; (3) sanctification; (4) the gift of the Spirit (Ezk. 36; Jer. 31; Is. 43); (5) resurrection; (6) eternal life.

XLV. To these spiritual promises pertain (1) remission of sins and justification. As this derogated the law causally in itself considered, so it is ascribed to faith in Christ (Acts 13:39; Rom. 4:7) and was claimed by the fathers (as Abraham, David and others, Ps. 32; Rom. 4); although it would be less felt on account of the interposed cloud of the law and the payment not as yet actually made. (2) Adoption, attributed to the Israelites, not only as external (Rom. 9:4), but also internal, without which the former would have been useless (Gal. 4:2); although it was connected with a servile condition on account of the minority of children. They were children who could and were bound to invoke God as their Father (Job. 34:36; Is. 63:16), but minors subjected by their Father to the ferule and rods of schoolmasters (Gal. 4:2, 3); who were not admitted to so great familiarity with the Father as to penetrate into his intimate counsels. (3) Sanctification, which is everywhere commanded and promised under the Old Testament (Lev. 26; Is. 1). (4) The gift of the Spirit, included in the promise made to Abraham (Gal. 3:13, 14) and found to have been promised frequently elsewhere (Is. 44:3; Ezk. 36:26, 27; Zech. 12:10). However this was not in the same manner as under the New Testament (speaking commonly of the state of the whole church) whether intensively as to degree or extensively as to gifts (either ordinary or extraordinary), which with respect to the church are peculiar to the New Testament. The effusion of the Spirit was due to the glory of Christ after he entered into heaven (Jn. 7:39). Such was the Spirit as was the nature of the covenant: (a) the Spirit of illumination, but not so clear and distinct as in the New Testament, and moreover joined with ignorance of the various circumstances of the mode, as it appeared in believers and in the apostles themselves in the time of Christ before the outpouring of the Holy Spirit; (b) the Spirit of adoption or sonship (because otherwise the believers of the Old Testament could not have known infallibly that they were children of God, which however they did know, when they invoked God as their Father, Is. 63:16); yet it was not purely such, but mixed with slavery and moreover not of full emancipation, who on account is called "the spirit of bondage" (Rom. 8:15), not absolutely, but relatively (inasmuch as by it believers were made certain of their own adoption, but not fully as to feeling and use); (c) the Spirit of consolation and of hope, but in the same manner (inasmuch as each was connected with some fear and the terror of death and of the curse which the law threatened); (5) the resurrection of the dead, which Christ deduced from the formula of the covenant; (6) eternal life, also included in that formula as the apostle gathers from the same (Heb. 11:10), not to mention the various prophetic oracles by which it was promised, of which we have spoken before in the question concerning the unity of the covenant.

What is the new dispensation?

XLVI. Thus far the old dispensation; the new succeeds, the administration of the covenant without the law and ceremonies after the appearance of Christ. It is called "new" not as to the substance of the covenant (which is the same in both) but: (1) as to the circumstances and mode, being manifested without a veil and the law (in which way that covenant appeared as if new or renewed), also because it sets forth Christ not to be exhibited but as exhibited, in which way it can be called new both intensively as to degree of light and extensively as to amplitude, extending itself indiscriminately to all nations; (2) as to the excellence and glory of this dispensation which far surpasses the old (2 Cor. 3:9, 10), as new is elsewhere taken for what is remarkable and superior (Rev. 5:9; Ps. 33:3); (3) as to perpetual duration, by which it happens that it is as it were always new, while those things which ought to cease are called old.

It consists: (1) in the incarnation of the Messiah; (2) in the abrogation of the ceremonial law; (3) in the outpouring of the Spirit; (4) etc.

XLVII. It consists (1) in the advent of the Messiah, his manifestation in the flesh and the fulfillment of the whole law by him (namely, of its ceremonies, prophecies and the entire righteousness prescribed by God in the law). (2) In the abrogation of all the ceremonies and of the whole legal dispensation by which the covenant of grace was veiled. (3) In the effusion of the Holy Spirit, both visible (as to extraordinary gifts) and invisible and perpetual (as to the ordinary gifts necessary for salvation to every believer, which is stated as a peculiar benefit of the New Testament in Joel 2:28-32). First, with respect to the extraordinary gifts: although enjoyed by certain persons under the Old Testament, yet as they were very few did not belong to the church. With respect to the ordinary gifts, which are both greater intensively (as to degree of light, trust, consolation) and extensively (as to parts because it teaches all things [Jn. 16:13; 1 Jn. 2:20] and as to object because it teaches all from the greatest to the least [Heb. 8:11]).

XLVIII. (4) In the calling of all nations, which is peculiar to the New Testament as to the full knowledge of circumstance and of mode. This was not attended to by the ancients who thought that the Gentiles would be brought into the old dispensation; and as to actual execution which could take place while the former worship stood. (5) In adoption, which in the New Testament not only as to the thing is such as it was in the Old, but also as to mode, condition and effects because: (a) in the New Testament it is proposed as having been acquired through Christ (Jn. 1:12); (b) it is purely such without the schooling, servitude and fear, and thus not of childhood, but of adult age and of emancipation, conjoined with the highest boldness (*parrēsia*) and confidence (Rom. 8:15). (6) In liberty, not only spiritual (which also existed in the Old Testament), but also external, by which we are free from the legal ceremonies (Col. 2:20-22) and besides are become the servants of Christ alone and not of men (Gal. 5:1). (7) In sanctification, which is greater in the New Testament as to higher illumination of the intellect (as to mode), which is not external and ceremonial (which even a hypocrite may have), but internal (as to efficacy), which is greater on account of the greater measure and virtue of the Spirit and as to the motives, which are far stronger, being drawn from the example of Christ. (8) In eternal life, which belongs to the New Testament: (a) as to actual aquisition obtained by the blood of Christ (which in the Old Testament was only moral); (b) as to the actual entrance of Christ as man into heaven, as the true sanctuary, into which he entered as a forerunner, not only for himself, but also for us (Heb. 6:20); (c) as to a far more illustrious manifestation (2 Tim. 1:10), which in the Old Testament was more obscure (Heb. 9:8)—hence confidence and hope is far greater, all fear of death being removed, entering now within the veil (Heb. 6:19); (d) as to the more frequent promises, which regard solely eternal life, those being removed which have reference to this life and its prolongation (which were far more frequent under the Old Testament).

The adjuncts are: (1) posteriority of time; (2) dignity and perfection; (3) perpetuity.

XLIX. The adjuncts of this dispensation are: (1) posteriority of time, not indeed as to substance (which was the same from the beginning) but as to circumstances and mode; (2) dignity and perfection by which in comparison with the old, it is far more worthy and perfect and such as becomes the manly age; (3) perpetuity because this economy is the last until the final advent of Christ, when it will be changed into the immediate and direct communion with God by which God will be all in all.

Eighth Question: The Difference Between the Old and the New Covenants

How the old and new covenants differ from each other: whether essentially (as to substance of doctrine) or accidentally (as to the manner of dispensation). We make distinctions.

I. As the Old and New Testaments have a multiple signification, so the proposed question ought to be answered in different ways, and the varying opinions (even of the orthodox) on both sides be reconciled.

II. Sometimes the Old and New Testaments are considered in relation to the writing and by this name the prophetic and apostolical writings are designated (delivered to the church by men of God either before or after the coming of Christ, 2 Cor. 3:14). In this sense, the New Testament is said to have been veiled in the Old and the Old Testament unveiled in the New. But we do not now treat of them under this relation (*schesei*), but with regard to the doctrine delivered.

How the Old Testament is taken broadly.

III. In this sense, the Old Testament is taken most especially in two ways, either broadly or strictly. Broadly, it denotes in general the whole dispensation under which the fathers lived from the beginning of the world until Christ. It contained the doctrine of grace delivered to the ancients, promising salvation and life to the people openly (indeed, under the condition of perfect obedience rendered to the moral law and the threatening of transgressors with death, together with the intolerable burden of ceremonies and the yoke of the most restricted Mosaic polity); reservedly, however, under the condition of repentance and faith in the Messiah about to come. In this respect, the Old Testament embraces three things most especially: (1) old doctrine, partly legal and partly evangelical; (2) an old servile form of worship and ecclesiastical service, laborious and shadowy; (3) the old method of external polity bound to one people and place.

Strictly.

IV. Strictly, however, it denotes the covenant of works or the moral law given by Moses—the unbearable burden (*abastaktō*) of legal ceremonies being added, absolutely and apart from the promise of grace. The former was signified properly and of itself (if the scope and intention of the lawgiver be considered) because in that first economy he joined together these three things by giving the old covenant or legal dispensation, not to abolish the promises, but to lead unto Christ. The latter is accessory and accidental, springing from an ignoring of the true end and the devising of a false. The true end was Christ for righteousness to every believer (Rom. 10:4), but the self-righteous Jews did not obtain this end because it was proposed under a veil (2 Cor. 3:14), i.e., under a wrappage of types and of figures because the promise of grace on account of Christ was clothed with legal rites. Hence they invented a false end, maintaining that the law was given in order that by its observance they might be justified before God and be saved (Rom. 10:3-5). Against this error the apostle everywhere disputes from that hypothesis which takes the law strictly and opposes it to the promise.

The new covenant is taken either broadly or strictly.

V. The new covenant is also taken in a twofold manner either broadly, inasmuch as it stands for the covenant of grace in general made with sinners, which existed under the Old Testament as well before Christ appeared as under the New after he had been manifested; or strictly, for the covenant of grace promulgated after the manifestation of Christ in the flesh, which should continue to the end of the world.

VI. Those of our party (as Rollock, Piscator, Trelcatius and others) who make two covenants diverse in substance, take the old covenant strictly, not only separating the promise of grace from it, but opposing the one to the other. In this sense, Paul seems to take it frequently (as 2 Cor. 3; Gal.4), so that the old covenant is the covenant of works and the new the covenant of the gospel and of faith. On the other hand, they who maintain only one (as Calvin, Martyr, Ursinus) take the word covenant more broadly, as embracing also the promise of grace (although somewhat obscurely). Because that promise was dispensed in different ways before and after Christ, they distinguish it into two—the old and new—by a distribution not of genus into species (as the former), but of subject according to accidents (which the others do not deny); thus they differ only as to the different use of terms, but not as to the thing itself (as Calvin observes, ICR, 2.7.2, pp. 350-51).

Opinion of the Lutherans concerning the difference between the old and new covenants.

VII. In assigning the difference between the Old and New Testaments the Lutherans differ also from our men and a question was agitated by them on this subject growing out of the sacramental controversy. They maintain that these two covenants are not only to be distinguished in substance, but also that the promise of grace is to be excluded from the old covenant. They accuse our party of error in setting forth the nature of the old covenant. Brochmann says, "Lutheran theologians unanimously teach that by the name of Old Testament is properly and in Scripture phrase signified that legal covenant which God made with the Israelites under the ministry of Moses" ("De Veteri et Novo Testamento," 2, Q. 4 *Universae theologicae systema* [1638], 2:283). He adds also that the question between us is "whether that gratuitous covenant entered into with the believing fathers in the first time of the fall, is the very same in substance with the New Testament" (ibid., p. 284). This, he says, is asserted by us, but denied by them.

VIII. However, we readily grant that the Old Testament and the Mosaic covenant taken strictly and absolutely as to the legal relation (*schesin*) differ in entire substance from the New. Hence the law and Moses are opposed to grace and to Christ (Jn. 1:17) and by Paul the letter and the Spirit, the ministration of condemnation and of righteousness (2 Cor. 3:6, 7). So we maintain that taken broadly and with the other evangelical relation (*schesei*) (clothed, namely, with its pedagogical circumstances), it did not differ as to substance, but only as to manner of dispensation.

IX. They take for granted that the old Mosaic covenant is so restricted to the moral law and its ceremonies and polity that the promise of grace is neither open nor impliedly contained under it. The contrary is evident from various considerations: (1) from the author of the covenant itself, who was the God of Abraham, Isaac and Jacob (i.e., as joined with the people by the Abrahamic covenant) and indeed acting from the gratuitous adoption and love of the people (Dt. 4:6-8; 7:6-8)—which is not of the legal, but of the evangelical covenant; (2) from the threefold matter, both the kind of doctrine (which was so legal in the commands of morals, as to be also evangelical in the promises of Christ and his grace) and the form of worship (which was wholly shadowy and typical referring to Christ) and the mode of polity (which was subordinate both to the doctrine and the worship, inasmuch as it ought to distinguish the people from whom Christ was to spring, and among whom he was to be preached and suffer); (3) from its twofold form, external, which was the legal obligation both of the people to keep the law and of God to give life (if the law was obeyed) and internal, in the gratuitous promise according to which God would be to the people for a God and the people in turn would be to him for a people (Lev. 26:11, 12; 2 Cor. 6:16); (4) from three effects: (a) the preparation of the sinner for seeking Christ by the moral law (Rom. 10:4; Gal. 3:24); (b) the showing of him by the ceremonial law (Heb. 10:12; Col. 2:16, 17); and (c) the offering of the same by the promise of grace connected with both.

X. Nor can they deny this if they wish to be consistent. As Brochmann in the same place confesses, they acknowledge that before Christ appeared in the flesh, there existed already in the church of God the doctrine concerning Christ, gratuitous reconciliation by Christ and that the fathers of the Old Testament were saved in no other way than by the grace of Christ alone. Nor do they deny that both covenants under the Old and New Testaments treated of Christ, the God-man (*theanthrōpō*); but they hold that this was in a different manner. Now this being posited, who does not see that the difference is only in the mode of dispensation, not in the very substance of the doctrine?

XI. To no purpose, however, does the author add in the same place: "There is as great a difference between the old covenant of grace and the New Testament, as there is between a promise and the fulfilment of a promise; between signification and exhibition; between a figure and the body itself; between an image and the thing designated by it (to wit, the old exhibited Christ only in promise and various types; but the new exhibits the body itself, the thing promised to the fathers and represented by types)" (Brochmann, "De Veteri et Novo Testamento," 2, Q. 4 *Universae theologicae systema* [1638], 2:284). Although we concede that this is true with respect to the complement of the promise (which referred to the manifestation of Christ in the flesh, the actual expiation of sin and the acquisition of salvation, which was to be made only under the New Testament), we deny that it can be said with respect to the application of salvation and the participation of the benefits of Christ and the fruit of his death and satisfaction, which were not withheld from the fathers. In this sense, they are rightly said to have had the thing signified and promised, the body itself and the living image of the legal shadows; not in virtue of the law, but of the promise. This he voluntarily acknowledges when he says, "The fathers did not stop in these signs, but lifted their hearts to the thing adumbrated in the signs, as Abraham who saw the day of Christ (Jn. 8:56) and Moses who preferred the reproach of Christ to the treasures of Egypt (Heb. 11:26)" (ibid., p. 285).

Sources of explanation.

XII. It is one thing for the old covenant strictly taken to differ essentially from the new. The apostle had this in mind in the allegory of Sarah and Hagar (Gal. 4:24), the former generating to freedom, the latter to bondage. He disputes against the false apostles who confounded the law and the gospel, which is referred to also in 2 Cor. 3:6, 7, in the antithesis between "the letter" and "the Spirit," "the ministration of condemnation" and "of righteousness." It is however another thing (when broadly considered as to economy) to be opposed as to substance, which we deny.

XIII. That which is grown old does not forthwith differ essentially from that which endures, if the growing old is only as to the mode and circumstances of the dispensation, not as to the thing itself. The Old Testament even broadly taken had become old as to the gospel relation (*schesin*), not with respect to what was essential to it (since Christ is the same "yesterday, today, forever," Heb. 13:8), but with respect to the circumstances and mode of dispensation, which was more obscure and harsher on account of the infancy of the church. To this also belongs the carnal worship prevailing under the Old Testament (which was to be abrogated).

XIV. What was established only by the blood of animals differs essentially from that which was established by the blood of Christ. But although the Old Testament is said to have been dedicated by the blood of calves and goats (Ex. 24:3, 4; Heb. 9:18, 19), this must be understood only as to the letter. As to the mystical sense, it was also dedicated by the blood of Christ, since by that typical blood the true blood of Christ (by whose efficacy and merit alone the ancients could be saved) was adumbrated (Mt. 26:28).

XV. There is not the same opposition throughout between the Old and New Testaments as there is between the law and the gospel. The opposition of the law and the gospel (in as far as they are taken properly and strictly for the covenant of works and of grace and are considered in their absolute being) is contrary. They are opposed as the letter killing and the Spirit quickening; as Hagar gendering to bondage and Sarah gendering to freedom, although the law more broadly taken and in its relative being is subordinated to the gospel. But the opposition of the Old and New Testaments broadly viewed is relative, inasmuch as the Old contained the shadows of things to come (Heb. 10:1) and the New the very image (*tēn eikona*).

XVI. Those do not agree in substance. Some of their sacraments are significative and exhibitive at the same time; others only significative. In the Old Testament, the sacraments were not only significative, but in their way also exhibitive of the thing signified. In this sense, circumcision is called a "seal of the righteousness of faith" to Abraham (Rom. 4:11*) and the fathers are said to have drunk Christ (1 Cor. 10:4). Nor is it an objection that Christ was not as yet incarnate and therefore could not be exhibited. Although he was not physically exhibited by incarnation, still he was morally exhibited in the promise by the reception of faith (which is "the substance of things hoped for" [*tōn elpizomenōn hypostasis*]).

XVII. Moses and Christ can be compared with each other in three ways: (1) relatively, as type and prototype because Moses prefigured Christ in various particulars, whom on that account he predicts would be a prophet like unto himself (Dt. 18:15); (2) comparatively, as the lesser is compared with the greater and the servant with his master (Heb. 3:4-6); (3) by way of dissimilarity and opposition, inasmuch as the law was given by Moses and grace and truth by Jesus Christ (Jn. 1:17). Grace is opposed to the curse of the moral law and the truth to the shadows and figures of the ceremonial law; or it is called true grace as not concealed under typical and carnal figures.

Opinions of the Reformed concerning the difference between the Old and New Testaments. They differer: (1) as to time.

XVIII. The orthodox maintain that the difference between the Old and New Testaments (broadly considered) is only accidental, not essential (as to the circumstance and manner and degree of the thing); not as to the thing itself, which was the same in each. This was proved before and is shown further: (1) as to time because the Old preceded Christ, while the New follows him. The former referred to Christ to be manifested and to come, while the latter refers to Christ already manifested and exhibited. Hence Christ pronounces the eyes of the apostles happy because they saw those things which the prophets and kings desired to see and yet did not see (Lk. 10:23, 24).

(2) As to clarity.

XIX. (2) As to clearness and obscurity because in the New the mysteries are far more clearly set forth, the veils and shadows of ceremonies and types being taken away. Hence the apostle says of the gospel that "we with unveiled face [*anakekalymmenō prosōpō*, by antithesis to Moses, who veiled his face (v. 7), a symbol of legal obscurity] behold the glory of the Lord in a mirror" (2 Cor. 3:18). The Old Testament was wholly symbolic and figurative. It had a shadow of things to come and not the very image of the things (Heb. 10:1). But the New (in which grace "has appeared [*epephanē*] to us," Tit. 2:11) is plain and open. Hence the time of the Old Testament is compared to the night (on account of the Sun of righteousness not as yet having arisen) and the time of the New to the day (in which the dayspring from on high has arisen). Here we must remark that although the same heavenly inheritance and promise of eternal life occurs in each, still it is differently set forth in the Old and New Testaments. In the New Testament, it is set forth clearly, openly and simply (*nude*) without any wrappings. But in the Old, it is rolled up in types and earthly pledges (among which, after the covenant was made with Abraham, the inheritance of the land of Canaan was most prominent). That this was typical, both reason itself dictates (since the possession of no earthly and finite good however excellent can satisfy and make the soul happy, but only the fruition of the eternal and infinite God himself) and Paul expressly testifies (Heb. 4).

3. As to easiness

XX. (3) As to easiness because administration and service (*latreia*) was far more burdensome in the Old than in the New Testament (whose sacraments are few in number, august in signification, very easy of observance). Here belong the words of Augustine: "The first sacraments observed in accordance with the law were prophetical of Christ about to come which, when fulfilled by the advent of Christ, were done away with and on this account done away with, because fulfilled . . . and others were instituted greater in efficacy, more useful, easier to be performed, fewer in number, revealed as it were by the righteousness of faith and to the sons of God called into liberty, the yoke of bondage being removed, which suited a people hard and given to the flesh" (*Reply to Faustus the Manichaean*, 19.13 [NPNF1, 4:244; PL 42.355]). For indeed the signs added to the word carried with them the genius of the word. The word was not so much of the gospel, as of the promise (*epangelias*); not announcing Christ manifested, but foretelling him to be manifested. Thus the sacraments were types of things to come, not memorials of things past (as are ours, 1 Cor. 11:24); handwritings, not mere receipts; a commemoration of sin, not a commemoration of a sacrifice already offered for sin. Nor is the objection of any force that the blood of victims far more clearly and easily adumbrated the death of Christ than the symbols of bread and wine in the Eucharist; and that there is a greater analogy between flesh and flesh than between flesh and bread. That signification is not to be drawn simply from a physical analogy or as to the physical being of things, but especially as to the moral being and from the divine institution (which is far clearer in the New Testament than in the Old). Before, the death of victims and the blood of lambs were required to prefigure the death of Christ still future; but after it happened in the New Testament, it was unnecessary. It neither ought any more to be adumbrated by the blood of victims as future, but it is sufficient that its commemoration be made in the communion with and application of it (which are better represented by the symbols of bread and wine).

4. As to sweetness.

XXI. (4) As to sweetness because in the Old Testament the law and its perfect obedience was more frequently urged (not indeed to the simple exclusion of gospel promises, but still with this intention—that by that rigorous exaction of obedience, the people still in infancy might be held under guardianship as it were and be compelled to seek Christ), while in the New, the gospel promises are more frequent (still not to the exclusion of the law impelling to offer new obedience by the grace of regeneration). Nor ought the severe burden of the cross (imposed by Christ upon his people in the New Testament) to be brought as an objection here. Besides not being wanting to the pious of the Old Testament (as this is the lot of believers in this world), still it ought not to be so much a burden as an honor to the disciples of Christ (Gal. 6:14), the yoke of

Christ being easy and light (Mt. 11:30). Here belongs the gift of the Holy Spirit, who, although not denied even under the Old Testament to the fathers, yet exercised his power more sparingly and less fully then, in accordance with the time and mode of revelation. Now, however, he exercises it far more richly and with greater fulness. As the revelation of grace is greater and more extended, he ought to be communicated under the New Testament according to the prophecy of Joel (2:28), whose fulfillment Peter claims for the first Pentecost (Acts 2:17, 18).

5. As to perfection.

XXII. (5) As to perfection, for although the Old Testament had an essential perfection as to the substance of the covenant of grace, still it did not have an accidental perfection as to degree. The whole of that economy was typical and shadowy, differing from the New not less than a shadow from the very image (*skia tē eikoni*); a thin shadow and rude outline from a living and express image. Hence the apostle attributes weakness to it (*astheneian*, Heb. 7:8-10), while treating of the imperfection of the Levitical priesthood. The latter having been abrogated, another according to the order of Melchizedek was to be raised up, since perfection was not in the former (whose weakness and unprofitableness [*anōpheles kai asthenes*] the apostle proves both from the infirmity and morality of the high priest and the pollution of sin [from which he was not free] and from the imperfection of the sacrifices and ablutions, which did not reach the conscience and soul, only of legal holiness and of outward operation; nor could the sacrifices of themselves expiate sin with God, Ps. 40:7, 8). And so it was necessary that all these with the tabernacle and the earthly sanctuary should be abrogated, that the way might be opened to the heavenly sanctuary. This also is the case with respect to the worship which flourished under the Old Testament. It was altogether shadowy and carnal, if compared with the worship predicated by Christ and instituted by the apostles (Jn. 4:23) and is no longer confined only to one place as before, but must be performed with "the Spirit" (without carnal types, Heb. 9:10) and "in truth" (without the Mosaic shadows, Col. 2:17; Heb. 10:1).

6. As to freedom.

XXIII. (6) As to freedom because under the Old Testament the spirit of bondage unto fear prevailed (Rom. 8:15). For although the fathers were sons of God and under that name masters and heirs, still they did not differ from servants (as to the external dispensation). As infants and minors, they were held under the severe and rigid schooling of the law (as under tutors and governors by whom they were driven to duty through fear of punishment and by threatenings and stripes, rather than by promises and the love of virtue, Gal. 4:1, 2). Hence although the right of freedom belonged to them in virtue of the covenant of grace and the gospel promises, still they obtained a very small sense and use of it, the threatenings and intolerable (*abastaktō*) yoke of the law bringing them into bondage and filling them with terror (which caused them to be terrified at the appearances of God and to hold as a comon saying, "We shall die because we have seen God"). But in the New Testament, it is a time of freedom because the covenant of grace which genders to freedom is fully revealed (Gal. 4:26). In it is proclaimed through the gospel Jubilee liberty to the captives (Is. 61:1, 2). The spirit of bondage unto fear is no longer given unto us, but the Spirit of adoption and so of liberty unto confidence, by which we cry, "Abba, Father" (Rom. 8:15). "Where the Spirit of the Lord is, there is liberty" (2 Cor. 3:17)—not only of internal communion, which the fathers possessed, but also of external dispensation; not only the liberty of filiation, which belongs also to infants, but also of emancipation, which belongs only to adults (not only as to its right and use and inchoate and imperfect sense, but total and full as to full sense and use, by which, as they are put in possession of the goods, so they have a full knowledge and enjoyment of them for their consolation and the fulness [*plērophorian*] of faith).

7. As to amplitude.

XXIV. (7) As to amplitude because the Old Testament was restricted to one nation—salvation was then only of the Jews (Jn. 4:22); "he hath not dealt so with any nation" (Ps. 147:19, 20). But the New is extended to all indiscriminately, so that in every nation he that "feareth him, and worketh righteousness, is accepted with him" (Acts 10:34, 35). It is restricted within no limits, nor is the worship of God any longer bound to a certain place, but in every place is equally acceptable to him (provided it be sincere and pure). Before, the Gentiles were said to be "afar off" and "aliens from the covenant" (Eph. 2:12). But now, the wall of separation having been broken down, a union has been made of two (to wit, of the Jews and Gentiles in one body) so that they are no longer two, but one (v. 14). Thus in Christ there is no more "Greek nor Jew, Scythian nor barbarian, male or female, but Christ is all, and in all" (Col. 3:11).

8. As to duration.

XXV. (8) As to duration because the Old had become antiquated and should continue only until the time of reformation (*diorthōseōs*, Heb. 9:10; Jer. 31:31). The overthrow of the Jewish republic, the confusion (*confusio*) of the tribes and the irreparable destruction through so many ages of the temple (in which that worship was performed) evinces this even openly. However, the New Testament is immutable and will perpetually endure until the consummation of the ages (*heōs synteleias tou aiōnos*). As perfection is characteristic of its administration, another revelation is not again to be expected, nor any other priesthood and sacrifice in addition to that of Christ, who was made a Priest and confirmed by a solemn oath in virtue of an "endless life" (Heb. 7:16). Hence the gospel is called "everlasting" (Rev. 14:6).

Ninth Question: The Surety of the Covenant of Grace

Whether Christ under the Old Testament had only the relation of a surety giving security or also of a surety promising it. The former we deny; the latter we affirm.

I. In order that the nature of the covenant of grace may be more fully understood, the nature and mode of the suretyship upon which it is founded must be examined more closely. Not that we may inquire into the mediatorial office of Christ (which we will treat about afterwards in its proper place), but only that the manner of the suretyship made by him under the Old Testament may be more thoroughly examined (concerning which the question may be agitated).

II. Moreover, here at the outset, we ought to come back to what we before observed—that this covenant of grace (instituted between an offended God and sinful, guilty man) could not have been ratified except by the intervention of a mediator, to reconcile the parties at variance with each other and perform the office of a surety, not only in the name of God (promising that he would fulfill the promises of the covenant, if we would fulfill its conditions—as, following Socinus, Curcellaeus falsely quibbles); but also to God for us—that he will fulfill all those conditions for us, which being performed, the inheritance according to the testament will come to us (most especially as to the fullest satisfaction to be given to divine justice for our sins). Nor does any controversy exist here among the orthodox, but only with the Socinians and their associates (against whom we will argue when we treat of the satisfaction).

Statement of the question.

III. Thus, the question agitated here properly respects the manner of the sponsion made by Christ under the Old Testament—whether it has only the relation of actual security or also of the promise of it. For there are some who make this another among other differences between the Old and New Testament—that Christ was indeed under that a giver of security, but not a promisor of it, i.e., he actually gave security indeed for the elect, but in such a way that there was not an actual transference of the debt to him; nor were the fathers freed from the guilt of sin, but God retained for himself the right of inflicting punishment upon them, if Christ should desert his bail and not make satisfaction to him. Just as in the civil law a difference is wont to be made between the one actually giving security and promising it: "He is the fidejussor who is so under obligation for another that the other nonetheless remains obligated even until the fidejussor or surety shall have made payment." Hence Justinian observes: "The obligation of the Fidejussors is an addition to the principal obligation" (*Institutes* 3.20* [trans. P. Birks and G. McLeod, 1987], pp. 110, 113). Now he is called an expromissor "who takes upon himself another's obligation, the guilty being set free or in that name not being bound, since he deserved to be bound."

IV. But the common opinion of the orthodox (with whom we agree) is that the sponsion of Christ from the time it was made, had not only the relation of fidejussion (*fidejussionis*) but of expromission (*expromissionis*), by which for that very reason the fathers were truly freed from the punishments due to them. Nor do we think that we should anxiously distinguish here between a fidejussor and expromissor. For the use of these words is not so different as to prevent their being often used promiscuously among lawyers, so that fidejussio has the same meaning as expromission. Cujacius says, "An expromissor is said as if a Fidejussor." "And in the Velleian decree *expromissio* is contained in the word *fidejussio*." "These have the same meaning: *fide jubere*, *judicium pro alio suscipere*, *expromittere*" ("Observationum et Emendationum," 13.35 *Opera* [1609], 4:327). Hence it ought not to appear surprising if, in describing the sponsion of Christ, the words *fidejussio* and *expromissio* are interchanged. Although this difference ought to have place in the civil law strictly speaking, still we do not think in this argument it is fitting to have recourse to political tribunals, that the nature of Christ's suretyship may be explained according to legal formulas. It is evident that there is a very wide difference between the court of earth and the court of heaven, and we here treat not of the human, but of the divine judgment, not of pecuniary debt and a mortal creditor, but of a penal debt and of God, the Judge and ruler of the world. Nor do we treat of an ordinary sponsor and mere man but of an extraordinary and the God-man (*theanthrōpō*), who, as a giver of his own life (*antipsychos*), substituted himself in our place and took upon himself the punishment due to us (a surety which the civil laws do not describe). Hence neither by *fidejussio* nor by *expromissio* (such as occur in human courts) do we think the surety of Christ can be sufficiently explained since its perfection is greater than both. Meanwhile, if we must conform to their usage and employ their words (since others do not occur), we say that it comes nearer to *expromissio* than to *fidejussio*, as it comprehends eminently and most perfectly whatever of perfection and efficacy *expromissio* has. Nor are various reasons wanting.

V. First, from the nature of the suretyship of Christ. Since that sponsion is nothing else than the perfectly absolute and immutable will of Christ, of substituting himself according to the eternal counsel of the Father in the place of the elect, and of making satisfaction for their sins, it necessarily implies by that very thing a real transference of the debts to him and the full deliverance and immunity of those for whom he agreed. Thus *fidejussio* as distinguished from *expromissio* cannot have place here simply, but *expromissio.* For the fidejussor is appointed only to insure confidence concerning the payment (not precisely his own) so as to promise that he will pay absolutely, but that the creditor may be made sure of the payment, where the principal debtor can be supplied still for paying it or at least where he still remains obligated and can and should first be applied to before the fidejussor. But here the case is evidently different. For as the elect were not so absolutely by paying, satisfaction could never be demanded of them. Thus by the suretyship and substitution of Christ in their place, they were freed according to the counsel of God, so that the payment could no longer be demanded of them (which Christ by his agreement took upon himself). In this he truly performed the office of an expromissor, who takes another's obligation upon himself so that the payment is demanded and expected from him alone, the original debtor no longer remaining bound. He so bound himself to the payment by his agreement that from him alone it could be demanded. The elect, who were the original debtors, were freed from all personal obligation and on that account no longer bound, so that if they should wish to pay for themselves, they would deservedly incur the crime of despisers of the Messiah, endeavoring to establish their own righteousness in addition to the acquired righteousness of God. This was the crime of the Jews (Rom. 9:31, 32; 10:3).

VI. Now that such is the sponsion of Christ, Scripture itself not obscurely demonstrates when it testifies that God "laid on him the iniquity of us all, the chastisement of our peace was upon him, and with his stripes we are healed" (Is. 53:5, 6). But how can the sins of men be said to have been cast upon Christ, if his sponsion was not absolute by a true transference of the debt upon him and the liberation of the guilty? Nor should it be said that "Jesus only took on him the sins, when he prepared himself for the sacrifice; and that God laid sins on him because they were actually exacted from him." It is one thing to demand of Christ a debt for present payment; another to lay iniquities upon him, and impute them to him. A debt can be imputed to the surety long before it is demanded for present payment. Isaiah does not teach that sins were then laid on him when they were actually demanded of him; but on this account sins were exacted of Christ by the endurance of punishment because they had already been imputed to him as surety in the counsel of God.

VII. Ps. 40:7, 8 has a reference to this. Christ declares that he came to do the will of his father, i.e., to offer the sacrifice of his own body in place of the legal victims which God rejected as useless. Why then did he manifest so great alacrity and promptness in fulfilling this office, unless even then his sponsion was absolute and simple, implying a true translation of our debts upon him? Nor does it help the matter to reply "that these words are by Paul referred to Christ's coming into the world" (Heb. 10:5). Although Christ could use these words of himself when coming into the world this does not hinder them from being applicable to himself at the time in which the psalmist speaks. Yea, this is necessarily supposed because he is speaking of the eternal and immutable will of God by which Christ (all the legal sacrifices being rejected) was constituted a surety and his satisfaction alone decreed and promised even from the very beginning—as it is written in the volume of the book (to wit, of the Scriptures). To this is added the reply of Christ himself by which he received the call of God and testifies that he is prepared to execute his will. The expression "the Lamb slain from the foundation of the world" (Rev. 13:8), has the same reference, designating the efficacy and certainty of his sponsion. Thus a sacrifice to be made only after many ages is considered as already offered.

VIII. Second, the nature of the thing itself demands this, whether God (to whom the sponsion ought to be made) is considered or the surety (who was bound to make it) or the elect themselves (for whom he agreed) or the nature of the security itself is attended to. As to God, his justice demanded a true expromissor and not a mere fidejussor. As it could not look for payment from the first debtors, so it could only acquiesce in the absolute sponsion of the Son, nor was it agreeable to him that Christ at the same time with the elect should remain bound by the same decree, since for this very reason he was given as a surety to them that on this very account they might be set free. Nor could his wisdom (foreknowing the sure payment to be made by Christ alone) hold under obligation as debtors and regard as still chargeable those from whom the payment had never been sought. Yea, since the works of God are known to him from eternity (Acts 15:18) by the light of omniscience that sponsion was observed by God not only as future, but even as present, yea, as actually performed; and its efficacy gave the same benefits to the fathers which we enjoy, which a mere *fidejussio* could not have conferred.

IX. The quality of the sponsor implies this. As he is God, infinite and most perfect, his sponsion ought to be most perfect and to involve whatever perfection can be conceived to be contained in an expromissor for the liberation of debtors. In addition, since he is such a sponsor as was neither invented nor given by men, but by God himself (yea, who from eternity offered himself to the Father and substituted himself in the place of sinners without their consciousness and desire; who was alone about to give payment according to the immutable decree of God, whose certainty was confirmed by various promises and sealed by many types), he could not have accomplished this unless even then he had fulfilled the functions of an expromissor and not only those of a fidejussor. Hence such was the efficacy and effect of that sponsion that in virtue of it the fathers were wholly freed from all punishments so that the payment could no longer be demanded of them. The learned men with whom we argue have not been able to deny this. Hence the very celebrated Cocceius: "The effect of the sponsion was that sin, after it was committed, was not imputed to the heirs written in the testament, whether there could not be in God the will to punish sin in them, since what had been laid on the surety ought both to rest upon and be demanded from him,

Is. 53:6, 7" ("Summa Theologicae," 35.2 *Opera omnia* [1701-06], 7:239). "For he became the surety of those for whom he was substituted; their sins were laid upon him" (s. 134+).

X. Third, the elect themselves for whom the sponsion was made demanded an expromissor and not only a fidejussor. Their surety ought to be given for life (*antipsychos*) (as was said before) who would substitute himself for the guilty to endure the punishment they deserved and in this way deliver them (which a mere fidejussor could not do, who promises only to assure the creditor that he will receive the payment, but not exactly his own). Again, as the elect were not more by paying, so neither could a payment be expected from them forever; yea, neither according to the decree of God was it ever to be demanded. On this account, the surety was bound to take the payment absolutely upon himself and thus actually to bear the relation of expromissor. Finally, since they were not only about to be saved by Christ, but are in reality saved and received into heaven in virtue of the suretyship of Christ, it does not suffice for Christ to have been a fidejussor (who does not draw after himself the personal liberation of the original debtors); but he ought necessarily to have the relation of expromissor, who acquires absolute deliverance for those for whom he provides security. Otherwise it would be said that they had been freed and yet remained under obligation; that they were esteemed just before God and yet were always under guilt (which is absurd [*asystaton*]).

XI. Fourth, the nature of that suretyship implies this. The absoluteness and immutability contained in an expromission is far more perfectly and eminently apprehended in the sponsion of Christ. For if in the former the surety alone is bound for the payment (the primary debt no longer remaining under obligation) and if from him alone the debt is demanded and the payment expected, here equally the suretyship of Christ excludes the proper payment of the elect because he bound himself so absolutely to the payment that in virtue of it they are freed from all personal obligation and from him alone the payment could be sought and expected. This is further confirmed by the end of the sponsion itself (which was no other than the absolute deliverance of the elect) and since this could not fail to take place, it ought necessarily to put on the nature of an expromission and not only of a fidejussion.

Sources of solution.

XII. Nor can it be said that God has always reserved to himself the liberty or right of exacting the payment from the elect or the original debtors. Since the sponsion of Christ was absolute from the immutable decree of God (by which he was substituted in the place of the sinner and alone was bound to bear the punishment they deserved), it cannot be conceived how (that decree concerning the requiring of punishment from the sponsor alone standing) men can still remain bound and God reserve to himself the liberty of exacting the payment from them. It is true indeed in the civil court that a creditor has the right of seeking a debt from two joint criminals; either from the original debtor or from his surety. But when after the debt is contracted and one becomes a debtor by not paying, a sponsor intervenes (who takes upon himself all the burden of discharging the debt and whose faith the creditor follows), by that very thing the first debtor is relieved of all demands. Otherwise the creditor would act against the admission of a sponsion and would seem to call in question the honesty of the sponsor. So here, because Christ by his sponsion took upon himself the burden of paying for sinners, God by that very thing laid aside the will of exacting the debt from them. This neither the divine equity could endure (that two should remain bound), when content with the satisfaction of one and in absolute obligation to it, he had fully acquiesced in it. Nor could his wisdom and truth endure that the debt should be demanded from those for whom (by an absolute decree) a sponsor had been constituted and in whom they are justified and exempted from all punishment. Nor could his goodness and mercy endure, holding as guilty and debtors those for whose deliverance he placed himself as sponsor at the bar of God.

XIII. To no purpose is it replied that "he could always have demanded payment from the elect (the satisfaction not having been made as yet) on the supposition that Christ would not stand to his suretyship and promises, but might desert his bail." This is to imagine what is evidently absurd (*asystaton*). Indeed when the sponsion or appearance of deceitful and inconstant man is concerned, his desertion is not feared without reason. And hence creditors so admit the fidejussion as not to relinquish their own right against the debtors, but retain it and in default of the payment promised by the sponsor, require that. But what danger of the desertion of bail can be conceived in Christ—most true, most powerful and the best? Yea, what possibility of it? How could his absolute promise made in the eternal decree of God and after it in the oracles of the Old Testament ("Behold I come to do thy will," i.e., to make satisfaction for those whom thou gavest to me) be recalled without by that very thing the immutable decree of God being rescinded and election to salvation being changed or being consistent with the punishment of the elect? Since this is plainly impossible (*adynaton*), the hypothesis whence it is deduced must necessarily be absurd also.

XIV. Although under the Old Testament, the payment had not as yet been made, it does not follow that the fathers were still so bound to it that it could be demanded from them. The payment was to be made only by the sponsor, from whom alone it must be sought and expected, according to God's eternal decree and covenant. However, on account of the union subsisting between us and Christ (while Christ has satisfied for us) it is just the same as if we ourselves had made satisfaction by him (2 Cor. 5:15, 21); still less accurately could the faithful under the Old Testament be said to have been bound to the payment to be made by the Mediator. But Christ, on the contrary (as from eternity constituted the sinner's sponsor), was bound to satisfy for them in virtue of his sponsion. Indeed what one does by another, he is considered to have done by himself if he substitutes him by whom he is said to act (in his own place) and gives to him the authority and power of doing something by himself. But here the case is evidently different. For neither did we put Christ in our own place; yea, we did not even form any such idea, but he was freely given to us. Nor could we give to him any power or ability to do what he did for us.

XV. As it is not derogatory to Christ, the God-man (*theanthrōpō*), to be called "sin" and "a curse" in time, so it is not repugnant that from eternity he was bound to the actual endurance of that curse in the nature to be assumed (which is to take upon himself the vicarious guilt of the elect). If it was not unbecoming for Chirst to become our Mediator, neither (by parity of reasoning) could it be unbecoming for him to perform all those things which the reason of his office and of the salvation of men (for whom he undertook these functions) demanded. Nor is

Christ to be regarded here as simply the *Logos*, but economically as the future God-man (*theanthrōpos*).

XVI. There is not the same reason for the transference of a pecuniary debt to a sponsor as of a penal debt. The former can be absolute and full as to every relation of debt because it does not matter who pays, but only what is paid; not the persons, but the money is considered. While in criminal actions where the person is regarded, the obligation cannot be transferred as to all its parts to the surety, but only as to some part (to wit, as to the certain punishment to be inflicted upon the surety in place of the accused, not however as to the personal obligation or punishment to be borne in his own person). Our sins are said to have been laid upon Christ in the former sense, not however in the latter; nor was our personal obligation transferred to Christ, but graciously dissolved. Hence although our sins may be called Christ's, as to the imputation of guilt, they do not cease to be ours as to ownership and commission. And as he substituted himself in our place, so whatever he paid he is properly said to have paid for us and in our name. For when anyone binds himself as a substitute (*antipsychos*) to suffer for the sins of another, it is always necessary that he should suffer in that one's place to satisfaction; nor can any other be here conceived than a vicarious payment by a gracious acceptation.

XVII. Although we call Christ an expromissor, we do not on that account hold that he was a mere expromissor or that a judicial transference was made here. This differs in various particulars from the sponsion of Christ and especially in this—that by it the obligation can become another's as to all its parts because pecuniary debts can be entirely transferred to another; nor is it necessary that the payment of them should be said to be made in the place of another (which does not have place in criminal actions, as has already been said). Also in this—that where by transference the delegated debtor is bound for the payment, no remission is made, the obligation remaining to the payment of the same thing which is due. This is not the case in this business where a vicarious punishment only and not a proper and personal punishment is paid for us. But this only we urge in order to explain the perfection and efficacy of Christ's suretyship (which cannot be sufficiently understood by fidejussion alone), so that here the suretyship of Christ is always to be considered as far more perfect and excellent than any civil expromission.

XVIII. When Christ is called the "surety" (*enguos*) of the new covenant (Heb. 7:22), his suretyship is not to be restricted to fidejussion alone. Besides the fact that the words of Paul are referred no less to the time of the New Testament (when no one denies that he was an expromissor), the word itself (according to the received use) denotes not only a mere fidejussor, but also an expromissor. *Enguos, anadochos*, but *anadechesthai* is the proper act of an expromissor (Hesychius, *Hesychii Alexandrini Lexicon* [1860], 2:6), who receives upon himself and acknowledges as his own a debt, according to Budaeus ("Commentarii linguae Graecae," *Opera omnia* [1557/1969], 4:3); cf. Martinius in his *Lexicon Philologicum* [1697], p. 24 on the words *engyē, sponsio, expromissio, anadochē.*

XIX. There is a difference between the legal and irrational (*alogōn*) victims and the heavenly and divine victim. Guilt could not be placed upon the former before they were offered because the transference was made by sinners according to God's appointment (without any consent of theirs) for the expiation of his sin.

But there was nothing to hinder the transference being made to Christ before he was actually offered, since he voluntarily undertook that office by the decree of God. Yea, it was necessary that his voluntary promise and sponsion should precede the oblation that the fruit of it might flow out to the Old Testament believers, who by faith should apply to themselves the power of Christ's merit, even then effectual for their deliverance.

XX. Although the ceremonial law with its sacrifices in its legal relation (*schesei*) was like a handwriting which inculcated the right of the violated covenant of works, on that account however it did not intimate that the suretyship of Christ was a mere fidejussion and that believers still remained bound under guilt. In its evangelical relation (*schesei*) (insomuch as it was a type of Christ), it shadowed forth the deliverance from guilt and the justification given in Christ, the surety. Hence circumcision is called the seal of the righteousness of faith (Rom. 4:11) and the Rock was Christ (1 Cor. 10:4). Whoever wishes to examine the subject further should consult the very celebrated Leydecker, an Utrecht theologian and professor, who pursues this argument fully and solidly (*Vis Veritatis*, Cont. 1, 2 [1679], pp. 72-120).

TENTH QUESTION: THE STATE OF THE FATHERS UNDER THE OLD TESTAMENT

Whether the fathers under the Old Testament can be said to have been still under the wrath of God and the curse of the law, and to have remained under the guilt of sin even until the death of Christ; nor had aphesin *or a full and properly so-called remission of sins been made, but only a* paresin. *We make distinctions.*

I. As the preceding question about the surety of the covenant of grace under the Old Testament was occasioned by the present (which refers to the state of the fathers under the Old Testament), the decision of that will also conduce greatly to the elucidation of this.

Statement of the question.

II. However, that we may not wander from the question and that our men may not fall into error (either in defect by depressing too much their privileges or in excess by extolling them unduly, as is frequently done), it must be observed: (1) that the inquiry does not concern the actual obtainment of reconciliation and of the remission of sins by the payment of a ransom (*lytron*) made in the death of Christ. It is agreed on both sides that this should only then be made and was made under the New Testament in the fulness of times. Rather the question concerns the moral application of that payment to be made at the time appointed of God, in the true and full remission of all the sins of believers, so that the debt could not any more be demanded of them.

III. (2) The inquiry does not concern the virtue and efficacy of the law considered in itself (as to justification)—whether remission was enjoyed by the fathers through the legal victims regarded in their absolute being or in their legal relation (*schesei*). All agree that this could not be, on account of the weakness (*adynamian*) of the law (Heb. 7:18, 19; 10:1-3). And in this sense, it is true that believers considered in themselves (and inasmuch as they were under the law) were under guilt and could have a conscience of sin. Rather the question concerns the efficacy of grace and of Christ's sacrifice shadowed forth by the legal victims—whether they obtained in the internal dispensation of the covenant of grace a full remission of all sins in virtue of the future death of Christ.

IV. (3) The inquiry does not concern the sense of remission of sins and the peace and consolation flowing thence as to degree—whether it was less under the Old Testament and greater under the New. No one denies this gradual distinction. As the light was obscure and the measure of the Spirit more sparing, so there was less sense of remission and less consolation. Yea, there was also the fear of death and the spirit of bondage from the severity of the legal economy (as has been fully shown before, Question 7). Rather the question is—whether (this difference being acknowledged) it ought on that account to be said that the fathers were still under guilt and the curse of the law and had not a true taking away (*aphesin*) of sins or a full remission of them, but only a letting-go (*paresin*) and passing by (in which they could be still bound to the handwriting and to the payment of the debt).

V. (4) The inquiry is not—whether they had the remission of sins and justification, which results from a payment actually made and which has connected with it absolute freedom from the handwriting, the annunciation of righteousness brought in and of the death of Christ for the destruction of sin. For no one can deny that this is the privilege peculiar to believers of the New Testament (in whose times the payment was actually made by Christ) and the handwriting (which was against us) blotted out on the cross. But the question is—whether such a justification alone deserves the name remission (*apheseōs*) and not that also which was granted to the fathers on account of the payment to be certainly made by Christ. This we maintain.

VI. Therefore, the question returns to this—whether under the Old Testament the sins of the fathers were so translated to Christ, the surety, that in virtue of the payment to be made in his own time, they obtained a true and full remission of all their sins and from a sense of it (if not full and perfect, still true and real), they could have a tranquilized conscience and enjoy solid consolation. Or whether (notwithstanding the suretyship of Christ) the fathers still remained under the curse of the law and the conscience of sin and were accused of it and the payment could always be demanded from them. And if any remission was granted to them, it had the relation of a passing by (*pareseōs*) rather than of removal (*apheseōs*). The former we assert; the latter, however, the learned men with whom we deal assert.

VII. For as they hold that Christ, the surety, was only a fidejussor, not an expromissor (as we have said before), who underwent security for the elect that they always remained bound, until the payment should be made; so they maintain that the fathers were still under guilt and the wrath of God on account of the delay of the expiatory sacrifice and remained (even up to the satisfying death of Christ) under the malediction of the law and the conscience of sin. Nor had they *aphesin* (i.e., a full and properly so-called remission of sins), but lived under a *paresei* (to wit, a connivance, dissimulation and pretermission, rather than under a full remission). Hence they determine that no sin was properly remitted under the Old Testament; that remission belongs to the New Testament and is promised, as a thing not of the older time, but of these latter times; and their justification on account of a certain imputation of sin and the wrath (which is wrought) had the relation only of passing by *pareseōs*.

VIII. We do not deny that an important distinction comes between the state of the believers of the Old and of the New Testament: such as exists between infants and minors, who are retained and strictly treated under tutors and schoolmasters; the same with adults and the emancipated, who both know their own goods and are admitted to a free use and enjoyment of them. We also concede that the law (by its threatenings) terrified the consciences of sinners and held them under a slavish yoke. Still we do not think that it can be truly said that the fathers were still under the wrath of God and the guilt of sin and could not have a tranquilized conscience from a full remission of sins.

Proof that the fathers were not under guilt: (1) from the suretyship of Christ.

IX. First, this is repugnant to the suretyship of Christ, which denotes the true transference of sins upon himself (as was proved in the former question) and consequently the true and absolute deliverance of the elect from all guilt and personal obligation. For these also mutually follow each other, so that when he is made sin for them, they are made the righteousness of God in him; when he is burdened, they are freed; when sins are laid upon him for his condemnation, they are taken away from them for their justification.

2. From the nature of the covenant of grace.

X. Second, it is repugnant to the nature of the covenant of grace under which the fathers lived. For since it implies the communion of the covenanted with God and the communication of all spiritual goods required to full felicity (and so of salvation itself) either we must say that the fathers were excluded from it or if they were received into it (as cannot be doubted), they must necessarily by that very thing have been freed from the curse of the law (and so of God) and from the guilt and sense of sin and admitted to the favor of God and a participation of salvation. Otherwise reconciliation can consist with wrath, blessing with cursing and a state of justification with the guilt of sin (which everyone sees to be absurd [*asystaton*] in the highest degree). If the curse of the law still sounded in the ear of those ancients, it does not at once follow that they were still under it because it was not set before them on this account that they might remain under it, but that by its threatenings they might be impelled to seek the remedy of grace in Christ, who by the intervention of his suretyship and in virtue of his future death, "which profited before it took place" (as Bernard aptly says), freed them from the curse of the law.

3. From the guilt of sin.

XI. Third, it is repugnant to the guilt of sin, under which they maintain the fathers still were. For since it involves a twofold obligation—either to a personal punishment to be endured by the sinner himself or to a punishment due to sin in general—if they were under guilt, it had reference either to one or to the other or to both. Yet neither can be said. They were not under it as to personal obligation because such an obligation is incompatible (*asystatos*) with the redemption and salvation of believers, which delivers man from all personal punishment. For although it was not transferred properly to the surety because it was a personal and proper punishment (which cannot be transferred to another) still it was so relaxed and dissolved by the sponsion of Christ that it cannot bind believers anymore. Nor can it be said that they were under guilt as to obligation to punishment in general because that was laid upon the surety and by it Christ was so bound to a vicarious payment that a full immunity of them followed from his obligation.

4. From the justification and salvation of the fathers.

XII. Fourth, it is repugnant to the justification and salvation of the fathers. For if they were justified and saved (as is acknowledged on both sides), how can they be said to have been still under guilt and the sense of sin? Now that justification and remission of sins was granted to them, not only do the clear promises of God given to them concerning it plainly prove (Ex. 34:7; Pss. 32:1; 51:3, 4; 65:3; 85:2, 3; 103:3; 130:4; Is. 1:18; 44:22; Mic. 7:18, 19), but also the examples of Abraham, David, Daniel and others (on whom this grace was bestowed) indubitably demonstrate. Nor should we here have recourse to prophecy, as if Pss. 32, 51 and 103 were prophetic, referring to the time and believers of the New Testament. It is evident that David applies them to himself and to believers in his own time. Yet no consolation could return to them, if these blessings only after many ages were to be bestowed upon the pious, who were to live under the New Testament. To no purpose is it also added that it is not denied that justification was given to the fathers, but only that justification which results from a payment actually made. No one denies that such an absolution was reserved for the New Testament. And if nothing else is meant, the whole controversy could easily be settled. But besides the fact that it is at variance with Scripture usage to take the word "justification" in this sense, the question will always recur—whether the remission granted to them was not plenary and *aphesis* properly so called. Or whether it only had the relation of a pretermission (*pareseōs*).

5. From justifying faith.

XIII. Fifth, it is repugnant to the nature of the justifying faith which the fathers had. For since it consists most especially in the fiducial apprehension and application of the righteousness of Christ and of his most perfect satisfaction (whether as already made or as infallibly to be made), followed by peace with God, boldness (*parrēsia*) in approaching him, tranquility of conscience and solid consolation in life and death, it cannot be conceived how one possessed of such faith can be said to have been still under guilt and a sense of sin and under the curse of the law. And it seems harsh and little consistent with the grace of God bestowed upon them (in which they so often glory and exult) to think so of them. Consider carefully here the examples of Abraham, Jacob, Job, David, Hezekiah and others, who frequently testify their confidence in God and the joy and consolation flowing from it; yea, and are proposed as an example to the believers of the New Testament (Rom. 4:3-5; Gal. 3:6; Heb. 11:2; 2 Cor. 4:13). For although it is true that this confidence and consolation was less in them as to degree (on account of the more rigorous economy under which they lived), still it cannot be doubted that their faith was the same as to species (with the effects inseparable from it).

6. From their sanctification.

XIV. Sixth, it is repugnant to their sanctification. For if by sanctification, they were delivered from the dominion of sin in virtue of the death of Christ working retroactively (as it did), they ought also to have been freed from its guilt by justification, since guilt and the dominion of sin mutually follow each other and establish and take away each other in turn. For as no one can be freed from guilt by justification without being immediately freed from its dominion by sanctification (which necessarily follows justification and cannot be torn asunder from it), thus he who is freed from its dominion ought first to have been freed from guilt, the cause of dominion.

7. From the distinction between pareseōs **and** apheseōs.

XV. Seventh, the distinction urged between *paresin* and *aphesin* (that *paresis* was only under the Old Testament but *aphesis* peculiar to the New) is without a solid foundation. (1) It is certain that these two words (although differing in sound; yea and obtain sometimes a diverse signification) are still promiscuously used by approved authors when they treat of the remission of sins. Buddaeus says *parienai* means "to indulge," "to permit," "to pardon" ("Commentarii linguae Graecae," *Opera omnia* [1557/1969], 4:762). Hesychius interprets *pariēmi synchrōnō, aphiēmi* and *paresin* by *aphesin* and *synchōrēsin* (*Hesychii Alexandrini Lexicon* [1861], 3:286 and 283). (2) In this affair, *aphesis* is everywhere ascribed to the fathers of the Old Testament, for the verb *aphienai* and the noun *aphesis* answer to the verb *ns', kphr, slch* and the nouns *slychh* and *kphrh*, by which the remission granted to them is expressed. "Blessed are they whose transgressions are forgiven" (*hōn aphethēsan hai anomiai*, Ps. 32:1); "and forgave the iniquity of my sin" (*kai su aphēkas tēn asebeian tēs kardias mou*, v. 5). Thus, "forgavedst the iniquity of thy people" (*aphēkas tas anomias tō laō sou*, Ps. 85:2); "for he will abundantly pardon" (*hoti epi poly aphēsei tas hamartias hymōn*, Is. 55:7). Nor can the very many other passages be understood differently which everywhere promise remission of sins to believers (Ex. 34:7; Pss. 65:3; 130:3; 103:3; Mic. 7:18, 19).

XVI. (3) If this distinction held good, neither could John the Baptist (before the actual expiation made by the death of Christ, which *aphesis* is said to follow) have baptized *eis aphesin hamartiōn* (Mk. 1:4). Nor could Christ have said with propriety to the paralytic and to the sinful woman "Your sins are forgiven" (*apheōntai soi hai hamartiai*, Lk. 5:20; 7:47), or have commanded the disciples to pray for *aphesei* of sins, adding his promise (Mt. 6:12, 14). Nor could Peter have rightly asserted that all the prophets gave witness to Christ, that every believer in Christ would receive *aphesin hamartiōn* (Acts 10:43) in his name. For that these things are to be understood of believers of the New Testament (who were to believe when Christ had come) not of those who lived under the Old Testament (as the Remonstrants hold) is at variance with all reason. Yea, it is repugnant to the scope of the prophets' testimony concerning Christ, who did not say this only for our sake, but also for the believers of the Old Testament to whom they wrote and to whom no less than to us it belonged to believe in the Messiah and to be saved by him. Hence Peter does not speak of those "who would believe," but of "believers"; indeed of all—"whosoever believeth on him" (*panta ton pisteuonta eis auton*). Finally, Paul ought not to have ascribed *aphesin* to the justification of the ancients (as he does however, Rom. 4). If there is any difference between *aphesin* and *paresin* it ought to have been shown there (if there is any). He is so far from doing this that by the very same words he sets forth their justification and ours.

XVII. (4) *Aphesis* ought to be granted where there is a plenary remission from every obligation, penal and personal, for remission can be nothing else than a pardoning and not punishing, that no one may be called to trial or the punishment due be demanded of him. Now it cannot be denied that such a remission was granted to the fathers, since they were made partakers of salvation. To no purpose is it objected that a plenary and emphatic remission supposes the payment made. It suffices for remission that liberation be granted from all punishment on account of the payment, whether made or still to be made. For although a real expiation cannot be made except by a payment actually made, nothing hinders remission (its fruit) from being granted to the believer in virtue of a payment still future, which before God (on account of its certainty) is considered as made.

Sources of explanation.

XVIII. The passage of Paul (urged above all others in confirmation of the *paresin* where he says, "Whom [Christ] God hath set forth to be a propitation, through faith in his blood, to declare his righteousness" *dia tēn paresin tōn progegonotōn hamartiōn tē anochē tou Theou*, Rom. 3:25) is not well brought forward here, however it may be explained. Whether the preposition *dia* is understood causally with some and signifies "on account of," indicating the impulsive cause of the propitiation instituted by God, and set forth in the gospel, and *paresis* being referred to the time to which the forbearance (*anochē*) of God is assigned: or is understood finally with others and as meaning the same as *eis* ("to"); so that *paresis* is the end why Christ is set forth to be a propitiation, or that *dia tēn paresin* is put for *dia tēs pareseōs*, "through the remission." If we follow this latter sense (which is the more common and more in accordance with the words and scope of Paul), *paresis* will be the same as *aphesis;* as if you said a relaxation, the metaphor being taken from the bonds by which sins, as it were, have bound us under the power of Satan, should be unloosed by the propitiation of Christ. Thus many versions, the French, the Dutch, the English, the Italian have it, and orthodox interpreters have thus far explained it (as Calvin, Martyr, Bullinger, Piscator, Pareus and others). The meaning will be that God set forth Christ to be a propitiation through faith in his blood, for this purpose—to declare his righteousness by or on account of the remission of preceding sins (i.e., which had been committed before under the Old Testament in the time of the patience of God). He mentions indeed especially preceding sins, not to the exclusion of present and future, but in order to amplify the power of Christ's redemption (which was efficacious not only to the expiation of present, but of preceding sins also). As to the present, it was sufficiently clear. But it was a difficult and a momentous question—What was the case with the fathers before the advent of Christ? It seemed almost incredible that the effect of remission existed before the cause and that sins were remitted before they were expiated. Therefore Paul asserts that the propitiation of Christ did thus extend backwards. He testifies: "Christ is the mediator of the New Testament, that by means of death he might expiate the transgressions that were under the first testament" (Heb. 9:15). Although Christ is said to have been set forth as a propitiation for the remission of preceding sins, it does not follow that they were not as yet remitted to the believers of that time because although it was only then obtained, it could be applied before.

XIX. If the former sense be retained, *paresis* will denote indeed a passing by and a dissimulation of sins, whose punishment he willed not to exact under the Old Testament, but deferred to the advent of Christ, in the meantime *en tē anochē*, bearing with the sins in forbearance and, as it were, overlooking them (*hyperidōn*, Acts 17:30). But then it will have reference not so much to the fathers, as to Christ, the sponsor, from whom he willed not to exact punishment from the beginning but left unpunished the sins laid upon him until the fulness of time. That *paresis*, however, did not prevent the fathers even then from rejoicing *aphesei*, obtaining a full remission of their sins in virtue of the future expiation. Thus the sense flows along clearly (to wit, that God set forth Christ to be a propitiation, through faith in his blood, to declare his righteousness, on account of the passing by [*paresin*] and deferring of the punishment of preceding sins, committed in the time of the forbearance of God, which he on this account deferred, not that he might leave them altogether unpunished, but that in his own time he might punish them in Christ, and show his righteousness against sin, which had not been so clearly shown under the forbearance [*anochē*], sin not having been as yet punished).

XX. The promise of the remission of sins is so ascribed to the days of the New Testament (Jer. 31:34), as the remaining promises of the covenant are ascribed to them; for example, that "God will be our God" (v. 33), which evidently was granted to the ancient people. Nor can it be denied that remission was already under the Old Testament because it is promised under the New, any more than the covenant of grace itself, which is said to have been established only in these last days. These promises, therefore, are not to be understood absolutely and simply (as if they were in no manner), but relatively and comparatively because they were to be far more clearly and efficaciously set forth under the New Testament, not as to substance, but as to mode and degree. Since remission was given under the Old Testament through Christ about to die, now it is given through him dead (i.e., the actual expiation having been made). (2) Remission under the Old Testament was dispensed through sacraments and sacrifices (which designated an expiation still to be made), but now under the New Testament, sacrifices having been abrogated, it is sealed by the sacraments as having been made. (3) It was formerly given ordinarily with less consolation, joy and certainty than now under the New Testament, on account of the clearness of the gospel, the removal of the legal yoke and the power and abundance of the consoling and joy-inspiring Spirit poured out after the exaltation of Christ. (4) Formerly it was given more sparingly and to fewer persons, but now it is more copiously dispensed and poured out indiscriminately upon all of every nation and rank. Thus far therefore this blessing is rightly promised, as peculiar to the New Testament. But the argument is badly drawn from the distinction of economy and manner of dispensation to an essential and intrinsic diversity, such as is here made between *paresin* and *aphesin*.

XXI. It is one thing to be justified by the grace of Christ from all things (from which men could not be justified by the law); another for that justification to be conferred at length only upon us under the New Testament. The former is mentioned in Acts 13:39, but not the latter because there is not here an opposition of the Old Testament (widely taken) to the New, but of the external ceremonies of the law to the internal communion of Christ (partakers of which the ancients were, beyond controversy). Thus nothing else is meant than that believers have the verity in the grace of Christ, only the shadow of which occurred in the external economy of the Mosaic Law (as Paul elsewhere testifies that ceremonies were a shadow of things to come and that the body is in Christ, Col. 2:17).

XXII. When Paul says, "Where remission of sins [*aphesis hamartiōn*] is, there is no more offering for sin" (Heb. 10:18), it is rightly argued from the position of the remission of sins to the position of the sole sacrifice of Christ, promised in the covenant of grace (by the intervention of which such a remission was acquired even to the exclusion of any other sacrifice of the same order or the repetition of it). For to no other end was it instituted than to acquire remission and to no purpose is it applied where sin has already been remitted. But falsely would anyone thence gather that remission had not been given for the sins under the Old Testament as long as the legal obligations were repeated somewhat frequently. It is evident that by such obligations remission could not be gained and therefore they were repeated to show that by them the expiation of sin was impossible (or as long as the oblation of Christ had not been made, because it is certain that its moral efficacy went before its actual existence). Again, *aphesis* can be taken metonymically for its foundation or meritorious cause (to wit, the actual expiation through the blood of Christ) since (this having been made), the sacrifices of the Old Testament (shadowing it) ought really to have ceased (as also all other expiatory sacrifices of that kind, which are incompatible [*asystata*] with the sacrifice of Christ).

XXIII. Although the payment ought not to be made under the Old Testament (and so neither was sin sealed up, nor iniquity actually expiated, nor the righteousness of ages yet brought in), still these things derogate nothing from the truth and certainty of the justification of the believers of that time. The payment was most certainly to be made by the surety (according to God's decree) in virtue of which they could obtain remission of sins, as moral causes are accustomed to act before they are actualized. Thus, the actual obtainment of remission of sins is one thing; the application of it as certainly and infallibly about to be, another thing. The former took place only under the New Testament, but the latter obtained already under the Old Testament. Christ was bound to take away sins meritoriously by a satisfaction, but God had already taken them away efficaciously from the believers of the Old Testament by remission.

XXIV. If remission of sins was gained by no one under the Old Testament by the Levitical sacrifices in their absolute being (considered under the legal aspect), it does not follow on this account that it was not obtained by the fathers through the sacrifice that was to be offered in its time (which was signified and sealed by those sacrifices). And if Paul says that perfection (*teleiōsin*) could not come by the law (which had only a shadow of good things to come, Heb. 10:1), as a consequence he denies it to the fathers, who were under the law; not in virtue of the law, which was weak in the flesh (Rom. 8:3), but by the grace and merit of Christ, of which they also were partakers.

XXV. Although the ceremonial law with its often repeated sacrifices was like a handwriting (which taught in a legal form [*schesei*] what believers were by nature and what sin deserved, by inculcating the right of the violated covenant of works, so that it was made in this respect a remembrance [*anamnēsis*] of sins, Heb. 10:3), still this did not hinder it (in its evangelical form [*schesei*]) from shadowing forth to them the future expiation of their sins by the blood of Christ and from sealing justification in him. In this respect, to the fathers rightly observing it, it could be in the place of a receipt which they would use for themselves to confirm the account of the handwriting against them. Thus while from one side it rebuked the guilt of sinners and threatened the deserved death to strike them with terror; from the other, it shadowed forth the death of the Mediator and sealed his grace for the consolation of the pious. The victims were therefore the remembrancers (*anamnēsis*) not only of sins, but of the remission of sins. They reminded them not only that they were sinners (and therefore worthy of death from the legal aspect [*schesei*]), but also that they have remission of sins in Christ.

XXVI. The "conscience of sins" of which Paul speaks (Heb. 10:2) cannot be of sin still resting upon the fathers and keeping them from all communion with God. For the suretyship of Christ, apprehended by faith, would prevent this from being the case. Rather it is the conscience of sin not as yet actually expiated, or capable of being expiated by the legal sacrifices, which on that account were repeated that believers might testify that they used them indeed as symbols of God's appointment. Yet they did not have true remission except from the suretyship of Christ and his future sacrifice, so that what the law could not do, that they obtained by the grace of Christ. Thus they did not indeed have that tranquility of conscience which arises from the ransom (*lytrō*) fully paid by the surety; nor was such a receipt given to them as is in the rising of Christ from the dead. But nevertheless they had as much as was sufficient to really tranquilize the conscience in the suretyship of Christ received by faith. For by it they could be certain that all their sins were blotted out of the account and carried to the account of Christ because he had taken these also upon himself and for them had constituted himself a debtor to suffer punishment; indeed so that they should be free from all personal obligation and the debt never be demanded of them. The conscience certainly cannot acquiesce unless it be actually expiated by a worthy sacrifice. There suffices for its acquiescence and enjoyment of its tranquility, the divine and unrepentable (*ametamelētos*) promise of the grace of God and the irrevocable substitution of a most sufficient surety accepted in the court of God, whether the ransom (*lytron*) is still to be paid by the surety or has already been paid.

XXVII. The actual expiation of sin is not necessary to its remission. It suffices that it be promised and will certainly be accomplished. I confess that where we treat of the proper and personal payment of pecuniary debt, there is not a cancelling of the debt, unless the payment is made. But it is different with a vicarious satisfaction in a penal debt, in which the sponsion alone (provided it be infallible) is sufficient for the liberation of the accused.

XXVIII. It is one thing for sin not to have been expiated as yet under the Old Testament; another for believers to have been still under the guilt of it. Sin indeed was as yet unexpiated and was to be expiated. But believers nevertheless were not under its guilt, which had been transferred to Christ. They therefore lived under guilt still existing, but not under guilt resting upon them. Rather it was transferred to Christ by God's appointment and by him taken upon himself (from which, in consequence, the pious were delivered). And as guilt no longer touched believers, so neither the curse, the consequent of guilt. The obtainment of deliverance from the curse of the law took place only by Christ, who redeems us from the curse of the law, being himself made a curse (*katara*, Gal. 3:13). But the fruit and application had already been granted to the fathers in virtue of his future death.

XXIX. It is one thing to live under a legal economy; another, however, to be under the law as a covenant or to be of the works of the law. The fathers are rightly said to have been under the legal economy, but not in like manner can they be said to have been under the law as under a covenant for seeking righteousness and life under it (or to be of the works of the law). As many as are under the law in this manner are under the curse (Gal. 3:10), which cannot be said of believers.

XXX. The time of the New Testament is called "a time of favor" and "a year of favor" (Is. 49:8; 61:2), not absolutely and simply, as if the fathers were under the wrath of God, since they lived under the same covenant of grace and were saved by the same grace of Christ with us; but relatively and comparatively, as to the clearer, fuller and more efficacious manifestation of grace. The legal pedagogy being abrogated (which was somewhat rigid) and the intolerable (*abastaktō*) yoke of ceremonies having been removed (by which they were pressed as to external dispensation), we experience far more excellently the grace and benevolence of God in Christ.

XXXI. Since the Devil has no power over man except from sin, either as to its guilt (by accusing him before God) or as to its dominion (by tempting him and holding him under a state of sin) or as to its punishments (afflicting and tormenting him, in accordance with the avenging justice of God), it cannot be truly asserted that the fathers were still under the power of the Devil. They were delivered both from the guilt of sin by justification and from its dominion by sanctification and from the punishments following it by the redemption of Christ and the power of the covenant of grace. Now although sin was not as yet abolished (i.e., expiated by an actual expiation through Christ), still it was abolished with respect to believers by remission (already granted in virtue of the transference of it to the surety and of the satisfaction to be made by him). Hence although he might throw up to believers their sin and tempt their consciences by this scruple (as he does still every day), yet he could not moreover obtain the rule over them, because they could easily overcome that temptation and repel the accusation from faith in the Redeemer promised to them and the grace to be obtained through him. This can be gathered from the notable example of Joshua representing the whole people (Zech. 3:1, 2). In the justification of Joshua, Satan is said to have stood at his right hand that he might oppose him as an accuser; yet the Son of God, our Redeemer, the true Jehovah, intercedes powerfully for him and pleads his cause against the unjust Accuser. Yea, he sharply rebukes him and teaches that he has no right over him anymore on account of God's election and redemption (by which he had become as "a brand plucked out of the fire," not only of the Babylonian captivity, but also of the infernal, of which that was a type). "The Lord rebuke thee, O Satan; even the Lord that hath chosen Jerusalem rebuke thee: is not this a brand plucked out of the fire?" (Zech. 3:2). And so far from the divine justice favoring his power in accusing believers of the Old Testament, he earned the severest rebuke from the Father, the Judge, and from the Son, the surety (as the very celebrated Leydecker fully demonstrates in the above cited book; cf. *Vis Veritatis* [1679]). To this volume we refer the reader who desires to gain a deeper knowledge of the whole of the controversy and others pertaining to it (which that most learned author distinctly and solidly handles).

XXXII. Now from these things (without adding more), it is sufficiently evident what is to be held as to the state of the fathers of the Old Testament (to wit, that they were sons, partakers equally with us of the same covenant of grace and of all its benefits and of salvation, but sons still in their minority [Gal. 4:2], having neither a full knowledge and feeling nor use of their goods; but held strictly like slaves under the legal bondage so that thus their state differs from ours, not as to the thing itself and the essence of saving doctrine [which in each case is the same], but as to degree and the different mode of dispensation). In this simplicity (which is abundantly sufficient for salvation), we think we ought to acquiesce. Thus there is no necessity for giving ourselves any further trouble in solving the various less necessary questions usually agitated here. These can break the bonds of peace and divide the souls of brethren in contrary pursuits (with great offense to the pious and injury to faith).

ELEVENTH QUESTION: THE LIMBUS OF THE FATHERS

Whether the souls of the fathers of the Old Testament were immediately received into heaven after death or were cast into limbo. The former we affirm; the latter we deny against the papists.

Statement of the question.

I. This question lies between us and the papists who (the more easily to defend their hypothesis concerning the imperfection of the Old Testament) maintain that the fathers who lived under it were not immediately admitted into heaven, but were detained in limbo until the coming of Christ. Now by the term *limbus*, they mean the upper part of hell and as it were the extremity; the metaphor being taken from a garment whose extremity or border (which runs along the extreme part) is called *limbus*, according to Virgil: "Clad in a Sidonian robe with embroidered border" (*Aeneid* 4.137 [Loeb, 1:404-5]).

II. The papists make a fourfold hell. They assign the first to the eternal punishment of sense and loss of the wicked, which is called by them hell by way of eminence (*kat' exochēn*). They make the second of temporal punishment of sense and loss, which they call purgatory. To the other two they give the common name of limbo. They hold the one to be eternal for the mere punishment of loss (for infants dying before baptism), which they call the "limbus of infants" (*Limbus Infantum*). The other is assigned to the temporal punishment of loss (for the fathers who died before the death of Christ), called by them the "limbus of the fathers" (*Limbus Patrum*). Thus Alstenstaig says on this word: "Limbus according to Gerson, is the upper part of hell, in which they were kept to be saved as far as the debt of the first parent should be paid by the death of Christ" (*Lexicon theologicum* [1619/1974], p. 498; cf. Gerson, "De Articulis Fidei," Exp. 5 *Opera Omnia* [1987, repr.], 1:238; Thomas Aquinas, cf. *Innocentii Quinti . . . in IV Libros Sententiarum Commentaria ex Manuscriptis . . . Thomae Aquinatis*, Dist. 45, Q. 1*, Art. 2 [1652/1964], 4:432-33; and Bellarmine, "De Purgatorio," 2.6* *Opera* [1857], 2:396-97).

III. On the contrary, the orthodox assert that the souls of the fathers were immediately received into heaven after death, where they enjoy happiness and are free from both kinds of punishment, both that of loss and that of sense.

Reasons against limbo: (1) from the formula of the covenant.

IV. The reasons are: (1) the formula of the covenant of grace under which the fathers lived does not suffer them to be hurled into a limbo, but demands that they should be admitted into heaven. For since God promised that he would be their God, not temporarily, but eternally (nor is he the God of the dead, but of the living)—the fathers must necessarily still live even after death, at least as to some part of them (i.e., as to the soul), not with any kind of life, but with a happy and heavenly life, necessarily included in this promise (as has been proved before, Question 2). Christ expressly teaches this. When speaking of the dead fathers he says "All live unto him" (*pantes autō zōsi*, Lk. 20:38), not only in the mind and power of God because he can recall them to life and was really about to do this according to his decree; but they live because they are before him always and enjoy a divine life. This is both "from him" (as the beginning) and terminates "on him" (as its object and end). Now who would say that they live in God who being thrust into hell are without the vision of God and feel the punishment of loss (at least the temporal).

2. From the example of Lazarus.

V. Second, the ancients immediately after death were received into the bosom of Abraham, as appears from the example of Lazarus (Lk. 16:22, 23). Therefore they were also received into heavenly joy. For "the bosom of Abraham" can be referred to no other thing than to eternal life; this is shadowed forth under the symbol of a sumptuous feast, in allusion to a custom of the ancients in which they were accustomed so to recline at their feasts that the one rested his head on the bosom of the other. This is said of John, because Christ reclining upon the higher part of the couch had John next to him, who is therefore said to have leaned upon his bosom (Jn. 13:23). Thus nothing is more natural than that it should be said here that Lazarus was to Abraham what John was to the Lord; in the heavenly feast especially since Christ elsewhere clearly unfolds this mystery when he says, "Many shall come from the east and the west, and shall sit down with Abraham, and Isaac, and Jacob, in the kingdom of heaven" (Mt. 8:11), i.e., shall enjoy with him the celestial banquet. "To sit down with Abraham" and "to be in the bosom of Abraham" are the same except that to be in the bosom is a mark of greater love because not all shall recline upon his bosom, as Maldonatus aptly remarks on this passage (*Commentaria in quatuor evangelistas* [1863], 2:287-88 on Lk. 16:22). Now mention is made of Abraham rather than of Jacob or any other saint; both because he was the father of believers in whose bosom (i.e., most loving embrace) they are collected who partake of the fruit of the same faith with him, as sons come together in the bosom of their father when they are graciously received by him; and also on account of his liberal hospitality during life, so that the hospitality of the good but wealthy Abraham may be opposed to the inhospitality of the wealthy provider of the feast.

VI. Hence it is evident that to no purpose does Bellarmine maintain that the bosom of Abraham is nothing else than limbo and that the souls of Abraham and of Lazarus were in the same abyss with the soul of the provider of the feast, distinct indeed from each other, but having nothing solid interposed, but only a great gulf (*mega chasma*) ("De Purgatorio," 2.6* in *Opera* [1857], 2:396). For first, our interpretation concerning the reclining in the heavenly banquet being established, this figment falls to the ground. Hence, after mention of this sitting down, it is added that others shall be cast out "into outer darkness" (*eis to skotos exōteron*, Mt. 8*:12)—the similitude being taken from a magnificent banquet in which on the inside the ceiling glitters with lamps, but outside there is nothing but the blackness of night. Thus whatever is outside the kingdom of heaven (where the eternal light shines) will be darkness. Again, in the bosom of Abraham good things are received and consolation is given to Lazarus for the torture he had suffered. Thus "the alternate changes of evil and good things are compensated by an ample retribution" (Tertullian, *De Idolatria* 13.14-15 [trans. J. H. Waszink and J. C. M. van Winden, 1987], pp. 46-47). But in limbo neither can this good be possessed, nor any place for consolation be had because there is the punishment of loss and exclusion from the face of God. Third, if Abraham was in hell, how can it be said that the abyss was so profound that there could be no passage from one to the other? How could Lazarus be said to have been carried away (*apenechtheis*) to a different place from hell, where the rich man is said to have been? Fourth, the Roman Ritual itself favors our opinion. For among other things which the clergy ought to sing, as soon as the funeral enters the church, they sing, "May Christ who called receive thee and angels carry thee into the bosom of Abraham" ("Caput 8: De Exspiratione*," *Rituale Romanum* [1944], p. 141). In reality the whole of this discourse (whether it be a history or a parable or a history parabolically described) must be understood not according to the letter (*kata to rhēton*) and historically, but parabolically, for neither tongues nor speech nor fingers can belong to souls.

3. From the thief.

VII. Third, the thief is admitted into paradise before the ascension of Christ according to his promise, "Today shalt thou be with me in paradise" (Lk. 23:43). Nor should it be said here that "today" must be construed with the preceding verb ("I say") and not with what follows ("shalt thou be with me") so that the meaning is "today I say unto thee, thou shalt be with me in paradise" (to wit, at the last judgment) because the construction will not suffer this. In vain would this be added because no one speaks except in the present time and it is clear that Christ refers to the words of the thief, "Remember me when thou comest into thy kingdom" (v. 42). Nor should it be said that paradise is limbo (as Maldonatus holds), because it appears from Scripture that paradise is located in heaven as a place of delight and of eternal happiness (2 Cor. 12:2, 4; Rev. 2:7). Nor should it be said that the thief requested only this—that Christ should remember him in paradise—because it is not absurd to say that Christ gave more to him than he asked, as the most kind Father is accustomed to do above what we seek. Nor is this a privilege peculiar to the thief and not common to others since faith and repentance (to whom this is given by Christ) is common to all true believers. Hence Bellarmine rightly proves from this passage that the saints immediately after death enjoy the vision of God ("De Sanctorum Beatitudine," 1.7 *Opera* [1857], 2:437-38).

4. From Enoch and Elijah.

VIII. Fourth, Enoch and Elijah were translated to heaven (Heb. 11:5; 2 K. 2:11). For although this was peculiar to them that they were bodily whirled into heaven, it was not singular that they were spiritually admitted into it; yea, they were the solemn pledges to the pious of the heavenly glory to be at length obtained. Nor if the letter said to have been written from Elijah to Jehoram (2 Ch. 21:12) was handed to the king only after Elijah's death, does it follow that it was written after his translation. It is one thing for it to have been written after his translation; another to have been given only then. The emptiness of the figment concerning the translation of Enoch and Elijah to a terrestrial paradise, also concerning their return to war against Antichrist has been elsewhere exposed (Volume I, Topic VIII, Question 7, Section 9).

5. From the consolation of the ancients.

IX. Fifth, the ancient believers waited for a heavenly city (Heb. 11:10) and had a great consolation and certain hope of glory in death (which would not have been the case if they had as yet to be hurled into hell). How could Jacob have testified that he waited with such earnestness the salvation of the Lord (Gen. 49:18) and David that he committed his spirit into the hand of the Lord (Ps. 31:5), if they should still be far off from the face of God and were to be glorified only after many ages? Nor can it be said that David thus commended to God the perfection of life because the words can bear no other meaning according to the style of Scripture than to deliver the soul to God (as is evident from the example of Stephen, Acts 7:59).

Sources of explanation.

X. What is said of "the sepulcher" and "death" (Gen. 37:35; 42:38)—that Jacob was about to go down with sadness (*lsh'vl*) ("into the grave") is falsely drawn to limbo. *Sh'vl* or *hadēs* is the grave into which men descend after death.

XI. "The pit wherein is no water," from which the ancients were to be sent forth by the blood of the covenant (Zech. 9:11), ought not to be drawn to limbo since this may be said partly literally concerning deliverance from the Babylonian captivity and the miseries accompanying it (from which the Jews were not yet entirely freed); partly mystically, concerning the spiritual captivity under sin from which Christ frees us by the efficacy of his blood, by which the covenant of grace is ratified (as it was the foundation of all deliverances even temporal).

XII. It was not the real Samuel who was seen by the woman (1 S. 28:12), but only his apparition (*spectrum*) (to wit, a demon personating the prophet), who came out of the earth to terrify Saul, as Satan himself often transfigures himself into an angel of light. For no right or dominion belongs to demons over the souls of the pious whom God has received into the eternal tabernacle that they may rest from their labors (otherwise their condition after death would be worse than in life, in which, armed with faith, they are safe from all the assaults of Satan). Besides, if it was Samuel himself, he would not have suffered Saul to worship him; nor could it be said that God had not answered Saul consulting him—neither by priests nor by prophets, because he had answered then by the prophets. Nor is there anything important as to the mistake in the name of Samuel given to that apparition; it could be so called on account of similitude, as images are usually called by the names of the things themselves of which they are images (as Augustine fully proves *ad Simplicianum*). Nor is there any importance in this that it predicted future things because this could be done by divine revelation for the punishment of men (as the same Augustine and after him Lyranus observe; cf. *De diversis questionibus ad Simplicianum* [PL 40:101-48]).

XIII. It is said that no one ascended into heaven before the Son of man descended from heaven (Jn. 3:13), not as to local ascension to the beatific vision because Enoch and Elijah had already been translated even bodily, but as to a mystical ascension (i.e., a knowledge of heavenly things to be made manifest to men). As "to ascend into heaven" (Rom. 10:6) is to know divine mysteries (cf. Prov. 30:4). In this sense, it is said that no one has ever seen God, but the Son, who is in the bosom of the Father, he has revealed him to us (Jn. 1:18); and "neither knoweth any man the Father, save the Son, and he to whomsoever the Son will reveal him" (Mt. 11:27).

XIV. "The way into the holiest of all" is said not to have been manifested before the ascension of Christ (Heb. 9:8); not that it was entirely concealed, but (1) that it was not so clearly made known. Therefore the fathers went into heaven through Christ (in whom they believed) because he is the way of entrance into heaven, but who was not yet clearly known because he had not yet come. (2) Again, it was not known to any of the Gentiles, as in the New Testament. (3) It was not as yet manifested by the actual ransom (*lytrō*) of Christ (which had not yet been paid), but only as to efficacy of merit. (4) Time is not compared with time here, but rather the Mosaic sacrifices with the sacrifice of Christ, to intimate that they could not open heaven to us, which was granted to the blood of Christ alone. (5) If Christ is said to have been the first who entered into heaven, this is to be understood not as to time, but as to causality because the entrance of Christ was the true cause of the fathers' no less than of our entrance into heaven.

XV. The "prison" (*phylakē*) mentioned in 1 Pet. 3:19 ("by which [Spirit] also Christ went and preached unto the spirits in prison" [*tois en phylakē*]) cannot mean the limbo of the fathers. He speaks of those which "sometime were disobedient" (*apeithēsasi pote*), while Christ by his prophetic Spirit through Noah preached repentance to them. Rather it denotes the infernal prison (as in Rev. 20:7) in which (in the time of Peter) they were held shut up on account of their resistance to the preaching of Christ by Noah (to wit, to those who are in prison now [*tois en phylakē ousi*], not who were formerly there).

XVI. Although it can be said that the ancients received some increase of knowledge and consolation after the exhibition of Christ in the flesh and his ascension unto heaven (as is said of the angels, Eph. 3:10), it does not follow that they had been altogether excluded from heaven and from beholding the face of God; but only that their beatitude was not yet fully consummated. To this some refer the words of the apostle: "God having provided some better things for us, that they without us should not be made perfect" (Heb. 11:40). And to this Calvin seems to have had respect by the mirror or act of watching in which he says the fathers were said from a desire of Christ not to exclude them from the fruition of beatitude and the vision of God, but to mark the desire and earnest expectation (*apokaradokian*) of the advent of Christ, to which also the angels are said to have looked (1 Pet. 1:12) (*Epistle of Paul . . . to the Hebrews and the First and Second Epistles of St. Peter* [trans. W. B. Johnston, 1963], p. 293 on 1 Pet. 3:19).

XVII. The promise sometimes denotes the first advent of Christ in the flesh promised in the Old Testament; sometimes the second in glory promised in the New. The ancients died without "receiving the promise" (Heb. 11:39)—namely, concerning the former advent of Christ, which was reserved for us without them. But believers still wait for the promise (*epangelian*)—namely, to be brought in the latter advent of the Lord (Heb. 10:36, 37)—which they also themselves are about to receive; but not without us for what we now expect will be common to us with them. Thus God has set before us "something better" (*kreitton ti*) with regard to the former advent, in which we alone rejoice.

TWELFTH QUESTION

Whether the Sinaitic legal covenant, made by Moses with the people of Israel on Mount Sinai, was a certain third covenant distinct in species from the covenant of nature and the covenant of grace. We deny.

Various opinions concerning the Sinaitic covenant.

I. The opinions of theologians vary on this subject. Some maintain that the Sinaitic covenant was a covenant of works; others that it was a mixture of the covenant of works and the covenant of grace; others that it was properly neither a covenant of nature nor of grace, but a third covenant distinct from both in its whole species and was instituted to minister to the covenant of grace (and for this reason properly called "subservient"). Finally others (with whom we agree) say that it was a covenant of grace, but promulgated with the law and lying under it (which was sanctioned in the unusual manner of terror and servitude, in accordance with the state of the Israelite people and the age of the church at that time).

Opinion of Cameron on the threefold covenant.

II. That celebrated man, John Cameron, seems to have been the first among our men to introduce an opinion concerning a threefold covenant ("De Triplici Dei cum homine foedere theses," *Opera* [1642], pp. 544-51). The most learned Amyrald embraced this and laboriously endeavors to prove it in "Theses Theologicae de Tribus Foederibus Divinis" (in *Syntagma Thesium Theologicarum* [1664], pp. 212-31). Their followers agree with them maintaining that there are three covenants (properly so called) which God has made with man: the first natural, made with innocent Adam in the earthly paradise; the second, of grace, entered into with fallen men in the gospel; the third, the legal covenant, confirmed through Moses with the Israelites on Mount Sinai. The latter is called the "ancient" or "subservient" covenant because God made it with them to prepare them for the covenant and inflame them with a desire of the promise and of the gospel covenant and at the same time of restraining them from wickedness by throwing (as it were) a rein over them, to the time in which he was to send the Spirit of adoption and govern them by the law of liberty.

III. Now they hold that such was the nature of this covenant that in various particulars it agrees with and differs from the covenant of nature and the covenant of grace. It agrees with the covenant of nature: (1) as to the contracting parties because in both they are God and man; (2) as to the stipulation which is annexed to both; (3) as to the promise which is the same in kind. It differs: (1) as to the object because the covenant of nature was entered into with all men, the legal with the Israelites alone (the former with man in a state of innocence; the latter with a part of the fallen human race); (2) as to the promise, which in the first was life to be passed in the earthly paradise, in the latter a happy life in Canaan; (3) as to the stipulation, the former binds to obedience due to the law of nature, the latter to ceremonies also; (4) as to foundation, the covenant of nature rests upon creation and general conservation, but the legal covenant rests upon the election of the Israelite people and their deliverance from Egypt; (5) as to end, the end of the former was more properly the exaction of duty from man;

of the latter, preparation for Christ from a conviction of man's weakness; (6) as to the mediator, the former was without one, the latter could not be entered into without a mediator.

IV. It agrees with the covenant of grace: (1) in the author because the author of both is God; (2) in the object (to wit, man—a sinner); (3) in the mediator, who is found in both; (4) in the end—the end of both is to show sin and to lead to Christ. It differs: (1) as to the relation (*schesin*) of the author, for in the legal God is considered simply as rebuking sin and approving righteousness alone, but in the evangelic, as pardoning sin and renewing righteousness in man; (2) as to stipulation—for that of the former is "Do this and live"; of the latter, "Believe and thou shalt be saved"; (3) as to the mediator, who in the former was Moses a mere man; in the latter Christ, the God-man (*theanthrōpos*); (4) as to the object, man stupefied by sin was the object of the former; the conscience terrified by sin was the object of the latter; (5) as to the effects, the former gendered to bondage, the latter to liberty; that led to Christ indirectly, this directly. That was a handwriting (*syngraphē*) against us, this a disburdener (*seisachtheia*); the one restrains from sin, but with compulsion, while the other restrains with spontaneous inclination (cf. Cameron, "De Triplici Dei cum homine foedere theses," *Opera* [1642], pp. 544-51).

Common opinion of the orthodox concerning the threefold covenant.

V. However, we recognize only two covenants mutually distinct in species (to wit, the covenant of works, which promises life to the doer; and the covenant of grace, which promises salvation to believers). Although we confess that the Sinaitic covenant as to mode of dispensation was different from both, still as to substance and species we deny that it is constituted a third covenant and hold that it was nothing else than a new economy of the covenant of grace. It was really the same with the covenant made with Abraham, but different as to accidents and circumstances (to wit, clothed as to external dispensation with the form of a covenant of works through the harsh promulgation of the law; not indeed with that design, so that a covenant of works might again be demanded with the sinner [for this was impossible], but that a daily recollection and reproaching of the violated covenant of works might be made; thus the Israelites felt their sin and the curse of God besides hanging over them and acknowledged the impossibility of a legal righteousness; driven away from that hope, they so much the more ardently thirsted for the righteousness of redemption and were led along by the hand to Christ). Hence in it there was a mixture of the law and the gospel: the former to strike terror into sinners and press upon the neck of the stiff-necked (*schlērotragēlou*) people; the latter to lift up and console the conscience contrite and overpowered by a sense of sin.

Statement of the question.

VI. The question is not whether the cause of salvation was different under the Old and New Testament. They with whom we argue confess that it was the same in both and that the fathers were saved in no other way than by Christ. The question is not even whether a multiple diversity occurs between this legal and evangelical covenant as to economy. This we acknowledge on both sides and have proved before. Rather the question is whether the diversity was essential and such that it may be called, besides a new covenant strictly, distinct in species as much from the covenant of nature as of grace (which they hold and we deny).

Reasons against a threefold covenant: (1) from Scripture, which mentions only two covenants.

VII. The reasons are: (1) the Scripture tells us of only two covenants, nowhere however of three. Now we are not to distinguish where the Scripture does not. In Gal. 4:24, under the allegory of Sarah and Hagar, Paul points out two covenants: the legal which genders to bondage; the evangelical, which leads to freedom. In Heb. 8 (from Jer. 31), two covenants are in like manner enumerated: the old which was violated and made void; the new which is eternal and immutable. Thereupon the apostle institutes an antithesis between the law of works and the law of faith; the letter that killeth and the Spirit that maketh alive (which he could not have done with sufficient accuracy, if there was a certain third covenant distinct from both).

2. From the modes of obtaining happiness, either by works or by faith.

VIII. (2) There can be so many and no more covenants as there are ways and modes of obtaining happiness and communion with God (which is the proper end of the institution of a covenant). Now there are only two such modes: either by personal and inherent or by imputed obedience; either by works or by faith. The former by the law, whose formula is "Do this and live"; the latter by the gospel, whose voice says, "Believe and thou shalt be saved." Nor can there be any middle way of happiness. Therefore in vain is a third covenant feigned which belongs neither to works nor to faith.

3. Because the Sinaitic covenant was a covenant of grace. This is proved: (a) from Dt. 7 and 29.

IX. (3) The Sinaitic covenant is no other than the covenant of grace entered into before with the fathers. This appears (a) from Dt. 7:11, 12 where Moses promises to the keeping of the covenant made with the fathers. Also from Dt. 29:10-13 where he renews the covenant made in Horeb, that he would be a God of the people according to the oath sworn unto the fathers, Abraham, Isaac and Jacob. This teaches most clearly that for no other end was this Sinaitic covenant made than to confirm the preceding covenant.

b. On the part of God.

X. (b) The parties to this covenant prove the same thing. There is here no other formula on the part of God than that which is found in the covenant of grace. He covenants with the Israelites as their God and also as the God of Abraham, Isaac and Jacob (Ex. 3:6; Acts 3:13). This is the very substance of the covenant of grace on God's part, embracing in itself the whole communication of God towards the perfecting and glorifying of sinful man (Lev. 26; Jer. 31; Mt. 22; 2 Cor. 6). Hence he is set forth not only as the God of his people, but also as their Redeemer (Ex. 20:2); as the merciful pardoner of sins (Ex. 34:6, 7); as a sanctifier, promising circumcision of the heart (Dt. 30:6, 8); as a faithful husband, having a marital care for his people (Ezk. 16:8, 9; Jer. 3:14; Hos. 2:20); as a kind father, who begets sons, nourishes and cherishes them with paternal affection (Dt. 32:6, 8-10; Is. 1:2, 3; Hos. 11:1); as a gracious king, who placed his sanctuary in the midst of the people that he might dwell and walk with them (Ex. 25:8; 29:45, 46; Lev. 26:11, 12), i.e., might hold communion with them, deeming them worthy of his gracious presence for direction in difficulties, protection in dangers, blessing in adversity and consolation in griefs. Now since so many and so great blessings could not be obtained from God except in virtue of a covenant of grace, the Sinaitic covenant (in which he so exhibited himself) can be no other than a covenant of grace.

c. On the part of the Israelites.

XI. (c) The Israelites, who were the other contracting part, sustained no other relation than what pertains to the covenant of grace, while they are considered both antecedently in themselves as sinners and exposed to death in a most miserable state (which is described by a virgin recently born lying in her own blood, Ezk. 16:4-6); and consequently from grace, as "the seed of Abraham" to whom the promises in Christ were made (Gal. 3:16)—as "the people of God" who obtained mercy (Hos. 2:1; Rom. 9:25; 1 Pet. 2:10); as *sglh* and *laos periousios* a peculiar treasure, above all people (Ex. 19:5), i.e., beloved of God above others, whom he claims as peculiar to him and whom, with great zeal, he cares for and guards like treasures of the most precious things. It is evident that all these relations (*scheseis*) pertain to the covenant of grace per se.

XII. It is confirmed by this—that the Israelites with whom God stipulates were already under the Abrahamic covenant (which was a covenant of grace). By it, they were saved in Christ. Therefore they could not be under a legal covenant. For no one can be at the same time under two covenants distinct in their whole species. Nor is it of any account to say that the legal subserved the covenant of grace, because it could do this by reason of economy, but not by reason of the covenant because it is opposed to and incompatible (*asystaton*) with grace.

d. From the circumstances of the covenant.

XIII. (d) There are very many circumstances in that giving of the law (*nomothesia*) which are purely evangelical—as that Moses having read the book of the covenant took the blood of the victims with which he sprinkled the people saying, "Behold the blood of the covenant which the Lord hath made with you" (Ex. 24:8). The apostle teaches this was not free from mystery (Heb. 9:20), to denote the blood of sprinkling (Heb. 12:24) and the sprinkling of the blood of Christ (both upon the altar for the satisfaction of justice and the expiation of sin; and upon the people for the application of his merit, the remission of sin and justification). An indubitable proof of this was the approach of the elders (who represented the whole people) to God (Ex. 24:10, 11), whom they not only "saw," but "did eat and drink before" (i.e., were admitted into communion with him [which had before been so strictly forbidden them] and enjoyed his good things). This could not have been done by the legal covenant (which keeps the sinner off), but must necessarily have been done by the gospel in virtue of the blood of Christ. And further, the twofold manner of legislation (which God wished to enter upon) must here be especially observed: the first terrible, related in Ex. 19, where barriers were placed around the mountain and Moses alone permitted to approach God; the other sweet, in which the covenant is made with the blood of victims and the elders with Moses are called up the mount that they may enjoy the sight and communion of God (Ex. 24:10, 11). The former has a legal relation (*schesin*); the latter an evangelical. These two relations (*scheseis*) are always conjoined in that dispensation. The latter is the more important and principal; the former accessory and ministerial.

XIV. Here belongs the fact that Paul describes the gospel righteousness of faith (Rom. 10:6-8) in the same words by which Moses had set forth the doctrine delivered to the people in the Sinaitic covenant (Dt. 30:11, 12, 14). Not only allusively and by way of imitation (*mimēsin*) transferring and adapting to the righteousness of faith what was said of the legal, but properly and by direct proof, both because he had designated the righteousness of the law in another manner that "the man which doeth those things shall live by them" and because the facility of observation of that word does not pertain to the law (which is a dead letter) but to the gospel (whose word is not only imperative, but also operative by the power of the vivifying Spirit). Here is meant the word not so much of the law as of the gospel, by which God (in the same place) promises pardon to penitents and circumcision of heart, i.e., "word of faith which we preach" (as the apostle explains in the same place). "But the righteousness which is of faith speaketh on this wise, Say not in thine heart, Who shall ascend into heaven? [for] the word is nigh thee, even in thy mouth, and in thy heart" (i.e., the whole doctrine of salvation, which is in the heart by faith, but in the mouth by confession). Now how could Paul have said this unless he had recognized that covenant, by virtue of which such promises were given, to be not so much legal as evangelical?

4. From the ceremonial law, which was wholly typical.

XV. (4) The ceremonial law (which made a part of that covenant) shows that all things in this covenant were mystical, typical, representative and symbolical of the covenant of grace and of all its parts (which accordingly were contained under them, as the truth under figures, Col. 2:17). This appeared most of all in the sacrifices which (for no other reason than as types of the sacrifices of Christ) expiated sins. Hence, "an offering made by fire is said to be of a savour of rest (*rych nychvch*) unto the Lord" (Lev. 1:9, 13, 17), i.e., most acceptable, which makes God (provoked by sins) rest and pleases him. Since however that expiation could not be made by the victim's own virtue (Heb. 9:9, 10), it must necessarily be made by another, namely by Christ prefigured. Nor does it help the matter to say that this worship belonged to external purity and immunity from temporal punishments in the court of earth. Although this was a use of ceremonies (inasmuch as they are considered absolutely and in themselves), they ought to have another (inasmuch as they were as figures and images). For thus they were as moral instruments by which (perceived by faith) the believers of the Old Testament perceived the thing at the same time as the apostle ascribes to them (1 Cor. 10:2-4).

5. From the sacraments of the Old Testament.

XVI. (5) The two sacraments of the covenant of grace already made with the fathers were conjoined to the Sinaitic covenant (to wit, circumcision and the Passover, which prevailed under that dispensation until Christ and were added as seals to confirm it, Jn. 7:22, 23; Dt. 16:1, 2). This could not have been done if it had been a third new covenant, distinct in entire species from the covenant of grace. For it is absurd to add the sacraments of the covenant of grace to a certain different covenant, whether it be called one of works or subservient.

6. From absurdity because it would derogate from the Abrahamic covenant.

XVII. (6) If the Sinaitic covenant was purely legal, it follows that God by this covenant derogated from the Abrahamic covenant because a posterior covenant derogates from a prior. Nor could place have been given for another covenant if that former had always stood. Now so far from derogating from the former covenant, it was rather made for its confirmation. Hence the apostle shows that the law (given four hundred and thirty years after the promise was given to Abraham, Gal. 3:17) could not make it of none effect. It was added only on account of transgressions, until the seed should come to whom the promise was made (v. 19). This proves that the law pointed away to Christ as the end to which it looked; if not by itself and in its own nature, at least in the intention and design of the lawgiver. To say that this covenant subserved the covenant of grace is really to say that it was not a covenant, but only a dispensation. A covenant properly so called has the power of binding by itself the contracting parties, nor is it directed to another. If therefore that dispensation had respect to another (as it really did), it is a proof that it was not a different covenant in species, but only a different mode of economy, adapted to the time, place and state of the persons.

Sources of explanation.

XVIII. The Mosaic covenant may be viewed in two aspects: either according to the intention and design of God and in order to Christ; or separately and abstracted from him. In the latter way, it is really distinct from the covenant of grace because it coincides with the covenant of works and in this sense is called the letter that killeth and the ministration of condemnation, when its nature is spoken of (2 Cor. 3:6, 7). But it is unwarrantably abstracted here because it must always be considered with the intention of God, which was, not that man might have life from the law or as a sinner might be simply condemned, but that from a sense of his own misery and weakness he might fly for refuge to Christ.

XIX. Although the Sinaitic and the legal covenants are opposed in Jer. 31 to the new covenant, it is not necessary that this opposition should be as to essence, but it can be as to accidents or diversity of economy (as a man is opposed to himself, as standing and sitting). If remission is promised under the new covenant, it does not follow that the fathers under the old were without it, no more than from the fact that God promises to be the God of future believers under the New Testament, it can lawfully be inferred that he was not the God of the fathers. These promises are not to be understood absolutely and simply, but relatively and comparatively with regard to greater clearness and efficacy. Again, if a specific opposition be urged, then the covenant is viewed, not in its whole latitude, but only as to the legal relation (*schesin*) and in contradistinction to the gospel—so as to designate what the law can or cannot do absolutely and in itself, separated from the gospel.

XX. The Sinaitic covenant was not without Christ because (1) Moses testified of him (Jn. 5:45, 46; Lk. 24:44; Acts 3:22, 23; 26:22, 23); (2) he is contained implicitly under the promise of a peculiar treasure, royal priesthood and holy nation (Ex. 19:5, 6 compared with 1 Pet. 2:9, 10)—for without Christ, sinners cannot obtain these privileges (as was said before); (3) in the preface to the decalogue, God is set forth as the God of the people and the deliverer from Egypt (which could be done only through Christ); (4) the ratification of the covenant by the blood of victims typified the blood of Christ; (5) the legal types and shadows chiefly pointed to no other than Christ; (6) the principal scope and spirit of the law was Christ, without whom it is nothing else than a corpse and a letter that kills (Rom. 10:4; Gal. 3:24).

XXI. The law is said "to be not of faith" (Gal. 3:12), not as taken broadly and denoting the Mosaic economy, but strictly as taken for the moral law abstractly and apart from the promises of grace (as the legalists regarded it who sought life from it). For it is proved that faith was taught even in the Sinaitic covenant: (1) because Christ, its object, was contained in it; (2) because God cannot be worshipped, as required in the first commandment, without faith, which purifies the heart, works through love and makes us acceptable to God (Acts 15:9; Heb. 11:6); (3) because the Sinaitic covenant by convincing man of his sin and weakness impelled him to seek Christ by faith, since by the law "God hath concluded all under sin, that the promise by faith of Jesus Christ might be given to them that believe" (Gal. 3:22); and "the law was our schoolmaster to bring us unto Christ, that we might be justified by faith" (v. 24); (4) because Paul describes the righteousness of faith (Rom. 10:6, 7) in the same words as Moses declared the precepts of the law (Dt. 30:11-13), to teach that they are not simply legal, but also evangelical. Nor if it is said in Gal. 3:23 that "faith" should be revealed (to wit, comparatively), as to clearer manifestation, does it follow that it was not revealed absolutely under the Old Testament.

XXII. The specific difference of a covenant cannot make a diversity of condition, expressed by the law and gospel—of the former imperfect obedience; of the latter in faith. It was not required in the same way, nor for the same end. For faith in Christ is demanded primarily and intended chiefly, but perfect obedience (under punishment of death and the curse) only subordinately and relatively to faith and the righteousness of faith. By convincing man of his sin and weakness, it forced him to seek a remedy in Christ by faith (as we have already said). Again, these two conditions are proposed because they are necessary to the salvation of the sinner: perfect obedience in Christ to fulfill the righteousness of the law (*to dikaiōma tou nomou*), without which the justice of God did not permit life to be given to us; faith however in us that the perfect obedience and satisfaction of Christ might be applied to us and become ours by imputation. Thus what was demanded of us in the covenant of works is fulfilled by Christ in the covenant of grace. Nor is it absurd that in this way justification takes place by works and by faith—by the works of Christ and by our faith. And thus in sweet harmony the law and the gospel meet together in this covenant. The law is not administered without the gospel, nor the gospel without the law. So that it is as it were a legal-gospel and an evanglical-law; a gospel full of obedience and a law full of faith. So the gospel does not destroy the law, but establishes it (Rom. 3:31) by giving us Christ, who perfectly fulfilled it. And the law is not against the gospel, since it refers and leads us to it as its end.

XXIII. Although Moses can in a measure be called a mediator in the Sinaitic covenant (because he acted the part of an internuncius by standing between Jehovah and the people [Dt. 5:1] who however could not reconcile the people to God), it does not follow that the covenant of which he is called the mediator was different in species from the covenant of grace, in which such a reconciliation is brought about. He was only a typical and external mediator, not a primary and true one from whom alone (his sponsion made and accepted by God) he had his whole power and efficacy to the reconciliation of sinners and their deliverance from the eternal curse and reception of heavenly life. Moses could (according to the relation [*schesin*] of internuncius which he sustained) in his manner give the covenant effect to a certain point by acting as the interpreter of the will of the parties so that by the intervention of their consent the covenant itself might be entered into. But he could not institute further reconciliation per se (which pertained only to Christ, who should be the peacemaker [*eirēnopoios*]).

XXIV. The promise of the land of Canaan given to the people was not primary and principal, but only secondary and less principal (added by way of proposition [*prothēkēs*]; of addition to the primary concerning God about to be their God and indeed as a pledge and symbol of the heavenly Canaan [of which it was a type, Heb. 4], to which the fathers looked [Heb. 11:15, 16]). Therefore, a specific diversity of covenant cannot (except falsely) be inferred from the diversity of that promise from the one given to us in the gospel. Rather only a diversity of dispensation may be inferred which even the other differences between the Old and New Testaments here adduced concerning the spirit of bondage (of which we have spoken before) imply.

XXV. It is one thing to speak of the law in itself (which had the form of a covenant of works and was enacted not with the end of making alive, but to convict of transgression, extort the confession of debt and lead to Christ); another concerning the Sinaitic covenant itself, in which the law was enacted. In the former sense, the law is called a handwriting against us and the minister of condemnation (2 Cor. 3:9; Col. 2:14); but in the latter sense, that covenant had the lively oracles (*logia zōnta*, Acts 7:38) and contained the saving promises of the grace of Christ.

THIRTEENTH TOPIC

THE PERSON AND STATE OF CHRIST

FIRST QUESTION

Has the promised Messiah already come? We affirm against the Jews.

I. Since Christ is the Mediator of the New Testament and the cause and fountain of all the blessings which flow to us from the covenant of grace, the doctrine concerning the covenant could never be rightly understood without a knowledge of Christ. Since two things in him should be most especially attended to (his person and office), we must speak first of his person before we pass to his office.

The first question, concerning the advent of the Messiah.

II. Now that we may the more easily inquire into the person of Christ, two questions must be premised: the first concerns the advent of the Messiah *in thesi*, from which it will appear that the Messiah, who was to come, has already come; the second concerns his person *in hypothesi*, or who he is, that we may know he is no other than Jesus of Nazareth, the son of Mary.

Who was promised from the beginning, but not immediately sent for a twofold cause: (1) both with respect to Christ;

III. We take for granted here that in which all agree: first, that the Messiah was promised immediately after the fall from the very beginning of the world as the only means of salvation; second, that although promised from the beginning, he was not to be sent immediately, but only after a long interval of time, for which most wise dispensation a multiple reason can be rendered, whether we regard Christ himself or men themselves. With respect to Christ: first, this conduced to his dignity, that before he came into the world, various heralds should announce beforehand his coming as of a supreme ruler—"The greater the judge approaching, the longer the line of heralds preceded" (Augustine, Tractate 31, *On the Gospel of John* [NPNF1, 7:190; PL 35.1638]). Thus faith might rest beforehand upon him and the way be prepared not only by various types, but also by concordant testimonies of prophets. Second, the long expectation of so great an event should render this benefit the more acceptable among men that the nativity (which was to surpass all miracles and all measure of intelligence) might produce by so much a more constant faith in us, as its declaration had preceded the more ancient and richer (as Leo says, *Sermon XXIII*, "On the Feast of the Nativity, III" [NPNF2, 12:133-34; PL 54.202]).

2. And with respect to men.

IV. With respect to men, the magnitude of evil required this, that the conscience (convicted of the multitude and heinousness of sins and of the inability of nature and the uselessness of all human means which could be devised), the necessity of a remedy might appear and the patient, feeling his weakness, might cry out to the physician and seek the aid of grace, as Augustine expresses it. God left men to a long expectation of himself that he might see whether he would fall by his own fault or could raise himself up by his own strength. On this account, God, during that whole time of his forbearance (*anochēs*), suffered sin to increase and in a measure to abound that the abundance of grace might thus be more illustrious. Still he did not wish that advent to be put off until the end of the world, lest by so long a delay the knowledge and reverence of God might fade away from the minds of men and desperation swallow up faith. Besides the dispensation of grace was to be distinguished from that of glory, nor ought the work of reparation to be contiguous to that of perfection. Its own age and time (*kairos*) or season was to be assigned to each work; and the first advent of Christ was not to be confounded with the second.

Statement of the question.

V. The question here concerns the time of the first advent. With regard to this, it is not only to institute a permissible inquiry but also necessary for the safety (*asphaleian*) of our faith. For this cause the Holy Spirit in the Old Testament wished to indicate it by certain unmistakable marks that believers might recognize him coming and no one could urge the pretext of ignorance in their rejection of him. Nor are the modern rabbis to be listened to who (the more easily to extricate themselves from the arguments with which we invincibly demonstrate from Scripture that this time has already gone by) have sought the following refuge: that no certain time for the advent of the Messiah is defined beforehand in Scripture, but that God kept that as a secret for himself alone that he might send the Messiah whenever he chose. Hence they severely prohibit inquiries into the time of the Messiah and anathematize any who attempt to compute the time of the Messiah—"Let their inflated bones be broken, who compute the periods of times" ("Sanhedrin," 97b, BT, p. 659). If anything else, this surely is the proof of a desperate cause. For who can believe it possible that there could be found among them those who could deny a thing so clear, so constantly believed among the people from every past age, so desired and expected (unless struck with blind error of mind and warped by prejudice)? They are so possessed by the spirit of contradiction as to think no comment so foreign that they cannot take it in their teeth, provided it is farthest from the sense which seems to be able to favor our Jesus.

VI. When in truth we dispute concerning the time of the advent of the Messiah, it must be observed: (1) that we do not treat of such a time or of such signs and marks of it as strike our senses unwittingly and which can be wholly unknown to anyone (such as the Jews wish and are usually called mathematical and physical: for example, the Messiah will come, the sun standing on the meridian; or during an eclipse of the sun at full noon; or on a mountain of God elevated above the other mountains). Rather we discuss the marks of time which they call historical, capable of being known by facts and events and such that they should be observed with attention and apprehended by faith. (2) That we do not do this that we may prove the precise article of that time (for instance: the year, the month, the week, etc.) appointed by God and what it was (for there is no necessity for this). But we do this only that we may prove broadly (*en platei*) that a certain time was appointed for the advent of the Messiah, and such that it can be known by the clearest facts and events (for this is now sufficient after all those events have taken place). (3) That we do not treat of any marks whatever of which mention is made in Scripture, but of those which serve for convincing the Jews and which have an essential connection with the Messiah's advent, so that they would not exist unless the Messiah had come. Because they exist, on that account, we must believe that he has come.

VII. Thus the statement of the question is reduced within these limits—whether the promised Messiah has already come; or is he truly still to come and to be expected by us. Has the time of that advent appointed beforehand by God already gone by and elapsed; or has it not yet come? The Jews maintain the latter with great obstinacy. We however assert the former, resting upon invincible reasons.

1. Demonstration of the advent of the Messiah drawn from the time of Shiloh.

VIII. The first demonstration is from the determination of the time in which the advent of the Messiah ought to take place. For if the time fixed for the advent of the Messiah has already come, the Messiah himself also must have come. Now that it has come and passed by is most clearly gathered from various characteristics. The first is drawn from the oracle of Jacob where the Messiah's advent is connected with the taking away of the Jewish scepter. "The scepter," says he, "shall not depart from Judah, nor a lawgiver from between his feet, until Shiloh come" (Gen. 49:10). Hence we thus argue—If the scepter was not to be taken away from Judah until Shiloh (who is the Messiah) comes, it follows that he has most certainly come because that oracle has been fulfilled long ago and the Jewish scepter has been taken away; nor have the Jews any rulers. To confirm the argument against the cavils of the Jews, two things must be proved: (1) that by Shiloh here the Messiah is meant; (2) that it refers to the taking away of the political dominion and authority of the Jews.

IX. First, Shiloh can be no other than the Messiah. For whatever may be the origin and signification of the word, it is certain that no other one is here designated. This is true whether it is explained by *apestalmenon, mittendum* (according to the Vulgate, as if it was to be read *shylvch*); or by "his son" (i.e., as Kimchi sets it forth—*bnv,* who shall be born [*mshlvch*] from "the afterbirth" of a woman, like all who are born); or that it may be derived from the Arabic tongue where *shvl* is "a flowing forth of blood"—"until the flowing forth [*shlvch*] of his blood" (i.e., the seed which should flow from it, according to Louis de Dieu, *Critica Sacra* [1963], p. 22 on Gen. 49:10); or the word is derived from *shlh* which means to do happily and prosperously, "until the harbinger of peace" or "the peace maker and peaceable" comes (as Oleaster, Avenarius and others hold); or the word is said to be composed of *shv,* signifying "office," and the affix *lv* (i.e., "office to him") because offices were to be imposed upon him (as Rabbi Salomon Jarchi maintains; cf. *Pentateuch with . . . Rashi's Commentary* [trans. M. Rosenbaum and A. M. Silberman, 1965], 1:245). Or finally it is explained by *'shr lv* "whose is" (supply, the kingdom), which seems to be the most appropriate opinion of all and best suited to this passage. Thus the meaning is, the kingdom will not be taken away from Judah "until he comes to whom it belongs." So the paraphrases of Onkelos and Jerusalem understood it: "until the Messiah comes, whose is the kingdom" (cf. Walton, *Biblia sacra polyglotta* [1657], p. 271 on Gen. 49:10 and *Das Fragmententhargum: Thargum jeruschalmi zum Pentateuch* [ed. M. Ginsburger, 1899], p. 25). The Septuagint translates it *ta apokeimena autō* or *hō apokeitai* (as Justin, Irenaeus, Tertullian). And light can be thrown upon this place from Ezk. 21:27 where the crown of Jechoniah is described: "And it" (supply crown) "shall be no more until he come [*'shr lv*] whose right it is." However, in whatever way it may be explained, it can be applied best to the Messiah, especially since immediately a mark of the Messiah is subjoined (to wit, that "unto him shall the obedience" or "the gathering of the people be"—which is everywhere ascribed to the Messiah, Gen. 22:17, 18; Is. 11:10; Mic. 4:1). The connection also demands it. For as he ascribes to Judah the prerogative and dominion over his brethren and the children of his father, so he says of the Messiah (who was to spring from him) that not only would his brethren worship him, but all the people would obey him also.

X. It can apply to no other. Not to Moses because the royal power was not as yet with Judah, nor could it have been transferred from Judah to Moses. Not to Saul, who ought to have been annointed in Shiloh, by whom the scepter was removed from Judah and transferred to the tribe of Benjamin. For (a) Saul was not anointed in Shiloh, but first in Ramah, solemnly chosen in Mizpeh and afterwards confirmed in Gilgal (1 S. 9; 10:17; 11:14); (b) before Saul the royal scepter had not yet been in Judah; yea, a kingdom had not yet been established in the midst of the people in any particular tribe; (c) while Saul was reigning the scepter was transferred to Judah and David, not therefore taken away from him; (d) neither the obedience nor the expectation of peoples could be to Saul. Not to David (in whom the tribe of Judah was about to be preferred) was transferred the royal dignity because it is not said that the scepter would be transferred, but taken away; nor did the scepter cease where it first began. Not to Jeroboam, who should have been crowned in Shiloh, because he was anointed in the city of Shechem, not in Shiloh (1 K. 12:1, 25); nor was the kingdom then removed from Judah; yea, it continued for a long time and they alone were reckoned also true kings. Not to Nebuchadnezzar, who would be sent to take away the kingdom on account of the sins of the people, because: (a) all the words of Jacob in this oracle are referred to the benediction of Judah, while that transportation was a punishment, not a blessing. (b) It is not true that the scepter was then taken away absolutely because it is certain that many of the chief men were carried away to Babylon and that the Jews lived according to their own laws with the consent of the king and had their own head (*aichmalōtarchēn*) or prince of captivity (*r'sh glvth*) elected from Judah. Finally the ancient Jews acknowledge that the word must be understood of the Messiah: (a) the Chaldee Paraphrase, Onkelos, Jonathan, Jerusalem—"Until King Messiah [*mlk' mshych'*] comes" (cf. Walton, *Biblia sacra polyglotta* [1657], p. 271 on Gen. 49:10; *Targum Pseudo-Jonathan of the Pentateuch* [E. G. Clarke, 1984], p. 62; *Das Fragmententhargum: Thargum jeruschalmi zum Pentateuch* [ed. M. Ginsburger, 1899], p. 25); (b) the Talmudists—"What is the name of the Messiah? Let the house of Rabbi Schelah teach us: Shiloh is his name, as it is written until Shiloh comes" ("Sanhedrin," 98b, BT, 2:667); (c) the rabbis—"Until Shiloh, that is, king Messiah comes" (*Genesis Rabbah* [ed. J. Neusner, 1985], 3:358). Rashi (*Pentateuch with . . . Rashi's Commentary* [trans. M. Rosenbaum and A. M. Silbermann, 1965], 1:245) and Rabbi Bechai (*Beor al ha-torah*: Bereshith, pp. 382-83) have the same thing.

XI. (2) Second, that it treats of the taking away of the Jewish kingdom is gathered from the word *shbt*, which cannot be referred here to any other than the distinctive mark of kings (to wit, "the rod" or "scepter," the symbol of royal majesty).

Hence the Septuagint translates *archōn*, Aquila *skēptron* (Origen, *Hexapla* [PG 15.324]); Symmachus *exousia* (ibid. [PG 15.325]). Falsely do the Jews say that a "rod of correction" is meant here, as in Prov. 22:15* (i.e., "affliction" and "oppression"), so that the sense is: "Oppressors shall not cease to afflict Israel until the Messiah comes who will deliver them." But on the other hand: (a) such a rod must be understood as is proper to "the lawgiver" (*mchvqq*, who is here joined) as it belongs to a king to have a scepter and to make laws (*skēptron de t'ēde themistas*, as Homer says, *Iliad* 2.205 [Loeb, 1:64-65]). Now what has the lawgiver to do with a rod of oppression? (b) The patriarch would thus have prophesied concerning the punishments and not the blessings of Judah, the opposite of which is evident from the words "Judah, thou art he whom thy brethren shall praise" (Gen. 49:8). Victory is promised to him, the prerogative of honor among brethren, the strength of a lion and the peaceable possession of prey. How can these be consistent with a prediction of affliction? Besides, since a rod of correction ought to be common to all the tribes, there was no reason why it should here be referred to the tribe of Judah alone. (c) It is not true that oppression never ceased in that tribe, since it flourished through many generations from David to Zedekiah. (d) The same words occur in Zech. 10:11, *ysvr shbt*, which the Septuagint translates *skēptron Aigyptou periairethēsetai* ("the scepter of Egypt shall depart away"). (e) The ancient Jews take the word as we do: "He shall not cease (*shbtv*) exercising dominion" (*Targum Onkelos to Genesis* [ed. M. Aberbach and B. Grossfeld, 1982], pp. 284-85); "Kings and Princes shall not cease" (cf. Walton, *Biblia sacra polyglotta* [1657], 3:130 on Zech. 10:11); "Kings shall not cease" (*Das Fragmententhargum: Thargum jeruschalmi zum Pentateuch* [ed. M. Ginsburger, 1899], p. 25). Concerning principality and dominion, it is thus explained by "Sanhedrin" (cf. 5a, BT, p. 16); Bereschit Rabba (*Genesis Rabbah*, 98.8 [trans. J. Neusner, 1985], 3:356-57); Ramban 1 ult. Jad. cap. 4+; Rabbi David Kimchi on the word *shbt* (*Seser ha-shorashim* [1847], pp. 365-66).

XII. Not without reason however is the taking away of the kingdom from Judah laid down as a mark of the Messiah's advent. The taking away of (*arsis*) the one is the establishing (*thesis*) of the other; the removal (*aphairesis*) of the kingdom from Judah is the founding of Christ's kingdom. For since the Jewish republic was primarily instituted on account of Christ to preserve the tribe from which the Messiah was to spring, the republic could not be overthrown, nor ought the tribe to be dissolved until the advent of the Messiah. Besides since that polity was shadowy and earthly (to which the promises were not directly made), it could not continue forever, but its glory ought to be abolished (*katargeisthai*) and give place to the mystical and eternal kingdom of Christ. It makes little difference, however, whether the particle *'d ky* ("until") is taken exclusively to mean that the scepter ought to have ceased before the Messiah's advent; or inclusively with the meaning that the empire would not cease until the Messiah came and that he would come before the taking away of the scepter. The force of the argument always remains against the Jews. For if it is true that the advent of the Messiah is joined with the removal of the scepter from Judah, it cannot be doubted that he has come, since for so long a time that scepter has been removed, all judicial power entirely taken away, the city destroyed and the people scattered (as the Jews themselves are forced to acknowledge). See Rabbi David Kimchi: "These are the days of exile, in which we now live, nor can we have a king, nor a prince out of Israel, since indeed we are under the sway of the Gentiles" (*Commentary of*

... *Kimhi on Hosea* [ed. H. Cohen, 1966], p. 31 on Hos. 3:4); and Manassah (ben Israel)—"This punishment we now suffer . . . living without a king, without a prince, without a government" (*Conciliator* [1972], 1:93).

XIII. Now there is no necessity for wearying ourselves in seeking the precise article of time in which that power was taken away from the Jewish people, provided it is evident (which is most certain) that it is now taken away and has been for many ages in the past. For although chronologists vehemently contend about it among themselves and there is a great discrepancy in their opinions, some maintaining that the scepter was taken away under Pompey, others under Vespasian, others (which is far more satisfactory) hold that it was not the work of one moment, as the republic was shaken by various changes under Pompey and Herod and at length overturned under Vespasian; still there is no need to decide this intricate question to strengthen our argument against the Jews. Its own force always remains from this—that it is established beyond all shadow of controversy that all authority has been for a long time taken away from the Jews, so that there are not days or years, but ages from the time of the fulfillment of this oracle. Hence it necessarily follows either that it was false and deceitful (which it is even impious to think) or that the Messiah has already come.

XIV. Nor are the Jews to be heard who have invented the tale that the scepter still remains in Babylon in those who rule over the people there. Manasseh (ben Israel) strives to confirm this from Benjamin, who relates that at Baghdad he saw with his own eyes among the Israelites a certain ruler born of the family of David, carried in a chariot amid the acclamations of the people (*Conciliator* [1972], p. 98). These are the sheerest figments of their brains, contrary to the opinion of the rabbis before quoted; contrary to the report of all who have travelled over the world or have written upon the subject (who maintain a deep silence concerning those rulers). And if there was any truth in it, is it to be believed even for a moment that the remaining Jews scattered throughout the world would remain in the miserable bondage under which they groan? Hence the testimony of Benjamin (as a false forger of fables and often convicted of lying by the learned L'Empereur) should have no authority with us (*Itinerium D. Benjaminis cum versione et notis . . . L'Empereur* [1633] and *Itinerary of Benjamin of Tudela* [ed. M.N. Adler, 1907], pp. 39-40). This can with the more certainty be said because the tribes being now confused, it is impossible to know certainly who are of the tribe of Judah, who of another.

XV. The principal difficulty as urged by the Jews remains—it cannot be gathered from this passage that the Messiah has already come, otherwise he ought to have come before the Babylonian captivity because in it the scepter was taken away from the Jews and never afterwards returned to them. For its solution we premise: (1) that it is not possible always to assign the certain and indubitable points of time in which the flower and glory of kingdoms continue or in which they fall off or are overthrown. As the establishment and dignity of kingdoms is not obtained together and at once (but little by little and successively), so the decline and fall do not take place in one moment, nor in a sensible and open manner, but by degrees and imperceptibly and insensibly. Thus it may the more quickly be perceived after it has happened than observed while it is. Therefore this is not to be restricted to a particular point of time, but ought to be considered broadly (*en platei*) in a certain latitude of time. (2) It is one thing for a royal family (having the right to reign) to continue; another for kings to be actually reigning. For the latter might be abrogated, while the former remained (as if a kingdom should be occupied tyrannically by anyone, the lawful heirs having been expelled—the possession [*ktēsis*] remains, while the use [*chrēsei*] is taken away). (3) It is not necessary to the fulfillment of the oracle that the highest dignity should always have been held by the tribe of Judah. It is sufficient to preserve its truth, if any sway and principality flourished in it because these words ("the scepter shall not depart, nor a lawgiver . . .") are to be taken disjunctively, not conjunctively. The meaning is the Jews would not be deprived of both until the Messiah should come, but one or the other would always be retained, if not the scepter, still a lawgiver and judiciary power and legislation (*nomothesian*). (4) It is not even required that dominion should always exist in a continued and uninterrupted series. It is sufficient for the denomination always to be (as although the Spanish kingdom may have passed over to the House of Austria, it does not cease to be called the Spanish Crown).

XVI. These positions being established, I say that the continuation of the scepter and of power in Judah can be clearly demonstrated: (1) from David up to the Babylonian captivity through 470 years; (2) during the captivity, first in Jehoiachin whose "head Evil-merodach did lift up, and set forth his throne above the thrones of the other kings" (2 K. 25:27, 28); second, in Daniel who was of the tribe of Judah and of royal blood (Dan. 2:25; 5:13); third, in the Aechmalotarchs ("governors of captivity") who were in the captivity. Hence Ramban: "Aechmalotarchs held the place of kings because it is said, the scepter shall not depart" (lib. ult. Iad. c. iv+); Rabbi Solomon, "The scepter shall not be taken away, these are the rulers of the exile, who govern the people by permission of the Persian kings" ("Sanhedrin," 5a, BT, 1:16). (3) After the Babylonian captivity, in Zerubbabel, a nephew of Jehoiachin, and Nehemiah, whom Eusebius affirms to have been of the tribe of Judah (cf. Joseph Scaliger, *Animadversiones in Chronologica Eusebii in Thesaurus Temporum* [1968], 2:98). Hence the Nehemiah who is numbered among the priests (Neh. 10:1) must have been a different person, so that it is evident from 7:5, 7 that there were two Nehemiahs. (4) From Nehemiah to Herod, a space of 335 years, the proof is more difficult because the canon of Scripture is wanting. Still it can be gathered from these three things: (a) as to the Maccabees although they were of the tribe of Levi, it did not cease to be called the Jewish kingdom because as the tribe of Judah alone returned from the captivity with the tribe of Benjamin (which was an accession to it), thus the kingdom and the republic was in the tribe of Judah and they who presided, although they might be from a different tribe, yet because they received the scepter from the tribe of Judah and in it and in its name wielded it, it could truly be said that the scepter was held by Judah because the imperial majesty always remained with it (as it was with Rome when Spaniards and Thracians were elected emperors); (b) in the Aechmalotarchs ("governors of captivity," of whom above); (c) in the great council, whose power was always great, as Josephus informs us, whence a royal throne is ascribed to this college of senators (AJ, 14.9*.167-72 [Loeb, 7:536-41) (Ps. 122:5; 2 Ch. 19:8); the president is called *ngydh* and in the Jewish books he is everywhere called *nsy'* and was always of the tribe of Judah, as the Jewish chronology testifies. And since the tribe of Judah alone with the accession of Benjamin returned, there is no doubt that of this tribe at least a majority of the council was composed, with whom the government was until (Judea having been conquered by the Romans) that power was worn away little by little and at length wholly taken away. Thus the fall of the Jewish republic can be viewed under these three steps: the first, under Pompey, who began in the year 60 before Christ; the second, by whom it was carried on, 10 years before Christ, when, Archelaus having been sent away, Judea was reduced to the form of a province; the third, in which it was consummated under Titus, the temple being destroyed and the city overthrown.

The second demonstration, from the weeks of Daniel.

XVII. The second demonstration is drawn from the weeks of Daniel. The passage reads: "Seventy weeks are determined upon thy holy city, to finish the transgression, and to make an end of sins, and to make reconciliation for iniquity, and to bring in everlasting righteousness, and to seal up the vision and prophecy, and to anoint the most Holy. Know therefore and understand, that from the going forth of the commandment to restore and to build Jerusalem unto the Messiah the Prince shall be seven weeks, and threescore and two weeks. . . . And after threescore and two weeks shall Messiah be cut off" (Dan. 9:24-27). Hence we thus argue: If after seventy weeks of years (i.e., after four hundred and ninety years from the permission of the return of the people), the Messiah should be manifested and slain to accomplish the work of redemption, he must of necessity have come long ago because already four times and more have flowed by since this prophecy. Now the former is true from the words of the prophet; therefore the latter also is true.

XVIII. To elucidate the arguments, three things must be proved: (1) that it refers to the Messiah; (2) that these are weeks of years and not of days; (3) that wherever we fix their commencement, this time has already expired. For if these are established, it will be invincibly evident against the Jews that the Messiah has already come. As to the first, that it refers to the Messiah is clear (a) from the open designation of him (v. 25), which name in this is ascribed to Christ alone absolutely by way of eminence (*kat' exochēn*) as peculiar to him, nor do we find it ascribed to anyone either ruler or priest, except with some addition, either of Lord, or of an affix, or of a proper name. (b) The Messiah is called *ngydh* (i.e., "prince" and "leader"), which is appropriate to Christ alone, as it is ascribed to him (Is. 55:4 and Mic. 5:2 compared with Mt. 2:6); therefore he calls him a leader by way of excellence because he surpasses all other kings and priests. (c) The works which it is said here will be performed in the time of the Messiah can pertain to no other than Christ alone: such as the making an end of sin, the expiation of iniquity, the bringing in of everlasting righteousness, the sealing of prophecy. (d) Jews explain the passage of the Messiah (Rabbi Saadia a Gaon, *Daniel im Targum, in loc.* [Dan. 9:24-27]; Rabbi Nachman Gerundensis, *Perushe ha-Ramban* [1963], p. 233 on Dan. 9:24-27 and others, as Manasseh ben Israel observes, *De Termino Vitae* [1639], pp. 165-80). (e) It is said of the Messiah that he shall confirm the covenant in the middle of the week and be cut off, which is appropriate to no one but Christ.

XIX. What Rabbi Solomon Jarchi says on Dan. 9 is worthless—that there are many Messiahs, but one only the son of David by way of excellence (*kat' exochēn*), of whom the passage cannot be understood. Cyrus (who is called "the Shepherd of God" and the "Messiah," Is. 44:28; 45:1). Rather v. 25 discusses Herod

Agrippa, v. 26; the ark and other furniture of the temple in Jerusalem, v. 24. For (1) since the Scripture in one and the same place speaks of the Messiah three times without any mark of distinction, no reason can be given why many are here to be feigned and that one excluded who alone is the true one (concerning whom alone the Holy Spirit wished to speak for the consolation of Daniel and the afflicted people). (2) Cyrus is indeed called "God's anointed" (Is. 44:28; 45:1) on account of the singular benefit to the people of God, to perform which he was appointed by the providence of God; but no one can say that he was the principal redeemer of the Israelites (concerning whom Daniel speaks). Again he speaks of the Messiah who was to come after seven weeks and sixty-two weeks, while Cyrus died before the first week. Hence Aben Ezra and other rabbis reject this comment. (3) With no more propriety is what is said in v. 26 referred to Herod Agrippa. For besides the fact that Daniel is absurdly feigned in the same place to bring forward another Messiah more than five hundred years after the death of the first, that last Agrippa (who reigned in Trachonitis) never had any power in Jerusalem or in Judea; so far is it that anyone should dream of his being a Messiah of the Jews. Nor (unless falsely) is he said to have been slain before the city was taken by the Romans, since even to the end of his life he lived on most friendly terms with them and, as far as he was able, assisted Vespasian in subjugating the Jews. (4) The holy of holies mentioned in v. 24 cannot be applied to the ark or altar, but it is a person who should be anointed. Now the ark was indeed sprinkled every year with blood, but is never said to have been anointed with oil. Add to this that in the second temple the Jews hold there was no ark and oil of anointing. Thus it cannot suit any other than our Christ, who was not only the holiest of all, but the very holiness itself of Israel, anointed by the Holy Spirit with the oil of gladness above his fellows (Lk. 1:35).

XX. Second, the weeks here mentioned are not of days, but of years (concerning which Lev. 25:8 treats), so that seven years should be reckoned in each week after the prophetic custom (Ezk. 4:6). The reason is manifold: (1) 70 weeks of days would be too restricted and would not make a year and a half, which would little suit so illustrious a prophecy, not to speak of its fulfillment; (2) nothing happened within that space of what the angel predicted, nor could Jerusalem be said to have been built in seven weeks (which took many more years); (3) the style here is prophetical (Ezk. 4:3-6; Rev. 12:6; 13:5). Elsewhere also it is taken in the same sense (Gen. 29:27) and where weeks of "days" are meant, the word "days" is added (Dan. 10:2; Ezk. 45:23). Here however there is no mention made of years because the angel speaks obscurely on purpose in order to preserve the prophetic custom. To no purpose do the Jews (pressed by the force of truth) have recourse here to "weeks of ten years" or "Jubilees." (1) By no approved author (nor in the whole of Scripture) is any mention made of such weeks, but only either of days or of years; hence it appears that they are gratuitiously forged. (2) The scope of the Holy Spirit is here clearly repugnant to it (which is to console Daniel and the people, crushed by a weight of sorrow, from the near approach of the Messiah after 70 weeks); but how frigid would this consolation have been—that he was to come only after three thousand five hundred years! (3) Daniel puts the advent of the Messiah before the destruction of the city and temple; yea, he subjoins that calamity as a consequence of the Messiah's death, as the most deserved punishment of so great a crime; but these fablers put the Messiah's advent three thousand years after the destruction of the city.

XXI. Therefore, God's purpose was to console the people in their most severe captivity and to confirm their faith; not only by designating its end, but also by promising a far more excellent redemption which was to be revealed after the interval of a longer time, not of 70 years, but of 70 weeks of years, that thus the grace of God may be compared with his judgment and the 70 weeks of years with the 70 years, during which the Jews suffered punishment. And so the angel answers the discourse of Daniel (who had spoken of the end of the 70 years), "Thou hast spoken of the term of the captivity and the end of the seventy years. However, I announce to you not only that near temporal deliverance, but promise a far more excellent one after 70 weeks of years that thus the mercy of God may surpass by sevenfold his judgment and the magnitude of grace absorb the magnitude of the calamity." For after the fulfillment of those proximate seventy years, God predetermined seventy weeks, not of days, but of years (to wit, four hundred and ninety years) for the duration of the people and of the city. Within these weeks, the Messiah (Lord) will come, who will expiate and abolish sin by his death, establish a gospel righteousness (which will last forever), fulfill and finish the prophecies, seal the vision and himself be consecrated most holy by the anointing of the Holy Spirit (whom he will receive without measure [*ametrōs*]) for an eternal king and head of his church.

XXII. Third, concerning the beginning and end of the weeks, interpreters contend with each other with great zeal. Nor is the reconciliation easy. But it is not necessary that we should worry ourselves in solving these most serious difficulties. Without this, the argument remains ever invincible against the Jews. For from whatever point their commencement is taken—whether from the first year of Cyrus, in which the Jews were permitted to return and build their city (as Beroaldus and Calvin hold from Ezr. 1:1); or from the second year of Darius Nothus, from Ezr. 6 (as Scaliger, Junius, Calvisius); or from the seventh of Artaxerxes Longimanus, of whom Ezr. 7:1, 13, 14 (as Capellus, Bullinger, Helvicus and others maintain); or from the twentieth, from Neh. 2:1 (as Julius Africanus, Torniellus, Ussher); or from any other point (for we do not now indeed make this controversy ours and leave the Jews free to follow whatever opinion they may prefer)—wheresoever the beginning of these weeks is taken, we maintain that it is clearer than the noonday sun that they have long ago passed by. Nor does an interval of some years or of a century come between, but of many centuries. The chronological question therefore being removed from the hinge of our controversy, this is to be retained as certain and indubitable—that the beginning is to be placed in the liberty to return and build the city proclaimed to the people by the edicts of the kings of Persia; and the end in the destruction of the city and the last desolation of the people. Within these boundaries all things predicted here must of necessity have happened, both those relating to the advent of the Messiah and the restoration and final fall of the city (which the thing itself cries out happened long ago).

XXIII. Not badly do some think that the beginning and end of these weeks ought not to be restricted here to a certain point or article of time, but should be understood widely (*en platei*) and with a certain latitude, so that the four edicts which were given in succession for leading back the people from captivity and the restoration of the city may be taken together and reckoned in the place of one (since the latter are, as it were, interpretations and, as they commonly say, amplifications of the first one; as our age is likewise known by different edicts made on account of religion). Therefore our minds are not to be tortured by the useless labor of seeking some indivisible point in which these things were fulfilled, since God does not wish us to stick to a point, but to regard the importance and substance of the events themselves. Therefore, as he wished that various things should here be embraced together which have a certain mutual connection that they might be observed by one glance (as it were) of our mind (to wit, the advent and death of the Messiah, the siege and overthrow of the city, the destruction of the temple and the abrogation of the Jewish worship, the distress and desolation of the people), they necessarily demand a certain latitude of time within which to be fulfilled. So that whatever things are here predicted from the deliverance of the captives and the restoration of the city to the ruin and destruction of the same ought to have taken place within the limit of these seventy weeks.

XXIV. The Jews (who miserably twist themselves in order to avoid this argument) betake themselves to the distinction between an absolute and hypothetical prediction that the prediction of Daniel concerning the advent of the Messiah is hypothetical, provided the people would not retard his coming by their sins and that on account of the sins of the people he did not come in the time announced beforehand by Daniel. But (1) this is a mere assumption, nor is there the slightest shadow of an indication of any condition in the oracle or in Daniel or elsewhere. (2) The advent of the Messiah flowed from the mere grace and mercy of God and its primary design was the taking away of the sins of the people. Hence nothing on the part of man could delay it and least of all sin, since that advent was destined by God especially for the removal and destruction of sin. (3) If any sin retarded the Messiah's advent, it should have been more heinous than any others which had been committed before. But we read of no other peculiar transgression committed by them which surpassed their former wickedness, if you except the guilt of the crucifixion of the Messiah, which they say was not a sin. But in the former temple, idolatry, homicide, adultery and all kinds of the most heinous sins raged among the people (according to the testimony of the prophets), notwithstanding which the promise concerning the Messiah's advent was made. While after the time fixed for the advent of the Messiah, idolatry ceased among them as well as other crimes (except stubborn unbelief, which they do not acknowledge). No one imputes to them anything above the preceding sins. Therefore a reason for such a delay cannot be drawn here.

XXV. Nor can the cavil of the Jews have place here—that they really should suffer on account of their sins a severe and prolonged captivity, but that it would at length come to an end, no differently than the Babylonian captivity. For what comparison can there be between the Babylonian captivity and the present most bitter dispersion of the Jews? What has an exile of 70 years in common with an exile of 16 centuries? In the former there was a hope of restoration and a designation of the end; here however there is no such thing. Then the body of the nation still stood using its own laws; now they live under a foreign power and laws. Then the tribes were still distinct and the priestly and royal families could be distinguished; now all things among them are confused and disturbed, so that no shape either of a polity or church appears, but a horrible example of the divine curse in these remnants miserably wandering about.

The third demonstration, from the glory of the second temple.

XXVI. The third demonstration is drawn from the glory of the second temple, during the existence of which the Messiah ought to come. For this was the prerogative of the second temple—that the Messiah (the Prince of Peace) should dignify it with his presence. Since, then, the second temple has for a long time been destroyed, it is a most certain proof that the Messiah came long ago. That mark is gathered from the twofold oracle of Haggai and Malachi, where it is clearly presented: "Yet once, it is a little while, and I will shake the heavens, and the earth, and the sea, and the dry land; and I will shake all nations, and the desire of all nations shall come: and I will fill this house with glory, saith the Lord of hosts" (Hag. 2:6, 7); and "The glory of this latter house shall be greater than of the former" (v. 9). Mal. 3:1 confirms the same thing: "Behold, I will send my messenger, and he shall prepare the way before me: and the Lord, whom ye seek, shall suddenly come to his temple, even the messenger of the covenant, whom ye delight in." Hence we argue thus—the second temple shall not be destroyed until the Messiah comes; therefore it is a certain mark that the Messiah has come, when that temple is destroyed. For in the former passage it is said that he would shortly come after the temple which was begun while Haggai was prophesying had been erected and then the temple would be filled with greater glory than the former. In the second passage, it is said that he will suddenly come to his temple—the one which was erected when Malachi prophesied. But how could it be said that he would come at once, if he was not to come except after some thousands of years?

XXVII. Moreover it is clear that the Messiah is referred to in both passages. (1) In Malachi because it treats of him who was to be sent and come into his temple as Lord and angel of the covenant; who was to have Elijah as a forerunner; and who was sought and expected. Now to whom except the Messiah can these things belong? Nor do the more learned Jews question it (as Rabbi David Kimchi, Aben Ezra and Maimonides, who refer it to the Messiah (cf. *Twelve Prophets* [ed. A. Cohen, 1948], p. 349 [on Mal. 3:1] and *Maimonides' Mishneh Torah* [ed. P. Birnbaum, 1985], p. 328). (2) So in Haggai, what is said of the shaking of heaven and earth and of all nations that they might come to their desire, can be referred to no other (whether by "the desire of the nations" is designated "the desired out of the nations," i.e., as many as were to be chosen out of the nations and called to Christ, answering to the oracle of Jacob, who said the gathering of the peoples would be to him; or, what seems more suitable, the Messiah himself is understood, who, far more truly than Daniel, is a "man of desires," "altogether [*epipothētos*] desirable," whom believers wished for with ardent longings). Again, what he adds concerning the greater glory of the second temple belongs here because from no other source could this come forth than from the presence of the Lord of the house, who was to bring peace—not a corporeal (of which we do not read of the Jews enjoying much under the second temple, as they themselves confess), but a spiritual and heavenly (which the Messiah, the Prince of Peace, was to bring and which the angels herald, Lk. 2:14).

XXVIII. To no purpose do the Jews wish the greater glory of this second house to be referred to the external things which rendered it conspicuous; or to the duration because the second was to stand 420 years (i.e., ten years longer than the first); or to the splendid gifts and sacrifices which Darius, Artaxerxes and other kings contributed to the erection of the temple; or to the additions of Herod, who raised up the temple more gloriously (as Josephus holds, AJ 15.380-87 [Loeb, 8:184-89]); or at least adorned it, according to Hegesippus. To no purpose, I say, is this adduced. (1) Such external and insignificant things do not compose the glory of God's house, nor would God for things so small speak so augustly and magnificently, as that he would move heaven and earth and do wonders. (2) God expressly says that he was unwilling to place that glory in these perishable things: "Mine is the silver and the gold"—as much as to say, If I wished, I could adorn this temple with gold and silver as the temple of Solomon was adorned; for mine is all gold, as in Ps. 50:10-12. But I will adorn it with a far more precious thing (to wit, with the presence of my Son, who is the glory of Israel). (3) Whatever additions or ornaments were made by Herod in the temple could never equal (much less surpass) the glory of Solomon's, which was rendered conspicuous above others by these most special ornaments of the temple (which the Jews confess were wanting in the second): the ark of the covenant, the perpetual fire, the sacred oil, the spirit of prophecy, and the Sheckinah or presence of God on the mercy seat.

XXIX. What they add concerning the erection of a third temple to which these things belong is just as spurious. It is treated of that temple which the Jews saw, which is called "this house" (*hbyth hzh*); otherwise no consolation could arise thence to Zerubbabel and his companions building the temple, whom nevertheless the Lord wishes to comfort by this argument—that this house would be filled with a greater glory. Nor if Herod is said to have restored that house is he therefore to be considered as having built an entirely new one. For it is always reputed to be the same as the temple of Zerubbabel. Finally, to no purpose is it feigned that an entirely new temple is to be built, since it was so destroyed as to leave no remaining hope of its restoration. They who attempted it under Hadrian or Julian failed in their attempt, prohibited by heaven.

The fourth demonstration, from the signs: (1) with respect to the Jews, the fall of the republic.

XXX. The fourth demonstration is drawn from the signs which should accompany the Messiah's advent: with respect to the the Jews, the fall of the Jewish republic and polity and the rejection of the people; with respect to the world, the end of false oracles; with respect to the church, the calling of the Gentiles. Since all these have for a long time been fulfilled, it is necessary that the Messiah must also have come. (1) With respect to the Jews, the sign was the fall of the republic. For since the Messiah was to spring from the Jews, the republic could not be destroyed before his advent. It is evident that the Messiah ought to have come to that people, distinct in their tribes and families; to that land and to the temple in which he was expected in daily worship. Now since the republic has been scattered for many ages and the people wretchedly dispersed through all parts of the world—driven out of their country and land, all government overthrown, the city levelled with the ground, sacrifices abolished, the temple destroyed, all the tribes confounded without any hope of return, not for 70 years only (which was the length of the Babylonian captivity), nor for 200 (during which their Egyptian bondage lasted), but sixteen hundred and more—what else do all these things cry out except that the Messiah has already come and that he is not to be expected anymore? If the miserable nation would more attentively consider them, they would find in themselves and in their own condition enough to force them to acknowledge their own error and perfidy. For what other cause can be assigned? Why for so many ages should they be thus neglected, experience so hard a fate, be scattered so widely as exiles, so pitiable a sport to the whole human race? For they anxiously expect their Messiah and weary themselves with daily vows and prayers; nor are they so polluted with the worship of idols or other sins of the Gentiles as their ancestors. Verily there must necessarily be another cause which permits this people (formerly beloved of God) to wander so miserably. It can be none other than the impious rejection of the true Messiah and the horrible slaughter and apostasy from the true faith, in which they persevere even up to the present time. Nor are the Jews to be listened to here who commonly make the objection that this advent was deferred on account of both their own sins and those of their fathers, which they committed under both houses. Since it is treated here not of one or another oracle, but of the constant tenor of the prophets and prophecies, no certainty would remain if it were not afforded in this chapter (on which all the rest depend). Again, if he promised anything formerly to his people, we do not read of its ever having been denied on account of their sins (as is evident from the deliverance out of Egypt and Babylon, which God fulfilled exactly at the appointed time, although the people were no less burdened with sin than now). Why, therefore, shall not the same thing be said to have occurred in this remarkable promise, in which the good of the whole nation was contained, while nevertheless the fulfillment of so great a promise would now be deferred beyond sixteen centuries and no hope of its fulfillment remain? Third, if on account of the sins of the people, the advent of the Messiah is deferred, then he will never come, since they will never be free from all wickedness. But so far from their sins hindering or delaying the advent, they ought rather to accelerate it, since he comes to take them away.

2. With respect to the world, the destruction of idolatry.

XXXI. With respect to the world, the destruction of false oracles and of pagan idolatry (which the prophets frequently predicted would be destroyed in the time of the Messiah, Is. 2:18, 20; Zech. 13:2). Profane history informs us that oracles ceased at the advent of Christ. Hence in the time of Tiberius questions arose why the oracles had become dumb, why the demons did not work as before. So sudden and amazing was that change that it was formidable and stupendous to the very adversaries of the Christian cause. Porphyry complains that the angry gods gave no response after Jesus came (cf. Eusebius, *Preparation for the Gospel* 179d [trans. E.H. Gifford, 1903], 1:197). Cicero testifies that in his time oracles had ceased and mentions an absurd cause to account for it (viz., the age of the place from which the exhalations arose, under the influence and excitement of which the Pythian priestess uttered her oracles, *De Divinitate* 2.57.117 [Loeb, 20:502-3]). Plutarch, who lived in the time of Trajan (i.e., a hundred years after Christ) published a treatise on the cessation of oracles. He relates that Epitherses, sailing past the Echinadian islands, heard a voice announcing—Great Pan is dead (to wit, in the time of Tiberius when Christ was crucified; cf. "Obsolescence of Oracles," *Moralia* 419C [Loeb, 5:401]). And under Augustus to one consulting the oracle of Apollo as to who should reign after him, he is said to have replied, "A Hebrew boy ruling over the happy gods commands me to leave this temple and to go to Hades immediately."

Fifth demonstration, from the confessions of adversaries.

XXXII. The confessions of the Jews themselves furnish the fifth argument. Among which is (1) the celebrated tradition of the house of Eli (for which see "Sanhedrin," 97a, BT, 2:657). This distributes the times of the world into three periods and concludes its whole duration within six thousand years. It gives the last two thousand years to the kingdom of Messiah: two thousand to Inanity, two thousand to Law, two thousand to the Messiah. Nor does it help them to reply that the time of the advent has already passed, but was deferred on account of the sins of the people. Since the promise was not conditional (as has already been said), but absolute, so far was it from being deferred on account of the sins of the people that it ought rather to have been accelerated to take them away. Nor does it help them to reply that he was indeed to come in the two thousand years (*dischilian*), but it is not said whether he was to come in the beginning or at the end of them. For two thousand years are assigned to him in the same manner in which the other two thousand are assigned to Inanity and to the Law (i.e, that the duration of the Law would take its beginning after the Inanity and ought to fill up two thousand years). Thus the Messiah's advent ought to commence at the end of the two thousand years of the Law in order to continue through another two thousand years. (2) The opinion prevailed among the Jews at the time of Christ that the Messiah was on the point of coming (to whom the minds of believers were directed). Hence Simeon and Anna are said to have waited for the consolation of Israel (Lk. 2:25, 38) and the Samaritan woman testifies of her belief that the Messiah would shortly come (Jn. 4:25); also various false Christs arose at that time. In addition, we have the report of pagan predictions, by which the Gentiles themselves were agitated. Here belong these declarations of Josephus, who says, "Then was fulfilled the oracle (*chrēsmon*) concerning a King who was to spring from their land and rule over the world" (JW 6.312 [Loeb, 3:466-67]); and of Suetonius, "An old and constant opinion gathered strength in the whole East that it was fated that at that time persons arising from Judea should possess the sovereign power" (*Lives of the Caesars: The Deified Vespasian* 8.4.5 [Loeb, 2:288-89]). That this indeed did not pertain to Vespasian (whatever Suetonious may say), but to Christ, who was born and suffered a little before the time of Vespasian, the thing itself declares. Whoever will carefully consider all the prodigies which occurred about the time of Christ's birth (related by Orosius and others) can easily discover that nature then was in labor with a king who was to come from the east, to whom as many as wished to be saved ought to submit (*Seven Books Against the Pagans* 7.1-4 [FC 50:283-92]). Anyone who desires more, may consult Raimundi, who has collected the testimonies of the Jews on this subject (*Pugio Fidei* 2.10 [1687/1967], pp. 394-403).

Sources of explanation.

XXXIII. Elijah, who was to precede the Messiah, is not the Tishbite literally, but John the Baptist analogically and figuratively (on account of the resemblance between him and Elijah in zeal and fervor for he was to come in the spirit and power of Elijah [Lk. 1:17; Mt. 11:14] as the Messiah is often called David, Jer. 30:9; Hos. 3:5).

XXXIV. The "end of days" or "the last days" (Is. 2:2) in which the Messiah was to come, do not denote the end of the world, but the fulness of times (*plērōma kairōn*) or the last dispensation (after which no other is to be expected, but eternity alone). Therefore it is called the end of days not absolutely, but comparatively in relation to the preceding times because they ought to bring an end to the Old Testament. Until that time all things were (so to speak) suspended and the people were commanded always to look forward to the Messiah and to keep their hope alive (not to rest in present shadows). But by the advent of Christ, a fulness of days is given in which the church is to be restored to her integrity.

XXXV. When it is said "the mountain of the Lord will be exalted above the other mountains" (Is. 2:2) in the time of the Messiah, this oracle is not to be understood properly and literally (which could not be said without absurdity), but mystically concerning the exaltation of the church (which is constantly designated by the Mount of the Lord and Mount Zion, inasmuch as in it shone the majesty of God, who willed to place his sanctuary there). Hence the sound of the gospel was heard through the whole world (which should carry us even to heaven) and a standard raised up for all nations. So in Bereschit Rabba: "The great mountain, i.e, Messiah." So also Aben Ezra: "That mountain, Messiah, is to be most highly exalted in the midst of the nations" (*Commentary of Ibn Ezra on Isaiah* [trans. M. Friedlander, 1873], 1:14). What is added concerning the confluence of all nations to it (v. 3) does not prove that there ought to be only one religion in the world at the time of Christ. Rather the meaning is—there will be a catholic church to be collected indiscriminately from all peoples, professing one religion and one faith in Christ (which is even fulfilled under the New Testament).

XXXVI. The peace which the Messiah was to bring should not be an earthly and corporeal peace (which Christ openly teaches was not to be expected by his followers, Lk. 12:51; Jn. 14:27), but a spiritual peace, which Christ purchased for us by his death and was preached through the gospel. And if it is said, "The wolf shall dwell with the lamb" (Is. 11:6), this must be understood figuratively of the calling and conversion of the Gentiles, by which nations most hostile to Christ before (like wild animals) should be reckoned among the sheep of Christ; and savage and cruel men (like beasts) should be tamed and made so gentle as to cherish mutual communion and so live that they (whom a desire of injuring had agitated) would contend in reciprocal duties, devoting their attention to the common advantage (designated by the change of swords and spears into ploughshares and pruning hooks, instruments of agriculture employed in time of peace for the benefit of man, Is. 2:4). Nor did this escape Maimonides, who teaches, "These and other like things, written concerning the things which belong to the Messiah, are allegories" (*Maimonides' Mishneh Torah* [ed. P. Birnbaum, 1985], p. 328 on 2 K. 12).

XXXVII. If the "light of the sun should be sevenfold" greater in the time of the Messiah, as also "the light of the moon as the light of the sun" (Is. 30:26), this cannot be understood literally. Besides the fact that no one could endure the brightness of the sun, so there would be no night on account of the brilliancy of the moon. The Lord makes his sun to shine upon the good and the evil; yet here happiness is discussed which cannot be common to the wicked. But they are to be explained figuratively, either historically of the greatness of the joy which the Jewish church (delivered from the Babylonian captivity) would experience; or mystically of the greatness of glory, knowledge and gladness which the Messiah (who was to come to heal the wounds of the church) would bring to it, when the dark shades of the law should disappear and the light of the gospel shine far, very far surpassing the feeble light of the Old Testament.

XXXVIII. Ezk. 41 and the following chapter do not mean that the temple at Jerusalem would again be restored, but the mystical temple of the church shadowed forth under the symbol of the old Temple of Solomon. Fulfillment of the latter is to be sought not in the carnal and earthly, but in the spiritual and heavenly Jerusalem; in that, namely, which John describes in words drawn from this sketch of Ezekiel (Rev. 21:22)—to be begun in this life indeed by the temple of grace, to be finished however in another by the temple of glory in heaven.

XXXIX. When it is said, "In Messiah's days Judah shall be saved and Israel shall dwell safely" (Jer. 23:6), it does not mean Israel according to the flesh, a remnant of which only was to be saved (as the Jews themselves acknowledge from Jer. 3:14 and Is. 8:14; cf. "Sanhedrin," 111a, BT 2:762). Rather it refers to Israel according to the spirit, to whom alone the promises were made (Rom. 9:4), under whom the whole church of the elect and of believers is meant.

XL. The advent of the Messiah cannot be called in question from the fact that Gog and Magog (whom he was to subdue) have not as yet appeared. It is a mere assumption that the Messiah ought to conquer them. What is said in Ezk. 38:2ff. concerning Gog and Magog is falsely drawn to this purpose. For it is evident that the Messiah is not spoken of there and it is clear that this is to be referred to the cruel oppressors of the Jewish church after the Babylonian captivity (such as the kings of Syria and the people of Asia Minor so called, either from Gyges, king of the Lydians, or from the Scythians and Tartars so called [Gen. 10:2] who formerly occupied Asia Minor and Syria). Hence in Asia, Hierapolis was called Magog (according to Pliny, *Natural History* 5.19* [Loeb, 2:282-83]) not far from the Euphrates; and in Syria, Scythopolis, to the east of the Lake of Tiberias, was formerly called Bethsan. Eusebius mentions this: "The Scythians overran Palestine and occupied Baisan" (i.e., Bethsan) "which they called from their own name, Scythopolis" (*Eusebi Chronicorum Canonum* [ed. A. Schoene, 1967], 2:88).

Second Question

Is Jesus of Nazareth the true Messiah? We affirm against the Jews.

Statement of the question.

I. After having proved in the preceding question that the Messiah has already come, we must now inquire farther into his person that we may know who he is and demonstrate that he can be no other than Jesus of Nazareth, the son of Mary. As, however, this is the principal foundation of our religion and the fulcrum of our faith, on that account this argument must be weighed with the greater accuracy that we may stop the mouths of Jews (the most bitter enemies of the Christian name) who use every effort to overthrow this saving truth.

II. The question is not Has the Messiah come? This has been proved. Rather the question is—Is Jesus of Nazareth (whom we believe and preach as the Messiah) that true and proper Messiah promised by God, who was to come for the salvation of men? The Jews obstinately deny it; we constantly affirm and invincibly demonstrate it.

That Jesus of Nazareth is the Messiah is proved from his criteria.

III. First, all the criteria (*kritēria*) of the Messiah by which God wished to designate him in the Old Testament to confirm our faith (those which refer to his birth as well as to his person and state; or doctrine and works) belong to him. Thus they either belong to no one or they suit him. As to his birth, whether we attend to the time of his nativity and his forerunner, or the place or tribe and family or manner, it is evident that all meet together and have their fulfillment in him (as can easily be shown by parts), not as to the particulars separately (in which way they would prove nothing), but connectedly as to all (which furnish a solid argument).

1. The first demonstration, from the birth of Jesus.

As to the time.

IV. (1) As to the time, the Messiah ought to be born at the time in which the royal and legislative power was to be taken away from the Jews after the 70 weeks of years (i.e., after the lapse of 490 years from the Babylonian captivity); also in the time in which the house of David would be in the lowest contempt and (as it were) a trunk cut off even to the roots (Is. 11:1). Now that our Jesus did appear at that time has both been proven above and the thing itself declares.

2. As to his forerunner.

V. (2) As to his forerunner; a forerunner ought to precede the Messiah's advent to prepare the way for him according to the prophetic oracles (Is. 40:3; Mal. 3:1). "Behold, I will send you Elijah the prophet before the coming of the great and dreadful day of the Lord" (Mal. 4:5). Thus it seems to have been fulfilled in John the Baptist, who was the voice of one crying in the wilderness, who went before Christ in the spirit of Elijah to prepare the way for him (Mt. 3:3; 11:14; Lk. 1:17); not only preaching repentance, but also giving a clear testimony to Christ and distinguishing him when present with a divine eulogy. In this sense, he is called the greatest of all the prophets and the first of evangelists (Mt. 11:9, 11). Having fulfilled his mission, he yielded to Christ and concluded the Old Testament (Mt. 11:13).

3. As to the place.

VI. (3) As to the place, the Messiah was to be born at Bethlehem according to the prediction of Micah: "But Thou, Bethlehem Ephratah, though thou be little among the thousands of Judah, yet out of thee shall He come forth unto me that is to be Ruler in Israel; whose goings forth have been from of old, from everlasting" (5:2). The Chaldee Paraphrase, Rabbi Solomon Rashi and Kimchi acknowledge that it treats of the Messiah and the Pharisees and scribes confess it in their answer to Herod's inquiry (Mt. 2:5, 6) (cf. *Biblia sacra polyglotta* [1657], 3:74 on Mic. 5:2; cf. also Johannis Buxtorf, *Biblia Sacra Hebraica and Chaldaica* [1619], *in loc* [Mic. 5:2]). Now everyone knows that Jesus was born in Bethlehem. That no one might suppose this happened by chance or by the purpose and compact or deliberate counsel of Joseph or Mary, God wished to bring about the thing by his remarkable providence to carry out his own prediction, the parents of Jesus not only being ignorant and not thinking of it, but desiring the contrary. For no other purpose did he prompt Caesar Augustus (the empire being now settled, enjoying everywhere profound peace and thinking of nothing less than fulfilling the prediction pertaining to the Messiah) to make a registration of the whole Jewish world, than that this oracle might be fulfilled and so it might be established by an indubitable argument that Joseph belonged to the family of David. For his family was obscure and now reduced to the lowest condition of life; he exhibited no signs of a royal descent. To no purpose does Manasseh ben Israel (departing with the more modern Jews from the ancient) hold that "Bethlehem is called the native place of the Messiah because he was to spring from David, a Bethlehemite, so that not the actual but the original nativity of the Messiah is demonstrated" (*Conciliator* [1972], 2:228 on Mic. 5:2). It speaks of a ruler about to be born at Bethlehem, which cannot be referred to the birth of David (already a long time past) without absurdity. Nor does what is added concerning his goings forth from of old prove this because this belongs to the eternal generation of the Messiah from the bosom of the Father by which he is the Son of God, as the nativity at Bethlehem denotes the temporal birth from the bosom of his mother.

4. As to tribe and family.

VII. (4) As to tribe and family, the Messiah was to spring from the tribe of Judah and the family of David according to the predictions (Gen. 49:10; Is. 11:1; 2 S. 7:13, 14) and from the confession of the multitude (Jn. 7:42). Hence he is frequently called "David" by the prophets. That this was fulfilled in our Jesus is evident both from the place of his nativity already mentioned (which was the house of David, whither the parents of Jesus should take themselves, so as to prove that they had sprung from that family) and from both genealogies of Christ which we have in Matthew and Luke. Nor can it be objected that the family of Joseph does not prove Jesus to have sprung from the family of David, since according to our hypothesis he was not his father. From the law, wives were to be taken from the same tribe and family (Num. 36:8), which although it would not be absolutely universal, ought to be the case where the virgins were to succeed to the patrimony (*epiklēroi*) (like Mary). Nor is it a hindrance that Mary is called a cousin (*syngenēs*) of Elizabeth (Lk. 1:36) because this might have arisen from the fact either that one of the ancestors of Mary had taken a wife from the tribe of Levi or some priest had taken a daughter from the blood relation of Mary.

5. As to the manner of birth.

VIII. (5) As to the manner of nativity, he should be born of a virgin from Isaiah's prophecy: "Behold, a virgin shall conceive, and bear a son, and shall call his name Immanuel" (Is. 7:14). This has so great weight that even alone it is sufficient to establish this mystery. But that it may be vindicated against the cavils of the Jews, the scope of the prophet is to be observed, which is to confirm the people against the fear with which they were agitated on account of Rezin and Pekah, kings of Syria and Israel who were besieging Jerusalem. On that account, God commands the prophet to approach the king (together with his son) and order him (fear being laid aside) to rest assured concerning the preservation and deliverance of himself and the people. And that he may be the more thoroughly persuaded of the truth of this promise, the prophet gives to him the choice of some sign to be sought either from heaven or from the earth. However, since Ahaz impiously refused the sign and many remnants of believers still survived, for their consolation and confirmation (as also for the conviction of Ahaz) he adds: God (notwithstanding the wickedness of the king) will give them a double sign—future and present: the future in Immanuel to be born of a virgin in his proper time (v. 14); the present in Shearjashub his son (v. 16), before whose adolescence the destruction of both kings would take place.

IX. It is clear that the prophecy can be understood of no other than the Messiah because: (1) it speaks of a child who was to be Immanuel and Lord of the earth (v. 14; 8:8); (2) of him who was to be born of a virgin; (3) of him who was to be for an unheard-of and wonderful sign. This cannot apply to Hezekiah, the son of Ahaz, because he had been born and was not about to be born. Again Hezekiah's birth was not from *ʿlmh* ("a virgin"), but from the wife of Ahaz; nor is it called miraculous; nor do we read of its being set forth anywhere else as a peculiar sign. Nor can it apply to Shearjashub, the son of the prophet; or to the other mentioned in chapter 8 called Maher-shalal-hashbaz. The former had already been born, having been led by Isaiah to the king (nor was his birth miraculous and from a virgin, although the imposition of his name was symbolical); the latter is distinguished from Immanuel (8:8) and he was born not of *hʿlmh* ("the virgin"), but of *hnbyʾh* ("the prophet"). Nor can it apply to any other ordinary child because this style is not common, nor are common things predicated of him. Rather it is the promise of a remarkable sign to be manifested not in a woman, but in a virgin. Hence it follows that this oracle could have reference to or be fulfilled in no other than Jesus of Nazareth.

X. Although the sign given here by the prophet was to be manifested only after many ages, still it could nonetheless conduce to the confirmation of the deliverance once promised. (1) It is not an absurd and unusual thing for future things to be employed as the sign of a proximate future thing (as appears from Ex. 3:12; 1 S. 2:34; 1 K. 22:25, 28; Jer. 44:29 where consequent signs are given, as also antecedent, and the events of prophecies are set forth in signs, Dt. 18:21f.). (2) It is not unusual in Scripture by mentioning great promises to procure faith for lesser promises, especially when those greater do not stand firm without the faith of the lesser (which is the case here). For since the Messiah ought afterwards to spring from the royal family of David and that too while the republic still existed, it is clear that neither that land (for which Ahaz so greatly feared) could wholly yield to the power of the enemy, nor the house of David be entirely destroyed. Hence the argument could be from similarity (*a simili*) or from the lesser to the greater (*a minori ad majus*). God will certainly fulfill the principal promise concerning the Messiah; therefore much more will he grant what is less (to wit, deliverance from the kings). (3) It is customary for the prophets to confirm all special promises by the general promise concerning the Messiah because it is the foundation of the rest, in whom all the promises are yea and amen (2 Cor. 1:20). (4) The promise of proximate deliverance is not only founded on the future sign (namely the Messiah, who was to be born of a virgin after many years), but also on the present (to wit, the son of the prophet already born, whom he had led with him to the king). To him, v. 16 properly refers: "Before this child" (pointing [*deiktikōs*] to him) "shall know to refuse the evil and choose the good" (i.e., has reached the years of discretion) "the land shall be delivered" (as in truth scarcely four years had elapsed before these kings were destroyed); or on the son who was to be born a little afterwards, of whom Is. 8:3, 4 speaks.

XI. Now although we never find Jesus of Nazareth addressed as Immanuel, still no less can it be said that he was to be so called. The verb *qrʾ* in Scripture is often put for "to be"; as when it is said "he shall be called wonderful, the counsellor"

(Is. 9:6) and "Jehovah our righteousness" (Jer. 23:5)—not so much to intimate with what name he was to be distinguished, as what he was really to be (whether as to his person, God-man [*theanthrōpos*], or as to his office, Mediator) who was to reconcile God to us. Hence Chrysostom well remarks on this passage: "It is usual for Scripture to put the things which happen in place of the names: they shall call him Immanuel, therefore, signifies nothing else than, they shall see God with men" (*Homilies . . . on Matthew* 5.3 [NPNF1, 10:32; PG 57:56-57]). If a certain ignorance is ascribed to Immanuel, it is of pure negation (which could be the case with Jesus, Lk. 2:40); not of deparaved disposition (which is sinful), from which he was always free. What is added concerning butter and honey denotes the usual bringing up of others, using ordinary food (which is included under butter and honey because the land of Canaan flowed with milk and honey).

XII. That *ʿlmh* here denotes a "virgin" and not any woman is evident: (1) from the origin of the word from *ʿlm* ("to hide") denoting the state of a virgin—hidden from the sight and communication of men; *ʿlmvmh* ("hidden from") and not known by man (as it were). Hence virgins were called among the ancients *katakleistoi* and *apokryphoi* (2 Mac. 3:19) because they were concealed and kept at home. (2) The authority of interpreters who cannot be suspected by the Jews: the Targums, Onkelos and Jonathan (cf. Walton, *Biblia sacra Polyglotta* [1657], 3:20 on Is. 7:14), and the Septuagint, which translates it *parthenos*, although Symmachus and Theodotion (in favor of the Jews) render it "young woman" (cf. Origen, *Hexapla* [PG 16:1653-54] on Is. 7:14). (3) Evident reason demands it because it treats of a divine and wonderful sign whose birth is no less wonderful than the name. But what kind of a sign is this, so common, so natural and ordinary a thing as for a woman to conceive and bear after intercourse with a man? (4) The ordinary use of the word in Scripture in six other passages where it occurs (Gen. 24:43; Cant. 1:3; 6:8; Ex. 2:8; Ps. 68:25; Prov. 30:19). In this last passage, to no purpose do the Jews maintain that a "prostitute" is meant because after the words "the way of a man *bʿlmh* is hidden," it is immediately added, "such is the way of an adulterous woman"; the employment of the mark of similarity shows that a similarity, not an identity, is denoted. The sense is that the way of a man to a maid is hidden (to wit, the arts by which men strive to gain the affections of virgins, whether for honest marriage or for corruption). She can also be called a virgin antecedently, who was such before; not consequently or by report (*doxastikōs*) and opinion (*synchōrētikōs*), whether because she is esteemed such or because she wished to be considered such (which cannot be the case here).

XIII. Moreover that Mary, who gave birth to our Jesus, was a virgin, not only the gospel history testifies, but even fame itself declares. For if this was not true, how could it happen that a virgin should lie about so great and so incredible a thing and that the apostles (who could easily have been convinced of its falsity) should dare so boldly to declare it, no one denying? If she really was taken in adultery (as some of the more modern Jews blasphemously assert), why was she never charged with it by the Pharisees and scribes? Why was she not brought to trial according to law and a punishment inflicted, so that the fame of the son would be struck through the side of the mother? But she survived her son, no one inquiring into his life.

The second demonstration, from the marks of the Messiah's person and state.

XIV. The second demonstration is drawn from the criteria of his person and state. (1) That the Messiah would be God is with certainty gathered not only from the predictions (which ascribe this name to him), but also from the divine works which he had to perform in executing the work of redemption. And that Jesus, the son of Mary, was both the Son of God and God, is indubitably proved both from the various divine works done by him (as will be proved hereafter) and from the testimony of Christ himself, who so often proclaims himself as the Son of God. And if he had falsely claimed this for himself, is it to be supposed that God (the jealous vindicator of his own glory) would have suffered his glory to be given to another? Would not so great a crime (a greater than which cannot be conceived) have been visited by some severe punishment? If an angel was so severely punished for affecting equality with God, what would have been done to this usurper and seizer of the nature of divinity itself? Now Jesus was not only not punished by God, but crowned with the highest glory and majesty. In a short space of time, he filled the whole world with his doctrine and erected a most powerful empire.

XV. (2) The Messiah is described as to be invested with a threefold office (for which reason he was to be anointed, Dan. 9:24): the prophetic from Dt. 18:15; Is. 61:1, 2; the priestly from Ps. 110; the regal from Pss. 2:6; 45:6, 7; Zech. 6:12, 13. Now we behold this fulfilled in our Jesus, who performed the office of prophet (in preaching the gospel); of priest (in the offering up of himself); and of king (in the establishment of a heavenly kingdom, as will be proved in the proper place).

XVI. (3) A twofold state is assigned to him: the first, of humility and suffering, in which he was to die; the second, of exaltation and glory, in which it behooved him to rise again and ascend to heaven (as is evident from Pss. 22, 110; Zech. 9:9; Is. 53). Now that this very thing is noticed in Jesus of Nazareth appears from the gospel history which describes his sufferings and glory, the state of emptying (in which he humbled himself even to the death of the cross) and the state of exaltation (in which being raised from the dead he has obtained a name above every name and sat down at the right hand of the majesty on high, Phil. 2:6-9; Heb. 1:3). This can be more fully shown as to all the circumstances of suffering and glory predicted of the Messiah in the Old Testament (which we find exactly fulfilled in Jesus under the New).

Third demonstration, from the doctrine of Christ and his works.

XVII. The third demonstration is derived from the doctrine and works of Christ. Since from the prophetic oracles the Messiah was to proclaim an acceptable year and to bring in the saving doctrine of the gospel to heal the contrite heart and preach liberty and redemption to the captives, who considers the doctrine preached by our Jesus and does not see that he most fully accomplished this in himself? He has brought the gospel to us from heaven, which shines everywhere with the brightest rays of divinity, and in which by disclosing to us the most perfect will of God (both as to precepts and promises) instituted a religion than which there never was a purer and more divine. In every part, it breathes piety and love and ministers to the glory of God and the salvation of men.

XVIII. Also so great and so many were his works that none more illustrious or more or greater could be desired or expected from the Messiah, according to the confession of the multitude—"When Christ cometh, will he do more miracles than these which this man hath done?" (Jn. 7:31). Hence Jesus so often appeals to his works as the most certain sign of his call (Jn. 4:36; 7:37, 38; 10:37; 15:24); yea, being asked by John, through his disciples, whether he was the Messiah who was to come (*ho erchomenos*), he rests the proof that he is upon no other thing than the multitude and magnitude of his miracles. He answers by a work, not by words; by a deed quicker than by a speech (Mt. 11:4, 5) because the Messiah was to be a wonder worker (*thaumatourgon*) distinguished by miracles (as Isaiah teaches): "Your God will come and save you. Then the eyes of the blind shall be opened, and the ears of the deaf shall be unstopped" (Is. 35*:4, 5). For if the law was glorious with signs and wonders, why should the gospel not be (2 Cor. 3:7, 8)? And if the Messiah should be wonderful (*pl'*) in his person, then he should be no less in works. Now that Christ made himself illustrious by such works, the Jews themselves cannot deny. Josephus calls him "a doer of wonderful works" (*paradoxōn ergōn poiētēn*, AJ 18.63* [Loeb, 9:48-49]). Some examples of this are related in the Talmud. Julian himself, the chief enemy of the Christian name, could not deny it. His miracles could not have been more clear because they were not done secretly in a corner and a retired place (which impostors seek); but openly and publicly, in the sunlight, at the corners of the streets and at crossroads, in every place and before the eyes of most bitter enemies. Not more, for John says they were so many that if every one should be written, even the world itself could not contain the books that should be written (Jn. 21:25). Not greater (in respect of nature), because they were not only dreadful portents and prodigies, striking terror (such as were the legal signs), but saving benefits from which men not only did not turn away, but flew in crowds to see and examine. They were not common signs and wonderful such as could be wrought by human or diabolical art; but grand, unusual and such as could be performed by divine power alone (such as raising of the dead, the curing of those born blind and those with incurable [*aniatōn*] diseases, etc). In respect of the object, they were not particular signs or restricted to certain species of things, but universal, testifying his power and dominion over all creatures in heaven and on earth, in the waters, on demons, on men, on trees, etc. In respect of the manner, he did not have to exert great efforts to perform them, but he wrought them by a word or a nod alone; now without means, then with them (for the most part useless in themselves; yea, contrary); now nearby, then afar off—yea, even when absent.

XIX. What reply did the Jews make? That others also had wrought miracles? But do we read of any other having wrought so many, so great and in that manner? Or that they were only wonders and not true miracles? But what is a true miracle except what surpasses the powers of the whole finite and created nature (such as the raising of the dead, the healing of incurable and desperate diseases, the casting out of demons, etc.), which we know were frequently done by Christ? That they were sheer impostures by which he deceived and trifled with men? But why was this never charged against him by the Jews, his most implacable enemies, who eagerly seized every opportunity of destroying him? Why did they not unmask the impostor and mountebank? On the contrary, who was ever farther removed from the arts of an impostor? They seek hiding places and retreats and shun the light, the more easily to impose upon the simple. But Christ worked openly and publicly, before innumerable witnesses, great and small, learned and unlearned, so that there could be not even a suspicion of fraud. They eagerly pursue empty, ridiculous and useless things. But Christ works nothing except what is holy and beneficial. They work for the sake of filthy lucre and to acquire glory or to deceive. But what like this do we find in Christ, who directed all things to the salvation of his people insofar that he willed to become poor that we from his poverty might be made rich? They are the slaves of the basest passions and serve the flesh and the devil. But Christ, the master of piety, proposed this one thing to himself—the production of holiness in our souls. That Christ wrought these miracles by the power of magic, as was often objected against him by the Pharisees when they slandered him by saying that by the power of Beelzebub, the prince of devils, he cast out devils? But why can the Jews suspect this of Jesus, the Nazarene, who was considered the son of a carpenter, more than of Moses, who (educated at the court of Egypt) could have acquired the profoundest knowledge of the magical art? Again who would suspect even slightly, either that any magician could, or that any devil would perform so many works which were pure blessings bestowed upon the human race? Who can believe that the Devil was willing to arm Christ for his own destruction and the overthrow of his tyranny? Nor could it have been done by collusion because friends enter into collusion and not enemies. Now the Devil had no more deadly enemy than our Jesus and his religion (which tended to the total destruction of the works of the Devil and to breathe piety and holiness into the soul). Finally, if he was a magician, why was he never brought to trial for magic and convicted by the senators in the Sanhedrin, all of whom the school of the Jews asserts were most skillful in detecting the magical arts? Why were crimes anxiously sought against him, when the single crime of magic would have been sufficient to secure his condemnation according to the law (Ex. 22:18)?

XX. But if the works which Christ did in the days of his flesh proclaim him to be the Messiah, no less effectually is this very thing proved by those which he accomplished after his resurrection and ascension into heaven by the mission of the Holy Spirit and the work of Christianity. First, the resurrection of Christ itself affords a clean testimony to him, since in it he was (as it were by a solemn decree) approved of God and declared to be his Son, credited by believers and acknowledged by enemies. Hence he adduces no other argument more illustrious and certain of his divinity and call: "Destroy this temple," says he (speaking of the temple of his body), "and in three days I will raise it up" (Jn. 2:19). To the Jews seeking a sign, he would give no other than his resurrection under the type of Jonah (Mt. 12*:38-41). And verily unless Jesus had been sent of God and unless he had been the anointed of the Lord (as he professed himself to be), who can believe that God, the most jealous vindicator of his own glory, would have exerted his power in raising him, to confirm so great a fraud and imposture and would have crowned so great an impiety with so large a reward? Add to this in the second place the wonderful and unheard-of mission of the Holy Spirit which happened expressly both in the time and place before predicted by Christ himself, with which the apostles were so filled that they were changed into new men and said and did such things as not only struck the spectators and hearers with astonishment and wonder, but by a most powerful affecting force drew them wonderfully to the faith and obedience of Christ. From whence could so great a miracle proceed except from God giving his testimony to Christ? That men of a low condition, vulgar and unlearned (*agrammatoi*), seemed as if in one moment to be transformed into most learned and eloquent men, acquainted with all tongues and endowed with a knowledge of the greatest things, who so pleaded the cause of their master intrepidly and with great energy (*energeia*) and boldness (*parrēsia*) of speech, strongly advocating religion not with counterfeit and far-fetched arguments, but with arguments of clear truth and greater than all exception, that in multitudes and crowds (as it were) men flocked to the gospel, notwithstanding threats, edicts, prisons, tortures and all kinds of severe punishments?

It is confirmed from the calling of the Gentiles and the founding of Christianity.

XXI. However, this was afterwards made more clear in the calling of the Gentiles and the founding of Christianity through the whole world. For the calling of the Gentiles was the peculiar work of the Messiah according to the prophetic oracles (Gen. 17:5; 49:10; Pss. 2:8; 22:27, 30; 68:31, 32; 47:7-9; 110:2, 3; Hos. 1:10, 11; Joel 2:28; Is. 2:2, 3; 11:10; 42:1, 4; 49:6; 54:1, 2 and in many other places). The thing itself exclaims and the monuments of histories testify that this was done by the gospel, so that in a short space of time it was spread over the whole world and nations from all sides flowed to Christ and emperors and kings cast their crowns and scepters at his feet. Thus no reason can be given why we should not believe our Jesus to be the true Messiah even from this mark alone.

Notwithstanding the various obstacles: (1) on the part of Christ;

XXII. For unless Jesus was the true Messiah and his doctrine truly divine, how could it have happened that he should be received as the Messiah and faith be given to his doctrine in the world, notwithstanding so many and so great obstacles (almost insuperable)? How could this have happened on the part of Christ himself (the founder of the religion), on the part of the doctrine itself to be preached, of the preachers themselves and their manner of teaching? For if Christ himself was regarded the chief and head of the religion, he was a man common in appearance (as he was supposed the son of a craftsman), of no dignity and name or rank; yea, despised by the higher class of his own people and loaded with all manner of insults and at length taken captive, bound like a slave, scourged and made to bear his own cross; like one convicted of treason against both God and man, nailed to the accursed tree. Now who could suppose that God would have used so common and so miserable (as he seemed) a creature to perform so great a work? Certainly this was the greatest stumbling block (*scandalum*) to the Jews and to the Greeks foolishness, which to the called was the highest power and wisdom of God (1 Cor. 1:18).

2. From the nature of the doctrine.

XXIII. The nature of the doctrine confirms it, which was such that it ought rather to have repulsed than allured men. Not only because it condemned all other contrary religions that had prevailed through the ages and had become strong through long practice and demanded their utter extirpation as empty, false, unworthy of and hostile to God; but also because it contained precepts most displeasing and most troublesome to the flesh—self-denial, love of enemies, the bearing of evils (even of a most oppressive cross) and abstinence from all vices and pleasures. It taught mysteries absurd and inaccessible to reason (such as that the God of glory and the prince of life was crucified). Now if he was God, what was more absurd? if man, what was more empty? It promised either little or nothing in this world but the honor of martyrdom and the burden of the cross (Mt. 16:24; Jn. 15:18, 19; Acts 9:16). Now who can so persuade and secure resources? Is it credible that so many nations would give their consent to such oppresive and difficult precepts, would undertake such labors without any reward, without any of the allurements of pleasure (yea, with the immediate loss of all things most pleasing to them), could be drawn to a ruinous virtue, unless they had been most thoroughly persuaded of the divinity of that doctrine? We wonder at Alexander the Great conquering the world with a few soldiers; at Joshua more, capturing Jericho by trumpets. But who will not wonder at Christ above others, who conquered the world by tongues, whose voice (although there was no speech by nature to them as to the heavens) went into all the earth (Rom. 10:18)? The word was foolishness to men. It was dreadful and such as ought to repel men. It both conciliates the mind and draws the heart. There was in it no art of persuasion, no embellished and enticing words. But still there was in it "the most powerful demonstration of the Spirit" (*apodeixis pneumatos kai dynameōs*, 1 Cor. 2:4). Nor is it to be supposed that the part which is called the foolishness of preaching was concealed and spread over with different colors. Nay, it was openly set before all (as Paul himself testifies, who openly professes that he was determined to know nothing else among them than Jesus Christ and him crucified). It was opposed by innumerable enemies, not by external and foreign only, but by carnal man himself, who leaves nothing undone to drive it from him. And yet it broke through all these obstacles and triumphed over man and his resistance. Cicero wonders that Romulus in an age still rude got himself to be esteemed a god (*The Republic* 2.10 [Loeb, 16:124-27]). But how much more is it to be wondered that our Jesus in a most literary and refined age, by the preaching of the word alone, procured belief in himself as God, so that on account of that confession his disciples were prepared to undergo every evil. Caligula, Nero, Domitian, while living were worshipped with divine honors; but when dead were exposed to a thousand insults. Jesus, when living, was esteemed the most helpless and miserable of mortals; after death, he obtained divine glory and now is raised above all kings. What could have been the cause of so great a change? No other than a persuasion of the divinity of his doctrine.

3. From the condition of the heralds.

XXIV. The condition of the heralds adds not a little weight to this demonstration. They were few—twelve in number; of the common people—obscure, fisherman, tax-gatherers; whom neither their family had made illustrious, nor power or resources enviable, nor favor dear, nor the smiles of the great agreeable, nor learning or eloquence famous or capable of winning the minds of mortals; who were deficient in all the things usually required to persuade men. Who can believe that it could have come to pass that by such men so great things could be done; and that to them would yield so many synagogues, so many schools, so many bands of philosophers, so many exalted geniuses, so many tribunals and scepters, if he whom they preached had not been the true Messiah? Few, they are sent to innumerable persons; ignorant to the learned; speechless to the most eloquent; simple to the shrewd; unarmed to the armed; without resources to the most powerful—yet notwithstanding they draw all after them. Let all the authors of the most celebrated ancient sects who applied all the power of genius to become renowned throughout the world and to whom nothing was wanting for the propogation of their systems in all directions, be compared with these. Yet who was there of them all who drew after himself (I do not say so many followers), but even the thousandth part? Thus God wished to put his treasure in earthen vessels that the excellency of the power might be of God, not of men; that piety and religion should owe nothing of their increase to the world, but that it might depend wholly upon God.

4. From the manner of teaching.

XXV. Finally, the manner of teaching evidently proves this very thing. For it was not labored and curious, adorned with ornaments of style and enticing words and composed to deceive, but simple, unaffected and equally obvious to the unlearned and learned so that all suspicion of fraud and deception might be absent. On this account, they neither used violence to compel the dissentient; nor treachery to deceive the imprudent; nor threats to terrify the reluctant; rather they desired a free faith or none. They thought it worthy of God in Christ to lead, not bodies, but souls in triumph. If they had resorted to forcible means, if they had wished to found religion by arms or legions, if with blood and slaughter (as the impostor Muhammad erected and supports his tyranny), it ought not to have appeared astonishing if they had met with success. But for the whole world in arms to be subdued by unarmed and weak men, of no power and authority, by persuasion alone, this indeed manifestly proves the divinity both of the author and of the doctrine by which it was accomplished. For to ascribe this work to the Devil, what else would it be than for the Devil to wish to be author of his own destruction and to conspire for the fall of his own kingdom? This no man in his senses would say.

XXVI. If the conversion of the world and the founding of Christianity (amidst so many intervening obstacles) are a certain proof of the verity of the Messiah, no less clear a testimony of the same truth is its conservation and propagation. For so many ages it has not been destroyed although Satan and the world have used every effort to overthrow it from the very foundation, but it is the more strengthened and increased and has always struck its roots deeper. On the other hand, other religions and systems (which were sustained by the authority of princes, the subtlety of philosophers and the eloquence of orators) have finally been abolished. Who does not judge the work to be not human but divine; and thus who does not judge its author to have been really what he professed to be—the Lord's Christ?

The fourth demonstration, from absurdities.

XXVII. The fourth demonstration is deduced from absurdities. (1) If Jesus was not the Christ (as he professed himself to be), his name and doctrine could never have risen among the kings and rulers who endeavored to suppress them, but his glory would have been buried with the names of others who were false christs; especially since it was supported neither by the power and authority of the world nor by the wisdom of the age. (2) If Jesus were not the Christ, of all who had lived (forgive the blasphemy) he would have been the most ignominious, who so often asserted concerning God, himself and us the greatest falsehoods and even confirmed them by an oath—

than which falsehood no greater or more dangerous can be. And yet it is acknowledged (even by the Jews, the heathen and Mohammadans themselves) that the most perfect purity of life, joined with honesty of soul, shone in him (which entirely takes away a suspicion of the same). (3) If Jesus was not sent of God, God (the most zealous vindicator of his own glory) would either have foretold this by a prophet that men might guard against such an imposture or would have confronted him by raising up prophets; or by the things themselves and the progress of time would have fulfilled what Gamaliel said, "If the work is not of God, it will be destroyed." Now in the progress of the ages, his fame was not only not extinguished and destroyed, but his doctrine increased and filled the whole world (as water leaping from a fountain with confluent streams, which reached only to the ankles before, is raised up to the knees and covers the breast and the head).

Sources of explanation.

XXVIII. When Christ says that he came not to send peace to the earth, but a sword (Mt. 10:34), the meaning is not that Christ would be the efficient cause of war per se, but the accidental cause (on account of the wickedness of the world, which, not enduring the gospel, would resist him, and excite wars against his professors). This is not opposed to the peace which the Messiah was to bring into the world according to the prophetic oracles (Is. 2:4; 11:6, 7; Mic. 4:3): (1) because it is not an earthly, but a mystical and heavenly peace; (2) not with the world of the wicked and the seed of the serpent (with whom an irreconcilable [*aspondon*] war should be, Gen. 3:15), but with believers among themselves, who laying aside hatred and enmity ought in Christ to be reconciled and to become one. (3) If wars are seen among Christians, this does not arise from the doctrine of Christ, but from the depravity of men.

XXIX. The destruction of idolatry (which was predicted for the time of the Messiah) ought not to take place in one moment, but little by little and by various degrees (which we behold has even happened). (1) The religion of Christ openly and professedly condemns idolatry most severely. (2) By it, it was even entirely extirpated in all the assemblies which truly professed the doctrine of Christ. (3) It is taken away every day in the world by the preaching of the gospel and if any among Christians still retain it (either wholly or in part) by that very fact they show that they are not the church of Christ, but of Antichrist (which is the greatest obstacle to the conversion of the Jews).

XXX. If John the Baptist sent to Jesus to inquire, "Art thou he that should come" (Mt. 11:2, 3), he did not do this because he was in doubt concerning him (since in a remarkable manner he had been convinced of it and had given such express testimony to him, Jn. 1:29, 32-34), but that he might confirm his own disciples (not as yet sufficiently persuaded and who besides were too strongly attached to their own master, by seeing and hearing him).

XXXI. So far from it being necessary for Christ to be approved and received by the synagogue, his rejection had been plainly predicted: "The stone which the builders refused" (Ps. 118:22); "Who hath believed our report?" (Is. 53:1). "When the son of David shall come," says Rabbi Judah, "wise men will be rare in Israel, the wisdom of the Scribe shall rot, and the schools of the theologians shall be dens of infamy" ("Sanhedrin," 97a, BT 2:655).

XXXII. If Jesus abrogated the ceremonial law, it does not follow that he was a violater of the law, but the finisher (*teleiōtēn*) and consummator—for by fulfilling he abrogated it. Nor, moreover, was he even opposed to that law because it was not given to continue forever, but until the time of restitution (*diorthōseōs*). Nor was he opposed to the counsel of God, who had decreed this change from eternity. If it is said that ceremonies and sacrifices should still exist under the Messiah, this is to be understood mystically as to the internal verity of gospel and spiritual worship, not literally as to the external figure (in accordance with the style of the Holy Spirit, who in a changed state retains the ancient name and describes gospel mysteries by legal terms).

THIRD QUESTION: THE NECESSITY OF THE INCARNATION.

Was it necessary for the Son of God to become incarnate? We affirm.

Words by which the incarnation is designated in Scripture.

I. Before we speak of the question, we must briefly notice the various words used to designate the mystery of the incarnation both in Scripture and among the ancients. In Scripture, it is called *phanerōsis en sarki* ("manifestation in the flesh," 1 Tim. 3:16); *sōmatos kasartismos* ("adaptation" or "preparation of a body," Heb. 10:5); *kenōsis* ("emptying" and assumption of the form of a servant, Phil. 2:7); *epilēpsis* ("taking on" of the seed of Abraham, Heb. 2:16); *epiphaneia* ("appearing," 2 Tim. 1:10).

And by the fathers.

By the fathers, it is now called *oikonomia* as distinguished from *theologia* because it was the work of a wonderful dispensation; then *enanthrōpēsis*, *ensōmatōsis*, *ensarkos parousia*, more commonly *sarkōsis* or *ensarkōsis*, a word undoubtedly taken from Jn. 1:14 when the *logos* is said to have been "made flesh." Here the word "flesh" is not to be taken strictly for one part of man, but broadly and synecdochically for the whole human nature, including the soul with the flesh. And thus is more clearly insinuated the greatness of the divine mercy and love towards men, since God condescended to such a degree as to be willing not only to associate with himself the soul (which is the nobler part of man), but assumed what is the meanest and most weak in us (to wit, this fragile and mortal flesh).

Of the necessity of the incarnation.

II. However as this mystery is unascertainable by reason and is known only by the aid of revelation, various questions are wont to be agitated about it. The first treats of its necessity. This again can be distributed into various heads: (1) Would it have been necessary for the Son of God to become incarnate, even if man had not sinned? (2) Was it necessary for the Son of God to become incarnate for us and was there no other mode of salvation possible with God? (3) Was it necessary for our own mediator to be God-man (*theanthrōpon*)? Concerning these we will speak separately under three propositions.

First proposition, the incarnation was not necessary except on account of sin.

III. First proposition: As the Son of God became incarnate only on account of sin, so it would not have been necessary for him to become incarnate if man had not sinned. It is opposed to the old Scholastics, who rashly and without Scripture authority asserted it (as Alexander of Hales, Occam, Bonaventure and others). Osiander, a Lutheran, in a former century interpolated their error. In recent times, the Socinians renew the same for no other object than to seek from it some support for their most pestilent heresy concerning the metaphorical redemption of Christ and the improper satisfaction.

It is proved: (1) from Scripture.

IV. Our reasons are: (1) no other end of the advent of Christ and of his incarnation is ever proposed (whether in the Old or in the New Testament) than that he might save his people from sin. If he is promised, it is only after the fall (Gen. 3:15) and to bruise the head of the serpent. If he is shadowed forth, it is by sacrifices appointed for the expiation of the sins of men. This the angel clearly confirms in the New Testament (Mt. 1:21), as do Zachariah (Lk. 1:67ff.), Simeon (Lk. 2:30, 34), John the Baptist (Jn. 1:29), Christ himself (Mt. 9:13; 20:28), the apostles, Paul (Gal. 4:4, 5; 1 Tim. 1:15; Heb. 2:14) and John (1 Jn. 2:1, 2; 3:8).

2. From his office, which has respect to sinners only.

V. (2) His office is occupied only with sinners. As a Prophet, he teaches sinners and calls them to faith and repentance (Is. 61:1, 2; Mt. 9:13); as a Priest, he gives himself as a ransom (*antilytron*) for sins (1 Tim. 2:6; Is. 53:10; 1 Jn. 2:2) and prays for transgressors (Is. 53:12; Jn. 17); as a King, he governs his people and defends them against the Devil, the world and the flesh that they may not be snatched out of his hands (Jn. 10:28; Rom. 8:35, 38, 39). In one word, he was incarnated that he might be a Mediator. And yet there would have been no need of a mediator, if there had been no sin.

3. From the impelling cause of the mission of Christ, which was love towards fallen men.

VI. (3) The impelling cause of the mission of Christ was the love and kindness of God towards men—not upright, but fallen (Jn. 3:16). This love is far more strongly commended when it is declared that he was sent for this end alone—that he might free us from the chains of sin—than if he had come for any other cause (Rom. 5:6-8).

4. From the fathers.

VII. (4) The fathers frequently confirm this: "If the flesh did not need to be saved, the word of God would by no means have been made flesh" (Irenaeus, *Against Heresies* 5.14 [ANF 1:541; PG 7:1161]); "There was no cause for the coming of Christ, the Lord, except to save sinners, remove diseases, remove wounds; neither is there cause for medicine" (Augustine, *Sermon 175*, "De Verbis Apostoli [9]" [PL 38:945]); "If Adam had not sinned, there would have been no need for our Redeemer to take on him our flesh" (Gregory the Great, *In Librum Primum Regum* 4.1.7 [PL 79:222]).

Sources of explanation.

VIII. Christ is called "the firstborn of every creature" (Col. 1:15), not as if rational creatures were produced after his model, but both in respect of eternal generation and in respect of dominion (which belongs to him in them). All things are said to have been created in him and on account of him as God, not as man. He is said to be the first in all things (v. 18), in dignity, not in time. Nor is man said to have been made after the image of God because he was formed after the model of Christ, but because he was created after the essential image of God, which consists in wisdom and holiness (as Paul teaches, Eph. 4:24; Col. 3:10).

IX. It is one thing for the marriage of Adam and Eve to have been a sign and type of the marriage of Christ with the church (according to the secret intention of the Holy Spirit); another for it to have been known by Adam and to be set forth by him as a prophecy of such wedlock. The former is granted, not the latter. And if the apostle does apply to Christ the words of Adam (Eph. 5:31), it does not follow that they were uttered by Adam for that end, but can properly be referred to him only allegorically on account of the resemblance (*similitudinem*).

X. If Christ was not to be incarnate before the consideration of sin, the church would not have been without a head (*akephalos*). He would have been its head (no more than of the angels) not in respect of humanity, but by the right of divinity and creation.

XI. The demonstration of love towards the human race by the Son about to be incarnate without respect to sin and the expiation of sins by him (incarnate) cannot be considered as subordinated ends, since such a subordination is at variance with Scripture. Scripture proposed no other end of the mission of Christ than the salvation of sinners, nor is it right to push our inquiries further, since Scripture is silent.

XII. God does not subtract from human nature that good of which it is capable by a natural capacity (which arises from the principles of nature itself), but he can take away from it that of which it is capable according to obediential power or the want of repugnance to receive all that God wishes. Such is the capacity of the hypostatical union in the human nature.

XIII. The goodness of God (communicative of itself) could be a sufficient motive to influence him to the production of creatures, but not for the incarnation of the Son of God (which extended further to their restoration).

Second proposition, sin being posited and the decree of God concerning the salvation of men, it was necessary for the Son of God to become incarnate. Statement of the question.

XIV. Second proposition: It was not only suitable, but necessary (sin and the decree of God concerning the redemption of men being supposed) that the Son of God should become incarnate in order to accomplish this work. (1) The question does not concern a simple and absolute necessity on the part of God for God could (if he had wished) leave man no less than the Devil in his destruction. Rather the question concerns a hypothetical—whether the will to save men being posited, the incarnation was necessary; or whether it could have been brought about by some other means. (2) Again, the question does not concern the necessity of the decree for no one denies that on the supposition of God's having decreed this, it ought necessarily to have been done. Rather the question concerns the necessity of nature—whether (the decree being set aside and antecedently to it) it was necessary for the Son of God to become incarnate in order to redeem us. (3) The question does not concern the necessity of fitness because all confess this was in the highest degree fitting to the divine majesty—that his precepts might not be said to have been violated with impunity. Rather the question concerns the necessity of justice—that in no other way could the justice of God have been satisfied and our deliverance brought about (which we assert).

XV. I know that some of the ancients (whom many of the Scholastics follow here) were of a different opinion—that other possible ways were not wanting to

God. Augustine: "Another possible way was not wanting to God, under whose power all things equally lie, but there was not and could not be another more suitable way of healing our misery" (*The Trinity* 13.10 [FC 45:388]). Various Scholastics agree with him here: Thomas Aquinas, ST, III, Q. 1*, Art. 2, pp. 2026-28; Lombard, *Sententiarum* 3, Dist. 2 (PL 192/2:759-60); Bonaventure, "Liber III. Sententiarum," Dist. 20, Q. 6 *Opera Theologica Selecta* (1941), 3:422-24. Nor are there wanting men on our side who incline to this: Peter Martyr, *Loci Communis*, Cl. 2, c. 17.19 (1583), p. 419; Tilenus, Disp. II, "De Incarnatione," *Syntagmatis Tripertiti Disputationum Theologicarum* (1618), pp. 398-408; Kimedoncius, *Of the Redemption of Mankind* 1.5 (1598), p. 9 and above others Twisse, who lays out his strength to prove this with great pains. But there were not wanting also some of the fathers and Scholastics who acknowledged this necessity: Athanasius, *On the Incarnation of the Word;* Anselm, *Cur Deus Homo;* Ambrose on Heb. 9+. With them many of our men agree (especially after the rise of Socinus) and their opinion we also embrace as the truer and safer.

XVI. The reasons are: (1) as God cannot deny his own justice, he could not free men without a satisfaction being made first. Satisfaction could not be made to infinite justice except by some infinite ransom (*lytron*); nor could that infinite ransom (*lytron*) be found anywhere except in the Son of God. Now that the exercise of that justice was necessary (not free or arbitrary, depending upon the good pleasure of God alone), we have proved in Volume I, Topic III (concerning God), Question 19.

XVII. (2) If it could have been done in any other way, it is not credible that the most wise and good God would have entered upon this counsel, which seemed to be little suitable to his wisdom and goodness. For if he could free men by word alone, was it becoming to his wisdom to accomplish so easy a thing with so much labor and as it were to move heaven and earth? Would he have done by more, what he could have done by fewer? And who can believe that the Father would have wished to send down from heaven his most beloved Son (in whom all his delight [*eudokia*] centers) unnecessarily to put on our flesh and to expose him to a thousand trials and at last to a most excruciating death for us? Verily the wisdom and goodness of God will not suffer us to believe that this was free to him, but a certain ineluctable necessity must have intervened.

XVIII. Nor is it to be supposed that in holding this, we wish to limit the omnipotence of God or to define what he can do with supreme right toward his creatures. We only show from Scripture what God can or cannot do according to ordinate power and right tempered by virtues. The other things belonging here will be spoken of hereafter when we treat of the necessity of the satisfaction.

Third proposition, the work of salvation required a God-man.

XIX. Third proposition: The work of redemption could not have been performed except by a God-man (*theanthrōpon*) associating by incarnation the human nature with the divine by an indissoluble bond. For since to redeem us, two things were most especially required—the acquisition of salvation and the application of the same; the endurance of death for satisfaction and victory over the same for the enjoyment of life—our mediator ought to be God-man (*theanthrōpos*) to accomplish these things: man to suffer, God to overcome; man to receive the punishment we deserved, God to endure and drink it to the dregs; man to acquire salvation for us by dying, God to apply it to us by overcoming; man to become ours by the assumption of flesh, God to make us like himself by the bestowal of the Spirit. This neither a mere man nor God alone could do. For neither could God alone be subject to death, nor could man alone conquer it. Man alone could die for men; God alone could vanquish death. Both natures, therefore, should be associated that in both conjoined, both the highest weakness of humanity might exert itself for suffering and the highest power and majesty of the divinity might exert itself for the victory.

XX. (1) It behooved him to be man in respect of the justice of God, which required sin to be punished in the same nature in which it had been committed, according to the oracle—"The soul that sinneth it shall die" (Ezk. 18:4). It also behooved him to be God, to add an infinite value to his sufferings. (2) In respect of the office of Christ, he ought to perform the office of Mediator in order to reconcile men to God. Therefore he ought to be between both and like Jacob's ladder join heaven and earth by a participation of the nature of both. As a Prophet, he ought as man to be taken from his brethren that he might become familiar with men and we might approach freely to him. But as God, he ought to send the Spirit into our hearts and write the law upon our minds to make us taught of God (*theodidaktous*). As Priest, he should be man because every high priest is taken from among men (Heb. 5:1) as he who sanctifies and they who are sanctified are all of one (Heb. 2:11); but as God to reconcile man to God, satisfy divine justice, abolish sin and bring in an everlasting righteousness, which no mortal could do. Also, the victim to be offered ought not to be angelic because it could not die, nor a brute, but rational and human; yea, more than human and celestial who should offer himself through the eternal Spirit and add an infinite weight and merit to the truth of his sufferings. As King, he ought to take humanity from us to become united to us; but this was to be united to divinity, by which he should exercise dominion, not over bodies only, but also over souls; not for a time, but forever; not over one nation only, but over the whole world.

XXI. (3) In respect of us, he should be man that by right of relationship and as a brother and our *g'l* he might deliver the captives and slaves of Satan (Lk. 1:71, 74) and unite us (freed from our former marriage under the law and covenant of works) to himself in the covenant of grace by an eternal and indissoluble bond (Rom. 7:4; Eph. 5:25). Also he should be God that by right of ownership and dominion, he might redeem us and claim us for himself. We have need of like feeling (*homoiopatheia*) in the one dying and of sympathy (*sympatheia*) in the one living. He should be man to be able to endure all the punishment due to us as of like passions (*homoiopathēs*). He should be God to be able as a merciful Priest to sympathize in our sufferings and to succor us when tempted. The evil by which we were pressed was such that none but a man could endure it, no one except God could free us from it. And the good which was to be conferred on us (to wit, righteousness and life) was such that although man was to receive it, still none but God could put us in possession of it.

XXII. Hence it is that when the Scripture speaks of Christ, it almost always joins these two relations (*scheseis*) and attributes things to him which teach that he was truly God-man (*theanthrōpon*). If he is called the seed of the woman (which belongs to man), the bruising of the serpent is ascribed to him (which belongs to God). If he is called the seed of Abraham, it is added in the same place that he is the seed in whom all the nations of the earth were to be blessed.

If as Prophet he should be taken from among his brethren, still he was such a Prophet as must be listened to under penalty of death (Dt. 18:19). He is a child born in time as man, but also a Son who is the Father of eternity as God (Is. 9:6). The offspring of David according to the flesh, but Jehovah our righteousness according to the Spirit (Jer. 23:6). A son to be born of a virgin, but whose name would be Immanuel (Is. 7:14). The Angel of the Covenant sent by God for the work of salvation, but the same one, the Lord who comes into his temple (Mal. 3:1). A citizen of Bethlehem to be born in an obscure place, but a ruler whose goings forth are from eternity (Mic. 5:2). A Priest, but forever; a King whose kingdom shall have no end. The seed of David according to the flesh, but the Son of God according to the spirit of sanctification (Rom. 1:3, 4).

FOURTH QUESTION

Whether only the second person of the Trinity became incarnate and why.

I. In the wonderful mystery of the incarnation which the apostle deservedly calls "without controversy great" (1 Tim. 3:16), four questions especially come under consideration: (1) the person assuming; (2) the nature assumed; (3) the mode of assumption by hypostatical union; (4) its effects. Here we dispute of the first.

Statement of the question.

II. The question is not whether the whole Trinity was active in the mystery of the incarnation. For since external works are undivided according to a received axiom of theologians, this work of incarnation (which is external) cannot but be a common one in respect of the whole Trinity. Hence the Father is said to have sent the Son (Jn. 3:16) and the Holy Spirit to have conceived the Son in the womb of the virgin. Yea, three persons were necessarily required for this work. One, to sustain the majesty of God, the author of all things and the supreme Judge, the offended party. The second, to act as Mediator between God and men and make satisfaction for men. The third, to carry out the work of salvation in us. To the first is said to belong the destination of salvation; to the second, its acquisition; to the third, its application and consummation. Therefore, the question is not Does the incarnation pertain in any way to the sacred Trinity? Rather the question is only whether it was terminatively and appropriatively incarnated. Although originally and principiatively as to efficiency the work of the whole Trinity, yet not subjectively and appropriatively as to terminus (in which sense it belongs only to the Son).

III. The question is not Was it necessary for God to become incarnate (as this has been proved already); nor whether the three persons could be incarnated. For the unity of the Mediator necessarily required a unity of person. Rather the question is Which person of the Trinity took this upon himself? The first or third or only the second? We assert the last.

IV. The reasons are: (1) the Scripture ascribes this to the Son alone, not to the Father or the Holy Spirit. The *Logos* only is said to have been made flesh (Jn. 1:14); the Son of God, who was in the form of God, took on him the form of a servant (Phil. 2:6, 7*; Heb. 2:14, 15); of the Son it is said he took part in flesh and blood and was made like unto us in all things, sin excepted.

V. (2) The Father could not be incarnated, for as he was the first in order he could not be sent by anyone or act as mediator to the Son and the Holy Spirit.

Nor was it fitting that he, who was the Father in divine things, should become the Son in human things by being born of a virgin. The Holy Spirit could not, who was to be sent by the Mediator to the church (Jn. 16:7), and yet he could not be sent by himself. Thus there would have been two sons, the second person by eternal generation and the third by an incarnation in time.

VI. (3) The Son alone could rightly undertake this function: (a) that he who is between the Father and the Holy Spirit should be Mediator between God and men. (b) It was fitting that he who was the Son by nature should make us adoptive sons by grace, that we might be coheirs with him who is heir of all things. (c) It was his to recreate (*anaktizein*) whose it was to create; that the Word, by which all things were made in the first creation, should reform us after his image in the second. The image of God obscured by sin and all but destroyed, could not be repaired in us better than by him who was the image of the invisible God. (d) No other was more fit to make our reconciliation than he who was the well-beloved (*agapētos*) Son of the Father, in whom he was well pleased (*eudokēse*, Mt. 3:17).

Sources of explanation.

VII. Although the divine nature may properly be said to have been incarnated in the Son, it does not follow that the whole Trinity became incarnate. The divine nature is said to be incarnate, not immediately and considered absolutely in itself, but mediately in the person of the Son, or under that reduplication insofar as it is determined and characterized in the person of the Son. Thus the incarnation is a work not natural, but personal, terminating on the person, not on the nature. Thus the whole divine nature indeed is well said to be incarnate, not because it is incarnate in all the persons, but because there is nothing wanting to the person of the Son of God as to the perfection of his divine nature. This particular incarnation of the one person without the incarnation of the rest does not hinder either that relation (*schesis*) between the persons themselves (because since it denotes a distinction and an opposition as to beget and to be begotten, it does not offer an impediment, but rather removes it) or the relation between the person and the essence (because since it does not abolish the distinction of persons, nor hinder one person from being distinguished from the others, much less does it hinder one from being incarnate without the others).

VIII. If incarnation is ascribed in some places to God (as 1 Tim. 3:16; Col. 2:9), this must be understood of the divine nature not absolutely and in itself, but relative to the characteristic of the Son by which he is distinguished from the Father and the Holy Spirit. And the fathers hold this, who affirm that the divine nature is incarnate (to wit, in one of the hypostases [*en mia hypostaseōn*] and in the hypostasis of the Word [*en hypostasei logou*]). Thus John of Damascus explains this phrase (*Exposition of the Orthodox Faith* 3.6 [NPNF2, 9:50-51]), as does Lombard (*Sententiarum* 3, Dist. 2 [PL 192/2:759]).

IX. Although the essence (on account of its perfect simplicity) cannot be divided into parts, still because it is one way in the Father (to wit, unbegotten [*agennētōs*]), another way in the Son (in whom it is begotten [*gennētōs*]), another way in the Holy Spirit, on this account the human nature could be assumed according to the one mode of subsisting which constituted the one person of the Trinity; thus it could not be assumed according to the rest (which constitute the remaining persons) since these modes differ not only in reason (logically), but also in the thing (really).

X. There is a difference between the intuitive vision in the blessed and the hypostatical union in Christ. The former is terminated first and by itself on the divine essence as it is common to the three persons because it ought to reach the thing as it is in itself (i.e., God ought to be seen and known by the blessed as he is and so at the same time one and three). But the human nature ought not to be united hypostatically to the whole Trinity. It was sufficient for it to be conjoined with the divine nature, not in all its extent and as belonging also to the Father and the Holy Spirit, but as it is characterized and determined in the person of the Son.

XI. If our divines have not admitted the phraseology of the Lutherans (who assert that the divine nature was incarnate), it is not because they absolutely and simply deny that the divine nature was incarnate and say that only a mode of subsistence (*tropon hyparxeōs*) was incarnate without the divine nature (as they are unjustly ridiculed). But they object to it only as a less accurate way of speaking, consistent neither with Scripture nor with the truth of the thing (unless it is explained with dexterity).

Fifth Question: The Nature Assumed

Was the human nature assumed by the Logos like ours in all respects (sin excepted) and his flesh taken from the substance of the blessed virgin; or did it come down from heaven? The former we affirm; the latter we deny against the Anabaptists.

Various errors concerning the humanity of Christ: of the Manichaeans.

I. As the divinity of Christ was attacked by the fury of various heresies, so Satan has raised up many enemies against his humanity. The Manichaeans and Marcionites maintained that Christ was a man not truly, but only apparently (as a phantom). Thus they converted his humanity into a specter. The Valentinians held that indeed he had a body, but one sent from heaven, not one received from the virgin. They also believed that the body of the virgin was like a channel through which the body of Christ passed. The Apollinarists believed indeed that he had flesh, yet not that he took it from the virgin; rather in the incarnation something of the Word was turned into flesh and the divinity informed the flesh in place of the soul.

Of the Valentinians.

Of the Apollinarists.

Of the Anabaptists.

II. Treading in the footsteps of all these, the modern Anabaptists deny that Christ took flesh and blood from the substance of the blessed virgin (*Protocol . . . de Gansche Handelinge des Gespreckes te Franckenthal . . . Gaspar von der Heyden*, Art. 3 [1571], p. 125 and *Protocol . . . handelinge des gesprecks tho Emdden . . .* G. *Goebens*, Art. 11-13 [1579], pp. 290-360). On this negative opinion, the Dutch and German churches agree—that Christ did not take flesh and blood from the substance of Mary; but they do not agree in the affirmative—whence he received it. The Germans confess their ignorance. The Dutch, however, more clearly profess that the flesh of Christ was from the Word of Life, from the seed of the Father (which seed is the Word of God).

Statement of the question.

III. The question is not Did Christ have flesh and was he and can he be called man? But Was he a man like unto us in all things, sin excepted? And did he receive flesh from the blessed virgin and from no other source? This they deny; we affirm.

That Christ is a true man like us is proved: (1) because he is called man, and Son of man.

IV. The reasons are: first he is everywhere called man and Son of man, which could not be said with truth if he had not had a nature like ours (i.e., taken from men). Nor if the angels (who appeared in human form) are sometimes called men according to appearance (*kata doxan*) because they seemed to be such to those to whom they appeared, does it follow that the same can be said of Christ. Nowhere is it said of them that they were sons of man, that they were made flesh, that they were partakers of flesh and blood.

2. Because he is called the seed of the woman and of Abraham, the fruit of the womb.

V. Second, he is called "the seed of the woman" (Gen. 3:15), "the seed of Abraham" (Gen. 12:3; 22:18), "the son of Abraham" (Acts 3:25), "the son of David and the fruit of his loins" (Lk. 1:32; Rom. 1:3), "the seed of the virgin and the fruit of her womb" (Lk. 1:31, 42), "made of a woman" (Gal. 4:4). Now how could he be distinguished by these names unless he had a nature like ours, taken from the very substance of a woman and a virgin? Nor can it be said (1) he is called the son of Abraham or of David because he was promised to them; for thus he might equally be called the son of all believers, to whom also he was promised. (2) He is the son of David in the same way in which he is said to be the son of Joseph. He is called the son of Joseph only equivocally because he seemed to be such in the opinion of others (as "we supposed" [*hōs enomizeto*], as Luke says, 3:23), but he ought to be called the son of David properly and univocally, having sprung from the fathers and from the seed of David according to the flesh (Rom. 1:3; 9:5). (3) Or he is called the fruit of Mary's womb because he was conceived in it, not from it. By womb, there is not denoted only the place of conception, but also the matter (as explained in Rom. 1:3 and Gal. 4:4 when he is said to be "made of a woman"). Nor if Christ was Mary's Lord according to the Spirit, does it follow that he could not be her son according to the flesh. (4) Or the spiritual, not the natural seed is meant because such a seed ought to be understood in virtue of which he should spring from the fathers according to the flesh (Rom. 9:5).

3. Because he was made flesh and our brother.

VI. Third, he was made a partaker of flesh and blood and from this is called our brother (Heb. 2:10, 14, 16). Nor can flesh and blood be taken simply for infirmity, but the truth of the human nature is necessarily implied. It treats of the man (referred to in Ps. 8) who ought to taste death for all, who is our brother and ought to be like us in all things (v. 17); who was of one blood with us ("for both he that sanctifieth and they who are sanctified are all of one" [v. 11], to wit, of the same mass or human nature which he calls flesh and blood [v. 14]) as the high priest in the Old Testament sanctifying the people was of the same nature with the people (Heb. 5:1); or the firstfruits is of the same nature with the remaining fruit. And further he teaches that Christ is a fit person to suffer for us and by his suffering to sanctify and redeem us as our Goel. But how could he be said to be either one with us or be set forth as our brother like us in all things, if he had not a human nature or flesh consubstantial (*homoousion*) with ours? Nor is it an objection that this nature also was common to reprobates, since Christ took it on for the sake of his children; nor could he have taken on any other than that common to all.

4. Because he took on the seed of Abraham.

VII. Fourth, "he took on him the seed of Abraham, not angels" (Heb. 2:16*). The verb *epilambanesthai* properly means to take hold of and assume (or to take on) and rightly refers to the assumption of nature into the unity of person. Thus the sense is—the Son of God assumed not an angelic, but a human nature from the posterity of Abraham and indeed according to the promise. The scope of the apostle and the connection show this to be the genuine sense, for he intends to prove the truth of the human nature of Christ and its consubstantiality (*homoousian*) with us by a participation of flesh and blood (which was necessary in every way for redemption) and because he had said that he partook of flesh and blood that he might deliver us (v. 14, 15). He now teaches how and whence he partook of that flesh (to wit, by assuming the seed of Abraham, i.e., not human nature in general, but in particular a nature derived from Adam, according to the promise made to him). Nor do the things urged by Socinus and others to escape its force disprove this interpretation. (a) "The Apostle did not say *epelabeto* ('in the past') but *epilambanetai* ('in the present') since the act of the assumption of the nature is momentaneous, not continuous." Since the hypostatical union perpetually lasts and is preserved and its conservation is a certain continued production of the thing, he speaks with propriety in the present. Besides an enallage of the present for the future frequently occurs (especially in narrations of public events), so that the things seem not so much to have passed as to be going on. (b) "He would prove the same thing by the same, for to be made like us (which follows) is the same as to assume our nature." But the following words ("wherefore it behooved him") contain not so much an inference from what is here asserted as an affirmation of the necessity of the thing there asserted (on account of what follows—"that he might be a high priest"). (c) "The seed of Abraham is a collective expression denoting many believers (Rom. 4:16; Gal. 3:29)." But "seed" is also spoken as often of one individually, and here Paul peculiarly teaches it should be understood (Gal. 3:16).

VIII. The verb *epilambanesthai* cannot be referred here to simple help and protection because it nowhere has such a sense. Nor does the passage Rom. 15:7 belong here. It is one thing *proslambanein eis doxan* ("to receive to glory"); another *epilambanein sperma* ("to take the seed"). There Christ is said to receive as unto glory or to make us partakers of heavenly glory; here, however, that he takes on him the seed or becomes partaker of flesh and blood. (2) From this assumption (*epilēpsei*), the angels are excluded; but from the care of Christ, the head (exalted in his office), the angels (who are members of the church triumphant) are not excluded (Heb. 12:22). (3) Christ assumed the seed on earth (as a comparison of what goes before and of what follows teaches); therefore not at length in heaven (as our opponents maintain).

5. From the genealogy of Christ.

IX. Fifth, the genealogy of Christ is given, in which he is said to have sprung from the fathers according to the flesh (Mt. 1; Lk. 3; Rom. 1:3). This would be untrue, if he had taken on the substance of flesh from any other source than the blessed virgin.

6. Because sin ought to be punished in the nature that sinned.

X. Sixth, if Christ was not made like us in all things as to identity of nature, he could not truly redeem us, since sin must be expiated in the same nature in which it was committed.

Sources of explanation.

XI. Christ is called "the Lord from heaven" (1 Cor. 15:47), not in respect of the matter of his body, but in respect: (1) of the person of the Logos (*Logou*) and of the divine nature which manifested itself in flesh; (2) of the efficient cause (to wit, of the Holy Spirit, from whom the humanity was conceived); (3) of the condition of Christ's life on earth, which was not terrene and earthly, but divine and heavenly; in holiness and power, not in the body. The antithesis instituted in Jn. 3:31 and 8:23, when Christ is said "to come" and "to be from heaven," but men "from the earth" does not prove that his flesh descended from heaven, but only opposes bare and mere men sprung from the earth to Christ, the God-man (*theanthrōpō*). Christ is opposed to Adam (1 Cor. 15:45-47), not in respect of flesh, according to which he is called the son of Adam (Lk. 3:38), but in respect of his person and office as the Lord from heaven. He is opposed to mere and animal man as the author of righteousness and life is opposed to the author of sin and death.

XII. A similitude may be either of external appearance only, or of internal truth and of natural properties. Christ is said to have been made in the likeness of man (Phil. 2:7), not in the former, but in the latter sense (as Adam is said to have begotten Seth in his own likeness, Gen. 5:3). And Elijah is said to have been "subject to like passions as we are" (*homoiopathēs hēmin*, Jam. 5:17), who yet had human affections truly and not only apparently. And if Christ is said in the same passage (*schēmati*) to have been "found in fashion as a man," the truth of his human nature is not on that account denied, but more strongly intimated because *hōs* marks not only likeness but reality (as often elsewhere, Jn. 1:14; 2 Cor. 3:18). Nor if he is said to have been found in external fashion as a mere man and a sinner like others, is it denied that he was a true man as to identity of nature. Finally, who can deny that he was a man, who was found in fashion as a man and humbled himself even unto death?

XIII. The consubstantiality (*homoousion*) of Christ with us consists in identity of nature and essential properties, but not in the relation of subsistence which was wanting to the human nature. Therefore, the singular human nature of Christ was complete physically in its substantial being as to its integral parts, but not metaphysically as to the mode of subsistence.

XIV. The same one who after the resurrection ascended into heaven, had descended from heaven (Eph. 4:9), as to person, not as to both natures of the person. He descended as Logos (*Logos*) by a remarkable manifestation; he ascended as God-man (*theanthrōpos*). Nor is it necessary for the ascension to answer entirely to the descent on account of the diversity of the subjects. The one is true and local; the other is only metaphorical. "The bread which cometh down from heaven" adumbrated by the manna formerly (Jn. 6:33) does not signify the human nature in the abstract, but the person in the concrete. It is called such now in relation to the divine nature when he is said to have come down from heaven; then in relation to the human, as when the flesh of Christ is said to be given for the life of the world. The bread which gives is the person of Christ; the bread which is given is the flesh of Christ.

XV. Those who suppose women are begotten without impregnation (*asporous*) and deny that they actively concur in generation, not only oppose themselves to physicians, but also contradict the Scripture, which asserts that the power of generation is bestowed upon the female as well as upon the male (Gen. 1:28) and ascribes seed to them (Gen. 16:10; 24:60). Hence there is granted a consanguinity between uterine brother and sister, although born of distinct fathers (Lev. 18:9, 10).

XVI. Christ does not deny that Mary was his mother simply (Mt. 12:47, 48), but prefers spiritual mother and brothers to carnal in order to testify that he esteems them more highly.

XVII. Christ is said to have been conceived of the Holy Spirit, not materially, but energetically (*dēmiourgikōs*) and efficiently (as the preposition denotes here the efficient cause because by his extraordinary power and operation he was conceived and not the matter out of which he was conceived).

XVIII. The "Son of the living God" cannot be called the son of Mary according to that in which he is the Son of God. But because he assumed the human nature from her into unity of person, he is rightly and truly called also the son of Mary in this respect. Thus Mary can truly be called *theotokos* or "mother of God," if the word "God" is taken concretely for the total personality of Christ consisting of the person of the Logos (*Logou*) and the human nature (in which sense she is called "the mother of the Lord," Lk. 1:43), but not precisely and abstractly in respect of the deity. Thus she is called the mother of God specificatively (i.e, of him who is God), but not reduplicatively (as he is God).

XIX. Whatever is born of flesh is flesh (Jn. 3:6), to wit, according to the order of nature in a natural way, or by ordinary and univocal generation; but not beyond the order and in a supernatural way, which is the case here. Hence although Christ sprang from Adam, a sinner, still he did not draw from him sin either imputed or inherent because he did not descend from him in virtue of the general promise—"increase and multiply." Rather he descended from him in virtue of the special promise concerning the seed of the woman. And although he was in Adam as to nature, yet not as to person and moral state or federal relation, by which it happens that all the posterity of Adam (Christ excepted) partake of his sin.

Sixth Question: The Truth of the Incarnation and the Hypostatical Union

Did the Son of God assume human nature into the unity of his person? We affirm against the Socinians.

I. In the Christian religion there are two questions above all others which are difficult. The first concerns the unity of the three persons in the one essence in the Trinity; the other concerns the union of the two natures in the one person in the incarnation. Now although they mutually differ (because in the first the discussion concerns the unity of essence and the Trinity of persons, while the other concerns the unity of the person and the diversity of natures), still the one greatly assists in the understanding of the other. For as in the Trinity, the unity of essence does not hinder the persons from being distinct from each other and their properties and operations from being incommunicable, so the union of natures in the person of Christ does not prevent both the natures and their properties from remaining unconfounded and distinct.

Statement of the question.

II. The question does not concern the truth of the human nature because that is acknowledged on both sides. Nor does it concern the truth of the nature or of the hypostasis of the Son of God because we have considered it elsewhere. Rather the question concerns the truth of the incarnation—whether the Son of God assumed the human nature into unity of person, so that the same one who was the Son of God became by the hypostatical union the Son of Man. This the orthodox assert; the Socinians deny.

III. The question does not concern the physical and essential union of two things to constitute one third nature (as the soul is united to the body to constitute a man). Not concerning the schetic (*schetikē*) and relative union consisting in the union of souls and the consent of wills, such as the union of friends. Not concerning a parastatic (*parastatikē*) union by mere standing by, such as that of the angels with bodies assumed. Not concerning an efficient (*drastikē*) union, as to general efficacy and sustentation by which all things are in God and we move, live and have our being in him (Acts 17:28). Not concerning the mystical union and grace of believers with Christ. Not of the substantial (*ousiōdei*) or essential union of the persons of the Trinity in one essence. Rather the question concerns the hypostatical union by the assumption of human nature into unity of the person of the Logos (*Logou*). This is so called, both in respect of form (because it is in the person of the Logos [*Logou*]) and in respect of the term (because it is terminated on it). Thus the union is personal, but not of persons, as the union of natures, but not natural. If at any time it is called *physikē* (natural union) by the fathers (as by Cyril, "Anathema 3," *Explicatio Duodecim Capitum* [PG 76:299]) it must be understood in a sound sense, so that not so much the relation of union is regarded as the extremes of union (for the extremes united are two natures).

IV. This union can be viewed either in respect of the principle or in respect of the terminus. In the former sense, it is attributed to the whole Trinity, by the power of which such union is made (to wit, by a transient action of God by which he united in the person of the Logos, the humanity of Christ). In the latter, it belongs to the Logos alone because it is terminated on him. Although the person of the Logos may well be said to have been incarnate, yet the Trinity itself may not because the incarnation is not terminated on the divine nature absolutely, but on the person of the Logos relatively.

V. By this union, therefore, nothing else is designated than the intimate and perpetual conjunction of the two natures—the divine and human—in the unity of person. By this, the human nature (which was destitute of proper personality and was without subsistence [*anypostatos*] because otherwise it would have been a person) was assumed into the person of the Logos (*Logou*), and either conjoined with or adjoined to him in unity of person, so that now it is substantial with the Logos (*enypostatos Logō*). For it is sustained by him, not by a general sustentation (by which all creatures are sustained by God), but by a special and personal sustentation, inasmuch as it is united into one person with the Word. Now although the human nature may rightly be said to be substantial with the Logos (*enypostatos Logō*) (because it was assumed into the unity of the person and is sustained by it), yet less accurately is it said to subsist with the subsistence of the Logos (*Logou*) because then the human nature would be a divine person.

VI. The human nature in the God-man (*theanthrōpō*) can be called both its adjunct and part in a sound sense. Adjunct, not that it is adjoined or adheres to it as the accident to the subject or a garment to the body, but because to the Logos (*Logō*) (existing without flesh from eternity) it was conjoined in time in the unity of person. It may be called a part also analogically and in a wider sense; not as if the person of Christ is compounded or consists of two incomplete natures, as parts properly so called (which would savor of imperfection); but because it subsists not in one, but in two natures and agrees with both; not accidentally, but essentially. Hence it is said to be composed (*syntheton*) rather of number than of parts because in it many things numerically (to wit, the human and divine natures) exist. If it is called the instrument of the Logos (*Logou*) by some, this is not done in respect of existence, but of operation because he assumed it on account of operation and works by it.

VII. This assumption, therefore, was not made for the completion of the person of the Logos (*Logou*) as such reduplicatively, since it was most perfect in itself from eternity, but of the person of the God-man (*theanthrōpou*) or Mediator specifically; not to the acquisition of new perfection in respect to the Son of God intrinsically, but to the communication of perfection with respect to us and to working extrinsically, in order that by that nature he might perform what was necessary for our redemption.

VIII. When the person of the God-man (*theanthrōpou*) is called by the fathers compound (*hen prosōpon syntheton ek theotētos epouraniou, kai anthrōpinēs sarkos*, as the fathers of the Synod of Antioch+ speak against Paul of Samosata), there is not meant a composition properly so called (as if the human and divine natures were as incomplete parts for the constitution of the whole). Rather an improper is meant inasmuch as that is said to be compounded which consists of different things; not physical of these (i.e., of essential parts) as man of soul and body; not accidental with these (i.e., of subject and accident), but hyperphysical and extraordinary (i.e., of this nature taken to this individual, incommunicable subsistence in which one of the extremes fills up and perfects, the other is filled up and perfected). Nor is it absurd that the divine nature in this way comes into composition with another because this is not after the manner of a part properly so called, but after the manner of assuming another nature. Thus it may be said to compose something with another not essentially, but personally; nor for its intrinsic perfection, but only for its extrinsic operation.

IX. Although we recognize in Christ a twofold union, one personal (of the two natures, the divine and human in one person), the other natural (of the soul and body in the one human nature), still falsely are we charged by some Lutherans with holding a twofold hypostatical union in Christ and thus favoring Nestorianism. These two unions differ from each other in many ways: (1) in kind, because the one is physical, the other is hyperphysical; (2) in the terminus, because there is a nature, here a person; (3) in the subject, which there is the human nature alone, here both natures; (4) in the adjuncts, because that is separable and was dissolved by the death of Christ, while this is inseparable—what the Logos (*Logos*) has once assumed he never laid aside.

X. The question therefore returns to this—Was it a true incarnation? That is, did the Son of God, the second person of the holy Trinity, join together with himself in unity of person, not a person, but a human nature; not by conversion and transmutation, but by assumption and sustentation, so that the Son of God was made the Son of man and our Mediator and is truly God-man (*theanthrōpos*)? The Socinians deny this. They teach that in Christ there is only one nature; that he is man not only true, but also mere and simple, whose whole prerogative, consequently, was in the excellency of his attributes and office, not of his nature. On the other hand, we affirm it.

The hypostatical union is proved: (1) from Jn. 1:14.

XI. The reasons are first, "the word was made flesh" (Jn. 1:14), where distinct mention is made: (a) of two extremes (to wit, the Word, which is shown to be a divine person from what goes before, where he is said to be God and with God and to have made all things [vv. 1, 3], and flesh, which denotes synechdochically the human nature); (b) of the union by which they were mutually joined together; not as by conversion and change (of which the immutable God is incapable), but by assumption, by which (remaining the same in himself, to wit, true and eternal God) he was made what he was not before by partaking of flesh and blood, according to that well-known phrase—"I am what I was" (to wit, God) "nor was I what I am" (namely man) "now I am called both" (to wit, God and man).

XII. Nor can the impious gloss of Socinus be allowed by which (about to corrupt this most lucid passage) he maintains that the verb *egeneto* is to be translated not by "was made" (as by the common consent of interpreters it is usually translated), but by "was" (as it is used elsewhere in this sense in Jn. 1:6—*egeneto*, "there was a man sent from God," and Lk. 24:19). The gloss is openly contrary to the text, where John clearly distinguishes the being of the Logos (*tou Logou*) from the being of the flesh; that which was Christ from eternity from that which he was made in time. The former he signifies by the verb *ēn* (*en archē ēn ho Logos*, "in the beginning was the Word," v. 1), without any indication of beginning or of origin. Even in the beginning, he was the Word, he was with God and he was God. The latter he denotes by the verb *egeneto*, which designates a beginning and origin because in the fulness of time God sent forth his Son *genomenon* (made of a woman, Gal. 4:4), who is elsewhere said to be made (*genomenos*) of the seed of David (Rom. 1:3). Nor if the verb *ginomai* is elsewhere taken in a different sense, does it follow that it cannot be used in this sense here (which the connection imperatively demands). To no purpose does he add that by the word "flesh," the humble and abject condition of Christ is denoted. For thus are connoted his infirmities that the human nature may always be supposed (which is the subject of them), so that the word may be said to be made flesh (i.e., a weak and poor man like unto us in all things).

2. From Phil. 2:6, 7.

XIII. Second, "Christ, being in the form of God, thought it not robbery to be equal with God; but made himself of no reputation, and took upon him the form of a servant, and was made in the likeness of men: and being found in fashion as a man" (Phil. 2:6-8*). Here various arguments lie concealed, not only for proving the divinity of Christ (as was shown in Volume 1, Topic III, Question 28, Section 2), but also the truth of the incarnation. (a) Express mention is made of the two natures of Christ—the divine (both by the form of God [*morphēn Theou*], which he is said to have had, and by equality with God, which he did not think it robbery to attribute to himself); the human (by the form of a servant [*morphēn doulou*] which he took on and the likeness of a man, in which he was made). (b) Of the union of these two natures in one person—the same one who was in the form of God is said to have taken on him the form of a servant and to have been made in the likeness of men; not only to have appeared in the form of a servant, as formerly under the Old Testament he appeared in the form of a man by clothing himself for a time with this form, as with a garment or symbol of his presence, but that he took on that form to indicate the true assumption of our nature into personal union. Here also belongs the verb *ekenōse*, which is not to be taken simply and absolutely (as if he ceased to be God or was reduced to a nonentity, which is impious even to think concerning the eternal and unchangeable God), but in respect of state and comparatively because he concealed the divine glory under the veil of flesh and as it were laid it aside; not by putting off what he was, but by assuming what he was not. And as the verb *ekenōse* properly implies he emptied himself out or seemed to be emptied of all that glory which is rightly called the fulness of the deity, that he might take on our vile nature (which is mere vanity and, as it were, nothing with respect to God, and in it the most abject and miserable condition of a slave), and so from almighty to weak, from most rich to poor (2 Cor. 8:9), from the Lord of angels the servant of men, from a most glorious and happy state, which he enjoyed with the Father, he entered into a most sad condition, in which he was made a worm, no man, a reproach of men and despised of the people (Ps. 22:6), without form, without comeliness (Is. 53:2), and cut off and, as it were, brought to nothing, according to the prediction in Dan. 9:26.

XIV. Our adversaries labor in vain to escape the force of this passage by saying: (1) "*morphēn Theou* does not designate the divine nature (which cannot be emptied), but the excellence and dignity of the human nature, seen in the working of miracles and in those rays which shone out from under the veil of flesh." First, in this sense Christ would have taken on the form of a servant before he had been in the form of God. This is directly contrary to Paul, who asserts that Christ had already subsisted in the form of God when he received the form of a servant and existing as such he had emptied himself, the form of a servant having been assumed. Second, the form of God here is "to be equal with God," which cannot be said of any excellence of angelic nature, much less of the human nature. The apostles wrought stupendous miracles; yea, greater than even those of Christ (Jn. 14:12) and yet they cannot on that account be called equal with God. Third, God cannot be emptied by a diminution of glory, but by its concealment (*occultationem*); not in the sight of God intrinsically, but extrinsically as to men. (2) With no better success do they hold that "the form of a servant does not connote the human nature of Christ, but only the most abject condition of Christ because having received the form of a servant he is said only to be made after the likeness of a man, i.e., as if a man, not however that he was made a man simply." Things that ought to be connected are separated, for the servile condition of Christ (designated by the form of a servant), does not exclude the truth of the human nature, but supposes it because he could not enter that servile state except in a human nature. If he is said to have been made in the likeness of men, the specific identity of the human nature is not denied, but only the numerical. Otherwise Seth would not have been of the same nature with Adam because he is said to have been made in his likeness (Gen. 5:3).

3. From 1 Tim. 3:16.

XV. Third, "God was manifested in the flesh" (1 Tim. 3:16), where two natures (a divine and a human) are connoted coalescing in the person of Christ by his incarnation. Otherwise the same Christ could not be called God and flesh; "to be manifested in the flesh" is the same as elsewhere "to be made partaker of flesh and blood" (Heb. 2:14); "to be made flesh" (Jn. 1:14); and "to come in the flesh" (*en sarki erchesthai*, 2 Jn. 7). God is said to be manifested not essentially (*ousiōdōs*) but hypostatically (*hypostatikōs*) (to wit, in the person of the Logos [*Logou*]), not by some sign of his presence given to men (as in the burning bush [Ex. 3:2] or in the pillar of cloud and fire [1 K. 8:10, 11]), nor by a human form assumed only for a time (as in Gen. 18), or by shadowy phantoms (*phasmata*), in which way false gods rendered themselves visible, "clothing themselves with bodies" (as Servius says, *In Vergilii Carmina Commentarii* [1961], 2:157 [on Aeneid, 7:416]), *heautous eidopoiountes eis anthrōpous*, as Heliodorus expresses it (*Les Ethiopiques*, 3.13.1 [trans. J. Maillon, 1960], 1:115). But he is manifested "in flesh" (i.e., in mortal and miserable human nature). He does not say simply that the divinity in the abstract, but "God" (*Theon*) in the concrete was manifested (to wit, the person of the Logos [*Logou*] was manifested because incarnation is not of the divine nature absolutely, but of a person).

4. From Rom. 1:3, etc.

XVI. Fourth, from the passages where two natures in the person of Christ are clearly set forth: "He was made of the seed of David according to the flesh; and declared to be the Son of God with power, according to the spirit of holiness, by the resurrection from the dead" (Rom. 1:3, 4). The limitation according to the flesh and Spirit denotes his two natures, the one according to which he was made of the seed of David (viz., the human), the other divine according to the Spirit of holiness, by which he was declared to be the Son of God by his resurrection (the indubitable argument of his divinity). Nor if "according to the flesh" is elsewhere taken in a sense a little different, either for corruption (as to "walk according to the flesh," Rom. 8:1) or for external form which strikes the senses (as "to judge according to the flesh," Jn. 8:15), does it follow that it cannot here signify Christ as to the human nature. For both the seed of David and the anthesis of the Spirit necessarily demand this. Nor if the same man can be said to be born according to the flesh and according to the Spirit (as is said of Isaac, Gal. 4:29), ought it forthwith to be denied that elsewhere a twofold nature is designated. It is one thing for a limitation to be added to an agent as to mode of generation (in which sense Isaac is said to have been begotten "according to the Spirit," although he was begotten according to the flesh, because in virtue of a special promise he was brought forth in a supernatural manner); it is another for it to be added to the subject as to the natures of which it is constituted (as in this passage).

XVII. The same limitation is added when it is said, "of the fathers, as concerning the flesh, Christ came, God blessed forever" (Rom. 9:5). Here the human nature is designated, according to which he must spring from the fathers, and the divine, according to which he is God blessed forever. So in 1 Pet. 3:18, it is said "being put to death in the flesh" (i.e., having suffered in the human nature), but "quickened by the Spirit" (i.e., raised up by the divinity, by that eternal Spirit by which he offered himself to God, Heb. 9:14). Thus, "God" is said "to have purchased his church with his own blood" (Acts 20:28). Here the words "his own" (*idiou*) show that the nature which suffered truly belongs to that divine person which is said to have purchased the church.

XVIII. Although the human nature of Christ is a first substance (intelligent and perfect in substantial being), it is not at once a person because it does not possess incommunicability and proper subsistence (as the soul separated is a singular intelligent substance, yet not a person because it is a partial being, incomplete, which does not subsist, but must be adjoined to another). The want, however, of proper personality does not derogate from the truth and perfection of the human nature of Christ because we measure the truth of human nature from the matter, form and essential properties, not from the personality. Hence the definition of a nature differs from that of a subsistence. Finally, personality is neither an integral nor essential part of a nature, but as it were the terminus. Because it shares in an uncreated subsistence, on that account it is far more perfect than if it subsisted by itself separated from the Word.

XIX. The Son of God did not assume man as one entire, incommunicable subsistence, but a human nature (i.e., man specifically so called). And as often as Christ is called a man or the Son of man in the Scripture, it is a name not of the nature, but of the person denominated from the other nature.

XX. God and man are either regarded in the abstract (to denote the divinity and the humanity) or in the concrete (to designate the person, which is God and man at the same time). In the latter sense, they are not disparate, but diverse (which can belong to one subject). But in the former sense, they are truly disparate (which can never be predicated of each other in turn). Although it may properly be said the man is God, improperly, however, would it be said—the humanity is divinity. Now although such disparates cannot be one in number ordinarily and physically, nothing hinders this from being held theologically and in that extraordinary God-man (*theanthrōpou*).

XXI. We do not think much labor should be devoted to explain the nature and representation of the propositions used in this mystery, such as "God is man" and "man is God." Nothing similar occurs in the universe and in this sense they are well called "unusual"; not disparates, by which a disparate is predicated of a disparate (because no person is divided from itself); but identical where one thing is predicated of itself not formally. In this sense, they can be called synonymical by a logical consideration and tropical by a rhetorical consideration. Synonymical because subject and predicate are taken concretely for the unity of person; so that the sense is: The person who is God, is also man. Thus the lowest species is predicated of an extraordinary and singular individual. Tropical because the subject and predicate indeed designate the same person, but in different respects (*kat' allo kai allo*) (i.e., as to deity and humanity). This tropical predication, therefore ("God is man" and "man is God"), is not to be resolved into this proper—The deity is God; the humanity is man—as the adversaries falsely object. Rather it is to be resolved into this: Christ (God according to the deity) is man according to humanity (and in turn). As God is said to have suffered (i.e., Christ who is God according to the deity suffered) not in the deity, but in the flesh.

XXII. The communication of the hypostasis of the Logos (*Logou*) made flesh can be understood in three ways: either effectively (as if it effected in the flesh another hypostasis); or transitively, so that it may be maintained that he formally transferred his own hypostasis into the flesh; or assumptively because he assumed flesh into the same hypostasis and united it to himself. In the former way, the phrase is heterodox and Nestorian. For if he had formed another hypostasis, there would be two hypostases and consequently two persons. The second is no less heretical because thus the flesh would formally subsist in the subsistence of the Logos (*Logou*) and thus be truly a person. Besides a personal property is simply incommunicable. But in the third sense, it is true and orthodox (viz., the Logos [*Logos*] may be said to have communicated his own subsistence to the flesh by assuming it into the unity of his own hypostasis so that the flesh is not a hypostasis, but real [*enypostatos*]; not existing separately, but sustained in the Logos [*Logō*] [as an instrument and adjunct personally joined to it] in order to accomplish the work of our redemption).

XXIII. Contradictories cannot agree in the same subject, in the same manner and in the same respect. But to be dependent and independent, finite and infinite belong to Christ in different respects (*kat' allo kai allo*): the former with respect to the human nature; the latter with respect to the divine.

XXIV. A local infinite distance can hinder the union of two natures, but not an infinite distance of perfection (such as exists between the human and divine natures).

XXV. If the Son of God assumed our nature, nothing on that account was added to him intrinsically to perfect his nature (which already had in an eminent degree all the perfection of humanity). Only extrinsically was something adjoined to it for the work of redemption.

XXVI. He who is made what he was not before transmutatively, is changed; but not forthwith, he who is only made what he was not assumptively. Therefore, the change (if there were any here) is in the human nature (which in an extraordinary and special manner is sustained by the Logos [*Logō*]), not in the person of the Logos (*Logou*) (who, always existing the same, united it to himself).

Seventh Question

Was the hypostatical union of the two natures in Christ such that neither the person is divided nor the natures confounded? We affirm against Nestorius and Eutyches.

Two rocks are to be shunned about the hypostatical union, Nestorianism and Eutychianism.

I. Although the mode of the hypostatical union is positively unspeakable (*arrētos*), still it is not badly designated negatively when it is denied to have been made either by a division of the person or by a mixture of natures. These are the two principal rocks to be avoided here: Nestorianism on the one side, which divides the person; and on the other, Eutychianism, which confounds the natures.

II. In opposition to this twofold error, the fathers in the Council of Chalcedon (451 A.D.) said that the union was made *adiairetōs* and *achōristōs* ("indivisibly and inseparably") against Nestorius; and *atreptōs* and *asynchytōs* ("without change and confusion") against Eutyches. The two natures were so united in the one person that they were neither converted the one into the other, nor confused so that from two a certain third nature composed of both resulted. Rather they remained unconfused, each with its own properties.

The opinion of Nestorius is examined.

III. The first error is that of Nestorius, Patriarch of Constantinople, who of the two natures of Christ invented two persons. On this account, he denied that the blessed virgin could be called the "mother of God" (*theotokon*) or "God-bearer," but only the mother of Christ (*Christotokon*); and that Christ was not God (*Theon*), but only a man possessed by God (*anthrōpon theophoron*). Thus he made two Christs—one of whom was crucified by the Jews; the other, however, who was not. Hence he repeatedly reiterated this, "Why dost thou glory, O Jew? thou hast crucified a man, not God." Nor did he acknowledge any other union (*henōsin*) of natures than an accidental, both as to standing-by (*kata parastasin*) and simple habitation (inasmuch as the Word dwelt in the man Christ, as in his temple); and as to grace (*kata charin*) and good will (*eudokian*) (inasmuch as God acquiesced in the highest degree with and was pleased with this man); and as to energy (*kat' energeian*) by operation (inasmuch as he was the instrument of God in those wonderful works which the Son of God wrought); and as to like will (*kata tautoboulian*) and affections (with respect to the consent between the will of man and God in Christ); and as to worth (*kat' axian*) and equal honor (*isotimian*) with respect to the dignity bestowed upon the assumed flesh.

IV. Now although there are not wanting those who (more favorable to Nestorius and more unjust to Cyril) can proclaim the former orthodox because he indeed distinguished natures in Christ, but did not separate them (and therefore was unjustly condemned in the Council of Ephesus), but proclaim the latter a heretic and thus do not hesitate to oppose themselves to the (thus far) constant opinion in the Reformed churches; still we do not think that this novel comment and that lordly (*kyrian*) opinion can be demonstrated by any solid argument (*doxan*). Yea, there are not a few which prove its vanity. (1) No one can readily presume that Nestorius did not think what is charged upon him by unanimous consent, both by the three ecumenical councils (of Ephesus, Chalcedon and Constantinople) and by writers of ecclesiastical history and heresiologists; yea, even by the Caesarean laws themselves, which order the books of Nestorius to be burned and devoted to utter destruction and call down the severest punishment upon those who dare to possess or read such writings or books (*Corpus Iuris Civilis, II: Codex Iustinianus*, 1.5-7 ["De summa Trinitate"], pp. 6-10). (2) The twelve sections or excommunications of Cyril approved by the Synod of Ephesus (given by Forbes, *Instructiones Historico-theologicae*, 2.6 [1645], pp. 82-84) clearly prove this. (3) For no other reason did Nestorius deny that Mary could be called the Mother of God (*theotokon*) than because he denied that two natures coalesced in the one person. Vincentius Lerin, his contemporary (placed outside of the parties), testifies of this. He relates that three years after the Council of Ephesus, he had written, "Nestorius with the opposite disease to that of Apollinarius, while he feigns that he distinguishes two substances in Christ, suddenly introduces two persons and with unheard of wickedness maintains that there are two Sons of God, two

Christs—one God, the other man" (*Commonitories*, 1.12* [FC 7:289; PL 50.654-55]). If Nestorius used doubtful and equivocal phrases to cover up his error (which can admit however a sound sense), it does not immediately follow that he was orthodox or that the fathers (who thoroughly knew his meaning) forced a wrong construction upon his language. If Cyril sometimes used harsher phrases which seemed to approach to Eutychianism in refuting Nestorius (as is frequently done by those, who opposing one error, appear to glide into another) it cannot thence be inferred that he had improper views of this mystery and favored Euthyches. As when he so often says "one nature" belonged to the incarnate Logos (*Logou*), he does not mean that the humanity and divinity coalesced in one nature, since in the same place he maintains that the union was made "without confusion" (*asynchytōs*). Rather he says this in opposition to Nestorius because there is one *hyphistamenon* ("subsistent") by which "the Word is united to the flesh according to hypostasis" (as the Anathema expresses it). Whatever it may be, the question is historical, of fact, not of right. This does not hinder us from rejecting as fundamental the error attributed to Nestorius. It is so rejected by all the orthodox, who assert that the hypostatical union was indeed made with a distinction of natures, but without a division of the person (relying upon various reasons).

And is rejected.

V. First, the passages which show that the Son of God was born of a virgin prove this. Since this cannot be understood of the divine (which is uncreated and eternal), but of the human nature (which had a beginning in its own time), it is rightly concluded that the divine and human nature in Christ constitute only one person concerning which are correctly predicated whatever things belong to the divine and human nature. "That holy thing which shall be born of thee shall be called the Son of God" (Lk. 1:35); "God sent forth his Son, made of a woman" (Gal. 4:4).

VI. Second, the passages in which one person consisting of two natures is described prove this. It is said, "Christ, made of the seed of David according to the flesh, and the Son of God according to the Spirit of holiness" (Rom. 1:3, 4*); "God, blessed forever and man, sprung from the fathers" (Rom. 9:5); "God manifest in the flesh" (1 Tim. 3:16); "who, being in the form of God, humbled himself and took upon him the form of a servant" (Phil. 2:6, 7).

VII. Third, the passages which ascribe diverse properties and operations to the one Christ prove it: as that the Son of man, who came down from heaven, yet is in heaven (Jn. 3:13); the Lord of glory was crucified (1 Cor. 2:8); God purchased the church with his own blood (Acts 20:28); all the fulness of the Godhead dwells in him (Col. 2:9). This could not be predicated of him unless the two natures had coalesced in the one person.

Sources of explanation.

VIII. Where there are two natures complete (in their substantial as well as their subsistential and incommunicable being) there are two persons. Now in Christ there are not two natures complete as to subsistence and incommunicable. If in Peter and Paul two singular natures constitute two persons, it does not follow that the same is the case with Christ. The two natures in men have incommunicability with singularity, but not in Christ because the human nature is determined to the assumption of the Word, to whom it is personally united. Nor does it follow that the word "man" is predicated equivocally of

Christ and of us, but only that the word "man" is taken at one time specifically for human nature (as it is predicated of Christ), at another personally (as it is attributed to us).

IX. Actions and passions belong to individual incommunicable subsistences denominatively. Yet they may also be ascribed formally to one or the other nature. Thus suffering and death properly and formally belong to human nature, but denominatively to the person according to the other nature.

X. A temple cannot be physically and materially the same with him who dwells in it; but metaphorically and mystically it is denied (as the soul is said to be in its own body as in a temple or tabernacle, although constituting the same person with it). The humanity of Christ is in this latter sense called the temple of the divinity, not in the former sense. Thus the distinction of natures is indeed well denoted, but not the division of the person.

XI. Mary is rightly called the Mother of God (*theotokos*) in the concrete and specifically because she brought forth him who is also God, but not in the abstract and reduplicatively as God. Although this is not expressly stated in the Scriptures, still it is sufficiently intimated when she is called the mother of the Lord (Lk. 1:43) and the mother of Immanuel. If the blessed virgin brought nothing to the person of the Logos (*Logou*) absolutely considered, still she can be said to have brought something to the person of the incarnate Logos (*Logou*) economically considered, inasmuch as she gave the human nature which he took into the unity of person.

XII. The title Mother of God given to the virgin was perverted by superstitious men into an occasion of idolatry, as Paul Sarpi observes. "Because the impiety of Nestorius divided Christ, constituting two sons and denying that he, who was born of the virgin Mary, is God; the church, in order to implant the catholic truth in the minds of believers, decided that the words, Mary, the Mother of God (*Maria theotokos*), should be more frequently inculcated in the churches of the East as well as of the West. This, instituted indeed solely for the honor of Christ, by degrees began to be shared with the mother and at length was referred entirely to her alone" (*History of the Council of Trent* 2 [1620], p. 181). Although, I say, this most gross error either arose from or was increased by this occasion, it derogates nothing from the truth because the abuse and error of the papists ought not to take away the lawful use of this name.

Eutychianism.

XIII. A second rock to be avoided here is Eutychianism. It is opposed to the former and is so called from Eutyches, the abbot of a monastery in Constantinople, who while ardently opposing Nestorius (dividing the person of Christ into two) confounded the two natures into one and was condemned by the Council of Chalcedon. Here belong the two adverbs *atreptōs kai asynchytōs* ("without change and confusion"), by which is intimated that one nature is neither changed nor converted by the hypostatical union into the other. Nor are the natures so confounded or mixed with each other that each of them does not retain its own properties and conditions.

XIV. The reasons are: (1) the opposition of the two natures in Christ is frequent in Scripture (Rom. 1:3; 1 Pet. 3:18; Heb. 9:14; Jn. 1:14; Phil. 2:6, 7, 11); (2) two wills are ascribed to him ("not my will, but thine, be done," Lk. 22:42). Nor does it follow that there are two willing because the will belongs to the nature, while willing belongs to the person; nor is it evident that the will follows personally forthwith because in God there are three persons, but only one will. (3) Contraries are ascribed to Christ, which could not be if there were not two natures in him (as that he would depart from the world and remain with us forever; that a child was born, who is the Father of eternity; that he suffered death and was made alive; in the form of God and in the form of a servant, etc.).

Sources of explanation.

XV. Although the efficient cause of the operations of Christ is one alone, still the exciting cause is twofold—the divinity and humanity. The work upon which both exciting (*egergēma*) causes exert their power is one, but the action (*energeia*) is twofold.

XVI. What coalece in one nature are not to be distinguished, but not what coalesce in one subsisting substance (as the two natures in Christ coalesce indeed in the same subsisting substance, but not in the same nature, which consists of two, like the soul and body). If the fathers sometimes employ this similitude in describing the hypostatical union, it does not follow that it holds good in every respect. They agree indeed in this—that as the body and soul form one person, so the divinity and humanity; and as the soul operates through the body (as the organ substantially united to itself) so also the divinity through the humanity. But they differ in this—that the soul and body form a person as parts and incomplete natures. But the divinity is properly neither a part nor an incomplete nature. Finally, from the soul and the body a certain third nature arises; but not from the divinity and humanity.

XVII. It is one thing to speak of the whole Christ; another to speak of the whole of Christ. The whole Christ is God and man, but not the whole of Christ. Whole in the masculine (*totus*) denotes a person in the concrete, but whole in the neuter (*totum*) a nature in the abstract. Therefore it is rightly said that the whole Christ is God or man because this marks the person; but not the whole of Christ because this marks each nature which is in him.

EIGHTH QUESTION: THE COMMUNICATION OF PROPERTIES

Were certain properties of the divine nature formally communicated to the human nature of Christ by the personal union? We deny against the Lutherans.

Effects of the hypostatical union with respect to the human nature are: the grace of eminence and habitual graces.

I. The effects of the hypostatical union are twofold: some refer to the human nature of Christ; others to the person subsisting in both natures. To the former are commonly ascribed both the grace of eminence (which is the dignity of human nature above all creatures, arising from the union of the same with the divine nature, by which flesh is a property of the Son of God—which can be said of no other creature) and habitual graces (to wit, those remarkable gifts which the divine nature bestowed upon the human, which although the highest and most perfect in their own order, still were not simply infinite, but according to the capacity of the recipient in the order of created gifts; yet they were greater than in any angels or saints, both in the dignity of the subject and in the perfection of parts and of degrees). Hence it is said, "God giveth not the Spirit by measure unto him" (Jn. 3:34).

With respect to the person: (1) a communication of attributes; (2) communication of office; (3) communication of honor.

II. With respect to the person the effects again are threefold: (1) a communication of attributes and of the properties of each nature to the person; (2) communication of office and of effects, by which the mediatorial works bearing upon our salvation are ascribed to the person acting according to both natures; (3) communication of honor and of worship due to the God-man (*theanthrōpō*).

Communication of attributes.

III. The communication of attributes (concerning which we now dispute) is an effect of the union by which the properties of both natures became common to the person. Hence the phraseology (or the manner of speaking) concerning Christ arises, by which the properties of either nature are predicated of the person of Christ, in whatever manner it is denominated. This is done either directly, when what belongs to the divine nature is predicated of the person denominated from the divine nature, and what belongs to the human nature of the person denominated from the human nature (as when the Word is said to have been in the beginning with God and God [Jn. 1:1]; when the Son of man, it is said, must be delivered to death and crucified [Lk. 9:22]). Or it is done indirectly, as when what belongs to the deity is predicated of the man Christ and to the humanity of Christ as God (as when suffering is ascribed to God [Acts 20:28] and ubiquity [which is proper to deity] is ascribed to the Son of man [Jn. 3:13]).

It can be called "real."

IV. This communication is not only verbal, but is rightly called "real"; not indeed with respect to the natures (as if the properties of the one nature were really communicated to the other), but with respect to the person, which consists of two natures really unified and claims the properties of both for itself. For although the union of the natures with each other is real, it is not necessary that the properties of the natures should be communicated to each other in turn. It suffices that they be communicated to the whole subsisting substance on account of that union.

It is considered either in the concrete or in the abstract.

V. That communication can be considered either in the abstract (in respect of nature), or in the concrete (in respect of the person). The words "concrete" and "abstract" are not to be spoken in the abusive sense of the Lutherans (with whom abstract is the human nature abstracted or separated from the deity, while concrete is the human nature as united to the Logos [*Logō*]). This is repugnant to the common use of philosophers and to the nature of the thing, according to which the human nature can never be separated from the Logos (*Logō*). But they are used here in accordance with the received use in the schools, as abstract is the name of a nature or of a form which is in another whether essentially or accidentally (as deity, humanity). The concrete is a person or subject having that form or nature which is expressed by the concrete words "God," "man."

Statement of the question.

VI. The question here does not concern communication in the concrete or (as they call it) of a nature to the person. That is acknowledged on both sides. Rather the question concerns communication in the abstract or of nature to nature—whether the properties of the divine nature were really and truly communicated to the human nature by the hypostatical union. This the Lutherans hold; we deny.

Its origin.

VII. The origin of the controversy is to be traced to another controversy concerning the Lord's Supper. For to retain the bodily presence, the Lutherans could not find sufficient support in the words of Christ and felt that they were heavily pressed by the article of his ascension. Thus they betook themselves to ubiquity. Now although Luther afterwards wished it discarded (relying upon the words of Christ alone), still Brentius and others (who renewed the sacramentarian controversy after the death of Luther) recalled the comment of ubiquity as the prow and stern of their cause. And because it was objected to them that ubiquity is an attribute of God and on that account incommunicable to others, they have gone so far as to say that some divine properties in virtue of the hypostatic union were transfused into the human nature of Christ. Hence in the Conference at Maulbrun (Maulbroon) they maintained that the personal union formally consists in the communication of properties or in the communication of subsistence, whose consequent effect is the communion of properties ("Die Maulbrooner Formel," in *Zwei Actenstude zur Genesis der Concordienformel* [Th. Pressel] in *Jahrbucher fur Deutsche Theologie* [1866], p. 652). This opinion is now held by almost all of them. Still it did not please Luther, who urged the communication of properties only in the concrete, not in the abstract. "The catholic belief is this, that we confess the one Christ to be true God and man. From this truth of double substance and from the unity of the person follows what is called the communication of attributes, so that the things which belong to man may rightly be said concerning God and on the other hand those which belong to God may be said of man. It is truly said, This man created the world, and this God suffered" ("Disputation de divinitate et humanitate Christi," in *Werke* [Weimar, 1932], 39:199). And concerning the last words of David: "These forms of speech they call the communication of attributes (i.e., when that which is proper to either nature and concerning it is said separately in the abstract, still in the concrete is ascribed to the person)" (*Works* [1955], 15:341, cf. p. 293). With this agrees Paul Eberus, a Wittenbergian Divine, in his book on this subject (*Vom heiligen Sakrament des Leibs und Bluts unsers Herrn Jesu Christi* [1562]).

VIII. The question again is not—whether the properties of the human nature were communicated to the divine nature (which the adversaries confess cannot be done). Nor—whether all the properties of the divine nature were communicated to the human nature. But whether only certain of them were communicated (as omnipresence, omniscience, omnipotence and the power of making alive). This they assert; we deny.

It is proved that there is no communication of attributes in the abstract: (1) because the divine essence cannot be communicated.

IX. The reasons are: (1) the divine essence cannot be communicated to a creature because a created thing cannot be made an uncreated, otherwise it would be God. Therefore none of the essential properties of God which are identified with the divine essence may be communicated. The same nature would be at the same time created and uncreated, immense and finite, which is contradictory. Nor is the contradiction removed by saying by an act of nature it agrees with the human nature that it be created and finite; but by an act of the person it is uncreated and immense. (a) Personality is not an act, but the mode of a thing. If the act of a person agrees with the humanity of Christ, it will undoubtedly be a person. Nor do these propositions cease to be true—"the Word was made flesh" and "the man is God"—if the divine essence does not communicate itself to the human nature. Their truth is not founded upon the communication of properties in the abstract, but on the personal union of the two natures in the concrete. By regeneration, we are made partakers of the divine nature (2 Pet. 1:4), not formally, but analogically by reason of the gifts.

2. Because properties are not communicated.

X. Second, what is proper to one cannot be communicated to another; otherwise it would cease to be proper and become common to that to which it is communicated. The reply is vain that it cannot indeed be communicated by participation (*kata methexin*), but (*kata syndyasin*) by a union of both, as occurs in subjects coupled together (*syndedyasmenois*). For *syndyasis* is not in natures united in the abstract, but in a person or whole consisting of natures united in the concrete. (2) "The properties can be communicated and still remain properties, since to God alone they belong by nature, but to the human nature by grace." What is made common to another in whatever way communicated can no longer be a property. Nor can the diversity of the human nature of Christ from other created things favor this communication, which cannot have a place in them. It consists in the excellence of gifts, the dignity of office and the assumption into the person of the God-man (*theanthrōpou*); not in the communication of attributes.

3. Because either all ought to be communicated or none.

XI. Third, either all the properties of the divine nature were communicated or none because they are inseparable and really one. Now of things which are really one, one being communicated, the other is necessarily communicated. Besides if on account of the hypostatical union certain properties were communicated to the flesh (since the Logos [*Logos*] united himself to the flesh), all the properties of the Logos (*Logou*) ought also to have been communicated (unless we wish to divide the Logos [*Logon*]). Nor can a reason be given why some are communicated, others not. For if they say that it is repugnant to human nature to be eternal, why is it not also repugnant to it to be omnipresent? And yet on the hypothesis of the Lutherans, all are not communicated; therefore none are. Nor can it be answered that there is a difference between God's attributes: that some are energetical (*energētikas*), exerting themselves outwards in peculiar operations, and the communication of them was necessary to the mediatorial office; others inoperative (*anergētikas*), not needing to be communicated. For such a difference holds good only in respect to effect and to us, not really in themselves and intrinsically where no such difference can be granted on account of the perfect simplicity of the essence; nor even a diversity in communication. Nor are they helped by the distinction between mediate and immediate communication, by which all the divine properties are said indeed to be communicated mediately in the hypostasis of the Logos (*Logou*) (which is communicated to the flesh), but immediately only some. Besides the formal communication of the hypostasis made to the flesh being taken for granted (as will afterwards be proved), it is not treated of a mediate but of an immediate communication by which all the divine properties ought to be predicated of the human nature according to that hypothesis because there ought to be an equal relation of all the properties with each other. I confess that they are distinguished into communicable and incommunicable, but we know that this is to be understood not formally (in which sense all are equally incommunicable), but only analogically.

4. Because the properties of the flesh are not communicated to the Logos.

XII. Fourth, if, on account of the union the divine properties are communicated to the flesh, then the properties of the flesh ought in turn to be communicated to the Logos (*Logō*). The union is reciprocal. However, they are unwilling to admit this. Nor can the distinction of the nature assuming and assumed remedy this difficulty. The foundation of a reciprocal communication is not assumption, but the union itself, which is reciprocal (as the divine is united to the human nature, so the human is united to the divine). Thus also it would demand a reciprocal communication, not in the concrete only, but also in the abstract. Nor can a difference be derived from this—that the human nature indeed needed the communication of these attributes, but not the divine nature. The human nature did indeed need exalted gifts for the performance of its own work, but not attributes of God (which would rather have destroyed the human nature and transformed it into deity).

5. Because there would thus be a confusion of natures.

XIII. Fifth, if a real communication of properties is granted in the abstract, there will be granted also a levelling and confusion of natures (which error was condemned long ago in Eutyches). The consequence is evident from the meaning of confusion, which takes place when two things or more and their properties are communicated (i.e., are made common). Nor does it help them to reply that a levelling is not made because the human nature does not derive from itself omnipresence. That one thing may be made equal to another, it is not necessary that it of itself and by itself should not be equal to that to which it is made equal. Communication is absurdly opposed to equalizing and confusion, which cannot be made without communication. Nor was it ever heard that those things which are already on an equality are made equal; or those things which are confounded, are confounded. Nor was Eutyches ever charged with believing that the flesh of Christ was made divine by itself and from itself; yea, not even that can be thought by those who are endowed with reason. For how could it be made divine if it had been already divine from itself?

6. From the hypothesis of the Lutherans.

XIV. Sixth, if the union was made (the natures themselves and their properties remaining unconfounded and entire and distinct, as the Lutherans acknowledge) a communication of properties could not have been made in it. For what is communicated does not remain proper. Nor can it be said that the properties always remain distinct because they belong to the divinity peculiarly (*idiōs*) and by nature and to the humanity by grace. Whatever is the mode of having, they maintain that they are really and truly possessed by the human nature so that they can lawfully be predicated of it and on that account remain no longer proper to the Logos (*Logō*).

nope

7. Omnipresence is impugned.

XV. Seventh, we thus argue against the omnipresence of Christ's human nature: (1) to whom omnipresence is not communicated either in a state of humiliation or in the state of exaltation. It is not absolutely communicated to him because there are only two states of Christ, the Mediator. And yet in neither is it communicated: not in humiliation because the gospel testifies that he was not everywhere, but now in this, then in that place and that he passed from place to place (Jn. 6:24; 11:15; Mk. 6:6). Not in exaltation because it was not granted while he lived on earth: "I know that ye seek Jesus, which was crucified. He is not here: for he is risen, as he said. Come, see the place where the Lord lay" (Mt. 28:5, 6); "Behold my hands and my feet, that it is I myself" (Lk. 24:39*). Nor was it granted after rising to heaven because (a) he foretold that he would go out of the world and no more be present here: "For ye have the poor always with you; but me ye have not always" (Mt. 26:11); "I came forth from the Father; and am come into the world; again, I leave the world, and go to the Father" (Jn. 16:28); "Now I am no more in the world" (Jn. 17:11), i.e., in a short time I will not be. (b) He really departed from this world (Lk. 24:51; Acts 1:9). (c) He now exists in heaven, nor will he return until the day of judgment: "Whom the heaven must receive until the times of restitution of all things" (Acts 3:21); "For if he were on earth, he should not be a priest" (Heb. 8:4); "The Lord shall descend from heaven" (1 Thess. 4:16*).

XVI. It cannot be replied: (a) "The human nature had omnipresence in the state of humiliation in the first act, but it did not exert or declare itself." This takes for granted the very thing to be proved. Nor would the Scripture absolutely and simply deny that Christ was everywhere, if this was to be understood only with a restriction and a limitation. (b) "Christ left the world as to visible and familiar conversation with his followers and servile condition, not however as to real and substantial presence, according to which he says that he will be with his disciples even until the end of the world." As Scripture teaches no invisible presence of the body of Christ anywhere, so the words of Christ exclude any presence of his body according to which it is said that he will leave the world (i.e., the earth) and ascend into heaven. Nor if it is said metaphorically of the Logos (*Logō*) that he came from the Father and came down from heaven, is there the same relation of leaving the world as to the flesh (which is properly attributed to him). He promises indeed that he will always be with his disciples as to the Spirit, not as to the flesh. (c) "There are three respects in which the body of Christ can be viewed: first according to the properties of its nature; second according to the glory of its resurrection; third according to the grace of personal union. In the former modes it is only in one place, but in the latter it is everywhere." From the third respect no more than from others does the omnipresence of the body follow because (united to the deity) as much remained as the body remained.

XVII. (2) The omnipresence of Christ's body cannot stand with various articles of faith. For if it is feigned to be omnipresent in virtue of the personal union, it could neither be conceived in the womb of the virgin, nor be born and come to light outside it, nor die. For the soul could not be separated from the body, or be buried (because it was already in a sepulcher), or rise again (because it was acting outside of a sepulcher), or ascend into heaven (where it was living already); nor could it descend from heaven to earth at the judgment, if it was to be everywhere present. Nor can it be said that Christ in the state of humiliation did not exhibit the majesty communicated to his flesh, but subjected it to locality and to the other conditions of this world. It is taken for granted (not proved) that there is a communication of majesty. Finally, locality depends upon the freedom of the will and does not flow from a necessity of human nature. The history of the ascension teaches that its departure was not only an intermission of companionship and conversation, but a translation of his body from earth to heaven and from a lower to a higher place (Mk. 16:19; Acts 1:1-11).

XVIII. (3) It is repugnant to the nature of the body, which is circumscribed and finite, has parts outside parts and ought to be of itself visible and palpable. Nor can it be objected: (a) "that it is unjust to subject a glorious body to the laws of a common nature." Glory does not destroy or change a nature, but only adorns and perfects it. (b) "That the body of Christ is circumscribed by a property of nature and in a physical mode, but uncircumscribed by reason of the union and in a hyperphysical mode." This distinction has a foundation neither in Scripture nor in the nature of the thing; yea, it is absurd and ridiculous because one body is held to be receptive of contrary properties—locality and illocality. The mode in truth is brought forward to no purpose when the thing is not recognized. (c) "The body of Christ was sometimes invisible (*aphanton*) and unseen (*aoraton*)" (Mk. 16:12; Lk. 24:31; Jn. 8:59). This happened not by a separation of visibility from the body, but partly by a miraculous evasion or withdrawal, partly by a holding (*retentionem*) of the eyes that it might not be recognized.

8. Omniscience.

XIX. Eighth, against the omniscience we thus argue: that nature cannot be called omniscient which is ignorant of anything, advances in knowledge and is finite. Now such is the nature of Christ, which did not know the day of judgment (Mk. 13:32), progressed in wisdom (Lk. 2:40, 52) and is finite and limited (and on that account irreceptive of the infinite).

9. Omnipotence.

XX. Ninth, against omnipotence. Omnipotence is not communicated to that which recognizes another more powerful than itself, on which falls a certain passive power. The one who is omnipotent, the same is impassible and immortal. Now Christ (according to the human nature) was passive and mortal and had need of the sustentation of the Father (Mt. 26; Jn. 17). Nor ought it to be said that Christ did this according to economy (*kat' oikonomian*) (because he humbled himself), but not from necessity or indigence. Although it is true that the Son of God assumed our nature from economy and not from necessity, yet it is false that the human nature of Christ did not need simply divine help for its conservation.

10. The power of making alive.

XXI. Tenth, against the power of making alive. Whoever has the power of making alive in himself is God because it belongs to God alone to make alive: "With thee is the fountain of life" (Ps. 36:9). And the life of God is nothing else than his very active essence, which cannot be communicated to a created nature. Finally, if human nature had that vivifying power, it cannot be said to be dead because the life of God cannot be extinguished, nor the personal union be dissolved.

Sources of explanation.

XXII. "From the real union of two natures in Christ to a communication of properties between the natures, the consequence does not hold good." The real union of natures does not take away their difference; yea, rather establishes it, since they cannot be said to be actually united (which in union are not distinct). Nor does this imply a real communication of properties with respect to natures, but with respect to the person (which consists of two really united and claims the properties of both for itself).

XXIII. From "the whole Christ to the whole of Christ" or "from the person of Christ to the natures, the argument does not hold good." Nor can what is attributed to the person be at once predicated of the natures because the person indeed claims for itself the properties of both natures, but one nature does not claim for itself the properties of the other, which belong to the person. Otherwise the natures would be confounded. Hence we can easily reply to Mt. 18:20 and 28:20 because they treat of the person in the concrete, not of the human nature in the abstract.

XXIV. "From the assumption of human nature into the unity of person an argument is not well drawn to the formal communication of the hypostasis of the Logos (*Logou*), nor to a communication of attributes in the abstract." The assumption of nature can take place without a communication of hypostasis. A hypostatic sustentation is sufficient that the human nature (which is in itself without subsistence [*anypostatos*]) may be made substantial in the Logos (*enypostatos Logō*) and be sustained by it. Hence indeed it follows that it has no subsistence, nor subsists in the manner proper to a person, since not even in union is it a person; but nevertheless, it subsists (or rather is sustained) in the Logos (*Logō*).

XXV. When "the fulness of the Godhead" is said "to dwell in Christ bodily (*sōmatikōs*)" (Col. 2:9), a communication of attributes in the abstract cannot be inferred. (1) It treats of Christ in the concrete, not of the nature in the abstract. (2) If it referred to the human nature as the temple of the Godhead (Jn. 2:19), nothing could be elicited thence for a communication of attributes. For it is one thing to dwell in the apostolic sense; another to communicate in the Lutheran sense. "To dwell bodily" with the apostle signifies that the whole fulness of the Godhead (i.e., the divine essence with the whole plenitude of its perfections) was united to the human nature; not in a shadowy fashion or by efficacy only or proximity (as in the types of the Old Testament and in believers and in other obscure and imperfect revelations), but truly and personally, just as a body is opposed to its shadow (Col. 2:17) and *sōma* with the Greeks often means "person." But to communicate (in the Lutheran sense) denotes to give and transfuse really into the humanity the whole fulness of the Godhead. It is evident that this cannot be the meaning here because since the fulness of the Godhead is nothing else than the very essence of God with all its attributes, if the fulness of the Godhead was communicated to the flesh, the flesh would be the Godhead itself and all the properties would equally be communicated to it (contrary to their own hypothesis).

XXVI. An indivisible (*adiairetos*) and permanent (*adiastatos*) union does not forthwith demand that wherever one of those united is, there the other must also be (unless when we speak of those things which are mutually equal and of which one does not exceed the other, which cannot be said of the deity and humanity of Christ). Thus what is in that whole (which is everywhere) ought indeed to be everywhere (if it is in the omnipresent whole by equalization or of such a union as exists between things equally infinite); but not where a finite nature is united to an infinity, its own finitude being retained.

XXVII. If the Logos (*Logos*) is anywhere out of the humanity by separation, so that it is separated from it, it can be said with truth that the man would be nowhere. But if it is anywhere out of the humanity by non-inclusion, it cannot be said with propriety that the man is nowhere because the Son of God is a man, not by a local coexistence of the humanity with the deity, but by a hypostatical union of the human nature—made not with a place, but with the Logos (*Logō*). On this account, the Logos (*Logos*) existing on earth is most truly man and has the human nature personally and most intimately united with it, although it is not present on earth. Therefore where the humanity of Christ is not, still there Christ the man may be said to be, inasmuch as the Logos (*Logos*) (there existing) sustains the humanity (although not existing there, but elsewhere).

XXVIII. "The ubiquity of the human nature being denied, a separation or division of the two natures in Christ does not immediately follow." It is one thing for the Logos (*Logon*) to be without the flesh by non-inclusion and in this sense it is conceded because it is not included in it, being infinite. It is another thing to be out of it by separation (which is denied) because although it is not included still it is nowhere separated from the flesh. This proposition—"the Word somewhere is not man"—admits of a twofold sense: it either signifies "the Word has deserted the human nature somewhere" and in this sense it is false because the Word once assumed, never dismissed; or it signifies that the "Word is somewhere where the flesh of the Word is not." And so it is true according to the word of Christ ("me ye will not have always," i.e., according to the humanity). Elsewhere he says, "I will be with you even unto the end of the world" (namely, according to the deity).

XXIX. Although Christ sits at the right hand of God (which is everywhere), it does not follow that Christ according to the flesh is everywhere. (1) The right hand of God is one thing; the sitting at the right hand is another. The first is the omnipotence and majesty of God. The latter, however, is the kingly office of the Mediator. It cannot straightway be said of him who sits at the right hand, whatever is said of the right hand. Otherwise, as the right hand of God is eternal and immense and so he who sits at the right hand ought to be such, even the church itself (which is said to sit at the right hand of her spouse, Ps. 45:9) could claim that for herself. (2) The phrase is not proper, but metaphorical and figurative. It indicates the name of the office proper to the person, not the everywhereness (*pantachousian*) or property of nature (to wit, the empire and domination bestowed upon Christ over the church and the world, as the apostle interprets it—"For he must reign," 1 Cor. 15:25). Now to reign is not of this or that nature, but of the person of the God-man (*theanthrōpou*). (3) Christ is not said to sit everywhere, but in heaven only (Eph. 1:20; Heb. 8:1). For the sake of this, he is said to have ascended into heaven, where the phrase ("in the heavens") is the determination of the place which Christ ascending occupied (Jn. 14:2, 3; 17:13); it is not a signification of heavenly glory, which is sufficiently expressed by the word "sitting."

XXX. Christ is said to have ascended into heaven that he might "fill all things" (Eph. 4:10). He does not fill all places with his body, but the members of the church with the gifts of the Holy Spirit (which sense the antecedents and consequents necessarily demand). In the antecedents (from Ps. 68:18), he shows that the end of the exaltation is the effusion of the gifts of the Holy Spirit (Eph. 4:8). This opinion (illustrated by an antithesis) he immediately repeats (vv. 9, 10 and what he there said, "to give gifts," he calls "to fill all things"). In the following, he declares the exaltation from its effects showing how Christ (being exalted) fills the members of the church (named in its teachers) expressly with his own Spirit.

XXXI. When it is said, "In whom are hid all the treasures of wisdom and knowledge" (Col. 2:3), that does not pertain to the human nature of Christ, but either to the mystery of the gospel by reason of signification (concerning which Paul had treated in the preceding verse) or to Christ himself. It is not so much by reason of the subject or of the wisdom with which Christ was endowed, as with regard to the object because in the acknowledgement of him all saving wisdom consists.

XXXII. The Spirit is said to be given (*ametrōs*) unto Christ "not by measure" (Jn. 3:34); not absolutely, as if the gifts of the Holy Spirit (bestowed upon him according to the prediction, Is. 11:2) were simply immense, as the knowledge and wisdom of God are simply immense. Rather they are given comparatively as to us and all the members of Christ, who from his fulness as their head receive grace for grace (Jn. 1:16). Thus what are disjoined in others (as to this one, one gift is given; to that one, another "according to the measure of the gift of Christ" [*kata to metron tēs dōreas tou Christou*, Eph. 4:7], i.e., which Christ willed to bestow upon us) in him are found conjoined because Christ is all in all (Col. 3:11). What in others are always imperfect, in him are most perfect. Hence he is said to be "anointed with the oil of gladness above his fellows" (Ps. 45:7; Heb. 1:9) because it behooved him to be the "firstborn among many brethren" (*en pasi prōteuein*, Rom. 8:29).

XXXIII. Since the universal judgment is a work of the mediatorial office, it is ascribed to the person according to both natures, not according to one only. Therefore the distinct operations of each nature concur to it, the divine indeed by omniscience and omnipotence, the human by the return to judgment and the sensible and visible acts of judgment described in Mt. 25:31-46. When it is said "And hath given him authority to execute judgment also, because he is the Son of Man" (*hoti hyios anthrōpou*, Jn. 5:27), the particle *hoti* is to be taken not so much reduplicatively (for "inasmuch as") so that Christ not only as God, but also as man may be called a Judge appointed by God (as the apostle has it, Acts 17:31), as causally (by "because") to mark the cause of the bestowment of this authority upon the Son—namely the office of Mediator which he entered through the incarnation. Thus the Son of man denotes here not the human nature in the abstract, but the person in the concrete, relative to his office; nor does it signify anything else than that such a power was given to him because he is the Messiah (who is called by Daniel the "Son of man," 7:13) to whom Daniel saw the empire and power given by the Ancient of Days (since he is that person who was chosen for so great and so sublime a mediatorial work).

XXXIV. Christ does not speak of that which was communicated to the human nature by the Logos (*Logō*) in the personal union (Mt. 28:18), but only shows what was given to him by God, the Father, for the execution of his office, not in the union, but after the resurrection. (2) He does not speak of the power (which is an essential property of God), but of the delegated power (which is a personal function of the Mediator); he does not say *pasa dynamis*, but *pasa exousia*, to denote the right and authority of commanding and judging. Hence he immediately adds, "Go ye therefore and teach." If all power requires omnipotence for its exercise, it is not necessary that he who has all power should forthwith have omnipotence with respect to both natures. It suffices that it belongs to the person as to one nature. (3) He does not say to "the human nature," but "unto me," to designate the person in the concrete, not the nature in the abstract. (4) Although nothing can properly be given to the deity as to essence, still there can be economically, both as to office (that he may undertake and execute it according to the will of the Father) and as to manifestation (that the glory of the deity, which had been concealed in the form of a servant, may now be revealed and become conspicuous to all, Jn. 17:5).

XXXV. He who works miracles by a proper and physical virtue ought to be omnipotent. But Christ as man did not work them by his own power, but after the manner of a moral instrument. Therefore he ought to concur to a miraculous work by contributing what is his own, but the infinite virtue by which properly the miracle was produced belonged to the divinity alone (Mk. 5:30). The miracles are ascribed to Christ in the concrete, not to humanity in the abstract.

XXXVI. The flesh of Christ is said to be vivifying (Jn. 6:48), not efficiently (by producing eternal life by itself), but meritoriously (by acquiring a right to life for us by his death). Again in similes, synecdoche must be acknowledged by which the work properly belonging to the person according to both natures is ascribed to the flesh or to the blood by a synecdoche of the part.

XXXVII. Although to the person denominated from one nature is ascribed what belongs to the one nature, still a false idea would be derived that it is ascribed to the subject, what does not belong to it; for example, suffering and death are ascribed to God—which do not belong to him (Acts 20:28). It is not ascribed to God as the subject of inhesion, but to the person (which is God) as to the subject of denomination (which suffices to remove a false conception).

XXXVIII. The various distinctions brought forward by Lutherans to reconcile the contradictions which occur in their opinion, cannot solve the knot and involve a multiple contradiction. (1) It is of the act of the person and of the nature that the human nature (as to the latter) should be finite, but omnipresent as to the former. (a) But this is to no purpose because the act of a person cannot belong to the nature which is not a person. And if a personal act belonged to the flesh of Christ, it would actually be a person. (b) Personality is not a divine act, but the mode of a thing distinct from its essence and existence. (c) A divine act cannot be ascribed to the human nature (which is not God). (d) That personal act either destroys the act of the nature or not. If the former, the flesh would cease to be flesh because an act of the nature is the nature itself. If not, then the flesh of Christ could always be called infinite and circumscribed within a certain space (which is incompatible [*asystaton*] with its ubiquity).

XXXIX. (2) The reason of a physical and of a hyperphysical (or majestic) mode is the same. (a) A hyperphysical mode does not destroy a nature, but adorns it. But the mode of being everywhere destroys it and on that account is antiphysical. (b) The body of Christ by the union did not lose quantity and so neither its mode nor dimension. (c) If by mode of majesty is meant only that most excellent glory (which the flesh assumed in the hypostasis of the Logos

[*Logou*]), it brings in indeed a prerogative of the flesh above every other creature; but not a communication of divine properties. If, however, a collection of all divine attributes is meant (since that majesty is nothing else than deity), it would follow that the deity itself is communicated to the flesh of Christ.

XL. (3) They are wont to distinguish in Christ a twofold being—local, according to which it is in a certain space; and illocal, according to which it was from the beginning of the incarnation everywhere. But this is done absurdly: (a) since the relation of time is no less connected with the body than the relation of place, there will be granted in Christ a twofold being, a temporal and not-temporal (or eternal) which however they do not maintain. (b) Locality and illocality are contradictories which cannot belong to the same thing; nor do diverse respects assist anything. For since the hypostatical union does not take away the nature of the body, it does not abolish its local being and so cannot give it an illocal being because what leaves one part of the contradiction cannot at the same time ascribe to it the other.

XLI. (4) They distinguish "possession" (*ktēsin*) and "use" (*chrēsin*), "by itself" and "as to another thing" (*kat' allo*). They hold that the deity of Christ is omnipresent by itself, according to possession (*kata ktēsin*) and as to the first and second act at the same time; but the humanity only as to another thing (*kat' allo*) and according to use (*kata chrēsin*). But this is false, (a) because such distinctions take away the subject itself (concerning which we treat). They all tend to this—that omnipresence in some way or other belongs to the body of Christ because it cannot remain a body if it is omnipresent. (b) In earthly things, possession (*ktēsin*) or proprietorship can often be distinguished from the use of a thing, because he who has the *chrēsin* or use of a thing does not always have the ownership. But this is not so in divine things. No other is omnipotent by use than he who is such by ownership (since God does not give his own glory to another). (c) If by "being everywhere as to another thing" (*kat' allo*) is meant only omnipresence with respect to the concrete or person, it will be a true sense, but an unsuitable locution. If, however, it implies the omnipresence given to the flesh in virtue of the union, it is an absurd distinction, involving an incompatibility (*asystata*) that the same subject is at the same time circumscribed and uncircumscribed.

XLII. The examples of the soul (which communicates life to the body) and of fire (which communicates to the heated iron the capability of burning and of shining) do not favor the communication of properties. The life which is produced in the body by the soul is not a property of the soul, but the effect. The power of shining and of burning in the heated iron is not in the iron, but in the fire latent and included in the pores of the iron.

Ninth Question: The Twofold State of Christ

Was Christ the Mediator bound to perform his office under a twofold state? We affirm.

The twofold state of Christ: of humiliation and of exaltation.

I. Thus far we have treated of the person of Christ. Now we must speak of this state in which he ought to fulfill the office committed to him by the Father. This is commonly held to be twofold: the one of emptying and humiliation; the other of exaltation and majesty; of suffering and of glory; of battle and of triumph; of the way and of the goal; of death and of life.

Its truth.

II. The following demonstrate the verity of both. (1) The oracles of the Old Testament in which he is foretold. In Ps. 8 mention is made of his being made a little lower than the angels (which is the emptying) and of a crown of glory and of honor (which is the exaltation). In Ps. 110:7, it is said of the Messiah, "He shall drink of the brook in the way; therefore shall he lift up the head." By the "brook" is denoted the multitude, weight and short continuance of the sufferings of Christ. For waters are everywhere the symbol of calamities (Pss. 69:2, 14, 15; 32:6; Job 21:20; 34:7; Is. 51:17), in opposition to the river of pleasures of which God gives his people to drink in grace and glory (Ps. 36:8*). Also by "drinking of the brook," the communion of sufferings is denoted (which were to be borne by Christ in his journey through this life, which was the way to glory). By "the lifting up of his head," however, is indicated the glory which followed his sufferings by the ordination of God and the necessity of our salvation (Lk. 24:26; Phil. 2:9). Thus "the stone which the builders refused is become the head stone of the corner" (Ps. 118:22), i.e., Christ, who is often compared to a stone and to a foundation (Is. 28:16; 1 Cor. 3:10), contemptuously rejected by the scribes and priests, to whose care was committed the building of the church, as useless and hurtful to the edifice, is constituted by God as the head of the church and as a cornerstone, who unites and sustains both walls, the Jewish and the Gentile. In Is. 53, the twofold state of the Messiah is so graphically painted that Isaiah seems rather an evangelist relating events than a prophet predicting the future. Hence Christ demonstrates from the prophets the verity and necessity of both states (Lk. 24:26, 27); and 1 Pet. 1:10, 11 says the prophets diligently inquired of the sufferings and the glory that should follow. (2) The various passages of the New Testament in which the fulfillment of the oracles is set forth (Phil. 2:7-9; 2 Cor. 13:4; 1 Cor. 15:3*, 4; Heb. 2:9; 1 Pet. 3:18; 1 Tim. 3:16).

Its necessity: (1) on the part of God.

III. Its necessity is evinced on the part of both God and Christ, and on our part, and on the part of the salvation to be bestowed on us. (1) On the part of God because to reconcile God to us and to obtain the fruits of saving grace, two things were to be done: first, satisfaction was to be made to offended justice by the suffering and death of Christ; second, the gifts of grace were to be poured out upon men (which was done in the exaltation, Eph. 4:8).

2. On the part of Christ.

(2) On the part of Christ because he must sustain a twofold relation of surety (to satisfy for us) and of head (to vivify and govern us in union with himself). In respect of the former, he must act for us with God by doing and suffering all that we owed. In respect of the latter, he must act in the name of God towards us that by imparting to us the benefits of the covenant he might draw us into communion with him. His threefold office also demanded this. The priestly consists of two parts: satisfaction on earth; intercession in heaven. As to the kingly, he must first by a struggle acquire for himself a people before he can be carried to the throne and take the reins of government. As a prophet, he must first be a minister of circumcision among his brethren before he can be raised to heaven as the light of the Gentiles and the teacher of the world.

3. On our part.

IV. (3) On our part, we are pressed by two evils brought upon us by sin: guilt in the sight of God and pollution in ourselves. Guilt could not be taken away except by the blood of Christ (which was a ransom [*antilytron*] for our souls); pollution could not be washed away except by the grace of the Spirit, who was the fruit of his exaltation (Jn. 16:7).

4. On the part of salvation.

V. (4) On the part of salvation, two things were required for its fruition: (a) acquisition; (b) application. To the acquisition, a state of humiliation was necessary because it could not be acquired except by death. To the application, however, a state of exaltation was necessary because it could not be applied except through the efficacy of life. In the one, he merited for us a right to life; in the other, he actually confers it upon us. In the first, the righteousness of Christ exerted itself for our reconciliation with God. In the other, the power of Christ exerted itself against the Devil and sin. In both, he accomplished the work which the Father gave him to do.

VI. Although Christ was in a state of humiliation, yet not such a state of humility as to prevent him from emitting many rays of his divine glory for the strengthening (*asphaleian*) of our faith: whether in the miracles he wrought or in the wonderful things which happened to him (such as were seen in his nativity, baptism, transfiguration and death).

VII. If it is asked—According to what nature are humiliation and exaltation to be ascribed to Christ?—we answer that this is properly said of the person and is to be referred to both natures (but with a great difference). To the human nature, indeed, as to real depression and exaltation in itself. To the divine, however, only in respect of concealment and of manifestation, relative to the flesh as a veil (by which it was covered and whence it brought itself forth). Emptying properly belongs to the human nature, inasmuch as he took upon him our weaknesses and suffered and died. Exaltation, however, belongs to it inasmuch as by rising it laid aside all weaknesses and assumed a glory which it had not before. But as to the deity, it was not lessened in the humiliation, nor increased in the exaltation. But emptying is ascribed to it as to concealment and restraining of glory and majesty under the form of a servant. But exaltation is ascribed to it as to manifestation (*kata phanerōsin*) and unfolding when (the veil of the weaknesses of the flesh being removed) that glory which he had from eternity and had been concealed for a time under that veil, shone forth in the person of the Mediator, exalted above all heavens (Jn. 17:5).

VIII. The Son of God is said to have emptied himself (Phil. 2:6, 7) not by an abdication of the deity (for he remained always equal with God, Jn. 5:17, 18), but by a concealment of it under the servile form. He became poor (2 Cor. 8:9), not by a loss of heavenly riches, which he always retained (since the fulness of the Godhead was in him and the treasures of wisdom and knowledge were laid up in him, Col. 2:3, 9), but by a hiding of them under the weak and needy flesh (Mt. 8:20; Eph. 4:9).

TENTH QUESTION: THE BEGINNING OF THE CHRISTIAN ERA
What was the natal year, month and day of Christ?

Dignity of the Christian.

I. Although there are various epochs (both sacred and profane) by which times are wont to be marked, still there is not one which approaches the dignity of the Christian era. The nativity of the Savior is unquestionably the chief of all epochs. To it all preceding times look as their happy and prosperous center and from it all posterior times flow as from a fountain to the end of the ages. "The generation of Christ," says Leo, "is the origin of the Christian people, and the birthday of the head is the birthday of the body, and while we adore the birth of the Savior we are found to celebrate our own beginning" ("On the Feast of the Nativity," 6.2 [NPNF2, 12:137; PL 54.213]).

When it commenced.

II. Now although the excellence and utility of that era is so great, still it is true no less than wonderful that Christians have only lately thought of settling and using it. For before the seventh century, we do not read of the Lord's birthday being applied to the designation of any business either civil or ecclesiastical. Justinian, it is true, who reigned 500 years after Christ, by an edict concerning the notation of times and the documents of public acts wished a fourth mark from the emperors to be added to the ancient designations of times from the building of the city, from the names of consuls, from taxes (*Corpus Iuris Civilis, III: Novellae* 47 [ed. R. Schoell, 1968], pp. 283-85). But he says not a word about a Christian era. Nor with the fathers and the councils held in those early ages is there any mention of it. First Dionysius Exiguus, a Scythian monk or Roman abbot, indignant at his own and former ages that in the Paschal Cycles, which proclaimed the times of the Passover and of festivals, the years were specially designated from the persecution under Diocletian (having expunged this mark of a heathen and most cruel persecutor), substituted the birth of Christ in his private calendar about the time of Justinian (A.D. 532). Having been discovered, this was followed by the Venerable Bede in the seventh century after Christ and by many others (but privately). For neither in any public acts either sacred or civil did the era of Christ begin to be employed before the time of Charlemagne, 800 years after Christ.

III. However after that time Christians may agree in the use of an era drawn from the birth of Christ, still it cannot be said how much both chronologists and theologians disagree with each other in fixing the certain and true beginning of that era. Some refer it to one, others to another year. About this, a twofold question is agitated which must be distinctly examined: (1) concerning the true terminus of the natal year; (2) concerning its month and day.

Various opinions concerning the natal year.

IV. As to the first, it would be tedious to enumerate here all the opinions of chronologists; much more laborious, if not altogether impossible, to reconcile them with each other. In passing, we note only the principal ones. Scaliger, Calvisius and Helvicus refer the natal year of Christ to the year of the world 3947; of the Julian period 4711; of the founding of the city 750; of Nabonassar 745; of Augustus for the assassination of Julius Caesar 41; of the calendar corrected by Julius 43; of the kingdom of Herod 33 and of his life 70 (from the consuls Lucius Cornelius Lentulus and M. Valerius Messalinus). Lansbergius agrees in the years of the city and the Julian and Nabonassar, but adds three to the years of the world, bringing it down to the year 3950. Petavius holds it to be 3979. Salianus (running out still further) extends it to the year of the world 4052. Torniellus subtracts one. Not to mention others (who depart more or less from this)—the vulgar era of Dionysius commences about the year of the world 3949.

Three marks of the natal year given in Scripture.

V. However, as these are rather chronological than theological matters, we think that anxious labor should not be spent upon it. Nor do we believe that it contributes much to the security (*asphaleian*) of our faith to know precisely in what year Christ was born, provided we hold that in his nativity the marks of the time predicted by the prophets truly concur. And thus various involved questions agitated here being dismissed, it suffices now indeed to observe that it is most safe to acquiesce in what the Scripture wished to relate to us on this subject for the confirmation of our faith. It sets before us rather the common marks of the birthday of Christ than the special. These circumscribe indeed in some measure the natal time and nowhere, however, precisely designate the year. Three principal marks are given in the New Testament from which a judgment can be formed of the time of Christ's birth. The first in the notation of the kingdom of Herod, in whose days he is said to have been born: "Jesus was born in Bethlehem, in the days of Herod the king" (Mt. 2:1). The second in the designation of the taxing of the whole world, instituted by Cyrenius, governor of Syria, by a decree of Augustus (Luke 2:1, 2). The third in the concurrence of the fifteenth year of Tiberius and the thirtieth of Christ, when he was baptized (Lk. 3:1, 23). Christ is said to have been about thirty years of age (*hōs etōn triakonta*) after he was baptized by John, to whom the word of God is said to have come in the fifteenth year of Tiberius Caesar. But all these marks are general and indefinite. They indeed teach that Christ was born in the days of Herod and in the time of the taxing first made by Cyrenius, but they neither designate precisely the year of Herod's reign, nor that of the taxing. Two things only are certain and indubitable. First, that Christ was not born either before the sway of Augustus and the reign of Herod, or afterwards. Second, that his nativity fell upon the last times of Herod, since after the death of Herod Christ is said to have returned from Egypt, still as a young child (*paidion*, Mt. 2:20), i.e., in a tender age. Finally, that the death of Herod is immediately subjoined as God-inflicted (*theēlaton*), after the snares laid for Christ and the most cruel massacre of children at Bethlehem.

VI. If it is inquired why the Holy Spirit wished to stop in these more general marks and did not transmit anything more special concerning the natal year (which he could easily have done), the answer is easy. It was unquestionably: (1) that it might be evident that the hinge neither of faith nor of salvation turned upon the exact computation of times. It suffices for us that Christ was truly born at the time designated by the prophet, although the particular notation of the year is not perceived. Now it does not belong to us to define with danger, what can be unknown without danger. (2) He wished also in this way to present more clearly the harmony of both Testaments. For as in the Old Testament, the advent of Christ is designated by the fall of the scepter of Judah and of Jewish independence (*autonomias*) (without a more special and precise designation of it), so his nativity is said to have occurred under the reign of Herod and the empire of Augustus. This eloquently indicates that the scepter had been taken away from Judah and the fulfillment of the times (by which the advent of the Messiah had been circumscribed) had been exhibited.

VII. And although the natal year itself is not precisely designated, it must not therefore be supposed that the fidelity of the gospel history is endangered. The accurate determination of time can be unknown without detriment to truth, when the question—Is it?—is acknowledged by all (as is the case here). For although there is disagreement among divines about the notation of the time, still all confess (even the Jews themselves) that Christ was born at a certain time. A general designation, therefore, made by Scripture can suffice here; nor should we labor much for anything further. It is better here to refrain (*epechein*) and to speak soberly, than to affirm anything rashly.

The question concerning the natal day and month.

VIII. The other question respects the natal month and day, about which there are three principal opinions. The first, which throws it upon the 25th of December (which is the common opinion of the papists and is received also by our men), which the Christian church follows. The other throws it upon the end of September which is the opinion of Scaliger, Calvisius, Beroald and others. But the reasons for neither are demonstrative, only probable, founded for the most part upon conjecture.

The first opinion, which places it upon the 25th of December.

IX. The principal foundation of the first opinion is drawn from Chrysostom on Lk. 1. The conception of both John and Christ happened on the two equinoxes; the nativity, however, on the two solstices. John was conceived on the autumnal equinox and born on the summer solstice (namely in the month of June). Christ however was conceived six months after on the vernal equinox and born in the winter solstice (which was supposed to fall according to the calendar of Eudoxus and Meton on the 25th of December). Now that John was conceived in the month of September in the autumnal equinox, he gathers from this—that the angel Gabriel foretells to Zacharias the conception of John on the tenth day of the seventh month, called Tishri (which answers to our September). This was the day of expiations on which Zacharias (supposed to have been the high priest) entered the holy of holies according to the law and burnt incense before the ark (Lk. 1:9). Having performed this duty, Zacharias went home and Elizabeth conceived in the beginning of October. Six months after (in the beginning of April, Lk. 1:26), Christ was conceived and born in nine months (at the end of December).

X. But it is not difficult to demonstrate that this foundation is rather weak. It rests upon a false hypothesis—that Zacharias was a high priest who must burn incense on the day of expiations. This is rejected by more than one reason from the text itself. For if Zacharias was a high priest, why does Luke say nothing about it, calling him not a high priest (*archierea*), but only "a certain priest" (*hierea tina*) (to wit, of the crowd of priests)? How is he said to have performed his priestly duty in the order of his course (*ephēmerias*) (which belonged to ordinary priests who daily served the altar and after a service of a week departed home), not indeed the office of the high priest, who (attached to no order) could be employed about any sacred duties at any time? Why is he said to have obtained by lot that service (*leitourgian*) of burning incense, when to the high priest alone that solemn ceremony belonged officially without the lot?

XI. Nor is the contrary proved either from the fact that he is said to have entered the temple to burn incense (because to burn incense outside of the veil and the sanctuary belonged to any priests chosen to it by lot, as the altar of incense was placed outside of the veil and the holy place [Ex. 30:6]); or from the fact that the people waited outside of the temple (Lk. 1:21) because it was usual for them to await in the court the return of the priest, since the priest alone was allowed to enter the holy place. Therefore the people (after their usual custom) waited for Zacharias while he performed the sacred duties that fell to him by lot. Nor is the contrary proved from the fact that the angel appeared to him on the right side of the altar of incense. This was not within the veil toward the ark, but outside of the veil at the side of the altar of incense, where the allotted priest burnt incense daily morning and evening.

The second opinion refers it to the autumnal equinox or the end of September.

XII. The second opinion is that of Scaliger, Calvisius and others, who think Christ was born in the autumnal equinox or about the end of the month of September. To prove this Scaliger thinks he can bring a demonstration from "the course" (*ephēmeria*) mentioned in Luke 1:5 (to wit, from the distribution of the families of priests who ought each in his own order by turns to devote himself to the divine service, according to the order established by David [1 Ch. 24:7-18] by which they were distributed into twenty-four classes and by lot thrown by David the first class fell to the family of Jehoiarib, the second to the family of Jedaiah [in which Zacharias was] and the rest to the other families there mentioned). And because in two hundred and twenty-four years, all the courses returned to the same days, by the help of this sacred circle the courses of particular families can be investigated most certainly. However, the calamity of the Babylonian captivity, the idolatry of various kings of Judah and the neglect of divine worship (and so of the priestly orders in the temple) introduced confusion into this order. Judas Maccabaeus (purging the temple from the pollutions of Antiochus) so restored this order of the courses that Josephus testifies they were never interrupted up to the last siege of Jerusalem by Vespasian (cf. JW 6:269-70 [Loeb, 3:454-55]). According to this computation of the heiratic circle, Zacharias (in the eighth class of Abia) entered upon his course on July 21, one hundred and sixty years (and one hundred and ninety-two days) after the dedication festival of Maccabaeus. It was finished on July 28, after which day (Zacharias returning home) Elizabeth could conceive John the Baptist in the beginning of August and was hid (according to Luke) five months. In the commencement of the sixth (to wit, January), after visiting Elizabeth, Mary conceived Christ, who after nine months or in the beginning of October near the autumnal equinox, brought him forth.

XIII. But this demonstration, however subtle and ingenious, does not seem sufficiently solid. It rests upon so many hypotheses, one of which slipping away, the whole edifice falls so that it cannot obtain a ready assent. Here it is specially taken for granted that a restoration of this order was made by Judas Maccabaeus and was never afterwards disturbed nor interrupted. But besides the fact that nothing is said of the restoration of this order (1 Mac. 4), by what argument can we be persuaded that no interruption ever took place afterwards (as Josephus holds) while so many chances could have disturbed this order (ibid.)? For example, if any family had been tainted with legal pollution, if any one of the twenty-four families had perished or was not present and other things of that kind. And whence will it be certainly evident that the families always remained in the same order, since they are not always enumerated in the same degree? Add that it is also supposed (without sure foundation) that Elizabeth conceived at once one or two days after the return of Zacharias, since Luke simply says this happened "after those days" (*meta tautas hēmeras*), which implies a certain latitude of time.

XIV. Besides this demonstration of Scaliger, other arguments are urged to the confirmation of this opinion, but of no greater weight. For instance that Christ ought to be born at the time when the shepherds could live out of doors (*agraulein*) and pass the night in the open air (*dianyktereuein en hypaithrō*); such however was not the time of winter. But this reason seems less strong to Casaubon (*De rebus sacris et . . . exercitationes . . . Baronii*, 2, Anni I, Num. 14 [1614], p. 174) because we are not to form our judgment from France or Germany concerning Judea and other warmer and more southerly countries, especially since in colder and more northerly countries this is also the case (as in England, where there is no fear from wolves or other wild beasts, the flocks are accustomed during the whole year to pass the night in the fields). Why then couldn't the shepherds in Judea (far warmer) live (*agraulein*) in the fields keeping watch over their flocks?

XV. Now although the time of the census instituted by Augustus seems less fit if it is the winter, it does not follow that it ought to be another time. For that time is to be sought from no other source than the will of the emperor, at whose pleasure all things were done. Yea, such subjection to those harsh commands was a part of the Jewish servitude. Nor were the Jews held in such estimation by the Romans that they would consult their advantage or disadvantage.

XVI. It was not necessary for Christ to be born at the same time of the year in which the world was created (namely in the autumn). Nothing hindered the world from being renewed by Christ, even though his nativity occurred at another time. Nor should the promulgation of the gospel Jubilee be made in the same time as the legal. Any year and any season under the Messiah is the acceptable year of the Lord and the day of salvation.

Opinion is withheld.

XVII. The third opinion is that of those who suspend (*epechousi*) their judgment maintaining that the natal month and day of Christ can or ought to be fixed by no one, since the Scripture is silent and we read of nothing being settled concerning it in the first ages of the Christian church. With them we agree, that we may not rashly define what cannot be solidly defined; but may be ignorant of what the Scripture wishes us to be ignorant (which might easily have pointed out that year, month and day, if it had seemed necessary for our consolation and faith). Hence we think that no controversy should be waged over this argument. And as we judge the celebration of the natal anniversary to be most pious and useful, still we think the precise observance of the 25th of December rests rather upon the custom and the long practice of the church than upon any apostolic command or example. He who wishes more may consult

Ussher's Annals (*The Annals of the World* [1658]), Spanheim's Doubts (*Dubia Evangelica* [1639]), Baillie's Chronology (*Operis historici et chronologici* [1668]), and others of our teachers who have treated this argument fully.

ELEVENTH QUESTION: THE CONCEPTION AND NATIVITY OF CHRIST

How was Christ conceived from the Holy Spirit and born of the blessed virgin?

The first degree of Christ's humiliation in the conception.

I. The first degree of Christ's humiliation and emptying is to be sought in his conception and nativity (which are two parts of his incarnation). For although there were not obscure proofs of his glory in both, it is certain that here is opened the great mystery of Christ's emptying—the eternal and most glorious Son of God willed to let himself down even to lay hidden within the recesses of a maternal womb and assume weak and mortal flesh.

II. The conception or *syllēpsis* (Lk. 1:31), called also *gennēsis* (Mt. 1:18), is that by which Christ was invisibly formed in the womb of the blessed virgin, without the concurrence of man, but by the power and overshadowing of the Holy Spirit alone: "That which is conceived in her is of the Holy Ghost" (Mt. 1:20). In this a twofold principle must be remarked: an active—the Holy Spirit; a passive—the blessed virgin.

Its active principle is the Holy Ghost.

III. The active principle was not a man (as in ordinary generation) because the conception should be such as to permit the virginity of the blessed virgin to remain pure and inviolate. It was also one by which Christ should be free from all taint of sin, which is usually propagated and contracted by ordinary generation. But the Holy Spirit alone (Mt. 1:18; Lk. 1:35) not to the exclusion of the other persons of the Trinity, who undividedly concur to this also as to other external works of the same kind; but appropriatively inasmuch as the consummation and fecundation of things is usually ascribed to the Holy Spirit (as those of creation and government are ascribed to the Father, those of redemption and wisdom to the Son). This was done in order that the generation of Christ might answer to our regeneration and have the same cause.

IV. Now the Spirit acts here not materially, but only efficiently; by power (*dēmiourgikōs*); not by seed (*spermatikōs*); by might (*kat' exousia*); not by intercourse (*kata synousian*), so that he was conceived from the power of the Spirit, not from the substance of the Spirit; not by generation, but by blessing and consecration (as the ancients express it). Thus the preposition *ek* marks the efficient cause, as often elsewhere when "all things are said to be from God" (Rom. 11:36) and the pious are said to be "born of God" (*ek tou Theou*, 1 Jn. 3:9), not indeed the material cause (as when it is ascribed to the virgin of whom he is said to have been born).

He, however, can not be called the father of Christ.

V. And hence we can readily answer the question asked here by Socinians—Can the Holy Spirit be rightly called the father of Christ since he is said to have been conceived from him? For since the title of father requires generation from the substance of the generator (and the generation of a nature similar to its own) and neither occurs here, it is clear that the Holy Spirit cannot be called the father of Christ. Besides, Christ is called "without father" (*apatōr*, Heb. 7:3) in respect of his humanity; and God is called Father—his Father alone and that peculiarly (Jn. 1:18; 5:17). A father does not proceed from, nor is he sent and given by the son, as the Spirit is said to proceed from, to be sent and given by Christ. Now it is one thing to form by his own power something from matter assumed from some other source; another to generate from his own substance. The Holy Spirit did the former, but not the latter (which belongs to a father).

VI. With no better success do the Socinians maintain (in order to destroy the divinity of Christ) that he is only called the Son of God on account of his extraordinary conception by the Holy Spirit. (1) As has been proved, he was the Son of God already before his conception by the Holy Spirit (Jn. 1:1, 2; Ps. 2:7; Prov. 8:24) and on account of this very thing the believers of the Old Testament were actually sons and heirs. (2) He is called the Son of God according to the divine nature, opposed to the human (Rom. 1:3, 4; 9:5; 1 Pet. 3:18). (3) As he is called the Son of man because he is begotten from man of the race of Adam, so he ought to be called the Son of God, not because he was conceived of the Holy Spirit in respect of his humanity, but because he was begotten of God in respect of his divinity. Otherwise the perpetual and immediate antithesis which occurs between these two names could not stand.

VII. Nor can this be evinced from Luke 1:35, "The Holy Ghost shall come upon thee" *dio kai* "therefore also that holy thing which shall be born of thee, shall be called the Son of God." The particles *dio* and *kai* are not marks of a consequent, as if he is the Son of God because he is begotten of the Holy Ghost. For before he was conceived, he is said to have already been and subsisted (Jn. 1:2; Phil. 2:6). Rather they are marks of a consequence, in respect of manifestation because his eternal filiation was declared *a posteriori*. Here pertain the following arguments: (1) it is not said "he will be" (*estai*), but "he shall be called" (*klēthēsetai*) (i.e., manifested and acknowledged to be the only begotten Son of God [Jn. 1:18], as in John 1:14 "We beheld his glory, as of the only begotten"). (2) It is not expressed in the masculine gender (*ho gennōmenos*) but in the neuter (*to gennōmenon*) to indicate not that the man who shall be born shall be called "the Son of God," but thus separately shall something essential in Christ be called (namely, his divine nature or person). This is well denoted by the neuter gender as a subsistence (*hyphistamenon*).

VIII. If believers are called Sons of God on account of the grace of regeneration, it does not follow that Christ was distinguished by name on account of his miraculous conception. There is one reason for believers who analogically (only on account of a participation of moral virtues) are said to be born of God; another for the only begotten Son of God, who was begotten of his essence and is said to be equal to him in all things.

IX. Moreover that operation of the Holy Spirit on the virgin is expressed by two words in Scripture—*epeleusin* and *episkiasin*. "The Holy Ghost shall come upon thee, and the power of the Highest shall overshadow thee" (*epeleusetai epi se, kai dynamis hypistou episkiasei soi*, Lk. 1:35), by which that wonderful and most powerful efficacy, working the mystery, is designated. By *epeleusin* is denoted the presence of the Holy Spirit and his action in general; not the common and ordinary exerted in the conception of all (Job 10:8; Ps. 139:15), but the extraordinary and heavenly (as the Spirit of the Lord is said to come to the help of those who are appointed to a great and extraordinary work [Jdg. 14:6]; and the Spirit came upon the apostles when he was sent from heaven in the form of tongues of fire to sanctify and prepare them for the work of the gospel [Acts 1:8]). By *episkiasin* is peculiarly meant the mode of that operation, which was: (1) most powerful for protection and defense (that the blessed virgin might not be consumed by the divine majesty); (2) most efficacious for fecundation that she might conceive in her womb without any help from man (as a bird is said to cover, cherish and set upon her eggs that by her heat the young may be hatched—in allusion to the creation, in which the Spirit is said to have brooded over the waters, Gen. 1:2; thus this fetus (it may be said) will spring from that virtue from which the world took its beginning; (3) secret and incomprehensible, which can neither be tracked by the reason, nor expressed in words. To this there is a reference in the shadow of the cloud upon the tabernacle (Ex. 40:34*, 35) and in the cherubim covering the ark (2 Ch. 5:8). Thus God wished to bring over a shadow, the mark of a secret and incomprehensible energy (*energeias*), that we might not too curiously pry into the mode of this mystery. So the angel aptly responds to the blessed virgin, who looked upon the matter as impossible because she had not known a man. This should not seem wonderful to her, since it was not to be by human aid, but by the power of God (to whom nothing is impossible) and in a manner wholly strange (which it was becoming in her to admire, not search into).

X. Now there were here two principal operations of the Holy Spirit: (1) the preparation of the material; (2) the formation of the body of Christ from the material prepared. First, he should by a suitable sanctification prepare the material separated from the substance of the virgin, not only by clothing it with that power and elevating it to that activity which would suffice for generation (without the semen of a man), but also by purging it from all taint of sin that it might be without guile (*akakos*) and pure (*amiantos*) and thus Christ might be born without sin. Thus there is no necessity to have recourse to the immaculate conception of Mary. For although there is no creature of whatever power possessed who can bring a clean thing out of an unclean (Job 14:4), still the power of God is not thus to be measured (with whom nothing is impossible and who calls those things which are not).

XI. The second operation was in the formation of Christ's body, to which pertains its organization, animation and the union of both body and soul with the Word. This the apostle expresses by *katartismon:* "a body hast thou prepared me" (*sōma katērtisō moi*, Heb. 10:5). For by the incarnation, the body of Christ was so formed and prepared by the Holy Spirit that in it he might perform a servile ministry, obey the Father and be sacrificed.

Was the body of Christ formed in a moment or successively?

XII. If it is inquired (as by the Scholastics), How was this accomplished by the Holy Spirit? In a moment or successively? it can be distinctly answered that three things occur here: (1) the preparation of the material from which Christ's body was formed; (2) the formation of the body from that material suitably prepared; (3) the perfection of the same body brought little by little to a just quantity by its own increase. As to the first and third, all agree that it was performed successively. But as to the second, which concerns the formation of the body, theologians dispute with each other, some advocating a momentaneous, others a successive formation (with whom we also agree).

XIII. (1) Momentaneous formation of the entire body of Christ and its conjunction with the soul is feigned without Scripture (in which no trace is found of such a miraculous formation). Yea, spaces of time are expressly mentioned in this affair and the acts of conception, generation and birth are distinctly enumerated, and the ordinary time is ascribed to them (Lk. 1:26, 38, 56, 57; 2:6). (2) Christ, in assuming the human nature, is said to have been made like unto us, not even infirmities excepted (but sin alone). Therefore it ought to be formed not in a moment, but according to the ordinary way, little by little. (3) Outside of the womb, it grew like other bodies; therefore there should be no difference as to its formation in the womb (as even the gestation was the successive and ordinary one of nine months, which would have been to no purpose if it had been formed and perfected in a moment). For if Christ's body was perfected in a moment, it could equally be born in the same moment; nor would the blessed virgin have had to endure the pains and labors of ordinary gestation.

XIV. It must not be thought that this dogma advances anything unworthy of the Holy Spirit. Although he could without delay and in a single moment have formed completely the body of Christ, still nothing hinders his having operated here successively (as he usually proceeds from imperfect to perfect in the works of nature and of grace). Nor is it of importance to inquire curiously at what time the soul was united to the body, the Logos (*Logos*) to the flesh. It is enough for us to believe that the human nature from the time it began to be never existed apart from the Logos (*Logō*), but was assumed by and hypostatically united to him. And if the soul could not be poured into the body unless already organized and completely formed (a point on which physicians are not agreed among themselves), it does not follow that the Logos (*Logon*) could not at once unite the flesh to himself, since his work could not be constrained either with the soul present or absent. Nor is it more absurd for the body of Christ (not as yet animated) to be united to the Logos (*Logō*), than for the same (when lifeless in the sepulcher) to remain conjoined with the same (as theologians acknowledge was done in the death of Christ).

XV. From this miraculous conception of Christ by the Holy Ghost arises the absolute holiness of Christ and his exemption from all sin, both imputed and inherent. Nor is it an obstacle that he is called the son of Adam (Lk. 3:38) in whom all are said to die (1 Cor. 15:22). The communion of sin pertains only to Adam's natural posterity, who were to spring from him in the ordinary way; not to him who descended from him in a manner evidently extraordinary. And as the grace of the holy conception preserved him from a participation of pollution, why should it not have exempted him from the guilt (which is wont to be imputed to his natural heirs alone according to God's ordering)? And if Christ could be in the loins of Abraham with Levi and yet not tithed with him, what is to prevent his having been in Adam and yet not having sinned with him and in him?

The nativity of Christ was ordinary.

XVI. The nativity from the blessed virgin follows after the conception of Christ, which took place in the time of parturition fixed and defined by nature. This parturition, although it was miraculous because of a virgin, still may well be called natural because she labored in the manner usual with mothers. Hence she cannot be said to have brought forth without pain. For since she was not without sin, she ought to endure the punishment of sin also in this particular and primeval lot of mothers: "In sorrow thou shalt bring forth children" (Gen. 3:16) and "A woman when she is in travail hath sorrow" (Jn. 16:21); even less (with the papists who derive thence the penetrating of bodies) ought it to be affirmed that Mary brought forth with a closed womb. The Scripture expressly states the contrary (Lk. 2:22, 23, when it applies to Christ the passage "Every male that openeth the womb," Ex. 13:2) and also the nature of the thing itself (not allowing of this penetration and the existence of two bodies in one place). Nor moreover is the virginity of Mary called into doubt. It did not consist in this—that Christ was born from a closed womb—but that she was a virgin untouched by man.

XVII. The passage concerning "the shut gate" (Ezk. 44:2), through which none could enter except the prince, is falsely adduced here. Besides being allegorical and on that account not argumentative (as our opponents confess), it is foreign to the subject discussed here. For the building shown to the prophet was not a type of the blessed virgin, but a type of the universal church. The gate of heaven (closed on account of sin) lies open to the church and is unbarred by Christ, its High Priest and Prince.

XVIII. From this nativity, Christ is well called the son of Mary, as from the eternal generation he is styled the Son of God. Nor did that twofold filiation in Christ (one with respect to the Father in heaven, the other with respect to his mother on earth) constitute a twofold son, but a single person to whom that twofold relation comes (since one and the same subject is receptive of many relations).

XIX. Here two questions are specially asked: (1) Why must Christ be born of a virgin? (2) As she was a virgin before and in parturition, was she a virgin afterwards? To the first it is replied in general that this was necessary for the fulfillment of the ancient oracles which expressly predicted it (Is. 7:14) and which on that account usually described the Messiah by the seed of the woman and the fruit of the womb. But in particular, various reasons are wont to be assigned for that dispensation. (a) A new mode of generation was suitable for a new man and an extraordinary person demanded an extraordinary birth. Before, the first man had been created immediately by God; afterwards, Eve had been drawn from a man without a woman. After that, all men are ordinarily born of a man and woman. A fourth mode remained for displaying the admirable wisdom of God in the production of men—that a man should be born of a woman without a man (which was fulfilled in Christ alone). To this, some refer the passage: "The Lord hath created a new thing in the earth, A woman shall compass a man" (Jer. 31:22, viz., in her womb). (b) He wanted him to be born of a woman like other men to prove that he was a true man. He was unwilling that he should be of the semen of a man "that we might believe he was also something other than a man," as Ambrose expresses it (*de Sacr. Incarn.*+)—the former pertained to our necessity; the latter to his dignity. (c) It was not becoming that the same son should have two fathers, but as he acknowledged no mother in heaven (as the Son of God), so he should acknowledge no father on earth (as the Son of man) and thus might truly be without father (*apatōr*) and without mother (*amētōr*). (d) If he had been conceived from the semen of a man, he could not be said to have been conceived of the Holy Spirit and would be a natural son of Adam and thus the inheritor of all his evils. Therefore, in order that it might be evident that he had nothing in common with sin (which is derived to us by ordinary generation), he ought to be born in an extraordinary manner.

XX. If indeed you ask with the virgin—"How could this be?"—the reply of the angel ought to be sufficient for us—"With God nothing shall be impossible" (Lk. 1:37). "If a reason is asked," says Augustine, "it will not be astonishing; if an example is demanded, it will not be singular. Let us grant that God can do something which we confess our inability to investigate; in such things the whole reason of the deed is the power of the doer" (*Letter 137*, "To Volusian" 2.8 [FC 20:24; PL 33.519]). Nor ought this to seem absurd either to the Jews or the Greeks, since among themselves various things no less absurd and impossible to reason are proposed. Cyril of Jerusalem follows these up excellently (*Catechetical Lectures* 12 (NPNF2, 7:72-81).

Was Mary always a virgin before as well as after parturition?

XXI. As to the second question, about the virginity of Mary, the question does not concern the time of or the time antecedent to the birth. For all Christians agree that she was a virgin before and in the birth. But we treat of the time following the birth—whether she always remained a virgin afterwards. This is not expressly declared in Scripture, but yet is piously believed with human faith from the consent of the ancient church. Thus it is probable that the womb in which our Savior received the auspices of life (whence he entered into this world, as from a temple) was so consecrated and sanctified by so great a guest that she always remained untouched by man; nor did Joseph ever cohabit with her.

XXII. Hence Helvidius and the Antidicomarianites (so called because they were opponents [*antidikoi*] of Mary) are deservedly rebuked by the fathers for denying that Mary was always a virgin (*aei parthenon*). They held that she cohabited with Joseph after delivery; yea, also bore children from him. As Augustine remarks, they rely upon the shallowest arguments, i.e., because Christ is called the "firstborn" of Mary (cf. *De Haeresibus* 56, 84 [PL 42.40, 46]). For as Jerome well remarks, she was so called because no one was begotten before him, not because there was another after him. Hence among lawyers: "He is the first whom no one precedes; he is last, whom no one follows." The Hebrews were accustomed to call the firstborn also only begotten; Israel is called "the firstborn of God" (Ex. 4:22), although the only people chosen of God. Thus "the firstborn" is said to be "holy unto God" (Ex. 13:2), who first opened the womb, whether others followed or not. Otherwise the firstborn would not have to be redeemed until after another offspring had been procreated (the law shows this to be false because it commands it to be redeemed a month after birth, Num. 18:16).

XXIII. (2) Not more solidly have they been able to elicit this from the fact that in the New Testament certain ones are called "the brothers of Christ." It is common in Scripture not only for one's own and full brothers by nature to be designated by this name, but also blood relatives and cousins (as Abraham and Lot, Jacob and Laban). Thus James and Joses, Simon and Judas are called brothers of Christ (Mt. 13:55) by a relation of blood. For Mary (who is called their mother by Matthew and Mark) is called by John the sister of the Lord's mother. However what is said in Jn. 7:5 that "neither did his brethren believe in him" must be understood of more remote blood relations.

XXIV. (3) Nor is it derived better from this—that Joseph is said "not to have known Mary till she had brought forth her firstborn son" (Mt. 1:25). The particles "till" and "even unto" are often referred only to the past, not to the future (i.e., they so connote the preceding time, concerning which there might be a doubt or which it was of the highest importance to know, as not to have a reference to the future—cf. Gen. 28:15; Pss. 122:2; 110:1; Mt. 28:20, etc.). Thus is shown what was done by Joseph before the nativity of Christ (to wit, that he abstained from her); but it does not imply that he lived with her in any other way postpartum. When therefore she is said to have been found with child "before they came together" (*prin ē synelthein autous*), preceding copulation is denied, but not a subsequent affirmed.

XXV. Although copulation had not taken place in that marriage, it did not cease to be true and ratified (although unconsummated) for not intercourse, but consent makes marriage. Therefore it was perfect as to form (to wit, undivided conjunction of life and unviolated faith), but not as to end (to wit, the procreation of children, although it was not deficient as to the raising of the offspring).

XXVI. However, although her virginity may piously be believed to have been perpetual, still a vow of virginity is falsely ascribed to her by the papists. For she could neither promise at the same time virginity to God and marriage to Joseph nor vow childlessness (*ateknian*) as a thing pleasing to God (which she knew was both cursed in the law [Dt. 7:14] and at variance with the custom of her nation and mentioned with an opprobious epithet by her cousin Elizabeth [Lk. 1:25]). Again, she could have vowed it neither before, nor after her espousal. Not before, for if she had taken such a vow, why then did she marry (since otherwise she could the more safely keep her virginity)? And with what conscience could she abuse the name of marriage to deceive Joseph and by suffering herself to be joined to a husband have despised the sacred covenant of wedlock without trifling with God? Not afterwards, because the vow would have been worthless without the consent of her husband (which can be proved by no argument).

XXVII. Nor do the words of Mary establish such a vow ("How shall this be, seeing I know not a man?," Lk. 1:34) as if she would indicate her moral inability from a vow, not her natural ability ("I know not," i.e., I am not accustomed to know, nor can I); indeed, not nature, nor the law prohibiting, but the vow (as Maldonatus holds, *Commentaria in quatuor evangelistas* [1863], 2:44 on Lk. 1:34). These words are falsely wrested to a vow of which there is not the slightest trace. They are only those of one wondering on account of the novelty and greatness of the thing and inquiring about the mode. For it could not but be wonderful to a virgin that immediate conception and birth should be foretold, no mention being made of the consummation of marriage or of her spouse Joseph, just as if they were already married (while she herself was conscious of her virginity and knew as yet no husband).

XXVIII. If it is further inquired why Christ wished to be born not only from a virgin, but of a virgin espoused, various reasons are adduced by the fathers with respect to Christ himself, to his mother and to us. With respect to Christ, that no one might think him illegitimate and born in adultery, that his genealogy might be known in the usual manner from the man Joseph (who was supposed to be his father) and of which parents he was born; finally, that he might have Joseph as his protector and guardian in infancy. With respect to his mother, that her reputation and safety might be consulted, lest she should be considered an adulteress and according to the law be stoned to death, and that she might have a man to care for, defend and protect her. With respect to us, that our belief concerning the birth of Christ from a virgin might be the more confirmed, when Joseph also himself testified it of his own wife.

TWELFTH QUESTION: THE GRACES AND GIFTS BESTOWED ON CHRIST

What graces were bestowed on the human nature of Christ? And did he have faith and hope? We affirm.

Statement of the question.

I. The question does not concern the eternal grace which is in God (to wit, the love and benevolence with which he embraced Christ and will embrace him forever; in which sense Christ is called the beloved [*agapētos*] Son in whom the Father is well pleased, Mt. 3:17). Nor does the question concern the grace of union by which humanity was assumed by the Logos (*Logō*) into union with his person. Rather the question concerns habitual graces or the gifts and perfections bestowed upon the human nature, in virtue of the hypostatical union.

Proof that graces were bestowed on Christ truly and fully.

II. That such graces were truly and most fully bestowed on Christ, Scripture teaches in many passages: as in Is. 11:2 where it is said, "The Spirit of wisdom and understanding shall rest upon him." And to this end, he is often called just, holy, innocent: Is. 53:11; Lk. 1:35; Acts 3:14; Heb. 7:26. Here belong the passages in which he is said to be anointed with the Holy Ghost and with power (Acts 10:38), anointed with the oil of gladness (Ps. 45:7), which can pertain only to the gifts of the Spirit, wonderfully rejoicing his soul. The plenitude of these is also designated when Christ is said to be "full of grace and truth" (Jn. 1:14) and to have received the Spirit without measure (*ametrōs*, Jn. 3:34).

III. Still it must not be supposed that this plenitude is simply infinite, both because the humanity is finite in itself and cannot be receptive of the infinite and because this grace is a created thing (to which therefore it is repugnant to be infinite). But it must be understood relatively: (1) in respect of the graces which are communicated either to angels or to men, than which the graces of Christ are far greater. In others there is a "fulness of sufficiency," inasmuch as they obtain from God as much grace as suffices for their salvation. But in Christ it is a "fulness of abundance," which suffices not only for himself but for others also, so that we all can drink of his fulness (Jn. 1:16). (2) In respect of degrees, because the graces of Christ had all degrees—whatever can be possessed from the law of God (beyond which there can be nothing) or to which nothing among men can be found equal numerically or internally. Nor is it an objection that there is no finite thing which cannot be said to be made equal to another. This indeed holds good in those things which are of the same kind and relation. The grace of Christ is not such in respect of the graces of other creatures because his was universal, but these are particular.

IV. These gifts of the Holy Spirit in their fulness, whether extensive (as to parts and species) or intensive (as to degrees) are enumerated by Is. 11:1, 2: wisdom, understanding, counsel, might, knowledge, fear. To these the Scholastics add (from the Vulgate, but without foundation and necessity), piety, which is already included in the fear of God. In this number, all are not contained, since elsewhere mention is made of other gifts; but the principal ones are pointed out which were specially required for the administration of the office imposed upon Christ. Nor is the Spirit with his gifts said to be only conferred upon Christ, but "will rest upon him." By this is denoted not only a true and real communication, but also a continuance and permanence of the gifts, since Christ possesses them not as an act and as a certain transient or perishable movement, but as permanent and fixed (which he most freely used as often and in whatever measure he pleased).

Did Christ have faith and hope?

V. A question is plied here by the Scholastics—whether Christ had faith and hope. And not a few of them, and especially Feuardentius (*Calvinismus exorcizatus sive Theomachia* 8 [1563], pp. 327-425), write to Calvin that he ascribes faith to Christ. This Feuardentius calls an impious error and contrary to Scripture. But that faith is not simply to be denied to Christ, the Scripture in more than one place shows when it calls Christ faithful (Heb. 2:17; 3:2). Peter applies to Christ the words of Ps. 16—"My flesh shall rest in hope" (Acts 2:26). Christ, calling the Father his God (Mt. 27:46), testifies to his faith in him. But it cannot belong to him in all that formality in which it belongs to men, since in that manner it involves imperfection.

And how?

VI. Faith, therefore, is ascribed to Christ, not inasmuch as it is a fiducial apprehension of the mercy of God. In this sense, it belongs to sinners only; nor is it ascribed in respect of mode of knowledge, as much as it is opposed to the obscurity of an enigma (inasmuch as it is opposed to sight [*eidei*, 2 Cor. 5:7], which cannot be done without imperfection, from which Christ is free). Rather it is ascribed to Christ as to substance of knowledge and assent to a thing known (i.e., to the doctrine revealed of God) and as to trust, which rests in the goodness of God providing all things necessary for us.

VII. The same must be said about hope. Whatever perfection is in it as to certainty (by which we firmly rest upon the divine promise concerning a future thing) is rightly ascribed to Christ; but what involves a defect and imperfection (inasmuch as it is a still obscure expectation of a thing not yet possessed, Rom. 8:24) ought not to be ascribed to him.

VIII. Although the soul of Christ even from the beginning rejoiced in happiness and enjoyed God himself in virtue of the hypostatical union, still he had not as yet its fulness (on account of the necessity of suffering). Rather he should at length obtain it after his resurrection and ascension when (being made an attainer) he was fully glorified both as to soul and body. Thus nothing hindered him from believing in God and hoping for the glory promised to him (Heb. 12:2).

Thirteenth Question: The Knowledge of Christ's Soul

From its very creation was the soul of Christ so filled with knowledge that it could be ignorant of or learn nothing? We deny against the papists.

I. The Scholastics distribute the knowledge of Christ into three principal species—blessed, infused and acquired—according to the threefold light of glory, grace and nature. They term that blessed by which Christ sees God according to essence, as the saints behold his face in heaven. To them, infused is that by which (by a supernatural habit) he knows heavenly things and whatever can be seen through the light of grace. Acquired is that by which he understands whatever can be known by the light of nature or of reason. But less rightly because beatific knowledge (which belongs to those who have attained) cannot fitly be ascribed to Christ while still sojourning upon earth, as will be seen hereafter. Therefore we acknowledge a twofold knowledge of Christ's human nature while on earth—infused and acquired or experimental. He received the infused by the grace of the Holy Spirit sanctifying his gifts (referred to in Is. 11:1, 2). The acquired is the actual knowledge which Christ gained both by ratiocination, by drawing conclusions from the principles of infused knowledge, and by his own experience (Heb. 4:15; 5:8).

Statement of the question.

II. We dispute here with the papists concerning the nature and extent of this knowledge: not concerning the knowledge of Christ glorified, but living on earth; not whether omniscience was given to him through the grace of the union (which we have refuted before); not whether he labored under a gross ignorance of many things (which is calumniously charged against us by our opponents) because thus he could not be freed from sin, not the least shadow of which do we acknowledge to have been in him.

III. But the question returns to this—Was the soul of Christ from the beginning imbued with so great knowledge in virtue of the hypostatical union that he was ignorant of nothing or could learn nothing *de novo*? This the papists affirm. "The common opinion of Catholics always was that Christ's soul from its very creation was filled with knowledge and grace, so that he learned afterwards nothing which he did not know before" (Bellarmine, "De Christi Anima," 1.1* *Opera* [1856], 1:266). However, we deny it. We acknowledge that Christ as God was indeed omniscient, but as man we hold that he was endowed with knowledge, great indeed beyond all other creatures, but yet finite and created, to which something could be added (and really was added).

The orthodox opinion is proved: (1) from Lk. 2:52.

IV. The reasons are: (1) Christ is said to have "increased in wisdom and stature" (Lk. 2:52). Now where perfection is, there is no increase. Nor can it be said that he increased only in the opinion of men (as Bellarmine holds, "De Christi Anima," 5 *Opera* [1856], 1:269) because more and more every day he disclosed his wisdom. As he truly increased in years and as to stature, so also with an increase of gifts as to knowledge, as Toletus clearly proves. Hence Ambrose says, "As he grew in the age of a man, so he grew in the wisdom of a man" (*The Sacrament of the Incarnation of Our Lord* 7 [72] [FC 44:247; PL 16.872]). Stapleton acknowledges the same on this place ("Antidota . . . in Lucae Cap. II," *Opera* [1620], 3:157 on Lk. 2:52). It is confirmed by this—that he is not said only to have increased with men, but also "with God" (which cannot be referred to a mere opinion, but carries with it the truth of the thing).

2. From Mark 13:32.

V. (2) Because "the Son" is said "not to know the day of judgment" (Mk. 13:32). Not by any means (as the Logos [*Logos*] or Son of God) could he be ignorant of the day, which he himself had predetermined with the Father (Acts 17:31); nor (as he made time) could he be ignorant either of its beginning or of its end; but as man and with respect to his human nature only (as the ancients in this way freed themselves from the objection of the Arians drawn from this against the divinity of the Son). Nor only because he did not know it to tell others (as Bellarmine, Becanus, Tirinus and others wish). This savors of Jesuistical equivocation. For who (without being guilty of falsehood) can absolutely deny that he knows what he does know because he was bound not to reveal it to others? Again, in this sense there would be scarcely anything which Christ might not be said not to know because he does not reveal his mysteries to the Gentiles and the Turks. Yea, the Father himself might be said to be ignorant of the day of judgment, since he reveals it to no one. Nor only because he knew indeed theoretically, but not practically and according to experience. Neither did the Father himself know it in this way since it had not yet arrived. But simply because the Word had not revealed this to him. And, moreover, Christ wished in this way to restrain the curiosity of his disciples that they should not dare to penetrate beyond what they ought, or weave anxious questions concerning the time of that judgment, since the members ought not to strive after that knowledge which was not granted even to the head, according to his humanity. Nor on this account are two Christs to be maintained, one of whom knew while the other was ignorant of the day of judgment, but only two natures in the one Christ, which as they are joined in union with the person, so also they retain their properties unconfounded (as many things are said of the whole Christ or person which do not pertain to the whole of Christ or to both natures, but only to one or the other of them). Therefore these propositions can be true at the same time, but in different respects (*kat' allo, kai allo*): Christ was ignorant of the day of judgment and Christ was not ignorant of the day of judgment. The opposition is made between natures most intimately connected, one of which is not included in the connception of the other. But it is different with propositions which are made concerning things differing not by a real, but only a formal distinction and which are such that the one is subordinated to and included in the other. Hence it cannot with propriety be said that a man is ignorant of something as to his animal being which he knows according to his rational being (because the rational is included in the animal).

3. From Heb. 2:17.

VI. (3) Because he was made "like unto us in all things" (Heb. 2:17) "sin excepted" (4:15). Nor can the ignorance which we ascribe to Christ form an exception here. Although ignorance of a depraved disposition and universal of things which it is necessary to know is properly reckoned among vices (from which Christ was free), still not the negative and particular of a certain thing unnecessary for that state and time. The words of Athanasius refer to this: "As a man he did not know, for ignorance is proper to men" (*hōs anthrōpos ouk oiden, anthrōpōn gar idion to agnoein*," "Contra Arianos, Oratio quarta," *Opera omnia* [1627], 1:496).

Sources of explanation.

VII. If Christ is said to know all things (Jn. 21:17; Mt. 11:27), it either pertains to his divine knowledge or, if extended to the human, ought not to be understood absolutely. Otherwise omniscience would have to be ascribed to his human nature (which our opponents do not hold). Rather it ought to be understood only relatively and comparatively with respect to the knowledge of men, than which it was far more perfect.

VIII. "The treasures of wisdom and knowledge" which are said "to be hid in Christ" (Col. 2:3) do not prove that there was in him all manner of knowledge in every time, always and absolutely; but that there was all that knowledge which could belong to the design of his mediatorial office, which was altogether superior to the knowledge of men and angels. In addition (as has been seen elsewhere), this can be referred best either to the person of Christ or to the gospel, concerning which he had just spoken.

IX. Christ, as the Son of God, had a right to all paternal goods from the incarnation itself, but he could be without a possession of some for a time by a voluntary dispensation. He should indeed be filled with all the gifts necessary to the performance of his mediatorial work; but in their own order and degree according to the economy of the divine will. The anointing was indeed made from the very moment of conception, but the acts of this anointing were dispensed through intervals of time, as also through various objects (as the divine nature in Christ at first repressed in some measure his majesty and as it were concealed it under the veil of the flesh, which afterwards broke forth more clearly in his exaltation). Thus the Spirit of wisdom (with which he was anointed) restrained its own acts and did not at once pour forth its rays in all their fulness upon the intellect of Christ. Hence although he had a most full (yes, an infinite) knowledge, still he did not communicate the whole of it to the man Christ.

X. A thing can conduce to the end of the incarnation in two ways, either mediately in a common manner or immediately in a singular manner. Although the ignorance of Christ was negative, it cannot be said to have been useful to the end of the incarnation singularly and immediately (as his death and resurrection was necessary). It is enough that it was such mediately and in a common manner that Christ might declare himself to be truly a partaker of our nature with its guiltless (*adiablētois*) infirmities, since this ignorance is a condition annexed to our animal nature.

XI. Our opinion is falsely compared with the heresy of the Agnoetae. There is nothing common to us and them, who ascribed ignorance to the Word or to Christ as he is God (cf. Alphonsus de Castro, *Adversus omnes haereses*, Bk. 5, Haer. 8 [1556], pp. 151-52 and Isidore, *Etymologiarum* 8.5.68 [PL 82.304]). Hence Nicephorus teaches that they were the shoot of Arianism (*Ecclesiasticae Historiae* 12.30 [PG 146.839-46]).

Was Christ at the same time a traveller and an attainer? The negative proved.

XII. Hence it can clearly be gathered what we must decide about the other question here urged by the papists—Was Christ at the same time a traveller and an attainer? This they maintain the more easily to deny that spiritual sufferings were felt by the soul of Christ. However, we deny it. These states are so opposed as to be incompatible (*asystatoi*) with each other. A traveller is on the road; an attainer is at the goal. The traveller labors and suffers; the attainer enjoys perfect happiness after his toils are finished. Since therefore he was here on the road to run the race set before him (in order to accomplish the work of our redemption, in which he was exposed to various trials and struggles; yea, sustained both the curse and the weight of the wrath of God), he could not at that time enjoy the benefit of an attainer in the most full happiness of human nature. This he obtained only by his exaltation, although he was always endowed with most perfect holiness without any taint of sin.

no beatific vision because he "runs the race set before him"

XIII. The happiness of those who have attained is a glorious and joyous state, free from pain and shame. The whole history of the life, suffering and death of Christ exclaims that such a glorious (Phil. 2:7, 8), happy state (Mt. 20:28; Lk. 9:58), free from pain or shame (Mt. 26:39; 27:31) did not belong to Christ on earth, but that it became his only after his death and departure from this world (Lk. 24:26; Phil. 2:8, 9).

Sources of explanation.

XIV. Because he is united most intimately with God, he ought to be on all sides and and in every way perfect with respect to holiness so that no taint of sin should be found in him. But not as to happiness, which can be evident even from the example of the body of Christ united with the Logos (*Logō*) (which could not be called perfectly happy since it was liable to suffering and death). The union therefore of his soul with God implies indeed the possession of happiness, but to be enjoyed at once or constantly always. According to the dispensation of God, suffering should precede his glory and happiness.

XV. The intrinsic and essential glory and happiness of the deity differs from the extrinsic and participated. With the divine nature, intrinsic and essential glory and happiness (which implies a communion of all divine perfections) was communicated by the hypostatical union to the person, the God-man (*theanthrōpō*). But to the human nature should be communicated only the external and participated. This does not adhere to the deity, but flows from it as an effect into the creature; indeed it flows as an accident which could sometimes be absent and sometimes be present.

XVI. If Christ is said to have seen the Father (Jn. 6:46), it does not treat precisely of the human nature, but of the person of the Logos (*Logou*), which as it was always united intimately to the Father could not but always enjoy his beatific vision. If the soul of Christ was more closely united with the deity than the souls of the blessed, it does not follow that he enjoyed the benefit of the saints made perfect. By a dispensation, he abdicated this right that he might fulfill the office of surety (which suretyship does not come in between the souls of the saints in heaven and their union with God).

FOURTEENTH QUESTION: THE SUFFERINGS OF CHRIST

Did Christ suffer only corporeal punishments for us in the body or in the soul, but only as to its lower and sensitive part? Or did he in truth also bear the spiritual and infernal punishments of sin themselves (in the superior as well as in the inferior part) properly in himself and from a sense of God's wrath? We deny the former and affirm the latter against the papists.

I. As the suffering of Christ is the principal part of the ransom (*lytrou*) paid for us by him and the special foundation of our confidence and consolation, it should also be the primary object of our faith and the theme of meditation, that with Paul we may count all things for loss but the knowledge of the crucified Jesus. We should attend to it more diligently as Satan the more impotently rages to obscure the truth of those sufferings and to deprive us of their saving fruit.

State of the question.

II. We do not inquire here whether Christ suffered anything. For there were formerly some who (since they supposed it unbecoming the divine glory of Christ to be affected with pains and sorrow) proceeded so far as to say that the body of Christ was impassible and on that account did not suffer truly but only apparently (*kata doxan*) (which was the heresy of the Aphthartodocetae, of whom Nicephorus speaks, *Ecclesiasticae Historiae* 17.29 [PG 147.295]). To these Hilary seems to approach not a little, when he maintains that the human nature in Christ (on account of its union with the Word) was exposed to no sufferings (cf. *The Trinity* 10.23 [FC 25:414-16]). However if that is the opinion of Hilary (which is here alleged in excuse by Lombard), it is as if he took away from Christ not so much the sense of suffering as the cause and desert of suffering (*Sententiarum* 3, Dist. 15.7 [PL 192/2.788-89]). Still this opinion was long ago condemned as contrary to the truth of the gospel history and our redemption, so that there is no necessity to bring it back again on the stage. Rather it is inquired concerning the nature and subject of the sufferings (to wit, What were the sufferings and in what subject? Were they in the body only or also in the soul? And if in the soul, were they only in its inferior part which is called the sensitive, or also in the higher and rational?).

The spiritual sufferings of Christ are proved: (1) from Scripture.

III. The papists (in order to defend their dogma concerning the perfect happiness of Christ's soul during the entire state of humiliation and to be able to reconcile it with the history of his passion) maintain that Christ suffered in body, not in soul. If they are pressed, they distinguish the lower and sensitive from the higher and rational soul. As to the former (to which they refer affections and perturbations), they grant that Christ suffered; but as to the latter, by no means. Or if he suffered anything in it, it did not suffer properly and in itself from a sense of God's wrath, but only through proximity (*dia parastasin*), or sympathetically (*dia sympatheian*) (on account of the union of the soul with the body). On the other hand, the orthodox refer Christ's sufferings to the soul as well as the body; to the higher part as well as to the lower. In the body indeed, he endured corporeal pains and agonies and a temporal death most cruel above all others; and in the soul, he endured spiritual and internal agonies (to wit, that most heavy and most dreadful weight of the divine wrath and the curse [*kataran*] due to us).

IV. The reasons are: (1) Scripture ascribes the sufferings of Christ to both parts and especially to the soul, when it says the soul of Christ was troubled (Jn. 12:27), "exceeding sorrowful" (*perilypos*) and as it were overwhelmed (Mt. 26:38); not therefore only in its lower, but also in its superior part. On this account, even the more since the soul is impartible (*ameristos*) and indivisible, one quality could not be affected without all the others sharing in it. Now the weight of that sorrow is demonstrated from this—that it is said to be "even unto death" (i.e., extreme) to denote the "weight of tribulation" (as the gloss has it). This is described by *taraxin* (trouble of soul, Jn. 12:27), by *adēmonian* (Mt. 26:37) and "amazement" (*ekthambēsin*, Mk. 14:33), when the soul (as it were) yields under horror and faints under the pressure of sorrow through an agony (*agōnian*) (to wit, such anxiety and anguish of mind as forces out a bloody sweat, Lk. 22:44) and the most fervent prayers which he offered to the Father with strong cryings and tears—that that cup might pass from him (when he had need of an angel as a comforter). Now whither should that extreme dejection and perturbation, that horror and exceeding fear, that severe conflict with the sense of the divine wrath and curse be referred unless we say that these sufferings were not only in the body, but in the soul; nor solely in the inferior, but also in the higher part of the soul unless we wish Christ to have been inferior to innumerable martyrs, who not only patiently and calmly, but also with joy and exultation endured bodily death and the most dreadful torments.

2. From the necessity of salvation.

V. (2) The necessity of our salvation required this. For as we had sinned in soul and body, so Christ, the surety, must suffer in both parts in order to pay a sufficient ransom price (*lytron*) to the divine justice and to redeem the soul and body. It is confirmed by this—that the sufferings denounced against sinners by the law are not only bodily and external, but principally spriritual and internal in a sense of the divine wrath and curse (Lev. 26; Dt. 27, 28; Gal. 3:10, 13). Hence Irenaeus says, "With his own blood the Lord redeemed us, who gave his own soul for our soul and his own flesh for our flesh" (*Against Heresies* 5.1 [ANF 1:527; PG 7.1121). Hence he is called not only *antilytron*, but also *antipsychos*, who pledges and exchanges soul for soul.

VI. (3) The punishment of desertion, suffered by Christ (of which he complained, Mt. 27:46) was not a bodily, but a spiritual and internal suffering. It arose not from any torment (however dreadful) which he could feel in his body (for many of the martyrs might have experienced such, who nevertheless are not said to have complained of this desertion), but from a most oppressive sense of God's wrath resting upon him on account of our sins. Now this desertion is not to be conceived as absolute, total and eternal (such as is felt only by demons and the reprobate), but temporal and relative; not in respect of the union of nature (for what the Son of God once assumed, he never parted with); or of the union of grace and holiness because he was always blameless (*akakos*) and pure (*amiantos*), endowed with untainted holiness; or of communion and protection because God was always at his right hand (Ps. 110:5), nor was he ever left alone (Jn. 16:32). But as to a participation of joy and felicity, God suspending for a little while the favorable presence of grace and the influx of consolation and happiness that he might be able to suffer all the punishment due to us (as to withdrawal of vision, not as to a dissolution of union; as to the want of the sense of the divine love, intercepted by the sense of the divine wrath and vengeance resting upon him, not as to a real privation or extinction of it). And, as the Scholastics say, as to "the affection of advantage" that he might be destitute of the ineffable consolation and joy which arises from a sense of God's paternal love and the beatific vision of his countenance (Ps. 16); but not as to "the affection of righteousness" because he felt nothing inordinate in himself which would tend to desperation, impatience or blasphemy against God.

VII. (4) Christ was made a curse for us (Gal. 3:13), while the curse due to us was laid upon him on account of the suretyship undertaken; not only "cursed" (*epikataratos*), but "a curse" (*katara*)—the abstract being put for the concrete for a heightening (*epitasin*) because he endured the whole curse which the law denounced against sinners. This assuredly does not respect only the body, but especially the soul, which can be affected by such a sense. Not a few papists have acknowledged this; cf. Maldonatus, *Commentary on the Holy Gospels: Matthew* (1888), 2:446 on Mt. 26:37; Ferus, *In sacrosanctum Iesu Christi evangelium secundum Matthaeum* (1559), pp. 376-77 on Mt. 27:46 and others.

Sources of explanation.

VIII. Although the Scripture for the most part ascribes salvation to the cross, blood and death of Christ, this is not done to the exclusion of spiritual and internal sufferings, but synecdochically denominating the whole from the sensible and external part exposed to the eyes. Nor can the cross or death be mentioned without involving by that very thing the notion of the curse annexed to them because the death was no other than that denounced by the law.

IX. Although internal and spiritual torments could not be figured in species and in particular by the death and shedding of the blood of victims, still they could in general be contained under them. For since fire is a symbol of divine wrath, there is nothing to prevent this consuming of the sacrifices by fire from being referred to the sense of divine wrath which Christ endured in his soul. Thus the blood of the sacrifices (as the seat of life) can best be called also a symbol of the soul. Besides a particular type was not wanting in the sufferings of David described in Pss. 22 and 69, which were not only external, but also internal.

X. It is not necessary that the sacraments should represent all parts of the sufferings of Christ; it suffices that they exhibit a certain part which could be signified by such symbols (but from which the rest are easily gathered) since they necessarily accompany each other in Christ; nor can the death of Christ be shadowed forth without the curse connected with it being presented to our minds.

XI. The sacrifice of Christ is called "the offering of his body" (Heb. 10:10) not in an opposition of the body to the soul (which he is also said to have laid down for us, Is. 53:10; Jn. 10:15), but by an antithesis to the Levitical sacrifices so often repeated (of which the apostle was speaking). Hence this kind of expression was most suitable.

XII. And hence can be clearly gathered what is to be judged concerning the sufferings of Christ—whether they are properly called gehennal and hellish, as our men hold. For since hell in Scripture denotes not only the sepulcher or place of the damned, but also their extreme condition of misery and calamity (as Arias Montanus well observes, *Biblia sacra Hebraice, Chaldaice, Graece et Latine* [1572], 7:183), and "infernal pains" are put for the most grievous, nothing hinders the sufferings of Christ from being called (in this sense) infernal on account of their dreadfulness and intensity.

XIII. Nor yet moreover could you rightly say either that he entered the place of the damned or was damned. He could indeed bear the punishments of those deserving to be damned, but not of the damned so that he entered into the infernal place prepared for them (from which no one can return) or that he was devoted to eternal punishment because the eternity of the punishments we deserved was compensated abundantly in Christ by their weight and extremity.

XIV. Much less should despair such as the damned feel be ascribed to Christ. It is not of the essence of punishment in itself considered and as it is inflicted by the Judge. Rather it is of the vice of the subject suffering, which when it considers the eternity of the most dreadful evils and the impossibility of escaping from it, cannot but fall into desperation (which was most foreign to Christ, who although he felt the dreadfulness of the torments inflicted upon him, still was certain of their happy end and his own deliverance). Hence appears the falsity of the atrocious calumny most unjustly charged by our opponents upon Calvin—as by Bellarmine ("De Christo Anima," 8 *Opera* [1856], 1:271-75); Genebrardus

(*Psalmi Davidis* [1606], p. 79 on Ps. 21 [22]:1); and Maldonatus (*Commentary on the Holy Gospels: Matthew* [1863], 2:551-54 on Mt. 27) and by others—because he says on Mt. 27:46, "but it is absurd that a voice of despair should escape from Christ" (John Calvin, *Harmony of the Gospels* [trans. A.W. Morrison, 1972], 3:208). For who does not see that it is an objection which he proposes to himself from the words of Christ ("My God . . .") and which he so explains as to prove most clearly that he was always farthest removed from desperation and full of confidence? "The solution," he says, "is easy, although the sense apprehended the destruction of the flesh, still faith stood fixed in his heart, by which he beheld a present God, concerning whose absence he complained" (ibid.). Now if faith was fixed in his heart, how could despair fall upon him? This he still more strongly confirms in ICR 2.16.5, 12, pp. 507-10 and 517-20, as will appear from an inspection of the passage. But if we wished to recriminate, how much more justly might this be fastened upon our opponents, of whom not a few are found to be guilty of this charge (as Maldonatus, *Commentary on the Holy Gospels: Matthew* [1863], 2:552 on Mt. 27:46)? Ferus, on the same passage, expressly ascribes despair to Christ (*In sacrosanctum Iesu Christi evangelium secundum Matthaeum* [1559], p. 376 on Mt. 27:46); cf. also Cusanus *de Cruciatibus Christi*+ and others. See our "Disputation on the Satisfaction," *Opera* (1848), 4:554.

XV. With similar calumny that great man of God is accused of saying that Christ "was damned" because he says "he was constituted in such a damnation" that he complained of being deserted of God (*Catechismus Ecclesiae Genevensis* [1545], CR 34.28-32). But: (1) who does not see that "damnation" is put here for "condemnation," according to the most customary style of the French language at that time? (2) If Christ is called "a curse," why cannot damnation be ascribed to him? (3) The fathers and some of our opponents have so spoken: Cyprian, "He was damned that he might free the damned; he suffered that he might heal the sick; he feared to make us secure" ("De Passione Christi" [attributed to Cyprian] in Arnold Carnotensis, *Opera*, p. 49 in Cyprian, *Opera* [ed. John Oxoniensem, 1682]); Gregory Nazianzus, "He united that which was condemned that he might free the whole from condemnation" ("Fourth Theological Oration, Second on the Son," 21 [NPNF2, 7:317; PG 36.131]); Athanasius, "There was need for the very Judge, who made the decree, to fulfill himself the sentence in the form of the condemned" (*de Incarn.*+); Gregory the Great, "He assumed the form of a condemned man" and "condemns him for sinners who is without sin" (*Morals on the Book of Job* 3.14* [1844], 1:148-49; PL 75.612-13). The Vulgate uses the word *damnatio* as does the Louvain Version of the year 1533. Cusanus uses the same word (*Exercit.* lib. xi+).

Fifteenth Question: The Descent of Christ to Hell

Was the soul of Christ, after its separation from the body, translated to paradise immediately? Or did it descend locally to hell? The former we affirm; the latter we deny against the papists and Lutherans.

I. The question concerning Christ's descent into hell is twofold: the one with the papists and some Lutherans, who hold a local descent of Christ; the other among the orthodox themselves concerning the true sense of the article—

whether it is to be referred to the spiritual anguish of Christ or to his burial and his most abject state under the dominion of death. We are now to examine the first and will speak of the last immediately afterwards.

Statement of the question.

II. The papists maintain that the soul of Christ from the time of its separation from the body straightway descended locally to hell until the resurrection. In the Catechism of Trent, it is proposed to be believed: "Christ being now dead, his soul descended into hell, and remained there just as long as his body was in the sepulchre" (*Catechism of the Council of Trent*, Art. 5 [trans. J. A. McHugh, 1923], pp. 62 and 64). And that no one might think this was only done by virtue and power and not by essence (as Durandus held, cf. *Sententias theologicas Petri Lombardi Commentariorum*, Bk. 3, Dist. 22, Q. 3, 4 [1556], p. 215), it is added in the same place, "It is to be entirely believed that the soul itself really and by presence descended into hell." However they wish him to have descended thither for the purpose of freeing the souls of the fathers of the Old Testament detained in limbo and of carrying them with him to heaven.

III. The Lutherans agree with them in asserting the substantial descent of Christ into hell; not only into limbo, but into the very place of the damned, to show his victory there and exhibit his triumph. On this account, they wish it to be referred to the state of exaltation and not to that of humiliation (as Brochmann determines, "De Servatoris Nostri Jesu Christi," Sect. 14, Q. 6, 7 in *Universae theologicae systema* [1638], 1:920-23).

IV. Hence the question took this form—whether Christ descended locally into hell or only to the limbo of the fathers and to purgatory for the purpose of leading out the souls of the pious or to the very place of the damned to openly exhibit his victory. This our opponents hold; we deny.

V. First, the soul of Christ immediately after its release from the body mounted up into paradise, according to the promise made to the thief, "Today shalt thou be with me in paradise" (Lk. 23:43). In vain (1) do our opponents wish the words to be understood of the deity only, with which the soul of the thief was to be in paradise. They involve the futurition in paradise or the translation not only of the soul of the thief, but also of Christ; that as Christ and the thief truly suffered, so they were to be carried together also into heaven, that both conditions might be common to both. And thus they were consolatory not only in order to the thief, but also to the Lord himself that in a short time they would both emerge from their distresses. Thus in the same manner, they might be in heaven as to their souls as they were on the cross together as to their bodies. Hence Cyprian: "The thief was made a partaker of the kingdom, who had been made by his confession a colleague in martyrdom" ("De Passione Christi" [attributed to Cyprian] in Arnold Carnotensis, *Opera*, p. 50 in Cyprian, *Opera* [ed. John Oxoniensem, 1682]). The words themselves prove this. Christ does not say, "I will be with you" (which designated the presence of the deity in paradise), but "thou shalt be with me," in order to promise him the fellowship of his humanity. Fellowship with Christ in his kingdom is promised. Now this cannot be understood of the deity (which concedes to no one such a privilege), but of Christ, the God-man (*theanthrōpō*), who calls believers into a share of his kingdom. (2) No better do others wish the word "today" to be referred to the words of Christ, not to the introduction into paradise. Thus the sense is, "Today I say to you," that thou shalt be with me in paradise. As Suarez well remarks, this is an elusion, not an interpretation. For there was no need for Christ to indicate this, which the verb of the present tense and the expression of Christ itself sufficiently indicated. Rather he wishes to encourage the thief (constituted in agony and breathing after the grace of Christ) by this consolation that his petition would be fulfilled on that very day. (3) Thomas Aquinas also gratuitously feigns, "Paradise here denotes generally the place of happiness, wherever it may be, in which they are said to be who enjoy the divine glory; whence the thief as to place was in hell with Christ, as to reward in paradise; so that paradise is wherever Christ is and wherever God is seen" (ST, III, Q. 52*, Art. 4*, p. 2305). But what is this except to mingle heaven not only with earth but also with hell? Thus the thief on the cross would have been already in paradise because he was there with Christ. Christ, however, speaks of that paradise, where he was not then. Finally, in no other way is paradise to be understood than as Scripture elsewhere speaks of it: as the seat of the blessed (2 Cor. 12:4; Rev. 2:7), which Bellarmine ("De Sanctorum Beatitudine," 3 *Opera* 2:426) and Suarez ("Commentaria . . . in tertiam partem D. Thomae," Q. 52, Dist. 42 in *Opera Omnia* [1856-78], 19:697-743) acknowledge. The thing itself proves this because the promise of Christ ought to answer to the petition of the thief, "Remember me when thou comest into thy kingdom." To which Christ answers, "Today shalt thou be with me in paradise" (i.e., in my kingdom).

VI. Second, the soul of Christ was in the hand of the Father: "Father, into thy hands I commend my spirit" (Lk. 23:46). Therefore it was not in hell because according to the style of Scripture the hand of the Father is not to be understood with respect to power (according to which the hand of God is everywhere, Ps. 139:7-10) or as it is the terrible hand of God, the Judge; but as the consoling hand of the Father of mercy with respect to glory and grace; or the condition of the blessed usually described by being in the hand of God. It is confirmed by this—that Christ by this phrase wished to proclaim that nothing more remained to be done by him, both as to freeing others and as to undergoing new torments. But as the body was about to enjoy its repose in the sepulcher, so the soul also was about to rest from all its labors and be bathed in the greatest joys. For to commit or commend the soul has a relation to foregoing labors. Christ, however, could not have said "I commend my spirit," if after death he was yet to descend into hell and suffer the most grievous burdens. (3) He commends his spirit to the hand of his Father in the same manner as David and Stephen commended their souls because these were the very words of David before (Ps. 31:5), from whom Christ took them, and of Stephen afterwards (Acts 7:59), who imitated Christ himself; yea, as Peter recommends all believers to commit their souls to the faithful Creator (1 Pet. 4:19*); not assuredly that they may descend into hell, but be received into heaven (as the ordinary gloss has it, "Into thy hands I commend my spirit that you may receive it, leaving the body"). Hence among the fathers the hand of the Father and hell are opposed. Cyril of Alexandria says, "The innocent above, the guilty below; the innocent in heaven, the guilty in the abyss; the innocent in the hand of God, the guilty in the hand of the devil" (*De exitu animi* [PG 77.1082]).

VII. Third, if according to the soul Christ truly and locally descended into hell, either that was done to suffer something there or to free the fathers or to

Saints are in heaven, not in limbo

preach the gospel to the dead or to show his victory to the devils. But the first cannot be said because he finished all things on the cross (Jn. 19:30) and by one offering he perfected forever them that are sanctified (Heb. 10:14). Not the second because they were already admitted into heaven; nor were they ever in a fictitious limbo, as was proved before. Not the third because preaching the gospel belongs only to the state of this life, not to the condition of death. If Peter says, "The gospel was preached to the dead" (1 Pet. 4:6*), this is not to be understood in the compound sense (as if he had preached to the dead as such because since they are not in the state of the way, they need no more any preaching), but in the divided sense (i.e., to them who are now dead, but who formerly lived when the gospel was preached to them). Not the fourth because that descent ought to be penal, not triumphal and belongs to the state of humiliation, not of exaltation.

VIII. Now that such was the descent of Christ various arguments prove. (1) According to the style of Scripture, a descent into hell signifies the most terrible adversities and most exquisite pains (Gen. 37:35; Job 14:13; Pss. 6:5; 86:13; 130:1). (2) The passages which speak of the descent into hell denote his extreme misery, not a triumph (to wit, in which he was not on that account to be left, but to be freed by the Father, Acts 2:30, 31). (3) The descent into the lowest parts of the earth is opposed to his ascension above all the heavens, which is a part of the exaltation (Eph. 4:9). Therefore it ought to be a part of his humiliation.

Sources of explanation.

IX. The "heart of the earth" in the style of the Hebrews means nothing else than what is within the earth, for *lb* is put for *thvdh* (which is the middle) and what is internal is often called the middle, whether it is in the middle or not. The borders of Tyre are said to have been "in the midst of the seas" (Ezk. 27:4) because washed on all sides by the sea; the mountain is said to have "burned unto the midst of heaven" (Dt. 4:11), i.e., up to the middle region of the air. Thus "to be in the heart of the earth" (Mt. 12:40) means nothing else than to be within the earth whether that be nearer or more remote from its surface. In this way is intimated the state of Christ's body in the sepulcher (which was in the earth, in which it rested until the third day).

X. When Christ is said to have "descended into the lower parts of the earth" (*eis ta katōtera merē tēs gēs*, Eph. 4:9), a local descent is not implied, but his humiliation and manifestation in the flesh which he assumed on earth, so that it is nothing else than to descend to the earth (which is the lowest part of the universe) by a construction sufficiently known to the Hebrews, in which the governing word stands for the apposition—"in the lowest parts of the earth" (Ps. 139:15), i.e., in the earth, which is the lower part with respect to heaven. Thus not the parts of the earth are compared with each other, but the heaven and the earth, parts of the universe. Nor do the words of the text admit of any other meaning. There is an opposition between the ascent from earth to heaven and the descent from heaven. However, as the ascent has the earth as the point from which and heaven as the point to which, so in turn the descent has heaven as the point from which and the earth as the point to which. This Cajetan saw, who by the lower parts of the earth wishes to be understood "the earth which is the lowest part of the world as distinguished from the lower parts of the heaven which are in the air. And thus he would more clearly have expressed it, because he descended first to the lower part of the earth."

XI. When Peter says "the soul of Christ was not to be left in hell" (Acts. 2:27 from Ps. 16:10), a local descent cannot be understood, but the detention in the sepulcher because this is referred by Peter to the resurrection. This is gathered: (1) from the connection "my flesh," says he, "shall rest" (i.e., in the sepulcher) "in hope, because thou wilt not leave." (2) From the phrase added for explanation, "Neither wilt thou suffer thine Holy One" (i.e., me) "to see corruption" (to wit, in the body), which otherwise it would undergo if left in the sepulcher. (3) From a comparison with Acts 13:34, 35 where God is said to have raised up Christ from the dead that he might not see corruption. Nor is this opposed either by the word *psychēs*, which as Emanuel Sa (*de phrasibus Scriptura+*) remarks, is put by a synecdoche of a part for the whole, for the whole person itself frequently elsewhere (Pss. 3:2; 17:13; Acts 7:14) or of a part for a part, for the body itself (Lev. 19:28; 21:1, 11; Num. 5:1; Lk. 6:9) as Virgil ("We bury the soul in the tomb," *Aeneid* 3.68 [Loeb, 1:352-53]), or by the word *hadēs*, which evidently is often put for the sepulcher, as will be proved hereafter.

XII. The passage in Peter, when "Christ quickened by the Spirit" is said "to have preached unto the spirits in prison" (*tois en phylakē*, 1 Pet. 3:19), does not favor the local descent into hell. (1) Peter does not speak of "the soul," but of "the Spirit." Therefore it cannot be understood of any descent of the soul. For that Spirit cannot here be taken for the soul but for the deity is gathered from the preceding verse. No other Spirit is meant than he by whom he was quickened. This cannot be said of the soul, neither subjectively because that only is quickened which can die (which cannot apply to the soul), nor efficiently because quickening is a work of infinite power. On this account, the deity itself must necessarily be understood. This is often thus designated elsewhere (Rom. 1:4; Heb. 9:14; 1 Tim. 3:16) where he is said to have been "justified by the Spirit," which Cajetan, Gagnaeus, Thomas Aquinas, Lyranus and others understand of the deity and the Holy Spirit. (2) It treats of the *apeithēsasi* (i.e., rebellious spirits) who did not obey those giving them good advice (such as the fathers cannot be called, whom they wish Christ to have led out of limbo [in which they were detained] to heaven). Nor can it be said that they indeed were unbelieving at first but afterwards repented because this is not in the text, but is rather opposed to it. For eight only are said to have been saved, the rest to have perished. Yet if some had repented, Peter would not have called them *apeitheis*. (3) There is no mention here of liberation, but only of preaching. (4) The "prison" (*phylakē*) treated of here is taken only in two ways in Scripture, either for a nightly guard or for a prison in which the guilty are detained (Lk. 3:20). Since, in truth, it cannot be used here in the first sense, it ought necessarily to be taken for a prison (as the interlinear Gloss says, "the prison of darkness and unbelief"). Nowhere in Scripture is any place called a prison where happy spirits are contained. (5) The preaching is not said to have been made to the spirits being in prison, as if they were in prison at the time of the preaching. For to what purpose would it have been made since there is granted no exit from it? But it is said to have been made formerly in the time of Noah (in which God's patience waited for men) to them who (at the time in which Peter writes) are in prison. Hence Peter does not say *ekēryxe tois pneumasi en phylakē* but *tois en phylakē pneumasi ekēryxe*. Thus the substantive verb must be supplied, not as the Vulgate has it *iis qui in carcere erant* as if they were in prison at the time of the preaching, but *tois ousi* ("who are," to wit, at the time of the apostle's writing). For that *pote* Peter does not join with the words *en phylakē*, but with *apeithēsasi* in this manner, *tois en phylakē pneumasi apeithēsasi pote*, clearly distinguishing the times in which they were rebellious in the days of Noah and in which they were thrust into prison on account of their rebellion. Thus the meaning of the passage is plain, as our Beza has most happily explained it. "Christ," says he, "whom I said was quickened by the Spirit, having gone, not by a change of place, but by a certain special manifestation of his presence, by revelation and operation, as God is often said to come in Scripture, not literally but figuratively and metaphorically; not in the body, which he had not yet assumed, but by that very Spirit or divine power by which he rose again and was quickened, and inspired (by which the prophets spoke, 1 Pet. 1:11) preached to those spirits, which are now in the prison of hell, where they suffer the punishment of their rebellion to his preaching in the time of Noah."+ This Andradius saw, saying that this is the meaning of the passage—"in which Spirit (coming long before) he preached to those spirits who now in prison pay the deserved penalty of their former unbelief, since they never wished to believe Noah telling them of their duty and building an ark by God's command" (*Defensio tridentinae fidei catholicae* 2 [1580], p. 294).

XIII. If Christ is said by the resurrection "to have been loosed from the pains of death" (Acts 2:24), it does not follow that he endured pains up to the moment of his resurrection and that his soul departed into hell, where he could be affected by such pains. The passage can be understood in two ways: (1) that "the pains of death" by a grammatical figure (*hen dia dyoin*) are put for a painful death. Christ, it is said, "will baptize with the Holy Ghost and with fire" (as Mt. 3:11), i.e., with spiritual fire, as Virgil, "I sing of arms and men," i.e., the armed man (*Aeneid* 1.1 [Loeb, 1:240-41]). It is certain that the death of Christ was connected with the most exquisite pains, nor was that death resolved except in the moment of the resurrection. (2) The passage to which Peter alludes (Ps. 18:5) employs the expression *chbly mvth*, which properly denotes cables and chains by which the man is detained as a captive in death, from which he is released by the resurrection. Thus there is no need to invent in addition any suffering of the soul after death. However, Peter, following the Septuagint, retains the word *ōdinas*, which can connote both the torments he suffered in death and the chains of death, by which in a measure he was bound in the sepulcher. Thus the meaning may be "whom" (namely, Christ) "God hath raised up, having loosed the chains of death because it was impossible that he should be always holden [*krateisthai*] like a captive by it."

XIV. The triumphal song which Paul sings (after Hosea, 1 Cor. 15:54, 55) is rightly referred to the resurrection of Christ, by which he began to triumph over sin, death and hell. But it cannot pertain to a descent into hell, which was the lowest degree of his humiliation, in which he seemed to be only not swallowed up by death.

Sixteenth Question

May the descent into hell be rightly referred to infernal torments and to a most abject state under the dominion of death in the sepulcher? We affirm.

I. By the preceding question, the false opinion of the papists concerning the local descent of Christ into hell was refuted. Now its true and genuine sense must be given. About this again the orthodox do not altogether agree among themselves, some referring it to the spiritual anguish and hellish torments which he suffered (as Calvin, Beza, Danaeus, Ursinus and others, even various confessions of the churches), others maintaining that it pertains to his burial and three days' detention in the sepulcher (as Zanchius, Piscator, Pierius and others).

Statement of the question.

II. However, we must observe before all things that we do not inquire concerning the origin of this article—whether it was contained from the beginning in the Apostles' Creed and constantly acknowledged and received by the churches. For it is evident that no mention is made of it in the Nicene Creed and in the Roman, according to Ruffinus (*A Commentary on the Apostles' Creed* 28* [NPNF2, 3:553-54]). The ancients who published confessions and set forth the rule of faith (such as Irenaeus, Origen, Tertullian, Augustine and others) say nothing about it. Also it is referred by Ruffinus only to the end of the fourth century. This article does indeed occur in the Athanasian Creed, but the article of burial being omitted is a clear proof that they were considered as one and the same thing. So it is very probable that this article was transferred from the Athanasian to the Apostles' Creed and at first perhaps was placed in the margin for the purpose of explication; then from the margin into the text itself where it was afterwards retained and incorporated with it. But this question being now dismissed, we treat here only concerning its true sense (about which all do not agree).

III. However, since there is no other cause for this discrepancy than the ambiguity of the word *sh'vl* and *hadēs* and the manifold sense of the phrase "to descend into hell," these must be briefly discussed. The word *sh'vl* is spoken in Scripture in four ways: (1) for a sepulcher (Pss. 16:10; 49:15); (2) for the place of the damned (Lk. 16:23); (3) for the greatest torments (Pss. 18:5; 116:3); (4) for extreme humiliation (Is. 14:15). Hence to descend into hell is used in four ways: (a) it denotes to be buried (Gen. 37:35; 42:38); (b) to descend into the place of the damned (Num. 16:33); (c) to feel infernal pains (1 S. 2:6); (d) to be extremely humbled (Mt. 11:23). According to this fourfold signification, there can be a fourfold meaning of this article. So that it may be referred either to a local descent into the place of the damned (as the papists and Lutherans hold and refuted by us already); or to the burial of Christ, or to his infernal sufferings, or to the extreme degree of his humiliation.

The reasons for the burial and the state of the dead.

IV. They who hold that this article does not differ from his burial rest especially upon these reasons: (1) that Peter (from Ps. 16:10 in Acts 2:31) seems clearly to refer to the burial of Christ, "David seeing this before, spake of the resurrection of Christ, that his soul was not left in hell." (2) Everywhere in Scripture *sh'vl* is put for the sepulcher and to descend into hell for to descend into the sepulcher (as Arias Montanus, Emanuel Sa and other papists and lexicographers teach). (3) In various creeds mention is made of a descent into hell, no mention being made of the sepulcher (as in the Athanasian Creed, which evinces that they were taken by him for one and the same thing). And here can be referred the fact that Paul mentions Christ's death, burial and resurrection according to the Scriptures (1 Cor. 15:3, 4), but says nothing of his descent into hell. However he would have spoken of it if he had believed that such an article meant anything else than his burial.

V. Still it is not probable that this article is the same as the burial. (1) It would be a tautology (*tautologia*) scarcely to be endured in so succinct and brief a creed. (2) It cannot be said that this article was appended to the former concerning the burial to explain it, since it is more obscure than the former. Thus it is not to be referred precisely to the burial, but to the state of death or his detention in the sepulcher under the dominion of death (as this phrase is often used to describe the state of the dead; cf. Gen. 37:35 where Jacob, bewailing his son Joseph whom he believed to have been torn in pieces by wild beasts, says, "I will go down" *lsh'vl* "unto my son mourning"; not indeed into a sepulcher because he supposed he had been torn in pieces by wild beasts and not buried, but simply to death or the state of the dead). Thus "in death there is no remembrance of thee, in *sh'vl* who shall give thee thanks?" (Ps. 6:5; cf. Job 17:13-15; Pss. 30:3; 49:15; Is. 14:11, 19, 20).

VI. Also, the passage of Peter (Acts 2:27) drawn from the oracle (Ps. 16:10) seems necessarily to demand this: "Thou wilt not leave my soul *eis hadou*" (supply *oikon*, employed by him to prove the resurrection). He says this prophecy was fulfilled by the resurrection of Christ, so that the meaning is: "Thou wilt not leave my soul" (i.e., my life) or "me in death, but wilt raise me up from death by the resurrection." Here belongs what is said in v. 24 concerning "the pains" or "chains of death" by which he was holden as a captive by death (from which he was released by the resurrection). It was impossible (both on account of the glory of his divinity and on account of the holiness of his humanity) to be held any longer by it.

Reasons for the torments.

VII. But neither is the other opinion to be repudiated which understands this descent of the extreme sufferings of Christ endured both in the garden and on the cross. It agrees (1) with the style of Scripture, which usually designates the most grievous torments by "hell" and the "pains of hell," as we have already said; (2) with the creed, that the most weighty and special sufferings of Christ be not passed over in silence (which would be the case, unless the descent of Christ into hell be understood of the internal sufferings of his soul). For the preceding articles speak only of the external sufferings of the body.

Reconciliation of the two opinions.

VIII. If it is asked which of these two opinions ought to be retained, we answer both can be admitted and be made to agree perfectly with each other. Thus by the descent into hell may be understood the extreme degree of Christ's suffering and humiliation, both as to soul and body; and as the lowest degree of humiliation as to the body was its detention in the sepulcher, so as to the soul were those dreadful torments he felt. And thus this last article will be apposite for expressing the last degree of Christ's humiliation, whether as to disgrace of body or as to anguish of soul. Nor should it seem wonderful if these two parts (mutually diverse from each other) should be joined together in one and the same article. It is not unusual in Scripture for a single sense to put on various relations (*schesin*) and for many things to be embraced together, especially when the things are mutually subordinated and connected with each other. Since this phrase may be referred now to abjection of the body, then to griefs of the soul (and Christ should have undergone both conditions), it was not without reason that the ancients added this article to the preceding in order to set forth more distinctly this state of Christ.

Sources of explanation.

IX. The constant and indissoluble union of the human nature with the divine in Christ does not hinder him from being able to suffer both in soul and in body the punishment due to us. The union with the Word causes him indeed to be always holy and free from all sin; but not that he should be always happy and glorious (since he came that he might suffer). Christ always had the glory of person as God-man (*theanthrōpos*); but he ought not to always have the glory of human nature (which he was to obtain only after his resurrection) because he was to be tempted in all things equally with us and be made a curse for our salvation.

X. As he is properly said to be damned who in hell endures the punishment due to his own sins, this term cannot be applied to Christ, who never suffered for his own but for our sins; nor did he suffer in hell, but on earth. Still there is no objection to saying that the Son of God was condemned for us by God, just as elsewhere he is said to have been made a curse (*katara*) and malediction for us. Nor is it more absurd to say that Christ was condemned than that the Lord of glory suffered and was crucified and for our sake was crucified and chastened (as is so often said).

XI. The vision of God belonging to the saints in heaven by glory differs from that of believers on earth by grace. They who see God in the former manner can be subjected to no further punishments and pains because they are in their native country, constituted in a state of happiness. But it is not the same with believers who, although they see God by faith, do not cease to be exposed to various afflictions. Christ on earth (as man) saw God in the latter sense, and far more perfectly than believers; but this vision did not hinder him from suffering and complaining that he was forsaken of God.

Seventeenth Question: *The Resurrection of Christ*

Did Christ rise by his own power? We affirm against the Socinians.

Statement of the question.

I. The first degree of Christ's exaltation is put in his resurrection. Concerning this, the question is here moved by the Socinians. Not indeed concerning its truth, for although the Jews call it into doubt (yea, even dare to deny it), it was proved by so many witnesses and testimonies and confirmed by so many signs and miracles that still to doubt concerning it is an inexcusable incredulity, especially after the irrefragable testimony of the apostles, who in giving it were neither deceived themselves nor wished to deceive others (nor could they, as was proved Volume I, Topic II, Question 4). The miracles which followed the resurrection of Christ prove that he lives and reigns gloriously in heaven (to say nothing now of the justice of God, the glory of Christ and our salvation, which necessarily demanded it, according to the prophecies uttered concerning it). Rather the question relates to its manner—Did he rise again by his own or by another's power?

II. For the Socinians, as they say Christ was a mere man (*psilou anthrōpon*), so they maintain that Christ did not raise himself by his own power, but was raised by God's power. Hence Socinus calls this doctrine "ridiculous, absurd and impossible" (cf. *De unigeniti filii Dei existentia* [1626], pp. 58, 59). The Racovian Catechism says it is "a notable error" (cf. "Of the Kingly Office of Christ," Sect. VII, *Racovian Catechism* [1818], pp. 361-64). But the orthodox ascribe the cause of the resurrection to Christ himself no less than to the Father. Since the power of the Father and the Son is the same, they think that by the same the Father raised Christ and Christ raised himself.

Proof that Christ raised himself: (1) from Jn. 2:19.

III. First, Christ expressly ascribes this to himself: "Destroy this temple" (speaking of the temple of his body) "and in three days I will raise it up" (Jn. 2:19). In Jn. 10:18, he testifies that "he has power to lay down his life and to take it again." This he could not have said if he had not the power of rising again from the dead. Nor if the former passage is tropical is it less weighty because it is clearly explained by Christ.

2. From Rom. 1:4.

IV. Second, the Scripture mentions the resurrection of Christ among the principal arguments by which his divinity is proved. In Rom. 1:4, Paul says that he was *horisthenta* (i.e., "declared" as it were by a public decree and proved to be the Son of God, powerful or "with power, according to the Spirit of holiness, by the resurrection from the dead"). Now this could not be said of a passive resurrection in which Christ was merely passive (as this cannot be said of Lazarus, Jairus' daughter and others raised by God). Hence we must necessarily understand here an active resurrection by which he raised himself by his own power of divinity, which not only the parallel passages (in which the divine nature of Christ comes to be denoted by Spirit, 1 Pet. 3:18; 1 Tim. 3:16; Mk. 2:8), but especially the antithesis (which is to the flesh) clearly proves—designated by "the spirit of holiness." For as he is called the Son of David according to the flesh (*kata sarka*, i.e., in respect of his human nature); according to the Spirit (*kata Pneuma*, i.e., according to his divine nature), he is said to be declared to be the Son of God by his resurrection. Otherwise the antithesis would be faulty, nor would he show according to what the Son of God was not made of the seed of David.

3. From John 5:21.

V. Third, Christ does the same works equally with the Father and "quickeneth whom he will" (Jn. 5:21). Now if he can quicken whom he will, what place can there be for doubting that he also raised up himself? It is confirmed by this—that he calls himself the resurrection and the life: "I am the resurrection, and the life; he that believeth in me, though he were dead, yet shall he live" (Jn. 11:25). Here the abstract put for the concrete intimates that he is the principal cause of resurrection and the very fountain of life, who by giving life to others is himself self-living (*autozōē*) and the author of his own resurrection.

4. From Col. 1:18.

VI. Fourth, he is the "firstborn from the dead" (Col. 1:18), which implies not only the prerogative of order, but also the virtue and power of him rising again, as having by nature what his other brethren obtain only by the grace of adoption.

Sources of explanation.

VII. Although the resurrection of Christ is often ascribed to the Father (Rom. 6:4; Acts 2:24; 13:30; Eph. 1:19, 20), it does not follow that it cannot be ascribed to the Son because whatever the Father does, the Son in like manner does (Jn. 5:19); and as the resurrection is an outward work, it ought to be undivided to the whole Trinity. But there is a peculiar reason why it is ascribed to the Father, on account of the obligation which Christ took upon himself, from which he ought to be released by the Father (as Judge), who, as he had delivered up Christ to death for our sins, so he ought to raise him up again for our justification—in order to testify that a full satisfaction had been made by him. Otherwise when it is treated of the confirmation of the vocation of Christ and the vindication of his divinity, the resurrection is more frequently ascribed to him (as we have said).

VIII. It is absurd and ridiculous that a mere man (*psilon anthrōpon*) who has died, should raise himself from the dead. But that the God-man (*theanthrōpon*) should raise up his humanity by virtue of his divine power is so far from being absurd that to deny it is blasphemous and wicked.

IX. Christ could have obtained his resurrection from the Father by prayers offered by himself as man (Heb. 5:7), and yet have effected it as God by the same power with the Father. For since Christ could raise Lazarus and others (since the Father had given to the Son to have life in himself and the Son, as the Father, quickens whom he will), who would wish to deny him the power of recalling himself to life?

X. Moreover when Christ raised himself up, it must not be supposed that he penetrated with his body the stone placed over the sepulcher (as the papists wish in order to defend their error). For the spiritual body which rises is no more converted into a spirit than the body into a soul. And divine power manifests itself not in destroying but in conserving the natures of things. Materiality and finitude do not belong to the infirmities of animal life, but to the essential properties of the body. The creature could therefore have yielded to the Creator in his resurrection this side of a penetration of its dimensions; or Christ employed the ministry of an angel to remove the stone from the mouth of the sepulcher before he could come forth (Mt. 28:2)—not from indigence, but indulgence in order to testify that his power was attended by ministers from all creatures; or because being still constituted in the state of obligation, he willed to wait for the sentence of the Father to be intimated to him by an angel.

Eighteenth Question: The Ascension of Christ

Did Christ ascend properly by a local movement from the lower places to the supreme heaven of the blessed; or metaphorically by disappearance? We affirm the former and deny the latter against the Lutherans.

Statement of the question.

I. This question is introduced on account of the Lutherans and those who ascribe ubiquity to the body of Christ. For the more easily to evade the argument drawn from the ascension of Christ to prove the circumscription of Christ's body, they deny that Christ truly and properly ascended; but only figuratively, inasmuch as he withdrew his visible presence from the world (although he still remains in the world invisibly). And the heaven into which he ascended (they maintain) is not the highest or third heaven (called the heaven of the blessed), but the heaven of the beatitude and kingdom of God (which is everywhere); cf. Brentius, "De Ascensu Christi," *Operum* (1579-90), 8:1029ff.

II. It is true that they are not entirely agreed among themselves. For some (as Brochmann, "De Servatoris Nostri Jesu Christi," Sect. 16 in *Universae theologicae systema* [1638], 1:937-48) do not deny that the ascension of Christ consists in a true and real transference and movement from the lower parts of this world upward and in a change of place; yea that he also entered into heaven (which he proves from various passages of Scripture). But what that heaven is cannot be conceived or explained by any mortal. He holds it as certain that there is not a certain corporeal place constituted above the visible heavens and separated from this earth by a local distance. It is defined not so much by local situation as by joy and glory.

III. On the contrary, we maintain that Christ went up locally, visibly and bodily from the earth into the third heaven or seat of the blessed above the visible heavens; not by a mere withdrawal of his visible presence or familiar intercourse, but by a true and local translation of his human nature. There he will remain until the day of judgment, so that although he is always present with us by his grace and Spirit and divinity, yet he is no longer with us by the bodily presence of his flesh.

Proof that the ascension of Christ was made by a local movement.

IV. It is proved (1) from the history of the ascension, which intimates a true and real change of place. It is said that "he was received up into heaven" (*anelēphthē eis ton ouranon*, Mk. 16:19); that "he was parted from them, and carried up into heaven" (*diestē ap' autōn, kai anephereto eis ton ouranon*, Lk. 24:51); "while they beheld, he was taken up; and a cloud received him out of their sight" (Acts 1:9, 10). Here is described the point from which (*terminus a quo*) of that ascension (to wit, the earth and Mount Olivet in particular); through what (the air and the clouds); to what (heaven): the words describing it (*analēpsis, anaphorē, diastasis, eparsis*) indicate a real translation and change of place. Nor is it of any use to reply that these things are said only of the familiar and earthly intercourse and conversation and not of his real, invisible presence, which was taken away from believers, which the solemn promise of Christ confirms (Mt. 28:20). The words themselves sufficiently teach no less the real presence of his body on earth, than that his familiar intercourse was removed, since indeed they necessarily suppose a translation from a lower place to a higher.

V. Second, he is said "to have left the world, and to have gone to the Father" (Jn. 16:28), which could not be said if he had withdrawn only his visible presence from the world. And the circumstances of the passages show that a local presence is meant, partly from the antithesis of the *terminus a quo* and *ad quem*—"I leave," he said, "the world" (i.e., the earth) "and go to the Father" (i.e., I ascend into heaven); partly from the opposition of his "coming" and of his "departure"—"I came into the world" by the incarnation, now "I leave the world" as to the flesh (namely, according to which he is said to have been taken up [*analēphtheis*] and seen by his disciples going into heaven [*poreuomenos eis ton ouranon*, Acts 1:10, 11]). If he is said to have come into the world as Logos (*Logos*) by manifestation only and not by a change of place, the same thing cannot be said of his flesh because there is one method for his divinity, which (since it is immense) cannot change its place; another, of his humanity, whose property it is to pass from one place to another.

VI. Third, the heaven into which Christ was carried is described to us as a certain place into which he has entered and into which we are to enter after him. It is called "his Father's house," in which are many mansions, whither Christ has ascended "to prepare a place for us" (Jn. 14:2, 3); "the third heaven and paradise" (2 Cor. 12:2, 4); into which Christ enters as our forerunner (Heb. 6:20); towards which we ought to raise our eyes "seeking those things which are above, where Christ sitteth at the right hand of God, and not those things which are upon the earth" (Col. 3:1, 2). Falsely, therefore, Brentius and other Lutherans maintain that heaven to be nothing else than happiness itself (which is incomprehensible to us). It is one thing to seek what that heaven is; another, however, to seek its quality.

Sources of explanation.

VII. Christ is said to "have ascended above all heavens" (Eph. 4:10) (to wit, the visible—namely, the aerial heaven) and the firmament (to wit, in order that he might enter into the third heaven or paradise). For he is said so to have ascended above all heavens that nevertheless he is said to be in heaven (Eph. 1:20). Nor if he is said to have ascended thither "that he might fill all things" is this to be understood of the filling of all places by omnipresence of body, but concerning the filling of all the members of his church by an effusion of the gifts of the Spirit (as it is explained in the same passage).

VIII. Christ was in the midst of the seven candlesticks and thus on earth (Rev. 1:13) by his Spirit, grace, protection and government; but not by a bodily presence. Nor did John see him walking by ocular vision on the earth, but only by intellectual and ecstatic vision (as is denoted in v. 10, when he is said to have been "in the Spirit" [*en pneumati*, i.e., in an ecstasy]; as in Acts 10:10, in which way also Paul beheld him standing near him, Acts 23:11).

IX. The same one who descended, also ascended (Eph. 4:10), as to person, but not as to nature. For the divine descended, but the human ascended—the former indeed metaphorically and figuratively (because it could not do otherwise); the latter, however, properly and locally, so that it is truly in heaven (where it was not before) as it is no more on earth (where it had been before). Although Christ did not descend properly and locally from heaven (because as Logos [*Logos*] he is everywhere), it does not follow that that heaven is not local, but allegorical, since such things are attributed to it as cannot square with anything but a true and proper place. In these locutions, therefore, the trope is not in the word "heaven," but in the words "coming" and "descending."

X. Although Christ departed by ascension to the Father (who is everywhere), it does not follow that that ascension is nothing else than a departure to supreme happiness (which is everywhere in the Father, not in any particular place). He is said to have departed to the Father, not that he was everywhere with the Father, but thither where he was to be crowned with glory and honor (namely, to heaven, where God has his throne and where Christ himself is to remain even until the consummation of all things). Thus when he says that he goes away, he intimates a change of place; when he adds that he goes away to the Father, he intimates a change of condition, fitting to the human nature.

XI. Although believers are happy wherever they may be (because they are always with God), still their happiness is not perfect until they are received into heaven (into which Stephen, breathing after Christ, looked). Hence Paul, although he was with Christ already by faith, still wishes (having left the earth) to go away to heaven and to be with him by sight (Phil. 1:23). And believers who are said to sit now in heavenly places with Christ by faith and hope are as yet absent from him and their home (2 Cor. 5:6).

XII. As it is said of Stephen, that he saw Christ in heaven, while "he saw the heavens opened, and Christ standing on the right hand of God" (Acts 7:56), namely, gifted with an extraordinary sharpness of sight by the Holy Spirit, in the same way Paul could have seen him (Acts 9:27). Hence in Acts 26:19, he calls it a "heavenly vision." And "the light which from heaven is said to have shone around him" (v. 13) was indeed a symbol of his glorious majesty, but not a proof of the presence of his body on earth or in the air. If Paul is said to have been in the way when he saw the Lord, it does not follow that Christ (seen by Paul) was also in the way.

Nineteenth Question: Christ's Sitting at the Right Hand of God

What is the session of Christ at the right hand of God? According to what nature does it apply to Christ and does it pertain to the relation of situation? We deny.

I. This question is necessary on account of the Lutherans, who, to prove the omnipresence and omnipotence of the human nature of Christ, maintain that he (according to his human nature) sits at God's right hand. However, that it may be more easily understood, we must first speak briefly of the sitting itself. Hence it can be gathered with little trouble how it belongs to Christ.

The sitting at God's right hand must be understood not literally, but figuratively.

II. The sitting at God's right hand can be understood not properly and literally (since God has neither a right nor a left hand), but figuratively and metaphorically to denote the supreme dignity and sway of Christ. The metaphor is taken from the custom of kings and chiefs, who are accustomed to place on their right hand those to whom they concede the nearest degree to them, both of honor and of power in governing. This phrase is understood of the nearest degree of honor in 1 K. 2:19, where Solomon, about to show his mother special honor, places her on his right hand. And in Ps. 45:9, the wife of the king (i.e., the church) is said to stand upon the right hand of the Messiah (i.e., in the next degree of dignity to him). It is used of dominion or the administration of a kingdom (Mt. 20:21) where the mother of the sons of Zebedee seeks that they might sit on the right and left hand of Christ in his kingdom (i.e., obtain the chief offices).

III. Hence the nature of Christ's sitting at the right hand of the Father may easily be discerned. For two things are specially designated here: (1) the supreme majesty and glory by which he was most highly exalted by God and received a name above every name (Phil. 2:9, 10; Heb. 1:3); (2) the supreme dominion which he powerfully exerts over all creatures and which he shows especially in the government and defense of the church. The latter is explained by Paul in 1 Cor. 15:25 where he explains the sitting at the right hand of Ps. 110:1 by "reigning" (*basileuein*): "he must reign, till he hath put all enemies under his feet." Thus that sitting is set forth by the subjection of all things under his feet (Eph. 1:22); and "who is gone into heaven, and is on the right hand of God; angels and authorities and powers being made subject unto him" (1 Pet. 3:22).

Sitting is properly not of natures, but of a person.

IV. From this declaration of the session of Christ, it is easy to gather how it belongs to Christ or what is the subject of that sitting. Whether it is the human nature simply, as the Lutherans hold (for the purpose of defending their hypothesis of the everywhereness [*pantachousia*] of Christ's body). Or the divine nature (as others). Or the person (which is the received opinion among the orthodox). We follow the latter maintaining that sitting properly belongs to the person of Christ according to both natures (but with a certain distinction).

V. The reason is—sitting at the right hand is not a property of the nature (either of the divine or of the human), but a property of the dignity of the person (to wit, the glorious state of Christ's person and the administration of the mediatorial office, whose works [*apotelesmata*] are common to the whole person with respect to both natures). Hence the Logos (*Logos*) does not say to the flesh, Sit at my right hand, but the Father says this to the Son (called to the mediatorial office). And the power is here to be distinguished from its exercise. For the subject of power is the person or Christ, the God-man (*theanthrōpos*), manifested in the flesh, not the natures simply. For that power is not an absolute accident necessarily inhering in the natures, but a simple relation (as royal power belongs neither to the soul nor the body of a king, but to the compound being). The subject of its exercise, however, is each nature: the divine by its own omnipotence and omnipresence; the human, on the other hand, by those remarkable gifts and that glory by which he excels all creatures.

VI. Therefore, the sitting in this way of the person consists in that supreme glory and power granted to him by his exaltation, by which he was exalted as the King and head of the church. In respect of the human nature, it consists in the glory and honor with which he was adorned above all creatures and of which he was before destitute. In respect of the divine, however, it consists in the manifestation of the power and majesty which he had concealed before under the veil of the weak flesh and the servile condition.

VII. As the passion, death and crucifixion so pertain to the human nature subjectively that they are attributed to the person also denominatively (in which sense actions and sufferings belong to compound beings), so the sitting (which implies a real communication of honor and glory with respect to the human nature) denotes also a relation of dominion and power which is proper to the person.

VIII. When Christ is considered theologically, as Logos (*Logos*) simply, it is rightly said to be the right hand of God inasmuch as he partakes of the same omnipotent essence of God with the Father. But when considered economically as Mediator, he is rightly said to sit at the right hand of God. In the former sense, the right hand of God is spoken of the divine omnipotence, but in the latter metaphorically of the empire and dominion which properly belongs to the person. It can also be ascribed to the divine nature in time, if not as to the new bestowal of a thing not yet possessed, still as to the manifestation of a thing possessed indeed before, but as yet concealed.

IX. Although to the exercise of the power granted to Christ, omnipotence and omnipresence are required, it does not follow that these were given to Christ's human nature. It is sufficient that they belong to the person (*supposito*) of Christ by reason of the divine nature. And thus the human nature was made partaker of that dominion, but after the manner of a creature (such as it always remains). The power and operations of the deity, by which he gloriously administers his kingdom, are divine—equal to God because he himself as God is equal with the Father. But the actions of humanity are indeed more perfect than the actions of other creatures, though not equal to the divine because he sits indeed at the right hand of God according to both natures (yet the truth of both natures being preserved).

When did Christ begin to sit at the right hand of God?

X. Hence we can readily respond to the question moved here concerning the time of Christ's sitting—When did he begin to sit? From eternity? as Thomas Aquinas, Maldonatus and others wish who interpret the sitting of the Son's equality with the Father; or from the very moment of his incarnation? as Brentius and his followers, who explain that sitting of the personal union of the flesh with the Logos (*Logō*) and the communication of properties to the flesh; or only after his resurrection and ascension? which we hold with the orthodox.

XI. First, Scripture expressly places the sitting of Christ after his resurrection and ascension (Eph. 1:20; Mk. 16:19; Heb. 10:12; 1 Pet. 3:21, 22). Second, it is the fruit of his humiliation and death (Heb. 1:3; 12:2). Third, he could not administer the mediatorial kingdom gloriously, unless his enemies had been conquered on the cross and in the ascension.

XII. Christ indeed as Logos (*Logos*) was from eternity with the Father, but he cannot on that account be said to have sat down at the right hand of God (in the sense in which that sitting is ascribed to him after the resurrection according to his glorious state as Mediator). He reigned as Son over the kingdom of nature, but not as God-man (*theanthrōpos*) over the economic kingdom. Christ as Mediator can be said in a certain sense to have sat down at the right hand of God as without flesh (*asarkos*) even before the incarnation; thus from the beginning of the world because he always was the head and King of the church who governed and defended it (Ps. 2:6; Heb. 13:8). But "with flesh" (*ensarkon*), he sits only after his passion and resurrection (Lk. 24:26). He had indeed the right of the kingdom from the hypostatical union, but he did not obtain the actual possession until after his ascension (Ps. 110:1; Acts 2:34-36).

XIII. The time of sitting *a posteriori* has no limit because it ought to be forever (*eis to diēnekes*, according to the apostle, Heb. 10:12). Nor do the words of Ps. 110:1 hinder where it is said he will sit "until (*'dh khy*) his enemies are made his footstool." It is known that this particle so asserts a certain time, concerning which it is treated and of which it can be doubted, as not to deny a continuation into the future (as appears from Gen. 28:15; Mt. 28:20; 1 Tim. 4:13). Thus the dominion of Christ is here asserted in the midst of enemies (i.e., in a most perilous time). But it is not denied as to the future because his kingdom ought to be eternal. There ought indeed to be a change in the manner of reigning, but not in the kingdom itself (as will be seen in the proper place).

XIV. Moreover the sitting of Christ at the right hand of the Father does not denote the situation or position (*ubicationem*) of Christ's body, since it is the state of his person. Nor can this be charged upon us unless slanderously, as if the right hand of God were with us a place and the sitting at his right hand a certain local situation. The heaven in which he is said to sit at the right hand of God is to us the place in which (as in a royal palace and a sanctuary not made with hands) he sits at the right hand of God. But no one of us says the right hand of God is a place.

XV. However, the error which the Ubiquitists falsely charge upon us, we deservedly ascribe to them according to their own hypothesis. From the session of Christ at the right hand of God, they infer the ubiquity of the body of Christ for the reason that the right hand of God is everywhere. This they cannot conclude without supposing and conceiving the right hand of God after the manner of a certain place and the session after the manner of a local situation.

XVI. To the argument drawn from the session of Christ at the right hand of God for his ubiquity, besides what has already been said in Question 8, Section 29 (and to say nothing of the form of the syllogism, which is clearly faulty on account of the four terms, when from the right hand of God, which is everywhere, it is concluded that he who sits at the right hand of God ought to be everywhere). However, since the right hand of God and sitting at the right hand of God widely differ (nor ought he who sits at God's right hand to be wherever that right hand is, especially since that sitting is not the designation of a local situation, but the bestowal of dominion and glory), it is certain: (1) that the state and office of the person is here confounded with a property of his nature because ubiquity is a property of his nature, while the sitting upon the right hand is a state and office of the person. (2) That a figurative and metaphorical locution is confounded with a proper one; for the sitting at the right hand is said figuratively, while the being everywhere is understood properly. (3) Glory and dignity are confounded with omnipresence; for what is glorious must not forthwith be omnipresent, if omnipresence destroys its proper nature (which is the case here). To make the body omnipresent is to say the body is not a body. (4) That the flesh of Christ is confounded with his dominion, so that the essence of the flesh extends as widely as his kingdom and dominion (which is indeed true of God, but not of the flesh in like manner however highly glorified). Nor is there need for the flesh to be present wherever he reigns, no more than a king ought to be bodily present in all the provinces of his kingdom, especially since Christ is everywhere present as to person with respect to his divine nature.

XVII. Although the receiving of a name above every name belongs in its own measure to the assumed nature also, still it must be so understood that the properties of the natures be preserved according to the Scriptures. Thus the Son is also glorified according to the flesh, but not so as to make the flesh equal to the Logos (*Logō*). Nor do we divide Christ or ascribe two glories and powers to him, than when saying man was made after the image of God and afterwards became corrupt, on that account either make the body equal to the soul or lower the soul to a level with the body in ignominy.

XVIII. It is one thing to say Christ is present everywhere, equal in glory with the Father and fills all things; another to ascribe this to the flesh of Christ. What is said of the person in the concrete cannot be (nor ought to be) forthwith applied to the natures in the abstract. For although it is true that the man Christ is God, still you would improperly say that this flesh is divinity. For not by commixture or confusion, but by an unconfused and unmixed union of the two natures, the Son of God was made man.

XIX. It is one thing for a glorified body to be made spiritual as to qualities with regard to splendor, activity, thinness and the like; but another to be made a spirit or to be changed into the nature of a spirit—and a spirit immense and infinite. The body of Christ, by its exaltation to and session at the right hand of God, was indeed made spiritual as to qualities, but was not changed into a spirit as to substance or essential properties, much less into an omnipresent spirit.

XX. For the rest, a certain diversity may seem to exist between our divines in the explanation of Christ's session at God's right hand. Some make it consist in four things: (1) in the equality of the Logos (*tou Logou*) or person of the Mediator with the Father, which he did not indeed receive in the session, but manifested in the time of humiliation; (2) in the perfection of his mediatorial office, by which he was constituted King and head of the church; (3) in the perfection of the humanity of Christ raised to the highest glory; (4) in the perfection of honor and worship, by which Christ is worshipped and adored as Lord and King of the church. Others make it solely in the communication of honor and dominion bestowed upon him after his ascension. This is not so much a dissent in reality as in the manner of teaching. The first group considers that session more broadly and describes it not only from the proper form, but also from the beginning or foundation (viz., equality with the Father, without which it would not have been capable of receiving such great honor and dominion from the antecedents and consequents which are necessarily conjoined with it). The others, however, view it more strictly—simply as to the form of session, which consists properly in the perfection of the mediatorial office, by which Christ, crowned with glory and honor, rules in the midst of his enemies.

FOURTEENTH TOPIC

THE MEDIATORIAL OFFICE OF CHRIST

First Question
In what sense is the name "Mediator" applied to Christ?

I. After the discussion concerning the person and state of Christ, we must now treat of his mediatorial office, on account of which he was made God-man (*theanthrōpos*) and ought to sustain a twofold state. Here the meaning of the term "Mediator" (usually applied to him in this business) must first be explained.

Derivation of the word "Mediator."

II. "Mediator" (in Greek *mesitēs*) is derived from *medius*. He is commonly so called who is the middle one between parties at variance and who intervenes (*mesiteuei*). For a "mediator is not of one" (as the apostle says, Gal. 3:20), but of more contending with each other (viz., in order to reconcile them). Hence Suidas explains *mesitēn* by *eirēnopoion*. He is also called by the Latins *Sequester*, as Tertullian uses the word to designate Christ (*Against Praxeas* 27 [ANF 3:624; PL 2.192]). Moreover he is a *sequester* who is the middle one between two altercating parties and by whom the matter in controversy is settled. He is so called from *sequendo* because each of the contestants follows his decision.

III. However, as the mediation of Christ can be viewed either in relation to his person or to his office or inasmuch as he is the middle one or because he mediates, the mediation is distinguished into two kinds: the first of which they call substantial, by which Christ is the middle one between God and man; the other efficacious and operative, by which he performs the duty committed to him by the Father. The former marks the state of the person; the latter his operation. The former designates the union of natures; the latter the execution of the office in the person. But that former (as less proper) is not attended to by us here, only the latter (which belongs to this topic).

In how many ways is he thus called?

IV. Therefore Christ is properly called Mediator by act and exercise because he exercises the office of Mediator to establish a union between God and men, separated from each other on account of sin. Now as a Mediator among men is various, either as a mere internuncius (the interpreter of each party, as Moses is called a mediator in the Old Testament because he stood between God and the people, Dt. 5:5); or as an arbiter, who is selected by the litigants and has power over the whole affair to settle it, not by strict justice, but equitability (*kat' epieikeian*); or as an intercessor and advocate, who entreats and intercedes for one party with the other; or as a surety and satisfier, who conciliates the discordant by making satisfaction to the offended party and going security for the future fidelity and obedience of the offending party, so that no cause of disagreement may afterwards arise between them. Thus according to these various relations (*scheseis*), Christ is rightly called a Mediator.

Christ, the Mediator, as an internuncius.

V. First, he was an internuncius by reason of his doctrine inasmuch as he was the interpreter of both parties and especially inasmuch as he declared the will of God to men (Jn. 1:18; Lk. 4:18). In this sense, he is called the "angel of the covenant" (Mal. 3:1) and "Counsellor" (Is. 9:6).

As arbiter.

Second, he can also be called an arbiter (as Ambrose on 1 Tim. 2—cf. *Ambrosiater/Pseudo-Ambrose: In Epistolam B. Pauli ad Timotheum Primam* [PL 17.493] and Augustine on Ps. 103, *Ennaratio in Psalmum CIII: Sermo IV* 8 [PL 37.1383] call him) because in procuring our reconciliation with God he acted not with strict justice, but tempered justice with grace and mercy.

As intercessor.

Third, because we had to deal with an offended supreme power, he must perform the office of intercessor and patron to plead our cause before God against the Devil and obtain the necessary grace for us (in which sense he is called an "advocate"—*paraklētos*, 1 Jn. 2:1).

As pacificator.

Fourth, as the discordance between us and God arising from sin could not be removed without a satisfaction to the justice of God and the expiation of sin, our Mediator ought to sustain the relation not only of internuncius and intercessor (as Socinus held), but especially of a reconciler and peacemaker (*eirēnopoiou*) who would procure peace for us with God by his own blood and, by paying a ransom (*antilytron*) for us, free us from the guilt and dominion of sin. Because it was not sufficient to have once reconciled men to God, if after that the same discordance could be renewed by the sin of man, the same one ought by the efficacy of his own suretyship to establish firmly the reconciliation once made that we might be forever united to God. The first and second modes belong to his prophetic office, the third and fourth to his priestly and kingly office.

VI. As a mediator ought to act for both sides (both with God offended and with offending man) in order to remove the obstacles to reconciliation, he really acted in both ways—both by satisfying and interceding for us with God (as a Priest) and for God with us by teaching and directing us (as a Prophet and King)—first by acting for us, then by working in us (as was more fully explained before in Topic XII on the covenant of grace, Question 2, Section 16). Hence all these acts are distinguished into impetratory (by which that reconciliation was acquired and which depend upon it) and applicatory and conservatory (by which all of them are applied and conserved). By the former, Christ is the Mediator and Savior by merit; by the latter, he is the Savior and Mediator by efficacy.

Statement of the question.

VII. Our controversy here is with the Socinians, who, to overthrow the whole doctrine of the satisfaction, confess that Christ is a Mediator, but only (1) of divine institution or revelation by which he declared the way of salvation consisting (according to them) in obedience to God's commands; (2) of example because he entered the same way with and exhibited a most perfect example to his own; (3) of confirmation because he unalterably fixed that obedience by his own death and passion. On the contrary, we (although not denying that Christ sustains these relations) still deny that in them alone consists his mediatorial office, but especially in the relation of reconciliation and satisfaction inasmuch as he was a peacemaker (*eirēnopoios*) who (peace having been made by blood) reconciled us to God.

Proof that Christ is a peacemaker.

VIII. The reasons are: (1) Scripture describes him not as a mere internuncius but as a true peacemaker (*eirēnopoion*) and pacificator and his mediation as a redemption and reconciliation. He is called Mediator (inasmuch as he gave himself a ransom [*antilytron*] for us, 1 Tim. 2:6) who, having made peace (*eirēnopoiēsas*) through the blood of his cross, reconciled God to us (Col. 1:20); also a pledge-giver (*enguos*) and surety of the new covenant (Heb. 7:22) who ought accordingly to pay and to satisfy for us; and a Mediator to procure for the called redemption by his death and obtain eternal salvation by his blood (Heb. 9:12, 15). Hence the blood of sprinkling (*rantismou*) is joined to the Mediator in allusion to the blood of legal victims dying for sinners (Heb. 12:24). All these imply not a simple declaration, but a true satisfaction (as will be proved more fully under the proper head).

IX. (2) The necessity of salvation required this since the variance between God and man caused by sin had rendered men haters of God (*theostygeis*, Rom. 1:30, i.e., not only "haters of God" actively, but also "hated by God" passively); that could not be taken away simply by doctrine or by example, but demanded a true ransom (*lytron*) by which not only man could be reconciled to God by repentance and the desire of holiness (as the Socinians maintain), but also God to man, with whom (on account of the nature of his vindicatory justice) he was deservedly angry and who therefore could be appeased only by an adequate satisfaction (by the substitution of a Mediator in his place who, by devoting himself for him, might receive upon himself the punishments due to him and by bearing them free him from them).

X. (3) If Christ was Mediator in no other way than by teaching and example, he would be placed in the same rank with the prophets and apostles—those especially who suffered martyrdom, manifested the way of salvation by their teaching and example and set forth to us the whole counsel of God (Acts 20:27). Nevertheless, the apostle denies this can be said when he calls Christ our only Mediator (1 Tim. 2:5). (4) He would be a Savior in no other way than morally and accidentally because the salvation of each individual would really depend upon himself, who would obey the divine commands (as will be shown more fully when we treat of the satisfaction).

Sources of explanation.

XI. Christ is called a Mediator "to give testimony" [viz., to the truth] "in due time" (*eis martyrion kairois idiois*, 1 Tim. 2:6) not only because he gave testimony to gospel truth by prophecy, but in addition because by his own death, he assured us of the benevolence obtained for us and of the reconciliation made with God. Or *martyrion* may be understood passively, concerning the thing to which testimony ought to be given because concerning it all men of God ought to bear testimony.

XII. The similitude between Moses and Christ does not at once imply parity—that Christ was Mediator in no other way than Moses, as an internuncius (Dt. 5:5; Acts 7:38). He was only a typical mediator and so far more imperfect than the antitype, Christ (yet he was a true and properly so-called mediator). He was a mere man, but Christ the God-man; he indeed communicated the oracles of God to the people, but did not reconcile the people to God or by his own blood appease the wrath of God, since he trembled greatly at the voice of God, the lawgiver (Heb. 12:21). But Christ made peace by his own blood and gave himself to God as a surety (*enguon*) for us. And so, as a partial and inadequate type, Moses could represent Christ in some functions of a mediator (for instance, as to prophecy and kingdom), but not as to all and especially as to the sacerdotal functions which were signified by other types (to wit, by the priests and victims).

XIII. Nor does Gal. 3:19 help our adversaries. Here the law is said to have been given "in the hand of a mediator" (*en cheiri mesitou*). Besides the fact that it can rightly be referred to Christ (which most of the Greeks and Latins, both ancient as well as more modern [and among them our Calvin, *The Epistles of Paul . . . to the Galatians* (trans. T.H.L. Parker, 1965), p. 62] have done), both because nowhere else is the name Mediator given to any other than Christ, who is also called the only one (1 Tim. 2:5) and because Moses is elsewhere (Acts 7:35) said to have been ordained a ruler and a deliverer of the people *en cheiri* ("in the hand"—viz., by the authority and direction *angelou*—"of an angel," to wit, of that one who appeared to him in the burning bush, the eternal Son of God). The latter is said to have given Moses the "lively oracles" (*logia zōnta*, v. 38, viz., the law which he delivered to the people). So that the sense is either that the law was delivered to the Israelites by the hand (i.e., the power and direction of the Mediator, Christ, preparing that people in this way for his advent) or that Christ by bringing forward the law with his own hand interposed himself as a surety, who would both perfectly fulfill the law at some time and by drawing the curse of the law upon himself, free us from it. If it is referred to Moses (as pleased Epiphanius and others, whom Beza follows here—cf. *Annotationes maiores in Novum . . . Testamentum: Pars Altera* [1594], p. 329 on Gal. 3:19) because *en cheiri* denotes ministry rather than supreme power (which would be less suitable to Christ) and because it is evident that the law was given by Moses (Jn. 1:17), as elsewhere it is said to have been given from God "by the hand of Moses" (Lev. 26:46), our opinion suffers nothing from this source because Moses may be called only a typical mediator, just as the law was a type of the gospel. Not that he was like Christ in all respects, but that he slightly shadowed him forth in certain respects only. But what is added, "a mediator is not of one, but God is one" (*mesitēs de henos ouk esti, ho de theos heis esti*, Gal. 3:20), that we may say something in passing concerning an obscure and difficult passage, can thus be illustrated not inappropriately from the scope of the apostle (which is to show that life and justification are not given by the law because since in bringing them in there was need of a Mediator, it appears thence that it is not the bond of our union with God, but rather the sign of our alienation from and disagreement with him). For he says "a mediator is not of one" (viz., party), but of many or at least of two, and they at variance. For where a union exists, there is no need of the interposition of a mediator. However, what is added ("but God is one") refers not so much to the unity and simplicity of God as to his constancy and immutability, no less in his nature than in his purposes and decrees (i.e., constant and always consistent). Since therefore he had prescribed in the law perfect righteousness for the attainment of life (which could not be given to him by sinful man), it is evident that the union between these two discordant parties (to wit, God and man) could not be effected by the law, but by the sole righteousness and satisfaction of Christ, which the gospel announces to us (as the apostle had intimated, v. 13). Certain ones, following the Ethiopic interpreter, give this explanation: "a mediator is not of one, but God is one" (viz., of the two parties at variance). But this seems somewhat cold because no one could be ignorant that God is one of the disagreeing parties, since it would treat concerning a mediation with himself.

Second Question

Is Christ a Mediator according to both natures? We affirm against the papists and Stancar.

I. This question lies between us and the papists, who, the more easily to foist in many mediators, hold that Christ was a Mediator according to his human nature alone (as they assert following Lombard, *Sententiarum* 3, Dist. 19.7* [PL 192/2.797-98]; Thomas Aquinas, ST, III, Q. 26, Art. 2, pp. 2159-60; Bellarmine, "De Christo," 3 *Opera* [1856], 1:290; Becanus, *Manuale controversiarum* 3.2 [1750], pp. 420-21 and others). Stancar follows them on this point. He opposed somewhat vehemently (Andreas) Osiander, his colleague in the Regiomontane (Konigsberg) Academy, who maintained that Christ was not Mediator except according to his divine nature and thus we are justified by his eternal and essential righteousness (not sufficiently distinguishing the efficacy of Christ from his merit). Stancar fell into the opposite error of the papists, affirming that Christ is Mediator only as to his human nature.

Statement of the question.

II. The question is not whether the person of the Mediator is divine. For our opponents do not deny this. Rather the question is whether the acts or sufferings of the Mediator proceeded from it according to the human nature alone. Or according to both. The papists distinguish between a principle-which (*principium quod*) and a principle-by-which (*principium quo*) or a formal principle. The former they say is a *suppositum* or person, not a nature. The latter, however, they hold to be only his human nature. "For although he was God," says Bellarmine, "who suffered, obeyed and satisfied, still he did all this in the form of a servant, not in the form of God" ("De Christo Mediatore," 1 *Opera* [1856], 1:290).

III. Four things must be accurately distinguished here in reference to the actions of Christ, as John of Damascus pointed out (*Exposition of the Orthodox Faith* 4.18 [NPNF2, 9:90-92]). (1) He is one that works (*ho energōn*), the agent or principle which acts (which is the *suppositum* or person of Christ). (2) The activity (*energētikon*) or formal principle by which he acts—that by which the agent or person of Christ works (to wit, the two natures, each of which works without any confusion). (3) The energy (*energeia*) or operation which depends upon the principle-by-which and partakes of the nature of its own principle, so that it is divine if the principle-by-which is the divine nature, but human, if it is the humanity. (4) The effect (*energēma*) or accomplishment (*apotelesma*) which depends upon the principle-which and is the external work, which we call mediation. There is therefore a twofold principle of mediation—a common and a proper. The common is one (namely, the person of the Mediator); the proper, however, is twofold (to wit, the divine and the human nature—the divine, indeed, the proper and formal principle of the divine actions; the human of the human actions). Not thus also are the proper actions to be ascribed to the formal principles or natures (as if they act separately), for each form acts with the communion of the other which is proper (to wit, the Word working what belongs to the Word and the flesh prosecuting what belongs to it, as Leo has it, *Letter 28 [10]*, "To Flavian" (FC 34:98; PL 54.767). Thus one is the principal agent (to wit, the person of Christ) and one the issue (*apotelesma*) or mediatorial work. But it is worked by two natures as two principles; whence flow two energies (*energeiai*) or operations concurring to that one work.

IV. Again the actions of Christ can be viewed in a threefold order as Christ can be regarded under a threefold relation (*schesei*)—either as God, or as man, or as God-man (*theanthrōpos*). Some are merely divine, which he effects only as God (such as creation and conservation). Others are merely human (such as eating, walking and sleeping). Others are mixed, which are called theandric (*theandrikai*) (such as redemption, to accomplish which both his divine and human natures concurred). Therefore the question is—To which class of these acts does mediation belong? To the merely human (as the papists hold) or to the theandric (*theandrikas*) (which we assert)?

Proof that Christ is Mediator as to both natures: (1) from Acts 20:28.

V. The reasons are: (1) Scripture ascribes the mediation of Christ to both natures—"God purchased the church with his blood" (Acts 20:28); "The Lord of glory was crucified" (1 Cor. 2:8); "He offered himself through the eternal Spirit" (Heb. 9:14). These indicate not only the dignity of his person, but also the efficacy of the sacrifice which proceeded from the divinity. For although these may be explained by the communication of attributes, still they designate that they partook of the divinity no less than of the humanity; each nature contributing what was its own—the human indeed the substance of the work (or passion); the divine, its infinite value and price.

2. From the parts of the mediation of Christ.

VI. (2) All the parts of the mediatorial work demand both natures. Christ is Mediator as to the same nature in which he is a Prophet, Priest and King. And yet according to both, he could and was bound to exercise that threefold office. It is evident first from prophecy.

Prophecy.

For as a Prophet, he must reveal the Father to us and manifest his will. And yet who could reveal the Father to us except the Son, who alone knows him (Mt. 11:27)? Who could declare his will and disclose the divine wisdom hidden in a mystery except the one who is in the bosom of the Father (Jn. 1:18)—the Word (*Logos*) and eternal Wisdom of God? Men indeed interpret the divine will and bring it to us, but only ministerially; but to act as a supreme and *anypeuthynon* ("not accountable to human criticism") interpreter of heavenly matters (and that too not only by an external suasion and preaching, but by an internal illumination and persuasion) belongs to God and not to man. Again, as a Prophet he ought to inscribe the law upon the heart and thus teach efficaciously as to give a new heart and open the mind to understand the Scriptures that believers may be truly taught of God (*theodidaktoi*, Jn. 6:45). This he could not do as man, but only as God. To him alone, it much more belongs to write on the heart than on stone.

The priestly.

VII. As a Priest, he was bound to satisfy divine justice perfectly for us. To intercede for sinners, he must abolish death by his own death (and him who had the power of death), to reconcile us (alienated from God) and unite us to him forever. Now who but God could oppose infinite merit to the infinite demerit of sinners and pay a ransom (*antilytron*) of infinite value to the justice of God? Who but God could bear the unbearable (*abastakton*) weight of wrath and not be crushed by it? Who but God had power to lay down life by a voluntary death and to take it up again by resurrection (Jn. 10:18)? Who but God could, through the eternal Spirit, offer himself (fulfilling at the same time the functions of priest and victim, Heb. 9:14), overcome death by death, vanquish Satan, obtain eternal redemption by his own blood and save his people forever (Heb. 7:25)?

And the kingly.

VIII. As King he ought to rule the universal church by the scepter of his word, send the Holy Spirit with all his gifts, effectually call, open hearts, bruise Satan, place all the enemies of salvation under his footstool and glorify his church. Now who could do all this except one furnished with invincible power (i.e., the true God)? Therefore in whatever manner Christ, the Mediator, is viewed, he must perform this office no less according to the divine than the human nature.

3. From his humiliation.

IX. (3) He ought to be Mediator according to the same nature in which he humbled himself and assumed the form of a servant. For he humbled himself for no other reason than that he might perform this office. Now he emptied himself according to the divine nature, not by a real diminution of his essential glory, but by an external hiding of his accidental glory.

4. From the mediation in the Old Testament.

X. (4) He ought to be a Mediator according to that nature in which he could work as Mediator even from the beginning of the world, since he ought to be the same yesterday, today and forever. Now he could not work according to the human, but only according to the divine nature, according to which (as he already existed) he could govern his church and enrich it with all gifts necessary to salvation.

5. From the effects of his mediation.

XI. (5) The principal effects of Christ's mediation (redemption and salvation, remission of sins, the gift of eternal life) belong equally to the divine and human natures. These are of such a kind as to be works and blessings of God alone. Nor ought it to be said that these acts depend upon the man Christ after the manner of an instrument, but on the Trinity as on the principal cause. Christ has not only the relation of an instrument (for thus he would work no more than his ministers, to whom such works are sometimes ascribed), but also of a principal cause, meritorious as well as efficacious. Hence Augustine says, "The divinity without the humanity is not the Mediatrix, nor the humanity without the divinity; but between the divinity and humanity alone, the Mediatrix is the human divinity and the divine humanity" (*Sermo* 47, "De Ovibus," 12 [21] [PL 38.310]).

XII. (6) Since the incarnation was made with unconfounded properties, it belongs to the acts no less than to the natures. The acts pertaining to mediation must therefore be ascribed to the divinity as the formal principle, since Christ became incarnate that he might be a Mediator. It is absurd then that the divinity of Christ should have refrained from the work on account of which Christ was most especially sent. If it exerted itself in miracles, much more did it distinguish itself in the work of redemption (more illustrious than all miracles); nor did it flash forth in so many miracles for any other cause than that by this very thing he might prove himself to be the true Savior.

Sources of explanation.

XIII. When the man Christ is said to be Mediator (1 Tim. 2:5), he is not proved to be so only as to his human nature. (1) The exclusive, as man only, is not added. (2) This is introduced exegetically not to exclude his divinity, but to include his humanity in order that we may approach him with greater confidence as being partaker of the same nature with us and because he was about to speak immediately of his delivery to death. (3) The argument of Romanists concludes nothing, unless it is supposed that wherever the concrete name of God occurs or of man attributed to Christ in the Scriptures, his divine or human nature is there designated (which cannot be said since the concrete denotes the person, not the nature). (4) The name of God used in this connection is taken personally to designate the Father economically, between whom and men Christ is the Mediator. If it is taken more widely for the whole Trinity, still his divine nature is not excluded from the mediation. For it is one thing for Christ to be a Mediator according to his divine nature absolutely, inasmuch as it is common to the three persons; another, according to the divine nature regarded economically with respect to his voluntary humiliation.

XIV. There is nothing absurd in an offended party becoming voluntarily a mediator in a different respect. Christ sets himself forth to us as such in the parable (Mt. 21:37) and wishes this to be done by his people (Mt. 5:24; 18:16). Nor is it unusual that the offended should institute a reconciliation with the offending (as God with our first parents [Gen. 3; 2 Cor. 5:18-20], the Israelites with the Benjamites [Jdg. 21] and David with his rebellious subjects [2 S. 19:12]; as a senator pleading the cause of the accused who is to be reconciled to the senate—which Menenius Agrippa formerly did between the Senate and the Roman people). Hence nothing hindered Christ as God-man (*theanthrōpon*) (considered economically) from being a Mediator to himself, as he is God essentially (*ousiōdōs*). For although God the Son (or *Logos*) does not differ from Christ the Mediator (or person) or his nature considered in itself and absolutely, still he does differ by economy and in relation to the mediatorial office. Since it is one thing for God to be the Son; another for him to be a Mediator; one thing to be offended as God, another as God-man (*theanthrōpōn*) to act as Mediator. Thus the mediation will always be to another, both because the Son and the Word differ from the God-man (*theanthrōpō*) (if not by nature [*physei*] at least economically [*oikonomia*]) and because the Son differs from the Father, with whom he is appropriatively called a Mediator—first personally because he is a different person from the Father; second by way of dispensation because the Son alone, not the Father, was made man and humbled himself.

XV. Although the mediatorial office belongs to Christ as to the divine nature, it does not follow that the Father and Holy Spirit are mediators equally with the Son. Mediation belongs to the nature, not as it is common to the persons, but as it is characterized and subsists distinctly in the person of the Son. External operations belong indeed to the whole Trinity and are common to all the persons, as they have the relation of one common principle, but that person on whom any operation terminates does not cease to hold the relation of an individual principle (as appears from the incarnation, which although originally belonging to the whole Trinity, still belongs terminatively to the Son alone, from whom as from the terminus, this work is denominated). The same must be said about his mediation.

XVI. The unity of a result indeed proves a unity of the principle-which (*principii quod*), but not always of the principle-by-which (*principii quo*). For the same work can proceed from various formal principles, but in different respects (*kat' allo kai allo*). For example, speech is one work produced by man as a common principle which, however, has two formal principles, the body and soul. Thus here we have distinct energies (*energeiai*) but one effect (*energēma*). Hence you would improperly infer that there followed a confusion of operations and by consequence of natures.

XVII. Although the office of a priest and intercessor is to serve, it does not follow that the divine nature in Christ is inferior to the Father. It follows only that Christ was made less than the Father not in nature (*physei*), but in economy (*oikonomia*); not absolutely and in himself, but in respect to a voluntary dispensation through which he humbled himself of his own accord.

XVIII. Although to lay down life is passively to die and to take it up is to rise again (and both may properly be said of the human nature), still if these phrases are taken actively (as they necessarily should be—see Jn. 10:17, 18 where the reference is to the power of laying down and taking up his own life again) or to the will over life and death, then to lay down life is to freely dispose of his own life as Lord of his own members and to take it up again is to raise himself up (which belongs not to the human nature, but to the divine).

XIX. In the sacrifice of Christ, the substance of the work must be distinguished from its value and dignity. The human nature alone contributed the former, but the divine nature ought to contribute the latter. Thus the humanity furnished the victim, the divinity the Priest (in which sense Christ is said to have offered himself through the eternal Spirit, Heb. 9:14). Now although the efficacy and value of a sacrifice is not in itself a real and physical act, still we must acknowledge that in a real action these always proceed from a real agent. If, therefore, the efficacy is from the divine nature as such, we must infer that the divine nature as such wrought in Christ, the sacrifice, and that the divinity took part in the mediatorial work.

XX. A mediator ought to be the middle one between dissenting parties; not negatively by a removal of extremes, but positively by a participation of their natures (for he could not be a Mediator for uniting men with God unless he had communion with both). Therefore, as he joined two natures in his person by a hypostatical union, so he must unite them in his office by a mystical union of will and operations. Therefore it is not sufficient for mediation that someone differs from both parties, for thus the angels could be mediators as standing apart from God and men. Rather there is required an equal distance and proximity (i.e., he should approach to and recede from him with whom the mediation is as much as from him for whom it is). Now Christ is not equally distant from God and man as a just man (as Bellarmine holds), for he differs from God by essence, but from sinful men only by qualities. Therefore, that there may be found both the distance and the proximity of a mediator, it must be sought in Christ, the God-man (*theanthrōpō*), who as he approaches to God and recedes from us (in respect of his divinity), so he approaches to us and recedes from God (in respect of his humanity).

XXI. When the fathers deny that Christ is Mediator insofar as he is God, they mean nothing else than to indicate the necessity of the hypostatical union in Christ, the Mediator, to show that he is a Mediator, not simply as he is God, but as God manifest in the flesh.

XXII. Although Moses, the mediator of the Old Testament, was only a mere man, it does not follow that Christ also could have performed this office according to his human nature. A typical mediator, who is a mere internuncius, differs from one who is a true peacemaker (*eirēnnopoios*), who could reconcile us to God only by an infinite price (*lytrō*) (such as Christ must be).

XXIII. Although Christ is proved to be a Mediator according to his divine nature, the Logos (*Logos*) is not on that account rendered inferior to the Father, nor is his consubstantiality (*homoousia*) denied. For it is one thing to make the persons unequal according to essence (with the Arians); another to distinguish the Son from the Father according to a voluntary economy by which he emptied himself. This they falsely pervert who calumniously charge us with Arianism.

Third Question

Is Christ the Mediator of angels? We deny.

Statement of the question.

I. Theologians vary in their opinions on this point. Some think that Christ can and ought to be called the Mediator of angels, but only of their conservation and confirmation, not of their redemption. For it happened that while other angels fell, these stood and so were confirmed in their righteousness received at creation so that they could never fall afterwards. On this account, they distinguish a twofold misery: one actual, the other potential; the former pertaining to evil angels and fallen men, the latter to angels and men in innocence capable of falling. To prevent this potency from exerting itself in acts, they maintain that as many as stood must have been confirmed and that this could be done by no other than Christ.

II. Although this opinion (thus explained) involves no absurdity and seems to contribute to the amplification of the glory of the Mediator, Christ, still the contrary opinion (which denies that Christ is the Mediator of angels) seems to us more true and agreeable to the sacred Scriptures. Thus if the angels were confirmed (as it was necessary they should be in order that they might be placed beyond the danger of a fall), they obtained this through a new grace of God (superadded to the always mutable state of nature) and by the Son of God—not as Mediator, but as Creator and Conservator, by whom and in whom all things are said to subsist (Col. 1:17).

Christ is not the Mediator of angels.

III. The reasons for this opinion are: (1) the Scriptures call Christ the Mediator between God and men, but never between angels. (2) There is no need of a Mediator where there is no discord; for a mediator is not of one (according to Paul, Gal. 3:20), yet there was no disagreement between God and the angels. (3) Christ is not joined with angels, but with men because he did not take on angels, but the seed of Abraham. Here the apostle gives the reason for the incarnation of Christ, undoubtedly because he must save men, not angels. (4) He is the Mediator of those of whom he is the propitiation (*hilasmos*, 1 Jn. 2:2), which does not pertain to angels. (5) If he had been given as a Mediator to angels, he must have been given to man in his state of innocence (which cannot be said since mediation pertains to the new covenant and was specially designed for taking away sin).

Sources of explanation.

IV. Christ is called the Mediator of the whole church of men, collected from all nations (Jewish as well as Gentile), but not of angels (who are distinguished from the church, Eph. 1:21, 22). Therefore although they can belong to the assembly of the glorified (Heb. 12:22, 23) and be fellow servants with believers (equally serving God), they cannot be properly called members of the church (who constitute the mystical body of Christ redeemed by him).

V. Although Christ became (in the economic kingdom of Mediator) the head and King of the angels (above whom he was exalted, so that he uses them as ministers for the salvation of believers [Heb. 1:14] and they are under him as their Lord whom they are bound to worship [Heb. 1:6; Phil. 2:10]), still he could not rightly be called their "vivifying head" in respect of a vital influx (which is diffused by the regenerating Spirit of Christ upon men alone, redeemed by the blood of Christ and effectually called).

VI. Although the angels could not merit glory strictly speaking (since it is beyond the merit of any creature whatsoever), it is not immediately necessary that Christ should merit it for them because God covenanted to reward them irrespective of their desert.

VII. All medicinal and liberating grace flows from the Mediator in the order of redemption. But there is not the same will for confirming and conserving grace, which belongs to the order of creation, for conservation is the function of him who created.

VIII. The passages of Scripture adduced from Job 4:18; 15:15; Eph. 1:10 and Col. 1:20 were answered in Volume I, Topic IV, Question 8, Sections 14-16.

Fourth Question: The Unity of the Mediator

Is Christ alone our Mediator with God? We affirm against the papists.

I. Our controversy here is with papists who (to establish more strongly their fiction of the invocation of saints) maintain that departed saints perform the office with God of mediators and intercessors for the living. They conciliate to us the favor of God not only by their prayers, but also by their merits.

Statement of the question.

II. The question is not about simple praying or intercession improperly so called—consisting in the mutual interchange of the prayers of some for others among the living. For we acknowledge that believers can pray for others and pastors especially ought to perform this office for the people with God. Rather the question relates to mediation properly so called, by which one may be considered as interceding by his own virtue and not only offering prayers to God, but also commending those offered to God and making them acceptable by his own merits.

III. The question is not whether the saints are our mediators with God in an equal degree with Christ. For this the papists avoid saying and on that account make a distinction between a primary and secondary mediator—a mediator of redemption and of intercession. But the question is whether in any sense they can properly be called our mediators. This they affirm; we deny.

IV. The question comes to this—whether besides Christ the saints are our mediators with God, who not only intercede for us with their prayers, but who conciliate his favor to us by their patronage and merits. Or whether Christ alone discharges the office of Mediator and Advocate for us. This we assert; our adversaries contend for the former.

V. In the priestly office of Christ, two parts are usually distinguished—satisfaction and intercession. The papists are not ashamed to ascribe both to the saints. As to intercession, we know it is ascribed to the saints when they contend that their prayers are offered by them; yea, they demand that pardon should be granted to them on account of their prayers and that they should be answered. The Roman Missal on the Festival of Saint Thomas: "God, for whose church the glorious Pontiff fell by the swords of the wicked, grant, we beseech thee, that all who implore his aid may obtain the salutary effect of his petition" (*Missale Romanum ex decreto Ss. Concilium Tridentinum* [1570], p. 31). And in the same for the Innocents: "O Lord, let not the pious prayers of thy saints be wanting to us, to recommend our service and obtain thy indulgence for us" (ibid., p. 30). On the Feast of All Saints: "We beseech thee to bestow, on account of multiple intercessors the abundance of thy propitiation desired by us" ("Proprium Missarum [Commune Sanctorum]," p. 116 in ibid.). And as to satisfaction, we know that blessings are demanded from God through the merits of the saints. On the Festival of Bishop Nicolas, they seek to be delivered from the flames of hell through his merits and prayers ("Proprium Missarum [December #6]," p. 4 in ibid.). On the Festivals of Pope Leo, Athanasius and Basil, we read: "By his interceding merits, absolve us from all our sins" ("Proprium Missarum [April #11]," p. 33 in ibid. for Pope Leo; ibid. [May #2], p. 39 for Athanasius; ibid. [June #14], p. 49 for Basil). On the octave for Peter and Paul: "That by the merits of both we may obtain eternal glory" ("De sanctis apostolis Petro et Paulo [Commune Sanctorum]," p. 23 in ibid.). Nor did Bellarmine differ from them. "It is not absurd," he says, "if holy men are said to be our redeemers in some way." In the same place, he adds not inaptly are holy men said in some way to redeem our faults by their sufferings ("De Indulgentiis," 1.4 *Opera* [1859], v. 4, Pt. 2, p. 120). Hence the same writer is convicted of falsehood when he denies that he worships saints as mediators, but only that they may add their prayers to ours ("De Romano Pontifice," 3.21 *Opera* [1856], 1:459-64).

Proof that the saints are not mediators: (1) from 1 Tim. 2:5.

VI. We wage war against the mediation of saints. First with the express words of Scripture, which ascribe this office to Christ alone: "One God, one Mediator between God and man, the man Christ" (1 Tim. 2:5). Here one Mediator is spoken of (not many) and he Christ (who gave himself as a ransom [*antilytron*] for us), not any saint or angel. To no purpose is the reply: (a) that he is said to be one, not the only one. The word *heis* often denotes not only one, but also the only one (as by Homer, *ouk agathon polykoiraniē, heis koiranos estō, heis basileus*, *Iliad* 2.203-5 [Loeb, 1:64-65]; and by Virgil, "One safety to the conquered," i.e, the only, *Aeneid* 2.354 [Loeb, 1:318-19]). The same is true frequently in Scripture (Eph. 4:6; Rom. 3:10, 12; 1 Tim. 3:2, 12), which Bellarmine does not deny ("De Christo," 1.3 *Opera* [1856], 1:156-59). The discourse of Paul also demands this signification because the Mediator (*heis mesitēs*) is said to be one in the same way in which God (*theos*) is said to be one (*heis*); not only one, but also the only one to the exclusion of any other.

VII. Second objection: "that he refers to the Mediator of redemption, who is only one, but not to the Mediator of intercession, who can admit associates." We answer: (a) the distinction is unknown to the Scriptures which mention one only Mediator, not many. (b) The distinction between the Mediator of redemption and of intercession is false because no one can be a mediator of intercession who is not mediator of redemption also. For these two functions—propitiation (*hilasmos*) and intercession (*emphanismos*)—are the two parts of mediation, belong to the same office and ought never to be separated, since they are joined in Scripture (1 Jn. 2:1, 2; Rom. 8:34; Heb. 7*:25), even as under the law it belonged to the priest to enter into the holy place and make supplication for the people (to whom it belonged to offer sacrifice). (c) Romanists themselves do away with this distinction while they acknowledge the saints to be redeemers in a certain manner and hold that they not only pray for our salvation, but also obtain it for us by their own merits. Hence they seek from them that very thing which they seek from Christ the Redeemer—remission of sins and eternal life (and that too in virtue of their merits, as was seen before). This everyone sees belongs assuredly to redemption. Nothing is more frequent among them than to call the blessed virgin a redemptress and deliverer from sins. (d) Paul treats not only of a Mediator of redemption, but also of intercession because he treats of the offering of prayers which ought to be made for all men; nor can they be rightly made except in the name of Christ, who alone is our Mediator.

VIII. Third objection: "Paul speaks of a primary, principal and immediate Mediator, but does not on that account exclude secondary, ministerial and mediate, just as although God alone is called good and Christ the one Master, this does not prevent others from being teachers, and others good." We reply: The distinction is unwritten (*agraphos*); yea also contrary to what is written (*antigraphos*), for the Scripture nowhere proposes to us many mediators or recommends believers to them. Since it ascribes this office to Christ alone, by that very fact it teaches that no others share (*akoinōnēton*) it with him. Nor is the similarity adduced applicable here, for God is called good so that his goodness is peculiar to him alone by way of eminence (*kat' exochēn*); nor can it belong to any other except analogically and in a far different manner. And if Christ sends teachers to us, still no one can or ought to give them the name of "Master," which belongs to Christ alone.

2. From 1 John 2:1.

IX. Second, "If any man sin, we have an advocate with the Father, Jesus Christ the righteous: And he is the propitiation" (1 Jn. 2:1). Here are three arguments: (a) he is called *paraklētos* or an advocate in the singular (which John would have said falsely if there were more and not one only); (b) this Advocate is expressly called Jesus Christ the righteous so that no other can arrogate this office to himself; (c) he is such an Advocate as to be also the *hilasmos* or propitiation for sins. And yet no one but Christ did this. The reply is useless that Christ is indeed called an advocate, but not the only one. For although the exclusive particle is not added expressly (*diarrēdēn*), still it is necessarily included in the epithets added, both of the righteous and the propitiation (*hilasmou*). Again, if he had recognized many advocates, why did he mention Christ alone and not add others to whom they might have recourse? Here belongs the passage, "I am the way, and the truth, and the life; no man cometh unto the father, but by me" (Jn. 14*:6); and "Neither is there salvation in any other" (Acts 4:12).

3. Because this is derogatory to Christ.

X. Third, the mediation of saints casts disgrace upon Christ, as if he was not alone sufficient and needs to associate others with him in this office (which cannot be said without grievous blasphemy). Nor does it help the matter to say that injury is not done to Christ because the saints receive from Christ the power to intercede and to petition. It is assumed that Christ merited for and willed to confer upon them such a power to intercede and obtain salvation for us (which the Scriptures have never said and cannot be proved by any reasoning). If Christ is a perfect Mediator, who by himself can exactly fulfill all the parts of that office, what need was there to form others for himself? Nor ought the reply to be made that no prejudice is thence created against Christ because the saints are not so much mediators of God and men as mediators of men to Christ (as Hessel [Estius] remarks, *In Omnes Pauli Epistolas* [1859], 2:660 on 1 Tim. 2:5). Thus there would be need of a mediator to a Mediator, while on the contrary he directly (*amesōs*) and most kindly calls us to himself and does not refer us to others: "Come unto me" (Mt. 11:28). Besides, these mediators to Christ would either require another Mediator to give them access to him or they would not. If they would, the question again arises whether with this third there would be need of another mediator. And thus on to infinity. If they would not, no reason can be given why these mediators to Christ should be more readily trusted by us than Christ himself. For he follows us not with a lesser but with a far more ardent affection and was made like unto us in all things that he might sympathize with our weaknesses (Heb. 2:17).

4. Because they cannot know our necessities.

XI. Fourth, the saints cannot know our necessities and try the reins and heart in order to have our thoughts and desires disclosed to them distinctly and accurately (without which they cannot discharge the office of mediators and intercessors). As to the exception of our opponents in reference to the knowledge of the saints, see it discussed before, Topic XI, on the law, Question 7.

5. Because this dogma savors of heathen superstition.

XII. Fifth, this dogma savors of heathen superstition and has sprung from the errors of the Gentiles who distinguished their gods into primary and secondary (who were of a lower order [demons] and were mediators between the supreme gods and men). "God," says Plato, "is not approached by men, but all intercourse and communication between the gods and men is carried on by demons" (*Symposium* 203 [Loeb, 3:178-79]). Hence they distributed provinces, cities, arts, diseases among the demons and assigned various offices to different ones (just as the adherents of the pope set saints over empires, cities, arts and diseases and acknowledge them as patrons and tutelary gods to whom they may continually have recourse).

Sources of explanation.

XIII. From the communion of saints to the communication of offices among them, the consequence does not hold good. The saints admitted into heaven indeed have communion with the living inasmuch as they are members of the same mystical body. But on that account, there is not granted a communication of offices, since they neither share in our necessities, nor can they hear and answer our thoughts and prayers; nor have we any more intercourse with them in virtue of which we might implore their assistance.

XIV. Not everyone who prays to God for us is at once a mediator with God; otherwise we would have almost as many mediators as brethren. And while Scripture most frequently mentions the mutual prayers of men, still it never teaches that men are mediators with God. Therefore, he is to be called a Mediator first who not only prays in general, but also prays for individuals; second, who prays in virtue of his own merits and obtains for us remission of sins and salvation. This can be said of Christ alone.

XV. It is one thing for Moses and Samuel while living to pray for the people; another for the same when dead to discharge this office for them. In Jer. 15:1, there is no exhortation to the intercession of the deceased, but the uselessness of their prayers is shown hypothetically (if they should still be among the living and should pray for the people, as was frequently done by them: "Though Moses and Samuel stood before me, and should pray for the people, yet my mind could not be toward this people"). The meaning is—If Moses and Samuel were still alive and should supplicate for this people, they could effect nothing by their supplication as they had formerly appeased God by their prayers (Ex. 32:14; 1 S. 7:9). Therefore he intimates the salvation of that people to be desperate and their destruction certain and settled. Compare: "Though these three men, Noah, Daniel, and Job, were in it, they should deliver but their own souls by their righteousness" (Ezk. 14:14*). Thus the reference here is not to the prayers of the dead, but of the living (if they should return to the people).

XVI. What is said about the harps and golden vials in the hands of the twenty-four elders (Rev. 5:8, 9) does not favor the intercession of saints. If this is referred to deceased saints, it will not signify the prayers which they offer for the living, but their doxology to God (*tēn eis theon doxologian*), as Aretas and Andrew of Caesarea observe (to wit, praises of God and incense of the act of grace which they continually offer to God; cf. *Commentarius in Apocalypsin* [PG 106.261] on Rev. 5:7, 8). This is immediately explained in the following verse by "the new song." Thus what is said these golden vials full of incense were are the prayers of saints (*hai eisin hai proseuchai tōn hagiōn*, "which are" [i.e., symbolically designate] "the prayers of saints," to wit, of those who had the harps and golden vials); or indefinitely of all the saints whose prayers are described by the odors. However, if we refer it to the praises and prayers of living saints (as is more probably true, nor does Estius object) nothing will be thence elicited for the prayers of the departed (cf. *Biblia Magna Commentariorum Literalum* [1643], 5:1137 on Rev. 5:8). Thus is described undoubtedly the evangelical worship of praises and prayers by words taken from the legal service so that harps (instruments of praises) denote the praises and the golden vials the prayers of believers offered from a heart purified by faith. Thus they show that they are truly kings and priests (as they afterwards say), for harps are becoming to kings (as to David), but vials to priests.

XVII. Although with earthly kings there is the need of agents and mediators to admit us to their presence, it is not so with the heavenly King who calls us immediately to himself (nor ever dismisses believers to the saints). If an earthly king should invite his subjects directly to himself, who would not approach him freely and with confidence? Who would wish princely patrons to secure an approach to him?

XVIII. The passages here adduced to favor the intercession of saints (Job 5:1; 19:21; 33:23; Ex. 32:13; Zech. 1:12; Rev. 8:3; Tob. 12) have been discussed in Topic V, on the angels, Question 9 and Topic II, Question 7.

XIX. It is one thing to pray for the church in general; another to pray for individuals. Although the saints should pray in general for the church militant (which they know is still assailed by adversaries and exposed to various struggles), it would not at once follow either that they pray for individuals (whose necessities and prayers they do not know) or that they are their mediators (who can obtain for them the grace of God by their own prayers and merits).

XX. The passage where Judas Maccabaeus is said to have seen in a vision Onias, the priest, and Jeremiah (who were then dead) praying for the Jewish people (2 Mac. 15:14) cannot help our opponents. (1) This is an apocryphal book crammed with fables (as Romanists themselves confess). In particular, Pope Gelasius admits First Maccabees alone, rejecting the Second (cf. *Conciliorum sub Gelasio* [PL 59.158]). (2) The passage proves only that the saints pray in general, not particularly after the manner of mediators. (3) Romanists themselves hold that the fathers before the death of Christ were still in limbo excluded from the face of God; therefore they were not suitable ones to pray for others.

XXI. "The cry of the souls under the altar" (Rev. 6:9, 10) does not pertain to intercession for others, but to prayers for themselves. They do not say, "Why do you not deliver our brethren?" but, "Why dost thou not avenge our blood?" Nor ought this to be understood properly (since souls do not cry) but allegorically—to denote their desire for the last judgment and resurrection (as Ambrose and Bernard thought, "Sermon 3," *In festo omnium Sanctorum* [PL 183.468-71]); or a manifestation of the wickedness of tyrants to be deservedly punished by God and of the innocence of the martyrs to be rewarded (as elsewhere the voice of the blood of Abel is said to cry out from the earth [Gen. 4:10] because the death and slaughter of the martyrs, always fresh before God, demands the avenging of divine justice, as Lyranus observes, *Biblia sacra cum Glossa ordinaria* [1545-1603], 6:1517 on Rev. 6:9, 10).

XXII. From the mutual prayers of the living to prayers of the departed for the living, the consequence does not hold good. Among the former, there is a mutual communion of offices and necessities; there is none between the dead and the living. The former are enjoined and praised in Scripture, but the latter by no means. Nor does the perfection of charity (with which the saints are blessed) conduce to their praying for us particularly because the condition of that life does not allow of it.

FIFTH QUESTION: THE THREEFOLD OFFICE OF CHRIST
Why ought Christ to sustain a threefold office of Mediator?

What is the mediatorial office of Christ?

I. The office of Christ is nothing else than a mediation between God and men, to discharge which he was sent by the Father into the world and anointed by the Holy Spirit. It embraces all that Christ ought to do from his mission and calling towards an offended God and offending men, reconciling and again uniting them to each other.

And instituted with how many degrees? (1) predestination;

II. The institution of this office is resolved especially by three degrees: (1) by the predestination of Christ; (2) by his mission; (3) by his calling. The first grade is in the eternal predestination of a Mediator, by which God selected and appointed his own Son as a Mediator to reconcile the elect to himself and accomplish the work of salvation (referred to in 1 Pet. 1:20; Acts 2:23; Rev. 13:8). The second in his mission, by which, according to the eternal decree of predestination, he was not only promised under the Old Testament, predicted in various prophecies, adumbrated by types and exhibited as the Mediator of the church, but in the fulness of times was sent into the world to take upon himself our nature, that in it he might accomplish the work demanded of him (which mission is mentioned in the gospel with the greatest frequency; not by a change of place, so as to come where he was not before, but by an extraordinary manifestation of his presence in the flesh, in which he visibly appeared and worked).

2. By his mission.

3. By his calling, which consists in unction.

III. The third grade consists in his vocation, by which he was consecrated to enter upon that office referred to in Is. 42:6: "I the Lord have called thee in righteousness" (cf. Ps. 110:4 and Christ himself, Jn. 10:36). Now this vocation embraces two parts: unction and inauguration. Unction, from which sprung the names of Messiah and Christ (which by way of eminence [*kat' exochēn*] was peculiar to our Redeemer, although others also are called improperly anointed and christs by reason of their prophetic or priestly or kingly office), denotes two things: (a) consecration to office, which belongs to the person of Christ even according to his divine nature, by which he was really consecrated to the office of Mediator (Ps. 2:6), usually designated in Scripture by the word "sanctification" (Jn. 10:36); (b) the bestowal of all the graces and gifts necessary to the execution of that office (relating only to his human nature), by which he is said to have been anointed with the oil of gladness above his fellows and gifted with the Spirit immeasurably (*ametrōs*) (Ps. 45:7; Is. 61:1, 2; Jn. 3:34).

And in inauguration.

IV. Inauguration is that by which (although by right of birth and by the benefit of the hypostatical union, he was really the Lord and heir of all things) he willed to be inaugurated into his office in a solemn manner (even as hereditary kings are accustomed by a solemn inauguration to be put in full possession of their kingdom in order that they may be acknowledged by all). Now this was done first in the baptism of Christ (Mt. 3:17) where in an illustrious and clearly extraordinary manner he was consecrated to the public exercise of his office. This was confirmed not only by the opening of the heavens and the sending down of the Holy Spirit upon him, but also by the voice from heaven testifying to the excellence of his person and office. To the person, being called the Son of God, not adoptive (many of whom God has), but the natural, only begotten and proper (who moreover is called "beloved" [*agapētos*] and most dear). To his office, since it is said that in him the Father is well pleased (*eudokētai*) (i.e., the Father not only entirely acquiesces in Christ and clearly delights in him, but also in him and on account of him we please and are acceptable to God, Eph. 1:6). Moreover the excellence of that office is clearly demonstrated by this—he was not constituted our Mediator without an oath, "The Lord hath sworn" (Ps. 110:4). From this Paul infers the superiority and eternity of the priesthood of Christ above the Levitical priesthood (Heb. 7). Second, in the transfiguration, in which he was in like manner confirmed in his threefold office by a heavenly voice (Mt. 17:5). Third, the inauguration was fully made after his resurrection and exaltation when "he was made both Lord and Christ" (Acts 2:36); "a name was given him which is above every name, that at the name of Jesus every knee should bow" (Phil. 2:9, 10); when all power is given him in heaven and on earth (Mt. 28:18); and when he sits on the right hand of the majesty on high (Heb. 1:3).

Manner of the threefold office of Christ.

V. This mediatorial office of Christ is distributed into three functions, which are so many parts of it: prophetic, priestly and kingly. These Christ sustained not separately, but conjointly (which is granted to him alone). For what in others were divided on account of their infirmity are united in Christ on account of his supreme perfection (since the dignity and burden of these functions were so great that no mortal could alone discharge them). There could indeed be kings and priests (as Melchizedek), kings and prophets (as David), priests and prophets (as sometimes the high priests), but we never meet with anyone who alone perfectly fulfilled these three. This was reserved for Christ, who alone could sustain the truth adumbrated by these various types. However if Moses is read of as adumbrating him (because he was not only a prophet of God and a leader and deliverer of the people, but also before the inauguration of Aaron had sometimes officiated as a priest, as in Ex. 24:4-6, 8), this was done out of order and only to an act. It cannot nor ought it to be adduced as an example.

It rests: (1) upon the Scripture;

VI. Various causes can be assigned for this distribution: (1) the Scripture is wont to designate Christ by this threefold name, setting him forth now as a Prophet (Dt. 18:15, 18; Is. 61:1, 2), as the Wisdom of the Father and the Word (*Logon*) through whom God addresses us, then as a Priest (Ps. 110:4 and frequently in the epistle to the Hebrews) and again as a King (Pss. 2; 110:1; Is. 9:6, 7; Lk. 1:32, 33). These three offices are described not only separately, but they are also conjointly set forth (as in Is. 9:6). He who is called a child by reason of his human conception and a Son by reason of his eternal generation is termed "Wonderful" (by reason of person), "Counsellor" (in respect of prophecy), "Father of eternity" (in respect of priesthood) and "Prince of Peace," upon whose shoulders the government is placed (in respect of his kingdom). Thus in Is. 61, a threefold end of the anointing of Christ is pointed out: "to preach good tidings unto the meek" (which belongs to a prophet); "to bind up the broken-hearted, and to comfort all that mourn" (which belong to a priest); "to bring liberty to the captives, and to exercise the vengeance of God" (which belong to a king, Ps. 110). The royal dignity of Christ and his victory and triumph over his enemies is asserted through the whole Psalm. Prophecy is built up in Ps. 110:2 when it is said that the scepter of his word shall go out of Zion. The priesthood is taught in v. 4: "The Lord hath sworn, and will not repent, Thou art a priest forever." Of the man, whose name is the Branch, who, it is said, shall build the temple of the Lord by the word of the gospel (Zech. 6:12-14), which belongs to a prophet, it is said he shall rule upon his throne (the function of a king) and a priest shall sit upon his throne (the same one who will be a king, will also be a priest). "And the counsel of peace shall be between them both" (i.e., between these two dignities, the royal and priestly). For one and the same person shall be king and priest, who will acquire peace for the church by his priestly office and defend it by his kingly office.

VII. Thus in the New Testament these three offices are often joined together as in Jn. 14:6 when Christ is said to be "the way, the truth, and the life"—the Way leading, the Truth teaching, the Life saving. The Way in his priesthood, when by his own blood he opened a way for us to heaven (Heb. 10:20); the Truth in his prophetic office because he reveals to us the word of the gospel, the only saving truth; the Life in his kingly office by which he quickens and protects us through his efficacy; the Way in death, the Truth in the word, Life in the spirit. Hence Emissenus on this passage: "I am the Way because no one comes to the Father except by me; I am the Truth because no one knows the Father except from me; I am the Life because no one lives except in me"+. The same is shown in the celebrated passage where Christ is said to be made of the Father unto us "wisdom, righteousness, sanctification and redemption" (1 Cor. 1:30). He is said "to be made" (i.e., appointed by God to be Wisdom to us, i.e., the infallible author and teacher of heavenly wisdom by prophecy); righteousness (i.e., the bestower of eternal and infinite righteousness by which we are freed from guilt and justified before God through his priesthood); sanctification (i.e., the cause of true and spiritual holiness by which we are freed from the dominion and purged of the corruption of sin through his kingship and redemption [which exerts itself in these three]—or, if it is taken strictly, as he is redemption from misery and death). Thus God is said to have spoken to us by his Son as by a supreme Prophet (Heb. 1:2, 3) who, after having purged our sins as a Priest, sat down on the right hand of the majesty on high as a King.

2. On the threefold misery of men.

VIII. Second, the threefold misery of men introduced by sin—ignorance, guilt and the tyranny and bondage by sin—required this conjunction of a threefold office. Ignorance is healed by the prophetic; guilt by the priestly; the tyranny and corruption of sin by the kingly. Prophetic light scatters the darkness of error; the merit of the Priest takes away guilt and procures a reconciliation for us; the power of the King removes the bondage of sin and death. The Prophet shows God to us; the Priest leads us to God; and the King joins together and glorifies us with God. The Prophet enlightens the mind by the Spirit of illumination; the Priest by the Spirit of consolation tranquilizes the heart and conscience; the King by the Spirit of sanctification subdues rebellious affections.

3. On the nature of the salvation to be conferred.

IX. Third, the nature of the salvation to be bestowed required the same. For three things are altogether required for it—annunciation, acquisition, application—that it might be revealed to us (to whom it is unknown by nature), that it might be acquired for us and applied when acquired. Therefore Christ by his threefold office ought to accomplish these three things: to announce salvation to us through the teaching of a Prophet; to acquire the promised salvation through the merit of a Priest; and to apply it when acquired through the efficacy of his Spirit as a King.

4. On the acts of a Mediator.

X. Fourth, the acts of a Mediator could not be performed otherwise. For two things were necessary: that he should act for us with God (*ta pros ton theon*) and for God with us (*ta pros hēmas*). By satisfying and interceding for us with God, he acted as a Priest: "For every high priest is ordained in things pertaining to God, that he may offer both gifts and sacrifices" (Heb. 5:1). By speaking and working for God to us, the former by announcing the grace of God and our duty, in which he acted as a Prophet; the latter by a powerful redemption from all our enemies and the efficacious procurement of a full salvation, in which he acted as a King.

5. On the fulfillment of types.

XI. Fifth, the symbolic anointing of the Old Testament. There was a threefold anointing of men under the Old Testament, obliged to be consecrated by a sacred anointing (to wit, prophets, priests and kings—as in the cases of Elisha [1 K. 19:16*], of Aaron [Ex. 29:7] and of kings frequently). Now as all the types related to the one Christ and obtained their fulfillment in him, Christ must exhibit the truth of that threefold office in himself, but far more perfectly than in the others—not only by reason of the conjunction of these three parts (which no man could fulfill at the same time, as we have already seen), but also by reason of the eminence and dignity, both of his office and of his gifts.

6. On the three attributes of God.

XII. Sixth, this is also clearly intimated in the three principal perfections of God, which exercised themselves towards us in the work of redemption—wisdom, mercy and power (since the Son, as a Prophet, reveals to us the wisdom of God, merits his mercy for us as a Priest and draws forth his power for our deliverance and salvation, as our King). Hence arises the object of the three cardinal virtues—faith, hope and charity. For faith embraces the doctrine of the Prophet; hope builds upon the merit of the Priest; and charity subjects itself by a voluntary obedience to the scepter of the King.

XIII. These three offices, however, are so united in Christ that they not only exercise their distinct operations, but the same act proceeds at the same time from the three (which not a little increases the wonderfulness of the thing). Thus the cross of Christ (which is the altar of the priest, on which he offered himself as a victim to God) is also the school of the prophet, in which he teaches us the mystery of salvation. Hence the gospel is called the word of the cross and the "trophy of the king," on which he triumphed over principalities and powers (Col. 2:15). "The gospel is the law of the prophet" (Is. 2:2, 3), "the scepter of the king" (Ps. 110:2), "the sword of the priest," by which he penetrates even to the dividing asunder of soul and spirit (Heb. 4:12) and an altar upon which the sacrifice of our faith ought to be placed. Thus the Spirit (who as a Spirit of wisdom) is the effect of prophecy, as a Spirit of consolation is a fruit of the priesthood, as a Spirit of strength and glory is a gift of the king.

Sixth Question

Was Christ caught up into heaven before beginning his public ministry in order to be taught there by the Father? We deny against the Socinians.

Statement of the question.

I. The opinion of Socinians—as Smalcius (*De Divinitate Jesu Christi* 4 [1608], pp. 10-15), Ostorodt (*Unterrichtung . . . hauptpuncten der Christlichen Religion* 16 [1612], pp. 91-96), the Racovian Catechism (cf. "Of the Prophetic Office of Christ," *Racovian Catechism* 5 [1818], pp. 170-72)—is that Christ (being a mere man) was at first uninstructed in and ignorant of that doctrine which he was to promulgate by his ministry for the salvation of men. On this account, when he was thirty years old and having been baptized by John, before he could enter upon his public ministrations, he was caught up into heaven. There he was taught most perfectly by God himself about his will and thus returning to earth began fully and sufficiently to declare the same doctrine to men. The time of that translation (although they do not dare to fix it precisely), they think can be best referred to the stay which he made fasting in the desert for forty days and nights. Their object is to escape the passages of Scripture by which we prove that Christ existed before he was born of the virgin—besides the fact that he is said to have come forth from the Father and to have descended from heaven.

II. The orthodox reject this translation of Christ to heaven as purely fictitious, found nowhere in Scripture and recognize no other descent from heaven in the days of his flesh than the metaphorical one made by his incarnation.

Proof of the orthodox opinion.

III. The reasons are: First, the silence of Scripture, which mentions it nowhere. It does indeed mention one ascension into heaven and entrance into the holy place after his resurrection (Heb. 9:12), but we find not the slightest trace of any other. The passages adduced here have a different reference, as will hereafter be proved. Now what could be the cause of this silence if it really happened, since it would greatly conduce to the commendation of Christ's doctrine? Why should it rather mention the carrying away of Christ by the tempter to a lofty mountain, than his translation to heaven by God himself? Nor can it be replied here that the evangelists did not mention that translation because it was done secretly and not openly, since they mention only things which they saw or had heard. They would therefore have to be silent concerning the resurrection of Christ, which occurred when no one was present except the guards; nor could Matthew have described the transfiguration (of which he was not an eyewitness [*autoptēs*]). Therefore they were bound to relate not merely what they themselves saw and heard, but what was revealed to them by the Holy Spirit concerning the deeds of Christ (which conduced to the instruction of believers).

IV. Second, Christ did not need such a translation to gain a knowledge of mysteries, neither according to his divine nature (because he was the Word [*Logos*] of the Father [Jn. 1:1] who was in his bosom and who therefore beheld all his secrets), nor according to his human nature. According to the latter, he received the Spirit without measure (Jn. 3:34), by whom he was sufficiently instructed in his office and treasures of wisdom and knowledge were laid up in him (Col. 2:3). It is confirmed by this—that while still a child of twelve years he gave wonderful proofs of his wisdom, teaching in the temple and disputing with the Pharisees (Lk. 2:47). Also at his baptism (before that fictitious translation), the Father testified from heaven that he was well pleased with him. But how could he be well pleased with him who did not yet understand his will? Third, if Christ had ascended into heaven after his baptism, Scripture ought to put his ascent before his descent. On the contrary, it puts the descent before his ascent (Eph. 4:9).

Sources of explanation.

V. It is one thing for Christ to have ascended to heaven properly and locally in respect of his humanity; another to have ascended metaphorically and mystically by a sublime knowledge of heavenly mysteries. Christ is not said to have ascended in the former sense ("No man hath ascended up to heaven, but he that came down from heaven, even the Son of man which is in heaven," Jn. 3:13) because the same one who ascended is said to have descended (thus he could not be said to be still in heaven), but concerning the mystical ascent (as he is said to ascend up to heaven who penetrates the secret of heaven [Prov. 30:4] because as far as heaven is distant from earth, so far are divine counsels distant from human [Is. 55:9]). That which is near us is obvious and plain and said not to be in heaven (nor for us to ascend thither, Dt. 30:12; Rom. 10:6). Thus the sense will be, No one knows heavenly things and is acquainted with the divine counsel except himself. The connection teaches that this must be the meaning because in the preceding verse he had treated of the revelation of mysteries: "If I have told you earthly things, and ye believe not, how shall ye believe if I tell you of heavenly things?" And in order to give the reason why he can both teach heavenly things by his own right and no one can know them (except he instructs them), he adds, "No man hath ascended up to heaven." But as to the words "the Son of man is in heaven," this must be understood of the person in the concrete, not of the human nature in the abstract.

VI. When Christ is said to have descended from heaven and to have come forth from the Father (Jn. 6:38; 16:28), it treats of his metaphorical descent by his manifestation in the flesh; not that he was where he was not before, but that he would work there. There is no allusion to a local descent according to his humanity, nor is Christ ever said to have returned from heaven, but only to have gone thither. If the Son of man is said to ascend where he was before after his resurrection (Jn. 6:62), this is not to be understood of his humanity, but only of his divinity where the Word (*ho Logos*) was before when he was with God (*pros ton theon*, Jn. 1:1).

VII. Although Christ utters those things which he was taught by the Father (Jn. 8:38) because he speaks what he heard (Jn. 3:32) and does nothing which he did not see the Father working (Jn. 5:19) to indicate that the Son has an intimate knowledge of all the works of the Father, it does not follow that he had been caught up into heaven in order to hear and see such things. He had this from intimate communion with the Father, on account of which he is said to be in the bosom of the Father (Jn. 1:18) and (because in his bosom) to reveal him to us.

VIII. Although Christ was not carried up into heaven, he is not on that account to be reckoned inferior to Moses and Paul, who were that they might be taught of God. (1) Although they were carried up thither, Christ was taught of God in a far more excellent manner in virtue of his hypostatical union. (2) There is a difference between servants and their Master. They had need of special and extraordinary instruction to gain that knowledge of which they were deficient. But Christ, from the moment of conception (anointed by the Holy Spirit), knew these things most fully. (3) Moses is not said to have been carried up to heaven, but to have been carried up to a mountain. Paul is indeed said to have been rapt into the third heaven, but whether in the spirit or in the body cannot be told (as Paul confesses he did not know himself).

SEVENTH QUESTION: THE PROPHETIC OFFICE OF CHRIST

In what does the prophetic office of Christ consist; or what are its parts and what is its mode?

In how many ways may prophecy be taken.

I. The first part of Christ's office is prophecy. It is taken here not broadly and improperly for any knowledge and celebration of God, as it is in Joel 2:28 when it is said believers under the New Testament will prophesy; or for public instruction, which belongs to interpreters of sacred things; or to the public teachers and ministers of the church, in which sense "the spirits of the prophets are subject to the prophets" (1 Cor. 14:32); or more strictly, concerning those whom God called immediately and out of their rank, not only to teach the people, but also to replace the corrupted worship of God and foretell many future things. This is the most ordinary signification of the word in the Old Testament, claimed by Moses in a certain peculiar manner (Num. 12:6-8), as will hereafter be seen.

And in what sense it is applied to Christ.

But it is taken most strictly and properly for that full and august revelation of the mysteries of salvation which Christ (as the highest teacher of the church) has exhibited to us.

It is not comprehended under the priesthood or under the kingship.

II. Some would wish this prophetic office to be comprehended under the kingly (to which legislation belongs) or to be contained under the priestly (to which the power of prophesying and the faculty of consulting God and giving responses was annexed). But they do not speak with sufficient accuracy because this did not hinder these three offices from being formerly distinct. As in reality it is one thing to be an ordinary pastor, but another to be a prophet; one thing to hear responses, another to bring forward new things not heard or sought. Prophets were raised up extraordinarily either to instruct or to renew the worship of God (whose words pious kings and priests eagerly received). They were also taken from another tribe than that of Levi (to which pertained the priesthood) and were consecrated for this end especially: that they might deposit the sacred canon with the church, which word is not of priests or of kings, but of prophets (2 Pet. 1:19), upon which the church ought to be built (Eph. 2:20). Thus there are in Christ the parts of a prophet, of a priest and of a king (as has been shown before).

The necessity of it is proved.

III. The necessity of this office appears from three things. (1) From the necessity of a revelation because there can be no knowledge of God and divine things without a revelation, for the natural man does not receive the things of God (1 Cor. 2:14) and no saving revelation is given except through Christ (Jn. 1:18; Mt. 11:27). Nor could reason or the law disclose to us the mystery of piety, but Christ alone in the gospel. (2) From the method of salvation because no means of salvation was given except faith: "Faith however cometh by hearing, and hearing by the word of God" (Rom. 10:17). (3) From the oracles of the Old Testament which promise that prophecy, which must necessarily be fulfilled.

And the truth.

IV. The Scripture often teaches the truth of the prophetic office of Christ: in the oracle of Moses, "The Lord thy God will raise up unto thee a prophet" (Dt. 18:15), which Peter teaches us pertains to Christ (Acts 3:22); where it is said a Spirit is given to Christ by the Father that he might "bring forth judgment to the Gentiles" (Is. 42:1-3, 6), i.e., act as a prophet among the Gentiles and by the just laws of the gospel and the just worship of God, lead them to true righteousness. Hence he is said to have been given "for a covenant of the people, for a light of the Gentiles, to open the blind eyes." This is confirmed in 49:12, but especially in 61:1, 2 where he is introduced saying, "The Spirit of the Lord God is upon me; because the Lord hath anointed me to preach good tidings unto the meek." He teaches this was fulfilled in himself (Lk. 4:21). Here belong the brief descriptions of Christ when he is called the "angel of the covenant" (Mal. 3:1), "Counsellor" (Isa. 9:6*), the eternal "Wisdom," which calls men (Prov. 9:1); "the Word" (*Logos*) by whom God speaks to us (Heb. 1:1), "Master" and "Teacher" (Mt. 23:7, 8), who alone is to be heard (Mt. 17:5)—which opinion prevailed to such an extent among the Jews that it passed even to the Samaritans—"Messias cometh [and] he will tell us all things" (Jn. 4:25). If Christ is distinguished from a prophet (Jn. 1:21), he is not on that account absolutely denied to be a prophet, but he is shown to be more than a prophet. He is not absolutely denied to be a prophet, but "the Prophet" (*ton Prophētēn*) (namely, that illustrious prophet whom the Jews supposed would come before Christ; or one of the prophets whom they thought would be resuscitated at the coming of the Messiah).

Its nature is considered either in matter of doctrine or in the mode of preaching.

V. The nature of this prophecy must be considered principally in two respects; (1) in the matter of the doctrine preached; (2) in the mode of preaching. The matter comes under three heads: exposition of the law; promulgation of the gospel; and foretelling of future events. For as the work of prophets was resolved principally unto these three parts—explanation and application of the law, inculcation of the promises of grace and foretelling of future events revealed to them by God—so Christ most perfectly fulfilled these three by interpreting most truly the law according to the intention of the lawgiver, preaching the gospel and predicting future events for the consolation of the church.

The first part of prophecy in the explication of the law.

VI. The first part of the prophetical office respects the doctrine of the law, in explaining and inculcating which he labored both that man (convicted of his own weakness) might fly the more eagerly on that account to Christ (as to a sacred anchor, where he might be safe from the lightnings and malediction of the law) and that he might vindicate it from the false interpretations and glosses of the Pharisees of his day and restore the meaning intended by God the lawgiver. Also in inculcating the spiritual and inner obedience of the heart which the spiritual law demanded, rejecting the outward righteousness which the Pharisees supposed to be sufficient (Mt. 5-7); subordinating the ceremonial to the moral law and the service of the former to that of the latter as better (Mt. 12:1ff.); and in rejecting the traditions of the elders as useless and offensive to God (Mt. 15:3; 23).

VII. Whether Christ in this explication of the law corrected the old law as imperfect and added new precepts to it (as the Socinians and Romanists pretend) has already been discussed in Topic XI, on the law, Questions 4 and 5 (which consult).

Whether Christ can be called a legislator.

VIII. To the question (wont to be agitated here) whether Christ is or can be called a legislator. We answer in a few words that Christ can be viewed in two ways: either absolutely and theologically (inasmuch as he is the Word [*Logos*] and the same God with the Father and the Holy Spirit); or relatively and economically (inasmuch as he is the God-man [*theanthrōpos*] and the Mediator between God and men). In the former respect, he is the one legislator who can save and destroy (Jam. 4:12). In the latter, he is neither properly a legislator, as Moses was (because he is opposed to Moses and his law as the author of grace and of truth, Jn. 1:17); nor principally because his principal office was to reveal to us the mystery of the gospel. Still nothing hinders our calling him a legislator secondarily and less principally, both because he was the restorer and vindicator of the law and because he is King and head of his church. Now it belongs to kings to make laws. Hence he is called "lawgiver" (*mchqq*, Is. 33:22) and the doctrine of Christ has also its own law, which prescribes to us faith and obedience in life. In this sense, the law is subordinated to the gospel and the gospel itself is called the law of faith, the royal law of liberty, the law of the Spirit and of life. Still our divines rightly deny (against Romanists and Socinians) that Christ is a lawgiver, inasmuch as a legislator denotes him who introduces new laws and new moral precepts not contained in the law itself (nor having their foundation in it).

IX. Although faith in Christ (which is prescribed in the gospel) can be called new in respect of its object (which is revealed in the gospel alone), still it belongs to the law in respect of act and of obligation because we are bound to believe in God and all his word. Repentance also belongs to the law; not as it was made for the first man, but as repeated for the sinner and illustrated by the gospel; and materially, if not formally, because it teaches and prescribes the mode of repentance.

The second, in the preaching of the gospel.

X. Another part of the prophetical office (and indeed the principal) is the preaching of the gospel or the annunciation of the grace brought in by Christ. Hence the gospel is called "the doctrine of Christ" (Acts 13:12) and "the testimony of Christ" (1 Cor. 1:6; Rev. 1:2). This is so not only because Christ is the proper object of that doctrine (1 Cor. 2:2), but also because he is its principal cause and primary author. The gospel, however, we do not understand here broadly for any promise of grace (which had place also in the Old Testament), but strictly for the completed gospel, which contains the manifestation of Christ in the flesh. There Christ teaches that he is a person, not only the Son of man (Mt. 8:20; 9:6), but also the Son of God (Jn. 3:16; 5:19; and elsewhere); that in office he is that Christ who was promised under the Old Testament

(Mt. 16:16)—Prophet (Jn. 10:11, 14), Priest (Jn. 10:15; 17) and King of his church (Jn. 18:36, 37)—who came to minister and to lay down his life as a ransom (*antilytron*) for many (Mt. 20:28); to save his people from their sins (Mt. 1:21); and to institute a new evangelical worship differing from the old legal worship, both as to place (because God selects no peculiar place for his worship now as formerly) and as to the mode of worship (because he wishes to be worshipped in Spirit and without carnal ceremonies, and in truth [without the shadows of the Mosaic law] and that too because he is a Spirit [therefore with a worship more adapted to his nature]).

Third, in the prediction of future events.

XI. The third part is the foretelling of future things. These are general: such as the prediction of the destruction of Jerusalem and of the end of the world (Mt. 24); the calling of the Gentiles (Jn. 4:21); and the abrogation of the ceremonial worship to give place to the spiritual and evangelical (Jn. 4:23; Jn. 10:16); of the future cross and the almost continual persecution of believers (Mt. 24; Jn. 15:20; 16:20, 22). However these predictions were tempered with the sweetest promises of the gracious presence of Christ and of the Holy Spirit in the midst of calamity (Jn. 14:18; 17:9), of the happy end of afflictions (Jn. 16:20, 22). The foretelling may also be special with respect to his own suffering, crucifixion, death and resurrection (Mt. 16:21; 26:23); the offense and flight of his disciples; Peter's denial and martyrdom; the treachery of Judas; the advent of false christs and imposters, and of false prophets. The apocalyptic prophecies belong here also in which Christ suggested to his servant the things which would happen even unto the end of the world, whether with respect to the struggles and calamities of the church or with respect to her victories and triumphs.

The mode of prophecy: (1) immediate and mediate.

XII. The mode of the prophecy of Christ is attended to in various particulars. (1) In the twofold mode of teaching, both immediate by himself in the days of his flesh and mediate by his ministers before his incarnation by the prophets in the Old Testament (who spoke under the influence of the prophetic spirit of Christ, 1 Pet. 1:11; 2 Pet. 1:21). Hence he is said to have preached by the Spirit in Noah (1 Pet. 3:19). And if God is said to have spoken unto us by his Son in these last days (Heb. 1:2), this must be understood not simply but comparatively (i.e., in a visible manner and by him as in the flesh [*ensarkon*]). Also after his advent by apostles and pastors—the former extraordinarily called and inspired with the gift of infallibility for a time; the latter called by the ordinary ministry of men, endowed only with common inspiration (even unto the end of the world). (2) In the external and internal, by which he not only outwardly reaches the ears of the body by his word, but also inwardly turns and opens the heart by his Spirit and leads it into all truth (Jn. 16:13). In this sense, the words of Christ are said to be "spirit and life" (Jn. 6:63), not only in respect of an understanding of the words spoken concerning the eating of his flesh (which were not to be taken grossly and carnally, but spiritually and mystically), but also in respect of the unconquerable efficacy which it exerts in the conversion of the heart. Hence the gospel is said to be written not on tables of stone, but "in fleshly tables of the heart" (2 Cor. 3:3)—the privilege of the new covenant in which God was to write the law upon the heart and believers were to be taught of God (*theodidaktoi*, Is. 54*:13).

2. External and internal.

3. In the various characteristics.

XIII. (3) In the various characteristics which attended his preaching: (a) in teaching, he everywhere exerted the highest authority, becoming a supreme and infallible teacher, not customary with other inferior teachers, for he taught as one having authority (*exousian echōn*), not as the Scribes and Pharisees (Mt. 7:28, 29). Thus no one could resist him and they were compelled to acknowledge that no one had so spoken (Jn. 7:46). (b) Admirable wisdom by which he so tempered his doctrine that he vindicated it from the cavils of his opponents and often vanquished them with their own weapons (Mt. 21:23-46). To this add that divine knowledge by which he was proved to be acquainted with the heart (*kardiognōstēn*) and fully informed of the future. (c) Generous liberty without respect of person (*prosōpolēpsian*) in teaching the truth of God and reminding each one of his duty. (d) Remarkable eloquence by which gracious words proceeded out of his mouth (*logoi tēs charitos*, Lk. 4:22) and excelled all others, so that majesty vied with simplicity, loftiness with sweetness. (e) Unconquerable constancy making no account of the authority and influence of his adversaries, whose crimes he the more sharply rebuked the more they strove to impose upon the simple with the mask of sanctity (Mt. 23:5). (f) Most ardent zeal (an example of which is given in Jn. 2:15, 16), moved by which he did not seek a retreat, but spoke openly also often neglecting the taking of food (Mk. 3:20; Jn. 4:32).

4. In the efficacy of his doctrine.

XIV. (4) In the evidently divine efficacy of his doctrine, by which Christ taught outwardly indeed with the greatest gravity and majesty (by which his hearers were especially moved). His preaching was clearly different from that of the Scribes (Mt. 7:29). But inwardly he powerfully insinuated himself into their minds and affected them in wondrous ways, converting or convincing some, exercising over all a greater than human power (Jn. 7:46; Lk. 24:32). Hence we infer that it was necessary for our Prophet to be furnished with divine power, since he not only surrounds us with light, but also supplies eyes, opens our hearts and irradiates our minds with heavenly brightness (2 Cor. 4:6).

5. In the authenticity and perfection of his doctrine.

XV. (5) In the authenticity and perfection of doctrine which was such that after the revelation of doctrine which Christ made, no other is to be expected hereafter (as the apostle shows, Heb. 1, 2). If the Spirit is said to be about to teach the church after Christ, this is not to be referred to a greater perfection extensively and objectively, but intensively and subjectively. Hence it is said that "he will take of the doctrine of Christ" (Jn. 16:14) because he was to teach nothing else than what had been proposed already by Christ and belonged to his person and office.

6. In holiness of life and miracles.

XVI. (6) In holiness of life and working of miracles. For he established and confirmed his doctrine not only by a most perfect holiness of life and a wonderful patience, but also by various stupendous miracles, both in order to vindicate the divinity of his person and to seal the truth of his doctrine. For he who by his own power did so many and such great works surpassing the strength of all created nature must have been clothed with divine power, since he performed works which God alone can do. It is evident that the same one spoke the words of God and we must believe that he introduced a self-credible (*autopiston*) and divine doctrine. For neither is falsehood becoming in the highest power, nor can we suppose that God would lend his power to an impostor or false prophet. I know that the adversaries of Christ urge many objections to throw discredit upon the miracles of Christ, but we have already shown that they are futile and most false; cf. Topic XIII, Question 2, Sections 18, 19.

How Christ differs from other prophets.

XVII. And hence can clearly be gathered the multiple difference existing between Christ and other prophets. For (1) they were only servants in the house of God (who spoke in Christ's name), from whom they received their commands. But Christ is a Son and Master (Heb. 3), the chief Shepherd (*Archipoimēn*, 1 Pet. 5:4) and supreme Master, Teacher of teachers, by whose Spirit all who speak are influenced and who alone is to be heard as the arbiter of faith (Mt. 17:5). (2) They could preach externally only, but nothing further. John baptizes with water, Paul plants and waters, but cannot give the increase. On this account, they are said to be "nothing" (1 Cor. 3:7) in respect of internal power and efficacy. But Christ operates both externally and internally, writes the law itself in hearts and "baptizes with the Spirit and fire" (Mt. 3:11), i.e., inspires an internal efficacy and operates within by his Spirit with action like fire—whose property it is not only to purge of dross and to wash the external surface as water, but also to penetrate deeply within. (3) Others were illuminated with divine light, but by a passing brilliance (*coruscationem*) and by way of transient act; hence they could not reveal future or secret things as often as they pleased. But Christ illuminates like a permanent habit (which he could use as often as he wished; although as long as he was on earth it did not pertain absolutely to all future things, but to those which the claims of his office and of our salvation required; hence he is said to have been ignorant of the day of judgment, Mk. 13:32). (4) To the others the Spirit was given only by measure; but to Christ he is given without measure (*ametrōs*, Jn. 3:34). The Spirit is said to have rested upon him with all its gifts (Is. 11:1, 2). The treasures of wisdom and knowledge are hid in him (Col. 2:3). (5) Others are called for a certain time; Christ, however, is called forever.

XVIII. God manifested himself to the others in various degrees (*polymerōs*) and in divers manners (*polytrotōs*), by visions and dreams, by immediate and secret inspiration and various other modes, to whom either asleep or awake he exhibited himself; either to the internal senses in a phantasy or to the external eye or to the ears or to the mind itself by an intellectual representation, in rapture and ecstasy. But Christ knew all things most perfectly; not what he received from another source, but what he himself saw and heard in the bosom of the Father (Jn. 1:18). Hence the revelation made by Christ in these last days (as most perfect and on that account the last) is opposed to the other revelations made through the prophets (Heb. 1:2).

And by name from Moses.

XIX. But Christ was not only superior to other prophets, but even to Moses himself (although far more excellent than the others and holding familiar intercourse with God and whom God addresses not in vision and enigmas, or in a dream [as others], but mouth to mouth, i.e., in his presence and most familiarly as a friend talks to a friend, Num. 12:8). It is indeed said that he would be like unto Moses (Dt. 18:15) and such also he was in various particulars. Moses and Christ from their very birth were badly treated—Moses by Pharaoh, Christ by Herod. Moses delivered the people from Egypt, Christ from sin; Moses was a mediator between God and the people, Christ between God and men. Both confirmed their doctrine by miracles, both fasted forty days, both had their faces illuminated with a divine splendor. But still Christ was far greater than Moses. The latter was only a servant in the house of God, but Christ is a Son and Lord (Heb. 3). Moses promulgated the law, Christ the gospel. Moses was a simple internuncius, but Christ a true peacemaker (*eirēnopoios*). Moses had glory in his ministration. But what was the glory of his countenance (*katargoumenēn*) when it passed away? Yet the glory of Christ is constant and eternal (2 Cor. 3:11).

XX. The object of the prophetic office (inasmuch as Christ exercised it immediately) was the Jews, for which reason he is called "the minister of circumcision" (Rom. 15:8). He professes that he was sent to the lost sheep of the house of Israel (Mt. 15:24). However, inasmuch as he exercised it mediately in the Old Testament, it was the same Jews (Rom. 9:4), with the exception of a few Gentiles, who were called as the firstfruits of the Gentiles: such as Melchizedek, Jethro, Rahab, Naaman and the like. But in the New Testament it is all nations indiscriminately who are called to a participation in salvation.

EIGHTH QUESTION: THE PRIESTLY OFFICE OF CHRIST

Whether Christ was a Priest of true name who began his priesthood on earth. Or was he so called only figuratively, who fulfilled his office in heaven after his ascension and not before? We affirm the former and deny the latter against the Socinians.

I. The second part of the mediatorial office of Christ is his sacerdotal dignity, the basis of all the benefits which Christ purchased by his death. Because various controversies are waged by various parties, we must treat this distinctly. So that we speak first of the Priest, then of the priesthood as to its double grade (to wit, satisfaction and intercession).

What is the priesthood of Christ?

II. The priesthood of Christ is the function of the mediatorial office according to which he performs those things with God which must be performed for sinners; both by offering himself up once as a victim for them and by interceding for them always with the Father. The great excellence of this function appears from the fact that no mystery was either predicted by clearer prophecies or adumbrated by more frequent types.

Concerning Christ, a Priest.

III. Our first controversy is with the Socinians, who, although they confess with the mouth that Christ is a Priest, yet in fact deny it by changing his priesthood from a proper to a figurative one in order thus the more easily to overthrow the verity of his satisfaction. Thus the Ravocian Catechism ("Of the Priestly Office of Christ," Sect. VI, *Racovian Catechism* [1818], pp. 349-59), Smalcius (*De Divinitate Jesu Christi* 23 [1608], pp. 134-40) and Vokelius (*De vera Religione* 3.37 [1630], pp. 144-47) explain themselves. First, they deny that Christ was properly a Priest, but is called so only figuratively and analogically. Nor does this office differ from the kingly in any other way than that the latter is the power and the former is the will to help us—that as King he is able, as Priest he also wills to assist us. Second, they maintain that he was not a Priest on earth, but became so only at last in heaven and that his death was not strictly an oblation or sacrifice, but a preparation for that sacrifice to be offered at length in heaven. Third, that no expiation of sin was made by any sacrifice offered on earth, but that the expiation (accomplished in heaven) is our deliverance, both from punishment (that we may not be damned on account of our sins) and from sins (that we may not serve them).

IV. The orthodox on the contrary constantly affirm that Christ is a real Priest and his priesthood one properly so called (which he performed partly on earth by the offering up of his body [both a true and real sacrifice for the expiation of our sins] and performs partly in heaven by interceding for us). Thus the priesthood is formally distinguished from the kingship: the former consisting in the offering of sacrifice and in intercession; the latter in the government and defense of the people acquired by the offering (which is proved distinctly).

1. Proof that Christ was a true Priest.

V. First, that Christ was a real Priest who offered a sacrifice properly so called appears: (a) because he is frequently called a Priest (Ps. 110:4; Heb. 5:5 and many times in chaps. 7-10); also he is reckoned among priests properly so called (Heb. 5:1) appointed to offer gifts and to do what ought to be done with God. Nor is the fact that his priesthood is contradistinguished from the Levitical priesthood (Heb. 7, 8) opposed to this because the consequence (from the negation of the species to the negation of the genus) is not valid. Hence it is gathered that this priesthood differs from the Levitical and is far more excellent; but it would be wrong to infer from this that his priesthood is improper and figurative. On the contrary, because it transcends the Levitical priesthood, it ought to be most proper and perfect, just as the priesthood of Melchizedek did not cease to be a true priesthood, although widely differing from the Levitical. (b) All priestly acts are ascribed to him—oblation and intercession (Heb. 7:27; 9:24; 10:7). (c) He was adumbrated by various types, both common (such as were the Levitical priests, who failed in various particulars) and special, in Melchizedek, who in a peculiar manner signified him (as will be seen hereafter). As therefore these were true priests, Christ must necessarily have also been a true and properly so-called Priest.

2. And was such even while on earth.

VI. Second, that he was a Priest while on earth and not just when in heaven is evident not only from the fact that on earth he was called to the priesthood (Mt. 3:17; Heb. 5:5) and because he already exercised on earth priestly acts by the offering of prayers (Jn. 17; Heb. 5:7, 8) and the sacrifice of himself (Eph. 5:2; Heb. 1:3; 10:6, 7) in which he gave himself a ransom (*antilytron*) for us and made an expiation of sin; but also because the priest, who was a type of Christ, did not become a priest when he entered into the holy place, but he was also a priest before the offering of a victim (which the apostle teaches obtained its fulfillment in Christ, Heb. 9:11, 12). It is confirmed from the nature of the priesthood, which is ordained for the offering of gifts and sacrifices for sins (Heb. 5:1). Yet this ought to be done not in heaven, but on earth because victims are not offered elsewhere. Again where there is a true sacrifice, there a true priest should be; but on the cross a true sacrifice was offered (according to the apostle, Heb. 7:27; 9:25, 28), which cannot be referred to the intercessory offering made continually in heaven. (a) It treats of an offering which corresponds with the offering of victims, made under the Old Testament by killing them and shedding their blood. (b) It treats of an offering made once for all (*ephapax*) and which consists in the suffering and death of Christ, not of that which is made continually in heaven—for that which is made to the end of the world cannot be said to be made once. (c) The discourse concerns that in which he visibly appeared, which ought to be understood of the days of his flesh on earth and not of his stay in heaven (where he now remains invisible until he returns to judgment). (d) That offering is meant which ought to have preceded his sitting down at the right hand of God since it is indeed said after he had offered one sacrifice for sins, he sat down on the right hand of God (Heb. 10:12) where the one offering is opposed to the sitting down forever. Now if that offering consisted in Christ's bearing the yoke for us, it would no longer be one offering (*mia thysia*), but an offering (*thysia*) equal with his sitting down (*eis to diēnekes*). Nor could that session be said to have followed that offering, since it would consist most especially in it.

3. That the priesthood is distinguished from the kingship.

VII. Third, that the priesthood is distinguished from the kingship formally. It does not consist only in a general will to assist us, but in the special will of offering a body divinely prepared for him as a sacrifice for our sins (as is evident). Although the kingly and sacerdotal offices in Christ unite amicably to the same common end (to wit, the salvation of men), still they are distinguished by peculiar functions (as among men the censer and the scepter, the headband and the crown differ). Kings are set over men by God to rule, defend and keep them in duty. But priests are appointed for men with God to offer gifts and oblations for sins (Heb. 5:1). Thus the formal acts of the priesthood of Christ are oblation and intercession, but of his kingship the defense, government and deliverance of the church. A king acts for the people and against enemies; a priest acts in the name of the people with God. The ability to protect his own and conquer enemies is the property of the kingship, but that of the priesthood is righteousness to appease God and satisfy the law. Hence the types of the priesthood and of the kingship were different in the Levitical priesthood and in the Davidic kingship. Falsely then is the priesthood made to consist only in the will to assist us (which belongs to the kingship as well as to the priesthood) since Scripture expressly makes it consist in the offering of his own body (Heb. 10:5-7) while expiation (properly so called) follows. This is made not only through the pardoning of sins by a certain absolute power, but through a true and proper satisfaction made by the blood and death of the surety on earth.

Sources of explanation.

VIII. When Paul says, "If Christ were on earth, he should not be a priest, seeing that there are priests that offer gifts according to the law" (Heb. 8:4), he does not wish to deny absolutely that Christ was a Priest while on earth (for this he at length asserts and confirms in chapters 7, 9 and 10). Rather he means it relatively, concerning one of the acts of that priesthood (namely, his appearance before and intercession with the Father), which could not be done elsewhere than in heaven. Thus this pertained to the present time in which the apostle was speaking, so that the sense is—If Christ were now on earth, he could not be a priest, since indeed in the Old Testament the high priest did not always remain in the outer court, but it behooved him sometimes to enter the holy place with blood. For if he had not done this, he would not have fulfilled all the parts of his office. But it does not follow that if the entrance of Christ into heaven was requisite for the continuance and consummation of that priesthood, it was requisite for its constitution. On the contrary, he would not have entered into heaven if he had not already been a Priest.

IX. Although the priesthood could not be accomplished on earth, it does not follow that it could not be begun there; nor do the things which pertain to the continuance belong straightway to the constitution of the priesthood. It is one thing for his priesthood not to be perfect and consummated on earth (which we grant); another for him not to have been truly and perfectly a Priest while on earth (which we deny). Yea, even for entering upon the former, he ought to have been already actually a Priest. Aaron was perfectly a priest even when he was remaining in the outer court, although he had not fulfilled all the parts of his office.

X. The suffering and death of Christ ought indeed to have been preparatory and antecedent to his intercession, which was the other part of his priesthood, to be performed in heaven. But they could not be called a preparation for the priesthood to be administered only in heaven, since in that death was properly contained a sacerdotal offering and delivering up of Christ for us.

XI. In Heb. 5:5, it is not taught when Christ was constituted a Priest, but by whom (to wit, by the Father, who acknowledged him as his Son). Therefore, it marks the divinity, not the time of his calling. If the declaration of Christ's priesthood pertains to the resurrection, it is not at once to be denied that he was already a Priest. For the thing is not to be confounded with the manifestation of the thing. Other things bearing upon this subject can be found in the Disputation, "De Satisfactionis Christi Veritate," Part VI, Section 19-33 in *Opera* [1848], 4:574-82.

Ninth Question

On the nature and unity of Christ's priesthood and why it is said to be according to the order of Melchizedek.

The twofold typical priesthood a figure of Christ's priesthood.

I. The nature and dignity of Christ's priesthood cannot be better understood than from a comparison of the twofold typical priesthood by which it was adumbrated in the Old Testament (to wit, the Levitical and the Melchizedekian—both of which indubitably had a reference to Christ and obtained their fulfillment in him; although in the latter, its far more perfect image was exhibited than in the former). Hence it is said to have been after the order of Melchizedek and not after the order of Aaron.

Comparison and difference between the Levitical and Christ's priesthood.

II. For although the Levitical priesthood was principally instituted for no other end than to adumbrate the priesthood of Christ (and the similarity can be traced in various things), still it is certain that the latter was far more august and perfect than the former and that they differ in many respects, whether we regard the persons or institution or efficacy or perfection and duration.

1. As to the persons.

III. For with regard to the persons, the Levitical priests were taken from the tribe of Levi alone; but Christ was to spring from the tribe of Judah (Heb. 7:13, 14). They were mere men; he the true and eternal Son of God. They were sinners who had need to offer for themselves; he was holy and immaculate who ought to offer only for us and not for himself (Heb. 7:26, 27). They differed from the victims which they offered and had to make expiation with others' blood; he was at the same time Priest and victim who delivered himself up for us and by his own blood entered into the holy place, having obtained eternal redemption for us. They were many (because individuals could not fulfill all the parts of that office), but Christ (because he most perfectly performed all things by himself) stands alone, needing neither a successor nor a vicar.

2. As to institution.

IV. (2) In respect of manner of institution although each was instituted by God, still the method of institution was far different. The Levitical was indeed without an oath, but the priesthood of Christ was with an oath (*meta horkōmosias*, Heb. 7:20, 21; Ps. 110:4) inasmuch as the sanction of an oath being employed the heavenly Father promised to Christ an eternal and unchangeable (*ametamelēton*) priesthood. The former "after the law of a carnal commandment" (*kata nomon entolēs sarkikēs*, Heb. 7:16) (i.e., various external and corporeal ceremonies having been employed, which were changeable and to be abolished); the latter "after the power of an endless life" (*kata dynamin zōēs akatalytuo*, i.e., not by that law and omen, that being soon about to die he would transmit the priesthood to others coming after him, but being consecrated through the Holy Spirit with a heavenly virtue and inaugurated to immortal life, he would be a Priest forever).

3. As to efficacy.

V. (3) With respect to efficacy; the Levitical was weak (*asthenes*) and useless (*anōpheles*), having by itself no power to expiate sin and purge the conscience (Heb. 9:13, 14; 10:3, 4). On this account, the law is said to have made nothing perfect (Heb. 7:19). Now what frequently offered and innumerable victims could not do, this single victim once offered accomplished (Heb. 10:10). The priesthood of Christ is most efficacious, both for justification through the infinite merit of his righteousness and for sanctification through the power of the Spirit. Hence all legal victims being rejected, God acquiesced in this sacrifice alone (Heb. 10:6-8; 1 Jn. 1:7).

4. As to perfection.

VI. (4) With respect to perfection; because the Levitical was inefficacious, it was on that account also imperfect, inasmuch as the same sacrifices had to be repeated every year and every day (Heb. 10:11). But because the priesthood of Christ was of infinite value and efficacy, on that account it was most perfect and exhaustive; so that the offering having been made once, it neither can nor ought to be repeated (as the apostle fully teaches, Heb. 10).

5. As to duration.

VII. Finally, as to duration; for the Levitical was temporal, both with respect to the order (which was to continue for a certain time only and afterwards to be abolished, Dan. 9:27; Heb. 7:16) and with respect to the persons (who being mortal, could not live long, but had need of successors to succeed in place of the defunct; so that from one to another the priesthood might be transmitted). But as Christ is immortal and living forever, he thus has an eternal and unchangeable (*aparabaton*) priesthood in which he has no predecessor or successor and which he administered not only on earth, but also (always living) exercises perpetually in heaven that he may plead for us (Heb. 7:24, 25).

What was the priesthood of Melchizedek?

VIII. The other typical priesthood (but far more excellent than the preceding and from which the priesthood of Christ is denominated) is that of Melchizedek, whose history Moses briefly relates (Gen. 14:17-24). David merely mentions the type (Ps. 110:4) and the apostle more fully unfolds it in his epistle to the Hebrews. However, since this argument is difficult to explain (*dysermēneuton*, Heb. 5:11) and light comes to us from no other source for gaining a knowledge of the mystery, we ought undoubtedly to acquiesce in those things which God wished to reveal to us in this place.

Who was Melchizedek?

IX. We should say something concerning his person, although it is easier to say who he was not than to describe who he was—the silence of Scripture imposing silence upon us here in a certain manner and checking our curiosity. First (negatively, *kat' arsin*), we cannot agree with those who make Melchizedek not a man, but the Holy Spirit (as some ancient heretics who on that account were called Melchizedekians, mentioned by Epiphanius, *Panarion* 55 [PG 41.971-90]; and Sixtus Senensis, *Bibliotheca Sancta* 5, anno. 90 [1575], 2:33). Or they make him the Son of God himself, manifesting himself to Abraham in this prelude to his future incarnation, as Cunaeus held (*De Republica Hebraeorum* 3.3 [1666], pp. 273-94). (a) There is no greater reason for understanding symbolically what is related of him in Gen. 14 than what is related of the other kings of Canaan. (b) Moses removes all doubt from us when he so expressly describes him by name, residence (a well-known place in Palestine), and office and actions. (c) Christ could not be called a priest after the order of Melchizedek unless he could be distinguished from him; nor could Melchizedek himself be considered truly like unto the Son of God (*aphōmoiomenos*, Heb. 7:3) unless he differed from Christ as the type from the prototype. Nor does his being said to be without father (*apatōr*) and without mother (*amētōr*) prove that he was not a mortal man. This is to be understood not absolutely, but comparatively; not so much positively as if he were such simply, as negatively because Scripture is silent concerning it (as will afterwards be seen). In no other way is to be understood what is said in Heb. 7:3—that he abides a priest continually. He was alone (having no successor) and testimony is given to him "that he liveth" (v. 8) because Moses (mentioning neither his birth nor death) seems, as it were, to set him forth as immortal. Thus a true and properly so-called eternity may in a certain manner be adumbrated.

X. Second, nor can we yield to those who think he was Shem, the son of Noah (as most of the Jews hold, an opinion embraced by Jerome, *Letter 73*, "To Evangelium" [PL 22.676-81] following Epiphanius, *Panarion* 55.6 [PG 41.982-83], and by many others). He could not be said to be without father (*apatōr*), without mother (*amētōr*) and without descent (*agenealogētos*), since his genealogy, birth and death are so accurately given. Nor can any reason be given why Moses should have changed the name. Again Canaan did not yield to Shem in inheritance, but to the Canaanites (Gen. 10:15, 19). Finally, Melchizedek had nothing in common with the Levitical race; otherwise Levi would have received no less tithes in

Shem than he had given in Abraham. Nor is it credible that the grandfather would receive tithes in the grandson or that the patriarch could be called a stranger in the country of his grandfather and under his eyes. Hence Josephus and Philo openly reject this opinion of their own comrades.

XI. Therefore the third opinion only is seen to be retained by us. It maintains that Melchizedek was a true man, sprung from men, king of Salem, who lived in the time of Abraham and held a kingly with a priestly office. To seek further who he was, is to pry into that which God has not been willing to make known to us. Yea, if this could be known and perceived, there would be no place for a type and mystery, the whole reason of which depends on this—that God for some wise purpose was unwilling that the race, birth and death of so great a man should be designated. In other cases, this is usually done intentionally, as often as reference is made to public persons (to wit, priests or kings). Nor can any other reason be given why that was not done than the special reason of a mystery (which the apostle follows up in the epistle to the Hebrews).

What is the order (taxis) of Melchizedek?

XII. This much was to be premised in order that the true reason of this figure may be known. For a clearer knowledge of it, we must first ascertain what the psalmist (Ps. 110:4) and after him Paul (Heb. 7:17) mean by *taxin Melchisedek*. The Hebrew word *dhbrthy* Paul translates by *taxin*, which denotes "an order," "custom" or "condition." Thus *y* here is paragogical, not an affix (as in Ecc. 3:18, *dhbrth bny 'dm*, "the condition of the sons of men"). Thus *taxis Aarōn* designates nothing else than the condition of the Aaronic priesthood prescribed by the law, as we gather from v. 16 where what he had said *kata tēn taxin* is interpreted "not after the law of a carnal commandment" (*ou kata nomon entolēs sarkikēs*) and what he said *kata taxin Melchisedek*, he explains by "after the power of an endless life" (*kata dynamin zōēs akatalytou*). Thus nothing else is denoted than the condition of the Melchizedekian priesthood and the agreement and similarity existing between it and the priesthood of Christ in this respect (as the apostle expresses it, "after the similitude" [*kata tēn homoiotēta*, v. 15]).

Christ agrees with Melchizedek: (1) in name and (2) in origin.

XIII. Now this similitude is made to consist of various particulars by the apostle: (1) in the name because he was called Melchizedek, king of Salem, which the apostle interprets to mean "king of righteousness" and "king of peace" (Heb. 7:2). Both of these properly belong to Christ, who is "Jehovah our righteousness" and the "Prince of Peace." (2) In origin because Melchizedek is described to us by Moses as without father (*apatōr*), without mother (*amētōr*) and without descent (*agenealogētos*, v. 3), not absolutely and simply, as if he were positively such (which the common condition of men, from the race of whom it was before said he had sprung, rejects); but relatively, in respect of the Mosaic description. For Moses speaks of Melchizedek as if he had fallen down from heaven, making no mention of his birth or death or of his parents, so that the true eternity of Christ might in a certain manner be adumbrated by such silence. Therefore, he is said to be without father (*apatōr*) and without mother (*amētōr*) not in nature (as a natural man and a son of Adam), but in economy (as a mystical man and a figure of the second Adam)—just as he is considered here not according to generation, but commemoration (because we find nothing about his parents in Scripture). In like manner, that he lacked "beginning of days" and "end of life" because it preserves a deep silence concerning his nativity and death. That he is without descent (*agenealogētos*) because his race is nowhere described, "whose father nor mother are written in the genealogies" (as the Syrian rightly explains it), i.e., for whom neither ancestors nor posterity are given in Scripture, so that it cannot be told from whom he sprang or who were to spring from him. For *genealogein* is to enumerate the race and family of anyone as *genealogein theous* is to "weave the genealogy of the gods" (according to Justin Martyr, cf. *Hortatory Address to the Greeks* 2 [ANF 1:274; PG 6.245-46]). But what only shadowily and imperfectly are found in him are truly and perfectly fulfilled in Christ: whether in respect of person or of office. For as to person, he was truly without father (*apatōr*) as man, truly without mother (*amētōr*) as God; as to office, neither born of a father who was a priest, nor from a mother who had sprung from priests. Nor do we read of his having either a predecessor or successor in this office (in which manner he is truly without descent [*agenealogētos*]).

3. In duration.

(3) As to duration because he is set forth as immortal, since no mention is made of his death by Moses (Heb. 7:8). But this is said most truly of Christ because he is a priest forever according to the power of an indissoluble law (Heb. 7:16).

4. In office.

XIV. (4) As to office because in him were united two offices—the regal and the priestly. The same King of men was the Priest of the most high God. This was not allowed under the Old Testament, in which God so circumscribed the limits of both these offices that one and the same person could not ordinarily exercise both. But this was truly fulfilled in Christ, who is described to us as a King and Priest (Ps. 110).

5. In dignity.

(5) As to dignity because he is set forth to us as superior to Abraham in that he is said to have blessed him (to wit, with a customary and priestly blessing according to which the lesser is blessed by the greater [Heb. 7:7], which Abraham himself publicly acknowledged by paying tithes to Melchizedek, which evidently were due to God only and to his ministers, Gen. 28:22). Thus Christ obtained a far more excellent office than the Levitical. Even though Christ was to spring from Abraham (as did Levi), he cannot be said to have paid tithes in him (as Levi is said to) because he was there only according to the flesh and the human nature, not according to the person and divine nature (which are here to be specially regarded).

6. In unity.

(6) As to unity because Melchizedek is set forth as the only one, having neither predecessor nor successor. Thus Christ is the sole Priest of the New Testament, who needs neither vicars nor successors. He lives forever, having an unchangeable (*aparabaton*) priesthood, as opposed to the Levitical priests, who (infirm and mortal) had to be many (Heb. 7:22, 23, 28).

XV. These are the principal heads of that similitude which show the priesthood of Melchizedek to be far more excellent than the Levitical. But Romanists deny that in these the reason of that order is to be constituted, but say it must be sought in the "bloodless sacrifice of bread and wine" which is offered daily in the Mass after the oblation of Melchizedek by the ministry of the priests of the New Testament, who were instituted by Christ for that purpose. But neither the blessing and tithing can constitute that distinction since both would be done by the Levitical priests; nor its unity and lack of succession because we read of no one having succeeded Abel (nor is the family of Job or of Elijah mentioned). But this reasoning is of no avail. (1) Although the things ascribed to Melchizedek may be found separately in others, yet nowhere except in him can they be found united. (2) Blessing and tithing in general pertained also to the Levitical priests, but not in the manner in which they are ascribed to Melchizedek, since he is said to have received tithes from and to have blessed Abraham (and in him the Levites as a superior blesses inferiors). (3) Abel cannot be called without father (*apatōr*), without mother (*amētōr*), or without descent (*agenealogētos*), nor is the family of Job and Elijah passed over in absolute silence. Besides these were not priests (of whom we are now treating).

Whether many priests after the order of Melchizedek may be granted. It is denied.

XVI. But let us see further, how falsely is obtruded a priesthood of the New Testament after the order of Melchizedek exercised by the ministers of Christ in the sacrifice of the Mass. This is plainly gathered from various sources. First, in this is constituted by the apostle the distinction between the Levitical and Melchizedekian priesthood—that they indeed were many simutaneously as well as successively; he however was alone, who should have neither partner nor successor. "And they truly," says the apostle in Heb. 7:23, 24, "were many priests, because they were not suffered to continue by reason of death: But this man, because he continueth ever, hath an unchangeable priesthood." This certainly could not be said if the Melchizedekian priesthood admitted of many mortal and infirm priests succeeding him, no other than the Levitical priesthood.

XVII. Nor does it avail to reply here with Bellarmine, "Paul does indeed exclude priests of the same order and dignity, but not inferior priests who, in respect of Christ, are really servants. No one indeed can succeed Christ in the same order because he lives forever, but nothing prevents others from being instituted under him as his vicars and servants; so that although Christ is our only Shepherd and Teacher (Mt. 23:8) still there can be other inferior teachers and shepherds without detriment to him" (lib. 1 de Missa, cap. 25+). (a) This distinction openly contradicts what the apostle says: The priesthood of Christ is unchangeable (*aparabaton*, Heb. 7:24), i.e., not only perpetual, but one which cannot be transmitted to another. Now if there could be many secondary priests, they would have a joint priesthood transmitted from Christ to them. (b) It is at variance also with the type. The priesthood of Melchizedek was such that it had no adjuncts (whether as successors or vicars and secondary priests), but was included in Melchizedek alone, every other being excluded. Therefore, since Christ is a Priest after the order of Melchizedek, he ought to be alone so that no one can be associated with him in this office under any name whatsoever (or pretext, partner, successor or secondary priest). For if the figure is restricted to one person, why not the verity with a better right? And if from the fact that Melchizedek had no successor the conclusion holds good that neither does Christ have any, then why not from the fact that he had no inferior is it not equally concluded that Christ has none? It is confirmed by this—that in the calling of Aaron mention is always made of his sons and posterity, but with respect to Melchizedek mention is made of the person himself for no other reason than to show that the Aaronic priesthood was assigned to one family, but the Melchizedekian to one person. (c) These secondary priests are either of the same species with the primary or they are of a diverse species; but neither can be said. Not the latter because thus the sacrifice which they offer would be different from the sacrifice of Christ (which our opponents do not allow). Not the former because thus they ought to be kings and priests, without fathers (*apatores*), without mothers (*amētores*), without descent (*agenealogētoi*) and to have a perpetual and unchangeable (*aparabaton*) priesthood (which could not be transmitted to another) and in which they would have neither predecessors nor successors (and the like, in which that order of Melchizedekian priesthood consists according to the apostle). Everyone sees that this cannot be said of them. Again, they ought to be ordained with an oath and after the power of an endless life (as Christ); to be pure and immaculate, not having need to offer for themselves, but only for the people, who should themselves be priests and victims; offer only once, not daily; not be prevented by death from remaining to minister in the true sanctuary (namely, heaven) as is said of Christ; but how different from them appears by itself. (d) If there are not under the New Testament priests of the same dignity and order with Christ because the reason for which there were many under the law does not now exist (i.e., "the necessity of dying"), so neither can there be many unequal and secondary because the reason for which there were many under the law ceases (i.e., infirmity) because one could not execute so many functions. On this account, he was obliged to have many associates to relieve him. But neither reason has place in Christ (immortal and most perfect), who therefore is neither prevented by death from continuing nor by infirmity is he unequal to so great an office (which is the reasoning of the apostle, Heb. 7:23, 24, 28).

XVIII. Nor can the contrary be proved by the instance (taken from the prophetic office of Christ) which can admit of secondary pastors and teachers, although Christ remains always the supreme pastor and teacher of the church. (a) A prophet who treats with men in the name of God differs from a priest who treats with God in the name of men. As to the former, Christ, remaining in heaven, requires ministers who (making up for his bodily presence) may visibly address men and frequently reach them; but as to the latter, since Christ is always present with the Father and the sacrifice once offered is of indefinite virtue, he does not require ministers to sacrifice in his place. (b) Christ, who calls himself our highest teacher, ordained apostles and ministers to preach (Mt. 28:19; Eph. 4:11), but we nowhere read of his having ordained inferior priests. (c) Inferior pastors under Christ do not impugn any type, as secondary priests would. (d) When Christ is called the only teacher, it ought to be understood to the exclusion of all others because he teaches externally and internally and because he brought us the gospel from heaven. Thus pastors teach nothing which they have not received from him (which can apply to no mortal). But this cannot be said of his priesthood because on the hypothesis of our opponents priests ought to be of the same order with Christ.

2. It was not instituted by Christ.

XIX. Second, that priesthood we do not anywhere in the New Testament read of as having been instituted either by Christ or by his apostles. Paul enumerates various orders of sacred offices both ordinary and extraordinary (Rom. 12; 1 Cor. 12; Eph. 4), but concerning priests of the New Testament he preserves a deep silence. Now is it credible that

Paul, who so accurately set forth all that belongs to the sacred ministry (even the more minute and less necessary, as is seen in the epistles to Timothy and to Titus), would have omitted this species and part of that office which is special and primary and in comparison with which the rest seem to be of small importance? Thus Christ does indeed call his own to the apostleship and ministry, to teach, preach the gospel and administer the sacraments; but nowhere does he command them to perform the priestly office and to offer him daily as a propitiatory (*hilastikon*) sacrifice. Nor is it favored by his commanding his disciples in the institution of the Eucharist to "do this in remembrance of him," because this applies to all believers (according to Paul's interpretation, who explains it by eating the bread and drinking the cup: "As often as ye eat this bread and drink this cup, ye do shew the Lord's death till he come," 1 Cor. 11:26*). Hence Bellarmine acknowledges this to be common to all Christians ("De Sacramento Eucharistae," 4.16 *Opera* [1858], 3:430-32). Again, it is an unheard-of thing that the same words can apply to two diverse and greatly separated sacraments, which would be the case here (namely, to the institution of the Eucharist and of a priesthood). Also, it gratuiously assumes that "do" is here put for "sacrifice." Nothing can be more foreign to the mind of Christ, who is found here to have neither observed nor enjoined upon his apostles any rite of sacrificing (as will be more fully shown in the proper place).

3. This priesthood can belong to no man.

XX. Third, this priesthood according to the order of Melchizedek is accompanied by such characters and marks as can belong to no one but Christ: that he is a Priest called and ordained by God with an oath (Heb. 7:21); having no need to offer for himself, but for the people (Heb. 7:27); who should offer not often, but once only; not the blood of another, but his own to take away sin (Heb. 9:26); who by his own blood ought to enter into the holy place, having obtained eternal redemption (Heb. 9:12); who is able to save them to the uttermost that come unto God by him, seeing he ever lives (Heb. 7:25); finally, who to perform all these duties is holy, undefiled and separate from sinners (Heb. 7:26).

4. Because Paul does not speak of it.

XXI. Fourth, the apostle, who so earnestly treats of the resemblance between the priesthood of Melchizedek and of Christ, says not a word about this bloodless sacrifice, or offering of bread and wine, in which they make this resemblance particularly to consist. He would not have omitted this if he had agreed in opinion with the papists. Nor must it be said here with Bellarmine that this did not fall in with the design of the apostle, which was to extol the excellence of Christ's priesthood above the Levitical. If the apostle intended to institute a comparison of this twofold priesthood, could or ought he to have omitted its most important part? Or that the mystery of the Lord's Supper was too deep to be perceived by the Hebrews, which the apostle calls "hard to be understood" (*dysermēneuton*, Heb. 5:11). For if this was the reason, he ought to have said nothing about so many other mysteries, no less difficult; yea, far more difficult than the mystery of the Lord's Supper (for example, the divinity of Christ, his incarnation, sacrifice, etc). Yea, in 6:1 the apostle testifies that the Hebrews ought not to remain in the rudiments of religion but, leaving the principles of the doctrine of Christ, to go on unto perfection.

5. Because the priesthood of Aaron and of Melchizedek do not differ in this respect.

XXII. Fifth, thus the priesthood of Aaron and of Melchizedek would not differ in this particular while they are set forth by the apostle as most diverse, since in the former also there was the offering of bread and wine (Ex. 29:24; Lev. 2; Num. 28:5, 12), where similar offerings are enjoined, not only as a certain part of another sacrifice or a seasoning of it, but also as an offering by itself (Lev. 2:1, 2). Yea, the Melchizedekian would be thrown below the Levitical priesthood, if what constituted there a part of the sacrifice, constituted here the whole sacrifice. Nor does it help the matter to reply that the Melchizedekian differed in this from the Levitical—in that the latter offered sacrifices of all kinds, bloody and bloodless; but the former only a bloodless. For so far from any excellence being given to the Melchizedekian, on the contrary the Levitical would have to be considered far more excellent for this very reason. Besides Christ would thus rather have to be called a Priest after the order of Aaron, than of Melchizedek, since he offered both a bloody and bloodless sacrifice in this sense—a bloody upon the cross, a bloodless in the Lord's Supper.

Sources of explanation.

XXIII. We find nothing in the history of Melchizedek (Gen. 14:17-24) from which we can infer that he offered a bloodless sacrifice of bread and wine to God. Nor does what is said concerning "the bringing forth bread and wine" for Abraham (returning from the slaughter of the kings) belong here. He is not treating of a sacerdotal function, but of the regal munificence by which he wished to recruit the wearied soldiers of Abraham and to entertain his victorious friend with a royal feast. This was the custom in those ancient times, to offer bread and wine to those returning from battle and victorious for the purpose of refreshing them (as Fagius remarks on Gen. 14:18, "Annotata ad Genesim," *Critici Sacri* [1660], 1:183). An example of this occurs in Jdg. 8:5, where the inhabitants of Succoth went out with loaves of bread to meet Gideon after he warred against the Midianites. Thus according to the Hebrew style, "bread" signifies all kinds of food and "to eat bread" with anyone is to sit at table and enjoy social intercourse with him. That this was the meaning of Moses in this place is proved: (1) from the word *hvtsy'*, which is "to bring forth," "to bring into the midst," "to draw out," "to lead out," not "to offer." Hence the Septuagint translates it uniformly by *agein*, *exagein*, *ekpherein* and never by *thyein*. Nor does it admit of any other meaning in Jdg. 6:18. Yea, if it could be taken in any other place in Scripture for a sacerdotal action, it would not follow that it must be taken here likewise in such a sense. (2) The nature of the thing demands this because a sacrificial offering demands some altar erected for this purpose, of which we find no mention made by Moses (as elsewhere he does carefully note this when he speaks of the sacrifice of Noah, Abraham, Jacob and others). Hence it is clear that this offering was not made to God for a sacrifice, but to Abraham for a feast. (3) Thus Josephus explains it, "Melchizedek here made presents to Abraham's army and furnished it with a great abundance of necessary things" (*echorēgēse de hyotos ho Melchisedek tō Abraam stratō xenia, kai pollēn aphthonian tōn epitēdeiōn paresche*, AJ 1.181 [Loeb, 4:88-89]). The Septuagint translates it by *exēnegēe*. In many versions (for instance the Complutensian) *autō* is added exegetically—"brought forth to him bread and wine" (*exēnenken autō artous kai oinon*). Thus Onkelos renders it (cf. Walton, *Biblia* *sacra polyglotta* [1657], p. 55 on Gen. 14:18). The Vulgate (which is authoritative with Romanists) has *protulit.* Jerome and Ambrose on this passage inform us that the old Hebrews so understood it (*Letter 73*, "To Evangelium*" [PL 22.678]; *De Abraham* 1.3.16-17 [PL 14.448-49]). Cajetan confesses that nothing is written here concerning a sacrifice or oblation, but concerning the bringing forward and drawing forth of bread and wine (which Josephus says was done for the refreshment of the victors, AJ 1.179-82 [Loeb, 4:88-91]).

XXIV. The instances adduced by our adversaries do not prove the contrary. (1) That the cause of oblation is at once given (drawn from the priesthood) when it is added, "For he was the priest of the Most High God." In the Hebrew, it is not a causal particle, but a copulative: as it is rendered by Pagninus, Montanus, Vatablus and the Septuagint, *hēn de hiereus.* Nor does it refer to what precedes, so as to render the reason why he brought forth bread and wine (since he did it as a friendly and confederate king), but to what follows in order that it may be understood by what right he blessed Abraham and received tithes from him. Nor if a Sophpasuch is added, does it show that the discourse is ended, but only the verse (as is frequently the case elsewhere, Ps. 95:7, 8; Gen. 23:17, 18; Jer. 33:10, 11). (2) That there was no need for the bread and wine to be appropriated to supplying the wants of Abraham's soldiers because they were now sated with booty (v. 24). It does not follow, Pererius himself being judge: "There seems to be little strength in this confutation because either Melchizedek did not know this, or if he did, he nevertheless wished by this gift to declare his benevolence towards Abraham and special delightful pleasure at his victory" ("Quinta Disputatio quae est tertia de Melchisedec," *Commentarium et disputationum in Genesim* [1601], 3:192 on Gen. 14). Besides all spoils are not eatable, capable of being eaten. (3) That nowhere else is mention made of Melchizedek's sacrifice, nor is its rite described except here. Therefore these words can with propriety be made to favor it, even if they are referred to a feast (that it is a sacred and religious feast) to prove his communion in the true worship of God, as was customary after sacrifices. But there was no more necessity for Moses to treat of the sacrifice of Melchizedek than of his genealogy and parents. For besides the fact that the priesthood is more extensive than the sacrifice (since praying and blessing belong to it), the design of the Holy Spirit was not to recount all the acts of Melchizedek's priesthood, but those only in which he excelled the Levitical priests (which could not be done by the reason of a sacrifice which was common to them). The mystical silence of Scripture on this as on other things was to intimate that Christ had nothing out of himself by which a sacrifice could be denoted because he ought to be both the Priest and the victim. What is added concerning the sacred and religious feast which followed his sacrifice (that the bread had been sacrificed before it was set before Abraham) is a mere supposition, not a trace of which occurs in the account given by Moses. Yea, it introduces inconsistencies (*asystata*). For since a sacrifice (as Bellarmine confesses) secures the destruction of the thing sacrificed, if the bread and wine were once destroyed in sacrifice, how could they be suitable for reception by men? The flesh of animals could indeed be eaten after their immolation, in which they suffered a destruction of themselves (i.e., death). But the same cannot be said of inanimate things which cannot be destroyed, except when they are either consumed or evaporated by the flames so that they cannot be used for food anymore.

XXV. Eternity of priesthood does not immediately infer the perpetuity of the offering of the sacrifice; as if the priesthood would be unoccupied, if a sacrifice was not offered continually by him. But it suffices that the sacrifice be perpetual in respect of efficacy and continual application. Thus the sacrifice of Christ once offered (which ceased with the act of offering), still abides continually in respect of eternal power and value because his blood is always living and fresh before God. Therefore, although the act of sacrifice ceased on earth, the priesthood is not on that account unoccupied, since a priest is not ordained only for offering, but also for interceding and executing other functions; yea, if Christ were now on earth, he would not be a priest (Heb. 8:4). Nor is it necessary that a priest should always have something new to offer (Heb. 8:3). It is only necessary that he should have offered at some time (as the Levitical priests, the sacrifice having been performed, did not cease to be priests). If an oblation is required, it is not always a repetition of the sacrifice, but a most efficacious representation of it by intercession—like the high priest who (the offering having been made in the tabernacle) carried the blood of expiation into the holy of holies interceding for the people.

XXVI. Since the apostle says that Christ is a Priest forever without any mention of a sacrifice, the eternity of his priesthood cannot consist in this, but is referred by the apostle to three other causes: (1) the eternity of his person because Christ, as the Son of God, lives forever (Heb. 7:3, 16, 17); (2) the power and efficacy of his sacrifice, which always abides and extends to all believers of every time (Heb. 7:25; 10:10, 19); (3) the perpetuity of his intercession because he always lives to intercede for us (Heb. 7:25).

XXVII. The Christian religion cannot be without some external and visible sacrifice by which the wrath of God was once appeased and sin expiated; but it is not necessary that that external sacrifice should be offered daily. It suffices that once offered, it has an eternal power and efficacy (which is the case with the sacrifice of Christ).

XXVIII. If it is said anywhere by the prophets that there would be priests and Levites under the New Testament, either it refers to a spiritual and mystical priesthood (which is common to all believers, through which having been made a royal priesthood they ought to offer spiritual victims acceptable to God through Christ [1 Pet. 2:5; Rom. 12:1; Heb. 13:15]; in which sense it is said in Is. 61:6, "Believers shall be named priests and ministers of God"); or the gospel ministry is meant, which is expressed by a legal phrase on account of the analogy of both. For as God employed the ministry of priests to conserve the method of divine worship, so in the Christian church he willed to use the sacred ministry by which the elect might be led to Christ and having been led might constantly persevere in his service. Thus the passage is to be understood where he says, "God will take of the Gentiles for priests and for Levites" (Is. 66:21), i.e., sacred ministers. However, as Levites are not to be understood properly here (of the tribe of Levi), so neither is the word "priest" to be understood properly, but mystically.

XXIX. If the ancients were accustomed sometimes to call gospel ministers priests, this was not done by them to denote that any real and properly so-called external sacrifice could be granted in the church besides the bloody sacrifice offered on the cross (for they were accustomed frequently to apply the same name to believers themselves). But this is especially true for a twofold cause.

First, ministers consecrate themselves to the work of the ministry. Second, by preaching the gospel, they (as it were) slay the people of God and offer them to God as a sacrifice well pleasing to him (*euprosdekton tō Theō*). Paul refers to this when he says that he "ministered the gospel of God" (*hierourgein to euangelion*) that "the offering up of the Gentiles might be acceptable, being sanctified by the Holy Ghost" (Rom. 15:16). Thus there is a sacrifice, but a mystical and figurative one, not a proper and visible one.

XXX. The distinction between a bloody and bloodless offering is absurd (*asystatos*). For (1) if Christ offered himself not only as a bloody but also as a bloodless sacrifice and is daily offered as a sacrifice, there is not one alone, but there are many sacrifices of the same Christ, against the express testimony of Scripture (Heb. 9:25; 10:10, 14). (2) Thus the argument of the apostle that Christ would have to suffer often (if there was a necessity of offering himself often) fails. (3) It is repugnant to the oracle of Paul testifying that without the shedding of blood there is no remission of sin (Heb. 9:22). Hence since the proper quality of a sacrifice is to be bloody, whoever holds to any bloodless sacrifice of Christ, by that very thing denies the true sacrifice of Christ.

XXXI. The taking away of the daily sacrifice (discussed in Dan. 8:11) ought to be referred historically and literally to the persecution of Antiochus (Epiphanes), who profaned the temple and caused the legal worship and especially the daily sacrifice to cease; but mystically (if the reference is to Antichrist) the daily sacrifice cannot pertain to the Mass because it was a bloody sacrifice which was usually offered twice a day and only in one place (which cannot be said of the Mass, but of the sacrifice of Christ, which is continually before God for a propitiation and before believers for their consolation). It can truly be said to have been taken away by Antichrist (by the institution of the sacrifice of the Mass incompatible [*asystatou*] with it).

XXXII. The "pure offering" spoken of by Malachi (1:11) can no more be referred to a sacrifice properly so called, consisting in an offering of bread and wine, than the incense mentioned in the same place. However, as it is clear that by this incense we are to understand mystically the prayers and praises of believers (which are often so designated, Ps. 141:2; Rev. 5:8), so by the pure offering nothing else is meant than the spiritual worship of God to be established among the Gentiles by the preaching of the gospel, the expression being accommodated to the legal worship as everywhere else (Rom. 12:1; 15:16; 1 Pet. 2:5; Phil. 4:18).

Tenth Question: The Necessity of the Satisfaction

Was it necessary for Christ to make satisfaction to divine justice for us? We affirm against the Socinians.

I. As the priesthood of Christ (according to the apostle's description and the Levitical types) is divided into two principal parts (*hilasmō* or the satisfaction given for us on the cross; and *emphanismō* or his appearing and intercession for us in heaven, 1 Jn. 2:2; Heb. 9:12), the doctrine of Christ's satisfaction (as the primary and most important part of the great mystery of piety and the principal foundation of our faith and hope) must be established before all things, defended and confirmed against the fiery darts of Satan, with which it is assailed by innumerable adversaries.

II. Whatever relates to the controversy concerning it can be reduced under five heads: (1) its necessity; (2) its truth; (3) its unity and perfection; (4) its mode and parties; (5) its object. We will discuss these distinctly in as many questions.

In what sense the word "satisfaction" is used here.

III. The satisfaction here discussed, is not taken widely for a simple and indiscriminate reparation of injury (as when one purges and excuses himself to him who has suffered injury). Rather it is taken strictly for the payment of a debt, with which is paid what another owes and with which he satisfies the creditor or judge who requires the debt or punishment.

Statement of the question: concerning its necessity.

IV. Concerning the necessity of a satisfaction, there are three principal opinions of theologians. The first of those simply denying it (as the Socinians, who not only deny that Christ satisfied for us, but also affirm that it was not at all necessary, since God both could and would gratuitously remit sin without any satisfaction; cf. Socinus, *De Iesu Christo Servatore*, Pt. I. 1 [1594], pp. 1-11). The second, that of those distinguishing between an absolute and hypothetical necessity; as to the latter, maintaining constantly (in opposition to the Socinians) the necessity of a satisfaction because God so decreed it. They also add a necessity of fitness to this because it is most fit that satisfaction should be made to divine justice that his commands may not be said to have been violated with impunity. As to the former, they deny that it was thus necessary absolutely because if God had wished, there were other modes of liberation possible to him. This appears to have been the opinion of Augustine (*The Trinity* 13.10 [FC 45:388-90]) and some of the Reformers, especially those who wrote before the time of Socinus. The third, that of those affirming, who maintain its absolute necessity, so that God not only has not willed to remit our sins without a satisfaction, but could not do so on account of his justice. This is the common opinion of the orthodox (which we follow).

God cannot forgive w/o satisfaction

V. However because our adversaries wrong us in many ways by their perverse explanation of our opinion, certain principles must be first laid down from which the whole doctrine concerning the satisfaction of Christ can be the more easily perceived and great light thrown upon both this question and those which follow. These have reference either to sin, for which a satisfaction is required; or to the satisfaction itself which is to be made; or to God, to whom it is to be rendered; or to Christ, by whom satisfaction is made.

VI. First, sin, which renders us guilty and hated of God and binds us over as debtors to punishment, may be viewed under a threefold relation (*schesei*) either as a debt, which we are bound to pay to divine justice, in which sense the law is called "a handwriting" (Col. 2:14); or as an enmity, whereby not only are we haters of God (*theostygeis*), but God himself looks upon us with hatred and indignation; or as a crime by which, before God, the supreme Ruler and Judge of the world, we become worthy of everlasting death and malediction. Hence sinners are sometimes called "debtors" (Mt. 6:12), then "enemies [*echthroi*] of God" (both actively and passively, Col. 1:21), and again "guilty before God" (*hypodikoi tō theō*, Rom. 3:19). Hence we infer that three things were required for our redemption—the payment of the debt contracted by sin, the appeasing of divine hatred and wrath and the expiation of guilt.

VII. And hence secondly, the nature of the satisfaction to be made for sin may be easily perceived (viz., in which these three relations [*scheseis*] at the same time concur): the payment of the debt, the appeasing of the divine wrath (by reconciling us with him) and the expiation of guilt (by the endurance of punishment). But as the principal relation to be attended to in sin is its criminality, so satisfaction has relation (*schesis*) to the punishment imposed by the supreme Judge.

VIII. However, a twofold payment (noticed by jurists) must be accurately distinguished here. One "by the very act of payment sets at liberty" the guilty and the debtor, when the very thing is paid which is in the obligation, whether the payment is made by the debtor himself or by a surety in his name. Another in which "the mere act of payment is not sufficient to liberate the debtor." For the payment is not the same thing precisely which is demanded in the obligation, but an equivalent, which although it does not by the very deed take away the obligation, yet being admitted (when it might be refused) is regarded as a satisfaction. In a pecuniary and a penal debt, this is evident. In a pecuniary debt, the payment of the debt by the very act frees the debtor (by whomsover the payment is made) because the person who pays is not attended to here, but only what is paid. Hence the creditor (payment being received) is not said to have treated the debtor with indulgence and to have forgiven the debt because he has received just as much as was due to him. But in a penal debt the case is different because the obligation regards not only things but persons (i.e., not only what is paid, but also him who pays, so that the punishment may be borne by the transgressor). For as the law demands individual personal obedience, so it also exacts a like punishment. Therefore in order that the guilty person may be freed by another's or a vicarious satisfaction, the act of the judge and ruler ought to come in. That act is called "relaxation" (in relation to the law). In relaxation to the debtor or guilty person, it is called pardon because his personal punishment is dispensed with a vicarious punishment admitted and accepted in its place. However, because the subject under discussion (sin) does not have only a relation to debt, but also to criminality, the satisfaction is not of that kind (which by the act itself frees the debtor) unless the forbearance (*epieikeia*) and remission of the Judge comes in. The very thing itself which is in the obligation is not paid (viz., a personal enduring of the punishment), which the law according to strict justice (*akribodikaion*) demands, but only a vicarious suffering. Hence it clearly appears how well remission and satisfaction here agree with each other whatever outcry our opponents may raise against it. For in the enduring of punishment suffered by Christ, there is satisfaction, but in the admission and acceptance of a substitute, remission. The former respects Christ, from whom God demands a punishment, not numerically but specifically the same with that which we owed. But the latter respects believers, whom God frees from punishment in their own persons, while he admits a substitute. Thus we see how admirably mercy is tempered with justice—justice since it is exercised against sin and mercy exercised towards the sinner. Satisfaction is made to the justice of God by a surety and remission given to us by God.

IX. Third, this reasoning is fortified from a consideration of the relations (*schesis*) of God, to whom satisfaction is to be made. As we have here a threefold relation of sin (as we have said), so God can be regarded either as the creditor or as the Lord and offended party or as the Judge and ruler. But in this affair, although both the former hold their own place here, yet the third is chiefly to be attended to. Since God is not merely a creditor here (who may at pleasure remit

2 senses of payment

punishment ↓ satisfies justice

substitution ↓ mercy

what is due) nor merely the offended party and Lord (who may do as he will with his own without injury to anyone), but the Judge and ruler of the universe, to whom alone belongs the infliction of punishment or deliverance from it because (as all jurists acknowledge) this belongs only to the supreme magistrate and the highest power (*tēs hyperechousēs exousias*). For although the creditor may demand his debt and the offended party restitution and compensation for his loss, yet the power to compel payment or exact punishment, no one has except the judge (who is established in authority). Here it is rightly to be held against our adversaries, whose capital error (*prōton pseudos*) is this—that sin is here to be regarded as a simple debt and God as a mere creditor, who can at will either exact or remit the punishment without a satisfaction. It is certain that God here sustains the character of Judge and ruler of the world. He has the rights of majesty to maintain and professes to be the guardian and vindicator of his laws. Therefore he has the claims not only of a creditor or Lord (which he can assert or remit at pleasure), but also the right of government and of punishment (which is natural and indispensable).

X. But here again the punishment itself (which the judge exacts) is to be accurately distinguished from the manner and circumstances under which it is enforced (for they widely differ). For as to the punishment itself in general, the right of God in this respect is plainly indispensable, being founded on the very justice of God. But as to the manner and circumstances of the punishment that it may be demanded from such a person and in such a way, it is not equally of natural right, but of positive and free right. For a certain forbearance (*epieikeia*) can be admitted here from the goodness of a most wise God, either in relation to time by the delay of punishment; or in relation to the degree by mitigation; or in relation to persons by a substitution. For although the person sinning entirely deserves punishment and can justly be punished, yet it is not so necessary and indispensable that for certain weighty reasons it may not be transferred to a surety. And in this sense, it is said by theologians that punishment should necessarily be inflicted impersonally upon every sin, but not therefore personally upon every sinner (since God can indeed through his singular grace exempt some from it by the substitution of a surety in their place).

XI. But that we may conceive it possible for God to do this, he is to be regarded not as an inferior and subaltern Judge appointed by law (who cannot dispense with its rigor by transferring the punishment to another), but as the supreme and *anypeuthynos* ("not accountable to man") Judge, who as he wills satisfaction should be made to his justice by the punishment of sin, so through his infinite wisdom and unspeakable mercy he can relax somewhat of the extreme rigor (*akribodikaiō*) of the law by exempting sinners from the due punishment and transferring it to a substitute. And hence we discover to whom the satisfaction is to be made—whether to the Devil detaining (as Socinus with a sneer asks) or to God as supreme Judge. For since the Devil here is only the servant of God, the keeper of the prison (who has no power over sinners unless by the just judgment of God), satisfaction is not to be rendered to him, but to God, the Judge, who primarily and principally holds them. We may add that it is falsely supposed here that in the suffering of punishment there must be some person to whom the punishment shall be rendered; as in a pecuniary debt, money is counted out to the creditor. It is sufficient that there is a judge who may exact punishment in order to preserve the majesty of the laws unimpaired.

XII. Fourth, the person himself who makes satisfaction is to be considered here. For as sin is to be viewed in the threefold relation of debt, enmity and crime (and God in the relation of creditor, offended party and Judge), so Christ must put on a threefold relation: a surety who can pay the debt for us; a Mediator and peacemaker (*eirēnopoiou*), to take away enmity and reconcile us to God; and a Priest and victim, to substitute himself in our place for a penal satisfaction. Again the satisfaction exacted by the justice of God principally demanded two things: (1) that it should be paid by the same nature which had sinned; (2) that nevertheless it should be of an infinite value and worth to take away the infinite demerit of sin. Two natures were necessary in Christ for the making of a satisfaction—a human, to suffer; and a divine nature, to give an infinite price and value to his sufferings.

XIII. Finally, since the substitution of Christ in our place must be made, its justice must be demonstrated that it may be evident in what case and under what conditions such a substitution of the innocent for the guilty can be lawfully made (which at first view appears to be not only unusual, but also unjust). Although a substitution (which is frequently made in a pecuniary debt) occurs more rarely in a penal debt; nay is sometimes prohibited (as among the Romans sureties were forbidden in capital punishment because no one is master of his own members and because the commonwealth would suffer detriment in such cases)—yet it was not absolutely unknown among the heathen. The examples of the friends—Damon and Pythias, one of whom voluntarily entered himself bail for the other to Dionysius in a capital cause; and of (M.) Curtius, Codrus and (Publius) Decius, devoting themselves for their country—sufficiently prove this (as also the right, practiced by the most humane people, of killing hostages [when the princes had failed in their promises], who on this account were called substitutes [*antipsychoi*]). Paul alludes to this when he says "for a good man some would even dare to die" (Rom. 5:7). The Scriptures often give it support, not only from the imputation of sin (by which one bears the punishment due to another), but also from the public use of sacrifices, in which the victim was substituted in the place of the sinner and suffered death in his stead. Hence the imposition of hands and the confession of sins over the head of the victim.

XIV. But that such a substitution may be made legitimately and without any appearance of injustice, various conditions are required in the surety, all of which are found perfectly in Christ. (1) A common nature that sin may be punished in the same nature which is guilty (Heb. 2:14). (2) The consent of the will that spontaneously and willingly (without compulsion) he should take that burden upon himself: "Lo, I come to do thy will" (Heb. 10:9). (3) Power and dominion over his own life so that he may rightfully determine respecting it: "No man taketh it from me, but I lay it down of myself. I have power to lay it down, and I have power to take it again" (Jn. 10:18). (4) The power of bearing all the punishment due to us and of taking it away as much from himself as from us. Otherwise, if he could himself be held by death, he could free no one from it. That Christ, God-man (*theanthrōpō*), possesses this power, no one can doubt. (5) Holiness and immaculate purity, that being polluted by no sin, he might not have to offer sacrifice for himself, but only for us (Heb. 7:25-27).

XV. On the basis of these conditions, it was not unjust for Christ, the righteous, to substitute himself for us, the unrighteous. For thus no injury is done to anyone. Not to Christ himself, both because he willingly took the punishment upon himself and because he had the power to determine concerning himself and the power to raise himself from the dead. Not to God, the Judge, because he willed and ordered it; nor to his natural justice, for this was satisfied by the punishment of the surety. Not to the empire of the universe, deprived of its best citizen by the death of an innocent person; for Christ, freed from death, lives for evermore. Nor by the life of the surviving sinner injuring the kingdom of God, because he is converted and made a new creature by Christ. Not to the divine law, for the most perfect fulfillment of all its demands made by Christ was foreseen and our twofold union with Christ (natural and forensic or mystical) by which, as he becomes one with us and we with him, so he may justly take our sins and evils upon himself and impart to us his righteousness and blessings. And thus there is neither an abrogation nor a derogation of the law, but an explication according to forbearance (*kat' epieikeian*), so that what was due to us in strict justice is transferred to Christ by the special grace of God.

XVI. These things were premised in order to lucidly discuss the proposed question, which is whether it was necessary that Christ should make satisfaction for us (absolutely on the part of justice as well as hypothetically in virtue of a decree of God). Whether it was not altogether necessary that Christ should make satisfaction for us, God being willing to remit sin gratuitiously and without any satisfaction; or whether it was rendered necessary only hypothetically on account of God's decree. The Socinians acknowledge no kind of necessity here. Some of the old theologians and some members of the Reformed church urge a hypothetical necessity only. They think it is sufficient for the refutation of heretics. But we (with many) retain both and hold that the satisfaction of Christ was necessary as much on the part of the justice as of the will of God. Still we do not urge a necessity simply natural, which is neither voluntary, nor admits of any modification in its exercise. Rather we urge a moral and rational necessity which as it flows from the holiness and justice of God and cannot be exercised except by the intervention of free will, so it admits of various modifications on account of the wisdom and clemency (*epieikeia*) of God (provided there is no infringement of the natural rights of deity).

The necessity of a satisfaction is proved: (1) by the justice of God.

XVII. Many arguments evince that there is such a necessity for the satisfaction of Christ. First, the vindicatory justice of God; for since this attribute is natural and essential to God (as has been proved, Volume I, Topic III, Question 19), upon which the natural and eternal right of God, the Judge, is founded (with which he can no more dispense than deny himself), its exercise must be necessary on the supposition of sin, although it becomes free by an intervention of the will. This is especially true since it does not consist in an act merely gratuitous and not due, like mercy (by which, whether it is exercised or not, injustice is done to no one), but in the due act of giving to each what is his own, from which God cannot abstain without detriment to his justice. But since this justice is nothing else than the constant will of punishing sinners, which in God cannot be inefficient (to whom belongs supreme majesty and infinite power), it necessarily demands the infliction of punishment either on the sinner himself or on the surety substituted in his place. Nor to this right can be objected either the relation of God's liberty (which is exercised only in matters of positive right, not in such as are of natural right) or the relation of mercy because, while it may release the sinner from punishment, it does not demand that sin itself shall remain unavenged.

2. By the nature of sin.

XVIII. Second, the nature of sin; for since it is a moral evil differing intrinsically and essentially from holiness (as has been shown Topic XI, on the law, Question 2), there is also a natural and necessary connection between it and physical evil (as they follow each other necessarily and since physical and penal evil cannot exist without moral evil, either personal or imputed, so moral evil cannot exist without drawing after it physical evil). Moral and physical good, holiness and happiness are indissolubly united together, not only by reason of divine wisdom (to which it is fitting that those things should go together which belong to the class of good or evil), but also by reason of goodness and justice. For as by the former, he cannot help being favorably disposed towards the good because he is good and kind to his own image; so the wicked cannot but be miserable because he is just. And this the rather because if he gives any blessing to the holiness of the creature, he does it from mere liberality without any merit on their part; but when he punishes the sinner, he renders to him what he owes and what he has merited by his sin.

3. By the sanction of the law.

XIX. Third, the sanction of the law because it threatens death to the sinner (Gen. 2:17; Dt. 27:26; Ezk. 18:20; Rom. 1:18, 32; 6:23). Since God is true and cannot lie, these threatenings must necessarily be executed either upon the sinner himself or upon a surety. To no purpose do our opponents reply that the threatening is hypothetical, not absolute (i.e., may be released by repentance). Because this takes for granted what is to be proved—that there is any such condition, either understood or expressed. Nay, as the penal sanction of the law is a part of the law itself, since the law itself is natural and indispensable (as was proved in the proper place), this sanction must also be immutable. We must not confound here particular and economical threatenings, nor such as are paternal and evangelical, denounced against men by a peculiar dispensation to recall them to repentance. Such threatenings may be revoked in case of repentance. Of this kind were those denounced against Hezekiah (Is. 38) and against the Ninevites (Jon. 3). The former should not be confounded with judicial threatenings and the immovable sanction of the law, which is founded on the very nature of God and to which men's consciences restipulate.

4. By the preaching of the gospel.

XX. Fourth, the preaching of the gospel (which announces the cruel and bloody death of the Mediator and surety who suffered for us) proves the same things most powerfully from the event *a posteriori*. For since God does not unnecessarily multiply things (nor do his wisdom and goodness permit us to believe that the Father could expose his most innocent and beloved Son to an excruciating and ignominious death without some weighty and indispensable necessity; nor can any reason for the necessity of such an unusual dispensation be conceived and rendered besides the satisfaction which must be paid to his justice for us), everyone must perceive that it was absolutely necessary. I know that other causes of that accursed death are here adduced by our opponents, so as to confirm Christ's doctrine and to set an example of all kinds of virtues, especially of love and constancy. But since he had confirmed his doctrines by numerous miracles and through his whole life had given the most illustrious examples of all these virtues, who could bring himself to believe that God for that one cause alone would expose his only begotten Son to such dreadful torments? Therefore (without all doubt) there was another cause for that dispensation (viz., the relation of justice itself to which he ought to make satisfaction). To this Paul bears witness when he says, "God hath set forth Christ to be a propitiation for our sins, to declare his righteousness" (*eis endeixin tēs dikaiosynēs autou*, Rom. 3:25), which was so inexorable as not to suffer our sins to be remitted except by the intervention of the death of Christ.

XXI. Again if God by his word alone was able and willing to remit our sins without the intervention of a satisfaction, how is it that Paul so often refers our salvation and justification to the blood of Christ, i.e., when he professes that "we are justified by the redemption which is in his blood" (Rom. 3:24), that "we have redemption in his blood, namely, the remission of sins" (Eph. 1:7) and that "he has reconciled all things to God by the blood of the cross" (Col. 1:20)? For there was no need of the shedding of his blood, if remission depended solely upon the will of God. Thus the apostle would say falsely what he so often says in the epistle to the Hebrews—that the blood of bulls and goats (i.e., legal sacrifices) could not take away sins (i.e., abolish their guilt and obtain their pardon) and that the oblation of Christ alone was sufficient to take away guilt without any sacrifice. For what could be taken away easily without any sacrifice at all could surely be taken away by the blood of legal victims. And if the will of God alone is necessary, why does Paul never refer to it, but always rises to the nature of the thing itself (as when he asserts that it was impossible for the blood of bulls to take away sins [viz., because sin is so abominable and hateful to God], that its stain could not be washed away by any blood except that of the Son of God himself)?

5. By the greatness of God's love.

XXII. Fifth, if there was no necessity that Christ should die in order to satisfy justice, the greatness of God's love in not sparing his own Son, but delivering him up for us all (which the apostle so strongly commends, Rom. 5 and 8) will be not a little diminished. For if there was no obstacle to our salvation on the part of justice, it would indeed have been great grace in God to have pardoned our sins, but it would have fallen far below that stupendous (*hyperbolēn*) love which, though justice inexorably demanded the punishment of sin, yet the desire of our salvation overcame (a tempering of justice with mercy being found for this purpose in his storehouse of amazing wisdom). Nor can Christ be said to have appeased the wrath of God if he (without exacting any satisfaction) could by a mere volition have appeased his own wrath.

6. By the glory of the divine attributes.

XXIII. Finally (1) our opinion concerning the necessity of a satisfaction does not derogate from any of the divine attributes. Not from God's absolute power because God cannot deny himself and his attributes; nor can he act in such a way as to give the appearance of delighting in sin by holding communion with the sinner. Not from his perfectly free will because he wills and can will nothing contrary to his own justice and holiness (which would be greatly injured should sin remain unpunished). Not from his boundless mercy, for this is exercised towards the sinner though satisfaction is demanded from the substitute. On the contrary, it tends to illustrate the glory of the most excellent attributes of God: of his holiness, on account of which he can hold no communion with the sinner without a previous satisfaction, by which both his guilt is removed and his pollution purged; of his justice, which so inexorably demands the punishment of sin that God even willed to punish it in his own Son that it might not go unpunished; of his wisdom, which found out what was impossible to every created intellect—a wonderful tempering of justice and mercy by which mercy can be exercised towards us without any detriment to justice; of his love, in not sparing his own Son in order that he might spare us. (2) It tends to the increase of piety by increasing our dread of sin (which is so great an atrocity that it could be washed out only by the blood of the Son of God) and by inflaming our hearts with a mutual love towards God that we might, according to our strength, love him who so dearly loved us.

Answers to objections.

XXIV. Although God demanded a satisfaction necessarily, it does not follow that he did not act freely. The necessity was not physical, but moral and rational springing from the hypothesis of sin (which he willed to permit) and of his decree concerning the salvation of men (on the basis of which he could not help acting consistently with his justice). For if God wishes to address men, he cannot avoid speaking the truth and yet he does it voluntarily.

XXV. It is one thing to remit from his right; another to remit from his justice. God can relax his right, but not absolutely. He can do it only insofar as his justice will allow (to wit, he cannot act unjustly). Justice, however, does not suffer sin to be pardoned without a satisfaction because then the majesty of the laws would be violated and sin would not receive its due. (2) It is not lawful always to remit from his right if it is public, not private right; judicial, not imperial; natural, not free; honest, not expedient. Now the right of punishment in God is not the private right of a creditor or master; not free and positive; not of private advantage, but of public honesty; the right of a ruler and Judge founded in his very nature (as we have already seen). And on this account, God could not dispense with that right (although he is not amenable to law) because he is a law to himself. Otherwise he could also pardon the sins of the impenitent, they remaining so (which nevertheless heretics deny). Nor if by such a dispensation injury would be done to no one, could God do it because his justice and the majesty of his laws would be tarnished.

XXVI. Satisfaction and remission are incompatible when used in reference to the payment of a pecuniary debt, whether made by the debtor himself or by another because in it regard is had not to the person who pays, but to what is paid (if just as much is paid as is owed). But this is not equally the case with the payment of a penal debt because here regard is had not only to what is paid but also to the person who pays. It is granted also in reference to a personal payment because he who pays his own debt has no need of remission; but it is granted in reference to another's and a vicarious payment (with which we are dealing here) because although justice is satisfied by a satisfaction, yet because it is another's and not a personal satisfaction (which the law demanded in strict justice) the act of the Judge is here required. By accepting the vicarious punishment of the surety, he remits from the guilty party the personal punishment which he was bound to suffer.

XXVII. The grace of God and the merit of Christ are not opposed, but subordinated because they are viewed here in different respects (*kat' allo kai allo*): grace in respect of us, both in the giving of the surety and in the acceptance of his satisfaction for our justification; but merit in respect of God's justice, which could not leave sin unpunished (which the apostle asserts are in the highest degree consistent with each other, Rom. 3:24, 25).

XXVIII. Although the remission of God and of men are similar in various points as to the thing (and most especially in the sincere and genuine pardon of offenses), it does not follow that they are exactly similar. Men are private persons to whom the right of punishment does not necessarily belong, but God is a Judge whose prerogative it is to punish sinners.

XXIX. If God promises remission of sins in the new covenant, this does not deny but supposes the satisfaction of Christ because it is promised in the name of Christ (Acts 10:43), i.e., through his virtue and merit. Nor is there any remission without the shedding of blood (*haimatekchysia*, Heb. 9:22). And if the elders are said to have obtained pardon by faith (Heb. 11), Christ is necessarily included (whom faith regards as its proper object); indeed inasmuch as he was crucified who ought to lay down his life as a sacrifice for sin (Is. 53:10) and to be made a sin offering (2 Cor. 5:21) and a curse (*katara*, Gal. 3:13). For other matters bearing upon this point, see Volume I, Topic III, Question 19; and Disputation 1 and 2, on the Necessity of Satisfaction ("De Satisfactionis Christi Necessitate," in *Opera* [1848], 4:385-435).

Eleventh Question: *The Truth of the Satisfaction*

Did Christ truly and properly satisfy God's justice in our place? We affirm against the Socinians.

I. The necessity of the satisfaction having been asserted, we shall now discuss its truth, which is not only called in question by the Socinians, but expressly denied. They appear willing to retain the word "satisfaction" and indeed in order to conceal their real views often use it, but in a far different sense from that of the orthodox (as will appear from the statement of the question).

Statement of the question.

II. The question does not concern a satisfaction of any kind whatsoever and improperly so called, by which Christ may have fulfilled all the conditions imposed upon him by the divine will in order to procure our salvation. For thus far they do not deny, but admit the satisfaction of Christ (as Crellius professes in his book against Grotius: "Responsio ad Librum Hugonis Grotii de Satisfactione Christi," 6 *Opera* [1656], 4:126-46). But the question concerns a penal satisfaction properly so called by which he not only fulfilled the will of God, but also his justice (Christ having taken upon himself our sins). This the Socinians deny; we affirm.

III. Second, the question does not concern a metaphorical satisfaction which is effected by the balancing of the account of the injured party, which precariously obtains some favor through the mere indulgence of God. Rather the question concerns a true and proper satisfaction made by the payment of a full price and which meritoriously obtains the liberation of the guilty on the ground of justice. This we preach from the word of God, but they reject.

IV. Third, the subject in controversy is not whether Christ died for us advantageously (i.e., for our good). Our opponents willingly admit that his death in various respects promotes our interests. Rather the question is whether he died for us substitutively (i.e., in our place, that by being substituted in our place, he suffered the punishment due to us). We affirm that he did.

V. Finally, the question is not whether Christ is our Savior either on account of his doctrine announcing to us the way of salvation or on account of the example of his life. He confirmed it by both his virtues and his miracles. Or on account of the communication of his efficacious power, because he will assuredly bestow on us this salvation in his own time. For Socinus grants all this to Christ (*Praelectionis theologicae* 21 [1627], p. 129). The question is whether he was most properly our Savior by his satisfaction and merits. Our opponents have openly fought against this doctrine; the orthodox have constantly defended it.

The truth of the satisfaction is proved: (1) by the redemption of Christ.

VI. The first argument is drawn from those passages in which Christ is said to have redeemed us—indeed at the price of his blood. For where the price (properly so called and indeed perfectly sufficient) is paid, there necessarily a true and properly so-called satisfaction has been made. A price indicates a relation (*schesin*) to distributive justice. The passages are various: "Ye were redeemed by a price" (*ēgorasthēte timēs*, 1 Cor. 6:20); "Ye were redeemed from your vain conversation, not by corruptible things such as silver and gold, but by the precious blood of Christ, as of a lamb without spot" (1 Pet. 1:18*, 19); "Christ gave himself for us, that he might redeem us from all iniquity" (Tit. 2:14); "In whom we have redemption through his blood" (Eph. 1:7); "The Son of man came to give his life a ransom for many" (*lytron anti pollōn*, Mt. 20:28). The name Jesus was given to him "because he saves his people from their sins" (Mt. 1:21).

VII. Although the word "redemption" is sometimes used in Scripture for a simple deliverance which is procured without the payment of any price (as Moses is called *lytrōtēs*, "a deliverer," Acts 7:25) and God is said to have redeemed his people out of Egypt (Dt. 7:8; Ps. 77:15 and elsewhere), it does not follow that it is to be taken in the same sense in this argument. Many things prove that it is to be understood properly and strictly. (1) This is the primary and specially proper signification of the words *lytroun* and *apolytroun*, from which we must not depart unnecessarily. This is not denied by our adversary. "To redeem anyone properly signifies nothing else but to free a captive, by paying a price to him who detains him" (Socinus, "De Iesu Christo Servatore," 2.1 *Opera omnia* [1656], 2:141). (2) The condition of man, who is to be redeemed, demands this since he is a captive not only of Satan and death, but also of sin (as to both its guilt and its pollution), and therefore of the divine law and justice. He is condemned of God (*hypodikos tō theō*) and a child of wrath and cannot be released but by a satisfactory payment. (3) Such is the redemption procured by the price mentioned in 1 Cor. 6:20. But why should the apostle use *lytrou* and *timēs* (price of redemption and punishment) if no price was paid? The reply—that this is said figuratively because we are freed from the power of sin—is taking for granted the very thing to be proved. Nay, the contrary is evident from this fact—that the price is compared to things very precious (as gold, silver and jewels, which have a relation to price truly and properly so called, 1 Pet. 1:18). (4) Not only is *lytrou* mentioned, but also an *antilytrou*, which does not denote any price in general, but one equal to the debt, securing a commutation of the debtor and a true compensation for the debt. This is the force of the preposition *anti*, which denotes substitution here. Aristotle uses the same word *antilytroun* to denote the redemption of a life by substituting another in its place (*Nicomachean Ethics* 9.2.4 [Loeb, 19:524-25]).

VIII. Hence it is evident that this redemption is not merely a gratuitous manumission (such as that of slaves who are freed by their masters) nor simply an act of power and bravery by which captives are taken out of the hands of an enemy, nor a bare exchange (such as that of prisoners of war). It is a real satisfaction such as a surety makes who pays in full for the debtor. For although there is a gratuitous liberation in respect of us who are saved freely and by the grace of God (Rom. 3:24; Eph. 2:8); and there is also liberation here in respect of the Devil, from whose tyranny we are delivered by the power of Christ, victorious and triumphant (Col. 2:15); and an exchange in respect of Christ, who was substituted in our place; yet in respect of God, the Judge, a real and perfect satisfaction was made.

2. Because Christ died for us.

IX. The second is drawn from those passages in which Christ is said to have died for us, not only for our good and advantage, but also in our place by a substitution properly so called (Rom. 5:6, 7; 8:32; 1 Pet. 3:18). But that this and no other is the sense of the phrases in this affair is gathered from the following reasons. (a) This is the ordinary signification of the preposition *hyper*, which is used here and which (when applied to persons) denotes substitution among the Greeks (as in Rom. 9:3 *anathema hyper adelphōn*, i.e., in the place of the brethren); "Scarcely for a righteous man will one die" (Rom. 5:7), i.e., in his place, as the Syrian renders it by *chlph*. (b) It is elsewhere expressed by *anti*, "in the place of" (as in Mt. 20:28) and by *antilytron*, a price of redemption (as in 1 Tim. 2:6), which necessarily implies a substitution. Thus life is given for life as is proper according to the *lex talionis*, "an eye for an eye" (*ophthalmos anti ophthalmou*, Mt. 5:38). (c) He is said to have died for us in a manner peculiar to himself and incommunicable to all others, in which neither Paul nor Peter can be said to have died and been crucified for us (1 Cor. 1:13), yet either of them might be said to have died for our good (viz., for our edification and confirmation in the faith). Therefore a vicarious death is to be understood, which could happen in the case neither of the apostles nor of the martyrs. Though the apostles may be said to have even suffered for the church (Col. 1:24), yet it does not follow that the object of their death was the same with that of Christ. They suffered as martyrs to edify, confirm and console the church (as is explained in 2 Cor. 1:6, "Whether we be afflicted, it is for your consolation," *hyper tēs hymōn paraklēseōs*); but Christ laid down his life to redeem the church. And if we are commanded to lay down our lives for our brethren (1 Jn. 3:16) as Christ laid down his life for us, this means that we are not to refuse to undergo the danger of death; nay, constantly to court even death itself, whenever the glory of God, the salvation of our neighbor or the edification of the church seems to demand it (as was the case with the martyrs). Hence we may well infer that we should imitate the example of Christ in this respect; but it does not hence follow plainly that there are the same purposes of our death for our brethren as of the death of Christ for us. For neither can we pay a ransom (*antilyron*) for our brethren that we may free them from eternal death

(Ps. 49:7), nor with our blood can we reconcile them to the Father and purge them from sin (all of which Christ did). Therefore our death may in some respects be compared to that of Christ, but not in all: in relation to an example of love, but not in relation to the merit of satisfaction. The particle *kathōs* ("as") denotes similarity, not equality (as often elsewhere, Mt. 5:48; 6:12).

3. Because he bore our sins.

X. Third, from those passages in which Christ is said to have borne our sins and on account of them to have been afflicted, to have been wounded, to have died—"He bore our sins in his own body on the tree" (1 Pet. 2:24). This is taken from Is. 53, in which the Chaldee paraphrase (cf. Walton, *Biblia sacra polyglotta* [1657], 3:142, 144 on Is. 53) and the ancient Jews consider the prophet as treating concerning the Messiah: "He bore our griefs and carried our sorrows, he was wounded for our transgressions, the chastisement of our peace was upon him, the Lord hath laid on him the iniquity," i.e., the punishment "of all our iniquities"; and "when thou shalt make his soul *'shm*" ("an offering for sin," vv. 10ff.). That all this implies a satisfaction is gathered from various things. (a) From the phrase "bearing our sins"; for although "to bear" and "to carry" are sometimes figuratively used for taking away and pardoning (as in Ex. 34:7 and Num. 14:18), it does not follow that we are to understand them in this sense here. There are most weighty reasons why we ought not to depart from the primary and most usual signification, according to which (as Socinus himself acknowledges, *Praelectionis theologicae* 21 [1627], p. 129) "to bear sin" is the same thing as "to bear the punishment of sins." Not only is the verb *ns'* used, which refers sometimes to a simple taking away of sin, but also the word *sbl*, which denotes the carrying and bearing of an imposed burden and thus clearly intimates the suffering of punishment. (b) From the manner of bearing them, which is described by wounded and bruised (vv. 5, 6), and the laying of them upon him. This could not be said unless Christ took upon himself the punishment of sin. Also what is said by Peter that "he bore them in his body on the tree" (viz., suffering the punishment). (c) From the simile because he is said to have borne sin in the same manner in which victims bore sins, since indeed he is said to have laid down his life (*'shm*) as a victim for sin in v. 10 (viz., by enduring death and shedding his blood in the place of sinners). (d) All things which indicate a true satisfaction occur here: the moving and meritorious cause (viz., our sins, not his own); he was wounded for our transgressions (vv. 4-6); and the bearing of punishment because he hath borne our griefs (v. 4); the imputation of our sins to Christ by God as a Judge—"The Lord hath laid on him the iniquity of us all" (v. 6); the voluntary undertaking of Christ as our surety because he was afflicted and opened not his mouth (v. 8); an expiation for sin and a full payment of the debt; because he laid down his life for sin and was taken from prison and from judgment (vv. 8, 10). Now with what propriety could all this be said if Christ had laid down his life merely to exhibit an example of patience and love and not to make satisfaction for sin?

XI. Although we are indeed informed (Mt. 8:17) that this prophecy of Isaiah was fulfilled when Christ healed bodily diseases (which, properly speaking, he did not bear, but only took away), yet it does not follow from this that the same may also be said of sins, which are the diseases of the soul. The diseases of the body are to be viewed in a different light from those of the soul. For in healing the former, it was not necessary that Christ should himself become sick; the power of Christ alone was demanded. But to heal the latter, justice required in addition that he should bear and take them upon himself before he could take them away from us. Hence he is held forth by the prophet as wounded and bruised, which was not necessary to the healing of the diseases of the body, but to bearing those of the soul only. And hence it is easy to gather what the Holy Spirit had regard to in this prophecy and how it is said to have been fulfilled when Christ healed diseases of the body (viz., he treats primarily and directly concerning spiritual debility, languors and disease). He treats sin, the punishment of which was laid upon him that he might suffer its desert in our place; but because bodily diseases are a part of the punishment of sin, he also regarded these secondarily and subordinately because he had the power of healing them. Therefore what the prophet declares in general concerning all diseases, Peter applies in particular to the diseases of the soul and Matthew applies to the diseases of the body, not excluding, but rather including the curing of diseases of the soul. He demonstrates that, by removing the cause, the effect was taken away. Spiritual and physical maladies are intimately connected with each other; the former draw after them the latter, while the latter presuppose the former. So Christ is said to have borne both, but in different ways on account of their different natures; the former indeed by efficaciously taking them away only, not by undergoing them in his own person; but the latter in both ways, both by bearing them himself and by taking them away. If Matthew says that Christ healed the diseases of the body that the prophecy might be fulfilled, we may not legitimately infer that the Holy Spirit refers to them alone. It is well known that in Scripture a prophecy is said to be fulfilled not only when it is fulfilled most perfectly and ultimately, but also when it begins to be fulfilled as to some part of it.

XII. Here are to be referred those passages in which Christ is said to have been made "sin" and a "curse" for us (2 Cor. 5:21; Gal. 3:13). For how can he be said to have been "made sin" (i.e., an offering for sin) by God as a Judge (Lev. 5:9) and "a curse" (i.e., a subject of the malediction and curse) pronounced by the law against sinners (and indeed not for himself, who was always most holy and supremely beloved by his Father, but for us) unless having been substituted in our place, he took upon himself all the curse of the law due to our sins in order that he might bear it and by bearing take it away and thus procure for us a blessing with God (i.e., the remission of our sins) and a right to life? What has this to do with an example of patience or a confirmation of doctrine? Who does not see rather that here is taught a true substitution of Christ in our place and in consequence of this a true satisfaction and expiation of sin? Nor can it be objected that "Christ is said to have been made a curse, not because he properly bore that curse, which could not have been the case with him, a blessed and perfectly innocent being, but because he suffered the punishment of the cross, which, under the law, was accursed." For the very words of the apostle and the redemption from the curse of the law, which Christ procured for us by his death, evince the contrary. For how can he be said to have been made a curse (indeed for the purpose of redeeming us from it) unless he took it upon himself? Nor is it an objection to this that he is the only begotten Son and the ever-blessed God, because he did not endure the curse in and for himself as the Son of God, but as our surety for us (whose person he sustained) in respect of whom he who was blessed forever can be said to have borne the punishment of the malediction on account of our sins.

XIII. And hence we can clearly gather in what sense the expression is used "he was delivered for our offenses" (Rom. 4:25), i.e., not only occasionally (as Socinus contends) because our sins were the occasion of the death of Christ or finally (as if Christ died only that he might incline us to leave off the commission of sin or render us certain of its pardon); but meritoriously, so that our sins were the moving, meritorious cause for Christ's being delivered up to death that he might suffer the punishment due to them and take away their guilt. For he is said to have been delivered for offenses, as sacrifices were offered for sin, doubtless on account of their guilt and to take it away. Hence the guilt of our sins was the meritorious cause of the death of Christ and the expiation and removal of it the final cause.

4. From the sacrifice of Christ.

XIV. This is proved further from the sacrifice of Christ offered on the cross, concerning which the Holy Spirit so often speaks (Is. 53:10; Jn. 1:29; Eph. 5:2; and in the epistle to the Hebrews *passim*). For why should Christ be so frequently and so expressly set forth as truly and properly a Priest, far more excellent than all the Levitical priests, one who by his oblation appeased the wrath of God and obtained eternal salvation for us, unless a full expiation for sin has been made by his satisfaction and the truth of the old figures more clearly displayed? For since by these expiatory victims, neither were the doctrines confirmed, nor examples of obedience and love given, nor a covenant entered into, nor the wrath of God appeased by their own efficacy, they must have been instituted primarily to represent the sacrifice and satisfaction of Christ. This may be proved more particularly: (1) from the relation of Priest which Christ here sustains; for he was appointed in things pertaining to God (*en tois pros ton theon*) (viz., to appease him by an atoning [*hilastikō*] sacrifice); (2) from the relation of victim, substituted in the place of sinners to bear the punishment of death due to them, as evinced by the rite of imposing hands upon the head of the offering and making a confession of sin over it; (3) from the threefold effect of the sacrifice in respect to God, by *hilasmon* or the propitiation of his wrath; in respect to sin, by the expiation (*katharismon*) and removal (*hagnismon*) of its guilt; in respect to man, by the remission (*aphesin*) which followed from the propitiation of God and the expiation of sin. For neither could the person be freed and obtain pardon without the substitution of a victim, nor could God be appeased without the shedding of blood, nor could sin be expiated without the enduring of punishment.

XV. To no purpose is it here objected by Volkelius and others: (1) "that all propitiatory sacrifices did not prefigure the sacrifice of Christ; but only the solemn and annual, which was offered up on the day of expiation (Lev. 16) and which contained no satisfaction; since it could flow neither from the victims themselves, nor from the person of the chief priest." Paul opposes not some one propitiatory sacrifice, but all the sacrifices to that of Christ and hence he infers the abrogation of the former (Heb. 7:27; 10:4, 5, 11). Neither the perpetual sacrifice (offered up daily), nor other propitiatory offerings (*hilastika*) of lambs (which were of a private nature) could refer to anything else than the oblation of the immaculate Lamb of God for us. Nor is it an objection that they were not offered for all in common, but for individuals in particular. For as the sacrifices which were made for all in common signified that Christ was to make a propitiation for all his people, so those which were made for each individual were designed to show that every one of Christ's people (pressed with the burden of sin) should seek and obtain reconciliation through the sacrifice of Christ. Further, although those sacrifices did not in the sight of God contain a satisfaction properly so called (since the soul of man is of too great a value to be redeemed with the blood of bulls or of goats), yet they gave a typical and ceremonial satisfaction pertaining to the purity of the flesh (Heb. 9:13)—a satisfaction which was to be ascribed neither to the victims offered, nor to the priest offering separately, but to both joined by the ordination of God.

XVI. Second objection: "An expiation is nothing else than a full deliverance from the death of sin, which deliverance cannot be attributed to the death of Christ in the way of merit, but only in the way of example and declaratively." But here the cause is confounded with the effect and what belongs to the judge (who frees the prisoner) with what belongs to the surety (who pays the ransom). For the judge sets the prisoner at liberty, while the prisoner (or someone in his name) pays the price of his redemption. Hence it follows that the purging of guilt and the removal of the accusation are effected by the bearing of punishment either in the person of the accused or in that of another. Again, if the entire end answered by the death of Christ was to declare that an expiation was to be made, it effected nothing more than the victims under the law, which might (nay did) attest the same thing. Yet the apostle Paul expressly declares that they could not make expiation for sin. If there were any propriety in this objection, the expiation might be attributed no less to Christ's resurrection than to his death (which nevertheless the Scripture nowhere does). Besides, the declaration has regard to men; expiation has regard to God. The former pertains rather to his prophetic office; the latter to his priestly office. If expiation is sometimes attributed to God himself (as in Dt. 21:8 and Ps. 51:9), who nevertheless did not make satisfaction, we ought not therefore to infer that it is of the same nature with that of Christ as the victim. According to the different nature of the subjects to whom the expiation is attributed, it is to be differently understood. For in respect of God, to expiate is to admit of an expiation made by a priest through pardon and the remission of sin. But in a priest and victim, it is to effect reconciliation meritoriously by the shedding of blood and the enduring of vicarious punishment.

XVII. Third objection: "Sacrifices were offered up only for smaller sins, such as were committed either through heedlessness or error, but not for the more aggravated and willful, for which no sacrifice was instituted. But that Christ died for all sins without distinction." But this is supposed gratuitously, not proved. Nay, it is said expressly that the goat on the great day of annual atonement bore "all the iniquities" of the children of Israel (Lev. 16:21, 22). Elsewhere sacrifices are said to be offered up not only for those sins which are committed *bshghghh* ("through error"), but also for those committed "willingly" and which are denoted by *'shm, cht', ph‛l, phsh‛* and similar words. And though "the priest" is said to "have offered for the errors of the people" (*hyper tōn tou laou agnoēmatōn*, Heb. 9:6, 7), yet it does not follow that voluntary sins are excluded. The word *agnoēma* is used to denote sin of every kind because every sinner is ignorant. Hence they are called "fools" and *anoētoi* everywhere in Scripture. In the Septuagint, *agnoia* often answers to *phsh'* and *'shm*, which denote wickedness and rebellion. If we do not read of any sacrifices having been particularly instituted for some aggravated voluntary sins (such as homicide, idolatry, adultery, etc.) which were done with "uplifted hand" (*byd rmh*) and through pride, this was because God determined to punish them by a capital punishment and those who sinned thus had no need of this remedy, as their deaths were a satisfaction to the public.

5. From our reconciliation with God.

XVIII. Fifth, we argue from our reconciliation with God which Christ procured for us by his death. For since that reconciliation supposes the settling of the variance caused by sin between God and his creatures, this could not be effected without a satisfaction. The satisfaction (interposing) removes a twofold obstacle: on the part of God, whose justice must be satisfied; on the part of men, the guilt of whose sin must be expiated by suffering the punishment due to it. The apostle everywhere teaches us that Christ procured such a reconciliation for us (Rom. 5:10; 2 Cor. 5:18, 19; Col. 1:20, 21).

XIX. The objection of our opponents amounts to this—"that this reconciliation is effected by our conversion to God and not at all by appeasing the divine wrath because God is not said to be reconciled by us, but we are reconciled to God; nay, he is said to procure for us this reconciliation, which is a sign not of enmity, but of friendship." Many arguments refute this capital error (*prōton pseudos*). (1) Scripture sets forth a twofold enmity and alienation, not only on the part of man (who by sin has become a hater of God [*theostygeis*, Rom. 1:30] and an enemy in his mind by wicked works [Col. 1:21]), but also on the part of God by his wrath (which is revealed from heaven against all iniquity, Rom. 1:18). Hence men are by nature "children of wrath" (Eph. 2:1) and God is said to be of purer eyes than to behold iniquity (Hab. 1:13). Yea, he is said not to be able to bear evil (Ps. 5:4-6). As therefore there was an alienation on both sides, so there ought to be a reconciliation on both sides: on the part of God, by a turning away of his wrath; on the part of men, by a conversion—all which the apostle clearly teaches (2 Cor. 5:18, 19). In consequence of God's reconciling us to himself through Christ (v. 18), Paul shows that the apostles, in the name of Christ, exhorted sinners to be reconciled to God. (2) If reconciliation was nothing but conversion, then it should rather be said to proceed from Christ's glorious life than from his bloody death and no reason can be given why sanctification should be proposed by the apostle as the end of our reconciliation (Col. 1:22), since nothing can be the medium and end of itself. (3) Such a reconciliation is meant as is effected by "not imputing to us our sins," on account of their having been imputed to Christ (since he was made sin for us, 2 Cor. 5:18, 21) and by the substitution of Christ in our place that he might die for us (as we collect from the comparison instituted between him and the man who would dare to die for a good man [Rom. 5:7], which implies a satisfaction, not a simple conversion). (4) Reconciliation is effected by making peace through the blood of his cross (Col. 1:20) and by an atoning sacrifice (*hilasmon*, 1 Jn. 2:2). But this does not intimate mere conversion, but primarily the appeasing of the wrath of God (which is brought about by the death of a victim).

XX. Although the Scriptures commonly speak of our reconciliation to God, rather than of God's being reconciled to us (because those offending have need to be reconciled to the offended), yet this does not exclude but rather includes a reconciliation of God with us. For there can be no offense without the injuring of justice and this injury must be repaired before God can reconcile men to himself and admit them to the communion of his grace. Nor if God is said to have procured this reconciliation, does it follow that he was not angry with us but at peace and friendly to us because this indeed implies that he (moved towards us with a love of benevolence) decreed to procure for us a reconciliation, but not that he was forthwith to be deemed appeased and reconciled, only that he might become so, while yet (in the meantime) he could not but be offended at our sins.

XXI. In vain is it added that "Christ is called our propitiation (*hilasmon*) and expiatory (*hilastērion*) sacrifice, not because he appeased God (angry with us) but because he testified that he was already appeased and by no means angry with us." The blood of Christ was not shed to prove the remission of sin, but to obtain it, as was the case in the propitiatory sacrifices of the Old Testament dispensation. Otherwise, there would have been no need of Christ to die and to shed his blood, since this could have been sufficiently testified both by his doctrine and by his life. If the covering of the ark is improperly and declaratively called *hilastērion* (or an expiation because by it God declared his benevolence towards his people), we are not thence to infer that it was of the same nature with the expiation made by Christ, to whom this is attributed in the strictest sense of the word (not so much passively as actively because he made a propitiation by his blood). What was shadowed forth in the mercy seat only typically and symbolically (by the sprinkling of the blood of the victims), that Christ truly and properly effected by the shedding of his own blood. But although he obtained for us the application and fruit of that propitiation by his continual intercession in heaven, we may not therefore infer that he has made it only in heaven. Nor does Heb. 2:17 relate to this. For Christ is not there said to make reconciliation (*hilaskesthai*) in heaven or to expiate sins, but only that on this account it behooved him in all things to be made like unto his brethren that he might be a faithful High Priest in things pertaining to God and in this character make reconciliation (*ta pros ton theon eis to hilaskesthai tas hamartias tou laou*) (which he had done by his death and suffering, as the following verse intimates).

6. From the nature of Christ's death.

XXII. Sixth, the same doctrine is proved from the nature and adjuncts of the sufferings of Christ as well as from the form of death which he suffered (to which nothing was wanting for a full and true satisfaction). (1) Not the essence and kind of punishment because the death denounced by the law was endured by him; not a common and ordinary death, but a violent and most bitter, inflicted as a punishment and accursed of God himself. In that death, besides the greatest ignominy and the severest pains inflicted upon his most sacred body, his soul was seized with the most appalling terror and sadness, and he was agitated with such anguish and fear that he had need of a comforting angel to appear to him. Sweat flowed from his body like great drops of blood. He offered up prayers and supplications with strong crying and tears unto him who was able to save him from death (Heb. 5:7). He was forsaken by God the Father, though not by a dissolution of the union, nor by withdrawing a participation of holiness, nor by withholding his supporting power, yet by withdrawing from him the beatific vision, by suspending the joy and comfort and the sense and fruition of full felicity. Such things can have no other adequate cause except in vindicatory justice demanding from Christ a most full satisfaction for us (unless we say that Christ was more effeminate and timid than innumerable martyrs who have sustained the same most painful bodily death; nay, if possible, torments more intolerable and yet with unshaken fortitude with the greatest alacrity and without any indications of grief or terror). Such blasphemy Christian ears cannot endure. (2) Not the time because although the time of Christ's sufferings was but finite in duration, yet it was infinite in value in consequence of the dignity of the person suffering. (3) Not the identity of the person sinning because although the law demanded this according to strict justice (*kata to akribodikaion*), the gospel through fatherly kindness (*epieikeian*), admitted a substitution (as was said before). It is sufficient that sin be punished, even if the sinner is not always punished.

7. From the attributes of God.

XXIII. Seventh, a satisfaction being asserted, mercy is displayed in an astonishing manner (which is so great that God spared not his own Son that he might spare us); justice, that it might remain unimpeachable, demanded even the blood of the Son of God; wisdom found out a wonderful plan of reconciling mercy with justice and untied a knot which otherwise could never have been loosed—a plan by which the conscience of man, terrified by a sense of sin and of judgment and the divine curse, is tranquilized. But the atonement being taken away, what becomes of the truth of God which so uniformly threatens death and a curse against sinners? What becomes of justice which not only acquits the convicted sinner (sin being unpunished), but also bestows on him the most honorable rewards? Not a few absurdities follow: (1) that our redemption may be attributed no less to the death of the apostles and martyrs than to the death of Christ, since indeed they also confirmed by their blood the doctrines of the gospel and gave us illustrious examples of patience and obedience; (2) that Christ saved us by his life and miracles rather than by his death (since the preaching of his doctrines and the example of his life were far more illustrious); (3) that the priestly office is altogether taken away from this earth and confounded with his prophetic and kingly offices; (4) that believers under the Old Testament were not saved by Christ (whom the example of his virtues and the preaching of his doctrine did not reach).

Sources of explanation.

XXIV. Although the word "satisfaction" is not found expressly and identically (*autolexei*) in the Scriptures, it is sufficient that it is contained equivalently and implicitly in them under other words which either have no meaning or else denote a true and properly so-called satisfaction: such as *apolytrōsis*, *antilytron*, *hilasmos*, *timē*, *katara*, *thysia*, *prosphora* and the like (which we have mentioned above).

XXV. As Christ sustains a twofold relation (*schesin*) with respect to believers—of surety and sponsor (bound to make satisfaction for them)—and of head and Lord (operating in them by the animating and directing influence of his Spirit), so he proposed to himself a double end in his death and sufferings. The first, to pay the price of redemption for us to divine justice; the other, to set before us an example for imitation that we might follow in his footsteps. Hence his sufferings may be regarded either as satisfactory or as exemplary. Therefore although they are set before us as an example (1 Pet. 2:21) and his death for us is compared with the death which we ought to suffer for our brethren (God so commanding, 1 Jn. 3:16), it does not follow that there was not a true satisfaction in his death because the positing of one end does not exclude but supposes the other.

XXVI. It is one thing to speak of a personal satisfaction and payment; another to speak of another's vicarious satisfaction. The former takes away all remission and grace, but not so the latter. Thus a satisfaction can consist with grace so that favor is shown to one, while a satisfaction is demanded from another. Thus when remission and satisfaction are referred to the same thing, they are inconsistent (*asystatoi*) with each other, but not so when referred to different things. Satisfaction has God for its object; remission has men. Satisfaction is made to the justice of God and on that account sin is freely remitted. Thus justice and mercy kiss each other, while the former is exercised against sin, the latter towards sinners. Remission is gratuitous with respect to us because a just satisfaction is demanded of the surety, nothing is demanded of us (since a full payment has been made).

XXVII. If Christ makes satisfaction, he does not at once make satisfaction to himself strictly speaking as Christ, but as God and the Son of God. Thus not to the same one and according to the same one does he give and receive payment. He gives it as God-man (*theanthrōpos*); he receives it as the Word (*Logos*); he gives it as Mediator and receives it as a Judge. Now it is not absurd that the same person should make satisfaction to himself when the satisfaction is not of a private nature (by which a private loss is compensated or money that is due is paid) because thus he would take of his own and with it pay himself. Rather the satisfaction is of a public nature by which a public injury is repaired (as a judge who has violated the law may, as a private person, make satisfaction to himself as judge by suffering—either in his own person or in that of another—the punishment denounced by the law; such is the case here).

XXVIII. If Christ did not suffer eternal death, but only a temporal death of three days, still no less did he pay what we owed as to infinity of punishment. If it was not infinite as to duration, still it was such equivalently as to value on account of the infinite dignity of the person suffering. For it was the suffering not of a mere man, but of the true God, who purchased the church with his blood (Acts 20:28) so that what was deficient in finite time is supplied by the condition of the divine person (which added an infinite weight to a temporary passion). Yet we may not infer that as the person suffering was infinite, one drop of his blood was sufficient for our redemption. Although any suffering whatever might have infinite value subjectively by reason of the sufferer, still his death alone could possess infinite value objectively in respect of the Judge inflicting it. The dignity of the person can increase the dignity of the punishment endured, so that the more exalted the person is who suffers, so much the heavier is the suffering to be considered; yet it cannot satisfy that species of punishment denounced by the law. Death alone answers to and fulfills the demands of law and justice.

XXIX. Although despair and gnashing of teeth are joined together with the punishments of the damned, it does not follow that Christ in bearing the punishment due to sin was bound to suffer these. They are not essential to the punishment inflicted by the Judge or borne by a most holy surety. But they hold the relation of adjuncts which attend it, on account of the circumstances of the subject suffering, who when he sees the impossibility of escaping from the punishment inflicted on him, easily sinks into utter despair and gnashing of teeth. It was far different with Christ, who felt secure of his deliverance and resurrection and in the midst of his agonies always testified his confidence in God.

XXX. Although a death of infinite value was due for every individual sinner, still no less sufficient is it for redeeming all the elect. The nature of a pecuniary payment differs from that of a penal satisfaction. The former is estimated by the amount paid by whomsoever the payment is made; nor can it avail more than the individual for whom the payment is made. But because the latter is estimated by the dignity of the person satisfying, on that account the dignity of the price is increased in proportion to his dignity and it can avail for many as well as for one. Although money has no higher value in the hand of a king than in that of a captive, still the head and life of a king are of more value than the life of a vile slave (as the life of David was reckoned of more worth than that of half the Israelite army, 2 S. 18:3). In this way, Christ alone ought to be estimated at a higher value than all men together. The dignity of an infinite person swallows up and absorbs all the infinities of punishment due to us. (2) It is not a new thing that what is necessary for one should be amply sufficient for many (when we speak of things which are communicated without division). One sun (which is necessary to the illumination of individuals) is still sufficient for the illumination of all. One victim was sufficient both for the priest and for the people. The sins of all the people were expiated by one annual expiatory sacrifice, although as many expiations were required as there were Israelites because that one expiation was so for the whole congregation as that by the appointment of God it was for individuals also. (3) Scripture is so express on this subject that no one (unless he is willing to contradict the Holy Spirit) can deny it. For why should Isaiah teach that God laid on him the iniquities of us all (Is. 53:6) and Paul that one died for all (2 Cor. 5:14) and that by one offering of himself he has forever perfected them who draw near to God (Heb. 10:14) unless to indicate that the one death of Christ is sufficient to make a full satisfaction for all the elect (in the same manner as the disobedience of Adam made many sinners, Rom. 5:18, 19). Finally, one cannot satisfy for many who are of the same rank; but nothing hinders when they are different. One plebeian cannot satisfy for many plebeians; but a prince can satisfy for many plebeians. If this holds good among creatures who are all finite and mortal, how much more between creatures and their Creator, between whom there is an infinite distance?

XXXI. The rule laid down by Ezekiel concerning the punishment of the soul itself that sins (18:20) cannot be understood absolutely and simply. Otherwise all imputation of sin would be taken away (which the Scripture builds upon with so many examples). Rather it is to be understood relatively in the ordinary way of providence, not in the extraordinary way of grace. Or it is to be understood in a method peculiar to the Jews, with whom the Lord dealt in such a way as to stop their mouths and keep them from complaining that they had undeservedly suffered punishment on account of the sins of their fathers; but not in his common government of men, in which God testifies that he will visit the iniquities of the fathers upon the children (Ex. 20:5)

XXXII. So far is the doctrine of Christ's satisfaction from throwing open a door to impiety and spreading a couch for security and negligence that it is the most efficacious means of holiness and the death of sin itself (which Christ assigns as one among others of the ends for his death). "That being dead unto sin, we may live unto righteousness; that henceforth we may no more live unto ourselves, but to him who died for us and was raised again for our justification," as Paul so often reasons on this subject (Rom. 6; Tit. 2:14; 1 Pet. 2:24). See further the "Disputation of the Truth of the Satisfaction," Parts 1-9 (Turretin, *Opera* [1848-49], 4:439-663).

Twelfth Question: The Perfection of the Satisfaction

Was the satisfaction of Christ so perfect as to leave no room after it either for human satisfactions in this life or for purgatory after this life? We affirm against the Romanists.

I. In the preceding question, we argued against the Socinians. In this, we deal with the Romanists, who, although pretending to hold the unity and perfection of the satisfaction of Christ and often exclaiming that serious injustice is done them when they are charged with saying that "something was wanting to the sufferings of Christ, by which he expiated our sins, to make his satisfaction full and complete" (as Bellarmine expresses it, "De Indulgentiis," 2.14 *Opera* [1859], v. 4, Pt. 2, pp. 162-63), yet in reality in many ways weaken and overturn it by maintaining that it must be restricted to sins committed before baptism and to the guilt of fault (*reatum culpae*) and not of punishment (*reatum poenae*), or to eternal punishment and not to temporal (of which we shall speak presently).

Statement of the question.

II. We must remark at the very outset that a satisfaction made to God differs from one made to man. The latter is either private (which is called a reparation and is due to a wounded and offended neighbor) or public (which is called canonical because contained in certain canons and rules of the ancient church and is very frequently imposed in the external court for the correction of sinners and the removal of scandals). The former is properly said about the *lytrō* (the price of redemption) by which Christ made satisfaction for us as our surety. However it is improperly ascribed to satisfactory works by which men are pretended to satisfy for their own sins or for those of others. Here we are to treat not of the former, but of that which must be made to God for the satisfaction of justice and the expiation of sin. For the question is not whether the satisfaction of Christ excludes all human satisfactions, either private or public and canonical, which are imposed upon sinners for their correction and to remove scandals from the church (for this we think was often both properly demanded in the ancient church and may yet be laudably observed). Rather the question is whether, besides the satisfaction made by Christ, other satisfactions for sin are to be made to God and can and should be imposed upon believers. This we deny; our opponents affirm.

III. The question is not whether the satisfaction of Christ excludes the chastisements of believers, which are called medicinal and improper punishments (such as the correction administered to children in their father's house), for this we readily grant. Rather the question is whether it excludes the satisfactions or penal sufferings on their part which are intended not as medicine only or as a proof of their piety, but as a satisfaction to avenging justice imposed by God as a judgment, not domestic and paternal (such as a father exercises towards children in accordance with the rules of love and wisdom), but forensic (decreed by God as a Judge against the wicked according to the prescriptions of the law). This is the dogma of our adversaries which is impugned by us. They hold that although the satisfaction of Christ is of infinite value, yet various satisfactions are still to be made by believers, if not for guilt or eternal punishment (which they acknowledge are taken away by Christ), at least for temporal punishment. "If anyone shall affirm that, on account of the merits of Christ, there is no necessity that we should make any satisfaction to God, through temporal punishments inflicted by Christ and patiently borne by us, or through punishments enjoined by the priest, not voluntarily undertaken, such as penances, prayers, fastings, alms, and other pious exercises, and shall further say that the new life only is the best penitence, let that man be accursed" (Council of Trent, Session 14, chap. 8, Canon 13, Schroeder, p. 104).

IV. The Remonstrants also endeavor to weaken the perfection of this satisfaction not a little. For although they have not yet reached such a height of boldness as with the Socinians to reject the satisfaction entirely, still they labor with all their might to diminish and detract from its efficacy and fulness. They maintain that the satisfaction was not accepted by God on account of its inherent dignity, but merely through grace, so that it was not a true satisfaction, but only an imaginary payment. They mean that God forbore to punish after Christ had died, not because a real satisfaction had been made to him, but because it pleased him to be gracious and to receive the satisfaction of Christ as complete.

V. However, we think that the satisfaction of Christ was so perfect and sufficient that he most fully satisfied for all our sins by the one offering of himself, not only for our guilt, but also for both temporal and eternal punishment. Henceforth there are no more propitiatory offerings or satisfaction to be made for sin, either in this life or after it, although believers are often subjected to the chastisements of God to promote their penitence and sanctification.

VI. Such is the perfection of the atonement that it is adequate to the justice of God revealed in the word and to the demands of the law and answers to the miseries and necessities of those for whom it was made, not through the mere gracious acceptance of God (for thus the legal victims might also have availed to expiate sin, contrary to Heb. 10:4), but through a sufficiency of merit and condignity of work: (1) in respect to parts because it most fully satisfied all the claims of the law upon us: both as to obedience of life and the suffering of death, as to satisfactory virtue by which it has freed us from the guilt of death and the curse by enduring the punishments due to us, and as to meritorious power by which it has reconciled the Father to us, and has acquired for us a right to life; (2) in respect to degree, for Christ has not only done and suffered all that which the law demands, but so fully and perfectly as to mode and degree that nothing more in this respect can possibly be desired (on account of the dignity of the person satisfying and the severity of the punishment exacted). Hence follows the third relation (*schesis*), of the perfection in respect to its effects, which are viewed both in respect to God (in a perfect reconciliation with him, Rom. 5:10; 2 Cor. 5:18) and in respect to sin (in its perfect expiation and remission, Eph. 1:7; Heb. 1:3; 9:26); in respect to believers, in their full consummation and redemption (Heb. 9:12; 10:14) both as to deliverance from death and as to the acquisition of a title to life.

The perfection of the satisfaction is proved: (1) from the dignity of the satisfaction.

VII. Now that such was the perfection of this satisfaction many arguments prove. First, the dignity of the person satisfying; this was not only holy and most pure, but also truly divine in which all fulness dwells (Col. 1:19)—a fulness of the divinity, a fulness of office, a fulness of merit and graces. We cannot doubt that the satisfaction which he has made is one of infinite value and efficacy and therefore of such fulness and all-sufficiency that nothing can be added to it. For although his human nature (which was the instrument in the obedience and sufferings) was finite, yet the satisfaction itself does not cease to be infinite (relative to the person, which is here the efficient cause and to which they ought to be attributed). They ought to be attributed because action and suffering belong to subsisting substances.

2. From its unity.

VIII. Second, the oneness of the offering made by Christ establishes our view. For why does Paul so often assert that Christ has offered himself once for us (Heb. 7:27; 9:26; 10:10, 12, 14) and that by one offering of himself he has for ever perfected them that are sanctified? Why does he always set before us the obedience of Christ as the sole ground of our justification (Rom. 5:18, 19) unless this obedience is full and perfect? For as repetition implies imperfection, so on the other hand oneness necessarily implies the plenitude and full accomplishment of the object.

3. From the approbation of the Judge.

IX. Third, the approbation of God as Judge confirms it. For if God testifies by any proof that he is most fully satisfied, no one can distrust the perfection of the satisfaction, since this only can be asked—that it be approved and accepted by the supreme Judge who demanded the satisfaction. That it has been approved and accepted by God is evident not only from the appointment of Christ to the mediatorial office (whom the Father often declares to be his beloved Son in whom he is well pleased), but especially by his resurrection from the dead. The latter is not only an indubitable proof of his divinity (Rom. 1:4), but also a most certain pledge and evidence of a most perfect satisfaction. For unless he had most fully satisfied even to the last farthing, is it credible that God (the Judge whose inexorable justice demands full payment) would have liberated him and raised him to that supreme glory which was the reward of his perfect obedience (Phil. 2:9)? As a creditor does not liberate a surety from prison unless a full payment has been made, so neither could Christ be set free unless he had satisfied to the full. Therefore, since he rose again so gloriously and was raised by the Father himself, there is no room left for doubt concerning the perfection of the satisfaction and the full payment of the price of redemption (*lytrou*) (to the full discharge of which, the Father has given us indubitable testimony).

4. From its effects.

X. Fourth, the effects presuppose a satisfaction and consequently its sufficiency. For why is our reconciliation with God, or the appeasing of his wrath, or the expiation and remission of sins not partial, but full and complete; or the redemption and glorification of believers themselves attributed to the death and obedience of Christ (as is often done in Scripture, Col. 1:20; 2 Cor. 5:21; 1 Jn. 1:7; Rom. 3:24; 5:10; Heb. 1:3; 9:14; 10:14), if his satisfaction was not full and complete? For a perfect effect necessarily supposes a perfect cause.

XI. But this perfect satisfaction being thus established, the Roman dogmas of the sacrifice of the Mass, of human merit and satisfactions in this life and of the purgatorial punishments to be endured hereafter are at once overthrown. For such things cannot be allowed without either accusing his satisfaction of insufficiency or God of injustice (exacting a double price and a double punishment of the same sin). Hence whatever may be said by Romanists concerning the infinity and sufficiency of the satisfaction of Christ is overturned in fact by this comment of theirs.

XII. In vain do our opponents reply: (1) "that our satisfactions do not derogate from the infinity and satisfaction of Christ; nay, that the greater glory thence accrues to it, since all their virtue and efficacy is derived from the satisfaction of Christ, who not only has satisfied for us, but also gives us the power to satisfy for ourselves. Thus they are not allied causes and of the same order, but inferior and subordinate." The very thing to be proved is taken for granted—that Christ gives us the power of satisfying for ourselves. This is without foundation in Scripture and is repugnant to the nature of the thing, since it is one thing to make satisfaction, another to give the power to make satisfaction. Nay, these things are utterly inconsistent (*asystata*) with each other. For if he fully satisfied for us, why are other satisfactions demanded? Nor is either fellowship or subordination of causes admissible here (where the primary cause is solitary, admitting no others). So far is this doctrine from adding to the greater glory of Christ that it really offers him an indignity by resorting to other allied or subaltern causes than those which belong to him alone as our perfect Redeemer. Nor if believers are fellow workers (*synergoi*) with God (in the application of this salvation to which they are bound to contribute something) can they therefore cooperate with him in its acquisition (to which they can bring nothing).

XIII. (2) No better can they escape by distinguishing "between the guilt of sin and of punishment, contending that though Christ has fully satisfied for our sin, he has not fully satisfied for our punishment; or if for eternal punishment, at least not for temporal, which must be suffered by believers themselves, either in this or in the other life." Besides the fact that Scripture attributes a full and entire remission of all sins to the satisfaction of Christ, on account of which there is now no more condemnation to them (Rom. 8:1) and they will be fully perfected, the distinction is absurd (*asystatos*) (such being the connection between sin and suffering that sin being removed as the cause, the punishment itself [the effect of sin] is necessarily taken away). Nor is remission of sin anything else than deliverance from all punishment because punishment cannot be justly inflicted where there is no transgression, nor would it be just to demand the payment of a debt already either paid or remitted.

XIV. (3) They also hold that "Christ made satisfaction for temporal punishment, not immediately, but mediately inasmuch as he makes satisfaction in and by us." But (a) this is a rash assertion without any authority from Scripture; (b) it is dangerous because men are associated with Christ in making satisfaction and a part of the work of redemption is taken out of his hands (for redemption and satisfaction are equivalent terms, since there is no other way to redeem than by rendering satisfaction); (c) it is false and contrary to Scripture, which asserts that Christ by himself has satisfied for sin and that there is no further satisfaction to be made by others.

XV. Further this perfection of the satisfaction asserted by us destroys also the nominal atonement devised by the Remonstrants. For where a perfect payment is made there cannot be a place for the exercise of grace in accepting what is merely nominal. For in making payments, grace is not considered, but the fulness of the satisfaction, which arises not only from the dignity of him who pays but also from the equality and value of the price paid. This may also be further confirmed from the fact that Christ is said to have come to fulfill the righteousness (*dikaiōma*) or "the right of the law" (Rom. 8:3, 4, to wit, by doing what we ourselves could not do on account of the weakness of the law). Now if by the satisfaction of Christ, the righteousness of the law is fulfilled in us, it must be adequate to the claims of the law. For if it was received by God only through a gracious acceptation, not the righteousness of the law, but the righteousness of grace would have been fulfilled in us.

XVI. Further, a gracious acceptation cannot be granted because Christ received upon himself all the punishment due to us (Is. 53:6-8)—even that which was the most grievous, the curse (*kataran*) of the law itself (Gal. 3:13). Finally, if God might have accepted any imperfect satisfaction, there was no necessity for the Son of God to stand as our surety and be subjected to extreme tortures and a most painful death. For satisfaction to God could have been received from any other man.

Sources of explanation.

XVII. It is one thing to suffer for the church in order to purchase her by paying a price of redemption; another to do so in order to edify, console and confirm her by an example of constancy and obedience. Paul says that he himself suffered for the church (or the body of Christ, Col. 1:24) not in the former sense (for he elsewhere denies that anyone except Christ alone is crucified for us, 1 Cor. 1:13), but in the latter, as he himself teaches us—"for your consolation" (*hyper tēs hymōn paraklēseōs*, 2 Cor. 1:6). He says that he endured all things "for the elect's sake" (2 Tim. 2:10), not to redeem them from temporal punishment, but that (confirmed by his example) they may obtain salvation by Christ. Thomas Aquinas correctly remarks on this subject, "The sufferings of saints are profitable to the church, not indeed by way of redemption, but by way of example and exhortation" (ST, III, Q. 48, Art. 5, p. 2287).

XVIII. The sufferings of Christ (the remains of which Paul was bound to fill up, *antanaplēroun*, Col. 1:24) are not the personal sufferings of the natural Christ, but those of Christ mystical (i.e., of his body, the church), which, after the manner of Christ, are to be endured by every Christian, whose members they are, and which were allotted to Paul in particular. On this account, he says he fulfills in turn or for his share bearing with alacrity that part of the cross which Christ had placed upon him. Christ is often thus put for his body (Acts 9:4; 1 Cor. 12:12) and "the sufferings of Christ" denote the afflictions of believers (2 Cor. 1:5; Heb. 11:26), not only in relation to their origin (because Christ, as supreme director of the theater of life, imposes them upon us and calls upon us to suffer them, Acts 9:16; 1 Pet. 2:21; Phil. 1:29); not only in relation to their object (because they are laid upon us on account of Christ and his gospel), but also in relation to our union and communion with Christ (because as we are one with him, so our blessings and sufferings are common to us and Christ). He is affected by our sufferings no less than by his own, and we are called to participate in his sufferings that we may be conformed to him in his cross before we are conformed to him in his glory (Rom. 8:18).

XIX. It is one thing for a person to atone for his sins by a true satisfaction; another to interrupt their course by works of repentance and charity. Daniel recommends the latter to Nebuchadnezzar (4:27), not the former. The word *prq* does not primarily signify "to redeem," but "to bear away," "to break off," and hence "to deliver." Therefore he exhorts the king to repentance and a change of life in order to make reparation to men by beneficence for the injuries and oppressions he had practiced and to break off his course of sinning that it might be better for him and that he might obtain exemption from the punishments hanging over him on account of his crimes (as well as a longer continuance of peace in his empire—"if it may be a lengthening of thy tranquility"). Here are to be referred the various passages in which remission of sins is promised to repentance, not as a meritorious cause or a satisfactory punishment, but as a condition annexed.

XX. It is one thing to speak of punishments properly so called and satisfactory, inflicted by a judge for the satisfaction of justice; another to speak of punishments improper and castigatory or medicinal. We do not deny that the latter are often appointed to believers, not by God, the Judge, but by God, the Father; not from hatred, but from love; not for vengeance, but for healing; not for destruction, but for correction. Hence Cyprian says: "The Lord chastises the saints that he may advance their holiness, and he advances their holiness that he may save them"+. Thomas Aquinas says: "Before remission they are the punishments of sin, after remission they are the struggles and exercises of the saints"+. And Augustine happily explains the difference between the punishments of the wicked and the chastisements of the pious: "All, both good and evil, are equally afflicted, nor by their afflictions can they be distinguished because what both suffer is not a distinction. For a distinction of sufferers remains even in a similarity of sufferings and even though, under the same pains, there is not the same virtue and vice; for as in the same fire gold shines and stubble smokes and by the same fan the chaff is blown away and the wheat purged; nor are dregs to be confounded with oil, because both are pressed in the same press. Thus one and the same inrushing power proves, purifies and refines the good; oppresses, ruins and destroys the bad. Hence under the same affliction, the wicked detest and blaspheme God, while the righteous pray to and praise him. So much difference does it make, not as to the kind of punishments, but as to the character of those who suffer them" (CG 1.8 [FC 8:29; PL 41.21]).

XXI. Such chastisements sometimes indeed retain the name of punishments, but improperly. (1) Punishments in their own nature are inflicted by the supreme Judge upon miserable mortals on account of a violated law; so that even after being changed into believers, the old name is retained because (though not formally) they are materially the same. (2) There are many points of resemblance between them and punishments properly so called. First, they are grievous and troublesome to the flesh (which ought to subdue no less than proper punishments). Second, they are dispensed to believers not carelessly, but by the certain will of a gracious God in no other way than punishments are inflicted by the will of a Judge. Third, sin is the occasion of their infliction. Fourth, from the feeling of believers, who often apprehend God as an angry Judge. Fifth, both are proposed for an example. But the difference between them always remains—that in the punishments of the wicked, the satisfaction of his justice is intended by God (the Judge) as the end; while in the chastisements of the righteous, the correction of his disobedient children is designed by God, as a Father.

XXII. The death of David's child (inflicted upon him after the remission of his sin, 2 S. 12:14) was a fatherly and medicinal punishment, not a satisfactory and judicial punishment. For sin having been once remitted, no punishment could remain to be borne. Nor can we infer this either from the fact that it is said to have been sent upon him by God because, by his sin, he had given occasion to the enemy to blaspheme the name of the Lord. For thus the occasion and moving cause is indeed denoted, but not the final; or if the final cause is intimated, it is not the satisfaction of justice, but the reparation of the scandal given because it was becoming that the discipline of the house of God (which had been most basely violated) should be healed by a salutary example. Nor from this—that David deprecates it with great feeling and tears; for such is the constitution of our nature that it endeavors to escape whatever is painful and severe (just as a sick man deprecates the caustic powders, the pain of cautery and the bitterness of medicine, although nothing can be further from punishments than these).

XXIII. Although death cannot be inflicted upon believers to guard against the future, nor for our amendment; yet it does not follow that it is a punishment properly so called, imposed as a satisfaction. There are many other causes, both that the remains of sin in us may be destroyed (and thus we may pass from a natural and earthly state to one spiritual and heavenly) and that thus piety may be exercised and the Christian virtues may shine forth in the most brilliant manner; also because the necessity of dying for all may be a most powerful excitement to amend our life.

XXIV. The "judgment" which Peter says must "begin at the house of God" (1 Pet. 4:17) is not the legal judgment of vengeance proceeding from a wrathful judge, but a fatherly and evangelical judgment of chastisement; not for punishment and destruction, but for example and correction, that thus arrested by the Lord we may not be condemned with the world (as Paul says, 1 Cor. 11:32). The "revenge" mentioned by Paul (2 Cor. 7:11) is not properly a punishment of God as a Judge, but denotes either the canonical punishment of excommunication (inflicted by the church for the removal of scandal and for an example) or rather the exercise of repentance and contrition (in which a sinner is angry with and takes vengeance on himself for the offense committed).

XXV. Although those whose sins were remitted under the Old Testament dispensation still had to offer sacrifices for them, it does not follow that there is room for satisfaction after the remission of sin. Those sacrifices were not (properly speaking) a satisfaction for sin, but types of a future atonement to be made by Christ, through the efficacy of which that pardon was procured.

XXVI. When it is said "by mercy and truth iniquity is purged" (or "redeemed," Prov. 16:6), this does not favor human satisfactions, whether the truth and mercy of God are meant (as some hold, for he would not take away but assert the satisfaction of Christ) or the mercy and truth of man (as others maintain, for then the condition to which remission of sin is given would be taught—but not the cause on account of which it is given). For as judgment without mercy will be exercised against the unmerciful, so the merciful shall obtain mercy (Mt. 5:7). The word *kphr* does not properly signify here an expiation, but either a covering and remission only (which God bestows upon true believers and the merciful) or the taking away and removal of the power of sin (as elsewhere, Is. 28:18). The exercise of love and sincere piety removes the contrary vices. The following clause confirms this when it adds, "By the fear of the Lord men depart from evil."

XXVII. Although nothing defiled can enter into the kingdom of heaven, yet there is no need of any satisfaction (after Christ's) in this life, or of a purgatory in another to purge away pollution. In the moment when the soul is separated from the body, believers are thoroughly purged of the remains of sin by the Spirit of Christ. The other arguments usually adduced to prove human satisfactions or purgatory will be examined and disposed of in their proper place.

Thirteenth Question: The Matter of the Satisfaction

Is the satisfaction of Christ to be restricted to the sufferings and punishments which he endured for us? Or is it to be extended also to the active obedience by which he perfectly fulfilled the law in his whole life? The former we deny and the latter we affirm.

Statement of the question.

I. Concerning the matter and parts of the satisfaction, the opinions of theologians vary. Some restrict it to the sufferings or punishments which Christ endured for us. This opinion appears to have been first maintained by Cargius, a Lutheran minister, and after him by Piscator, a Reformed professor at Herborne and his followers. Some of these place the whole righteousness in the death of Christ; others comprehend in it all the sufferings he endured through the whole course of his life and call this his "passive righteousness." However the active righteousness (which they place in the obedience yielded by him to the precepts of the law), they suppose to have been necessary as a condition in the person of the Mediator to the performance of his office; but not forming a part of his satisfaction or his merits which are imputed to us.

II. But the common opinion and the one received in our churches is that the satisfaction of Christ, which is imputed to us for righteousness before God, embraces not only the sufferings which he endured either in his life or at his death, but also the obedience of his whole life, or the just and holy actions by which he perfectly fulfilled the demands of the law in our place. Thus from these two parts, the full and perfect price of our redemption proceeds.

III. The subject of controversy is not: (1) whether Christ perfectly fulfilled both the general law binding him to serve God and the special law commanding him to submit to death; and whether the obedience of his whole life was necessary to him for the execution of the work of salvation and useful to us and rendered for our good. For our opponents grant not only that Christ perfectly fulfilled both laws, but also that the obedience of his life was necessary both for him (as a condition required in the Mediator for the performance of the prescribed functions) and in many respects profitable for us. But we inquire whether it was also rendered in our place and whether it forms a part of the satisfaction which he made to God for us. This they deny and we affirm.

IV. (2) The inquiry is not whether the mere sufferings belong to the satisfaction. For our adversaries acknowledge that no suffering can be satisfactory without action, inasmuch as in order to its being acceptable to God, it must include an active obedience or voluntary oblation which unites the highest love with the most perfect righteousness and holiness. They even say that the observance of the whole law was contained in that one action in epitome (*kat' epitomēn*). Rather the question is whether with the obedience which he exhibited in his death (by enduring the punishment due to us) ought also to be joined the obedience of his whole life by which he fulfilled all righteousness and was perfectly conformed to the law. This we maintain and they deny.

V. (3) The question is not whether the original and habitual holiness of Christ was a quality and condition of the mediatorial person (both as man and as an Israelite; both as Priest and victim), which should be free from every stain. Rather the question is whether the righteousness of merit (which pertains to the execution of the office and is imputed to us for the remission of sins and for obtaining a right to life) arises from the punishments he endured. Whether it does not also flow from the holy actions which he did through his whole life and by which he most fully obeyed the law. Thus in Christ are to be distinguished what conduced directly and immediately to merit and satisfaction (as "that which merited" and what only pertained to them mediately as previous conditions; and "that by which he merited"). In the latter, we place the personal holiness of Christ.

VI. The question is reduced to this—Is the satisfaction of Christ made in our place to be restricted to his death alone (or at least to those sufferings which either preceded or accompanied his death)? Or does it embrace all that Christ did and suffered for us from the beginning to the end of his life? The learned divines mentioned before hold the former opinion; we maintain the latter.

VII. For a clearer understanding of our opinion we remark: (1) the satisfactory sufferings of Christ must be extended to all those which were inflicted upon him, not only on the cross, but also in the garden (yea, through his whole life). Here we cannot approve of the hypothesis of those who wish to restrict all the satisfactory sufferings of Christ to those which he endured during the three hours of the obscuration of the sun while he was on the cross and before he expired, by excluding the others from the satisfaction of justice (although they might pertain to the vindication of divine truth and to the accomplishment of the types). For however indubitable it is that those were the greatest agonies to which he was exposed during the time of darkness (*nychthēmerō*), still it is no less evident that the others were expiatory also. (a) The Scripture nowhere restricts his sufferings to the three hours of the cross, but speaks of them in general without any limitation (Is. 53:4, 5; 1 Pet. 2:21; 3:18; Mt. 16:21; Heb. 5:7; 10:8, 9). They even extend them to his whole humiliation and self-emptying (*kenōsin*, Phil. 2:6, 7). (b) The agonies Christ endured in the garden (which are described by the words "trouble" [*taraxin*], "heaviness" [*adēmonian*], "amazement" [*ekthambēsin*], and "exceeding sorrowful even unto death" [*perilypēsin mechri thanatou*] on account of the weight of divine wrath and malediction which he sustained) were the principal part of the spiritual punishments which Christ must suffer for us. (c) The contrary opinion wrests from pious souls (placidly resting in all the sufferings of their Savior as satisfactory) the consolation thence derived and snatches from them the innumerable evidences of his amazing love.

VIII. Neither ought the following objections to be made here: either what is asserted in Zech. 3:9, "I will remove the iniquity of that land in one day"; or what Paul says, "We are sanctified through the offering of the body of Jesus once for all" (Heb. 10:10). These do not restrict his propitiatory sacrifice to the cross. The inference to be drawn from them is not that Christ's antecedent sufferings are not satisfactory, but only that the satisfaction was consummated on the cross (of which this was the fruit—that all the sins of all the elect were blotted out on that very day). This is the reason why Paul synecdochically refers the expiation of our sins to the one offering of Christ. It was the last and most piercing of all his sufferings, without which all the other antecedent sufferings would have been insufficient (as the payment of the last farthing completes the satisfaction, which is followed by the cancelling of the bond and the giving of a receipt). Although he was inaugurated into his mediatorial office in the thirtieth year of his age, we may not infer from this that before that time he was neither a Priest nor a victim. By the same mode of reasoning, it would follow that before thirty years of age he was not a Mediator. If Christ was in favor with the Father and his well-beloved Son (nay, even sometimes in his life glorified), it is not proved that he did not then bear the wrath of God because these two are not incompatible (*asystata*) with each other. Nor did Christ (viewed in himself) ever cease to be most dear to the Father even in his excruciating tortures, although as our surety he bore a load of wrath on account of our sins and was made a curse for us. Nor was it necessary that the punishments imposed upon Christ should always be so intense and oppressive that they could admit of no mitigation at certain intervals, by which he might be animated the more to encounter bravely the conflict set before him.

IX. Second, we remark that in the actions and sufferings of Christ two things are to be distinguished: their substance and form. Their substance we call the actions and sufferings as such considered in the class of being; their formality, the same, inasmuch as they are regarded in the class of morals or as to right and righteousness (*dikaiōma*), which arise from them in relation to the tribunal of God. As to the former, the actions and sufferings are many and various; but as to the latter, it is one form only, under which they come to be considered (namely, the form of righteousness [*dikaiōmatos*], which is a certain whole composed of all his actions and passions taken together). Hence one action or passion alone cannot be called fully meritorious or satisfactory because the concourse of a perfect obedience is required for this. Although various degrees and acts may be observed in the obedience of Christ (which he commenced at his birth, continued through his whole life and consummated at his death), still it is unique as to the completion (*apotelesma*) of the work of salvation and as to the righteousness (*dikaiōma*) flowering out from it.

X. Third, we remark that the obedience of Christ has a twofold efficacy, satisfactory and meritorious; the former by which we are freed from the punishments incurred by sin; the latter by which (through the remission of sin) a right to eternal life and salvation is acquired for us. For as sin has brought upon us two evils—the loss of life and exposure to death—so redemption must procure the two opposite benefits—deliverance from death and a right to life, escape from hell and an entrance into heaven. The various passages of Scripture which clearly express this twofold benefit belong here: "reconciliation for iniquity and the bringing in of an everlasting righteousness" (Dan. 9:24) is ascribed to Christ; "liberation from the curse of the law and the bestowment of blessing" (Gal. 3:13); "freedom from the law, and the adoption of sons" (Gal. 4:5); "salvation from wrath, and the gift of life" (Rom. 5:10); "forgiveness of sins, and inheritance among them which are sanctified" (Acts 26:18).

XI. Now although these two benefits flowing from the obedience of Christ are indissolubly connected in the covenant of grace so that no one can obtain the remission of sin without acquiring a right to life, they are not on that account to be confounded as if they were one and the same thing. Rather they are to be distinguished because it is one thing to free from death, another to introduce into life; one thing to deliver from hell, another to bear into heaven; to free from punishment and to bestow a reward. If no one can be freed from death without also being made a partaker of life, it does not follow that a deliverance from the death we deserve is not to be distinguished from the acquisition of glory. There are many degrees of life as well as of holiness. The possession of life does indeed follow liberation from death; but not at once the possession of a happy and glorious life (just as liberty certainly follows deliverance from prison, but not immediately a diadem and a throne—as Joseph might have been freed from his bonds but not at once set over Egypt). Between death and life simply, there is no medium; but between eternal death and a happy and glorious life, there is a life of bondage in a state of pilgrimage (not of heavenly rest) in which man is still bound to the performance of duty.

XII. While we think these two benefits should be distinguished, we do not think it should be anxiously inquired (as some do) by what acts Christ made satisfaction or merited. They attribute the satisfaction to his sufferings, the merit to his actions alone, so that by the former he freed us from death and by the latter acquired for us a right to life. The Scripture nowhere appears to distinguish the obedience of Christ into parts, but sets it before us as a unique thing by which he has done everything which the law could require of us. Again, as Christ by the obedience of his life has rendered what was due from us (and to which we were otherwise personally bound), by that very obedience he has satisfied for us the demands of the law. As his passive obedience proceeded from unspeakable love to us (which is the fulfilling of the law), we cannot deny that it was meritorious, as it had the relation of a *lytrou* and *timēs* (or price) by which a right to life has been acquired for us. Therefore these things should not be curiously distinguished because both these benefits conjointly depend upon the entire virtue of the cause—the obedience of Christ. For neither could sin be expiated before the law was perfectly fulfilled, nor could a right to life be acquired before the guilt of sin was removed. Therefore he merited by making satisfaction and by meriting made satisfaction. Herein lay the utmost merit—that he performed an arduous and most difficult work (by his most perfect obedience), impossible to all other beings and by no means obligatory upon himself, by his most perfect obedience. By this obedience, he both manifested his amazing love to us and his submission to the Father and in all things conformed to the special law of his own calling. Yet it would have been of no avail to us had it not been sealed and consummated by his death. And the satisfaction is not to be ascribed only to the external oblation of his blood, but principally to an internal act—his spontaneous and unchangeable will by which we are said to be sanctified (Heb. 10:14); not only to the payment of a price (*lytrou*), but of the whole of the price (*lytrō*) (which is Christ delivering up and subjecting himself for us).

XIII. Nor is Socinus to be listened to here. He maintains that satisfaction and merit are incompatible (*asystata*) with each other because satisfaction is the payment of a just debt and merit is an undue work. Although this may rightly be said in respect to a proper satisfaction, it is not so in respect to a vicarious satisfaction in which a surety, while making satisfaction, can also merit both as to the debtor by paying (when under no obligation to do so) a debt for him—by an undue work acquiring for him freedom from the debt and thus graciously freeing him from all obligation—and as to the creditor (especially if a covenant has been made, such a payment having been stipulated) admitting it not only as a satisfaction for sin, but also as procuring a title to blessings not otherwise due. This is the case here as appears from Is. 53:10; Heb. 9:15; Col. 1:19, 20 and similar passages.

XIV. Fourth, we add that there are two things in the law—precepts, which prescribe duties; sanctions, which ordain rewards to those who keep the law and punishments to its violators. Also we note that man, who is under the law, can at the same time be bound both to obedience and punishment, not indeed in a state of upright nature, but in a state of sin (as was proved in Topic XI, on the law, Question 22, Sections 12, 13, etc.). For as he sustains a twofold relation (*schesin*) to God, both of creature and of a sinful and condemned creature, in the former he always owes obedience to God (nor can he ever receive a dispensation from it in whatever state he may be); in the latter, he is liable to punishment. On this account, it cannot be said that the same debt is paid twice. A penal debt is one thing, arising from past transgression; an obediential debt is another thing, arising from the indispensable obligation of the creature, extending to all times and from which the creature cannot be exempted even while suffering the punishment of its transgressions.

XV. Fifth, we add that there is a threefold subjection to the law—a natural, a federal and a penal. The natural arises from the law as a rule of holiness and belongs to the creature as a creature. Therefore, it is eternal and indispensable because in every situation, the creature is bound to be subject to God and to obey him. The federal depends upon the law as prescribing the condition for acquiring happiness and belongs to the creature in a constituted state (in which he entered into a covenant with him and prescribed the performance of duty under the promise of rewards and punishments). The penal belongs to the sinful and guilty creature who is bound to suffer the punishment denounced by the law. The first is absolute and immutable. As long as there is a Creator and a creature, so long must the creature be subject to the Creator (and God can no more dispense with this right than he can deny himself). The second is economical and mutable which, as relating to man in a constituted state, must continue in force as long as man continues in the state and no longer; but after he has finished life and reached the goal, he is freed from this subjection. The third is necessary and inevitable on the supposition of sin (which punishment always follows). The first is founded in the essential right of God and in his natural, underived and necessary authority (*autokratorikō*) over the creature and in the natural dependence of the creature upon him. The second is founded in his free right or voluntary dispensation, whereby it pleased him to enter into a covenant with his creature and promise life under this or that condition. The third is founded in his judicial right and vindicatory justice by which the sin of the creature is avenged. All rational creatures (angels and men) are subject to the law in the first way; Adam, in a state of innocence, in the second; devils and reprobate men in the third.

XVI. According to this threefold relation (*schesin*), it is easy to understand how Christ was made under the law (*hypo nomon*) and how he was subjected to the law—whether for himself or for us. For as a man, there is no doubt but he was subject to the law for himself as a rule of holiness by a common and natural subjection (under which angels and the saints in heaven are who are bound to love and worship God). But it does not at once follow from this that he was subject to the law as commanding the condition of happiness by an economical and federal subjection, so that he merited life by obedience (since he had already obtained that by virtue of the hypostatical union), much less by a penal subjection (for he was most holy and absolutely free from all sin). So that when he undertook this twofold office of fulfilling the law to acquire life, as much as to the precepts by doing as to the sanction by suffering, all this was to be done for us by a voluntary dispensation from the office of Mediator and in virtue of an agreement entered into with the Father himself that (offering himself as our surety) he would do and suffer in our place all those things to which we had been bound and which were necessary for our redemption.

Proof that the satisfaction consists in the obedience of his life: (1) from Rom. 5:19.

XVII. These remarks having been premised for a more ready understanding of the subject, we proceed to the confirmation of our opinion, which rests upon many passages of Scripture. (1) "For as by the disobedience of one many were made sinners, so by the obedience of one, are many made righteous" (Rom. 5:19). Here the satisfaction of Christ is referred to the obedience not only of his death, but also of his life. (a) He treats his whole obedience without any limitation; hence this obedience must be full and perpetual from the beginning even to the end of his life, but not incomplete and imperfect. (b) He treats an obedience which implies conformity to the law in every way, not only as to the sanction of punishment, but also (and indeed principally) as to the keeping of its commandments. (c) He considers what is called "the gift of righteousness" (v. 17), which cannot be said of the sufferings of Christ. (d) He considers what is opposed to the disobedience of Adam, but as that was a violation of the whole law, so also the former must be a fulfillment of the whole law. (e) He treats what was due from us, both as to punishment and precept. Nor does it help the matter to say "that the obedience is nothing else than the one righteousness" (*hen dikaiōma*, mentioned in v. 18, which is said to be "unto justification of life," *eis dikaiōsin zōēs*) and that the condemnation of sin under which we have fallen arose from one sinful act of Adam. The righteousness (*dikaiōma*) spoken of here does not signify only one act of righteousness, but the righteousness arising from a fulness of obedience. If by one sin guilt came upon all, righteousness does not pass from one act upon all because evil is from any kind of defect, but good requires a perfect cause.

2. From Phil. 2:8.

XVIII. Second, the obedience of Christ is to have been "even unto death" (*heōs thanatou*, Phil. 2:8), where not only is its intensity marked out as to degree (the greatest which can be rendered by a creature), but also its extension and duration (because from the beginning of life even to death he constantly persevered in it). This is evident both because that obedience is referred to the whole emptying (*kenōsin*) and humiliation of Christ (which appeared not only in his death but in his whole life) and from other passages where that obedience is described by the imprinting of the law upon his heart and his active observance of it (Ps. 40; Heb. 10:5). Elsewhere it is set forth as a race which Christ had to run (Heb. 12:1, 2) and as a work which he had to do (Jn. 17:4). These were not to be consummated by one act, but by a constant tenor of obedience through his whole life.

3. From Rom. 8:3, 4.

XIX. Third, Christ ought to be made in the likeness of sinful flesh that he might supply the inability (*adynamian*) of the law and fulfill in us the righteousness of the law (Rom. 8:3, 4). This impotence of the law is not to be understood subjectively as if it were in the law itself, but objectively in the sinner in relation to the law (for he could not keep even one of its commands). And thus the law is called weak, not as to the infliction of punishments, but as to the keeping of its commands. Christ, therefore, by supplying what the law could not do in us must accomplish what the law demanded of us and is called "righteousness" (*dikaiōma*) or the right of the law (viz., "a right to life") which arises from its fulfillment, not only as passive, but also as active. For since the law and commands of God are the same, punishments cannot be said to fulfill the law or its commands, but to satisfy the denunciations of the law. Who would say that a robber (capitally punished on account of his crimes) had obeyed the command or law of the king? Besides, since to act agreeably to law is a thing honest and praiseworthy, this cannot be asserted concerning the enduring of punishment, unless perchance one is to be praised because he is tormented in hell.

4. Because Christ fulfilled what was due from us.

XX. Fourth, the satisfaction of Christ ought to be extended to all that was due from us and that he ought to pay in order to obtain life for us. But the obedience of his life no less than the suffering of death was required for this; not only because the sinful creature is bound to both these, but also because both were necessary for the remission of sins and a right to life. For life is promised by the law, not to him who suffers, but to him who performs—"Do this and live." Therefore it would not suffice to have endured punishments by dying, unless the keeping of the commands was added. Nor must we rely here on the statement "that the method of legal and gospel justification is different. In the former, observation of the law was certainly required as the cause of life, but not so in the latter." The difference of our justification is not placed in the thing itself (which is the same in each case, viz., a perfect and numerically absolute righteousness, exactly answering to the conditions of the law concerning the manner of obtaining eternal life and to the eternal and immutable claims of God upon the creature—from which Christ could not derogate because he did not come to abolish but to fulfill the law, Mt. 5:17; Rom. 3:31), but only in the manner because what was due from us and was demanded under the law by personal obedience, that was demanded from Christ by the obedience of another.

5. From Rom. 1:17; 3:21; 5:18.

XXI. Fifth, the satisfaction of Christ is to be sought in his righteousness (as appears from Rom. 1:17; 3:21; 5:18; Phil. 3:9; Dan. 9:24). Hence justification is described by the imputation of righteousness (Rom. 4). But the righteousness of Christ does not consist in his sufferings, but in his actions; nor by suffering, but by doing do we obtain the righteousness of the law (as by sinning we contracted the guilt of unrighteousness). In this sense, Christ testifies that "all righteousness was fulfilled" by him (Mt. 3:15, viz., by doing the will of the Father as to all its parts). And Paul says, "Christ was made sin for us, that we might become the righteousness of God in him" (2 Cor. 5:21, i.e., in the same manner as those sins by which we violated the law were imputed to Christ, so the righteous actions by which he fulfilled it for us are imputed to us).

6. Because the righteousness of Christ is not divided.

XXII. Sixth, Christ is not divided (*memeristai*, 1 Cor. 1:13), so neither ought his righteousness to be divided, but to be bestowed on us whole (*holoklēros*) and undivided. The whole paschal lamb was to be eaten. In like manner, a whole Christ is to be received by us, both as to what he did and what he suffered. This tends to the greater glory of Christ and to our richer consolation, which they obscure and lessen not a little who detract from the price of our salvation a part of his most perfect righteousness and obedience and thus rend his seamless tunic.

Answer to objections.

XXIII. If our salvation and redemption are ascribed to the blood and death of Christ, this is not done to the exclusion of the obedience of his life because nowhere is such a restriction found. Elsewhere (as we have seen) it is extended to the whole obedience and righteousness of Christ. Rather it must be understood by a synecdoche by which what belongs to the whole is ascribed to the better part because it was the last degree of his humiliation, the crown and completion of his obedience (which supposes all the other parts and without which they would have been useless). For no righteousness merits unless it is preserved up to the very last breath, nor can any payment be perfect unless the handwriting is blotted out.

XXIV. Although the apostle attributes the blessedness of the saints to the remission of sins flowing from the shedding of blood (Rom. 4:6, 7), it does not follow that our righteousness and the whole and entire righteousness of Christ are founded in his passion alone. Paul does not argue from an equivalency, as if it was the same to impute righteousness and to pardon sins, but from a holding together (*allēlouchia*) and the indissoluble connection of the blessings in the covenant of grace by which it happens that no one's sins are pardoned without his obtaining immediately a right to life and becoming an heir of the kingdom of heaven. In like manner, Paul treats the love of our neighbor and the fulfilling of the law as the same thing (Gal. 5:14) because where the former exists, the other necessarily follows.

XXV. Although each obedience of Christ (that of his life as well as that of his death) was perfect in its kind, still neither alone could suffice for a satisfaction which required both the observance of commands and the enduring of punishments (by which liberation from death and a right to life might be procured). The positing of the one is not an exclusion, but an inclusion of the other.

XXVI. What one person owes for himself, he cannot pay for another if he is a private person. But this is not so if he is a public person who may act both in his own name and in the name of those whom he represents. Again he who pays what he himself owes cannot by the same thing satisfy for others, unless he has made himself a debtor for them. For although he may be a debtor, still because he voluntarily made himself a debtor in order to free another, while he pays what he owes, he satisfies for another. Thus Christ, who became man not for himself, but for us, must fulfill the law not for himself, but for us, in order to merit life (which he did). Third, although Christ (as to himself by a natural subjection) as a creature was under the law, still not by a federal and economical subjection in order that he might obtain life by the law and place himself as a surety in the place of sinners. This was a work of voluntary agreement and he owed no such thing for himself, neither as to person (because he is the theanthropic [*theanthrōpos*] Son of God and Lord of the law), nor as to his human nature (whether absolutely or respectively). Not absolutely, (1) because his human nature was adjoined to the person of the Logos (*Logou*) and as this was not subject to the law, so neither could the nature assumed by it be subject in that sense; and (2) because as in the assumption of human nature the humiliation of Christ consists, so also in those things which result from this assumption. Such is the subjection to the law, not respectively because Christ (as man) was not bound to the legal covenant, which pertained only to those whom Adam represented in that covenant (to wit, who naturally descended from him). Finally, he had no need to acquire for himself a right to life by his own obedience—this necessarily resulting from the union with the Word (*Logō*). Hence it follows that Christ owed all his federal obedience for us (as surety) because he represented our persons.

XXVII. Although Christ fulfilled the law for us as to obedience, it cannot be inferred that we are no longer bound to render obedience to God. It certainly follows that we are not bound to obey for the same end and from the same cause (to wit, that we may live by it, from our federal subjection). But this does not hinder our being bound by a natural obligation to yield the same obedience to God, not that we may live but because we live; not that we may acquire a right to life, but that we may enter upon the possession of the acquired right. Just as (though Christ died for us) we do not cease to be still liable to death—not for a punishment, but for salvation.

XXVIII. A righteousness of innocence (when one is accused of no fault) differs from a righteousness of perseverance (to which a reward is due for duty performed). The remission of sin brings in the former righteousness by taking away the guilt of sins committed, but does not on that account draw after itself the righteousness of perseverance, as if he who obtains it had really performed all duties. It is one thing to free a person from the punishment due to the omission of duty; another to reckon him really righteous with the righteousness of perseverance to which life is promised (as if he had omitted no good or committed no evil). The former is obtained by remission, but not the latter (which would be repugnant to the truth and just judgment of God). Remission of sin does not make it no sin, but prevents its imputation. It only takes away the guilt of sin and consequently its punishment, but does not remove its pollution. Thus to be considered as "having committed no evil and as having omitted no good" can be understood in two ways: either as to punishment, so that we can no more be punished than if we had really committed no sin and omitted no duty (in which sense it is true that by the remission of all sins we are placed in that state because we are freed from all the punishment due on account of it); or as to reward, so that he who is reckoned to have omitted no duty and to have committed no sin shall be judged by God to have done all things necessary for the obtainment of life. Thus it is false that he whose sins are remitted is to be viewed in that place because remission causes the removal of the punishment, but not that God should determine that the sinner is free from all delinquency and has fulfilled all parts of his duty and is righteous (which would be repugnant to the truth—as if the guilty is to be esteemed righteous because the judge has pardoned him, a suppliant and confessor).

XXIX. God cannot be accused of demanding a double payment of the same debt because since the law binds sinners to obedience and punishments (as has just been said), the actions and sufferings of Christ do not constitute a double payment, but only one and a unique righteousness (*dikaiōma*) by which liberation from death and a right to life have been acquired for us.

XXX. The law cannot be said to have been fulfilled by epitome (*kat' epitomēn*) in the voluntary suffering of Christ. It demands perfect obedience, not only by epitome (*kat' epitomēn*), but also as to each particular (*kath' hekasta*); not only as to degree and intensively, but also as to duration and extensively—from the beginning even to the end of life, which cannot be accomplished in one or another action.

XXXI. So far is the whole righteousness of Christ (which is imputed to us) from being well placed in his sufferings (and for this reason being rightly called active) that no righteousness is to be placed properly in suffering, but only in action. Nor can anyone be called righteous because he suffers, since pain is not a virtue. Besides, sufferings do not yield obedience to those commands of the law to which the promise of life is annexed, but they only satisfy its sanctions. Hence they cannot be called righteousness. If there is any righteousness in punishment, it is the righteousness of the punisher, not of him who is punished.

XXXII. Calvin, in many parts of his works, teaches the received opinion, especially in the following: "When it is asked how, sin having been removed, Christ has taken away the enmity between us and God and acquired a righteousness which has made him favorable and friendly to us, it may be answered generally that he has done this by the whole course of his obedience. This is proved by the testimony of Paul, 'as by the transgression of one, many were made sinners, so by the obedience of one, many were made righteous.' And indeed, elsewhere he extends the cause of pardon, which delivers us from the curse of the law to the whole life of Christ: 'when the fullness of time was come, God sent forth his Son, made under the law, to redeem them that were under the law.' Thus even in his baptism he declares that Christ fulfilled a part of this righteousness because he obediently performed his Father's command. Finally, from the time that 'he took upon himself the form of a servant,' he began to pay the price of liberation in order to redeem us. Nevertheless, that the Scripture may define more precisely the mode of salvation, it ascribes this as peculiar and proper to the death of Christ" (ICR, 2.16.5, p. 507). "Nor yet," he afterwards adds, "is the remaining part of his obedience, which he performed during his life, excluded, as Paul comprehends the whole from the beginning even to the end of his life when he says that 'he humbled himself and took upon him the form of a servant, and was obedient to his Father unto death, even the death of the cross.' And, indeed, his voluntary subjection occupies the first grade in his death also, because a sacrifice availed nothing, unless offered freely" (ICR, 2.16.5, p. 508). "I answer that accepting grace is nothing else but his gratuitous goodness by which the Father embraces us in Christ, clothes us with his innocence and causes us to accept it, that on account of it, he may esteem us as holy, pure and innocent. For it behooves the righteousness of Christ, which as alone perfect, so alone can stand in the sight of God, to be presented for us and to be set to our account in the judgment as offered by our Surety. Furnished with this, we, through faith, obtain perpetual remission of sin. By its purity, our defilements and stains of imperfection are washed away. They are not imputed to us, but as if buried they are hidden out of sight, nor will they rise against us in judgment" (ICR, 3.14.12, p. 779.). He confirms the same thing on the epistle to the Romans and the epistle to the Galatians (*The Epistles of Paul . . . to the Romans* [trans. R. Mackenzie, 1961], p. 118 on Rom. 5:19; and *The Epistles of Paul . . . to the Galatians* [trans. T.H.L. Parker, 1965], pp. 73-74 on Gal. 4:4).

XXXIII. The French Synods have repeatedly declared that the same truth should be retained inviolable, as the Privatensian (in the year 1612) and the Tonneinsian (in the year 1614), whose words are these: "Since man can find in himself, before or after his calling, no righteousness by which he can stand before the tribunal of God; he cannot be justified except in our Lord Jesus Christ, who was obedient to God the Father, from his entrance into the world even until his ignominious death on the cross: in his life and at his death, the whole law given to man having been perfectly fulfilled, as well as the command to suffer and lay down his life as a price of redemption for many, by this perfect obedience we are rendered righteous, inasmuch as the grace of God is imputed to us and received by faith, which he gives us; by this we are assured that, by the merit of the whole of this obedience, we have the remission of our sins and are rendered worthy of eternal life" (cf. Quick, *Synodicon in Gallia Reformata* [1692], p. 401).

Fourteenth Question: The Object of the Satisfaction

Did Christ die for each and every man universally or only for the elect? The former we deny; the latter we affirm.

I. The question concerning the object of Christ's death or the universality of the satisfaction and redemption has been (and still is) agitated by various persons. This imposes upon us a necessity of discussing it also in order that nothing may seem to be lacking in this treatise concerning the satisfaction of Christ.

The opinion of the Pelagians.

II. Among the ancients, it appears that the universality of redemption was contended for by the Pelagians and Semipelagians. Hence Prosper (concerning the remains of the Pelagian heresy) says, "This is their definition and profession that Christ died for the whole human race and that no one is excluded from the redemption effected by his blood" (*Letter to Augustine* 6 [ACW 32:43; PL 33.1005]). And among the damnable errors which they boasted of having found in Augustine was this also: "The Savior was not crucified for the redemption of the whole world." Faustus (Rhegiensis) says, "They wander far from the path of piety who say that the Savior did not die for all" (*De Gratia Dei et Libero Arbitrio* 1.4 [PL 58.789]). And Hincmar enumerates it as one of the errors of Gottschalk that he preached that Christ did not pour out his precious blood to God the Father for the redemption and salvation of all men, but for those only who are saved, or for all the elect (cf. Flodoard, *Historiae Ecclesiae Remensis* 3.15* [PL 135.180-81]). To the same purpose are the anathemas of the pretended Council of

Arles, recorded in the letter of Faustus, the standard-bearer of the Semipelagian council. But as Augustine in his time opposed himself to these, so did Prosper and Fulgentius (his disciples) and other preachers of the grace of Christ (pressing in their track) defend the truth bravely and heartily. The same was afterwards confirmed by Remigius, bishop of Lyon (*De Tribus Epistolis Liber* [PL 121.985-1068]) and the council Valentine III held in the year 855 (Canon 4, Mansi, 15:5).

Of the Jesuits.

III. The same controversy was afterwards renewed among the Romanists, some of whom defended the universality of redemption (with the Semipelagians), others its particularity (with Augustine and his genuine disciples). This controversy lay principally between the Jesuits and Jansenists, of whom the former (an offshoot of the Pelagians) warmly contend for the universality of Christ's death, while the latter with great firmness defend its particularity, following their founder, Jansen, who has argued this subject very largely and with great solidity in his *Augustinus* ("De Gratia Christi Salvatoris," 3.20 [1640/1964], pp. 369-80), his *Apologia Jansenii* published in 1644, Art. 17, 19, 20+ and in *Catechismo de Gratia*, c. 7, de Predesti. q. 65+.

Of the Lutherans.

IV. The controversy then passed from the Romanists to the Protestants, not only on account of the Lutherans, who with the Jesuits retain and contend for a universal satisfaction (as Eckhard, *Fasciculus controversiarum Theologicarum* 15.6 [1631], pp. 322-33; Brochmand, "De Gratia Dei," 2, Q. 17, 18, 19 in *Universae theologicae systema* [1638], 1:595-97 and others); but principally on account of the Arminians (known by the name of Remonstrants), who, about to recall popery indirectly and to contend for the idol of free will, drew most of their errors from Molinus, Lessius, Suarez and other Jesuits. This is among the rest concerning the universality of Christ's death and is placed among those that were rejected and condemned by the Synod of Dort, as may be seen in the second chapter of their "Rejection of errors concerning the Death of Christ" (*Acta Synodi Nationalis . . . Dordrechti* [1619-20], 2:139).

Of the Arminians.

V. The article in their remonstrance against the Synod of Dort is this: "The price of redemption which Christ offered up to his Father was not only in itself and by itself sufficient for the redemption of the whole human race; but was even paid for all men and every man by the decree, will and grace of God the Father; and, therefore, no one is particularly excluded by an antecedent decree of God from a participation of the fruits of the death of Christ. 2. Christ, by the merit of his death, has so far reconciled God the Father to the whole human race that the Father on account of his merit, his own justice and truth being preserved, can enter and wishes to enter into and sanction a new covenant of grace with sinful men exposed to damnation" (*Acta Synodi Nationalis . . . Dordrechti* [1619-20], 1:129). Therefore they hold: (1) that Christ, by the counsel of God, so died for each and every one that not only is his death sufficient in itself on account of its own intrinsic value, but was also offered up sufficiently for each and every one inasmuch as God willed that what was in itself sufficient for all should be paid either in the place or for the good of each and every one (or of the whole human race) so that by its intervention it comes to pass that God ever afterward willed to deal gratuitously with the human race and hence that the death of Christ was not a promise of the new covenant, but its cause and foundation. (2) That Christ, by his own intention and that of his Father, has obtained a restitution into a state of grace and salvation for all men and each man (those passed by as well as those who are saved), so that no one (on account of original sin) is liable to condemnation or will be condemned, but all are freed from the guilt of that sin. (3) That Christ, according to the counsel of his Father, underwent death for all without a certain and definite design of saving anyone in particular. Thus the necessity and utility of the atonement made by the death of Christ might be in every respect preserved, even if the acquired redemption should never be actually applied to any individual. (4) That Christ, by his satisfaction, merited salvation and faith for no one with such certainty that the satisfaction must be applied to them efficaciously for salvation, but merely acquired for the Father a plenary will and power to treat anew with men, to enter into a covenant either of grace or of works and to prescribe whatever conditions he chose. The performance of this depends entirely upon the free will of man, and therefore it could happen that either all or no one should fulfill them. (5) That the acquisition extends further than the application (as salvation was obtained for all, which is applied to a very few). All these can be gathered from the Collation published at the Hague (*Collatio scripto habita Hagae Comitis* [1615]) and from the Remonstrance against the Synod of Dort (in the declaration of their opinion concerning the second article).

Of the universalists.

VI. Those of our ministers who defend universal grace yield to this opinion, if not entirely yet in a great measure. For as they hold a universal philanthropy (*philanthrōpian*) and love of God towards the human race, so they think Christ was sent into the world by the Father through that love (as a universal remedy to procure salvation for each and every one under the condition of faith); and that Christ with that intention died for all under the same condition (although the fruit and efficacy of his death will be enjoyed by a few only to whom God by a special decree determined to give faith). In this manner, they teach that the decree of the death of Christ preceded the decree of election and that God in sending Christ regarded not some more than others, but appointed Christ as a Savior equally for all; yea that he did not absolutely intend so much salvation in him, as the possibility of salvation (viz., the removal of impediments which justice opposed to their salvation) by a satisfaction afforded to him and thus opened a door of salvation that God (being appeased) might make a new covenant with them in consistency with the claims of his justice and think of giving salvation to them. For this end he took care by a universal call that Christ so given and dying for all might be offered to each and every one. But because he foresaw that no one would believe (on account of the innate depravity of the heart), they contend that God (by another special decree) determined to give faith to some by which they might believe on Christ and certainly become partakers of salvation, the rest being left in unbelief and on account of it most justly condemned. In this they rightly differ from the Arminians. All this can be clearly gathered from their writings. Thus Cameron says, "The death of Christ belongs, under the condition of faith, equally to all men" (*Opera* [1659], p. 389 on Heb. 2:9). Testard says, "The design of giving Christ for a propitiation in his blood was the making of a new covenant with the whole human race and the possible call to salvation and the salvation of all men, justice no longer resisting" (*Eirenikon seu Synopsis Doctrinae de Nature et Gratia*, Th. 77* [1633], p. 54). And: "In this sense, indeed, no one can deny that Christ died for each and everyone, that his faith may stand in the word of God" (Th. 79, ibid., p. 56). Amyrald says, "The redemption of Christ is to be considered in two ways: either as absolute, inasmuch as some truly embrace it; again as it is affected by a condition, inasmuch as it is offered on these terms—that if anyone will embrace it, he shall become partaker of it. In the former mode, it is particular; in the latter, universal. In like manner, its destination is twofold: particular, inasmuch as it has a decree to give faith connected with it; universal, inasmuch as that decree is separated from it" ("Doctrinae de gratia universali," in *Mosis Amyraldi . . . Dissertationes Theologicae Quatuor* [1645], pp. 37-38). This he had more expressly taught previously: "Since the misery of man is equal and universal, and the desire which God has to free them from it by so great a Redeemer proceeds from the mercy which he has towards us as his own creatures fallen into so great ruin, in which his creatures equally lie, the grace of redemption, which he has procured for and offers to us, should be equal and universal, provided we are equally disposed to receive it" (*Brief Traitte de la Predestination* 7 [1634], p. 77).

VII. Though all agree that Christ died for each and every one, still they do not explain their meaning in the same way. For some say openly that Christ died conditionally for each and every one and absolutely only for the elect (as appears from the above extracts). Others, however, seeing the great absurdities pressing upon this view, abstain from such a manner of speaking and prefer to say that Christ did not die for men on condition that they would believe, but absolutely, whether they would believe or not. Thus the approach to salvation might be free to all who would believe and the way to a new covenant might be opened equally to all (viz., the obstacle of justice being removed by the death of Christ, an obstacle preventing God from being reconciled to men). Yet they all come to the same point when they say that Christ made satisfaction for each and every one and obtained reconciliation, remission of sins and salvation for them; of which (if many are deprived) the cause is not to be sought in the insufficiency of the death of Christ, or in a defect of his will and intention, but only in the unbelief of those who perversely reject the offered grace of Christ.

VIII. But the common opinion of the Reformed is that Christ (from the mere good-pleasure [*eudokia*] of the Father) was appointed and given as a Redeemer and head, not to all men, but to a certain number of men. By the election of God, these compose his mystical body. For these alone, Christ (perfectly acquainted with his call) in order to fulfill the decree of election and the counsel of the Father, was willing and determined to die; also to add to the infinite price of his death a most efficacious and special intention to substitute himself in their place and to acquire faith and salvation for them.

Statement of the question.

IX. Hence the state of the question is easily elicited. (1) It is not asked with respect to the value and sufficiency of the death of Christ—whether it was in itself sufficient for the salvation of all men. For it is confessed by all that since its value is infinite, it would have been entirely sufficient for the redemption of each and every one, if God had seen fit to extend it to the whole world. And here belongs the distinction used by the fathers and retained by many divines—

that Christ "died sufficiently for all, but efficiently for the elect only." For this being understood of the dignity of Christ's death is perfectly true (although the phrase would be less accurate if referred to the will and purpose of Christ). But the question properly concerns the purpose of the Father in delivering up his own Son and the intention of Christ in dying. Did the Father appoint his Son for each and every one and, did the Son deliver himself up to death with the design and intention of substituting himself in the place of each and every one to make satisfaction and acquire salvation for the same? Or did he resolve to deliver himself up for the elect only, who were given him by the Father to be redeemed and whose head he was to be? Therefore, the question hinges upon this—not what is the nature and power of Christ's death in itself, but what was the purpose of the Father in appointing him and the intention of Christ in undergoing it. Hence it is sufficiently evident that it is not here treated of the revealed will (*euarestias*) of God only, but of his secret will (*eudokias*) under which the death and mission of Christ fall (as all must agree).

X. (2) The question does not concern the fruits and efficacy of Christ's death—whether each and all will be actually made partakers of these. Puccius (cf. *De fide natura hominibus universa insita* [1577]) and Huberus (cf. *Christum esse mortuum pro peccatis omnium hominum* [1590]) formerly held this view. Our opponents acknowledge that these are to be extended to believers only. Rather the question refers to the design of God in sending his Son into the world and the purpose of Christ in his death. Were these such that Christ by substituting himself in the place of each and every one, made satisfaction and obtained the remission of sin and salvation for them all or for the elect only? They affirm the former; we affirm the latter.

XI. (3) We do not inquire whether the death of Christ gives occasion to the imparting of many blessings even to reprobates. For it is due to the death of Christ that the gospel is preached to every creature, that the gross idolatry of the heathen has been abolished from many parts of the world, that the daring impiety of men is greatly restrained by God's word and that some often obtain many and excellent (though not saving) gifts of the Holy Spirit. All these unquestionably flow from the death of Christ, since no place would have been given for them in the church unless Christ had died. Rather the question is whether the suretyship and satisfaction of Christ were (by the counsel of God and the will of Christ himself) intended for each and every one (as they hold); or for the elect only (as we assert).

Proof that Christ did not die for all: (1) from the restriction of his death to certain ones.

XII. The reasons are: (1) the mission and death of Christ are restricted to certain ones—to "his people," "his sheep," "his friends," "his church," "his body"—and never extended to all men severally and collectively. Thus Christ "is called Jesus, because he shall save his people from their sins" (Mt. 1:21). Elsewhere he is called "the Savior of his body" (Eph. 5:23), "the good Shepherd, who lays down his life for the sheep" (Jn. 10:15) and "for his friends" (Jn. 15:13). He is said "to die that he might gather together in one, the children of God that were scattered abroad" (Jn. 11:52) and "to purchase the church with his own blood" (Acts 20:28; Eph. 5:25, 26). Now if Christ died for each and every one, why do the Scriptures so often restrict his death to a few? How can he be said to be the Savior of his people and of his body simply, if he is the Savior of others also? How can he be said to have laid down his life for his sheep, for the sons of God and for the church, if (by the counsel of God and the intention of Christ himself) he died for others also? Would this be a greater proof of his love and a foundation for stronger consolation?

XIII. To no purpose is it here objected in general: (1) "that the Scripture, which in some places restricts the death of Christ to a few, elsewhere extends it to all." That universality (as will hereafter be shown) is not absolute, but limited; one which respects the classes of individuals, not the individuals of classes. (2) "That in those passages reference is made not to the acquisition alone, which considered separately is universal, but to the application, which is particular." Those bounds which the Holy Spirit uses in the texts cited above (such as "the Savior," "to lay down his life for some," "to give himself for some" and to save [*peripoiein*] some) properly denote satisfaction, the procuring and acquisition of salvation. Although they draw after them the application, they are no less efficacious since the acquisition and application are inseparable as being of the same extent (as will shortly be proved). (3) "That it can be said at the same time that Christ died for some absolutely and for all conditionally." This takes for granted what ought to be proved—that there was a twofold intention in Christ's death: one conditional which extended to all; the other absolute which was restricted to a few. Scripture never mentions this, but speaks of the application as conditional, yet never of the redemption. Nor would the nature of the thing allow this since (on their hypothesis) there was as yet no consideration of the elect in the decree concerning the death of Christ, according to which he died (indeed with the same intention with which the decree was passed, since the execution must answer to the destination; nor could there be any other affection and intention in Christ dying than in the Father destining). They hold that the elect were separated by a posterior decree from others. Again, who can believe that in the one most simple act by which God decreed all things (although we have to conceive of it by parts), there were two intentions so diverse (not to say contrary) that in one manner Christ should die for all and in another only for some? Nay, since Christ could not will to die absolutely for the elect without involving (by the law of contraries) a will not to die for the reprobate, it cannot be conceived how in one act he should will both to die for the reprobate and not to die for them. (4) "Although these passages speak of the elect, yet they are not to be understood concerning them exclusively of all others; as when Paul says that Christ was delivered for him, he does not exclude others from a fellowship in the same love (Gal. 2:20)." All the passages adduced, if not explicitly yet implicitly include an exclusion in the description of those for whom Christ died (which cannot pertain to others). Although the blessing is promised to the seed of Abraham (the particle "alone" not being added), still it may be sufficiently inferred from the nature of the thing. So all these passages tend to the same point—to amplify the remarkable love of Christ to his sheep for whom he delivered himself up to death. But if they have nothing peculiar in this affair above others, what reason can be given why that immense love of Christ (who lays down his life, pours out his blood and gives himself up) should be applied specially to them? Nor does the example of Paul apply here. He does not speak of this as a privilege peculiar to himself, but as one common to himself and other elect or believing persons to whom he sets himself forth as an example that they might predicate the same thing concerning themselves in the same state.

XIV. Not more solidly is it objected in particular: (1) against Mt. 1:21—"Although Christ is called the Savior of his people in a peculiar sense, on account of salvation being actually and really bestowed upon them, yet there is no reason why he should not be the Savior of others also, on account of having obtained salvation for them, although on account of their unbelief they will never be made partakers of it; in the same manner as Paul says, 'God is the Savior of all men, but especially of them that believe,' 1 Tim. 4:10)." It is gratuitous to say that Christ is the Savior of those for whom salvation is indeed acquired, but to whom it will never be applied. Even the very word "to save" denotes the actual communication of salvation, and Christ is Jesus, not only because he is willing and able to save and because he removes all obstacles out of the way of salvation, but because he does really and actually save his people, not only by his merit acquiring salvation for them, but also efficaciously applying it to them, which was the intention of God in sending Christ and the end of his mission (as the angel clearly intimates by the imposition of the name Jesus). Nor does the passage in Paul prove the contrary (1 Tim. 4:10). There the word Savior (*sōtēr*), which in the latter clause is taken strictly and properly with regard to believers (as denoted by the word "especially" [*malista*]), in the first clause is taken in its wider sense of a "preserver"—"in him we live and move and have our being" (Acts 17:28); as in Ps. 36:6 (to which passage Paul alludes), God is said to *sōzein*—"to preserve man and beast." Hence Chrysostom, Oecumenius, Primasius and Ambrose say, "He is the Savior of all at present" (i.e., as far as regards the present life), but of believers only "in the future" and as to eternal life; cf. Thomas Aquinas on this passage—"who is Savior of the present and future life because he saves with a bodily salvation as to all, and thus he is called the Savior of all men. He saves by a spiritual salvation also as to the good and is hence said to be the Savior especially of them that believe" (*Angelici Doctoris Divi Thomae . . . Commentaria in Epistolas omnes D. Pauli*, II/V [1856], p. 34 on 1 Tim. 4:10).

XV. (2) To the passage in Jn. 10:15, it ought not to be objected that "the sheep, for whom he laid down his life, were not the elect alone." For the passage clearly teaches that it can apply to none but the elect. Christ is speaking of sheep who hear his voice and follow him, whom he knows and dearly loves, whom he must bring into one fold under one Shepherd (vv. 15, 16), to whom he would give eternal life and no man shall be able to pluck them out of his hand. This can be said of no others than the elect, who are called sheep both antecedently (in virtue of their eternal destination to life) and consequently (in virtue of their call in time). Nor may it be objected "that he is said to have laid down his life for his sheep because they alone shall enjoy the fruits of his death, while it is of no use to others on account of their unbelief. Thus to die for some either signifies to die with this intention that they shall be profited in reality, which is true only of the sheep." The phrase "to lay down life for some" can no more be referred to the apprehension of the fruits of Christ's death, than when it is said he gave himself a ransom (*antilytron*) for all (which is extended to each and every one). Nor is there any reason why the former should be referred to the intention and effect at the same time, but the latter restricted to the intention and desire only of assisting. Nor can it be conceived what difference there is between the two. For he who wills to die for anyone that he may profit him, wills by that very thing that he shall be profited in reality. He will in reality profit him if he can, otherwise a reason would have to be given why Christ obtains what he intended as to his sheep, but fails in his intention as to the rest. Or "that he could not die for his sheep as such because then, they would have been his sheep before he died for them and acquired them for his own. Hence he laid down his life for them merely as sinners, which character belongs to them in common with others, and that hence he must have laid down his life for others also." Although they were not as yet actually his sheep, still they were so by destination. They were given to Christ to be redeemed and purchased by him as the Good Shepherd, who with his own blood must redeem them; therefore they were given to Christ by the decree of God before they were in his hands (Jn. 17:24). Nay, the very mission of Christ was founded upon that gift. "This is the will," says he, "of him who hath sent me, that of all which he hath given me I should lose nothing, but should raise it up again at the last day" (Jn. 6:39). Otherwise unless a fixed number of those to be saved had been contemplated by God when he determined to send Christ, the effect of his death would have been uncertain and this whole mystery of redemption might have been rendered utterly fruitless by the perverse obstinacy of man.

XVI. (3) The objection against Eph. 5:25 and Tit. 2:14 is not valid—"that although Christ is said to have delivered himself up for his people and for his church, yet it is not to be restricted to it alone, with the inference that he gave himself up for no others." An exclusion is intimated with sufficient plainness by the words themselves and the nature of the thing. (a) For such a delivering up is meant as arises from the love of Christ towards his church, as his spouse; but such a love necessarily includes an exclusion. So when Paul says in the preceding verse, "Husbands love your wives," although an exclusion is not expressed, it is sufficiently implied. Who would hear without indignation the adulterer plead thus in vindication of his crime—"It is indeed said, 'Husbands, love your wives,' but it is not said, love those alone"? (b) Such a giving of himself is here meant as has for its end the sanctification of his church and its salvation (i.e., the application with the procurement). This clearly belongs to none but the elect and the church alone. And since he delivered himself up for none except for this end, he can be said to have delivered himself up for no one who will not obtain that end.

XVII. (4) The objection is futile which is brought against Mt. 20:28, 26:28 and Heb. 9:28—that "many here is not opposed to all, but to one, and a few" (as is done in Rom. 5:19 and Dan. 12:2*) and that "many is often put for all." The many treated here are described by such marks as cannot be common to each and every one: that he gave himself a ransom for many (*lytron anti pollōn*); in place of many by an actual substitution; that he shed his blood for many for the remission of sins; that he offered himself to bear the sins of many (*eis to pollōn anenenkein hamartias*); for the actual abolition of sin. If many is sometimes opposed to one and a few (yea, is used also for all), it is not therefore necessary to understand it so everywhere. Nay, it is often so extended to many as to be a negation of all. Hence Jerome says, "He does not say that he gave his life for all, but for many, that is, for all those who would believe" (*Commentariorum in Evangelium Matthaei* [PL 26.150] on Mt. 20:28)—who are none other than the elect, in whom God works both to will and to do. The interlinear gloss adds "for many, not for all, but for those who were predestinated to life" (cf. *Biblia sacra cum glossa ordinaria* [1617], 5:339 on Mt. 20:28).

2. From the restriction of his death to those given to him by the Father.

XVIII. Second, Christ was given and died for no others than those who were given to him by the Father. However all men universally were not given to Christ, but only some. Therefore the truth of the major cannot be questioned. For since in the design of the Father (according to which Christ should die and truly did die) not only was Christ appointed as Redeemer, but he was also appointed for those for whose redemption and salvation he was to die. It is evident that he could die for none others than those who were in this sense given to him. And hence a twofold donation can be observed: one, of Christ to men; another, of men to Christ. Christ was given to men for the purpose of saving them and men are given to Christ that through him they might be saved. The former is referred to in Is. 9:6 and 49:6, and in all the passages in which Christ is said to be sent and given for us. The latter is referred to in others where mention is made of those given to Christ (as in Jn. 17:2, 6, 12; 6:37). Since, however, this twofold giving is reciprocal, each of them must also be of the same extent so that Christ is given for none but those who are given to him and all those are given to Christ for whom he is given. But the Scriptures in many places assert that not all men, but some men only were given to him (which is assumed in the minor) when it distinguishes them from other men: "As thou hast given him power over all flesh, that he should give eternal life to as many as thou hast given him" (Jn. 17:2); and "I have manifested thy name unto the men which thou gavest me out of the world: thine they were, and thou gavest them me" (v. 6); when it designates them by "the people whom he foreknew" (Rom. 11:2); heirs and children of promise (Rom. 9:8); the seed of Abraham, not carnal, but spiritual, both of the Jews and Gentiles (Rom. 4:13; Gal. 3:8, 16; Heb. 2:16); his people and body or the church of Christ (Mt. 1:21; Eph. 5:23); vessels of mercy afore prepared to glory (Rom. 9:23, 24); chosen in him and predestinated to adoption and to conformity to his image (Rom. 8:30; Eph. 1:4, 5); and the posterity of the second Adam, all of whom are to be quickened in Christ, in opposition to the posterity of the first Adam, in whom all die (1 Cor. 15:22, 23). From all these, it is evident that the object of the giving of Christ is so restricted to a limited number that it cannot be extended to each and every one.

XIX. To no purpose do they reply that "the giving of Christ was conditional, not absolute; that the law and condition was that men would receive by faith the benefit offered to them, and since this is not done by the greater part, it is no wonder that they derive no advantage from it." It is gratuitously supposed that there was such a conditional giving, since Scripture nowhere mentions this condition. For although faith is proposed as a means and condition necessary to the reception and enjoyment of this benefit, yet it does not follow that it was a condition to the giving of Christ (since it is itself a gift of grace and a fruit of this giving). Further, if the giving of Christ was founded upon any condition, it would either depend upon man or upon God. The former can be said by none but a Pelagian. If the latter be asserted, then it comes to this—that Christ is said to be given to us by God as a Savior on this condition, that he will give him to us by the production of faith or under the condition of faith (which faith, however, he who alone is able to give it, will not give—a glaring absurdity).

XX. Our view is still further confirmed by the connection of the twofold relation (*scheseōs*) which Christ sustains to us (viz., the relation of a surety and that of a head). He is our surety that by satisfying he may acquire salvation for us. He is our head that by his Spirit working in us he may apply this salvation to us. He is not given as a head to all men, but to his members only (i.e., to the elect, who are made actual partakers of salvation). He cannot be a surety or sponsor of any other than these since the reason for both relations (*scheseōs*) is the same; nor ought there to be a greater extension of the one than of the other. The same thing can be proved from the connection between the death and resurrection of Christ in which this same twofold relation exists. Indeed since he died as surety, he must rise again as head. However since there is the same reason for his death and resurrection, no other cause can be given why the former should be more extensive than the latter. Hence it is that Paul places these two as being of equal efficacy (*isodynamounta*) and extent: "Christ died for our sins and rose again for our justification" (Rom. 4:25); "he died for all, that they which live should not henceforth live unto themselves, but unto him which died for them and rose again" (2 Cor. 5:14, 15). He cannot be said to have died for others than those for whom he rose again because no one becomes a partaker of the fruits of Christ's death except by his resurrection. Now that he did not rise again as a head (to confer the salvation obtained by his death upon all) is self-evident.

3. From the connection between his satisfaction and intercession.

XXI. Third, the same truth is established by the connection between his satisfaction and the intercession of Christ. For since they are parts of the same priestly office, they must also be of the same extent. He should intercede for those for whom he made satisfaction; nor should he make satisfaction for others than those for whom he intercedes. The same thing must be the object as much of his propitiation (*hilasmou*) as of his appearance in the presence of God (*emphanismou*) as they are connected indissolubly by Paul and John (1 Jn. 2:1, 2; Rom. 8:34). Now Christ himself expressly declares that he does not intercede for all, but only for those who are given him by the Father: "I pray not for the world, but for them which thou hast given me" (Jn. 17:9). However, since to offer up prayers for anyone is much easier than to give blood and life for them, who will say that he dies for those to whom he denies his prayers? or that he would have denied his prayers to those for whose sake he was just about to pour out his blood at the very moment before his death?

XXII. Nor is it to be said here with the Remonstrants that "there is a twofold intercession of Christ, one universal, which is in respect of the whole world, concerning which Isaiah speaks (53:12), according to which he is said to have prayed for his persecutors (Lk. 23:34); another particular, which is in respect of believers, which is spoken of in Jn. 17 and Rom. 8." It is gratuitously supposed that a universal intercession can be granted. For as he is always heard by the Father (Jn. 11:42), if he would intercede for all, all would be actually saved. Nor is this universal intercession proved from Is. 53:12, where it is said that he would intercede for the transgressors; not for all, but for the many of whom mention is there made and whom he is said to justify (v. 11). Nor is it proved from Lk. 23:34. He does not pray for all those who crucified him, but for those who sinned from ignorance (as Christ adds there), who also obtained the fruit of his prayer (Acts 2, 3).

If Christ (from a humane affection and an impulse of love) prayed also for those who perished, it does not follow that the intercessory prayers which he offered up as Mediator (and in that special office) are to be extended to others than those elected and given him by the Father. To these Christ himself restricts his intercessory prayers.

XXIII. Nor does he escape better, who says that the world of unbelievers only is excluded from the prayers of Christ, those who are guilty of rejecting the gospel and hate believers (Jn. 10:14), but not the world beloved of God, for whom he gave his own Son (Jn. 3:16). But these prayers did not have any other object than to obtain the gift of perseverance for believers. Since that world is opposed to those given by his Father in election, it necessarily ought to be extended to all the reprobate, who were not given to Christ (and this antecedently to their unbelief), whether they should be disbelievers in the gospel presented to them or merely guilty of violating the law of nature. And since that reprobation was made from eternity, they could never be viewed in any other light by God. Nor does the world (whom God is said to have so loved as to give his Son) form any objection to this exclusion because (as will be seen in the proper place) this does not extend to all men universally, but indiscriminately to the elect. If he prays for the apostles, who were then believers and asks for them the gift of perseverance, it does not follow that he prays for believers only as such and in consequence of their faith. Nay he prays for all who would believe "that they may be sanctified through the truth and made perfect in one" (Jn. 10:19, 21). Since this cannot be done without the gift of faith, he must have prayed for faith to be given to them. Further, since he declares that he sanctifies himself for them that they also might be sanctified through the truth (and as none are sanctified but the elect), we must conclude that he meant those prayers for them alone that faith and other gifts necessary to salvation and perseverance might be bestowed upon them.

4. From the inseparableness of the gift of the Son and the gift of the Holy Spirit.

XXIV. Fourth, from the inseparable connection between the gift of the Son and the Holy Spirit. For since these two gifts (the most excellent of all) are given by God to us for salvation and are always joined in Scripture as cause and effect (Jn. 16:7; Gal. 4:4, 6; Rom. 8:9; 1 Jn. 3:24), they must be of equal extent and go together so that the Son is not given to acquire salvation for any others than those to whom the Spirit was given to apply it. Nor can any reason be adduced why there should be a greater extension of the gift of the Son than of the gift of the Spirit. Now it is evident that the Spirit is not given to all, but to the elect alone. Therefore the Son ought not to place himself as surety for others that a harmony may be maintained between the work of the Son and that of the Spirit. And here belongs the argument of Paul in which from the giving of Christ he infers the bestowal of all saving benefits: "He that spared not his own Son, but delivered him up for us all, how shall he not with him also freely give us all things?" (Rom. 8:32). The apostle reasons from the greater to the less (viz., he who gave his Son [which was undoubtedly the greater gift], how shall he not give faith and all other saving blessings, which is the lesser?). And this the rather because (as we shall presently prove) Christ by delivering himself up has merited for us all these gifts together with salvation. Hence we must conclude either that all things shall be given with Christ to the reprobate if he died for them; or if they are not given (which is granted by all), neither was Christ given for them. Nor can the knot be untied by alleging that the apostle treats of a special delivering up for believers. Besides the fact of the gratuitous assumption that there was a universal delivering up of Christ (as was said before); since faith is a fruit of that death, it cannot be put before it as an antecedent condition. Further, since according to the order laid down by our learned opponents themselves, the decree concerning the death of Christ was antecedent to the decree concerning the bestowal of faith, it cannot be conceived how at one and the same time and in the selfsame most simple act, he could be delivered up for all, and only for some.

5. From the supreme love of Christ.

XXV. Fifth, from the supreme love of Christ. He so dearly loved those for whom he died that a greater love cannot be conceived. "Greater love," says he, "hath no man than this, that a man lay down his life for his friends" (Jn. 15:13). And Paul so commends that love as truly wonderful and unheard-of among men: "For scarcely for a righteous man will one die: yet peradventure for a good man some would even dare to die. But God commendeth his love towards us, in that, while we were yet sinners, Christ died for us" (Rom. 5:7, 8). But this cannot be said of each and every man, since all can see that Peter was more beloved by Christ than Judas. It is inconceivable how it can be said that he loved those most dearly whom as an inexorable Judge he had already delivered up (or was about to deliver up by an irrevocable decree) to Satan to be eternally tormented. Nor can it be said that they treat of external acts of love. Besides the fact that external acts presuppose internal, if Christ exerted that exterior act to each and all (a greater than which cannot be granted), it follows that nothing more could be done by Christ for the elect than for the reprobate (which everyone sees to be absurd). Nor if he loves some of the elect more than others as to the internal gifts of the Spirit (a diversity of which is required for the perfection of his mystical body) does it follow from this that the greatest degree of love with which he is affected towards both should not be the laying down of his life for them.

6. From the nature of his suretyship.

XXVI. Sixth, from the nature of Christ's suretyship the same doctrine may be derived. For since it implies the substitution of Christ in our stead, so that he died not only for our good, but in our place (as was said before and invincibly proved against the Socinians), so that he transferred to himself by his suretyship all the debt of those whose persons he bore and took it away from them and as he effaced it most fully as if his own no less than if the sinners themselves had done this very thing, it cannot be conceived how they for whom he died and made satisfaction in this way could still be subjected to an eternal curse and obliged again to bear the deserved punishments. Nevertheless, this must be said if he died for others than the elect, since this openly impeaches the veracity and justice of God. For if the debt has been transferred to Christ in consequence of his suretyship and discharged by him, everyone must see that it has been so taken away from the first debtors that payment cannot anymore be demanded from them; rather they must forever afterwards remain free and absolved from all obligation to punishment. Pertaining to this are all the passages of Scripture which assert that our sins were so transferred to Christ that the chastisement of our peace was upon him and by his stripes we are healed (Is. 53:5, 6), also when he is said to have been made sin and a curse for us that we might be made the righteousness and blessing of God in him (2 Cor. 5:21; Gal. 3:13).

7. Because he procures salvation for those only to whom he applies it.

XXVII. Seventh, Christ died for those only for whom he obtained and to whom he applies salvation. But he procured salvation for and applies it to the elect alone. Therefore, he died for them only. The reason of the major rests upon a double foundation: that (1) the death of Christ was appointed by God in order that he might obtain salvation for us; (2) the procuring cannot be separated from the application. For the end of the acquisition cannot be other than the application and to no purpose would a thing be obtained which is never applied. Thence it follows that if salvation is obtained for all, it must be equally applied to all. If it is not applied to all, but only to the elect, then it was not obtained for all, but for the elect only. In vain it is objected: (a) that the death of Christ was not appointed so much to obtain salvation, as to remove the obstacle which justice interposed to prevent God from thinking about our salvation. For it would follow that Christ did not so much acquire redemption and salvation for us as the possibility of salvation only and placed it in the power of the Father to make a new covenant of grace with men. This was not long since condemned in the Remonstrants as injurious to the efficacy of his mediation. Therefore how can Christ be said to have given himself a ransom (*antilytron*) for us, to have obtained eternal salvation for us and other things of the same kind (which denote not only the possibility of salvation, but the salvation actually obtained by him for us)?

XXVIII. (b) Equally futile is the objection "that Christ obtained redemption for all with this intention—that it might be applied to all, provided they would not reject it." This cannot be said with regard to multitudes to whom Christ has neither been offered, nor even known by name. Then Christ would thus have proposed a fruitless object to himself concerning a thing which was not only never to happen, but also could not happen without his gift (which nevertheless he determined not to give them). As if this was the design of Christ—I wish to obtain redemption for all to the end that it may be applied to them, provided they believe; and yet to multitudes I am resolved neither to reveal this redemption, nor to give those to whom it is revealed that condition without which it can never be applied to them (i.e., I desire that to come to pass which I not only know will not and cannot take place, but also what I am unwilling should take place because I refuse to communicate that without which it can never be brought to pass as it depends upon myself alone). Now if this would not be becoming in a wise man, how much less in Christ, supremely wise and good? Nor if the defect of its application does not happen by the fault of Christ, but accidentally (viz., by the wickedness and unbelief of men), does it cease to be less injurious to the honor of Christ; as if he either could not foreknow or could not remove those impediments which obstruct the application of the salvation he obtained and thus make it fruitless. But they deny that it is vain because although it fails of success, yet it was not made rashly and undesignedly because however men act, Christ attained by his death what he principally intended (as pardon and salvation are now prepared for each man if he will only believe and repent—which the inexorable rigor of divine justice prohibited before). All this does not remove the absurdity because, since no other can be the object of the acquisition than the application, it cannot but be in vain if it does not accomplish this object. And Christ needed to die for men not only that salvation and pardon might be procured for them under a condition (which they could not comply with), but that they might actually obtain pardon and salvation.

XXIX. This may be more firmly established by the manner of the acquisition. For if it is extended to each and every one, it must be either absolute or conditional. The former cannot be asserted because then each and every one would undoubtedly be saved. Neither is the latter true: (1) because a conditional acquisition would not properly be an acquisition, but only the mere possibility of acquisition, provided the condition is complied with. (2) He acquired that condition either for all or for some only. If he acquired it for all, therefore all must be made actually partakers of salvation because such a condition could not be acquired except absolutely and unconditionally (and so to be conferred upon all). For a condition of a condition is not admissible, otherwise the thing would run into an endless chain of conditions. Nor can any condition be granted which would not coincide with the thing to be acquired. If for some only, the acquisition is not plenary and sufficient and is especially destitute of a necessary part of itself. Again, it would be vain and illusory (viz., done under a condition, impracticable and never to be performed and which God not only foresaw would never be complied with, but which he, who alone is able to give it, had decreed not to grant). Finally, Christ is thus feigned to have had a double intention in his satisfaction: first, conditional for all, then absolute for the elect (which can never either be proved from Scripture, nor reconciled with the unity and simplicity of the decree concerning the death of Christ).

8. Because he did not merit faith for all.

XXX. Eighth, Christ died for those only for whom he merited salvation and with salvation all the means necessary to obtain it—especially faith, repentance and the Holy Spirit, the author of both (without which salvation is unattainable). Now this cannot be said of each and all, for then all would undoubtedly be saved; rather it may be said of the elect only. Therefore . . . etc. That Christ merited faith for men by his death, many arguments prove. (1) He is called "the author and finisher of faith" (*archēgos kai teleiōtēs pisteōs*, Heb. 12:2; Acts 5:31). Now if he is the author of our faith, he must be the acquirer of it for he gives us nothing which he has not by his merit acquired for us. (2) He is the meritorious cause of salvation; therefore also of all the parts of which salvation consists. But faith and spiritual life (which he works in us) are the chief part of our salvation. (3) Christ is the cause and foundation of all spiritual blessings (Eph. 1:3), among which the first and most special is faith. Hence to believe on him and to suffer for his sake are elsewhere said to be given on the part of Christ (Phil. 1:29). (4) As Christ was to send us the Spirit, so he was also to merit him; hence the Spirit is proposed to us as one of the fruits of Christ's death (Jn. 16:7)—therefore also all his gifts and especially faith. Nor is the Spirit (as sanctifying and consoling) to be distinguished here from him as illuminating, as if Christ had merited the former only and not the latter. For since all these operations proceed from the same Spirit, he who acquired for us the Spirit (the author of these gifts) must also have acquired with him all his gifts. As faith is the principle and root of our sanctification, he who merited the sanctifying Spirit must also have merited faith itself, which purifies the heart. (5) Christ could not be a true and full Savior unless he had acquired faith for us (without which it is impossible to obtain salvation). And this was the constant doctrine in the Reformed churches—that Christ had merited for us faith no less than salvation, and that he is the cause of all the gifts bestowed upon us by the Father. Hence the venerable fathers of the Synod of Dort, in their exhibition of true doctrine, say, "Christ acquired for us faith and all the other saving gifts of the Holy Spirit, by his death" ("Secundum Caput: De Morte Christi," 8 in *Acta Synodi Nationalis . . . Dordrechti* [1619-20], 1:290). In their Rejection of Errors, they condemn "those, who teach that Christ by his satisfaction, merited for none certainly salvation and faith, by which his satisfaction is efficaciously applied for salvation, but that he only acquired for the Father a power, or an entire willingness, to enter into a new covenant with man, and to prescribe whatever new conditions he might wish, the performance of which depended upon the free will of man; and that thus it could happen, either that none, or all might fulfil them. For they think too meanly of the death of Christ, recognize in no way the primary fruit of or the benefit obtained by it and recall the Pelagian heresy from the shades of Orcus" ("Secundum Caput: De Morte Christi," Reiectio Errorum, 3 in ibid., 1:291).

XXXI. But to no purpose do some distinguish here the decree to deliver Christ up to death, from this death itself (which took place in time), so that the former was antecedent to the election of certain persons, but not the latter (which follows the decree of special election). For Amyrald himself, speaking of Christ's death in time, says, "Redemption ought to be equal because all ought to repent, as equally miserable creatures of God" (*Brief Traitte de la Predestination* [1634], p. 77). And the very nature of the thing proves this. For since the sense and affection of the Son must be the same with that of the Father for all (as the same author says, ibid., Part 2, p. 356), the death of Christ in time must be conformed to the eternal destination of the Father, as he would not make a satisfaction except according to the paternal prescription. Therefore since the decree of the Father concerning the delivering up of Christ to death arose from a common affection towards all men before any consideration of the election of some to faith, Christ himself, in his death, could have no other intention and end than to follow the design of the Father. Again, according to this conception, Christ in his death must have considered some as elect, others as reprobate. For since election is not without reprobation, Christ could not think about the election of some without at the same time thinking about the preterition and reprobation of others. If, therefore, he willed with a special affection to die for those whom he knew to have been elected (considered as such), he must also have nilled by some other affection to die for others whom he knew were reprobated as such. Nor do they help themselves by saying that Christ did not die for the reprobate in a compound sense and formally (inasmuch as they are reprobate), but in a divided sense and materially (for those men who in another moment of the decree are reprobated). For in addition to our inability to conceive how such abstractions can belong to a unique and most simple act of the decree of God, it would thus follow that Christ could not die for the elect as such (here we reason by the rule of contraries). And it appears inexplicable how Christ in his death could have regard to a first and fourth decree as to the elect (i.e., should have willed to die for them, considered both materially as men and formally as elect); while as to the reprobate, he dealt abstractly and considered them only as men, not as reprobates (for election and reprobation walk hand in hand and mutually imply each other).

XXXII. But because certain learned men have observed that their hypothesis (which makes faith not a fruit of the merit of Christ's death, but a gift of the Father) is pressed by various inconveniences, is an indignity to Christ and injurious to salvation, they have sought another way of escape by teaching sometimes that "Christ did obtain faith and repentance for all conditionally, for the elect absolutely." At other times, they say "that he did not obtain these in the way of satisfaction and of meritorious cause, but in the way of final cause, that faith might be given to the elect to bring them to Christ." But neither of these can be said with truth. Not the former because it cannot be conceived under what condition faith could be obtained for us, since it is itself a condition. But although faith is usually proposed after the manner of a condition (under which salvation is promised in Christ), yet it is also proposed after the manner of a benefit in the covenant of grace, which Christ obtained for us by his death. Hence Christ must be regarded as having acquired for us not only salvation if we believe, but also faith that we may believe. Not the latter because an acquisition in the way of final cause and not in the way of satisfaction and of meritorious cause is thus far a distinction unknown in theological schools. Since every acquisition properly so called is founded upon the satisfaction and merit of the obtainer. Then if Christ did not obtain for us faith in the way of meritorious cause, he did not merit faith. But neither can he be said to have obtained faith for some in the way of final cause, since no elect were yet attended to by Christ when God decreed that procurement (which he was to effect by his death). Again, either for all (for whom salvation is obtained in the way of satisfaction) faith is obtained in the way of final cause or not. If the former, all will be saved; if the latter, to what purpose is salvation acquired for them by way of satisfaction for whom faith is not acquired by way of final cause (without which salvation cannot be obtained)? Again he either obtained that faith for all by way of final cause or for the elect only. If for all, all therefore shall obtain it; if for the elect, Christ must by dying have done something more for these than for those, since nevertheless in the moment of the decree concerning his death he had an equal regard to all. So in whatever way this hypothesis is considered, difficulties will always remain. How can faith be equally acquired for each and every one which yet all do not equally obtain? Or if it has not been acquired for all, how vain and delusive is that acquisition of salvation which is made only on the condition of faith (which yet he who obtained the salvation knew it was not possible for the sinner to exercise without his grace and which he, who alone can give, has decreed not to give)? We must, therefore, come to this conclusion—either faith must be said to be in our power (as Pelagius held) or it must be said to have been obtained by Christ that it might be given to us by the Father.

XXXIII. Nor is the difficulty relieved by the example they bring forward of a prince paying the price (*lytron*) of redemption for all the captives, although he does not effect by it that all wish to be freed from captivity. A comparison should not fail in an all-important circumstance; for it is evident that the prince, although he might earnestly wish, is not able to give to the captive the will of applying the price (*lytron*) to himself. However Christ is able. But if a prince could be supposed, who could not only pay the ransom (*lytron*) for the captives, but could also give them the will to avail themselves of it (nay, further, suppose that the prince knew that they had not and could not have this will unless he bestowed it upon them, which yet he would not do); who would say that he seriously willed to liberate those captives and had given the ransom (*lytron*) with an intention and design to emancipate them? Again if the comparison is pressed, it may be easily repulsed. For as to the corporeal liberation of a captive, it does not suffice to pay a ransom (*lytron*), but it is also necessary to break off the chains which bind him in prison; otherwise the payment of the price will be ineffectual. So for the liberation of the soul from the spiritual captivity of sin, it is not enough to pay a ransom (*lytron*) to divine justice, but the chains of sin and unbelief (by which they are hindered from being able or even wishing to enjoy the liberty purchased) must also be unloosed and burst asunder.

9. From the expiation of all the sins of those for whom he died.

XXXIV. Ninth, if Christ died for all, then he expiated all their sins and therefore must have made satisfaction for unbelief and final impenitence (which prevent man from applying to himself redemption), and so they will no longer stand in the way of such an application; for on the supposition of satisfaction having been made for them, they must be pardoned. Nor can it be objected to this that "the blessing will be applied, if the condition on which redemption has been procured be complied with." It involves a contradiction that this condition should be complied with where the unbelief and impenitence are supposed to be final. And thus Christ is absurdly pretended to have died to expiate the incredulity of a man, provided he would not be unbelieving, but believe (as if I should say, I have found an infallible remedy for the cure of a blind or leprous person to be applied on this condition—that he will not be blind or leprous). Further, the want of the condition cannot hinder the application of redemption to unbelievers, since Christ is supposed by his death to have satisfied for that unbelief and therefore to have expiated this very failure. But since everyone must see that this cannot be said of the reprobate, it is clearly inferred that Christ did not die for them.

10. From various absurdities.

XXXV. Finally, if Christ died for each and every one, it follows: (1) that Christ died for multitudes on condition that they would believe, to whom neither Christ nor his death has ever been made known and who therefore could not believe. (2) That he died for those whom he knew were to be sons of perdition (whom God had passed by) and who would never to all eternity receive any of the fruits of his death and so exercised the greatest love towards those whom both he and the Father (by an eternal preterition and reprobation) intolerably disliked. (3) That he died for those who were already tormented in hell and actually damned without any hope of salvation and thus bore the punishment as surety in their place, who were already suffering punishment for themselves and must suffer it without end. (4) Christ would be called the Savior and Redeemer of those who not only never will be saved, but who never by any means can be saved. Or he would be called an imperfect and partial Savior, who by satisfaction is indeed the author of the acquisition, but not of the application;

since, nevertheless, he cannot be truly called the Savior of any but those whom he makes partakers of salvation and who are actually saved.

Sources of explanation.

XXXVI. Christ is nowhere in Scripture said to have died for all, unless in the same place a limitation is added from which it may be inferred that it is to be understood not universally of each and every one, but restrictedly according to the subject matter. Sometimes it refers to the multitude of the elect, which has its own universality. When it is said "that he died for all" (2 Cor. 5:15), they only are meant "who are also dead," not with a death "in sins," but with spiritual "sin." The object of the apostle is not to prove the corruption of individuals, but to demonstrate with what obligation believers are bound to their duty—whether as to justification through the imputation of the merit of Christ's death (as if they had made satisfaction in their own persons) or as to sanctification through the crucifixion of the old man by the efficacy of the cross of Christ, who live not unto themselves, but unto Christ; for whom Christ not only died, but also rose again and whom "the love of Christ constraineth." Expressions of this nature indicate that they can belong to no others than the elect and believers (to whom alone it belongs to die in Christ and with him, Rom. 6:6, 8). Thus in 2 Cor. 5:19, where God is said "to be in Christ reconciling the world to himself, not imputing their trespasses to them," no other world can be meant than those who are really reconciled to God and to whom he does not actually impute their sins. It is plain that this agrees with none but the elect. Hence they are pronounced blessed to whom the Lord does not impute sin (Ps. 32:2). In the same sense, "all are said to be made righteous by the righteousness and obedience of one," as all are made guilty by the transgression of one (Rom. 5:18, 19). Undoubtedly all those who "receive abundance of grace and of the gift of righteousness" (*tēn perisseian tēs charitos kai tēs dikaiosynēs*, v. 17) and who are really justified (v. 19) are no others than the elect and believers, who belong to and make up the whole body of Christ. For Adam is opposed to Christ, head to head: to wit, as sin and death have passed upon all who descend from Adam, so righteousness and life pass upon all who belong to the second Adam. This is elsewhere expressed by the apostle by the phrases dying and being made alive: "in Adam all die" (1 Cor. 15:22), i.e., all who die, die in Adam and on account of his sin; and "all in Christ shall be made alive," i.e., all who will be made alive either in grace or in glory, will be made alive no other way than in and on account of Christ. All those for whom Christ is said to have tasted death (Heb. 2:9) are "sons." They are either brought or to be brought to glory, the "captain" of whose "salvation" is Christ. They are "sanctified," whom he calls "his brethren" and "whom God has given him" (vv. 10, 11).

XXXVII. Sometimes a syncategorem "all" is used indefinitely and indiscriminately without a distinction (*diastolēn*) of nations, conditions, sexes, characters and other particulars. By it men are distinguished from one another, but not without all exception. Thus Paul sets it forth: "Whosoever believeth on him shall not be ashamed. For there is no difference [*diastolē*] between the Jew and Greek: for the same Lord over all is rich unto all that call upon him" (Rom. 10:11, 12*). Thus understand the passage "In him there is neither Jew nor Greek, circumcision nor uncircumcision, barbarian, Scythian, bond nor free: but Christ is all, and in all" (Col. 3:11), i.e., no difference of nation or condition promotes or hinders salvation, but Christ is all, i.e., bestows all things necessary for salvation upon all believers without any regard to nation or condition. This is explained in Rev. 5:9 when the twenty-four elders in their song say, "Thou hast redeemed us to God by thy blood, out of every kindred, and tongue, and people, and nation," i.e., from all the tribes of Israel and from men of all languages, whether they are civilized (who are usually called *laoi* or barbarous, to whom the word *ethnous* is frequently applied).

XXXVIII. The same meaning attaches to the passage (so often in the mouths of our opponents) where Christ is said "to have given himself a ransom for all" (*polythryllētou*, 1 Tim. 2:6). For all those are meant in whose place Christ substituted himself to bear the punishments due to them and to pay the price of their redemption; for all the orthodox have maintained against the Socinians that this is the import of the word *antilytron*. Now he cannot be said to have done this for each and every one; for thus no one could anymore be condemned and bear the punishment of his own sins. (2) Paul speaks of all those for whom Christ is Mediator by intercession and by satisfaction, for we have seen above that these are the two inseparable parts of his priestly office. And yet the Remonstrants acknowledge that he does not intercede for all men. (3) All those are denoted "whom God wills to be saved and to come to the knowledge of the truth." But experience teaches us that this cannot be said of each and every one, and it has been proved before by us (Volume I, Topic IV, Question 17, Section 34ff. where the subject is minutely examined). Thus the phrase cannot be understood universally of the individuals of classes, but indiscriminately and indefinitely of classes of individuals (i.e., of some men, as Beza rightly translates *tous pantas* here by *quosvis*—"some" of whatever nation, state and condition they may be; cf. *Annotationes maiores in Novum . . . Testamentum: Pars Altera* [1594], p. 444 on 1 Tim. 2:4). Calvin (on the passage) proves this by most solid reasoning: "The apostle simply means that no people of the world nor order of men is excluded from salvation because God wills the gospel to be offered to all without exception" (*The Second Epistle of Paul . . . to the Corinthians and . . . Timothy* [trans. T.A. Smail, 1964], pp. 208-9 on 1 Tim. 2:4). And afterwards: "The universal particle must always be referred to kinds of men, and not to persons; as if he had said, not only Jews, but Gentiles also, not only plebeians, but princes too, are redeemed by the death of Christ" (ibid., p. 210 on 1 Tim. 2:5).

XXXIX. The world for which Christ is said to have been sent and to have died (Jn. 3:16, 17; 4:42; 6:33) cannot be extended universally to the whole human race, since innumerable persons of that world perish. Rather it denotes either the universality of the elect or (indefinitely and indiscriminately) all peoples, Jews as well as Gentiles (as was proved at length, Topic IV, Question 17). Thus there is an allusion to the promise made to Abraham, that in his seed (i.e., Christ) all families of the earth should be blessed (Gen. 12:3; 26:4; 22:18); also an allusion to the nations, whose father he is said to have been made (Rom. 4:16). Now this belongs not to all men universally who are in the world, but to all the promised seed without distinction of nation. This appears in fact both from the fact that all are not justified and saved by faith (as its blessing is explained in Gal. 3:8, 16) and that Paul explains all that seed by that which is "of faith" (Rom. 4:16) and which "is called in Isaac" (Rom. 9:7). Thus the world for whose life Christ gave his flesh to death (Jn. 6:51) is none other than the world to which he is said to give life (v. 33). The bread of God is he which comes down from heaven and gives life to the world. This cannot be extended to all men universally and severally, since the giving of life imports its actual application and communication, which belong to the elect only. In this sense, he promises to give eternal life to his sheep (Jn. 10:28). Nor (unless absurdly) can that be said to be given which is only obtained for or offered to one, but never actually imparted. In this sense, Christ is said to be "the Lamb of God that taketh away the sin of the world" (Jn. 1:29). Since the word *airein* signifies not a simple taking, but also a taking away, the sins of the reprobate cannot be said to be removed entirely (which still remain upon them). No other world can be meant but that of the elect, made up of Jews and Gentiles indiscriminately, whose sins he is said to have borne in his own body on the tree that they, being dead to sin, might live unto righteousness (1 Pet. 2:24). These are said to be blessed because their transgression has been taken away (Ps. 32:1).

XL. When John says, "Christ is a propitiation for our sins, and not for ours only, but for the sins of the whole world" (1 Jn. 2:2), he does not wish to extend this to each and every one, but to those only who can console themselves by the intercession of Christ and the remission obtained through him (who are none other than the elect). For these only can Christ be an expiation (*hilasmos*) and propitiation, whose comforter (*paraklētos*) and Advocate he is with the Father (because these two are joined together by the apostle as equal and inseparable). Yet Christ is not an Advocate for all (as those learned divines confess on Jn. 17:9). Again, God must be actually propitiated and reconciled to those for whom Christ made a propitiation (unless we suppose that Christ failed in his purpose and poured out his blood in vain—contrary to the apostle, who asserts that he for whom Christ died cannot be condemned [Rom. 8:34]; this cannot be said of those who are excluded from the covenant and upon whom the wrath of God abides). Finally, the scope of the apostle (which is to console believers against the remains of sin) proves that this cannot be extended to all. For what solace can a man receive from that grace which is common to the elect and the reprobate, if he knows that Christ in dying has done nothing more for him than for the unbelieving and reprobate? Therefore, the phrase of John has no other reference than to the believing inhabitants of the whole world; or, as Calvin says, "The sons of God dispersed through the whole world" (*The Gospel According to John . . . and the First Epistle of John* [trans. T.H.L. Parker, 1961], p. 244 on 1 Jn. 2:2). This is true lest anyone should think that this blessing was to be restricted to the apostles alone or to the Jews alone or to those believers alone to whom John wrote his epistle. But it was much more extensive—as far as the world extends, to believers redeemed out of every tribe, tongue, people and nation (i.e., out of the whole world). It makes little difference whether by "our sins" are understood the sins of the apostles or those of then living believers of the Jews of the dispersion (to whom undoubtedly this epistle was directed with the epistles of Peter and James, and which on this account are called catholic because they are not inscribed to any particular city or person) as distinguished from those who had already believed before the time of Christ; or who would afterwards believe to the end of the world. For the question still comes to the same point—it is sufficient that the whole world cannot designate the universality of all men since John and those to whom he writes are distinguished from it (who nevertheless are included in the universality of men). This was the opinion of Calvin on this passage: " 'Not for our sins only' is added by way of amplification, that believers might be firmly persuaded that the expiation made by Christ extended to all who would embrace the gospel by faith" (ibid.). And afterwards: "The object of John was none other than to make this blessing common to the whole Church; therefore, under 'all' he does not comprehend the reprobate, but designates those who would afterwards believe and who were scattered over the various regions of the world. For then truly, as it is proper, the grace of Christ is illustrated, when he is preached as the only salvation of the world" (ibid.).

XLI. Although Christ came to save "that which was lost" (*to apolōlos*, Mt. 18:11) and saves none other than lost and miserable sinners, yet it is not necessary on this account that he should save all who are lost and sinners. Nay, he expressly testifies that he did not come to call those out of the lost who (ignorant of their own lost state) are swollen with a high opinion of their own righteousness, but those only who labor under the load of sins and feel their heaviness (Mt. 11:28). Hence he says that he indeed came to save "that which was lost" (*to apolōlos*) in order to mark the character and condition of those who will be saved, but not "all that which was lost" (*pan to apolōlos*) to designate their number.

XLII. It is one thing to perish actually and eventually, another occasionally and by reason of duty when he gives occasion to one of destroying himself and by which he would, if left to himself, perish. Paul, who speaks concerning the perishing of a brother for whom Christ died (Rom. 14:15; 1 Cor. 8:10, 11), does not mean actual perdition (as if one for whom Christ died could actually perish) since no one can snatch his sheep out of his hand (Jn. 10:28). Nor can anyone of those perish whom the Father gave him to be redeemed (Jn. 17:12) because they are kept by the power of God through faith (1 Pet. 1:5), especially since he speaks of "a brother" who although weak (Rom. 14:1), yet God is able to make stand (v. 4). Rather Paul means occasional perdition when by an unseasonable and preposterous use of Christian liberty in things indifferent the conscience of a weak brother is wounded and offended, and he is exposed to the danger of perishing, as far as in us lies. So the Scriptures often use words which denote an effect and action to designate the occasion or motive by which the thing could be brought about. Thus he is said to be guilty of adultery (as far as in his power) who has looked upon the wife of another man to lust after her (Mt. 5:28); and he is said to "make God a liar" (i.e., as far as he can) who does not wish to believe the word of the gospel (1 Jn. 5:10). Therefore a brother is said to perish by our knowledge when we do nothing to preserve him. This is expressed by destroying: "Destroy not a weak brother with thy meat" (Rom. 14:15).

XLIII. When false prophets are said "to deny the Lord that redeemed or bought them" (*ton autous agorasanta despotēn*, 2 Pet. 2:1), he cannot mean a redemption (properly so called) from the malediction of God and from eternal death. No one is so redeemed who was not given by the Father to Christ to be redeemed and who consequently will be kept by him and saved for ever as a member of his church and one of his peculiar people. Rather he means a liberation from error and idolatry by an external call of Christianity and a setting apart to the work of the ministry for which they were in a certain measure bought by Christ (as the Lord), who had acquired them and made them his own by calling them into his house (as masters formerly bought servants and employed them in domestic duties). That this is the meaning of the apostle is collected from various considerations: (1) he makes mention of a *despotou*, a word signifying a master and an owner rather than a Savior (to whom redemption properly so called belongs). (2) The word *agorazein* taken simply is used of any kind of deliverance and purchase. (3) The kind of redemption here meant is that through which those bought are said "to have escaped the corruptions that are in the world through the knowledge of God and our Savior," by which "they have known the way of righteousness" (vv. 20, 21*). This can belong to no other than a deliverance from the errors and idolatries of paganism and a calling to the truth, defecting from which through apostasy and the introduction of most pernicious heresies, they are said to deny their Master who bought them and called them to his service.

XLIV. One sanctification by the blood of the covenant is internal, spiritual and real, belonging to those who are actually redeemed and regenerated by Christ; another is external and apparent as to profession. The former necessarily supposes that Christ died for those who are thus sanctified; but not so the latter because many hypocrites obtain sanctification by reason of an external calling or a reception of the sacraments (to whom, nevertheless, Christ with his benefits does not belong, since they are destitute of faith). When Paul speaks of those who count profane the blood of the covenant wherewith they were sanctified (Heb. 10:29), he cannot mean the former sanctification, which is inadmissible upon the hypothesis of the Reformed, but the latter—such as belongs to those who (professing the gospel, sprinkled in the sacrament of baptism) renounced it by a denial of Christ and apostasy from the gospel. Just as he who takes the bread of the Eucharist unworthily is said to be guilty of the body and blood of Christ (1 Cor. 11:27, 29). Besides, since the expression of the apostle is hypothetical, not absolute, it points out indeed the connection of the antecedent with the consequent or what would happen to such as committed so great a crime. Yet it establishes nothing in reality with respect to those who are redeemed and true believers, no more than what he asserted in Gal. 1:8.

XLV. What each one is bound to believe absolutely and simply, at first and immediately without anything supposed, that is true, I grant. But not likewise what anyone is bound to believe with a certain limitation, mediately and on the supposition of various acts. But it is false that all men are bound to believe that Christ died for them simply and absolutely. In the first place, all those are not bound to believe this to whom the gospel has never been preached, to whom Christ has never been made known, but only the called: "For how can they believe in him of whom they have not heard? and how can they hear without a preacher?" (Rom. 10:14). Second, not even all the called are bound to believe absolutely and immediately that Christ died for them, but mediately (the acts of repentance and faith being supposed) because to no one but him who believes and repents does this command belong. And so far is this from being true with respect to the unbelieving and impenitent that he who orders them to believe this miserably mocks them since the wrath of God abides on them and they are bound to believe that they are condemned already (Jn. 3:36). Nor if they are bound to believe that Christ has died for them on the supposition that they would truly repent and fly to him, does it follow that this is absolutely and simply true whether they believe or not. Hence they who are ordered to believe are not all men simply, but relatively (to wit, "the weary" and heavy laden with the burden of sin, Mt. 11:28; "the thirsty" and they who feel their need of drink, Is. 55:1, i.e., who are penitent and feel their misery).

XLVI. Nor is the reply satisfactory here that "faith in Christ is demanded of all the called and that not a faith of any kind, but a true and justifying faith, which it cannot be unless it terminates on Christ as dying for me." Although faith in Christ is demanded (and certainly a true and justifying faith), it does not immediately follow that it is required as to the exercise of all its acts immediately and at the same time and especially as to the special and ultimate act of believing in Christ as having died for me. For although it is included in the acts of justifying faith, still it is not its first act which is immediately and in the first instance demanded of the called; rather it is the ultimate act which presupposes many others. That this may be understood more clearly, above all things the various acts of faith must be distinguished. First, one is direct, which has for its object the word of the gospel and Christ proposed in it, by which I fly to Christ and embrace his promises; another reflex, which has for its object the direct act of faith by which I am persuaded that I truly believe and that so the promises of the gospel belong to me. Again the direct act is twofold: one consisting in the assent which faith gives to the word of God and the promises of the gospel as true in relation to the giving of salvation to all who repent and by a living faith fly to Christ and embrace him; another in refuge and trust by which (acknowledging Christ as the only and all-sufficient Savior) we fly to him and rest in him that from him we may obtain both pardon of our sins and the possession of salvation. Now the faith commanded in the gospel is commanded as to the first and second acts (which are direct) before it is commanded as to the third act (which is the reflex) and necessarily supposes the two former as it cannot exist unless preceded by them. Hence we gather that in the aforesaid argument there are four terms: the major speaks of the direct act of faith which is commanded in the word (to wit, as to assent and refuge); the latter, however, concerning the reflex act as to the sense and assurance (*pepoithēsin*) of faith. For Christ is not revealed and promised in the gospel as having died for me in particular, but only in general for believers and penitents. Hence by consequence, the fiducial act in Christ being posited, I can and must infer that he died for me when by the reflex act I know and feel from the fiducial act that I have truly and sincerely fled to him. Now that the faith enjoined upon us in the gospel is not an immediate belief that Christ died for me in particular appears with sufficient clearness even from this—that when it is enjoined either by Christ or his apostles, no mention is made of its particular application to this or that man, but only of a general relation either to duty or to the blessings promised believers; as Peter in his remarkable declaration of faith (Mt. 16:16) professes nothing more than that he believes Jesus to be the Christ, the Son of the living God: "We believe and are sure that thou art Christ, the Son of the living God" (Jn. 6:69). Thus Paul demands no more of those who believe unto salvation than "to confess with the mouth the Lord Jesus and to believe with the heart that God raised him from the dead" (Rom. 10:9). So when the saints are commanded to believe in the name of the Son of God (Jn. 3:18; 1 Jn. 5:13), they are bound indeed to believe that Christ is the true Messiah and to fly to him as the only author of salvation to those who, through faith and repentance, betake themselves to him, but not that he died for them immediately (save after the preceding acts have been exercised).

XLVII. Hence it is evident that the command to believe in Christ embraces many things before we come to the ultimate consolatory act by which we believe that he died for us. First, we are commanded to believe all that the Scripture reveals to us concerning our misery and inability to secure our own salvation. Hence arises a salutary despair of ourselves and an acknowledgement of the necessity of a remedy. Second, they who thus despair of themselves are commanded to believe that Christ, the Son of God, is the alone all-sufficient Savior given by God to men, in whom they can obtain perfect salvation and remission of sins who sincerely fly to him and are led to repent seriously of their sins. Third, they who are thus contrite and penitent and despairing of themselves are commanded to fly and to come to Christ as the rock of salvation, to embrace his merit as all-sufficient, to incline and sweetly rest upon it, from it alone expecting remission of sin, righteousness and salvation. Fourth and finally they, who perceive that they do repent and rest upon Christ truly and solely, are then at length bound to believe that Christ died for them and that on account of his death their sins are remitted. From all this, it is quite plain that faith in Christ first presupposes a sense of misery and a desire of deliverance and that the command to believe does not respect all promiscuously, but all who feel their misery and desire deliverance from it, who hunger and thirst, who labor and are heavy laden, who are broken in spirit and contrite in heart (Mt. 11:28; Is. 61:1). Second, that this command does not immediately and in the first instance demand of us the faith by which we believe that Christ died for us, but the faith by which we fly to Christ, embrace him and rest upon him (which is nothing else than that movement by which the repenting sinner, dejected under a sense of his misery and aroused by the call of the gospel, renouncing every other remedy and trust, flies to Christ as the rock of salvation and with his whole heart earnestly desires and seeks the grace offered in the gospel). Or to express it more concisely, "the flying of the repenting sinner for refuge to God as the fountain of all grace and to Christ as the ark of safety opened in the gospel." If I am conscious that I have exercised this (which is the formal act of faith), then I can and ought to elicit the other act of faith by which I believe that Christ died for me (repenting and flying to him), which is called the consequent act because it follows the direct by which I believe in Christ and take myself to him as the only and all-perfect Savior; and the consolatory act because it pours into the soul of the believer unspeakable joy and consolation. Therefore since no one can have this special and reflex act of faith unless the other preceding acts have been exercised together with the desire of true repentance, it appears that all are not bound to believe that Christ died for them, but only believers and penitents (i.e., all who, through the knowledge of sin and a sense of the divine wrath, are contrite in heart, fly to Christ and seek from him remission of sins and rely on his merit alone for salvation).

XLVIII. In vain will anyone reply: (1) "that the command of faith in Christ embraces all its degrees and acts; and therefore that all those acts and among them the last, by which we believe that Christ died for us, is required of all to whom the command to believe is preached." Such is the nature and dependence of these acts upon one another that there is no place for the last without the former; nor for the third without the second; nor for the second without the first. Therefore, when the command to believe is announced, the first act is demanded of the sinner, not that he may stop there, but that having performed it, he may go on to the second (but not having performed it, by no means). For neither can he nor ought he to believe that Christ is his Redeemer who does not wish to believe that Christ is the Son of God and the Redeemer of men; nor should a man believe that he is his Redeemer in the hypothesis, who does not believe that he is the Redeemer of all who believe on him in the thesis; but who finds in himself the preceding acts (which are the foundation of this last), then and then only, can and ought to exercise that last one also.

XLIX. (2) "That as many as are commanded to believe in Christ are commanded to have justifying faith, since indeed no other can be saving; but justifying faith necessarily implies a particular application that we believe not only that Christ died in common for men, but for us in particular because otherwise it would not differ from the historical faith of reprobates; nay, nor from the faith of devils, who can believe the same thing." I answer that the justifying faith commanded in the gospel embraces indeed those various acts of which we have spoken, but each one in its own order. First, the direct and formal act called justifying, which consists in the practical judgment of the intellect concerning Christ as the sole and most perfect Redeemer of those who believe, repent and seriously fly to him; also in the refuge of the will flying to Christ and resting in him alone. Second, the reflex and consolatory act which follows of itself when the first is performed. For from the time that I feel myself persuaded by the gospel promise, fly seriously to Christ, expect righteousness and life from him alone and rest upon him, I can and should certainly infer that Christ died for me, since from the gospel I am assured that he died for all who believe and repent. Hence the answer is easy to the argument—Whosoever is bound to have justifying faith is bound to believe that Christ died for him. I deny that this is true of the immediate and direct act of faith; but I admit it to be true of the reflex and secondary act or in the compound sense (and the first act being presupposed), but not in the divided sense (and that first act being excluded). Nor therefore does the faith of believers agree with that of reprobates and devils. For although the reprobate can theoretically believe that Christ is the Son of God and the Redeemer of men, yet they are never so truly practically persuaded of it by a fiducial assent to the word of God that they fly to him and rest upon him alone. For if they were truly persuaded that Christ is the only and perfect Savior of believers and penitents (and that out of him there is no salvation), since the will necessarily follows the dictate of the practical intellect and all naturally seek happiness, it would be impossible for them not to fly to Christ and embrace him for salvation with their whole hearts. Hence it also appears that the faith of devils has nothing in common with that of the elect, since they know that Christ is given to men alone (nor can they elicit any fiducial trust in reference to him).

L. (3) "That no one can place his trust in Christ who does not know beforehand that Christ died for him or is his Savior. For man always is anxious about his salvation until he knows the intention of God and the will of Christ, whether the death of Christ was designed for him by the purpose of God." I answer that there are two parts or acts of Christian reliance; the first is in flying to Christ and receiving him; the latter is in the acquiescence and joy which spring from a sense of having received Christ. The former is the act of faith by which we fly to Christ as the only Savior, cleave to him and appropriate him to ourselves for salvation. The latter is the act by which flying to Christ and resting on him, we trust that we have (and to eternity will have) communion with him in his death and its benefits as well as acquiesce in him, being firmly persuaded that he died for us and by his death reconciled us to God. The former is called by some "faith on Christ"; the latter "faith respecting Christ." The latter regards Christ as having died for us, but not the former. For no one can know that Christ has died for him, unless he has first believed on him. For since he is promised only to believers and penitents, I must first fly to Christ and apprehend his merit with the desire of serious repentance before I can determine that his death belongs to me by the decree of God and the intention of Christ. Not that my faith makes Christ to have died for me (for his death went before all faith in the class of meritorious cause and the grace of faith is a fruit and effect of the death of Christ), but because it is a mark and condition from which I recognize *a posteriori* that Christ's death was from eternity destined for me. Nor if I cannot as yet determine that Christ died for me, must I on that account always remain anxious and my faith be wavering and unsettled. It may firmly rest upon the general promises of the gospel made to believers and penitents. Hence by certain consequence I can gather *a posteriori*, if I find in myself that faith and repentance that these promises belong to me.

LI. (4) "That by our hypothesis the foundation of the sinner's consolation is subverted because we are bound to proceed from a particular to a universal: Christ died for some; therefore he died for me. According to the laws of good reasoning, we should proceed from a universal to a particular: Christ died for each and every man; therefore, also for me." But (a) it is a gratuitous assumption that we proceed here from a particular to a universal (which everyone sees to be absurd). For we argue entirely from a universal (but in a certain order and respect) to a particular: Christ died for all who believe and repent; but I believe and repent; therefore he died for me also. (b) It is false that a ground of consolation can be drawn from the absolute universality of the death of Christ because no solid consolation can be drawn from that which is common to the godly and ungodly (nay to the innumerable multitudes who have been and shall be damned equally with those who shall be saved). For since he may be supposed to have died even for Judas and Pharaoh (who have perished notwithstanding), how can the fear of damnation be taken away from me by this? If you say that this fear may be taken away by faith, we must proceed to another syllogism concerning all believers (not concerning all men): Christ died for each and all who believe; but I believe; therefore he died for me, for whosoever believes on the Son shall not perish, but have everlasting life. This is precisely our method. (c) No solid peace can be derived from that which is insufficient for salvation which neither prevents, nor alone can prevent, the preterition or damnation of innumerable multitudes (such as universal objective grace is without subjective). What will it avail the sinner to know that no one can be a partaker of that death without faith? Will he not always be anxious to know whether he is of the number of those to whom God wills to give faith, since it is not given to all? May not all the difficulties (*scrupulus*) which can be opposed to particular mercy and redemption be equally urged against a particular decree of bestowing faith? Therefore if the conscience cannot be solidly established (except on the supposition of the universal mercy of the Father and the universal redemption of the Son), it never can be except on the supposition of a universal call and grace of the Spirit. If the difficulty thence arose—Who knows whether Christ died for me, because he did not die for all?—may it not also arise thence, Who knows whether God wills to give me faith and whether I am of the number of the elect or of those passed by? Besides the fact that all such difficulties arise from a desire to know what it is not given to man to know (since it becomes no mortal to search *a priori* into the secrets of election and reprobation), man should proceed here *a posteriori* and examine himself as to whether he has truly repented of his sins or not. If he has, he ought to entertain a sure confidence of the grace of God and his own election. If he has not as yet, he ought to use the means prescribed by God to hear, read, ponder the word and pour out ardent prayers to God for the obtainment of the gifts of repentance and faith. Nor can any difficulties be brought forward on this subject, the solution of which does not rest upon our learned opponents equally with us (unless with the Arminians they wish to recognize universal subjective sufficient grace, which dogma as evidently Pelagian, they have through the grace of God constantly thus far professed to reject). Therefore a solid foundation of consolation can be sought, not from the universality of the death of Christ, but from the universality of the promises with respect to those who believe and repent.

LII. Although the reprobates who do not believe the gospel will be deservedly condemned for their unbelief, it does not follow that they were commanded to believe that Christ died for them. There are various acts of incredulity besides that: for example, he who does not believe that Jesus is the Son of the living God and the Messiah sent by God, but a false prophet and an impostor or that faith in him is a condition necessary to salvation, is deservedly considered guilty of unbelief, although he may never have thought of Christ's dying for him. For belief in him (which Christ so often demands and for the want of which he rebukes the Jews) embraces many things; nor was it at once to be believed by individuals among the Jews that Christ was their Mediator and Redeemer; nay this could not be believed unless many other things had preceded. For they must first have believed that salvation was not in the law, or in legal ceremonies and works; that it was to be sought only in the Messiah promised by the prophets; that Jesus of Nazareth was that Messiah and that all believing in him would be saved. All these somewhat general acts of faith must have preceded the belief that Christ had died for him. Nor can it be said that all these acts are comprehended in the command to believe on Christ and especially the appropriating and special act. As we have said above, although all these acts are included, still they are commanded in a certain order, some before, others after; nor the latter without the former, but only after the former have been exercised; and on the supposition of the first acts not having been performed, there could be no place for the latter.

LIII. Although by the preaching of the gospel, God offers Christ to the called with his benefits, it does not follow that he must have died for them in order that the offer may not be insincere. He is not offered absolutely and simply, but under the condition of faith and repentance; not as a narrated truth which, whether believed or not, always remains true, but as a promised truth which is ascertained to be true only when its condition is complied with (as Cameron declared). From this it follows that there is an indissoluble connection between faith and salvation and that all are bound to faith who wish to enjoy Christ and his benefits, and who are called to Christ; but that God, by his eternal and immutable decree, has destined Christ to be the Savior of all who are called or that he intended that Christ by his death should acquire eternal salvation for each and every man, can in no way be inferred from this call. For the word of the gospel which is preached to the called does not declare his eternal decree concerning each of the called—namely, that in it he destined redemption through Christ and salvation for each and every man. Rather it indicates the command of God to them with a promise annexed; or what is the duty of those who wish to be partakers of the redemption and salvation procured by him. Nor are we to suppose that on this account such an offer is adverse to his decree. Although it does not answer to the decree concerning persons by which he destined Christ as the Savior of the elect alone and his death as the price of their redemption and decreed to bestow upon them faith (because the expression and execution of this decree is not the external call through the word, but the internal of the Spirit, which is therefore called calling according to purpose [*kata prothesin*]), still it answers most completely to the decree respecting things or respecting the order and means of salvation by which it pleased God to connect Christ and faith together and to offer him to all the called. Christ speaks of this decree in Jn. 6:40: "And this is the will of him that sent me, that every one that seeth the Son and believeth on him, may have everlasting life." Thus the conditional promises made to those who believe and repent show to all the called the connection of faith with salvation according to the ordination of God and who of them will obtain remission of sins and salvation (to wit, believers and penitents). But they no more make known that Christ died for all the hearers of the gospel than that they shall all believe and obtain pardon of sin. However from the remission which they who believe and repent obtain, it follows certainly that Christ died for them. It would also follow of the others, if they would believe and repent. But he reasons falsely who would infer hence that Christ died for all, on condition that they would believe, because he would argue incorrectly from the conditioned to the absolute.

LIV. We take pleasure in weaving here into a crown the judgment of Diodati and Tronchin, the very celebrated theologians deputed to the Synod of Dort, who, in the name of the whole Genevan Church, presented to the venerable Synod this as the common faith of the church never to be given up: "Christ, out of the mere good pleasure (*eudokia*) of his Father, was appointed and given to be the Mediator and Head of certain number of men, constituting his mystical body by the election of God" (*Acta Synodi Nationalis . . . Dordrechti*, Head II, Th. 1 [1619-20], 2:130). "For these, Christ, fully aware of his vocation, willed and decreed to die, and to add to the infinite value of his death a most efficacious and special intention of his will" (Head II, Th. 2, ibid.). And: "The universal propositions, which are found in Scripture, do not signify that Christ died for each and every man and made satisfaction for them according to his Father's purpose and his own intention. But they must be restricted to the totality of Christ's body; or to be referred to that economy of the new covenant, by which, without regard to any external distinction of peoples, the Son receives for his inheritance all nations, that is, to all nations and peoples in common, at his pleasure, he reveals and sends the grace of preaching, and out of them gathers his church, which is the foundation of the general call of the gospel" (Head II, Th. 6, ibid., p. 132). For other matters pertaining to this subject, see Topic IV, Question 17 and Topic XII, Question 6.

Fifteenth Question: The Intercession of Christ
Why and how does Christ intercede for us?

I. The other part of Christ's priestly office consists in intercession. Concerning this three things may be remarked: (1) its necessity; (2) its unity; (3) its mode and nature. Of its unity, we treated under the unity of the Mediator (Question 4). We must now discuss briefly its necessity and its nature or mode.

The necessity of Christ's intercession is proved: (1) from its institution by God.

II. Various arguments prove the necessity of his intercession. (1) The institution of God, who wished two parts to be in the priesthood—satisfaction and intercession; just as under the Old Testament the high priest was bound to do two things in virtue of his office—first, to offer a victim upon the altar of whole burnt offerings; second, to carry the blood of the offered victim into the holy place and to burn incense upon the altar of incense. Having finished his sacrifice on earth upon the cross, Christ must intercede in heaven. Hence Paul testifies if he were on earth, he should not be a priest (Heb. 8:4) because he ought not to exercise his service (*leitourgian*) in an earthly temple (one made with hands), but in the heavenly.

2. From the method of our salvation.

III. (2) The method of our salvation; it was not sufficient to obtain salvation once, unless it could be perpetually preserved and applied. Christ obtained the former by his satisfaction, but the latter he should procure by his intercession. By the former, he obtained salvation; by the latter he preserves it. By the former, he purchased the right to life and reconciled us to God; by the latter, he actually admits us to a participation of life and continually keeps us when once established in the grace of God.

3. From our unworthiness.

IV. (3) The consideration of our unworthiness; since we are not such as could approach God by ourselves (who is a consuming fire), it was necessary that a Mediator should interpose for our help to secure our access to God so that we might come with confidence to the throne of grace. And because we offend God every day, we need an advocate to intercede for us every day.

4. From the accusation of the Devil.

V. (4) The accusation of the Devil; for as he continually criminates and accuses us to God, we have need of a most efficacious advocate to plead our cause before God, against the charges of a most unjust adversary—to stop his mouth (Zech. 3:2) and to wash away the guilt of the crimes laid to our charge (Rom. 8:33).

What is intercession?

VI. Concerning the nature of his intercession, the Socinians err maintaining that it is to be understood figuratively and as properly belonging to his kingly office and that nothing else is meant by it than that "Christ, furnished with divine power, zealously accomplishes all things pertaining to the method of our salvation," as Volkelius expresses it (*De vera Religione* 3.38 [1630], p. 149). They wish this to be designated by the word "intercession" that it may appear that Christ has the power to govern us and to procure our salvation, not at all from himself, but from the Father. Thus they overthrow the whole priesthood of Christ, making him a pure King. But the orthodox think that a real intercession is to be held as a part of his priestly office, distinct from the kingly.

Christ intercedes as a Priest.

VII. The reasons are: (1) Christ is everywhere introduced as performing the office of intercession, not as a King, but as a Priest: "Christ is not entered into the holy places made with hands, the figures of the true; but into heaven itself, now to appear in the presence of God for us" (Heb. 9:24, 25). The apostle manifestly alludes to the high priest of the Old Testament, who, having offered the sacrifice, entered into the holy place with the blood of the victim to intercede for the people. Hence it is described by appearing (*emphanismon*) before the face of God, which cannot be referred to an exercise of his regal power, but properly to a priestly intercession.

VIII. (2) In the same sense, he is called our Advocate (*paraklētos*) with God (1 Jn. 2:1) that he may supplicate for the pardon of our sins and plead our cause as an Advocate and defender with God against the slanderous charges of Satan, "the accuser [*katēgorou*] of the brethren" (Rev. 12:10). The Holy Spirit is indeed distinguished by the same name (Jn. 14:26), but with a different meaning. For as the word sometimes signifies an adviser or teacher and master, sometimes an advocate, then again a comforter, Christ is properly called a *paraklētos* under the second notion on account of his intercession. But the Holy Spirit is so called under the first and third because they belong to him both as teacher and master (who must lead us into all truth) and as consoler to encourage us by the promises of grace and to excite in us groanings which cannot be uttered, by which we may cry unto God.

IX. (3) In Rev. 8:3, the intercession of Christ is represented to us by the angel with the golden censer, to whom was given much incense to offer with the prayers of the saints on the golden altar before the throne. These are truly sacerdotal, not kingly acts. For it is elsewhere proved that this can be referred only to Christ, the objections of our opponents being refuted.

X. (4) If his intercession is nothing else than an employment of the kingly power, these two offices (carefully distinguished in Scripture) would be confounded. Nor should Christ have been adumbrated by and compared with priests, but with kings only.

Sources of explanation.

XI. The intercession ascribed to Christ does not derogate from his glory because it is not supplicatory and after the manner of a request (like that of saints on earth and men praying for themselves); but an efficacious address after the manner of jurisdiction (as it is commonly called) by which Christ repeatedly represents to God his blood once shed that by its virtue and efficacy our sins may be pardoned and the gift of perseverance granted to us. This proves an economy of office, but does not lessen his glory. On this account, Paul claims both distinctly for Christ, his sitting at the right hand and his intercession for us (Rom. 8:34), in order to indicate that both properly belong to him: the former belongs to him as a King; the latter to him as a Priest.

XII. As the humanity of Christ does not hinder us from invoking and adoring him as a supreme and omnipotent King because he is not a mere man, but the eternal God equally with the Father; so his divine and regal power does not prevent him from interceding for us because he is God-man (*theanthropos*) and as such the Mediator between God and men.

What is the mode of his intercession?

XIII. As to the mode of his intercession: (1) the circumstances of prayer are not to be considered as belonging to it, as if he knelt after the manner of suppliants, raised his hands or eyes to heaven and prostrated himself before God (which would be inconsistent with the glory he obtained by his sitting down at the right hand of God); but only the substance of prayer, by which he declares and asks for the blessings necessary to us. (2) This intercession is made either in express words or interpretatively; more in things than in words by a representation of his death in heaven, in which the blood of Christ is said to speak (Heb. 12:24). (3) In whatever manner it is made, we must not suppose that it is made to obtain anything by way of new merit because Christ finished all things in his death (as he himself testifies, Jn. 17:4; 19:30, as does Paul, Heb. 7:28; 10:14). Rather we must hold that what he acquired for us by the merit of his death may be actually and efficaciously applied to us for salvation.

XIV. This intercession consists of various acts. (1) The appearing of Christ for us by which he places himself before God the Father as the only satisfier for our sins, representing the blood once shed (i.e., the merit of his death) and asking that at the sight of it he would pardon our sins and bestow upon us all blessings necessary to salvation, until he has conducted us into the possession of full felicity: "Father, I will that they also whom thou hast given me, be with me where I am; that they may behold my glory" (Jn. 17:24). Hence the Lamb is seen standing in heaven, as it had been slain (*hōs esphagmenos*, Rev. 5:6) because his blood is ever fresh and living (i.e., of eternal virtue and efficacy). (2) Our defense and protection against the thunderbolts of the law and the accusations of Satan, pleading our cause at the tribunal of God. (3) His suretyship for us by which as he demands grace from the Father and the gifts of the Spirit necessary to our perseverance, so in turn in our name he promises to God obedience and fidelity. (4) The offering of our persons and the sanctification of our prayers and of our entire worship, inasmuch as he presents all our prayers to God as spiritual sacrifices, perfumed with the most fragrant odor of his own sacrifice, so that in and through him they may be pleasing and acceptable to God (1 Pet. 2:5). Hence he is represented as an angel with a burning censer (Rev. 8:3) to whom is given much incense, that he should offer it with the prayers of saints. Elsewhere he is called an altar upon which all our sacrifices must be placed and on which alone the rational worship we render to God can be pleasing to him.

XV. Hence it appears how widely and greatly the prayers which believers offer for each other differ from the intercession of Christ. For Christ alone intercedes for us, relying upon his own merit and righteousness, by himself alone and on account of himself obtains what he seeks, approaches God by himself immediately and without any other intercessor, by himself stands in our place and appears before God, by himself offers to God our persons, prayers and actions. But believers neither rely upon their own merit, nor seek nor obtain anything by and on account of themselves, but only in the name of Christ. Nor do they dare approach immediately to God without Christ, nor presume to stand in our place before God, nor can they present to him our persons and prayers. Hence the Romanists unite the intercession of Christ with secondary intercessors with no less sacrilege than when they unite his sacrifice with secondary priests; nor is this crime diminished by their distinction between mediators of intercession and mediators of redemption (as has already been seen).

XVI. But when intercession is ascribed to Christ, it must not be so restricted to his human nature as to remove it wholly from the divine considered in personal union with it. Although it cannot belong to the latter with respect to essence absolutely (since it is one with the Father under this relation [*schesei*]), prayer cannot be predicated of it (by which he demands something from the Father). Still there is nothing to prevent our ascribing intercession to it according to the economy of grace because to pray is just as consistent with it as to take the form of a servant and to undertake the mediatorial work.

SIXTEENTH QUESTION: THE KINGDOM OF CHRIST

Whether the economical kingdom of Christ is temporal and earthly or spiritual and heavenly. The former we deny; we assert the latter against the Jews.

I. The third part of the mediatorial office is his kingdom (to wit, that dignity and authority with which he governs the church by his word and Spirit and defends and preserves it against all enemies). Its necessity, truth and nature must be considered.

Christ's kingdom is twofold: natural and economical.

II. But before all things we must distinguish the twofold kingdom, belonging to Christ: one natural or essential; the other mediatorial and economical. Christ possesses the former over all creatures with glory and majesty equal to that of the Father and Holy Spirit. The latter (according to the economy of grace) he administers in a peculiar manner as God-man (*theanthrōpos*). The former extends equally over all creatures; the latter is terminated specially on the church. That is founded on the decree of providence, this on the decree of election. That is exercised by Christ inasmuch as he is God (*Theos*) and the Logos (*Logos*); this inasmuch as he is God-man (*theanthrōpos*). Hence it is called his "mediatorial and economical kingdom" because it is a dominion peculiar to the Mediator and as it were his own according to the dispensation of grace. The other belongs to him by nature and is on that account called "natural." The mediatorial belongs to him from the free institution of God because he constituted him King over the church (Ps. 2:6).

The necessity of the mediatorial kingdom is proved.

III. The necessity of Christ's mediatorial kingdom depends upon three particulars: (1) the decree of God, who elected him from eternity; (2) the method of our salvation, which requires not only the annunciation of it by Christ as a Prophet and the acquisition of it by him as a Priest, but also the application and conservation of it forever by him as a King; (3) the most dangerous enemies (more powerful than the world and hell), against whom we need the protection and guard of a King; such, Christ alone can be, the Lord of heaven and earth, the King of kings and the Lord of lords (Rev. 17:14).

Its truth is gathered from prophecies and types.

IV. That Christ ought to be a true King appears not only from the first promise, concerning the seed of the woman which was to bruise the head of the serpent or concerning the victory to be gained by Christ over Satan (which clearly pertained to the kingly office of Christ particularly); it also appears from the various remarkable prophecies which ascribe this dignity to the Messiah (Pss. 2; 45; 72; 89; 110; Dan. 2; Jer. 23:5, 6; Zech. 6; 9; Is. 11). It also appears from the many illustrious types given concerning it, but especially in the kingdoms of David and Solomon who (all confess) above all others prefigured Christ: the former, Christ suffering and struggling; the latter, Christ victorious and reigning in peace.

It consists of two parts: destination and calling.

V. As the constitution of the kingdom is resolved into two parts—eternal destination and calling, and inauguration in time—so its administration and exercise consist principally in four things: (1) in the calling and gathering of the church; (2) the conservation and government of the same; (3) the protection and defense of it against all its enemies; (4) the full and perfect glorification of it, to be made on the last day. The first three pertain to this life through grace; the fourth to the future life in glory.

Statement of the question.

VI. The question here is not Ought Christ, the Messiah, to be a King? For the Jews agree with us that he should. Rather the question concerns the manner of that kingdom—whether it should be mundane and earthly, or spiritual and heavenly. The former is held by the Jews, who from an erroneous view of the prophecies concerning the glory of the Messiah, expect a temporal and earthly King. He will bring them (now exiles) back to their native land with a great slaughter of their enemies and will give them every kind of happiness. This opinion prevailed among the Jews even in the time of Christ, not only among their own leading men, but also among the apostles themselves, who hopefully anticipated earthly administrations and contended for supremacy; yea, even after his resurrection they asked him, "Wilt thou at this time restore again the kingdom to Israel?" (Acts 1:6). However because of the various allusions in the Old Testament to the sufferings of the Messiah (inconsistent with the glory of such a kingdom), the more modern Jews have invented a twofold Messiah—one of whom will be the son of Joseph, humble and poor and exposed to various persecutions; the other, the son of David, strong and powerful, who will reign with magnificence in the world. This delirium is easily refuted from the consent of the ancients (who recognized only one Messiah) as well as from the Scripture itself, which speaks of only one to whom two states would belong—humility and glory. Hence the orthodox infer that his kingdom is not mundane and earthly, but spiritual and celestial.

Proof that the kingdom of Christ is not earthly but spiritual: (1) from Gen. 49:10 and Dan. 9:26.

VII. First, from the prophecies of the Old Testament, the Messiah was to come when the scepter should be removed from Judah and the legislative power taken away (Gen. 49:10); as was actually the case in the time of Christ, the Jews being under the power of the Romans. Hence he could not be a temporal King because to be a King and to be subject to another are inconsistent. Daniel refers his appearance to the time when the city and temple were to be overthrown and no trace of them would remain (Dan. 9:26).

2. Because it was adumbrated by earthly kingdoms.

VIII. Second, the kingdom of Christ was adumbrated by various temporal kingdoms. Now corporeal and earthly things are not types of things both corporeal and worldly homogeneous with them, but of better and more excellent (namely, of spiritual things). The figure must be inferior to the thing figured by it; the shadow to the substance. Since the government of the Old Testament (adumbrating the kingdom of Christ) was corporeal, the kingdom of Christ must be spiritual.

3. Because the things pertaining to this kingdom are spiritual: the King; his throne; his scepter; his subjects.

IX. Third, all that pertains to this kingdom is spiritual, not mundane and earthly: (a) the King humble and poor (Zech. 9:9), who should come without form and comeliness as a rod out of the stem of Jesse (Is. 11:1); who came in the form of a servant to minister, not to be ministered unto (Mt. 20:28); who subjected himself to the authority of the Romans and paid tribute to them (which everyone sees to be incompatible [*asystata*] with an earthly kingdom). (b) His throne is not earthly and visible, but divine and heavenly; at the right hand of God where he should sit (Ps. 110:1). (c) His scepter is not material, but mystical (to wit, the word of the gospel, Is. 2:3). This is truly called "a scepter of strength" (Ps. 110:2) because it is the power of God unto salvation and the arm of the Lord (Rom. 1:16; Is. 53:1). (d) His subjects are not earthly and carnal men, but spiritual and heavenly; regenerated by the Spirit, born not of flesh, but of God (Jn. 1:13*), whose citizenship (*politeuma*) is in heaven (Phil. 3:20); a willing (*ndhbhvth*) people (Ps. 110:3), who would spring from the womb of the morning (i.e., from the light of the gospel) and spiritually adorned with the beauties of holiness.

The mode of his administration; laws.

(e) The mode of administration is entirely spiritual, not by might nor by power, but by his Spirit (Zech. 4:6; Hos. 2:18; 2 Cor. 10:4). (f) The spiritual laws are those which regulate not only the external, but also the internal acts of a man and transfer them from earthly and corporeal to heavenly and divine things—a service not carnal and bodily consisting in external ceremonies, but spiritual in Spirit and in truth (Jn. 4:24; Rom. 12:1; 1 Pet. 2:5).

Blessings.

(g) The blessings promised are not temporal (although they are sometimes represented by figures of them), but spiritual and heavenly: remission of sins, eternal righteousness, the gift of the Spirit, salvation and everlasting life.

4. From the end of the kingdom.

X. Fourth, the Messiah was to come for the purpose of abolishing the tyrannical kingdom of Satan (introduced by sin), to expiate sin and to bring in everlasting righteousness (Dan. 9:24). Now these things could only be done spiritually; for as Satan, the prince of this world, reigned among men through their errors and sins, so Christ is the King of the church (Satan having been conquered through the death of the cross, Col. 2:15) and reigns spiritually in the hearts of believers by faith, love and the practice of good works.

5. Because it is the kingdom of heaven.

XI. Fifth, the Messiah's kingdom is the kingdom of heaven (as it is everywhere in Scripture distinguished by this name and recognized by the Jews themselves), which therefore pertains not to the world, but to heaven. It is heavenly (a) in origin because not human power and wisdom, but divine providence alone inaugurated it; (b) in state because it consists entirely in things celestial, mystical and divine, and not in things earthly and corporeal; (c) in act because wholly occupied with the distribution of heavenly blessings (Rom. 14:17).

6. Because it is not of this world.

XII. Sixth, the kingdom of Christ is not of this world (Jn. 18:36). Christ does not deny that his kingdom is in this world, for he was appointed by God to rule in the midst of his enemies (Ps. 110:2); but he does deny that his kingdom is "of this world" and (as he adds in the end of the verse) "my kingdom is not from hence" (*enteuthen*). He does not say, "My kingdom is not" here, but "it is not" hence; "it is in the world" but "not of the world," as Augustine says ("Tractate 115," *On the Gospel of St. John* [NPNF1, 7:424; PL 35.1939]). It is not of the world as to origin because it is not constituted by the world and by men living in the world like the kingdoms of the world. Rather it has God as its sole and immediate founder, by whose authority it was erected and by whose power it is strengthened. It is not of the world as to mode because the kingdoms of the world consist of and are defended by a multitude of subjects, number of provinces, crowds of cities, abundance of riches, bristling forts, armed garrisons and other external means, without which they would necessarily fall. But the kingdom of Christ (as we have already said) is conducted in a spiritual manner, recognizes no other honors and resources than righteousness, holiness, peace of conscience, salvation and eternal life; no other arms than the word and Spirit; no other fortifications than the protection of God. Pilate had this understanding of it; he clearly perceived that no prejudice could be created from it against the empire of Caesar; otherwise he would not only have agreed with the accusation of the Jews charging Christ with rebellion against Caesar, but would have been the first to think of taking him out of the way. However since, having dismissed this accusation of the Jews and Christ's own confession concerning his kingly office, he pronounces him just and innocent and desires him to be cleared from condemnation (for he knew that for envy they had delivered him, Mt. 27:18), he sufficiently demonstrates that he did not believe it was a temporal kingdom opposed to the sway of Caesar which Christ ascribed to himself.

Sources of explanation.

XIII. When the angel says, "The Lord God shall give unto him the throne of David, and of his kingdom there shall be no end" (Lk. 1:32), he does not wish to teach that the kingdom of Christ would be temporal like that of David; but that the kingdom of Christ was typified by the kingdom of David, so that the kingdom of David ought to be perfected and consummated by Christ's kingdom, not temporally (because it is evident that it was to be taken away at the coming of Christ), but in a spiritual and mystical manner (as Christ himself is called "David"). Thus what is said concerning the eternity of his kingdom must be understood not as to the letter and type, but as the antitype and the truth itself (which ought to be fulfilled in Christ in a far more excellent manner).

XIV. Although temporal kingdoms are subjected to Christ, his kingdom ought not on that account to be temporal. They are not subjected to and administered by him temporally and in an earthly manner, but spiritually and divinely; even as the earth is under heaven and is ruled by him, it is not therefore done in an earthly but in a heavenly way. Indeed he reigns differently in the pious and the wicked: in the former by the sweet and healthful influence of the Spirit, as head; in the latter, by his own powerful virtue as Lord; but over both he exercises a spiritual, not an earthly sway.

XV. The various oracles concerning the restitution and perpetual duration of the government and kingdom of the Jews, adduced by the Jews to prove the temporal kingdom of the Messiah (such as Dt. 30:3-5; Ezk. 37:24, 25; Dan. 7:27; Mic. 4:6-8), neither can nor ought to be understood literally (*kata to rhēton*), but mystically and spiritually. (1) It is usual with the prophets to speak of the things of the New Testament in legal terms and under the covering of corporeal things to adumbrate things spiritual and heavenly. If these are pressed to the letter, they would give either no sense or an absurd one. (2) The promises given there concerning spiritual blessings cannot be fulfilled in the carnal, but in the spiritual Israel. (3) If Christ ought to have erected a temporal kingdom in Judea, he would not have suffered Jerusalem to be levelled to the ground, the temple to be overthrown and all that belonged to the Jewish state and polity to be abolished. (4) The reasons for the institution of the Jewish polity cease by the advent of Christ and by the calling of the Gentiles.

XVI. Although the Messiah is opposed to earthly kings (Ps. 2:6) and it is said that he will break them with a rod of iron (v. 9), it does not follow that his should be a worldly kingdom. Although it is not earthly, nothing prevents him from subduing earthly kings in a spiritual manner (as God is the conqueror of all monarchs in a spiritual manner). And what is added concerning the rod of iron must be understood metaphorically with this meaning, just as a potter's vessel is dashed in pieces when struck by an iron rod. Thus also these nations shall be broken by the word of the gospel, which is the scepter or rod of his strength. This is confirmed from this—that the things predicated of the Messiah in Ps. 2 are promised in Rev. 2:26, 27 to all who overcome to denote their spiritual power in the other world.

XVII. Ps. 72 must be understood immediately and literally of Solomon, a type of Christ; mediately, however, and mystically of Christ, his antitype. Thus in the explication, we must consider what things are consistent with and agreeable to the type and what to the antitype. As to the former, corporeal and earthly things are designated (such as he himself was); but as to the latter, spiritual and divine things are designated.

Seventeenth Question: The Eternity of Christ's Kingdom

Is the mediatorial kingdom of Christ to continue forever? We affirm.

I. The second condition of Christ's kingdom is its eternity, concerning which we have a controversy with the Socinians. In order to impair the dignity and divinity of our Mediator, they maintain that this kingdom will come to an end on the last day and its ultimate act will be the judgment of the whole world; then his kingdom and regal authority will be given up to the Father. With them agree (although with a different feeling and intention) those of the orthodox who think that Christ's mediatorial kingdom will end with the world in order that a place may be given to his essential kingdom alone, by which God will be all in all.

II. And although this question (as agitated among the orthodox) is problematic (concerning which either side can be taken without destroying the foundation of faith, provided that it is firmly held against the Socinians that Christ will forever be the King of his church—whether as Mediator or as God), still the affirmative appears to us to be the more suitable to the oracles of Scripture and the truer.

Statement of the question.

III. On the state of the question, we observe first—the mediatorial kingdom of Christ can be viewed either as to its very substance or as to the form and mode of administration. This can be either immediate and internal or external and mediate, carried on by the intervention of the ministry of angels and of men and occupied in protecting the church against enemies (by whom it is continually assailed on earth) and in dashing to pieces and utterly destroying them. The mode of administration can be changed and abrogated, the substance of the kingdom ever remaining. In this way faith (it is said) will be changed into vision, not as to substance of knowledge (which always remains the same; yea, will even be more perfect), but as to mode, inasmuch as faith will no longer rest upon the word and be attended with obscurity, but will behold God himself face to face. The question here does not concern the mode of its administration (which all confess will be changed), but only concerns the substance of the kingdom (which some contend will cease). We hold that it will remain forever.

IV. Second, mediation includes three principal parts: (1) the acquisition of salvation; (2) the application of it when acquired; (3) the conservation of it when applied. We are not treating of the first and second, for Christ so performs them in this life that there will be no more room for them in the life to come. In this sense, we readily grant that the mediation of Christ will cease because there will be no more need of acquisition or of any new application. But we treat of its conservation, in reference to which we contend that Christ will perpetually conserve the blessings obtained for us and so will reign forever over his church.

The eternity of Christ's kingdom is proved: (1) from 2 S. 7:12, 13; Lk. 1:33; Dan. 7:14.

V. The reasons are: (1) the Scriptures often predicate eternity of that kingdom (as in 2 S. 7:12, 13 where it is said "the throne of Christ will be stablished forever"; to which these words of Lk. 1:33 answer, "of his kingdom there shall be no end"; in Dan. 7:14, it is said "to the Son of man was given a kingdom, which shall not pass away, nor be destroyed"). Nor can it be objected: (a) that not an absolute, but a defined eternity is meant because it refers to Solomon, whose kingdom did cease. Although this may be said of the type (viz., of Solomon, who was a figure of Christ), it cannot apply to Christ, the antitype, to whom eternity properly so called belongs (which the words both in Samuel and in Luke designate). (b) That Christ will reign as God, but not as Mediator. Christ is referred to not as God simply, but as Mediator inasmuch as he ought to sit upon the throne of David (i.e., to fulfill in a mystery what David had in a figure, which belongs not to his essential but to his mediatorial kingdom).

2. From Dan. 2:44.

VI. Second, "this kingdom was never to be destroyed, nor left to other people" (Dan. 2:44). For reference is made here to the kingdom of Christ, which he should hold after the destruction of the four monarchies and kingdoms represented in the statue of Daniel. All Christians agree on this, whether by the fourth kingdom is understood the Roman Empire or the kingdom of the Seleucids and Lagids (i.e., from Lagos, father of Ptolemy I), the successors of Alexander (about which all are not agreed). It is said that it will never be destroyed, in opposition to earthly kingdoms which (of whatever nature or dignity they might be adumbrated by gold, silver, brass and iron [i.e., by metals of different value and price]) were to be overturned, whether by external violence or by internal discord and their own weakness (by which permanency is denied to earthly things). But this is such a kingdom that it can be overthrown neither from within nor from without, being fixed (*asaleuton*) and immovable (Heb. 12:28).

3. From the functions of mediation.

VII. Third, the various functions of the mediatorial office were to be perpetual. (a) As to prophecy because it is said that he will illuminate the saints forever; the city will not need the sun and the moon for "the glory of God will lighten it and the Lamb will be the light thereof" (Rev. 21:22, 23); and the Lamb shall feed them and lead them unto living fountains of water (Rev. 7:17). (b) As to the priesthood by a perpetual representation of his sacrifice as the foundation of the glory we shall possess that was not only to be purchased, but also conserved forever. For things are conserved forever because things are conserved by the same means and methods by which they are acquired. Hence it is called an "unchangeable" (*aparabaton*) priesthood (Heb. 7:24). (c) As to his kingdom, he will always reign in the church as her head and surety by an indissoluble (*adialyton*) union; not surely as God only, but also as Mediator. Hence it is distinctly set forth as "the kingdom of our Lord and of his Christ" (Rev. 11:15; 12:10) and the consummation of marriage is set forth by the marriage of the Lamb with the church (Rev. 19:7). Since this should be eternal and indissoluble, it involves the eternity also of the operation and relation of Christ as Mediator (as of a husband towards the church, his spouse).

4. From the bond of union with God.

VIII. Fourth, Christ is the bond of our perpetual union with God. For since the creature by himself can neither approach God nor continue in communion with him, it was necessary that as by Christ he once approached God, so by the same he should adhere forever to him through his power and efficacy. Nor can the members of Christ's mystical body derive life and glory from any other source than from the influx of the head, with whom they ought forever to remain united. Nor is 1 Cor. 15:28 ("God will be all in all") opposed to this because this must be understood with respect to external means which are available in this life (to wit, the word, the sacraments and the like), by which we see God in a mirror and enigmatically only and cleave to him by faith; intimating that God will immediately and by himself make us fully partakers of his own blessedness, but not to the exclusion of Christ, the head of the church, from whom all blessings in her are derived.

Sources of explanation.

IX. When it is said that Christ will sit at the right hand of the Father until the Father shall make his enemies his footstool (Ps. 110:1), the dominion of Christ (in which he ought to reign among his enemies) is indeed affirmed during the whole time of this life, yet the eternity of his kingdom in the world to come is not denied. Thus often in Scripture these particles *khy*, *'dh*, *achris hou* or *heōs hou* ("until," "even until") cover indeed the present or past time (concerning which a doubt might arise); but they do not deny and exclude the future. Thus it is said that Christ will be with his disciples even unto the end of the world (Mt. 28:20) to assure them of his presence in the midst of perils and trials, but not to the exclusion of his communion with them forever. The same meaning attaches to Gen. 28:15 and Ps. 123:2. Because, then, a doubt might arise how Christ could hold a kingdom in the midst of the assaults of so many enemies, the Holy Spirit wished to confirm our faith in this particular (the eternal duration of his kingdom not being denied).

X. The "kingdom" which "Christ will deliver up to God and the Father" (i.e., to God his Father, 1 Cor. 15:24) can be understood in two ways: either materially and subjectively for the church itself, constituting the mystical body of Christ; or for its subjects, as elsewhere the kingdom of Christ is often put for his people. Thus the sense is that Christ (the work of salvation having been consummated) will bring to the Father the church perfectly consummated and redeemed from all enemies, to be fully blessed according to the oracle of Isaiah. This is claimed for Christ: "Behold I, and the children which God hath given me" (Heb. 2:13); but still in such a way that he will always remain its head. Or it may be understood formally, not as to the very substance of the kingdom, but only as to the mode of its administration, which is concerned with collecting, governing and defending the church from her enemies (which will have no more place after all her enemies are vanquished). Thus he will deliver up the kingdom, not by a deposition and abdication of it, but by an exhibition of it as consummated. He will return it to God, who had delivered it to Christ (the method of administration entrusted to him) and will ascribe to his glory whatever he has done. What is expressed in the beginning of the verse concerning the "end" does not pertain to the end of his kingdom, but to the end of the world; the end of all Christ's enemies who will then be so overthrown that they can never recover themselves; the end of every power and empire, which Paul asserts will be abolished; the end, in fine, of all the instrumentalities which God appointed for the protection of the good and the restraint of the wicked (which will then cease because God will be all in all).

XI. The subjection attributed to Christ (1 Cor. 15:28) must not be referred to the person of the Son (as if from a King he would become a subject) because in this sense he always was and will be equal with the Father. Rather it must be referred either to his mystical body or the church (which is frequently designated by the name of Christ, 1 Cor. 12:12), which will then be perfectly subjected to God; not by a subjection of depression, but of glory and perfection so that as all things were subjected to the saints by God in the person of their head (Ps. 8:4-6; Heb. 2:5-8); so the head may be subjected to God in the person of his members. Or it may be referred to the humanity of Christ, which (as created) ought to be subjected to God forever; or to his office and mediation, according to which he should be subjected to the Father in heaven no less than on the earth, as inferior to him not by the deposition of his office, but by a subordination of it.

XII. It is said that "God will be all in all" (1 Cor. 15:28) exclusive of the external means—the word, sacraments and the like by which God communicates himself to us here. For he will then communicate himself to the saints without such means; we will no longer behold him in a mirror and darkly, but will see him most clearly face to face (but not to the exclusion of Christ, the head and Bridegroom of the church, who will always be the bond of our communion with God). Further, God will be "all in all," not absolutely and simply (as if even the devils themselves will be saved), but as to subject matter, with regard to believers and saints, whom he will make most fully to partake of his own happiness (in opposition to the manner in which he communicates himself to us with restrictions and limitations, in accordance with the condition of life; as to parts, but not as to degree; as to grace, but not as to glory). But then God will be all in all saints; as to fulness of blessings (which are required for every species of happiness) since God will give himself wholly to them; as to fulness of degrees that those blessings may be such as to admit of no addition as to intensity, no more than as to extent; as to fulness of subjects that to all the saints all these blessings and to individuals all things undividedly may be communicated, both in body and in soul for their perfect consummation.

XIII. The work of salvation having been finished and consummated, there is no further need of the economical mediation (which relates to the acquisition and application of salvation); but the truth of our union with Christ, the head, always remains, by which the benefits once bestowed are conserved forever.

XIV. Although Christ as Logos (*Logos*) with the Father and the Holy Spirit will exercise an essential kingdom over the saints, still this will not prevent him from reigning over them as God-man (*theanthrōpos*) and as Mediator; as now the kingdom of nature, which exists in the world, does not take away the kingdom of grace in the church.

XV. Nothing hinders the kingdom of Christ from being called at the same time both temporal and eternal; the former with respect to the mode of government which obtains in this life among enemies; the latter properly and by itself because it will never have an end, either as to the King himself or as to his subjects or as to his glorious administration (Dan. 7:14; Lk. 1:33; Rev. 21, 22).

Eighteenth Question: The Adoration and Worship Due to Christ as Mediator

Is Christ to be adored as Mediator? We distinguish.

I. Since among the effects and consequences of the hypostatical union is wont to be placed the honor of adoration and the religious worship due to Christ, the God-man (*theanthrōpō*), our Mediator, a controversy may be urged concerning it and has been urged before this; not only by the Socinians (who either deny that Christ ought to be adored or deny that his divinity can be proved from such adoration and worship), but also among the orthodox.

Occasion of the question.

II. Not only the Romanists gave occasion to the question (who diligently inquire concerning the adoration of the human nature of Christ; cf. Thomas Aquinas, ST, III, Q. 25, Art. 1-3, pp. 2153-56); also the Lutheran Ubiquitarians, who dispute concerning the adoration of the body of Christ, or of Christ according to his human nature and as he is Mediator (cf. Eckhard, *Fasciculus controversiarum Theologicarum* 6.12 [1631], pp. 134-40 and Balduinus in Cas. Consci. li. 2, c. 5+ and others); but especially the Socinians. For when the orthodox strive to prove the eternal deity of Christ and his consubstantiality (*to homoousion*) from the honor and adoration due to him, they (to escape this argument) make an exception to the consequence of the major by distinguishing between the worship and adoration which is given to the eternal God, the Father (as the first cause), and that which is given to Christ, the Mediator, as such (i.e., as the second, middle and subordinate cause of all that pertains to salvation). Each adoration is indeed divine, but not supreme; only the former and not the latter are supreme so that Christ is not to be acknowledged as the ultimate end of adoration (cf. "Of the Person of Christ," Sec. IV, Chap. 1, *Racovian Catechism* [1818], pp. 156-57; Socinus, "De Jesu Christi Filii Dei . . . adversus Andream Volanum," *Opera omnia* [1656], 2:371-422). Hence the argument proposed by them—the adoration given to Christ as Mediator does not belong to God as such (or because he is such) and consequently does not prove his deity or consubstantiality (*homoousion*); but adoration is given to Christ as Mediator, therefore . . . etc. This was answered by some through a denial of the minor. Hence arose the question concerning the adoration of Christ as Mediator, about which there is a division—some affirming and others denying.

III. Although we must confess that aside from the Socinian controversy concerning the adoration due to Christ (of which we have already spoken), this question (as agitated among the orthodox) is problematic and less principal (concerning which it may be disputed on both sides without injury to faith; yea, it even admits of much logomachy). Still it is easy for anyone to understand that it is of some importance (after the snares of the Socinians have been detected and their hiding place in that distinction concerning the worship of Christ as Mediator has been found out) that we should be able to dispute against them more strongly and successfully.

Statement of the question.

IV. That the state of the question may be more rightly held (in positing which various errors are usual), we observe: (1) that the question does not concern the adoration of Christ, the Mediator, nor what is the material object (if it is proper so to speak) of the adoration, to which the adoration is directed; for concerning this all the orthodox agree against the Socinians that Christ, the God-man (*theanthrōpon*), our Mediator, is to be adored with religious adoration and such as is due to God alone. Rather the question concerns the formal object or the relation under which Christ is to be adored—whether it is only the deity of Christ or also his humanity and mediation, or the mediatorial office. Whether he is to be adored as God only or also as Mediator. And because these particles—"as," "inasmuch as," "because," etc.—are accustomed to be taken more widely and specificatively (that the object about which something is done may be specified); or more strictly and reduplicatively (when it is limited by the relation according to which the predicate agrees with its subject), they are not taken here in the first, but in the latter sense. The question is not whether Christ as Mediator specificatively (i.e., who is Mediator) is to be adored, but reduplicatively (as such and under that formal relation).

V. (2) The question does not concern the motives and reasons on account of which Christ can and ought to be adored and worshipped. For all agree that these are to be sought not only from the preeminence (*hyperochē*) of his divine majesty, but also from the various benefits bestowed by him upon us, whether in creation or in redemption. Rather the question concerns the foundation which establishes adorability or concerns the ultimate term to which the adoration is directed and on which it terminates. Some make this the deity alone, others the Mediator also.

VI. For the decision of the question, four things must be accurately distinguished here: (1) the object which is adored; (2) the foundation or the formal relation under which he is adored; (3) the motive and reasons on account of which he is adored; (4) the adjunct without which he is not adored. The object is the person of the Mediator, not as God or man simply, but as God-man (*theanthrōpos*). The foundation of adoration is the deity alone because nothing besides God is to be adored. The motive is not the excellency of the divinity alone, but the various offices and benefits of Christ and especially the mediation itself. The adjunct is the body or his human nature, without which the person is not adored. We consider this subject under four propositions.

VII. First, "adoration is due to Christ, the Mediator, and properly belongs to the person of the Mediator, and pertains to it." Concerning this there is no dispute among the orthodox who (against the Socinians) defend the justice and necessity of the adoration of Christ from the express oracles of Scripture: Pss. 2:11, 12; 97:7; Heb. 1:6; Mt. 2:2, 11; 8:2; 9:18; 14:33; 15:25; 28:9, 17; Lk. 24:52; Jn. 2:23; 9:38; Acts 7:59, 60). This is so not only as he is the Logos (*Logos*) and the Son of God, but also as he is the God-man (*theanthrōpos*) and Mediator because faith is due to him as such and distinct from the Father (Jn. 14:1); worship is due to him as Judge and the Son of man (Jn. 5:22, 23), as God incarnate coming into the world (Heb. 1:6), as the Lamb (Rev. 5:12), as the Redeemer (1 Cor. 6:20), as Lord, who on account of his humbling himself is exalted and has obtained a name above every name, that at the name of Jesus every knee should bow (Phil. 2:7ff.); and as the spouse of the church (Ps. 45:11). Now this adoration is properly due to his person and belongs to it. "For honor is properly given to the whole subsisting thing," as Thomas Aquinas well expresses it ("actions and passions belong to individual, incommunicable subsistences," ST, III, Q. 25, Art. 1, p. 2153).

VIII. Second, "the foundation and formal relation of adoration is not either the human nature or the mediatorial office, but the divinity only." Nothing created is by itself adorable; only the divine essence, infinite, omniscient, omnipotent and eternal (which has supreme excellency [*hyperochēn*] and majesty above all things) can admit of legitimate adoration because it is a confession and celebration of omniscience, omnipresence and omnipotence (since God alone can know and hear prayers everywhere and can and will assist the suppliants and so it is an attribute [*idiōma*] and necessary consequence of divinity). Since this does not belong to the human nature (which is created and finite), it is not by itself and on account of itself adorable. Hence the Nestorians adoring Christ, as the Son of the blessed virgin, whom they distinguished from the eternal Son of God, were condemned as man-worshippers (*Corpus Iuris Civilis, II: Codex Iustinianus* 1.1.5ff. ["De Summa Trinitate"], pp. 6ff.). Hence we cannot agree with those who hold that the humanity of Christ should be so adored by itself as to be the terminus and object of the adoration, in order that they may gather from this that the divine attributes are really communicated to Christ's human nature. The same thing ought to be said of the mediatorial office. For since it is a work of God among creatures by which he is externally denominated and a contingent and temporary adjunct (which could be and not be), it cannot lay the foundation for legitimate adoration. Hence the adoration of the Mediator does not terminate in the mediation, but in the deity. For if I ask, Why may Jesus be adored? and the answer is returned, Because he is Mediator; it can be inquired further, Why may the Mediator be adored? No other answer can be given than that of the ancient Christians to the Arians: Because he is God consubstantial (*homoousios*) with the Father. Here is the ultimate terminus beyond which we cannot go.

IX. Third, "although mediation is not the foundation of adoration, still it has the relation of motive, on account of which it ought to be paid to Christ." For since the benefits of God move us to worship and glorify him and the redemption (conferred upon us by the mediation of Christ) is the most excellent of all blessings, it ought above all to impel us to adore our Redeemer. In this sense, Peter exhorts suffering believers "to commit their souls to God as unto a faithful Creator" (*hōs pistō ktistē*, 1 Pet. 4:19), where creation is brought forward as a motive for entrusting their souls to the hands of God. Thus it is said, "Thou art worthy, O Lord, to receive glory and honor: for thou hast created all things" (Rev. 4:11). Also it is said (referring to the Lamb), "Thou art worthy to take the book, and to open the seals thereof: for thou wast slain, and hast redeemed us to God by thy blood out of every kindred, and tongue" (Rev. 5:9). Hence if it is asked the reason on account of which Christ is worshipped, the proper answer is: Because he is the Mediator. So many and so great blessings flow to us from the mediation of Christ that worship and adoration cannot be denied to him without sacrilege.

X. Fourth, "although the human nature of Christ is not the object of adoration (terminating on it), still it is the inseparable adjunct without which adoration is not paid and which is adored with the Word." For as it enters into the constitution of the Mediator as God-man (*theanthrōpou*), the adoration cannot be paid to the Mediator without being extended in some manner to the human nature (which being intimately united by the hypostatical union to the Logos [*Logō*] has obtained such an eminence as to be adored with it). Augustine illustrates this by the simile of a king who is adored with his diadem and purple robes (Sermon 246, "De Verbis Domini [58]," PL 39.2200). However since the union of the Word with the flesh is far more close than that of a king with his clothing, nothing hinders our saying that the adoration of the Word is extended to the flesh also in its own way. This is rightly set forth by Athanasius to Adelphus against the Arians: "We do not adore a creature; by no means. For such errors belong to the heathen and Arians; but we adore the Lord of the creature, the incarnate Word of God. For although the flesh itself by itself is a part of created things, still it has become the body of God. Nor do we pay adoration to this body as separately distinguished from the Word, nor, when about to adore the Word, do we separate the Word far from the flesh, but since we know, as it is said, 'The Word was made flesh,' we acknowledge him as God even in the flesh" (*ho Logos sarx egeneto, touton kai en sarki genomenon epiginōskomen Theon*) (Letter 60, "To Adelphius" [NPNF2, 4:575; PG 26.1074-76]).

XI. And hence it is clearly gathered what is to be determined concerning the adoration due to Christ and concerning the celebrated question agitated about it. For if that particle limits the subject as to the foundation and term of the worship and the formal and proper relation in which adorability belongs to the Mediator, it is rightly said that Christ as Mediator is not to be adored because the mediation of Christ does not found and ultimately terminate our adoration, but the divinity only (which makes the person of the God-man [*theanthrōpou*] adorable). But if the same particle (as is often the case) is put for specifying the person to be adored or for indicating the reasons and motive by which we are impelled to the adoration, it cannot be denied that Christ in this respect should be adored as Mediator because both the person is adored and various motives are drawn for the adoration from the mediation itself. Thus those passages are to be interpreted which are adduced to favor the adoration of the Mediator.

XII. The Socinians can receive no help in opposing the eternal deity of Christ from this: that if he be adored as Mediator, he ought to be adored as man, since humanity is included in the conception of Mediator. Although the "whole" Mediator and God-man (*theanthrōpos*) is to be adored (i.e., the person of Christ, which is divine and consequently adorable); yet not at once the whole of the Mediator or whatever enters into the constitution of the person of the Mediator, so as to be a formal object of worship. It suffices that a Mediator cannot be conceived without determining him to be God. And so far from its following that the divinity of Christ cannot be proved from his adoration (because he is adored as Mediator), on the contrary we must necessarily conclude from this that he is God because he cannot be a Mediator without being God and the name and conception of Mediator involve his deity.

XIII. It cannot be denied that Christ is to be adored as Mediator because in this respect he is inferior to the Father. From that economical inferiority as to office and assumption of body, no detriment was done to his deity and essential adorability. For if he was made consubstantial (*homoousios*) with us in respect of his flesh, he always remained consubstantial (*homoousios*) with the Father in respect of his divinity.

XIV. The formal object of adoration (which contains in itself its cause) differs from the object of consideration, a certain relation of which is held in the adoration. Divinity is the first, but humanity is the second. Nor if one adoration alone is given to the person of the God-man (*theanthrōpou*) are the natures on that account confounded or made equal. For as the union does not confound the natures (nor the honor and glory of the natures in the one person of Christ), so the adoration no more confounds the natures and the honor due to them than faith. But as it regards Christ as God and man distinctly in the one person, so it ascribes to him according to both natures what belongs to him.

XV. Although the human nature or the flesh of Christ is not adored "by itself" (*kath' heautēn*), nor "on account of itself" (*di' heautēn*), because since it is a creature, it is not adorable by itself or in its own nature—"nothing created is adorable," says Epiphanius (*pan to ktiston ou proskynēton*, *Panarion* 64.8 [PG 41.1084])—still it is rightly said to be adored in the Logos (*Logō*), with whom it is personally united. Thus the ultimate term of adoration is not the flesh, but the deity, which is not only the proper object of adoration, but also its true and proper cause; both by reason of its infinite excellence (*hyperochēs*) and majesty (to which by itself adoration is due) and because all the efficacy of the mediation (however common to both natures) flows properly and originally from it.

XVI. If some of the orthodox have said, "The humanity or flesh of Christ is adorable," they do not understand it in this sense—as if it was the proper object which should terminate the adoration on itself and by itself. But inasmuch as it is the flesh of the Word (which is adored in the Word and with the Word), they mean to intimate that the worship which ought to be paid to Christ is not to be separated into various species. This was formerly done by the Nestorians, who professed to reverence Christ with one adoration as God, with another as man. This is done by the Romanists, who rendering supreme worship (*latreian*) to the deity, give inferior worship (*hyperdouleian*) to the humanity. Thus they pay to the humanity a lower worship than to the cross (to which they hold *latreian* is due).

XVII. To the argument of the Socianians—"Whoever is adored as Mediator is not the supreme God; but Christ is adored as Mediator; therefore he is not the supreme God"—whatever reply is made (whether by a negation, who wish Christ to be adored as Mediator) or by a destruction of the minor (which others wish), the doctrine of Christ's divinity stands untouched. For they, who deny that he is adored as Mediator with respect to his office, nevertheless firmly defend the adoration of the person of the Mediator with respect to his divine nature or inasmuch as he is the Logos (*Logos*). No less satisfactorily do others answer to the major, that so far from the inference from the adoration of Christ, the Mediator, being that Christ is not the supreme God, the invincible conclusion rather is that he is the true and eternal God—since a mere man could not be our Mediator, he must be God.

XVIII. We ought not to be so anxious concerning the relation under which we ought to adore Christ, but continually worship and reverence him in fact with devout submission of mind, with true faith and constant obedience as the eternal Son of God, our Redeemer, even to the last breath.

XIX. It is one thing for worship to be due to the name of Jesus formally considered (for the word itself); another materially (for the person signified by such a name) as the name of God is often put for God. When Paul says, "To Christ is given a name which is above every name, that at the name of Jesus every knee should bow" (Phil. 2:9*, 10), he does not take "name" in the former, but in the latter sense (as appears from the parallel passages, Is. 45:23 and Rom. 14:11, where the object of genuflection is said to be Jehovah and the very person of Christ, not his name—"every knee shall bow to me"). Hence the practice of the Romanists is not free from superstition. They uncover the head and bow the knee at the utterance of the name "Jesus," while the no less holy and venerable names "God" and "Christ" are not so received.

FIFTEENTH TOPIC

CALLING AND FAITH

FIRST QUESTION

What is calling and of how many kinds? Also, how do external and internal calling differ?

I. We have thus far spoken of the office of Christ. We must now treat of his benefits, which pertain to the application to us of the salvation acquired (which is begun here by grace and will be consummated by glory in heaven). The first of these is calling; not a special calling to some office (whether political or sacred, in which sense Paul frequently says that he was "called" to be an apostle, Rom. 1:1), but a general call to salvation. Its great excellence appears even from the fact that the church itself obtained its name from the word *klēsei* or "calling" (and is no other than "the assembly of the called").

What calling is. II. This calling is an act of the grace of God in Christ by which he calls men dead in sin and lost in Adam through the preaching of the gospel and the power of the Holy Spirit, to union with Christ and to the salvation obtained in him. In it, the two terms "from which" (*a quo*) and "to which" (*ad quem*) are to be considered. The term "from which" (*terminus a quo*) is the state of sin and condemnation in which we lie (Eph. 2:1); darkness (Eph. 5:8; 1 Pet. 2:9); the world (Jn. 15:19); and the things which are behind (to wit, earthly and mundane, Phil. 3:13). The term "to which" (*terminus ad quem*) is union with Christ (1 Cor. 1:9); holiness (Rom 1:7; 1 Cor. 1:2; 1 Thess. 4:7); marvelous light (1 Pet. 2:9); the kingdom of God (1 Thess. 2:12); eternal glory in Christ (1 Pet. 5:10); eternal life (1 Tim. 6:12).

III. Hence it is at one time called a "holy calling" (2 Tim. 1:9), not only by reason of the principle (because God the author of calling is holy, 1 Pet. 1:15), but also by reason of the end (because it tends to holiness). At another time, it is called the "heavenly calling" (*klēsis epouranios*, Heb. 3:1), the "high calling" (*hē anō klēsis*, Phil. 3:14) because it is from heaven and calls to heaven (in allusion to the Olympic games, in which the prize [*brabeion*] was not only suspended above the goal, but the athletes ran below and were crowned in a higher place where the judges [*brabeutai*] and superintendents sat, from which they urged the runners to the race by the voice of the herald).

Why so called. IV. If the question is asked why the Holy Spirit willed to employ this nomenclature for the description of this work, many answers can be given. (1) To designate the misery of man; for being separated and far removed from God by sin, he was to be recalled from his wanderings that he might return to God, just as God seeks and calls to the fleeing Adam, "Adam, where art thou?" (2) To point out the means which God uses in the conversion of men (to wit, the voice of the gospel and the preaching of the word, than which nothing fitter and better adapted to a rational creature could be given in order that man who is gifted with speech [*logikos*] might harmonize with the word [*logō*]). (3) To exhibit the various relations (*scheseis*) under which calling can be viewed: either as a certain new creation (in which God calls those things which are not as though they were, Rom. 4:17)—bringing us out of the nothingness of sin to life and shining into our hearts (in the same manner as he formerly commanded the light to shine out of darkness, 2 Cor. 4:6); or as a wonderful resurrection in which we are called by the almighty voice of Christ that we may arise from our sins (Eph. 1:20; 2:5), just as by his voice he raised Lazarus from the tomb, "Lazarus! Come forth" (and on the last day the dead will be raised by the sound of Christ's voice, Jn. 5:25); or as the supreme dignity of sons of God and a glorious office to which we are called, in union with Christ, as by calling dignities and offices are accustomed to be given to men in the world; or as a stadium and race course which is set before us (Phil. 3:14; Heb. 12:1), as the runners in the Olympic games were accustomed to be called to the race by the voice of a herald that they might press forward from the starting line to the finish line.

How distinguished.

V. However, this calling is distinguished in different ways by different persons. By some, it is made threefold: real by works, verbal by the gospel, spiritual by the Spirit. The first is extended to all in the world; the second is restricted to the called in the church; the third is peculiar to the elect and believers only. However it takes for granted that there is a calling to salvation by the works of nature (which we have already confuted).

Into external and internal.

VI. A twofold calling is therefore acknowledged by us, corresponding to the twofold state of the church—the visible and invisible (viz., an external and internal). The former takes place only by the ministry of the word and sacraments (which are external means of application). The latter, however, takes place with the additional internal and omnipotent power of the Holy Spirit. That knocks only at the ears of the body; this knocks at the heart also. That exerts only itself objectively; this works effectively also. That persuades morally; this persuades and draws efficaciously also.

VII. Now although they agree in various particulars both on the part of God calling (because each has God for its author, who calls men to his kingdom) and on the part of the men called (who are both dead and lost in sin as to internal qualities, and weak, unwise generally and ignoble as to external qualities, 1 Cor. 1:26); and on the part of the instrument, which in both is ordinarily the word; and on the part of the end, which is the glory of God and the salvation of the called; still they differ in several particulars. (1) With respect to the author; for in the external, God acts imperatively only, exacting from man duty, but giving no strength to perform it; but in the internal, operatively also with the command of duty supplying the necessary strength and working within what he enjoins without. (2) With respect to the mode; the former is done by the word only, the latter by the Spirit also. (3) With respect to amplitude; that belongs to many, this to few—"many are called, few are chosen." That is broader, extending even to the reprobate who are in the church (in which sense the gospel is compared to a threshing floor which contains chaff with the wheat and to a net, which gathers good and bad fish, Mt. 13:47). This is coextensive with election as its effect (which is therefore called "calling according to purpose," *kata prothesin*, Rom. 8:28) by which all the elect and they alone are called. (4) With respect to the event; that always remains inefficacious, this is efficacious and certainly attains its end: "Every man that hath heard, and hath learned of the Father, cometh unto me" (Jn. 6:45). (5) With respect to duration; that is temporal and revocable (as appears in the fickle [*proskairois*] and in apostates who return to their vomit); this, however, is immutable and not to be repented of (*ametamelētos*, Rom. 11:29). That constitutes the visible and external communion of the church in a profession of religion and the use of the sacraments; this constitutes the invisible and internal communion of the church in faith and love. From that they are called saints equivocally; from this properly and univocally.

Whether external and internal calling are distinguished only by the event.

VIII. A question is here agitated by our opponents about the distinction of this twofold calling—whether the internal and effectual calling is distinguished from the external only *a posteriori* and eventually; or whether it is also distinguished *a priori*, by reason of the will and the divine decree and the nature of calling itself. For the Lutherans think the internal and external on the part of the thing are one and the same, so that all externally called are also internally called. Being asked, however, how it happens that the external calling is efficacious in one and not in another, they reply that this arises from the will of man. The Arminians explain the matter more clearly. Calling is inefficacious in some but not in others, not because God works more in the latter, but because the good will of man superadds efficacy and because they freely receive the word which the others reject. But the orthodox hang that difference not on the free will of man, nor do they measure it by the event only, but seek it in the very decree of God and the nature of calling and the difference in subjective grace (which operates far more efficaciously in some than in others).

IX. The reasons are: (1) the internal calling is according to purpose (*kata prothesin*, Rom. 8:28) (depending therefore on God's decree) and is eternal and without repentance (*ametamelētos*, Rom. 11:29). It is not, therefore, efficacious only eventually. (2) The event itself depends entirely upon the decree of God, who so powerfully directs the calling that it accomplishes its own end in those who are elected ("As many as were ordained to eternal life, believed," Acts 13:48). (3) Otherwise man would make himself to differ—contrary to Paul ("Who maketh thee to differ? and what hast thou that thou didst not receive?" 1 Cor. 4:7). Nor would it be of "God alone who hath mercy, but of man that willeth and runneth" (Rom. 9:16); since nevertheless, God works in us to will and to do (Phil. 2:13). The objections brought forward by our opponents will be examined when we come to treat of the efficacy of calling.

X. Calling is again distinguished into ordinary and mediate, and extraordinary and immediate. The former God employs in the ordinary dispensation of his grace by the intervention of external means (or the ministry of men). The latter, however, is usually exercised beyond the order, with respect to certain individuals whom God immediately and of himself (without the intervention of men) calls and turns to himself (such as was seen in the thief, in Paul and others immediately called by God).

SECOND QUESTION: THE CALLING OF THE REPROBATE

Are the reprobate, who partake of external calling, called with the design and intention on God's part that they should become partakers of salvation? And, this being denied, does it follow that God does not deal seriously with them, but hypocritically and falsely; or that he can be accused of any injustice? We deny.

Statement of the question.

I. This question lies between us and the Lutherans, the Arminians and the patrons of universal grace, who (to support the universality of calling, at least as to the preaching of the gospel in the visible church) hold that as many as are called by the word are called by God with the intention of their salvation. For otherwise God would trifle with men and not deal seriously but hypocritically with them, offering them grace which, nevertheless, he is unwilling to bestow.

II. Now although we do not deny that the reprobate (who live in external communion with the church) are called by God through the gospel; still we do deny that they are called with the intention that they should be made actual partakers of salvation (which God knew would never be the case because in his decree he had ordained otherwise concerning them). Nor ought we on this account to think that God can be charged with hypocrisy or dissimulation, but that he always acts most seriously and sincerely.

III. To make this more distinct, we must remark: (1) the external call is extended to the reprobate as well as to the elect; but in a different manner—to the elect primarily and directly. For their sake alone the ministry of the gospel was instituted to collect the church and increase the mystical body of Christ (Eph. 4:12). They being taken out of the world, preaching would no longer be necessary because the word of God cannot return unto him void (Is. 55:11). But to the reprobate, it is extended secondarily and indirectly because, since they are mingled with the elect (known only to God, 2 Tim. 2:19), the call cannot be addressed to men indiscriminately without the reprobate as well as the elect sharing in it (in order that the end ordained by God may be obtained); as a fisherman in casting his net intends only to catch good fish, but indirectly closes in his net the bad also mixed with the good.

IV. (2) The end of calling can be considered in two ways: either on the part of God or on the part of the thing (which is called the end of the worker and the end of the work). Although each is conjoined in the elect, yet in others they are separated (as in the legal proclamation, the end of the thing is life by the law, but the end of God after man's fall cannot be the happiness of man, which through sin has become impossible to him by the law; rather the conviction of man's weakness and leading of him to Christ is the end of the law; so in the gospel call, the end of the thing is the salvation of man because by its nature it tends to the bringing of him to salvation by faith and repentance; but not at once with respect to all the called is it the end of God, but only of those to whom he decreed to give faith and salvation).

V. Further, that end on the part of God is either common to all the called or special with respect to the elect or the reprobate. And as to the common, we ought not to doubt that it is the demonstration of the mode and way of salvation and the promise of salvation to those who profess the prescribed condition. But the special with respect to the elect proceeds further (viz., to the actual bestowal of salvation upon those whom on that account he calls not only imperatively but also operatively; not only by prescribing duty, but by performing that very duty, working within us by his Spirit what he externally enjoins by his word). However with respect to the reprobate, his end is their conviction and inexcusability.

VI. Now as this calling springs from a threefold principle, so it obtains a threefold end. (1) It springs from the authority of a legislator who has the right to prescribe to man his duty. (2) It springs from the goodness and grace of a Lord who does not cease to bless the creature (although unworthy and guilty) by showing him the way of salvation and showering upon him various blessings. (3) It springs from the justice of a Judge who wishes to convict the stubborn and rebellious and to render them without excuse. Hence a threefold end flows. The first is the prescription of duty that he may know what God demands from him and what he owes to him (namely, to believe and repent). The second is the promise of blessing on the condition that he knows what God has determined to give to believers and penitents. The third is the detection of the wickedness of the heart (Lk. 2:35) and its inexcusability (Jn. 15:22), its stubbornness being supposed, so that both the man himself in his conscience and others may really know that the vengeance of God against that servant is just (who while he knows his master's will and ought to do it, still neither does nor wishes to do it, Lk. 12:47).

VII. Hence it appears that the question does not (in general) concern the end of calling on the part of the thing (which we do not deny to be salvation); but on the part of God; not whether God wills to bestow any grace upon reprobates above those who are destitute of this blessing (such as the heathen and other infidels), but whether he intends to give saving grace or salvation to them and calls them with this purpose, that they may really become partakers of it (and if it happens otherwise, it is beyond God's intention and accidentally). This our opponents maintain; we deny. Again, the question is not whether the event of external calling is the same with respect to all and whether all the called are affected in the same manner. For they, with whom we argue, confess that it is widely different and that those indeed who spurn the heavenly call (or do not proceed as far as saving repentance) are thus made inexcusable; that others, however, who obey, obey by the special grace of God (the power and efficacy of his Spirit turning their minds and souls to obedience—hence it appears that the salvation which they obtain was destined for them). Rather the question is whether the disparity of the event does not prove a disparity of intention in the caller. Or whether all are called with the intention and purpose that they should partake of salvation. This they assert; we deny.

Proof that God acts seriously in the calling of reprobates, although he does not intend their salvation.

VIII. The reasons are: (1) God cannot in calling intend the salvation of those whom he reprobated from eternity and from whom he decreed to withhold faith and other means leading to salvation. Otherwise he would intend what he knows is contrary to his own will and what he knew in eternity would never take place (and that it would not take place because he, who alone can, does not wish to do it). This everyone sees to be repugnant to the wisdom, goodness and power of God.

IX. (2) God does not intend faith in the reprobate; therefore neither does he intend salvation (which cannot be attained without faith). Now that he does not intend faith is gathered from the fact that he does not give it to them, nor did he decree to give it; nay, he determined to withhold it. It is of no avail to reply that God did not intend to produce it in the reprobate, but still he intends and wills that it should be possessed by them. That intention either respects the very futurition of the thing (in which sense God cannot be said to intend it because since it is not to be given to the reprobate, he would fail in his intention) or it respects only the will to give them this command (in which sense we do not deny that God intends this); but thus it is reduced under the approving and preceptive will of God (of which we do not treat here).

X. (3) Christ, in calling the reprobate Jews, testifies that he had as his proposed end their inexcusability (*anapologian*). It is said, "He came for judgment, that they which see might not see" (Jn. 9:39) (i.e., who profess that they see, still do not see and are more and more blinded). "If I had come and spoken unto them, they had not had sin: but now they have no cloak for their sin" (Jn. 15:22). Nor ought it to be said that Christ does not speak of the intention of God calling, but concerning the event of the call for God might have a most holy intention to which nevertheless the event would not at all answer. Nothing can happen to God accidentally and beyond his intention. Hence such an event ought to be intended by God from eternity. What is added—that they had not had sin, if Christ had not come—must not be understood absolutely and simply, but relatively (to wit, as to a despised and rejected gospel not announced to them—as was the case on that account to be guilty of sins committed against the law).

XI. (4) They who are called with the intention of salvation are "called according to purpose" (*kata prothesin*) because that intention is the act of election and the effecting of the purpose (*protheseōs*). Now it is certain that no reprobates are called according to purpose (*kata prothesin*) because thus they would both love God (Rom. 8:28) and be necessarily justified and glorified—for whom he called, them he also justified, etc. (v. 30), which cannot be said of them.

XII. (5) Salvation according to the intention of God is promised to none others than those having the prescribed condition: such as are weary and heavy laden (Mt. 11:28), thirsty (Is. 55:1), believing and penitent (Acts 2:38). Since this cannot be said of the reprobate, it cannot equally be said that they are called by God with the intention that they should be saved.

XIII. (6) It can no more be said that God calls each and every man with the intention that they should be saved, than that they should be damned. For a conditioned promise includes the opposite threatening, so that every unbeliever will be condemned as every believer is to be saved. Therefore as it is absurd to say with respect to the elect that God calls them with the intention that they should be damned (since he had decreed to fulfill the condition in them), so it is no less absurd to say that he calls the reprobate with the intention that they should be saved (since God knew they would never have that condition; nay, he, who alone can give, has decreed to withhold it from them). It can no more be concluded that God wills all to be saved for the reason that he promises pardon of sin and salvation to all promiscuously (if they repent), than that he nills the salvation of all for the reason that he denounces a curse and death upon all (unless they repent and believe).

Sources of explanation.

XIV. Although God does not intend the salvation of the reprobate by calling them, still he acts most seriously and sincerely; nor can any hypocrisy and deception be charged against him—neither with respect to God himself (because he seriously and most truly shows them the only and most certain way of salvation, seriously exhorts them to follow it and most sincerely promises salvation to all those who do follow it [to wit, believers and penitents]; nor does he only promise, but actually bestows it according to his promise); nor as to men because the offer of salvation is not made to them absolutely, but under a condition and thus it posits nothing unless the condition is fulfilled, which is wanting on the part of man. Hence we cordially embrace what is said on this subject by the fathers of the Synod of Dort: "As many as are called through the gospel are seriously called. For God shows seriously and most truly in his word, what is pleasing to him, to wit, that the called should come to him. He also seriously promises to all who come to him and believe rest to their souls and eternal life" ("Tertium et Quartum: De Hominis Corruptione et Conversione," 8 *Acta Synodi Nationalis . . . Dordrechti* [1619-20], 1:[302]).

XV. He, who by calling men shows that he wills their salvation and yet does not will it, acts deceitfully, if it is understood of the same will (i.e., if he shows that he wills that by the will of decree and yet does not will it; or by the will of precept and yet does not will it). But if it refers to diverse wills, the reasoning does not equally hold good. For example, if he shows that he wills a thing by the will of precept and yet does not will it by the will of decree, there is no simulation or hypocrisy here (as in prescribing the law to men, he shows that he wills they should fulfill it as to approbation and command, but not immediately as to decree). Now in calling God indeed shows that he wills the salvation of the called by the will of precept and good pleasure (*euarestias*), but not by the will of decree. For calling shows what God wills man should do, but not what he himself had decreed to do. It teaches what is pleasing and acceptable to God and in accordance with his own nature (namely, that the called should come to him); but not what he himself has determined to do concerning man. It signifies what God is prepared to give believers and penitents, but not what he has actually decreed to give to this or that person.

XVI. It is one thing to will reprobates to come (i.e., to command them to come and to desire it); another to will they should not come (i.e., to nill the giving them the power to come). God can in calling them will the former and yet not the latter without any contrariety because the former respects only the will of precept, while the latter respects the will of decree. Although these are diverse (because they propose diverse objects to themselves, the former the commanding of duty, but the latter the execution of the thing itself), still they are not opposite and contrary, but are in the highest degree consistent with each other in various respects. He does not seriously call who does not will the called to come (i.e., who does not command nor is pleased with his coming). But not he who does not will him to come whither he calls (i.e., did not intend and decree to come). For a serious call does not require that there should be an intention and purpose of drawing him, but only that there should be a constant will of commanding duty and bestowing the blessing upon him who performs it (which God most seriously wills). But if he seriously makes known what he enjoins upon

elect called by decree and all by precept

the man and what is the way of salvation and what is agreeable to himself, God does not forthwith make known what he himself intended and decreed to do. Nor, if among men, a prince or a legislator commands nothing which he does not will (i.e., does not intend should also be done by his subjects because he has not the power of effecting this in them), does it follow that such is the case with God, upon whom alone it depends not only to command but also to effect this in man. But if such a legislator could be granted among men, he would rightly be said to will that which he approves and commands, although he does not intend to effect it.

XVII. An absolute promise cannot be serious unless founded upon the will and intention of the promiser to give what is promised. But it is different with a conditioned promise. It suffices for the preservation of his sincerity that there be the intention in God to connect most certainly the thing promised with the condition, so that the latter nowhere occurs without the former attending it. Hence it happens that on account of this connection and dependence, the offer of salvation made to believers is most serious, for no one will have faith who will not most surely obtain salvation.

XVIII. The word of external calling ought to be the sign of some decree upon which it is founded; but not forthwith of a decree concerning the saving of individuals, but concerning the means and their connection with salvation. The foundation of calling in general (inasmuch as it is directed indiscriminately to men) is the decree concerning the collecting of a church by the word. The foundation of calling with respect to the elect is the special decree concerning the bestowal of the salvation acquired for them by Christ upon some certain persons. The foundation with respect to reprobates is the decree concerning the order and connection of the means of salvation and concerning the proposal and enjoining of these means upon men. Therefore the word of calling is the sign of that decree by which he made an indissoluble connection between faith and salvation (which because the word proposes, no simulation can be ascribed to God, since he proposes nothing which is not most true).

XIX. Since faith in Christ (which is prescribed to us in calling) is not prescribed to us as to all its acts together and at once, but by degrees and successively (and as to general and direct acts before the special and reflex acts; as to the acts of assent and refuge before the act of acquiescence in Christ as having died for me; nay, neither are these commanded except the antecedents being exercised), it is false to say that the promise of salvation with respect to us is made under a condition which cannot be fulfilled without falsehood. For that Christ is a true and perfect Savior of all flying to him seriously by faith and repentance (which is prescribed to be believed by men in the direct act of faith) can be believed without falsehood, even by those for whom Christ has not died.

XX. The promises and threatenings added to God's commands express nothing more concerning the mind and intention of God than the commands themselves (which show what is his preceptive will, but not what is his decretive will—which ought properly to be called the will of God). Therefore as the Holy Spirit employs these towards the elect as motives suitable to the human mind to bring about their conversion, so in no other way does he will they should serve with those whom God does not intend to convert and actually to bring to salvation than partly to exhibit the necessary connection between faith and salvation, partly to render them inexcusable.

XXI. The invitation to the wedding proposed in the parable (Mt. 22:1-14) teaches that the king wills (i.e., commands and desires) the invited to come and that this is their duty; but not that the king intends or has decreed that they should really come. Otherwise he would have given them the ability to come and would have turned their hearts. Since he did not do this, it is the surest sign that he did not will they should come in this way. When it is said "all things are ready" (Lk. 14:17), it is not straightway intimated an intention of God to give salvation to them, but only the sufficiency of Christ's sacrifice. For he was prepared by God and offered on the cross as a victim of infinite merit to expiate the sins of men and to acquire salvation for all clothed in the wedding garment and flying to him (i.e., to the truly believing and repenting) that no place for doubting about the truth and perfection of his satisfaction might remain.

XXII. Although the intention of pastors who call ought to be conformed to the intention of God (by whom they are sent to call men) in this—that they are bound from the order of God to invite all their hearers promiscuously to repentance and faith as the only way of salvation; and that they ought to intend nothing else than the gathering of the church or the salvation of the elect (in bringing about which they are co-workers [*synergoi*] with God). Still in this they also differ—the omniscient God distinctly knows who are the elect among gospel hearers and who are the reprobate. The former alone he wills to save individually, not the latter. However, ministers (being destitute of such knowledge) do not know to whose salvation their ministry will contribute, not being able to distinguish between the elect and the reprobate, charitably hoping well for all, nor daring to decide concerning the reprobation of anyone. Thus they address all the called promiscuously and indiscriminately even by God's appointment, still intending the salvation of no others than the elect (like God). Thus they do nothing in this ministry which does not answer both to the command and intention of God, although God (conscious of his decree) proceeds further than they and distinctly intends the conversion and salvation or the inexcusability of particular persons.

XXIII. The foundation of consolation is not weakened in the preaching of the gospel, although there is a certain diversity between the intention of God and that of the minister. However it suffices for its foundation that they agree in the general intention and primary object of gathering a church to God which he may sanctify and glorify and of calling all who repent and believe for that end to salvation. Now the diversity which occurs about the knowledge of individual reprobates or elect persons (whom God alone knows and not ministers) cannot overthrow consolation or furnish just cause of despair, no more than the particularity of election and the immutable decree of reprobation. For as the intention of God is not (the decree of reprobation being rescinded) to admit the reprobate by calling into communion with him; so neither ought that to be the intention of the ministers, who ought to intend properly the salvation of no others than the elect (although in accordance with charity, they can also wish for the salvation of others and to promote it as far as in them lies).

XXIV. It is one thing for God to indicate in his word (even to those who will not believe) that faith and repentance are the most sure and infallible means of obtaining salvation; another for God to make this internal declaration of his word with those who will not believe for this purpose—that they may actually believe and be saved. For if he seriously intended this end, he would add to the external preaching the internal power of the Spirit, without which it remains always inefficacious.

XXV. It is not indeed repugnant to the wisdom of God to will to command and to command actually what nevertheless he certainly knew would not be done by those whom he commanded. In such a command, he wills to unfold his right and man's duty, no less than his own goodness and justice. But it is repugnant for God simply and absolutely to will and intend what nevertheless he not only knew would never happen, but even what he himself decreed should never happen.

XXVI. Although God offers the word to the reprobate for this end—that by their obstinacy they may be rendered inexcusable—he does not therefore offer it that they may reject it, for this is a sin which God neither intends nor does. Rather he offers it that the latent perversity of their hearts may be manifest (Lk. 2:35) and that by this rejection of the word (arising from man himself), he may have the occasion of displaying his justice in the infliction of punishment. Now although man could not receive the word without grace (which God does not will to bestow upon him), he must not therefore be considered as calling in order that he may reject him. Rejection does not follow of itself from the nature of calling, but accidentally from the depravity of the man himself. For although he could not receive the word without grace, still the rejection springs from no other source than his stubborn wickedness.

XXVII. Man does not cease to be inexcusable although he does what God intended because he does not do what God commanded; as Herod and Pontius Pilate are nonetheless inexcusable although they did nothing but what the hand of the counsel of God had decreed before to be done (Acts 4:28). The decree is not the rule of our actions, only the precept.

XXVIII. To render man inexcusable, it is sufficient to take away from him the pretext of ignorance, not however to take away inability. For man is accustomed to plead ignorance, but never inability. For man (such is his pride) always persuades himself that he can do what is prescribed and is sufficiently convinced that he sins through stubborn depravity when he fails in his duty. The pretext of ignorance certainly ought to be allowed because it excuses, provided it is not affected and voluntary. However it is not so with regard to impotency, when it is voluntary and brought on (*epispastos*). A man is not bound to know what is not revealed. But he is bound to perform even that which through sin he is made unable to do; and consequently it can be exacted from him.

Third Question: Sufficient Grace

Is sufficient, subjective and internal grace given to each and every one? We deny against the Romanists, Socinians and Arminians.

Distinction between sufficient and efficacious grace.

I. Among the various distinctions of the grace employed in calling, that is the most common by which it is distributed into sufficient and efficacious (which gave rise to this question). Something must be premised concerning it that it may be evident in what sense it is proposed by our opponents and rejected by us, as in a sound sense it can be admitted by us.

In what sense it is used by Romanists.

II. Bellarmine distinguishes between sufficient and efficacious grace thus: "Sufficient grace is that by which God so calls, excites and is prepared to assist men by directing, protecting and cooperating, that the man thus excited can really will to believe, be converted, do good, although he does not in fact will to believe, be converted and do good; hence this grace remains inefficacious. The effectual is that by which God so calls, excites and is prepared to help man by directing, protecting and cooperating, that man thus excited and called, really and infallibly wills, believes, is converted and does good works" ("De Gratia et Libero Arbitrio," 1.2 *Opera* [1858], 4:273.)

III. But this division should be deservedly suspect by us. (1) It obtrudes upon us the Pelagian poison. For what he called "the possibility of believing" (given by the grace of the Creator to all men), according to the will of each one, that they call the sufficient help or grace given to all men for this purpose—that they may be able to believe if they wish. What he called help, grace, suasion, doctrine and law, this they call moral suasion and efficacious help. But whatever that help may be, they maintain that it is such that it depends upon the will of men to profit or not profit by it (if the man wills or does not will), which is pure and unmixed Pelagianism. (2) All grace sufficient for conversion ought to be efficacious; otherwise sufficient grace in fact would be insufficient (to produce whose effect certain other grace ought to be superadded). (3) Christ strikes at this distinction when speaking of efficacious grace (which he had given to the apostle to free him from the severe thorn by which he was afflicted). He calls it by no other name than sufficient ("My grace shall be sufficient for thee"), by this very thing showing that all the sufficient grace of God is also efficacious; otherwise this would not have brought a great consolation to Paul complaining of the grievous temptation by which he was assailed. Nor does it help the matter to say that some sufficient thing is efficacious, not all. For if it is a legitimate division, the members ought not to coincide and no sufficient grace ought to be inefficacious.

In what sense it can be admitted.

IV. Still we do not deny that in a certain sense the division can be admitted if a sufficiency, not absolute and simple is meant, but a relative sufficiency both with regard to external means and internal illumination for a knowledge of the truth and temporary faith (Heb. 10:26; Lk. 8:13) and for conviction and inexcusability (*anapologian*, Jn. 15:22). But for conversion, we recognize no sufficient grace which is not equally efficacious.

Statement of the question.

V. The question does not concern any kind of grace or help which can obtain in nature as well as in grace. For it is certain that God has nowhere left himself without excuse (*amartyron*) towards men in whatever state. Nor can it be denied that a convincing and coercing light can often be granted to the heathen by which they are restrained from many wickednesses and enormous crimes; and that the reprobate mingled with the elect are favored with the external preaching of the word and sometimes an internal illumination of mind by which they mourn over their sins and congratulate themselves at least for a time concerning the word admitted, as appears in the temporary. But the question here concerns salutary help and grace, sufficient for conversion.

VI. The question does not concern objective and external grace proposed to man by way of object (of which we treated in the preceding question), but concerns subjective and internal grace which is received by way of a faculty or act in man. The question does not concern the act and event itself—whether all actually believe. For all agree that innumerable persons remain unbelieving. Rather the question concerns the potency—whether they could believe. Not—whether that grace is bestowed upon all in equal measure. For our opponents acknowledge that the help of divine grace is not equally present to all, nor in any moment whatever is sufficient to the rising again from sin (as Bellarmine has it, "De Gratia et Libero Arbitrio," 2.2 *Opera* [1858], 4:298-99). But whether it is at least sometimes conferred upon individuals.

VII. The question returns to this—whether the gratuitous favor of God regards individuals so kindly as to communicate to all, whether heathen or Christians, infants or adults, reprobate or elect, in their state after the fall, according to place or time, mediately or immediately, ordinarily or extraordinarily, grace not of any kind whatsoever, but grace saving and sufficient for conversion; not external only, but subjective and internal. Our adversaries wish this; we deny it.

VIII. The Romanists maintain that help sufficient for salvation (according to place and time) is given to all, so that there is no one who does not sometime at least have this help, either immediately in the case of adults or mediately in the case of infants in the parents, who can procure baptism for their children. Bellarmine thus expresses it: "Sufficient help as to place and time is given to all mediately or immediately" ("De Gratia et Libero Arbitrio," 2.5 [Prop. 5] *Opera* [1858], 4:301).

IX. The Arminians (pressing in the same footsteps after the Socinians) assert that God (who had the universal will of saving each and all, and of redeeming the same) willed also by a universal call to bestow means sufficient for faith and repentance upon each and all. However, he does this in such a way that the use of these means should be subject always to the free will of man, in whose power it is to use or not use that grace, to believe or not. Nay, they seem to go somewhat further than the Romanists themselves. For the latter acknowledge that God was absolutely free in granting that sufficient grace to men and that there would be no injustice in him if he withheld it from all. But the Remonstrants contend that God was bound in the new covenant to supply that grace; that he might not labor under the unjust suspicion that he demanded something of us beyond our strength (as Arnoldus Corvinus expresses it against Molinaeus).

X. The design of both in adopting this Pelagian error is to offer incense to the idol of free will and to establish their dogma concerning the indifference (*adiaphoria*) of the will by proposing a grace such as can always be rejected or received by man. The principal foundations of this opinion are two: (1) God exacts nothing from man which cannot be done by him; (2) faith and repentance (which are the conditions of the new covenant) were not enjoined in the first covenant, nor belong to natural duty. Thus no one is bound to them, unless strength is again conferred upon him.

XI. However, the orthodox deny both that God is bound to bestow such grace upon all and that he wills in fact to confer it and actually to impart it to each one. Rather he bestows it only on those who are the called according to his purpose (*kata prothesin*) (viz., to the elect).

Proof that sufficient grace is not given to all.

XII. The reasons are: (1) saving grace is not extended beyond the decree, since it is its effect. But God did not decree that all should obtain salvation because as he loved Jacob, he hated Esau. As he elected some and destined them to salvation, so he reprobated others and destined them to wrath; as he pities certain persons, so he hardens others to whom no one would say that sufficient grace is given. Nor can it be replied that the decree of God is not absolute, but suspended on the good or bad use of free will. The very thing in question is taken for granted (and what we refuted in the proper place when we discussed the decree of reprobation).

XIII. (2) External objective grace is not common to all, as we have already seen. Therefore much less subjective and internal grace. Hence God is said in past ages to have permitted the Gentiles to walk in their own ways (Acts 14:16), which he still does as to the Turks, Persians and Indians. And yet who would say that sufficient grace is given to them whom God permits to walk in their own ways, when he winks at the times of ignorance?

XIV. (3) All men have not faith (2 Thess. 3:2), but only the elect (Tit. 1:1) (to wit, they who were ordained to eternal life, Acts 13:48). Now if sufficient grace is given to all, therefore also the grace of believing. Nor ought it to be replied here that grace is indeed given sufficiently on the part of God, but there is an obstacle in their perversity of will by which this one rejects the offered grace which another embraces. The question always recurs concerning the cause of that diversity—Whence does it happen that one receives grace above the other? For he either has it from himself or from a fuller grace of God. If from himself, therefore man (contrary to Paul) makes himself to differ. If from God, therefore the former grace cannot be said to be sufficient since he needs another superadded to the determination of the man. And if it was sufficient, why did it not remove the perversity of the one as well as that of the other?

XV. (4) The grace which is given to all is either equal and alike in all or unlike and unequal. If unlike, it cannot be called sufficient and universal, but some common, some particular. If alike and equal, why are its effects so unequal? You will say from the dissimilar dispositions of men and will because this one receives, that one rejects it. Therefore either the remedy was unlike (which did not heal both) or the disease of nature was unlike (as Pelagius held and the apostle denies, Rom. 3:12). And to whatever direction our opponents turn themselves, they must come to this—that unless discriminating peculiar grace is given to those who are converted, the discretion of man must be resolved into the free will of man on the assumption of sufficient grace which our opponents urge (which is the very error of Pelagius).

XVI. (5) Not a few of our opponents reject this dogma, as the entire school of Jansen, when he proves sufficient grace to be monstrous: "As explained by the more modern, it is a distinct kind of help from others which from the first fall of man until the day of judgment never had, nor will have any effect upon the human will" (cf. "De Gratia Christi Salvatoris," 3.3 *Augustinus* [1660/1964], p. 258). He shows from the nature of grace that sufficient grace according to the more recent sense is granted to none (ibid., 3.4, pp. 262-67). He proves that innumerable persons are destitute of that sufficient grace and that it was devised by Semipelagians (ibid., 3.10-12, pp. 300-23). In the following chapters, he refutes the arguments of the Jesuits for sufficient grace. Alvarez had already asserted this (*De Auxiliis divinae gratiae et humani* 8.71 [1610], pp. 497-505). It is also evident that this dogma was disapproved of by many others, such as Bennius, Osorius and Delphinus.

XVII. (6) To this sufficient grace either something is added that it may be efficacious or nothing. If anything ought to be added, then it is not sufficient. If nothing, then its efficacy will depend on man, not on God and his grace. And it will be called efficacious grace only from the event, not from its own nature. Thus that distinction will not be a distinction of grace, but of the event itself so that it will always be the same grace, which sometimes obtains the events, sometimes not.

XVIII. (7) To innumerable persons neither a heart to understand is given, nor eyes to see (Dt. 29:4), nor a knowledge of the mysteries of God (Mt. 13:11), nor the drawing of the Father (Jn. 6:44), which are the only means sufficient for conversion. Nor must it be said here that God on his part willed and was prepared to give that heart and eyes, but that man opposed it. The question is not what God was prepared to give, but whether he really gave it (which is here expressly denied). Nor could the rebellion of man stand in the way of its bestowal if he wished. Grace is given for no other purpose than to remove it; nor can it be removed without it. Nor is what is added any more conclusive that a clear and distinct knowledge of the mysteries of the gospel was indeed denied to others (which was granted to the apostles), but not on that account was all grace denied by which they can know those mysteries. For whatever grace was granted to them, it cannot be called sufficient since it is granted that it was given to them to know these mysteries. As to the drawing of the Father, since no one can come to Christ, except the Father draw him; and no one is drawn who does not come because whoever has heard from the Father and is taught, comes to him (as it is added in the same place)—it is evident that all are not drawn by the Father because all do not come to Christ. Consequently sufficient grace is not granted to them.

Sources of explanation.

XIX. It is one thing to suffice for conviction in the order of external means; another for conversion to suffice in the order of internal means. The words of Is. 5:4 ("What could have been done more to my vineyard, that I have not done in it?") treat of the first, not of the second sufficiency: (1) to wit, concerning external means and those indeed which are conferred not upon all, but only upon the called in the church; not of internal means because he compares himself to a vinedresser, who plants a vineyard in rich soil, surrounds it with a ditch, guards it with a hedge, erects a press and a tower (i.e., plants it with the word, cultivates it with kindness, girds it with protection and does all those things which are required from a careful vinedresser in order that the vineyard may bring forth good fruit); but he does not speak of the vegetation and vital influence which draws after it most certain conversion. (2) The Hebrew words *mh l'svth* must not be translated "what could I have done more," since God could have done something more by internally turning and renewing the heart; but "what was to be done" or "what ought I to do which I have not done," which could be desired by the best husbandman (i.e., in the order of external means which take away all pretext from sinners; not as to internal disposition which man ought to contribute from himself—nor is God bound to restore what has been lost by man's fault). Or it signifies that nothing remains to be done further after these means had been abused than to destroy it, as he adds in v. 5. (3) The expectation here ascribed to God after the manner of men must be understood in a manner becoming to him (*theoprepōs*), not to designate the weakness of an expecter and the uncertainty of the event, but as denoting only the exaction of duty and the patience and forbearance of God, who tolerates the sinner, giving him time for repentance, nor does he immediately (applying the ax) cut down the barren tree (Lk. 13:7). However, although he had not granted all the grace necessary for converting man (because he was not bound to that), still he could rightly expect grapes and justly complain concerning the unperformed duty because the equity of duty flowed spontaneously from the blessing of God. Nor did the Israelite church perform all that it could in this regard and what could be performed by man out of a state of grace—as to abstain from the more grievous sins and mourn over them (such as is attributed to the Ninevites themselves). He is not therefore said to have waited as if he was deceived in his expectation because he could not be ignorant of the result; but he waited that the heinousness of the sin might be intimated and the justice of inflicting punishment upon the people.

XX. When it is said "Christ stands at the door and knocks" (Rev. 3:20), it cannot be inferred that sufficient grace is granted to all. (1) He is there treating of those already called who were in the church, not of those about to be called. (2) That standing and knocking not only designates internal notions, but is properly referred to external exhortations (which are made partly by the word, partly by afflictions) of which he had spoken in the preceding verse. Therefore he knocks in different ways at the hearts of the elect and reprobate; at the former externally and internally by the word and by the Spirit so that, by knocking imperatively by the word, he may also open them operatively by the Spirit (as was the case with the heart of Lydia). At the latter, however, he only knocks externally by the word that they may understand their duty, the promised benefit, the heinousness of their sin and the justice of punishment if they neglect the voice of God. Nor is it absurd for God to knock, although he knows that man will not open. He does not cease justly to admonish man of his duty and to convict the rebellious of obstinacy.

XXI. Although men cannot come by their own strength, nor does God afford them the power to come (because he is not bound to that), still the calling is not unavailing because by calling he draws the elect to come to him, while he renders the reprobate inexcusable if they do not come. They are bound to come and yet are unwilling to come (which suffices for their just condemnation). Nor is it equitable that the sin of a man should profit him and so be unaccountable because he has made himself impotent by his own wickedness. This impotence, so far from excusing him, the rather aggravates and increases his guilt because it is induced (*epispastos*) and voluntary, by which as he cannot, so he does not wish to believe. The case is different with involuntary and merely natural inability in a blind or dead man, to see or act. When a man is destitute of faculties, he is not bound to exercise them. Now the obligation (by which the creature is bound to his Creator) can be expunged by no occasion, much less by the wickedness of man because man is never deprived of the faculty of understanding and will, but only of its good disposition.

XXII. It is absurd to say that sufficient grace is given to all, if not immediately at least mediately, because to him who does what he can, God will not deny grace and is prepared to give the light of the gospel to those who properly use natural light. (1) This dogma of the Pelagians can be confirmed by no passage of Scripture; nay, it is overturned by innumerable passages in which gospel grace is not ascribed to the good use of nature or to the merits of men, but to the sole mercy of God and his most free good-pleasure, (2 Tim. 1:9; Rom. 9:16; Eph. 2:1, 4; Is. 65:1). (2) God would be said to be prepared for that which he still knows never will happen and which he has himself decreed not to do because he knows the condition to be impossible to man. (3) The gospel would have been revealed to the wiser and more sincere among the heathen (who seemed better disposed towards it, while yet he had denied it to them), while he often bestowed it upon infants and the most corrupt (Mt. 11:25).

XXIII. Nor can they press the words of Christ into a confirmation of this dogma, where he promises to give more to him that has ("Whosoever hath, to him shall be given," Mt. 13:12) because he refers not to the gifts of nature, but of grace; not to the increase of the former, but of the latter. Nor can this be obscure to one duly considering the connection and design of the words of Christ in the two passages in which they occur. For in Mt. 13:12, Christ gives the reason why to the apostles it was given to know the mysteries of the kingdom of heaven, while to others it was not given: "Whosoever hath, to him shall be given, and he shall have more abundance; but whosoever hath not, from him shall be taken away even that he hath" (i.e., "what he seems to have" [*ho dokei echein*], as Luke explains, "shall be taken away," 8:18). Now these "not having" are designated by Mark by those "who are without" (Mk. 4:11); they are opposed to those having, who are within (i.e., to the true elect who are in the church). Thus Christ intimates that God's saving benefits are closely connected with each other, so that he who has received the first, the others will be added to him, until the measure of all gifts is complete in him (as in a chain from the drawing of the first link the rest must necessarily be drawn, Rom. 8:29).

XXIV. Thus in the parable of the talents (Mt. 25:29), the same expression is repeated and by "having" not only the possessor of, but also the one properly using the talents entrusted to him (both for his own and for the salvation of others) is meant. For he who makes no good use of what he has, has not for both himself and others. It is a common saying, "What he has is as much wanting to the avaricious man as what he has not." Hence Augustine says, "Everything which does not fail by being given away, while it is possessed and is not given, is not yet possessed in the way it should be possessed, and therefore is said not to be possessed" (CI 1.1* [FC 2:27; PL 34.19]). Hence it is evident that what belongs to the gifts of grace are falsely drawn to the gifts of nature; as if by a leap God would promise to one having in the state of nature a gift in the state of grace (as if apart from grace something could be done which has the power and effect of conciliating the grace of God). For it is clear that Christ meant nothing else than to describe the indissoluble connection of the gifts of grace and their progress and increase even to perfection.

XXV. It is one thing for the kindness, patience and longsuffering of God (by which he puts off the punishment of crimes on the part of the guilty) to invite man (in a state of sin) to repentance, inasmuch as he supplies the reasons and time for repentance; another for God (on his part and as far as he can) to give help sufficient for conversion to man through such patience. It is plain that this external longsuffering and tolerance of God is not sufficient to soften the heart of man and to give a better direction to his affections.

XXVI. In the new covenant, God is not bound to supply sufficient strength to man for fulfilling it that there may be an equality of credit and debt (as Bellarmine has it). There is not prescribed a different obedience and faith as to essence from that prescribed in the first covenant (for compliance with which man in the beginning had received sufficient strength). Since he lost this by his own fault, God is not bound to restore it to him by demanding the duty from him. The equality of credit and debt is to be estimated not according to the state of sin, but according to the state of creation. For what was then credited to man is wholly due to God (although by his own fault he is not able to pay). Whether Adam had the power to believe in Christ—about this we have a dispute with the Arminians; cf. Topic VIII, Question 2.

XXVII. The examples of the eunuch and Cornelius (drawn from Acts 8:26-39 and 10, as if on account of their good use of natural light, the light of grace was given to them) are not pertinent here. They cannot be reckoned among unregenerate infidels when the gospel was published to them, but among proselytes whom, already imbued with a knowledge of the Jewish religion, God willed to grant a further knowledge of the gospel and of Christ now revealed; so that they might not only believe generally in the promised Messiah, but particularly in Jesus of Nazareth as the true Messiah sent by God. Other things belonging here may be found in the preceding Question and in Question 6, Topic XII.

Fourth Question: Effectual Calling

Is effectual calling so denominated from the event (or from congruity) or from the supernatural operation of grace itself? The former we deny; the latter we affirm against the Romanists and Arminians.

Three opinions of the Romanists concerning effectual calling.

I. That the true nature and method of effectual calling may be ascertained, the discrepant opinions in reference to it must be considered. Bellarmine enumerates three principal opinions held by Romanists ("De Gratia et Libero Arbitrio," 1.12 *Opera* [1858], 4:290-94). The first is that of Molina, Lessius, Becanus and most of the Jesuits. They maintain that it is called "effectual calling" simply from the event. The second is that of Bellarmine, Suarez and others who follow them. They deduce it from its congruity. The third is that of the Thomists and Dominicans, who draw it from physical predetermination.

1. From the event.

II. Bellarmine says that the first makes "effectual calling to consist in the assent and cooperation of man; so that it is called effectual from the event because it brings about its effect, and does so because the human will cooperates with it; so that it is in man's power to render sufficient grace effectual." But this opinion brings back the very error of Pelagius, who transferred the principal cause of conversion to the free will of man. Hence it is properly rejected by Bellarmine himself and opposed by various arguments—especially by this: "If that opinion was true, free will would clearly make the difference between the believer and the unbeliever contrary to Paul, 'Who maketh thee to differ? and what hast thou that thou didst not receive?' (1 Cor. 4:7). For if two hear the same address and have the same internal inspiration, and one believes, while the other does not, could not he who believes say, 'I made myself to differ from the unbeliever because I willed to believe, he did not?' And yet the apostle says this could not be done." This argument entirely overthrows this most pestilential error and even alone can suffice to demonstrate its falsehood, so that we here dismiss the many others which are drawn from the total inability of man in reference to good and the insuperable power of grace (of which we will speak hereafter).

2. From congruity.

III. The second opinion (which Bellarmine rather insinuates than establishes at the end of chap. 12 cited above) is that of those who place the efficacy of grace in "the congruity of calling, to wit, in a certain external moral suasion, which can be rejected by the free will and still have an infallible effect because God uses that suasion, which he knows is congruous with their minds, whom he decreed to draw efficaciously, and which he certainly knows will not be despised by them" ("De Gratia et Libero Arbitrio," 1.12 *Opera* [1858], 4:293-94). These are the words of Bellarmine in the cited passage. Explaining his meaning more clearly, he teaches "that the efficacy of suasion results not so much from the vehemence of the persuasion as from the disposition of the will which God foresaw, namely when God so proposes something by internal persuasion that he sees the will to be fitted for consenting" (ibid., 4.11, p. 370). And in the same place he adds, "The infallibility of the thing does not arise from the vehemence of the divine motion, but from a foresight of the aptitude of the will itself" (ibid.). If it is asked in what that congruence of the will consists, Suarez says that some think it consists only in a certain proportion which there is between the illumination effected in such a way by God in a man of such a complexion, nature and condition; God however, comprehending these most exactly in each man, knew also what mode of calling was adapted to him so that if his heart was thus touched, he would consent. However, that calling should be a means accommodated to the efficacious intention of God (which the not being fulfilled confounds), and that congruity alone induces a certain moral certainty, to which it is not absolutely repugnant that the free will resists the calling thus congruous. He therefore says that every efficacious calling consists in this: "that God foreseeing by his infinite wisdom what each cause or will is about to work in every event and occasion, if it is constituted in it, also understands, when and to what call each will is about to yield assent if given to it. Hence when he wills to convert a man, he wills also to call him at that time and in that manner in which he knows that he will consent and such a calling is called efficacious because although from itself it does not have an infallible effect, still as it underlies such divine knowledge, it will infallibly secure it" ("De Concursu et Efficaci Auxilio Dei," 15.3+ *Opera* [1856-78], 11:231-41). Hence it appears that this congruity according to these authors consists principally in three things: (1) in suasion; (2) in such a contemporaneousness of suasion, in such a person so disposed, in such a place and time; (3) in middle knowledge, by which he foreknows how the will is about to incline itself, placed in such a time and on such occasions.

IV. But this opinion is deservedly discarded by the orthodox. First, it coincides with the first, which Bellarmine rejects (although he is inconsistent) because no less than the preceding it ascribes the efficacy of grace to man's will; thus the reason with which he solidly attacks the first opinion recoils upon himself. For if it is in our power to assent to and obey congruous calling or not (as he himself says while he suspends the efficacy of the call upon the disposition and aptitude of the human will congruously called, in that manner and at that time in which God foresaw that it would yield assent), surely not only the partial, but the whole cause of the difference will be from man and not from God. Nor is it difficult to show that no other efficacious cause can be assigned here besides the human will. For what cause can be assigned: prevenient and assisting grace? This is supposed to be common to the uncongruously and the congruously called (which leaves the free will in its own indifference). The congruity? But the whole of that congruity only induces from itself (as Suarez says) a certain moral certainty to which it is not absolutely repugnant for the free will to resist the calling thus congruous. The concourse of various circumstances and the suitableness of the time and of this place rather than that? But these are external adjuncts and accidents destitute of all causality. The foreknowledge of God? But since foreknowledge is not the cause of things and supposes its object, it does not make it. Man cannot be said to be about to do anything because God foreknew it, but God on this account foreknew it because man was about to do it (besides this, middle knowledge is a mere figment, as has been proved). Therefore no other cause for this difference and conversion can be given besides the pleasure and free will of man, who is called at that time and in the place in which God foresaw he would assent.

V. Second, this opinion supposes that there can be granted some aptitude for conversion in the unrenewed will. This is Pelagian and diametrically opposed to the Scriptures, which so often assert the absolute inability (*adynamian*) of man to good and are accustomed to express it by no other name than that of death. Now who would say that there is any aptitude and disposition in the dead man to raise himself? or in a nonentity to create itself?

VI. Third, it is repugnant to the action of God in the conversion of man, which consists not in a simple and bare moral suasion (which is merely objective), but in an omnipotent and irresistible power. It is nothing less than the very creation and resurrection of man, which therefore operates not only objectively, but also effectively with man (as we will soon prove). Now who can believe that to regenerate and resuscitate man, to take away his heart of stone and to give him a heart of flesh, is nothing else than to morally persuade to conversion (i.e., to invite to conversion by precepts, arguments, promises and threatenings; as when the orator, by an eloquent peroration, not only exhorts but also persuades)? But far different is the language of Augustine when he says, "Not by the law and doctrine sounding without, but by an internal and secret, a wonderful and ineffable power, God works in the hearts of men not only true revelations, but also good wills" (*On the Grace of Christ* 25 [24] [NPNF1, 5:227; PL 44.373]).

VII. Fourth, if the efficacy of grace depended upon the congruity of calling and the concourse of various circumstances, they would be converted who seem more fitted and disposed to receive the gospel and about whom more circumstances gathered. But on the contrary, God hides his mysteries from the wise and reveals them unto babes (Mt. 11:25). He calls nations alienated from Christ and the covenants, without God and having no hope, plunged in the densest shades of superstition and idolatry, and rejects the covenanted Jews to whom all the external helps for receiving Christ had been abundantly supplied, while no circumstances seemed to be wanting to their congruous calling: the knowledge of the law; the oracles of the prophets; the testimony of John the Baptist; the presence, miracles, death and resurrection of Christ established by so many most satisfactory arguments; the earnest zeal of the apostles in instructing them—which were all wanting to the Gentiles. Who would not have judged from these circumstances that the Jews were more congruously called and so ought the rather to be converted, while, on the contrary, it happened that very many of the Gentiles and very few and almost none of the Jews were converted? This miracle of grace Paul celebrates in the words of Moses and Isaiah: "But I say, Did not Israel know? First Moses saith, I will provoke you to jealousy by them that are no people, and by a foolish nation I will anger you. But Esaias is very bold, and saith, I was found of them that sought me not; I was made manifest unto them that asked not after me. But to Israel he saith, All day long I have stretched forth my hands unto a disobedient and gainsaying people" (Rom. 10:19-21*). Now what is the congruity of calling and aptitude to obedience in those not seeking?

VIII. Efficacious grace (by which the will is so moved as to yield its consent infallibly) can be called congruous in a certain sense, inasmuch as God, by efficaciously moving the will, moves it congruously to consent. As it is congruous to the nature of the will, there is no support given by this to the opinion of Bellarmine because that congruity is not derived from the disposition of the will itself or from the circumstance extrinsically approaching the efficacious help. Thus it varies according to the diverse circumstances and qualities of the subject and so the motion which is congruous with respect to one, is incongruous with respect to another and vice versa. But it brings with it that help which is called efficacious and which on that account is distinguished from the inefficacious (which is given to the unconverted). The objections commonly urged here will be solved more conveniently in the following question.

The third opinion, from physical predetermination.

IX. The third opinion is that of the Thomists and Dominicans, who make the efficacy of calling to consist in physical predetermination. They assert that efficacious grace is a physical and real action of God which determines the will to will and select the good breathed into it by exciting grace because God cannot physically predetermine the will without the will itself being determined and willing that to which it is determined—as that grace cannot fail in producing its effect. Thus Bellarmine explains their meaning ("De Gratia et Libero Arbitrio," 1.12 *Opera* [1858], 4:290-94). This opinion (although rejected by Bellarmine as destructive of free will) comes nearest to the truth, although perhaps it is less accurately expressed by a physical predetermination for the reason that it seems to confound the natural acts of providence (necessary from the condition of the second nature both to all agents and every state of man) with the supernatural acts of grace, which in the state of sin are the rational and moral mode of acting (which even in conversion is employed by God as fitting to nature). Hence Jansen brings forward various distinctions between the medicinal assistance of God and that physical predetermination ("De gratia Christi salvatoris," 8.3 *Augustinus* [1640/1964], pp. 822-25), as it is handed down by his defenders. Francis

Zumel far more suitably unfolds his own meaning and that of his associates: "That this efficacious grace of God properly proceeding efficiently from him, and moving us beforehand, and predetermining, on account of its priority of causality alone, should be called a physical predetermination, the authors of the opposite opinion think, of which word they were the first inventors; for before their time we spoke differently, saying that the actual grace of God moving us beforehand must be determined to be efficacious and that God properly moves us efficiently by the act of his grace. Wherefore there is no reason why they should repeat so often physical predetermination, which is not physical, that is, natural, but supernatural and divine; not exactly moral, but supernatural, efficient properly from the efficacy of divine grace, which perfects nature, does not injure the will, but itself is so much the more free and acts the more freely, as it is more subjected to the actual grace of God" ("Tam ad primam partem, quam ad primam secundae sancti Thomae," *Variorum Disputationum* [1609], 3:109).

The opinion of the orthodox expressed in five propositions.

X. The orthodox suspend the efficacy of calling neither upon the event, nor upon its congruity. But they derive it from the supernatural power of grace and the divine and ineffable motion of God, which so sweetly and at the same time powerfully affects the man that he cannot (thus called) help following God who calls and being converted. Although its nature cannot indeed be fully perceived by us, we embrace it in five propositions.

First proposition.

XI. The first proposition: "The ways of the Lord in grace as well as in nature are inscrutable (*anexichniastoi*). Nevertheless if we cannot understand the reason and the how (*to pōs*) of those things which God has willed to conceal from us, the thing itself and the fact (*to hoti*), which has been plainly revealed to us, is not on that account to be denied by us." For if in the order of providence, we cannot comprehend the reason of the counsels of God and the mode of his reasons and are compelled to confess that it is incomprehensible (*akatalēpton*), why can this not be said with far greater propriety concerning the ways of predestination and the mode of efficacious grace and the Holy Spirit operating in us? Especially since Christ testifies that the Spirit is like the wind which "bloweth where it listeth, and thou hearest the sound thereof, but canst not tell whence it cometh, and whither it goeth" (Jn. 3:8), to intimate that it operates in us in wonderful and ineffable ways; although its force is felt most powerfully, still its way cannot be known or explained. Therefore they are disappointed who would wish the mode of its operation to be accurately described to them and what its secret movements are, what and how great that heart-turning power of the Spirit acting in the hearts of the elect, and in what degrees and moments he carries forward his work. For this is felt by experience rather than capable of being explained by reason (no otherwise than a pregnant woman is ignorant of the way in which the vital fetus will be conformed and will grow). Still it is false to proceed from the ignorance of the mode not revealed in the Scriptures and unnecessary to be known by us in order to salvation, to a denial of the thing itself which is so clearly revealed in the Scriptures.

Second proposition.

XII. Second proposition: "The movement of efficacious grace in man is not after the manner of an act or only simultaneous concourse, but also after the manner of a principal and of previous concourse or predetermination." It is opposed to the old and new Pelagians, who, denying all previous concourse (in grace as much as in nature), maintain that God concurs in good no other way than by way of act (which indeed reaches the effect, but not the cause), so that the grace of God and the will of man must be conceived as two allied and coordinate causes in the production of the effect, like two horses drawing the same chariot. But as we have established the necessity of a previous concourse or predetermination in the way of providence (Topic VI, Question 5), we think it should be even more firmly held in the works of grace. For since the will by sin is become not only weak, but plainly impotent and dead (as was seen in its own place—Topic X, of the freedom of the will, Question 4—and will be proved further), God would in vain concur only by way of act or of allied cause with the free will in order to its conversion. By way of principle, he would flow into the will itself for its renewal and vivifaction in order that (itself being renewed and acted upon by God) it might act as a cause not allied and coordinate, but subordinate, drawing all its power and efficacy from the influx of grace (which the Scriptures usually designate by creation, regeneration, resurrection and similar phrases). Augustine frequently insinuates this: "A good will precedes many gifts of God, but not all; for what does not precede is itself in them" (*Enchiridion* 9 [32] [FC 2:397; PL 40.248]). He also says, "God, not by the law or doctrine sounding without, but by an internal and hidden wonderful and ineffable power, operates in the hearts of men, not only true revelations but also good wills" (*On the Grace of Christ* 25 [24] [NPNF1, 5:227; PL 44.373]). Thus Hugo St. Victor: "Repairing grace first produces a good will that it may exist; then inspires it, that it may be moved; first, it works it, then by it" (*On the Sacraments of the Christian Faith* 1.6.17 [trans. R.J. Deferrari, 1951], p. 106 [PL 176.274]).

Third proposition.

XIII. Third proposition: "As conversion can be considered under a twofold relation (*schesei*), either as habitual or as actual, so both God and man certainly concur, but in such a way that in both the glory of the whole action ought be ascribed entirely to God alone." Habitual or passive conversion takes place by the infusion of supernatural habits by the Holy Spirit. On the other hand, actual or active conversion takes place by the exercise of these good habits by which the acts of faith and repentance are both given by God and elicited from man. Through the former, man is renovated and converted by God. Through the latter, man, renovated and converted by God, turns himself to God and performs acts. The former is more properly called regeneration because it is like a new birth by which the man is reformed after the image of his Creator. The latter, however, is called conversion because it includes the operation of the man himself. Now although in the order of time, they can scarcely be distinguished in adults (in whom the action of God converting man is never without the action of man turning himself to God), still in the order of nature and of causality the habitual ought to precede the actual and the action of God the action of man. A thing ought to exist before it can work, and as the soul cannot elicit acts of the understanding and will (unless furnished with the natural powers of intellect and will in the sphere of being), so it cannot properly understand and will in the sphere of morals unless renewed by supernatural dispositions and habits. An evil tree cannot bring forth good fruit, unless from an evil it is first made a good tree. The second act necessarily supposes a first. Also an object which ought to be apprehended by a faculty requires the faculty itself (rightly disposed) antecedent to its reception. Therefore this is the first degree of efficacious grace by which God regenerates the minds of the elect by a certain intimate and wonderful operation and creates them as it were anew by infusing his vivifying Spirit, who, gliding into the inmost recesses of the soul, reforms the mind itself, healing its depraved inclinations and prejudices, endues it with strength and elicits the formal principle to spiritual and saving acts (in which sense we are said to be "the work of God [*poiēma theou*] created in Christ unto good works," Eph. 2:10). Also we obtain the new birth, from which acts of faith and love flow forth (1 Jn. 4:7; 5:1). Thus this habitual conversion consists in principles of action which God confers upon the faculties of corrupt man. They are supernatural qualities or habits and dispositions, from which results an active power of converting himself (such as the Scriptures mean by the "new heart," the "seed of God," "eyes," "ears," "mind" and the like denoting something inherent and permanent).

XIV. But because this first degree would be of no avail without the second, habitual is followed by actual conversion (by which man puts forth acts, God drawing forth from the healed and changed will itself the very act of believing and conversion and the soul itself thus moved freely eliciting its own act). In this sense, God is said to give not only the power of believing, but the belief (*to pisteuein*) or the act itself (Phil. 1:29) and "to will and to do" (*to thelein kai energein*, Phil. 2:13), inasmuch as the Holy Spirit excites the intellect and the will and the remaining faculties (endowed with new qualities and sanctified) to the eliciting of good actions. Just as in restoring sight to the blind, Christ did two things: he first opened their eyes and so restored the power of seeing; then he caused the man to see at the same moment. So in the resurrection of Lazarus, the soul was first restored to the body, then he elicited vital actions. Thus God by his omnipotent acting produces in the man (or in the will) new qualities; then he excites those faculties to action.

XV. However although in every instance God and man concur, still they concur in different ways. God is the sole cause of habitual conversion. He effects it by the heart-turning power of his Spirit without any cooperation from man. Here man (since it treats of his renewal) is only passive and subjective inasmuch as he is a mere subject receiving the action of God. But with respect to the actual, the principal cause is indeed God, but the proximate and immediate cause is man, who (excited by the Holy Spirit and imbued with the habits of faith and love) believes and loves. Hence although the act of believing is produced by God, yet because it is exercised by man as the proximate cause, it is ascribed not to God, but to man. Thus man holds himself here, both passively to receive the motion of prevenient and exciting grace (for the will does not act unless acted upon) and actively and efficiently because he actually believes and works under God. Still thus he is said to be the cause of his own conversion that he is not such from himself, but from grace, both because the power of believing is only from God and because the very act of believing depends upon God himself exciting the faculty to its operation. Hence nothing can be concluded from this for the power of free will.

XVI. Hence it appears that man is not like a log and a trunk in his regeneration, as our opponents falsely charge upon us. (1) The will is the receptive (*dektikon*) subject of grace; this cannot be said of a trunk. (2) The Spirit does not force the will and carry it on unwillingly to conversion, but glides most sweetly into the soul (although in a wonderful and ineffable manner, still most suitably to the will) and operates by an infusion of supernatural habits by which it is freed little by little from its innate depravity, so as to become willing from unwilling and living from dead. (3) The will so renewed and acted upon immediately acts, converting itself to God and believing.

XVII. Although the word and the Spirit have their own parts in this twofold conversion so that no one may feign for himself an enthusiastic regeneration because the Spirit does not act without the word (at least in the ordinary and common mode of acting which he employs with reference to adults). For that he can extraordinarily operate without the word by secret movements and internal operations (as was frequently the case with inspired [*theopneustous*] men), no one, I think, will disavow and deny. Still the method and causality of each is not the same. For the Spirit indeed is the principal efficient cause which acts in each conversion, both by infusing strength for acting well and by exciting to operation the strength conferred, thus captivating the mind unto the obedience of Christ and changing the strength (*rhopas*) and inclination of the will and affections—so that what in the gospel seemed repulsive and absurd to the natural man is now judged by the spiritual man to be most pleasant and wise and so most worthy of our love and admiration. But as to the word, although it also efficiently concurs both in the acts preceding regeneration and consequently in the actual conversion (which we hold is brought about by the Spirit through an infusion of habits), it properly obtains no efficiency; nor yet does it belong to the class of those instruments which reach to the effect itself than of those at whose presence the principal cause operates. And thus the Spirit is indeed rightly said not to work without the word, but not by the word only, but immediately and distinctly from the word (as will hereafter be more fully proved).

Fourth proposition.

XVIII. Fourth proposition: "The movement of efficacious grace is properly to be called neither physical nor ethical, but supernatural and divine (which in a measure includes both those relations [*schesin*])." It is not simply physical because it is concerned with a moral faculty which ought to be moved in a way appropriate to its nature; nor is it simply ethical, as if God acted only objectively and used mild suasion (as the Pelagians maintain). Rather it is supernatural and divine, rising above all these classes. In the meantime, it partakes somewhat of the ethical and the physical because the Spirit in our conversion operates both powerfully and sweetly, pleasingly and invincibly. It pertains to a physical mode that God by his Spirit creates, regenerates, gives us a heart of flesh and infuses into us efficiently the supernatural habits of faith and love. It pertains to a moral mode in that it teaches, inclines, persuades and draws to itself by various reasons as if by the chains of love. Hence Augustine is accustomed everywhere to express it by the phrase "delightful conqueror" (cf. *On the Forgiveness of Sins and Baptism* 2.32 [19] [NPNF1, 5:57; PL 44.170]) who has conjoined with the highest pleasantness and sweetness, the greatest efficacy and power which expels all the obstinacy of the heart. Thus neither that strength nor efficacy compels the man unwillingly, nor sweetly moves him now running spontaneously; but each joined together both strengthens the weakness of man and overcomes the hatred of sin. It is powerful that it may not be frustrated; sweet that it may not be forced. Its power is supreme and inexpugnable that the corruption of nature may be conquered, as well as the highest impotence of acting well and the necessity of doing evil. Yet still it is friendly and agreeable, such as becomes an intelligent and rational nature.

XIX. Nor ought this to seem amazing: (1) the servitude of sin that cannot be escaped (which holds him bound as if by the brazen yoke of sins) is however connected with his pleasures; and the impotence of acting well and the necessity of doing ill is most near and voluntary. (2) The sinner both as the subdued captive of sin is led under sin, is without strength (*asthenēs*) and is entirely destitute of strength for good; and as an enemy (*asebēs*) of God and impious, he feels the deepest enmity towards God and is accustomed to war against him (*antistrateuesthai*, Rom. 7:23), not only averse from God by impotence, but also averse by malignity. A more fitting remedy for this evil could not be employed than if the invincible grace of God should be imbued also with an incredible sweetness to overcome the weakness of man and correct his wickedness. For unless that grace by which we are converted were furnished with the highest power, sin (which has struck its roots so deeply in us) could not be overcome and rooted out. Unless the same would yield fruit of the sweetest joy so that the most loathsome delight of sin might be overcome by the opposite pleasure, the man would be drawn not voluntarily, but unwillingly and in a manner little suited to his nature.

XX. Scripture clearly intimates this when it usually describes the operation of grace in those terms which approach the physical mode and designate the supreme power of God (when it calls it "creation," "resurrection," "regeneration," "drawing," etc.) and which pertain to the ethical mode (as when it explains it by "illumination," "doctrine," "persuasion" and similar words). Nay it frequently joins together the relations (*schesin*) both of sweetness and efficacy in the same passages, as when the spouse joins "running" with "drawing" (Cant. 1:4*); Christ joins the "yoke" and the "burden" with "easiness" and "lightness" (Mt. 11:30); we are said to be drawn, but also at the same time to be taught (Jn. 6:44, 45); to be persuaded by the power of the Spirit, but also by the demonstration (1 Cor. 2:4); to be converted by the exceeding great power of God, but with an illumination full of joy (Eph. 1:18, 19); to be bound, but also to be enticed (?Jer. 20:7); to be constrained, but with the cords of a man (*philanthrōpias*) and with bands of love (Hos. 11:4; 2 Cor. 5:14)—by which as with golden chains believers being bound are drawn to Christ, far more truly than orators are said to draw men by their eloquence. Hence the same gospel by which we are converted is called both the "power" and "wisdom" (1 Cor. 1:18, 19, 24); or "the arm of God," than which nothing is stronger; and "honey" or "milk," than which nothing is more pleasant (Ps. 19:10; 1 Pet. 2:2). The same Spirit by whom we are renewed is a Spirit of strength and a Spirit of grace; a scepter of virtue and the oil of gladness; a Spirit of power (*dynameōs*) and of love (*agapēs*) (2 Tim. 1:7)—in order to designate its omnipotent and most friendly power.

XXI. And hence we can clearly gather how liberty in this affair conspires in a friendly manner with necessity. Our opponents are unwilling to acknowledge this. As often as they see the sweet operation of grace described, so often do they exclaim that it is not therefore invincible and as they say irresistible. As often as they hear its insuperable efficacy preached, then they vociferate that the liberty of the will is impaired and man converted into a trunk and log. But whoever attends to this twofold relation (*schesin*) of efficacious grace will readily perceive that these are not opposed to, but are in the highest degree consistent with each other: our calling is a work of divine omnipotence, that no one may make it resistible; and it claims us for itself by a loving and most tender necessity of persuasion, that no one may imagine it to be forced or involuntary. Such is the nature of the things which are usually presented to the mind that the more strongly they act, the more sweetly do they flow into the mind. Thus no power is greater than love, or necessity stronger than charity, which, poured upon us like oil, pervades us with the sweetest delight and like the strongest bond constrains us (2 Cor. 5:14). Thus the first truth can neither be known nor happily possessed, unless both with the highest freedom and with the strongest necessity. Thus the omnipotent and efficacious operation of the Spirit is not opposed to that sweet method by which God acts through precepts, exhortations and other things of the same kind; by which God speaks after our mode, although with all these he acts after his own.

XXII. However, whatever is that motion of efficacious grace, still it is such and so great that it is entirely invincible and insuperable; nor can any will of man resist God willing to convert him. This is the principal mark and properly the characteristic of efficacious grace by which it is distinguished from all the other gifts sometimes bestowed by God even upon the reprobate. For since the others can in different ways affect man and influence by illumination, coercing and even in some degree changing (at least as to external morality), this alone converts and recreates man; indeed with so great efficacy as infallibly to obtain its result and overcome any resistance of the will (which will be more fully demonstrated in what follows).

Fifth proposition.

XXIII. Fifth proposition: "Although the Spirit in effectual calling does not act without the word, still he does not act only mediately through the word; but he also acts immediately with the word on the soul, so that the calling necessarily produces its effect." I say the Spirit does not act without the word. For since (as we have just now intimated) God wills here to act in a manner suitable to a rational nature and, according to the apostle, "faith comes by hearing, and hearing by the word of God" (Rom. 10:17), it is evident that the word ought necessarily to concur with the Spirit for our conversion from the order of God and the constitution of the covenant of grace (Is. 59:21) and without it the Spirit does not work faith in adults. Nor is there any doubt that its wise and fit dispensation by a clear and solid proposition of the truth opportunely made, conduces greatly to the success of the good work. But whatever may be its efficacy, still it is not sufficient without the immediate operation of the Spirit. Nor can the word (proposed with whatever evidence and opportunity and clothed with whatever circumstances and supports) ever produce that effect unless the secret, ineffable and hyperphysical operation of the Spirit attends to affect the soul immediately and turn it by its omnipotent power. And no wonder, since two things are necessarily required for conversion: on the one hand, the object which is externally presented to the mind; on the other, the faculty which receives it within. And such and so great is the corruption introduced into the soul by sin that although there always remains in it a natural power of understanding and willing, still the moral habit or disposition of judging and willing properly has so failed that it can no longer be moved to a right exercise of itself by the presentation of the object (as it usually can in the natural order and in the instituted state of man) unless the faculty itself is first renovated. On this account, there is always need for a twofold grace in the conversion of man: the one objective and extrinsic, consisting in the proposition of the object; the other subjective, acting immediately upon the faculty to render it capable of receiving the object, not only that it may be able rightly to elicit its own acts in reference to it, but also to elicit them actually. Each depends upon the Holy Spirit working in two ways—both in the word and in the heart; in the word as the objective cause; in the heart as the efficient cause of faith. In the word, acting morally by the revelation of the object and suasion; in the heart, working efficaciously and hyperphysically by an infusion of good habits, the creation of a new heart and the powerful impression of the proposed object.

XXIV. That this was the opinion of the ancient church against Pelagius (who denied that immediate grace) is plainly gathered from Augustine. For Pelagius referred the whole operation of grace either to nature (which was the gift of God) or to the law and doctrine by which God illuminates the mind and demonstrates and teaches what we ought to do and persuades us of all that is good: "He assists us by his doctrine and revelation, while he opens the eyes of our heart, while he demonstrates the future to us that we may not be taken up with present things, while he lays bare the snares of the Devil, while he illuminates us with the multiform and ineffable gift of heavenly grace" (*On the Grace of Christ* 8 [7] [NPNF1, 5:220; PL 44.364]). The orthodox contend that a far different grace is to be acknowledged. "Not only that we may know the things to be done, but also do what is known; not that we may believe the things to be loved, but also love the things believed. This grace, if it must be called doctrine, is surely so called that God is believed to infuse it deeper and more intimately with ineffable sweetness, not only by those who plant and water externally, but also by himself who secretly gives its increase, so that he not only shows the truth, but also produces love. For thus God teaches those, who are the called according to his purpose, at the same time teaching both to know what to do, and to do what they know," as Augustine expresses it (ibid., 12 [13]-13 [14] [NPNF1, 5:222; PL 44.367]). And: "Therefore let them read and understand and confess that not by the law and doctrine sounding externally, but by an internal and hidden, a wonderful and ineffable power, God works in the heart not only true revelations, but also a good will" (ibid., 24 [25] [NPNF1, 5:227; PL 44.373]). This he confirms in the *City of God:* "The Holy Spirit operates internally that the medicine, administered from without, may be availing. Otherwise even if God himself, using the creature subdued to himself, should address in some human manner the human senses, whether those of the body or those which we have in sleep most like these, and would not rule and act upon the mind by a more inward grace, all the preaching of the truth would do no good to man" (CG 15.6 [FC 14:423; PL 41.442]). This very thing Prosper admirably pursues. "Persuading and teaching not only by this kind counsel and exhortation, as if grace had the rule of the law, but changing the mind within and reforming it and making a new out of a broken vase, by the power of creating; this not the admonition of the law, not the words of the prophet, not the nature furnished him accomplishes, but the one who made, restores" (*Carmen de ingratis* 14.335-41 [trans. C.T. Huegelmeyer, 1962], pp. 62-63 [PL 51.114]).

XXV. That this was the opinion of the fathers of the Synod of Dort is evident from what they held concerning the corruption and conversion of man against the Remonstrants, who explained the operation of grace by moral suasion (which was always resistible) nor recognized any other mode of acting than an objective and moral and mediate through the word (as they testify in *Collatio scripto habita Hagae Comitis* [1615]). They say, "We believe with the Word of God that the Spirit of God puts forth no strength in us for conversion, except by the Word, since this is the only seed of our regeneration" (ibid., p. 308). And on p. 314: "The efficaciousness of the power of God can be determined either as the efficient cause of our faith, which we here reject, or as the foundation upon which faith is built," i.e. (as they a little while after explain), "exciting faith by way of object" (ibid.). Episcopius more clearly unfolds this adding the corollary: "Whether any immediate action of the Spirit upon the will or mind is necessary or promised in the Scriptures, in order that anyone may be able to believe the word externally presented? We maintain the negative" ("Disputationum theologicorum," 46 *Operum theologicorum, pars altera* [1665], Pt. II, p. 437). He says elsewhere (contending after the Socinian Catechism—cf. *The Racovian Catechism*, Sect. V, chap. 6 [1818], pp. 284-88) "that anyone can, provided only he has the use of reason, without any peculiar immediate or internal enlightenment, most easily understand and perceive all the meanings of the Scriptures, which are necessary to be known, believed, hoped for, or done, in order to salvation" (?'Status controversiae de Perspicuitate S. Scripturae,' in "Institutiones Theologicae," *Opera Theologica* [1678], pp. 264-65.)

XXVI. In order to meet this most dangerous error, the fathers thus explain the mode of operation of grace: "When God follows out this his good pleasure in the elect, or works true conversion in them, he not only sees that the gospel is preached externally to them, and powerfully enlightens their minds by the Holy Spirit, that they may rightly understand and discern the things of the Spirit of God, but the efficacy of the same regenerating Spirit penetrates to the inmost recesses of the man, opens the closed heart, softens the hard heart, circumcises the uncircumcised, and infuses new qualities into the will, makes it alive from dead, from evil good, from unwilling willing, and acts upon and strengthens it, so that as a good tree it may bring forth the fruits of good actions. And it is that regeneration, new creation, raising from the dead, and vivification, so greatly spoken of in the Scriptures, which works in us without us" (*Acta Synodi Nationalis . . . Dordrechti*, Head III-IV, Theses 11 and 12 [1619-20], 1:303). And in the rejection of errors, the Synod condemns those who teach "in the true conversion of man, new qualities, habits, or gifts cannot be infused by God into his will, and so faith, by which we are at first converted, and in virtue of which we are denominated believers, is not a quality or gift infused by him, but only an act of man, nor can it in any other way be called a gift than with respect to the power of coming to him. For these things contradict the sacred letters which testify that God infuses into our hearts new qualities of faith, obedience and the sense of his love (Jer. 31:33; Is. 44:3; Rom. 5:5)" (ibid., Rejection of Errors, 6, p. 306). Also it condemns those who teach "that the grace by which we are converted to God, is nothing else than a mild suasion, or as others explain it, a most excellent mode of acting in the conversion of man, and best adapted to human nature, which is performed by suasion, and there is nothing to hinder even moral grace alone from making natural men spiritual; nay, God produces the consent of the will in no other way than by moral reasons, and in it consists the efficacy of the divine operation, which overcomes the operation that God promises eternal and Satan temporal good. For this is altogether Pelagian, and contrary to the whole of Scripture, which besides this, acknowledges also another and far more efficacious and more divine mode of acting of the Holy Spirit in the conversion of man: 'A new heart also will I give you, and a new spirit will I put within you' (Ezk. 36:26)" (ibid., Rejection of Errors, 7).

XXVII. This opinion Calvin frequently endorses against Pighius. For as the latter acknowledged with Pelagius no other means of our conversion than the external and objective, the former (on the contrary) maintains that God works in the elect in two ways: "externally by the word, internally by his Spirit" ("Defensio sanae et orthodoxae doctrinae . . . adversus . . . Alberti Pighii," CR 34.345). "Illuminating the mind by his Spirit, forming the heart to the love and worship of righteousness, that they may become new creatures; the Word exciting them to desire, seek and obtain the same renovation" (ibid.). And since he had brought forward the objection of Pighius, by which he supposed he had been bound and reduced to a contradiction (namely, that "either the preaching of the Word was prior or posterior to the action of the Spirit; that this second is inconsistent, because believers would to no purpose seek and long for regeneration, which they had already obtained; that the former is the case, and is not in accordance with my doctrine, which holds that man under the old nature is not able even to seek the good? . . . I, however, answer, the Word is preached to believers already regenerated, and that too efficaciously and with fruit, not that they may be born new creatures, but that they may grow and increase" (ibid.). And afterwards: "While Paul glories that the ministry of the Spirit was committed to him, he mutually reconciles these two things by one word, and declares what he meant by it: namely that God efficaciously inscribes upon the hearts of men by his Spirit, what by his mouth he speaks to their ears, not before, nor after, but at the same time. By preaching, therefore, the seed is sown; the Spirit of God however within causes it to strike root, germinate and fructify" (ibid.). And a little after: "Let us only retain that connection of the secret operation of the Spirit and of external preaching which Paul describes, and we will be freed from all difficulty" (ibid., p. 346). And after he had related how Pighius wished God to convert men, "By his goodness and patience, by not punishing them on the spot, but giving time and place for repentance; still by many means, exhortations, kindnesses, and chastisements urging, soliciting and stimulating them to the same," he adds, "here the whole and entire Pelagius discloses his sacrileges. For he holds to external means only, by which God invites men, and includes in these the whole grace of conversion; preserving a profound silence concerning the more inward motion of the heart, the renovation of the Spirit" (ibid., p. 384).

XXVIII. These propositions being thus established, if the question is now asked whether besides the objective and mediate grace by which the Spirit acts upon minds by the word preached with whatever opportunity and accompanied by whatever circumstances and helps, there is required another grace subjective and immediate by which he operates immediately upon the faculties themselves to dispose them to a saving reception of the word and by whose efficacy conversion is necessarily and infallibly brought about. We answer affirmatively, as the church formerly determined against the Pelagians and most recently against the Remonstrants.

Immediate grace is proved: (1) from the corruption of man.

XXIX. The reasons are first, because the magnitude of the corruption and impotence introduced by sin proves it. For if what the Scriptures teach concerning the most miserable condition of sinners and their total and absolute impotence for good is true (when they call them not only sick and weak, but "dead in sins," Eph. 2:1, 2; "blind," nay, even "darkness" itself, Eph. 4:18; 5:8; "who do not receive and cannot receive the things of the Spirit of God," 1 Cor. 2:14; "the servants of sin," Jn. 8:34; Rom. 6:19; "the enemies of God," Col. 1:21; "who are not and cannot be subject to his law," Rom. 8:7; in one word "who can neither think nor do anything good of themselves," Jn. 15:5; 2 Cor. 3:5), how can the hypothesis stand which maintains that nothing else is required for the conversion of a man than moral suasion and the proposition of the gospel object fitly and opportunely made? Now if nothing else is required to heal the soul, how is it said to be entirely impotent for good; nay, dead? Who could believe that the dead can be raised by the sole proposition (however opportunely made) of the object, which acts only morally and objectively? Who (on the contrary) does not acknowledge the necessity of some omnipotent grace to infuse new life into him and new powers for believing and working? And as for eliciting vision in the blind and the exercise of life in a dead man, a simple proposition of the object is not sufficient, but there is required first of all the restoration of the visual faculty which is corrupted and the renewal of life extinguished by death; so for the spiritual vision of faith, a revelation of the doctrine in the word is not sufficient unless the corrupt faculty is cured within and disposed to receiving the object. Nor is it sufficient for the resurrection of the dead man to excite him (as if buried in a deep sleep) by a loud cry, unless with the external voice an internal and almighty power is conjoined, which can restore life to him. I confess that the difference between spiritual and bodily blindness and death lies in this—that in the latter the visual and vital faculty has been wholly destroyed, but the rational faculty has only been corrupted and not extinguished by sin. But this does not hinder the impotence from being invincible in both, so that the man not only does not, but he even cannot will because although the natural power of understanding and willing remains in man, still the moral habit or disposition of understanding and willing properly is evidently lost. This cannot be restored by an objective presentation of the truth alone, but demands a real infusion of power. To say here (as the Remonstrants and others) that the state of the sinner is described by death, to denote not so much his impotency as his negligence and indifference (as they are often called "deaf" and "blind" who do not hear or see or who are unwilling to hear or see, although they might—the antecedent being put for the consequent because the dead and blind do nothing) —what is it but to do violence to Scripture and to change expressions (which it repeatedly uses to describe the greatness of our corruption) into mere hyperboles beyond all reason? For why should it so often propose to us the sinner as wholly weak (*asthenē*) and destitute of strength (who can neither know anything true, nor do anything good), if this was always in his own power and truly from himself (*ek tōn eph' hēmin*), so that there is not wanting to us the capacity of knowing but only the actual knowledge? Nor would the faculty need grace to confer that power or capacity of acting, but only to excite it by the presentation of the object. Now who does not see that in this way the truth of original sin taught in the Scriptures and constantly believed in the church would in a wonderful manner be obscured and destroyed?

XXX. Besides, it is evident that no object ever concurs to forming and disposing its own faculty to exercise itself, but supposes it disposed and rightly constituted (since indeed it cannot act on the faculty except by the apprehending power of the faculty itself, by which it may be received and which acts on it with a due proportion, which is here required). Whatever may be the presentation of the object in the mind, it will always be unavailing unless it is conceived as already disposed for it; not assuredly by the word (concerning the reception of which we are treating), but by the immediate action of the Spirit, who prepares the faculty. For if a thing can work before it exists and every second act supposes a first, how could man, a sinner, elicit the act of faith and love unless he had first received the moral principle and habit or disposition to believe and love (which he lost by sin)? Who would say that the faculty ought to act in order to be renewed and regenerated? Ought it not rather to be renewed and regenerated before it can act, since it can do nothing good unless begotten again? To no purpose is recourse had here to the natural faculty, which can always receive the object presented and is born fitted to be moved of itself by it. Although it can always understand and will as to being (*to einai*) and in the sphere of being, yet it can (as to well-being [*to eu einai*] in the sphere of morals) neither know anything true, nor do anything good on account of its congenital habit of sin and its invincible impotency to evil. And thus we must come to this—either to deny with Pelagius the total corruption of our faculties and their impotence for good, so that the soul can act on the word by its own strength to the acknowledgement of the truth; or to acknowledge the necessity of an immediate and subjective grace by which it is disposed to the reception of the truth.

XXXI. However, so far is the word proposed to the corrupt mind from being able to move it, that the word itself (if not by itself, at least by accident) confirms and increases those prejudices. The word of the cross preached to the natural man is a stumbling block and foolishness, according to Paul: "We preach Christ crucified, unto the Jews a stumbling block, and unto the Greeks foolishness" (1 Cor. 1:23); "The natural man receiveth not the things of the Spirit of God; for they are foolishness unto him: neither can he know them, because they are spiritually discerned" (1 Cor. 2:14). Here he teaches that the mystery of the gospel proposed by the Holy Spirit through the preaching of the word as the supreme wisdom of God (and is such really) can be regarded by the natural man in no other light than mere foolishness and so is rejected by him as a thing most worthy of the contempt and aversion of men. Now if such prejudices arise and are confirmed by the preaching of the word, how can it happen that they could be taken away simply by it? The Scripture sufficiently testifies that our original corruption consists not in mere prejudices and false ideas (otherwise infants in whom they are not found, would be free from that sin), but in depraved habits and in the general disorder of our faculties and in the total and highest propensity of the soul to evil born in all mortals (whence the prejudices take their rise), which the word (with whatsoever great evidence presented) never could change unless the heart-turning power of the Spirit intervened (who creates and reforms the heart anew and by taking the reason captive bends it into obedience to Christ).

XXXII. This very thing is still more clearly confirmed from the original corruption born with infants. For it is evident (as the Scriptures so often testify) that they are "children of wrath" (even as others), "dead in sins" (Eph. 2:1-3) and "conceived in iniquity" (Ps. 51:5), "unclean" and "born of the flesh" (Job 14:4; Jn. 3:6), who consequently cannot enter into the kingdom of heaven unless they are first regenerated (Jn. 3:5; Rev. 21:27). How then can they be purged of their uncleanness and be born of water and the Spirit (i.e., of water which is the Spirit; or of the Holy Spirit exercising the power of water; as it is elsewhere said, "Christ will baptize with the Spirit and with fire," i.e., with a fiery Spirit, Mt. 3:11), if no other than objective grace is granted through the knowledge of the truth (of which they are certainly not capable)? Surely we must either deny original sin in infants or we must hold that they are sanctified by immediate and real grace that they may be received into the kingdom of God. Examples of this are often seen, in Jeremiah, John the Baptist and others gifted with the Holy Spirit even before the use of reason. Now if such grace is infused into them that works their regeneration, why could it not be communicated also to adults for the production of the same work? For although the Spirit does not work in adults without the word, still nothing stands in the way of the Spirit operating in them distinctly from the word, as it operates without the word in infants by a most efficacious power. This is as easy and prompt to him as it is incomprehensible and wonderful to us, as Calvin remarks most excellently (ICR 4.16.18, p. 1341).

2. From the mode of operation of grace.

XXXIII. Second, the mode of the operation of grace in our conversion further invincibly proves this when it is described as a "creation," a "resurrection," a "new birth," the "taking away of the heart of stone" and the "giving of a heart of flesh," a "drawing," a "giving of the Spirit" and other like expressions. These imply the invincible and supreme power of God. For if the whole action of God consists in the clear proposition of the gospel opportunely made, why is omnipotence required for that? What is there in it surpassing the ordinary mode of man's acting? Is not this to obscure and almost reduce to nothing God's almighty action? To what purpose then are those magnificent words used by Paul to describe the omnipotence which God exerts in us when he says that it is "an exceeding greatness of power" (*hyperballon megethos dynameōs*), indeed "according to the working of his mighty power, which he wrought in Christ, when he raised him from the dead" (*kata tēn energeian tou kratous tēs ischuos autou*, Eph. 1:19*, 20), if God does not act otherwise than morally and objectively as men are accustomed to act? Can he be said to create us, if he does nothing else towards us than to teach and persuade? Verily the wisdom of God (which is accustomed to express things in the most appropriate words) does not allow us to believe that he willed to use such emphatic and efficacious phrases to describe so weak and mild an action; but demands that we say that a certain most efficacious power (if not physical, yet hyperphysical and most real) is denoted. Nor if the Scriptures order us to make to ourselves a new heart, does it follow that this depends on man, not on God; or that regeneration is begun by the work which God commands man to do and when man does it he little by little receives life, as the Remonstrants hold. That command denotes what he is bound to do, not what he is able to do. It is exacted from man while he is dead (which he does not unless vivified, God himself doing in us what he commands).

XXXIV. The similitude of generation, so often employed in this argument, has no little force. For as in man's generation or that of other things which are begotten, two things are necessarily required: the seed which comes from without and the internal virtue of the womb or of the earth, which receives and makes it alive (which the seed does not give but supposes). To no purpose would it be thrown into the earth or womb, unless an internal and vital force existed to receive and give it roots. Thus in regeneration with the word (which has the relation of the seed), there is required the internal and quickening power of the Spirit to dispose the heart to receive it so that it may not fall among thorns or rocky places and on the hard road where it will be either choked or immediately dried up, but on "good soil" (to wit, a "good and honest heart" [Lk. 8:15]—not however made such by its own nature, but by the Spirit through immediate grace). So the barren or effete womb (such as that of Sarah) could never have conceived from the seed unless with the seed should be given a certain internal power to strengthen the debility of the womb and render it capable of receiving the seed and of conceiving from it by its plastic (*plastikēn*) force. Paul testifies this of Sarah when he says, "Through faith she received strength to conceive seed" (Heb. 11:11). Thus the heart of man, which is not only barren and effete, but wholly dead and destitute of strength to conceive any good, could never conceive the fetus of a new creature unless the quickening power of the Spirit should be applied to it for conceiving.

3. From the passages in which grace is set forth as necessary for the reception of the word.

XXXV. Third, here pertain the various passages of Scripture in which grace is proposed as necessary for the reception of the word; as when the psalmist seeks "that his eyes may be opened, that he may behold wondrous things out of the law" (Ps. 119:18) and Paul prays for the Ephesians to be given "the Spirit of wisdom and revelation"; to wit, that the eyes of the understanding may be "enlightened," that they may know "the hope of his calling," and the "riches of the glory in the saints" (Eph. 1:17, 18). Christ is said "to have opened the understanding of the disciples, that they might understand the Scriptures" (Lk. 24:45). He is not said to have only "explained the Scripture" (*dianoixai tas graphas*) as he did to the disciples at Emmaus (v. 32) which belonged to external preaching; but to have "opened their understanding," which implies the power and efficacy of the Spirit operating within and illuminating the understanding. God is elsewhere said "to open the ear" (Is. 48:8; 50:5) for those whom he disposes to hear the word preached and see miracles, unless God gives eyes to see, ears to hear and a heart to understand (Dt. 29:3, 4). In the same sense, God is said "to have opened the heart of Lydia, that she might attend unto the things which were spoken by Paul" (*prosechein tois laloumenois hypo tou Paulou*, Acts 16:14). From this it is clear that the opening of the eyes and of the heart is set forth as a means to attention or understanding of the word and to obedience of faith, without which they could not be obtained. For if the heart ought to be opened to attend to the word, it could not therefore be opened by the word, but ought to be opened antecedently to the reception of the word. The nature of the thing itself demands this; for since attention to the word cannot be in a closed but in an open heart, it must necessarily be supposed to be open in order to attend to it. Nor can that opening be secured only by the word, since it could not secure that except as received into the heart by attention (which already supposes the opening). Therefore since that opening signifies the removal of all the obstacles which hinder the ingress and fruit of the word (which occur in the understanding and will, as well as in the affections), it ought necessarily to be made by grace as distinct from the word.

XXXVI. Vain is the objection urged here by the Remonstrants that this opening of the heart could be made also by the word, as elsewhere Paul is said "to have been sent to the Gentiles to open their eyes, and to turn them from darkness to light" (Acts 26:18). And thus it does not differ from attention, but is used for one and the same thing. Thus God is said to have opened their heart when they attended to the words of Paul. Nothing else is meant than that the preaching of Paul was efficacious and that the praise of this efficaciousness should be ascribed to God, the prime mover of all things. For although the opening of the heart is objectively ascribed to the word also in its own manner (inasmuch as it can be done by a moral cause because it usually takes place not without the word, but at its presence) and is ascribed to the ministers of the word instrumentally because they are the instruments employed by God in this work, still it cannot be brought about simply by the word or by the word presented by men of God, unless the word approaches with the internal power of the Spirit distinct from the word (by whose intervention the word presented from without to the mind may be received by it with faith). Luke distinctly declares this when he says that Lydia first "heard Paul" (i.e., was present at his preaching and received his word into her ears). For the orator would strike the ears in vain unless the Creator would unlock the heart. In vain would the word beat at the door of the heart closed by unbelief and ignorance, unless it were opened by the grace of God working the very thing which it enjoined. On this account, he adds that God opened her heart that she might attend to the things taught by Paul, marking the end and effect of that opening. And thus three things are here distinctly enumerated as occurring in effectual calling: (a) the action of Paul preaching; (b) the action of God opening the heart; (c) the action of Lydia with opened heart embracing the word by faith. These three flow spontaneously from the words of Luke, so that we are not to have recourse to the figure hendiadys—that the opening of the heart and the attention are used for one and the same thing (which everyone can see would be forced and unsuitable to the words of Luke). If elsewhere man is commanded to open his heart (Rev. 3:20), this is to denote his duty, not his strength. Again, it properly relates to those already called. Third, it is not done without the grace of God, which as it knocks acting objectively, so it opens the heart for itself working subjectively.

4. From the passages in which the power of the Spirit is distinguished from the word.

XXXVII. Fourth, immediate grace is favored by those passages in which the power of the Holy Spirit working in us is openly distinguished from the word: "Our gospel came not unto you in word only, but also in power, and in the Holy Ghost" (1 Thess. 1:5*). This could be said with very little fitness, if the Spirit would act in no other way than by the word and objectively. Thus elsewhere, speaking of the ministers of the word: "Paul plants, Apollos waters, but God gives the increase; neither he who plants, nor he who waters is anything, but God giving the increase. We are then co-workers with God" (1 Cor. 3:6, 7, 9). Here God and men not only are opposed, but the action of man planting and watering by the word is openly distinguished from the internal action of God giving the increase (i.e., the power to germinate, grow and bring forth fruit). Hence the planter and waterer are said to be nothing in virtue of their operation; not absolutely and simply, as if their ministry were useless, but comparatively with reference to God because they can contribute nothing besides the external work. This would be of no avail without God, who not only concurs with them in planting and watering externally, but (what is the principal thing in this work) produces life and increase, in which he has no fellow worker (*synergon*). And thus Paul exhorts the Corinthians to concord and to avoid the disputes and factions which were seen among them by occasion of their pastors. For since all are "one" (v. 8) (i.e., in office and work, serving one Lord with conjoined strength and laboring in the same business), it was not right that they should make parties or that on account of them they should be divided into factions. Hence Calvin with propriety infers "that God works in two ways in his elect, externally by the word, internally by the Spirit" (*Defensio sanae et orthodoxae doctrinae . . . adversus . . . Alberti Pighii* [CR 34.345]). And a little after: "By preaching the seed is sown that it may, however, take root, germinate and fructify; the Spirit of God works within" (ibid.). Here belong also the words of Cameron which clearly suppose immediate grace: "That the ministers of the gospel, however, are called co-workers with God must be understood differently. For thus a comparison is instituted between the outward preaching of the word and its power and efficacy in the minds of men, the former of which is indeed from God, but by the intervention of human work, the other comes immediately from the Spirit of God alone. In this appears a certain image of cooperation, man speaking without, the Spirit persuading within" ("Disputationis de Gratia et Libero Arbitrio," Th. 20 *Opera* [1659], pp. 332-33).

5. From the passages which speak of the internal action of God.

XXXVIII. Fifth, no less solidly do those passages establish this which ascribe to God a certain internal action in the conversion of man: when God is said "to work in us to will and to do" (Phil. 2:13); "to fulfil in us the work of faith with power" (2 Thess. 1:11); "to work in us that which is well-pleasing in his sight" (Heb. 13:21) and others of the same kind. To these ought also to be referred those in which God promises "to put his laws within us" and "write them in our hearts" (Jer. 31:33); "to give us a new heart" and "to put a right spirit within us, that we may walk in his statutes, and keep his judgments" (Ezk. 36:26, 27). These either have no meaning or they imply a certain intimate and most efficacious action upon our hearts. Nor can it be said that the mediate operation of the Spirit (which is made by the word) is rightly called internal also because it not only knocks at the ears of the body, but is borne also into the mind itself which it affects. For in the same way, the speech of any man addressing and teaching and persuading others, carried to the mind itself by the senses could be called internal (which, however, no one would say). For it is clear that by these expressions, an antithesis is presented between God's mode of acting and man's. Man's consists only in the external proposition of objects, while God intimately pervades the heart itself and immediately affects it. Nay, thus is the efficacy of the Spirit working in the covenant of grace best distinguished from God's mode of acting in the legal covenant. For in the latter, the Spirit indeed by God-inspired (*theopneustous*) men promulgated the law outwardly and moved also in some degree the mind itself within; but because he only commanded and did not operate or supply strength for acting, on this account it is called by Paul "the letter" (2 Cor. 3:6) "engraven in stones" (v. 3). But because in the covenant of grace, the Spirit not only commands duty by the preaching of the word, but intimately and immediately works docility and obedience, he is on that account said to write the law upon our hearts and to make us to walk in his precepts.

XXXIX. This very thing is more clearly proved from the gift of the Spirit, which is conferred upon us by Christ, who as he is distinguished from the word, so he operates distinctly from it. Not only is it a certain power which exerts itself in man, but a divine person who comes into our hearts that he may dwell in them as his temples (1 Cor. 3:16; 6:19) and abide with us forever (Jn. 14:16); but also because he exercises those operations in us which prove his intimate and immediate grace. For how could one and the same Spirit be said to work all things in us, both as to extraordinary and peculiar gifts and as to ordinary and those common to all believers (1 Cor. 12:11), to bear witness with our spirit that we are the sons of God, to speak and cry out in us, help our infirmities, intercede for us with unutterable groanings (Rom. 8:26), to establish and seal us unto the day of redemption (2 Cor. 1:22; Eph. 4:30), to search the heart, and like fire, oil, light, life penetrate to the inmost recesses of the heart and other things of this kind, if all his virtue extended no further than to a mediate action by the word and if he were not the immediate principle of regeneration, imbuing our souls with life, faith, holiness and joy? Yea, the antithesis instituted by Paul between the flesh and the Spirit (Rom. 8) demands that as the flesh is the internal and immediate principle of all sins in the carnal man, so the Spirit is the internal and immediate principle in the believing and regenerated man of all good works, by which they live and walk and regulate all their actions according to the word of God. Here belongs the passage that the Comforter will teach his people all things and will lead them into all truth (Jn. 14:26; 16:13). To prevent anyone from referring this to some privilege peculiar to the apostles, John extends it to all believers: "But ye have an unction from the Holy One, and ye know all things; nor have ye need that any man teach you; but the same anointing teacheth you of all things" (1 Jn. 2:20*, 27). By "anointing," it is clear that the Holy Spirit is meant, teaching believers not only externally by the word, but internally and immediately. In this sense, they are elsewhere called the "taught of God" (*theodidaktoi*, Jn. 6:45), not only because they are instructed by the word of Christ, but also because they are internally taught by the Father and drawn to Christ.

6. From its necessity and possibility.

XL. Sixth, if mediate grace is not to be admitted, it is either because it is unnecessary or because it is not possible, or because it does some violence to the human will and to free will. But no such thing can be said. Its necessity has been demonstrated already from the magnitude of our corruption and impotence and confirmed from the necessity of regeneration in infants (which cannot proceed from any other source). Its possibility is clear not only from the extraordinary and immediate conversions of those who straightway and as it were in one moment and in the twinkling of the eye and without the previous preaching of the word were renewed and drawn to Christ (as was the case with Zacchaeus, the robber and Paul); but also from God-inspired (*theopneustois*) men who had the secret and immediate inspirations of the Holy Spirit (as the prophets and apostles and other holy men, who spake as they were moved by the Holy Ghost [*pheromenoi hypo pneumatos hagiou*, 2 Pet. 1:21] and in whom the Holy Spirit spoke, and whom the Holy Spirit enabled to speak, Mt. 10:19, 20). For if immediate grace acted in them, why can it not act also in others, since the same Spirit who was the author of prophecy in the men of God is also the author of faith in believers? Hence also we gather that such grace is not repugnant to our liberty; for if it could operate without injuring the will and liberty of those holy men, why can it not equally act in believers (their nature and liberty remaining untouched)?

7. From absurdities.

XLI. Finally (not to offer more arguments which might be adduced further) the various absurdities, by which the opposite view is pressed, sufficiently demonstrate its falsity. For if no other operation of the Spirit in calling is granted except the mediate by the word and by moral suasion, the cause of the difference between the hearers of the same word (of whom some are converted, others remain unbelieving) will not depend upon grace, but on man (contrary to Paul, 1 Cor. 4:7). For since the word (by which grace alone is supposed to work) is often proposed equally to both at the same time and place, by the same preacher and with the same arguments and motives, nothing can occur here which is not common to both and consequently which can make a difference between one and another. Nor does it help the matter to recur here to the diversity of circumstances preceding or attending the word, which by God's Spirit are so aptly and opportunely arranged with respect to the one and not to the other that as to the former the effect necessarily follows, but not as to the latter. For although we confess that various circumstances concur to this work and are most wisely arranged by God and greatly contribute to the success of the good work, still we deny that this variety of circumstances or their concurrence can be called the proper and adequate cause of the difference. For all these circumstances (whatsoever they may be) have to do either with the object (i.e., the word) or with the subject (i.e., man). As to the object, no variety of circumstances can be granted on our hypothesis because we suppose the same word to be preached to both, by the same pastor, at the same time and place and in the same manner. As to the subject, they are either extrinsic and accidental only (having no necessary connection with the effect and which on that account cannot be the causes of the difference between the one and the other) or intrinsic and essential and on the positing of which it cannot but follow (such as those are which affect and dispose the subject differently). Now concerning these the question again arises whether the diversity they produce in the subject (such as, for example, attention, docility and submission of mind) are from nature or from grace. If from nature, Pelagius conquers and man makes himself to differ. If from grace (since this cannot depend upon the word, which we said was common to both), this itself is the immediate grace for which we contend (which was the cause of that difference).

XLII. Again, if a variety of circumstances produces a diversity of effect, then wherever they occur, a diverse effect also will follow and where they are alike, the same effect ought to exist. But the case is otherwise. For in various circumstances, the effect does not cease to be the same and in the same circumstances the effect is often different. How many are there to whom a happy birth, good instruction, blessings and castigations and similar good or evil things equally happen, who are nevertheless affected by them in different ways, either to good or to evil? How many also, who placed in circumstances plainly different, are still equally converted by grace? For example, the two robbers crucified with Christ were in the very same circumstances, the same object was presented to their eyes, the same words struck their ears and they seemed in all respects equal. And yet one believed and was converted; the other remained unbelieving and obstinate. What reason can be assigned for this difference? Or what was the different birth of each or instruction or different kind of life or other hidden circumstances? But besides these being taken for granted, they are not proved. If these were in the highest degree true, they would be of no avail because they could not give the true and proper cause of such a great difference. For the various circumstances which did not prohibit (when an equal occasion of acting badly was given) both from equally indulging in robbery, how could they have impelled the one to impiety and the other to faith when an entirely equal occasion for conversion to God was given? Therefore there could have been no other cause of that difference than the secret influence of the Holy Spirit, who in a similar state, still did not will to give similar grace, in order to show that he breathes where he wills and has compassion on those whom he wills and hardens whom he will. Again, how did it happen that at the same addresses of Peter and of Paul, at the same time and place, and with the same circumstances delivered to large crowds, still some of them believed and others remained unbelieving? No other reason can truly be given for this difference than an internal disposition of the mind, which if it is not from subjective grace, must be said to depend upon nature (contrary to the Scriptures).

XLIII. (3) If the efficacy of calling depends upon a concourse of circumstances which are opportunely arranged by the wisdom of God (as he sees is agreeable to the state, inclination and mental disposition of this or that one), Bellarmine and most Romanists with him rightly maintain that the efficacy of calling depends upon its congruity. For God, in calling man, "employs that suasion which he sees is suitable to the inclination of those whom he decreed to draw efficaciously . . . and as he sees the will to be fitted for consenting" (as we have already proved out of Bellarmine; cf. Section 3 above). However since this comment has thus far been constantly rejected as most false, how suspect ought that hypothesis to be which, if it does not plainly agree with it, still anyone can easily judge that it approaches very near to it?

XLIV. (4) If the entire action of the Spirit is dispensed by the word with certain circumstances, in no other way would Christians be brought into the church than philosophers into their schools; nor will the action of God, converting sinners, differ from the action of the orator drawing men by his eloquence to assent, or of a master teaching his disciple. For in both cases there will be a moral and objective action by which the doctrine is proposed and confirmed by various reasons fitted to persuade. In both, circumstances are sought and laid hold of whether from time or place or the state and disposition of persons, which may be more congruous and opportune for the production of the effect. In both, the arguments are carried not only to the ears of the body, but to the soul itself by way of knowledge (by which prejudices are driven from the mind and the truth impressed upon it). A difference cannot arise here from the nature of the object (which is far more excellent in the Christian system than in human systems). The question is not about the nature of the object, but about the mode in which it is received by man and works in him; or from the variety of reasons and motives which the Holy Spirit uses in the word to persuade (which is far more efficacious in the gospel than in philosophy, as drawn from the authority of God speaking; for in philosophy these are merely external, which can indeed make a gradual and accidental difference, but not an essential and specific difference, since the mode of persuasion by reasons remains the same in both). A difference cannot arise here from the concourse of circumstances which are not only observed by God, but so aptly arranged as to draw the effect necessarily after them (which cannot be done by man, in whose power they are not placed and on whom they do not depend). Although it belongs to God, as the supreme ruler and Lord, to arrange these circumstances, it belongs to man only to observe them and use them when presented. Hence it happens that he does not always persuade because he cannot obtain the concourse of these circumstances; still it is certain when he persuades that happens from no other source than from the concourse of these circumstances (which being presented he opportunely uses). Now who would say that the invincible grace of God does not differ in any way from the ordinary mode of acting of weak men? Why then is the Holy Spirit of grace so anxiously sought (as is usually the case) as often as the word is preached that he may internally dispose and open their hearts, while the pastor strikes the ears of the body, if his whole operation is limited to the arranging of circumstances?

XLV. (5) If the conversion of man must be ascribed to God, not to man, because with the presentation of the word he arranges the circumstances (from the concourse of which the infallible event follows), why should we not say with equal propriety that God is the author and cause of evil because he no less certainly arranges the objects by which the wicked are allured to vice and even certain vices and circumstances from which sin necessarily springs? Everyone knows that it did not happen without the providence and special dispensation of God that Judas was tempted by money, the Jews moved with hatred against Christ, and Herod and Pontius Pilate consented to give Christ up to death. For Peter testifies that they did nothing except what the hand and counsel of God (i.e., his efficacious counsel) had before decreed to be done (Acts 4:28). Nor can it be doubted that the selling of Joseph by his brethren and his being carried down to Egypt was brought about by the providence of God through the arrangement and concourse of all those circumstances (which drew that effect after them). Hence Joseph acknowledges that God himself sent him to Egypt and turned into good what his brethren had meant for evil (Gen. 50:20). Now if the providence of God (which is concerned about evil by the arrangement of objects and circumstances) did not make him the author of sin, why should the arranging of objects and circumstances which draw us to Christ make him the author of our conversion? And if the wicked (although impelled to evil by various temptations arranged by the singular providence of God) do not cease to be the authors of their own sin, why should believers (who are supposed to be drawn to Christ in no other way than by a proposition of objects and the arrangement and concourse of certain circumstances) not be equally the authors of their own conversion?

XLVI. From all these it is easy to conclude that the true cause of the difference between the hearers of the word can be no other than the hidden and immediate power of the Holy Spirit affecting some in preference to others. For whatever other reasons can be adduced, either from birth and temperament or from education or precepts and examples or from blessings and calamities or from other similar circumstances and aids, besides the fact that they can belong to unbelievers equally with believers, it is certain they are not such as have causality properly so called (which obtain the very effect and necessarily convert the heart of man, as they can in some degree move and excite it). I confess that the attention and docility by which men become "taught of God" (*theodidaktoi*, Jn. 6:45), which occurs in some rather than in others, is a cause of this difference. But since this cannot be from nature, but from grace (since we are all equally deaf to the voice of God, yea, also wholly dead), even from this is invincibly proved the necessity and truth of immediate grace.

Sources of explanation.

XLVII. The efficacy ascribed to the instrumental cause does not detract from the principal cause, nor does it exclude but suppose it. Therefore, all the praises bestowed upon the word (as that it is the seed of our regeneration, illuminates the mind, sanctifies the heart, as a two-edged sword pierces even to the dividing asunder of the soul, and the like) evince that conversion does not take place without the word and that the Holy Spirit employs it as a most efficacious instrument for its production. But they do not therefore imply that he works in any other way than by the word, since every objective presentation of the word (even the most efficacious) would always be useless without the immediate power of the Spirit (as has been seen).

XLVIII. Although the word is not sufficient for conversion without immediate grace, God cannot be therefore charged with employing insufficient means for producing the effect he intends, nor can sinners offer any pretext of an excuse. The word does not cease to be sufficient in its own order (to wit, on the part of the object). And if it remains inefficacious in the reprobate, that does not happen by itself from a defect in the word, but accidentally from the fault of man (which so far from excusing him, only aggravates his guilt the more).

XLIX. Although man in a state of sin is never destitute of the natural faculty of understanding and of willing (by which he is borne to the object proposed to him) and can in some measure receive it at least as to the force of its terms and a merely historical knowledge, still it is so corrupt that no moral capacity or disposition remains in it anymore for acting well (until by immediate grace it is disposed for the saving reception of the word and a practical knowledge of it).

L. Since the Spirit never acts immediately upon us without the word, his movement cannot be called brute and irrational (such as towards trunks and logs), but always conjoined with knowledge and light since that immediate operation has in view nothing else than to impress the proposed word upon the heart, captivating the blind reason into the obedience of Christ and so changing (*rhopēn*) by victorious delight the strength or propensity of the will to evil; that what was before followed with hatred and contempt as the highest evil is now pursued with the most ardent love as the highest good.

LI. The Spirit works immediately upon us, not so much before or after the word as together with it. Thus the conversion produced by the Spirit is effected in its own order by the word also: by it objectively and morally; by the Spirit efficiently, who on this account is called "the spirit of faith" (2 Cor. 4:13) inasmuch as the same object (which is presented externally by the word and is received by man at least theoretically and historically) is impressed upon the mind by the Spirit internally that it may be believed by it practically and savingly.

LII. As the word does not exclude the necessity of immediate grace, so neither does immediate grace exclude the use of the word and other external means, but supposes them. Although the word and the accompanying circumstances being taken away, conversion cannot ordinarily happen, it does not follow that when these are posited, conversion immediately follows (unless accompanied by immediate grace).

LIII. Though the impotence of man were purely moral, it would not follow that it could be healed by moral reason alone through objective grace solely. Nay, since it is inexpugnable in the sphere of morals, it demands some power stronger than a moral power (i.e., a hyperphysical and divine) to conquer it. Nor can a remedy be brought to it by moral reasons more than to one naturally dead by natural means. Nor if the suasion of the Devil's word alone begat that impotence can it forthwith be taken away by the sole suasion of the divine word. In his upright state, mutability was essential to man, by which he could easily be turned from good to evil. But in his corrupt nature, no strength anymore remains to rise from the vilest to the best estate. (2) It is gratuitously supposed that a merely moral impotence was contracted by sin, since it both is and may well be called physical also (as was proved Topic X, Question 4), both because it is in us by nature, and it is invincible and insuperable to man no less than merely natural; and because it introduces a real and physical disorder and corruption, not indeed into the substance of the soul itself (as Flaccius Illyricus held, whose comment is deservedly exploded, nor can it be charged upon us except most falsely), but into the faculties themselves, both the lower appetites (by a rebellion of the affections) and the higher faculties of the mind and will (through depraved habits born with them). These cannot (unless by a hyperphysical and most efficacious operation) be restored to integrity so as to be turned from sensible and corruptible good to the eternal and spiritual.

LIV. Immediate grace (as taught by the orthodox) has nothing in common with enthusiasm (*enthusiasmus*), but differs from it in various ways. (1) Enthusiasm seeks new revelations outside of the word; but immediate grace seeks none because it always attends the word (nor does it do anything else than impress it upon the mind). (2) In enthusiasm, the objects impressed upon the mind do not come from without, but are suggested internally by the Spirit through secret inspirations. But here the object is supposed always to come from without and to be drawn from the word. (3) Enthusiasm takes place by sudden movements which precede and often exclude meditation and reasoning themselves. But the operation of the Spirit does not exclude, but draws with itself reasoning and the grateful consent of the will. Finally (not to offer now any more points of difference), enthusiasm does not produce a change of heart but affects the mind while the will remains always unchanged. Hence it also falls upon the impious (as in the case of Balaam and others), but the operation of grace necessarily implies a change of heart and a desire for holiness.

LV. Since the Spirit, who operates immediately in us, is the same in all the elect (inspires them with a love of the truth and with obedience of faith, bestows upon them other gifts), he is falsely traduced as a private Spirit. This is most unjustly charged upon us by the Romanists.

LVI. Although deliberate and rational motions of the appetite suppose a previous knowledge of the intellect in a natural and well-consitituted order, it does not follow that it is always so in a perturbed order and in the state of sin. There are various undeliberate motions arising from corrupt affections which pervert the very judgment of the intellect; nay, impel and determine it to corruption according to the trite saying, "Each one judges as he is affected." Hence by the judgment alone intellects cannot be corrected, but they ought to be cured by immediate grace.

LVII. Although the mode according to which immediate grace acts in us can be neither perfectly conceived nor expressed, its truth must not on that account be denied. There are innumerable things, the truth of which cannot be denied by anyone and yet their mode can evidently be understood by no one.

Fifth Question

Whether in the first moment of conversion man is merely passive or whether his will cooperates in some measure with the grace of God. The former we affirm and deny the latter against all Synergists.

I. This question lies between us and the Romanists, Socinians, Remonstrants and other offshoots of the Pelagians and Semipelagians who, not to injure or remove the free will of man in calling, maintain that it has a certain cooperation (*synergeian*) and concourse with the grace of God. Hence they are called Synergists.

II. The question does not concern the second stage of conversion in which it is certain that man is not merely passive, but cooperates with God (or rather operates under him). Indeed he actually believes and converts himself to God; while being acted upon, he acts; and being regenerated and moved by God, he moves himself to the exercise of the new life. Rather the question concerns the first moment when he is converted and receives new life by regeneration. We contend that he is merely passive in this, as a receiving subject and not as an acting principle.

III. Again, the question is not whether man is able to convert himself without grace. The Romanists acknowledge the necessity of a certain prevenient and exciting grace; nor would anyone dare to assert this, unless he wholly denied the taint of original sin. Rather the question is whether he is able to cooperate with that exciting grace.

IV. The question is not whether any dispositions are necessary in man by which he may be prepared for conversion. We confess that in spiritual no less than in natural generation, we reach spiritual birth by many preceding operations and that God (who wills to perform that work in man not by violent seizures, or enthusiastical movements, but in a way suitable to our nature; and who carries it on not in one moment, but successively and by degrees) uses various dispositions by which man is little by little prepared for the reception of saving grace (at least in ordinary calling). Thus there are various acts antecedent to conversion and, as it were, steps to the thing (*gradus ad rem*) before he is brought to the state of regeneration, either external, which can be done by man

Aquinas on operating/cooperating grace

(such as to enter a church, to hear the word and the like), or internal, which are excited by grace in the hearts of those not yet converted (such as the reception and apprehension of the presented word, a knowledge of the divine will, a certain sense of sin, the fear of punishment and a desire of deliverance). Rather the question is whether in the very moment of conversion and as to the steps of the thing (*gradus rei*), man has anything from himself with which he can cooperate with efficacious grace so that the work can be ascribed not only to grace, but also to free will excited by grace. This the Romanists and other Pelagianizers affirm; we deny it with the orthodox. The latter recognize no efficient cause properly so called other than God himself regenerating or the Spirit of regeneration. And they make man to be regenerated the merely passive subject of the regenerating Spirit and of the new qualities infused by him (although after the new qualities have already been infused, he holds himself as the free active instrument of his own actions).

V. The Socinians (who with Pelagius deny original sin propagated in us by impure generation and assert that whatever depravity or taint is in us is contracted by frequent acts of sin and a certain custom of sinning) recognize no other regeneration than a change of a depraved custom and life and a reformation according to the doctrine of Christ (as Socinus, *De Baptismo aquae Disputatio* [1613] and Smalcius, *De Christo vero et Naturali Dei Filio* 2 [1616], pp. 13-18 define it). Therefore according to this, they hold that even in the first moment, man cooperates with God.

VI. As to the Romanists, the Council of Trent clearly expresses its own opinion: "If anyone says that the free will of man moved and excited by God cooperates not at all, by assenting to God exciting and calling, by which it disposes and prepares itself for obtaining the grace of justification and cannot dissent if it wishes, but as an inanimate something does not act at all and is merely passive, let him be anathema" (Session 6, Canon 4, "Concerning Justification," Schroeder, pp. 42-43). So too Tirinus: "To be excited, drawn, invited by God, is not free to me, for they are the motions sent to us immediately from God alone. Still I am free to consent or not to consent to him exciting and to follow or not to follow him drawing and exercising suasion" (*Theologicae elenchticae . . . controversiarum fidei*, Cont. 14, no. 4 [1648], p. 152).

VII. However because our adversaries frequently distinguish grace into "exciting and assisting, operating and cooperating, prevenient and subsequent," we must before all things ascertain in what sense it can either be admitted or ought to be rejected. If by exciting, operating and prevenient grace, they understand the first movement of efficacious grace by which we are excited from the death of sin to a new life and really converted before any cooperation and concourse of our will; and by assisting, cooperating, and subsequent, its second movement, which is cooperated with by the converted and assists them to act, we would readily admit this distinction. For we see that Augustine often employed it: "We read of both in the sacred writings, both his mercy goes before me and it follows me; it goes before the one unwilling that he may will successfully" (*Enchiridion* 9 [32] [FC 3:397; PL 40.248]). And in the same place, he tells us that it was rightly said by the apostle: "It is not of him that willeth, nor of him that runneth, but of God that showeth mercy, so that the whole is due to God, who both prepares a good will of man to be assisted and assists it when prepared" (ibid.). "That we may, therefore, will, he operates without us; when, however, we will, and so will as to do, he cooperates with us; still without him either operating that we may will or cooperating when we will, we have no ability to do the good works of piety" (*On Grace and Free Will* 33 [17] [NPNF1, 5:458; PL 44.901]). But it is employed in a different sense by them, so that by exciting, prevenient and operating, they mean only sufficient grace acting by illumination and moral suasion (which does not subject the free will to itself so as to efficaciously incline and determine it to acting, but is subjected to the free will so that it is always in its power to receive or reject that grace; to consent to or dissent from it), and by cooperating grace, that which cooperates with the yet unconverted will, and with which in turn the will not as yet converted cooperates. Bellarmine plainly intimates this when he says, "He calls all that they may come to him, not that they can come by the powers of nature alone, but to put them in mind that they should cooperate with prevenient grace" ("De Gratia et Libero Arbitrio," 2.3 *Opera* [1858], 4:300). The Synergists openly acknowledge this; cf. Jansen, "De gratia Christi salvatoris," 4 in *Augustinus* (1640/1964), pp.393-485, who treats this argument fully and shows how far they recede from the opinion of Augustine (who also uses this distinction).

VIII. However, we more fitly distinguish the grace of God, not into "grace giving to the grateful" or "making grateful" (to wit, the gratuitous love of God by which he follows us in Christ and to which we hold ourselves objectively); but "given to the grateful" (which embraces all saving benefits flowing into us from him gratuitously, giving as from a most copious fountain. Such grace inheres in us, into first that by which we are efficaciously called from a state of sin and brought into a state of grace (which is well called prevenient and operating, but in a sounder sense than by the Romanists) and second that by which being already converted we are strengthened and directed in the state of grace (which is appropriately called in an orthodox sense cooperating and subsequent).

The cooperation of man is impugned: (1) by his corruption.

IX. These points being fixed, we proceed to confirm our opinion and build it up on four principal arguments. The first is drawn from the greatness of our corruption, which excludes all cooperation on our part. We are by nature sinners and children of wrath, nothing but flesh, whose imagination is evil even from infancy (Jn. 3:6; Eph. 2:3; Gen. 6:5); who cannot even think anything good of ourselves (2 Cor. 3:5); dead in sins (Eph. 2:1); bearing a stony heart (Ezk. 36:26) and in general laboring under a total impotence to good (Rom. 5:6). Therefore we can neither cooperate nor dispose ourselves to conversion; cf. objections in Topic X, on free will, Question 4.

2. By the nature of regeneration.

X. (2) By the nature of regeneration; since this is a change or renovation of nature, it ought to be the work of God alone and not of man. Both because that regeneration is simply impossible for man (1 Cor. 2:14; Rom. 8:7; Jer. 13:23) and because as in the beginning he alone created man after his image, so in it he alone can reform him (Col. 3:10). And as in natural generation, children cannot beget themselves, or contribute anything to their birth, but are merely passive, so in supernatural regeneration no one can regenerate himself, but it is the work of our heavenly Father alone. Hence it is everywhere taken away from man and ascribed to God (Ps. 100:3; Jn. 1:12, 13; Jam. 1:18; 1 Pet. 1:3, 23; Jn. 3:5, 6; Tit. 3:5).

3. By the infinity of power required in it.

XI. (3) By the infinity of power required in it; it is a work of divine omnipotence, which on this account belongs to God alone and cannot be ascribed to the finite human will as its proper cause. Hence it is called a "creation" (2 Cor. 5:17) and a "resurrection" (Col. 2:12), which can admit of no cooperation (*synergeian*) anymore than they who are created and raised can cooperate in their own creation and resurrection.

4. By the attendant absurdities.

XII. (4) By the absurdities attending it; on this supposition, the glory of conversion is divided between the creature and the Creator and man would have in himself matter for glorying because he had made himself to differ and would possess something which he had not received. The falsity of this, however, the apostle Paul often and expressly testifies (1 Cor. 4:7; Eph. 2:8, 9; Rom. 3:27; 4:1, 2).

Sources of explanation.

XIII. First Corinthians 15:10 does not help the Synergists. (1) Paul treats of his own ministry, not of conversion. (2) He refers all the success of the work, not to himself, but to grace. Paul does not say that grace had labored with him that he might come with it into a fellowship of praise and of labor; but on the contrary, he refers to that which he had said concerning himself—that he had labored more than all (by which *epanorthosis* he wishes to give the entire praise to the grace which was with him). On this account, the words *hē charis tou theou hē syn emoi* are not to be rendered (with the Vulgate) "the grace of God with me" (supply "wrought," as a Lapide and Tirinus hold), but "the grace of God, which is with me" (which the force of the article intimates to signify that whatever labor he performed, he wished to be ascribed not to himself, but to the grace of God which was with him).

XIV. It is one thing to speak of the cooperation of men with God in the work of ministry; another of their cooperation in the work of conversion. In the former sense, they are called "co-workers with God" (*synergoi theou*, 2 Cor. 6:1; 1 Cor. 3:9) because God uses their labors and ministry in preaching the gospel and edifying the church, although in the bestowal of life and blessings and increase God has no co-worker (*synergon*, 1 Cor. 3:9*). But in the latter sense, no one can be called a fellow worker with God in the first stage of conversion, in which the power to believe is given unto us.

XV. When the Spirit is said "to help our infirmities" (Rom. 8:26), it does not refer to those about to be converted, but to converts and believers whose infirmities the Spirit assists, especially when he intercedes for them and teaches them to pray (not knowing how). If men are said to be assisted by God, it must not be referred to the first and prevenient grace by which they are converted, but to the concomitant by which, when converted, they are bound to promote and work out their own salvation.

XVI. It is one thing for man to have a free will; another to be able to cooperate with grace through his free will. We do not deny that man when first converted has free will, otherwise he would not even be a man. But we deny that he can cooperate with God or hold himself indifferent to the receiving or rejecting of his grace.

XVII. Although man cannot cooperate with God calling, it does not follow either that all diligence and zeal in the exercise and cherishing of faith is taken away or that the precepts and promises have no place; or that they are not to be praised who will to believe and repent and that they do not sin who are unwilling. (1) The diligence and zeal of man do not pertain to man's cooperating with God when he is first converted; but that, excited and converted by God, he may act and work out his own salvation. (2) The precepts and promises are rules of duty, not a measure of strength and no faculty is derived from the precept or strength from duty. For God most wisely admonishes man both of his duty and impotence by his commands and employs them as means to bring about what he commands.

XVIII. Although in his regeneration man preexists (which cannot be said of natural generation), he exists as the passive subject of another's operation, not as the principle of his own operation. And if he puts forth vital acts, they belong to the natural and animal life, not to the spiritual life of grace (in respect of which he is said to be wholly dead).

XIX. So far is the will of man from being injured by the grace of God (the cooperation of man having been excluded) that it is the rather made perfect when delivered from the bondage of sin into the liberty of grace (God, who made the will, not taking away its nature and mode of acting, but confirming it). Nor (unless absurdly) is it said to be turned into a log, since it is not only the rational (*logikon*) subject (which is capacious and conscious of grace), but also the living and moral instrument (which God uses to perfect actual conversion in him)—either of which cannot be said of a log.

XX. Although the Holy Spirit is repeatedly promised and given also to believers now renewed and converted (as to the progress and increase of regenerating grace [Lk. 11:13; Jn. 7:38, 39] to promote and perfect the good work which began in them; or to the confirmation and sealing of the same grace even unto the day of redemption and as to the gift of consolation, referred to in Eph. 1:13, 14), it does not follow that it is not also given to the unrenewed for regeneration, as the Spirit of regeneration and illumination. Yea, since regeneration cannot be produced except by the Spirit (Jn. 3:5, 6), who is the author of our spiritual life (Gal. 5:25), it is supposed necessarily to be given.

XXI. The actual mortification of the old and the vivification of the new man, consisting in the laying aside of vices and the emendation of life and morals (to which man cooperates), follows indeed habitual regeneration as its proper fruit (Gal. 5:22, 23; Col. 3:5) and cannot be separated from it. Still it is distinguished from it as the effect from the cause and an act from a habit (Eph. 2:10; Rom. 6:4; Ezk. 36:26; Jer. 32:39). For we are made new creatures by God that we may thus walk in newness of life.

Sixth Question

Whether efficacious grace operates only by a certain moral suasion which man is able either to receive or to reject. Or whether it operates by an invincible and omnipotent suasion which the will of man cannot resist. The former we deny; the latter we affirm against the Romanists and Arminians.

I. This is the principal hinge of the controversy, agitated after the Romanists by the Arminians concerning the mode of conversion (which was defined by the Synod of Dort, *Acta Synodi Nationalis . . . Dordrechti*, Head III-IV [1619-20], 1:297-300).

Statement of the question.

II. On the state of the question, it must be observed: (1) that the question is not whether grace concurs to the production of faith, but in what manner and how long it concurs. For the Arminians seem to grant all things to grace and confess that free will can do nothing of itself. But when they come to an explanation of the mode, according to which grace acts, then they maintain that it always so operates that man is free either to admit it or to reject it, either to draw or not to draw the bolt. Hence of two to whom the same grace is offered, if one is converted while the other remains unbelieving, the reason is not to be found (according to them) in the grace (which is the same), but in the disposition of the subject or man, because the one draws the bolt, the other does not (i.e., one rejects the grace which the other admits). Thus what they seem to give largely with one hand (preaching that the beginning, progress and complement of all our good is from grace), they secretly steal away with the other, maintaining that the mode of that operation is "resistible" (under which word they hide the consent and cooperation of the will by which man can always either reject or receive grace—i.e., make himself to differ).

III. Now although the expressions "resistibility" and "irresistibility" of grace are both barbarous and little adapted to unfold what is sought (for by them, that is called resistible which can be hindered), still since it is one thing to resist, another to overcome, we are compelled to use them *ad hominem* that we may draw off the mask from our adversaries (who under this novelty of words, endeavor to propagate the poison of an ancient heresy).

IV. (2) The question does not concern the power of resisting (or the inchoate and incomplete resistance)—whether man is able to resist God calling and actually resists him. For this we willingly grant and experience to our great detriment—that man not only can resist, but is not able not to resist. Rather the question concerns a total and complete resistance or the success of the resistance (to wit, whether man can so far resist, or actually does resist, as to conquer and overcome grace, and the will always remain undecided). This our opponents assert and we deny.

V. (3) The question does not concern external and objective grace—whether man can resist the word and other external means employed by the Spirit for his conversion. For no one denies that resistance can be so made to them that they often remain useless and inefficacious. Rather the question concerns internal and subjective grace—whether when God applies it for conversion, man can so struggle against it that the event intended by God does not follow.

VI. (4) The question is not whether grace is resistible in respect of the intellect or affections; for the Arminians confess that the intellect of man is irresistibly enlightened and his affections irresistibly excited and affected with the sense of grace. But it is treated of the will alone, which they maintain is always moved resistibly, so that its assent remains always free. There is granted indeed irresistibly the power to believe and convert itself, but the very act of believing and converting itself can be put forth or hindered by the human will because they hold that there is in it an essential indifference (*adiaphorian*) as to admitting or rejecting grace. The falsity of this has been demonstrated in its proper place. Thus we strenuously deny that efficacious grace is resistible in this sense.

VII. The question then returns to this—whether the mode of operation of efficacious grace is always resistible. That is—whether all the operations of grace being supplied (which God employs to effect conversion in us), still that conversion remains so in the power of man that he can close or not close the door (i.e., receive or reject it) and thus convert or not convert himself. This our opponents hold, while we deny. Nay, we maintain that efficacious grace so works in man that although he cannot help resisting from the beginning, still he can never resist it so far as to finally overcome it and hinder the work of conversion.

The irresistibility of grace is proved: (1) on the part of man;

VIII. The reasons are: first, on the part of man—he labors under a total and invincible impotence for good (as has been fully proved in Topic X, Question 4), which is expressed at one time by death, then by blindness, again by a heart of stone and similar phrases. As it cannot be overcome by moral suasion alone (acting only objectively), but requires an omnipotent power (operating effectively if not physically, yet supernaturally and divinely), it thus supposes nothing in man by which he can receive grace and render it efficacious from resistible. For what disposition can there be in a dead man for living, in one blind for seeing, in a stone for feeling? And as for the operation of the senses when they are impaired, the proposition of an object is not sufficient, but the healing of the impaired faculty itself is required antecedently in order that it may rightly apprehend the object and elicit its own act (as was shown above in Question 4). Thus in the faculties of the rational soul corrupted by sin, the proposition of a moral object does not suffice. There is required in addition an efficacious physical or rather hyperphysical renovation of the corrupted faculty.

2. On the part of God.

IX. Second, on the part of God converting—he employs in this work such efficacy and power, as is evidently insuperable (which on this account is described by the most emphatic [*emphatikōtatois*] terms and implies an invincible force and infallible success: as when he is said "to create" men [Ps. 51:10; 2 Cor. 5:17; Eph. 2:10]; "to regenerate" [Jn. 3:5; Tit. 3:5; 1 Pet. 1:3]; "to raise again" [Eph. 1:19, 20; 2:4, 5; Col. 2:12, 13]; "to take away the heart of stone and give a heart of flesh" [Ezk. 36:26]; "to draw" them [Jn. 6:44]). Therefore, as no one can resist a creator, begetter and raiser, so neither can they resist God converting. Although the action of God in our conversion does not agree in all respects with creation, resurrection and generation (and various differences occur here), the force of the argument cannot be broken. In similar metaphors, the circumstances are not to be pressed (in which there can be many disparities); rather the scope only is to be attended (which is no other than to describe the immense and invincible efficacy of grace which exerts itself in the conversion of men like the power which God employs in creation and resurrection). Nor do those magnificent descriptions of this operation (repeated so often by the apostle) have any other reference: as when he says, "God, who commanded the light to shine out of darkness, hath shined in our hearts, to give the light of the knowledge of the glory of God in the face of Jesus Christ" (2 Cor. 4:6*); and when he asserts that he employs in our conversion the same power which he used in raising Christ from the dead—"That you may know what is the exceeding greatness of his power he wrought in Christ, when he raised him from the dead" (Eph. 1:19, 20). Here Paul so extols the power of God that he seems never to satisfy himself. Not only does he mention power, but (that we should not suppose it was here common and ordinary) he adds greatness (*megethos*) of power and indeed exceeding power (*hyperballon*) (i.e., surpassing our comprehension). And as if this was not sufficient, he subjoins the omnipotent and invincible mode in which this immense power operates, not only by mild suasion, but "according to the working of the power of his strength" (*kata tēn energeian tou kratous tēs ischuos*) (i.e., of his mightiest strength, an example of which was seen in the resurrection of Christ), so that the same infinite power which exercised itself in the raising of Christ ought to operate equally in raising men from the grave of sin. Now if God acts no further in converting us than to leave man undecided, so that it is in his own power to admit or reject grace, what need was there for that piling up of words and with what appearance of truth could he say that that invincible power is exercised in us after the manner of the resurrection of Christ? Indeed either all these things have no meaning or they demonstrate the irresistibility and insuperable efficacy of grace.

X. Nor can it be said as the Remonstrants wish: (1) "that he treats of the resurrection of the body, not of the conversion of the soul." The scope and the connection of the words manifestly show that he treats of our conversion and by no means of our resurrection. This is confirmed where the apostle, returning to his proposition, says, "Even when we were dead in sins, he hath quickened us together with Christ" (Eph. 2:5), which cannot be understood of the resurrection; nor can the following: "we are his workmanship, created in Christ Jesus" (v. 10). Finally, if he had wished to denote the resurrection, he would not have said that power is exerted in us now; rather he would have said it will only be exerted in the future.

XI. (2) "That he treats not of the production of faith because he addresses believers who already believed, but of the conservation and increase of faith" (as in 2 Thess. 1:11). Although he addresses those who are already believers, it does not prevent him from recalling to their memories the manner in which they believed and the invincible power of God by which they believed (that on this account they might be the more excited to glorify God). Again, if so great a power is required in its conservation and increase, no less (yea, a far greater) is required for its production. (3) "That the act of conversion cannot depend upon God alone, as a resuscitation of the dead depends upon the raiser alone because it is enjoined upon and often ascribed to man himself." But although it is enjoined upon man as a debt due, this does not hinder God from claiming it as his peculiar work. God by commanding such things as he himself will give shows the obedience due and partly gives it also by commanding it. And although actual conversion is ascribed to man in the second stage (because being acted upon he acts), nevertheless habitual conversion is never ascribed to man in the first stage.

XII. The passages which explain our calling by a "drawing" clearly prove the same efficacy: "No man can come to me, except the Father draw him" (Jn. 6:44). For if anyone properly considers this expression, he will readily discover that it cannot consist with the faculty of dissenting if you wish. For he to whom that faculty is left can indeed be said to be "led," but not to be "drawn" (which indeed denotes no coercion and violence because from unwilling man becomes willing); rather it implies the infallibility of the event so that he who is drawn necessarily follows and cannot help coming—"Draw me," says the spouse, "and I will run after thee" (Cant. 1:4); and where he describes the effect of this drawing—"Every man therefore that hath heard, and hath learned of the Father, cometh unto me" (Jn. 6:45). In the latter, two things of the highest importance are taught: (1) the necessity of grace, without which it is impossible to come to Christ (i.e., to believe) because no one can come unless he is drawn; (2) the efficacy and insuperability of the same because whoever is drawn and taught by the Father comes to Christ. Augustine well remarks: "He does not say, 'hath led,' that we should understand there that the will in some way precedes. Who is drawn, if he is already willing? And yet no one comes unless he wills. Therefore he is drawn in wonderful modes that he may will, by him who knows how to work internally upon the very wills of men, not that men unwilling may believe (an impossibility), but that they may become willing from unwilling" (*Against Two Letters of the Pelagians* 1.37 [19] [NPNF1, 5:389; PL 44.568]).

XIII. It cannot be objected here: "All are indeed drawn who believe, but not they alone." The words themselves prove the contrary; for as by saying, "No one comes to Christ, except him whom the Father hath drawn" (Jn. 6:44), he proves that only those drawn by the Father come to Christ, so by adding, "Whoever hath heard, and hath learned of the Father, cometh unto me" (v. 45), he asserts that all who are drawn necessarily and infallibly come. These two propositions mutually help each other, so that they alone and all the drawn may be said to believe in Christ. No more solid is the objection: "That drawing is not irresistible because it is made by hearing and learning, neither of which can be done in an irresistible manner." The institution of men differs from that of God. Men do not draw by teaching since they can exercise suasion but not persuasion; while they who are taught of God are drawn (i.e., they necessarily follow and obey because they are taught not only mediately by the word, but immediately and internally by the Spirit [1 Jn. 2:20] and by being taught they are drawn). "His own pleasure draws each one," says the poet (Virgil, *Eclogue* 2.65 [Loeb, 1:14-15]). "The mind is drawn even by love," says Augustine ("Tractate 26.4" *On the Gospel of John* [NPNF1, 7:169; PL 35.1608]). Demonstration does not compel, but draws and influences by a friendly necessity. When God teaches, he demonstrates (i.e., not only exhorts and moves, but persuades and carries through); when man learns from God, he is not indeed drawn with twisted neck, but is conquered by the truth and vanquished by a triumphant delight, than which nothing is sweeter, nothing more efficacious. Hence he says all hearers come (i.e., not only obtain the power to come, but the act itself). Augustine properly remarks, "Every man that hath learned of the Father, not only can come, but comes, when now both the possibility and affection of the will and effect of the action is attained" (*On the Grace of Christ* 1.15 [14*] [NPNF1, 5:223; PL 44.368]). So that here the greatest sweetness is conjoined with the highest efficacy, the former indeed by doctrine and the latter by drawing (i.e., such a doctrine as is true forcible conviction [*peithananke*], which by influencing persuades and turns to obedience). Finally to no purpose is it added, "If the drawing signifies an action produced in man before he can come to Christ, he will be already converted before he comes to him (i.e., converted before he is converted)." For what hinders us from saying converted in the first stage (i.e., born again) before he is converted in the second stage? Yea, it is necessary for God to come to us before we can go to him that he may apprehend and prevent us by his mercy before we apprehend him—that he may be found of those not seeking him (Is. 65:1). For no one is a believer except the one who has obtained mercy from God.

3. Because God gives a new heart.

XIV. Third, the invincible operation of God is taught in the passages in which God is said to give us a new heart and to take away the heart of stone and to make us walk in his statutes: "A new heart also will I give you, and a new spirit will I put within you: and I will take away the stony heart out of your flesh, and I will give you an heart of flesh. And I will put my spirit within you, and cause you to walk in my statutes" (Ezk. 36:26, 27). Here the arguments are as weighty as the words are many. "I will give," he says, not only offer and prepare; a "heart," not only a mind, but the very sanctuary of the soul; "a new heart," not, I will patch up the old and change it into a better, but I will give an entirely new and another; not uniting mine with your heart, but removing wholly the hard, dry and totally senseless stony heart; "I will put in you an heart of flesh" (i.e., flexible, soft and obedient, endowed with active feeling); and that this grace may be more powerful and efficacious, "I will put my Spirit," not I will make it to pass like a stranger, but will put it as a Lord and ruler, not in your nostrils, but "within you" to exercise a governing power in you. And lest you should suppose that only the power of doing well is conferred upon you, I will procure the act itself; "I will cause to walk in my statutes," not I will exhort, but I will persuade; not I will impel that you may be able in the way you wish, but "I will cause you to walk," I will work in you to will and to do, I will cause you to do. Now what place could there be for such a magnificent promise if God acts in us only by mild suasion and resistibly? Who does not see that the invincible and insuperable grace of God cannot be expressed by different words? It is the same with the promise in Jer. 31:31ff. where God promises that under the new covenant he will write his law upon the hearts of his people that all may know the Lord. This assuredly denotes not a resistible, but an invincible action which most certainly obtains its effect. For God inscribing the law, it must be inscribed and believers must be taught and converted.

XV. Fruitless is the objection: (1) "that the grace of conversion cannot be described in these passages because God always gave to the elect even under the old covenant a new heart, while here a special blessing is promised peculiar to the new covenant." Although the giving of faith and a new heart is not a blessing peculiar to certain elect persons, but common to all, still some privilege must here be recognized with respect to believers of the New Testament dispensation—if not as to the thing, at least as to the mode and degree of the thing, inasmuch as he gives a new heart far more illustriously and solemnly and to a far greater number than under the Old Testament. Now what are not illustrious, sometimes the reason of them is not given in the Scriptures, as if they were not; as "the Spirit" is said "not yet to have been given" (Jn. 7:39) because he had not been given so gloriously and copiously. (2) "That a giving of the heart is commanded" (Ezk. 18:31). That is commanded as the duty of man which is promised as a blessing of God. By the precept is signified what man owes; by the promise whence he ought to expect what he cannot have from himself. Besides since such a command is addressed to those already called, they are not ordered to make a new heart for themselves so much in the beginning of conversion, as in its progress by the desire of sanctification and repentance. Finally, on the hypothesis of the Arminians, God commands also that we should have a spiritual understanding and affections kindled to spiritual good and yet they hold that these are breathed into us by God in an irresistible way. (3) "That these promises are not absolute but conditional" (Ezk. 11:18-21). A condition is indeed proposed and required by God, but this he himself supplies and creates in the elect by the secret power of the Spirit. The Spirit, therefore, is promised to those who put away the things that ought to be put away, not because they had done this before (for how could they do it before God removed the heart of stone, the cause of all these abominations), but that they may be endowed with the power of the Spirit so that this removal is a condition consequent, not antecedent (which itself also in this place is promised rather than demanded). The reason is plain. This promise contains the principle of all good in man and the cause of all that is demanded from him (to wit, the Holy Spirit, who not only perfects, but also begins in us every good work). (4) "That this promise was made to the whole people and yet in many was not fulfilled, since a hardening of Israel occurred." If not fulfilled in Israel according to the flesh (because all are not Israel who are of Israel, Rom. 9:6), still it was most certainly and infallibly fulfilled and is fulfilled every day in Israel according to the Spirit (who are the true people to whom the promise was made, whom God foreknew, Rom. 11:2; 1 Pet. 2:9).

4. Because God gives the very act of willing.

XVI. Fourth, God gives us not only the power of believing or of doing well, but the very act: "Unto you is given not only to believe on him, but also to suffer for his sake" (*to eis auton pisteuein, alla kai to hyper autou paschein*, Phil. 1:29); "It is God which worketh in you both to will and to do" (*ho energōn to thelein kai to energein*, Phil. 2:13); "May God make you perfect in every good work to do his will, working in you that which is wellpleasing in his sight" (Heb. 13:21). Here also belong other passages where it is said that faith is "the gift of God" (Eph. 2:8) and that "God gives repentance" (Acts 11:18). Now if God not only appeals to and exhorts, but himself works (*energei*) in us; not only works the power but the very act of willing and believing, who does not see that his action is irresistible which necessarily produces its own effect? For if man can always resist or can actually resist, this would undoubtedly be done because the will willed to resist. And yet how can the will will to resist (i.e., be unwilling to admit grace, in which God efficaciously works to will)? And this is that remarkable special grace granted to the elect in the covenant of grace, by which they not only can believe if they will, but will since they can. This the Catholics constantly maintain against the Pelagians: "God commands man to will; but the Lord works in man even to will: he commands him to do, but he works even to do" (Epist. Synod. Afric. Episcop.; cf. Fulgentius, Letter 15, "Episcopi Africani" 13 [PL 65.440]).

XVII. Nor must it be said here: (1) "An act is said to be given, when it is given so that we can perform it." On the contrary (from the canon of philosophers), "From the power to the act, the consequence does not hold good." God gave to Adam the power not to sin, but he did not on that account give him the act of not sinning; otherwise he never would have sinned. Nor must it be said: (2) "That action of God is not irresistible because it ought to be connected with the operation of man, who ought also to work out his own salvation and indeed with fear and trembling." The zeal and obedience of man does not exclude but supposes the necessity of irresistible grace—that man not only may be able to perform it, but may actually perform it according to the promise of the new covenant.

Fear and trembling are no more inconsistent with the irresistibility of the cause than with the certainty and infallibility of the event perceived by us (with which the very example of Christ teaches us it can consist: he, although sure of victory, still was seized with fear, as we read in Heb. 5:7, 8). And on this account the more because that is not a fear of uncertain doubt and distrust, but of humility and pious solicitude (which is one of the means by which God produces in us most efficaciously that willing and doing). Nor must it be said: (3) "The act of faith cannot be irresistibly effected because it would thus not be an action, but a passion." This divine action does not injure but strengthens the liberty of the will, and nothing hinders the same action from being performed freely (i.e., of his own accord by man) and yet being done by the invincible grace of God, which in the highest degree reconciles the infallibility of the event with the liberty of the will. For God so acts in us as not to overturn the singular nature of things, but to leave to each its proper method of acting: "Where the Spirit of the Lord is, there is liberty" (2 Cor. 3:17). Therefore in what way soever the act of believing is introduced by God, still because it is exercised by man, it is ascribed to man. Nor must it be said: (4) "Not faith, but salvation is said to be the gift of God" (Eph. 2:8). If salvation is the gift of God, then also faith itself, which is the first part of salvation. Again because believers are said to be "the work of God created in Christ" (v. 10), it necessarily includes faith as the principle of our regeneration; otherwise if faith were not the gift of God, man could glory in himself (contrary to the apostle). Nor must it be said: (5) "It treats of those already believing and converted for whom Paul prays" (Heb. 13:21; 2 Thess. 1:11). For if we cannot, even when converted, do the will of God unless he works it in us, how much less before and in conversion itself?

5. From absurdities.

XVIII. Fifth, we argue from the absurd consequences of the opinion of our opponents. (1) If grace always works resistibly in us so that it depends upon the free will of man to either use this or resist that, it will follow that in conversion more is to be ascribed to the will of man than to God and that he who uses grace rightly makes himself to differ from others (contrary to Paul, 1 Cor. 4:7) and has some cause for glorying. For if after all the operations of grace, the will of man is left in equilibrium, it necessarily follows that not God through grace, but man through free will is the principal cause of faith and conversion; he contributes what is the greater, God contributing the lesser. Again, if the will is left doubtful in order that it may determine itself, who does not see that man is properly the cause of his own distinction, since grace which is held to be common and resistible could not accomplish this? And since suasion acts only objectively, it cannot be considered the efficient cause, but man must be. And yet Paul, on the contrary, says, "Who maketh thee to differ from another? and what hast thou that thou didst not receive? Now if thou didst receive it, why dost thou glory, as if thou hadst not received it?" But although the apostle there treats of the difference between eminent teachers and those who had received fewer gifts, there is nothing to hinder it from being applied in the highest sense to the difference between believers. For the expression is general and what is said concerning one class of goods, the same is said truly of all others both natural and supernatural—especially of the grace of election, which is the greatest of all and the root and cause of the rest. Again from the lesser, if the believer can do nothing in acquiring or increasing his graces (concerning which he can glory), how much less in laying the foundation of faith, which is far more difficult?

XIX. (2) This opinion weakens the diligence of prayer and gracious actions. For why should believers seek from God the act of faith and conversion, if it depended not upon grace but upon their own free will? And how could they thank God for this gift if they owed it to their own will and not to the power of God? Nothing occurs more frequently with Paul than desires and prayers, no less than gracious actions (which he puts forth for the faith and conversion of men, Eph. 1:17; 3:16, 17; 1 Thess. 3:12, 13; 5:23; 2 Thess. 1:11; Heb. 13:21; Rom. 1:8; 1 Cor. 1:4, 5, 7; Eph. 1:3, 15, 16; 2 Cor. 1:3, 4; 2 Thess. 1:3). And yet if the act of faith is always in man's power (however great the grace of God employed), for what purpose is it sought from God or is thanks rendered for it?

XX. (3) The prescience of God would thus be rendered uncertain and doubtful. For if all these operations of grace having been exercised (by which the will was formed and fitted to be moved), yet the will on account of its innate liberty cannot be moved, he could not certainly know in what direction it would incline because there can be no certain knowledge of a thing which can be otherwise (as has been fully proved in Volume I, Topic III, Question 13, concerning middle knowledge, Section 12).

XXI. (4) The grace of Adam would thus be confounded with the grace of Christ. For it was given to Adam also to be able to stand, as to us it is given to be able to believe. Our condition, therefore, under grace will not be better than his lot in nature; or less exposed to chance and mutability. However it is evident that there is a great difference between nature and grace: the former always mutable, the latter always certain and immutable because in the former man was left in the hand of judgment, but in the latter he is guarded by the power of God. Nor has he only from God a help *sine qua non* (i.e., the power of acting well) but also a help by which (that is, the very act also to will what he can).

XXII. (5) Thus God will not operate more efficaciously in the conversion of men than Satan operates in their seduction because Satan also uses suasion, exhortations, promises and threats to pervert men. Nor can the reason of the difference lie in this—that God promises eternal and incorruptible goods and Satan only temporal and corruptible goods. Although they are false and perishable goods which he promises, still he exhibits them as true and eternal, ensuring the happiness of man (as when he promised our first parents that they would be as gods). Again, whatsoever goods are promised, the mode of action with God remains always the same, if he acts in no other than a suasive and resistible manner. Nor if Satan (acting resistibly) perverts far more, does it follow that God also acting irresistibly does not act stronger than he. The case of sin (in which man lies and to which he is most inclined by his own nature, even without the impulse of Satan) differs from that of holiness to which sinful man is so averse that he cannot be brought to it except by a certain omnipotent power. And although those are far fewer who feel it in comparison with the reprobate, Satan must not on that account be said to be stronger than God because this does not arise from impotence, but from liberty (according to which he decreed to exert that efficacy of grace only in these few).

Sources of explanation.

XXIII. It is one thing to resist the Holy Spirit externally commanding in the word; another, however, to resist him operating in the heart. One thing to resist the Spirit convincing and coercing only; another to resist him converting and renewing also. The Jews indeed are said to have resisted the Holy Spirit in the former way: not in the latter (Acts 7:51). This is clear from the following words ("Which of the prophets have not your fathers persecuted? And they have slain them which shewed before of the coming of the Just One?") and from the example of Stephen. For they resisted the Holy Spirit speaking by Stephen because they were unwilling to receive his word; nay, they rushed upon him like wild beasts (which is the force of the word *antipiptein*). It is indeed said that they were not able to resist the wisdom and the Spirit by which he spake (Acts 6:10, 11), but then to resist does not properly signify to be opposed to or to stand against, but to overcome or to conquer (as in Lk. 21:15). Although these Jews were convicted by the force of the truth by Stephen speaking by the Holy Spirit, it does not follow that the Spirit employed all that grace which was necessary for conversion. There was required in addition a circumcision of the heart or of the soul, which they are here said to have lacked (Acts 7:51), no less than their fathers (Dt. 29:4).

XXIV. Although the Holy Spirit had not decreed or intended to convert them, still no less can they be said to have resisted the Holy Spirit (not indeed intending their conversion, but prescribing their duty and showing the way of salvation and using all external means necessary for their conversion). Therefore they resisted the revealed will, which is the rule of duty; not the hidden will, which decrees events. Nor, if they could not believe without the special grace of the Holy Spirit, which was denied to them, does it follow that God could not justly complain of their contumacy. (1) They could not have opposed such or so great resistance to the Holy Spirit speaking in the prophets, as they did. (2) They were not the less bound to the prescription of duty and their voluntary and affected inability could not excuse them.

XXV. "The eyes to see and ears to hear" spoken of in Ezk. 12:2 cannot refer to the grace of conversion or the eyes of faith. For it is added in the same place concerning "the house of Israel" that it is a "rebellious house" which consequently did not have the "eyes of the mind" or the faculty of understanding and perceiving the things presented (which, on account of their own wickedness, they were unwilling to use). Otherwise if God had given to them the spiritual eyes and ears of the new man, they could not help seeing and hearing. Nor, if eyes to see and ears to hear (which he is said to have denied the people, Dt. 29:4) signify the grace of regeneration, does it follow that they are to be taken in the same sense here because the circumstances are diverse.

XXVI. It is one thing to resist God admonishing and calling externally; another to resist God intending conversion and calling efficaciously and internally. The former is asserted when the prophet says, "He had spread out his hands all the day unto a rebellious people" (Is. 65:2*); not the latter. The "spreading out of the arms" denotes the mild and benevolent invitation of God by which he allured them from without, whether by the word or by blessings, inciting them not occasionally, but every day by the ministry of his servants. But it cannot denote the powerful and efficacious operation by which the arm of the Lord is revealed to those who are taught of God and drawn by the Father and by which it is said that he manifested himself to those who asked not for him and was found of them that sought him not (which the prophet had said concerning the efficacious calling of the Gentiles, v. 1).

XXVII. Although Christ professes that "he had wished to gather together the children of Jerusalem, and they would not" (Mt. 23:37), it does not follow that grace is resistible. (1) Jerusalem is here openly distinguished from her children and by it are denoted the elders, scribes, priests and other leaders of the city (who are gifted with the better name of city [as Mt. 2:1, 3] and who wished to be considered the fathers of the people). Nor does Christ say that those whom he wished to gather together were unwilling to be gathered together. But only that Jerusalem was unwilling that her children should be gathered and "thou wouldst not" (*kai ouk ethelēsate*) (to wit, ye leaders). And thus Christ does not so much complain of those who being called had not come, as of those who resisted the calling of others as much as they could (the key of knowledge being taken away); not entering as to themselves and prohibiting others who entered (i.e., who desired to enter) as much as in them lay, as we read in Lk. 11:52. But still Christ did not cease, notwithstanding the resistance of the leaders of the city, to gather whom he wished, as Augustine has it (*Enchiridion* 24 [97] [FC 2:449-50; PL 40.277]). (2) Although Jerusalem is not distinguished from her children, but is taken for the inhabitants themselves, it would not follow that they resisted efficacious grace, both because not the decretive but the preceptive will is denoted (which repeatedly put them in mind of their duty) and because "gathering together" differs from "conversion." The former pertains to the external call by which men are collected into one by the word and brought into fellowship with the church. The latter pertains to the internal call wrought by the Spirit, whom men cannot resist. Christ indeed wished them to do what he commanded (i.e., it would be pleasing to him) and he had also decreed to command it. But still he was unwilling as to the event (i.e., he had not decreed that the thing which he had commanded should actually be done). For, if he had seriously wished it, no reason can be given why they would not have been gathered together, since no one can resist his will.

XXVIII. When the Pharisees are said "to have rejected [*athetēsai*] the counsel of God against themselves [*eis heautous*]" (Lk. 7:30), we are not to understand the decretive will, which is immutable and irrevocable (Is. 46:10; Heb. 6:17), but the preceptive will, which is often designated by the word *boulēs* or "counsel" (Prov. 1:24, 25; Acts 20:27; Rev. 3:18). They are therefore said to have despised the counsel of God to their own destruction, inasmuch as they rejected the command of God proposed by John by which he called them to faith and repentance, and thus closed the way of salvation shown to them by him and to their own great harm despised that grace of God.

XXIX. The curse, pronounced by Christ upon Chorazin and Bethsaida concerning their obstinacy and unbelief (Mt. 11:21), proves indeed that it was most aggravated and intolerable by an odious comparison with a most corrupt people who were considered by the Jews themselves as infamous and detestable above all others. But it cannot prove that the grace which Christ exercised towards those cities and which they so persistently resisted, was sufficient for conversion. Nor can it be gathered from his saying that the Tyrians and Sidonians would have been converted if the same mighty works had been done among them and a similar grace granted. (1) These words ought not to be understood so much properly of actual future conversion (which cannot be produced by miracles alone) as hyperbolically and popularly (to exaggerate the unbelief and impenitence of the

Jews themselves, which surpasses even the corruption of the most abandoned Gentiles). Such comparative exaggerations are familiar in the Scriptures. Thus the Lord addresses the prophet: "I have sent thee to the house of Israel; not to many people of a strange speech and of an hard language. Surely, had I sent thee to them, they would have hearkened unto thee" (Ezk. 3:5*, 6). Not that these Gentiles would really have been more inclined to hear the prophet, especially since they would not understand him; but to convict the Jews the more for their obstinacy. In the same sense, this prophet asserts that the Israelites were doubly worse than the Samaritans. He says, "Judah hath justified her sisters" (Ezk. 16:51) by sinning far more grievously than they (who had almost reached the climax of iniquity). For no other reason did Christ say, "If these should hold their peace, the stones would cry out" (Lk. 19:40). And nothing occurs more usually and frequently in ordinary conversation: If I had done this or that, I would either have softened rocks or taught brutes or the deaf would have heard and the blind have seen and the like. We do not mean that rocks could be softened or brutes could be taught or the deaf hear and the blind see, but by this odious comparison we mean to express the inflexibleness of the inexorable Judge and the stupidity of the scholar. Evidently in a like manner Christ says here that the Tyrians and Sidonians would have been converted if these miracles had been done among them, not to intimate that their conversion would take place on this supposition, but to set forth the greatness of the sin of the Jews; as if he would say, There is no nation so savage and of so stubborn a neck (I except neither Tyre, nor Sidon, nor Sodom itself) which would not have been converted or at least moved by so great signs and wonders as were done by me among you, against which you inhabitants of Chorazin, Bethsaida and Capernaum still harden yourselves. Further, the foundation of that curse is not necessarily in grace sufficient for conversion, which the Jews received and the Tyrians and others did not. But it must be sought either from the appearances (*ek tōn phainomenōn*) according to the probability of the thing and in a human manner by way of accommodation or from the certain knowledge of Christ with respect to the disposition of the subjects, which he knew was worse and more obstinate in the Jews than in the others; who as they had less light, had also sinned less and would be punished also more mildly. (2) It can also be rightly said that it is not treated here of saving and internal conversion, but only of external repentance. First, because it is expressed by "sackcloth and ashes" (which are external signs of repentance). It is one thing, however, to express conceived grief in sackcloth and ashes and to begin repentance in some manner; another to be converted by efficacious grace. Also because it is ascribed to the sight of miracles, which are only an external means and are not sufficient for conversion, unless an internal and heart-turning power accompanies them. Now although such repentance would not have been sufficient for their conversion and salvation, still it was sufficient for the condemnation of the Jews who, excited by so many miracles of Christ, did not put forth even the least motion of external repentance.

XXX. The act of obedience which is produced by that efficaciousness (which being posited, the act cannot but exist) does not cease to be free and so a true act of obedience, if that efficaciousness neither brings any violence to man, nor introduces a brute and physical necessity, but leaves to him his own spontaneity and purpose (*proairesin*) (which we maintain grace does). For man does not cease to will most freely what he wills, although he wills it necessarily; nor does the grace which makes him willing from unwilling, take away, but rather restores liberty because it is liberty willingly and with joy to serve God. The fundamental error (*prōton pseudos*) of our opponents is that liberty is placed in indifference (*adiaphoria*) and cannot consist with necessity (which we have frequently refuted by the example of the angels and saints in heaven, whose act of obedience is indeed necessary and infallible, but still most free).

XXXI. Although grace irresistibly inclines and bends the will of man, still we must not imagine any coaction here. (1) In coaction, the principle is only extrinsic, to which he who is compelled contributes nothing; while here there is also an intrinsic principle because grace is the soul of our soul (*anima animae nostrae*). (2) Coaction is not in congruity with nature, but conversion perfects nature. (3) It is impossible and absurd (*asystaton*) for the will to be forced because thus it would be nolition (*noluntas*), not volition (*voluntas*).

XXXII. Although no others can be converted than these who are actually converted, it does not follow that others are called to no purpose and hypocritically. There are different ends of that calling (as was said before), which free God from all deceit and hypocrisy.

XXXIII. One resistance is partial and incomplete (which can for a time be opposed and struggled against); another total and complete (which can not only for a time resist the operation of grace, but directly hinder and make it void). We do not deny that man can resist God calling. Yea, we confess that he cannot but resist with the former resistance, but not with the latter.

XXXIV. Whom God ordinarily calls by the word of the gospel alone, these he does not will to convert with that efficaciousness, which being posited, they cannot help believing and turning themselves. But it is not the same with those whom he calls at the same time by the word and the Spirit (which he does towards all the elect) because the Spirit applies all that efficaciousness which overcomes all resistance of the will. The Spirit concurs with the word and the word with the Spirit; not collaterally, as if the word does something which the Spirit does not do, but subordinately; not indeed by a successive ordination, so that the Spirit begins there at length where the efficacy of the word ceases, but by a simultaneous subordination, as that of the instrument to the principal cause (which is here the Holy Spirit, who works in two ways—both in the word and in the heart: in the word by suasion, in the heart by persuasion; in the word objectively, in the heart efficaciously). If the word alone concurred, its force would be wholly resistible; but because the word (in the elect) is never destitute of the Spirit, on that account grace never remains inefficacious in them.

XXXV. The irresistibility of grace can never induce security or negligence and a contempt of means because the irresistible and immediate action of God on the soul does not exclude but supposes the external means (which God uses to carry on this work).

Seventh Question: On Faith

In how many ways may faith be taken and how many kinds of it are enumerated?

I. As calling is to faith and faith is the first effect of calling by which man answers to the call of God, the discussion of calling rightly precedes the inquiry concerning faith (which is indissolubly connected with it). For as God calls by his word and offers the promise of grace, thus man responds by faith and receives and applies to himself the offered promise. The Scriptures often introduce this colloquy: "I will say, It is my people; and they shall say, The Lord is my God" (Hos. 2:23; Zech. 13:9; cf. Ps. 27:8; Jer. 3:22; Rom. 8:15, 16).

The necessity and dignity of faith.

II. So great is the necessity of faith in the matter of salvation that as Christ alone is the cause of salvation, so faith alone is the means and way to Christ. Hence it is celebrated as the bond of our union with Christ because he dwells in us by faith (Eph. 3:17); as the condition of the covenant of grace under which salvation is promised to us, the fruit of election (Tit. 1:1), the instrument of justification (Rom. 5:1), the principle of sanctification (Acts 15:9) and the infallible means of salvation (Jn. 3:16). Thus it is in some measure deservedly a universal virtue, which either formally includes or consequently and necessarily draws after it all the duties of the believer. Hence according to its various acts and relations (*scheseis*), it is compared rightly now to the eye (in respect of the knowledge of Christ), then to feet (in respect of approach and refuge), then to hands and mouth (in respect of reception and application).

Its homonymies.

III. However, faith (to premise a few things concerning the homonymy of the word) is taken in different ways in Scripture. Sometimes it is taken for the "fidelity" which we observe towards others, by which that which is said is done (as Cicero expresses it, "the constancy of words and deeds," *De Officiis* 1.28.98 [Loeb, 21:100-101]), which is the foundation of justice; this is often attributed to God (Rom. 3:3). Sometimes it is taken for the faith which we apply to others by an assent to a thing done or a future thing, resting upon the veracity of the speaker. Either it is taken objectively for the faith "which is believed" or the doctrine of the gospel (which is the object of faith [Gal. 1:23; 1 Tim. 1:19; Gal. 3:25] and its external profession [Rom. 1:8]). Or it is taken subjectively and habitually for the faith "by which it is believed," which is again distinguished by some into the faith "by which we believe God" or "by which we believe in God" (as Lombard observes, *Sententiarum*, III, Dist. 23.4 [PL 192/2.805]), so that to believe God is to believe that God is; to believe in God is to have faith in God speaking; and to believe in God is to place confidence in him. Hence Augustine says: "We believe Paul, but not in Paul" ("Tractate 29.6," *On the Gospel of John* [NPNF1, 7:185; PL 35.1631]). But this difference is not perpetual. For although to believe God and in God differ, Scripture often uses one for the other (as it is said of Abraham that "he believed God" [Rom. 4:3], where the topic is justifying faith; so elsewhere in various places).

Kinds of faith.

IV. Faith is more properly distinguished into that which is a bare assent to revealed and known truth, possessed even by devils (called "historical faith," which is referred to in Jam. 2:19). Or into that which with assent (of the goodness of the object) has come delight and joy, but which is evanescent, called "temporary [*prokairos*] faith," which is spoken of in Mt. 13:20. Or into that which indicates an assent to some particular promise concerning a miraculous event to be wrought above order either by us or in us or about us, called the "faith of miracles" (Mt. 17:20; 1 Cor. 13:2). Or finally into that which involves a fiducial apprehension of Christ and his benefits, called "justifying and saving faith" (of which the Scriptures are full). This distinction is founded both on the usage of Scripture (which repeatedly speaks in different ways of faith) and from its varied relation to the object. For when the object is offered to the mind simply under the idea of truth, the faith occupied about it is called historical; when it is proposed under the idea of a good in respect of some particular promise and as to an extraordinary and miraculous event, the faith of miracles apprehends it. When it is presented under the idea of a useful and pleasurable good, temporary faith is concerned with it. When, finally, it is exhibited under the idea of a moral good, it pertains to justifying faith.

V. Falsely, however, do our opponents maintain that these various kinds do not constitute a diverse, but one and the same faith, since they are mutually separable from each other (cf. Bellarmine, "De Justificatione," 1.4 *Opera* [1858], 4:464-65). For there is historical faith in devils and many unbelievers who still are destitute of temporary and justifying faith (Jam. 2:19), as they are also destitute of the faith of miracles, which they cannot work. In some, temporary faith is found in those in whom there is no justifying faith (Lk. 8:13), or the faith of miracles (Acts 8:19). In others is found the faith of miracles without justifying faith (as in Judas and in those spoken of in Mt. 7:22). In innumerable believers, there is justifying faith without the faith of miracles.

VI. Now although these various kinds of faith can concur in one subject (as in the case of the apostles and others, and then they are not many habits, but constitute one and the same faith at least by aggregation), it does not follow on its own part that they do not differ, since they may be so clearly distinguished by the formal object and the mode of operation. Thus saving faith can be said to contain eminently the faith of miracles because it can be raised by God so as to work miracles. But the faith of miracles does not reciprocally include justifying faith, since the former is found in various reprobates.

VII. Although saving faith is one and undivided (*isotimos*) in all, both on the part of the object (which was the same in the Old as well as in the New Testament as to substance, Eph. 4:5) and on the part of the subject specifically, this does not hinder the equivocal word "faith" from being distinguished in its equivocal senses (which constitute so many kinds of it).

Eighth Question: The Various Acts of Justifying Faith

How many acts does justifying faith include in its formal conception?

Various opinions about the acts of faith.

I. As the knowledge of habits can be derived from no other source more certainly than from the knowledge of their principle acts and of the object about which they are occupied, the nature of faith cannot be rightly perceived unless these two things are known: (1) of what acts it consists; (2) what is its object.

II. As to the acts, they are explained by theologians in different ways—some making more, others fewer. Some make only one, namely assent or persuasion. Others acknowledge only two—knowledge and assent. Others add a third (to wit, trust). Others a fourth also (to wit, confidence or the acquiescence of the will). These different opinions do not so much change the nature of faith as unfold it in different ways. And hence it is that some place faith equally in the intellect and the will; others only in the intellect formally and in the will only energetically (*energētikōs*) or effectively and consequently (or even principally in the will). And thus certain ones include all those acts formally in faith; others, however, suppose or infer some of them.

III. The more common and truer opinion recognizes three acts in faith: knowledge, assent, trust (*notitiam, assensum, fiduciam*). Although all the others can be referred to these, still that we may understand the whole subject more easily, we must treat more distinctly of them.

The direct and reflex act.

IV. First, a twofold act of faith comes into consideration—the one direct, the other reflex. The direct is occupied about the object itself presented in it, while the reflex is concerned with the direct act. By the direct act, man believes the promises of the gospel; while by the reflex he (looking upon his faith) knows that he believes. The direct act precedes; the reflex follows and such a subordination exists between them that just as the direct draws the reflex after it, so the reflex necessarily supposes the first (nor has it a place unless the direct has gone before: for example, a person cannot know that he believes, unless he really believes; he cannot know Christ as his own, unless he believes Christ was given for all believers and penitents).

Six acts of faith: (1) the act of knowledge.

V. Second, these acts of faith are not of one kind, but various and multiple according to its various relations. We can refer these to six and of these five are direct and one reflex. The first is the act of knowledge (*notitia*)—of all things to be believed by us, whether pertaining to our misery or to the grace of God. For as truth is the object of faith (and indeed not any truth, but the divine and supernatural truth revealed in the word of God), it requires above all knowledge for its apprehension; not only that by which we know what things are credible and by which we ascertain the literal meaning of words and terms (which is supposed for faith and can be gained by each one's private study, even by those who do not believe); but also that by which we know the divinity and infallible truth of the things to be believed (which constitutes the first act of faith, as will be proved further on against the Romanists).

2. Theoretical assent.

VI. The second is theoretical assent (*assensus*), by which we receive as true and divine what we know. This is called "historical," not from the object (because it is only of histories) or from the cause (to wit, sacred history), but from the mode in which anything is believed. As indeed philosophers observe three degrees of perfection in assent (to wit, firmness, certainty and evidence); firmness that it may be without hesitation; certainty that it may rest upon a certain and solid foundation; evidence that it may not rest upon another's testimony, but be proved either by the senses or by reason (as in science). The assent of faith indeed has firmness and certainty because founded upon the divine and infallible word; but not evidence because it is founded upon testimony, not reason (which the apostle points out when he says faith is the substance [*hypostasin*] and evidence [*elenchon*] to designate its firmness and certainty; but of things not seen [*tōn ou blepomenōn*] to intimate its lack of evidence, Heb. 11:1).

3. Fiducial and practical assent.

VII. The third act is fiducial and practical assent or a persuasion of the practical intellect by which we judge the gospel to be not only true, but also good and therefore most worthy of our love and desire; also the promises of grace to be most certain concerning the remission of sins and the bestowal of salvation upon all believers and penitents and so also upon me if I shall believe and repent. In this sense, *plērophoria* is ascribed to faith (i.e., a full persuasion of the power and will of God made known to us in his word [Rom. 4:21], the metaphor being taken from ships which are carried into port under full sail). Thus mention is made of "full assurance of understanding" (*plērophorias syneseōs*, Col. 2:2) by hypallage for "fully persuaded understanding" (*syneseōs peplērophorēmenēs*). In Heb. 10:22, the apostle wishes us to draw near with a true (i.e., an upright and sincere) heart "in full assurance of faith" (*en plērophoria pisteōs*, i.e., with a sure persuasion of mind and a firm trust of heart founded upon the word of God). Now this persuasion ought not to be only inchoate and half full (which sometimes exists in the reprobate also who receive the word with joy), but full and absolute, determining and drawing after it the will and beholding the gospel object and the promise of grace, not only as true and imbued with a certain good, but also as the highest good proposed to us in God and affording the sole and most sufficient means of salvation in Christ.

4. Act of refuge.

VIII. The fourth is an act of refuge arising from a persuasion by which we betake ourselves by an act of desire to Christ thus known by us, seeking in him pardon of sin and salvation. Because the desire of salvation and happiness is implanted in all, it cannot happen that man who knows he is most miserable and who is thoroughly persuaded that nowhere else than in Christ alone can the means of salvation be found and that he cannot obtain this salvation without coming to him and being united with him; it cannot happen, I say, because the desire of salvation and happiness is implanted in all, that he (going out of himself and his own righteousness, whose worthlessness he acknowledges) should not seriously and most ardently betake himself to Christ—desire, seek and endeavor to possess him in every way. This the Scripture at one time terms "approach" (*prosagōgēn*) and "access" to Christ (Mt. 11:28; Rom. 5:2; Eph. 2:18); at another "seeking" and "search" for God (Is. 55:6); then "hunger and thirst for righteousness" (Mt. 5:6; Ps. 42:1, 2; Rev. 22:17; Is. 55:1, 2), i.e., a most fervent desire to enjoy Christ and God (Ps. 84:1, 2; Cant. 1:2; 3:1). Frequent examples of this occur with David; with the spouse (Cant. 2, 5); in the prodigal son, who, feeling his own misery and coming to himself, determined to return to his Father—"I will arise and go to my Father"; in Paul counting all things loss "for the excellency of the knowledge of Christ, that he might be found in him, not having his own righteousness, which is of the law, but that which is through the faith of Christ" (Phil. 3:8*, 9*).

5. Act of reception and union.

IX. The fifth is the act of reception of Christ or of adhesion and union, by which we not only seek Christ through a desire of the soul and fly to him, but apprehend and receive him offered, embrace him found, apply him to ourselves and adhere to and unite ourselves to him. For as God freely offers his own Son in the gospel to the sinful soul, burdened and cast down and broken by a sense of his sins, and Christ offers himself with all his benefits and the fulness of salvation residing in him, so the soul (firmly persuaded of the fulness of salvation in Christ, seriously flying to him and earnestly desiring communion with him) cannot help embracing with the highest freedom of the will that supreme good offered, and the inestimable treasure, selling all for him (Mt. 13:44), resting upon Christ as the sole Redeemer and delivering and making himself over, and so firmly retaining him that he is prepared to lose anything else rather than reject him. This is the formal and principal act of justifying faith, usually termed "reception": "As many as received him" (i.e., "who believed on his name," Jn. 1:12); believers are said "to receive the gift of righteousness" (Rom. 5:17); "to receive Christ" (Col. 2:6); "I found him whom my soul loveth: I held him, and would not let him go" (Cant. 3:4); sometimes "meat and drink" (Mt. 5:6; Jn 6); the "putting on of Christ" (Gal. 3:27). And because the soul thus apprehending Christ reclines upon him and rests upon and cleaves to him, faith is also sometimes described as an act of "reclining" (Ps. 71:5; Is. 10:20; 48:2; 50:10; Mic. 3:11); as also an act of adhesion and binding closely, and of the most strict union by which we are bone of his bone and flesh of his flesh and one with him; and Christ himself dwells in us (Eph. 3:17) and we in him (Jn. 15:5). From this union of persons arises the participation in the blessings of Christ, to which (by union with him) we acquire a right (to wit, justification, adoption, sanctification and glorification).

6. Reflex act.

X. The sixth is the reflex act arising from a sense of faith by which the soul which has thus received Christ (turning itself back upon itself and seeing in its heart the direct act of persuasion, refuge and reception) concludes that it believes and, because it believes, that Christ certainly died for him and belongs to him with all his blessings and that he will assuredly be made happy by him. For since he is promised to all those weary with the sense of sin, those flying to and sincerely receiving him (i.e., truly believing in him), the believing soul cannot apprehend itself as weary and see itself in this way flying to Christ and resting upon him without immediately concluding that Christ is his and he is Christ's and that nothing can separate him from his love. An act of this kind occurs in Paul when he says, "I am crucified with Christ: nevertheless, I live; yet not I, but Christ liveth in me: and the life which I now live in the flesh, I live by the faith of the Son of God, who loved me, and gave himself for me" (Gal. 2:20). "I know whom I have believed, and am persuaded that he is able to keep that which I have committed unto him against that day" (2 Tim. 1:12).

7. Act of confidence and consolation.

XI. But seventh, an act of consolation and confidence follows this act—consisting in that joy, tranquility, peace, acquiescence and delight which arise from the possession of Christ, by which the believing soul leaning upon its beloved (Cant. 8:5) and conscious of its own most intimate union with Christ through faith and sure of its own mutual communion and love with him, piously exults and rejoices in the Lord, glories in adversity and courageously challenges and despises all enemies whatever (Rom. 8:38, 39); rejoices with joy unspeakable and glorious (1 Pet. 1:8); rests under the shade of the tree of life and satiates itself with its sweetest fruits (Cant. 2:3), certain that he who began the good work, will infallibly carry it on to perfection. We have an example of this in the spouse (Cant. 2:16; 7:10); in David (Pss. 16:7, 8; 116, 118); in Paul (Rom. 8:38, 39) and in all believers (Rom. 5:1, 2).

XII. And this last act does not enter properly into the essence of faith and constitute as it were its form, but flows from it as a necessary consequence and an inseparable effect. However the others properly belong to it and have their seat partly in the intellect, partly in the will: in the intellect, the act of knowledge and assent which, although required in faith, do not as yet constitute its formal act (which properly consists in persuasion, which belongs to the intellect); in the will, refuge and reception or adhesion.

XIII. However, it ought not to seem strange that faith is assigned to two faculties of the soul. For besides the fact that not a few unrenowned or mean philosophers acknowledge no real distinction between the intellect and the will, but wish the soul (as understanding and knowing) to be called intellect, but as willing and seeking will; it is no more repugnant for faith to belong to two faculties than either free will or the image of God (which have their seat partly in the intellect, partly in the will). Faith is not a unique and simple habit, but composed and aggregate. Therefore it cannot be comprehended by a single conception, but includes various conceptions subordinate to itself (which are well referred to both faculties).

XIV. And hence it appears that Bellarmine and other Romanists falsely place faith so in the intellect as to deny it to be in the will. For since it is evident that faith has for its object not only the true, but also the good, and consists especially in flying to Christ and receiving him, what room can there be for doubt that it pertains properly to the will also? Not a few of the Romanists themselves acknowledge this: "Faith belongs to the intellect and the affections" (Bonaventure, "Liber IV. Sententiarum," Dist. 9, Dub. 1 in *Opera Theologica Selecta* [1949], 4:199); "To believe pertains to the intellect as it is moved by the will to assent" (Thomas Aquinas, ST, II-II, Q. 2, Art. 2, p. 1180). So too Biel, Estius (*Guillemi Estii . . . in Quatuor Libros Sententiarum Commentaria* 3.23.2 [1680], v. III, Pt. 1, p. 62) and Altenstaig in his dictionary on the word *fides* (*Lexicon theologicum* [1619/1974], pp. 324ff.) and others.

NINTH QUESTION

Is faith assent without knowledge and can it be defined better by ignorance than by knowledge? We deny against the Romanists.

I. This question is discussed by us with the Romanists, who the more easily to subject the people to them by a blind obedience, not only keep them from reading the sacred Scriptures, but also exclude from the faith (imposed upon them) knowledge, referring it to a bare assent, so that it is better defined by ignorance than by knowledge, as Bellarmine says ("De Justificatione," 1.7 *Opera* [1858], 4:468-69).

Statement of the question.

II. The question is not whether faith is assent, which is acknowledged on both sides. Nor is the question whether it is a full and perfect knowledge of mysteries, both as to the reason (*to dioti*) and the fact (*to hoti*), so that we ought to believe nothing which we do not clearly and distinctly perceive. For as most gospel mysteries in the greatest degree escape the grasp of the reason, they can never be clearly and distinctly perceived by us as to the wherefore (*to dioti*) or the how (*to pōs*) or their nature and mode, but only as to the fact because they are truly thus revealed. Again, as sanctification is imperfect, so faith has its degrees by which it increases and grows, both as to knowledge and as to trust. In this sense, we do not deny that faith can be called in a certain sense implicit, both in children and the uninstructed (who have only an obscure knowledge) and in the more advanced (in whom the light is always mixed with darkness, who often can reach only the fact [*to hoti*], but do not rise to the why [*to dioti*]). Thus the faith of the Old Testament fathers could be called obscure and implicit with respect to ours on account of the obscurity of the revelation. But the question is whether faith in its conception includes knowledge; if not a full, still a true and certain knowledge in its own order.

III. The question is not whether faith is knowledge, which has evidence. For it is thus distinguished from knowledge, which has a certain and evident assent (which is founded upon clear and sure reason) and from opinion, which rests only upon probable reason. Faith denotes a sure assent indeed, but inevident; founded not upon reason, but upon the divine testimony. Rather the question is whether that assent is blind, destitute of all knowledge, so that it may be better defined by ignorance and to believe is to assent to things unknown. This is "implicit faith" (which they say suffices for the salvation of the laity if they believe what the church believes, although they may not know what the church believes, or what it ought to believe, or what church is to be believed). This is called "the faith of Carbonarius" because being asked what he believed, he answered, "What the church believes." Again being asked what the church believed, he said, "What I believe."

IV. The design of the Romanists is to keep the people in ignorance that the yoke of traditions and of all kinds of errors and superstitions may the more easily be placed upon them. For hence it happens that they keep the laity from reading the Scriptures, that they wish all sacred things to be retained in an unknown language so that they may deprive the laity of judgment concerning sacred things. Thus a thick ignorance and horrible darkness covers the whole papacy and a direful tyranny has been introduced; for there is nothing too false and absurd to be obtruded for belief under the title of the Catholic faith (indeed, untried [*abasanistōs*] and without any examination).

V. We hold that faith includes knowledge in its conception, not that faith is absolutely the same as knowledge, or that to believe is the same as to understand (as Bellarmine falsely states our opinion); but that since knowledge is the genus of all habits, while faith by his own confession is an intellectual habit, faith also ought necessarily to embrace knowledge that it may be true. Hence it appears that Bellarmine does not in good faith exhibit the meaning of Calvin when he says: "He says that the kingdom of heaven is entered not by ignorance, nor by a submission of our sense, but by a sure and certified knowledge," as can be collected from his words. For Calvin says: "The Scholastics fabricated the comment of implicit faith, under which name adorning gross ignorance, they perilously sport with the miserable people. Is this to believe, to understand nothing, provided you obediently submit your sense to the church? Not in ignorance, but in knowledge is faith placed and that indeed not only of God, but of the divine will. For neither from this do we obtain salvation either because we are prepared to embrace as true whatever the church may have taught, or because we leave to it the province of inquiring and of knowing, but when we recognize God the Father as propitious to us by the reconciliation made by his Son . . . By this knowledge, I say, not by the submission of our sense, we obtain entrance into the kingdom of God" (ICR, 3.2.2, pp. 544-45).

Proof that there is knowledge in faith: (1) from John 17:3.

VI. It is evident that knowledge is included in faith. (1) It is defined by knowledge: "This is life eternal, that they may know thee" (Jn. 17:3). Nor is this referred only to the intuitive knowledge in heaven, but it ought to be extended to the saving knowledge required on the way which Christ proposes as the certain and infallible means of obtaining that life and by which it is begun in us (1 Jn. 5:13). "By his knowledge shall my righteous servant justify many" (i.e., by faith which alone justifies us, Is. 53:11). Hence elsewhere its act is described by understanding: "Through faith we understand that the worlds were framed by the word of God" (Heb. 11:3). "And we believe and are sure that thou art that Christ, the Son of the living God" (Jn. 6:69). Here knowledge is added to faith to explain it, to intimate that it is placed in knowledge. Elsewhere faith is expressed by "full assurance of understanding" (*plērophorian syneseōs*, Col. 2:2) and by "knowledge of the truth" (*epignōsin alētheias*, 2 Tim. 3:7).

2. Because faith and the word are related.

VII. (2) Faith and the word are related (Rom. 10:17; Jn. 6:45). Therefore, where faith is, there knowledge ought to be because the word cannot be believed or received unless it be known; for as there is no desire of, so neither is there assent to what is unknown. And if faith is from the hearing of the word and from the instruction of the Father ("Whoever hath heard and hath learned of the Father cometh to Christ," Jn. 6:45), how can it be without knowledge? Can the believer be God-taught (*theodidaktos*) without a knowledge of the things which are taught by God?

3. Because the confession of faith is enjoined upon us.

VIII. (3) We are commanded to make confession of our faith and to give a reason for it: "For with the heart man believeth unto righteousness; and with the mouth, confession is made unto salvation" (Rom. 10:10). "Be ready always to give an answer to every man that asketh you a reason of the hope that is in you" (1 Pet. 3:15). Therefore knowledge is necessary in faith. For who will say that a confession can be made and a reason given for things unknown?

IX. (4) Knowledge is everywhere required in faith. Hence the "word of faith" is called the "wisdom and understanding" of believers (Dt. 4:6). "I am now come forth," said the angel, "to give thee skill and understanding. Understand the matter, and consider the vision" (Dan. 9:22, 23*). Christ commands us to "search the Scriptures" (Jn. 5:39), which cannot be done without that act of the mind by which knowledge is acquired. The Bereans are praised because they did not inconsiderately believe what they heard from Paul, but diligently investigated their agreement with the Scriptures, searching the Scriptures (*anakrinontes tas graphas*, Acts 17:11). And elsewhere Paul praises the Corinthians because they were enriched in all knowledge (1 Cor. 1:5), and challenges their judgment: "Judge ye what I say: I speak as to wise men" (1 Cor. 10:15). He enjoins upon the Colossians the knowledge and understanding of mysteries (Col. 2*:2*, 3*).

X. (5) Ignorance is convicted of being the mother of error and the cause of destruction: "My people are destroyed for lack of knowledge" (Hos. 4:6); "My people doth not consider" (Is. 1:3); "Be ye not as the horse, or as the mule, which have no understanding" (Ps. 32:9). The Sadducees are rebuked because "ye do err, not knowing the Scriptures" (Mt. 22:29).

Sources of explanation.

XI. It is one thing for the faith of miracles and the gift of interpreting the Scriptures to be distinguished as diverse gifts (*charismata*); another for justifying faith and knowledge to be distinguished. The former is said in 1 Cor. 13:2, not the latter. "All faith" (*pasa pistis*) is not put here distributively for every kind of faith, but collectively for a perfect and complete faith in all its parts and degrees (as if he said, Whatever faith belongs to wonder workers [*thaumatourgois*], if all that was brought together into one and was in me). Now that such a faith is meant appears not only from the article, which denotes a certain kind of faith, but also from the explanation added, "so that I could remove mountains" (i.e., perform truly wonderful and stupendous works, a proverbial saying from Mt. 17:20).

XII. What removes all vision, sensitive as well as intellectual, cannot be knowledge. Rather faith is that which moves from (*amovet*) sensitive vision and the intuition of glory, in which sense it is said to be "the evidence of things not seen" (*elenchos tōn mē blepomenōn*, Heb. 11:1), i.e., the proof (demonstration) of things which are either invisible and inaccessible to the senses, or which are hoped for as future, but not as yet seen (i.e., possessed). Still it does not remove the intellectual knowledge of the light of grace, since by it we have the eyes of the mind illuminated that we may know what is the hope of our calling and of the riches of glory (Eph. 1:18) and the things which are given to us (1 Cor. 2:12).

XIII. "Bringing into captivity the thought to the obedience of Christ" (2 Cor. 10:5) is not to be ignorant of Christ or his doctrine or to understand nothing about it. Otherwise Paul would to no purpose say to the Corinthians that he proposed to know nothing among them save Jesus Christ crucified (1 Cor. 2:2). Rather it is to have faith in Christ and his received doctrine and to subject itself to him, although it may seem absurd to worldly reason and wisdom (as in the case of Abraham, Rom. 4:20). This is the "obedience of faith" by which we believe God speaking, although we do not understand the wherefore (*to dioti*) of the things to be believed (provided we do know the fact [*to hoti*]).

XIV. Is. 7:9 cannot be brought in here as if the prophet wished to intimate that faith is only a step and the way to knowledge (as the Vulgate falsely translates, "If ye will not believe, ye shall not understand"). The Hebrew has a different meaning: "If you will not believe, surely ye shall not be established" (*'m l' th'mynv khy l' th'mnv*). Thus it is a rebuke of the incredulity of Ahaz and his court in this sense: If ye will not credit my words, it is for no other reason than because ye are not stable, but faithless in the covenant of God. Or what seems more suitable, it is a threatening of the punishment hanging over them: If ye do not believe the divine promise concerning the preservation of the city, surely you will not be established (to wit, against your enemies or in your land), but you will be taken away as captives, so that certain destruction awaits you.

XV. The lack of evidence ascribed to faith does not exclude all knowledge, but only that which is founded upon scientific means (i.e., upon sense or evident reason drawn from the nature of a thing). It is called "an inevident habit" not to the denial of all knowledge, but to the removal of the knowledge which comes from philosophical reasoning, since it rests upon testimony and the authority of the speaker. Therefore it excludes the knowledge of natural light, not of the supernatural revelation. It excludes knowledge philosophically so called, which is opposed to opinion; but not popularly, as it is opposed to ignorance. And although the judgment which rests upon the testimony and authority of another is not evident and scientific knowledge, still on account of that it ought not to be called ignorance rather than knowledge because we ought always to understand who and what testifies, that we may believe him.

Tenth Question

Is faith trust? We affirm against the Romanists.

I. We said that faith consists principally of three acts: knowledge, assent and trust. We have just now treated of knowledge against the Romanists. Now (the second being dismissed, about which there is no controversy) we must say a few words concerning the third, which is said to be placed in trust (*fiducia*) and concerning which we have a dispute with our opponents.

Twofold question concerning trust.

II. A twofold question occurs here: one with the Romanists, who deny that trust belongs to faith (which means only an assent to an unknown thing); the other among the orthodox themselves—not properly (whether trust pertains to faith), but under what relation it must be ascribed to it (whether of form or of effect). This must be discussed briefly before we pass to the other, which is of greater importance.

1. Among the orthodox, which may be reconciled.

III. The diversity existing among the orthodox arises from a diverse comprehension of trust, which can be taken in three ways. (a) For a fiducial assent or persuasion, arising from a practical judgment of the intellect concerning the truth and goodness of the gospel promises and the power, will and fidelity of God promising; as the synonym to it is "persuasion" (*peismonē*, Gal. 5:8) and in this sense "full assurance" (*plērophoria*) is attributed to faith (Col. 2:2; Heb. 10:22). (b) For the act of "flying to and reception of" Christ by which the believer (recognizing the truth and goodness of the promises) betakes himself to Christ, receives and embraces him and rests solely upon his merit. (c) For the confidence or acquiescence and tranquility of mind arising from the flying of the soul to Christ and his reception. For he who firmly rests upon Christ and embraces him cannot help acquiescing securely in him and trusting that he has found and received what he sought. In the first and second signification, trust is of the essence of faith and is well called by theologians its form. As will afterwards be proved against the Romanists, it is a fiducial apprehension of Christ offered with all his blessings in the word of the gospel. But in the third signification, it is rightly called by others not the form but the effect of faith because it springs from it, but does not constitute it.

IV. Hence the meaning of the passage of Paul readily appears where faith is distinguished from confidence (*pepoithēsei*) or trust: "By faith we have access with confidence to him" (Eph. 3:12). For *pepoithesis* here means "trust" inasmuch as it is the tranquility of conscience; or trust in him in whom faith is placed. The meaning is "believers in Christ" (i.e., planted in Christ by faith) have boldness (*parrēsian*, i.e., both boldness to preach the gospel intrepidly to everyone and spiritual security by which they freely dare to invoke God as their Father); also "free access to him with confidence" (*kai prosagōgēn en pepoithēsei*, to wit, of finding him and obtaining the things sought) "by the faith of him" (*dia tēs pisteōs autou*, i.e., which the faith in Christ procures).

2. Between us and the Romanists.

V. As to the other question, between us and the Romanists, it is inquired whether trust is included in the conception of faith; or whether it differs from it. The Romanists (in order to establish their comment concerning implicit faith and blind or bare assent) hold the latter, maintaining that faith is nothing else than a bare assent which does not have for its object the special mercy of God, but the whole word of God (as Bellarmine states it, "De Justificatione," 1.5-6 *Opera* [1858], 4:465-68). On the contrary, the orthodox think trust is so of the essence of faith that it cannot be called faith which is destitute of such trust.

Proof that faith is trust: (1) from the object.

VI. The reasons are: (1) from the object. The objects of justifying faith, proper and specific (as will be proved afterwards), are the promises of the gospel, which cannot be received except by trust because they are proposed not only as true, but also as good. The gospel is not only the object of contemplation of the intellect, but also the object of consolation of the heart (which faith cannot apprehend except trustingly). Hence as it is adumbrated by milk and food and the sweetest delights, so the faith (concerned with it) is well compared to spiritual eating, drinking and tasting (which cannot be without trust).

2. From the acts of faith.

VII. (2) From the acts of faith. For since (as was proved above) in the conception of faith is included an act of persuasion and the act of flying to and reception of Christ (which cannot exist without trust), from this very thing it is evident that trust cannot be separated from faith, but belongs to its essence. And even the word *plērophoria* (attributed to it) invincibly proves this. Here belong the passages in which faith is described as a fiducial apprehension of Christ and his satisfaction: "But as many as received him, to them gave he power to become the sons of God, even to them that believe on his name" (Jn. 1:12); "that they may receive forgiveness of sins by faith that is in me" (i.e., in Christ, Acts 26:18). Elsewhere faith is placed in this—"that we believe he was delivered for our offences, and was raised again for our justification" (Rom. 4:25); that by faith we apprehend him "as a propitiation set forth by God in his blood" (Rom. 3:25). By this act, it is distinguished from the other kinds of faith which either do not have respect to the promise of God or not in the same manner.

3. From the effects.

VIII. (3) From its effects. The properties and effects ascribed to faith cannot be bare assent, but necessarily suppose antecedent trust as the cause: such as peace of conscience (Rom. 5:1); access to God and to the throne of grace (Eph. 2:18; Heb. 4:16); boldness (*parrēsia*) by which we address God as our Father (Rom. 8:15; Gal. 4:6); confidence (*pepoithēsis*) as to the hearing of our prayers (Eph. 3:12); a holy boldness (*tharsos*) by which we are confident in all evils, glorying (*kauchēsis*) in the Lord (Rom. 5:11); and in adversity (Rom. 5:3). All these cannot be in the believer, except on the supposition of trust from which they spring.

4. From its opposites.

IX. (4) From its opposites. Distrust, hesitation, fear, pusillanimity (which are properly repugnant to trust) are opposed to it: "O thou of little faith [*oligopiste*], wherefore didst thou doubt?" (Mt. 14:31); "if ye have faith, and doubt not" (Mt. 21:21). It is said concerning Abraham that "he staggered not at the promise of God through unbelief [*apistian*]; but was strong in faith" (Rom. 4:20). Christ said to the fearful apostles in the storm, "Where is your faith?" (Lk. 8:25). James wishes him who seeks anything to ask it of God in faith, nothing wavering (Jam. 1:6). Here hesitation is manifestly opposed to trust, which is required in faith. Elsewhere Christ, in rebuking the lack of faith in his disciples, does not convict them of not assenting to the articles of faith, but of diffidence and fear for themselves.

5. From examples.

X. (5) From the examples of believers whose faith is commended for its trust; such as that of the Canaanite woman, "O woman, great is thy faith" (Mt. 15:28), namely by which she confided in the promise of Christ; of Abraham, who being fully persuaded (*pistei plērophorētheis*) is said to have believed in hope against hope (Rom. 4:18*); of the disciples, who left all to follow Christ because they knew that in him were the words of life (Jn. 6:68); of Paul, who believed that mercy was shown to him (1 Tim. 1:16).

Sources of explanation.

XI. Faith is called "the substance of things hoped for and the demonstration of things not seen" (*hypostasis tōn elpizomenōn, kai elenchos tōn mē blepomenōn*, Heb. 11:1), not only because it makes future goods subsist speculatively in the intellect by assent, but especially practically in the heart by trust and hope. Hence Paul explains the *hypostasin* of faith by boldness (*parrēsian*) and trust (Heb. 3:6, 14). Thus it is called the *elenchos* of things invisible because by a fiducial apprehension it places before the eye of faith as present, the things which are invisible to the eyes of the body. Thus he does not speak here of a merely logical and theoretical demonstration (such as science begets), but of a practical and fiducial, which prepares access to God (Rom. 5:2; Heb. 11:6). If among the acts of faith mentioned by Paul, a knowledge of creation is placed (Heb. 11:3), it does not follow that trust is excluded because the positing of the one is not an exclusion of the other. This is readily gathered from the examples of the faith of the fathers adduced by the apostle, which are not only speculative of the mind, but also fiducial of the heart, inasmuch as the fathers not only certainly assented to the promises of God, but also firmly trusted in them (as the examples of Noah, Abraham, Moses and others prove).

XII. What has for its object the whole word of God generically as well as specifically—that is not trust, I confess. But what has for its common and generic object the whole word of God can have the promises of grace as its proper and specific object. What fall under the former are believed by assent and what fall under the latter are believed by assent and trust together.

XIII. Although believing is sometimes taken for simply assenting, it does not follow that it is always so taken or that the whole nature of faith is contained in assent alone because in innumerable other passages belief embraces assent and trust.

XIV. So far is the example of Abraham (Rom. 4) from proving that faith is not trust, that it invincibly demonstrates that it is necessarily included in it because he could not be said to have been "fully persuaded [*plērophorētheis*] and to have believed in hope against hope," unless by trust (inasmuch as he conceived in his heart a firm trust in the truth and power of God, although all things appeared against it). Thus he could not be said "to have staggered not through unbelief" (v. 20) unless inasmuch as through the trust opposed to it he was strengthened against all those things which seemed to oppose the divine promise.

XV. If trust is called by the Scholastics "strengthened hope," this must be understood of the trust of hope, which differs from the trust which is peculiar to faith in various particulars. The former is only of a future good, but the latter of a present; or as if present, as also of a past. The former has for its object more the "thing of the word" (i.e., the promised goods); the latter rather the "word of the thing" or the promises of it—although they so differ that the one depends upon the other and they cannot be separated from each other.

faith is not hope (relevant to Aquinas)

ELEVENTH QUESTION: THE OBJECT OF FAITH

What is the object of faith in general and can what is false come under it? We deny.

I. Because various questions are agitated about the object of faith, we must distinctly discuss them. We do so in four propositions.

The first proposition, concerning the object of faith: that it ought to be true, not false.

II. First proposition: "The object of faith ought to be true and nothing false can come under it." The reason is that the word of God (which is most true) is the sole object of faith and cannot be exposed to any error or falsehood, no more than God himself (its author, who is the truth itself and who, as he cannot be deceived, so he cannot deceive anyone, not knowing how to lie). And yet if a falsehood could come under faith, the word of God could be false, the law would oblige us to believe a lie and divine faith would be a principle of deception (which is absurd). Hence Paul says the faith of the Corinthians would be vain and the apostles found to be false witnesses, if Christ had not risen and if what was false should be believed (1 Cor. 15:14, 15*).

III. The various examples adduced to prove that falsehood can come under faith prove nothing of the kind. The Ninevites were bound to believe that their city would be overthrown, not absolutely and simply, but only conditionally—unless they would repent (as is evident from the edict of the king proclaiming a fast: "Who can tell if God will turn and repent, and turn away from his fierce anger, that we perish not?" Jon. 3:9). Hezekiah ought not to have believed a falsehood when Isaiah threatened him with death because this word was not so much the prophetical prediction of a thing absolutely to happen, as a conditional threat to excite his humble deprecation of it. This he sufficiently perceived when straightway having turned to the wall, he prayed to Jehovah, who also heard his prayer, adding fifteen years to his life (Is. 38:2, 5). Or it was a declaration of the severity of the disease, which according to the natural order of things ought to result in such an event (unless God would deliver him miraculously).

IV. Adam was not bound to believe absolutely that in his state of uprightness he would possess eternal life; but only conditionally if he continued in obedience. This condition was not to be believed because it was not promised, but to be performed because it was commanded. If after his fall, he was bound to believe absolutely that he would die, he ought not equally to have believed before his fall that he would live. The cases are not the same. For in his innocent state, the condition was as yet to be fulfilled; while after the fall, the condition was in fact violated and so the threatening could be actually put in force. Meanwhile although after the fall he was bound to believe absolutely that he was exposed to death, he was bound to believe nothing distinctly concerning the event because it was not revealed to him.

V. According to the command of God concerning the sacrifice of his son (Gen. 22:2), Abraham was bound to believe what was strictly true—that God had commanded him to slay his son and to commit the event to God. But he was not bound to believe that Isaac would be slain by him (which was false; although perhaps he had reached that opinion because he did not sufficiently perceive the meaning and end of the command given to him); yet this was only human faith, not divine. Although by divine faith Abraham believed that God was able to raise up his son if he should die, it does not follow that he ought equally by divine faith to believe in his death; nor ought this to have lessened his alacrity in performing his duty because he was not obliged to attend to the event, but only to the duty enjoined upon him; nor could it hinder the trial of his faith, which was sufficiently evident in this, when notwithstanding all the obstacles in the way of the fulfillment of that command, he still girded himself to obey it, committing the event to God.

VI. The Israelites were not bound to believe absolutely from the promise of God that each and every individual would enter the land of Canaan without any condition; for the event taught that the condition of faith (although tacit) was always implied and since many were destitute of it, it is not strange that they were excluded from this blessing.

VII. Although we are bound to believe that God willed preceptively and approvingly what will never actually happen on account of the obstinacy of man, it does not follow that we are obliged to believe a falsehood. For we are not bound to believe that this will really happen or that God decreed it, but only that God willed to enjoin it upon man and that this is his duty (which is perfectly true).

VIII. In Jer. 4:10, God is not said to have deceived the people effectively by obliging them to believe a falsehood, but permissively (as words often are active in sound, but are permissive in meaning or declarative) allowing them to be seduced and deceived by the mouth of false prophets or judicially giving them up to a spirit of error. The words can be understood also interrogatively (although the mark of interrogation is wanting, as often elsewhere) with the meaning—Have you deceived the people? Can it be that you have duped the people with the vain hope and promise of peace, when you mean no such thing?

Second proposition: there is no other object of faith than the written word of God.

IX. Second proposition: "The object of faith is none other than the written word of God according to the measure of revelation." Faith (*pistis*) is one thing; knowledge (*gnōsis*) another. The latter is gained even from nature by beholding the works of God, but the former only from supernatural grace and revelation by the hearing of the word (which alone is the object of faith [*piston*]). Hence faith is said "to be of hearing" (Rom. 10:17). In 1 Cor. 1:21, Paul testifies, "Because the world" (i.e., the human race) "in the wisdom of God" (i.e., by a contemplation of the workmanship of the world in which the wonderful wisdom of God shines forth) "by wisdom knew not God" (to wit, unto salvation), "it pleased God to save them that believe by the foolishness of preaching" (i.e., by the gospel). This appears foolish in the judgment of men: substituting faith alone by which we believe the word for knowledge which arises from his works.

X. We say that this word as written is the object of faith, against the Romanists, who maintain that there is an unwritten (*agraphon*) word in the voice of the church which can establish our faith. We acknowledge no other God-inspired (*theopneuston*) word than the in-written (*engraphon*) and written; which, therefore, we are strictly prohibited adding to or taking anything from. Now although the word as to substance is always the same (which ought to be apprehended by faith), still not equally according to degrees because God willed to reveal it at sundry times (*polymerōs*) and in divers manners (*polytropōs*); now obscurely, as under the Old Testament, then more clearly, under the New. Hence the object of faith is not simply the word, but the word revealed in this or in that manner. Thus the measure of the revelation is also the measure of faith and indeed not in this sense—that faith always clearly sees what things are declared in the object and according as they are declared; but that it sees or is bound or is able to see no more than what is revealed.

Third proposition: the object is either material or formal.

XI. Third proposition: "The object of faith is either material or formal." The material are the things believed (namely the whole word of God and all its propositions, whether they pertain to the law or to the gospel). They become known to us by a divine and supernatural revelation; if not as to the why (*to dioti*) or the mode and reason, at least as to the fact (*to hoti*); either explicitly in so many words or implicitly and by necessary and evident consequences (which we have proved belongs to the word of God, Topic I, Question 12).

XII. A formal object implies a reason or cause under which things are believed (to wit, the principle itself of believing). This is not the authority of the church as Romanists hold (because although the church may be the motive to faith in those about to believe and the human instrument and means of it, yet it can never be called its principle, as we have already seen in the proper place), but the authority of God, the only one credible of himself (*autopistou*) as the first and infallible truth, revealing himself in the word, in which is granted the ultimate analysis of faith (as in its own formal object, which alone can establish divine faith because it rests in no one except God alone, Jer. 17:5, 7).

Fourth proposition: the object is either common or proper.

XIII. Fourth proposition: "The object of faith is either general and common or it is proper and special." The general is the whole word of God, which is proposed to us that it may be believed, whether in respect of histories (which narrate things done) or of prophecies (which predict things future) or of doctrines and precepts (which regard no differences of time) or of promises and threatenings (which are made to the pious or impious). All these fall under the object of faith, although in different ways according to the nature and condition of each.

XIV. Although primarily and of themselves, all things are not of faith which are contained in God's word (so as to belong to doctrines and articles of faith and that to know all those things is necessary to salvation), still it is of faith and necessary to salvation to believe all things were committed to writing by the inspiration (*theopneustōs*) of God for the fulness of the knowledge of the church.

XV. The proper and specific object of justifying faith, not as it is a theological virtue (under which respect the sole and entire word of God is embraced equally as true and infallible) but as it is a gospel condition, is the doctrine concerning Jesus Christ and the promise of the remission of sins and of salvation in his blood. This proposes for its object God, not simply as a Creator and Lord, but as a Redeemer and Father in Christ; as covenanted and ours, who wishes to be our God that he may bestow salvation upon us. And here God and Christ ought to be indissolubly joined together. God as the supreme good, in whom we are to be made happy; Christ as the only and infallible means by which we are to be led to God. Christ wished to signify this when he says that eternal life is placed in the knowledge (i.e., in the faith) of God the Father and of Jesus Christ whom he sent (Jn. 17:3). This is undoubtedly so because the Father cannot be savingly known unless by the Son, who also has manifested the Father to us and by his own blood prepared a way for us to him (Mt. 11:27; Jn. 14:6).

Is Christ only the secondary object of faith?

XVI. However when we say that God and Christ are the object of faith, we must take special care not to take this in a Socinian sense. In order to overthrow the divinity of Christ, they distinguish the object of faith into primary and secondary: the Father being the primary object, who is the first and supreme cause of our salvation; the Son the secondary object, who is only the second intermediate and instrumental cause of our salvation. Faith in the Father is terminated in him as the ultimate object, but faith in Christ is not terminated in him, but through him is directed to God and rests at length in him. The former is supreme divine worship, proper to God alone; the latter subordinate, mediate, divine worship, ascribed from grace. Thus Socinus speaks against Wujek ("Responsio ad libellum Jacobi Wuieki Jesuitae," 4 *Opera omnia* [1656], 2:557-67; cf. "Of the Person of Christ," Sect. IV, chap. 1, *Racovian Catechism* [1818], pp. 154-55).

XVII. We think that Christ is indeed to be distinguished from the Father in faith and its object in two ways: both in person, as he was eternally begotten of the Father; and in office, as he was made a Mediator between God and men. But as neither the order of subsistence in the divine persons nor the office he bears destroys the mutual equality of the persons (since they always remain mutually equal in essence [*homoousioi*]), so we hold that it does not introduce disparity whether of object or of religious worship in reference to it. Thus the faith is one by which we believe in God, the Father, and in God the Son, the God-man (*theanthrōpon*). The trust is one which is reposed in each, not diverse; one supreme, the other intermediate and only subordinate.

XVIII. The reasons are: (1) Christ is the true and eternal God with the Father, as was fully proved in the proper place. (2) Equality of honor and of worship is ascribed to him with the Father: "All men should honor the Son, even as (*kathōs*) they honor the Father" (Jn. 5:23), i.e., with equal worship because he made himself equal with God (v. 18) and proved himself to be so by his works (vv. 19, 21). Thus, "Ye believe in God, believe also in me" (Jn. 14:1) that your heart be not troubled. Why so? Because I am one with God the Father. If it were not so, he would neither have claimed to be God, nor have exhorted his disciples to trust in him no less than in the Father. Thus frequently elsewhere faith in Christ is required equally with the Father, and in the Apostles' Creed, the three persons of the Holy Trinity in the object of faith are distinguished in order but not in degree. Nor is one faith required in the Father, another in the Son, another in the Holy Spirit; but one and the same faith in the three persons of the one deity. (3) Faith in a mere man (such as the Socinians feign Christ to be) cannot be exercised without sacrilege (Jer. 17:5).

XIX. When Christ says, "He that believeth on me, believeth not on me, but on him that sent me" (Jn. 12:44), he does not wish to exclude himself from the primary object of faith, but he either speaks hypothetically (namely, according to the false opinion of the Jews, who believed that he was a mere man and taught without the command of God, as Jn. 7:16); or it is not to be understood absolutely, but comparatively (i.e., not so much or only in me, but also in him who sent me, as in Mk. 9:37).

XX. When Peter says, "Believers by Christ believe in God" (1 Pet. 1:21), he does not remove Christ from the embrace of the same object, but partly teaches the cause and author of faith, partly points out the order in which faith ascends to God; not immediately, but mediately through Christ the Mediator. But this order (established by the perfectly wise counsel of God) derogates nothing from the equality of the persons.

XXI. Honor and glory are said to be given to Christ exalted by the Father (Phil. 2:9-11) for worship, not as if he lacked it before (because faith in him and adoration had already been commanded [Ps. 2:12]; nay, he had it from eternity, Jn. 17:5), but inasmuch as in the flesh and with it he was declared and acknowledged as the Son of God, who before was concealed under the veil of the flesh as a mere man.

Twelfth Question

Whether the proper and specific object of justifying faith is the special promise of mercy in Christ. We affirm against the Romanists.

I. Although from what was said about trust in Question 10 it can appear that faith in its object regards principally special mercy, yet because the Romanists severely contest it (in order to impugn the certainty of faith more successfully and refer its formal conception to a rude and simple assent), a few words must be given to that question also.

Statement of the question.

II. Because the state of the question is often involved, observe (1) that the question does not concern the common and adequate object of faith, which is certainly the whole word of God (as was seen before), but concerns the special and proper object, and as it is distinguished from the remaining kinds of faith. This we hold to be the evangelical promise concerning Christ, the Mediator, and the special mercy granted in him to believers and penitents. For it so far properly justifies and saves, as it apprehends and embraces the merit of Christ revealed to it in the word of the gospel; and the believer firmly believes that remission of sins is obtained by the merit of Christ, not only for other believers, but also for him privately believing.

III. The question is not whether the special promise of mercy respects every single man to whom the gospel is proposed; but whether it respects each and every single believer to whom it is made. This is not sufficiently attended to by various persons, who from the fact that our theologians dispute against the Romanists that faith has for its object special mercy, infer that that special mercy pertains to every single one and that each one can apply to himself that promise as his own. It is one thing for the believer to be able and to be bound to apply such a promise to himself; another for a man to do it. For since the gospel promises are not given to men simply as such, but to men believing and repenting, no one but a believer and penitent can truly apply them to himself. Not that faith *a priori* causes such promises to pertain to them (since this depends antecedently on the election of God), but because it is the condition and instrument *a posteriori* by which according to God's order they ought to be made partakers of the promises and the argument from which they gather that they truly pertain to them.

IV. Special mercy can be viewed in three ways: either as it is promised in the word to all believers and penitents and as it is to be apprehended by them; or as it is actually conferred upon believers apprehending it and seriously flying to Christ; or as having already been bestowed in fact upon those who have apprehended it by faith. To this threefold relation (*schesei*) answers the threefold act of faith which is concerned with it. First, he who believes that remission of sins will be bestowed by the special mercy of God on account of Christ upon all who will believe and repent and so also upon me if I believe. Second, he who believes that remission of sins is actually bestowed in the present upon me believing and repenting. Third, he who beholds it as having been bestowed already in the past by which I believe that my sins have been forgiven me on account of Christ, in whom I know that I believe. The first is called an "act dispository" to justification because it disposes us to receive it; the second an "act justificatory" because the absolving sentence of our justification attends it; the third an "act consolatory" because it follows it. The first two are direct, which are carried into the promise; the third is a reflex, which is carried into a direct act. The former precede justification, if not in order of time, at least in order of nature as its cause; the latter, however, follows it as the effect. Now although they all pertain to justifying faith, still they are not equally essential to or inseparable from it. For the first two are so essential to faith that no one can be a true believer or obtain justification without them; but the third is not of equal necessity (at least as to its exercise) and rather belongs to the perfection of faith than to its essence (since it is certain that the believer can sometimes be without that feeling).

V. Hence it appears that the special application of promises is twofold: one which respects the remission of sins as a good to be certainly obtained; the other which beholds it as a good already bestowed. Each distinguishes justifying faith from historical; but the first alone is the principal act of the faith which justifies us, while the second follows it as its fruit. Historical faith regards the promise of the gospel merely theoretically without any application. But justifying faith goes further, causing the believing man to regard the promises as intended for penitents (of the number of whom he is). This application neither demons nor the impenitent can make. The other follows this application by a reflex act by which the believer, seeing that he has believed, is surely persuaded that his sins have been pardoned. The first application is the trust of adhesion, by which it happens that man, flying to Christ, rests upon and cleaves to him. The other is the "trust of sense," which rests upon the sense of Christ received and of remission obtained in him.

VI. And hence the answer to the question agitated here is easy—whether the object of saving faith is the remission of sins, either already obtained or still to be obtained. Hence our opponents take occasion to traduce our doctrine as absurd (involving us in a ridiculous circle)—as if we say that justifying faith (by which we obtain the pardon of sins) consists in this: that we believe our sins have been already pardoned—as Arnaldus, following Bellarmine, fully discusses (*Le Renversement de la Morale de Jesus-Christ* 2*.9 [1672], pp. 183-89). But it is easy to rid ourselves of such misrepresentations and calumnies. First, remission can be said to have been obtained by right through the death of Christ, in whose blood we have remission (Eph. 1:7); or in fact by the efficacious application of it to the heart. In the former sense, the object of faith is properly said to be the remission of sins already obtained (namely, by the merit of Christ). But in the latter sense, it is only remission about to be obtained because, since faith is the instrumental cause of justification, it ought to precede justification. And yet the trust of remission obtained necessarily follows it because the persuasion concerning anything done is always posterior to the thing done (which is its object and cannot be its cause). Second, the fiducial act (as we have already said) is twofold: one which precedes justification as its cause; the other which follows it as its effect. The former (which consists in a persuasion of the most full satisfaction of Christ made for the sins of all who believe, fly to and receive him) respects the remission already obtained by the merit of Christ, but to be really applied to me believing. The latter (which consists in the reflex act of faith and in the sense of justification) regards remission as already applied to me. By that, I believe that my sins will be pardoned in the future or are here and now in the present remitted. By this, however, I believe that my sins have already been forgiven me in the past. Hence to obtain the remission of sins, I ought not to believe that my sins have been pardoned (as they falsely charge upon us); but I ought to believe that my sins will most certainly be forgiven me (believing and repenting) according to the promise made to those who believe and repent (which afterwards, from a secondary and reflex act by the sense of faith, I believe have been pardoned).

Proof that the proper object of faith is the promise of special mercy: 1. because . . .

VII. These things being established, the question returns to this—whether the proper and specific object of faith is the promise of the special mercy of God in Christ. The Romanists deny this; we affirm it. The reasons are: (1) the object of faith is the same as that of the gospel, since these have a mutual relation to each other. Now the proper and specific object of the gospel is the promise of special mercy in Christ (Rom. 1:16; Jn. 3;16), since it has no other object than to set forth to us Christ crucified as the author of salvation to all who repent and believe, and thus our Messiah and Redeemer if we believe.

2. From faith.

(2) Faith has regard to the promise of grace. Now every promise implies a special application with respect to those to whom it is made. For although in general it is proposed to all believing, yet because all individuals are contained under the genus, whoever apprehends as true the general promise concerning the saving of all who believe, ought also to apply it to himself in particular, if he feels that he is of the number of those believing. However since it is certain that the believer can be sure of his own faith (as will be proved hereafter) nothing prevents him from rightfully and lawfully applying to himself the general promise as pertaining to himself. Yea, once the promises were made for no other end than that they should be received, every single person ought to apply them to themselves.

3. From the examples of the saints.

VIII. (3) The faith of the saints always principally had regard to special mercy in Christ. Paul testifies that he believes Christ loved him and died for him (Gal. 2:20); that Christ came to save sinners, of whom he is the chief (1 Tim. 1:15). He indicates the same thing everywhere for believers (Rom. 8:16, 32, 33; Eph. 1:3-5; 2 Cor. 5:1; Col. 1:5; 1 Pet. 1:2; 1 Cor. 2:12; 1 Jn. 3:2). Nor must we here have recourse to a certain special and extraordinary revelation, belonging to some and not to all. That persuasion is not founded upon any privilege of certain believers, but depends upon general foundations common to all believers (to wit, the nature of the covenant; the death and resurrection of Christ; the faithfulness of God and the like).

4. From the sacraments.

IX. (4) The sacraments, which are the seals of the promises, imply that particular application inasmuch as they were instituted for this end—that the general and indefinite promises might be applied and sealed to each particular individual. Hence they are proposed not only in general, but they are administered and proposed in particular to this or that individual, who is supposed to have faith. Now the reason of the sacraments is also the same as the promises. Nor is it any help to say with Bellarmine that the sacraments are infallible signs of salvation, not absolutely, but on their own part, if man does not interpose an obstacle. As we have already said, we speak here of the true believer, not of the hypocrite who shuts the door and to whom therefore the sacrament seals nothing.

5. From the sealing of the Spirit.

X. (5) They who are sealed by the Holy Spirit and have received the earnest of the inheritance can apply the promises to themselves; for no one is sealed unto an indefinite hope, but only he to whom the promise is peculiarly applied. Now the earnest is given not only that one may know that the salvation to be obtained by a few has been promised to all and with no choice, but that he may understand that he has been chosen among all and out of all, to whom the promise would be made certain. And this is predicated everywhere of believers (2 Cor. 1:21, 22; Eph. 1:13; 4:30; Rom. 8:16).

XI. (6) Justifying faith without special mercy would not differ from the faith of devils and the reprobate (to whom knowledge and assent can belong, but not trust in the divine promises).

object is special mercy

XII. Although the special promise of mercy with respect to individual believers in particular is not contained expressly and explicitly in the word, still it may be deduced from it implicitly and by necessary consequence. For he who says, Whoever believes shall be saved, says also that Peter and John believing shall be saved. As in the law special precepts are contained under the general and what is in general prohibited to all ought also to be applied in particular to individuals, thus what is promised to all in any class can and ought to be applied to individuals contained in that class. Again, since Christ has applied to various persons the promises in particular (as to the paralytic, the thief, the adulteress), so the Holy Spirit applies the same in particular to those who believe (Rom. 8:16); as gospel ministers do (Jn. 20:23) who are ambassadors for Christ (2 Cor. 5:20).

XIII. What the apostle says ("Faith is the evidence of things not seen," Heb. 11:1) proves indeed that in faith is required the knowledge and firm persuasion of the truth of the things proposed for belief; but does not deny that the trust in special mercy pertains to it. Yea, he necessarily supposes this when he says it is "the substance of things hoped for" (*hypostasin tōn elpizomenōn*). What he adds concerning the creation of the world (v. 3) and the building of the ark has the same bearing. For as redemption supposes creation, so the knowledge of the former supposes the knowledge of the latter (as justifying faith supposes historical faith). It is false however concerning Noah, that in the building of the ark he regarded nothing but the dreadful judgment of God in destroying the human race and did not think about the deliverance of himself and his own by special mercy. Nay, for no other reason did he build the ark than to provide for himself and his family. When the object of faith is said to be to believe that God is and is the rewarder of them that seek him (v. 6), it is evident that two things are necessarily joined together (which are gratuitously bestowed from special mercy): knowledge and assent in respect of the existence of God; and trust in the rewards.

XIV. Since Christ proposes himself to his hearers as the object of faith, he cannot be said to have required only a belief in his omnipotence or divinity without special mercy (which will not be shown elsewhere than in him). This appears from the example of the blind men who implored his mercy, "Have pity upon us, thou Son of David" (Mt. 9:27*); and of Peter and the apostles, who professed to believe that Jesus is the Christ and the Son of the living God (i.e., the Mediator who was about to conciliate the favor of God for us, as they elsewhere explain this, Jn. 6:69); of the centurion who not only believed that Christ could by his power, but that he also wished by his grace to cure his servant (Lk. 7:9); of Martha, who asserted that she believed Christ to be the Messiah who was to come for the salvation of men (Jn. 11:27).

XV. Although Christ healed the leper (not fully persuaded of his will, Mk. 1:40), it does not follow that justifying grace does not have regard to special mercy. For the case of a temporal blessing widely differs from that of an eternal blessing. If it was permitted the leper to doubt concerning the restoration of health (concerning which he had received no peculiar promise), it is not lawful for us also without a reflection upon God to doubt concerning a participation in the grace and salvation promised to all that believe. Again, although Christ, accommodating himself to human infirmity, mildly passes over and covers the defects, he does not on that account approve them since elsewhere he frequently rebukes his disciples for their doubts concerning his benevolence and their little faith (*oligopistian*, Mt. 8:26; 14:31).

XVI. The faith in the resurrection and divinity of Christ (demanded from the apostles, Rom. 4; 10:9; 1 Cor. 15; Acts 2:24; 4:10; 10:40) does not exclude, but supposes special mercy because in this is the foundation of our salvation and consolation—that God sent his Son into the world to die for our sins and to be raised for our justification.

XVII. Although the Apostles' Creed contains nothing explicit about special mercy, still it involves it sufficiently expressly, not only in the article about the remission of sins and eternal life, but principally where faith in God—the Father, Son and Holy Spirit—is described (which necessarily implies the fiducial apprehension of special mercy).

XVIII. Although the faith which justifies regards as its object the whole word of God and includes many things which are merely historical and dogmatic, still as it justifies, its proper object is special mercy because it cannot justify except as it regards the mercy of God in Christ.

XIX. So far is the faith in special mercy from doing away with preaching, the sacraments and good works, that it supposes their necessity because they are the means by which it is sealed and confirmed and increased in us. Nor is the grace of God a cushion of security or a cause of licentiousness, but the mother of vigilance and an incentive to holiness (2 Cor. 5:14; Gal. 2:20; Ps. 130:4).

XX. Although the faith of believers has been according to the measure of revelation, either more obscure or clearer in the Old and New Testaments, yet it always had for its object God's special mercy in Christ. Under the New Testament Christ clearly proclaimed himself to be the Messiah, the Savior of the world (Jn. 4:26), by the merit of his death (Mt. 20:28; 26:28) and by the efficacy of the Spirit (Jn. 4:14; 7:37), indeed to those who believe in his name (Jn. 3; 6). And if the apostles did not sufficiently understand what he said about his passion and death (Lk. 18:32-34), this must be ascribed to their weakness and their preconceived opinion about the temporal kingdom of Christ, which was afterwards corrected by him; but not to a defect in the revelation, which was sufficiently clear. As to the believers of the Old Testament, their faith (although more obscure) had also for its object Christ and the promises of grace in him (as is evident from Jn. 8:56; Lk. 10:24; Acts 10:43; Heb. 11; 1 Pet. 1:10, 11). And even the sole little clause of the covenant proves this. It could not be received by them in faith, unless they believed in the Messiah also, on whom that covenant was founded and in whom all the promises of God are Yea and Amen (2 Cor. 1:20).

Thirteenth Question

Whether the form of justifying faith is love or obedience to God's commands. We deny against the Romanists and Socinians.

Twofold question concerning the form of faith.

I. A twofold question is agitated here: (1) against the Romanists, who hold love to be the form of faith; (2) against the Socinians, who make its form to consist in obedience to God's commands. We must treat these clearly.

1. With the Romanists.

II. The Romanists (to prove that faith considered in itself does not justify, but borrows its whole power of justifying from love) distinguish faith into formed and unformed. They term that unformed which is separated from love, and formed that which is perfected by love as the form (which the Scholastics laboriously strive to establish; cf. Peter Lombard, *Sententiarum*, III, Dist. 23 [PL 192/2.805-7]). They hold indeed that there is in it whatever is necessary to belief, but that love ought also to be in it and concur with it to our vivification and justification before God. But because they see it can be opposed to them (that faith has its own internal form by which it is constituted and becomes true faith and is distinguished from others and so cannot be informed by love, which is a distinct virtue from it), they answer that love is not the essential form of faith. Rather since it adds some perfection to faith, it can metaphorically be called the form on account of its analogy to a form properly so called which in its own manner perfects the subject (as Gregory of Valencia expresses it, *Commentariorum theologicorum*, Disp. I, Q. 4 [1603-9], 3:329-46). Durandus sets it forth that love is not the form of faith according to its natural being; yea, it can be separated from it. But it is the form of faith as to its meritorious being, inasmuch as it deserves eternal life because the act of faith is not meritorious, except insofar as it is commanded by love (without which it does not have the relation of merit and by which man pleases God); cf. *Sententias theologicas Petri Lombardi Commentariorum*, Bk. 3, Dist. 23, Q. 8 (1556), pp. 220-21.

III. But this opinion rests upon a doubly false foundation. The first is that there is any true unformed faith. For since form gives being to a thing, it is absurd (*asystaton*) to say that there is an unformed faith. The other concerns the merit of faith and of works (as will be proved in the proper place), so that it is deservedly rejected as false and absurd. Nor can it be confirmed by the passage where faith is said by the apostle "to work by love" (*di' agapēs energoumenē*, Gal. 5:6) because this is not to be understood passively, as our opponents hold (so that faith may be said to be made operative by love [as if it borrowed its universal efficacy from love] because it rather bestows that upon the others as their cause and root, than receives from them), but actively, as the original word *energeisthai* is often taken elsewhere (Rom. 7:5; 2 Cor. 1:6; 4:12; Col. 1:29; Jam. 5:16), inasmuch as it is that which is produced by faith as the term, not which produces faith as the principle (i.e., which draws love after it and in producing this exercises and manifests itself). Thus Paul wishes to prove not that any faith whatsoever in Christ avails, but only the true and living which works by love and good works. Thus the actions of love are from faith imperatively, not elicitively.

IV. The opinion of our opponents receives no better support from Jam. 2:26 where "faith without works" is said to be "dead" because this must not be understood of the causality of works to the life of faith *a priori*, as if works made faith living, but of a declaration *a posteriori* because works demonstrate a living faith; as a body without spirit is said to be dead (i.e., it is known to be dead from the want of respiration and breathing; for here *pneuma* is used for *pnoē* or "respiration").

2. With the Socinians.

V. The Socinians, the more easily to overthrow the fiducial apprehension of Christ's satisfaction (in which the orthodox constitute the essence of faith) and thus retain the righteousness of works (as so expressly distinguished from the righteousness of faith in Scripture), hold that faith is nothing else than obedience to God's commands. Thus good works are not so much the fruit of faith as its form, as Ostorodt expresses it (*Unterrichtung . . . hauptpuncten der*

Christlichen Religion 2 [1612], p. 22). Volkelius places the third degree of faith in obedience to the commands of God: "The third," says he, "is to confide in Christ and through him in God, and so relying upon the hope of immortality, to accommodate himself wholly to the wish of God (i.e., of Christ) and thus also to obey the commands of God" (*De vera Religione* 4.3 [1630], p. 178).

VI. But on the other hand, faith cannot be obedience to the commands because thus two virtues would be confounded which are mutually distinct—"faith and love" (1 Cor. 13:13). The former is concerned with the promises of the gospel; the latter with the precepts of the law (which on this account is said to be the end or "fulfilling of the law," Rom. 13:10). The former is the cause, the latter the effect: "For the end of the commandment is charity out of a pure heart, and of faith unfeigned" (1 Tim. 1:5). That is the instrument of justification, while this is its consequent fruit. Hence in the matter of justification, faith and works are opposed as opposites and contraries (Rom. 3:28).

VII. Nor can it be replied that works (not any kind, but perfect and in every respect agreeing with the law) can be opposed to faith in justification. It is clear from Paul that all works entirely, whether perfect or not, are opposed to faith in justification and that faith does not justify as a work (which is the fundamental error [*prōton pseudos*] of our opponents, who thus confound the law with the gospel and the condition of the covenant of grace with a legal condition, as will be proved in the proper place).

VIII. Although to believe is to obey the command to believe prescribed in the gospel (1 Jn. 3:23), faith is not on this account rightly said to be obedience to God's commands in the sense of our opponents (who here understand by commands the precepts of the law which are to be done and fulfilled on our part by good works; not the commands of the gospel which enjoin upon us faith in the promises of grace). And if faith is called the "work of God" (Jn. 6:29), this was rather done imitatively (*mimētikōs*), regard being had to the petition of the crowd, who had asked "What shall we do, that we might work the works of God?" Faith was able to give them what they had vainly sought in the works of the law; as elsewhere the gospel receives the name of law and works of charity and beneficence are called a fast (Is. 58:6, 7) because they really accomplished what the Jews in vain sought by their hypocritical fasts.

IX. The faith by which Abraham was justified cannot be called obedience to commands (although obedience was prescribed to him as a condition, Gen. 17:1), for it is clearly taught to have been faith in the promise (Gen. 15:5, 6; Rom. 4:11, 13, 16). The walking before God spoken of in Gen. 17:1 is not a condition of the justification of faith, but its effect. Nor can the offering of his son also be said to be its cause because already thirty years before he had been justified (Gen. 15:6). Therefore, the causal particle "since" or "seeing that" (occurring in Gen. 22:16) is a cause or mark of consequence, not of a consequent.

Is love separable from faith? We deny.

X. Although love is not the form of faith but may be distinguished from it, it cannot on that account be said to be separable from it (as the Romanists contend; cf. Bellarmine, "De Justificatione," 1.15 *Opera* [1858], 4:483-87). It is the proper and immediate effect of faith, which cannot be separated from its cause. Hence it is said to work by love (Gal. 5:6) and to be dead without works (Jam. 2:20). Hence John asserts that the knowledge of God without his worship is false and deceitful: "He that saith, I know him, and keepeth not his commandments, is a liar, and the truth is not in him" (1 Jn. 2:4). He refers the gospel commandment to faith and love as two marks of true believers mutually inseparable (1 Jn. 3:23).

XI. Nor can the contrary be proved from 1 Cor. 13:2 because there the subject is the faith of miracles and not justifying faith, as we said before. Nor is it an objection that in v. 13 the subject is saving faith because it is not a conclusion arising from the preceding discussion, but a new argument and that too lastly from things related (to wit, from the cessation of faith and the duration of love). Nor can it be proved from Jn. 12:43 where it treats of the leaders believing in Christ. It could not be true justifying faith, since "they are said to have loved the glory of men, more than the glory of God" (which does not suit believers). Hence it was only in theoretical assent arising from the evidence of Christ's doctrine and the power of his miracles, not fiducial and practical. If in the same chapter belief in Christ is taken for true faith, it ought not to be taken here in the same way because the circumstances differ. Or from this that "one may say he has faith" which is without works (Jam. 2:14). It is one thing really to have faith; another "to say that he has it" (which the hypocrites do, priding themselves on an empty profession of faith). If faith ought to cease in heaven while love remains (1 Cor. 13:8), this must be understood formally as to the mode of cognition which will cease, not materially as the substance of knowledge which will be the same. For the knowledge which is commenced here by the hearing of the word in the light of grace will be consummated by sight in the light of glory.

Fourteenth Question: The Subject of Faith

Do infants have faith? We distinguish.

Statement of the question. The faith of infants.

I. Concerning the subject of faith a question is moved as to infants. There are two extremes: (1) in defect, by the Anabaptists, who deny all faith to infants and under this pretext exclude them from baptism; (2) in excess, by the Lutherans, who, to oppose themselves to the Anabaptists, have fallen into the other extreme, maintaining that infants are regenerated in baptism and actually furnished with faith, as appears from the Mompeldardensi Colloquy (*Acta Colloquij Montis Belligartensis* [1588], p. 459). "The round assertion of our divines is that actual faith is ascribed to infants with the most just right" (Brochmann, "De Fide Justificante," 2, Q. 10 in *Universae theologicae systema* [1638], 2:429).

II. The orthodox occupy the middle ground between these two extremes. They deny actual faith to infants against the Lutherans and maintain that a seminal or radical and habitual faith is to be ascribed to them against the Anabaptists. Here it is to be remarked before all things: (1) that we do not speak of the infants of any parents whomsoever (even of infidels and heathen), but only of believers, or Christians and the covenanted. (2) Nor do we speak of every single infant as if such faith is given to all without any exception; for although Christian charity commands us to cherish a good hope concerning their salvation, still we cannot certainly determine that every single one belongs to the election of God, but leave it to the secret counsel and supreme liberty of God. Since indeed the predestination of God makes a difference between children (Rom. 9:11) and the promise of the covenant was ratified (v. 8) not in the children of the flesh, but in the children of the promise, we therefore treat here indefinitely of infants of every order and condition (who pertain to the election of God, whom it is not for human judgment to distinguish).

Proof against the Lutherans that infants do not have actual faith: (1) because they do not profess the actual knowledge of anything.

III. We embrace our opinion in two propositions. The first is opposed to the Lutherans: "Infants do not have actual faith." The reasons are first because they have not an actual knowledge of anything. Hence they are said not to know good or evil, nor can they discern between their right and left hand (Dt. 1:39; Is. 7:16; Jon. 4:11). Nor ought the objection to be raised (a) "Still the knowledge of many things is born with us." It is one thing to have the principles and seeds of knowledge in the common notions implanted in us (which we grant); another to have actual knowledge (which we deny). (b) "Faith does not depend upon the use of reason; nay, it ought to bring reason into obedience to it" (2 Cor. 10:5). It is one thing for faith to depend on the use of reason as a principle; another for faith to suppose reason as its subject. The former we deny with Paul, who on this account wishes the reason to be captivated into the obedience of faith. The latter we hold with him, who wishes our spiritual worship to be reasonable (*logikon*, Rom. 12:1). Therefore where the use of reason is not, there neither the use or exercise of faith can be.

2. Because they are not capable of acts of faith.

IV. Second, infants are not capable of acts of faith, or of knowledge because intellect does not exist without action; nor are they capable of assent, which ought to be carried to the object known; nor of trust, which is concerned with the special application of the promise of grace. Therefore neither are they capable of faith, which consists of these three acts. Nay, it is most absurd (*asystaton*) that there should be a movement of the intellect or of the will without knowledge (which is always supposed for them).

3. Because they are not capable of the word.

V. Third, they are not capable of hearing and meditating on the word from which faith is conceived: "for faith cometh by hearing" (Rom. 10:17). Nor must it be said with Brochmann that God appointed baptism as a laver of water for the regeneration of infants in the word, as for adults he destined the hearing of the word. Although baptism is the external sign of regenerating grace (at whose presence God can give it to infants by the Spirit without the hearing of the word), still it cannot be said that actual faith is given to them (which cannot be such except insofar as it actually exerts itself about the hearing of the word).

Sources of explanation.

VI. The little children spoken of in Mt. 18:6 (who are said to believe in Christ) are not infants in tender age (*tenella aetate*), but children who already enjoy some use of reason. For the passage refers to those who can be "called" and "offended," which cannot apply to infants endowed with no knowledge of good or evil. Nor is there any disproof either in the name *paidiōn* (given to them) because it is general, signifying children of more advanced age as well as infants. Or in the word *brephous*, which we have in Lk. 18:15, because (aside from the fact that it is not found in Mt. 18 where children believing is treated), it can also be extended to the age capable of instruction—as Timothy is said "to have known the holy scriptures from a child" (*apo brephous*, 2 Tim. 3:15). Again, Christ by *paidia* who believe in him, can mean adults who are equal to infants in humility, innocence and modesty. Nor can it be concluded that infants and children are equal in spiritual intelligence, since age contributes nothing to faith. Although age contributes nothing to faith as the efficient cause per se, still it is required for it as a receptive subject (because a thing is received after the manner of the recipient).

VII. When the apostle says, "Without faith it is impossible to please God" (Heb. 11:6), he speaks of adults, various examples of whom he in the same place commemorates and whom alone the proposed description of faith suits (Heb. 11:1). Now it is different with infants who please God on account of the satisfaction of Christ bestowed upon them and imputed by God to obtain the remission of their sins, even if they themselves do not apprehend it and cannot apprehend it by a defect of age.

VIII. Although faith depends on the operation of the Spirit effectively, it can also depend in some measure on reason instrumentally and subjectively because it is the instrument by which the act of faith is elicited from a mind renewed by the subject in which it is received. Hence the use of reason being removed, there can be no actual faith.

IX. The cause of pedobaptism is not the actual faith of infants (of which they are no more capable than of that instruction by which adults are taught and are made the disciples of Christ, Mt. 28:19), but both the general command to baptize all the members of the church and the promise of the covenant made to parents and also to their children (Gen. 17:7; Acts 2:39). Nor does it thence follow that the sacrament is an empty ceremony to those using it without faith because this is the case only with adults, who are capable of faith and in whom on that account there ought to be a mutual stipulation on the part of God and man. But not in regard to infants, to whom the sacrament does not cease to be efficacious and ratified on the part of God, although on the part of man it cannot be known or received by faith.

X. It is one thing to obtain the fruit of baptism by an active sealing on God's part; another to be sensible of its fruit by a passive sealing on man's part. The former is well ascribed to infants, but not the latter.

XI. The examples of Jeremiah and John the Baptist indeed teach that infants are capable of the Holy Spirit and that he is also given at this age, but it cannot be inferred that they actually believed. Jeremiah is indeed said to have been sanctified from the womb as a prophet of God, and John is said to have leaped in his mother's womb at the presence of Christ, but neither is said to have actually believed. Besides, even if any such thing were ascribed to them, the consequence would not hold good; for this would be singular and extraordinary from which a universal rule ought not to be drawn.

XII. It is one thing to praise God subjectively and formally from knowledge and affection; another to praise him objectively and materially. Infants are said to praise God in the latter, not in the former sense (inasmuch as God, in the care and preservation of them, wonderfully manifests his own glory, Ps. 8:2).

Seminal faith is granted in infants.

XIII. Second proposition: "Although infants do not have actual faith, the seed or root of faith cannot be denied to them, which is ingenerated in them from early age and in its own time goes forth in act (human instruction being applied from without and a greater efficacy of the Holy Spirit within)." This second proposition is opposed to the Anabaptists, who deny to infants all faith, not only as to act, but also as to habit and form. Although habitual faith (as the word "habit" is properly and strictly used to signify a more perfect and consummated state) is not well ascribed to them, still it is rightly predicated of them broadly as denoting potential or seminal faith. Now by "seed of faith," we mean the Holy Spirit, the effecter of faith and regeneration (as he is called, 1 Jn. 3:9), as to the principles of regeneration and holy inclinations which he already works in infants according to their measure in a wonderful and to us unspeakable way. Afterwards in more mature age, these proceed into act (human instruction being employed and the grace of the same Spirit promoting his own work by which that seed is accustomed to be excited and drawn forth into act).

1. Because the covenant pertains to them.

XIV. The reasons are: (1) the promise of the covenant pertains no less to infants than to adults, since God promises that he will be "the God of Abraham and of his seed" (Gen. 17:7) and the promise is said to have been made "with the fathers and their children" (Acts 2:39). Therefore also the blessings of the covenant (such as "remission of sins" and "sanctification") ought to pertain to them (according to Jer. 31 and 32) and are communicated to them by God according to their state. In this sense (as some think), the children of believers are called "holy" by Paul (1 Cor. 7:14). This may with more propriety be referred to the external and federal holiness which belongs to them, according to which (because they are born of covenanted and Christian parents—at least of one) they are also considered to be begotten in "holiness" (i.e., in Christianity, and not in heathenism, which was a state of uncleanness [*akatharsias*] and impurity).

2. The kingdom of heaven belongs to them.

XV. (2) The kingdom of heaven pertains to infants (Mt. 19:14), therefore also regeneration (without which there is no admittance to it, Jn. 3:3, 5). Now although Christ proposes this to adults for an example of humility to show that they ought to be like children in disposition in order to enter the kingdom of heaven, still he does not exclude (but includes in that promise) infants themselves, from whom it commences.

3. The examples of infants who have been sanctified.

XVI. (3) There are examples of various infants who were sanctified from the womb (as was the case with Jeremiah and John the Baptist, Jer. 1:5; Lk. 1:15, 80). For although here occur certain singular and extraordinary things (which pertained to them alone and not to others), still we may fairly conclude that infants can be made partakers of the Holy Spirit, who since he cannot be inactive, works in them motions and inclinations suited to their age (which are called "the seed of faith" or principles of sanctification).

4. They have common notions.

XVII. (4) Infants draw from natural generation common notions (*koinas ennoias*), and theoretical as well as practical principles of the natural law; and if Adam had continued innocent, the divine image (which consists in holiness) would have passed by propogation to his children. Therefore what is to prevent them from receiving by supernatural regeneration certain seeds of faith and first principles of sanctification, since they are not less capable of these by grace than of those by nature?

Solution of difficulties.

XVIII. Although there seem to be in infants no marks from which we can gather that they are gifted with the Holy Spirit and the seed of faith (because their age prevents it), it does not follow that this must be denied to them since the reason of their salvation demands it and the contrary is evident from the examples adduced.

XIX. As before the use of reason, men are properly called rational because they have the principle of reason in the rational soul; thus nothing hinders them from being termed believers before actual faith because the seed which is given to them is the principle of faith (from which they are rightly denominated; even as they are properly called sinners, although not as yet able to put forth an act of sin).

XX. If any of our theologians deny that there is faith in infants or that it is necessary for their salvation (as is gathered from certain passages of Peter Martyr, Beza and Piscator), it is certain that this is meant of actual faith against the Lutherans, not of the seed of faith or the Spirit of regeneration (which they frequently assert is ascribed to infants). Peter Martyr, after saying that the Holy Scriptures do not say that infants believe, adds: "I judge that it is sufficient that they who are to be saved be determined by this—that by election they belong to the property of God, they are sprinkled by the Holy Spirit, who is the root of faith, hope and love, and of all the virtues, which afterwards it exerts and declares in the sons of God, when their age permits" (*Loci Communes*, Cl. 4, chap. 8.14 [1583], p. 826). Thus Calvin: "Yet how, say they, are infants regenerated, having a knowledge neither of good nor of evil? We answer, the work of God, even if we do not understand it, still is real. Further infants who are to be saved, as certainly some of that age are wholly saved, it is not in the least obscure were before regenerated by the Lord. For if they bring with them from their mother's womb innate corruption, they must be purged from it before they can be admitted into the kingdom of heaven, into which nothing impure and polluted enters" (ICR, 4.16.17, p. 1340). This he fully discusses in the following sections.

Fifteenth Question

Does temporary faith differ only in degree and duration or also in kind from justifying faith? The former we deny; the latter we affirm against the Remonstrants.

I. This question about the difference between temporary and justifying faith was raised by the Remonstrants. For in order to prove the apostasy of the saints, they employed principally the argument drawn from temporary believers. However since our theologians answered that they were not true believers and that their faith was not saving and justifying, but differing in its entire species from the faith of true believers, they (on the contrary) maintained that the difference is only of degree, not specific. Thus they differ from each other in duration and continuance alone and not in their very nature, as they express themselves: "Temporary (*proskairos*) faith is true justifying faith and pleasing to God, as long as it lasts; nor does it differ in kind from true faith which continues to the end" (Declar. Exhib.+). Although they do not doubt that they are alike in various particulars, the orthodox still maintain that the difference is specific and essential.

Temporary faith differs from justifying: (1) as to origin.

II. The reasons are (1) saving faith differs from temporary in origin and foundation. The former flows from the special grace of election when it is called "the faith of the elect" (Tit. 1:1); which is given only to those who are the called according to his purpose (*kata prothesin*, Rom. 8:28) and were ordained to eternal life (Acts 13:48). On the contrary, the latter depends upon common grace which bestows even on the reprobate certain blessings: not only external and temporal, but also spiritual and initial gifts (although not saving) as a testification of a certain general love and to increase their guilt on the supposition of their contumacy. Hence Paul, speaking of the apostasy of Hymenaeus and Philetus, says, "Nevertheless the foundation of God standeth sure" (2 Tim. 2:19), i.e., not on this account does the faith of true believers waver, being built upon the immovable foundation of the election of God.

2. As to the recipient subject.

III. (2) As to the subject receiving, both "of whom" (*hou*), which in justifying faith is an elect person (Tit. 1:1; Rom. 11:7); in temporary faith the reprobate (Mt. 24:11; 1 Jn. 2:19). And "in what" (*en hō*) (which in the former is a "good heart"; in the latter a "stony heart"). For temporary (*proskairos*) faith is in a "rocky," i.e., a stony and ungrateful heart "alone" (Mt. 13:20), but saving faith is received into "good ground" (v. 23), which is explained by a good and honest heart (*kardian kalēn kai agathēn*, Lk. 8:15), i.e., remarkably good (for the reduplication intensifies the expression after the manner of the Greeks). Since it cannot be from nature, such a heart ought to be given to us by grace, while it takes away from us the heart of stone and gives us one of flesh (Ezk. 36:26). Since this is not given to the temporary (who retain their stony hearts), for this very reason their faith ought to differ wholly in kind from saving faith.

3. As to internal principle and rooting.

IV. (3) As to internal principle and manner of rooting. For the principle of saving faith is the Spirit of regeneration and of adoption (Jn. 3:5; Rom. 8:15), but of temporary faith the Spirit of illumination (Heb. 6:4). The mode of rooting is deep in the former and superficial in the latter. Justifying faith is rooted intimately in the heart, consisting in a deep, most internal, vital, friendly and efficacious impression by which the word becomes implanted (*emphyton*) and tempered with faith (Jam. 1:21; Heb. 4:2). And believers are "rooted in love" (*errizōmenoi en agapē*, Eph. 3:17), "rooted in Christ" and "established in the faith" (Col. 2:7). Now temporary (*proskairos*) faith "has no root" (Mt. 13:21), i.e., it sticks to the uppermost surface of the soul (to wit, in the intellect); it does not penetrate to the heart, nor does it have true trust in Christ by whose power we are united to Christ as a solid and rich soil from which we draw the sap of life (Heb. 3:14; Rom. 11:17, 20).

4. As to their effects.

V. (4) As to their effects. For temporary (*proskairos*) faith as it is in stony ground and has no root, so it remains unfruitful (*akarpos*) and barren because the seed as soon as it sprung up was withered away (*phuen exēraithē*, Lk. 8:6). For it had no moisture, or root to draw it up, or deep earth (*bathos tēs gēs*), which a long root demands. But saving faith is productive and fruit-bearing, and they who have it are said to "bear fruit constantly" (*karpophorein en hypomonē*) and indeed abundantly (Mt. 13:23).

5. As to acts of faith: knowledge, assent, trust.

VI. (5) As to the essential acts of faith, knowledge, assent and trust. For in justifying faith, knowledge is deep, cleaving to the inmost heart; experimental, not derived from hearing alone, but confirmed by the sense of experience (1 Pet. 2:3; Phil. 1:9); "living and practical," bearing with it not only light, but also heat (1 Jn. 2:4). But in temporary faith, the knowledge is superficial and theoretical, making man wiser but not better. Assent in the former is certain and solid (in which there is "fulness of assurance" [*plērophoria tēs syneseōs*, Col. 2:2], so as to be carried into the things to be believed by an action as it were intuitive, placing before itself absent things as if they were present and invisible as if visible; for which reason it is said to be the "substance of things hoped for" (*hypostasis tōn elpizomenōn*) and "the evidence of things not seen" (*elenchos tōn mē blepomenōn*, Heb. 11:1). But in temporary faith, the assent is weak and slippery, connected with a perpetual hesitation and wavering. Hence it is said to be without root and readily yields to rising temptations and is prostrated (Mt. 7:26, 27). Trust in justifying faith is true and real, since it arises from the deepest knowledge and sense of God's grace (1 Tim. 1:5; 2 Tim. 1:5). On the other hand, temporary faith is blinded and weak, cleaving to the lips alone, and does not reach to the heart. Accordingly it is an empty presumption and confidence rather than a true trust; such as was exhibited in the young man (Mt. 19:16-22) and in various hypocrites rashly glorying in the grace and salvation of God. Nor is the reason obscure, since indeed these imagine that the salvation promised in the gospel belongs to them, either without any or with a false foundation; while without any examination of themselves (which they avoid as too troublesome and inconvenient), they proudly claim for themselves the grace of Christ and securely sink into a vain sleep, not inquiring, or wishing to inquire, what is the foundation of their imagination. Sometimes they seek it from a false conception of the universal mercy of God (and I know not what letting down of the gospel covenant) or from the external communion of the church and religious worship or from a certain moral honesty (because they are a little less wicked than the worst) or from a certain security of a sleeping and torpid conscience, which they feign to be the peace and consolation of the Holy Spirit (by which they falsely deceive themselves, as if they were sufficient signs of the grace of God). But true believers compare themselves far otherwise. Panting for the grace of Christ from an intimate sense of their own misery and apprehending it with a firm faith (but with submissive humility), still they do not dare to glory in it as if it were their own, except after they have both ascertained the marks of grace and made an examination (*kritēriōn*) of their own hearts and after they by diligent search have found in themselves the certain and infallible proofs and effects of grace.

VII. This is confirmed more strongly from the various acts of this faith pointed out before, whether as to the persuasion of the intellect or as to the refuge of the will and its reception of and adhesion to Christ. For persuasion in true believers is indeed certain and most true, springing from the manifestation of the truth and goodness of the promises of grace (which it regards as an inestimable treasure and deservedly values). But in the temporary (*proskairos*), it is uncertain and light, furnished to them by way of light (which although it is in some measure affected by the pleasure, newness and rarity of gospel truth, still they are never persuaded of its goodness as the highest and inestimable, on account of which all things ought to be deserted). Hence as often as other things are presented to the mind which allure with great appearance of pleasure or utility or which bring some evil to those professing such doctrine, it easily suffers the ideas of those truths which are opposed to their interests to be obliterated and another practical judgment is formed from the flesh concerning following the world and denying Christ. Hence it is not surprising if in the act of refuge they wonderfully differ from each other. For as justifying faith is plainly persuaded of its own most miserable condition and the supreme necessity and excellence of grace and regards God as the highest good, Christ as the only and most perfect Savior, it cannot help flying to him with the most fervent affection and zeal, and receiving and embracing him as offered absolutely and entirely, and being united to him by an indissoluble bond, and most constantly cleaving to him (1 Cor. 6:17), all other things being rejected, which could hinder this union and communion (Mt. 13:44; 19:27; Phil. 3:7-9), and prepared to do and to suffer anything to obtain and retain Christ (Lk. 9:23; 14:26, 27; Mt. 16:24, 25; Acts 15:26). But as the temporary (*proskairos*) has a slight and uncertain persuasion, it also coldly and remissly betakes itself to Christ and if it apprehends and receives him, it does this rather with the mouth than with the heart (Mt. 15:8). Or if it receives him in the soul, it is rather in the intellect through knowledge than in the will through love (Tit. 1:16). Or if in the will and heart, it never does this with the whole heart, but with a heart halved and divided between the world and Christ, so that it never delivers itself wholly to God, but wishes with Ananias (Acts 5:3) to keep back something (*nosphizein*) and to keep it for itself. Hence hypocrites are called "double-minded" (*dipsychoi*, Jam. 1:8), who have "a heart and heart" (i.e., adhering partly to God and partly to the world). Nor does it give itself absolutely and unlimitedly without any restriction (as should be the case with true believers), but conditionally and limitedly with a mental reservation, provided the profession of the truth does not interfere with their interests and they may be permitted equally with Christ to possess their own riches, honors, pleasures and other advantages of life. When it sees that these are incompatible (*asystata*), it rather recedes from Christ and basely deserts him than renounces the world and its pleasures (Lk. 18:23).

6. As to adjuncts and properties: joy.

VIII. The same difference is clearly proved from the two properties or fruits following faith: joy and consolation with sanctification and the desire of holiness. For saving faith generates solid and unspeakable (*aneklalēton*) joy in the heart from a most intimate sense of the presence of divine grace and the hope not to be deceived of future glory (which is such that it is constant and eternal and which no one can take away from us, Jn. 16:22). But temporary (*proskairos*) faith has some joy because it is said to receive the word "with joy" (*meta charas*, Mt. 13:20), but an evanescent and fleeting joy arising not from a true and fiducial apprehension of Christ, but either from the newness and rarity of doctrine (Jn. 5:35), which usually pleases the intellect, or from its sweetness and pleasantness (which promises freedom and salvation) or from its utility in obtaining the advantages of life (as is seen in those who followed Christ on account of the bread and the miracles wrought by him). Hence the circumstances being changed, as soon as the cross and persecution on account of the word succeeds, they are straightway offended and go back (Mt. 13:21).

As well as sanctification.

IX. Sanctification necessarily follows saving faith because it purifies the heart (Acts 15:9) and is efficacious through love (Gal. 5:6). So pathetically (*pathetice*) does it represent the incredible love of God towards us and the supreme love of Christ dying that it inflames the believer with a mutual love of his most kind Savior, so that he thinks nothing is preferable to living and dying again for him (2 Cor. 5:14, 15; Gal. 2:20); impresses upon the soul with such deep characters the form of virtue, so that it supposes nothing more beautiful for itself than to give all diligence to the cultivation of it; and so deeply inscribes the meditation of the promised happiness that he is prepared to try and endure all things for it (2 Cor. 4:16, 17). But temporary faith, deceiving man with a vain confidence, either plunges him into a deep sleep of security that indulging the flesh he snores loudly; or if by a superficial knowledge of gospel truth and of the good presented in the gospel, he is excited to any emendation of life and external change of acts for the better so as "through the knowledge of the Lord and Savior Jesus Christ he escapes in some measure the pollutions of the world" (2 Pet. 2:20), it does not penetrate even to the heart itself to purify it and introduce new habits of holiness. Hence as often as either the enticements of the world and of the flesh or persecution present themselves, they soon grow weary in their course of inchoate probity and return to their former wallowings. Then the true and good notions which the gospel had implanted in them are so led out from the mind that they readily prefer present pleasure and utility and the avoidance of impending loss to all the promises of the gospel and the desire for the piety prescribed by Christ.

7. As to the object.

X. As to the objects and the relation under which it is apprehended by faith. As the gospel object (besides the idea of truth) also has the threefold idea of virtuous, useful and delightful good (when it is proposed to us under the idea), either of pleasures of every kind or of riches and immense treasures or of supreme glory and perfection, faith is thence affected in different ways. Historical faith apprehends it simply under the idea of truth and temporary faith under the idea of a useful or pleasant good (which can bring to us either some memorable advantage or some uncommon pleasure). While justifying faith properly and primarily regards it under the idea of a moral good, although it does not neglect the other relations (*scheseis*) secondarily. As the soul, deeply imbued with the love of virtue, is either not agitated by disturbances or if sometimes it is tossed about by some vehement object, or either by the promise of good or the threatening of evil things, it immediately rises again by the consideration of the more excellent good which is presented to the mind. Thus that which is moved by the appearance of virtue is not drawn at all (or only languidly and coldly is held strongly entangled by the idea of the useful and agreeable), does not indeed fail as long as these two goods are conjoined. But when they are separated (as they are separated when, for example, the cross and persecution on account of Christ come upon them), then the impression of the moral truth and good becomes slight and self-love (*philautia*) induces the man to decide that the idea of the useful and agreeable should be followed.

Sources of explanation.

XI. If the temporary are sometimes called "disciples of Christ" and "sons of God," "faithful" and "believers," it is either according to opinion (*kata doxan*) (because they seem to be such in the opinion of others) and out of the judgment of charity (because by a profession of faith and reception of the sacraments, they mingle in the public society of the church); but not according to the truth of the thing. Hence Augustine says, "Certain persons are sons of God to God, who are not such to us, and there are certain others, who on account of grace received even temporarily, are called by us sons of God and yet are not such in the sight of God" (*Admonition and Grace* 9 [20] [FC 2:269; PL 44.928]).

XII. Faith is not true because it perseveres, but it perseveres because it is true. Thus perseverance is not the cause of the verity of faith, but the consequent and the effect—for because it has solidity and a deep root in the heart, on this account it is constant and perpetually endures. As from lightness arises liability to fall, so from solidity arises stability. For although duration does not properly constitute the essence of a thing, still it so follows it that from it a judgment can well be formed concerning the truth of a thing *a posteriori*. Duration is an index of truth, as truth is the principle of duration.

XIII. Nothing is said of the temporary (Mt. 13) which proves that their faith agrees in kind with justifying faith and differs only in degree. Not that "they hear the word, and immediately receive it with joy" because that reception is into the mind, not into the heart (as seed falling upon stony places is received indeed upon the upper surface of the earth, but does not penetrate farther). And the joy with which it is received is not solid and true, arising from a fiducial sense of God's grace, but from perishable things (to wit, the novelty and pleasantness of the doctrine or even the hope of earthly advantage). Not that "the seed springs up" (although it did not come to maturity) because that superficial germination as it takes place in a different kind of ground, so it ought to differ specifically from the intimate and true, which brings forth good fruit. Not that "they do certain good works," as is said of the Israelites that they seek God and are pleased with the knowledge of his ways (Is. 58:2); of the Jews, who exulted in the light of John the Baptist (Jn. 5:35); of Herod, that he did many things after hearing him (Mk. 6:20). These are no other than external good works (as to the substance of a work and moral virtue), but not truly such as to the truth of the thing and the manner according to which they ought to be done.

XIV. Heb. 6:4-6 does not prove that the apostates were true believers and that their faith was the same in kind as justifying faith. (1) The apostle speaks hypothetically, not absolutely; for *to parapesontas* is the same as if he had said "if they shall fall away" (*ean parapesōsi*). From the hypothetical to the absolute the consequence does not hold good, unless the condition be posited. Nor did the apostle threaten to no purpose because by such conditional threatenings God prevents the renewed from falling, frightening them by the fickleness of the apostate and

Holy Spirit can make on a partaker w/o justifying faith

exciting them to the desire of perseverance. And although the condition on God's part and as to the event is impossible, it would be very possible on the part of man left to himself. (2) Whatever is ascribed to them can be predicated of the unrenewed and reprobate, who can "be made partakers of the Holy Spirit" (if not as to the fundamental and saving gifts of conversion and consolation, still as to the initial gifts of illumination and conviction or even as to extraordinary, miraculous and ministerial gifts). They can be illuminated and have a knowledge of the truth, if not a practical and consoling, yet a theoretical and constraining. They can "taste the good word of God" with an outward and labial, but not an inner and radical taste. They can "taste the powers of the world to come," not so much by hope and joy (which are the first fruits of heavenly glory) as with respect to miracles (which are often termed powers and which were usually performed in the primitive church, which is called the future age, "the world to come" [as in Heb. 2:5] because it was such in the time of the fathers of the Old Testament). They can "taste the heavenly gift" as to a participation of faith, if not saving, still true in its kind and which could be obtained only from heaven. (3) These things are ascribed to them rather sacramentally and extrinsically (as to a profession of the truth and the reception of baptism), than spiritually and internally (as to the reception of faith without hypocrisy [*anypokritou*], which is the gift without repentance [*ametameletōn*] of the elect).

XV. Although the faith of the temporary is true in its own order because it truly receives the seed with joy and is not feigned by those who thus believe, who not only think they believe, but really and truly believe (hence they are even said "to believe," Jn. 2:23; Lk. 8:13), still it is not a true and living justifying faith, in which sense it is even called hypocritical because it is emulous of the faith of the elect and has an external resemblance to it (although destitute of its truth); and so great is its similarity to it often that a greater is not seen between an image and its prototype. Hence not only others who see them are easily deceived by them, but the believers themselves also are deceived and impose upon themselves; not feigning, but believing that they are truly believers (God alone, who searches the innermost recesses of the heart, knowing the truth). Still it is certain that there is a manifold and most essential difference (as was said before) which shows that they mutually differ not only in degree or duration, but in very kind and nature.

Sixteenth Question: The Perseverance of Faith

Whether the true believer can ever totally or finally fall from faith. We deny against the Romanists, Socinians, Remonstrants and others who favor the apostasy of the saints.

I. As there are two principal adjuncts of justifying faith—perseverance and certainty (the former implying its perpetual duration and incapability of being lost so that the believer never entirely falls from it; the latter involving subjectively its certain knowledge and sense)—so two questions arise thence. The first concerns perseverance; the other concerns its certainty. We must treat these distinctly.

II. The question concerning perseverance is agitated by us with the old and new Pelagians and Semipelagians, who agree in opposing and denying it. Such are the Romanists, Socinians, Anabaptists and Remonstrants, who, on this point (as in the others concerning grace), depart from the orthodox doctrine and were condemned by the Synod of Dort in Article 5 (*Acta Synodi Nationalis . . . Dordrechti* [1619-20], 1:311-17).

Statement of the question.

III. (1) The question does not concern believers and saints, who are such equivocally both from external calling and profession; who are sometimes so called, whether from their own presumption (on account of the initial gifts granted to them) or from the opinion of others (whom we confess not only can fail in their faith, but also really fail). Rather the question concerns those who are univocally and properly such, planted in Christ the Savior by true faith, to whom the fundamental and saving gifts of adoption, justification and sanctification were not only destined, but have also been conferred.

IV. (2) The question does not concern the possibility of failing on man's part and in a divided sense. For no one denies that believers considered in themselves as to the mutability and weakness of their nature, not only can fail, but could not help failing if left to themselves (especially on the approach of the temptations of Satan and of the world). But the question concerns the possibility of failing on God's part, as to his purpose in the compound sense and with regard to the event itself. In this sense, we say their defection is impossible, not absolutely and simply, but hypothetically and relatively.

V. (3) The question does not concern the act or exercise of faith—whether it can be interrupted and fail even as to time, which we every day sadly experience by the grievous falls of the saints. Rather the question concerns the essence of spiritual life and the state and habit of faith. Not whether it can as to facility and readiness of acting sometimes be diminished and very much injured and the spiritual life itself suffer a deep syncope, so as to seem only a little removed from death; but whether it can be weakened and destroyed so far as to be wholly taken away and to cease to exist; or concerning a total and final defection by which they can wholly fall from faith and eternally perish.

VI. (4) The question is not whether the believer can demeritoriously lose faith and break off the bond of communion with Christ (as far as in him lies), so that his separation from Christ and loss of faith is not prevented by himself (which no one denies); but whether he can in fact and effectively entirely lose faith and be separated from Christ (which we contend cannot take place on account of the intervening grace of God). (5) The question is not whether when he falls into enormous sins, he incurs the paternal indignation of God; is deprived of the sense of justification and adoption; loses that fitness and disposition for the kingdom of heaven which consists in the practice of faith and holiness; contracts damnable guilt, so that, while he continues in that state impenitent, he ought to consider himself liable to death and as certain to die unless he is converted (for all this we readily grant). Rather, the question is whether he falls into the hostile hatred of God, the Judge, by which his right to the kingdom of God is taken from him, the state of adoption and justification abrogated and the grace of faith and regeneration entirely rooted out of his heart. This our opponents hold; we deny.

VII. The question, therefore, returns to this—whether a true believer who is called according to God's purpose and truly justified, furnished with a faith not dogmatical and temporary, but living and saving, can (no less as to God and the event, than as to himself) lose faith, not only objectively (which believes), but also subjectively (by which he believes); not only demeritoriously, but effectively (totally); not only as to act and sense, but also as to habit and power, and finally remain in unbelief and impenitency and so cut himself off from a right to the kingdom of heaven and from the state of adoption and be eternally condemned. The Pelagians formerly affirmed this; the Romanists have until now; the Socinians, Remonstrants and others who follow them affirm it. The orthodox constantly deny it. They think that the habit of faith once enjoyed by the elect can indeed sometimes be strained or remitted, become stronger or weaker in reference to the inroads of sin, but so that it is never wholly and finally destroyed and lost, nor the grace of regeneration once bestowed upon man wholly taken from him.

VIII. Our opponents are distinguished into two classes. Some contend only for a temporary cutting off of faith and justification, so that faith may indeed totally fail, but not finally (being restored before death by the special grace of God, lest approaching death should meet the man destitute of faith). Others urge not only a total, but also a final apostasy of the saints and the excision of faith. Both are opposed by the same arguments.

Proof of the perseverance of faith: (1) from the election of the Father.

IX. The foundations of the orthodox opinion are various: (1) the election of God. This purpose is eternal and unchangeable (*ametatheton*, Heb. 6:17; Rom. 9:11), the foundation (*stereon*) firm (2 Tim. 2:19), efficacious both as to faith and as to the means indissolubly joined together with the end (Rom. 8:29, 30); nor can an immanent act of God be rescinded or changed either by the Creator (who is always consistent with himself and with whom there is no variableness or shadow of a turning) or by the creature (who has no power and strength over the Creator or his acts). Thus faith which is the fruit of that immutable election and the infallible means of salvation cannot help being firm and immutable (as we have already proved, Topic IV, Question 12).

2. From the nature of the covenant of grace.

X. (2) The nature of the covenant of grace. Since it is firm and immutable and can never be abrogated because it is founded upon God's grace alone and not on man's obedience (like the legal, which on that account was rescinded and made void), the blessings dependent upon it should also be perpetual and immutable; such as especially faith, justification and regeneration, which are its peculiar goods. This Jeremiah in the remarkable prophecy (31:32, 33; 32) excellently testifies where he not only asserts that God willed to make a new covenant with the church, by which he would bestow upon it all saving gifts (both of justification, by not remembering anymore their sins, and of sanctification, by writing the law upon the heart); but that he would also make them perpetual and eternal, both by pursuing them with his constant love (that he might not depart from them) and by putting his fear in them (that they might not depart from him). "I will make an everlasting covenant with them, that I will not turn away from them, to do them good," he says (32:40). "I will put my fear in their hearts, that they shall not depart from me." He does not say, I will exhort to fear and drive them to fear me, but "I will put" fear in order that they may not depart. He does this to teach that he will most surely bring about the execution of the covenant. For since only two things could render that covenant void (on the one side, a change in God's love; on the other, the inconstancy and instability of our fear and faith), God confirms us against both dangers when he promises on the one side the constancy of his love that he may not depart from us; on the other the perpetuity of our fear. Thus now we ought to fear neither that he will desert us, nor that we will desert him, since he promises that he will bestow both benefits; thus fulfilling not only his part, but also ours and taking care that we do not fail in our duty. Hence Augustine says: "God willed it to belong only to his grace, that man should come to him, and he willed it to belong only to his grace that man should not depart from him" (*On the Gift of Perseverance* 13 [7] [NPNF1, 5:530; PL 45.1001]).

XI. Here pertain those important promises concerning the guardianship and preservation of believers which are frequently met with in the Scriptures: "I will never leave thee, nor forsake thee" (Dt. 31:8; Heb. 13:5), which would be absurd and false, if he suffered us to fall from faith and salvation. "The mountains shall depart, and the hills be removed; but my kindness shall not depart from thee, neither shall the covenant of my peace be removed, saith Jehovah" (Is. 54:10). He draws a similitude from the firmest things to teach that the mountains would be moved before the love of God would depart and the covenant of grace entered into with the church be abrogated, which he calls an everlasting covenant and "the sure mercies of David" (*to hosia pista Dabid*, Is. 55:3)—which were promised to David or are founded on the mystical David and are Yea and Amen. "This is my covenant with them: My Spirit that is upon thee, and my words which I have put in thy mouth, shall not depart out of they mouth, nor out of the mouth of thy seed, from henceforth and for ever" (Is. 59:21). Here he promises to the church the perpetual presence of his word and Holy Spirit, which are the two means of ingenerating and conserving faith through all ages even unto the end of the world. "I will betroth thee unto me forever" (Hos. 2:19) points out the intimate and constant species of love and union by which he betroths us to himself in Christ by an indissoluble and eternal marriage (which ought not to continue only for a time and afterwards be made void [such as the first was, which the people had broken], but for ever). Of the same kind are these promises of the New Testament: "My sheep hear my voice, and I know them, and they follow me: and I give unto them eternal life; and they shall never perish, neither shall any pluck them out of my hand, because my Father, which gave them me, is greater than all" (Jn. 10:27-29*). He says that he gives eternal life (i.e., will most certainly give) so that no one will pluck them (neither by force nor by deceit; not even the Devil himself, who holds the empire of death; not the world, not the flesh, not prosperity, not adversity) out of his hand (i.e., from the power by which they are guarded) because God who gave them to him to be guarded and preserved is more powerful than all—angels, as well as men and every creature. Thus "upon this rock I will build my church; and the gates of hell shall not prevail against it" (Mt. 16:18). He promises firmness and perpetuity to the church and to its individual members (to wit, to those who are built upon Christ the immovable rock of ages, so that neither the power of death and the grave, which is often designated by *hadou pylas* [Is. 38:10; Job 38:17], is able to hold back and destroy them) because he who believes passes from death to life (Jn 5:24) and will certainly be raised again at the last day (Jn. 6:40). Nor will the assaults of Satan, who is the prince of this world and who here exercises his sway (as formerly princes sat in the gates of cities and there gave decisions), be able to prevail against them. There are innumerable promises of this kind which promise the protection of God and perserverance to the believer (as 1 Cor. 1:9; 10:13; Phil. 1:6; 1 Thess. 5:23, 24; 2 Thess. 3:3; 1 Pet. 1:5). Hence we infer, since God (who is faithful and constant in his promises) in his word so often and so expressly has promised perserverance to us, it cannot help being certain and indubitable.

XII. The exceptions of our opponents return to this: in general (1) "the promises of God are not always fulfilled, especially when they are not absolute, but conditional such as those are which always suppose a condition on the part of man, to which he may fail to respond." We answer first, the promises concerning the end are falsely confounded with the promises concerning the means. We do not deny that the former are conditional and are really such; but the latter are by no means because there are not granted conditions of conditions, otherwise the thing would go on to infinity; besides the condition would thus coincide with the promise (to wit, God would promise perserverance to man provided he perserveres, for this is his duty, not to be wanting to himself, which is nugatory; for to what good would he promise him what he already has?). However, we say that the promise is given to the believer that he may do his duty, not because he does it. Second, absolute can be understood in two ways: either as excluding means and equivalent to immediate; or as excluding a condition upon which it may rest. In the latter sense, it is certain that the promise of perserverance is not conditional because there is no condition which does not fall under the promise itself; but in the former sense, nothing prevents the promise requiring means by which it may be executed, since perseverance is not physical, but moral, perfected by man himself through the aid of grace. But these means are included in the very promise, so that they can be fulfilled by man. (2) "The defect is not on God's part, who does what he has promised, but on man's, who on account of supreme lightness of his will withdraws himself from what is offered." Hence God indeed fortifies us from external enemies, but not from ourselves and domestic perfidy. Here belongs the expression of Bellarmine: "Love does not cut us off, but we sometimes cut ourselves off from it" ("De Justificatione," 3.15 *Opera* [1858], 4:564). We answer, but this is a foolish refuge since Scripture makes mention of no condition as the cause of fulfillment of the promise. Rather it intimates only that God promises and affords the very conditions he requires. For otherwise to what purpose does he write the law in the heart, sustain with his hand, give escape from temptation, except that the will might not rush headlong into any wickedness and danger, or forthwith spring back from grace received? I confess that faith and repentance are required in the subject because the promise is given only to the believer, but the perseverance which is promised ought not at once to be supposed. (3) It is added, "The promises are made to the church, not to particular believers." But on the contrary, what is promised to the church, the body, regards also its individual true members who share in the nature of the body. Hence it is necessary that he who "is the Savior of the body" should save by the same help all who are members that the body may be complete and not diminished (*mutilatum*).

XIII. In particular, on the passages in Jer. 31, 32: (1) "That it treats of the bringing back of the people from the Babylonian captivity (32:37), not of perseverance which belongs to the elect alone, which is supposed to have been already granted to all believers of the Old Testament." We answer, although the prophecy can have this reference as to a temporal blessing, still it stretches further to the times of the New Testament as to the spiritual benefit. Christ himself so teaches when he applies to all the elect the fact that they were to be "taught" of God (*theodidaktoi*, Jn. 6:45), which the prophet had said concerning Israel. Paul also clearly testifies this in applying it to the covenant of the New Testament (2 Cor. 3; Heb. 8). Therefore, under the promise of restoration from captivity (which was made to the whole of Israel after the flesh) is included the promise of a renewal of the covenant of grace (which was made to the whole of Israel according to the Spirit, who in its own time should be entirely saved [Rom. 11:26], of whom he was the type; as it is usual with the prophets to connect these with each other). If perseverance was already granted to the elect under the Old Testament, it does not follow from this that it could not be promised anew (for the covenant of grace was also in existence). But still it is promised because it was to be renewed far more illustriously and efficaciously both on account of the abundance of blessings and on account of the head who was to come and because the types having been removed all things were to be proposed plainly. (2) "That the intention and end are pointed out, which God proposed to himself, but not the event, in order to denote the certain great and efficacious motion of God, which was to be by the many distinguished benefits with which he was to affect the people and soften their hearts and minds, so that it would not be his fault if the end was not fully obtained, and that God would do all in his power, as this could happen otherwise, because it was not to happen without their cooperation," as Collat. Hagi.+ cavil following Socinius (*Praelectiones theologicae* 12 [1627], pp. 45-47). We answer (a) the intention is falsely separated from the event, because God can never fail in his intention and end. (b) It is not treated here of the law or precept by which he prescribes to man his duty (which man through his depravity does not perform), but of a promise which he says he will fulfill: "I will write my law, I will put my fear in them, that they may not depart, I will cause them to walk in my precepts." (c) If nothing else was meant than that God would not fail or that he would as much as he could, therefore there was no prerogative of the new covenant, for he had already bestowed upon the people so many and such great blessings that nothing could be added above them (Is. 5; Jer. 25:4, 5). "Ye have seen," says Moses, "the signs . . . but the Lord hath not given you an heart" (Dt. 29:2, 4*). This is what was wanting and that which he promises to give. Nor is it only a promise, but a prediction and a prophecy; not only of the intention, but of the event itself. For what consolation could they have otherwise had from it?

XIV. As to the passages in Is. 54:10; 59:21; Hos. 2:19: "The promises were made to the church, and to the sons of God in a compound sense, as long as they will remain such, to show what God will do on his part (to wit, that he will not violate this covenant); but it cannot be inferred hence that such cannot become unbelievers." But since these promises bear upon this—that the church and believers (who are made such by regenerating grace) will be so preserved by God that they cannot perish, who does not see that the gift of perseverance of faith is necessarily included that they might never cease to be such and perish in fact? Nor does it imply only that God on his part would do what is required for the keeping of the covenant, but also that he would effect in us that we should never wholly cast aside that covenant. This appears both from its being compared with the covenant made with Noah (which was absolute, ever to endure and not conditional, Is. 54:9) and from its being set forth under the symbol of "espousal" (Hos. 2:19, 20) where no condition can have place in which Christ ought to prepare for himself his spouse (Ezk. 16; Eph. 5:25). Nor should it be added "this promise and the like belongs to the kingdom of glory." God should betroth his people to himself on that day in which he will provide for her corn and wine and oil, of which there will be no need in the kingdom of glory. Nor is it necessary that God should take care that we depart not from him, where there is no peril, no fear and not even the possibility of departing; where for being able not to sin (*posse non peccare*) (which was the case in paradise), it will be for ever not to be able to sin (*non posse peccare*) (which is the state and condition of the elect angels).

XV. As to Jn. 10:28, "Christ promises that no one shall be able to pluck his sheep while they are sheep, but it does not follow that they cannot cease to be sheep or by their sins escape out of the hands of the Father." But the argument of Christ supposes the sheep which are not plucked out will have eternal life. "I give unto them eternal life; and they shall never perish." This would be false if the sheep could perish, even if they be not plucked out. (2) The sheep which cannot be plucked out of the hands of Christ by the temptations of any enemies cannot cease to be sheep because no such change could be made except by some attempts of enemies. (3) The promise of Christ would be futile. For what would it help to be guarded from external enemies if danger always hung over us from internal enemies? Believers ought to fear not only from others, but more especially from themselves. The shepherd who promises to guard and keep the sheep absolutely will not discharge his duty if he permits them to wander and perish; but he ought to take care not only that they be not taken away from him by deceit and violence, but that they be not removed by disease or fault, or withdraw themselves from the fold by inborn simplicity and wander into devious paths.

3. From the merit and efficacy of Christ.

XVI. (3) The merit and efficacy of Christ, the Redeemer, who has purchased for them by his sacrifice (*hilasmon*) on earth not an evanescent blessing, nor applies it mutably by his intercession in heaven. For who can believe that Christ would have suffered; that they who were given him of the Father for an inheritance and peculiar property, whom he bought so dearly (not with gold, or with silver, but with his own precious blood and with dreadful tortures of soul and body and with an accursed death), having been plucked from him should pass over to the power of another and indeed of an enemy most hostile to him? Nay, as he is the Savior of his body, he cannot suffer any of them to perish who were given to him by the Father, but he guards them by his grace, continually dwelling in them and strengthening more and more the bond of union so that it can never be broken. Here belongs the passage of Paul: "God that spared not his own Son, but delivered him up for us, will give all things with him" (Rom. 8:32). Since he has given the greater, he cannot withhold the lesser; he gave his Son to enemies (which is the greater), how will he not give perseverance to friends now reconciled? But Christ himself testifes that this should be put beyond all doubt: "All that the Father giveth me shall came to me; and him that cometh to me I will in no wise cast out" (Jn. 6:37). "This is the Father's will which hath sent me, that of all which he hath given me I should lose nothing, but should raise it up again at the last day" (v. 39). Now how could this be carried out unless he would secure them not only against the perdition of death, but also from the perdition of sin, which is the surest cause of destruction? Hence he elsewhere asserts "that he had kept all those, whom the Father had given him, and none of them is lost" (Jn. 17:12) because he had joined them to himself by the closest union, from which flowed a fellowship of all his blessings and especially of his life through the Spirit. "Because I live," he said, "ye shall live also" (Jn. 14:19). Yes, he already lives in us (Gal. 2:20). On this account, he is called by the apostle "the leader and finisher of faith" (*archēgos kai teleiōtēs pisteōs*, Heb. 12:2); not only by merit, but also by efficacy because as he is the author of faith, he is also its preserver, who confirms it when produced in us by the word and the Spirit (by the gift of perseverance) and defends us against all temptations, and at last perfects and completes it with the crown of glory and immortality. And although the obedience of believers is required for this perseverance, it does not follow that it is not certain because it is so the duty of man as to be also the gift of Christ (by which he promotes and perfects faith in us, begun by giving the grace not only of believing, but also of persevering).

XVII. This is confirmed by the nature of the union of believers with Christ (as of the members with the head) which is not only intimate and most strict intensively, but also incapable of being dissolved (*adialytos*) extensively and of perpetual duration. Thus nothing can break that bond, or separate us from him (Rom. 8:38) because "he that is joined unto the Lord is one spirit with him" (1 Cor. 6:17) and from him has not only an influx of regenerating grace, but also of strengthening and preserving grace. Thus he is preserved not only from external assaults, but also from the internal assaults of the flesh and of sin (Phil. 1:6). Hence Augustine says: "That is not really the body of Christ, which will not be with him forever" (CI 3.32 [45] [FC 2:153; PL 34.82]). And as from the natural body of Christ now glorified it is impossible that one member can be torn away, thus from his mystical body no believer can be torn away. Hence believers planted in Christ by true faith may be said both as to the past to have now passed from death to life, and as to the present to have eternal life, and as to the future that they will not come into condemnation, nor will they perish forever (Jn. 5:24; 10:28). Now although that union is reciprocal, so that Christ not only remains in us, but we ought to remain in him (Jn. 15:5), that certainty is not removed because Christ himself causes us to remain, while he exhorts us to it making a privilege out of a duty. Hence the love of Christ is said to be "strong" (Cant. 8:6, 7, i.e., insuperable) as "death," which conquers all things, and "a jealousy cruel as the grave: the coals thereof are coals of fire" (i.e., of brightest flame) which God by the most powerful heat of his Spirit kindles to endure forever "so that many waters cannot quench that love." This could not be said if that love could be changed and that most close union produced by it could be dissolved.

XVIII. Paul magnificently sets forth this constancy of the union and love of Christ. For after saying "All things work together for good to them that love God, to them that are the called according to his purpose" (*kata prothesin*, Rom. 8:28) (which would not be true if anything could extinguish their faith and sanctity), he adds a reason drawn from the indissoluble connection of the blessings of God, of predestination with calling, of calling with justification, and of justification with glorification. Hence at the end he subjoins that full confidence (yea, and glorying) by which he challenges all the enemies of our salvation. He is most fully persuaded that nothing can ever separate us from the love of Christ. "Who shall separate us from the love of Christ? Shall tribulation, or distress, or persecution, or famine, or nakedness, or peril, or sword? Nay, in all these things we are more than conquerors (*hypernikōmen*) through him that loved us. For I am persuaded, that neither death, nor life, nor angels . . . nor any other creature shall be able to separate us from the love of God, which is in Christ" (vv. 35, 37-39*). But how could the apostle so boldly challenge all the enemies of our salvation and express full persuasion of the final perseverance of believers from their indissoluble union with Christ and the eternity of his love, if it were true that the Devil, the world and sin or any temptations could separate the justified believer from God's love and lead him to eternal destruction? Paul's glorying would undoubtedly be empty and the consolation he draws from it against all the assaults upon believers would be false. Nor can it be objected here either "that this was a special privilege of Paul, not common to others." For since in no other thing does he place his hope and confidence, than in the immutability of eternal election, efficacious calling, love and union with Christ (which are common to all believers), he does not mean to speak only of himself; nay, he expressly speaks in the plural, "Who shall separate us?" joining himself with others; or "that things are conditional, i.e., provided we do not separate ourselves from God by sin, or give ourselves up to our enemies; and on this account Paul does not mention sin, which nevertheless no one doubts can especially separate us from God." For besides the fact that in this way nothing would be said here of the believer which could not with equal truth be said of Adam (namely, that nothing could have separated him from the love of God if he had retained his righteousness), the discourse of Paul would afford a ridiculous meaning (namely, that nothing can separate us from the love of Christ provided only we remain in it [i.e., we will persevere if we persevere] because to remain in his love is nothing else than to persevere). As however it is useless to be safe from external enemies if danger of destruction is always impending over us from ourselves, so it would be absurd for him to glory as for a victory obtained (the hope of which depends on an uncertain condition of a both doubtful and perilous event). Hence, that the truth may be consistent with the apostle's glorying, the union of believers with Christ should be certain and indissoluble. Indeed, what could separate them from him? The Devil, the prince of this world? But as he had no power over Christ, so neither has he any over his members and he is greater who is in us than he who is in the world (1 Jn. 4:4). Could the world? But Christ has overcome the world (Jn. 16:33) and that we may overcome the world, he gives us faith which is the victory over the world. Could death and the grave? But he that believes in Christ shall not see death; yea, he has already passed from death to life (Jn. 5:24). Could Christ cease to love us or we to love him? But he pursued us with an eternal love and gives us his fear that we may not cease loving him. Could sin and the flesh? But he who is planted in Christ is dead and buried to it (Rom. 6:4). Finally, could the inconstancy of our will and the imaginary indifference of free will? But he in whom Christ lives is so constrained by his love that he no longer lives to himself, but is bound to serve him by an indeed close, yet still a sweet and pleasant necessity (2 Cor. 5:14).

XIX. The efficacy of his intercession also belongs here. Since this cannot be made void (Jn. 11:42), the perseverance he so anxiously seeks for them ought to be certain and indubitable. Thus he prays that Peter's faith fail not. "Satan hath desired to sift you, but I have prayed for thee, that thy faith fail not" (Lk. 22:31, 32*). Here two petitions are opposed: the one of Satan that he may sift Peter and the other apostles (i.e., tempt and disturb them, and by tempting and disturbing separate them from Christ—these two things occur in sifting, agitation and separation); the other of Christ, for Peter especially (as tried the more), not that his faith might not be tried and weakened, but that it might not fail; if not as to act (which ought to be interrupted), but as to habit. And that no one might say that this referred to Peter alone, he elsewhere prays for the other apostles; yea, and for all who would believe: "Holy Father, keep through thine own name . . . that they may be one, as we are" (Jn. 17:11); and "Neither pray I for these alone, but for them also which shall believe on me through their word" (Jn. 17:20). He had promised before that he would do this. "I will pray the Father, and he shall give you another Comforter, that he may abide with you forever" (Jn. 14:16). Not on earth only (once and again) does he pray, but in heaven, seeing he ever lives to make intercession for us (Heb. 7:25).

4. The guardianship of the Holy Spirit.

XX. (4) The guardianship and sealing of the Holy Spirit. The Spirit, who is given to us, ought to remain with us forever. "I will pray the Father, and he shall give you another Comforter, that he may abide with you forever" (Jn. 14:16). Here the perpetual indwelling of the Spirit is promised, not only as to intention, but also as to the event itself; not only in the apostles, but also in all believers, who in virtue of the covenant of grace (Is. 59:21) are made partakers of this gift (Gal. 4:6); not for a time, so that when once given it might be taken away from them, but forever that his grace may continually solace and sustain them even to the end (although unequally and in different degrees). Now how can this perpetual presence and indwelling of the Spirit consist with the total and final apostasy of the saints? This is further confirmed by the operation of the Spirit in us, which is described by "sealing," when he is said "to seal" us "unto the day of redemption" (Eph. 1:13; 4:30). For since this seal (*sphragis*) pertains to nothing else than confirming in the hearts of believers the certainty of God's promises concerning grace and salvation (as the seals applied to instruments denote their immutability), who does not gather from this the certainty of salvation and perseverance; unless we wish the testimony of the Holy Spirit to be fallacious and the sealing useless, even the thought of which is impious? Hence the fathers call that seal *akatalyton* ("indestructible") which is said to be impressed upon us, not for a certain time only, but "unto the day of redemption" (i.e., even to the end). And on this account, the argument binds the more when the mode of sealing is attended to, which is not only external by the sacraments, but also internal by consolation and sanctification (which are as it were so many parts of this seal and which on the one hand confirm the eternity of God's love in us, on the other hand persuade us to the constancy of our faith and obedience from the grace of God). Hence it is evident that in vain do our opponents reply that it is treated here of the sealing to salvation and not to faith. For by the very thing by which we are sealed to the certain obtainment of salvation, we are also sealed to the constant continuance of faith in us (which is a means of salvation). And if faith is supposed to be already in the sealed (for no one except a believer is sealed), the promise is not immediately made to be conditional (depending upon man's will) and not absolute. For it is one thing for faith to be supposed in the subject; another for persevering faith to be supposed (which comes under the promise).

5. From the nature of the gifts.

XXI. (5) The nature of the gifts bestowed upon us by the Spirit. Since these are without repentance (*ametamelēta*) and eternal, they do not allow the believer adorned with them to fall either totally or finally: "The gifts of God are without repentance" (*ametamelēta*, Rom. 11:29). Now if they are such as God will never repent of when once granted (i.e., he will never recall them), they must necessarily remain in us. How then could they be without repentance (i.e., immutable and constant), if man can lose them or wholly fail from them? Although the apostle here in the first place has reference to the calling of the Jews (many of whom fell and were destroyed), still no less valid does the argument of the apostle remain (to wit, although many of the Jews remain in unbelief, God cannot reject the people whom he foreknew would always be beloved on account of the fathers [nor can they wholly fail]; yet it would happen sometime that they would all be collected into the church of Christ because the gifts and calling of God are without repentance [*ametamelēta*]). Therefore what is true of the Jewish nation, the same ought also to hold good of the church and individual believers—that the calling and gifts of God once bestowed on them are without repentance (*ametamelēta*) and irrevocable, since the reason in each case is the same. Nor is it to be added, "Although God does not repent of his gift, still man can repent of the gift received or retained." These gifts and calling without repentance (*ametamelēta*) tend to confirm faith in man and cause him never to repent (entirely at least) of the accepted gift. On this account, perpetuity is ascribed to the Christian virtues; as to faith, when it is said our victory which overcomes the world (1 Jn. 5:4); to love because "it never faileth" (1 Cor. 13:8); to hope because "it does not make ashamed" (Rom. 5:5).

And spiritual life.

XXII. This is still further confirmed from the nature of the spiritual life which is generated in us by the Spirit. It is not liable to destruction or extinction (like the animal life), but is perpetual and eternal. On this account, believers in grace are said to have eternal life already: "He that believeth in me hath eternal life" (Jn. 5:24; 6:40). He does not say, shall have in the future, but has now in the present. "These things have I written unto you that believe on the name of the Son of God; that ye may know that ye have eternal life" (1 Jn. 5:13). And yet, if the life which we have here by grace is eternal, how can it be extinguished or fail? Can it happen that at last we may fall from the eternal life (into which we are translated by faith) into the eternal death from which we were translated? "Blessed is he that hath part in the first resurrection: on such the second death hath no power" (Rev. 20:6). Now although this spiritual life (no less than the animal) suffers its decays in the serious lapses of saints and does not always have the same tone and vigor, sometimes languishes and seems to be suffocated, still by no means is it entirely suffocated and extinguished; but by subsequent acts of repentance and faith it is renewed as often as the sinner struggles and from that fall (as if with collected spirit) is inflamed with a greater hatred of evil and a more ardent love of good.

XXIII. We must not omit here the important passage where the apostle most clearly proves our proposition (in which, eluding or corrupting, our opponents labor wonderfully hard). "Whosoever is born of God doth not commit sin; for his seed remaineth in him: and he cannot sin, because he is born of God" (1 Jn. 3:9). If anyone is born of God, he does not sin; whoever sins, is not born of God; yea, he does not see or know him (v. 6). He does not say simply one born of God sins not (i.e., the true believer) for the apostle recognizes sin in the saints and does not except even himself (1 Jn. 1:8); but "does not commit sin" (i.e., so that sin rules over him by which he would return wholly under the power of Satan) in the manner in which the unrenewed sin (with the desire and habit of sinning, sin reigning). Even as he is said "to do justice," not who does any work of justice, but who employs himself in a continual exercise of it; as he is said "to do medicine" who professes it and is engaged in its practice; "to do merchandizing," "to do art" who practice them. Nor is he said only "not to sin," but that he "cannot" even "do it"; not only because "he ought not" from his duty, for thus the unrenewed might be said not to be able to sin because he ought not; or because he cannot do it morally (i.e., he does it with difficulty) because thus the gradation of the apostle from the lesser to the greater is taken away. He does not sin and he cannot sin because not to sin is greater than to sin with difficulty. Rather it is said absolutely as to the event because this cannot be done from a twofold cause. First, on account of the internal principle itself because the "seed of God" (to wit, the implanted [*emphyton*] word and the Holy Spirit, by whose power we are born again) is not only for a moment, but "remains in him" (i.e., is in him permanently). For it is evident that existence alone is not meant here, but a constant abiding because it treats of an incorruptible seed, of regeneration to eternal life, of remaining (which does not permit the renewed to sin and by which the Spirit remains with him forever, Jn. 14:16). The believer ought to remain perpetually in the house and never be ejected from it (Jn. 8:35). Second, on account of the very generation accomplished by that seed because a birth from God has the conserving cause and effect of its own perseverance in him who is born; for the seed of God remains in him and helps to defend him from sin. That act of regeneration, in which is the foundation of relation because it cannot have been, cannot but be; for his seed which remains in him makes an eternal bond of relation, as the Son of God is always what he is once. And although that seed does not always bring forth fruit in the believer as to the second act, it does not follow that it does not remain as to the first act (as life remains in a tree during the winter when it can bear neither leaves nor fruit).

XXIV. Nor is it to be said here that the opinion of John is true in the compound sense, namely that he who is born of God cannot sin (inasmuch as he is born of God); still that he can sin in the divided sense, if he neglects the seed of God. For thus a causal is changed into a conditional. John does not say he that is born of God cannot sin inasmuch as he is born of God, but "because he is born" and because the seed remains in him (i.e., always perseveres and remains in him), whence he is born a son of God. Otherwise the statement of the apostle would be made frigid, asserting what no one could doubt. For neither the Devil himself, nor any wicked man commits sin according to what he was made by God. However more absurd is Bellarmine's explanation: "He that is born of God does not sin, as long as he continues a son of God" (i.e., he does not sin as long as he does not sin) ("De Justificatione," 3.15 *Opera* [1858], 4:564). Thus neither could Adam have sinned as long as he persevered. But John meant another thing—that believers avoiding sin (at least reigning sin) may in this way know that they are born of God (on whom it does not fall); not in the sense which our opponents charge upon us ("Do not sin, because ye cannot sin"—which is plainly ridiculous); but in another, which is the best ("Take care, brethren, not to indulge in sin because if anyone does so and thinks he is born of God he evidently deceives himself; for he who is born of God, is not accustomed to do so, nor indeed can he"). Moreover this impossibility does not exist on the part of man, but on the part of the seed preserving the believer from such a lapse and on the part of the spiritual birth (which is the cause of that perseverance and which excludes apostasy). Thus not to be able to sin and to be born of God are mutually related to each other, as cause and effect. Hence the proposition of the apostle cannot be identical; as if he should say, he who does not sin, does not sin; no more than this, he who is born of man uses reason. For the believer in the subject of the proposition is described by his origin, but in the predicate by an essential property.

From the various similes.

XXV. Here belong the various similes used by the Holy Spirit to shadow forth the perennial nature of that life; as when it is compared to "an incorruptible seed" (1 Pet. 1:23), not only in itself formally, but also in us effectively because it produces eternal life and always remains in the believer (1 Jn. 3:9). It is "a well of water springing up into everlasting life, of which whosoever drinketh shall never thirst" (Jn. 4:14); a vineyard which shall no more be pulled up (Am. 9:15); "a tree planted by the rivers of water, whose leaf shall not wither" (Pss. 1:3; 92:14). He not only says that this water remains, but is multiplied and made a perennial fountain springing up into eternal life (i.e., which springs up from the earth even to heaven and to God and eternal life and carries us along, as it descended from God to us), as waters usually rise to the height of their own source; "a house built upon a rock" which stands immovable against the winds, storms and inundations of waters (Mt. 7:25) and against which the gates of hell cannot prevail (Mt. 16:18). Now if the believer who is born of God could become a child of the Devil; if the water of saving grace could be entirely dried up; if the pious who is built upon the rock of ages could fall, how could it be called an incorruptible seed and water springing up into eternal life and a house built upon a rock?

XXVI. The objection to Jn. 4:14 is fruitless. First, "that it treats of eternal life, in which thirst is perfectly satisfied, not of the life of grace, in which it is blessed to thirst" (Mt. 5:6); "yea, we can also cease from drinking." The design of Christ is to show the prerogative of the spiritual water which he gives above the elementary water. First in this, that well water does not entirely quench the thirst, but the water of Christ so takes away the thirst that he who has once drunk never thirsts forever (to wit, with a thirst of total indigence, which belongs to the wicked [Is. 65:13], although he can still thirst with a thirst of desire and total fruition, which is always in believers [who are not as yet perfect, 1 Pet. 2:2, 3] in this life). Second, that well water does not remain in him who drinks, but passes off and disappears, hence he is again compelled to thirst. But the water of Christ is a permanent and perennial fountain, not only in respect of glory (where a fulness of this water will be given), but also in this life (where we begin already to drink of it). Hence he does not say this fountain is eternal life, but springs up into eternal life, to intimate that this perennial fountain has already begun in the heart of the believer in grace, until it leads him along unto eternal life; as elsewhere Christ says from him "who believes streams of living water shall flow forth" (Jn. 7:38), speaking of the gifts of the Holy Spirit who was to be given to believers. Second, "the word 'drink' is intensive, i.e., it denotes a continuous or at least final act, so that Christ did not mean, He who has once drunk and has once believed, but He who has continually and perseveringly done so, will live forever." But the words of Christ preclude this interpretation. He does not say, he who continually has drunk, but who has drunk (i.e., who has once truly drunk because having taken that one draught he causes him always to drink and because the water which Christ gives becomes a fountain). Christ gives this water, when it is once drunk. Therefore, where it is once drunk, it becomes there a fountain of water springing up to eternal refreshment. Otherwise if Christ meant only this—that as long as man drinks of that water he should not thirst—the same might have been said of any other drink—that as long as anyone drinks of it he shall not thirst.

6. From the judgment concerning the apostate.

XXVII. (6) The judgment, made in Scripture concerning the apostate, as if wholly different from true believers bears upon this subject. "They went out from us," says John, "but they were not of us; for if they had been of us, they would no doubt have continued with us; but that they might be made manifest that they were not all of us" (1 Jn. 2:19). As Augustine fitly remarks, "That is not really the body of Christ, which will not be with him forever" (CI 3.32* [45] [FC 2:153; PL 34.82]). And elsewhere: "They were not sons even when they were in profession and name sons" (*Admonition and Grace* 9 [20] [FC 2:269; PL 44.928]). Thus the apostle distinguishes "being in the church" as to external profession and the ecclesiastical body; and "being of the church" as to internal communion and the mystical body of Christ (which belongs to the elect alone). Now the apostate and antichrists (of whom John speaks) had indeed been among them in the Christian assembly and the visible church of believers by a profession of faith and communion of the sacraments; and had fallen from that communion, not so much by a change of place, as a change of doctrine and affection (as they are said to go out of the world, not who separate themselves from it in body, but in mind and affections). And because a great scandal could have arisen thence (as if the church had begotten such pests or true believers could fail), John meets the case when he adds they were not of the number of true believers, because if they had been of them, they would in like manner have remained constantly with them; but this happened in order that it might be manifested that not all who are in the church and who make a profession of faith are truly believers and members of Christ's body. The apostle could not have said this unless he had supposed it to be certain and indubitable that they, who had once been drawn into the mystical body of Christ and the invisible church, could not fail from it. For what is objected by some—that this going out denotes the apostolic mission (as if they had pretended they had been sent by the apostles, which, however, was not so) is so absurd as to need no refutation. Now although we do not deny that true believers can for a time recede from their external profession and fall into a denial of Christ (either from fear and weakness or an error of mind or from the hope of gain, from which fall they can rise), it cannot, therefore, happen that they should fall by a total lapse and from wickedness and a deliberate purpose of mind, from hatred and contempt of the truth, so as to become persecutors and seducers; yea, also antichrists (such as were these apostates concerning whom he speaks).

7. From the absurdities.

XXVIII. (7) From absurdities. The apostasy of saints being established (a) the decrees and gifts of God without repentance (*ametamelēta*) are suspended on the uncertain will of man. (b) The chain of the means of salvation which God has woven together for the sure consolation of his people is broken. (c) The doctrine of the gospel is turned into mere conjecture and the confidence and certainty of salvation is forthwith snatched from the distressed conscience. (d) The distinction between the reprobate and the elect is taken away, while these and those promiscuously are either admitted at random to the condition of those to be saved or are excluded. (e) The whole plan of salvation is rendered useless. For if it is possible for every believer to fall from faith, it might happen that there would be no elect. For if one falls, why not another? and for the same reason, why not all? Thus there could be no church and Christ had died in vain.

Sources of explanation.

XXIX. The examples adduced of those who are said to have fallen from faith do not prove the apostasy of the saints. It is either defection from temporary faith, not from saving faith (as those referred to in Mt. 13:21); or from external communion and the visible church, not the internal and mystical church. This is meant in those passages where mention is made of the covenant-breaking Israelites, who were broken off on account of unbelief (Rom. 11:20), who are contradistinguished from those elected unto glory and who have obtained salvation (Rom. 11:7) and the branches (which not bearing) do not remain in Christ, but are cut off and burned (Jn. 15:2, 6). They are said to be in Christ because they are in the society of the church and by baptism are initiated into Christ and in both their own opinions and the opinions of others seem to be planted in Christ, but who adhere to him rather by contiguity of external communion, than inhere by continuity of internal communion, and by the vivifying influx of the Spirit. Or they are said to be in Christ from a federal and sacramental sanctification—external, not intimate and real (alluded to in Heb. 10:29); or "from the faith which is believed" or the doctrine of the gospel and its profession; not, however, "from the faith by which it is believed" or the habit once given to the true believer (as it is said concerning the last days that some "shall depart from the faith" [1 Tim. 4:1], to wit, from the truth of the gospel, attending to deceiving spirits; and of Hymenaeus and Philetus [1 Tim. 1:19, 20; 2 Tim. 2:17] that "they have made shipwreck concerning faith" [*peri tēn pistin*], viz., departing from the pure and sincere preaching of the gospel, which for a time they had retained). In this sense, they are said "to have put away a good conscience" (to wit, the unclouded sincerity and affection of mind in retaining the purity of the gospel, which they cast aside, spreading the sail to ambition and their other affections, interpolating the true doctrine with various deadly errors—such as the denial of the last resurrection, saying that it had passed already). They are said to have put away a good conscience, not by rejecting what they had, but by not admitting it (as the word *to apōsasthai* used here primarily signifies the repulsion and rejection of a thing which is not held [as in Acts 13:46], not for the shaking off of a thing already possessed). It can also be observed that they are not said to have made shipwreck from faith but "concerning faith" (*peri tēn pistin*) (*circa fidem*, as the Vulgate renders it), so that the metaphor is taken from sailors and faith is here set forth as a harbor to which they steered the way; the doctrine of the gospel being received, it would have led them, so that in it they would have found peace of conscience and salvation (as Theophylact observes on this passage, *Commentarius in primam epistolam ad Timotheum* [PG 125.27 on 1 Tim. 1:19]). To arrive at which the course of navigation must be governed by a good conscience; casting this aside, they could not reach it. And thus they made shipwreck about it, not only not appealing to it, but running upon the dreadful rocks of error, where they truly made shipwreck (i.e., rushed headlong to destruction). Elsewhere faith is compared to a mark at which we aim and a goal towards which we run and about which they are said "to err concerning the faith" (*astochein peri tēn pistin*, 1 Tim. 6:21) who follow science falsely so called (*pseudōnymon gnōsin*).

XXX. The examples of the saints who fell into grievous and heinous sins do not prove that they fell totally and finally from the faith. It is one thing to fall into sin; another to come under the dominion of sin (as it is one thing to slip into the mud; another to throw oneself into and roll in it with pleasure)—in one there is the accident and weakness of sinning; in the other it is a purpose of life and resolution of the will. The saints sin in the first and not in the second way. If for a time they wander from the path of faith and truth, they do not wholly lose their purpose. In a shipwreck, they keep hold of a plank; in winter of the seed; in a paroxysm, the principle of reason; nor with the act does the habit perish, nor with the seduced affection is the purpose to return taken away.

XXXI. David sinned grievously and against his conscience; yea, in his twofold sin of adultery and homicide, he for some time was stupefied. Hence his faith was not only undoubtedly lessened, but even fast asleep so that he could not for a time perceive the sense of grace. But still he did not totally fall because he sinned not so much from deliberate wickedness and from habit, as from vehement desire and seduction of the flesh; overcome, namely, by his concupiscence (2 S. 11:2-4). Hence, being rebuked by Nathan, he at once recognized and confessed his sin and flew to the grace of God, and on this account the prophet soon announced the pardon of his sin. On this account, he so earnestly seeks, not that the Spirit might be restored to him, but that "the Holy Spirit might not be taken from him" and that "the joy of salvation might be restored unto him" (Ps. 51:11, 12). This proves that the sense of grace had indeed been interrupted, but not that grace had been taken entirely away. If David acknowledges that he is "a man of death" (2 S. 12:5) (i.e., exposed to death, who really deserved such a punishment on account of his sin), it does not immediately follow that he had wholly fallen from faith and from grace because from the demerit and guilt of sin to the event the consequence does not hold good. It follows indeed that he was in that state in which he was worthy of being smitten with death and separated from God; but not forthwith that he was actually and in fact separated (on account of the intervention of God's mercy). It is indeed certain that David can be said to have remained in death as to his guilt (as long as he remained in sin and was not turned) and that he had lost the fruit and sense of justification; but not moreover can he be said to have fallen absolutely from the grace of adoption and from his right to life, which belonged to him as a child of God. Therefore, what John says, that a murderer "abideth in death" and "has not eternal life abiding in him" (1 Jn. 3:14*, 15) must be understood of an impenitent and unconverted murderer (such as David was not).

XXXII. Solomon was a sad example of human frailty in those grievous sins by which he contaminated himself, by his unbridled license of polygamy and insane love of strange women. While a king he was the wisest of mortals, beloved of God, of so great worth that the business of building the house of God was committed to him, a type of Christ, who in the days of his youth had been regarded as a pattern of wisdom and justice. Now when old, he turns his heart away from God, and goes after idols, and becomes an architect of idols and temples of the Devil; who was before the master workman (*dēmiourgos*) of the temple of God (which so increases the heinousness of his sin that scarcely anything like it is found among the saints). In the meantime if it is thoroughly examined, it is not such as to compel us to believe that he fell totally from faith, so that its habit was not only weakened and very much diminished and stupefied, but wholly extinct. Yea, there are many things from which his penitence and perseverance can be inferred. (1) From the memorable promise made to David concerning him (2 S. 7:14, 15), as the type of Christ, which threatens him sinning with stripes, but does not take away grace (contrary to what was done to Saul). "I will be his father, and he shall be my son. If he commit iniquity, I will chasten him with the rod of men, but my mercy shall not depart away from him." A federal promise here is granted, not only of a kingdom (as Kimchi holds; cf. Johannis Buxtorf, *Biblia Sacra Hebraica et Chaldaica* [1619] on 2 S. 7:14), but of all the graces with which the father pursues his son (which is incompatible [*asystatos*] with desertion). (2) This is confirmed by that special love with which God is said to have embraced him (2 S. 12:25). Hence the name Jedidiah ("loved of the Lord") was given to him, for the love of God for his people is eternal (Jer. 31:3). (3) He was a distinguished type of Christ, which he could not be if he is to be placed in the number of apostates and reprobates. (4) In 1 K. 11:4, 6, where his sins are enumerated, it is said, "The heart of Solomon was not perfect with the Lord his God, as was the heart of David his father, nor did he fully follow after the Lord, as did David his father." Hence we can gather, although an uxorious man by love and indulgence towards his wives, he had departed from the true God, whether by tolerating the worship of idols and building temples to them by an idolatry only participative and indirect (as not a few of the Jews and Christians think); or by worshipping them himself or bringing idols into the temple (in which the true worship of God continued even when idolatry obtained); still he had not wholly abjured the worship of God. Hence Augustine joins him with Aaron, whom he says was "induced not to consent to the erring people in making the idol, but was bound to have stopped it" (CG 14.11 [FC 14:378; PL 41.419]). (5) Solomon is praised after his death when reference is made to Rehoboam: "For three years he walked in the way of David and Solomon" (2 Ch. 11:17). Here it treats of the imitation of piety, which the Holy Spirit would not have said if he had wholly fallen from faith. (6) The same thing is proved by his repentance, the testimony to which is not only the reformation of the church instituted in the last years of his life (2 Ch. 11:17), but especially his Ecclesiastes, which (it is the constant opinion of the Jews) was not only written by him (as can be gathered even from the title of the book when it is called, "The words of the Preacher, the son of David, king in Jerusalem," 1:1), but also after his fall at the end of his life (as is gathered from the sum of the book, which is nothing else than deep humiliation before God; a graphic description of the vanities and pleasures of all kinds which he had indulged in; express confession of his sin; an abnegation of his own wisdom, which he had abused (Ecc. 7:23); the woman by whom he was fascinated and seduced to detestable sin (v. 26); and the recalling of all desire to the fear of God alone, in opposition to the nothingness (*oudeneian*) and falsity of idols, as to the one thing necessary; and "the beginning and end" (*archēn kai telos*) of true wisdom (Ecc. 3*:11*, 12). Nor can these objections to this repentance of Solomon have any force—either that Scripture does not expressly mention it, because we have no explicit mention of the repentance of Adam, Lot, Samson and others (which nevertheless no one calls in question and the arguments adduced are sufficient to prove it); or that he did not remove the idols because it is said, "Josiah defiled the high places which Solomon had built for Ashtoroth, for Chemosh, and for Milcom" (2 K. 23:13). He might have left those high places to serve afterwards for worship, not idolatrous, but of the true God of Israel; as it is said of the people after the destruction of idolatrous worship by Manasseh that "the people did sacrifice still in the high places, yet unto the Lord their God only" (2 Ch. 33:17). Josiah wanted to destroy these in order the more thoroughly to purge the worship of God from all superstition.

XXXIII. That Peter grievously sinned by denying Christ and even confirming his denial by perjury cannot be doubted. But that faith in his heart was not wholly taken away (although the confession in his mouth was wanting) is solidly drawn: (1) from the prayer of Christ, who prayed for him "that his faith might not fail" (*ekleipē*, Lk. 22:32), which everyone believes was heard by the Father. Nor can this be understood only of a final defection because the words of Christ cannot be referred to time, but to the thing which is said to fail in whatever time that may happen (so that faith might not be entirely extinguished, but remain in him). Otherwise Christ would not have obtained his wish and Satan would have secured his purpose. (2) The manner in which Peter sinned shows that it was not a total defection because he sinned not from depravity and a deliberate purpose of mind, but from the weakness and fear of the flesh (which so occupied his mind, that neither in the first, nor the second, and hardly in the third denial could he collect his mind or think that he had sinned at all). (3) The grief and bitter tears which followed his fall at the look of Christ and the crowing of the cock show that faith had not entirely failed in him. Hence the Savior, by looking at him, did not infuse a new habit, but resuscitated him (preserved by the secret power of the Spirit). "And Peter remembered," as the text has it (i.e., returned to himself, whom fear had before distracted). Thus "the strength of his faith had been shaken," as Tertullian says (lib. de Fug. in Persec.+), but it was not shaken off; faith was moved, but not removed; debilitated, but not destroyed; obscured, but not extinguished. "Love not so much turned away, as conscience disturbed" (as Leo the Great says, Serm. 9, de Passi.+); "He loved within, him, whom he denied without" (although the affection fettered by fear lay torpid, faith remained in the first act, the fear of danger intercepted the second). Hence Theophylact says, on these words of Christ: "I have prayed for thee, said he, that thy faith fail not. For although for a time thou wilt be shaken, still thou hast the hidden seeds of faith; even if the attacking spirit shall tear off the leaves, still the root will live and thy faith shall not fail. I will not altogether leave thee" (*Enarratio in Evangelium Lucae* [PG 123.1074] on Lk. 22:32). Now although confession is an effect of faith (which follows it), it does not follow that where faith is it always and everywhere exerts itself; or that faith is straightway extinguished whose confession was not voluntarily rejected, but only oppressed by fear.

XXXIV. They, who do the works of the flesh with a full will and earnestness and persevere in them, are rightly said to have entirely fallen from faith. But believers cannot be said to sin in this sense (from 1 Jn. 3:19; 5:18) because they do not sin so much from depravity and a full consent of the will without reluctance, as from weakness and the impotence of the affections. And although those sins are committed not rarely from some previous deliberation against their conscience, still because that purpose (*proairesis*) does not so much arise from habit as from a vehement disturbance of the affections (in which there is always either an antecedent struggle or subsequent grief and a certain resistance of the conscience), it is evident that they cannot be called sins of bad habit and of pride (which are committed with an uplifted hand and shake all grace out of the heart). If resistance of conscience occurs even in the unrenewed sometimes, the same is not to be thought of the sins of believers because in the former the struggle is only between the appetite and reason (which represses sin rather than destroys it and induces a dread of punishment, not a loathing of sin); but in the latter, the struggle is between the flesh and the spirit (which always supposes some faith and grace in the heart). Hence Augustine says: "The sons of God, as long as they live mortally, struggle with death, and although it is said truly of them 'as many as are led by the Spirit of God are the sons of God' so by the Spirit of God they are excited and as sons make progress towards God, as also by their Spirit, the corruptible body principally exerting its influence, as sons of men by certain human motions they desert to themselves and on that account sin" (*Enchiridion* 17 [64] [FC 2:423; PL 40.262]). Hence as on account of the unwillingness of the flesh, the actions which follow the Spirit are never so purged from all taint as to have no fault and defect; so those in which the flesh preponderates are never so delivered up to indwelling sin, but that always by the opposition (either simultaneous or subsequent) of the Spirit and *ex post facto*, its tyranny and dominion is hindered and destroyed.

XXXV. Perseverance is either physical and ignorant of itself, arising either from hardness of the material or the nature of the form (such as exists in gold or in heaven). Or it is moral, arising from a purpose of mind and a constancy of will in retaining the object. To the first, exhortations and promises are altogether useless; but not equally to the second because they are the means by which it is promoted and fulfilled. Hence so far is our doctrine from taking away the use of exhortations and promises and threatenings concerning perseverance that their necessity is the rather more firmly established. For they are the means appointed by God to obtain it, inasmuch as by them God works faith, the fear of him, the desire of avoiding falls and, after their occurrence, of rising from them. If God has promised perseverance to believers, he has not promised it absolutely and without the means, but through means to be used by man himself; to be bestowed, so that God preserving man, he is bound also to preserve himself through the grace of the Spirit (1 Jn. 5:18). Hence believers are certain of their perseverance through faith in the promises, not through any external force (which retains them willing or unwilling and, even remaining in sin, in the way of salvation), but in the use of the means and in the practice of piety; while working out their own salvation with fear and trembling, they trust that God is he who works in them both to will and to do and who graciously perfects the good work he has begun. So that occasion of licentiousness and impiety is drawn falsely from this doctrine, since to indulge in wickedness and to have the effective grace of perseverance are incompatible (*asystaton*). Nay, he who has this hope purifies himself (1 Jn. 3:3) and should be fully persuaded that no one without holiness shall see God and that life can be attained in no other way than the way of piety. Therefore no other security arises from the certainty of perseverance in man than a spiritual certainty. This does not exclude, but supposes the use of means and ingenerates in our minds a fear not of distrust, but of solicitude and zeal in the constant use of these means.

XXXVI. The righteousness of the first institution in nature differs from that of restitution in grace. From the former Adam could fail because it was mutable; but we cannot fail from the latter, which is immutable and without repentance (*ametamelētos*).

XXXVII. The passage—"When the righteous turneth away from his righteousness, and committeth iniquity, all his righteousness that he hath done shall not be mentioned: in his sin that he hath sinned, in them shall he die" (Ezk. 18:24)—does not favor the apostasy of saints. (1) It is hypothetical, not absolute; (*bhshvbh tsdyq*) "when the righteous turneth away" (i.e., "if he turneth away"). However, it is known that a condition puts nothing in being, but denotes only a necessary connection of the antecedent with the consequent. If some possibility of defection be denoted on the part of man (when viewed in a divided sense), it cannot at once be inferred that there is a possibility in the compound sense on the part of the grace of God and as to the event. For what is possible with regard to the nearest and known cause is impossible with regard to the remote and hidden (which is in the decree of God). Here then, where God prescribes to man his duty and acts as a lawgiver, he does not disclose the event of the things decreed by him. As Lord of the world and dispenser of good and evil, he intends nothing else than to deliver the rules of his duty and to declare the rewards and punishments which hang over them from a compliance with or neglect of it (without any reference to the possibility or impossibility of the thing). (2) It treats there of the righteousness of the law and of works, not of the righteousness of the gospel and of faith (to wit, the prophet speaks *ad hominem* and according to the opinion of those whom he addresses here, who, as they were under the law, sought a legal righteousness from the law and wished to be justified by the works of the law). The Lord (in order to expose the vanity of this error and at the same time defend the justice of his providence against their calumnies) says the righteousness of the righteous profits him nothing, unless it is constant and perpetual. Otherwise if the righteous turns away, all his preceding works are in vain; he will die in his iniquity because when they looked into themselves, it ought not to seem wonderful to them if they should endure the punishments inflicted by the justice of God. Now such righteousness from which anyone falls (although it is not blinded and hypocritical and only as to external appearance, but also true in its kind), still cannot be considered as saving and vivifying (which is pleasing to God) because from the defection its vanity is demonstrated. If life is promised to the righteous, it does not follow that he speaks of perfect righteousness because life is promised to the persevering righteous (i.e., to one doing righteously), not just as the righteous failing from his righteousness exercises it, but sincerely, heartily and constantly (1 Tim. 1:5; Mt. 22:37).

XXXVIII. Judas is not said to have been of the number of those who were given to Christ to be saved because he was "a son of perdition" (*hyios apōleias*, Jn. 17:12) (i.e., then utterly lost and so worthy of perdition, who had brought it on himself by his own crime and was destined to perdition and destruction by God's eternal just judgment [Acts 1:16; 4:27, 28]; who is therefore opposed to the elect sons of God, who were given to Christ to be saved). Therefore *eimē* is not an exceptive but an adversative particle here for "but"—"None of those whom thou hast given me is lost, but (only) the son of perdition" is lost. He was not of the number of the given, but of the reprobate devoted to destruction (as it is often used elsewhere, Gal. 2:16; 1 Cor. 7:17; Gal. 1:7; Rev. 21:27).

XXXIX. It is one thing to fall from grace positively by a real privation of grace already received; but another to fall from it negatively by not obtaining it. They of whom Paul speaks are said in the latter, not in the former sense to "have fallen from grace" (Gal. 5:4), inasmuch as miserably desiring Judaism with Christianity and the law with the gospel, their own righteousness with the righteousness of Christ, deprived themselves of and so fell from it (as he says elsewhere of the Jews, Rom. 9:31). Since grace and merit are incompatible (*asystata*), whosoever seeks his righteousness either in whole or in part in the law, cannot help falling from grace.

XL. It is one thing to be delivered to Satan with the feaster (*Epulone* [i.e., the rich man of Lk. 16:19]) for eternal torment; another to be delivered with the incestuous Corinthian for the destruction of the flesh that the Spirit may be saved in the day of the Lord (1 Cor. 5:5). The believer can be delivered up in the latter, not in the former way. Excommunication does not simply exclude the fallen from the kingdom of heaven, but with this condition—unless they rise again by repentance (which that censure as a healthful medicine works in true believers through the grace of God, 2 Cor. 7:11). Hence the excommunicated does not cease in secret to be a member of Christ, although as to external discipline for a time he may be cut off from the external body of the church and from the communion of sacred things (to wit, excommunication is the rod of a pious mother over a bad son, whom she does not therefore regard as not a son because she whips him, but chastises him severely that he may reform and not cease to be a son altogether).

XLI. Although the saints on account of the grievous sins into which they slip, deserve exclusion from the kingdom of heaven and the abrogation of their justification and adoption, still it happens by the mercy of God that on this account neither their right to the kingdom of heaven is taken away, nor justification or adoption recalled, nor their state of regeneration effectively destroyed. The right to the kingdom is not founded upon our actions, but on the gratuitous adoption of God and our indissoluble union with Christ. Also the guilt of this or that sin does not abrogate the universal justification of preceding sins and the state of the person reconciled to God by Christ. The privilege of adoption does not depend upon us, but upon the mercy of God the Father alone. The grace of regeneration flows from the Spirit, who as he once implanted in our hearts that vivifying seed, so he impressed upon it a heavenly and incorruptible force and this he perpetually cherishes and preserves. Thus although sinful man can (at least for a time) lose the use of this right and the sense of justification, still he cannot fall from that right. Even if he were deprived of the solace of adoption, still he is not at once divested of that adoption so that he who had been made a son of God should become a child of the Devil and a servant of sin. And if that seed is latent in the heart and does not exhibit itself outwardly in the bearing of fruit, still it is not dead—life is always in the root. The act of faith can be intercepted, but the habit itself cannot be shaken off (as fire lies concealed under ashes; as life which suffers it decays; as a plant in the winter which neither flourishes nor bears fruit).

XLII. It is one thing for a believer sinning grievously to be damnable by his own merit (if regarded as to himself in a divided sense); another, if considered in the compound sense and as to God's decree. In the former sense, it is true that he is exposed to death and if he continues in that state, will certainly be condemned. But in the latter sense, it is rightly said that they will be absolved and saved (God so arranging the matter by his immense love and wisdom that he may not die in that state, but may be restored and return to the way by a renewed act of faith and repentance before he reaches the goal). Hence according to a double relation (*schesin*), these two propositions (although seemingly contrary) can be true at the same time. It is impossible that David (elected and a man after God's heart) can perish. It is impossible that David, an adulterer and murderer (if death should take him away in his impenitence) can be saved. The former by reason of God's decree; the latter by reason of the heinousness and demerit of his sin. But this difficulty divine providence and grace solves, taking care that David (or any of the elect) should not die in that state in which on account of impenitence he would be excluded from salvation.

XLIII. But if it is asked how faith can subsist in the believer together with such grievous sins? The answer is easy—just as contraries can remain in the same subject, but in a lower degree. As the flesh and the Spirit, although always struggling against each other, still cannot entirely drive each other out while we continue in this mortal state; and as the Spirit, while it prevails in the contest, depresses the flesh indeed, but does not wholly destroy it; thus when the flesh lusts against the Spirit and leads a man captive under the law of sin, it represses the power of the Spirit, but does not straightway destroy and shake it off. The highly sinful acts cannot (it is true) subsist with the opposed acts of righteousness: for example, the act of adultery with an act of chastity; an act of unbelief with an act of faith; an act of hatred with an act of love; but still they cannot destroy the habit itself. Thus nothing hinders faith and love from remaining in a sinning man, but as to the first act, not the second; as to the seed, not as to the fruit; as to the habit (but languishing and decreased), not as to its exercise and operations.

XLIV. Nor in this way (as our opponents cavil) is the idea of the virtues wholly corrupted because they are said to subsist with atrocious sins; so that those who also fall into unbelief ought to be called believers on account of the incapability of faith being lost; ought to be called righteous and holy, who pollute themselves with various contaminations of unrighteousness and impurity; chaste, who are adulterers, etc. Since there are always two principles in the believer (the flesh and the Spirit), nothing prevents their obtaining different names according to these different principles so that he may be called a believer and righteous on the part of God, who elected and redeemed him, and with regard to the Spirit; but he may be called an unbeliever and unrighteous on his own part and with regard to the flesh. Again, since a habit is perfected by an act and a virtue takes its denomination not so much from a latent habit as from the act exerting itself, it is absurd to call a believer falling into adultery or murder chaste or mild because he puts forth acts opposed to chastity and love (although the habit of love, but weak and languishing, can still remain in him). And this ought to be said on this account the more because although those seeds and habits of Christian virtues which remain in him are weakened, they are true in their own kind. Still they cannot be called saving and pleasing to God (who conciliates the nearest fitness to them for entering into heaven) because they obtain this only by reason of their acts, not by reason of their habits; nor does faith justify, unless by act; nor is love pleasing to God, unless as it is exercised.

XLV. It is one thing to fall from a state of grace, inasmuch as it denotes a blessing of God or the condition of children and a right to life (which God bestows upon them by efficacious calling and adoption); another, inasmuch as it denotes the duty of man or the aptitude and disposition to the kingdom of heaven by the practice of faith and the exercise of repentance, by which the believer is placed in that state that dying in it he will necessarily be saved. In this sense, the Romanists speak very much of the state of grace. We do not deny that in this latter sense the believer by his sins and especially his more heinous sins falls from a state of grace, inasmuch as he loses his disposition for the kingdom of heaven (for nothing impure can enter there) and enters into a state of condemnation according to the most just judgment of God, by which the unjust, robbers, fornicators, adulterers are kept out of the kingdom of heaven and handed over to eternal punishment. But in the former sense, it is rightly said that the believer does not fall from a state of grace because the right of sons once given to him is never taken away on God's part (although its use and sense can be interrupted for a time) and the seeds of grace and of virtue are never taken away from him.

XLVI. The kingdom of sin can be regarded either as to state universally or as to act partially. We do not deny that the believer can sometimes be under the partial reign of sin (i.e., as to act and as to certain sins in which he indulges). But we deny that he can be under the universal reign of sin as to state, so as to come absolutely under its power and that it reigns in him without any struggling against and resistance to it. The flesh is victorious in various contests, but neither totally, so that there is nothing any longer in man to resist it, nor finally, so as to be perpetually superior. Nay, as the Spirit always preserves the seed of grace in him, it at last comes out victorious over the flesh and causes the believer to gain the victory (*hypernikan*). In this sense, what was formerly said of the Romans can be said properly of the believer: "In engagements indeed they were sometimes overcome, but never in a war." For although there is in him something of both kingdoms (of sin and of grace, on account of the flesh and Spirit dwelling in us), there is said to reign in him, not the flesh (which is wounded little by little and destroyed), but the Spirit of grace (which is confirmed every day and made perfect).

XLVII. It is one thing to recede in some measure or to retrocede from grace (i.e., the gratuitous favor of God in Christ, and a saving influx); another to fall and to be discharged entirely from it. One thing to sin; another to perish wholly. One thing to remit or intermit an act of faith; another to shake off the habit itself. One thing to be deprived of the sense of justification; another to be disturbed from the state. The former we grant, but not the latter. Nor as often as the action is perverted, is faith at once overthrown; or as often as love is thrown off, is it shaken in the struggle with temptations. The fruit and leaves fall, while the sap of the fruit-bearing tree lies in the root. Nor does he who sometimes with

Nebuchadnezzar loses possession of the kingdom or with the leper is prevented from living in his own house, at once lose the right to it. As often as a father is angry with a prodigal son, he does not so often cast him out from the number of his sons; nor when he begins to severely chastise, does he cease to love him sincerely.

Seventeenth Question: The Certainty of Faith

Whether the believer can and ought to be certain of his faith and justification by a divine and not merely conjectural certainty. We affirm against the Romanists and Remonstrants.

I. After having proved the perseverance of faith against the apostasy of the saints, we must also demonstrate its certainty against the hesitation (*epochēn*) and doubt of the opponents of grace. However, a twofold certainty is usually ascribed to faith: first, concerning itself—by which each believer knows and is certain that he has justifying faith; the second, concerning the grace of justification and of salvation—by which the believer is certain that his own sins have been pardoned and thus that he is a partaker of salvation. We will dispute concerning both at the same time.

The opinion of the Romanists.

II. Our controversy here is with the same adversaries who oppose perseverance. The Romanists teach that the believer has no certainty save a conjectural certainty of his own faith; nor can any believer be certain that he believes in Christ with a true and not a hypocritical, with a living and not a dead faith, since all can variously both be deceived and deceive themselves (and often do). Bellarmine maintains this where he proposes to himself the proof of these four things: (1) that a certainty of faith cannot be held concerning one's own righteousness; (2) that no one is bound to have it, even if perchance he could have it; (3) that it is inexpedient for it to be possessed ordinarily; (4) that in fact it is not possessed, except by a few, to whom their own justification is specially revealed by God ("De Justificatione," 3.6, 8 *Opera* [1858], 4:541-42, 542-44). As to the certainty of grace, the Council of Trent denies "that anyone can know with the certainty of faith, which nothing false can fall under, that he has obtained the grace of God" (Session 6.9, Schroeder, p. 35). It denies "that those, who are truly justified, ought to determine with themselves without any doubt at all, that they are justified" (Session 6, Canons 13, 14, Schroeder, p. 44).

III. Now although our opponents quarrel as to the meaning of the decree of the Council, each party (those who contend for the certainty, such as Catarinus and Marinarus, as well as those who convict of intolerable arrogance the presumed opinion of the certainty of grace) draws the versatile opinion of the Council to suit their own view (as was done by Soto and Vega). The latter were both in the Council and endeavored to prove discrepant opinions from the Council. Still it is certain that the more common opinion of the Romanists is that of uncertainty, especially among the Jesuits, who teach that no one without a special revelation can be sure (with the certainty of divine faith) that his own sins have been pardoned because they perpetually suppose that this certainty rests upon one's own infirmity and indisposition. Hence they conclude that the certainty of justification is only conjectural, opinionable, deceitful (i.e., really no certainty at all). They do indeed distinguish between the certainty of faith and the certainty of hope or of trust. The certainty of faith, they say, is that which depends upon the word and promise of God alone and rests upon no other foundation. And thus of its own kind it is absolute and infallible and excludes not only all doubt, but also fear. The certainty of hope or of trust, however, rests upon a double foundation; partly on the divine promise on the part of God, partly on his own disposition on the part of man. In this respect, it does not exclude fear entirely, nor is it certainty simply, but relatively and conjecturally (inasmuch as anyone diligently examining himself collects from various signs and motions of the mind that he is drawn by a true repentance of sins and sincerely loves God, still it is [not] so great as to be sufficient to produce security, as Bellarmine explains it, "De Justificatione," 3.2 *Opera* [1858], 4:533-35; and Stapleton, "De universa iustificationis: De certitudine gratiae," 9.11 *Opera* [1620], 2:317-19). Now although while answering our arguments, they deny that they take away all certainty concerning one's own grace and concede that believers can be persuaded and certain of their own justification in the sight of God; nor is it necessary that they should continually doubt concerning the remission of their sins. Still when they dispute against us or address the people, they strive to prove by many arguments that believers are doubtful and uncertain concerning their own righteousness, not knowing whether they are in the grace of God, nor (except rashly) can they determine certainly and unhesitatingly that they have through Christ obtained the pardon of sin. Hence it is gathered that they either speak absurdities (*asystata*) or that all that certainty which they seemingly acknowledge is nothing else than a mere conjecture, which can take away from the mind neither doubt nor fear.

IV. It is not, however, for nothing that the Romanists so fiercely strive for the retention of their hesitation (*epochē*) and doubt. They understand that the whole business of popish traffic rests upon this once being established (also at the same time the constancy of saving faith)—the taxes, vows, pilgrimages, fraternities, supererogatory works, purgatory, sale of indulgences, trafficking of the Mass and other base merchandise (*aischrokerdeias*) of the popish kingdom immediately fall. For he who would be certain of his own salvation would betake himself neither to the patronage of the saints, nor to the merits of martyrs, nor to the absolution of priests (which is the executioner of the Roman tyrant).

The opinion of the Arminians.

V. The Arminians do not differ widely from the Romanists here. The members of the Conference at the Hague think "that it is laudable and useful to doubt, whether we will always be what we are now."+ Since indeed they fear, as they elsewhere explain themselves, lest such a certainty be like a cushion upon which they can gently recline themselves and sweetly sleep. "That certainty, therefore, is sufficient," as Corvinus says against Molinaeus, "by which believers know that they, if they persevere in the faith, will remain in the grace of God, and will obtain eternal life, which certainty is only conditional, not absolute" (*Petri Molinaei novi anatomici* [1622], p. 690).

The opinion of the orthodox.

VI. The orthodox opinion is that believers can not only be certain of their faith and of its truth and certainty with a certainty not human and fallible, but divine and infallible (which is greater or less as faith is found to be stronger or weaker); but they both can and ought to be certain of the grace of God and the remission of sins inasmuch as in serious contrition for their sins by true faith, they apprehend the promise of gratuitous mercy in Christ, rest in him fiducially and thus render their hearts secure. Still this security neither induces carnal confidence, nor excludes filial fear and pious solicitude, nor is it always placed beyond the risk of temptation or the fear of the contrary. Its foundation is partly the infallible promise of the gospel (Jn. 3:14-16; 1 Tim. 1:15), partly the infallible testimony of the Holy Spirit in the conscience of each one (Rom. 8:16). However that this opinion may be more clearly apprehended and freed from the slanders and cavils by which our opponents are wont to attack it as a cushion of impiety and the mother of security, it must be observed: (1) that the certainty we speak of has regard most especially to three things—past election that we may know that we belong to the number of the elect; present grace that we may be certain of the grace of God and of our faith (viz., that we truly believe and are in the grace of God); and future glory that we be persuaded of the possession of the glory and happiness promised by God. (2) That the certainty of past election and of future glorification depend upon the certainty of present grace. Since this is the bond of election and glorification (to wit, the fruit of the former and the means to the latter) whoever is certain that he is in the grace of God and in faith can decide that he was elected and will certainly be glorified. (3) That the certainty of present grace is not contained immediately in the word, but depends upon the testimony of the Holy Spirit and the vision of the heart; in the serious examination of itself and the experimental sense of the peculiar marks and effects of grace (such as grief for sin, desire of grace, repentance and the desire for holiness, abnegation of self and the love of God above all things and the like). For since such effects cannot be produced by the flesh, but by the Spirit, from this it can be evident that he who finds these in himself, is in a state of grace. (4) These effects do not always have an equal degree of perfection, but now a greater, then a lesser (as the believer is either in the beginning of his calling or exposed to grievous temptations, thence it happens that the act of this persuasion does not always have the same degree of certainty, but is now stronger, then weaker; yea, sometimes is wholly wanting). Still the believer emerging from the waves of oppressive temptations, not only raises up again the same trust and full confidence (*plērophorian*) (which had been almost suffocated), but also acquires a greater degree of it, virtue coming out of the trial stronger and more exercised (as when the clouds are scattered, the day is brighter; and after a disease the strength is more established).

Statement of the question.

VII. Hence the state of the question can easily be gathered. (1) The question does not concern a moral and conjectural certainty (which our opponents grant); nor an extraordinary certainty given to a few by revelation (which they admit also). Rather the question concerns a divine and infallible certainty which exists or can ordinarily exist in every believer; not from his own disposition or natural light, but from the grace of the Spirit by the energy (*energeian*) of faith, which, resting upon the external promises of the word and the internal testimony of the Holy Spirit, exerts itself in all more or less, but as much as suffices for true consolation. (2) The question is not whether that certainty can be in the believer without the use of means (i.e., the desire for holiness and the exercise of repentance and the actual purpose of living piously); much less is the question whether it can consist with an actual and direct purpose of sinning, so that the believer can determine that he is in grace and will most certainly be saved, while he has purposed to indulge in sin and in the lusts of the flesh. For we hold that these are not to be wrested apart from each other and that persuasion cannot proceed into act without the desire of holiness. For he gave his promises to those walking in that way alone, and there are the indubitable effects and signs (*gnōrismata*) of true faith and justification.

VIII. (3) It is not inquired whether this certainty can always show itself in act or always come forth in the same degree. For since it does not exist in us (as we have just said) without the use of means, it is certain that when these means are not used or when the contrary are used, the act itself cannot be put forth. Again, since the state of the believer is not equable as to the desire of holiness, but now weaker, then stronger and faith at one time is sick and infirm, at another healthy and vivid; now in trials and strugglings, then free from them; also, the persuasion which springs from it is not always in the same degree, but now vivid, then weak; at another time, as in the severest trials, none at all. Nor must we think that it is all over with the truth of faith. Although an elicited act of that certainty is necessary to the consolation of the believer, still it is not required for the truth of faith (as it may be elicited in single moments and he must be said at once to want faith who is destitute of that); for neither does fire always emit a flame, nor a fountain streams of water, nor a mother always feel the motion of the fetus. Thus although this persuasion arises from the nature of faith, it does not always (as it can and ought) exert its act, but it is sometimes suppressed—whether on account of the weakness of faith and its imperfection or from the severity of trials. But this does not prevent the foundation from always being in the believer and the principle from which (if he rightly considers his own state and the divine promise) he can deduce this actual full confidence (*plērophorian*).

IX. (4) The question is not whether the certainty which the believer has of his own faith and justification is always of the same reason altogether with that certainty which we have concerning those articles and doctrines of faith contained expressly in the word of God; so that by the same faith entirely, by which the doctrines of faith are believed, each believer is bound to believe that he is in the grace of God. For although each is true and undoubted, founded upon the double infallible testimony of the promise in the word and of the Spirit in the heart, yet each is not of equal necessity. For the former is altogether necessary in the believer and conduces to the truth of faith; nor can anyone remain a believer, and be considered as such and doubt concerning the articles of faith—for example, whether Christ is the true Messiah and the Son of God and the like. Rather the latter conduces only to its perfection; for neither is he who doubts whether he is justified on that account to be considered as lacking true faith, nor as being in the grace of God. The former is opposed to the doubt by which anyone doubts of the promises of God, whether they are true or not; the other to the doubt which concerns one's own salvation and remission of sins from a sense of their own infirmity. Therefore the question is whether this latter certainty (as it differs from the former) is divine and infallible or merely conjectural.

X. (5) The question is not whether this certainty has such a degree of certainty as excludes continually all dread of the contrary, but as at length overcomes and proves superior to it. For we acknowledge this confidence (with respect to innate imbecility), sometimes is agitated and fluctuates, especially in the early period of calling when believers are neophytes (*neophytoi*) or of little faith (*oligopistoi*) or under the cross and afflictions (especially if they are severe and lasting), or in the struggle with temptation, and in spiritual desertions, when the Spirit of consolation is sometimes so removed and the light of the divine countenance hidden, that in the excess of the mind sad complaints often fall from the believer: "I am cut off from before thine eyes" (Ps. 31:22); "The terrors of God do set themselves in array against me" (Job. 6:4). Although the sense of present grace and confidence of the future can for a time sleep in the sons of God, still we maintain that the believing soul surely struggles out from that abyss of temptations from the grace of God electing, redeeming, guarding and raising up (which restores to him the joy of his salvation and causes him at last [more slowly or quickly] to elicit that sense for his consolation).

XI. Hence the state of the question returns to this—whether the true believer can (not from a view of his own worth and disposition, but of the divine estimation and guardianship) be certain (not with a certainty only of the object, but of the subject; not of a conjectural moral opinion and hope, but of true and justifying faith, by the spirit of adoption excited in his heart from a legitimate examination of himself; not only concerning his present faith and justification, but also as to the future concerning his own salvation and glorification). The opponents deny; we affirm.

The certainty of faith is proved: (1) from the nature of faith.

XII. The reasons are: (1) from the nature of faith since it has a twofold act (as was seen above): a direct and a reflex. By the direct, it is borne into the promise itself, but by the reflex into its own apprehension and thus not only believes, but also knows that it believes (just as in the natural life, the soul not only understands, but is also conscious of its own operation and knows that it understands—which is the peculiar privilege of the rational soul). Thus in the spiritual life, the regenerate soul has this peculiarity—that it can not only elicit acts of faith and love, but also turning in upon itself, know that it elicits them and is thoroughly persuaded of them. Nor ought a reason to be sought for this persuasion more than of that by which man knows that he lives and understands. Yet because the false presumption of the flesh can counterfeit the true persuasion of faith, the truth of that persuasion can be gained further from the effects and fruits of true faith *a posteriori* (to wit, both from the sweetness of spiritual consolation and joy and from the desire for sanctification and repentance). For he who has discovered in himself both these effects of faith, ought not to doubt the truth of his faith. "And hereby we do know that we know him, if we keep his commandments" (1 Jn. 2:3*). If these marks are not so sensible as to be always clearly perceived by us; if the desire of sanctification grows cold; if joy is disturbed by an opposite doubt, the soul is not on that account to lose courage and despair of salvation, but to rise to the very first principles of sanctification. These are: (a) to feel internal corruption; (b) to be displeased with oneself on account of it; (c) to hate sin; (d) to grieve as often as we fall and offend God; (e) to avoid occasions of sinning and to use the means prescribed by God to excite the gift of God, such as prayer, meditation on the word and the like.

XIII. Further, not only the nature of faith, but the Scripture also proves this knowledge and sense of faith. Paul, speaking of himself, says, "I know whom I have believed, and am persuaded that he is able to keep that which I have committed unto him against that day" (2 Tim. 1:12). And John: "We do know that we know him" (*ginōskomen hoti egnōkamen auton*, 1 Jn. 2:3); "He that believeth on the Son of God hath the witness in himself" (1 Jn. 5:10). On this account, the apostles profess that they believe: "We believe and are sure that thou art the Christ, the Son of the living God" (Jn. 6:69). Christ claims this knowledge for them, "At that day ye shall know that I am in my Father, and ye in me, and I in you" (Jn. 14:20). Now Christ dwells in us by faith, nor are we in Christ except by faith. It cannot therefore be known that Christ is in us except we know that we have faith. And that no one might think this a privilege peculiar to the apostles, Paul extends it to all: "We have received the Spirit which is of God; that we might know the things that are freely given to us of God" (1 Cor. 2:12). Nor does Christ mean anything else when he promises to inscribe a "new name" on the white stone to be given to the victor, "which no man knoweth saving he that receiveth it" (Rev. 2:17). But how could that remarkable name of the sons of God (which the Holy Spirit writes in our renewed hearts as on a white stone—the most certain mark of our absolution and glorification) be said to be known to the believer alone, if he is involved in perpetual doubt (*epochē*) and cannot know anything certain concerning his state?

XIV. This very thing is still more strongly confirmed from the description of faith given in the Scriptures, which necessarily implies this certainty, as when it is said to be the "substance of things hoped for and the evidence of things not seen" (*hypostasis tōn elpizomenōn elenchos tōn ou blepomenōn*, Heb. 11:1). Here the Greek Scholiast observes that this is said inasmuch as it causes things not present to stand forth in some manner and invisible things to come into the sight; not of the eyes, but of the mind. For since things which are in hope are unsubstantial (*anypostata*) and do not have subsistence (as things not as yet before us), faith gives them a certain subsistence as to being known, causing them in some measure to be and be present by this very thing—because she believes them to be; and makes invisible things present to herself and sees them before her by demonstration (*elenchon*) (which Chrysostom says "concerning things which are very manifest"—*epi tōn lian dēlōn*, "Sermon 21," *On Hebrews* [NPNF1, 14:462; PG 63.151]). But how can it be called a substance (*hypostasis*) or a demonstration (*elenchos*) if believers ought to fluctuate in perpetual doubt and suspense (*epochē*)? Yea, he here points out a wonderful certainty—for both its degrees are various, and that is the highest which is in the present itself. Hence confidence (*pepoithēsis*, Eph. 3:12), boldness (*parrēsia*, 2 Cor. 3:12; Heb. 3:6; 4:16), full assurance (*plērophoria*, 1 Thess. 1:5; Heb. 6:11) are ascribed to faith, which either suppose or necessarily draw after them confidence, and are opposed to doubt and diffidence (Mt. 21:21; Jam. 1:6). Nor ought it to be replied "that these indeed conclude concerning the thing, but not concerning the person." As faith has these things in itself, it necessarily bestows the same upon those in whom it is severally. Thus they are not only true *in thesi*, but also *in hypothesi*. Nay, this cannot be ascribed to faith except relative to the subject in which it inheres and in which it is adapted to produce such certainty.

XV. Unless the believer could know his own faith, in vain would an examination of his faith be prescribed to him, as is frequently done: "Let each one examine himself" (1 Cor. 11:28) before coming to the supper (to wit, whether he truly believes in Christ and is such as he ought to be, who deals with such great mysteries). "Examine yourselves, whether ye be in the faith; prove your own selves. Know ye not your own selves, how that Jesus Christ is in you?" (2 Cor. 13:5). He here refers to what he had said in v. 3—that the Corinthians sought a proof (*dokimēn*) or evidence of Christ speaking in him; as if he said, Ye wish to find out whether Christ speaks in me, but I exhort and admonish you that before you seek this in us, to seek rather of yourselves and be willing to prove yourselves, whether ye are in the faith. Also whether ye know yourselves that Christ is in you (to wit, by the faith which ye find to be in you); for thus of me, by whose ministry ye have received faith, ye ought not to doubt that Christ speaks in me (namely, from the fruit of my apostleship among you and from the mutual relation between the faith of the people and the preaching of the minister). But why should the apostle exhort to this examination of their faith and to a knowledge of Christ dwelling and working in them, if no solid certainty could be gained concerning it? Nor can it be replied here "that he treats of the presence of Christ among them by miracles and not of his presence in them by justification." The very words prove the falsity of this interpretation. Paul does not direct them to look around out of themselves upon the proof of Christ's power and miracles, but to prove themselves whether they are in the faith and whether by faith they feel Christ dwelling in them. Nor do the following words indicate a different meaning ("except ye be reprobates") because this cannot be said of the faith in miracles, since he ought not at once to be considered a reprobate and as rejected who is deprived of it; rather it pertains to justifying faith.

XVI. The same thing is deduced from this—that individuals are bound to make confession of their faith (1 Pet. 3:15; Rom. 10:9). For how could they confess it sincerely and constantly, if they cannot be certain of it? I confess that not a few lie and act hypocritically in professing a faith which they do not have. But this does not hinder believers from making that confession truly and consequently having their faith clear, which otherwise they could not confess.

2. From the testimony of the Holy Spirit.

XVII. The second argument is drawn from the testimony and the seal of the Holy Spirit. It was not sufficient for God to preserve us to his glory, unless he would assure us of that preservation that we might give him thanks for it. Nor would it suffice for our consolation that we are in the grace of God unless we should feel the sense of it, since for happiness not only the possession of the good is required, but also the knowledge of that possession. Therefore he willed to give us the certainty of both: first in his word, which furnishes testimony to the truth of the promises; second in the heart, by the Spirit testifying of the truth of the application of them. However since that testimony cannot be uncertain and deceitful (as proceeding from the teacher of truth), the certainty also which he ingenerates is not merely conjectural and probable, but divine and infallible. To demonstrate this more efficaciously, the Scriptures employ not only one, but many similitudes which have a certain wonderful emphasis; especially if they are considered not singly, but collectively (*athroōs*) and all at the same time. Here belongs the fact that the Spirit is at one time set forth as "a Spirit of truth" who like a "teacher" leads us into all truth and makes us "God-taught" (*theodidaktous*, Jn. 6:45; 14:17; 16:13); at another as "a witness" who gives us infallible testimony of the grace of God and of Christ (Jn. 15:26; 16:14) as also concerning our state when "he witnesses with our spirit that we are the sons of God" (Rom. 8:16); not only to confirm the certainty of the object, but especially to produce a certainty of the subject, which is the design of a witness. Hence Chrysostom rightly says, "What doubt is left here? If a man, or an angel should make a promise, perhaps some might doubt, but if the supreme Essence, the Spirit of God, who causes us to pray, makes a promise to those praying, bestows the promise, giving the testimony to us within, what room is there for doubt?" ("Homily 14," *On Romans* [NPNF1, 11:442; PG 60.527]). Then as "a scribe" who writes the law and the covenant of God in our hearts (Jer. 31:33; 2 Cor. 3:3), to intimate that his testimony is not momentary and mutable, but a constant and perpetual act by which like a heavenly chancellor he records upon our hearts the diploma of our justification, by which the election of the Father and the redemption of the Son are confirmed in us. Again, as "a seal" by which believers are sealed unto the day of redemption (Eph. 1:13; 4:30), not only to confirm the truth of the promises of grace and their certainty in our hearts, as diplomas and royal letters are wont to be fortified with seals, that strong and indubitable authority may be won for them; but also that believers themselves may be sealed, both that they may be distinguished from others and know that they are declared to be in the number of those to whom the right to life is given and that they may know that they are under the seal of God (who will most surely be guarded by him until they arrive there). Then, finally, as "an earnest" (2 Cor. 1:22; 5:5; Eph. 1:14) by which God not only seals in us the certainty of the promises, but also gives us a certain pledge of his constant and eternal love (which he now makes a part of the future inheritance and of the consummated happiness which awaits us in heaven in intimate communion with our heavenly sponsor). This undoubtedly he would not have done unless he wished to make us certain of the plenary possession of the inheritance; as Chrysostom remarks on this passage, "For unless he had been about to bestow the whole, he would not have willed inconsiderately to leave the pledge, and cause a loss of it" (*ou gar ei mē emelle to pan didonai, eileto auton arrabōna parapheinai, kai apolesai eikē kai matēn*, "Homily 3," *On Second Corinthians* [NPNF1, 12:290; PG 61.411]). Moreover, that this certainty might be confirmed more and more in our minds, God willed that it should be a mutual pledge between himself and believers. For as he gave a divine earnest to our hearts, so also we commit to him our deposit like a pledge (2 Tim. 1:12). Both these pledges are given not for the security and confirmation of both, but only of one party (namely, of us); although possessed on both sides, both are conserved by the fidelity of only one party (namely, God).

XVIII. The objections of our opponents amount to this: (1) "The testimony of the Spirit is indeed certain and indubitable, but no one can be certain with a divine faith, but from conjectures only, which can be deceitful, whether what he feels in himself is really the testimony of the Holy Spirit, since many are wont here to deceive themselves; and he may be a wicked man who cherishes security unto destruction" (as Gregory of Valencia admonishes us). We answer that those who thus speak, sufficiently betray the fact that they have never felt in their hearts this testimony of the Spirit. He furnishes such indications of himself as not to permit true believers to doubt his presence (although hypocrites frequently deceive themselves here, taking a vain presumption of the flesh for a true persuasion of the Holy Spirit). And even the effects alone of the Spirit in us as much of consolation as of sanctification (which can by no means arise from the flesh, Gal. 5:19-22), sufficiently and more than sufficiently prove their cause (as fire from heat, life from motion and feeling and causes are most certainly known from their peculiar effects). (2) "That this testimony is only an experience of a certain internal sweetness and peace which cannot produce certainty, except a conjectural." We answer that although this testimony is experimental (founded upon the vision of the heart and a sense of grace), still it is none the less certain because it depends on an infallible principle. Nor is it only of a light and momentary agreeableness (which can deceive man), but of a most efficacious sweetness (which is called by Augustine "conquering" because it captivates the mind into the obedience of faith and ingenerates a full persuasion in our souls). (3) "That the gifts concerning which Paul says the Spirit bears witness (1 Cor. 2:12) are such, that they never could ascend into the heart of man; therefore the certainty of them cannot be gained." We answer that not even thus could any knowledge of them be gained, which Paul, nevertheless, testifies is given to believers by God's special grace. Therefore the apostle means nothing else than to show the divinity and excellence of the mysteries of the gospel and of the gifts which God bestows upon his own (which is so great that to no man or angel could they be known, unless God revealed them—to which neither the sharpness of the eyes [although that sense avails most in obtaining the knowledge of things], nor the attention of the ears, nor the sagacity of the heart or natural light could ever rise). (4) "The testimony of the Spirit is conditional provided we are not wanting to ourselves and on this account Paul exhorts the Ephesians not to grieve the Spirit, by whom they were sealed, which would not be necessary, if this testimony was indubitable." We answer that although the testimony of the Spirit cannot be granted in us without the use of means (i.e., the desire of holiness), it does not follow that it is doubtful and uncertain because even these means are promised to us by God and procured for us by the Spirit.

3. From the examples of the saints.

XIX. Third, from the examples of the saints. As "Abraham, the father of believers, against hope believed in hope, being not weak in faith, but being fully persuaded (*plērophorētheis*), that what he had promised, he was also able to perform" (Rom. 4:21). Now do these things accord with the doubt (*epochē*) of the Romanists or denote a conjectural certainty only? Do they not breathe a divine and infallible certainty? The same is proved by the words of Jacob panting after the salvation of the Lord and expecting it with confidence: "I have waited for thy salvation" (Gen. 49:18). Nor was David less confident in various psalms. "I have set the Lord always before me: because he is at my right hand, I shall not be moved. Therefore my heart is glad, and my glory rejoiceth: my flesh also shall rest in hope. For thou wilt not leave my soul in hell; neither wilt thou suffer thine Holy One to see corruption" (Ps. 16:8-10). For although this oracle refers directly and primarily to Christ (in whom alone it ought to be perfectly fulfilled, as Peter concludes, Acts 2:31), nothing prevents it from pertaining secondarily and consequently to David himself, who lawfully promised himself immunity from death because Christ by rising again procured immortality not for himself alone, but for all believers. The same thing he frequently confesses elsewhere: "Surely goodness and mercy shall follow me all the days of my life" (Ps. 23:6); "I shall never be ashamed" (Ps. 31:1; cf. Pss. 62:1, 2; 118:5). Paul frequently testifies the same thing, but especially in Rom. 8:38: "I am persuaded (*pepeismai*) that nothing shall be able to separate us from the love of God in Christ." Here he indicates a persuasion, not only moral and conjectural, but certain and not in the least deceitful, since it flows from election (vv. 29, 33), and from the power of the Holy Spirit (v. 26) and produces strong consolation (v. 31), by which he does not dupe himself by a mere opinion and hope, but raises himself with an indubitable confidence against all his enemies. He is certain not only that nothing will separate believers, but that nothing shall even be able to separate them from the love of God.

XX. To no purpose is it replied here: (1) "that these few remarkable men were made certain perhaps by a special revelation." But this is gratuitously assumed and refuted by Paul himself, who ascribes it to the faith of Abraham and not to a revelation (Rom. 4; Heb. 11:8-19). Nor does he ascribe it to him only as peculiar, but speaks of it as common to others and derives it from the immutable purpose of election; from the love of Christ; from his death and intercession (which are the blessings not of particular, but of all believers). (2) "That the words 'we know and are persuaded' do not necessarily include the certainty of divine faith, but a certain conjecture from signs." We answer that we do not deny that by internal signs and marks we are led into this knowledge, but the Holy Spirit seals to our consciences that these signs are not deceitful. John confirms this: "If our heart condemn us not, then have we confidence toward God. And hereby we know that he abideth in us, by the Spirit which he hath given us" (1 Jn. 3:21, 24*). In vain, however, would John say that we know and understand that we have the Spirit of God and that that Spirit is the proof of our communion with Christ, if we could have this only from deceitful and conjectural signs.

4. From the prayers of the saints.

XXI. From the prayers of the saints. Believers are commanded to seek the pardon of their sins from God; therefore they can be certain of it, since they know that their prayers are not in vain with God, but certainly obtain according to God's promise whatever they have asked in faith (Mk. 11:24; 1 Jn. 5:14, 15). Nor is it an objection that the prayers of believers are not always heard (as in the case of Paul, 2 Cor. 12:7-9) because it is one thing to seek from God temporal, another, spiritual things. Concerning the former, the promise is not definite, but conditional inasmuch as they are consistent with the glory of God and our salvation. Concerning the latter, however, it is absolute: "Ask and it shall be given you, whatsoever ye shall ask in my name, that will I do" (Mt. 7:7; Jn. 14:13). Now the apostle meets with the refusal of a bodily, not of a spiritual good. To no purpose is it added, It can be gathered from prayer itself that we are not certain of grace and salvation because no sane man seeks for what he possesses. For although we possess salvation by hope, still we do not as yet possess it as to the thing and perfectly; hence prayer comes in as the principal means of obtaining it. Nor if certain circumstances neglected in prayer can sometimes render them void, is all their certainty straightway removed. We speak of prayers rightly made, not defective prayers. The certainty is not founded upon the perfection of the prayers, but upon the affection of the heart. For God does not look at the merit, but the sincerity of the suppliant. The same thing is confirmed from the actions of graces which believers are bound to put forth on account of the blessings bestowed upon them in Christ—remission of sins and regeneration, etc. (Col. 1:12, 13; 1 Pet. 2:9). For who can fittingly give thanks to God for that benefit which he does not know and doubts whether it has reference to himself (i.e., that he is a partaker of it)? For he who gives thanks for that of which he is uncertain (whether it has been given to him or not) appears rather to trifle than to testify as a grateful soul.

5. From the fruits of the Spirit.

XXII. (5) From the fruits of the Spirit and of faith. "Being justified by faith, we have peace with God" (Rom. 5:1) and "The fruit of the Spirit is love, joy and peace" (Gal. 5:22). Peter says, "Believers rejoice with joy unspeakable and full of glory" (1 Pet. 1:8), which Paul says passeth all understanding (Phil. 4:7). Now what peace, what joy can be conceived in those who do not know whether they have God as an angry and hostile Judge, or appeased as a merciful Father; whether they are in a state of salvation or of eternal damnation; and who are agonized with perpetual doubt and distrust? Hence can that unspeakable joy arise except from an intimate and vivid sense of the divine love towards him and a certain trust in eternal blessedness and glory?

6. From absurdities.

XXIII. (6) From the absurdities which follow the opinion of our opponents. The doctrine concerning diffidence and uncertainty convicts God of falsehood (1 Jn. 5:10), casts aside the testimony of the Holy Spirit, contends with peace of conscience and the joy of the Spirit (which is peculiar to true believers), hinders true invocation (which ought to be made with faith) and leads to desperation. For he who is never certain of the grace of God does not have (when temptation arises) a place where he may fix his foot and whither he can betake himself that he may bind up the wounded or rouse the languid and dejected conscience. A striking proof of this is furnished by those miserable consciences (groaning under the popish tyrant) when they reach the jaws of death. You behold them continually trembling and anxious, having nothing to support them; while tossed about by the waves of doubts and fears, they never can reach the harbor of peace and tranquility, but miserably perish in the sea of temptation. But just as (certain consolation being proposed to the sinner in life and in death) the table (set up in the temple of God by the Roman moneychangers) is overturned; so the same consolation being cast out, it is introduced and hence a trembling and vacillating conscience gives place to will-worship and the sale of indulgences. Nay, hence the rich spoils and great gain to the Roman clergy, while souls trembling in extreme agony are made tribute-payers to agents, thrusting out pictured merchandise of merits and vain consolations from the sacrifice of the Mass, destined either to be mitigated or ransomed by the imaginary flames of Purgatory.

Sources of explanation.

XXIV. There is one certainty of perfect inherent righteousness; another of faith and grace or reconciliation with God through Christ and of the remission of sins. It is one thing to be puffed up with one's own righteousness; another to be cheered with the consciousness of gratuitous reconciliation. In the former sense, Solomon is to be understood when he says, "No one can say that his heart is clean" (Prov. 20:9). But not in the latter. For although no one can glory concerning the perfection of inherent righteousness (as the Septuagint has it, *tis kauchēsetai agnēn echein kardian*), it does not follow that the believer cannot glory concerning the grace of Christ imputed and apprehended by faith. This certitude does not depend upon the perfection of inherent righteousness, but upon the truth of the Spirit working within.

XXV. The examples of Job (Job 9:12, 15, 28; 31:14), of David (Ps. 19:13), of Paul (1 Cor. 4:4; 9:27), who do not dare to arrogate righteousness to themselves, show indeed that they acknowledged the imperfection of their holiness (which cannot stand the trial of the divine judgment for their justification). But they do not prove their uncertainty concerning God's grace and their own faith, which elsewhere they so magnificently proclaim: Job (13:15; 19:25); David (Pss. 32:5; 103:1-3; 118:17); Paul (Rom. 8:38; 2 Tim. 1:12; Gal. 2:20) and in many other passages.

XXVI. The clauses which seem to imply some doubt or uncertainty of grace—"Turn ye to me with all your heart, who knoweth if God will return and repent?" (Joel 2:12, 14); "Perhaps God will pardon thy sins" (Dan. 4:27); "Who can tell if God will turn and repent, and turn away from us his fierce anger?" (Jon. 3:9); "Repent of this thy wickedness, and pray God, if perhaps he may forgive thee" (Acts 8:22)—either do not treat properly of the remission of sin as to eternal punishment, but of a plenary relaxation of temporal punishment (which is not always granted even to those who repent); or they are not always the marks of those doubting, but rather of those expressing the difficulty of the thing on account of the heinousness of the sins and exciting the desire of believers to seek grace with so much greater zeal and animating them to obtain the wished for confidence. Examples of this kind often occur: 2 K. 19:4; Prov. 24:18; Ecc. 5:5; Jn. 5:46; 8:19; Rom. 11:21; Ex. 32:30. Or they set forth the condition under which remission is promised; as Acts 8:22, where "if" (*ei ara aphethēsetai*) is the same as "that" (*hina*) or "in order that (*hopōs dē*) it may be forgiven thee"; "if by any means (*eipōs katantēsō*) I might attain unto the resurrection" (Phil. 3:10, 11), i.e., in order that I might attain (in which sense Eustathius remarks that it is often used, *Commentarii ad Homeri Iliadem* [ed. M. van der Valk, 1971]).

XXVII. It is one thing to speak of the objective certainty of the faith which is believed (i.e., the doctrine delivered in the word), another of the subjective certainty of the faith by which it is believed (i.e., the habit which is in believers). The former ought to stand out and be elicited from the Scripture immediately and expressly; but the latter ought not to be in the Scriptures, but in the heart of the believer from the Scriptures and in accordance with it to be transcribed by the finger of God because it arises from a vision of the heart or from the sense and experience of the believer. Still the certainty of faith ought not to be considered as less. Because although this truth is not contained expressly in the Scriptures as to hypothesis, still it is deduced from and founded upon it as to thesis (according to the general rule of logicians according to which particular propositions are included in universal). Therefore since the Scripture says that all believers will obtain pardon of sin and salvation, by that very thing it leaves the believer to conclude that such remission and salvation are destined to him believing (seeing that feeling and experience do not change the rule in itself, nor render human if it is divine, but applies *in hypothesi* the general rule to a particular subject). Now although we do not hold that there is an equal necessity or degree of evidence of this twofold certainty (the revealed as well as the experimental, as was seen before), both do not cease to be of divine faith since each rests upon a divine and infallible testimony: the former indeed of the Spirit speaking in the word; the latter of the Spirit speaking in the heart (who is a witness beyond all exception).

XXVIII. As not every fear is incompatible (*asystatos*) with the certainty of grace, so neither is every fear either enjoined upon or removed from the believer. Servile fear is one thing; filial another. The former regards the punishment alone or sin on account of its punishments (which belongs to slaves, who attend solely to their own advantage or disadvantage). But the latter regards either sin alone or the punishment on account of sin (which belongs to sons and answers to the reverence and love of children towards parents). That is incompatible (*asystatos*) with certainty, and love is in this sense said to cast out fear (1 Jn. 4:18); and believers are said not to have received the spirit of bondage again to fear (Rom. 8:15). But this, so far from being incompatible with certainty, is the means by which it is produced and confirmed in us. For since the certainty of grace cannot exist in us with a purpose to sin and without the use of means, this fear (which has for its object the avoiding of sin and promoting the desire of holiness in us) cannot take away certainty, but rather posits it since certainty does not exclude the ends, but supposes the necessity of the means. Therefore if fear is recommended to us, it is not a servile fear which draws with it diffidence and doubt, but a filial fear which consists principally of three particulars: (1) filial reverence and humility in regard to God—opposed to Pharisaical pride and presumption; (2) solicitude, caution and watchfulness in regard to the Devil, in flying from all the temptations of sin and using all the means leading to holiness—opposed to the carnal security of the Epicureans; (3) a constant purpose to cleave to God more and more and to walk in the ways of the Lord far from the ways of the flesh and of the world—opposed to the license and frivolity of the wicked. Therefore this fear removes the false mode of certainty (which flows from carnal security and profane license), but confirms and increases the true. In this way, the more the believer (by pious solicitude) takes care not to wander from the path of holiness and more and more adheres to his God by constant obedience, so much the more will he also be persuaded of the grace and love of God and of his salvation.

XXIX. As often as "fear" (*phobos*) and "trembling" (*tromos*) are joined together in the Scriptures (cf. 1 Cor. 2:3; 2 Cor. 7:15; Eph. 6:5; Phil. 2:12), they do not indicate any doubt or uncertainty and diffidence; but they denote only humility and a letdown (*demissionem*) of the mind. This is clearly gathered even from the last passage, in which Paul commands us to "work out our salvation with fear and trembling," not assuredly of diffidence and doubt, since he adds at once "God works in us to will and do" (which rendered him altogether certain of grace), but of reverence and solicitude, by which the grace of God works out our salvation. Hence it is that fear is often joined with certainty and joy. Who more certain than Paul of the grace of God and of his own salvation (in which he exults, Rom. 8:38; 2 Tim. 4:6-8)? Yet who was more anxious on that account to avoid sin and promote his own sanctification (1 Cor. 9:27; Phil. 3:13, 14)? Thus we are commanded "to serve the Lord with fear and to rejoice with trembling" (Ps. 2:11), because joy without fear is pride, fear without joy is despair; both joined together add sure confidence with deep humility to the mind. Thus the believer fears on account of sin, rejoices on account of grace, fears on account of his own infirmity and threatening dangers and anxiously uses all the means that he may not slip into carnal security. Still he rejoices with confidence in the divine aid promised to him that he may not rush into despair. And if some passages exhort to fear and apprehension (as Prov. 28:14; 1 Pet. 1:17 and similar ones), they inculcate rather anxiety concerning the means, than doubt concerning the end. Such fear is not to be opposed to confidence towards the promises of Christ, but to the carnal presumption concerning our own strength.

XXX. Although the truth of faith depends upon the condition of a pure heart (Acts 8:37; Rom. 10:9, 10), it cannot be less certain because God, who requires faith from a pure heart (i.e., sincere and not in the least hypocritical, 1 Tim. 1:5), bestows upon and puts in believers such a heart by the grace of regeneration (Ezk. 36:26). The passages adduced from Jer. 17:9 and Prov. 20:9, which testify that the heart of man is wicked and inscrutable and no one can say his heart is clean, show only what the heart of man is by nature, not what it may be made by grace. The certainty of the believer is not therefore to be convicted of rashness and presumption, since it does not rest upon a natural and fallible judgment of the heart, but upon the judgment of the renewed heart, the testimony of the Holy Spirit (which proves the truth and sincerity of faith from its adjuncts and effects, according to criteria [*kritēria*] proposed in the word). This is true both by reason of the subject, when the heart is found to be good and honest (Lk. 8:15); not hard, but broken and contrite (Is. 51:1; 66:2; Ps. 51:17); not hypocritical (which covers, exterminates and conceals sin), but sincere (which confesses and suppliantly prays for the pardon of sin, Ps. 32:5); and as to the object and mode, when faith embraces the gospel, not on account of the novelty of its doctrines or the license to sin, but from Christian liberty and gratuitous justification (Rom. 6:2; 1 Pet. 2:15, 16). Also on account of God, the fountain of all good, and Christ, in whom all fulness of grace dwells; also as to its acts, such as contrition of heart and serious grief for sin on account of God, hunger and thirst or a desire for righteousness, a permanent sense of grace, a good conscience, carefulness to avoid falling and to approve itself to God more and more by the practice of holiness, not for a moment, but seriously and constantly. Still in these absolute perfection is not to be expected, but sincerity is to be looked for because Christ does not break the bruised reed, nor extinguish the smoking flax, and regards not so much the quantity as the quality of faith.

XXXI. What we are bound to believe with divine faith ought always to be believed as undoubted, when it is treated of truths immediately revealed and independent of us—such as articles of faith, the truth of which we cannot doubt under any pretext. But it is not so with the certainty which the believer has concerning the remission of his sins. This is not immediately revealed in the word, but arises from the inner experience and sense of the heart. This depends upon us and can be often dubious and uncertain, no less than the principle upon which it rests. Hence it is false that the true believer at any time can and ought to be certain of the remission of his sins, even when he lies in sin and indulges in the lusts of the flesh, because (as we have said) certainty is not granted without the use of means.

XXXII. Absolute certainty (which does not depend upon any condition which can render it uncertain), such as the certainty that God is and that the soul is immortal and the like, differs from conditional certainty, which depends upon some condition, such as the certainty in Hezekiah of his life being prolonged for fifteen years. This was promised to him and he could therefore be certain about it, but still under the condition that he would not deny himself necessary food, but would use the necessary means for the preservation of his life. Such is the certainty of the believer (of which we speak), which supposes the use of means as a condition, as we have said. The first certainty is incompatible (*asystatos*) with fear because it has for its object a truth independent of us; but the second not only does not exclude fear, but necessarily supposes it as the means for its confirmation.

XXXIII. The fear of a future evil (which ought necessarily to happen) cannot consist with certainty. But the fear of an evil which could happen (unless we guard against it in time) not only does not conflict with certainty, but serves to produce it while it induces solicitude and watchfulness, by which we take care not to fall into such evil. This is the fear which the Holy Spirit requires in believers.

XXXIV. Since the certainty which we urge ought to be always connected with the use of means, we search for it in vain in the impenitent sinner. And if the believer at any time was able to exercise a true act of that certainty, while he was in the way and practice of holiness, he cannot equally exercise it while indulging in the flesh or committing any grievous sin. He ought not to be ignorant that perseverance in sin is inconsistent (*asystaton*) with that certainty. Therefore he is never influenced to say, I was once certain of the grace of God, I ought therefore to be certain hereafter concerning it whatever I may do. As he did not put forth the act of certainty in the past (except by the use of means), so neither can he put it forth in the present except he be in the same state and not otherwise. And if the former act of certainty regards also the future, it regards it on the same supposition (to wit, if he uses the means and is in the way of holiness).

XXXV. The doubting of the saints is a mark of infirmity, not a support of uncertainty. It shows what may sometimes be done in fact, not what ought to happen in right. So that it is not to be praised and referred to the virtue of humility (as the Romanists hold), but to be striven against earnestly and to be deplored as a depraved weakness belonging to the remains of sin.

XXXVI. As the certainty of perseverance is the consolation of the laboring, not the mother of security (which can consist with the lasciviousness and slothfulness of the flesh), since it can be granted only to those walking in the path of holiness; so the want of this certainty ought not at once to produce despair (as if it was all over with their salvation when faith does not always elicit that act of certainty). This is properly the fruit of the soul confirmed in the Lord and of the exercised senses. Therefore those who are not as yet confirmed must press forward by degrees and perceptibly in the ways of the Lord, rather than endeavor to embrace and anticipate with one glance of faith those immense spaces of perseverance. And in this practice of faith, I prefer sometimes to hear the groans of the mourner than the laughter of one exulting (not so much by faith as by opinion). It often happens that they who presume deceive themselves, but they who sigh and with the publican are afraid to lift up their eyes, still have the thing itself which they do not see—behold that Jesus present whom they seek and do not recognize him. The others, however, afterwards perceive that which they think they have, wrested away from them.

XXXVII. The security of the flesh, which rests and loves to deceive the life with slothful ease, differs from the security of the believing and pious man who prays always and labors in the business of salvation. As in a city, the security of stupid men (who snore and are captured unawares when buried in sleep and wine) differs from the security of the watchful and aroused (who keep guard lest they be disturbed by an unexpected attack; nor can they be induced to desert their station by a panic terror or by an insane fear). Such is the holy security of the pious, which not only does not exclude watchfulness and the desire for piety, but necessarily supposes them as the certain means of their own preservation. The other things which belong here may be gathered from Topic IV, Question 13.

SIXTEENTH TOPIC

JUSTIFICATION

FIRST QUESTION

Is the word "justification" always used in a forensic sense in this argument; or is it also used in a moral and physical sense? The former we affirm; the latter we deny against the Romanists.

I. As in the chain of salvation justification follows calling (Rom. 8:30) and is everywhere set forth as the primary effect of faith, the topic concerning calling and faith begets the topic concerning justification. This must be handled with the greater care and accuracy as this saving doctrine is of the greatest importance in religion. It is called by Luther "the article of a standing and a falling church" (*Articulus stantis, et cadentis Ecclesiae*). By other Christians, it is termed the characteristic and basis of Christianity—not without reason—the principal rampart of the Christian religion. This being adulterated or subverted, it is impossible to retain purity of doctrine in other places. Hence Satan in every way has endeavored to corrupt this doctrine in all ages, as has been done especially in the papacy. For this reason, it is deservedly placed among the primary causes of our secession from the Roman church and of the Reformation.

II. However, although some of the more candid Romanists (conquered by the force of the truth) have felt and expressed themselves more soundly than others concerning this article (nor are there wanting also some among other divines who, influenced by a desire to lessen controversies, think there is not so great matter for dispute about it and that there are here not a few logomachies), still it is certain that up to this time there are between us and the Romanists in this argument controversies not only verbal, but real and many which are of great importance (as will be made manifest in what follows).

III. From a false and preposterous explanation of the word, the truth of the thing itself has been wonderfully obscured. In the first place, its genuine sense (and in this question most especially) must be unfolded. This being settled, we will be able the more easily to reach the nature of the thing itself.

***Homonyms of the verb* justificare.**

IV. The word *htsdyq*, to which the Greek *dikaioun* answers and the Latin *justificare*, is used in two ways in the Scriptures —properly and improperly. Properly the verb is forensic, put for "to absolve" anyone in a trial or "to hold" and to declare "just"; as opposed to the verb "to condemn" and "to accuse" (Ex. 23:7; Dt. 25:1; Prov. 17:15; Lk. 18:14; Rom. 3-5). Thus apart from a trial, it is used to acknowledge and to praise one as just and that too either deservedly (as when it is terminated on God, in which way men are said to justify God when they celebrate him as just [Ps. 51:4]; "wisdom" is said to be "justified of her children" [Mt. 11:19*; Lk. 7:35], i.e., acknowledged and celebrated as such); or presumptuously ([*doxastōs*] as the Pharisees are said to justify themselves, Lk. 16:15). Improperly it is used either ministerially, for to bring to righteousness (Dan. 12:3 where *mtsdyqy* seems to be exegetical of [*exēgētikon tou*] *mskylym* because while the preachers of the gospel instruct and teach believers, by this very thing they justify them ministerially [to wit, by teaching them the true way in which they can be justified] in the same sense in which they are said to save them, 1 Tim. 4:16). Or by way of synecdoche (the antecedent being put for the consequent) for "to free"; "he that is dead is justified from sin" (Rom. 6:7), i.e., freed. Or comparatively, where on account of a comparison between the sins of Israel and Samaria, Israel is said "to justify Samaria" (Ezk. 16:51, 52) and the sins of Judah increasing, Judah is said "to have justified Israel" (Jer. 3:11) because Israel was more just than Judah (i.e., her sins were fewer than the sins of Judah).

Statement of the question.

V. Hence arises the question with the Romanists concerning the acceptation of this word—whether it is to be taken precisely in a forensic sense in this affair; or whether it ought also to be taken in a physical and moral sense for the infusion of righteousness and justification, if it is allowable (so to speak) either by the acquisition or the increase of it. For they do not deny that the word *jusfiticatio* and the verb *justificare* are often taken in a forensic sense, even in this matter, as Bellarmine ("De Justificatione," 1.1 *Opera* [1858], 4:461-62), Tirinus (*Theologiae elenchticae . . . controversarium fidei*, Cont. 15, number 1 [1648], pp. 217-21) and Toletus (*Commentarii et annotationes in epistolam . . . ad Romanos*, Annot. 13 [1602], pp. 117-22) and not a few others. Yet they do not wish this to be the constant meaning, but that it often signifies a true production, acquisition or increase of righteousness; this is especially the case when employed about the justification of man before God. Hence they distinguish justification into "first and second." The first is that by which the man who is unjust is made just; the second is that by which a just man is made more just. Hence Bellarmine says: "Justification undoubtedly is a certain movement from sin to righteousness, and takes its name from the terminus to which it leads, as all other similar motions, illumination, calefaction; that is true justification, where some righteousness is aquired beyond the remission of sin." Thomas Aquinas says, "Justification taken passively implies a motion to making righteous, just as calefaction a motion to heat" (ST, I-II, Q. 113, Art. 1, p. 1144). Now although we do not deny that this word has more than one signification and is taken in different ways in the Scriptures (now properly, then improperly, as we have already said), still we maintain that it is never taken for an infusion of righteousness, but as often as the Scriptures speak professedly about our justification, it always must be explained as a forensic term.

Proof that the word "justification" is forensic.

VI. The reasons are: (1) the passages which treat of justification admit no other than a forensic sense (cf. Job 9:3; Ps. 143:2; Rom. 3:28; 4:1-3; Acts 13:39 and elsewhere). A judicial process is set forth and mention is made of an accusing "law," of "accused persons" who are guilty (*hypodikoi*, Rom. 3:19), of a "hand-writing" contrary to us (Col. 2:14), of divine "justice" demanding punishment (Rom. 3:24, 26), of an "advocate" pleading the cause (1 Jn. 2:1), of "satisfaction" and imputed righteousness (Rom. 4 and

5), of a "throne of grace" before which we are absolved (Heb. 4:16), of a "judge" pronouncing sentence (Rom. 3:20) and absolving sinners (Rom. 4:5).

VII. (2) Justification is opposed to condemnation: "Who shall lay anything to the charge of God's elect? It is God that justifieth. Who is he that condemneth?" (Rom. 8:33, 34*). As therefore accusation and condemnation occur only in a trial, so also justification. Nor can it be conceived how God can be said to condemn or to justify, unless either by adjudging to punishment or absolving us from it judicially. Toletus is compelled to confess this on Rom. 8:33: "The word justification in this place is taken with that signification, which is opposed to its antithesis, namely, condemnation; so that it is the same in this place to justify as to pronounce just, as a judge by his sentence absolves and pronounces innocent" (*Commentarii et annotationes in epistolam . . . ad Romanos* [1602], p. 441 on Rom. 8:33). Cornelius a Lapide, who otherwise earnestly strives to obscure the truth, still overcome by the force of the truth, acknowledges that God justifies (i.e., absolves from the threatened action of sin and the Devil and pronounces just).

VIII. (3) The equivalent phrases by which our justification is described are judicial: such as "not to come into judgment" (Jn. 5:24), "not to be condemned" (Jn. 3:18), "to remit sins," "to impute righteousness" (Rom. 4), "to be reconciled" (Rom. 5:10; 2 Cor. 5:19) and the like. (4) This word ought to be employed in the sense in which it was used by Paul in his disputation against the Jews. Yet it is certain that he did not speak there of an infusion of righteousness (viz., whether from faith or from the works of the law, the habit of righteousness should be infused into man), but how the sinner could stand before the judgment seat of God and obtain a right to life (whether by the works of the law, as the Jews imagined, or by faith in Christ). And since the thought concerning justification arose without doubt from a fear of divine judgment and of the wrath to come, it cannot be used in any other than a forensic sense (as it was used in the origin of those questions which were agitated in a former age upon the occasion of indulgences, satisfactions and remission of sins). (5) Finally, unless this word is taken in a forensic sense, it would be confounded with sanctification. But that these are distinct, both the nature of the thing and the voice of Scripture frequently prove.

Sources of explanation.

IX. Although the word "justification" in certain passages of Scripture should recede from its proper signification and be taken in another than a forensic sense, it would not follow that it is taken judicially by us falsely because the proper sense is to be looked to in those passages in which the foundation of this doctrine is formed. (2) Although perchance it should not be taken precisely in a forensic sense for "to pronounce just" and "to absolve in a trial," still we maintain that it cannot be taken in a physical sense for the infusion of righteousness, as the Romanists hold (as is easily proved from the passages brought forward by Bellarmine himself).

X. In Is. 53:11, where it is said Christ "by his knowledge shall justify many," it is manifest that reference is made to the meritorious and instrumental cause of our absolution with God (namely, Christ and the knowledge or belief of him). For the knowledge of Christ here ought not to be taken subjectively concerning the knowledge by which he knows what was agreed upon between himself and the Father (which has nothing to do with our justification); but objectively concerning that knowledge by which he is known by his people unto salvation (which is nothing else than faith, to which justification is everywhere ascribed). The following words show that no other sense is to be sought when it is added "for he shall bear their iniquities." This denotes the satisfaction of Christ, which faith ought to embrace in order that we may be justified.

XI. Nor does the passage in Dan. 12:3 press us. As we have already said, justification is ascribed to the ministers of the gospel, as elsewhere the salvation of believers is ascribed to them (1 Tim. 4:16; 1 Cor. 9:22). Not assuredly by an infusion of habitual righteousness (which does not come within their power), but by the instruction of believers by which, as they open the way of life, so they teach the mode by which sinners can obtain justification in Christ by faith. Hence the Vulgate does not translate it *justificantes*, but *erudientes ad justitiam.*

XII. "He that is righteous, let him be righteous still" (Rev. 22:11) does not favor our opponents so as to denote an infusion or increase of righteousness. Thus it would be tautological (*tautologia*) with the following words, "He that is holy, let him be holy still," because justification would not differ from sanctification. But it is best to refer it to the application and sense of justification; for although on the part of God justification does not take place successively, still on our part it is apprehended by us by varied and repeated actions, while by new acts of faith we apply to ourselves from time to time the merit of Christ as a remedy for the daily sins into which we fall. Nay, although it should be granted that the exercise of righteousness is here meant (as in a manuscript we have *dikaiosynēn poiēsatō*) that it may be opposed to the preceding words—"He that is unjust, let him be more unjust"—the opinion of the Romanists will not on that account be established.

XIII. "The justification of the wicked" of which Paul speaks (Rom. 4:5), ought not to be referred to an infusion or increase of habitual righteousness, but belongs to the remission of sins (as it is explained by the apostle from David). Nay, it would not be a justification of the wicked, if it were used in any other sense than for a judicial absolution at the throne of grace. I confess that God in declaring just ought also for that very reason to make just so that his judgment may be according to truth. But man can be made just in two ways: either in himself or in another; either from the law or from the gospel. God therefore makes him just whom he justifies; not in himself, as if from a sight of his inherent righteousness he declared him just, but from the view of the righteousness imputed—in Christ. It is indeed an abomination to Jehovah to justify the wicked without a due satisfaction, but God in this sense justifies no wicked one (Christ having been given to us as a surety who received upon himself the punishment we deserved).

XIV. Although certain words of the same order with justification denote an effecting in the subject, there is not the same reason for this, which otherwise barbarously has been received into Latinity to express the force of *htsdyq* and *dikaioun* (neither of which admit a physical sense). Thus we magnify and justify God, not by making him great from small or just from unjust, but only declaratively celebrating him as such.

Second Question

Is the impulsive and meritorious cause (on account of which man is justified in the judgment of God) inherent righteousness infused into us or good works? We deny against the Romanists.

I. Since it is evident from the preceding question that the word "justification" is forensic and is taken judicially here because it relates to the manner in which sinful man can stand before the bar of God and obtain the pardon of sin with a right to life, we must inquire before all things what is the foundation of this justification or what is the true and proper meritorious cause in view of which he is absolved by God from sin and adjudged to life. Concerning this we must first treat negatively (*kat' arsin*) according to the Pauline method in order that we may see in what it does not consist; second, we must treat affirmatively (*kata thesin*) to see in what it does consist.

Statement of the question.

II. However, we must premise here that God, the just Judge (*dikaiokritēn*), cannot pronounce anyone just and give him a right to life except on the ground of some perfect righteousness which has a necessary connection with life; but that righteousness is not of one kind. For as there are two covenants which God willed to make with men—the one legal and the other of grace—so also there is a twofold righteousness—legal and evangelical. Accordingly there is also a double justification or a double method of standing before God in judgment—legal and evangelical. The former consists in one's own obedience or a perfect conformity with the law, which is in him who is to be justified; the latter in another's obedience or a perfect observance of the law, which is rendered by a surety in the place of him who is to be justified—the former in us, the latter in Christ. Concerning the first, Paul says, "Not the hearers, but the doers of the law shall be justified" (Rom. 2:13); and "Moses describeth the righteousness which is of the law. That the man which doeth those things shall live by them" (Rom. 10:5). Concerning the other, he says, "The gospel is the power of God unto salvation to every one that believeth, for therein is the righteousness of God revealed from faith to faith: as it is written, The just shall live by faith" (Rom. 1:16, 17); and "Being justified freely by his grace through the redemption that is in Christ Jesus" (Rom. 3:24). Concerning both, he says, "That I may be found in Christ, not having my own righteousness, which is of the law, but that which is through the faith of Christ" (Phil. 3:9; cf. also Rom. 9:30, 31). Hence a twofold justification flows: one in the legal covenant by one's own righteousness according to the clause, "Do this and live"; the other in the covenant of grace, by another's righteousness (Christ's) imputed to us and apprehended by faith according to the clause, "Believe and thou shalt be saved." Each demands a perfect righteousness. The former requires it in the man to be justified, but the latter admits the vicarious righteousness of a surety. The former could have place in a state of innocence, if Adam had remained in innocence. But because after sin it became impossible to man, we must fly to the other (i.e, the gospel), which is founded upon the righteousness of Christ.

III. This being established, the question does not concern legal justification. For we confess that in it inherent righteousness is its meritorious cause, nor can it be obtained except by the perfect obedience of man. But because the law has now become weak by sin, this method of justification is impossible (*ek tōn adynatōn*). Thus we treat of the evangelical justification proposed to us in the covenant of grace, which we deny to be founded in inherent righteousness.

IV. The question is not whether inherent righteousness is infused into us through the grace of Christ, by whose intervention we are made partakers of the divine nature (2 Pet. 1:4) and obtain a true and real holiness pleasing and acceptable to God, by which we are properly denominated just and holy. For whatever the opponents may calumniously charge upon the orthodox (to wit, that "we allow of no inherent righteousness," as Bellarmine, "De Justificatione," 2.1 *Opera* [1858], 4:502, and others after him), it is surely a most foul calumny. Its falsity is proved from the writings of our divines whether public or private, in which everywhere and with common consent they teach that the benefits of justification and sanctification are so indissolubly connected with each other that God justifies no one without equally sanctifying him and giving inherent righteousness by the creating of a new man in true righteousness and holiness. But the question is whether that inherent righteousness (such as exists in believers on earth) enters into our justification, either as its cause or as a part, so that it constitutes some part of our justification and is the meritorious cause and foundation of our absolving sentence in the judgment of God. Romanists, as they pretend that justification consists of two parts—remission of sin and internal renovation of mind—so they assert that the cause on account of which God justifies us is the righteousness of God, which (infused into us) constitutes us internally righteous. For although they do not appear to exclude entirely the righteousness of Christ, inasmuch as they hold that by it he merited that God should communicate to us by the Holy Spirit internal righteousness and thus it is a condition of the formal cause (i.e., of inherent righteousness that it may be given to man), still they maintain that the right to seek life depends upon inherent righteousness and that on account of it God justifies us.

V. This is evident from the Council of Trent where "the justification of the wicked is said to be the translation from that state in which man is born a son of the first Adam, into a state of grace and the adoption of the sons of God by the second Adam, Jesus Christ, our Savior. This translation indeed, after the promulgation of the gospel, cannot be made without the washing of regeneration or a desire for it" (Session 6.4, Schroeder, p. 31). And: "Justification itself follows this disposition or preparation which is not only the remission of sin, but also sanctification and the renovation of the inward man by a voluntary reception of grace and gifts, by which a person who was unjust is made just and instead of an enemy becomes a friend, so that he is an heir according to the hope of eternal life" (Session 6.7, Schroeder, p. 33). And afterwards: "The formal cause of it is the righteousness of God, not that by which he is himself righteous, but that by which he makes us righteous; and by which, bestowed upon us as his gift, we are renewed in the spirit of our mind and are not only accounted, but are truly called and are righteous, receiving each of us righteousness in ourselves, according to our measure, which the Spirit distributes to everyone as he wills and according to the peculiar disposition and cooperation of everyone" (ibid.). And Canon 11: "If any man shall say that men are justified solely by the remission of sins to the exclusion of grace and charity which is shed abroad in our hearts by the Spirit and is inherent in them, or even that the grace by which we are justified is only the favor of God, let him be accursed" (Session 6, Canon 11, Schroeder, p. 43). From these declarations, it is evident that the Council held that inherent righteousness is the cause on account of which we are justified. Nor ought we to be deceived by their seeming distinction between the formal and meritorious cause: the one indeed being Christ's, but the other infused righteousness. Since they speak of justification before God, the formal cause cannot be distinguished from the meritorious cause because in this respect the formal cause is nothing other than that in view of which God frees us from condemnation and receives us to eternal life.

VI. On the other hand, the orthodox think far differently. For although they do not deny that inherent righteousness was purchased for us by the merit of Christ and by his grace conferred upon us so that by it we are and can be denominated truly just and holy, still they deny that it enters into justification in any way, either as a cause or as a part, so that justification may be said to be placed in it and by and on account of it man may be justified before God. For the righteousness of Christ alone imputed to us is the foundation and meritorious cause upon which our absolutary sentence rests, so that for no other reason does God bestow the pardon of sin and the right to life than on account of the most perfect righteousness of Christ imputed to us and apprehended by faith. Hence it is readily gathered that we have not here a mere dispute about words (as some falsely imagine), but a controversy most real and indeed of the highest moment. In it we treat of the principal foundation of our salvation, which being overthrown or weakened, all our confidence and consolation both in life and in death must necessarily perish.

VII. This appears more clearly when we come to the thing itself and the controversy is not carried on coldly and unfeelingly in scholastic cloud and dust (as if from a distance), but in wrestling and agony—when the conscience is placed before God and terrified by a sense of sin and of the divine justice, it seeks a way to stand in the judgment and to flee from the wrath to come. It is indeed easy in the shades of the schools to prattle much concerning the worth of inherent righteousness and of works to the justification of men; but when we come into the sight of God, it is necessary to leave such trifles because there the matter is conducted seriously and no ludicrous disputes about words (*logomachia*) are indulged. Hither our eyes must be altogether raised if we wish to inquire profitably concerning true righteousness; in what way we may answer the heavenly Judge, when he shall have called us to account. Truly while among men the comparison holds good; each one supposes he has what is of some worth and value. But when we rise to the heavenly tribunal and place before our eyes that supreme Judge (not such as our intellects of their own accord imagine, but as he is described to us in Scripture [namely, by whose brightness the stars are darkened; at whose strength the mountains melt; by whose anger the earth is shaken; whose justice not even the angels are equal to bear; who does not make the guilty innocent; whose vengeance when once kindled penetrates even to the lowest depths of hell]), then in an instant the vain confidence of men perishes and falls and conscience is compelled (whatever it may have proudly boasted before men concerning its own righteousness) to deprecate the judgment and to confess that it has nothing upon which it can rely before God. And so it cries out with David,

"Lord, if thou marked iniquity, who can stand?"; and elsewhere, "Enter not into judgment with thy servant, because no flesh will be justified in thy sight."

VIII. Here then is the true state of the controversy. When the mind is thoroughly terrified with the consciousness of sin and a sense of God's wrath, what is that thing on account of which he may be acquitted before God and be reckoned a righteous person? What is that righteousness which he ought to oppose to the judgment of God that he may not be condemned according to the strict demands of the law (*akribodikaion*), but may obtain remission of sins and a right to eternal life? Is it righteousness inhering in us and inchoate holiness or the righteousness and obedience of Christ alone imputed to us? Our opponents hold the former; we the latter. We are about to demonstrate this distinctly: (1) as to inherent righteousness; (2) as to imputed righteousness. Of the latter we will treat in the next question; of the former we speak now.

Proof that inherent righteousness cannot be the cause of justification: (1) because it is imperfect.

IX. That inherent righteousness cannot be the meritorious cause of our justification, we prove: (1) because no one is justified by an imperfect righteousness, since the judgment of God is according to truth and in it there is no room for a gracious acceptation; nor can deception consist with his law and justice. But inherent righteousness is not perfect, nor actual, nor habitual. Not actual because in many things we all offend (Jam. 3:2) and there is no one that sinneth not (1 K. 8:46), which Bellarmine himself does not deny ("De Justificatione," 2.16 *Opera* [1858], 4:530-32). Not habitual because the perfection and imperfection of an act depend upon the perfection or imperfection of the habit and our regeneration is always imperfect here (1 Cor. 13:12; Gal. 5:17). Nor ought it to be objected "that this absolute perfection was required under the law, but is not required under the gospel." The relaxation made under the gospel does not extend so far that an imperfect righteousness can be accepted for a perfect righteousness; for God cannot be satisfied except by a perfect righteousness. Rather it consists in this—that the vicarious and the alien righteousness of a surety is admitted for our own. Nor ought it to be objected "that righteousness is properly said to be perfect because it belongs to the works of God, which must be perfect because the work of the Rock is perfect" (Dt. 32:4). For the works which God does immediately by himself (which are rightly called perfect absolutely and simply) and the mediate works (which are performed by the intervention of creatures—such as the work of regeneration—which are not at once perfect because God operating according to our capacity promotes and perfects them little by little) differ.

2. Because works are excluded.

X. Second, our justification takes place without works; therefore also without inherent righteousness, which consists wholly in works or in habits from which works spring. The passages are obvious. Scarcely anything has been said more often and asserted more constantly; nothing certainly more fully argued: "By the deeds of the law, there shall no flesh be justified" (Rom. 3:20); "We conclude, that a man is justified by faith without the deeds of the law" (v. 28). This the apostle confirms in Rom. 4:6 and Gal. 2:16 and in many other places. Nor should it be replied here that all works are not absolutely excluded, but certain ones only (to wit, ceremonial); or if moral works are excluded, those only are meant which precede faith and grace and which are done by the strength of free will, not those which are done from faith and grace. Since the apostle absolutely and simply excludes all works without any exception, it does not become us to limit what he does not limit. The thing itself proves this also for he antithetically opposes faith to works in this matter. Hence it appears that all works entirely of whatsoever kind and not some particular ones are excluded. Otherwise he could not have simply opposed "one working" and "one believing," "to do" and "to believe," but a certain kind of working to other kinds.

Both ceremonial.

XI. This is demonstrated in particular (1) as to ceremonial works. For that law with its works is understood to be excluded by the apostle by which is the knowledge of sin (Rom. 3:20) and the whole world has become exposed to condemnation (v. 19). Concerning this it is said, "The man that doeth them shall live in them" (Gal. 3:12) and from the curse of which Christ redeemed us (v. 13). This must be understood of the whole law, especially the moral, not the ceremonial. (2) If the ceremonial law only would be excluded, not the moral (since it is the less principal part of the law), justification would have to be ascribed rather than denied to the law by reason of the moral law (which is much prior). (3) This objection is rejected by many Romanists—Lombard, Thomas Aquinas, Toletus, Pererius, Justiniani, Salmeron and others, as their commentaries clearly show. Lombard says, "Without any works of the law, even the moral" (*In Epistolam ad Romanos* [PL 191/1.1364] on Rom. 3:27). Thomas Aquinas says on this passage: "Without the works of the law, not only ceremonial, which do not bestow grace, but signify it, but also without the works of the moral precepts according to this, not by works of righteousness which we have done (Tit. 3:5)" ("Lectio IV Ad Romanos," *In Omnes Sancta Pauli Epistolas Commentaria* [ed. P. Marietti, 1917], 1:55-56 on Rom. 3:27-31). Augustine teaches expressly that Paul speaks of the whole law (*On the Spirit and the Letter* 13 [8] [NPNF1, 5:87-88]). Nor if the controversy between Paul and the false apostles arose from the use of circumcision and the observance of the ceremonial law (which they urged as necessary to justification), does it follow that the apostle speaks of it alone when he excludes the works of the law from it. He passes from a part to the whole, this hypothesis of the false apostles drawing with it a necessity of observing the whole law (as we see in Acts 15:5) and Paul himself testifies when he says that he who presses circumcision as necessary "is a debtor to do the whole law" (Gal. 5:3) because the law demands not a partial, but a perfect obedience in all. Hence because he saw that believers would thus slide back to the old covenant and depart from the new, he inveighs with so much warmth against this error as most pestilential.

And moral after grace.

XII. No better do others answer that it treats of works of the moral law done before faith and grace. (1) Paul excludes all works which are opposed to faith; yet all works without distinction are here opposed to faith, as working and believing are opposed (Rom. 4:5). (2) There was no necessity to exclude the works of the unregenerate, since it was acknowledged that they were sins, being done without faith (Rom. 14:23). (3) The examples of Abraham and David adduced by Paul (Rom. 4), inasmuch as they had been already converted and were believers, prove that works performed even after faith are excluded; as the apostle speaking of himself (now a believer) says, "I know nothing by myself; yet am I not hereby justifed" (1 Cor. 4:4). (4) All those works are excluded which could leave any reason for boasting to man (Rom. 3:27). And yet such are works done by faith which they hold to be meritorious. (5) The works of believers are effects which follow justification, not the causes which precede it. (6) The design of the apostle in the epistle to the Galatians was to dispute against the false apostles who joined together in justification, faith and works, the grace of Christ and their own merits. (7) If he had wished to exclude only the works of nature and not the works of grace, why does he so often and so carefully oppose works to faith absolutely? Why does he never oppose the works of nature to the works of grace, which would have greatly assisted in refuting the calumny of his adversaries by which they assailed his doctrine, as if by excluding works from justification he would open the door to sin: "Shall we continue in sin, that grace may abound?" (Rom. 6:1). And yet that inference would be founded upon no foundation at all, if Paul had wished to exclude only works done before faith. For who otherwise would gather that sin must not be indulged in after faith on this account because works antecedent to faith do not justify in the least? Now both kinds of works being excluded, it was easy to object this very thing, which the Romanists of the present day object to us (to wit, that it is useless to do good works if there is no merit in works; nay, we should rather sin that grace may abound). This objection of the profane, the apostle did not refute by a distinction between antecedent and subsequent works (which assuredly he ought to have done according to the hypothesis of our opponents); but by an explanation of sanctification and its indissoluble connection with justification.

3. Because justification is free.

XIII. Third, "our justification is free by the grace of God, through the redemption of Christ" (Rom. 3:24). Here the grace of God cannot denote the infused habit of love (as Bellarmine holds), but the favor and benevolence of God because we are said to be justified by his grace (*tē autou chariti*) (i.e., as the leading [*proēgoumenē*] and meritorious cause is placed in the redemption of Christ, the false is rejected by the particle "freely" [*dōrean*], which excludes all merit in us). (2) This grace is opposed to works and boasting (Rom. 11:6; Eph. 2:9). (3) We cannot be justified by the redemption of Christ otherwise than by the imputation of his righteousness. This is incompatible (*asystatos*) with inherent righteousness in the matter of justification; for if we are justified in another, we cannot be justified in ourselves. (4) Pererius confesses that *charin* here denotes rather the gratuitous goodness and kindness of God towards men (which is elsewhere called "kindness" [*chrēstotēs*] and "love" [*philanthrōpia*] toward man, Tit. 3:4). If the benevolence of God works good-pleasure (*eudokias*) in men (i.e., the good which he wills for them), it does not follow that he gives inherent righteousness that we may be justified by it. God does that good by distinct acts—the good indeed of imputed righteousness by the act of justification or inherent righteousness by the act of sanctification (as he has made Christ unto us both righteousness and sanctification, 1 Cor. 1:30).

4. Because justification consists in the remission of sins.

XIV. Fourth, according to Paul justification consists in the remission of sins (Rom. 4:8). Nor can it be done otherwise, since a sinner is concerned. And yet he whose sin is freely pardoned cannot be justified by inherent righteousness; nor is inherent righteousness remission of sins. Nor does he escape who says that it is not indeed remission of sins, but still it is connected with it in justification. It involves a contradiction to say that man is justified at the same time by inherent righteousness and by remission of sins, as it is most absurd (*asystaton*) for one to be justified in himself and in another (by a personal and by another's obedience).

5. Because justification is not by the law.

XV. Fifth, if justification were by inherent righteousness, justification will be of the law, not of the gospel, and the two covenants will be confounded which are nevertheless constantly opposed as diametrically opposite to each other. Legal justification takes place in no other way than by inherent righteousness, whether actual or habitual; gospel justification is to be sought not in us, but in another. This the apostle clearly teaches when he wishes "to be found in Christ" (to wit, in the judgment of God) "not having his own righteousness, which is of the law, but that which is through the faith of Christ" (Phil. 3:9) (i.e., not an inherent righteousness, arising from an observance of the law and which is called ours because it is in us and is perfected by our actions, but the righteousness of God and Christ, imputed to us and apprehended by faith).

6. Because this is derogatory to Christ and furnishes material for boasting.

XVI. Sixth, this derogates from the merit of Christ and is an argument for glorying and pride. For if the righteousness and merit of Christ most fully suffice for our justification, why are human merits sewed on? Is not injury thus done to Christ and material given to man for glorying in himself with God? Nor is this absurdity removed by saying that all this righteousness depends on Christ, who obtained that also for us and gave to it the power of meriting. Besides the gratuitous assumption that Christ merited for us the power of meriting (as will be seen in the proper place), whatever good man receives from God by grace (according to their hypothesis) does not exclude the concourse of free will (by whose intervention man may have some material for glorying in himself, while we ought to glory in the Lord alone). The Pharisee is no less condemned, although giving thanks to God he professes that he has all that he has from him, not from himself (Lk. 18:11, 12, 14).

7. Because it does not take away guilt.

XVII. Seventh, remission of sin requires the removal of guilt by the payment of the ransom (*lytrou*) due. And yet inherent righteousness can neither remove the offense to God or the guilt springing from it, nor compensate for the injury to the divine majesty. For besides the fact that it looks to the future (that man may perform his duty), not to the past (that he may compensate for the defect of duty by giving a satisfaction), it is impossible by a quality of finite virtue and worth for an offense of infinite indignity to be blotted out and compensated for.

8. From the testimony of Contarini and Bellarmine.

XVIII. Eight, we cannot omit here the remarkable testimonies of two cardinals, who, overcome by the power of the truth, agree with us. The first is Cardinal Contarini, who thus expresses himself: "Since we reach a twofold righteousness by faith, a righteousness inherent in us, and the love and grace by which we are made partakers of the divine nature; and the righteousness of Christ given and imputed to us, since we are planted in Christ and put on Christ: it remains to inquire, on which of these we ought to rest, and to think ourselves justified before God (i.e., reckoned holy and righteous). I truly think it to be said piously and religiously that we ought to rest, I say rest as upon a stable thing, which can certainly sustain us, upon the righteousness of Christ bestowed upon us, and not upon the holiness and grace inherent in us. For this our righteousness is inchoate and imperfect which cannot keep us from offending and from constantly sinning in many things. Therefore we cannot in the sight of God on account of this our righteousness be esteemed righteous and good, as it becomes the sons of God to be good and holy. But the righteousness of Christ given to us is a true and perfect righteousness. It is altogether pleasing in the sight of God. In it there is nothing that offends him; that does not in the highest degree please him. We must therefore rest upon this alone (sure and stable) and on account of it alone we must believe that we are justified before God, that is, considered righteous and called righteous" ("De Justificatione," *Casparis Contareni Cardinalis Opera* [1571], p. 592). From him Bellarmine does not differ much, who, after exerting all his strength in a defense of human merit, pressed by the consciousness of the truth, at length is brought to say "that on account of the uncertainty of personal righteousness, and the danger of vain glory, it is the safest to place our entire confidence in the mercy and kindness of God alone" ("De Justificatione," 5.7 *Opera* [1858], 4:615). To this proposition answers this clause of his will: "And I pray him to admit me among his saints and elect, not as an estimator of merit, but as a bestower of pardon."

Sources of explanation.

XIX. Christ by his obedience is rightly said "to constitute" us "righteous," not by an inherent but by an imputed righteousness as is taught in Rom. 4:6 and gathered from the opposition of the antecedent condemnation (Rom. 5:19). For they are no less constituted righteous before God who, on account of the obedience of Christ imputed to them, are absolved from deserved punishment, than they who on account of the disobedience of Adam are constituted unrighteous (i.e., are exposed to death and condemnation). If Adam constituted us unrighteous effectively by a propagation of inherent depravity (on account of which we are also exposed to death in the sight of God), it does not follow equally that Christ constitutes us righteous by a forensic justification at the bar of God by inherent righteousness given to us by him. The design of the apostle (which alone is to be regarded) does not have this direction. He only wishes to disclose the foundation of the connection between being exposed to death and the right to life, from our union with the first and second Adam, as to the thing (although the mode is different on account of the difference in the subject). The "abundance of grace and of righteousness" (*perisseia tēs charitos kai dikaiosynēs*, Rom. 5:17) does not denote habitual grace or inherent righteousness, but the abundance of divine mercy and the infinite treasury of righteousness, which believers obtain in the obedience of the Mediator. And this gift is said to be greater than the sin of Adam because the grace of God giving us the righteousness of Christ, not only took away the guilt of one transgression, but of all actual sins (as Thomas Aquinas well remarks on this passage). Nor does it press us more that we are said "to receive abundance of grace" (Rom. 5:17) because we receive it by the hand of faith, not that it becomes ours by way of infusion or of inhesion, but by way of imputation.

XX. "Justification" is not set forth as a genus, embracing under itself "ablution" and "sanctification" (1 Cor. 6:11), but on the contrary "ablution," which is adumbrated in baptism; as the more general word is set forth in the first place, containing under it justification and sanctification as two species, as frequently both these benefits are wont to be described by the one word—ablution, as much as justification (Ps. 51:2; 1 Jn. 1:7) and as much as sanctification (Heb. 9:14). What is added, however, concerning "the name of Christ" does not properly denote an invocation, which is made by it, but the power and efficacy of it—that "to be justified in the name of Christ" is nothing else than to be justified by and on account of Christ. For there is no other name by which we can obtain salvation.

XXI. Paul does not say that we are justified by regeneration (Tit. 3:5-7); nay, since he ascribes justification to the grace of God and takes it away from works, he shows that he is unwilling to ascribe it to righteousness inhering by regeneration, which is rather the fruit than the cause of justification. But his intention is to point out how God will have us saved by two benefits which he bestows upon us—regeneration, of which the Holy Spirit is the author in us; and justification, which we obtain by Christ, by which we are made heirs of eternal life. That denotes the way of salvation, this its cause.

XXII. The conformity to the image of Christ to which we are predestinated (Rom. 8:29) means indeed that we are made partakers of inherent holiness and righteousness like his; but it does not mean that we are justified by that inherent righteousness, as he was. For both our preceding sin and the imperfection of this righteousness in us renders such a justification impossible. For it cannot happen that they, who are the children of wrath by nature and who are never without sin, can be justified in the same manner in which he was justified, who knew no sin and in whose mouth no guile was found.

XXIII. Although Abel and Noah were righteous and did good works, still they were not on that account justified by their own inherent righteousness and good works. Nay, Paul testifies that they were righteous by the righteousness of faith (Heb. 11): Abel in that by faith he offered a more excellent sacrifice, by which he also obtained witness that he was righteous (v. 4). Noah became heir of the righteousness which is by faith (v. 7), which is no other than the righteousness which God imputes through faith (Rom. 4:5, 6). From this flowed the good works which they performed.

XXIV. Since justification is described in the Scriptures by remission of sins and the imputation of righteousness, it cannot be called a motion from sin to righteousness, such as occurs in illumination and calefaction. And this is the fundamental error (*prōton pseudos*) of our opponents, who convert a forensic and judicial action (which takes place before God) into a physical or moral action (which takes place in us).

XXV. When believers seek to be justified by God according to their righteousness (Pss. 7:8; 17:1; 18:20), we must not understand it of a personal righteousness (of which they elsewhere confess they are destitute, Pss. 130:3; 143:2), but of a righteousness of the cause (which they maintained and on account of which they suffered persecution from the wicked); or if personal righteousness is understood by it, it is not universal and absolute (which is found in no mortal), but particular as to certain acts in which they can conduct themselves well by the grace of God (such as was the action of Phineas which was imputed to him for righteousness) and comparative, not relative to God, but to the wicked (who undeservedly slandered them).

XXVI. The proportion of man to the highest good is either from the prescription of the law ("Do this and live") or from the assistance of grace. In the former sense, man in innocence would have had a proportion to the highest good. But by sin, that way having been shut up, another was to be sought in Christ, who by fulfilling the law for us, acquired for us a right to the highest good or eternal life. When therefore life is said to be given to the pious and righteous, the quality or disposition of the subject is denoted (which ought to possess life), not, however, the cause of such a good (i.e, how happy they ought to be, not why and on account of what).

XXVII. Although in those to whom the satisfaction of Christ is imputed, the habit of righteousness is also infused (which we reach only in the other life and by this habit we begin to be righteous morally and inherently), still we cannot be called righteous relative to the divine judgment. For we are constitued righteous in the divine court only insofar as we can remove the accusation with which we are charged—of sin past as well as present. Now such an inchoate habit of righteousness cannot remove such an accusation, whether by making it false (because it is evident that we always have sinned and so are guilty) or by expunging it through a suffering of the punishment due (because it cannot have the relation of a satisfaction for sins committed by which their guilt may be taken away). For it tends to this—that we may not sin hereafter; but it cannot make us not to have sinned so that we do not need another's righteousness imputed to us for our justification.

Third Question

Is the righteousness and obedience of Christ imputed to us the meritorious cause and foundation of our justification with God? We affirm against the Romanists and Socinians.

I. The false and pretended impelling and meritorious cause of our justification (which is placed by the Romanists in inherent righteousness) having been rejected, the true and genuine cause must now be exhibited from the Scriptures (to wit, the righteousness and obedience of Christ imputed to us by God). That the truth and mode of this may be the more clearly seen and more strongly retained against the cavils of our opponents, the following things must be premised.

The opinion of the orthodox concerning the imputation of Christ's righteousness.

II. First, we suppose that justification is a forensic act of God (as has already been proved), not as a creditor and a private person, but as a ruler and Judge giving sentence concerning us at his bar. (2) Justification is the act not of a subordinate Judge, who is bound to the formula of the law, but of a supreme magistrate and prince, to whom alone belongs, in virtue of his autocratic (*autokratorikō*) right, the showing of favor to the guilty and the relaxation of the rigor of established laws. (3) That God does not here sit on the throne of justice that he may act according to the strict justice of the law (*kata to akribodikaion nomou*), but on the throne of grace that he may act according to the gospel forbearance (*epieikeian*). (4) That he so acts from mercy as not to do injury to his justice, which (since it cannot suffer his laws to be violated with impunity and sin to go unpunished) necessarily requires some satisfaction (*lytron*) to be made to it.

III. Hence it follows (5) that God cannot show favor to, nor justify anyone without a perfect righteousness. For since the judgment of God is according to truth, he cannot pronounce anyone just who is not really just. However, since no mortal after sin has such a righteousness in himself (nay, by sin he has been made a child of wrath and become exposed to death), it must be sought out of us in another, by the intervention of which man (sinful and wicked) may be justified without personal righteousness. Human courts often justify the guilty, either through ignorance (when the wickedness is not known and lies concealed) or by injury (when it is not attended to) or by iniquity (when it is approved). But in the divine court (in which we deal with the most just Judge, who neither holds the guilty as innocent, nor the innocent as guilty) this cannot occur. Therefore he who is destitute of personal righteousness ought to have another's, by which to be justified. For although God (as the supreme arbiter of affairs and the sovereign Lord of all) has the power to remit the punishment of sinners, still he cannot (because he is most just) thus favor the sinner, unless a satisfaction is first made by which both his justice may be satisfied and punishment taken of sin. Since this could not come from us who are guilty, it was to be sought in another, who (constituted a surety in our place by receiving upon himself the punishment due to us) might bestow the righteousness (*dikaiōma*) of which we were destitute.

IV. The gospel teaches that what could not be found in us and was to be sought in another, could be found nowhere else than in Christ, the God-man (*theanthrōpō*); who taking upon himself the office of surety most fully satisfied the justice of God by his perfect obedience and thus brought to us an everlasting righteousness by which alone we can be justified before God; in order that covered and clothed with that garment as though it were of our first-born (like Jacob), we may obtain under it the eternal blessing of our heavenly Father.

V. Further, as long as Christ is outside of us and we are out of Christ, we can receive no fruit from another's righteousness. God willed to unite us to Christ by a twofold bond—one natural, the other mystical—in virtue of which both our evils might be transferred to Christ and the blessings of Christ pass over to us and become ours. The former is the communion of nature by the incarnation. By this, Christ, having assumed our flesh, became our brother and true Goel and could receive our sins upon himself and have the right to redeem us. The latter is the communion of grace by mediation. By this, having been made by God a surety for us and given to us for a head, he can communicate to us his righteousness and all his benefits. Hence it happens that as he was made of God sin for us by the imputation of our sins, so in turn we are made the righteousness of God in him by the imputation of his obedience (2 Cor. 5:21).

VI. Just as Christ sustains a twofold relation (*schesin*) to us of surety and head (of surety, to take away the guilt of sin by a payment made for it; of head, to take away its power and corruption by the efficacy of the Spirit), so in a twofold way Christ imparts his blessings to us, by a forensic imputation, and a moral and internal infusion. The former flows from Christ as surety and is the foundation of our justification. The latter depends upon him as head, and is the principle of sanctification. For on this account, God justifies us because the righteousness of our surety, Christ, is imputed to us. And on this account we are renewed because we derive the Spirit from our head, Christ, who renews us after the image of Christ and bestows upon us inherent righteousness.

VII. However, because we treat here of the imputed righteousness of Christ, we must remark further that the word "impute" (which is in Hebrew *chshbh;* in Greek *logizesthai* or *ellogein*) can be taken in two ways, either properly or improperly. That is said to be imputed to anyone improperly which he himself has done or has, when on that account a reward or punishment is decreed to him. As sin is said "to be imputed" to the wicked (2 S. 19:19), when the reward of iniquity is imputed to them; and the judgment exercised by Phinehas "was counted unto him for righteousness" (Ps. 106:31), i.e., it was pleasing to God and gained for him the praise of holy zeal and the covenant of a perpetual priesthood. Properly is to hold him who has not done a thing, as if he had done it. In turn not to impute is to hold him who has done a thing as if he had not done it; as Paul desires the fault of Onesimus to be imputed to him (which he himself had not committed, Philem. 18) and asks that the fault should not be laid to the charge of those who forsook him (which they had committed, 2 Tim. 4:16). From this twofold acceptation of the word, a twofold imputation arises (about which Paul speaks)—of grace (*kata charin*) and of debt (*kat' opheilēma*): "Now to him that worketh is the reward not reckoned of grace, but of debt. But to him that justifieth the ungodly, his faith is counted for righteousness" (Rom. 4:4, 5), viz., of grace. For the foundation of imputation is either in the merit and dignity of the person, to whom a thing is imputed; or it is out of it in the grace and mercy alone of the one imputing. The first is the legal mode, the other is the evangelical. Hence we gather that this word is forensic. It is not to be understood physically of an infusion of righteousness, but judicially and relatively, of gratuitous acceptance in the judgment of God (which also appears from the force of the word *logizesthai* and *ellogein*, which is drawn from accountants).

VIII. But here we must accurately distinguish between imputed and putative or fictitious in order to meet the calumny of our opponents who traduce this imputation as a mere fiction of the mind about a thing not existing. For it is a thing no less real in its own order (to wit, judicial and forensic) than infusion in a moral or physical order; as the imputation of a payment made by a surety to the debtor is in the highest degree real (to wit, by which he is freed from the debt and delivered from the right which the creditor had over him). Hence it is evident that this judicial act of God does not lack truth because he does not pronounce us righteous in ourselves (which would be false), but in Christ (which is perfectly true); nor does it lack justice because there is granted a communion between us and Christ, which is the solid foundation of this imputation.

IX. Therefore when we say that the righteousness of Christ is imputed to us for justification and that we are just before God through imputed righteousness and not through any righteousness inherent in us, we mean nothing else than that the obedience of Christ rendered in our name to God the Father is so given to us by God that it is reckoned to be truly ours and that it is the sole and only righteousness on account of and by the merit of which we are absolved from the guilt of our sins and obtain a right to life; and that there is in us no righteouness or good works by which we can deserve such great benefits which can bear the severe examination of the divine court, if God willed to deal with us according to the rigor of his law; that we can oppose nothing to it except the merit and satisfaction of Christ, in which alone, terrified by the consciousness of sin, we can find a safe refuge against the divine wrath and peace for our souls.

meaning of "impute"

X. Now although we hold that there is nothing in us which can be opposed at the bar of God for justification, still one would improperly conclude from this what our opponents falsely and slanderously charge upon us—that we recognize no inherent righteousness in believers and by reason of which they are truly reckoned righteous and holy with God. Thus that we teach that believers always remain wicked and unjust in themselves, and that the righteousness of Christ is imputed to us solely to cover our sins and not to take them away. Hence they take occasion to traduce our doctrine concerning the imputation of Christ's righteousness as impious and execrable. As we just now said, however, we hold these two benefits to be inseparable: that no one is justified by Christ who is not also sanctified and gifted with inherent righteousness (from which believers can truly be denominated holy and righteous although not perfectly in this life).

Statement of the question.

XI. From these principles, the state of the question can be readily gathered. First, against the Socinians it is inquired, Are the righteousness, obedience and satisfaction of Christ imputed to us for righteousness? For as they deny that the obedience and satisfaction of Christ were rendered for us, so they reject the imputation and application of that obedience and satisfaction and explode it as a human invention (Socinus, "Tractatus de Justificatione," *Opera omnia* [1656], 1:601-27; Ostorodt, *Unterrichtung . . . hauptpuncten der Christlichen Religion* 36, 37 [1612], pp. 294-328; Smalcius, "De Justificatione," *Refutatio Thesium D. Wolfgangi Frantzii*, Disp. IV [1614], pp. 91-154). The orthodox, however, think the obedience and satisfaction of Christ are imputed to us for righteousness inasmuch as they are reckoned ours by the gratuitous mercy of God and on account of them we are absolved from sin in God's court and pronounced just.

And with the Romanists.

XII. But against the Romanists, the question is not: (1) Is the righteousness of Christ the formal cause of our justification (i.e., is it the form by which man is constituted just inherently, as the Romanists understand it describing justification by the infusion of righteousness)? For since we have already proved that it is a forensic, not a physical act, the question regarding the internal formal cause is fruitless (which pertains to the blessing of sanctification). Rather the question concerns the meritorious and impulsive cause of the divine judgment or our absolving sentence. Not, Is the righteousness of Christ our formal and inherent righteousness subjectively? But, Is our righteousness real and sufficient imputatively, by which, if we are not formally righteous by inherent righteousness, still we are formally justified by the imputation of it, so that apart from it there is no other material of our righteousness before God?

XIII. (2) The question is not Is the righteousness and merit of Christ imputed to us? For this the Romanists do not dare to deny. The Council of Trent says, "Christ by his most holy suffering on the cross merited justification for us, and satisfied God, the Father for us, and no one can be just, unless he to whom the merits of the suffering of our Lord Jesus Christ are communicated" (Session 6.7*, Schroeder, p. 33). Hence Vasquez says, "We grant there are imputed to us for a certain effect, not only those things that are in us, as sin, faith and righteousness, but also some things that are without us, as the merit and obedience of Christ, because not only the things that are in us, but also those without, in view of which something is given to us are said to be reckoned among our things for some effect, as if they were truly ours" (*Commentariorum ac Disputationum in primam secundae . . . Thomae*, II, Disp. 222.1 [1631], p. 637). Bellarmine also acknowledges this: "If the Protestants mean only this that the merits of Christ are imputed to us because they are given to us of God, and we can offer them to the Father for our sins, since Christ undertook the burden of satisfying for us, and reconciling us to God, the Father, their opinion is correct" ("De Justificatione," 2.7 *Opera* [1858], 4:518). And yet we mean nothing else; for what he adds ("that we wish the righteousness of Christ to be so imputed to us that by it we are called, and are formally righteous," ibid.), he supposes falsely and gratuitously from his perverse and preposterous hypothesis concerning moral justification. But the question is To what is that imputation made? To justification and life, as we maintain; or only to the infusion of internal grace and inherent righteousness, as they hold? That is, are the merits of Christ so imputed and communicated to us as to be the sole meritorious cause of our justification and that there is no other righteousness on account of which we are acquitted in the sight of God (which we contend for); or are they so imputed as to be the conditions of a formal cause that is of inherent righteousness, so that man can be gifted with it; or of an extrinsic cause which deserves the infusion of righteousness by which man is justified, so that not the merit of Christ properly, but inherent righteousness acquired by the merit of Christ is the proper and true cause on account of which man is justified (which they maintain)? They so limit the benefit of the imputation of Christ's merits to obtaining the effect of infused grace that this imputation is made for no other end than to merit for us infused grace, in virtue of which we obey the law and, being righteous in ourselves, are justified; as Vasquez, in the passage cited, observes—cf. *Commentariorum ac Disputationum in primam secundae . . . Thomae*, II, Disp. 222.3 [1631], pp. 639-42). Hence Bonaventure denies that the causality of justification or of the remission of sins properly belongs to the death or resurrection of Christ, but only "by way of intervening merit," which is reduced to the material cause, while he determines the formal cause to be infused love ("Liber III. Sententiarum," Dist. 19, Art. 1, Q. 1 in *Opera Theologica Selecta* [1941], 3:392-94). From these it is evident that the question here is Are the righteousness and satisfaction of Christ so imputed to us by God as to be the only foundation and meritorious cause in view of which alone we are acquitted before God of our sins and obtain a right to life? Our opponents deny; we affirm.

XIV. However, there is no need to remark that by the righteousness of Christ we do not understand here the "essential righteousness of God" dwelling in us (as Osiander with Schwenkfeld dreamed, opposing himself to Stancar his colleague, who acknowledged Christ as Mediator only according to his human nature—which error was exploded and perished with its author). That righteouness could not be communicated to us subjectively and formally which is an essential attribute of God without our becoming gods also. And the Scripture everywhere refers the righteousness of Christ, which is imputed to us, to the obedience of his life and the suffering of his death, by which he answered the demands of the law and perfectly fulfilled it. If we had need of an infinite righteousness, it should not be such in essence, but only in value and merit. If Christ is Jehovah, our righteousness, and if he is made to us righteousness by the Father, this is not said with respect to essential righteousness, but to the obedience which is imputed to us for righteousness. This is called the righteousness of God because it belongs to a

Bellarmine holds that Adam's sin imputed

divine person and so is of infinite value and is highly pleasing and acceptable to God. By this righteousness then, we understand the entire obedience of Christ—of his life as well as of his death, active as well as passive (as we have already proved, Topic XIV, Question 13).

Imputed righteousness is proved: (1) from Rom. 5:18, 19.

XV. Now that this righteousness of Christ is the foundation and meritorious cause of our justification, we prove: (1) because by the righteousness and obedience of one, Christ, we are consitituted righteous—"As by the offense of one" (supply "guilt") "came upon all men to condemnation, even so by the righteousness of one" (*di' henos dikaiōmatos*) (supply "the blessing redounded") "upon all men unto justification of life. For as by one man's disobedience many were made sinners, so by the obedience of one shall many be made righteous" (Rom. 5:18, 19). Here it is clear that the one transgression (*hen paraptōma*) is opposed to the one righteousness (*heni dikaiōmati*) and the disobedience of one man (by which men are constituted sinners and guilty before God by the imputation of that sin) is opposed to the obedience of one, Christ, by which the elect are constituted righteous (i.e., are justified before God; not assuredly by inhesion, but by imputation). (a) The act of one cannot be made the act of many, except by imputation. (b) The righteousness (*dikaiōma*) upon which justification of life (*dikaiōsis zōēs*) rests, demands a perfect and absolute righteousness (which cannot be said of inherent righteousness). (c) The condemnation (*katakrima*) to which the justification of life (*dikaiōsis zōēs*) is opposed, is not a physical, but a forensic and judicial act. In vain does Bellarmine maintain that the obedience of Christ is indeed the efficient but not the formal cause of justification, as the disobedience of Adam constituted us sinners, not formally but efficiently. We are not treating of an infusion of righteousness or of renovation (as we have just said), but of a juridical constitution which cannot take place except by imputation (since it is of another's, not of a personal righteousness). Again, Bellarmine himself testifies the contrary when he says, "The sin of Adam is so imputed to his posterity, as if we had all committed the same sin" ("De amissione gratiae," 4.10 *Opera* [1858], 4:160). And: "The sin of Adam is communicated to us in the manner in which what passes over can be communicated, to wit, by imputation; for it is imputed to all who are born of Adam" (ibid., 5.17, p. 227). Nor if we are constitued unrighteous and guilty by sin propagated from Adam, ought we at once to be justified by inherent righteousness communicated to us through regeneration by Christ because there is a very different reason for each. And Paul here institutes the comparison between the first and second Adam in the thing and not as to the manner of the thing.

2. From Rom. 4:3.

XVI. Second, faith is said to be imputed to us for righteousness. "Abraham believed God, and it was counted unto him for righteousness" (Rom. 4:3); not the faith itself or the act of believing formally, as if it were righteousness with God (as the Remonstrants hold, against whom we will dispute hereafter) because thus justification would not be without works, since faith itself is a work; but objectively and relative to the righteousness of Christ, which faith apprehends and applies to itself. The apostle calls this "the righteousness of faith which is through the faith of Christ" (Phil. 3:9) "in which alone he wishes to be found" (viz., at the bar of God). For it is to be sought nowhere else than in

Christ, who is Jehovah our righteousness, and who of God is made unto us righteousness. It is confirmed by this—that Paul in the same place explains the imputation of faith for righteousness by "the imputation of righteousness without works" (Rom. 4:6). Hence it is surely evident: (a) that justification consists in the imputation of righteousness, that no one may suppose this phrase was invented by us; (b) that this righteousness cannot be inherent, given to us by infusion, both because it is said to be without works and because what is inherent is opposed to what is imputed. On that account, it is opposed by Paul to his own righteousness which is of the law (Phil. 3:9) and is elsewhere called "the righteousness of God," which is manifested without the law (Rom. 3:21, 22). This is so because it is subjectively in a divine person and so of infinite value; and originally because it is from God, since it is given to us freely by God; and terminatively because it leads to God and is approved by him and can alone sustain the examination of his judgment. Therefore whoever by faith applies that righteousness to himself is said not to come into judgment, but to have already passed from death to life (Jn. 5:24), i.e., to be justified.

3. From 1 Cor. 1:30; 2 Cor. 5:21.

XVII. Third, Christ is the righteousness by which we are justified. For on this account he is said to "be made of God unto us righteousness" (1 Cor. 1:30) and we are said to be made the righteousness of God in him: "God hath made him to be sin for us, who knew no sin; that we might be made the righteousness of God in him" (2 Cor. 5:21). From this it is evident: (a) that Christ is our righteousness before God, not surely inherently (because the righteousness of one cannot pass over into another), but imputatively; (b) we are made the righteousness of God in him, just as he is made sin for us. Now Christ was made sin for us, not inherently or subjectively (because he knew no sin), but imputatively (because God imputed to him our sins and made the iniquities of us all to meet on him, Is. 53:6). Therefore, we also are made righteousness, not by infusion, but by imputation. Augustine well expresses this: "He, therefore, was sin, that we might be righteousness, nor ours, but God's, nor in us, but in him, as he demonstrated sin, not his own, but ours, nor in himself, but in us constituted in the likeness of sinful flesh, in which he was crucified" (*Enchiridion* 13 [41] [FC 2:406-7; PL 40.253]). The objection is fruitless that "Christ is said to have been made righteousness, as he was made wisdom and sanctification, not surely imputatively, but effectively." For even if he was equally made to us of God all these as to merit because he acquired all these blessings for us, still he was not made in the same manner as to bestowal, but diversely according to the diversity of the gifts (even the nature of the thing demands this). For if he was made righteousness in no other way than sanctification (i.e., effectively), Paul would be guilty of tautology, since in this way justification and sanctification would not differ. Therefore he is made wisdom and sanctification to us effectively by illuminating and regenerating us; but righteousness imputatively by imputing to us his righteousness. Bellarmine cannot deny this when he says that Christ can rightly be said to be made righteousness meritoriously "because he satisfied the Father for us, and gives and communicates that satisfaction to us, when he justifies us, so that he can be called our satisifaction and righteousness, as if we ourselves had satisfied God" ("De Justificatione," 2.10 *Opera* [1858], 4:523). This he confirms on 2 Cor. 5:21: "The righteousness of Christ is imputed to us as to the satisfaction, which he made for us" (ibid., p. 574). Nor can that which our opponent adds in the same place help his cause when he says: "But not on this account can we be reckoned righteous, if the stains and corruption of sins truly inhere in us" (ibid.). For if the righteousness of Christ is imputed to us (as he had already confessed), then certainly we are considered righteous in him; for no one imputes righteousness to him whom he does not count righteous. And if the satisfaction of Christ is imputed to us, then our debts for which he satisfied are not imputed, but are remitted. Falsely also he holds "that the righteousness inhering in us is here called the righteousness of God because it is given to us of God; or also because it is the image and effect of the righteousness of God" (ibid.). For the little clause "in him" stands in the way; for how could it be said to be in Christ, if it was in us? Contarini acknowledges this: "The righteousness of God in him, since his righteousness is made ours, is given and imputed to us" (cf. "De Justificatione," *Casparis Contareni Cardinalis Opera* [1571], p. 592).

4. From the suretyship of Christ.

XVIII. Fourth, justification takes place on account of the suretyship of Christ and the payment made for us by him—which cannot be done without imputation. For as a payment made by a surety for a debtor cannot help him except by imputation (inasmuch as the payment made by a surety is applied to him as if it had been made by himself), the cancelling of the debt follows and the deliverance of the debtor. Thus since Christ undertook to be our surety and paid in our place, who does not see that the payment made by him and the ransom (*lytron*) given is imputed to us for full absolution (i.e., is considered by God as if it had been given by us)? In this sense, we are said to be "justified by the death and blood of Christ" (Rom. 5:9) because the merit of his obedience and death was that in view of which God was reconciled and gave to us the pardon of sin. In the same sense, he is said "to have been made a curse and sin for us, that we might be made a blessing and righteousness in him" (Gal. 3:13; 2 Cor. 5:21) because the curse and punishment of sin which he received upon himself in our stead secures to us blessing and righteousness with God in virtue of that most strict union between us and him by which, as our sins are imputed to him, so in turn his obedience and righteousness are imputed to us. Just as under the law the punishment which the victims suffered in the place of sinners was imputed to them for the expiation of sin and their liberation.

5. From Rom. 8:3.

XIX. Fifth, Christ justifies us by that by which he frees us from the condemnation of the law and fulfills in us its right to life. "For what the law could not do, in that it was weak through the flesh, God sending his own Son in the likeness of sinful flesh, and for sin, condemned sin in the flesh: that the righteousness of the law might be fulfilled in us" (namely, our justification by the law having become impossible through sin, God restored this benefit to us in Christ). Being made like to sinful flesh (yet without sin), he offered himself for us as a victim for sin and having made a most full satisfaction condemned sin (i.e., perfectly expiated it) in the flesh for this end—that the condemnation of sin might give place to our justification and the righteousness of the law (*to dikaiōma nomou*) (i.e., the right which it has) whether as to obedience or as to punishment is fulfilled in us (not inherently, but imputatively); while what Christ did and suffered in our place is ascribed to us as if we had done that very thing. Thus we are considered in Christ to have fulfilled the whole righteousness of the law because in our name he most perfectly fulfilled the righteousness of the law as to obedience as well as to punishment.

6. From Rom. 4:5.

XX. Sixth, our justification is "a justification of the ungodly but to him that worketh not, but believeth on him that justifieth the ungodly, his faith is counted for righteousness" (Rom. 4:5). A justification of the ungodly cannot be made by infusion, but by imputation. For although he that is justified does not remain wicked, but is renewed by the grace of Christ, he cannot be said to be justified by that renovation (which is the effect following justification, not the cause which precedes it). And faith, by which man is justified and is made righteous in Christ, does not prevent him from being and being called wicked in himself, inasmuch as he is opposed to the one working as he who has nothing upon which he can rely before the divine tribunal for his justification and so is "ungodly," partly antecedently, partly with respect to justification; not however concomitantly, still less consequently.

XXI. Various testimonies of the fathers could be gathered together here. By their vote, they approve our opinion, but we omit them from a desire to be brief. It will be sufficient to quote the words of Bernard because he often asserted this saving doctrine with exceeding skill: "Another's righteousness is assigned to him who wanted a personal righteousness" (*Contra . . . Errorum Abelardi Epistola* CXC 6.15 [PL 182.1065]). And a little after: "If one died for all, therefore all are dead; that the satisfaction of one might be imputed to all, as that one bore the sins of all" (ibid.). And: "My merit then is the compassion of the Lord; I am not wholly destitute of merit, as long as he is not wanting in mercy" ("Sermon 61 [5]," *Song of Solomon* [trans. S.J. Eales, 1984 rep.], p. 368; PL 183.1073). And a little after: "Shall I sing of my righteousness? O Lord, I will make mention of thy righteousness alone, which is also mine. Shall I fear that one righteousness is not enough for both? It is not a short garment which according to the prophet cannot cover two" (ibid.). And: "Not to sin is the righteousness of God; the righteousness of man is the indulgence of God" ("Sermon 23* [15]," ibid., p. 141; PL 183.892).

Sources of explanation.

XXII. Christ ought not only to restore the goods lost in Adam, but also to remove the evils contracted through Adam. Now there were two—guilt and corruption of nature—to which two goods should be opposed: the imputation of righteousness to take away guilt before God; and a renovation of nature to heal inherent corruption. Again, Christ not only restored the lost goods, but in a far more excellent way. We lost mutable righteousness, but an immutable righteousness is restored to us. We lost only an inherent righteousness and there is given us an imputed righteousness with an inherent, without which we could not be made partakers of the inherent. Otherwise if nothing was restored in Christ than what had been lost in Adam, pardon of sin would not be given to us in Christ because it was not lost in Adam.

the debt really is paid

XXIII. What is imputed to anyone by a mere gracious acceptation, that is not really paid, but is considered as paid; but what is imputed on account of a true payment made by another supposes the thing to be paid. Now the imputation of the righteousness of Christ (of which we speak) is not to be understood in the first sense (the improper sense, for an imputation which takes place without any payment at all whether of the debtor or of the surety); but is to be understood in the latter sense inasmuch as it is founded in another's payment (that of Christ the surety).

XXIV. Although we are justified by the imputed righteousness of Christ, it does not follow that we are no less righteous than Christ and are thus considered like Christ, saviors and redeemers of the world; and that Christ on account of our unrighteousness imputed to him can be called a sinner. The dignity of the head ought always to remain his own, that the members may be conformed to the head; but in their order and not that they should become the head. Thus although as to imputation we are truly righteous in the sight of God, still Christ is righteous in a far more perfect manner. We are such relatively in him and indeed precariously and dependently; Christ, however, is such infinitely, originally, inherently and subjectively. (2) Indeed we can (on account of Christ's righteousness imputed to us) be said to be redeemed and saved passively, but not to be redeemers actively because he alone can be a Redeemer whose righteousness is imputed to another; not he who needs the imputation of another. (3) Christ cannot (on account of our sin having been imputed to him) be called a sinner (which implies inherent corruption), but only a victim for sin, who received on himself the punishment due to sin. Thus guilt was to be taken away, not its pollution.

XXV. Where two contrary physical forms and qualities exist under the same genus, there it is certain that the denomination should be made from the intrinisic (which affect the subject more), than from the extrinsic. Now inherent righteousness and imputed righteousness are not under the same genus. The former indeed is in the class of relation, but the latter is under the class of quality. Thus nothing is to hinder the subject from being denominated from both under a different respect (*schesei*). For when the inherent quality is regarded, he is said to be a sinner and wicked; but when the external and forensic relation is considered, he is said to be righteous in Christ. It is indeed true that no one can be called righteous inherently by another's righteousness because if it is inherent, it is no longer another's. But still he can be said to be justified imputatively, since every day among men a debtor (on account of the payment made by a surety) is said to be free and discharged. Augustine beautifully explains this: "It is surely just, that they whom the devil held as debtors, should be discharged believing in him whom he killed without any debt" (*The Trinity* 13*.14 [FC 45:395; PL 42.1028]). Hence it is evident that the example of the Ethiopian adduced by Bellarmine (who is to be denominated rather from the blackness of his body than from the whiteness of his garments) is improper (*aprosdionyson*) since we are not speaking here of an inherent quality or of an adhering garment, but of a juridical relation given to him by the Judge. Besides, the Ethiopian always remains an Ethiopian in the same manner; yet the believer does not remain wicked, but is converted.

XXVI. Although God justifies us on account of the imputed righteousness of Christ, his judgment does not cease to be according to truth because he does not pronounce us righteous in ourselves subjectively (which would be false), but in another imputatively and relatively (which is perfectly true). Thus God truly estimates the thing and judges it as it is; not in itself and in its own nature, but in Christ.

XXVII. The spouse is said to be "all fair" (Cant. 4:7) in two ways: (1) in her head and husband imputatively, when all her pollutions are so covered by his righteousness that there is no more condemnation in her; nor does God see in her anything as to practical and penal knowledge which he can reprehend; (2) in herself inherently because she has been perfectly renewed by the Spirit, if not with a perfection of degrees, still with a perfection of parts and of grace which will at length be crowned by a perfection of glory.

XXVIII. Although the imputed righteousness of Christ is maintained by us to be the foundation of our justification before God, it does not on that account cease to be purely gratuitous on our part. It is a mere gift of God's mercy because the sponsor is given to us of God and was substituted in our place and because his obedience and righteousness (which we ourselves ought to have rendered from the rigor of the law) is reckoned ours and imputed to us by God. And what is more, the righteousness of the law is fulfilled in us (Rom. 8:4) and justification thus ceases to be of the works of the law performed by us, that still it is not made against it, but in accordance with it and the law is not only not made void but is rather established by faith (Rom. 3:31).

XXIX. Although justification can be called extrinsic objectively (inasmuch as it is the imputation of righteousness which is formally without us), still it is ours terminatively. Nor is it more absurd for the righteousness of Christ to be extrinsic to us and yet to be imputed to us than it is absurd for our sins to be extrinsic to Christ and yet to be imputed to Christ for punishment; or (*ad hominem*) than it is absurd for the satisfaction of saints to be imputed to others, as the Romanists maintain.

XXX. As the disobedience of Adam truly consitituted us sinners by imputation, so also the righteousness of Christ truly justifies us by imputation. Thus "imputed" is properly opposed to "inherent," but not to "true" because we do not invent an imputation consisting in a mere opinion and fiction of law; but one which is in the highest sense real and true. Yet this truth belongs to imputation, not to infusion; is juridical, not moral.

XXXI. The righteousness of Christ is rightly said to be imputed to us for righteousness, not that it may be reckoned righteousness (which was already so before), but that what was before another's may be made ours and that on account of it we may be pronounced righteous and received to eternal life.

Fourth Question

Does justification consist only in the remission of sins? Or does it embrace also adoption and the right to life? The former we deny and affirm the latter.

I. We have discussed the meritorious cause or the foundation of justification. We must now treat of its form or parts. In this matter, the opinions of theologians vary.

Statement of the question.

II. Some contend that the whole of justification is comprehended in the remission of sin alone, so that God is to be considered as justifying us when he pardons our sins and absolves us from all punishment. They also hold this opinion who maintain that Christ's passive righteousness alone is imputed to us. However, others make justification to consist of two parts: remission of sin and imputation of righteousness. The former removes punishment from the sinner; the latter renders him worthy of the reward or of life.

III. But neither opinion seems to us to explain this subject with sufficient accuracy. Not the first because (as we shall afterwards say) absolution from punishment is not sufficient for a full justification, but the communication of a right to life is also required. If the orthodox sometimes assert that justification is contained in the remission of sins alone, it does not follow that they do not also acknowledge the right to life under it. For they speak thus against the Romanists, who hold that to justification pertains not only the remission of sins, but also an internal renovation of the soul and an infusion of righteousness. Against these they well maintain that the whole of justification consists in the remission of sins, under which they embrace also the right to life, exclusive of the renovation of man or the infusion of righteousness.

IV. But neither can the second opinion be received simply because in it are falsely joined the remission of sins and the imputation of righteousness, as if they were parts answering to each other: remission indeed the first; imputation of righteousness another. However they do not in turn correspond with each other as a part to a part, but as a cause to an effect and a foundation to that which rests upon it and depends upon it. For if we wish to philosophize correctly, God does not remit our sins and afterwards impute righteousness, but he first imputes righteousness and afterwards on account of that imputed righteousness, remits our sins. For a satisfaction and a ransom (*lytron*) must necessarily intervene in order that remission may be granted by God without detriment to his justice and that it may be the foundation of the absolving sentence which is made in favor of the elect. If by the imputation of righteousness, theologians mean nothing else than the bestowal of a right to life (as it is certain many do), they hold that indeed truly, but do not express themselves with sufficient accuracy.

V. Thus then we believe the thing may be more readily and clearly conceived. Christ having been destined and given of God to us as a surety and head, in virtue of this union it happens that whatever was done by him (or endured for the perfect fulfillment of the law as to its precepts as well as to its penal sanction) is reckoned ours, as done in our place, and is imputed to us by God as if it had been performed by ourselves. From this imputation of his most perfect righteousness flow two benefits—both remission of sins and the bestowal of a right to life or adoption (in which two the whole of justification is contained). Thus the imputation of righteousness is the foundation and the meritorious cause of justification, while adoption and absolution are two parts of justification and effects of the imputation of righteousness which are inseparable from each other. For as pardon of sin cannot be granted nor a right to life be conferred, except on the supposition of the imputation of righteousness (by the intervention of which God can without prejudice to his justice free from punishment and bestow life), so, such imputation being posited, both these benefits flow necessarily from the double property of this righteousness, inasmuch as it has a satisfactory and meritorious power at the same time. By reason of the former, imputed righteousness is the foundation of the remission of sins; by reason of the latter, it is the cause of the right to life.

Remission and the right to life, the two parts of justification.

VI. Now many reasons prove that these two benefits must be joined together here, whether we attend to the law (which was to be fulfilled) or regard our necessity, or the nature of things, or the voice of Scripture. For as the law contains a sanction of two parts—on the one side the punishment of death to transgressors; on the other, the reward of life to the obedient—so the righteousness of the law (which by the justification of Christ is fulfilled in us) cannot be obtained except with the remission of sins (which involves a liberation from punishment). We have a right to life which Christ acquired for us most perfectly by his obedience.

VII. Second, the necessity of salvation demanded this very thing. Two evils were conveyed to us by sin: (1) that we were made guilty before God; (2) that we were made enemies and aliens from God, the fountain of life—the guilt of death into which we enter and the privation of life which we lost. And thus we could not be restored to integrity unless the guilt of death were taken away by the remission of sins and a right to life were given by adoption. As happiness is placed not only in a privation of evil, but most especially in the possession of good, it was not enough to be delivered from evil or death, unless also the right to good or life had been conferred.

VIII. Third, the nature of the thing proves it. It is one thing to redeem from punishment; another to assign a reward also. It is one thing to deliver from death; another to bestow life and happiness. It is one thing to bring out of prison; another to seat upon a throne. The former takes away evil, but the latter superadds good also; as if a fugitive slave should not only be acquitted of the punishment due, but also raised to the dignity and right of a son. For although these two things are connected together indissolubly from the covenant of grace, still from the nature of the thing they could be separated; as Adam, although innocent from the beginning of his creation and worthy of no punishment, still was not at once worthy of a reward until he had perfected the round of obedience, so it was not absolutely necessary that he whose sins have been remitted and who is delivered from the guilt of death, should straightway be gifted with a crown of immortality (since, if it pleased God, he might have afterwards directed man to work by which he should obtain the reward). Liberty certainly necessarily follows deliverance from prison, but not immediately the crown and throne. Joseph freed from his chains ought not on that account to be set over Egypt. Mephibosheth, brought out from squalor and thirst, was not immediately to be carried to the king's table. Thus two things must be distinctly conceived of in this benefit: the pardon of sin committed with a deliverance from the curse of the law; and a bestowal of the reward or blessing.

IX. In many places, Scripture connects and distinguishes these. "Christ was made under the law [*hypo nomon*] to redeem them that were under the law" (Gal. 4:4, 5) (to wit, as to the curse that we might receive the adoption of sons; i.e., the right to life which flows from adoption). Paul elsewhere confirms this: "by which faith we receive forgiveness of sins, and inheritance (*klēron*) among them which are sanctified" (Acts 26:18) (i.e., a right to eternal life with other saints). Here belongs the gradation between peace and glory which he weaves together when he says that "being justified we have peace with God, and rejoice in hope of the glory of God" (Rom. 5:1, 2). Peace has reference to deliverance from punishment and glorying supposes the bestowal of a right to life, which is the foundation of our hope. On this account, he joins together "the being saved from wrath" and "glorying in God" (Rom. 5:9, 11). This very thing Daniel had already intimated when he ascribes to the Messiah, who was about to come, "a propitiation of iniquity" (by whom remission would be obtained) and "the bringing of an everlasting righteousness" (by whose power a right to life would be given, Dan. 9:24). Nor does Christ mean anything else when he promises believers "a transition from death to life" (i.e., not only deliverance from death, but also the possession of life). John means the same thing when he says that Christ not only "washes us from sin" by obtaining their pardon, but also "makes us kings and priests" who obtain the right to happiness and glory (Rev. 1:5, 6).

X. Hence it appears that they are deceived who hold that the remission of sins and the imputation of righteousness differ only by reason of the diverse terms from which (*a quo*) and to which (*ad quem*); as it is not the covering of nakedness and the putting on of a garment, for this reason that sin and righteousness are contraries (*ameta*), one of which being posited the other is taken away. For it is far otherwise with these things, as we have already said. They are so to be joined together, as still not to be confounded, but to be distinguished as really differing from each other; or if the imputation of righteousness is put for a right to life, it is with respect to remission after the manner of a part, constituting with it the form of justification. Hence they are not to be compared with each other as the covering of nakedness and the putting on of a garment (which are really one and the same thing), but as deliverance from punishment and royal dignity in a guilty person.

XI. Sin and righteousness are indeed direct contraries (*ameta*), but not the righteousness which signifies perseverance in righteousness and perfection itself. For it is one thing to be free from corruption, but another to have persisted in duty and to have acquired merit. Adam had the former, not the latter. Thus between death and life there is no middle ground; but between eternal death and a happy life the middle ground is the mortal and animal life, a pious and holy life—but on earth, not in heaven, under the obligation of meriting by obedience. So many things could still come in between the flames of hell and the joys of heaven, deliverance from punishment and the possession of the reward; the punishment of slaves and the dignity of sons. Who, therefore, confers upon us (who were slaves adjudged to eternal punishment) adoption and an inheritance, will he not also wonderfully increase the benefit? It was much for us to be manumitted and to be made freedmen; now to be pronounced children and heirs, this is the climax and crowning blessing of mercy.

XII. When Paul argues from the remission of sins to the imputation of righteousness (Rom. 4:5-7), he does not do this on account of their equivalency, as if these two do not differ from each other and signify one and the same thing. Rather he does it on account of the undivided connection between both because remission of sins can be given to no one, except on account of the imputation of righteousness and imputation of righteousness is given to no one without his sins being forthwith pardoned.

XIII. Although he who obtains the remission of all his sins (of omission as well as of commission) is freed from punishment (which he deserved on account of those sins) and thus far can be pronounced righteous (or rather justified and acquitted), still, accurately speaking, he cannot on that account be considered to have omitted nothing really good and to have committed nothing evil. God by remission reckons a man not unrighteous, not because he judges him never to have sinned and to be without a stain, but because he forgives and pardons the guilty whatever evil he has committed. However to pardon and, on account of rectitude of conduct (*katorthōmata*), to reckon worthy of a reward and to honor, are far different. See what was said in Topic XIV, Question 8, Section 28 and following.

Fifth Question: The Remission of Sins

Does remission of sins consist in an absolute removal of them? Or in the pardon of them? And after the guilt is remitted is a certain punishment retained? Or is it wholly remitted? The former we deny; the latter we affirm against the Romanists.

I. Because various questions are wont to be agitated concerning the remission of sins, we must touch briefly upon them under three propositions.

The first proposition, concerning the remission of sins, which is not the abolition of them, against the Romanists.

II. The first: remission of sins does not consist in a removal of the corruption or depraved quality, but in a gratuitous pardon of the criminality and guilt arising from it. This is opposed to the Romanists, who, to support their hypothesis concerning physical justification by infusion, maintain that remission of sin consists in a real taking away of it, as to corruption as well as to guilt. Thus an infusion of righteousness always succeeds remission, as light always follows the scattering of the clouds of darkness.

III. But the following arguments prove the falsehood of this opinion. (1) The mode of speaking and the proper signification of remission among men, which does not imply the extinction of sin, but only the pardoning of it (as a prince, by remitting a crime, does not take it away, but only pardons it and frees it from the punishment due on account of it). (2) The synonymous phrases of Scripture teach the same thing when remission is expressed by a "covering" (Ps. 32:1). Not that they are not, but that in the sight of God the Judge, they do not come into condemnation. For this reason, we ought to put on Christ that his righteousness may cover our sins before God. By a "not imputing" (Ps. 31:2) that on account of them we may not be punished as we deserve. By a "not remembering" (Jer. 31:34) that God may not deal with them practically according to his justice in punishing them. By a "blotting out" (Pss. 51:1; 103:12; Acts 3:19; Col. 2:14) not of the corruption but of the guilt, as a creditor expunges from his account book a debt from which he wishes to release the debtor by destroying and blotting out the very handwriting that it may no longer have any force. Even so God destroys the sins which are written in his book and for which we are accountable (*hypodikoi*) when he pardons them by freeing us from the guilt which attached to us on account of them. By a "casting of them behind his back" and "throwing them into the sea" (Mic. 7:19) that they may no more come into judgment. By a "purging" by way of propitiation and of offering (*hilasmou*, Heb. 1:3; 9:14) that the guilt of sin (which makes us hateful and abominable to God) may be cleansed; in allusion to the sprinkling (*rhantismon*) of the old sacrifices, which did not take away inherent pollution, but adhering guilt. By a "turning away" of "his face" (Ps. 51:9) and a "putting away" (2 S. 12:13) and similar phrases which rightly mean a juridical pardoning of guilt, not a real removal of pollution.

IV. (3) If remission of sin was the taking away of inherent corruption, as the former is perfect, so also the latter ought to be perfect (which is repugnant to Scripture, which testifies that sin always remains in us and belongs to the experience of saints, who always complain of the struggles of the flesh and the Spirit). (4) If not to impute sin is to expel it and to infuse righteousness; from the opposite, to impute sin will be to infuse sin. The falsity of this appears from the case of Christ, to whom sin was imputed, but not infused.

Sources of explanation.

V. Although by remission of sins actual guilt or the obligation to punishment is taken away, potential guilt is not immediately taken away or the intrinsic merit of sin (which flows from its inherent corruption) because remission consists only in this—that the guilty person is freed by the Judge from the actual punishment due to him, not however immediately from all vitiosity. Hence Paul indeed says there is no condemnation to them which are in Christ (Rom. 8:1), but he does not say there is nothing condemnable or worthy of condemnation. For as long as sin remains in us (now it remains as long as we live), there is always something condemnable, although on account of the interceding grace of the Judge it does not any more actually condemn us.

VI. There is a theoretical covering of sinners which belongs to omniscience, according to which it is certain that nothing can be covered by God except what he wholly destroys and abolishes; another practical (which has respect to the exercise of justice and thus can be covered by him)—what is still in the subject, when God does not see it so as to notice it, is blotted out of his book so that it may not come into account. Thus sins are said to be covered before God not because they are absolutely taken away (as they are not), but because they are not allotted to punishment. Hence Augustine says, "Therefore, why does he say his sins are covered? In order that they might not be seen. For what was it for God to see sins except to punish them?" ("Sermo ad Plebem," *Ennaratio in Psalmum XXXI: II* [PL 36.264]).

VII. Although the remission of sins is expressed by various phrases (which denote a real taking away), it does not follow that they imply a total abolition of sin because in remission there is something real, since by it the actual obligation to punishment and the punishment itself are really and truly taken away from the person. Again, these phrases (such as "to take away," "to bear away," "to remove," "to wash out," "to purge sins") are partly explained by others which signify the removal of guilt (not however the nonexistence of sin) and are partly drawn from the effect of sacrifices, which was the propitiation and purgation of sin; not by a removal of its corruption, but by a taking away of the guilt and a giving away (*condonationem*) of the punishment.

VIII. Although we do not deny that sin is really abolished in those to whom it is remitted, it does not follow on that account that remission itself consists in that abolition. The former is concerned only with the guilt of sin, the latter with its pollution; the former considers sin with its relation or obligation to punishment, the latter as a quality inherent in the subject; that is performed at the same time and at once, this little by little and successively. Nor does an infusion of righteousness forthwith follow remission of sin from the nature of the thing, as he who remits another's debt ought not at once to give a new sum of money to him. We pardon the sins of others, nor on that account do we expel them from them, since there is one action which is done concerning someone and about him objectively, another which is done in someone subjectively.

Second proposition: remission is total with respect to guilt as well as to punishment.

IX. Second proposition: remission of sin is total and absolute with respect to guilt as well as to punishment. This is also against the Romanists, who urge a partial and not a total remission of guilt, but not of punishment; or of eternal, but not of temporal punishment. "If anyone says that after justification is received, criminality is so remitted to any penitent sinner and the guilt of eternal punishment destroyed, that no exposedness to temporal punishment to be taken away either in this world or in the future remains, before he can gain access into the kingdom of heaven, let him be accursed" (Council of Trent, Session 6, Canon 30, Schroeder, p. 46).

X. For guilt to be remitted while the punishment is not remitted is absurd (*asystaton*) because there is no punishment without guilt and remission of guilt is nothing else than deliverance from punishment. (2) It is repugnant to Scripture which nowhere speaks of the remission of sin except on the supposition that no punishment of it is exacted; otherwise a great disturbance would be introduced into the Scriptures and nothing could be considered fixed and certain in them. Also great darkness would be poured over both the divine promises and threatenings, as often as either remission of sin is promised or denied (whether it is only of the guilt or also of the punishment; and whether of all or of a certain part of each). Again, how could God be said to cast behind his back, not to impute, to destroy, not to remember, if he still exacts the punishment of them (i.e., recollects and imputes them to punishment)? (3) The common manner of speaking does not suffer it to be said that his sin has been remitted from whom some punishment of sin is exacted. For thus anyone might be said at the same time and at once "to let go" (*aphienai*) and "to keep hold" (*kratein*) of something (which is a contradiction); as no one would say that a debt had been remitted to a person from whom the payment of it is still required. (4) The nature of remission, which is entirely gratuitous, cannot allow this because what is obtained by the payment of any price, cannot be called gratuitous. (5) The justified cannot have peace with God according to Paul (Rom. 5:1), if they are still to be disturbed in life or after death. (6) In believers after the reception of justification, there is no condemnation (Rom. 8:1). Therefore no punishment remains, since condemnation is the devoting to punishment.

XI. (7) This hypothesis supposes either that Christ has not fully satisfied for us or that God demands the payment of the same debt twice (both of which are impious and blasphemous). Nor can it be replied, "Subordinates are not at variance because the satisfactions of men depend upon Christ's satisfaction, and from it have the power of satisfying; that Christ satisfied immediately for the guilt and exposedness to eternal death, mediately, however, for temporal punishment also, inasmuch as he furnishes the grace by which we ourselves make satisfaction to God." (a) It is gratuitously supposed that our satisfactions can be subordinated to Christ's satisfaction, since they are expressly opposed to it. For if righteousness came by the law then Christ is dead in vain (Gal. 2:21). (b) This mediate satisfaction is unheard-of in Scripture, which never says that Christ satisfied that he might acquire for us the power to satisfy, but by himself (*di' heautou*) made expiation for sins, and thus reconciled us to God and freed us from the curse of the law, being made a curse for us. Now how could Christ be said to have borne our sins in his own body on the tree (i.e., their punishment) and to have freed us from the curse and to have blotted out and taken out of the way the handwriting which was against us (Col. 2:14) and by one offering to have perfected forever them that are sanctified (Heb. 10:14), if believers are still bound by the guilt of some punishments for which they are yet to make satisfaction? Finally, the mode of speaking does not suffer it to be said that he made satisfaction for us, unless he has cancelled our debt with his own money.

XII. No less absurd is the answer "Our satisfactions are required that the satisfaction of Christ and the remission acquired by him may be applied to us." Although the satisfaction of Christ must be applied to particular believers to avail them, this ought to be done by the word and sacraments externally, by the Spirit and faith internally; but it cannot be done by satisfactions which ought to be offered to God, not to men. Nor have we ever heard it said that the remission of a debt is applied by an exaction of it and that this rests upon the debtor in order that he may enjoy the payment made for him by his security, so that the money which the sponsor paid for him, he also should pay out of his own funds to the creditor afterwards (or certainly some part of it). Again, if (in order that Christ's satisfaction for temporal punishments may be applied to us) our satisfactions are required, why are they not equally necessary in order that the same may be applied for guilt and eternal punishment? Or if they confess that they are not required for that application, why should they be required for the other, since no reason for the difference can be assigned? Finally, if Christ's satisfaction ought to be applied by our satisfaction, our satisfaction again would have to be applied by another satisfaction and so on to infinity.

XIII. What Scripture sometimes says of the exercise of judgment against the church and believers (1 Pet. 4:17; 1 Cor. 11:32 and elsewhere) does not favor the error of the Romanists. The judgment of a vindictive judge is one thing; the judgment of paternal chastisement is another. The one is legal, the other evangelical; the one proceeding from wrath and hatred, the other from love and mercy; the one for destruction and death, the other for correction and salvation; the one is exercised against the wicked and rebels, the other towards the pious and believers, not to destroy, but to teach and make them more cautious afterwards. Hence Augustine says, "What you bewail is medicine, not a punishment; chastisement not condemnation; be unwilling to repel the rod, if you do not wish to be repelled from the inheritance" (Psalm 103* [102].17 [20] [NPNF1, 8:508; PL 37.1332]). The former is incompatible (*asystaton*) with remission, not the latter.

XIV. Although afflictions of themselves and in their own nature are truly the punishment of sin according to the threatening of the law (Lev. 26), still on account of our gratuitous reconciliation with God in Christ they cease to be punishments (*timōriai*). They become either fatherly chastisement (1 Cor. 11:32; Heb. 12:8); or necessary evidences (*dokimasiai*) that we may be manifested to ourselves and to others (Jam. 1:2, 3); or witnesses (*martyria*) or testimonies concerning the truth of doctrine (Acts 5:41). On this account, they are reckoned even among the blessings of God (Ps. 94:12; Job 5:17; Phil. 1:29; Heb. 12:6, 7). They are connected with joy (Acts 5:41; Jam. 1:2; Heb. 12:11). They have glorying as an attendant (Rom. 5:2, 3). Therefore if they are still called punishments after the remission of sin, this is not said properly because they are without the formal reason of punishment (to wit, that it should be inflicted from the wrath of the Judge as the avenging of sin and the destruction of the sinner). Rather it is said improperly, both because they were of themselves the punishments of sin and because they tend to the destruction of the flesh and of the old man.

XV. This full and total remission of sins being established, the treasury of papal indulgences sinks and that most foul trafficking of the mystery of iniquity is swept away. For if the remission granted to believers is entire and total, freeing them from all guilt and punishment, why are necessary satisfactions further invented (either personal or another's) for the taking away of punishment, if not eternal at least temporal? I dismiss the various arguments, which prove not only the weakness but also the falsity of that error (concerning which we will speak in the proper place) from which it will appear that this comment is not only unwritten (*agraphon*), but also contrary to what is written (*antigraphon*) and unreasonable (*alogon*) and filled with innumerable contradictions and impieties. Hence it should not seem amazing if this occasioned (as is well known) the work of the Reformation in the year 1519 at Zurich by Zwingli; in the year 1517 at Wittenberg by Luther, who could not endure that most disgraceful traffic in sacred things.

XVI. Nor ought we to recur to the indulgences of the fathers, which have nothing in common with the modern papal indulgences (as they cannot be ignorant who have any knowledge of the ancient discipline). Since it is evident that in the ancient church very severe canonical punishments and satisfactions were imposed upon public sinners by penitential canons, specimens of which can be seen not only in the canons of the councils of Elvira, Ancyra and Nicea, but also in the decrees of Burchard, Ivo and Gratian (which were not rendered properly to God in the court of heaven as a satisfactory punishment for their sins, but only to the church itself for the extinction and reparation of the scandal by which it was injured). But since on account of that rigor many were reduced to desperation and relapsed into Gentilism, a modification of indulgences was introduced, which sinners obtained either by the intercession of martyrs or received from their bishops (their serious grief being regarded lest they should be swallowed up of sadness), by which, the severity being relaxed, they were restored to communion before the time required by the canons and a dispensation of canonical punishments was granted to them, as may be seen in Cyprian, *Letters* 15, 16, 17 (ACW 43:90-98); Canons 5 and 11 of the Council of Nicea (cf. Hefele, 1:386-87, 416-17); Canons 21 and 22 of the Council of Ancyra (A.D. 314) (Hefele, 1:220-21); and Canon 37 of the Council of Agathensis (Agde/Agatha, A.D. 506) (Hefele, 4:82). Afterwards most persons withdrawing from the yoke of the penitential canons, partly changes and partly redemptions of canonical satisfactions were introduced. Hence a fast of three days was redeemed by a recitation of fifty psalms, and by the feeding of some destitute person, or by three denarii from him who did not know the psalms (Burchard, *Decretorum* 19 ["Ex Poenitentiali Romano"] [PL 140.949-1014]). This gate of redemptions, however, being once opened, the sale of indulgences at length began in the eleventh century under Urban II. To make them of greater importance, various comments were devised concerning their value and efficacy, not only in the court of earth (as to canonical punishment), but also in the court of heaven and as to the satisfaction to be rendered to divine justice for sins. Hence it is evident how much these indulgences differ from the ancient, which were nothing else than relaxations of canonical punishments and dispensations from their severity for the consolation of private persons and the common edification of the church. However the modern are held to be relaxations of the satisfactory punishments of divine justice.

Third proposition: remission is extended to all sins.

XVII. Third proposition: "Remission is extended to all the sins entirely of believers, of whatever kind they may be, future as well as past and present, but in their own order." This question is moved with regard to future sins—are they also remitted at the same time and at once with the past and present sins? For there are some even of our theologians of great reputation who think that in the justification of the sinner all his sins (the future equally with the past) are at the same time and at once remitted, both because the righteousness of Christ, which is the foundation of our justification, is wholly (however great it is) imputed at once and at the same time to us and because justification ought to leave no room for condemnation (Rom. 8:1). Nay, being justified, they have peace with God (Rom. 5:1) and are called blessed (Ps. 32:1). This could not be said if they could still be subjected to condemnation on account of future sins not remitted.

XVIII. We think the difficulty can be overcome by a distinction. All sins (future as well as past) cannot be said to be remitted at the same time and once formally and explicitly because as they are not accidents of a nonentity, so as long as the sin is not, punishment is not due to it; and since it is not due, it cannot be remitted (as a debt not yet contracted cannot be cancelled). Besides for the remission of sin there is required a confession and repentance of it, which cannot be made unless it has been committed. Hence we are ordered to seek remission of sins every day, which is to be applied to sins committed, not to anticipate their perpetration. But because in justification the righteousness of Christ is applied to us (which is the foundation upon which the remission of all our sins rests) and because from the covenant of grace God promises that he will not remember our sins, nothing prevents us from saying that in this sense sins are remitted eminently and virtually because in the righteousness of Christ imputed to us is the foundation of that remission. And thus all our sins are remitted by God, whether past or present or future, but with respect to the time in which they are committed; so that past and present are actually remitted, the future when they are committed will most certainly be remitted according to God's promise. Thus the state of justification remaining undisturbed and the acceptation of the person remaining uninterrupted and the general remission of sins already committed, the following and future as to particular absolution are not actually pardoned before their commission; nay, before they have been repented of either generally or particularly.

XIX. I confess if we regard the eternal purpose of God in which all things, even the future, appeared to God as present (Acts 15:18) and the merit and acquisition of Christ, who offered to God a perfectly sufficient ransom (*lytron*) for the expiation of all our sins, so that as to the promise given by God in the covenant of grace concerning their remission, remission under this relation (*schesei*) can be said to be extended to all sins whether past or future. But if the actual remission itself is regarded, which is made by an intimation of the absolving sentence in the heart of the believer and penitent, it can be referred only to sins already committed. Thus to take away the guilt of subsequent sins, there is required a particular application of remission, not only as to the sense and assurance of remission, but also as to the true and real forgiveness itself.

XX. As the person whose sins are pardoned can be considered, either as to the state of grace (in which he is constituted by justification) or as to the particular acts (which he can afterwards commit), so remission can be viewed in two aspects: either generally as to state (according to which God receives the believing and penitent sinner into grace on account of Christ and bestows upon him the pardon of all the sins of which he is guilty); or specially as to particular acts of sin into which he afterwards falls, for taking away the guilt of which a particular absolution is needed. Not that the state of justification into which he is translated can be dissolved or remission once bestowed be abrogated, because God remains always his Father, but a Father angry on account of sins recently committed (which although they cannot constitute him a "child of wrath" on account of the immutability of calling and justification, still they make him a "child under wrath," so that he deservedly incurs the fatherly indignation of God and has need forthwith of a new justification or particular remission of these sins through faith and repentance).

XXI. Although the justified believer has not as yet the formal remission of future sins, he does not cease to be happy and free from actual condemnation because he has the foundation from which he can infer with positive certainty that it is prepared for him according to God's promise. If the whole righteousness of Christ is at the same time imputed, its entire fruit does not flow out to us at once, but successively in proportion to the inrushings of sin (for the remission of which the believer ought to apply that ransom [*lytron*] to himself every day).

Sixth Question: Adoption

What is the adoption which is given to us in justification?

The other part of justification, adoption.

I. The other part of justification is adoption or the bestowal of a right to life, flowing from Christ's righteousness, which acquired for us not only deliverance from death, but also a right to life by the adoption with which he endows us. For on this account, he is said to have been made under the law (*hypo nomon*) by an economical subjection that he might redeem us from the bondage of the law and confer upon us the adoption or the right of sons (Gal. 4:4, 5). On this, the right to life depends because "if children, then heirs" (Rom. 8:17). John says "to them who received him," i.e., "who believed on his name, he gave power to become the sons of God" (1:12). Here *exousia* does not signify authority or power because it has reference here to inferiors; nor faculty or potency by which a person can make himself a son. Rather it signifies *axiōma* (i.e., the dignity and right of sons).

In how many ways adoption may be taken.

II. However adoption here is not taken by us (as it is elsewhere) for an external calling and reception into the covenant (such as was formerly the case with the Jews, whose is said to be the adoption, Rom. 9:4). Nor for the sense and use of adoption which is made by emancipation, such as belongs to believers of the New Testament, who because they are made adults and are no longer minors are said to have received the Spirit of adoption and are no longer called servants, nor are held in the manner of servants, but are sons and heirs who rejoice in this right (Gal. 4:5). Nor for the full manifestation of adoption, which will occur in the resurrection. In this sense, believers are said to wait for the adoption (i.e., the resurrection of their bodies, Rom. 8:23). Rather it is taken for a juridical act of God by which from his mere mercy, he adopts into his family through faith in Christ those whom he elected to salvation from eternity and bestows upon them the name and right of sons as to inheritance.

What is adoption?

III. However as the word "adoption" is derived from a custom received among men, so the action itself has a multiple analogy with civil adoption (although it differs also in various things and is better). Adoption is defined by lawyers as a "lawful act imitating nature introduced for the consolation of those who have no children." Thus there is required here: first an adopter, who can have the authority of a father who (destitute of children) supplies the defect of nature by law and receives a stranger into his own family and promises to him paternal favor; (2) the person adopted, who passes from his father's family into another and (his state being changed) changes his name and life and has a right to the paternal goods and especially to the inheritance; and in turn binds himself to all the duties of filial obedience. Thus in this matter, adoption is not an act of nature, but of a gracious will which our heavenly Father wished to exercise towards us. In this sense, he is said "to have begotten us of his own will" (Jam. 1:18) and the very name adoption (*hyiothesias*) denotes this voluntary and most free disposition of God. By it God transfers us strangers and foreigners (who were the servants or slaves of Satan) from the family of the old Adam and the power of darkness and admits us into his own family and the kingdom of light and gives us the dignity of sons. He not only bestows upon us the glorious name of dearly beloved sons (1 Jn. 3:1; Rev. 2:17; 3:12) with the distinctions and honors pertaining to them, but also gives us a right to all his goods of grace as well as of glory. All this comes under the name of inheritance as acquired not by any merit, but given by the mere grace of the Father to us in virtue of our adoption by him. And we in turn (answering by faith to this great love) bind ourselves to filial worship and obedience to him (2 Cor. 6:18; 1 Pet. 1:15, 16; Mal. 1:6, 8).

How it differs from human adoption.

IV. Of whatever kind may be the analogy, still a great and remarkable difference always intervenes. For what the law does among men, this is a work of mere good will (*eudokias*). That was sought out for the solace of childlessness to supply a defect of nature; but this was made for our consolation only, not for God's, who was perfectly well pleased with his only begotten Son. That was ordained for the succession to the goods of a deceased father, but this only for a participation in the goods of a Father living forever. That can give the name, the titles and distinctions of sons, but not the mind and qualities. But in this, God by adopting changes the heart, and to whom he gratuitously gives the right of sons, he also impresses upon them the mind and character of sons by the Spirit of adoption. That does not make them good, but supposes them to be so; for neither would a man adopt anyone as a son unless he perceived in him something lovely. But this is a work of mere grace which does not suppose anything good in us who were enemies, rebels and most corrupt. Thus God adopts us, not because we are good, but to make us good.

V. Here belongs the testamentary disposition which the Father is said to have instituted for giving us the inheritance. It is nothing else than the final and immutable will sealed in the Scriptures and confirmed by the blood and death of Christ, by which he pronounces elect believers his heirs. Christ clearly intimates this: "I appoint" (*diatithemai*, or give by a will) "unto you a kingdom, as my Father hath appointed (*dietheto*) unto me" (Lk. 22:29). "And for this cause he is the mediator of the new testament," says Paul, "that by means of death, for the redemption of the transgressions that were under the first testament, they which are called might receive the promise of eternal inheritance" (Heb. 9:15). The goods left by this testament do not pertain only to "the inheritance of this world" (Rom. 4:13), according to which all things are ours (1 Cor. 3:21), but it is especially the inheritance of heaven or of the kingdom of heaven (Mt. 25; Jam. 2:5). Thus it is the inheritance of God himself, who (as he is the highest good) is often called our portion and inheritance (Gen. 15:1; Ps. 16:5; Jer. 10:16), as believers are the portion and inheritance of God (Ps. 33:12).

VI. Now although this privilege as to the thing is common to all the believers of the Old Testament, no less than to those of the New, who were both sons of God and had a right to the heavenly inheritance (to which after death they were admitted), still it is certain that the condition of believers of the New Testament as to the mode is far better in this respect: they are no longer in an infantile age, held like slaves under teachers and the rudiments of the world, when they were not able to have either the sense or the use of their right, animated by the spirit of bondage. But now being adults and emancipated by Christ, they are admitted to the sanctuary of the Father and have a full sense and fruit of their right, the Spirit of adoption being received, in virtue of which they can confidently cry out, Abba, Father. Paul refers to this when he says, "Christ was made under the law, to redeem them that were under the law" (to wit, under the curse of the moral law and under the yoke of the ceremonial law) "that we might receive the adoption of sons" (Gal. 4:4, 5). Not that only by which we are separated from the children of wrath and of the Devil, but also that by which we far excel infants, who do not differ from slaves. This is more copiously proved in Topic XII, of the covenant of grace, Question 10.

VII. From these positions, it is gathered that to no purpose do some anxiously ask here how justification and adoption differ from each other, and whether adoption is by nature prior to justification (as some hold, who think it is the first and immediate fruit of faith by which we are united and joined to Christ; or whether posterior to and consequent upon it, as others). For since it is evident from what has been said that justification is a benefit by which God (being reconciled to us in Christ) absolves us from the guilt of sins and gives us a right to life, it follows that adoption is included in justification itself as a part which, with the remission of sins, constitutes the whole of this benefit. Nor can it be distinguished from adoption except inasmuch as it is taken strictly for remission of sins, since in its formal conception it includes also acceptation to life, which flows from the imputation of Christ's righteousness.

VIII. Nor is adoption here to be confounded with our union with Christ. For although it necessarily flows from it as its cause and foundation (since from union with Christ depends the communion of all his benefits, of justification and of sanctification and of glory), still it cannot (if we wish to speak accurately) be identified with it. Rather it stands related to it as an effect to its cause. Hence it is that, being united to Christ as our head and the first-begotten of God, his most perfect righteousness becomes ours by the imputation of God and the reception of faith, upon which depend both absolution from sins and the adoption or acceptation to life and the inheritance which is the right of sons. For as many as obtain that dignity are not only received into God's family to be members of his house (Gal. 6:10), to be always under the fatherly protection of God, depending upon him for nutrition, education and perpetual conservation, but have a right to the inheritance (Rom. 8:17), i.e., the possession of all the goods of the Father and the enjoyment of God himself (which is our inheritance).

Christian liberty flows from adoption.

IX. From this adoption springs Christian liberty, which is not an immunity from all laws (divine and human) and a license to live according to our pleasure and to indulge the lusts of the flesh (as the Libertines profess, changing liberty into licentiousness); not an exemption from the civil obligation of subjection and from the tributes and jurisdiction of magistrates (as the various Anabaptists maintain and which the Romish clergy claim for themselves against the express teachings of Scripture); but it is a spiritual and mystical manumission obtained for us by the blood of Christ, by which from the spiritual bondage of the law, of sin, of the world and Satan (by whose chains we were before bound), we are brought into the liberty of the sons of God (as it is treated in Jn. 8:32, 36; Rom. 6:15, 22; 8:2, 3; Gal. 3:13; 4:6, 26; 5:1; Heb. 2:15 and elsewhere); through which being called into fellowship with God (as our Father) and with Christ (as our brother), we obtain dominion over the creatures and are heirs of the kingdom of Heaven.

SEVENTH QUESTION: THE JUSTIFICATION OF FAITH

Does faith justify us properly and by itself or only relatively and instrumentally? The former we deny; the latter we affirm against the Socinians, Remonstrants and Romanists.

Justification—active and passive.

I. Since justification can be viewed either actively (on the part of God who justifies) or passively (on the part of man who is justified), a twofold handling of it can also be adopted: either with respect to the benefit itself conferred upon us by God and of the righteousness imputed to us; or with respect to its reception and application made by faith (of which we now treat).

Statement of the question.

II. However, it is not controverted whether faith justifies—for Scripture so clearly asserts this that no one dares to deny it. Rather we inquire regarding the manner in which it justifies, in describing which there is an amazing discrepancy of opinions.

The opinion of the Socinians.

III. All our opponents agree in this—that faith justifies properly and by itself and so is our very righteousness—but with some differences. For the Socinians maintain that faith or the act of believing is the cause of our justification so that there is no other immediate and formal righteousness by which we are just before God than our faith; also justification is a universal affection of faith—"Not because it is considered such by the gracious acceptation of God; by which it pleased him to reckon faith for perfect righteousness, or for a perfect fulfillment of the law, no otherwise than formally under the legal covenant, the perfect obedience of the law was that universal righteousness upon which life depended" (as Socinus, *De Iesu Christo Servatore* [1594] frequently expresses it; Smalcius, *Refutatio Thesium D. Wolfgang Frantzii* [1614]; Volkelius, *De vera Religione* 4.3 [1630], pp. 175-84). The Remonstrants agree with them on this point in their Confession, c. 21+ (cf. *The Confession or Declaration of the . . . Remonstrants* 18* [1676], p. 211).

And of the Romanists.

IV. The Romanists hold that faith is the disposing and cause *sine qua non*, which not only disposes to righteousness, but also begins and merits righteousness itself. "If anyone says that the wicked are justified by faith alone, so that he understands nothing else to be required to cooperate for obtaining the grace of justification and is necessary from no part, to be prepared and disposed with the motion of his own will, let him be accursed" (Council of Trent, Session 6, Canon 9*, Schroeder, p. 43). Bellarmine says, "Faith justifies as the beginning and root of justification because it is the first motion towards God, for it behooves one approaching God to believe that God is" ("De Justificatione," 1.13 *Opera* [1858], 4:479). This opinion is founded upon a false hypothesis—as if justification consists in an infusion of righteousness and is a certain physical motion which demands previous dispositions in the subject before the introduction of the form.

The opinion of the orthodox.

V. However the orthodox differ wholly from them. They teach that faith is the organic and instrumental cause of our justification and that justification is ascribed to it, not properly and by itself (inasmuch as it is a work or as if it was the righteousness itself by which we are justified before God; or as if by its own worth or by the indulgence of God it deserves justification in whole or in part), but improperly and metonymically (inasmuch as Christ's righteousness, which faith apprehends, is the foundation and meritorious cause on account of which we are justified). So that it is said to justify relatively and organically: relatively because the object of faith is our true righteousness before God; organically because faith is the instrument for receiving on our part and for applying to ourselves, that righteousness.

Proof that the act of believing is not our righteousness.

VI. Two things therefore must be done by us here. First, negatively (*kat' arsin*), the false mode of the justification of faith (introduced by the Socinians and Romanists) must be removed. Second, affirmatively (*kata thesin*) the true and genuine sense must be established. As to the former, faith or the act of believing is not considered as our righteousness with God by a gracious acceptation: (a) because what is only the instrument for receiving righteousness cannot be our righteousness itself formally. Now faith holds here only the relation (*schesin*) of an instrument, as is evident both from its proper act (which is instrumental and consists in the reception of Christ [Jn. 1:12] and the acceptance of righteousness [Rom. 5:17] and of the remission of sins [Acts 26:18]); and from the subordination of the causes of justification to the same effect (to wit, the grace of God, the redemption of Christ and faith). This is alluded to by Paul in Rom. 3:24 where faith cannot sustain any other meaning than that of an instrument, since the grace of God holds the relation of an efficient principle and the redemption of Christ that of the meritorious cause.

VII. (b) Because faith is distinguished from the righteousness itself which is imputed to us, both because it is said to be "of faith" and "by faith" (Rom. 1:17; 3:22; Phil. 3:9) and because Christ with his obedience and satisfaction is that righteousness which is imputed to us (Is. 53:11; Jer. 23:6; 1 Cor. 1:30; 2 Cor. 5:21; Gal. 3:13, 14), which faith indeed apprehends as its object, but with which it cannot be identified. Hence Scripture nowhere says that God willed to count our faith for righteousness, but that he made Christ unto us righteousness; that he is Jehovah our righteousness and that we are the righteousness of God in him.

VIII. (c) Because we are not justified except by a perfect righteousness. For we have to deal with the strict justice of God, which cannot be deceived. Now no faith here is perfect. Nor can it be said that it is not indeed a perfect righteousness of itself, but is admitted as such by God and considered such by a gratuitous lowering of the law's demands. For in the court of divine justice (which demands an adequate and absolutely perfect payment), there cannot be room for a gracious acceptation which is an imaginary payment. Again, since our justification is a forensic and judicial act (where God shows himself just, Rom. 3:25), it does not admit of a gracious acceptation (which never proceeds from the authority and sentence of the Judge, but from the voluntary and private stipulation of the parties).

IX. (d) If faith is counted for righteousness, we will be justified by works because thus faith cannot but have the relation of a work which justifies. And yet it is clear that in this business Paul always opposes faith to works as incompatible (*asystata*) and two antagonistic (*antidiērēmena*) means by which man is justified either by his own obedience and in himself, by the law, or by another's obedience by the gospel. Nor does the difference between these modes of justification consist in this—that in the former a perfect obedience and in the latter an imperfect is accepted of God as perfect, since the mode of justification would be always the same—by works. Rather the difference consists in this—that since in both cases a perfect righteousness is required, in the former from the strictness (*akribodikaiō*) of the law God demands a personal righteousness, here from the forbearance (*epieikeia*) of the gospel he admits another's (to wit, the righteousness of Christ). Thus faith cannot be said to justify properly and by itself unless we slide back to the old covenant and return to legal justification.

X. "The faith of Abraham," it is said, "was imputed to him for righteousness" (Gen. 15:6; Rom. 4:3). Not properly because in this way he would have been justified by works (which the apostle denies in the same place). But (1) relatively and metonymically, so that faith is taken for its object (Gal. 3:25), i.e., for that which faith believes (to wit, that the promise concerning the seed [from Gal. 3:16], not so much bodily as spiritual, which he received by faith, was the foundation of his justification). This is confirmed by the circumstance that what does not inhere and what is contradistinguished from works is here said to be imputed. Thus in this sense faith is said to be imputed for righteousness by a hypallage because righteousness is imputed by faith, as the apostle declares in equivalent terms (Gal. 3:5, 6; Rom. 3:22). Nor is this to wrest the Scriptures and to express coldly the power and efficacy of faith, as Forbes falsely charges upon our theologians (*A Treatise Tending to Clear the Doctrine of Justification* 4 [1616], p. 10). Nay, no more clearly and truly can the genuine sense of that imputation be set forth. For since that thing which is imputed to us for righteousness ought to be our righteousness before God (i.e., that on account of which God justifies us); nor can faith be that (as we have already said and as he himself does not deny when he recognizes it to be the instrumental cause); it is clear that this phrase cannot be taken properly, but only metonymically with regard to the object. Nor is anything more usual in Scripture than for a faculty to be taken for its object. This does not prevent (2) faith from being said to be imputed for righteousness organically because it is the instrumental cause which apprehends the righteousness of Christ by a metonymy of the effect for the efficient, as it is elsewhere called eternal life (Jn. 17:3; 12:50), i.e., the instrumental cause of life.

XI. In vain, however, does Arminius contend that the righteousness of Christ is not imputed for righteousness, since it is that very righteousness itself (to wit, supposing that is not properly righteousness which is imputed to us for righteousness). He falsely confounds to impute for righteousness by gracious acceptation that which is not a righteousness and to impute to a person for righteousness that which he did not have. The first sense has no place here, only the latter. Accordingly what Abraham had not is said to be imputed to him for righteousness and the righteousness of Christ is imputed to us (i.e., reckoned ours), which was not ours. Thus imputation does not deny the truth of the thing or the perfection of the righteousness, but only the truth of the possession by ascribing to a person what was not properly his.

XII. What is said concerning anyone in Scripture ought to be altogether in him, but according to the manner which it teaches itself. Now the manner in which justification and salvation are ascribed to faith, does not consist in its own proper efficiency (as if our faith wrought or effected them), but they are placed only in its fiducial apprehension and application. Nor otherwise are we said to please God by faith (Heb. 11:6) and to be purged of sin (Acts 15:9), than because it applies to us the righteousness and blood of Christ, who purges us from sins and makes us acceptable to God.

XIII. It is one thing for blessings to be conferred according to faith (i.e., under the condition of faith) under which they are promised in the word and which we acknowledge with the Scriptures; another for faith to justify properly and by itself or to count faith itself for righteousness and thus to impute it for righteousness to the believer. There faith holds the relation of an instrument. Here, however, it holds that of a principal cause and foundation (which we deny).

2. Faith does not justify dispositively.

XIV. Second, against the Romanists we prove that faith does not justify dispositively or meritoriously, as the beginning and root of righteousness. (1) The Holy Spirit nowhere ascribes to faith the beginning or only a part or disposition to justification, but the whole and entire justification. (2) Thus the antithesis of the apostle between works and faith would not hold good, since faith would always justify like a work. (3) Justification, as being a forensic act, takes place at once and in a moment (*en atomō*); nor can it admit of a beginning and progress. (4) Thus we could be said to be justified "on account of faith" (*dia tēn pistin*). The Scripture never says this, but always either "by faith" (*pistei*) or "through faith" (*dia tēs pisteōs, ek pisteōs*) as by an instrument. If in various passages these prepositions—"by" and "through"—have a causality properly so called (as when they are connected with the death and blood of Christ), it does not follow that they have the same force when used concerning the justification of faith. Nay, since it is evident that a man cannot be justified by two righteousnesses (one in himself, the other in Christ), if the righteousness and blood of Christ is the proper cause of his justification, this cannot be ascribed to faith, but only the instrumental cause. (5) This opinion falsely supposes that justification is a physical motion inhering in the subject, which needs previous dispositions by which it may be acquired so as to be introduced into the subject. But this is false since it is a forensic act (as was proved before) to which man holds himself objectively, not subjectively. And although faith is required on the part of man for receiving this benefit, it does not follow that it has the relation of a disposition by which the sinner is disposed to the infusion of righteousness.

Sources of explanation.

XV. Faith is viewed in different lights: either in the act itself of justification or in the person of the justified or in the effect of justification. In the person of the justified, it is well called "the beginning of righteousness"; not imputed but inherent because it is the root of all virtues. Thus in the effect of justification, it is the principle and cause of new obedience; but in the act of justification, it can be nothing else than an instrument apprehending and applying to man that which justifies. Thus he is justified not by the merit of faith, but only by it as a means. instrument

XVI. Although justification is drawn away from works as to merit and a properly so-called efficiency, it does not follow that the same is ascribed to faith in the same manner. Nay, because it is taken away from works, it cannot for the same reason be ascribed to faith because it would thus justify as a work; nor could we be said to be justified without works. It therefore suffices (in order to save the opposition of the apostle) that faith should be substituted by him in the place of works because by faith we most surely obtain what the Jews in vain sought in works (although it acts here not meritoriously, but only instrumentally).

XVII. Faith is said to save us (Lk. 7:50), not by meriting something in order to justification, but only receptively and organically because it was the instrument receptive of that benefit. Nothing is more frequent than by a metalepsis to ascribe to an instrument the effect of the principal cause (as when "the gospel" is said "to be the power of God unto salvation," Rom. 1:16; the diligent hand is said to increase the house; the plough to enrich the farmer; the hand of the giver to relieve the poor; and the like). If elsewhere the greatness of the faith of the Canaanite woman to whom Christ granted the sought-for blessing is extolled (Mt. 15:28), its merit and efficiency is not on that account denoted. Believing, she was certainly healed because, faith being the medium, God bestowed this blessing upon her; but believing, he healed her, not on account of the fact that faith properly speaking effected or merited the healing.

XVIII. Therefore the true mode of the justification of faith is no other than instrumental. (1) Its proper act consists in the reception of Christ and his righteousness, as was said before. (2) It justifies in no other manner than by its being directed to the death and obedience of Christ (to wit, by apprehending and applying Christ to itself as a ransom [*antilytron*] given for us and a propitiation [*hilasmon*] for sin, 1 Jn. 2:2). (3) Faith in the Scriptures is described by "eating," "looking" and "touching," which have only an instrumental causality, not a proper efficiency (as the looking at a serpent did not cure per se, but relatively to the brazen serpent; nor does eating nourish except by food thrown into the mouth). (4) Justifying faith stands related in no other way to justification than as the faith of miracles stands related to the working of miracles; not effectively, but organically by apprehending the special promise given concerning them.

XIX. Not without reason, however, is this ascribed above all other things to the believer because it alone of all the virtues can subsist with grace as consisting in the mere reception and apprehension of an object placed beyond itself. Hence it is said to be "of faith, that it might be by grace" (Rom. 4:16), to wit, as man owes this entire blessing to God, he has no reason for glorying in himself. For if he were justified by works or inherent righteousness, he would seem to have something in which to glory; but when he is justified by faith (which gives nothing to God, but only receives) all glorying is excluded. This Toletus well explains when he gives the reason why the Scripture ascribes justification to faith alone: "Namely, because in faith it is more manifested that man is justified not by his own virtue, but by the merit of Christ. For as in beholding the serpent God placed healing in the desert, because the looking indicated more that the men were healed by the virtue of the serpent, not of any personal work or medicine; so faith shows that sinners are justified by the virtue and merit of Christ, in whom believing they are saved, not by any virtue and merit of their own. And it is the reason why justification is ascribed to faith especially by Paul, who strives to exclude from justification the works of the law, and human merit or efficacy, and to place it in the virtue and merit of Christ alone. Therefore he makes mention of faith in Christ. This neither repentance, nor love, nor hope have, for faith is carried more immediately and distinctly to it, by whose virtue we are justified" (*Commentarii et annotationes in epistolam . . . ad Romanos*, Annot. 17 [1602], p. 177 on Rom. 3:22).

XX. Although the sacraments are external means and instruments applying (on the part of God) the promise of grace and justification, this does not hinder faith from being called the internal instrument and means on the part of man for receiving this benefit offered in the word and sealed by the sacraments.

XXI. What justifies as an instrument does not forthwith justify as a work, although that instrument is a work. It is one thing for it to be a work and another to justify as a work. What justifies as a work ought to be the meritorious cause of justification, but what justifies as an instrument does not justify meritoriously, but only apprehensively and receptively; not by giving, but by receiving. Therefore the action of faith justifies us, but not as an action simply (as if it were our righteousness with God), but in relation to its object inasmuch as it receives Christ. As the extension of the beggar's hand is indeed the act of the beggar prescribed by the rich man, still as an act it does not enrich the beggar, but insofar as in this way he applies the gift of the rich man to himself and makes it his own.

XXII. Although faith is called "the work of God" (Jn. 6:29), it does not follow that it justifies as a work. Although it is enjoined by God (and in this sense is called the work of God and is due from man that he may obtain life), it is not on this account due as the meritorious cause of that life, but only as a means and instrument receptive of the righteousness of Christ, which is the true cause of life. And thus it is so called by Christ imitatively (*mimētikōs*) and by allusion to the Jewish sense, who sought life by the works of the law: "What must we do," said they, "that we may work the works of God?" To this legal question Jesus answers, not legally, but evangelically (yet in a legal style, taking the legal phrase from the expression of the Jews and applying it to his discourse): "This is the work of God that ye believe"—intimating that no further work was necessary to acquire salvation, but that faith was substituted in the place of all works for the reception of it (as if he said, work earnestly, only believe—this is work, this is labor). Evidently as to a sick man seeking by what medicine he is about to be healed, if the physician answers, this is the medicine which I prescribe to you; keep quiet and confide in me—he does not wish to intimate that that rest and confidence are any remedies to cure him, but he means only this—there is no need of medicine. Thus the Scripture often ascribes the names of things (to which men attribute falsely a great efficacy and value) to those things which are truly efficacious and valuable; as the gospel is called law because what the law sought, the gospel gives; what the Jews vainly sought in the law is obtained by the gospel. Thus regeneration is called circumcision (Phil. 3:3); believers are called sons of Abraham; love and piety are called fasting (Is. 58:6, 7); and faith is called a work.

XXIII. But we think it ought not to be anxiously inquired whether faith stands here in the relation of an instrument or also of a condition, as some think. Both may be ascribed to it, provided the condition is not understood as that in view of which God justifies man in the legal covenant. For in this sense, it cannot be called a condition, unless we agree with the Socinians and Remonstrants, who hold that faith or the act of believing is admitted by God by a gracious acceptation for a perfect righteousness (which we have just now refuted). Rather it is taken broadly for all that is required on our part to obtain this benefit—whether it has the relation of a cause properly so called or only instrumental. For thus as that condition has the relation (*schesin*) of an instrument, so the instrument has the relation of a condition on our part without which justification cannot be granted. Moreover concerning the manner in which faith concurs to justification and concerning its threefold act—dispository, justificatory and consolatory—see what was said in Topic XV, Question 12, Section 4.

Eighth Question

Does faith alone justify? We affirm against the Romanists.

I. This question also lies between us and the Romanists, who not only corrupt the true mode of the justification of faith by making the instrumental cause meritorious or at least dispositive, but by connecting with it the other virtues both as attendants and companions in this act. Hence arose the controversy concerning "faith alone justifying" (*sole Fide Justificante*), which as it is of no less importance than the preceding, so it is agitated with no less warmth of spirit.

Origin of the question.

II. This question is not of recent birth. Even from the very beginning of the Christian religion, this was asserted by the false apostles or Judaizing Christians. They did not with full front attack the faith as the Pharisees, but on the side by a deadly mixture associating the law with the gospel, Moses with Christ and faith with works in the matter of justification, so that man should be justified not by faith alone, but at the same time by works also. Against them the apostle disputes in his epistles to the Galatians, Philippians and Colossians. This is urged by the Romanists of this day, who hold that with faith, fear, hope, love, penitence, the purpose of a new life concurs to justification. "If anyone shall say that the wicked are justified by faith alone, so as to understand that nothing else is required to cooperate for the obtainment of the grace of justification and is necessary from no part, that he should be prepared and disposed by a motion of his own will, let him be accursed" (Council of Trent, Session 6, Canon 9, Schroeder, p. 43). This is more fully set forth in chapters 5 and 6, where the mode and necessity of preparation for justification are treated (ibid., pp. 31-33).

Statement of the question.

III. But that the state of the question may be the more easily understood, we must remark that a twofold trial can be entered into by God with man: either by the law (inasmuch as he is viewed as guilty of violating the law by sin and thus comes under the accusation and condemnation of the law); or by the gospel (inasmuch as he is accused by Satan of having violated the gospel covenant and so is supposed to be an unbeliever and impenitent or a hypocrite, who has not testified by works the faith he has professed with his mouth). Now to this twofold trial a twofold justification ought to answer; not in the Romish sense, but in a very different sense. The first is that by which man is absolved from the guilt of sin on account of the righteousness of Christ imputed to us and apprehended by faith; the other is that by which he is freed from the charge of unbelief and hypocrisy and declared to be a true believer and child of God; one who has fulfilled the gospel covenant (if not perfectly as to degree, still sincerely as to parts) and answered to the divine call by the exercise of faith and piety. The first is justification properly so called; the other is only a declaration of it. That is justification of cause *a priori;* this is justification of sign or of effect *a posteriori*, declaratively. In that, faith alone can have a place because it alone apprehends the righteousness of Christ, by whose merit we are freed from the condemnation of the law; in this, works also are required as the effects and signs of faith, by which its truth and sincerity are declared against the accusation of unbelief and hypocrisy. For as faith justifies a person, so works justify faith.

IV. The question does not concern justification *a posteriori* and declaratively in the fatherly and gospel trial—whether faith alone without works concurs to it (for we confess that works come in here with faith; yea, that works only are properly regarded because it is concerned with the justification of faith, which can be gathered from no other source more certainly than by works as its effects and indubitable proofs). Rather the question concerns justification *a priori*, which frees us from the legal trial, which is concerned with the justification of the wicked and the perfect righteousness, which can be opposed to the curse of the law and acquire for us a right to life—whether works come into consideration here with faith (as the Romanists hold) or whether faith alone (as we maintain).

V. (2) The question is not whether faith alone justifies to the exclusion either of the grace of God or the righteousness of Christ or the word and sacraments (by which the blessing of justification is presented and sealed to us on the part of God), which we maintain are necessarily required here; but only to the exclusion of every other virtue and habit on our part. Hence the Romanists have no reason for accusing us of confusion (*akatastasias*) in this argument as if we ascribed justification at one time to the grace of God, at another to the blood of Christ and then again to faith. For all these as they are mutually subordinated in a different class of cause, consist with each other in the highest degree.

VI. (3) The question is not whether solitary faith (i.e., separated from the other virtues) justifies (which we grant could not easily be the case, since it is not even true and living faith); but whether it "alone" (*sola*) concurs to the act of justification (which we assert); as the eye alone sees, but not when torn out of the body. Thus the particle "alone" (*sola*) does not determine the subject, but the predicate (i.e., "faith only does not justify" [*sola fides non justificat*], but "faith justifies alone" [*fides justificat sola*]). The coexistence of love in him who is justified is not denied; but its coefficiency or cooperation in justification is denied. (4) The question is not whether the faith "which justifies" (*quae justificat*) works by love (for otherwise it would not be living but dead); rather the question is whether faith "by which it justifies" (*qua justificat*) or in the act itself of justification, is to be considered under such a relation (*schesei*) (which we deny).

VII. Hence the question returns to this—Does faith justify, not as it is objectively the doctrine of salvation, but subjectively as it assents to that saving doctrine and applies it to itself; not as the promise to do something, but as we rest upon the promises in Christ as sufficient; alone (*sola*), not by reason of existence (i.e., solitary without faith and love), but in respect to function or efficiency; not by way of preparation with other virtues or of merit, but relatively after the manner of an instrument, apprehending the satisfaction of Christ and fiducially applying it. The Romanists deny; we assert.

Proof that faith alone justifies: (1) from Rom. 3:28.

VIII. First, man is justified by faith without works; therefore by faith alone. The reason of the consequence is manifest because there are not more modes of justifying than these two—by faith and by works. Thus, one being removed, the other must not only necessarily be left, but also left alone. Otherwise the enumeration would not be legitimate. Now why would the apostle so often and so expressly institute an antithesis between faith and works in this matter, if works could concur with faith in any way to the act of justification? Would he not in this particular have occasioned believers to err by removing works absolutely and simply from it, if they contribute anything towards it? Let the various passages in which exclusives are employed be carefully examined and the thing will be clearer than the midday sun: "We conclude that a man is justified by faith without the deeds of the law" (Rom. 3:28); "By grace are ye saved, through faith; and that not of yourselves: it is the gift of God: not of works" (Eph. 2:8); and more clearly, "knowing that a man is not justified by the works of the law, but by the faith [*ean mē dia pisteōs*] of Jesus Christ" (Gal. 2:16). Here it is certain that the particle (*eimē*) is adversative and exclusive (as often elsewhere, Mt. 12:4; 24:36; Mk. 13:32; Jn. 17:12; Rev. 9:4; 21:27) from the force of the immediate opposition of faith and works, which mutually displace each other. Nor can the Romanists themselves deny this. Estius says the most learned interpreters follow this opinion (which Salmeron, Justiniani and others confirm). To no purpose, therefore, do others pretend that *ean mē* is here exceptive, with the meaning that a man is not justified by works, except as faith in Christ approaches to works. This is the very thing which Paul opposes against the false apostles, who maintained that not works alone could justify a man, but faith mingled with works (so that justification might be ascribed partly to faith and partly to works, which Paul frequently asserts is inconsistent [*asystaton*]—as Salmeron and Estius acknowledge). No better is the explanation of Cornelius a

Lapide, who thinks that only the works of the law are excluded here, but not the works of hope, fear and love, which faith begets and produces, and which are under faith as daughters under a mother. We have seen above that all works are entirely excluded by Paul; not only the ceremonial, but also moral; not only those performed before grace, but also those performed from grace in the renewed.

2. Because it alone apprehends the righteousness of Christ.

IX. Second, by that alone are we justified by which the righteousness of Christ is applied to us, who satisfied the law for us. Now this is done by faith alone; nor does it belong to love or to hope. Not to hope, which does not apprehend, but expects the thing promised. Not to love, which is concerned with the fulfillment of a command, not with the apprehension of a promise.

3. Because Abraham was justified by faith alone.

X. Third, we also are justified in the same way in which Abraham, the father of believers, was justified because what was written concerning him pertains not only to him, but to us also (Rom. 4:24). And yet Abraham was justified by faith alone: "Abraham believed in the Lord; and he counted it to him for righteousness" (Gen. 15:6), not of debt, on account of works preceding faith or subsequent to it, but of grace so that he might not have wherein to glory. For if "Abraham were justified by works, he hath whereof to glory; but not before God" (Rom. 4:2), to wit, he has no matter for glorying (*kauchēma*) (which is to be drawn from the preceding verses). The argument is from the destruction of the consequent to the destruction of the antecedent. If Abraham was justified by works, he hath whereof to glory in himself as if he had contributed something of his own to which a reward was due in the judgment of God. And yet he hath not whereof he can glory in himself before God. Therefore he was not justified by works. Nor can it be said here that works preceding faith are excluded; not those done from faith on account of which he could have had glory before God, as he is called a friend of God. For this is to gainsay openly and to contradict Paul to his face, who expressly testifies that Abraham had not whereof to glory before God. For it is gratuitously and most falsely supposed that only works antecedent to faith are excluded. But he excludes all works entirely without distinction and indeed the works of Abraham not only as an unbeliever, but also a believer (since this was said of him when he was already a believer and renewed). Again, he excludes all debt (v. 4); therefore, he also excludes every work. Finally, if he had not wished to exclude works done from faith, he ought not to have opposed "one working" to "one believing" simply, but one working without faith to one working from faith (which, however, he nowhere does).

4. From Rom. 3:24, 25.

XI. Fourth, we are justified gratuitously and by the grace of God; therefore by faith alone because faith alone can consist with grace (Rom. 3:24, 25). Nor is Bellarmine to be listened to, who wishes the particle "freely" not to exclude merits absolutely, but proper merits (or those which are from us, not from God). For merits arising from prevenient grace (which are called by them merits of congruity) are not opposed to grace, unless we wish grace to contend with grace. Nor does it follow hence that a man who is justified freely is justified by faith alone because as gratuitous justification does not exclude faith (because it is by grace), so neither ought it to exclude repentance and love, which are from grace. For as we have already remarked, the particle "freely" excludes entirely all merits; for whatever is freely given, that is acquired by no merit. Nor can the grace which is undue subsist with merit, which makes the pay due: "If by grace, then it is no more of works: otherwise grace is no more grace. But if it be of works, then it is no more grace: otherwise work is no more work" (Rom. 11:6). Now although faith is not excluded in justification, it is not on that account excluded from grace (for thus works done from grace would not have to be excluded). But because it alone above other virtues has a power receptive of and applicatory to the righteousness of Christ (and so supposes man to be a sinner and destitute of all righteousness), it excludes all merit.

5. From Rom. 1:17.

XII. Fifth, "the righteousness of God is said to be revealed from faith to faith; as it is written, The just shall live by faith" (Rom. 1:17). Here the apostle intends to prove that the gospel is the power of God (i.e., the sole most efficacious instrument for salvation) in opposition to the weakness of the law (Rom. 8:3; Heb. 7:19) because in it is the righteousness of God—not formally and subjectively (which is in God), but effectively (which is given to us by God); not inherent, because it is said to be manifested without the law by faith (Rom. 3:21), and to be imputed without works (Rom. 4:6), but imputed (which is opposed to man's righteousness and his own works, Rom. 10:3, 4; Phil. 3:9). Thus the most perfect righteousness of Christ (which alone can bear the scrutiny of the divine trial as being divine and infinite, which is the cause and foundation of life and salvation) is revealed from faith to faith (i.e., is announced by the gospel, so as to be apprehended by faith alone because nothing besides faith can concur in the reception of it). Hence he does not say "from faith to works," but "from faith to faith" so that to faith alone this office is wholly ascribed. That Paul may prove this doctrine to be neither absurd nor new, he confirms it by the prophecy of Habakkuk where he says, "The just shall live by his faith" (2:4). Now although this prophecy refers also to a temporal blessing (viz., deliverance from the Babylonian captivity, which they would obtain by the intervention of faith in the divine promise; hence it is referred to by Paul in Heb. 10:38 to support believers in afflictions), still because the declaration of the prophet is general concerning faith in the promises of God, it is rightly applied specially to faith in Christ; and on this account the more—that the prophets and pious Jews regarded the promise of the Messiah as the foundation of all promises. Hence Paul (as best knowing the mind of the Holy Spirit) refers it (in Gal. 3:11 and in this place) to justification in order to teach that by faith alone man obtains the righteousness which brings eternal life to him. "The just shall live by faith," whether the "by faith" (*to ek pisteōs*) be referred to the just with this meaning—he who by faith is just—or to life, meaning—the just lives by faith. They amount to the same thing and each is true—that both he who by faith is just, obtains salvation; and again he who is just, obtains salvation by faith. In vain, therefore, is it said that Paul understands a living faith and that it alone is not such, but with works. Although living faith is never alone in the person who is justified, still it is alone in the very act of justification—to the production of which the other virtues can contribute nothing, faith alone claiming this privilege for itself (as we have said before). No better do others wish that life to be referred to the works by which faith proves itself alive. The design of the prophet is to teach that faith alone is the means of obtaining salvation, both temporal and spiritual. And Paul says that this righteousness by faith is manifested without the law; which cannot be said of the righteousness of works, but only of the righteousness of faith; which is said of the man believing, not of one working.

Sources of explanation.

XIII. It is one thing for love and works to be required in the person who is justified (which we grant); another in the act itself or causality of justification (which we deny). If works are required as concomitants of faith, they are not on that account determined to be causes of justification with faith or to do the very thing which faith does in this matter.

XIV. Although the whole force of justifying on the part of man is in faith as to the act of apprehension (so that other virtues contribute nothing to it with faith), it does not follow that faith can justify when they are absent as well as when they are present—yea, even when the opposite vices are present. It is one thing to justify without virtues (i.e., separated from them—which we deny); another for it to justify alone, but not separated from them. As it does not follow, the hand alone writes and the eye alone sees—therefore as much when torn from the head and the other members as in the body; the sole force of respiration is in the lungs—therefore the lungs can respire torn out from the liver and other viscera as well as when connected with them (which everyone sees to be absurd). There are hundreds of things of this kind which have a certain proper efficacy and effect, which still, when separated from their adjuncts, lose all their power. Natural potencies are connected as to existence, but disjoined as to operation. Light and heat in the sun are most closely connected together, but still the light alone illuminates, the heat alone warms. Therefore, although the other virtues do not justify with faith, still faith cannot justify in their absence, much less the opposite vices being present. For faith cannot be true except in connection with the virtues (which if they do not contribute to justification, still contribute to the existence and life of faith, which the presence of vices would destroy).

XV. It is one thing for the love of the sinner to be the cause of the remission of sins *a priori;* another to be the effect and proof *a posteriori.* The latter is affirmed in Lk. 7:47, not the former. We gather this: (1) from the scope of the parable, which is to demonstrate which of two debtors, whose debt the creditor had cancelled, ought to love the creditor most (to wit, in token of gratitude); (2) from the answer of Peter, "I suppose that he, to whom he forgave most," where love is placed as following, not as going before remission; (3) from the end, where a small remission is put as the cause of a small degree of love, "To whom little is forgiven, the same loveth little" (v. 47); (4) from v. 50, where salvation is ascribed to the faith, not to the love, of this woman, "Thy faith hath saved thee." Nor does the particle *hoti* stand in the way because (as is known) it is so often only ratiocinative, not causal—the cause of the consequent, not of the consequence, so as to intimate that thence is known and gathered that many sins were forgiven her because she loved much.

XVI. When John says, "We know that we have passed from death unto life, because we love the brethren" (1 Jn. 3:14), he teaches that love is a proof and sign of our justification from which we know that we have passed from death unto life. For he who is in love is in God (who is love) and he who is in God, cannot be in death. But he does not mean that love is the cause of that translation (which is elsewhere ascribed to faith, Jn. 5:24). Hence Lorinus and Gagnaeus on this passage well remark that "the causal article denotes the cause, not of the thing but of the knowledge." On this account even the more, that since God loved us first (not we God, 1 Jn. 4:10), the justification by which God loved us ought to precede our love.

XVII. Christ promises "the love of the Father" to those who love him (Jn. 14:23), not affectively and as to its beginning (as if the love of the Father then begins, since he loved us before, 1 Jn. 4:10), but effectively and as to continuance and increase because he will prove his love by distinguished blessings and console them by a new manifestation of himself. But this has nothing to do with justification because to love Christ and to keep his commands belongs to a man already constituted in grace and justified.

XVIII. The "fear of the Lord" (to wit, filial and reverential) is a consequence of justification, not a previous disposition to it. It is not called "the beginning of wisdom" (Ps. 111:10) as if it initially disposes to wisdom, but because it is its head and perfection, as it is said to be in Ecc. 12:13, which begins from it (Prov. 9:10) and ends in it. If it is said *apōtheisthai hamartēmata* (Sir. 1:21), this ought not to be understood of a positive expulsion (as if it introduced either meritoriously or dispositively remission of sins), but of a negative expulsion because he who fears God does not indulge in sins, nor give ear to their solicitations.

XIX. It is one thing for hope to concur to salvation; another for it to concur to justification. The former is asserted in Rom. 5:5 and 8:24 when hope is said not to make us ashamed; yea, also to save us. For the expectation of salvation is founded upon a hope so certain to be fulfilled in its own time, as if we already possessed salvation itself. But not the latter because the object of hope is not the remission of sins, but the fulfillment of the promised salvation.

XX. Although remission of sins is promised to repentance (because it ought to accompany faith and be in him who is justified as a certain condition requisite from him because God cannot pardon sin to an impenitent), it does not follow that it can be said to justify with faith because it contributes nothing (neither meritoriously, nor instrumentally) to the act of justification.

XXI. It is one thing for eternal life and the heavenly inheritance to be referred to works as meritorious or instrumental causes of our justification; another as effects of faith and qualities and dispositions requisite in the subject to be glorified. As it is one thing to seek "why" (*quare*) life is given to believers; another "upon what" (*quibus*) or "upon what qualities" (*qualibus*) it depends. The former we deny because our works of whatever kind cannot merit life, nor have they the relation of an instrument for apprehending it. But the latter we grant. Nor is anything different gathered from Mt. 25:34, 35, where works are not adduced by the Judge as "the foundations of the right" which they obtain to eternal life. The proper cause of that right is indicated in the preceding verses, when they are called "ye blessed of my Father," who ought "to inherit (*klēronomein*) the kingdom" (i.e., possess it by a title of inheritance). Rather they are adduced as arguments and testimonies indubitable *a posteriori*, from which the truth of their faith could be proved, and the equity of the sentence pronounced (as the particle *gar* is not causal [*aitiologikē*], but only ratiocinative).

XXII. Since Paul and James were inspired by the same Spirit, they cannot be said to oppose each other on the doctrine of justification, so that one should ascribe justification to faith alone and the other to works also. The reconciliation is not difficult, if the design of each be considered and the natures of faith and of justification (concerning which both treat) be attended. Paul disputes against the Pharisees, who urged the merits of works; James disputes against the Libertines and Epicureans, who, content with a profession of faith alone, denied not only the merits of works, but also their necessity. Against the former, Paul rightly urges faith alone for justification. Against the latter, James properly commends the necessity of works for the confirmation of justification. Paul speaks of a living and efficacious faith; James of an idle and dead faith which cannot be demonstrated by works (2:18); Paul of justification *a priori* and constitutively; James of the same *a posteriori* and declaratively; Paul properly constitutes the former in faith alone; James rightly places the latter in works, by which the reality of our faith and justification is declared not only before men, but also before God. Therefore, when faith is said "to have wrought with works in Abraham, and by works to have been made perfect" (v. 22), this ought to be understood in relation to the efficacy of faith, which exerted itself by works and by which also it was consummated and made perfect. It ought not to be understood essentially, for this it has by its own nature (but declaratively) because it is proven to be perfect and sincere; just as "the power of God" is said to be "made perfect in our weakness" (2 Cor. 12:9), i.e., known and declared to be perfect. See what else belongs to this point in our "Disputatio . . . De Concordia Pauli et Jacobi," *Opera* (1848), 4:731-52.

XXIII. It is one thing for works to be connected with faith in the person of the justified; another, however, in the matter of justification. The former we acknowledge and will afterwards prove, when we discuss the necessity of good works; but the latter we deny with Paul—nay, we maintain that they are wholly incompatible (*asystata*) with faith.

XXIV. Augustine says rightly, "Good works do not precede the one to be justified, but follow the one justified" (*Faith and Works* 14 [FC 27:247; PL 40.211]). A person is justified freely by faith without works (Rom. 3:24); yea, justification is of the wicked (Rom. 4:5; 5:6). No good works can be granted which precede his justification as causes, but only which follow as the effects and fruits springing from the faith of remission (Lk. 7:47; 1 Tim. 1:5). If calling (by which faith and holiness are infused) is prior to justification, it does not follow that holiness no less than faith is prior to it because holiness is indeed infused, but in its own order and by faith (Acts 15:9). Faith however concurs to justification before it does to sanctification. If remission is sometimes promised to repentance, this is indeed promised to it as a condition not antecedent or concomitant by reason of contrition, but only consequent as to new obedience.

Ninth Question: The Time of Justification

Was justification made from eternity or is it made in time? Is it an undivided act taking place at one and the same time?

I. The opinions of theologians about this question vary. Some maintain that it is an immanent act in God which was performed from eternity; others that it is transient, terminating in us and which takes place only in time and in this life. And there are some who hold that it is postponed to the last and decretory day, in which all must stand before the solemn and public tribunal of Christ to hear the sentence of absolution or of condemnation from his lips. Now although there is an agreement on both sides in the substance of the thing and a disagreement only in the mode of the thing, still it is of no little importance to the accurate knowledge of the subject to know what is the true opinion to be held here.

II. The first opinion is that of those who hold that justification preceded our birth and was made in eternity because they conceive it to be an immanent and internal act in God. However, as nothing new can happen to God in time, they think it was made in him from eternity and is ascribed to faith only as to cognizance and sense because it leads us into the knowledge of him and makes us certain of it.

Our justification is not made from eternity.

III. But although we do not deny that our justification was decreed even from eternity (as nothing takes place in time which was not constituted by him from eternity), still we do not think (speaking accurately) justification itself can be called eternal. The decree of justification is one thing; justification itself another—as the will to save and sanctify is one thing; salvation and sanctification itself another. The will or decree to justify certain persons is indeed eternal and precedes faith itself, but actual justification takes place in time and follows faith.

IV. Second, Paul expressly confirms this in the chain of salvation, enumerating in order the benefits flowing to the elect from the eternal love of God where he puts calling before justification as something antecedent: "Whom he called, them he justified" (Rom. 8:30). Nor have those various passages a different meaning in which we are said to be justified through and by faith, than that faith is a something prerequisite to justification. This could not be said if justification was done from eternity. For it is weak and foreign to the meaning of Paul to refer these things to the sense of justification only.

V. Third, the nature of the thing itself proves this. For since justification or remission of sins necessarily involves a deliverance from the obligation to punishment which sins deserved and no one can obtain it without faith and repentance, it is evident that such a justification could not have been made from eternity, but only in time—when the man actually believes and repents. Otherwise it would follow that he who is justified and consequently has passed from death unto life and become a child of God and an heir of eternal life, still remains in death and is a child of wrath. He who is not yet converted and lies in sin, remains in death (1 Jn. 3:14) and is of the Devil (1 Jn. 3:8) and in a state of condemnation (Gal. 5:21).

VI. Finally, since justification is a blessing of God, while a blessing cannot pass to us and be actually bestowed upon us, except in time, it is clear that it is not to be conceived of after the manner of an immanent and internal act in God, but after the manner of a transient act arising from God and passing over and terminating upon the creature (not that it may subjectively inhere in him, as the Romanists falsely hold because this pertains to sanctification; but that it may adhere to him and the creature has an objective relation to it, while the absolving sentence is intimated to him by the Holy Spirit). If grace is said to have been given to us in Christ before the world began by reason of "destination" (2 Tim. 1:9) because from eternity God decreed to give it to us in time, it does not follow that it can be said to have been really bestowed because the decree indeed causes us to obtain in time a right to life certainly and infallibly, but not that we can say we already obtained it actually. It causes that we should be justified, but not to be already justified.

It does not take place only at the last day.

VII. But as justification cannot be conceived to have taken place from eternity before the ages, so neither ought it to be thrown forward to the consummation of the world as others hold—as if God only then exercises properly the act of a Judge, both in the pardon of believers and in the condemnation of the wicked. For thus the declaration of justification is falsely confounded with justification itself. For although we are told the heavenly Judge will then sit on his throne of glory to exercise the last solemn act of judgment (as much in grace as in justice, in the sight of heaven and earth), this does not prevent that judgment from commencing in the present life. Nay, this must necessarily be supposed, since that final judgment is nothing else than a public and solemn manifestation of preceding judgments. And as Scripture everywhere sets before us the examples of God's judgments, public as well as private over the wicked and rebellious (such as the flood, the destruction of Sodom, the overthrow of the Egyptians and the like), to refer these to mere chastisements of God, tending towards the improvement and salvation of those upon whom they were sent, is to contradict the whole tenor of Scripture and rashly to confound the medicinal chastisements of believers (which are sent upon them for instruction [*paideian*] by God as a merciful Father) with the punishments of the wicked (which are inflicted by God as an angry Judge, to punish [*timōrian*] and avenge himself of their sins)—which has thus far been unheard-of in theological schools. So that he is evidently a stranger to the Scriptures who does not know that God is often set forth as justifying believers in this life; as is evident from the examples of Abraham (Gen. 15:6), of David (Ps. 32:1, 2, 5; Rom. 4:6, 7), of the sinful woman (Lk. 7:48), of the publican (Lk. 18:14) and of all believers (Rom. 5:1). Not to say now that that opinion is hurtful to the consolation of believers, which springs from no other source more certainly than from a sense of the grace of God and his justification. For how else could they have the confidence in which they glory and exult on account of their justification and enjoy unspeakable (*aneklalētō*) peace and joy?

But it takes place in this life in effectual calling.

VIII. This opinion then being dismissed, we embrace the middle one, which makes justification to take place in this life in the moment of effectual calling, by which the sinner is transferred from a state of sin to a state of grace and is united to Christ, his head, by faith. For hence it is that the righteousness of Christ is imputed to him by God, by whose merit apprehended by faith he is absolved from his sins and obtains a right to life. This absolving sentence, the Spirit pronounces in his heart when he says, "Be of good courage, son, thy sins are pardoned."

IX. Further, this justification can be regarded in different ways: (1) actively on the part of God intimating by the Spirit the absolving sentence in the heart of the believer and judicially from the throne of grace (Heb. 4:16), pronouncing it upon us; and passively on our part, inasmuch as we admit and receive that absolving sentence delivered in the court of conscience by the Holy Spirit with faith, joy and the protestation of gratitude.

X. Second, universally as to state, when we are first received into union with Christ and his righteousness is imputed to us by God and received by faith. For then in passing from a state of sin into a state of grace, the guilt of all preceding sins is actually taken away and a remedy given to us in the righteousness of Christ against future sins. And specially as to particular acts of sin into which we afterwards fall, which also need a particular absolution. As often as it is intimated to us in the court of conscience, so often the believer is by repentance turned again to God and by faith applies to himself Christ's righteousness. In this sense, we are commanded to seek remission of sins every day; not only with regard to the sense, but also with regard to the thing itself because sins cannot be forgiven unless committed (as we remarked before).

XI. Third, justification can be viewed in a twofold aspect (*schesei*): either as to the "eternal destination" in the decree, in which sense grace is said "to have been given to us in Christ before the world began" (2 Tim. 1:9) and God is said to have "predestinated us unto the adoption" (Eph. 1:5); or as to its execution in time which again can be regarded on the one hand as to obtainment, which was made by the death of Christ on the cross (referred to in Rom. 5:9, 10: "We were justified and reconciled to God by the blood of Christ"; and "Christ reconciled all things to God through the blood of the cross," Col. 1:20). Elsewhere Christ is said to "have been raised again for our justification" (Rom. 4:25) because as in him dead, we are dead, so in him raised and justified, we are justified (i.e., we have a sure and indubitable pledge and foundation of our justification because for no other cause was he justified by the Spirit [1 Tim. 3:16] except that we might be justified in him). Nor in a different sense does Paul say, "God was in Christ, reconciling the world unto himself, not imputing their trespasses unto them" (2 Cor. 5:19); to wit, inasmuch as in Christ dying, the Father had the foundation of reconciliation by which he was made more propitious to the world of the elect, collected as well from the Jews as from the Gentiles, so that he does not impute to them their sins (which he imputed to Christ), but by absolving them from their sins, he may justify them also in him. On the other hand it may be viewed as to application, which is made in the heart by an intimation of the absolving sentence (referred to in Mt. 9:2). Or it may be viewed in general as to the state of the believer when he is first called; or in particular as to the act when he obtains the pardon of particular sins; or as to the sense and certainty of it, arising in us from a reflex act of faith (called consolatory); or finally, as to its declaration, which should be made immediately after death (Heb. 9:27) and publicly on the last day (which is not so much justification, as a solemn declaration of the justification once made and an adjudication of the reward, in accordance with the preceding justification).

XII. Hence it is evident in what sense justification can be called an undivided act; not on our part and with respect to the sense of it (which is produced by various and repeated acts according as this sense can be interrupted; or increased or diminished, by reason of interfering sins); but on the part of God, not only by reason of his decree (by which our justification was decreed) and by reason of his merit (by which he obtained it), but also by reason of the application when the absolving sentence is intimated to us. This is done by a unique act, not by many successive acts, just as inherent righteousness is wont to be infused into us (although this act is often applied to particular everyday sins).

TENTH QUESTION
The unity, perfection and certainty of justification.

I. Unity, perfection and certainty are the three principal adjuncts of justification concerning which disputes exist. Of these we must speak briefly because we have elsewhere discussed them partially.

The unity or equality of justification among believers.

II. Unity can be regarded in two ways: either relative to believers among themselves; or absolutely with respect to him who is justified. In the former sense, it is said to be "one in species" or "equal in all believers" of all times and places because God justifies all believers in the same manner (viz., by his grace and the merit of Christ through faith). "Seeing it is one God," says the apostle, "which shall justify the circumcision by faith, and the uncircumcision through faith" (Rom. 3:30), i.e., who justifies the Jews as well as the Gentiles by faith. For since all are liable to sin and condemnation (v. 19), and destitute of the glory of God (v. 23), there is no other method of justification than by faith. The apostle proves this fully in the same place and confirms it by the examples of David and of Abraham (Rom. 4); as also of all the saints of the Old Testament mentioned in Heb. 11, who by faith are said to have pleased God (v. 6), to have obtained witness that they were righteous (v. 4) and to have become heirs of the righteousness which is by faith (v. 7). Nor either in the Old or New Testament can there be found any dissimilar example of a person justified in another way. Hence Peter says, "To him give all the prophets witness, that through his name whosoever believeth in him shall receive remission of sins" (Acts 10:43). Through the grace of Christ, we shall be saved, even as they (Acts 15:11). Christ is the same yesterday, today and forever (Heb. 13:8); he is the Way, and the Truth and the Life; no one can come to the Father except by him (Jn. 14:6).

III. For the objections brought forward here by the Socinians against the identity of the justification of the believers of the Old and New Testaments, see Topic XII, Question 5 concerning the unity of the covenant of grace (where they are discussed).

IV. Now although the same benefit as to substance was common to the believers of the Old Testament no less than to those of the New (as they had true remission of sins in and on account of Christ), still there was a multiple difference as to degree and sense. It is far more clearly revealed and more fully and efficaciously felt by us now; as was proved in the same place and in Question 12.

The numerical unity of the same in particular believers.

V. Second, the same justification is one numerically in individuals. It is not promoted successively after the manner of sanctification by repeated acts, but is finished in one judicial act and brings to the believer the remission of all sins. Hence the Romanists (from their fictitious hypothesis concerning physical justification by an infusion of righteousness) falsely make it twofold: the first, that by which a man from being unjust is made just by an infusion of righteousness; the second, that by which from being just he is made more just by the increase of righteousness. The foundation having been once overturned (as was done above), whatever is built upon it falls. Nor does the passage in Rev. 22:11 favor this error because (as we have already said), it does not treat of the infusion of righteousness, but either of the sense and declaration of righteousness once gained (which is retained by the exercise of righteousness) or of its special application to everyday sins.

VI. The distinction between active and passive justification points out indeed the truth of the terms "from which" and "to which" (viz., of God who justifies and of man who is justified), but does not change the degree or species. For by the same sentence by which God justifies us (while he intimates it to the conscience), we are also passively justified when it is received by us through faith.

VII. The blessing of justification and the right to it differ from the feeling and the knowledge of it. There is no cutting off or renewal of the former because it is a gift without repentance (*ametamelēton*). The latter, however, may be interrupted and restored according to the various increases and decreases of sanctification. And although that sense may be interrupted in grievous sins and be recovered by various and repeated acts, still the blessing of justification remains always in him the same.

VIII. Although our justification will be fully declared on the last day (our good works also being brought forward as the sign and proof of its truth, Mt. 25:34-40), still falsely would anyone maintain from this a twofold gospel justification—one from faith in this life (which is the first); the other (and second) from works on the day of judgment (as some hold, agreeing too much with Romanists on this point). The sentence to be pronounced by the supreme Judge will not be so much a new justification, as the solemn and public declaration of a sentence once passed and its execution by the assignment of the life promised with respect to an innocent person from the preceding justification. Thus it is nothing else than an adjudicatory sentence of the possession of the kingdom of heaven from the right given before through justification. And if works are then brought forward, they are not adduced as the foundation of a new justification to be obtained then, but as signs, marks and effects of our true faith and of our justification solely by it.

IX. It is one thing to apply justification often and to extend it to sins of daily occurrence (in which sense we are commanded to seek remission of sins every day); another to repeat and renew justification often. The former we grant, but not the latter. Nor is there need that a new justification should take place as often as the believer falls into a new sin. It is sufficient that the justification once made (which if not formally, virtually and generically contains the remission of all sins) be applied and extended specifically and determinatively to this or that sin by an intimation of the Holy Spirit and the apprehension of faith.

X. Although remission of sins ought to be applied often to daily sins, yet falsely would anyone thence gather that sins once discharged revive and return again by subsequent sins (as some of the Romanists hold), since it is an unchangeable (*ametamelēton*) gift of God. Nor does the parable of that ungrateful servant (who, after a greater amount had been yielded to him by his master, wished to deal cruelly with his fellow servant who owed him far less and who on that account was delivered to the tormentors till he should pay all that was due unto him [which is recorded in Mt. 18:23-35]) prove this. It pertains to nothing else than to show that the remission of sins proposed conditionally does not belong to him in whom the condition is lacking. The design of the parable (which is to be regarded here simply) is no other than to teach that the mercy of God is not exercised towards the unmerciful; nor are sins pardoned by God, except to those who forgive the offenses of others. To show this the more efficaciously, the master is opposed here to his servant, an immense sum to a minute and the highest clemency to extreme inhumanity.

2. Perfection.

XI. (2) Perfection belongs to justification, according to which it is so full and absolute intensively (both with respect to evils taken away and blessings acquired) that it is free as to itself from increase and decrease. Nor does it admit of more and less, although as to the apprehension and sense of it our faith advances so gradually as to have even its progressions and defects. If the faith by which we are justified is active and remitted, it does not follow that justification itself is equally intermittent because it does not justify by itself and properly, but only instrumentally and relatively; as the beholding of the brazen serpent did not cease equally to heal, although some looked at it more intently and strongly than others.

3. Certainty.

XII. (3) Its certainty is twofold: one of the object in itself by the immutability and perseverance by which God never recalls the pardon once given (on account of the immutability of his grace, justice and promise confirmed by an oath, Heb. 6:17, 18). For the gifts of God bestowed upon the elect and the calling according to his purpose (*kata prothesin*) are without repentance (*ametamelēta*, Rom. 11:29). Hence God never condemns and disinherits those whom he has once justified and made heirs. The other is the certainty of the subject, which refers to the sense of justification. Although it is possible from the nature of faith (yea, even necessary to bring peace and consolation to our souls), still it is not always in the same degree—but more perfect or imperfect according to the proportion of faith, so that there never was a believer (not even excepting Abraham [Gen. 17:17], or David [Ps. 42:5, 11]) who did not have to struggle with doubts concerning grace. How each of these certainties belong to justification has already been shown fully, when we discussed the perseverance and certainty of faith; cf. Topic XV, Questions 16 and 17.

SEVENTEENTH TOPIC

Sanctification and Good Works

First Question
What is sanctification and how is it distinguished from justification, yet inseparable from it?

I. As Christ was made to us of God righteousness and sanctification (1 Cor. 1:30)—not dividedly, but conjointly; not confusedly, but distinctly—so the benefit of sanctification immediately follows justification as inseparably connected with it, but yet really distinct from it.

Homonyms of sanctification.

II. The word "sanctification" is not used here broadly for any separation from common use and consecration to a sacred use, as it is often taken in Scripture as to sacred things (made either by institution, such as the sanctification of the seventh day; or by the relation of sign, such as the sanctification of the elements in the sacraments; or by manifestation, as God is said to be sanctified by men [1 Pet. 3:15]); or for federal sanctity by external calling, as Israel is said to be holiness unto the Lord (Jer. 2:3). Rather, it is used strictly for a real and internal renovation of man by which God delivers the man planted in Christ by faith and justified (by the ministry of the word and the efficacy of the Spirit) more and more from his native depravity and transforms him into his own image. Thus with separation from the world and sin and consecration to the service of God, it implies a renovation of his nature.

III. But because this real change of man is made by various degrees, either by efficacious calling (which carries with it the donation of faith and of repentance by faith and a translation from a state of sin to a state of grace); or by regeneration (which bespeaks a renovation of the corrupt nature); or by the infusion and practice of holiness, hence sanctification is now extended widely to the whole state of the believer and embraces also calling itself. In this sense, Paul, in his epistle to the Hebrews, often designates believers by "those who are sanctified" (*tous hagiazomenous*, Heb. 2:11; 10:14). It is also taken more strictly and properly for renovation after the image of God. This follows justification and is begun here in this life by regeneration and promoted by the exercise of holiness and of good works, until it shall be consummated in the other by glory. In this sense, it is now taken passively, inasmuch as it is wrought by God in us; then actively, inasmuch as it ought to be done by us, God performing this work in us and by us.

Sanctification does not consist in a change of morals alone.

IV. However, this does not consist in a correction of life and morals alone (as the Socinians maintain, who, denying original corruption and whatever taint and depravity is in us, say it has been contracted by frequent acts of sin and by a certain habit of sinning, and contend that regeneration and sanctification are nothing else than "a change of a bad habit and of life, and reformation according to the doctrine of Christ;" cf. Socinus, lib. de Bapt.+ and Smalcius, *De Christo vero et Naturali Dei Filio* 2 [1616], pp. 13-18). Rather it consists in a change and renovation of the nature itself (corrupted by original sin) by which depraved qualities and habits are cast out and good ones infused so that the man desists from evil acts and strives for good.

V. The reasons are: (1) the Scripture extends sanctification not only to acts, but to the renovation of the nature itself (1 Thess. 5:23). Paul prays for the Thessalonians "the sanctification of their whole spirit and soul and body"; by "spirit," he means the higher part of the soul and by "soul," the lower, which the Scripture elsewhere denotes by a renovation of the mind and will (Eph. 4:22-24) and of the sensual appetite (Tit. 3:5; Gal. 5:24).

VI. (2) It is expressed elsewhere by "the giving of a heart," "creation," "generation," "resurrection," "putting on the new man." These phrases demand not only the correction of life and of acts, but a renovation of the whole nature. (3) This sanctification ought to be common to infants no less than to adults, so that they can enter into the kingdom of God (in whom however a change of acts does not take place). (4) As the corruption of sin infects the whole nature (not only as to acts, but also as to habits), so sanctification ought to include a reformation of the whole nature, habitual as well as actual.

VII. An habitual change in qualities (by which we are made new creatures) differs from an actual change in life and morals (by which we are demonstrated to be such). God makes us first new creatures by regeneration; then we show that we are regenerated by our new obedience (as these acts are distinguished in Eph. 2:10; Ezk. 36:26; Jer. 32:39). In the former manner, we are said to be new creatures *a priori;* in the latter *a posteriori.*

VIII. The actual laying aside of vices and the correction of life and morals follow regeneration, as its proper effects (Gal. 5:22, 23; Col. 3:5). But regeneration itself is not properly such a deposition, but its cause (which consists in a renovation of the corrupt nature and restoration to the image of God).

Sanctification is distinguished from justification.

IX. However, this sanctification must be carefully distinguished from justification because the conforming of them gave rise to the principal errors of the Romanists on the doctrine of justification, as we have already seen. For although they agree in their author (God), in the meritorious cause (to wit, the righteousness of Christ, which purchased for us both these benefits, when he came with water and blood, 1 Jn. 5:6), in the general design (God's glory and our salvation), in the instrumental cause (to wit, faith by the reception of the one and by the production of the other), it is certain that in many respects they differ, as Scripture has frequently distinguished these benefits (1 Cor. 1:30; 6:11; Tit. 3:5; Rev. 22:11). Nor could Paul so often have denied that we are justified by works if justification is the same as sanctification; nor could it with any show of justice have been objected to him that his doctrine relaxed the desire for holiness, if "to justify" is the same as "to sanctify."

X. Therefore, they differ in many ways: (1) as to their object. Justification is concerned with the guilt of sin; sanctification with its pollution. (2) As to their form. The former consists in the judicial and forensic act of remission of sin and imputation of righteousness; the latter in the physical and moral act of the infusion of righteousness and internal renovation. (3) As to the recipient subject. To the former, man holds himself objectively on the part of God acquitting; to the latter, on the part of God renewing subjectively. (4) As to degrees. Justification is given in this life fully because we are plainly reconciled to God, so that being justified by faith we have peace with God (nor is there any condemnation to believers); but sanctification is indeed begun in this life, but is perfected only in the other. That takes place at once; this, however, by degrees and successively. (5) As to order. That is prior at least in the order of nature because God sanctifies those only who are reconciled and justified by faith; this, however, follows.

XI. Although Paul does not make express mention of sanctification in the chain of salvation, it does not follow that it is included in the word justification, as if it were identical with it. It is far more fitly included either under calling (which is the beginning of sanctification) or, what we think is truer, under glorification (which is its consummation and complement—as sanctification is the beginning of glory). Hence it is frequently designated by the word "glory" (Rom. 3:23; 2 Cor. 3:18).

XII. Although by sanctification we are made righteous habitually, still we are not made righteous imputatively or rather justified; nor can the etymology prove this, as we have seen before.

XIII. If sanctification purges us from all sin, this must be understood only as to the pollution inhering in us and not as to the guilt adhering before God and making us liable to his judgment.

XIV. Although sanctification depends upon the same cause as justification (to wit, the blood and death of Christ), they ought not be the same on that account. The cause does not produce it in the same manner. For it is related materially to justification, inasmuch as it is the material and foundation of our justification drawing that immediately after itself; but with respect to sanctification, only efficiently and mediately, inasmuch as it is the external impelling cause by which God is moved to give unto us the Holy Spirit, the author of sanctification. Thus in baptism each benefit is sealed to us, but each according to its own fashion (*schesin*). There we put on Christ as righteousness and sanctification (Gal. 3:27): righteousness, which takes away the guilt of sin and covers; sanctification, which every day removes and washes away that pollution. The blood of Christ (of which the water is the symbol) has a twofold power—to purge the guilt before God (inasmuch as it is a ransom [*lytron*] or price of redemption) and to purge the pollution in us (inasmuch as it is a bath or laver [*loutron*] of sanctification by the Spirit).

Sanctification is not to be separated from justification.

XV. Although we think that these two benefits should be distinguished and never confounded, still they are so connected from the order of God and the nature of the thing that they should never be torn asunder. This is clearly evident even from this—that they are often set forth in one and the same word as when they are designated by the words "cleansing" and "purging" and "taking away," not only in different places, but also in the same context (as Jn. 1:29, when "the Lamb of God" is said "to take away the sin of the world," i.e., both by taking away its guilt and punishment by the merit of his blood and by taking away its pollution and taint by the efficacy of the Spirit; and in Rev. 1:5, Christ is said "to wash us from our sins," both as to justification and as to sanctification; in which sense "the robes of believers" are said "to have been made white in the blood of Christ" [Rev. 7:14] because having been shed upon the cross it produced remission of sins, which was accomplished under the law by the shedding of blood, and because being sprinkled upon the heart it purges the conscience from the dead works of sin).

The truth of this connection proved: (1) on the part of God.

XVI. Now the necessity and truth of this connection is gathered on the part of God justifying, of Christ redeeming, of the Spirit regenerating and of justification and the faith by which we are justified. (1) God joined these two benefits in the covenant of grace, since he promises that he will not remember our sins and that he will write his law in our hearts (Jer. 31:33, 34). Nor does the nature of God suffer this to be done otherwise. For since by justification we have a right to life (nor can anyone be admitted to communion with God without sanctification), it is necessary that he whom God justifies is also sanctified by him so as to be made fit for the possession of glory. Nay, he does not take away guilt by justification except to renew his own image in us by sanctification because holiness is the end of the covenant and of all its blessings (Lk. 1:68-75; Eph. 1:4).

2. On the part of Christ.

XVII. (2) Christ sustains a twofold relation (*schesin*)—that of a surety and of a head. As a surety, he justifies us and as a head, he sanctifies us. By reason of the former, his death is the meritorious cause of justification; by reason of the latter, it is the exemplary cause of sanctification (Rom. 6:4, 5; 8:29; 1 Pet. 2:21). Therefore, as Christ is given to no one for a surety to whom he is not given for a head, so no one is justified by the merit of the surety (Christ) who is not sanctified by the efficacy of Christ (the head) after his image. It is not sufficient that Christ died and lives for us, unless he also mortifies the old man in us after the likeness of his own death and vivifies the new man, so that what was done in the head is done in the members. Besides from the death (by which we are justified), not only is the Spirit acquired, but also the principal motives to sanctification are derived. These are: (a) the foulness of sin, which can be washed away by nothing else than the blood of Christ; (b) God's hatred of sin, who spared not even his own son to avenge it; (c) the unspeakable love of Christ, whose love ought so to constrain us that we should no longer live to ourselves but to him who died for us (2 Cor. 5:14, 15); (d) the right which Christ acquired in us by dying (Rom. 14:8, 9; 1 Cor. 6:20), which demands that we should glorify him with our body and spirit. Finally, this is the principal end of Christ's death—that being dead to sin we should live unto righteousness (1 Pet. 2:24; Tit. 2:14).

3. On the part of the Spirit.

XVIII. (3) The Spirit, who is given to us, has a twofold name: the "Spirit of adoption" who seals our justification; and the "Spirit of sanctification" who begins and carries it forward. Hence his operation is usually twofold: the first by consolation, when he testifies that we are the sons of God (Rom. 8:16); the other by sanctification, when he makes us cry out, Abba, Father (v. 15). On the part of God, he descends into us and confirms his promises, while on our part he makes us ascend to God to the execution of our duty.

4. On the part of faith

XIX. The very faith by which we are justified demands this. For as it is the instrument of justification by receiving the righteousness of Christ, so it is the root and principle of sanctification, while it purges the heart and works through love (Gal. 5:6). Justification itself (which brings the remission of sins) does not carry with it the permission or license to sin (as the Epicureans hold), but ought to enkindle the desire of piety and the practice of holiness. With God, it is a propitiation that he may be feared (Ps. 130:4); speaks peace to his people that they may not turn again to folly (Ps. 85:8). Thus justification stands related to sanctification as the means to the end. And to this tends the whole economy of grace, which for no other reason has dawned upon us, unless "that, denying ungodliness and worldly lusts, we should live soberly, righteously, and godly" (Tit. 2:12).

5. On the part of the sacraments.

XX. The sacraments prove the same thing, being administered to seal the benefits of Christ. Baptism, which is administered for the "remission of sins" (Acts 2:38), is also a "laver of regeneration" (Tit. 3:5). And if in the supper is exhibited to us the body of Christ broken and his blood poured out for the remission of sins (Mt. 26:28), in the same place the body and blood are exhibited as the aliment of spiritual life, which consists in sanctification (1 Cor. 10:16).

XXI. Although the justified believer falls into various sins, often so grievous that the progress of his sanctification is for a long time interrupted (nay, itself not a little weakened), it does not follow that sanctification itself is torn away from justification. For if actual sanctification is taken away, still habitual sanctification is not; nor is the seed of God ever removed, but remains always in us (1 Jn. 3:9), as we have already proved concerning the perseverance of faith. He who sins does not act in a holy manner; but still he who does not exercise the act of holiness can have the habit of holiness remaining in himself, although weakened and infirm.

XXII. It is one thing to be purged from old sins sacramentally and conditionally; another really and absolutely. They (of whom Peter speaks, 2 Pet. 1:9) were purged from sin in the former sense, but not in the latter, on account of a defect of the required condition (viz., faith). Thus they could be called neither justified nor truly sanctified. See more on this subject in a later question concerning the necessity of good works.

SECOND QUESTION: THE PERFECTION OF SANCTIFICATION

Is sanctification so perfect in this life that believers can fulfill the law absolutely? We deny against the Romanists and Socinians.

I. Among the questions concerning sanctification agitated between the orthodox and the ancient and modern Pelagians, are two principal ones: the first referring to its origin, the other to its perfection. However, because we have fully treated of the former when we disputed concerning effectual calling (dismissing it), we proceed to the other, which was formerly and is now agitated with great warmth of feeling.

The origin of the question.

II. It is well known that this is enumerated also among the many heads of the Pelagian hydra—that he contended that the believer can in this life live without sin and so can perfectly fulfill the law and be constituted in a state of sinlessness. Hence he is often called "the preacher of sinlessness" by

Jerome (*Against the Pelagians* 1.25 [NPNF2, 6:461; PL 23.542]). Augustine thus describes this error: "The Pelagians go so far as to say that the life of the righteous in this world has no sin, and from these in this mortal existence the church of Christ is made up, so as to be wholly without wrinkle and without blemish, as if it was not the church of Christ, which throughout the world cries out to the Lord, Forgive us our debts" (*De Haeresibus* 88 [PL 42.48]). To this error the fathers strongly opposed themselves. Among others were Jerome (Letters 133, "To Ctesiphon" [NPNF2, 6:272-80]; and in three books against the Pelagians, *Against the Pelagians* [NPNF2, 6:448-83]); and Augustine (*On the Forgiveness of Sins and Baptism* 2 [NPNF1, 5:44-68], Letter 89, "To Festus" [FC 18:34-40], CG 14.9 [FC 14:366-73], *On Man's Perfection in Righteousness* [NPNF1, 5:159-76], *Enchiridion* 17 [64] [FC 2:423] and elsewhere in many passages).

III. The same question was renewed in this century by the Neopelagians, Romanists, Socinians and Anabaptists, who, to pave the way for the merits of works, maintained that the law can be perfectly fulfilled by the renewed. Hence among the Romanists themselves, a fierce contest about this article sprang up between the Jansenists and Jesuits. Thus of the five famous propositions of Jansen (condemned by Innocent X), this was also: "Some commands of God are impossible to righteous persons, willing and striving according to the present strength which they have; grace also is wanting to them, by which they would become possible" (cf. "Errores Cornelii Iansenii de gratia," in H. Denzinger, *Enchiridion Symbolorum* 1092/2001 [1963], p. 445). Now although in distinct questions we might treat of the imperfection of sanctification and the impossibility of fulfilling the law, yet because they belong to the same and are proved by the same arguments, they are here joined together by us.

Statement of the question.

IV. That the statement of the question may be rightly ascertained, we remark: (1) that the question does not concern (a) the perfection of sincerity, which consists in this—that a person may serve God with an enlightened and whole heart. For this we think ought to be found in true believers, as it is ascribed to Job when he is said to be "perfect and upright, and one that feared God, and eschewed evil" (Job 1:1). Hezekiah also claims it for himself (Is. 38:3). (b) Nor does the question concern the perfection of parts, as much subjective with respect to the whole man, who ought to be sanctified wholly, in body as well as in soul and spirit (1 Thess. 5:23); as objective, with respect to the whole law as to all its commands. For this also we believe is required of the believer, as it is predicated of Zacharias and Elizabeth (Lk. 1:6). (c) Nor does the question concern comparative perfection, which is ascribed to some believers more advanced than others. In this sense, the believers of the New Testament are called "perfect" (*teleioi*, 1 Cor. 2:6) with respect to the believers of the Old, who are called "children" (*nēpioi*, Gal. 4:1); also with respect to Christian believers who made greater progress than others in faith and piety and who have their senses exercised to distinguish good and evil above others, who still have need of milk and who are engaged with the rudiments of religion (spoken of in Phil. 3:15; Heb. 5:13). (d) Nor does the question concern evangelical perfection, which is with the covering of grace and with paternal forbearance (*epieikeia*) when all things are counted as done, when what is not done is pardoned (viz., covered by the righteousness of Christ, in whom we are said to be perfect, Col. 2:10). For we recognize all these species of perfections. But the question concerns legal perfection—absolute in all parts, so that nothing is wanting to it, either as to degree or as to parts, intensively and extensively.

V. (2) It is not inquired concerning an absolute and total impossibility, according to which it is said that a certain thing cannot be done, either because it involves a contradiction (since it is repugnant to the nature of God) or because it suits man in no state. For in this sense, we do not say that the commands of God are impossible to man, because they were both possible to man in a state of nature and would be possible to man renewed in the state of grace (if God should will to give such and so great a measure of grace as to take away all the corruption of his heart); and they will be possible in glory. But it is inquired concerning a relative impossibility in relation to our state and the order of God, who, although he could, still did not will to give us here a perfection of sanctification, for the most weighty reasons; both that thus the state of the way and of our native country (the church militant and triumphant) might be distinguished and that in this way the desire of holiness may be the more strongly excited and we may know that we are not to be idle in the work of sanctification (since something is always to be done, nor are there ever wanting enemies against whom we must fight).

VI. (3) The question is not whether the works of the righteous are truly good (which our opponents press here extraneously), for this belongs to another question concerning the truth of good works (where it will be shown in what sense the works of believers are truly good and are still called sins). Rather the question is Are they so perfect as to answer to the law; and do they have nothing in them which it can reprehend?

VII. The question returns to this—Can the renewed believer so carry on his own sanctification as to attain perfection (not only as to parts, but also as to degrees); and can he fulfill the law (not only mildly [*epieikōs*] and evangelically, but also strictly [*akribōs*] and legally) and so copiously satisfy the divine law as to live not only without crime, but also without sin; and the law have nothing which it can accuse and condemn in him, if God should enter into judgment with him? The opponents affirm; we deny.

VIII. It is not to be concealed, however, that the Romanists speak on this subject confusedly; nor do they exhibit their meaning with sufficient plainness. Bellarmine indeed sets forth the state of the question sophistically when he says the question is "whether men, justified and by the assistance of God's grace, can so fulfill the law that their works are not only not to be called sins, but also merit that they should be called truly and properly righteous persons" ("De Justificatione," 4.10 *Opera* [1858], 4:585). He slanderously charges our theologians with teaching "that the divine law is wholly impossible even to a just man" (ibid.) and thence "infer that there is in us no true actual righteousness, but all the works of the just are mortal sins from their very nature" (ibid.). For it is far different to say that the law is clearly impossible to man (which denotes every kind of impossibility) from saying that the believer cannot fulfill the law fully (which intimates a relative impossibility). We do not say that the law is absolutely impossible to believers, but only as to the strictness (*akribeian*) of the law. It is one thing that there is in us no actual righteousness and that our good works are from their own nature mortal sins (which they falsely charge upon us); another that this righteousness is not perfect and that good works (although they are sins accidentally on account of the remains of the flesh inhering in us) are still in themselves truly good (which we hold).

good works are not mortal sins
L truly good

IX. The Council of Trent seeks a shelter in general words when it says, "If anyone should say the commands of God are impossible to be observed by the justified man, constituted under grace, let him be accursed" (Session 6, Canon 18, Schroeder, p. 44). And lest someone might understand an absolutely perfect observance of them, Canon 23 pronounces "an anathema upon those who teach that a person once justified can in his whole life avoid even venial sins, except by the special privilege from God" (Schroeder, p. 45). Here it seems indeed to recognize that a perfection of all kinds cannot be afforded the believer except by a special privilege (which Stapleton, Andradius, Tapper and others do not deny). But what they seem (pressed by the force of truth) to give with one hand, with the other they at once take away when they cease not to urge the absolute possibility of the law and by various arguments laboriously strive to prove it, as Bellarmine ("De Justificatione," 4.10, 11ff. *Opera* [1858], 4:585ff.). Nor can they think and speak otherwise according to their hypothesis concerning justification and the merit of works (works of supererogation and gospel counsels), which necessarily suppose a perfect and absolute observance of the law. For how could a person be justified by works otherwise or do more than and above what the law demands? And thus it must be said they even utter absurdities (*asystata*) when they thus speak or raise a smoke before us and do not fully explain to us their meaning. However we prove the imperfection of our sanctification and the impossibility of fulfilling the law.

The imperfection of sanctification and the impossibility of fulfilling the law proved: (1) from the remains of sin.

X. First, from the remains of sin. Where sin dwells, there perfect sanctification cannot be, nor a fulfilling of the law. And yet in believers, whoever they may be, sin always dwells: "If we say that we have no sin, we deceive ourselves, and the truth is not in us" (1 Jn. 1:8); "In many things we offend all" (Jam. 3:2); "There is no man that sinneth not" (1 K. 8:46); "Who can say, I have made my heart clean, I am pure from my sin?" (Prov. 20:9). To say here with Bellarmine, "These sins are only venial, beyond, but not contrary to the law" ("De Justificatione," 4.14 *Opera* [1858], 4:591), is to suppose what is to be decided (*to krinomenon*) (which we have refuted in the proper place, when we proved that all sin is mortal and so against the law, as true lawlessness [*anomian*]; and that none is venial which is beyond it). Nor does he escape better, who shall have said with the same (ibid., 4.12, pp. 587-88) that these are different questions: Can the commands be kept? and Can man live without sin? To the former, Augustine always answered affirmatively, but to the latter he answered negatively. Two questions, which amount to the same thing, are falsely distinguished. For no one can obey the commands, except by living without sin; nor can anyone live without sin, unless he keeps the commandments. Nor do we find Augustine, when answering Pelagians, distinguishing these two questions. He does indeed distinguish between the two: "Has any of the renewed been without guilt?" (to which he answers affirmatively); and "Has anyone of them been without sin?" (to which he answers negatively; cf. *On the Grace of Christ* 1.53 [48] (NPNF1, 5:235). But when treating of the fulfilling of the law, as he maintains that no one is without sin, so he holds that no one can in this life fulfill the law; cf. *On Man's Perfection in Righteousness* (NPNF1, 5:159-76).

2. From the struggle between the flesh and the Spirit.

XI. Second, this very thing is confirmed by the "struggle between the flesh and the Spirit" which perpetually occurs in believers in this mortal life, and forces out of them so many groans and lamentations. For since the flesh is opposed to the law of God (neither is subject to it, nor indeed can it be, Rom. 8:7), it is evident that as long as the flesh remains in us (it remains, however, as long as we are here), neither is our sanctification perfect, nor can the law be fulfilled by us. Paul graphically describes this struggle in two places: "The flesh lusteth against the Spirit, and the Spirit against the flesh: and these are contrary the one to the other: so that ye cannot do these things that ye would" (Gal. 5:17); and "I am carnal, sold under sin" (Rom. 7:14); "The good that I would I do not: but the evil which I would not, that I do" (v. 19); "But I see another law in my members, warring against the law of my mind, and bringing me into captivity to the law of sin which is in my members" (v. 23). Hence he breaks forth into this sad complaint: "O wretched man that I am! Who shall deliver me from the body of this death?" (v. 24). These indeed are not the expressions of a man perfectly fulfilling the law and having an excess of merit, but of one groaning under the burden of sin, and panting for deliverance. And since lust is a sin forbidden by the law (as the apostle testifies in the same place), how can he fulfill the law who is always exposed to the motions of lust and who always feels it struggling and warring in his members against the Spirit?

XII. I know that Socinus replies here that Rom. 7 does not treat of Paul as renewed, but as constituted under the law. For in his little book concerning the meaning of this chapter, he speaks thus: "In my judgment we must avoid as the pestilence itself, believing that this passage (Chap. 7, Epistle to the Romans), pertains to Paul himself now renewed; for I affirm that in this passage Paul describes a man destitute of the grace of Christ, and relying on the law itself" (cf. "De loco Pauli . . . in Epistola ad Rom. cap. septimo," *Opera omnia* [1656], 1:112). Thus the contest between the appetite and the mind and intellect is described because he holds the will to be the middle one, which in this contest sometimes helps the appetite, sometimes the mind. Arminius agrees with him. There are also some of our theologians who incline to this opinion. On this account, they invent a certain new and third state between the state of nature (in which man is as yet unrenewed) and the state of grace (in which he is now renewed)—viz., a state under the law and the spirit of bondage in which the man is not as yet renewed, but neither wholly unregenerated. Rather he is imbued with some knowledge of the law and possessed of the spirit of bondage, in which he experiences these alternating changes, in which he sometimes seems to approach to the good from his knowledge of the law and, by the impulse of the spirit of bondage, to recede from it and so be driven to sin from his incapability of resisting corrupt appetites. But whatever both maintain, we cannot recede from the opinion commonly received among the orthodox, which is that Paul speaks of himself as renewed and that this severe struggle (often occurring between the old and new man, the flesh and spirit) is here described by him.

XIII. There are various reasons which prove it: (1) from the notation of the time. Paul does not speak in a past tense (as before in v. 9), but in a present tense—"I am carnal" (v. 14); "I do not the good I would, I delight in the law of God" (v.

19, 22*). Now when he wrote this, he was no more under the law, but under grace. (2) He treats of him to whom the willing of good and the nilling of evil (or a hatred of sin) belongs: "For what I would, that do I not; but what I hate, that do I" (v. 15) and "For to will is present with me; but how to perform that which is good I find not" (v. 18). Now this belongs only to the renewed, in whom God works both "to will and to do" (*to thelein kai to energein*) although they are not always allowed to carry out what they wish (for us, to others who can think nothing good, how can they be said to will it?). (3) He treats of him who consents to the law of God in the inner man and who delights in it (v. 22), from which delight arises service—"With the mind I serve God" (v. 25). But who would say that any other than a believer delights in the law of God and according to it serves God; or that the inner man is any other than the new man? He is frequently designated as such (Eph. 3:16; 2 Cor. 4:16; 1 Pet. 3:4). (4) He speaks of him in whom are distinguished two principles: one according to which he does the evil which he would not; the other according to which he does not perpetrate evil, but sin dwelling in him perpetrates it, and according to which he serves God (vv. 17-19). Now it is evident that this can be said only of the believer, who has within him the old man and the new man, the flesh and the Spirit. (5) He treats of him who groans on account of his misery and who seeks and wishes for deliverance and congratulates himself and gives thanks when he has obtained it (vv. 24, 25)—which refer to no one except the renewed person. (6) A middle state between the regenerate and unregenerate is a pure invention, as if there were a middle ground between the child of God and the child of the Devil, between a living and a dead man. Nor can this be referred to the state under the law because those who lived under it were either reprobates (who were under it as a covenant and so under its curse, Gal. 3:10); or renewed (who were under it as a dispensation, in which although more sparingly and obscurely, still the grace of the regenerating Holy Spirit was granted to them).

XIV. Paul ascribes nothing here to himself which cannot be found in the renewed. Not his saying that "he is carnal and sold under sin" (v. 14) because this is not to be understood absolutely, but comparatively and relatively; as Paul calls the Corinthians "carnal, and not spiritual" (1 Cor. 3:1) because they still exhibited in their actions many remains of the flesh and the old man. Not a universal sale and captivity as to state, as if he were still under the dominion of sin, because thus he would neither delight in the law of God according to the inner man, nor could he be said to serve God with his mind; rather a particular captivity and selling as to certain acts, in which sense the flesh is said to lust against the Spirit, so that we do not what we would (Gal. 5:17). Nor when he says "sin dwells in him," because it is one thing to dwell, another to reign. That denotes the presence of sin as it exists in the believer even unto the end, but this denotes its tyranny and dominion, which is overcome by the Spirit of Christ. Not that "he wishes for deliverance" from "the body of death," since the believer is freed from the law of sin and death. For an inchoate deliverance and a perfect deliverance differ: one is from the curse of the law and exposure to death; the other from the dominion of sin and mortality (which attends it). The believer has already obtained the first, but he as yet expects and wishes for the other.

XV. Although a struggle between the appetite and reason often occurs in the unregenerate, such as in the Medea of the poet, who said, "I see the good, approve it too, and yet the wrong pursue" (Ovid, *Metamorphosis* 7.20-21 [Loeb, 1:342-43]), still there is a great difference between this and the struggle of the flesh and the Spirit of the renewed (of which Paul speaks). (1) As to their causes, the struggle of the unrenewed arises from the dictation of the conscience (or the strictures of the natural light, which have their seat principally in the intellect) and from the fear of punishment; the struggle of believers arises from the new and supernatural quality or principle of the Holy Spirit, which is spontaneously borne along to those things which are good; not only from a slavish dread of punishment, but from a filial reverence of God. (2) As to their subject, the light of the unregenerate is merely theoretical, remaining in the intellect and not reaching to the heart. But the light of grace (granted to the renewed) not only inheres in the governing (*tō hēgemonikō*) or superior part of the soul, but passes also to the concupiscible (*to epithymētikon*) or its lower part. (3) As to their objects, the contest of the unregenerate is occupied only about the more gross sins, which all abominate by the natural light; while the contest of believers is occupied with those also which (in the external court of men) are neither subjected to punishment, nor to any rebuke. (4) As to their effects, the former struggle can consist with the daily practice of sin and if it sometimes causes that good be done or evil avoided, still it can never arise to this—that it should be well done—and so represses rather than destroys sin; hence at last the reason with its light yields and is conquered. But in the struggle of believers, the flesh is bruised and mortified to such a degree that even if it cannot be eradicated absolutely and as yet exerts itself in many acts, still it cannot prevail, but is at length overcome by the Spirit, who makes believers more than conquerors (*hypernikan*).

3. From Acts 15:10.

XVI. Third, the impossibility of fulfilling the law is proved from Acts 15:10, where it is called an unbearable (*abastakton*) yoke: "Why tempt ye God, to put a yoke upon the neck of the disciples, which neither our fathers nor we were able to bear?" For if it could not be borne, how could it be fulfilled by anyone? In vain does Bellarmine reply that it refers to the ceremonial and not to the moral law. (1) If this could be said of the ceremonial, still more strongly could it be said of the moral law. (2) The ceremonial law of itself could not be called an unbearable (*abastakton*) yoke; yet this is properly referred to the moral, which could never be fulfilled by anyone and which places under a curse those who live under it. (3) The question which was moved respected the whole law; not only the ceremonial, but also the moral (Gal. 5:3). Nor is it an objection that the apostolic decree seems to treat only of the ceremonial law. The question arose indeed on the occasion of the ceremonial law, but Peter seeing that it extended further, speaks of the whole law, showing its impossibility because it was a yoke, which neither they nor their fathers were able to bear.

XVII. It is confirmed by this—that the law demands an obedience of all kinds, as much with regard to the internal affections as with regard to the external effects; not only as to parts, but also as to degree, that we may love God with our whole mind, heart and strength; that the true method of loving him should be without measure (as Bernard expresses it). Since it is evident that this cannot be fulfilled by any mortal (as everyone is convinced), it follows that the law in this sense is impossible to man. Nor can it be excepted that only a sincere and unfeigned love is meant; although a sincere love will be accepted by God through a paternal indulgence, still it does not cease to demand a perfect love in every respect (such as is due from a rational creature).

4. From the petition for the remission of sins.

XVIII. Fourth, we are commanded to pray daily for the remission of our sins. Now if it was possible for the renewed to fulfill the law of God, it is possible for the same not to need the remission of sins and not to be bound to say according to the command of the Savior, "Forgive us our debts." For in whom no transgression of the law is found, in him no cause of remission is understood and so no necessity of seeking remission is discovered. Augustine frequently employs this argument against the Pelagians: "Whoever says that this petition 'Forgive us our debts' is not necessary to any, even a holy man, both knowing and doing the will of God, greatly errs" (*On Forgiveness of Sins and Baptism* 3.23 [13] [NPNF1, 5:78; PL 44.200]). And elsewhere: "They who contend that there are or were in this life righteous persons, having no sin at all, presumptuously and most openly contradict the Lord's Prayer" (*Against Two Letters of the Pelagians* 4.27 [10] [NPNF1, 5:429; PL 44.629]). Nor is the objection of Bellarmine of any value—that these are only venial sins, which are beyond, not contrary to the law. As we have already said, this distinction is futile and absurd (*asystatos*). For where there is need of remission, there transgression has gone before; where transgression is, there also is lawlessness (*anomia*).

5. From the examples of the saints.

XIX. Fifth, from the examples of the saints. The saints everywhere openly acknowledge and confess this inability (Job 9:3, 20, 28; 15:15); David (Pss. 32:5; 130:3; 143:2); Solomon (Prov. 20:9; 1 K. 8:46); Isaiah (Is. 64:6); Daniel (Dan. 9:5, 6); Paul (Rom. 7:14; Phil. 3:13); John (1 Jn. 1:8); James (Jam. 3:2). Nor can any example of a sinless (*anamartētou*) man be given, if you except Christ. Let our Pharisees and Perfectionists go and put up for sale the perfection of their holiness; yea, their works of supererogation also (i.e., let them impudently allege that they are more righteous and holy than all saints).

Sources of explanation.

XX. The yoke of Christ, described as easy and light (Mt. 11:30), is not the law of Moses taken strictly (which is by itself an unbearable [*abastakton*] yoke), but partly the doctrine of the gospel concerning faith and new obedience (which the Holy Spirit works in us, thus rendering it easy and light); partly the yoke of the cross (called "light" because God does not permit us to be tempted beyond our strength, 1 Cor. 10:13; 2 Cor. 4:17). It is called "easy" because the consolation of the Holy Spirit so tempers the cross, as to elicit from it the sweetest fruits of righteousness and joy.

XXI. The commandments of God are said "to be not grievous to the believer" (1 Jn. 5:3), not as to the perfect possibility of obeying the law or the sinlessness (*anamartēsian*) of man, which John expressly denies (1 Jn. 1:8). But both with respect to imputation and the remission of sins because the perfect obedience of Christ is imputed to us by faith, to whom at once (1 Jn. 5:4) the victory is ascribed and our defects are covered; thus "all things are reckoned as done, when whatever is not done is pardoned," as Augustine has it (*Retractions* 1.19 [18] [FC 60:80-81; PL 32.615]). And with respect to renovation because the Holy Spirit renews the hearts within and works a true and sincere love in them, by which as a willing people (Ps. 110:3), not by compulsion and by the spirit of bondage, but spontaneously and sweetly, they are impelled by the Spirit of adoption to duty; nor are they any longer held bound by the unbearable (*abastaktō*) yoke to obtain life by a perfect observance of the law, but are placed under the sweet yoke of Christ, which prescribes obedience as the testimony of a grateful soul.

XXII. If any are said in the Scriptures to have fulfilled the commands of God and to have loved him with their whole hearts and to have been perfect (as is said of Noah, Gen. 6:9; of David, Ps. 119:10; Josiah, 2 K. 23:25; Asa, 2 Ch. 15:17; Zacharias and Elizabeth, Lk. 1:6 and others), this must be understood not absolutely and simply of a legal perfection of love and obedience (as well intensive as extensive—which is incompatible [*asystaton*] with the sins ascribed to them), but relatively and restrictively concerning an evangelical obedience (which marks a sincere and unfeigned [*anypokriton*] obedience); or comparatively, both with respect to the wicked (who lie wholly in sin) and with respect to those less holy. If Zacharias and Elizabeth are called "righteous before God" (*enōpion ton theou*), this indeed denotes that their righteousness and piety was not clouded and hypocritical, able to stand before men, but true and sincere, which approved itself to God himself. But we cannot thence infer that it was absolutely pure, since in the same place the unbelief of Zacharias is rebuked. Nor more, when they are said to have "walked" (*amemptoi*) in the commandments of the Lord, for this indicates only that they lived without complaint and reprehension before men. It is one thing to be absolutely sinless (*anamartēton*), but another to be "blameless" (*amempton*). Paul demands that a bishop should be *anepilēptos* (incapable of being attacked) which is the same as *amemptō* (blameless); not that he should be without sin (which is impossible), but that he should be without reproach and rebuke.

XXIII. The law is absolutely and perfectly possible to those who keep the commandments absolutely and perfectly; and they are with propriety said to fulfill the commandments, who love in the same manner. But since no one so loves and keeps the commandments (because we know only in part [1 Cor. 13:9], and love in part and in many things we offend all, Jam. 3:2), no one can claim this privilege for himself. And what is said in Jn. 14:23 and Rom. 13:8 is to be understood in no other way than concerning a sincere observance in this life and a full and perfect observance in the other.

XXIV. What is impossible simply (*haplōs*) and in its own nature binds no one. But the commandments of the law are impossible only in a certain sense (*kata ti*) in our state as sojourners—on account of the intervening vice of our nature. As a creditor does not lose the right of demanding a debt of the debtor (even if he cannot pay it), so the rights of God are not lessened although man by his own fault is no longer able to pay. Again God does not enjoin the law upon believers as if it was absolutely possible to them, but that by knowing their duty and their own inability to perform it, they may the more ardently seek the help of grace. "God does not command impossibilities," says Augustine, "but by commanding he admonishes us both to do what we can and to seek what we cannot" (*On Nature and Grace* 50 [43] [NPNF1, 5:138; PL 44.271]). And Bernard: "The Preceptor knew that the weight of the precept exceeded our strength, but he judged it useful from this very circumstance to put them in mind of their own insufficiency, and that they might know to what end of righteousness they ought to rely for strength. Therefore by commanding impossibilities he does not make prevaricators, but humble persons, that every mouth may be stopped and the whole world become subject to God" ("Sermon 50 [2]," *Song of Solomon* [trans. S.J. Eales, 1984 rep.], p. 303; PL 183.1021).

XXV. What pleases God in and by itself (on account of a perfect conformity with his law) is perfectly just; but not in like manner what pleases him through and on account of Christ (as good works please him not because they are perfect and absolutely good, but because they are done in the faith of Christ—by whose obedience all our corruptions and defects are covered and pardoned).

XXVI. When Paul says, "I can do all things through Christ which strengtheneth me" (Phil. 4:13), it must not be understood absolutely, but in accordance with the subject matter (to wit, those things which relate to bearing patiently and moderately whatever the condition of the present life). For the apostle does not speak there of a perfection of morals or of the sinlessness of Pelagius, but of the constancy of the pious mind in bearing prosperity moderately and adversity courageously and patiently. "All things are possible to him that believeth" (Mk. 9:23), not simply that he can be without sin, but relatively as to any either ordinary or extraordinary blessing to be obtained from God.

Third Question: The Necessity of Good Works

Are good works necessary to salvation? We affirm.

I. Since the practice and desire of good works pertain to sanctification, it cannot be better ascertained than by getting a proper knowledge of their nature. Now there are four principal questions concerning them: their necessity, truth, perfection and merit. We must treat of these individually. Having already in the preceding question spoken of their perfection, we now take up their necessity.

Three opinions concerning the necessity of good works.

II. There are three principal opinions about the necessity of good works. First is that of those who (sinning in defect) deny it; such were formerly the Simonians and the modern Epicureans and Libertines, who make good works arbitrary and indifferent, which we may perform or omit at pleasure. The second is that of those who (sinning in excess) affirm and press the necessity of merit and causality; such were the ancient Pharisees and false apostles, who contended that works are necessary to justification. These are followed by the Romanists and Socinians of our day. The third is that of those who (holding the middle ground between these two extremes) neither simply deny, nor simply assert; yet they recognize a certain necessity for them against the Libertines, but uniformly reject the necessity of merit against the Romanists. This is the opinion of the orthodox.

Statement of the question.

III. Hence it is evident that the question here does not concern the necessity of merit, causality and efficiency—whether good works are necessary to effect salvation or to acquire it of right. (For this belongs to another controversy, of which hereafter). Rather the question concerns the necessity of means, of presence and of connection or order—Are they required as the means and way for possessing salvation? This we hold.

IV. Although the proposition concerning the necessity of good works to salvation (which was thrust forward in a former century by the Romanists under the show of a reconciliation in the Interimistic formula, but really that imperceptibly the purity of the doctrine concerning justification might be corrupted) was rejected by various Lutheran theologians as less suitable and dangerous; nay, even by some of our theologians; still we think with others that it can be retained without danger if properly explained. We also hold that it should be pressed against the license of the Epicureans so that although works may be said to contribute nothing to the acquisition of salvation, still they should be considered necessary to the obtainment of it, so that no one can be saved without them—that thus our religion may be freed from those most foul calumnies everywhere cast most unjustly upon it by the Romanists (as if it were the mistress of impiety and the cushion of carnal licentiousness and security).

The necessity of good works is proved: (1) from the command of God.

V. Now although this necessity has already been established in part (Question 1 where we treated of the connection between justification and sanctification), it is still further proved both from the command of God and from the nature of the thing itself and the condition of the believer. For since the will of God is the supreme and indispensable rule of our duty, the practice of good works cannot but be considered as highly necessary (which the Lord so often and so expressly recommends and enjoins in his word). There is no need to refer to passages for they are so numerous. Let the following be specially consulted (1 Thess. 4:3, 4; 1 Jn. 4:21; Jn. 13:34; Mt. 5:16; 1 Pet. 1:15, 16; 2 Pet. 1:5-7, 10; Rom. 6:11, 12; 12:1, 2ff.). And so far from leaving to each one the license of living according to his pleasure, it openly condemns and abhors it (Rom. 6:1, 2, 15; Gal. 5:13; 1 Thess. 4:7; 1 Pet. 2:16) and declares that believers are "debtors" who are bound to new obedience by an indissoluble and indispensable bond (Rom. 8:12; 13:7; 1 Jn. 4:11), not only by the necessity of the precept, but also by the necessity of the means.

VI. This can be demonstrated more clearly from the nature of the thing and the state and condition of man, whether we look to the covenant of grace entered into with him or attend to the doctrine of the gospel which he professes; or to the state of grace in which he is placed; or to the benefits which depend on it, past as well as present and future. All these draw after them the absolute necessity of good works.

2. From the covenant of grace.

VII. And as to the covenant, everyone knows that it consists of two parts: on the one hand the promise on the part of God; on the other the stipulation of obedience on the part of man. For as God promises in it to be our God, he wishes that we also in turn should be his people. And as that promise includes every blessing of God, so the obligation denotes the duties of all kinds owed by man to God (as was seen when we treated of the clauses of the covenant). Although God by his special grace wishes these duties of man to be his blessings (which he carries out in them), still the believer does not cease to be bound to observe it, if he wishes to be a partaker of the blessings of the covenant.

VIII. However, the promise of grace flows from the three persons of the holy Trinity. All concur in the work of redemption and hold a peculiar relation (*schesin*) according to the mode of operation proper to each. The first, indeed, of the

Father adopting us into his family; the second, of Redeemer and head, redeeming his people and uniting them to himself as his purchase and body; the third, of Comforter and sanctifier consecrating us for temples to himself. Thus a threefold necessity of worship and obedience arises that we may live worthily as the sons of God, members of Christ and temples of the Holy Spirit: that we may adore and worship the Father (1 Pet. 1:15, 16; Mal. 1:6; Eph. 5:1); that we may glorify the Redeemer with all our soul (1 Cor. 6:20) and serve him as a "peculiar people zealous of good works" (*periousios zēlōtēs kalōn ergōn*, Tit. 2:14); that we may venerate with great zeal the Spirit dwelling in us and, living in the Spirit, walk also in the Spirit (Gal. 5:25), nor suffer his temple to be polluted (1 Cor. 6:15, 19). This is sealed to us in baptism (administered to us in the name of the whole Trinity) and procured by our union with Christ. It cannot be true and saving unless it draws after it conformity with him (to which we were predestinated, Rom. 8:29) that with him we should die to sin and live to God (Rom. 6:11), walk as he walked (1 Jn. 2:6) and himself both be formed and live in us (Gal. 2:20; 4:19).

3. From the gospel.

IX. Third, the word of God or the gospel which is proposed for our belief as a rule of faith and of life proves this necessity no less. It is not a doctrine merely theoretical (which feeds the mind with fruitless knowledge), but practical (which affects the will itself and renews it). On this account, it is called the "mystery of godliness" (1 Tim. 3:16); the light which transforms (2 Cor. 3:18); truth which sanctifies (Jn. 17:17), which makes us not only wiser, but also better (Jn. 13:17); the seed of our regeneration (Jam. 1:18; 1 Pet. 1:23); the law of the Spirit and of life (Rom. 8:2), which by freeing us from the law of sin and of death, still does not make us without the law, but under the law to Christ (1 Cor. 9:21; Gal. 2:19). Here belongs also the religion we profess, which demands not a mere profession of the truth, but principally the practice of piety and love (Rom. 2:28, 29): "Pure religion and undefiled before God and the Father is this, To visit the fatherless and widows in their affliction, and to keep himself unspotted from the world" (Jam. 1:27).

4. From the state of grace.

X. Fourth, the state of grace and of liberty into which the gospel transfers us demands this. It is a spiritual freedom from the curse of the law, the tyranny of Satan and the yoke of sin, but not a carnal license. It does not remove us from obedience to God, but joins us by a stronger bond to him: "Being then made free from sin," says Paul, "ye became the servants of righteousness" (Rom. 6:18); "As free, and not using your liberty for a cloak of maliciousness, but as the servants of God" (1 Pet. 2:16), viz., in whose worship our true liberty consists because "to serve God is to reign." Christ, by freeing us from the curse and rigor of the law, still did not free us from the obligation to obedience, which is indispensable from the creature. Grace demands the same thing. The greater it is, the more effectually it obliges us to gratitude, so that it not be turned into lasciviousness (*aselgeian*, Gal. 5:13; Jd. 4), but that it be referred to the desire of holiness (Tit. 2:12). Hence, the apostle infers that we must not remain in sin "because we are not under the law, but under grace" (Rom. 6:14, 15).

5. From the blessings of God.

XI. Fifth, all the benefits of God tend to this, whether regarded as to the past in eternal election or as to the present in grace, or as to the future in glory. For all these are destined to or conferred upon us for no other reason than to promote the work of sanctification. On this account, good works are set forth to us as the effects of eternal election (Eph. 1:4); the fruit and seal of present grace (2 Tim. 2:19; 2 Cor. 1:21, 22; Jn. 15:4; Gal. 5:22); and the "seeds" or "firstfruits" and earnests of future glory (Gal. 6:7, 8; Eph. 1:14; Rom. 8:23). Hence these are called "the nurseries of hope, incentives of love, signs of secret predestination, presages of future bliss, the way to the Kingdom, but not the cause of reigning" (Bernard, *Tractatus de Gratia et Libero Arbitrio* [PL 182.1030]). Scripture frequently testifies this concerning election (Jn. 15:16; Eph. 1:4; 2 Thess. 2:13, 14); redemption (Lk. 1:74; Tit. 2:14; 1 Pet. 2:24; 2 Cor. 5:14, 15); calling (2 Pet. 1:10; 1 Pet. 2:9; Phil. 3:14); faith (Gal. 5:6; Acts 15:9); justification (Pss. 130:4; 85:8; Eph. 2:8-10); regeneration (2 Cor. 5:17; Col. 3:1, 2).

XII. This very thing is no less expressly delivered concerning future glory. For since good works have the relation of the means to the end (Jn. 3:5, 16; Mt. 5:8); of the "way" to the goal (Eph. 2:10; Phil. 3:14); of the "sowing" to the harvest (Gal. 6:7, 8); of the "firstfruits" to the mass (Rom. 8:23); of labor to the reward (Mt. 20:1); of the "contest" to the crown (2 Tim. 2:5; 4:8), everyone sees that there is the highest and an indispensable necessity of good works for obtaining glory. It is so great that it cannot be reached without them (Heb. 12:14; Rev. 21:27).

XIII. Finally, there are three things, the necessity of seeking which above all others devolves upon us (to wit, the glory of God, the edification of our neighbor and our own salvation). It is known the practice of good works contributes to these in the greatest degree. Thus it easily appears that they are necessary above all things (Mt. 5:10; Phil. 1:11; Rom. 15:2; 2 Pet. 1:10).

Sources of explanation.

XIV. Works can be considered in three ways: either with reference to justification or sanctification or glorification. They are related to justification not antecedently, efficiently and meritoriously, but consequently and declaratively. They are related to sanctification constitutively because they constitute and promote it. They are related to glorification antecedently and ordinatively because they are related to it as the means to the end; yea, as the beginning to the complement because grace is glory begun, as glory is grace consummated.

XV. Although we acknowledge the necessity of good works against the Epicureans, we do not on this account confound the law and the gospel and interfere with gratuitous justification by faith alone. Good works are required not for living according to the law, but because we live by the gospel; not as the causes on account of which life is given to us, but as effects which testify that life has been given to us.

XVI. Believers are a willing people who ought not to be impelled to good works by necessity (*ex anankēs*) (viz., by a necessity of compulsion), but spontaneously and voluntarily (*hekousiōs*). But still, works do not cease to be necessary by the necessity of means and of debt. Although all coaction is necessity, not all necessity is coaction. The calumnies wont to be drawn against the necessity of good works from our doctrine concerning perserverance and the certainty of faith have been discussed in Topic XV, Questions 16 and 17.

Fourth Question: The Truth of Good Works
What is required that a work may be truly good? Are the works of the righteous such? We affirm.

What are good works?

I. When we speak of the truth of good works, we do not mean works simply moral as they are contradistinguished from spiritual and supernatural by some. In this sense, those are called moral by them which are such as to external discipline or external act (which they commonly term the substance), constituting civil and external discipline or righteousness. Aristotle unfolds these in his *Nicomachean Ethics*. Spiritual are those which are such as much as to substance as with regard to circumstances. The former are called good equivocally (*homonymōs*) and as to external appearance only; but the latter univocally (*synonymōs*) and as to essence, inasmuch as they have in themselves a supernatural goodness truly pleasing to a reconciled God and Father and are ordained by him to receive the rewards of this as well as of the future life (of which we here treat).

II. In such works, the matter and form must be considered. The matter are all the actions of man depending upon his intellect and will and pertaining to the will (*to thymikon*) and the appetite (*to epithymētikon*); those which are said to be the first motions by philosophers, whether they are done without delay or with delay. These are commonly called morals—whether with pleasure or without it; whether with or without deliberation and with the consent of the will. The form is the accordance with the law and will of God, with respect to the substance of the action as well as with respect to its circumstances.

III. By the substance of an action, we do not mean only the act external to the inducement, but both the internal and external act at the same time (if indeed each is connected together); or the internal only, if the external cannot be held. These two acts are so mutually related that the external act is not properly good without the internal (as is apparent in hypocrites), but the internal can exist without an external because goodness is properly constituted in the will and intention. Again, the external does not increase the goodness of the internal by itself, but accidentally, inasmuch as it either continues or conserves the act of the will.

IV. By circumstances we mean all the modifications which attend actions of this kind, so that the work may not only be good, but also that it be done well according to the command of God. In this sense, it is commonly said, "God loves not so much the adjective as the adverb"; also good requires an entire cause, embracing not only the substance of the action, but also the circumstances. Hence a thing good in itself may still become evil and be turned into a sin, if it is not well done (as prayer, charity, etc.).

What is required in good works and what they are.

V. However, to constitute this goodness, four things are specially required: a principle, rule, mode, end. (1) That the work may be done from the faith of a renewed heart because "whatever is done without faith is sin" (Rom. 14:23). (2) That it be done according to the prescription of the law and the will of God revealed in his word, which is the sole rule of faith and life. (3) That it be done in a lawful mode (i.e., not only externally, but also internally) because the law (which is spiritual, Rom.

7:14) regards not only the external motions of the body, but principally the internal actions of the mind. (4) That it be done to the glory of God, the sole object to which we ought always to look; and to which all things should be subordinated (1 Cor. 10:31)—not only with a virtual and habitual, but also with an actual intention. For since it is an intention, it ought to be the most explicit of the highest good and be interrupted by no other intention.

Hence it follows that the virtues of the heathen were not good works.

VI. Hence we infer (1) that the virtues of the Gentiles (however illustrious), still cannot be said to be good works, whatever the Pelagians formerly and the modern Socinians, Romanists and especially the Jesuits maintain. These are not willing that "the works of unbelievers should be sins or the virtues of philosophers should be vices," as we read in the Bull of Pius V and of Gregory XIII (cf. "Bull 111.25," *Magnum Bullarum Romanum* [1965], v. IV, Pt. 3, p. 427) and in Bellarmine ("De Gratia et Libero Arbitrio," 5.9 *Opera* [1858], 4:391-94) and Trininus (*Theologiae elenchticae . . . controversiarum fidei*, Cont. 12, no. 5 [1648], pp. 569-83). To these Jansen with his whole school strongly opposed himself in his *Augustinus*. For although they might have some external goodness (by reason of the external act and object, which was good), still they sinned in three things: (a) as to the principle, which was not a renewed but an impure heart, although imbued with some knowledge of virtue and vice from the dictation of the natural law; (b) as to the mode because the internal obedience of the heart was wanting; (c) as to the end because direction to the glory of God was required, which they did not have in view. Moreover no difference can be determined between the most wicked and the more virtuous of them (as between Fabricius and Cataline) because a difference always remained between them. "Not because the one was good," says Augustine, "but because the other was worse and Fabricius was less wicked than Cataline; not in having true virtues, but not deviating as much from true virtues" (*Against Julian* 4.3.25 [FC 35:190; PL 44.751]). There it was better for them to cultivate this civil virtue, than to loosen the reins to the appetite of the flesh, by which if they could not obtain the reward of glory, still they would have to expect a less severe punishment (as those failing only in the mode of acting, sinned less than others who sinned in the very substance of the deed). But because we have treated of this question in Volume I, Topic X, Question 5, we add no more.

Nor is a good intention sufficient.

VII. Hence also it is evident that the Romanists err when they hold those to be good works which are obtruded upon God (not commanding and requiring) which Paul calls will-worship (*ethelothrēskeia*) and condemns (Col. 2:23). For when it is treated of the worship of God, we must not only abstain from things forbidden, but also from things not commanded; nay, such works are forbidden just because they are not commanded: "What thing soever I command you, observe to do it: thou shalt not add thereto, nor diminish from it" (Dt. 12:32); "Remember all the commandments of the Lord, and do them: and seek not after your own heart" (Num. 15:39*). He exclaims in Is. 1:12, "Who has required this at your hands?" And: "In vain do they worship me, teaching doctrines, which are the precepts of men" (Is. 29:13).

VIII. Nor can the diluted comment of good intention favor this error, as if what is done contrary to or beyond God's command can be a good work because it is done with a right intention. For that is falsely termed a good intention which is opposed to God's intention. Saul indeed pleaded a good intention when, being commanded to destroy the Amalekites utterly, he spared the king and reserved the fattest sheep for sacrifices; but this was not received as an excuse and Samuel testifies that God wished obedience, not sacrifice no matter with what good intention offered. This same good intention destroyed Uzzah, when he reached out his hand to support the ark shaking in the wagon. Christ, speaking of his persecutors, says, "They think that they do God service, whosoever killeth believers" (Jn. 16:2). The worst religions applaud themselves in the highest degree and cover their works with a good intention.

IX. Further with regard to the question here agitated between us and the Romanists—whether the works of believers are and can be called truly good. We must distinguish between truly good and perfectly good. We have proved before that the latter cannot be ascribed to the works of the saints on account of the imperfection of sanctification and the remains of sin. But the former is rightly predicated of them because although they are not as yet perfectly renewed, still they are truly and unfeignedly renewed. While the Romanists are unwilling to make this distinction, they falsely charge us with denying that the works of believers are truly good because we maintain that they are imperfect, since the truth and perfection of works are notwithstanding most diverse and the former can be granted without the latter.

The works of believers are truly good.

X. That the works of believers are truly good is proved: (1) because they are not performed only with the general concourse of God, but by a special motion and impulse of the Holy Spirit, who dwells in the hearts of believers and excites them to good works. Hence these works are usually ascribed to him as the primary cause (Ezk. 36:27; Gal. 5:22; Rom. 8:9, 10; Phil. 1:6; 2:13). Nor are they done only by the Holy Spirit exciting and impelling, but also by the qualities of infused grace mediating (which overcome the order of nature). Hence Paul ascribes all his works to the grace of God (1 Cor. 15:10) and Christ asserts that we can do nothing without him (Jn. 15:5). Now what is produced by the Spirit and the grace of Christ must be truly good. Nor does the flesh, which still remains in us, hinder this because its presence can indeed take away the perfection of sanctification, but not its truth.

XI. (2) Such works please God; therefore they are truly good. For what is properly and by itself sin, cannot please him. The passages are obvious (1 Pet. 2:5; Heb. 11:4-6; 12:28; Rom. 12:1; 14:18; Phil. 4:18). I confess that the first cause of their acceptance is Christ, in whom we are pleasing to God (Eph. 1:6) because the person is rather pleasing to God and is reconciled to him by the Mediator. In this sense, God is said to have had respect to Abel rather than to his sacrifice (Gen. 4:4). But this does not hinder God from being pleased with the works also, on account of the true goodness which occurs in them (flowing from the regeneration of the heart and the restoration of the divine image). For wherever God beholds his own likeness, he deservedly loves and holds it in honor. Thus not without a cause is the life of believers (regulated according to holiness and righteousness) said to please him.

XII. (3) A reward is promised to them, which could not be done if they were not truly good. For although works have nothing in themselves which can deserve and obtain such a reward (which on this account is merely gratuitous, as will soon be shown), still they have a certain ordination and aptitude that they are ordained to a reward, both from the condition of the worker, who is supposed to be a believer (i.e., admitted into the grace and friendship of God), and from the condition of the works themselves, which although not having a condignity to the reward, still have the relation of disposition required in the subject for its possession. This condition being fulfilled, the reward must be given as, it being withheld, the reward cannot be obtained. For as without holiness, no one shall see God and, unless renewed by water and the Spirit, cannot enter the kingdom of heaven (Jn. 3:5; Heb. 12:14); so, holiness being posited, glory is necessarily posited from the inseparable connection existing between them.

XIII. Our affirmation that all works (even the best) are not free from sin in this life does not destroy the truth of the good works of believers because although we affirm that as to mode they are never performed with that perfection which can sustain the rigid examination of the divine judgment (on account of the imperfection of sanctification), still we maintain that as to the thing they are good works. And if they are called sins, this must be understood accidentally with respect to the mode, not of themselves and in their own nature. So there always remains a difference between the works of the renewed and the unrenewed. The latter are essentially and specifically evil and so destitute of those circumstances and conditions which are requisite to the essence of a good work (which accordingly are only good as to sight and appearance). On the other hand, the former are essentially good works because they have all things from which the goodness of an action results and so are truly and not apparently such (although as to degree they may fail and have blemishes mixed up with them).

XIV. Although the works of the renewed are said to be sins, and so faith (by which we are justified) can be called a sin under a certain relation (*schesei*) (as also the prayer by which we seek the pardon of sins), it does not follow that man is justified by sin and by sin obtains the remission of sins. We do not say that the act of believing itself or of praying is a sin, but only that there are defects and blemishes connected with it. Thus the work of faith is not the instrument of justification with respect to such imperfections, but with respect to the act itself (which is produced by the Holy Spirit and under that reduplication). Nor by sin do we seek or obtain the remission of sin, as our opponents foolishly infer; but we seek it by and on account of the merit of Christ, the duty, not the fault of our prayer mediating as the condition required from us.

XV. Although it is granted that all the works of the renewed are tainted by some sin, the apostle could rightly say, "I am conscious of no evil," because he does not speak here of the course of his whole life, but concerning a ministry faithfully completed. Nor does he boast that the work of his ministry had been so completed by himself that no fault had interfered with it on the part of the flesh, but that he had done nothing deceitfully and impiously to wound his own conscience. For otherwise, he professes that he did not do the good that he would, but rather the evil he hated (Rom. 7:19).

XVI. Since God works in us all our good works as far as they have any goodness in them and not as far as they have any imperfection or taint in them (in which sense they spring from the flesh), we say truly that every good work is marred by some sin and yet we deny truly that God is the author of this faultiness or sin.

XVII. Nor is it absurd (*asystaton*) and inconsistent for the same work (good and bad) to be called worthy of a reward and punishment in different respects (*kat' allo kai allo*). Inasmuch as the good arises from the Spirit, it may be evil according as the flesh is mixed with it—good with respect to the act, evil with respect to the viciousness cleaving to it. Nor ought believers by works of this kind to be said to serve God and Satan, or to be the sons of God and of Satan. They only are said to serve the Devil and are called his children, who live under the dominion of darkness; not they who have shaken off this dominion and produce good works, although tainted in some measure with the vice of the flesh. Thus Paul professes that he serves Christ, and is reckoned among the sons of God, who confesses that he serves the law of God with his mind, but the law of sin with his flesh (Rom. 7:25).

Fifth Question: The Merit of Works

Is there a merit of congruity or condignity? Do good works merit eternal life? We deny against the Romanists.

I. That the doctrine of the merits of works may be more clearly held, we must premise a few things concerning the word "merit" and the verb "meriting," from which a decision concerning the thing itself can be more easily arrived at.

The word "merit" is taken broadly and strictly.

II. The word "merit" is used in two ways: either broadly and improperly; or strictly and properly. Strictly, it denotes that work to which a reward is due from justice on account of its intrinsic value and worth. But it is often used broadly for the consecution of any thing. In this sense, the verb "to merit" is often by the fathers put for "to gain," "to obtain," "to attain." Augustine says: "The sinner ought not to despair of himself because Paul obtained (*meruisti*) pardon" (Sermon 170, "De Tempore [49]" [PL 38.927]). Ambrose says: "O Water! which hast merited to be the sacrament of Christ, which dost wash all things, and art not washed" (*Expositio Evangeli . . . Lucam* 10.48 [PL 15.1907-8] on Lk. 22:11, 12). Hence from Gregory the Roman church sings, "O happy guilt, which merited to have such a Redeemer" (cf. *The Roman Sunday Missal for America* [1933], p. 255). The Romanists do not deny the abuse of this word. Cassander says: "The word 'to merit' in the ancient ecclesiastical writers means almost the same as to obtain or is fit and suitable to obtain" ("Hymni Ecclesiastici," in *Georgii Cassandri . . . Opera* [1616], p. 179). He proves this from a passage of Cyprian, who renders Paul's expression, "I obtained mercy" (*alla kai eleēthēn*, 1 Tim. 1:13) by *misericordiam merui* and adds in the same place, "If this meaning of the word is retained, many things which seem to be rather harsh will appear to be more mild and suitable." Vega says: "It does not escape me that the word is used by the fathers where there is nothing of merit, either of congruity or of condignity" (*De Iustificatione Doctrina Universa* 8.8 [1572/1964], 1:189). In the same sense, the authors of the Augsburg Confession use the word "merit" (cf. *Book of Concord*, Art. 6 [ed. T.G. Tappert, 1959], p. 32), as also the Apology, Art. 20 (ibid., p. 228), as Bellarmine acknowledges ("De Justificatione," 5.1 *Opera* [1858], 4:603-4). From this time, the verb "to merit" and the word "merit" have been more frequently used in this improper sense. The later doctors of the schools now swelling with superciliousness, the phrases of the fathers being received badly and contrary to their meaning, they began to say that men properly merited eternal life by their works and that good works are meritorious of eternal life, not only from the covenant, but also by reason of the work itself.

Threefold merit according to the Romanists: congruity, worth and condignity.

III. The Romanists commonly define "merit" as an action to which some reward is due. Some make two, others three kinds: of congruity, worth and condignity. The merit of congruity they apply to a work morally good, done from the free will unassisted by grace (to wit, that is congruous and suitable to the divine goodness to infuse the grace of justification into those morally disposed and doing what they can). The merit of worth they hold to be the suitableness or aptitude of the worker to obtain that which he deserves; as the reason for the name is drawn from the person working rather than from the work itself, inasmuch as he is considered by God worthy to merit eternal life. Finally, the merit of condignity they maintain to be a good work done from free will assisted by grace which is such as to be altogether worthy of such a reward, not only from agreement, but also on account of the intrinsic value of the work and the equality between the work and the reward. But many of the more modern Romanists (as Bellarmine and others) reduce these three kinds to two, on this account most especially—the Vulgate renders the word *axion*, from which they wish to draw merit, now by *dignum* (as in Rev. 3:4), then by *condignum*. Thus in this respect, there is no difference between them (Bellarmine, "De Justificatione," 5.16 *Opera* [1858], 4:627-29). Hence some are said to be merits of grace from congruity; others merits of glory from condignity.

IV. Still we must confess that to many of the Romanists this distinction is less pleasing and seems incongruous. They think there is no merit of congruity, among whom are Thomas Waldensis, and Paul Burgensis, as Bellarmine tells us ("De Justificatione," 5.16 *Opera* [1858], 4:628). Stapleton says: "Merit of congruity with respect to first grace was long ago exploded; nor was it ever received by the more respectable Scholastics, as by Thomas in his *Summa* and later writings, and his followers" ("De universa iustificationis: De peccato originali," 2.4 *Opera* [1620], 2:50). Becanus acknowledges that "the merit of congruity has not properly the relation of merit, but only of a certain suitableness, and therefore it is not necessary to dispute about it, because nothing certain can be affirmed of it" (*Summa Theologicae Scholasticae* 2.5*.5.1 [1651], p. 509). Still because it is as yet retained by many others (as by Vasquez, Cajetan and others) and is the commonly received opinion among them, its emptiness must be briefly demonstrated.

What is merit; and what are its conditions?

V. That this may be done more readily, the definition of merit properly so called must be premised and the conditions required for it must be considered. Biel defines merit to be "a work imputable to praise" (i.e., worthy of praise) (*Canonis Misse Expositio* 59* [ed. H. Oberman and W. Courtenay, 1965], 2:440). If our opponents would be content with this meaning, there would be no controversy. For no one denies that the good works of the believer are worthy of praise. Bellarmine enumerates seven conditions of a meritorious work: (1) that it be a good work; (2) a free work; (3) done in obedience to God; (4) by man as a sojourner (i.e., acting among the living); (5) by a justified person and a friend of God; (6) that it proceed from love; (7) that it has the promise of God annexed. But although all these conditions are required in a good work, still they do not suffice to render it meritorious because in true merit Bellarmine himself acknowledges something additional is required (to wit, an intrinsic worth and value) when he says that that is merit to which a reward is due by way of justice, not only distributive but also commutative, so that there may be a just equality between the work and the reward ("De Justificatione," 5.10-16 *Opera* [1858], 4:618-29).

VI. To true merit, then, these five conditions are demanded: (1) that the "work be undue"—for no one merits by paying what he owes (Lk. 17:10), he only satisfies; (2) that it be ours—for no one can be said to merit from another; (3) that it be absolutely perfect and free from all taint—for where sin is, there merit cannot be; (4) that it be equal and proportioned to the reward and pay; otherwise it would be a gift, not merit (which Bellarmine himself acknowledges [ibid., 5.17, pp. 629-31] according to the meaning of the Council of Trent); (5) that the reward be due to such a work from justice—whence an "undue work" is commonly defined to be one that "makes a reward due in the order of justice."

There is no merit in general.

VII. From these we readily gather that there now can be no merit in man with God by works whatsoever, either of congruity or of condignity. (1) They are not undue, but due; for whatever we are and can do, all this we owe to God, whose debtors we are on this account called (Lk. 17:10; Rom. 8:12). (2) Not one is ours, but all are gifts of grace and fruits of the Spirit (Jam. 1:17; Phil. 2:13; 2 Cor. 3:5). (3) They are not perfect, but alloyed as yet by various impurities (Rom. 7:18; Gal. 5:17, 18; Is. 64:6). (4) They are not equal to future glory because there is no proportion between the finite and temporary and the infinite and eternal (Rom. 8:18; 2 Cor. 4:17). (5) The reward promised to them is purely gratuitous and undue and so to be expected not from the internal merit of the work and its intrinsic worth, but only from the most free estimation of it by the one who crowns it (Rom. 6:23; 4:4; 11:6). Hence also it appears that there is no merit properly so called of man before God, in whatever state he is placed. Thus Adam himself, if he had persevered, would not have merited life in strict justice, although (through a certain condescension [*synchatabasin*]) God promised him by a covenant life under the condition of perfect obedience (which is called meritorious from that covenant in a broader sense because it ought to have been, as it were, the foundation and meritorious cause in view of which God had adjudged life to him).

Neither of congruity.

VIII. In particular, the following arguments disprove merits of congruity. (1) Nothing good can be either thought or done by sinful man not as yet renewed (as has already been fully proved when we treated of free will and effectual calling). (2) Grace which is due is not grace. Now the grace given to us is wholly gratuitous, preceding and anticipating all our acts and dispositions and in reference to which man stands merely passively (as Paul constantly teaches, Rom. 9:16; Eph. 2:3, 5, 9, 10; Tit. 3:5; 1 Cor. 3:3, 5, and has been shown by us in the cited place). (3) Thus man would give something to God first (contrary to Paul, Rom. 11:35) and have something which he had not received (against the same, 1 Cor. 4:7). (4) Enemies and those without God (such as we all are before grace, Eph. 2:11, 12; Tit. 3:3) can deserve nothing. (5) Either this merit arises from all works or from some only. No one would say from all, nor from some because thus he who would sin in one, would not be guilty of all (contrary to Jam. 2:10).

IX. To no purpose is the saying of Christ "whosoever hath, to him shall be given" (Mt. 13:12) wrested to prove the merit of congruity. There (as we have already observed), the reference is not to gifts of nature, but to those of grace; not to the moral virtues or disposing acts of the unrenewed, but to the increase of true faith according to the grace of election (v. 11). That God is said to be well pleased (*euaresteithai*) with the sacrifices of beneficence (Heb. 13:16) teaches indeed that God is pleased with such victims and gratefully regards them, but by no means that he is regarded by them (as the Vulgate barbarously translates it). Besides, it treats of the works of believers, who are already in grace, not of the acts of the unrenewed. If God did sometimes reward the virtues of the Gentiles or the unrenewed by certain temporal blessings in order to testify how acceptable true righteousness is to him, it does not follow that they deserved such a reward from congruity.

Nor of condignity.

X. As to merits of condignity, the Romanists differ in opinion. Three principal ones are enumerated. The first is that of those who wish the good works of the righteous to be meritorious of eternal life from condignity by reason of the work, even if no divine agreement would exist. Bellarmine ascribes this to Cajetan and Dominic de Soto ("De Justificatione," 5.17 *Opera* [1858], 4:629), which Vasquez, Michael Bayus and many Thomists follow, as Becanus observes (*Summa Theologicae Scholasticae* 2.5.5.1 [1651], p. 510). Another is that of Scotus and his followers, who pretend that good works proceeding from grace are not meritorious from condignity by reason of the work, but only by reason of the divine covenant and acceptance. The third is that of those who, joining the first two opinions, determine works to be meritorious neither simply in themselves, nor only from the covenant, but with respect to the covenant and the work at the same time (which Bellarmine embraces and which he holds to be that of the Council of Trent, although nothing certain can be drawn from it). It is indeed certain that the Council expressly asserted merits. But in this, the sly cunning of the fathers exercised itself that, conscious of the Scholastic contests concerning the reason and mode of merit, they were still unwilling to decide the pending controversy and employed their usual stilted style that they might in some way or other gain the favor of both the contending parties. "If anyone should say that the good works of a justified person are so the gifts of God, that they are not also the good merits of the one justified, or that the one justified by good works, which are done by him through the grace and merit of Jesus Christ, whose living member he is, does not truly deserve an augmentation of grace, eternal life, and the obtainment of that eternal life, if he dies in grace, and even the increase of glory, let him be accursed" (Session 6, Canon 32, Schroeder, p. 46).

XI. Now although they who embrace the second opinion (acknowledging no merit except from agreement) err less dangerously than others and come nearer the truth, still they cannot be excused. First they greatly abuse words, calling that merit of condignity which in no way deserves that name (if we wish to follow the ordinary method of speaking). For who would say that a work of condignity merited eternal life which by itself is not worthy of so great a reward, but to which that reward is liberally promised above its own worth? Again, this manner of speaking is not only abusive, but also very dangerous (to wit, favoring Pharisaical pride, which affords the occasion of making grievous mistakes in the thing itself—to wit, ascribing too much to our works and not a little diminishing the glory of the divine mercy, which has evidently been the case in the Roman church).

Statement of the question.

XII. But because the more common opinion of the Romanists is that which Bellarmine follows (who builds the merit of works partly on the covenant, partly on the intrinsic worth of work), being about to dispute against this we ought above all things to investigate the state of the question. The question is not (1) Are good works pleasing and acceptable to God and do they obtain from God the reward of life? For this we willingly grant to our opponents, provided a gratuitous and not a due reward is meant. (2) The question is not Is it lawful to work with a view to the reward? For we do not deny that this can be done, a twofold caution being used. First, that it be the view of the reward as a gratuitous boon and not as a due price. Second, that it be not regarded alone or primarily and principally, but less principally and secondarily after the glory of God (which should be regarded here by us above all things).

XIII. (3) The question is not Do works have any relation to eternal life? And is there any suitableness and proportion between good works and eternal life? For we confess that there is a relation of order and of connection, such as exists between the means and the end, the way and the goal, the contest and the crown, the antecedent and the consequent. Also there is a fitness and proportion as it were between things of the same order, such as between sowing and the harvest, the firstfruits and the mass, the beginning and the completion of a thing. Rather the question is Do they have the relation of a cause properly so called? And is there between them a proportion of equality and of commensuration? This we deny.

XIV. (4) The question is not Ought God by agreement to pay a reward to good works? For we do not deny that God from the time he gave the promise is necessarily bound to fulfill it and thus is made in a certain measure a debtor, not to us, but to himself and his own faithfulness. Rather the question is Do works, from their intrinsic value and worth, merit and obtain the reward promised by God and by the virtue of which they can be said to effect salvation itself? Our opponents affirm; we deny.

XV. Our opponents unfold their meaning thus: "It is more agreeable to the Catholic doctrine that the value and dignity of eternal life should first be ascribed to the works of the just without any agreement and favor" (Vasquez, *Commentariorum ac Disputationum in primam secundae . . . Thomae*, Disp. 214.4 [1631], 2:559). And a little after he adds, "The works of the just derive no accession of worth from the merits of Christ or from his person" (ibid.). Bellarmine says: "It is more honoring to have something from merit, than from a gift alone" ("De Justificatione," 5.3 *Opera* [1858], 4:605). He dared to assert that God is a debtor and under obligation to man: "Not from the promise alone but even from our work God is made a debtor" (ibid., 5.17, 18, pp. 629-32, especially p. 631).

Proof that there is no merit of condignity: (1) on the part of God giving life.

XVI. But this proud and Pharisaical doctrine, the Scriptures frequently and severely condemn. (1) On the part of God giving the life, when it calls eternal life the gift of God; not a gift of any kind whatsoever, but a charisma (*charisma*) which is a truly gratuitous gift (*apo tou charizesthai*) and is opposed to a debt (Rom. 4:4). "The wages of sin," says the apostle "is death, but the gift of God is eternal life" (Rom. 6:23). The force of the argument increases from the antithesis of the wages and the gift. For the just relation of the opposition would seem to demand that as he had said "the wages of sin is death," thus on the other hand he would say, "but the wages of righteousness is eternal life." Nor ought he to have spoken otherwise, if he had believed with the Romanists that life is acquired by our merits. But why did the apostle violate the law of antithesis and say in an inverted phrase, "The gift of God is eternal life" unless it was to show that they held the most diverse relations—that life and death are indeed the ultimate end of man, but the condition of each is not equal; that death is acquired by true merit (i.e., by sins), to which from distributive justice death is due. But eternal life is not acquired by righteousness in like manner; it is given to no merit, but is a gratuitous gift, conferred from pure liberality. This Augustine well remarks: "Since he could have said, the wages of righteousness is eternal life, he preferred to say, By grace is eternal life, that we might hence understand, that God brings us to eternal life not for our merits but by his compassion" (*On Grace and Free Will* 21 [9] [NPNF1, 5:452; PL 44.893]). The same is the teaching of those various passages where salvation is said to be from mercy: "Who crowneth thee with loving kindness and tender mercy" (Ps. 103:4); "By grace are ye saved" (Eph. 2:8, 9); "According to his mercy he saved us" (Tit. 3:5). For since mercy is free and undue, if salvation is of mercy, it cannot be from our merits.

XVII. To no purpose is it replied that eternal life is said to be grace, not because it is not of the reward of merit, but because the merits themselves are of grace. These are incompatible (*asystata*): to give a thing from grace and to give it from merit. For merit makes a thing due, while grace supposes it undue. Therefore whatever is given from grace cannot be given from merit, otherwise grace would not be grace. Bellarmine himself does not deny this when he says in weighing merit and assigning the due reward, a certain commutative justice is exercised (i.e., that in which beyond all consideration of persons a due equality according to quality is preserved in giving and receiving); cf. "De Justificatione," 5.14, ibid., pp. 623-26.

2. On the part of Christ.

XVIII. (2) On the part of Christ meriting. Christ most fully merited life and salvation for us; hence there can be no room for our merits (Acts 20:28; Heb. 9:12; Acts 4:12). The reason of the consequence is drawn from various sources. (a) The theandric (*theandrikai*) and redemptive actions (such as his is) are so proper to Christ, as to be plainly incapable of being shared (*akoinōnētoi*) with others because they belong to the duty demanded of him alone. (b) What is by itself and immediately most sufficient for the acquisition of any right has no need of the connection of another thing in order to the acquisition of it. Now that such is the merit of Christ, no one can deny. (c) This openly derogates from the merits of Christ. For since to merit is to obtain a right which was not possessed before, if men ought to merit life by their works, it follows that before their merits they had no right to it and thus Christ did not perfectly merit it (which cannot be said without blasphemy). He confesses that celestial goods do not belong to him who wishes to obtain them by his own merits. He rejects the title of heir who wishes to be a buyer.

XIX. I know that it is objected here: (1) that our merits are not to be opposed to the merits of Christ; since they spring from them and whatever praise they have, the whole of it redounds to the praise of the merits of Christ. Nor are our merits required on account of the insufficiency of Christ's merits, but on account of their greatest efficacy, since he obtained this from God that we might be able of ourselves to obtain life by our own merits (as because God uses the sun to light the world, there is not any imbecility in God, but his omnipotence, who could not only do this by himself, but also give to a created thing the power to do it). We answer: But these things are gratuitous inventions. For our merits cannot be laid side by side with the merits of Christ, neither as associated causes (in which there is not the dependence of the one upon the other, as they maintain there is between Christ's merit and ours and which produce the effect partially, not totally—which cannot be said of Christ, who is not only the author, but also the finisher of salvation); nor as subaltern and subordinate causes because merit of itself does not indicate a relation to another merit, but rather a respect to a reward. (2) It is absurd (*asystaton*) to say that our merits arise from the merits of Christ because as it cannot be said another redemption is born of the redemption of Christ; so neither is another merit generated from his merit; and as Christ did not produce other christs secondarily, so neither did his merit produce other secondary merits. (3) Most falsely also is Christ said to have merited the power of meriting because thus Christ would not have merited immediately beatitude itself, but only mediately (contrary to the Scriptures, Jn. 10:28; Heb. 9:15). Again, if the merit of Christ is most sufficient of itself, why is there need to patch it up with human merits? For what can be done by fewer ought not to be done by more; nor can a place be granted for new merits where the merits of Christ have fully acquired the right we seek. (4) The simile of the sun is wholly dissimilar. It is one thing to speak of efficient causes, which have a mutual subordination; another to speak of meritorious causes, which can suffer no such subordination; one thing to speak of the order of nature, in which God willed to institute such a concatenation between the first and second causes; another of the order of grace, in which he wished Christ alone to be the unique and singular cause of our salvation (Acts 4:12).

3. On the part of believers.

XX. (3) On the part of believers who, since they are the servants of God, can do nothing which they do not owe; on that very account they cannot merit anything. The words of Christ are express: "When ye shall have done all those things which are commanded you, say, We are unprofitable servants: we have done that which was our duty to do" (Lk. 17:10). Here there are as many weighty reasons as there are words. (a) Christ speaks hypothetically and by way of concession (*synchōrētikōs*), "When ye shall have done," not that there is anyone who can fulfill the law, since in many things we offend all (Jam. 3:2), but even granting there is one, still he would be an unprofitable servant (as Cajetan, Jansen and Stella explain it). (b) Christ does not mean that they thus speak only through humility and modesty (although it is not really true), for he does not wish us to be so humble as to lie, but from the truth of the thing and a sense of our own infirmity, which the reason added by Christ (that they did what was their duty to do) sufficiently evinces. (c) Christ does not speak here of a servant who is a simple mercenary, serving his master for stipulated wages, and to whom after his work is done pay is due; but one who is a slave, who belongs wholly to his master, so that he is bound to give to him his labor entirely and assiduously (such as were the Roman and Jewish slaves of that time, as Bellarmine, Salmeron and Barradas understand it). (d) They are called "unprofitable servants," not only such as they are of themselves or in a state of nature, but such as they are in a state of grace because the apostle addresses those who are supposed to do those things which no one can do of himself. (e) He calls them not only useless to God (who does not need our service [Ps. 50:12] and to whom our good does not reach [Ps. 16:2]), but also useless to themselves (as Maldonatus and Alphonsus de Castro explain it). Since therefore it is here treated concerning God (who owes nothing to his servants), and concerning men, who (as slaves) can merit nothing from their master, and concerning works which are due, it is incontestably proved that there can be no merit with God.

XXI. Although Bellarmine turns himself in all directions to escape the force of these arguments, he is at last forced to take refuge in Augustine's explication of the words of our Lord. He evidently agrees with us when he says, "We can be called unprofitable servants, when we have kept all the divine commands, since we do nothing beyond what we ought and can seek no just reward thence" (Ser. 3 de verbis Dom.+). This strangles our opponent completely. Nor does what he adds afterwards remove the difficulty, "Unless God had willed to enter into a liberal covenant with us; for we are in our condition the slaves of God and if he willed, he could oblige us without any reward to whatsoever works he pleased." For the gratuitous covenant (which he condescended to make with us) does indeed make God a debtor to his own faithfulness for the fulfillment of his promise; but not that anything is due to our works as if they were meritorious, since he crowns his gifts in us, not our merits.

4. On the part of works.

XXII. (4) On the part of the works. Since these are destitute of the conditions of true merit (as we have said before), they cannot merit anything, not only because they are due and not ours, but also because they are imperfect and finite, having no proportion to eternal glory (which Paul testifies when he says, "The sufferings of this present time are not worthy to be compared with the glory which shall be revealed in us," Rom. 8:18). "Our light affliction, which is but for a moment, worketh for us a far more exceeding and eternal weight of glory" (2 Cor. 4:17). Here the apostle expressly professes that afflictions are not worthy (or as the Vulgate has it *condignas*). Now if the afflictions which we suffer for Christ's sake (which belong to a far more noble virtue) are not condign, how much less the actions? And if there is no condignity, where then is the merit of condignity? The apostle demonstrates this more clearly by the comparison instituted, when he opposes momentary affliction, or its shortness (*to parautika*) to the eternity of glory, for "weight of glory" (*to baros doxēs*, 2 Cor. 4:17) he puts for "exceedingly heavy glory" (*doxan bareian kath' hyperbolēn*) (to wit, excellent above measure and solid and true, where he alludes to the word *kbhvdh*, which signifies "glory," not that which weighs down, but that which is solid and permanent).

Nor can it be said here that the apostle speaks of the substance of works, not of the absolute proportion which can intervene on account of the worth of love, whence they proceed (as the sufferings of Christ, although temporal, had a proportion to glory on account of the dignity of the person; and the temporal delights of sinners are most worthy of eternal punishment). It is taken for granted that Paul speaks only of the substance of works and not of their absolute proportion. Nay, he could not have spoken of their condignity without speaking of their proportion, nor can the worth of love bring with it any merit, since the whole of it however great it may be (as being due) is not meritorious. The simile of the sufferings of Christ is clearly no simile at all, for the infinity of his person gives an infinite worth to his sufferings, although finite in themselves. But our works can have no meritorious worth either as to substance or as to mode. The sins of the wicked are also rightly said to deserve an infinite punishment on account of the infinity of the offended majesty; but our works have nothing meriting glory either in whole or in part.

5. On the part of eternal life or glory.

XXIII. (5) On the part of eternal life or glory. It is called "an inheritance" (which does not fall under merit), but depends upon the gratuitous adoption of God. If good works are required for entering upon this inheritance, it does not follow that they merit the inheritance. The inheritance is one thing, the addition of the inheritance another; eternal life one thing, its possession another; as the right to the promised land was one thing, the actual introduction to it another. That was bestowed upon them in the title of the inheritance from the grace of God alone; but they could not be put in possession of the land until the Canaanites were driven out. Thus the right to life is given to us by God from adoption, but it cannot be entered into and obtained by the way of good works. Therefore the causes of the inheritance must be distinguished from its conditions: works are conditions, but not merits. If eternal life is elsewhere said to be a reward, it does not follow that it is acquired by merits because it is known that a reward from debt differs from a reward from grace, such as is this of ours. Hence Paul calls glory "the reward of the inheritance" (Col. 3:24), i.e., the reward which is an inheritance and so merely gratuitous.

Sources of explanation.

XXIV. From a reward to merit, the consequence does not hold good. One reward is of debt; another of grace (Rom. 4:4). As Ambrose remarks, one of liberality and of grace; another the due wages of virtue and the remuneration of labor ("To Justus" [FC 26:105-15]). Life is promised to works as a reward, but as a gratuitous and undue reward (which is the gift of God, Rom. 6:23) and an inheritance (as has been said) obtained not by the right of merit, but by the privilege of sonship—however, the exercise of good works coming in as a necessary condition. On this account, it is proposed as wages and a reward in order to excite believers to diligence, not to foster pride; but this gratuitous reward (which follows our labors) no more proves merit than the buying in the prophet proves a price and money (Is. 55:1, 2). Hence what is called *misthos* (Mt. 5:46; 6:1) is elsewhere called *charis* (Lk. 6:32); and children (or the fruit of the womb) are called a reward, who nevertheless are the gift of God (Ps. 127:3).

XXV. Strict justice of equality, which has reference exactly to the equality of a work, differs from the justice of faithfulness tempered by mercy, which regards the truth of the divine promise and the covenant which God condescended to make with us. God presents life to our works from the justice of faithfulness, by which he is faithful and true in fulfilling his promises; but not from the justice of equality, as regarding the merit of the work (which Durand acknowledges, *Sententias theologicas Petri Lombardi Commentariorum*, Bk. 2, Dist. 27, Q. 2 [1556], pp. 152-53). This is so not because it is just to pay the due reward to our merits, but because it is just for God to stand to his promises and not suffer the death of Christ to be made void.

XXVI. God will give "according to works" (*kata ta erga*), not "on account of" (*dia*), to denote the proportion of quality, not of equality—that it may be well with the good, evil to the wicked, as it is explained in Rev. 22:12: "I will give to every man according as his work shall be" (*hōs to ergon autou estai*). Yet that the work will not be commensurate with the promised reward by condignity. Gregory the Great observes this: "It is one thing to give according to works; another on account of them. For in this expression 'according to works,' the very quality of the works is understood, so that his retribution is glorious whose works have appeared to be good" ("Psalm 7.11," *In Septem Psalmos Poenitentiales* [PL 79.651]).

XXVII. The causal particles *gar* and *dia* ascribed to good works (Mt. 25:35; Rev. 7:15) are not causal, but ratiocinative (as often elsewhere: Mt. 16:2, 3; Jn. 16:27; 1 Cor. 10:5). These point out the cause of the consequence, not of the consequent; the marks of those who will be saved and the testimony of faith and eternal election, but not the meritorious cause of salvation. Thus they are the arguments and proofs *a posteriori* of the just sentence in the absolution of believers, not causes and foundations *a priori*. For the elect are said to receive the kingdom "prepared from eternity" by the grace of God, not secured in time by the merit of works, so that they possess it by "the title" of "inheritance," as "sons blessed of the Father," not as servants who have made themselves worthy of such a reward by their own works.

XXVIII. Worth of person differs from worth of a work. Believers are said to be worthy, but not their works. (2) One dignity is said to be proper, founded upon a person's own works, another depends upon the worthiness and acceptance of another. The worth of perfection and of merit (everywhere denied to works) differs from the worth of aptitude and of fitness, according to which believers are said to be worthy of the kingdom of heaven (Mt. 10:11; 2 Thess. 1:5; Rev. 3:4), i.e., fit and suitably disposed to possess it. Thus the word *axios* is often used (as in Mt. 3:8; Acts 26:20). Therefore, they are worthy, not from the internal worth of their works, but from the divine estimation of them. This makes them worthy from unworthy (Col. 1:12) by reason of the white robe of Christ's righteousness, with which they are clad (Gal. 3:27), and of the divine adoption, not by reason of inherent righteousness, which is perfect in no one in this life. The apostle does not mean anything else when he says that the pious are counted worthy (*kataxiōthēnai*) of the kingdom of God, not by their own merits, but by the grace of God in Christ (2 Thess. 1:5). For his grace is all our sufficiency (*hikanotēs*) and worth (*axia*). Hence *kataxiousthai* in Scripture is sometimes the same as *charisthēnai* (Acts 5:41; Phil. 1:29). Salmeron holds that "we are said to be worthy where the inheritance is given to no merit of ours" ("Disputationes in Epistolam Pauli ad Colossenes," Disp. II, *Comentarii in evangelicam historiam et in Acta Apostolorum* [1602-4], 15:321).

XXIX. It is one thing for good works to please and delight God (which we acknowledge); another for good works to appease him and to obtain from him something by way of merit. The former is declared when Paul says, God is well pleased (*euaresteisthai*) with the sacrifices of beneficence (Heb. 13:16), i.e., delights in and gratefully receives them; not, however, the latter as the Vulgate barbarously translates it by *promereri.* So "the reasonable service" (*thusia euarestos*, Rom. 12:1) is one which is acceptable to God; and Enoch is said "to have pleased God" (*euarestēkenai tō theō*, Heb. 11:5) as the Vulgate itself has it.

XXX. Although life is rendered to good works no less than death to evil works, still it is not in the same manner that good works have the same causality with respect to salvation as evil have in respect to condemnation. The evil deserve damnation of themselves as undue and ours, but the good do not equally deserve salvation, since they are due (not ours) and imperfect. Besides any transgression of the law subjects a man to the divine malediction; but in meritorious works a perfection of all kinds both of parts and of degrees is required, for more things are required for the constitution than for the destruction of a thing.

XXXI. A promise makes the thing promised due, yet not from the worth of the work, but from the fidelity of the promiser. (2) Not every promise under the condition of a work implies merit, but only if it is the condition of an undue work and has a just proportion to the reward, which cannot be the case with our works. Augustine says, "The Lord made himself a debtor to us, not by receiving anything from us, but by promising all things" (*Ennaratio in Psalmum CIX** 1 [PL 37.1445]).

XXXII. Since respect of persons (*prosōpolēpsia*) has place only in debts and in judicial matters, not in gratuities, he cannot be called a respecter of persons (*prosōpolēptēs*) who gives a reward without merits and who gives greater rewards to lesser works. Otherwise the householder would truly have been a respecter of persons who gave those laboring a shorter time in the vineyard the same pay with others who had labored through the whole day (Mt. 20:1-16).

XXXIII. The word *katergazesthai* (used by Paul in 2 Cor. 4:17, speaking of the relation of afflictions to glory) does not properly denote efficiency and merit, but the way and the means, inasmuch as glory follows and obtains momentary affliction; as with the Greeks it is often the same as *kratēsai* ("to possess and to obtain"). The law is said "to work wrath" (*katergazesthai*, Rom. 4:15), not because it deserves or properly effects it, but because it follows the law accidentally on account of man's transgression of it (Phil. 2:12). The same word denotes the desire to promote sanctification and by it to receive and obtain, but not to deserve salvation.

XXXIV. Nothing in favor of merit can be elicited from the passage of Paul (2 Tim. 4:8). (1) Not from "the crown of righteousness," by which he designates glory. This can be understood of "the righteousness of God" because life is given from a promise and it is a part of righteousness to stand by promises. Bernard sets it forth at the end of his book on grace and free will: "It is just that he should render what he owes, but he owes what he has promised, and this is the righteousness of which the apostle speaks—the promise of God" (*Tractatus de Gratia et Libero Arbitrio* 14.51 [PL 182.1029]). If it be referred to the righteousness of man, it is not so much to the righteousness of the person as of the cause (for which the contest is engaged in); not to legal righteousness (which Paul everywhere excludes), but to evangelical righteousness (which sets aside all merit). Thus he alludes to the crowns given to victors, whether in war or in the games (which supposed indeed the necessity of a contest as the antecedent condition; but not as the cause properly so called or merit). Nay, these crowns were called "donatory" because they were given rather according to promise than from the performance. (2) Not from this—that God is called "the righteous Judge" (*dikaios kritēs*). He is not a legal Judge who cannot give a crown of righteousness, except on account of an absolutely perfect running and contest corresponding exactly with the strict justice (*tō akribodikaiō*) of the law (which is given to no one in this life). But he is an evangelical Judge, who enters into judgment not with mercenaries, but with sons; not according to strict justice (*kata to akribodikaion*), but according to forbearance (*kat' epieikeian*). Nor does he freely crown our merits, but his own gifts, gratuitously given. Now it is one thing to give a crown according to the righteousness of veracity and of goodness according to a promise (by which he is veracious and faithful); another to give it according to the righteousness of obligation and debt (by which he is bound from the performance of men). (3) Not from the verb *apodounai* because (as is well known) it is often used for the simple *dounai* (Mt. 27:58; Lk. 4:20; 9:42; Acts 4:33 and elsewhere). However Paul here employs this verb rather than the simple verb, not on account of a proportion of equality existing between the work and the reward; but on account of the twofold relation (*schesin*) to the promiser and the worker because the reward is given both after the promise and after the past work. But because the promise is absolutely gratuitous and undue and the work due, finite and imperfect (the reward infinite and eternal), *to apodounai* cannot designate the merit or worth of the work.

XXXV. To the passages of the fathers which our opponents are accustomed to use, these answers in general can be given. (1) To no purpose are those passages adduced in which mention is made of beatitude as the crown, reward and pay, in which they testify that God will render to each man according to his works because we have already said that this does not imply merit. (2) Merit with them is often a consecution and obtainment of any thing, even of a thing gratuitous and undue. Bellarmine himself acknowledges this when he confesses that Augustine calls merit any good act on account of which we receive something else ("De Gratia et Libero Arbitrio," 1.14 *Opera* [1858], 4:295-97). (3) That they are accustomed to call prior grace the merit of later and the later the reward of the prior, not on account of any relation of true merit, but on account of that order which God instituted and by which he wished that graces should follow themselves and succeed each other in turn. (4) If certain more difficult expressions are met with when they speak rhetorically and declamatorily that men may be the more effectually incited to the desire of good works, they are to be explained by other passages in which, treating this argument dogmatically and professedly, they confess that no merit can be granted towards God and that all things are received from him gratuitously.

XXXVI. Innumerable passages could be brought together here from which this is evident. But it will be sufficient to quote only a few out of the many. Chrysostom, although often too prone to launch out into the praise of the strength of nature, was still far from an opinion of merit. "The apostle saying the wages of sin is death, has not preserved the same order about good things, since he does not say, the reward of our works, but the gift of God, showing that not by themselves are they freed, nor do they receive a debt, nor a compensation and wages of labor, but that all is done by grace" ("Homily 12," *Epistle to the Romans* [NPNFl, 11:417; PG 60.496] on Rom. 6:23). "Why does he call it an inheritance? Showing that no one obtains the kingdom by his good and rightly performed actions. . . . For no one has proved that he has thus regulated his life as to be thought worthy of the kingdom, but whatever that is, it is his gift. Moreover he said, when ye shall have done all things, say, we are unprofitable servants, for we have done what we ought to have done" ("Homily 2," *Homilies on Colossians* [NPNFl, 13:266; PG 62.312] on Col. 1:12). Jerome says, "Then we are righteous when we confess that we are sinners, and that our righteousness consists not in our own merit, but in the mercy of God" (*Against the Pelagians* 1.13 [FC 53:247; PL 23.527]). Augustine says, "Christ alone underwent punishment for us without evil merit that we through him might obtain undue grace without good merit" (*Against Two Letters of the Pelagians* 4.4 [6] [NPNFl, 5:419; PL 44.613]). And: "He preferred to say, the gift of God is eternal life, that we might understand that God brings us unto eternal life not on account of our merit, but through his own mercy" (*On Grace and Free Will* 21 [9] [NPNFl, 5:452; PL 44.893]). And: "Sins are thine, merits are God's, and when the reward shall have come, he will crown his gifts, not thy merits" (Psalm 70 [71] [NPNFl, 8:324; PL 36.895]). Bernard says, "My merit, therefore, is the compassion of God, I am not wholly destitute of merit, as long as he has compassion" ("Sermon 61 [5]," *Song of Solomon* [trans. S.J. Eales, 1984 repr.], p. 368; PL 183.1073). The Council of Orange says, "God loves us such as we will be by his gift, not such as we are by our merit" (Canon 12, Hefele, 4:159).

XXXVII. Nay, in the very church of Rome itself not a few passages are found which are opposed to merit, as when the church says, "From no action of ours do we have confidence" ("Collect for Sexagesima Sunday," *The Roman Sunday Missal for America* [1933], p. 127); and "Receive not as in an estimator of merit, but as a bestower of pardon" (*The Roman Sunday Missal for America* [1933], p. 513). Pope Adrian says he rests upon a broken reed and a wounded hand who trusts in his own righteousness. Vega (following Thomas Waldensis) says, "He is a sounder theologian, a truer Catholic, and agreeing more with the sacred Scriptures, who simply excludes merits" (Opusculum 4, "De Meritis in Generali," *De Iustifications Doctrina Universa* [1572/1964], 2:782). Hence Bellarmine ("De Justificatione," 5.7 [prop. 3] *Opera* [1858], 4:615) and after him Tirinus (*Theologicae elenchticae . . . controversiarum fidei*, Cont. 16, number 12 [1648], p. 389) return to this at length after all their labor, so as to say, "On account of the uncertainty of our own righteousness and the danger of vain glory, it is safest to rely upon the mercy of God alone and in his kindness." Now if this is said truly (as it is altogether most true), why do they not (being about to withdraw themselves from the danger of vain glory) lay aside wholly that Pharisaical opinion concerning merit that they may with Paul seek the only righteousness which is by faith in Christ (Phil. 3:9)? Why do they not, the word and doctrine of merit being cast aside, suffer us to rely upon Christ's merit alone and place our confidence in God's mercy alone, if this is the safest course? But we have determined to follow what is the safest.

XXXVIII. Here belong the public formulas for consoling the sick and troubled used in the church of Rome which clearly confirm our doctrine concerning the obtainment of salvation, not from works, but from the mercy of God alone. Among these that one ascribed to Anselm is remarkable. For among the questions which he prescribes for the weak and dying is this final one: "Do you believe that you cannot be saved except by the death of Christ?" The sick man answers, "I do." Then it is said to him, "Come then, while breath remains in you, have confidence in no other thing; trust yourself wholly to this death, cover yourself entirely with this alone. . . . And if the Lord God would wish to judge you; say, O Lord, I place the death of our Lord Jesus Christ between thee and between me and thy judgment" (cf. St. Victor of Paris, *Consuetudines* 67, ll. 71-75 [Corpus Christianorum Continuatio Medaevalis 61:260]). The Ordo Baptizandi+, published at Venice in the year 1575, can also be consulted and the *Preceptorium* (1501) of Nicholas of Lyra put forth at Cologne (1499) where many other things of the same kind can be found.

Question concerning aureolas.

XXXIX. From what has been said it can easily be inferred what we must determine on the question concerning aureolas agitated here by the Romanists. Are there "halos of glory" in heaven assigned to certain ones above others; for instance to virgins, teachers and martyrs? This is the opinion of Thomas Aquinas and of the Scholastics. By aureola, they mean a joy arising from works which have relation to a certain surpassing victory and which is an accidental reward added to the essential gold or reward (i.e., to the joy with which anyone rejoices in his union with God). They seek a foundation for it in the relation of the fight to the crown for the crown is due to the contest. Therefore, where there is a special reason of the contest, there is a special crown, which is called an aureola. And since the reward ought to correspond with the merit, some excellence in the reward ought to answer to the excellency of the merit and this is called an aureola.

XL. But the folly of this figment is evident: (1) from all the arguments by which we have destroyed merit universally—for what is denied of a whole class is also denied of all its species. And if man cannot do what he ought (as was said before), how could he merit anything beyond the common reward? (2) Rashly and gratuitously is this asserted without any support from the Scriptures. And who constituted these seraphic doctors distributors of eternal rewards? Or where did they learn that aureolas are to be expected by virgins, martyrs and teachers?

XLI. Although a crown is promised to the strife and victory, it does not follow that it is due to it from merit (as has been said), but from grace. The contest is not only due, imperfect and unequal to the crown, but wholly from grace. As therefore every battle is fought by grace, thus also the special battle is fought from special grace. Hence to fight such a contest is not a proof of greater merit, but of greater grace. And because more is given from God to one thus contending, he is more indebted to God, not God to him.

XLII. Although different degrees of glory are recognized, so that God from grace will reward the labors and suffering of the pious not only with temporal but also with celestial rewards, still nothing can be gathered thence in favor of aureolas because glory as well as all degrees of it are wholly gifts of grace and the pure charisma (*charisma*) of God (which is incompatible [*asystaton*] with merit).

XLIII. The promise which is given to him that overcometh of the hidden manna and the white stone (Rev. 2:17), so refers to the martyrs as to pertain no less to all believers, who have a continual contest with the Devil, the world and sin. If such a reward is promised to him that overcometh, it does not follow that it is due to his merit. What is said of teachers "who shall turn many to righteousness that they shall shine as the stars" (Dan. 12:3), can indeed teach that there are different degrees of glory, but not that this difference will arise from a different proportion of merit. Nay, since whatever virtue was in them was entirely from grace, it cannot be meritorious.

XLIV. The "virgins" (alluded to in Rev. 14:4) are not proper, but metaphorical (i.e., true believers), who as "a chaste virgin" (2 Cor. 11:2) ought to keep their faith with Christ (their spouse) inviolate, worshipping God purely, without any guilt of idolatry (which is spiritual fornication and adultery), who are on this account opposed to Babylon, the mother of harlots and her followers, who commit fornication with her. However, it is clear that this pertains not only to the single but also to the married.

XLV. The "great reward" promised to those who suffer persecution (Mt. 5:12) denotes indeed the excellency of the reward promised, but as it is promised gratuitously, it is to be given so gratuitously as not to be rendered to any merit of their own. And it is said to be such not relatively to the small and lesser reward of others; but in comparison with the small and few works done by those to whom that reward is to be given because the reward is truly great and most abundant in comparison with the small labor. For our sufferings are not to be compared in worth with the glory to be revealed (Rom. 8:18).

We have now said enough on this subject. God grant that, dismissing a vain confidence in our own merit, we may rest in the most perfect merit of Christ alone and so keep faithful to him and fight the good fight even unto the end that we may receive a crown of righteousness; due not to our merit, but most graciously promised to us from the heavenly rewarder. To him, the author and finisher (*archēgō kai teleiōtē*) of our salvation, the one and triune God, "from whom, by whom and to whom are all things, be praise and glory world without end." Amen.

Topic 13,9 ~~B~~ 18–22
- personhood denied of humanity of Xp
- instrument

13, 7, 15 - soul/body is very dominant analogy
13, 8, 1 - habitual grace/eminence
14, 2 - Christ's mediation
- 2 actions/apotelesmata
- instrument denial (381)

argument mediation is one of the "theandric", saving works
Christ does → it cannot be limited to his humanity
+ plus, divinity is not "unminded"

14, 4 - mediation of intercession ; satisfaction denied to the saints
- Saints do not know our needs
- mystical body does not entail communio offices

14, 8 (p. 401) - Christ's Doctrine furnished w/ divine power
- clothed with divine power - God alone can do these works

Turretin - "weak" necessity for satisfaction (422)

Great analysis of PSA (9.14, loc. 11)
instrumental humanity infinite effect (440)

Sacrament of confession criticized (441)
; "temporal punishment"

positive quote of Aquinas on martyrs (442)

*** Suffering of mystical body (Col 1:24) (442)
***